The Encyclopedia of the American Theatre 1900-1975

Edwin Bronner

SAN DIEGO • NEW YORK
A. S. BARNES & COMPANY, INC.
IN LONDON:
THE TANTIVY PRESS

Encyclopedia of American Theatre text copyright ©1980 by
A. S. Barnes and Co., Inc.

The Tantivy Press
Magdalen House
136-148 Tooley Street
London, SE1 2TT, England

All rights reserved under International and Pan American Copyright Conventions.
No part of this book may be reproduced in any manner whatsoever without written permission from the publisher, except in the case of brief quotations embodied in reviews and articles.
First Edition
Manufactured in the United States of America
For information write to A. S. Barnes and Company, Inc.,
P.O. Box 3051, San Diego, CA 92038

Library of Congress Cataloging in Publication Data

Bronner, Edwin, 1926-1976
The encyclopedia of the American theatre, 1900-1975.

1. Theater—United States—Dictionaries.
2. Theater—United States—Reviews. 3. American drama—20th century—Bibliography. I. Title.
PN2266.B68   792'.0973   75-2439
ISBN 0-498-01219-0

1 2 3 4 5 6 7 8 9   84 83 82 81 80

Preface

Most of the conventions used in the encyclopedia are self-explanatory. To conserve space, symbols and abbreviations are employed throughout. Each play's title is followed by the New York opening date, the name of the theatre, and the number of performances.

For example, the notation for *Abie's Irish Rose* (5/23/22, Fulton, 2,327) tells the reader immediately that the play opened on May 23, 1922 at the Fulton Theatre and ran 2,327 performances.

Abbreviations which appear most frequently are A (Author), C (Cast), D (Director), and P (Producer).

Introduction

This book contains information about plays produced on- and off-Broadway from 1900 to 1975. The plays were written (or adapted) by American or Anglo-American authors. In preparing each entry, my primary concerns were accuracy, clarity, and comprehensiveness. Consider, as a random example, that stylish comedy, *The Firebrand:* What was it about? Who appeared in it? Who wrote it? When and where did it open? How long did it run? Was it ever musicalized? Was there a screen version? If so, what was the title? And who were the stars?*

By consulting *The Encyclopedia of the American Theatre,* the answers to these (and other) questions may quickly and easily be found. The purpose of this book, therefore, is to bring together, in one convenient source, information usually found only by consulting a dozen or more esoteric or fairly inaccessible volumes.

Here then, arranged alphabetically by title for easy reference, are the plays of our American Theatre.

Edwin Maduro Bronner
San Francisco

---

*The Firebrand dealt in lighthearted fashion with the escapades of Benvenuto Cellini. Joseph Schildkraut, Frank Morgan, Edward G. Robinson, and Nana Bryant appeared in leading roles. Edwin Justus Mayer was the author. The play premiered October 15, 1924 at the Morosco Theatre for a run of 287 performances. It was musicalized by Kurt Weill and Ira Gershwin as *The Firebrand of Florence* (1945) with Earl Wrightson, Lotte Lenya and Melville Cooper heading the cast. The screen version was retitled *The Affairs of Cellini* (United Artists, 1934) and starred Fredric March and Constance Bennett with Frank Morgan, Fay Wray, and Louis Calhern prominent in supporting roles.

Abbreviations

A:	Author
Ad.:	Adapted (Adapter)
b/o:	Based On
C:	Cast
CD:	Costume Designer
CH:	Choreographer
D:	Director
deb.:	N.Y. Stage Debut
i.a.w.:	In Association With
L:	Lyricist
M:	Musical Score (Composer)
O/B:	Off-Broadway
P:	Producer
R:	Revived*
Rep.:	Repertory Production
SD:	Scene Designer
SV:	Screen Version (S)**

*Notable or especially interesting revivals and return engagements are listed. Credits are not repeated if substantially the same cast, producer, and director were involved.

**Studios and distributors represented by talking picture versions (or notable silent screen versions) of plays include:

AA	Allied Artists
BV	Buena Vista
Col	Columbia
Fox	Fox Film Corp.; 20th Century-Fox
MGM	Metro-Goldwyn-Mayer; Metro
Par	Paramount; Famous-Lasky
RKO	RKO Radio
U	Universal
UA	United Artists
WB	Warner Bros.; First National

A

Abe and Mawruss

See *Potash and Perlmutter in Society*.

Abe Lincoln in Illinois (10/15/38, Plymouth, 472)

Robert E. Sherwood's Pulitzer Prize play dealing with the life of Lincoln (Raymond Massey) from young manhood to his farewell speech at Springfield when he departs for Washington to become the sixteenth President of the United States. In twelve episodes covering thirty years, and using Lincoln's own words whenever feasible, the author explores the complex and contradictory character of this ungainly, heroic figure who was summoned to greatness almost against his will. "One of the most stirring of American plays . . . should become an American classic" (Richard Watts, Jr., *Herald Tribune*). "It isn't easy to account for the feeling of rising excitement I had throughout the twelve scenes . . . I suppose it was just the surprise and gratitude and somehow the sorrow of seeing a very great man exactly as he must have been" (Wolcott Gibbs, *The New Yorker*). *Abe Lincoln in Illinois* was the first production sponsored by The Playwrights' Company in which five leading American dramatists—Maxwell Anderson, S. N. Behrman, Sidney Howard, Elmer Rice, and Robert E. Sherwood—banded together to produce their own plays. The success of the Sherwood play got the organization off to an auspicious start. Canadian-born actor Raymond Massey received the best notices of his career in the title role. C: Muriel Kirkland, Adele Longmire, Howard da Silva, Albert Phillips, Arthur Griffin, Lewis Martin, Calvin Thomas, Herbert Rudley, Wendell K. Phillips. Making their Broadway debuts in the production: Kevin McCarthy, Joseph Wiseman. D: Elmer Rice. SD: Jo Mielziner.

R: (1/21/63, Anderson, 40) by the Phoenix Theatre, with Hal Holbrook as Lincoln. D: Stuart Vaughan.

SV: RKO, 1940, Raymond Massey, Ruth Gordon, Gene Lockhart, Mary Howard, Howard da Silva, Harvey Stephens (directed by John Cromwell).

Abide with Me (11/21/35, Ritz, 36)

Clare Boothe's first play, a gloomy psychological melodrama about a sadistic dipsomaniac (Earle Larimore) who is finally shot to death by his old servant (Maria Ouspenskaya). "A gratuitous horror play" (*New York Times*). "At the end of the play, Miss Boothe sprang out like a gazelle to cries of 'Author! Author!'—which were audible to no ears but her own" (*Herald-Tribune*). *Abide with Me* ("It abode with nobody," said the authoress) opened on Broadway two days before Miss Boothe's marriage to publisher Henry Luce. The play gave no indication whatever of Clare Boothe's flair for satiric comedy, as evidenced by *The Women* (1936), *Kiss the Boys Goodbye* (1938), and *Margin for Error* (1939). C: James Rennie, Cecilia Loftus, Lee Patrick, P: Pearson and Baruch i.a.w. A. H. Woods. D: John Hayden.

Abie's Irish Rose (5/23/22, Fulton, 2,327)

A Jewish boy marries a Catholic girl, thus setting into motion three acts of slapstick, sentimentality, and family feuding. This was the basic plot of *Abie's Irish Rose,* a phenomenon unique in the annals of the American theatre. First called *Marriage in Triplicate,* the script was rejected by every manager who read it. Author Anne Nichols realized that in order to get a Broadway hearing, she would have to produce the play herself. She assembled a nondescript cast, hired a relatively unknown director (Lawrence Marston), and invested her life savings of $5,000 in the shoestring production. Ridiculed by most of the critics, the play struggled to survive during its early weeks. (To keep the show going, Miss Nichols borrowed $30,000 from gambler Arnold Rothstein.) Shortly thereafter, the comedy began to catch on with the public. By the time it was through, eleven million people had paid twenty-two million dollars for the privilege of watching love conquer all. The play ran five years (2,327 performances) in New York, establishing a new long-run record up to that time. As for Anne Nichols, her $5,000 investment netted her a reputed five million dollars, or an average of one million dollars per year in profits. For the record, the members of the original cast were: Robert B. Williams, Marie Carroll, Alfred Wiseman, John Cope, Bernard Gorcey, Mathilde Cottrelly, Howard Lang, Harry Bradley, and Dorothy Grau. R: (5/12/37, Little, 46) by Anne Nichols, with Bernard Gorcey and Alfred Wiseman once again in the cast. The play ran five weeks instead of five years. A subsequent revival (11/8/54, Holiday, 20) lasted less than three weeks on Broadway.

    SV: Par, 1929, Nancy Carroll, Buddy Rogers, Jean Hersholt; UA-Bing Crosby Productions, 1946, Joanne Dru, Richard Norris, Michael Chekhov, Eric Blore.

Abraham Cochrane (2/17/64, Belasco, 1)

Highly discursive, loftily literary soap opera about an enigmatic stranger (Bill Travers) who sets out to seduce a friend's discontented wife. C: Ann Harding, Nancy Wickwire, Olympia Dukakis, John Griggs. A: John Sherry. P: Fried and Jacobson. D: Harold Stone.

Absence of a Cello (9/21/64, Ambassador, 120)

The difficulties encountered by a brilliant (but broke) physicist and his unconventional family when, with a job in view, they pretend to be conformists. Literate, bright, and cheerful comedy by Ira Wallach b/o his novel of the same name. C: Fred Clark, Ruth White, Murray Hamilton, Ruth McDevitt, Charles Grodin, Mala Powers, Lee Kurty. P: Ellis and Britton. D: James Hammerstein. *Note: Absence of a Cello* was produced in London during the 1968–69 season as *Out of the Question.* The cast was headed by Michael Denison, Gladys Cooper, and Dulcie Gray.

Accent on Youth (12/25/34, Plymouth, 229)

Delightful comedy about a middle-aged dramatist who can't help manipulating life and looking at it from a playwright's viewpoint. Cyrano fashion, he even composes a successful love scene that wins for a young rival the hand of his attractive secretary. In the end, however, the playwright concludes that youth is not everything. As for the secretary, she discovers that an exhausting life with a young athlete is infinitely less pleasurable than a comfortable, orderly existence with an older man. Hence, she eagerly resumes her relationship with the wise and sophisticated dramatist. "A light and literate comedy with an almost Oscar Wildean humor" (*World-Telegram*). C: Nicholas Hannen, Constance Cummings, Irene Purcell, Theodore Newton, Ernest Cossart, Ernest Lawford. A: Samson

Raphaelson. P: Crosby Gaige. D: Benn W. Levy. SD: Jo Mielziner.

SV: Par, 1935, Sylvia Sidney, Herbert Marshall, Philip Reed; 1950, *Mr. Music,* Bing Crosby, Nancy Olson, Charles Coburn, Ruth Hussey, Marge and Gower Champion, Peggy Lee, Groucho Marx; 1959, *But Not For Me,* Clark Gable, Carroll Baker, Lilli Palmer, Lee J. Cobb.

Accused (9/29/25, Belasco, 95)

A famous lawyer (E. H. Sothern) finds his beautiful client guilty of murder, but succeeds in having her acquitted anyway. Lush melodrama in the David Belasco (P/D) manner, plus a chance to view noted Shakespearean actor Sothern (of Sothern and Marlowe) in modern dress. Adapted and extensively revised by George Middleton from a play by Eugene Brieux.

Achilles Had a Heel (10/13/35, 44th Street, 8)

Weird fable about the rivalry between a Negro elephant keeper (Walter Hampden in blackface) and a vindictive white zoo attendant. This pretentious allegory by Martin Flavin, author of such popular successes as *Broken Dishes* (1929) and *The Criminal Code* (1929), was a resounding failure. C: Sylvia Field, John Wray. In bit roles: starlet Virginia Grey, writer Roland Kibbee. P: Walter Hampden. D: Walter Hampden, Martin Flavin, Howard Lindsay.

Acquittal, The (1/5/20, Cohan & Harris, 138)

A plucky young reporter (William Harrigan) insinuates himself into the home of an acquitted murderer, goads him to commit suicide, and winds up consoling the murderer's attractive widow (Chrystal Herne). Trim, well-acted suspense melodrama. A: Rita Weiman. P: Cohan and Harris. D: Sam Forrest.

Ada Beats the Drum (5/8/30, Golden, 46)

Flighty Midwesterner (Mary Boland) persuades her down-to-earth husband (George Barbier) and dim-witted daughter (Nydia Westman) to accompany her to Europe to "soak up culture." There they become involved with assorted fortune hunters and phonies. Cute comedy by John Kirkpatrick. P: John Golden. D: Geoffrey Kerr.

SV: MGM, 1937, *Mama Steps Out,* Alice Brady, Guy Kibbee, Betty Furness.

Adam and Eva (9/13/19, Longacre, 312)

A family of selfish wastrels is told that father's big rubber business has gone snap. Of course, Dad is really solvent but the experience of earning a living does positive wonders for each member of the family. Ingratiating comedy by George Middleton and Guy Bolton was one of the popular successes of 1919. C: Otto Kruger, Ruth Shepley, Berton Churchill, Roberta Arnold, Reginald Mason, Ferdinand Gottschalk. P: F. Ray Comstock.

Adam Had Two Sons (1/20/32, Alvin, 5)

A couple of wild boys of the road escape from a San Francisco prison camp and, trailed by a detective, head for Panama. Glum, unconvincing melodrama with Paul Kelly, Preston Foster, Raymond Hackett, and Raquel Torres. A: John McDermott. P: Aarons and Freedley. D: Melville Burke.

Adding Machine, The (3/19/23, Garrick, 72)

Elmer Rice's expressionistic fantasy about the life and death of Mr. Zero (Dudley Digges), a nameless cog in the vast machinery of business. Tied to a soulless job and a shrewish wife (Helen Westley), this underpaid, overworked bookkeeper murders his boss in resentment and panic when he learns he is to be replaced by an adding machine. After his execution and burial, Mr. Zero reaches the hereafter, consisting largely of a great adding machine. But even Heaven has no use for this browbeaten cipher and he is forced to return to earth again to the same old treadmill existence. C: Edward G. Robinson, Margaret Wycherly, Louis Calvert. P: The Theatre Guild. D: Philip Moeller. SD: Lee Simonson. M: Deems Taylor. Despite muted but generally favorable reviews, *The Adding Machine* failed to make much of an impression on Broadway. However, with the passage of time—and the spread of automation—the play's reputation has grown, and it has been widely restaged throughout the world.

Note: Elmer Rice said that *The Adding Machine* flashed into his mind "as though a switch had been turned or a curtain raised . . . I saw the whole thing complete: characters, plot, incidents, even the title and some of the dialogue. Nothing like it ever happened to me before or since. I was actually possessed . . . It was as close to automatic writing as anything I have known."

SV: British, 1969, Milo O'Shea, Phyllis Diller.

Adrea (1/11/05, Belasco, 123)

The tragic misadventures of a blind princess (Mrs. Leslie Carter) on a mythical island in the Adriatic during the fifth century A.D. Fanciful, bombastic spectacle-drama from the David Belasco (P/D) show shop. C: Tyrone Power, Sr., Charles A. Stevenson, R. D. McLean, Claude Gillingwater. A: David Belasco and John Luther Long.

Adrea. **Scene with Mrs. Leslie Carter (1905).** *Courtesy Museum of the City of New York Theatre and Music Collection.*

Adventure (9/25/28, Republic, 22)

Soldier of fortune (John Litel) settles in Wyoming, opposes wicked cattlemen. Poky Western drama. A: John Willard. P: Bernard Steele. D: Bernard Steele and Rollo Lloyd.

Advise and Consent (11/17/60, Cort, 212)

Melodrama of Washington wheeling and dealing surrounding the appointment of a Secretary of State accused of having once had communist leanings. An unscrupulous senator attempts to blackmail the chairman of the investigation committee into supporting the nominee, thereby forcing the chairman to commit suicide to shield his family from a homosexual incident in his past. In the end, principles prevail over pragmatism, and the Senate turns down the controversial nomination. ". . . a big, bold, rough, tough, mean, ornery, and very exciting show . . ." *(Herald Tribune)*. ". . . a loaded condemnation of the liberal position" *(New York Times)*. "A curiously hollow melodrama . . . lively but . . . strangely aimless" *(Post)*. C: Richard Kiley, Ed Begley, Chester Morris, Henry Jones, Kevin McCarthy, Staats Cotsworth, Judson Laire, Conrad Bain, Woodrow Parfrey, Barnard Hughes, Wilson Brooks. A: Loring Mandel b/o the Pulitzer Prize novel by Allen Drury. P: Fryer and Carr i.a.w. John Herman. D: Franklin Schaffner. SD: Rouben Ter-Arutunian.

SV: Col, 1962, Henry Fonda, Charles Laughton, Don Murray, Walter Pidgeon, Peter Lawford, Gene Tierney, Franchot Tone, Lew Ayres, Burgess Meredith, Paul Ford, George Grizzard, Inga Swenson, Paul McGrath, Will Geer, Edward Andrews, Betty White, Eddie Hodges, Tom Helmore, Paul Stevens (directed by Otto Preminger from a screenplay by Wendell Mayes).

Advocate, The (10/14/63, ANTA, 8)

Earnest but loosely structured, undramatic retelling of the Sacco-Vanzetti courtroom case. C: James Daly, Paul Stevens, Martin Brooks, Dino Fazio (deb.), Dolph Sweet, Tresa Hughes, John Cecil Holm, Wilson Brooks, Barnard Hughes. A: Robert Noah. P: Ellis and Hammerstein. D: Howard da Silva. SD: Ralph Alswang.

Affair of Honor (4/6/56, Barrymore, 27)

Feeble costume antic about a lecherous British major (Dennis King) who lusts after a pretty tavern wench (Betsy Palmer). A: Bill Hoffman. P: The Theatre Guild i.a.w. Theatre 200. D: Robert Douglas.

Affair of State, An (11/19/30, Broadhurst, 24)

To forestall a revolution, the beautiful but childless Archduchess Alexa (Florence Eldridge) must promise the people an heir to the throne. To make good her promise, a handsome young lieutenant is pressed into service. Sniggering sex comedy by Robert Buckner, co-author of *The Primrose Path* (1939) and future Hollywood scenarist *(Jezebel, Yankee Doodle Dandy*, etc.). C: Wilfrid Seagram, Moffat Johnston (D). P: Benjamin David.

After All (12/3/31, Booth, 20)

The efforts of the younger generation to break away from home, and resolve their respective romantic involvements, was the theme of this slight and unsuccessful comedy-drama by Anglo-American author John Van Druten. Humphrey Bogart had the unrewarding role of Duff Wilson, whom the heroine (Margaret Perry) loved and almost lost, while British actress Helen Haye played the matriarch who ruled the family roost with an iron hand. C: Patricia Calvert, Walter Kingsford. P: Dwight Deere Wiman. D: Auriol Lee.

SV: MGM, 1932, *New Morals for Old,* Robert Young, Myrna Loy, Margaret Perry.

After the Fall (1/23/64, ANTA, 208)

Arthur Miller's controversial autobiographical 1964 drama. The controversy centered mainly on one of the major characters—a self-destructive, sexually attractive entertainer and cult personality named Maggie—obviously patterned after Miller's second wife, Marilyn Monroe. The action of the play takes place "in the mind, thought and memory of Quentin" (Jason Robards, Jr.), a successful New Yorker in the throes of emotional crises. Recalling entanglements with blacklisting, and the wreckage of two marriages, Quentin attempts to piece together fragments from his past in a soul-searching monologue directed at an unseen listener who may be a psychiatrist, or God, or Quentin himself. Commissioned to serve as the first production of New York's Lincoln Center Repertory Company, *After the Fall*—Mr. Miller's first new play in almost a decade—generated considerable interest. Critical opinions as to the merits of the drama were sharply divided, however. Some reviewers reviled the work as "shameless exhibitionism" and felt that the memory of the late Marilyn Monroe had been desecrated. Among the naysayers were Robert Brustein (*The New Republic*) and Walter Kerr (*Herald Tribune*). Brustein called it "a confessional autobiography of embarrassing explicitness . . . a three-and-one-half-hour breach of taste," and added: "Mr. Miller is dancing a spiritual striptease while the band plays *mea culpa*." Said Kerr: "*After the Fall* resembles a confessional which Arthur Miller enters as a penitent and from which he emerges as the priest. It is a tricky quick change . . . but it constitutes neither an especially attractive nor especially persuasive performance." C: Barbara Loden, Salome Jens, Ralph Meeker, David J. Stewart, Zohra Lampert, Mariclare Costello, Michael Strong, Patricia Roe. P: Repertory Theatre of Lincoln Center. D: Elia Kazan. SD: Jo Mielziner. M: David Amram.

After Tomorrow (8/26/31, Golden, 78)

Financial and domestic crises delay a young couple's impending marriage. Gimmicky 30's drama. C: Ross Alexander, Josephine Hull, Donald Meek, Barbara Robbins, Joseph Sweeney. A/D: Hugh Strange and John Golden (P).

SV: Fox, 1932, Charles Farrell, Marian Nixon.

Agatha Sue I Love You (12/14/66, Henry Miller, 5)

Ramshackle comedy about a couple of down-on-their-luck gamblers. C: Ray Walston, Corbett Monica, Renee Taylor, Betty Garde, Lee Lawson. A: Abe Einhorn. P: Judith Abbott and Edwin Wilson i.a.w. Valando and Pransky. D: George Abbott.

Age of Innocence, The (11/27/28, Empire, 209)

A titled socialite (Katharine Cornell) falls in love with her cousin's husband (Rollo Peters), but their affair is doomed by the conventions of the elite society (New York, 1870's) in which they live. Dawdling drama adapted from Edith Wharton's Pulitzer Prize novel by Margaret Ayer Barnes (who won the Pulitzer Prize herself in 1930 for her novel, *Years of Grace*). C: Franchot Tone, Arnold Korff, Stanley Gilkey. P: Gilbert Miller. D: Guthrie McClintic.

SV: RKO, 1934, Irene Dunne, John Boles, Julie Haydon.

Aged 26 (12/21/36, Lyceum, 32)

A "romantic drama" dealing with the tragically brief life of John Keats. Cruelly attacked by the critics for his long poem

The Age of Innocence. **Katharine Cornell and Arnold Korff (November 27, 1928).**
Courtesy Museum of the City of New York Theatre and Music Collection.

Endymion (1818), the twenty-three-year-old poet is befriended by Byron, Shelley, and the beautiful Fanny Brawne, with whom he falls hopelessly in love. The play ends as Keats sets sail for Italy. There he will die of tuberculosis at age twenty-six. This frequently engrossing biographical drama was written by Kentucky-born authoress Anne Crawford Flexner. C: Robert Harris, Linda Watkins, Kenneth MacKenna, Anthony Kemble Cooper, Lloyd Gough, Leona Powers. P: Richard Aldrich. D: Harry Wagstaff Gribble. SD: Stewart Chaney.

Ah, Wilderness! (10/2/33, Guild, 285)

Eugene O'Neill's only comedy, an affectionate portrait of family life in 1906 Connecticut. What plot there is revolves around Nat Miller (George M. Cohan), a wise and tolerant father whose teenage boy Richard (Elisha Cook, Jr.) is flirting with radicalism and sending erotic poetry to his next-door sweetheart. Nat's facts-of-life talk with his son, and Richard's subsequent coming to manhood, bring the play to a happy conclusion. "The tenderest and most amusing comedy of boyhood in the American Drama" (George Jean Nathan). George M. Cohan, appearing for the first time in a play not of his authorship, gave an immensely engaging performance in *Ah, Wilderness!*, as did Will Rogers in the West Coast production. The characters and story of this comedy came to O'Neill in a dream. Although he was working on a tragic drama (*Days Without End*) at the time, he put it aside and wrote *Ah, Wilderness!* while it was fresh in his mind in about five weeks. "My purpose," said O'Neill, "was to write a play true to the spirit of the American small town at the turn of the century.... It's the way I would have

Ah, Wilderness! **Scene from Act IV (1933).** *Courtesy Museum of the City of New York Theatre and Music Collection.*

liked my boyhood to have been. It was a sort of wishing out loud." C: Gene Lockhart, Eda Heinemann, Marjorie Marquis, William Post, Jr., Ruth Gilbert. P: The Theatre Guild. D: Philip Moeller. SD: Robert Edmond Jones.
R: (10/2/41, Guild, 29). C: Harry Carey, William Prince, Tom Tully, Ann Shoemaker, Enid Markey. Dennie Moore, Zachary Scott (deb.). D: Eva Le Gallienne.
Musicalized by Bob Merrill, Joseph Stein, and Robert Russell as *Take Me Along* (1959) with Jackie Gleason, Walter Pidgeon, Eileen Herlie, Robert Morse, Una Merkel, Susan Luckey, Arlene Golonka, Peter Conlow, Valerie Harper.
SV: MGM, 1935, Wallace Beery, Lionel Barrymore, Eric Linden, Mickey Rooney, Aline MacMahon, Cecilia Parker (directed by Clarence Brown from a screenplay by Albert Hackett and Frances Goodrich); 1948, *Summer Holiday*, Mickey Rooney, Walter Huston, Frank Morgan, Gloria De Haven, Marilyn Maxwell, Butch Jenkins, Anne Francis (directed by Rouben Mamoulian).

Alias Jimmy Valentine (1/21/10, Wallack's, 155)

A reformed safecracker allows himself to be betrayed when he uses his old burglar tools to open the bank vault in which his fiancee's niece is trapped. Crackerjack crook melodrama, topnotch in every department. *Alias Jimmy Valentine* was adapted by Paul Armstrong from a short story by O. Henry. O. Henry was paid $500 for the dramatic rights. Armstrong made $100,000 in royalties from the play. C: H. B. Warner, Laurette Taylor. P: Liebler & Company. D: Edward E. Rose.
R: (12/8/21, Gaiety, 46) by George Tyler. C: Otto Kruger, Margalo Gillmore, Mary Boland, William Ingersoll, Emmett Corrigan. D: Hugh Ford.
SV: MGM, 1928, William Haines, Lionel Barrymore; Republic, 1936,

Return of Jimmy Valentine, Roger Pryor, Charlotte Henry; 1942, *Affairs of Jimmy Valentine,* Dennis O'Keefe, Ruth Terry.

Alias the Deacon (11/24/25, Sam H. Harris, 277)

A lovable rogue straightens out assorted problems in a small town and then goes on his way. What used to be called "an audience show." As such, okay. C: Berton Churchill, Mayo Methot, Donald Foster. A: John B. Hymer and Le Roy Clemens. P: Samuel Wallach. D: Winchell Smith and Priestly Morrison.

SV: U, 1934, *Half a Sinner,* Berton Churchill, Joel McCrea, Mickey Rooney; 1940, Bob Burns, Mischa Auer, Dennis O'Keefe, Peggy Moran, Jack Carson, Ed Brophy.

Note: A silent version (U, 1927) featured Jean Hersholt, Ralph Graves, and Ned Sparks.

Alice in Arms (1/31/45, National, 5)

A soldier (Kirk Douglas) and a civilian (Richard Coogan) vie for the affections of a former WAC lieutenant (Peggy Conklin). "A mild, skimpy and completely uneventful little comedy . . ." (*Sun*). A: L. and M. Bush-Fekete and Sidney Sheldon. P: Choate and Elkins. D: Jack Daniels.

Alice in Wonderland (12/12/32, Civic, 119)

Excellent adaptation by Eva Le Gallienne (P/D) and Florida Friebus of the children's classic, combining both *Alice in Wonderland* and *Through the Looking Glass.* The critics lavished praise upon the entire production: the Irene Sharaff costumes and settings (faithfully reproduced from the original Tenniel drawings), Richard Addinsell's melodic score, Remo Bufano's extraordinary masks and marionettes. Presented originally in Rep., the production later was moved from O/B to the spacious New Amsterdam Theatre where it enjoyed a successful run. Standouts in a large company: Josephine Hutchinson (Alice), Richard Waring (White Rabbit), Burgess Meredith (Dormouse, Duck, and Tweedledee), Joseph Schildkraut (Queen of Hearts), Howard da Silva (White Knight), Leona Roberts (Red Queen), Florida Friebus (Cheshire Cat). Fifteen years later, Miss Le Gallienne revived the Lewis Carroll fantasy (4/5/47, International, 100), recreating her role of the White Queen. This time her company featured Bambi Linn (Alice), Julie Harris and William Windom (alternating in the role of the White Rabbit), Eli Wallach (Duck), Richard Waring (Mad Hatter), Philip Bourneuf (White Knight), Henry Jones (Humpty Dumpty), Margaret Webster (Red Queen and Cheshire Cat), Raymond Greenleaf (Duchess). This revival was welcomed by both press and public. R: An avant-garde version of *Alice,* developed by the Manhattan Project as a horror tale, was an O/B success

Alice in Wonderland. **Josephine Hutchinson as Alice and Eva Le Gallienne as the White Queen (1932).** *Courtesy Museum of the City of New York Theatre and Music Collection.*

(10/8/70, Extension, 119) under the direction of André Gregory. P: Austin and Smith.

SV: Of the several screen versions of *Alice in Wonderland*, perhaps the most interesting (if not the most successful) was Paramount's 1933 production directed by Norman McLeod from a Joseph Mankiewicz-William Cameron Menzies screenplay. The star-studded cast included: Charlotte Henry (Alice), Gary Cooper (White Knight), Cary Grant (Mock Turtle), W. C. Fields (Humpty Dumpty), Richard Arlen (Cheshire Cat), Edward Everett Horton (Mad Hatter), Louise Fazenda (White Queen), Edna May Oliver (Red Queen), Alison Skipworth (Duchess), Skeets Gallagher (White Rabbit), Jack Oakie (Tweedledum), Roscoe Karns (Tweedledee), Charles Ruggles (March Hare), Ned Sparks (Caterpillar), Polly Moran (Dodo Bird); also Leon Errol, Ethel Griffies, Sterling Holloway, May Robson, Mae Marsh, Raymond Hatton, Jackie Searle, Ford Sterling.

Alien Corn (2/20/33, Belasco, 98)

Trapped in a frustrating teaching job in a bleakly provincial women's college, would-be concert pianist Elsa Brandt (Katharine Cornell) finds the strength of character to leave the stifling academic environment and take up her rightful vocation. A splendid performance by Miss Cornell was the greatest asset of this understated drama by Sidney Howard. C: Siegfried Rumann, James Rennie, Luther Adler, Lily Cahill, Charles Waldron, Richard Sterling, E. J. Ballantine. P/D: Guthrie McClintic. SD: Cleon Throckmorton.

Alison's House (12/1/30, Civic, 42)

Pulitzer Prize drama by Susan Glaspell suggested by events in the life of Emily Dickinson. The family of a noted American authoress debates destroying her unpublished poems that reveal the dead woman's love for a married man. In the end, the family decides to preserve the poems for posterity. Several critics voiced dismay at the Pulitzer award to this over-literary closet drama of limited popular appeal. C: Eva Le Gallienne (P/D), Alma Kruger, Donald Cameron, Josephine Hutchinson, Florida Friebus, Leona Roberts, Walter Beck, Howard da Silva, Robert Ross. *Alison's House* was presented O/B at Miss Le Gallienne's Civic Repertory Theatre. When Lee Shubert moved the production uptown, Gale Sondergaard succeeded Eva Le Gallienne in the leading role. The play lasted two weeks on Broadway.

All Dressed Up (9/9/25, Eltinge, 13)

Scientist tests truth drug on his dinner guests with unanticipated results. Intriguing premise prosaically handled. C: Norman Trevor, Kay Johnson, James Crane, Eliot Cabot. A: Arthur Richman. P: A. H. Woods. D: Guthrie McClintic.

All Editions (12/22/36, Longacre, 23)

Silly farce about a public relations counsel (Walter Greaza) and his zany clients. A: Charles Washburn and Clyde North (D). P: Juliana Morgan.

All God's Chillun Got Wings (5/15/24, Provincetown, 43)

Eugene O'Neill's study of miscegenation and racial hatred dealt with the marriage of a Negro lawyer (Paul Robeson) and a white girl (Mary Blair), and the tragic consequences of this union. Unable to withstand the scorn of society, the girl suffers a reversion to childhood. In an intensely moving final scene, she asks her husband if God will forgive her, and he replies: "Maybe He can forgive what you've done to me; and maybe He can forgive what I've done to you; but I don't see how He's going to forgive—Himself." Years ahead of its time, this shattering portrait of a man and woman trapped in a corrosive love-hate relationship ran into censorship trouble even before its O/B opening. During rehearsals, the company received a steady stream of poison-pen letters and warnings of legal action. O'Neill himself was the target of threats from the Ku Klux Klan. It is not a "race problem play" O'Neill declared in a letter to the press. "It is primarily a study of the two principal characters, and their tragic struggle for happiness." Nevertheless, the storm of protest continued unabated. "*All God's Chillun* received more publicity before production than any play in the history of the theatre," said director James Light. The New York police did their best to close the production before it opened. They succeeded in keeping from the stage the children who were to act in the first scene, but the parts were read by the director, and the rest of the play went on without difficulty. *All God's Chillun Got Wings* received sharply divided notices: "Likely to take a permanent place in the American theatre" (Robert Welsh, *Telegram-Mail*). "A very tiresome play" (Heywood Broun, *World*). Concerning Mr. Robeson's performance, however, there was unanimous agreement: "One of the most thoroughly eloquent, impressive and convincing actors that I have looked at and listened to in almost twenty years of professional theatre-going" (George Jean Nathan, *American Mercury*). "The man brings a genius to the piece" (Laurence Stallings, *World*). Robeson later (1933) played the role in London opposite Flora Robson.

All Good Americans (12/5/33, Henry Miller, 39)

Comedy by Laura and S. J. Perelman. A chic fashion designer, working in France, tries to decide whether to marry a struggling writer or a respectable businessman. "For the thousandth time *All Good Americans* tells the thin story of American expatriates in Paris. . . . Neither the story, dialogue, nor acting can pull the play into the line of the moderately worthwhile" (*Theatre Arts*). C: Hope Williams, Fred Keating, Eric Dressler, Mary Philips, James Stewart. P: Courtney Burr. D: Arthur Sircom. SD: Mordecai Gorelik.
SV: MGM, 1934, *Paris Interlude*, Robert Young, Madge Evans, Otto Kruger, Una Merkel, Ted Healy.

All in Favor (1/20/42, Henry Miller, 7)

High jinks in a Washington Heights boys' club. ". . . makes youth the stuff no one can endure" (*New York Times*). C: Raymond Roe, Arnold Stang, Frances Heflin, Bobby Readick. A: Louis Hoffman and Don Hartman.* P: Elliott Nugent (D), Robert Montgomery and Jesse Duncan.

---

*Longtime Hollywood writer-director-producer with a long list of credits, mainly comedies.

All My Sons (1/29/47, Coronet, 328)

Arthur Miller's first Broadway success; this 1947 drama received sharply divided notices. Having sold defective airplane parts to the government during World War II, a small-town manufacturer throws the blame on his partner and rationalizes his own guilt in the matter. Confronted with the revelation that his unsavory business ethics caused the death of twenty-one combat pilots (including his own son), the manufacturer commits suicide in expiation. ". . . a pitiless analysis of character that gathers momentum all evening and concludes with both logic and dramatic impact" (*New York Times*). "More indignation than craftsmanship . . . the offering merely stammers to a climax" (*Herald Tribune*). An almost classic example of the thesis play, *All My Sons* was frequently forceful but patently contrived. "I felt I had to perfect conventional technique first and *All My Sons* was an exercise," said Arthur Miller. The purpose of the play, according to the author, was "to bring a man into the direct path of the consequences he had wrought." Miller's *Death of a Salesman* two years later (1949) was a far more powerful and artistically mature drama on the same theme—the problem of moral responsibility. C: Ed Begley, Arthur Kennedy, Karl Malden, Beth Merrill, Lois Wheeler. P: Harold Clurman, Elia Kazan (D), Walter Fried i.a.w. Herbert H. Harris. SD: Mordecai Gorelik.

SV: U, 1948, Edward G. Robinson, Burt Lancaster, Mady Christians, Howard Duff, Lloyd Gough, Frank Conroy, Louisa Horton, Arlene Francis, Henry Morgan.

All Over (3/28/71, Martin Beck, 42)

Drama of a death watch conducted by the family and friends of a man who is slowly expiring offstage. Starkly identified only as *Wife, Doctor, Son*, etc., the characters sit about the stage discussing his imminent death, and have at each other in numerous lively quarrels. This is as close as the play gets to any sort of action. The characterizations are surprisingly one-dimensional: the loyal wife, rebellious daughter, sassy nurse. Little is learned about any of them despite the great amount of talk, nor is the dying man drawn in any detail. He is supposed to be famous, but the reason is never disclosed. By the end of the two acts, when the doctor reports the great man dead by announcing "it's all over," the audience is too bemused to care. On the positive side, the dialogue displays Albee's unique eloquence, but in *All Over* it has no cumulative impact. Though the play concerns the universal subjects of love and death, it is too foggy to stimulate the intellect and too cold to stir the emotions. Critical opinion was widely divided, ranging from the raves of Clive Barnes and Harold Clurman to the pan of T. E. Kalem of *Time*, who referred to Albee as the "club bore." The play proved attractive to star players. The big names in the New York cast were echoed in other productions, most notably in the London staging headed by Angela Lansbury and Peggy Ashcroft. A: Edward Albee. C: Jessica Tandy, Colleen Dewhurst, Betty Field, Madeleine Sherwood, George Voskovec, Neil Fitzgerald, James Ray, John Gerstad, Charles Kindl, Allen Williams. D: John Gielgud. SD: Rouben Ter-Arutunian. P: Richard Barr, Charles Woodward, Edward Albee.

All Rights Reserved (11/6/34, Ritz, 31)

Wife of literary lion writes a sexy bestseller under a *nom de plume*. Inept and tiresome 30's comedy. C: Violet Heming, William Harrigan, Thurston Hall, Louis Jean Heydt. A: Irving Kaye Davis. P: Joseph Pollak. D: Melville Burke.

All Soul's Eve (5/12/20, Maxine Elliott's, 21)

The spirit of a dead woman takes possession of the body of an Irish girl. Intermittently effective fantasy by Anne Crawford Flexner. C: Lola Fisher, Cyril Keightley, Walter Kingsford. P: John D. Williams. D: Homer Saint-Gaudens.

All Summer Long (9/23/54, Coronet, 60)

Portrait of a complacent midwestern family—blustering father (Ed Begley), bumbling mother (June Walker),* brainless daughter (Carroll Baker)—whose river bank house is threatened by erosion. The two brothers (John Kerr and Clay Hall) work together to make a retaining wall to save their home from the rising river. They fail, the house crumbles, and the family has to flee for its life. This Robert Anderson drama, b/o Donald Wetzel's novel *A Wreath and a Curse*, received mixed reviews and closed after a modest seven-week run. P: The Playwrights Company. D: Alan Schneider.

CD: Anna Hill Johnstone. SD: Jo Mielziner. M: Albert Hague.

———

*Mother of John Kerr.

All That Glitters (1/19/38, Biltmore, 69)

Practical joker (Allyn Joslyn) passes off a high-priced call girl (Arlene Francis) as a South American princess. One of the flimsier comedies from the George Abbott (P/D) show shop. C: Everett Sloane, Barry Sullivan, Edith Van Cleve, Judson Laire, Jean Casto. A: John Baragwanath and Kenneth Simpson.

All the Girls Came Out to Play (4/20/72, Cort, 4)

An unfunny comedy about a couple of fellows living together in suburbia. The bored wives of the neighborhood suppose them to be homosexuals, their particular attention focusing on the husky young blond who wears few clothes. Actually, he's a composer under house arrest till he finishes a new show score, and robustly heterosexual. The inevitable occurs when the ladies make his acquaintance, and the neglectful husbands who've been cuckolded plot revenge on the seducer. Critical reaction was murderous. "*All the Girls Came Out to Play* closed Saturday after four performances too many" (Joseph Mazo, *Women's Wear Daily*). A: Richard T. Johnson and Daniel Hollywood. C: Dennis Cole (deb.), Bill Britten, Jay Barney, Fred Nassif, Conrad Fowkes, Charlotte Fairchild, Susan Bjurman, Peg Shirley, Michael Murphy, Bette Marshall, Christine Jones, Don Simms. D: John Gerstad. SD: Leo B. Meyer.

All the King's Men (2/4/29, Fulton, 33)

Stepmother finally learns to care for her husband's young son. Maudlin 20's drama by Fulton Oursler. C: Mayo Methot, Grant Mitchell. P: Lew Cantor. D: Priestly Morrison.

SV: RKO, 1936, *Second Wife*, Lila Lee, Conrad Nagel.

All the Living (3/24/38, Fulton, 53)

Two idealistic doctors experiment with a new drug formula to help treat the mentally defective. A state hospital for the insane was the setting for this absorbing 1938 drama by actor Hardie Albright b/o Dr. Victor Small's book *I Knew 3000 Lunatics*. Produced by Cheryl Crawford and directed by Lee Strasberg, *All the Living* was a *succes d'estime* but a box-office failure. C: Leif Erickson, Sanford Meisner, Charles Dingle, John Alexander, Elizabeth Young, Alfred Ryder. SD: Harry Horner.

All the Way Home (11/30/60, Belasco, 333)

Doleful drama (set in rural 1915 Tennessee) dealing with the reactions of an expectant mother (Colleen Dewhurst) and her six-year-old son to the sudden death of her young husband (Arthur Hill) in an automobile accident. Despite inadequacies in the play's structure, and its lack of dramatic action, this chronicle of family life generated considerable emotional force in its best scenes. The production was noteworthy in that critics and audiences joined in an effort to keep it running when it seemed doomed at the box office. Adapted from the Pulitzer Prize novel *A Death in the Family* by the late James Agee,* the play won both the Pulitzer Prize and the Drama Critics Circle Award. C: Lillian Gish, Aline MacMahon, John Megna, Thomas Chalmers, Art Smith, Clifton James, Lenka Peterson, Dorrit Kelton, Lylah Tiffany. A: Tad Mosel. P: Fred Coe i.a.w. Arthur Cantor. D: Arthur Penn. CD: Raymond Sovey. SD: David Hays.

SV: Par, 1963, Jean Simmons, Robert Preston, Pat Hingle, Aline MacMahon, John Cullum, Thomas Chalmers (directed by Alex Segal).

---

*Noted film critic and Hollywood scenarist (*The African Queen, The Quiet One*, etc.).

All You Need Is One Good Break (2/9/50, Mansfield, 32)

Overwritten tale of a Bronx wastrel who fancies himself a big-time gambler. ". . . exceptionally dreary . . . a dismal swamp of words" (*Post*). C: John Berry, Lee Grant, J. Edward Bromberg, Gene Saks. A: Arnold Manoff. P: Monte Proser and Joseph Kipness i.a.w. Jack Small. D: Berry and Bromberg.

Alley Cat (9/17/34, 48th Street, 8)

Married man (Alan Dinehart) falls in love with brassy young dress designer (Audrey Christie). Vapid 30's comedy-drama. C: Evelyn Varden, Kay Strozzi, Mozelle Britton. A: Alan Dinehart (D) and Samuel Shipman b/o a play by Lawrence Pohle. P: Margaret Hewes.

Allure (10/29/34, Empire, 8)

Sadist finds enjoyment in mentally torturing her crippled sister. Sibling rivalry melodrama was an almost total misfire. C: Edith Barrett, Florence Williams, Guido Nadzo, Robert T. Haines, Jess Barker. A: Leigh Burton Wells, P: Dreyfuss and Gernhardt. D: Clifford Brooke.

Aloma of the South Seas (4/20/25, Lyric, 163)

Red-blooded American tries to resist wiles of sultry native lass. Meretricious junk. C: Vivienne Osborne, Frank Thomas, George Gaul, William Gargan (deb.). A: John B. Hymer and LeRoy Clemens. P: Carl Reed. D: A. H. Van Buren.

SV: Par, 1941, Dorothy Lamour, Jon Hall, Lynne Overman, Katherine DeMille, Philip Reed.

Note: The silent version (Par, 1926) of this sarong saga starred Gilda Gray and Percy Marmont.

Amazing Dr. Clitterhouse, The (3/2/37, Hudson, 80)

In order to study the criminal mind at first hand, a psychologist (Cedric Hardwicke) joins a gang of crooks. Ingenious melodrama had a moderate New York run, was a great hit in London. The play was written by Barré Lyndon, Anglo-American author whose screenplay credits include *The Lodger, Hangover Square, Night Has a Thousand Eyes, War of the Worlds*, etc. C: Clarence Derwent, Frederic Worlock, Helen Trenholme. P: Gilbert Miller. D: Lewis Allen.

SV: WB, 1938, Edward G. Robinson, Humphrey Bogart,* Claire Trevor, Donald Crisp, Allen Jenkins, Gale Page (directed by Anatole Litvak from a screenplay by John Huston and John Wexley).

---

*Bogart invariably referred to this film as *The Amazing Dr. Clitoris*.

Ambush (10/10/21, Garrick, 98)

A Jersey City clerk (Frank Reicher) sees his ideals and standards of decency ambushed by the behavior of his promiscuous daughter (Florence Eldridge) and money-mad wife (Jane Wheatley). Well-constructed, grimly realistic domestic drama by Arthur Richman. P: The Theatre Guild. D: Robert Milton.

SV: WB, 1931, *The Reckless Hour,* H. B. Warner, Conrad Nagel, Dorothy Mackaill, Joan Blondell.

Amen Corner, The (4/15/65, Barrymore, 84)

James Baldwin's play about a storefront preacher in Harlem and her family conflicts. Beautiful performance by Beah Richards as the lady evangelist. "It is a flawed work, but with a poetic honesty and power" (*Cue*). P: Mrs. Nat King Cole. D: Frank Silvera.

American Born (10/5/25, Hudson, 88)

Minor George M. Cohan (A/P/D) opus in which a Wisconsinite (Cohan) goes to England and teaches the British a thing or two about the good old U.S.A. "A cretonne grab bag of sentimental situations and vaudeville gags" (*Sun*).

American Dream (2/21/33, Guild, 39)

Chronicle of a greedy New England industrialist family from 1650 to the Depression years of the 1930's when the American dream turned sour. Vivid, frequently absorbing dramatic trilogy by poet George O'Neil. C: Douglass Montgomery, Stanley Ridges, Claude Rains, Gale Sondergaard, Josephine Hull, Lee Baker, Helen Westley, Leona Hogarth, Edith Van Cleve, Erskine Sanford, Sanford Meisner. P: The Theatre Guild. D: Philip Moeller. SD: Lee Simonson.

American Gothic (11/10/53, Circle in the Square, 77)

Bleak OB period drama (19th-century New England) about a troubled marriage and subsequent divorce, and of the grim revenge the unhappy heroine finally takes on her ex-husband's second wife. ". . . compact, detached and overwhelming in the first act . . . discursive and thin in the second" (*New York Times*). C: Jason Robards, Jr., Clarice Blackburn, Jean Stapleton (deb.). A: Victor Wolfson b/o his novel, *The Lonely Steeple*. P/D: Jose Quintero.

American Landscape (12/3/38, Cort, 43)

The ghosts of American patriots return to earth to persuade a Connecticut businessman not to sell his estate to a German-American bund. Stagebound fantasy by Elmer Rice (A/D) seldom cast its intended spell. C: Charles Waldron, Isobel Elsom, Charles Dingle, Donald Cook, George Macready, Sylvia Weld, Theodore Newton, Phoebe Foster. P: The Playwrights' Company.

American Tragedy, An (10/11/26, Longacre, 216)

Generally effective dramatization of Theodore Dreiser's landmark novel about an ambitious but callow factory worker who meets and falls in love with a wealthy young socialite. His future seems assured until a drab working girl he seduced becomes pregnant. She drowns in what appears to be an accident, but a subsequent court finds the young man guilty of murder in the first degree. C: Morgan Farley, Miriam Hopkins, Katherine Wilson. A: Patrick Kearney. P: Horace Liveright. D: Edward Goodman.

SV: Par, 1931, Phillips Holmes, Sylvia Sidney, Frances Dee (directed by Josef von Sternberg); 1951, *A Place in the Sun*, Montgomery Clift, Elizabeth Taylor, Shelley Winters, Keefe Brasselle, Raymond Burr, Anne Revere (directed by George Stevens).

Note: Publisher Donald Friede (of the firm of Boni and Liveright) took Theodore Dreiser to see the play early in its run. Dreiser was enthralled. "He would not get up in the intermission," Friede recalled. "He would not talk. He just sat there. And when the curtain went down on the death-cell scene, he turned to me and I could see that there were tears in his eyes. 'The poor boy!,' he said. 'The poor bastard! What a shame!'"

See *Case of Clyde Griffiths*.

American Way, The (1/21/39, Center, 244)

George S. Kaufman and Moss Hart's lavish patriotic extravaganza depicting the fortunes of a German immigrant (Fredric March) and his wife (Florence Eldridge) from their arrival at Ellis Island in 1896 to the rise of the Nazi movement in the United States in 1939. The play's thesis—democracy will survive as long as men are willing to die for freedom—was effectively dramatized within the framework of an eye-filling, bountiful spectacle. The production employed 222 actors, seven stage managers, an enormous amount of scenery, and special music composed and arranged by Oscar Levant. *The American Way* was a popular success from its first performance. "No audience that I can remember in my time on the stage aisle has been so shaken with emotion . . ." (*Journal-American*). "An expensive stage show . . . that rises now and then to moving heights by reason of its honest acting and playing" (*News*). C: McKay Morris, Ruth Weston, Hugh Cameron, David Wayne, Alan Hewitt, Adrienne Marden, Whit Bissell, Allen Kearns, Le Roi Operti, Dick Van Patten, James Russo, Bobby Barron. P: Sam H. Harris and Max Gordon. D: George S. Kaufman and Hassard Short. CD: Irene Sharaff. SD: Donald Oenslager.

Among the Married (10/3/29, Bijou, 44)

A wife opts for the double standard in marriage when she catches her philandering husband and best friend *flagrante delicto*. Uneven 20's comedy by Vincent Lawrence (A/D). C: Frank Morgan, Katherine Wilson, Peggy Allenby. P: Philip Goodman. A successful West Coast production of this play (November, 1929) starred Edward Everett Horton, Florence Eldridge, and Mary Astor.
  SV: MGM, 1931, *Men Call It Love*, Adolphe Menjou, Leila Hyams, Norman Foster, Hedda Hopper, Mary Duncan.

Among Those Sailing (2/11/36, Longacre, 7)

Young fellow is torn between two sisters, one married and the other single. Vapid 20's comedy-drama. C: William Harrigan, Ruth Weston, Selena Royle. A: Laura Walker. P: A. J. McGoldrick. D: Robert Milton.

Amorous Antic, The (12/2/29, Masque, 8)

Love among the bohemian set; weak triangle farce by Ernest Pascal (A/D). C: Frank Morgan, Alan Mowbray, Phoebe Foster. P: Sam H. Harris.

Amourette (9/27/33, Henry Miller, 21)

Irate father pursues runaway daughter. Dull period comedy by Clare Kummer. C: Francesca Bruning, Byron McGrath, Arthur Aylesworth, Mildred Natwick. P: Peters and Spiller. D: Leo Bulgakov.

And Be My Love (1/18/34, Ritz, 4)

Tepid teacup comedy about an aging Casanova. C: Barry Jones, Lily Cahill, Renee Gadd, Maurice Colbourne, Rita Vale. A: Lewis Galantiere and John Houseman. P: Maurice Colbourne (D) and Barry Jones.

And Be My Love (2/21/45, National, 14)

Amorous antics of an elderly actor and a middle-aged widow. ". . . tasteless, tactless and tiresome. . ." (*Journal-American*). ". . . a stupefying bore, a very opiate of a play" (*PM*). C: Walter Hampden, Lotus Robb, Esther Dale, Violet Heming, Jed Prouty. A: Edward Caulfield. P: Arthur J. Beckhard (D) i.a.w. Victor Hugo-Vidal.

And Miss Reardon Drinks a Little (2/25/71, Morosco, 108)

Static drama of three middle-aged sisters. All schoolteachers, one drinks excessively, one teeters on the edge of lunacy, and the third has moved up to an administrative post, reinforcing her natural dignity and self-possession. The crux of the plot is whether the peculiar sister (Julie Harris) will be sent to an institution. The signing of her commitment papers is discussed at great length, but though the pen is poised, they remain unsigned at final curtain. Momentum does not build as the play progresses, there is little character development, and nothing much has changed, or even happened by the end of Act III. The theme of *And Miss Reardon Drinks a Little* is the familiar one of apparent eccentricity masking the profoundest sanity, but the execution here is unpersuasive. Marvelous notices went to the cast, particularly to Estelle Parsons as the drinking sister of the title. Rae Allen, as a clumsily devious visitor, won the Tony Award for Best Supporting Actress, Straight Play. Much of the dialogue is funny, though too liberally laced with four-letter words, but the play is ultimately without point. A: Paul Zindel. C: Julie Harris, Estelle Parsons, Nancy Marchand, Bill Macy, Rae Allen, Virginia Payne, Paul Lieber. D: Melvin Bernhardt. P: James B. McKenzie, Spofford J. Beadle, Seth L. Schapiro, Kenneth Waissman and Maxine Fox. SD: Fred Voelpel.

And Stars Remain (10/12/36, Guild, 57)

Discovering that her sympathies lie with the downtrodden, a young socialite (Helen Gahagan) rebels against the dictates of her ultra-conservative family. Clifton Webb made his legitimate (nonmusical) theatre debut in this confused, verbose comedy-drama by Julius and Philip Epstein. (The brothers Epstein went on to become leading Hollywood scenarists with such scripts to their credit as the Academy Award-winning *Casablanca*).

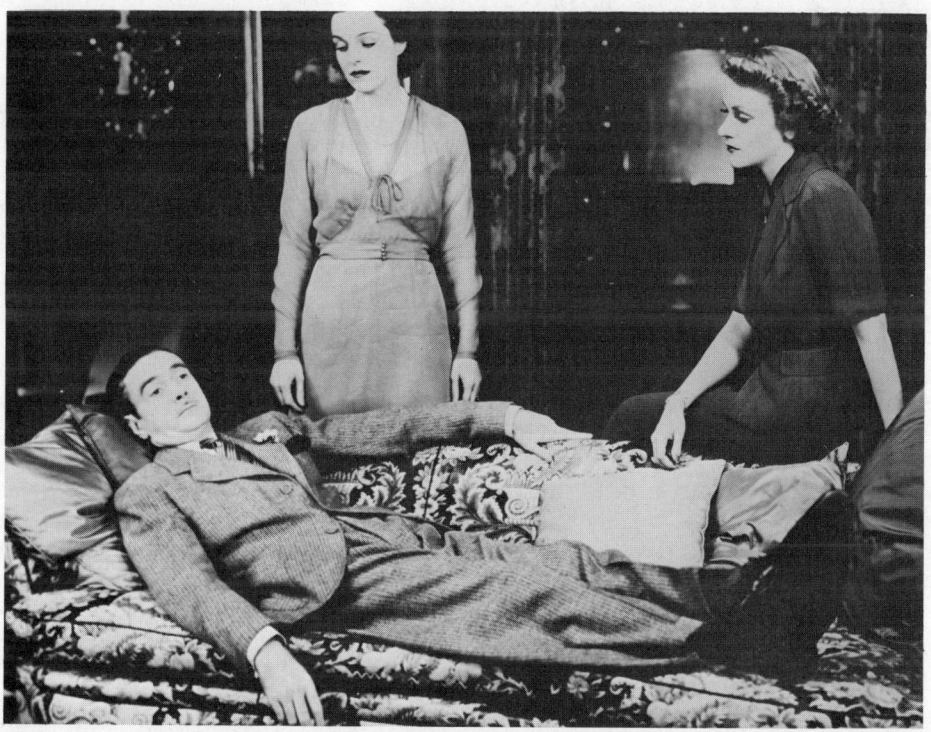

And Stars Remain. **Clifton Webb, Helen Gahagan, and Claudia Morgan (October 12, 1936).** *Courtesy Museum of the City of New York Theatre and Music Collection.*

C: Charles Richman, Claudia Morgan, Ben Smith. P: The Theatre Guild. D: Philip Moeller. SD: Aline Bernstein.

And Things That Go Bump in the Night (4/26/65, Royale, 16)

Terrence McNally's first Broadway play. All about a bitch-mother (Eileen Heckart) and her sadistic offspring hiding in their underground shelter from an unspecified "it" that is "moving west," and of the unsuspecting male visitor to their bomb-shelter home who is driven mad with lust for the handsome son (Robert Drivas) of the family. ". . . one of those off-bleat stupefactions that make the modern stage look like the queerest wing of a nuthouse" *(Time)*. C: Susan Anspach, Marco St. John, Clifton James, Ferdi Hoffman. P: Theodore Mann and Joseph E. Levine i.a.w. Katzka-Berne, Inc. D: Michael Cacoyannis. SD: Ed Wittstein.

Andersonville Trial, The (12/29/59, Henry Miller, 179)

Reconstruction of a famous post Civil War military inquiry—the court-martial (and subsequent conviction) of Henry Wirz (Herbert Berghof), charged with criminal responsibility in the death of thousands of Northern soldiers while serving as commander of the infamous Confederate prison at Andersonville, Georgia. "A provocative study of the moral issues involved in the conflict between man's obligation to authority and to his conscience" *(Post)*. C: George C. Scott, Albert Dekker, Russell Hardie, Ian Keith, Robert Carroll, Robert Gerringer, James Greene, Frank Sutton. A: Saul Levitt. P: Darrid, Saidenberg and Hollywood. D: Jose Ferrer. CD/SD: Will Steven Armstrong.

Angel in the Pawnshop (1/18/51, Booth, 85)

Pixilated young girl (Joan McCracken) seeks refuge in hockshop run by kind-hearted Irish pawnbroker (Eddie Dowling). ". . . balderdash . . . a tedious theatrical what-not" *(Herald Tribune)*. A: A. B. Shiffrin. P: Eddie Dowling and Anthony B. Farrell. D: John Larson CD/SD: John Blankenchip. M: Will Irwin.

Angel Island (10/20/37, National, 21)

Murder strikes during a search for buried treasure on an isolated isle. Some capable performers were squandered in this murky George Abbott (P/D) mystery melodrama. After three weeks of dwindling business, *Angel Island* disappeared from view. C: Arlene Francis, Lea Penman, Betty Field, Carroll Ashburn, Doro Merande, Edith Van Cleve, Clyde Fillmore, Eric Wollencott, Louise Larabee, Joyce Arling. A: Bernie Angus.
SV: PRC (Producers Releasing Corp.), 1945, *Fog Island,* George Zucco, Lionel Atwill, Veda Ann Borg, Jerome Cowan, Sharon Douglas.

Angels Kiss Me (4/17/51, National, 2)

Doleful drama about the unhappy marriage of a brash extrovert and a wealthy manic-depressive. ". . . more like pulp fiction than living theatre." C: Alan Manson, Maryanna Gare. A: Scott Michel. P: Trudi Michel. D: Ramsey Burch.

Animal Kingdom, The (1/12/32, Broadhurst, 171)

In this successful comedy by Philip Barry, nonconformist publisher Tom Collier (Leslie Howard) looks upon the two women in his life and finds it difficult to discover which is the wife and which the mistress. His wife Cecelia persuades him to publish popular tripe and alienates him from his friends, while his former mistress, Daisy Sage, remains spiritually and intellectually his equal. In the final scene, Tom recognizes the resemblance of his home to a high-class bordello and decamps to rejoin Daisy, his "real" wife. "This eminently disinterested department takes the liberty of feeling very proud of what Mr. Barry and Mr. Howard have created" *(New York Times)*. At Philip Barry's insistence, an unknown actress named Katharine Hepburn played the key role of Daisy Sage in the prior-to-Broadway tryout of *The Animal Kingdom*. There were differences of opinion from the outset. Before the New York opening, producers Gilbert Miller (D) and Leslie Howard fired Hepburn, and brought Frances Fuller in to replace her. C: William Gargan, Lora Baxter, Ilka Chase, Harvey Stephens.

SV: RKO, 1932, Leslie Howard, Ann Harding, Myrna Loy, William Gargan, Neil Hamilton, Ilka Chase, Henry Stephenson; WB, 1946, *One More Tomorrow,* Dennis Morgan, Ann Sheridan, Jack Carson, Alexis Smith, Jane Wyman, Reginald Gardiner, John Loder, Marjorie Gateson, Thurston Hall, John Abbott.

Anna Christie (11/2/21, Vanderbilt, 177)

Pulitzer Prize drama by Eugene O'Neill. A Swedish prostitute (Pauline Lord) visits her seafaring father (George Marion) and his barfly-mistress (Eugenie Blair) and falls in love with Mat (Frank Shannon), a blustering Irish stoker who, like her father, is unaware of Anna's sordid past. The play hints at Anna's regeneration through marriage, but ends ambiguously; fate ("dat ole davil sea") and the characters' inner natures will not allow them to remain settled for long. "A rich and salty play that grips the attention from the rise of the first curtain and holds it fiercely to the end" (Alexander Woollcott, *New York Times*). *Anna Christie* had been tried out by George C. Tyler under the title of *Chris Christopherson* with Lynn Fontanne as Anna, but the play was withdrawn for repairs in Philadelphia. The revised and retitled script was presented by Arthur Hopkins (P/D) who cast Pauline Lord as the bewildered and tragic heroine. The role elevated Miss Lord to stardom. Robert Edmond Jones' settings also were ac-

Anna Christie. **Pauline Lord, George Marion (1921–22).** *Courtesy Museum of the City of New York Theatre and Music Collection.*

corded much praise. "I never liked it so well as some of my other plays," O'Neill confessed years later. "In telling the story I deliberately employed all the Broadway tricks which I had learned in my stage training." O'Neill boasted that the writing of *Anna Christie* had been "too easy" and that he would never write such a play again. R: (1/9/52, City Center, 30) by N.Y.C. Theatre Co. and Harald Bromley. C: Celeste Holm, Kevin McCarthy, Art Smith, Grace Valentine, Arthur O'Connell, Robert Anderson. D: Michael Gordon. Musicalized by Bob Merrill as *New Girl In Town* (1957) with Gwen Verdon, Thelma Ritter, George Wallace, Cameron Prud'homme.

SV: MGM, 1930, Greta Garbo, Marie Dressler, Charles Bickford, George Marion.

Note: A silent version (WB, 1923) starred Blanche Sweet.

Anna Lucasta (8/30/44, Mansfield, 957)

Anna Lucasta, a young prostitute, marries and tries to settle down to small-town respectability, but her past catches up with her. The play ends happily (if unconvincingly) when her husband pursues his runaway bride and persuades Anna that he loves her despite her past. "... an interesting but curiously uneven play" *(Sun)*. Philip Yordan's melodramatic variation on the *Anna Christie* theme was originally written with a Polish family background. Produced with an all-black cast in a tiny Harlem basement, *Anna Lucasta's* structural defects were masked by vigorous acting and adroit staging. Transferred to Broadway, the play was an overnight hit. C: Hilda Simms, Earle Hyman, Frederick O'Neal, Canada Lee, Alvin Childress, Alice Childress, Rosetta LeNoire, Georgia Burke. P: John Wildberg. D: Harry Wagstaff Gribble.

SV: Col, 1949, Paulette Goddard, Oscar Homolka; UA, 1959, Eartha Kitt, Sammy Davis, Jr., Frederick O'Neal, Rex Ingram.

Note: Philip Yordan's writer-producer film credits range from *The Harder They Fall* to *The Battle of the Bulge. Anna Lucasta* was his only Broadway play.

Anne of England (10/7/41, St. James, 7)

A court feud between the Duchess of Marlborough (Flora Robson) and her venomous cousin (Jessica Tandy) helps bring about the defeat of the Churchills during the reign (1702–14) of Queen Anne (Barbara Everest). Sumptuously produced historical drama, adapted by Mary Cass Canfield and Ethel Borden from a play by Norman Ginsbury. "A pallid chronicle play . . . a ponderous bore" *(Herald Tribune)*. C: Leo G. Carroll, Frederic Worlock, Reginald Mason. P/D: Gilbert Miller.

Anne of the Thousand Days (12/8/48, Shubert, 288)

Maxwell Anderson's chronicle of a tempestuous period in England's history, the years (1526–36) when Henry VIII (Rex Harrison) broke off religious ties with Rome, seized the wealth of the church, and executed all who stood in the way of his marriage to Anne Boleyn (Joyce Redman). Disappointed by Anne's inability to give him a male heir, Henry casts his roving eye elsewhere and offers Anne the choice of death or exile. She chooses the former, thus ensuring the succession to the throne of her daughter Elizabeth. "A robust and vivid play" *(Sun)*. Drastically overhauled during its pre-Broadway tryout (where it was rated a hopeless failure), *Anne of the Thousand Days* opened on Broadway to general critical acclaim. C: Percy Waram, John Williams, Viola Keats, Harry Irvine, Russell Gaige, Wendell K. Phillips, Louise Platt, Monica Lang, Walter Matthau (deb.). P: The Playwrights Company and Leland Hayward. D: H. C. Potter. CD: Motley. SD: Jo Mielziner. M: Lehman Engel.

SV: British, 1970, Richard Burton, Genevieve Bujold.

Anniversary Waltz (4/7/54, Broadhurst, 615)

Troubles mount when Father (Macdonald Carey) inadvertently reveals that he and Mother (Kitty Carlisle) lived together in sin before legalizing their union. Despite mixed reviews, this heavy-handed farce prospered on Broadway for 615 performances. C: Howard Smith, Phyllis Povah, Warren Berlinger, Andrew Duggan. A: Jerome Chodorov and Joseph Fields. P: Joseph M. Hyman and Bernard Hart. D: Moss Hart. SD: Frederick Fox.

SV: UA, 1959, *Happy Anniversary*, David Niven, Mitzi Gaynor, Carl Reiner, Loring Smith, Patty Duke, Monique Van Vooren, Elizabeth Wilson (directed by David Miller).

Another Language (4/25/32, Booth, 348)

Domestic comedy-drama about a dominating mother of four married sons and the one daughter-in-law who opposes her tyranny. A first play by Rose Franken, author of *Claudia* (1941), *Another Language* was a substantial success. "Steadfastly authentic . . . constantly wise and interesting" (*American*). C: Dorothy Stickney, Margaret Wycherly, John Beal, Glenn Anders, Margaret Hamilton. P/D: Arthur J. Beckhard. R: The return engagement (5/8/33, Waldorf, 80) featured Patricia Collinge and Esther Dale in the roles originally played by Dorothy Stickney and Margaret Hamilton.

SV: MGM, 1933, Helen Hayes, Robert Montgomery, Louise Closser Hale, William Farnum.

See *The Hallams*.

Another Part of the Forest (11/20/46, Fulton, 182)

Lillian Hellman's prologue to *The Little Foxes* showing the ruthless Hubbard clan twenty years earlier (1880), bound together by greed in a household seething with hatred, frustration, and treachery. The leading characters are Marcus Hubbard (Percy Waram), a southern traitor and profiteer; his half-demented wife Lavinia (Mildred Dunnock); and their three children: the wily Benjamin (Leo Genn), the weakling Oscar (Scott McKay), and the calculating Regina (Patricia Neal), a true opportunist who will go wherever the power lies. The major thrust of the play centers around Ben's repeated attempts to obtain control of the family fortune. When he stumbles upon his father's terrible secret (complicity in the deaths of seventeen young Confederate soldiers), Ben blackmails Marcus into handing over the reins of power and becomes the new family tyrant. " . . . a witches' brew of blackmail, insanity, cruelty, theft, torture, insult, drunkenness, with a trace of incest thrown in for good measure . . ." (*New York Times*). " . . . one of the most fascinating plays of the contemporary American theatre" (*Post*). *Another Part of the Forest* marked the Broadway debut of Patricia Neal as Regina, the girl portrayed as a woman by Tallulah Bankhead in *The Little Foxes* (1939). Other standouts in a uniformly excellent company were Margaret Phillips as Birdie, the poverty-stricken aristocrat, and Jean Hagen (deb.) as a town trollop. C: Bartlett Robinson, Beatrice Thompson, Paul Ford. P: Kermit Bloomgarden. D: Lillian Hellman. CD: Lucinda Ballard. SD: Jo Mielziner. M: Marc Blitzstein.

SV: U, 1948, Fredric March, Ann Blyth, Edmond O'Brien, Dan Duryea, Florence Eldridge, John Dall, Betsy Blair, Donna Drake, Fritz Leiber (directed by Michael Gordon).

See *The Little Foxes*.

Another Sun (2/23/40, National, 11)

Play by columnist Dorothy Thompson and actor Fritz Kortner (D) dealing with the plight of World War II refugees trying to make a new life for themselves in New York City. "Awkwardly, aimlessly written, missing almost all the excitement inherent in its theme" (*Sun*). C: Hans Jaray (deb.), Celeste Holm, McKay Morris, Arnold Korff, Herbert Rudley, Leo Bulgakov. P: Cheryl Crawford.

Antonia (10/20/25, Empire, 55)

Opera star (Marjorie Rambeau) leaves the ha-cha-cha life in Budapest and retires to a farm, but the lure of the bright lights is too much for her. George Cukor made his Broadway directorial bow with this tedious romantic drama adapted, and extensively revised, by Arthur Richman from a play by Melchior Lengyel. C: Philip Merivale, Ilka Chase, Lumsden Hare, George Renavent. P: Charles Frohman, Inc.

Any Wednesday (2/18/64, Music Box, 982)

Frothy four-character sex farce about a lecherous millionaire (Don Porter), his kooky mistress (Sandy Dennis), his deceived wife (Rosemary Murphy), and an irate salesman (Gene Hackman). The salesman acts as catalyst when he accidentally discovers that the tycoon has ensconced the pretty, young mistress in his corporation's executive suite, and is writing off the expense as a tax-deductible entertainment item. ". . . a neat, nice and awfully funny comedy" (*Women's Wear Daily*). *Any Wednesday*, which almost folded during its out-of-town tryouts due to producer-director-cast disagreements and generally negative reviews, opened on Broadway without advance interest or enthusiasm. It turned out to be the surprise hit of the theatre season and ran a highly profitable 982 performances. It was author Muriel Resnik's first play. She later sold the screen rights to Warner Brothers for three-quarters of a million dollars. P: George, Granat, Erskine, Katz and Specter. D: Henry Kaplan. CD: Theoni V. Aldredge. SD: Robert Randolph.

    SV: WB, 1966, Jane Fonda, Jason Robards, Dean Jones, Rosemary Murphy (directed by Robert Miller).

Anybody Home (2/25/49, Golden, 5)

Dashing bachelor threatens the marriage of a restless wife and her stuffy husband. "My new candidate for the worst-play-ever-produced-on-any-stage honors" (*Sun*). "I herewith publicly apologize to the author of any play which in the past I may have described as the worst I ever saw" (George Jean Nathan). C: Donald Curtis, Phyllis Holden (P). A: Robert Pyzel. D: Ralph Forbes.

Anything Might Happen (2/20/23, Comedy, 64)

Nice cast—Roland Young, Estelle Winwood, Leslie Howard—trapped in a feeble, virtually plotless triangle comedy by Edgar Selwyn (A/P/D).

Apology (3/22/43, Mansfield, 8)

The life of a ruthless businessman as explained by a lady lecturer (Elissa Landi). ". . . a dull and obvious fantasy, with about as much depth as a guppy bowl" (*Herald Tribune*). A: Charles Schnee. P/D: Lee Strasberg.

Appearances (10/13/25, Frolic, 23)

Negro defends himself against a false charge of rape. Well-intended but clumsy 1925 drama by black playwright Garland Anderson. P: Lester W. Sagar. D: John Hayden.

Apple, The (12/7/61, Living Theatre, 64)

Jack Gelber's avant-garde O/B oddity in which actors using their own names invent various characters and improvise haphazard irrelevancies. A disjointed, self-indulgent bit of abstract nothingness. C: Julian Beck (SD), James Earl Jones, Fred Miller. P: The Living Theatre. D: Judith Malina.

Apple of His Eye (2/5/46, Biltmore, 118)

Comedy about the May-December romance between an elderly Indiana farmer (Walter Huston) and the pretty young girl (Mary James) who comes to tend his house and remains to fall in love with him. ". . . a placid, slow-motion and flimsy little play. . . . It isn't worth Walter Huston's time" (*Sun*). C: Doro Merande, Mary Wickes, Joseph Sweeney, Arthur Hunnicutt, Tom Ewell, Clare Woodbury, Roy Fant. A: Kenyon Nicholson and Charles Robinson. P: Jed Harris (D) i.a.w. Walter Huston.

Note: Apple of His Eye marked Walter Huston's last Broadway appearance.

Applesauce (9/28/25, Ambassador, 90)

Amiable little farce about a small-town backslapper who tells people what they want to hear. C: Alan Dinehart (D), Walter Connolly, Gladys Lloyd. A: Barry

Conners. P: Richard Herndon.
SV: WB, 1936, *Brides Are Like That*, Ross Alexander, Anita Louise, Gene Lockhart.

Apron Strings (2/17/30, Bijou, 226)

After his mother's death, a young man finds his life governed by a series of letters which that good woman left behind for his instruction. Having no vices or weaknesses, this upright lad is forced to cultivate them in order to at last break free of his mother's apron strings. Pleasant homespun comedy. C: Roger Pryor, Jefferson De Angelis. A: Dorrance Davis. P: Forrest Haring. D: Earle Boothe.
SV: U, 1931, *Virtuous Husband*, Elliott Nugent, Jean Arthur.

Arab, The (9/20/11, Lyceum, 53)

Handsome desert sheik tames spoiled heiress. Edgar Selwyn (A/D) played the sheik in this crude "romantic melodrama." P: Henry B. Harris.
SV: MGM, 1933, *The Barbarian*, Ramon Novarro, Myrna Loy, C. Aubrey Smith, Edward Arnold, Reginald Denny.

Are You Decent? (4/19/34, Ambassador, 188)

Liberated female decides to become a mother without benefit of clergy. Execrable comedy. "Excuse me for mentioning it, but a play called *Are You Decent?* opened last night" (John Mason Brown, *Post*). C: Claudia Morgan, Eric Dressler, Lester Vail. A: Crane Wilbur. P: Albert Bannister. D: Dmitri Ostrov.

Argyle Case, The (12/24/12, Criterion, 191)

A quick-witted detective (Robert Hilliard) investigates the murder of a capitalist. Lively whodunit with the detective in the case patterned after William J. Burns, early director of the FBI and founder of Burns International Detective Agency. A: Harriet Ford and Harvey O'Higgins (in cooperation with William J. Burns). P: Klaw and Erlanger. D: Robert Hilliard and Gustav Von Seyfferitz.
SV: WB, 1929, Thomas Meighan, H.B. Warner, Lila Lee, Zasu Pitts.

Aries Is Rising (11/21/39, Golden, 7)

Dreadful comedy about a would-be starlet and her doting mother. Co-authored by Caroline North and celebrity arbiter-chronicler Earl Blackwell. C: Blanche Sweet, Constance Collier, Mary Mason, John Craven, Bernardine Hayes. P: Irving and Dolan. D: Robert Ross.

Arizona (9/10/00, Herald Square, 140)

When an Arizona rancher is threatened by massacring Indians, a brave lieutenant gets through the Indian lines and brings the Cavalry to the rescue. *Arizona*, a smash hit melodrama by Augustus Thomas, started a vogue called "the western." Its success spawned an endless series of imitations on stage (and subsequently, of course, on screen). C: Theodore Roberts, Vincent Serrano, Walter Hale, Edgar Selwyn, Eleanor Robson, Louise Closser Hale. P: La Shelle and Hamlin.
R: (4/28/13, Lyric, 40) by William A. Brady. C: Dustin Farnum, William Farnum, Vincent Serrano, Chrystal Herne, Elsie Ferguson. D: Augustus Thomas.
Musicalized by Sigmund Romberg as *The Love Call* (1927).
SV: Col, 1931, *Men Are Like That*, John Wayne, Laura La Plante. A subsequent Columbia release (1940) with William Holden and Jean Arthur retained little but the title of the play.

Arms and the Girl (9/27/16, Fulton, 77)

Comedy that tried to extract laughter from the plight of American idlers stranded amidst the ruins of Belgium during the early days of World War I.

Ruth Sherwood (Fay Bainter), a piquant young charmer from Indiana, blandly introduces a fellow American (Cyril Scott) as her fiancé to save him from being shot as a spy by the conquering Germans. Naturally, to allay the suspicions of the Prussians, a mock wedding and honeymoon must then be arranged. The story, according to the reviewer for the *New York Times,* started out as "an amusing little romance" that curdled as it approached its climax: "The climax is so silly that it suggests not merely fatigue, but a sheer paralysis of the faculty of invention." A: Grant Stewart and Robert Baker. P: William Harris, Jr. D: Paul Dickey.

Around the Corner (12/28/36, 48th Street, 16)

Charles Coburn starred in this humdrum comedy-drama about the problems of a Depression-era family in the Midwest. C: Merle Maddern, Milburn Stone, Lillian Emerson. A: Martin Flavin. P: Lodewick Vroom. D: Bertram Harrison.

Arrest That Woman (9/18/36, National, 7)

Prostitute becomes involved in a murder case. Old-hat courtroom melodrama. C: Doris Nolan, Hugh Marlowe (deb.). A: Maxine Alton. P: A. H. Woods. D: Ira Hards.

Arsenic and Old Lace (1/10/41, Fulton, 1,444)

The famous farce about a pair of gentle Brooklyn spinsters (Josephine Hull and Jean Adair) whose hobby is murdering lonely old men and burying the bodies in their cellar. The arrival of a sinister nephew (Boris Karloff), with a body of his own to dispose of, triggers a series of gleefully ghoulish complications. "The theatre, which is several thousand years old, has never produced anything like *Arsenic and Old Lace.* And in case you're not impressed by the fact that it's different and unusual, you might like to know it's also screamingly funny" (*PM*). ". . . so sidesplitting and terrific that it can be guaranteed to make even dramatic critics care for the theatre" (*Post*). This bizarre mixture of mayhem and merriment was written by former music teacher and actor Joseph Kesselring. Originally titled *Bodies in our Cellar,* the play was, from all accounts, a straightforward melodrama of the creaking door, shrieks-in-the-night variety. Producers Howard Lindsay and Russel Crouse took the script under their wing. There was much speculation at the time that Lindsay and Crouse played pivotal roles in restructuring and rewriting the Kesselring opus, a charge vigorously denied by all three gentlemen. In any event, *Arsenic and Old Lace* proved to be the biggest surprise hit of the wartime years. It was shrewdly staged and splendidly acted, especially by Josephine Hull as Abby Brewster, the more fluttery and scatterbrained of the two pixilated poisoners. Boris Karloff made his Broadway debut in the play as Jonathan Brewster, the old ladies' congenitally nasty nephew ("the kind of boy who liked to cut worms in two with his teeth"). The celebrated screen bogeyman suffered terrible pangs of stage fright during rehearsals, and begged to be relieved from his contract. By opening night, however, Karloff was in fine form, and received notices to gladden the heart of any actor. The role of Jonathan subsequently was played by such movie menaces as Bela Lugosi and Erich von Stroheim, with Raymond Massey inheriting the part in the 1944 screen version. C: Allyn Joslyn, Helen Brooks, Edgar Stehli, John Alexander, Anthony Ross, Henry Herbert. D: Bretaigne Windust. SD: Raymond Sovey.

SV: WB, 1944, Cary Grant, Priscilla Lane, Raymond Massey, Peter Lorre, Jack Carson, Josephine Hull, Jean Adair, James Gleason, Edward Everett Horton (directed by Frank Capra).

As a Man Thinks (3/13/11, Thirty-Ninth Street, 128)

Under the ministrations of a "mental healer" (John Mason), an errant wife (Chrystal Herne) is reunited with her family. Compact, effective 1911 drama by Augustus Thomas (A/D). P: Messrs. Shubert.

As Good as New (11/3/30, Times Square, 56)

When a husband cheats on his wife with her best friend, she retaliates by taking a lover. Meandering comedy by Thompson Buchanan. C: Otto Kruger, Vivienne Osborne, Majorie Gateson. P: Charles Dillingham. D: Stanley Logan.

SV: WB, 1934, *Easy to Love,* Mary Astor, Adolphe Menjou, Genevieve Tobin, Edward Everett Horton, Hugh Herbert, Guy Kibbee, Patricia Ellis, Hobart Cavanaugh.

As Husbands Go (3/5/31, Golden, 148)

Restless wife gives up British lover to remain with dull but devoted husband. Popular, shrewdly written Rachel Crothers (A/D) domestic comedy. C: Lily Cahill, Jay Fassett, Catherine Doucet, Roman Bohnen, Geoffrey Wardwell. P: John Golden.

SV: Fox, 1934, Warner Baxter, Helen Vinson, Warner Oland.

Ask My Friend Sandy (2/4/43, Biltmore, 12)

Book publisher (Roland Young) is talked into giving away his fortune by a brash young soldier (Norman Lloyd). ". . . sleepy and slow and not funny" (*New York Times*). "Norman Lloyd as Sandy reminded us of a very talkative parrot in an Army uniform" (*Post*). A: Stanley Young. P/D: Alfred de Liagre, Jr.

Assassin, The (10/17/45, National, 13)

Misguided attempt by Irwin Shaw to dramatize, in semidocumentary fashion, the murder of Admiral Darlan. ". . . loose, talky and theatrical" (*Sun*). C: Frank Sundstrom, Roger De Koven, Harold Huber, Karl Malden, Clay Clement, Carmen Mathews. P: Carly Wharton and Martin Gabel (D). SD: Boris Aronson.

Note: Jean François Darlan, French admiral, advocated collaboration with Germany. He subsequently went over to the Allied cause and was appointed high commissioner in French North and West Africa. He was assassinated in December 1942.

At Bay (10/7/13, 39th Street, 119)

An amateur detective (Guy Standing) rescues a District Attorney's daughter (Chrystal Herne) from the clutches of a blackmailing lawyer. "Excellent melodramatic entertainment" (*New York Times*). A: George Scarborough. P: Messrs. Shubert.

At 9:45 (6/28/19, Playhouse, 139)

Who shot Judge Clayton's son? Fair Owen Davis mystery melodrama; few surprises. C: Harry Green, Clifford Dempsey, Nedda Harrigan. P: William A. Brady. D: John Cromwell.

At War with the Army (3/8/49, Booth, 151)

Slapdash farce about training camp life and the problems, military and romantic, of a harried first sergeant (Gary Merrill). Highlight: a recalcitrant soft drink machine suddenly coming to life and emptying itself in jackpot fashion. "It is a comedy with funny things, rather than a funny comedy" (*Post*). C: Sara Seegar, Mike Kellin, Tad Mosel, Maxine Stuart, Sally Gracie. A: James B. Allardice. P: May, Rosenfeld, and McCallum. D: Ezra Stone.

SV: Par, 1950, Dean Martin, Jerry Lewis, Polly Bergen.

The Auctioneer. **Scene with David Warfield from the revival production (September 30, 1913).** *Courtesy Museum of the City of New York Theatre and Music Collection.*

Auctioneer, The (9/23/01, Bijou, 105)

A Jewish auctioneer (David Warfield) inherits a modest fortune, loses it in a swindle, and finally regains it through the efforts of his prospective son-in-law. Sentimental hokum, very nicely acted by Warfield, a former dialect comedian of Weber and Fields' Music Hall, here making his debut as a Broadway star. Thanks to such stage successes as *The Auctioneer* (together with prudent investments), David Warfield amassed twelve million dollars before his death in 1951. A: Lee Arthur and Charles Klein. P/D: David Belasco.

Auntie Mame (10/31/56, Broadhurst, 639)

More a series of freewheeling revue sketches than a play, this immensely popular fabrication recounts the now-familiar tale of a madcap adventuress who takes her orphaned nephew under her wing and introduces him to the bohemian life in America, c. 1928–46. Along the way, Auntie Mame finds time to marry (briefly) into southern gentility, and to expose the family of her nephew's fiancée as stuffy nitwits. But primarily the show was designed as a cartoon-styled portrait of a lovable lunatic, a tailor-made vehicle for the bravura comedic talents of star Rosalind Russell. Greer Garson and Beatrice Lillie (who played Mame in the 1958 London production) succeeded Miss Russell on Broadway; Sylvia Sidney and Constance Bennett were among the ladies who essayed the role on tour. C: Polly Rowles, Peggy Cass, Marian Winters, Robert Smith, Robert Higgins, Jan Handzlik, Cris Alexander, James Monks. A:

Jerome Lawrence and Robert E. Lee, b/o the novel by Patrick Dennis. P: Fryer and Carr. D: Morton DaCosta. SD: Oliver Smith.

Musicalized by Lawrence and Lee and Jerry Herman as *Mame* (1966) with Angela Lansbury, Beatrice Arthur, Jane Connell, Willard Waterman.

SV: WB, 1958, Rosalind Russell, Forrest Tucker, Coral Browne, Fred Clark, Roger Smith, Patric Knowles, Joanna Barnes, Jan Handzlik, Lee Patrick, Willard Waterman, Connie Gilchrist (directed by Morton DaCosta from a screenplay by Betty Comden and Adolph Green); 1974, *Mame*, Lucille Ball, Beatrice Arthur, Robert Preston, Jane Connell, Bruce Davison, Don Porter, Audrey Christie, John McGiver (directed by Gene Saks from a screenplay by Paul Zindel).

Autumn Garden, The (3/7/51, Coronet, 101)

Lillian Hellman's introspective comedy about a group of unhappy, discontented middle-aged idlers in a summer resort on the Gulf of Mexico. The play's catalyst is a bustling, self-important artist (Fredric March) who likes to meddle in other people's affairs. It is he who forces the other characters to accept the fact that what they have now become is what they made of themselves in earlier years. "An intelligent comedy" (*News*). "A room full of men and women arbitrarily suffering from nothing but the calendar. . . . A diffuse and somnambulistic play" (George Jean Nathan). C: Florence Eldridge, Ethel Griffies, Kent Smith, Jane Wyatt, Colin Keith-Johnston, Carol Goodner, Joan Lorring, James Lipton, Margaret Barker. P: Kermit Bloomgarden. D: Harold Clurman. SD: Howard Bay.

Autumn Hill (4/13/42, Booth, 8)

Counterfeiters take over the home of a New England spinster (Beth Merrill). Dull melodrama by John Harris and Norma Mitchell, coauthor of *Cradle Snatchers* (1925) and *Post Road* (1934). P: Max Liebman. D: Ronald Hammond.

Avanti! (1/31/68, Booth, 21)

A stuffy American businessman visits Italy to claim the body of his recently deceased father, and falls in love with the kooky daughter of his late dad's mistress. This 1968 comedy* by Samuel Taylor had its share of bright lines, but the play's overall impression was somewhat less than satisfactory. Standout performance: Keith Baxter as a cheerfully amoral Italian bisexual who is, at all times, perfectly willing to accommodate the heroine—or the hero. C: Robert Reed, Jennifer Hilary, Betsy von Furstenberg. P: Morris Jacobs and Jerome Whyte i.a.w. Richard Rodgers. D: Nigel Patrick. SD: Donald Oenslager.

SV: UA, 1972, Jack Lemmon, Juliet Mills, Clive Revill (directed by Billy Wilder).

---

*Produced in London (1975) as *A Touch of Spring* with Hayley Mills, Peter Donat, and Leigh Lawson in the leading roles.

Aviator, The (12/6/10, Astor, 44)

A neurasthenic young fellow (Wallace Eddinger), afraid of anything that goes up (including elevators), becomes a pilot. Primitive but funny farce. A: James Montgomery. P: Cohan and Harris. D: Sam Forrest.

Musicalized by Louis A. Hirsch as *Going Up* (1917) with Frank Craven, Donald Meek, Ruth Donnelly, Edith Day, Marion Sunshine.

SV: WB, 1930, Edward Everett Horton, Patsy Ruth Miller; 1931, *Going Wild*, Joe E. Brown, Walter Pidgeon, Frank McHugh, Ona Munson, Lawrence Gray.

Awake and Sing! (2/19/35, Belasco, 184)

Clifford Odets' first full-length play; probably the most successful treatment of bourgeois Bronx life ever written. *Awake and Sing!* deals in Chekhovian terms with the disintegration of the Bergers, a lower middle-class family struggling to survive the Depression in a Bronx tenement. Here frustration and argument are the norm, and life is "printed on dollar bills." The dominant characters in the play are Bessie, the grasping, abrasively disagreeable mother, and Ralph, the idealistic son who desperately wants a chance to break free from the unjust coercion of the family. In the end, the suicide of his wise and loving grandfather frees Ralph from the tyranny of his mother. "A well-balanced, meticulously observed, always interesting and ultimately quite moving drama" (John Mason Brown). A harsh and turbulent protest against the injustices of the capitalist system, *Awake and Sing!* gained for twenty-nine-year-old Clifford Odets the reputation of being America's most promising young playwright and a possible successor to Eugene O'Neill. This was a promise not borne out by Odets' later work. C: Stella Adler, Jules (John) Garfield, Luther Adler, Morris Carnovsky, Art Smith, Phoebe Brand, J. Edward Bromberg, Sanford Meisner, Roman Bohnen. P: The Group Theatre. D: Harold Clurman. SD: Boris Aronson. Revived O/B (5/27/70, Bijou, 41) with a cast headed by Joan Lorring, Robert Salvio, Salem Ludwig, and Bill Macy. D: Arthur Seidelman.

Awake and Sing, by Clifford Odets. **Stella Adler and J. E. Bromberg (1935).** *Courtesy Museum of the City of New York Theatre and Music Collection.*

Awakening of Helena Richie, The (9/20/09, Savoy, 120)

Lugubrious tale of a young woman (Margaret Anglin) abandoned by her selfish lover. A: Charlotte Thompson, based on a novel by Margaret Deland.

Awful Truth, The (9/18/22, Henry Miller, 146)

Lucy Warriner (Ina Claire) has to summon her first husband to satisfy prospective husband number two that no hint of scandal accompanied her divorce. Lucy and husband number one fall in love anew and end up at the altar once again. Highly entertaining comedy. C: Bruce McRae, Paul Harvey, Raymond Walburn, Cora Witherspoon. A: Arthur Richman. P: Charles Frohman, Inc.

SV: Pathe, 1929, Ina Claire, Henry Daniell, Paul Harvey; Col, 1937, Irene Dunne, Cary Grant, Ralph Bellamy; 1953, *Let's Do It Again*, Jane Wyman, Ray Milland, Aldo Ray.

B

Bab (10/18/20, Park, 88)

Helen Hayes' first starring role on Broadway. Gossamer-thin little comedy about an 18-year-old subdeb and the havoc she raises when she fabricates a love affair for herself. The years following *Bab* found Helen Hayes cast in nothing but comedy-type ingenue roles "until," sighed Miss Hayes, "I was squeezing cuteness out of my grease paint tubes and scooping charm out of my cold cream jars. It became a compulsion to get away from all that!" A: Edward Childs Carpenter, adapted from the novel by Mary Roberts Rinehart. P: George C. Tyler. D: Ignacio Martinetti.

Baby Cyclone (9/12/27, Henry Miller, 187)

A young married couple (Spencer Tracy and Nan Sunderland) engage in a heated tug of war over the wife's pet Pekingese.

Baby Cyclone. Charles McCarthy, Natalie Moorhead, Spencer Tracy, Nan Sunderland, and Grant Mitchell (September 12, 1927). *Courtesy Museum of the City of New York Theatre and Music Collection.*

Airy bit of nothing by George M. Cohan (A/P), who wrote the role of the long-suffering husband especially for Tracy. "Spencer Tracy does the outstanding work of the evening, making the role ... both amusing as farce and credible as characterization" (*New York Times*). C: Grant Mitchell, Georgia Caine. D: Sam Forrest.

Baby Mine (8/23/10, Daly's, 287)

To win back her errant husband, a wife pretends she has become a mother. When a bumbling friend arranges to "borrow" a baby, the complications begin. Absurd situation farce tickled the 1910 national funny bone and had a highly profitable Broadway engagement. C: Ernest Glendinning, Marguerite Clark. A: Margaret Mayo. P: William A. Brady. R: (6/9/27, 46th Street, 12) by John Tuerk. C: Humphrey Bogart, Lee Patrick, Roscoe ("Fatty") Arbuckle.

Baby Want a Kiss (4/19/64, Little, 145)

That celebrated film couple, Paul Newman and Joanne Woodward, came to Broadway in this comedy which tried to satirize the American Dream of Success but, despite witty lines, never found a satisfactory mode for doing so. With hints along the way of Albee, Ionesco, and Pirandello, the shred of plot has an unsuccessful writer (James Costigan) hosting a reunion for old friends Paul and Joanne, here called Emil and Mavis, famous movie stars. The three characters talk and talk, in the process exposing the pretensions of the illustrious pair amusingly but not incisively. The ultimate effect is blurry. ". . . more fun for those who are in it than those who were at it" (*News*). A: James Costigan. P: The Actors Studio. D: Frank Corsaro.

Bachelor Father, The (2/28/28, Belasco, 264)

Amusing comedy about an old codger (C. Aubrey Smith) who sends for three of his illegitimate offspring, from different parts of the world, and installs them in the ancestral manse in Surrey. C: June Walker, Geoffrey Kerr, Viola Roache, Rex O'Malley. A: Edward Childs Carpenter. P/D: David Belasco.
SV: MGM, 1931, Marion Davies, C. Aubrey Smith, Ralph Forbes, Raymond (Ray) Milland.

Bachelor's Baby, The (12/27/09, Criterion, 192)

A baby-hating bachelor becomes the guardian of a four-year-old child. Sentimental comedy-farce by and with Francis Wilson. P: Charles Frohman.

Back Here (11/26/28, Klaw, 8)

A tough Irish sergeant (Melvyn Douglas), recuperating from battle wounds in a veterans' hospital, has his faith restored when he finds true love with a taxi dancer. Painfully mawkish 20's drama. C: Peggy Shannon, Jean Dixon, George Meeker, Kitty Kelly. A: Olga Printzlau. P: William A. Brady i.a.w. I. H. Herk. D: Victor Morley.

Back Pay (8/30/21, Eltinge, 79)

Fannie Hurst tearjerker about a prostitute (Helen MacKellar) with "a crêpe de chine soul" who gives up everything to nurse her blinded sweetheart. When he dies, she renounces the easy life to clerk in a department store. P: A. H. Woods. D: E. F. Bostwick.
SV: WB, 1930, Corinne Griffith, Grant Withers, Montagu Love.

Bad Girl (10/2/30, Hudson, 85)

The marital problems of a moist-eyed Bronx typist (Sylvia Sidney) and the irresponsible young fellow (Paul Kelly) she weds and eventually reforms. Moderately successful tearjerker by Vina Delmar and Brian Marlow b/o Miss Delmar's best-selling novel. P: Robert

Bachelor Father. **(February 28, 1928).** *Courtesy Museum of the City of New York Theatre and Music Collection.*

Newman. D: Marion Gering.
SV: Fox, 1931, James Dunn, Sally Eilers.

Bad Man, The (8/30/20, Comedy, 320)

Pancho Villa, here called Pancho Lopez, sets an American girl free from her cruel husband by the simple expedient of shooting him. ". . . occasionally exciting and almost continuously amusing" (Alexander Woollcott, *New York Times*). A big factor in the success of *The Bad Man* was the excellent performance given by Holbrook Blinn in the role of Lopez, the *sympatico* Mexican bandit. C: Frank Conroy, Frances Carson, Edna Hibbard, James Bell, Chief White Hawk. A: Porter Emerson Brown. P: William Harris, Jr. D: Lester Lonergan.

SV: WB, 1930, Walter Huston, Sidney Blackmer, James Rennie; Par, 1934, *The Trumpet Blows*, George Raft, Adolphe Menjou; WB, 1937, *West of Shanghai*, Boris Karloff, Ricardo Cortez, Beverly Roberts; MGM, 1941, Wallace Beery, Lionel Barrymore, Ronald Reagan, Laraine Day, Henry Travers, Tom Conway, Chill Wills.

Bad Manners (1/30/33, Playhouse, 8)

Young girl (Margaret Sullavan) moves into the apartment of a middle-aged playboy (Bert Lytell). The relationship—platonic at the outset—ends in love and marriage. Woefully thin comedy by Dana Burnet and William B. Jutte. P/D: Brady and Wiman.

Bad Seed, The (12/8/54, 46th Street, 334)

A mother discovers that her angelic-seeming nine-year-old daughter has calmly committed three cold-blooded murders. The mother herself turns out to be the child of a celebrated mass murderess, and it is the thesis of the play that the instinct for killing had been passed on to the granddaughter. "Geneticists are likely to quarrel with its theme of wholly hereditary evil [but] . . . it is a genuine fourteen-carat, fifteen-below chiller" *(Herald Tribune)*. C: Nancy Kelly, Patty McCormack, Henry Jones, Eileen Heckart, Evelyn Varden, Thomas Chalmers, Lloyd Gough A: Maxwell Anderson b/o the novel by William March. P: The Playwrights Company. D: Reginald Denham. SD: George Jenkins.

SV: Filmed by Warner Brothers (1956) with substantially the same cast as appeared in the Broadway stage production. The screen version was directed by Mervyn LeRoy.

Badges (12/3/24, 49th Street, 104)

Bumbling young fellow (Gregory Kelly) solves mystery involving a pretty girl (Lotus Robb) and a gang of clever stock and bond thieves. Reasonably lively comedy-melodrama by Max Marcin and Edward Hammond. P: Jules Hurtig. D: Edgar MacGregor.

SV: Fox, 1929, *The Ghost Talks*, Helen Twelvetrees, Charles Eaton, Clifford Dempsey, Stepin Fetchit.

Ballad of the Sad Cafe, The (10/30/63, Martin Beck, 123)

Edward Albee's dramatization of Carson McCullers' southern-gothic novella in which an ex-convict husband is in love with his mannish wife, the wife with a hunchbacked dwarf, and the dwarf with the husband. No good comes to any of the three characters. Each is destroyed by the one he loves, and by the unpredictability of love itself. "The play is not only dark inside, it is emotionally impenetrable. . . . In spite of vivid things in it, it ends as speculative grotesquerie" *(Herald Tribune)*. C: Colleen Dewhurst, Lou Antonio, Michael Dunn, Roscoe Lee Browne, William Prince, Enid Markey, Jenny Egan, John C. Becher, Roberts Blossom. P: Lewis Allen and Ben Edwards (SD). D: Alan Schneider. M: William Flanagan.

Ballyhoo (1/4/27, 49th Street, 7)

Playboy falls in love with circus bareback rider. Dreary true-confessions yarn. C: Minna Gombell, Eric Dressler, Hugh O'Connell. A: Kate Horton. P: Russell Janney. D: Richard Boleslawski.*

---

*Hollywood director (1930–37); films include *Rasputin and the Empress*, *Clive of India*, *Theodora Goes Wild*, etc.

Banco (9/20/22, Ritz, 70)

Rakish gambler (Alfred Lunt) pursues his ex-wife and wins her back. Tiresome comedy. C: Lola Fisher, Edward G. Robinson, Charlotte Granville. A: Clare Kummer, from a play by Alfred Savoir. P: William Harris, Jr. D: Robert Milton.

Barber Had Two Sons, The (2/1/43, Playhouse, 24)

Dismal anti-Nazi melodrama about a Norwegian mother (Blanche Yurka) and her two sons, one a patriot, and the other a traitor. "The plot thickened until it curdled" *(Post)*. A: Thomas Duggan and James Hogan. P: Jess Smith. D: Melville Burke.

Barber of New Orleans, The (1/15/09, Daly's, 27)

Miscegenation in old Louisiana, c. 1800. Tasteless mixture of drama, comedy, and melodrama. C: William Faversham, Berton Churchill, Percy Waram. A: Edward Childs Carpenter. P/D: Faversham.

Barchester Towers (11/30/37, Martin Beck, 37)

Social crises erupt with the appointment of a new bishop in an English cathedral town. Dawdling dramatization of the Anthony Trollope novel was not one of Ina Claire's happiest vehicles. C: John Williams, J. M. Kerrigan, Damian O'Flynn, Effie Shannon, Ruth Matteson, Florence Edney. A: Thomas Job. P/D: Guthrie McClintic. SD: Jo Mielziner.

Barefoot in Athens (10/31/51, Martin Beck, 30)

Maxwell Anderson's historical play dealing with the last days of Socrates when he faces charges of treason against the state. "...a drama of absorbing interest" (*Post*). "Most of it is not only barefoot but heavy-footed and slow" (*New York Times*). C: Barry Jones, Lotte Lenya, Philip Coolidge, George Mathews, William Hansen, Daniel Reed, David J. Stewart. P: The Playwrights Company. D: Alan Anderson. SD: Boris Aronson.

Barefoot in the Park (10/23/63, Biltmore, 1,532)

Neil Simon's featherweight frolic about the marital difficulties of Manhattan newlyweds (Robert Redford and Elizabeth Ashley) as they try to cope with life in a tiny, unfurnished, fifth-story walkup apartment. Critical kudos were accorded all concerned, including Mike Nichols for his impeccable staging and Mildred Natwick for her portrayal of a delightfully daffy mother-in-law. "The funniest comedy I can remember" (*Journal-American*). "Breezy, amiably idiotic and irresistibly funny" (*Herald Tribune*). Neil Simon's second Broadway play, *Barefoot in the Park* tried out in Bucks County under the title *Nobody Loves Me*. It seemed "dismal to me," said its author. When it reached New York, it lasted 1,532 performances, making it the eighth longest-running nonmusical offering in Broadway history. C: Kurt Kasznar, Herb Edelman, Joseph Keating. P: Saint Subber. CD: Donald Brooks. SD: Oliver Smith.

SV: Par, 1967, Robert Redford, Jane Fonda, Mildred Natwick, Charles Boyer, Herb Edelman, Mabel Albertson, Fritz Feld (directed by Gene Saks).

Barker, The (1/18/27, Biltmore, 225)

Fast-talking pitchman (Walter Huston) tries to break up the romance of his college-educated son (Norman Foster)* and an exotic snake charmer (Claudette Colbert). Colorful, entertaining melodrama of carnival life; good supporting performance by George Barbier as the flustered, sputtering owner of the tent show. A: Kenyon Nicholson.** P: Charles L. Wagner i.a.w. Edgar Selwyn. D: Priestly Morrison.

SV: Fox, 1933, *Hoopla*, Clara Bow, Preston Foster.

---

*Film director Norman Foster (*Journey Into Fear, Rachel and The Stranger,* etc.) married leading lady Claudette Colbert in 1928. They were divorced in 1935.
**Kenyon Nicholson gathered material for *The Barker* by the simple expedient of joining a traveling carnival. Nicholson later co-authored the 500-performance comedy hit *Sailor, Beware!* (1933).

Barnum Was Right (3/12/23, Frazee, 88)

Exuberant young man turns dilapidated old homestead into ritzy resort. Silly farce. C: Donald Brian, Marion Coakley, Enid Markey, Lilyan Tashman. A: Philip Bartholomae and John Meehan (D). P: Louis Werba.

SV: U, 1929, Glenn Tryon.

Bat, The (8/23/20, Morosco, 878)

Of the hundreds of pre-World War II mystery plays, none was more popular than *The Bat*, a shivery concoction laced with comic relief that ran on Broadway for 878 performances. It told the complicated tale of a wise dowager and her

frightened maid who foil an unknown killer in the spooky mansion that they've rented for the summer. Hidden somewhere in the house is the loot from a recent bank robbery. Four different people arc after the money, including an archcriminal known only as The Bat. In the end, it is the supposed detective who turns out to be the notorious criminal. C: Effie Ellsler, May Vokes, Edward Ellis. A: Mary Roberts Rinehart and Avery Hopwood, from Miss Rinehart's novel, *The Circular Staircase*. P: Wagenhals and Kemper. D: Collin Kemper. R: (1/20/53, National, 23) by James Elliott. C: Lucile Watson, ZaSu Pitts, Shepperd Strudwick, Harry Bannister. D: Jonathan Seymour.
SV: UA, 1931, *The Bat Whispers,* Chester Morris, Una Merkel; AA, 1959, Vincent Price, Agnes Moorehead.

Battle, The (12/21/08, Savoy, 144)

A multimillionaire (Wilton Lackaye) manages to instill the capitalist virtues in his socialist-minded son (H. B. Warner). "*The Battle* is a capital and labor play written from the point of view of capital. [It] proves nothing, but its argument and action are entertaining" *(New York Times)*. C: Josephine Victor, Elsie Ferguson. A: Cleveland Moffett. P: Liebler and Co. D: Hugh Ford.

Battleship Gertie (1/18/35, Lyceum, 2)

Young seaman (Burgess Meredith) becomes involved with Japanese spies and a dim-witted female stowaway in Pearl Harbor. This 1935 naval comedy-farce was presented by Courtney Burr, producer of the smash hit nautical comedy, *Sailor, Beware!* (1933). In this case, lightning did not strike twice. *Battleship Gertie* was a two-performance disaster. C: Boyd Crawford, Helen Lynd, Harry Davenport, Horace MacMahon. A: Frederick Hazlitt Brennan. D: Arthur Sircom. SD: Boris Aronson.

Be Your Age (2/4/29, Belmont, 32)

Amorous widow (Spring Byington) undergoes rejuvenation treatment, then makes a play for the doctor. Silly comedy-drama. C: Romney Brent, Halliwell Hobbes. A: Thomas P. Robinson and Esther Willard Bates. P: Richard Herndon. D: Ira Hards.

Be Your Age (1/14/53, 48th Street, 5)

Comedy about a widower's attempts to break up the May-December romance of his schoolgirl daughter and a middle-aged Lothario. ". . . bathed in clichés of thought, action and writing" *(Post)*. C: Loring Smith, Conrad Nagel, Hildy Parks, Dean Harens, Lee Remick (deb.). A: Mary Orr and Reginald Denham (D). P: Alexander H. Cohen and Joseph Kipness i.a.w. M. K. Bauer. SD: Ralph Alswang.

Beaucaire (12/2/01, Herald Square, 64)

The adventure-loving Duc d'Orléans (Richard Mansfield) masquerades as a lowly barber. Roguish costume comedy by Booth Tarkington and Evelyn Greenleaf Sutherland. P/D: Mansfield. Musicalized by Andre Messager as *Monsieur Beaucaire* (1919) with Marion Green in the title role.
SV: Par, 1946, *Monsieur Beaucaire,* Bob Hope, Joan Caulfield, Joseph Schildkraut, Constance Collier, Reginald Owen.

Beautiful People, The (4/21/41, Lyceum, 120)

An indigent father, a son who writes novels consisting of one word, and a daughter who talks to mice live harmoniously together in a rickety mansion in San Francisco's Sunset District. Various friends wander in and out of this hospitable domicile. Eventually, a long-absent son comes home, and the play ends. William Saroyan wrote, produced, and directed this fanciful "fantastic comedy" which was nominated best play of the year by six leading New York drama critics. Other reviewers, such as the *New York Sun's* Richard Lockridge, found *The Beautiful People* only mildly amusing and at times "downright foolish." Most of the major characters were portrayed by unknown, inexperienced actors. Chorus girl Betsy Blair played the mice-loving sister, choreographer-dancer Eugene Loring was her brother, and artist Don Freeman impersonated the older brother who finally returns to his loving if somewhat unusual family. C: Curtis Cooksey, E. J. Ballantine.

Beauty Part, The (12/26/62, Music Box, 85)

S. J. Perelman's loosely connected satirical sketches in which a Candide-like youth, seeking to make his way in the arts, finds the hand of materialism sullying every aspect of American culture. This disjointed but often excruciatingly funny lampoon of twentieth-century cultural affectations was notable in that it enabled Bert Lahr (playing six different roles) to give one of the great comedic performances of his career. The New York newspaper blackout of 1962–63 was in large part responsible for keeping the production from reaching the audience it merited. *The Beauty Part* closed after a brief run of little more than ten weeks. C: Larry Hagman, Alice Ghostley, Charlotte Rae, David Doyle, Bernie West, Patricia Englund, William Le Massena, Arnold Soboloff, Sean Garrison. P: Michael Ellis i.a.w. Edmund Anderson. D: Noel Willman. SD: William Pitkin. CD: Alvin Colt.

Beclch (12/16/68, Gate, 48)

A merciless white queen (Jean David) torments her African subjects until the time for her ritual destruction arrives. "Exotic and fascinating" *(Newsday)* OB symbolic drama by Rochelle Owens, author of *Futz!* (1968); directed by Don Signore.

Beekman Place (10/7/64, Morosco, 29)

Lackluster drawing-room comedy about a temperamental violinist whose extramarital past catches up with him. Written, directed, and co-produced by Samuel Taylor, author of *The Happy Time* (1950), *Sabrina Fair* (1953), *The Pleasure of His Company* (1958), etc. C: Fernand Gravet, Arlene Francis, George Coulouris, Leora Dana, Laurence Luckinbill, Carol Booth, Mary Grace Canfield. P: Stevens, Taylor, Bonfils-Seawell. SD: Oliver Smith.

Bees and the Flowers, The (9/26/46, Cort, 28)

Divorcée tries to conceal a second marriage from her teenage children. "An exceedingly silly comedy . . ." *(PM)*. C: Barbara Robbins, Russell Hardie. A: Frederick Kohner and Albert Mannheimer (D). P: Mort Singer, Jr.

Before Morning (2/9/33, Ritz, 28)

Glamorous actress, suspected of poisoning her ex-lover, is blackmailed by a nefarious physician. Run-of-the-mill whodunit. C: Jessie Royce Landis, McKay Morris, John Litel, Louise Prussing, Louis Jean Heydt, Hugh Buckler, Clyde Fillmore. A: Edna and Edward P. Riley. P: Bannister and Norman. D: William B. Friedlander.

Before You Go (1/11/68, Henry Miller, 29) 29)

Caught in a thunderstorm, a homely bookkeeper (Marian Seldes) seeks shelter in the dingy Greenwich Village apartment of a lonely department store buyer (Gene Troobnick). How they reach for mutual understanding, and find love, provides the substance of this two-character comedy-drama. "Wry, perceptive, honest, sad, funny, and tender . . ." *(Time)*.

A: Lawrence Holofcener. P: Peregrine Productions. D: Mark Gordon.

Before You're 25 (4/16/29, Maxine Elliott's, 23)

When a radical editor lands in jail for his views, his pregnant common-law wife goes to live with his family. Discovering the joys of bourgeois life, she persuades her left-wing lothario to marry her and embrace a more conservative life style. Billed as "a gay comedy," but commonplace dialogue and characterization limited its mirth quota. C: Eric Dressler, Mildred McCoy, Josephine Hull, Ernest Glendinning. A: Kenyon Nicholson. P/D: Lawrence Boyd.

Beggar on Horseback (2/12/24, Broadhurst, 224)

"It's probably twenty years since I saw it for the sixth or seventh time and I'd like to see it again," Ogden Nash wrote this editor some years ago. The play Nash made reference to was *Beggar on Horseback,* an expressionistic dream fantasy by George S. Kaufman and Marc Connelly that remains to this day one of the brightest feathers in the cap of the American theatre. In the play, a struggling young composer (Roland Young) falls asleep and dreams what might befall him should he proceed with his plans to marry the daughter of a millionaire. In his dream, the bride's wedding bouquet is made of bank notes; his life is spent in manufacturing widgets (shades of *How To Succeed In Business Without Really Trying!*); he murders his impossible in-laws and is thereafter condemned to work in an art factory and produce made-to-order masterpieces. When he awakens from his nightmare, he is glad to break off the match and return to his equally impecunious sweetheart. This sprightly and imaginative satire on standardization, conformity, and big business materialism was hailed by critic Alexander Woollcott as "a small and facetious disturbance in the rear of the Church of the Gospel of Success." It was the best of the Kaufman-Connelly collaborations. C: George W. Barbier, Spring Byington, Kay Johnson, Osgood Perkins, Greta Nissen. P/D: Winthrop Ames. M: Deems Taylor. R: (5/14/70, Lincoln Center, 52) by The Repertory Theatre. C: Leonard Frey, Susan Watson, Biff McGuire. D: John Hirsch.

Beggars Are Coming to Town (10/27/45, Coronet, 25)

A gangster (Paul Kelly) seeks to square accounts when he returns, after fourteen years in prison, to find that his erstwhile partner (Luther Adler) has swindled him. ". . . written, played and staged like a Hollywood movie of the vintage of 1928" *(World-Telegram).* C: Dorothy Comingore, Adrienne Ames, Herbert Berghof, Tom Pedi, George Mathews, E. G. Marshall, Arthur Hunnicutt. A: Theodore Reeves. P: Oscar Serlin. D: Harold Clurman, CD: Ralph Alswang. SD: Jo Mielziner (with technical advice from restaurateur Vincent Sardi).

SV: Par, 1948, *I Walk Alone,* Burt Lancaster, Kirk Douglas, Lizabeth Scott, Wendell Corey, Marc Lawrence.

Behavior of Mrs. Crane, The (3/20/28, Erlanger's, 31)

Wife agrees to give spouse a divorce provided that he and his mistress find her a new husband. Promising comic notion handled without wit or flair. C: Margaret Lawrence, Isobel Elsom, Charles Trowbridge, Walter Connolly. A: Harry Segall. P: Eugene Parsons. D: Bertram Harrison.

Behind Red Lights (1/13/37, Mansfield, 176)

Murder in a high-priced whorehouse. Sleazy 30's melodrama by Samuel Shipman and Beth Brown b/o a novel by the latter. C: Dorothy Hall, Hardie Albright,

Bruce MacFarlane, Beatrice Kay, Edward Andrews. P: Jack Curtis. D: A. H. Van Buren.

Behold the Bridegroom (12/26/27, Cort, 88)

A spoiled and willful girl (Judith Anderson) comes too late upon the man who might have redeemed her. Interesting but uncertain George Kelly (A/D) character study. C: Jean Dixon, John Marston, Lester Vail, Thurston Hall. P: Rosalie Stewart.

Behold This Dreamer (10/31/27, Cort, 58)

Sensitive youth (Glenn Hunter) finds life in a mental institution preferable to life with his prosaic wife and family. Interesting comedy-drama billed as "a paradox in five scenes." A: Fulton Oursler and Aubrey Kennedy b/o Oursler's novel. P: George C. Tyler. D: Frederick Stanhope.

Believe Me, Xantippe (8/19/13, 39th Street, 79)

After committing a crime, a brash young man (John Barrymore) wagers he will be able to evade arrest for an entire year. He not only wins the bet, but also the sheriff's daughter. Entertaining farcical melodrama; a Harvard Prize Play by Frederick Ballard. C: Henry Hull, Mary Young, Katherine Harris, Theodore Roberts. P: William A. Brady. D: John Craig.

Bell, Book and Candle (11/14/50, Barrymore, 233)

A beguiling young witch (Lilli Palmer) casts a spell over an attractive publisher (Rex Harrison), but loses her occult powers when she falls in love with the man she hexed. Set in contemporary Manhattan, this airy fable by John Van Druten (A/D) was one of the comedy hits of 1950. "Completely enchanting . . . a wonderfully suave and impish fancy" *(New York Times)*. C: Jean Adair, Scott McKay, Larry Gates. P: Irene M. Selznick. SD: George Jenkins.

Note: The national touring company starred Rosalind Russell and Dennis Price and, subsequently, Joan Bennett and Zachary Scott.

SV: Col, 1958, James Stewart, Kim Novak, Jack Lemmon, Hermione Gingold, Ernie Kovacs, Elsa Lanchester (directed by Richard Quine).

Bell for Adano, A (12/6/44, Cort, 296)

Paul Osborn's dramatization of John Hersey's Pulitzer Prize novel concerning the efforts of an idealistic army administrator (Fredric March) to bring the tenets of American democracy to an occupied Sicilian town. "Well-written, well-acted, well-staged . . ." *(Journal-American)*. This 1940s drama, which played to capacity audiences throughout its run, marked an auspicious producing debut for former talent agent and artists' representative Leland Hayward. C: Margo, Everett Sloane, Tito Vuolo, Alexander Granach, Leon Rothier, Bruce MacFarlane, Harold J. Stone, Phil Arthur. D: H. C. Potter. CD/SD: Motley.

SV: Fox, 1945, John Hodiak, Gene Tierney, William Bendix, Richard Conte, Glenn Langan, Henry Morgan, Stanley Prager (directed by Henry King).

Bellamy Trial, The (4/22/31, 48th Street, 17)

Who killed the beautiful but wicked Madeleine Bellamy? Placid courtroom melodrama by Frances Noyes Hart and Frank E. Carstarphen b/o Mrs. Hart's novel. C: E. E. Clive (P/D), Philip Tonge, Viola Roache, Ian (John) Emery, Wilfrid Seagram.

SV: A part-talking screen version of the Frances Noyes Hart novel was filmed (MGM, 1929) with Leatrice Joy, Betty Bronson, and Edward Nugent heading the cast.

Belt, The (10/19/27, New Playwrights, 48)

Sputtering attack on Henry Ford and the deadly monotony of Detroit's factory system. Interesting premise shrilly and unconvincingly developed. Produced by the radical-oriented New Playwrights Theatre (backed by millionaire art patron Otto Kahn). C: Ross Matthews, Lawrence Bolton, Franchot Tone (deb.). A: Paul Sifton. D: Edward Massey.

Berkeley Square (11/4/29, Lyceum, 227)

"Berkeley Square—I thought it would look like this!" murmurs Peter Standish (Leslie Howard) appreciatively, seeing the home of his ancestors for the first time. Transported back to the year 1784, but knowing the future, young Standish is constantly making *faux pas*. He falls in love with Helen Pettigrew (Margalo Gillmore), the daughter of the household. When she dies, he returns to the present, but his soul is linked indissolubly to the past. "A transcendental theme . . . easily the finest play now to be seen in New York" (Heywood Broun, *Telegram*). P/D: Gilbert Miller and Leslie Howard. John Balderston (A) based his artful metaphysical fantasy on *A Sense of the Past*, an unfinished story by Henry James. A man with an abiding passion for the eighteenth century (he maintained that Betsy Ross was his great-great-grandmother), Balderston nurtured a lifelong interest in supernatural themes. The success of his play *Dracula* (1927), followed by the even greater success of *Berkeley Square*, prompted a flood of screenwriting offers. Balderston's subsequent Hollywood credits include such classics in the horror *genre* as *Frankenstein, The Bride of Frankenstein, The Mummy, Mad Love,* and *The Mystery of Edwin Drood*.
SV: Fox, 1933, Leslie Howard, Heather Angel. Colin Keith-Johnston, Irene Browne, Beryl Mercer; 1951, *I'll Never Forget You,* Tyrone Power, Ann Blyth, Michael Rennie, Dennis Price.

Berlin (12/30/31, Cohan, 25)

To retrieve some incriminating documents, the nefarious World War I head (Sydney Greenstreet) of the German Secret Service relentlessly pursues a British spy (G. P. Huntley, Jr.) and his girl (Helen Vinson) throughout the city of Berlin. Mediocre 1931 melodrama. A: Valentine Williams and Alice Crawford. P: Moore and Reed. D: Fritz Feld.

Bernardine (10/16/52, Playhouse, 157)

A gang of teenagers daydream about the wooing and winning of their dream girl Bernardine (the boys' name for their ideal of femininity). However, when one of the lads finally meets a real Bernardine, the would-be conquest turns out to be a friend of his mother, and the affair is over before it begins. ". . . a bit rickety as to structure [but] . . . a little sweetheart of a comedy" (*News*). Written by Mary Chase, author of *Harvey* (1944). C: Johnny Stewart, John Kerr, Warren Berlinger, Michael Wager, Beverly Lawrence, Peggy Cass. P: Irving L. Jacobs. D: Guthrie McClintic.
SV: Fox, 1957, Pat Boone, Terry Moore, Janet Gaynor, Dean Jagger, Walter Abel.

Best Laid Plans, The (3/25/66, Atkinson, 3)

Stale sex comedy about a thoroughly conventional career girl who poses as a beatnik. C: Marian Hailey, Edward Woodward, Kenneth Mars, Polly Rowles, Cynthia Harris. A: Gwen Davis. P: Hillard Elkins i.a.w. Donald J. Mitchell. D: Arthur Storch.

Best Man, The (3/31/60, Morosco, 520)

Gore Vidal's witty, trenchant comedy-drama dealing with political infighting in a battle for the presidential nomination.

Top contenders: William Russell (Melvyn Douglas), a liberal intellectual accused of being indecisive, and Joseph Cantwell (Frank Lovejoy), a ruthless, power-hungry young senator with a homosexual incident in his past. Masterminding the match: a peppery ex-President (Lee Tracy) who tries unsuccessfully to persuade Russell to make political capital out of the dirt he has uncovered. Instead, the high-principled Russell sabotages Cantwell's "dirty tricks" campaign by withdrawing from the race and supporting a middle-of-the-road candidate. ". . . a breezy melodrama . . . both comic and exciting. . . . One of the pleasures of *The Best Man* is the sardonic consistency with which it recalls characteristics of current politicians—the fastidiousness and wit of Adlai Stevenson, the belligerent political guile of Harry Truman, Richard Nixon's soap-opera with wife and dog to convince the country of his honesty" *(New York Times)*. C: Leora Dana, Kathleen Maguire, Ruth McDevitt. P: The Playwrights Company. D: Joseph Anthony.

SV: UA, 1964, Henry Fonda, Cliff Robertson, Lee Tracy, Margaret Leighton, Edie Adams, Ann Sothern, Gene Raymond, Kevin McCarthy, Shelley Berman, Mahalia Jackson, Howard K. Smith, John Henry Faulk, Richard Arlen, George Furth (directed by Franklin Schaffner).

Best People, The (8/19/24, Lyceum, 144)

Poor little rich girl falls in love with her chauffeur while her playboy-brother opts for a chorus girl; their upper-crust parents try to smile bravely through it all. Entertaining comedy by David Gray and Avery Hopwood. C: Charles Richman, Margaret Dale, Gavin Muir, Frances Howard, James Rennie. P: Charles Frohman, Inc.

SV: Par, 1930, *Fast and Loose*, Miriam Hopkins, Carole Lombard, Frank Morgan, Charles Starrett, Ilka Chase.

Best Years (9/7/32, Bijou, 45)

Domineering mother almost ruins her daughter's life. Dull 30's comedy-drama. C: Jean Adair, Katherine Alexander, Harvey Stephens. A: Raymond Van Sickle. P: Elizabeth Miele. D: Priestly Morrison.

Bet Your Life (4/5/37, Golden, 8)

Comedian Willie Howard coauthored this anemic 30's farce about the tribulations of a sweepstakes winner (Lew Hearn). P: Ben Stein. D: A. H. Van Buren.

Note: When *Bet Your Life* closed after one week of dismal business, coauthor Fritz Blocki rewrote the script. Six weeks later (5/24/37) the revised comedy opened at the 49th Street theatre with a new title, *Money Mad*. It lasted one performance.

Between Two Worlds (10/25/34, Belasco, 32)

Tough-minded Bolshevik (Joseph Schildkraut) seduces wealthy but naïve American girl (Rachel Hartzell) on an ocean liner. Presumably both learn something from the encounter. According to Elmer Rice (A/P/D) the play was "in every sense a failure."

Beverly Hills (11/7/40, Fulton, 28)

Sex-starved actresses, double-dealing agents, and idiot producers hamper the efforts of an ambitious wife to land a choice screenwriting job for her weak-willed husband. "The characters are all unpleasant enough to be the butts of sardonic jest, but it takes more than that to provide satire. Wit helps, for one thing" *(Sun)*. *Beverly Hills,* a short-lived entry of the 1940 season, was coproduced and directed by Otto Preminger. It was the first of three Hollywood satires to open on Broadway in the space of one week. *Quiet Please* and

Glamour Preferred were the other two exhibits. All three comedies were failures. C: Helen Claire, Ilka Chase, Clinton Sundberg, Violet Heming, Enid Markey, Doro Merande, Effie Afton, Fred de Cordova, Lea Penman, William Talman. A: Lynn Starling and Howard J. Green. P: Laurence Schwab and Otto Preminger.

Beware of Widows (12/1/25, Maxine Elliott's, 57)

Determined widow (Madge Kennedy) finally wins the man of her choice. Inconsequential Owen Davis comedy-drama. P: Crosby Gaige.

Bewitched (10/1/24, National, 29)

Aviator (Glenn Anders) rescues a lovely sorceress (Florence Eldridge) from an enchanted castle, awakens to find it was all a dream. Fanciful yarn by Edward Sheldon and Sidney Howard remained resolutely stagebound, never cast its intended spell. P/D: John Cromwell.

Beyond the Horizon (2/2/20, Morosco, 111)

Eugene O'Neill's first full-length play; generally credited as marking the coming of age of the American theatre. New England farmer Robert Mayo (Richard Bennett), filled with wanderlust and hating the farm on which he was born, is about to leave home on a long sea voyage. Ruth Atkins (Helen MacKellar) persuades Robert to stay and marry her, while Robert's prosaic brother Andrew (Edward Arnold), who really loves the farm, goes on the planned trip. All three fail in their search for meaning in life, none more cruelly than Robert, who dies

Beyond the Horizon (1920). *Courtesy Museum of the City of New York Theatre and Music Collection.*

without having seen beyond the horizon. ". . . memorable tragedy, so full of meat that it makes most of the remaining fare seem like the merest meringue . . . the play has greatness in it" (Alexander Woollcott, *New York Times*). George M. Cohan told this editor that *Beyond The Horizon* was his favorite play of the twentieth century. When I asked Cohan the reasons for his choice, he replied: "Because of its remarkable character study; because it is not a cut and dried story with the usual happy ending, but a realistic, truthful document: honest, sincere, inspiring." O'Neill's initial Broadway production was first presented at a special matinee performance. When the play was put on for a regular run, the roles of Andrew and Ruth were played by Robert Kelly and Elsie Rizer, with Richard Bennett continuing in the role of Robert. *Beyond The Horizon* won for O'Neill his first of four Pulitzer Prizes. P: John D. Williams. D: Homer Saint-Gaudens. R: (11/30/26, Mansfield, 79) by The Actors Theatre. C: Robert Keith, Aline MacMahon, Thomas Chalmers.

Bicycle Ride to Nevada (9/24/63, Cort, 1)

The final disintegration of novelist Sinclair Lewis, here called Winston Sawyer (Franchot Tone), ravaged by alcohol and tormented by awareness of his creative decline. ". . . hopelessly maudlin . . . painful rather than dramatic" (*Post*). A: Robert Thom; b/o the novel *Dangerfield* by Barnaby Conrad (onetime secretary to Sinclair Lewis). P: Roger L. Stevens and Herman Shumlin (D) i.a.w. Morris and Hale. SD: Howard Bay.

Big Chance, The (10/28/18, 48th Street, 120)

Crude, propagandistic World War I comedy-drama purporting to show that Sherman was wrong and war is swell. A group of moral derelicts—Tenderloin idlers, drunks, panhandlers, and racetrack touts—are strengthened and redeemed when they hear the call to arms and enlist in the service of their country. "*The Big Chance,* with all its crudities, brings a mood of courage and cheer into the somewhat dreary atmosphere of our wartime dramatics" *(New York Times)*. C: Willard Mack, Mary Nash, John Mason, Katherine Harris Barrymore, William E. Meehan, Ramsey Wallace. A: Grant Morris and Willard Mack. P: A. H. Woods. D: W. H. Gilmore.

Big Fight, The (9/18/28, Majestic, 31)

Jack Dempsey as heavyweight champ Tiger Dillon, beset by a crooked manager, smitten by a cute manicurist. Climax: the big fight in Madison Square Garden. Guess who wins. A compendium of prizefight clichés, this 20s curio demonstrated conclusively that Dempsey was a better pugilist than performer. C: Estelle Taylor (Mrs. Jack Dempsey), Roy Hargrave, Jack Roseleigh, Victor Kilian, Arthur Vinton. A: Milton Herbert Gropper and Max Marcin. P: Sam H. Harris and Albert Lewis. D: David Belasco. SV: World-Wide, 1930, Guinn "Big Boy" Williams, Lola Lane.

Big Fish, Little Fish (3/15/61, ANTA, 101)

Excellent comedy-drama about a gentle middle-aged bachelor (Jason Robards, Jr.) whose seedy Manhattan apartment has become a refuge for a group of crotchety, parasitic second-raters of both sexes. They have grown to rely on his understanding and tolerance and he, conversely, is equally dependent on them to feed his psychological needs. So strong is this mutual bond that when he is offered a well-paying publishing-house job overseas, the leechlike hangers-on are fiercely indignant at the thought that he would dare desert them. The editorial assignment falls through, but the barnacle-encrusted "Big Fish" heads for Europe anyway, leaving his school of minnows behind. "Funny and yet strangely profound . . . first class theatrical fare"

(*Journal-American*). C: Hume Cronyn, George Grizzard, Martin Gabel, Ruth White, Elizabeth Wilson, George Voskovec. P: Lewis Allen and Ben Edwards (SD) i.a.w. Joseph E. Levine. D: John Gielgud.

Note: Big Fish, Little Fish was a first play by Anglo-American novelist-playwright Hugh Wheeler (*A Little Night Music, Irene, Candide*). At the core of the drama was an old accusation that hangs over the hero: when he was a brilliant young professor at a girls' college he had been accused of seducing a trustee's daughter who, when jilted by him, committed suicide. However, when the play had its first tryout in Philadelphia, the girls' school was a boys' school and the trustee's daughter was the trustee's son. Despite many changes made in the script before the Broadway opening, several traces of the original situation seemed to linger on, prompting more than one critic to complain of a certain aloofness and "disquieting elusiveness" surrounding the central character.

Biggest Thief in Town, The (3/30/49, Mansfield, 13)

Complications ensue when a small-town undertaker (Thomas Mitchell) and doctor (Walter Abel) steal the body of the town's wealthiest citizen, and discover that there's still a little life left in the corpse. "... about as funny as a funeral" (*New York Times*). Originally intended as a socially significant drama, this Dalton Trumbo play was rewritten by its author during the pre-Broadway tour and turned into a farce-comedy. To little avail: the show closed after thirteen performances. C: Rhys Williams, Lois Nettleton (deb.), Robert Readick, Russ Brown, William J. Kelly. P: Lee Sabinson. D: Herman Shumlin.

Note: Screenwriter Dalton Trumbo (*Thirty Seconds Over Tokyo, Exodus, Spartacus, Hawaii*, etc.) was one of the "Hollywood Ten" who were blacklisted for refusing to tell the Un-American Activities Committee whether they were or were not Communists.

Big Hearted Herbert (1/1/34, Biltmore, 154)

Penny-pinching businessman is reformed when his long-suffering wife finally rebels and turns their comfortable home plain to the "nth" degree. Enjoyable domestic comedy by Sophie Kerr and Anna S. Richardson. C: J. C. Nugent, Elizabeth Risdon, Alan Bunce. P: Eddie Dowling. D: Dan Jarrett.

SV: WB, 1934, Guy Kibbee, Aline MacMahon; 1940, *Father is a Prince,* Grant Mitchell, Nana Bryant.

Big Knife, The (2/24/49, National, 109)

Clifford Odets' melodrama about a high-salaried screen star (John Garfield) trapped in a net of Hollywood corruption and scandal. Having permitted his press agent to go to jail on a homicide charge of which he was guilty, the actor is blackmailed by his wicked studio boss (J. Edward Bromberg) into signing an onerous $3,400,000 long-term contract. The play concludes with the star committing suicide by slashing his wrists and drowning himself in the bathtub of his Beverly Hills home. "Overwrought and overwritten, a play with enough plot and sub-plot for an old-time Bowery thriller" (*Sun*). C: Nancy Kelly, Paul McGrath, Theodore Newton, Reinhold Schunzel, Joan McCracken, Leona Powers, Frank Wilson, William Terry. P: Dwight Deere Wiman. D: Lee Strasberg. SD: Howard Bay.

SV: UA, 1955, Jack Palance, Ida Lupino, Rod Steiger, Shelley Winters, Ilka Chase, Wendell Corey, Everett Sloane.

Big Lake (4/11/27, A.L.T., 11)

First play by Lynn Riggs, whose *Green Grow the Lilacs* (1931) was musicalized as *Oklahoma!* (1943). Two young Oklahomans, mistaken for a murderer and his moll, meet death with nobility and heroism. ". . . simple, direct, bitingly true" *(News)*. C: Helen Coburn, Frank Burk, Grover Burgess, Stella Adler, Frances Williams, Harold Hecht. P: American Laboratory Theatre. D: George Auerbach.

Big Night (1/17/33, Maxine Elliott's, 7)

In order to land a big order, a salesman arranges for his pretty wife (Stella Adler) to romance an out-of-town buyer (J. Edward Bromberg). Acid, frequently witty Dawn Powell script suffered from a lumbering, heavy-handed approach. *Big Night* was a big failure. C: Lewis Leverett, Phoebe Brand, Roman Bohnen, Clifford Odets, Russell Collins. P: The Group Theatre. D: Cheryl Crawford. SD: Mordecai Gorelik.

Big Pond, The (8/21/28, Bijou, 47)

A young Frenchman (Kenneth MacKenna) must make good in the U.S. rubber business before he can marry the boss's daughter* (Lucile Nikolas). Transplanted to America, he becomes such a go-getter that he wins the approval of his prospective father-in-law (Harlan Briggs), but loses the girl. Moderately diverting comedy by George Middleton and A. E. Thomas. P: Edwin H. Knopf (D) and William P. Farnsworth.
SV: Par, 1930, Maurice Chevalier, Claudette Colbert, George Barbier.

---

*This role was to have marked Katharine Hepburn's Broadway debut, but she was fired for incompetence after one performance of the pre-Broadway tryout.

Big Time Buck White (12/8/68, Village South, 124)

A militant black lectures a social club on the meaning of race pride and liberation. Trenchant O/B thesis-drama with Dick Williams (D) in the title part. A: Joseph Dolan Tuotti. Musicalized by Oscar Brown, Jr. as *Buck White* (1969) with Cassius Clay (a.k.a. Muhammad Ali) making his Broadway debut in the leading role.

Big Two, The (1/8/47, Booth, 21)

Postwar romance between an American newspaperwoman (Claire Trevor) and a Russian army captain (Philip Dorn) in occupied Austria; written by Hungarian-American playwright L. Bush-Fekete* and his wife Mary Helen Fay. ". . . a haphazard and unsettled mixture of romantic comedy, political preachment and frenzied melodrama" *(Sun)*. C: Felix Bressart, Eduard Franz, John Banner, E. A. Krumschmidt, Walter (Jack) Palance. P: Elliott Nugent and Robert Montgomery (D) i.a.w. David Bramson. SD: Jo Mielziner.

---

*Hollywood screenwriter since the mid-1930's; Ernst Lubitsch's *Heaven Can Wait* was b/o his play, *Birthday* (unproduced in America).

Big White Fog (10/22/40, Lincoln, 64)

In a quixotic quest to help found a new African republic, a Chicago black (Canada Lee) loses his money, his family, and finally his life. Well-written, frequently stirring O/B drama by pioneer black playwright Theodore Ward. P: Negro Playwrights Company. D: Powell Lindsay.

Billy Budd (2/10/51, Biltmore, 105)

Sensitive adaptation of Herman Melville's classic allegorical tale of treachery in the 18th century British navy, and of a pure-in-heart sailor confronting unyielding evil in the person of a brutal ship officer. These inevitable adversaries ultimately destroy one another, thus proving Melville's thesis that neither absolute good nor absolute evil can survive in this world. ". . . a horrifyingly candid drama . . . has size and depth as well as color and excitement" *(New York Times).* C: Dennis King, Charles Nolte, Torin Thatcher, Guy Spaull, James Daly, Jack Manning, Jeff Morrow, Lee Marvin (deb.). A: Louis O. Coxe and Robert Chapman. P: Chandler Cowles and Anthony Brady Farrell. D: Norris Houghton. SD: Paul Morrison. The Melville novella was musicalized as *Billy* (1969) by Glassman, Dante, and Allan with a cast headed by Laurence Naismith, Robert Salvio, John Devlin, John Beal, George Marcy, and Dolph Sweet.

SV: AA, 1962, Terence Stamp, Robert Ryan, Melvyn Douglas, John Neville and Peter Ustinov (who also directed).

Note: Billy Budd originally was produced O/B (1/29/49, Lenox Hill, 7) in "a more poetic and austere form" as *Uniform of Flesh.*

Biography (12/12/32, Guild, 267)

Charming, unconventional portrait painter Marion Froude (Ina Claire) is pursued by a middle-aged conservative and a young radical. Marion, representing the liberal viewpoint, defends the wisdom of cultivating the greatest possible tolerance for all points of view, and ends by refusing both men. One of the wittiest comedies of the American theatre, *Biography* was an unqualified triumph for author S. N. Behrman and star Ina Claire. C: Jay Fassett, Earle Larimore, Arnold Korff, Charles Richman. P: The Theatre Guild. D: Philip Moeller. SD: Jo Mielziner.

SV: MGM, 1935, *Biography of a Bachelor Girl,* Ann Harding, Robert

Biography. **Ina Claire, Jay Fassett, unidentified actor, and Arnold Korff (1932).** *Courtesy Museum of the City of New York Theatre and Music Collection.*

Montgomery, Edward Arnold, Edward Everett Horton, Una Merkel.

Bird Cage, The (2/22/50, Coronet, 21)

Melvyn Douglas (miscast) and Maureen Stapleton in Arthur Laurents' lurid melodrama about the machinations of a ruthless nightclub owner. Miss Stapleton played Douglas's browbeaten, alcoholic wife. ". . . chiefly sound and fury . . . vigorous, cluttered and rather exhausting . . ." (*Post*). C: Eleanor Lynn, Sanford Meisner, Laurence Hugo, Jean Carson, Mike Kellin, Heywood Hale Broun. P: Fried and Nordenson. D: Harold Clurman. CD: Ben Edwards. SD: Boris Aronson. M: Alec Wilder.

Bird of Paradise, The (1/8/12, Daly's, 112)

Pretty Hawaiian princess (Laurette Taylor) falls in love with fickle American scientist (Lewis Stone). When he tires of her, she hurls herself into the crater of a volcano. Inane escapist nonsense became a big stock company and road show hit. A/D: Richard Walton Tully. P: Oliver Morosco. Musicalized by Rudolph Friml as *Luana* (1930).
SV: RKO, 1932, Dolores Del Rio, Joel McCrea, John Halliday, Creighton Chaney (Lon Chaney, Jr.), Skeets Gallagher; Fox, 1951, Debra Paget, Louis Jourdan, Jeff Chandler, Everett Sloane.

Birthright (11/21/33, 49th Street, 7)

When Hitler comes to power, a German-Jewish family find themselves trapped in a sudden whirlpool of hate. Earnest, intermittently effective 1933 drama; written by future Hollywood writer-producer Richard Maibaum, staged by screenwriter-producer-director Robert Rossen. C: Montagu Love, Sylvia Field, Alan Bunce, Edgar Stehli, Don Beddoe, Thais Lawton. P: Irving Barrett and Robert Rossen.

Bishop Misbehaves, The (2/20/35, Cort, 120)

Paying an unexpected visit to a roadside pub, a mystery-loving bishop (Walter Connolly) investigates a crime, metes out retribution, and sets the course of two young lovers (Jane Wyatt and Alan Marshal) on a smooth road. Fairly diverting melodramatic comedy. A: Frederick Jackson. P: John Golden. D: Ira Hards.
SV: MGM, 1935, Edmund Gwenn, Maureen O'Sullivan.

Bitter Stream (3/30/36, Civic, 61)

An Italian farmer rebels against Il Duce's totalitarian regime and becomes a martyr in the cause of freedom. Stagebound drama b/o the internationally acclaimed anti-Fascist novel *Fontamara* by Ignazio Silone. C: Albert Dekker, Lee J. Cobb. A: Victor Wolfson. P: The Theatre Union. D: Jacob Ben-Ami and Charles Friedman. SD: Cleon Throckmorton.
Note: Silone fled Italy in 1931, but returned in 1944 in time to witness the capture and shooting of Benito Mussolini by Italian partisans.

Black Boy (10/6/26, Comedy, 39)

Sketchily written drama about the rise and fall of a black prizefighter (Paul Robeson). A: Jim Tully and Frank Dazey. P: Horace Liveright. D: David Burton.

Black Monday (3/6/62, Van Dam, 16)

Problems of desegregation in a small Southern town. Earnest but heavy-handed O/B drama by television and screen writer Reginald Rose (*Twelve Angry Men,* etc.). C: Nancy Coleman, Yaphet Kotto, Billie Allen. P/D: William Hunt.

Black Pit (3/20/35, Civic, 86)

A coal miner, forced to work as a company spy, betrays his fellow workers and is ostracized. *Black Pit* was written by screenwriter Albert Maltz (*This Gun for Hire, The Naked City*, etc.). "Maltz creates no response but ennui, and disappointment at his inability to make a vigorous subject live vigorously" (*Theatre Arts*). C: Alan Baxter, Millicent Green, Howard da Silva, George Tobias, Martin Wolfson, Anthony Ross, Frances Bavier, Vincent Sherman. P: The Theatre Union. D: Irving Gordon.

Black Sheep (10/13/32, Morosco, 4)

Iconoclastic writer disrupts his middle-class family when he returns home after a seven-year absence. Woefully weak comedy by Elmer Rice (A/P/D). C: Donald MacDonald, Ann Shoemaker, Jean Adair.

Black Souls (3/30/32, Provincetown, 13)

Visiting an all-black college in the South, a senator and his nymphomaniac daughter are sexually aroused by various members of the staff. Shrill, frequently repellent 1932 O/B melodrama. C: Juano Hernandez, Rose McClendon. A: Annie Nathan Meyer. P: William Stahl. D: James Light.

Black Tower, The (1/11/32, Harris, 73)

Insane sculptor (Walter Kingsford) embalms humans in stone. Fairly effective gooseflesh exhibit. A: Ralph Murphy and Lora Baxter. P: Ben Stein. D: Sidney Salkow.

Black Velvet (9/27/27, Liberty, 15)

Odious melodrama about an elderly southern bigot (Arthur Byron) who causes trouble for blacks, whites, and mulattos alike on his old plantation. A/D: Willard Robertson. P: M. J. Nicholas.

Black Widow (2/12/36, Mansfield, 7)

A deranged doctor (Lucille La Verne) takes to murdering pregnant girls and stuffing their bodies into an incinerator. When a couple of smart detectives (King Calder and Keenan Wynn) finally corner the fiend, she throws herself into the fiery furnace. Laughably inept shocker. C: Joanna Roos, Stanley Smith, A. H. Van Buren. A: Samuel John Park. P: Thomas Kilpatrick. D: Miriam Doyle.

Black-Eyed Susan (12/23/54, Playhouse, 4)

Sniggering sex farce about a young wife (Dana Wynter) who sets out to seduce her neurologist (Vincent Price). ". . . shoddy, sleazy, leering, vulgar, blatant, ill-mannered, coarse, witless, feckless, insulting, discouraging and unfunny" (*News*). C: Everett Sloane, Kay Medford, Charles Boaz. A: A. B. Shiffrin. P: Gordon W. Pollock i.a.w. Hart and Goodman. D: Gregory Ratoff.

Bless You, Sister (12/26/27, Forrest, 24)

The life and loves of evangelist Aimee Semple McPherson (here called Mary MacDonald), dramatized in a series of generally ineffective vignettes. *Bless You, Sister* was written by future screenwriters John Meehan (*Boys Town, Valley of Decision*) and Robert Riskin (*It Happened One Night, Mr. Deeds Goes To Town, Lost Horizon*), and was co-directed by John Meehan and George Abbott. C: Alice Brady, Charles Bickford, Robert Ames. P: A. and R. Riskin.

SV: Col, 1931, *The Miracle Woman*, Barbara Stanwyck (directed by Frank Capra).

Blessed Event (2/12/32, Longacre, 124)

The life of a scandal-mongering Broadway columnist (Roger Pryor) is threatened when he reveals the pregnancy of a gangster's girlfriend (Isabel Jewell). Rowdy, highly entertaining comedy, with the play's central character obviously patterned after Walter Winchell. C: Matt Briggs, Allen Jenkins, Lee Patrick, Jean Adair, Herman Mankiewicz, Lynn Root. A: Manuel Seff and

Forrest Wilson. P: Sidney Phillips and Harlan Thompson (D).
SV: WB, 1932, Lee Tracy, Dick Powell, Mary Brian, Ned Sparks, Ruth Donnelly, Allen Jenkins, Frank McHugh, Emma Dunn.

Blind Alley (9/24/35, Booth, 118)

Superb melodrama about a deranged criminal who uses a psychology professor's home as a hideout. The professor has only one viable weapon against this cold-blooded killer—his knowledge of psychoanalysis. Aided by the killer's fear of insanity, the psychiatrist probes the gangster's sick mind, leading him step by step toward self-awareness and thus, inevitably, toward self-destruction. Brilliantly acted by Roy Hargrave as the fugitive and George Coulouris as the psychology professor, *Blind Alley* was a faultlessly crafted exercise in suspense. A: James Warwick. P: James R. Ullman. D: Worthington Miner.
R: (10/15/40, Windsor, 63) by Elkins and Taylor. C: Roy Hargrave, James Todd, Lila Lee, Bernardine Hayes. D: J. B. Daniels.
SV: Col, 1939, Chester Morris, Ralph Bellamy, Ann Dvorak, Melville Cooper, Joan Perry, Rose Stradner, Marc Lawrence; 1948, *The Dark Past*, William Holden, Lee J. Cobb, Nina Foch, Adele Jergens.

Blind Mice 10/15/30, Times Square, 13)

Assorted romantic problems in a residential home for working girls. Talky comedy-drama by Vera Caspary and Winifred Lenihan (D), with Claiborne Foster heading an all-female cast. P: Crosby Gaige.
SV: Par, 1931, *Working Girls*, Paul Lukas, Buddy Rogers.

Blood and Sand (9/20/21, Empire, 71)

Elaborate, lethargic tale of the life and loves of a bullfighter (Otis Skinner), based on the novel by Blasco-Ibañez. C: Catherine Calvert, Cornelia Otis Skinner (deb.). A: Tom Cushing. P: Charles Frohman, Inc.
SV: Fox, 1941, Tyrone Power, Rita Hayworth, Linda Darnell, Nazimova, Anthony Quinn, John Carradine, J. Carrol Naish.

Blood Money (8/22/27, Hudson, 64)

Upright young couple (Thomas Mitchell and Phyllis Povah) almost sacrifice their lives trying to keep one hundred thousand dollars from a gang of crooks. So-so 20's melodrama. A: George Middleton b/o story by H. H. Van Loan. P: Mrs. Henry B. Harris. D: Ira Hards.

Blood, Sweat and Stanley Poole (10/5/61, Morosco, 84)

To pass a written test in the peacetime army, an unlettered officer (Darren McGavin) enlists the aid of a private with a high I.Q. and a psychological aversion to army life. With his help, the officer manages to retain his rank and also to wreak revenge on a venal captain (John McMartin). In the role of the bumbling but brainy draftee, twenty-one-year-old Peter Fonda made an impressive Broadway debut, but the play itself, a gagged-up comedy by James and William Goldman, proved only intermittently satisfactory. P: Roger L. Stevens and Fields Productions i.a.w. Lyn Austin. D: Jerome Chodorov.

Bloodstream (3/30/32, Times Square, 28)

Interesting, well-acted 1932 melodrama about a group of rebellious black prisoners trapped in a coal-kine disaster. C: Frank Wilson, John Cecil Holm, Ernest Whitman. A: Frederick Schlick. P: Sidney Harmon. D: Sidney Salkow.

Blow Ye Winds (9/23/37, 46th Street, 36)

Henry Fonda returned to Broadway in this cliché-ridden 1937 comedy-drama about the on-again-off-again romance of a ne'er-do-well sailor and a woman scientist. Fonda's typically understated performance as the amiable loafer won the critics' praise, but the play itself was dismissed as "listless, loquacious, and monotonous." *Blow Ye Winds* was written by novelist-screenwriter Valentine Davies, author of *Miracle on 34th Street, Bridges at Toko-Ri,* etc. C: Doris Dalton, Edgar Barrier, Edgar Stehli, Blaine Cordner. P/D: Arthur Hopkins.

Blue Boy in Black, The (4/30/63, Masque, 23)

A pretty black maid (Cicely Tyson) sets out to seduce her married employer. Intermittently effective O/B satire on race relations. C: John Hillerman, Alice Drummond, Billy Dee Williams. A: Edmund White. P/D: Ashley Feinstein.

Blue Denim (2/27/58, Playhouse, 166)

A fifteen-year-old youth discovers he is to become the father of his high-school sweetheart's child. His inability to confide in his well-meaning but obtuse parents leads to near tragedy. This touching and believable, if occasionally contrived, comedy-drama was written by James Leo Herlihy and William Noble, and was staged by Joshua Logan. C: Burt Brinckerhoff (deb.), Carol Lynley (deb.), Chester Morris, June Walker, Pat Stanley, Warren Berlinger. P: Wolferman and Hammerstein. SD: Peter Larkin.
SV: Fox, 1959, Brandon de Wilde, Carol Lynley, Macdonald Carey, Marsha Hunt, Warren Berlinger (directed by Philip Dunne).

Blue Flame, The (3/15/20, Shubert, 48)

Silent screen vamp Theda Bara came to Broadway in this preposterous horror yarn—indisputably one of the worst plays ever written. Scientist John Varnum (Alan Dinehart) brings his fiancée Ruth Gordon (Theda Bara) back to life after she has been fatally struck by lightning. Bereft of soul, the resurrected Ruth becomes a sultry she-devil who slinks around luring innocent men to their doom. Before her exotic blandishments have run their course, the audience is treated to a comprehensive catalog of vice, 1920's style, including seduction, burglary, murder, blasphemy, the cocaine habit, infidelity, and white slavery. ". . . an actress who is so bad that she entertains rather than affronts. Some of her more heated passages are delivered with all the fervor of a lady demonstrating pancake flour in the food section of a department store. . . . The audience was something between reverent and amazed" (Percy Hammond, *Tribune*). A: George V. Hobart and John Willard, from a play by Leta Vance Nicholson. P: A. H. Woods. D: J. C. Huffman and W. H. Gilmore.

Blue Ghost, The (3/10/30, Forrest, 112)

Silly mystery-comedy set in a haunted castle; nondescript cast. A: Bernard J. McOwen and J. P. Riewerts. P: Jimmie Cooper. D: Stephen Clark.

Blue Mouse, The (11/30/08, Lyric, 232)

Ambitious businessman hires a beautiful chorus girl to pose as his wife and compromise his boss. Frothy farce, extensively revised and Americanized by Clyde Fitch from a play by Engel and Horst. C: Mabel Barrison, Harry Conor. D: Clyde Fitch. Musicalized by Harry Carroll as *The Little Blue Devil* (1919) with Lillian Lorraine and Bernard Granville.

Bluebeard's Eighth Wife (9/19/21, Ritz, 155)

A wealthy American playboy (Edmund Breese) has divorced seven wives. His eighth bride (Ina Claire) schemes to ensure that she will be his last marital fling. Scintillating comedy set in Paris and Biarritz was extensively revised by

Charlton Andrews. Adapted from a play by Alfred Savoir. P: William Harris, Jr. D: Lester Lonergan and Robert Milton. SV: Par, 1938, Gary Cooper, Claudette Colbert, David Niven.

Blues for Mister Charlie (4/23/64, ANTA, 148)

James Baldwin's inflammatory tale of a militant young Negro's return to a small Southern town, his subsequent murder by an illiterate white racist, and of the tragic events that follow in the wake of this crime, climaxing with the acquittal of the white man. Adapted from his novel of the same name, Mr. Baldwin's first stage work—a shrilly discordant hymn of hate to the white race—won praise from most of the first-string critics. More polemic than play, *Blues for Mister Charlie* did nothing whatever to better the cause of race relations. C: Al Freeman, Jr., Pat Hingle, Rip Torn, Diana Sands, Ralph Waite, Rosetta Le Noire, Percy Rodriguez, Ann Wedgeworth, Joe Don Baker. P: The Actors Studio. D: Burgess Meredith.

Body Beautiful, The (10/31/35, Plymouth, 4)

Country girl comes to New York in search of a career, becomes a fabulously successful burlesque queen. Raffish, short-lived comedy by Robert Rossen (A/D), Hollywood writer-producer-director (*All the King's Men*, *The Hustler*, etc.). C: Polly Walters, Oliver Barbour, Garson Kanin, Arlene Francis (deb.). P: Sidney Harmon. SD: Boris Aronson.

Book of Charm, The (9/3/25, Comedy, 34)

Country bumpkin buys a handbook on how the smart set conducts itself. By following the book's advice, he impresses the town and wins back his girl. Stale comedy of the "Ain't we cute" school. C: Kenneth Dana, Lee Tracy, Elizabeth Patterson, Mildred MacLeod. A: John Kirkpatrick. P/D: Rachel Crothers.

Boom Boom Room (11/8/73, Vivian Beaumont, 37)

The adventures of a go-go dancer and her search for identity and love. If the task is difficult the unfortunate girl cannot be blamed for her psychic confusion. Her mother tried to abort her, her father may have sexually abused her, and as an adult, her world is peopled by a lesbian dance captain, an alcoholic lover, a drearily shy boy friend, a homosexual who earns a living as a sperm donor, and other misfits and eccentrics. Throughout the action, several dancers gyrate in cages hung about the stage. The unencouraging ending finds the girl heading for New York to become a topless dancer. The critics praised Madeline Kahn's virtuoso performance of the hapless heroine. For the play itself, they variously expressed themselves as exasperated: "a long and tedious Expressionistic play" (Douglas Watt, *New York Daily News*); bemused: "a very strange and unusual play. It seemed to me somewhat obscure" (Richard Watts, *New York Post*), or ecstatic: "a near masterpiece, theatrically thrilling, awesome in its humanity" (Martin Gottfried, *Women's Wear Daily*). Revised after its Broadway run, the play opened O/B 11/20/74 for 31 performances newly titled *In the Boom Boom Room*. A: David Rabe. C: Madeline Kahn, Charles Durning, Charlotte Rae, Robert Loggia, Mary Woronov, Frederick Coffin, Peter Bartlett, Michael Kell, Warren Finnerty, Margaret Davies, Cissy Colpitts, Madeleine Swift, Lani Sundsten, Barbara Monte-Britton. D: Julie Bovasso and Joseph Papp. P: Joseph Papp, New York Shakespeare Festival Lincoln Center. SD: Santo Loquasto. CD: Theoni V. Aldredge.

Boomerang, The (8/10/15, Belasco, 522)

The romantic problems of a young doctor and his first patient. Sprightly, engaging, extremely popular comedy. C: Arthur Byron, Ruth Shepley, Wallace Eddinger, Martha Hedman. A: Winchell Smith and Victor Mapes. P/D: David Belasco.

SV: Par, 1929, *The Love Doctor*, Richard Dix.

Borak (12/13/60, Martinique, 31)

O/B verse-drama about a Civil War officer (William Swetland) whose sense of duty compels him to order the execution of his own son (Andrew Prine). "An uncommonly thoughtful and provocative play" (*New York Times*). A: Robert D. Hock. D: Allen Fletcher.

Border-Land (3/29/32, Biltmore, 23)

Amateur spiritualist traps murderer during seance. Typical, resolutely routine 30's thriller. C: Lester Vail, Catherine Doucet, Howard Lang, Lenita Lane, Alan Campbell, Edgar Barrier. A: Crane Wilbur. P: Philip Gerton. D: Frank McCormack.

Born Yesterday (2/4/46, Lyceum, 1,641)

The long-run comedy hit by Garson Kanin (A/D) in which Billie Dawn* (Judy Holliday), the dumb blonde mistress of a millionaire junkman (Paul Douglas), is tutored in the social and intellectual graces by a liberal writer (Gary Merrill) with whom she falls in love. Billie is smartened up to such an extent that she turns on her protector ("You're just not couth!") and, together with the crusading journalist, puts a stop to the profiteer's power-grabbing ploys. "An uproarious delight" (*Herald Tribune*). "Brilliantly written, brilliantly acted and brilliantly staged" (*Journal-American*). *Born Yesterday* was Garson Kanin's first play and it was written for screen star Jean Arthur. When Miss Arthur took ill during the Boston tryout, unknown Judy Holliday was rushed in as a last-minute replacement and became an overnight star. Sports announcer Paul Douglas also got his big Broadway break in this 1940's version of the Pygmalion story. As roughneck racketeer Harry Brock, Douglas received notices to gladden the heart of any actor, and this was only his second show. (He had played a bit part as a radio announcer ten years earlier in *Double Dummy,* a short-lived farce of the 1936 season.) Kudos also went to Donald Oenslager (SD) for his appropriately hideous $235-a-day Washington hotel suite. *Born Yesterday* was a gold-plated bonanza for everyone connected with it, and especially for producer Max Gordon. The play returned a $1,080,000 profit on a $37,000 investment.

SV: Col, 1951, Judy Holliday, William Holden, Broderick Crawford (directed by George Cukor).

---

*Hollywood actress Jean Parker played this role in the West Coast company. Lon Chaney, Jr. played Harry Brock.

Boss, The (1/30/11, Astor, 88)

The reform and domestication of a ruthless labor boss (Holbrook Blinn) by the daughter (Emily Stevens) of a rival contractor. Suggested by the muckraking exposés of Lincoln Steffens and Ida Tarbell, *The Boss* was a stageworthy if melodramatic study of labor-management problems and big-city political corruption during the first decade of the twentieth century. A: Edward Sheldon. P: William A. Brady. D: Brady and Blinn.

Both Your Houses (3/6/33, Royale, 120)

Maxwell Anderson's Pulitzer Prize-winning satire on American politics. A newly elected congressman, at work on a big appropriations bill, is pitted against a group of old-time politicians. The young idealist tries to draw up a reasonably honest bill but, realizing the hopelessness of his cause, turns around and makes the bill so outrageously dishonest that he feels certain it will instantly be killed. Instead, the bill is so pleasing to all parties that it goes through both Houses, and its

Both Your Houses. (1933). Courtesy Museum of the City of New York Theatre and Music Collection.

author is hailed as a political genius. This keen-witted and incisive portrait of Washington corruption was not a solid hit despite good reviews. The 1933 bank holiday and the Depression were among the reasons cited at the time for the play's moderate Broadway run. C: Shepperd Strudwick, Walter C. Kelly, Mary Philips, Morris Carnovsky, Robert Strange, J. Edward Bromberg, Russell Collins, Joseph Sweeney, Jerome Cowan, Jane Seymour.

Bought and Paid For (9/26/11, Playhouse, 431)

A pretty telephone operator meets and marries a self-made millionaire who insists upon his marital rights by smashing down his wife's bedroom door. She leaves the brute, but he seeks her out, begs forgiveness, and they are reunited. Julia Dean and Charles Richman played the leading roles in this steam-heated melodrama by George Broadhurst, but it was Frank Craven who turned the play into a hit with an enormously engaging performance of a parasitical shipping clerk. P: William A. Brady. D: Edward Elsner.
R: (12/7/21, Playhouse, 30). C: Helen MacKellar, Charles Richman, William Harrigan. D: John Cromwell.

Boundary Line, The (2/5/30, 48th Street, 37)

Conflict between a sensitive poet and his shrewish wife is resolved when he finally leaves her and heads for the open road. Soporific drama by Dana Burnet (A/D). C: Otto Kruger, Katherine Alexander, Winifred Lenihan, Charles Trowbridge. P: Jones and Green.

Box Seats (4/19/28, Little, 28)
A fallen woman struggles to keep her daughter respectable. " . . . a shopworn and prolix narrative" (*New York Times*). C: Joan Storm, Patricia Barclay, George Barbier, Elizabeth Patterson, Paul Guilfoyle, Millard Mitchell, Harold Elliott. A/D: Edward Massey. P: Gordon Leland. SD: R. N. Robbins.

Boy Friend, The (6/7/32, Morosco, 15)
A slippery character known as the Eel (Brian Donlevy) comes to New York to protect the good name of his dumb chorus girl sister. Noisy, tiresome farce-comedy. A: John Montague. P: Carl Hunt (D) and George Miller.

Boy Meets Girl (11/27/35, Cort, 669)
Uproarious lampoon of Hollywood during its heyday; written by Bella and Samuel Spewack, produced and directed by George Abbott. The basic story line dealt with the marvelously irreverent screenwriting team of Law and Benson (read Hecht and MacArthur), and of their wild-eyed schemes to make a movie star out of a waitress's illegitimate baby. Crammed with rapid-fire gags, zany characters, and delightful plot convolutions, *Boy Meets Girl* took Broadway and the country by storm. C: Allyn Joslyn (deb.), Jerome Cowan, Royal Beal, Joyce Arling, Charles McClelland, James MacColl, Everett Sloane, Garson Kanin.
SV: WB, 1938, James Cagney, Pat O'Brien, Marie Wilson, Ralph Bellamy, Dick Foran, Frank McHugh, Ronald Reagan.

Boy on the Straight-Back Chair (2/14/69, American Place, 38)
Creditable O/B study of a young mass murderer. Presented by The American Place Theater, directed by Lee Von Rhau.

Boy Who Lived Twice, A (9/11/45, Biltmore, 15)
Weird mumbo-jumbo about "soul transference" between identical twins. ". . . inexpert and befuddled . . . a clumsy variation of *Here Comes Mr. Jordan*" (*Sun*). C: Claire Windsor, Vaughan Glaser. A: Leslie Floyd Egbert and Gertrude Ogden Tubby. P: Hall Shelton. D: Paul Foley.

Boys in the Band, The (4/15/68, Theater Four, 1,000)
A fascinating, often viciously funny look at the homosexual subculture, the event being a birthday party being held in honor of one of the members of the New York encampment, momentarily threatened by the surprise arrival of a seemingly straight friend. Skillful delineation of character and a deadly accurate ear for dialogue distinguished this script by Mart Crowley (his first professionally produced play). Expertly acted by an all-male cast, *The Boys in the Band* went on to become one of the most successful productions in off-Broadway history, and was equally successful in many other cities throughout America and Europe. Written in five weeks, the play was said to have netted the author more than a million dollars. C: Kenneth Nelson, Cliff Gorman, Leonard Frey, Laurence Luckinbill, Frederick Combs, Keith Prentice, Reuben Greene, Peter White, Robert La Tourneaux. P: Richard Barr and Charles Woodward, Jr. D: Robert Moore. SD: Peter Harvey.
SV: National General, 1970, with substantially the same cast that appeared in the New York production. Directed by William Friedkin.

Brass Ankle (4/23/31, Masque, 42)
A southerner (Alice Brady) learns she has mixed blood when she gives birth to a Negro boy. To shield her husband and daughter, she pretends to have had an affair with a black servant. Her husband

kills her and the baby. Somber tragedy of miscegenation by DuBose Heyward, author of *Porgy* (1927) and *Mamba's Daughters* (1939). P: James W. Elliott. D: Harold Winston.

Brass Ring, The (4/10/52, Lyceum, 4)

A middle-aged businessman returns to Paris in a vain effort to recapture his lost youth, but learns that his routine job and suburban family back home are what really count. "An extremely pleasant evening in the theatre . . ." *(Herald Tribune)*. ". . . a triumph of hack work in playwriting . . . a steady flow of workshop clichés" *(New York Times)*. C: Sidney Blackmer, Carol Goodner, Paul Ford, Douglas Watson, Bethel Leslie, Conrad Janis, Patricia Benoit. A: Irving Elman. P: Donald Wolin i.a.w. Donald Flamm. D: Stanley Gould.

Brat, The (3/5/17, Harris, 136)

Intrigued by a street urchin who says *erl* for *oil* and *goil* for *girl,* a blasé novelist takes her to his posh estate to study her reactions at firsthand. Little Miss Fixit then proceeds to solve everyone's problems. Routine, utterly predictable comedy. C: Lewis Stone, Maude Fulton, Edmund Lowe. A: Maude Fulton. P/D: Oliver Morosco.
SV: Fox, 1931, Sally O'Neill, Alan Dinehart (directed by John Ford from a screenplay by S. N. Behrman); 1940, *Girl from Avenue A,* Jane Withers.

Bravo! (11/11/48, Lyceum, 44)

Serio-comic stage piece by Edna Ferber and George S. Kaufman (D) dealing with the plight of Central European theatre refugees trying to gain a foothold in America. The two leading characters were patterned after a Ferenc Molnar-like Viennese playwright and his actress-inamorata. ". . . has incidental gaiety, nostalgia and charm, but rarely comes to complete life" *(Post)*. C: Oscar Homolka, Lili Darvas, Fritzi Scheff, Kevin McCarthy, Frank Conroy, Edgar Stehli, Jean Carson, King Calder. P: Max Gordon.

Breaks, The (4/16/28, Klaw, 8)

Wicked farmer rapes his young housekeeper, kills himself when she runs off and leaves him. Dismal, disjointed drama by J. C. and Elliott Nugent. C: J. C. Nugent, Sylvia Sidney, Elliott Nugent. P: Richard Herndon. D: J. C. Nugent and Alan Dinehart.

Breeze From the Gulf, A (10/15/73, Eastside Playhouse, 48)

A boy growing up is the subject of this effort by Mart Crowley, author of the 1968 hit, *The Boys in the Band*. *Breeze* follows the life of Michael Connolly (Robert Drivas) from age fifteen to thirty, and is told in powerful style almost too punishing to be other than depressing. Weighed down by a drunkard father (Scott McKay) and a neurotic mother addicted to drugs (Ruth Ford), Michael deteriorates from Catholic altar boy with religious ideals to disillusioned cynic whom we may infer is homosexual. Though sincere and deeply felt, the exposition and development of the play were not dramatically rewarding enough to compensate for its wearying melancholy. "There can be no doubt that the intensity of the author's feeling comes from the heart. . . . The acting is forceful and believable" (Richard Watts, *New York Post*). ". . . obviously been a painful play to attempt to write. . . . Miss Ford is superb. . . . McKay is first-rate. . . . Drivas brings considerable appeal to the vague role of Michael" (Douglas Watt, *New York Daily News*). C: Robert Drivas, Scott McKay, Ruth Ford. D: John Going. P: Charles Hollerith, Jr. and Barnard S. Straus.

Brewster's Millions (12/31/06, New Amsterdam, 163)

Young man (Edward Abeles) must spend

one million dollars immediately if he is to receive major inheritance. Extremely amusing farce-comedy based on George Barr McCutcheon's story. A: Winchell Smith and Byron Ongley. P: Thompson and Dundy. D: Smith and Thompson.

SV: British, 1935, Jack Buchanan, Lili Damita; UA, 1945, Dennis O'Keefe, June Havoc, Helen Walker, Eddie "Rochester" Anderson, Gail Patrick, Mischa Auer; British, 1961, *Three on a Spree,* Jack Watling, Carole Lesley.

Note: A silent version (Par, 1921) starred Fatty Arbuckle.

Bridal Quilt (10/10/34, Biltmore, 5)

Kentucky hillbilly becomes smitten by New Jersey socialite. Humdrum comedy by actor Tom Powers (A/D). C: Blaine Cordner, Claudia Morgan, Eleanor Lynn, James Todd, Lester Vail. P: Vera Murray.

Bridal Wise (5/30/32, Cort, 128)

Young boy brings his divorced parents together again. Entertaining comedy by Albert Hackett and Frances Goodrich. C: Madge Kennedy, James Rennie, Raymond Walburn, Jackie Kelk, Blyth Daly, Lew Payton. P: Sigourney Thayer. D: Frank Craven.

Bride of the Lamb (3/30/26, Greenwich Village, 103)

Ina Bowman (Alice Brady), the repressed and unhappy wife of an alcoholic dentist in the heart of the midwestern bible belt, meets a handsome tent evangelist (Crane Wilbur), traveling as "a go-getter for the Lord." Their affair culminates in the poisoning of her husband and in Ina's mental breakdown. The final curtain finds Ina introducing everyone to her new bridegroom, Mr. Christ. Bold Freudian study of small-town eroticism and religious frenzy, with Miss Brady splendid as the guilt-ridden heroine. Produced O/B by Alice Brady i.a.w. Robert Milton (D); written by William Hurlbut.

Bride of Torozko, The (9/13/34, Henry Miller, 12)

Anti-semites try to prevent the marriage of a Jewish girl (Jean Arthur) to a simple Hungarian lad (Van Heflin). However, the girl turns out to be Catholic and the wedding, presumably, takes place as scheduled. "I can recall few more sluggish entertainments" *(World-Telegram).* "In spite of the fact that she is still wasted on a play that is unworthy of her, Miss Arthur is a young actress who matches her charm and beauty with sincerity and skill" *(Post).* C: Sam Jaffe, Lionel Stander, Victor Kilian. A: Ruth Langner b/o a play by Otto Indig. P: Gilbert Miller and Herman Shumlin (D). SD: Stewart Chaney.

Bride the Sun Shines On, The (12/26/31, Fulton, 79)

On her wedding day, the giddy bride-to-be (Dorothy Gish) discovers it is the woman-shy church organist (Henry Hull) she really loves. Modest comedy, adeptly acted. C: Nicholas Joy, Sam Wren, Fania Marinoff, Armina Marshall. A: Will Cotton. P: New York Repertory Company. D: Knowles Entrikin.

Brief Moment (11/9/31, Belasco, 129)

The bumpy marriage of a weak-willed socialite and a cabaret singer was examined in pedestrian fashion in this disappointing comedy by S. N. Behrman. Alexander Woollcott (deb.) provided some amusing moments as the hero's testy, corpulent friend. Woollcott played the entire part lolling on a sofa, uttering such Algonquinesque sagacities as: "Vitality is tiresome to live with. I once lived with a girl who had vitality and she wore me out. Nowadays I go in for languor." C: Francine Larrimore, Robert Douglas,

Brief Moment (Belasco Theatre, November 9, 1931). *Courtesy Museum of the City of New York Theatre and Music Collection.*

Louis Calhern, Paul Harvey. P/D: Guthrie McClintic.
SV: Col, 1933, Carole Lombard, Donald Cook, Gene Raymond, Monroe Owsley.

Brig, The (5/15/63, Living Theatre, 177)

Written by ex-Marine Kenneth H. Brown, this semidocumentary recorded the brutal treatment of a group of prisoners in a Marine Corps stockade, climaxing in the attempted escape of the men, and the resulting sadistic retaliation by the Marine Corps guards. A harrowing, essentially undramatic stage editorial; presented O/B with a nondescript cast by The Living Theatre. D: Judith Malina. SD: Julian Beck.

Bright Boy (3/2/44, Playhouse, 16)

A Machiavellian, revenge-seeking youngster vows to square accounts with his prep-school classmates, and does. David Merrick made his Broadway producing debut with this 1944 comedy-drama. The play was coproduced by Arthur J. Beckhard (D). ". . . talky, anticlimatic and occasionally downright dull . . ." *(New York Times)*. C: Donald Buka, Carleton Carpenter, Liam Dunn, Ivan Simpson. A: John Boruff.

Bright Honor (9/27/36, 48th Street, 17)

Problems of a rebellious plebe at a military school. Interesting but predictable 30's comedy-drama. C: Charles Powers, Leon Ames (deb.). A: Henry R. Misrock. P: Kirkland and Grisman. D: Anthony Brown.

Bright Rebel (12/27/38, Lyceum, 7)

Ponderous historical romance about the life of Lord Byron (John Cromwell) with special emphasis on his ill-fated marriage to Anne Isabella Milbanke (Francesca Bruning). A: Stanley Young. P/D: William Kilcullen.

Bright Star (10/15/35, Empire, 7)

An egocentric (Lee Tracy) marries a wealthy girl (Julie Haydon) who is deeply in love with him. His self-centered drive for success wrecks the marriage and brings on his wife's death. Despite its somewhat soapy plot line, this play by Philip Barry contained shrewd character observation, polished dialogue, and several highly effective scenes. Shabbily treated by the critics, *Bright Star* flickered out after seven performances. C: Jean Dixon, Louis Jean Heydt. P/D: Arthur Hopkins.

Brighten the Corner (12/12/45, Lyceum, 29)

Wheezy farce about the complications that ensue when an eccentric uncle (Charles Butterworth) mistakes a comely young woman for his nephew's wife. Written by John Cecil Holm, coauthor of *Three Men on a Horse* (1935); Butterworth's last Broadway appearance. P: Jean Dalrymple. D: Arthur O'Connell.

Brightower (1/28/70, John Golden, 1)

A drama that explores the individual's right to privacy. Daniel Brightower, a famous author with strong overtones of Hemingway, commits suicide because he fears he's going insane. His death is described publicly as an accident. A great writer, a legend in his own time, he is not allowed to rest in peace. A biographer is soon on the widow's doorstep, attempting to ferret out secrets of the great man's life. Flashbacks showing Brightower's decline are alternated with scenes of the widow trying to protect his life from exploitation. Author Dore Schary is against invasion of privacy, but his dramatization of this point-of-view brought blistering attacks from the critics. "If you want to know why serious drama is dying on Broadway, take *Brightower* as an object lesson. Its pompous noodle is filled with illusions of artistry, and its quality of writing wouldn't make an agony column" (Clive Barnes, *New York Times*. ". . . a parody of the ludicrous" (Martin Gottfried), *Women's Wear Daily*). "He [Schary] should have named him Ernest Hemingway, stuck to the facts and have done with it" (Douglas Watt, *New York Daily News*). To his credit, Schary has enjoyed happier moments on Broadway, notably as author of *Sunrise at Campobello* and adapter of Morris West's *The Devil's Advocate*. Though there was but one performance, Geraldine Brooks as the widow was memorable enough to earn a Tony nomination for Best Actress. A: Dore Schary. C: Robert Lansing, Geraldine Brooks, Arlen Dean Snyder, Martha Galphin, Paul McGrath, Will Hussung, Richard Buck. D: Mel Weiser. P: Michael Byron and Mel Weiser. SD: Tom Munn.

Brittle Heaven (11/13/34, Vanderbilt, 23)

Poetess Emily Dickinson (Dorothy Gish) falls in love with the husband (Albert Dekker) of her best friend, novelist Helen Hunt Jackson (Edith Atwater). "Most of the characters are bare, even of outline. . . . Even Dorothy Gish, who touches the part of Emily affectionately and sympathetically, cannot give it life" (*Theatre Arts*). A: Vincent York and Frederick Pohl b/o Josephine Pollitt's biography of Dickinson. P: Dave Schooler. D: Clarence Derwent.

Broadway (9/16/26, Broadhurst, 603)

Phenomenally successful melodrama about a gallant, small-time hoofer and his chorus girl sweetheart who become embroiled in a bootlegging murder. "The most completely acted and perfectly directed show I have seen in thirty years of professional playgoing" (Percy Hammond, *Tribune*). *Broadway* was the first play to convincingly depict the garish atmosphere of backstage nightclub life. The script had been turned down by every New York manager until unknown producer Jed Harris decided to take a chance

with it. Opening to rave reviews, the play ran seventy-six weeks and grossed more than two million dollars. C: Lee Tracy, Sylvia Field, Eloise Stream, Paul Porcasi, Joseph Calleia, Robert Gleckler, Edith Van Cleve, Millard Mitchell. A/D: Philip Dunning and George Abbott.
SV: U, 1929, Glenn Tryon, Evelyn Brent; 1942, George Raft, Pat O'Brien, Janet Blair, Broderick Crawford, Marjorie Rambeau. S. Z. Sakall.
Note: James Cagney understudied Lee Tracy in the leading role of hoofer Roy Lane during the New York run of *Broadway*.

Broadway Boy (5/3/32, 48th Street, 7)

Poorly written, skimpily mounted comedy about the problems of a would-be theatrical producer. "*Broadway Boy* sets out to show the difficulties of producing a show on a shoestring with such verisimilitude that one wonders how it ever got itself produced" (Robert Benchley, *The New Yorker*). C: Roy Roberts, Clarence Derwent, Roberta Beatty. A: Wallace A. Manheimer and Isaac Paul. P: Barton Slater. D: Jacob A. Weiser.

Broadway Interlude (4/19/34, Forrest, 12)

The relationship of a young playwright and his actress-fiancée is threatened when they fall under the baleful influence of flamboyant theatrical producer David Belasco (here called Grant Thompson). Heavy-handed backstage comedy-drama by Achmed Abdullah and William Almon Wolff b/o a novel by Faith Baldwin and Achmed Abdullah. C: Robert Emmett Keane, Arthur Pierson, Sally Starr, Dorothy Knapp. P: Theodore Hammerstein (D) and Denis Du-For.

Broadway Jones (9/23/12, Cohan, 176)

Brash young playboy (George M. Cohan) learns humility when he inherits his uncle's business. Breezy Cohan (A/D) comedy. P: Cohan and Harris.
Musicalized by Cohan as *Billie* (1928) with Joseph Wagstaff and Polly Walker.

Broken Chain, The (2/19/29, Maxine Elliott's, 30)

Plodding drama about the problems of an orthodox rabbi (Frank McGlynn) burdened with a rebellious son and daughter. A: William J. Perlman. P: Jacob A. Weiser. D: Mark Schweid.

Broken Dishes (11/5/29, Ritz, 165)

A "pale, gawky and uncertain ingenue" named Bette Davis made her Broadway debut in this lightweight domestic comedy by Martin Flavin. Flavin admitted the unknown actress was given the part "over my dead body!" but changed his mind about her after the second week of rehearsals. "This new girl is going to be good," he said. He was right. In *Broken Dishes*, Bette Davis played the role of Elaine Bumpsted, daughter of a henpecked father (Donald Meek) and an overbearing mother (Eda Heinemann), who asserts her independence by marrying the boy (Reed Brown, Jr.) she loves. P: Marion Gering (D) and Oscar Serlin.
SV: WB, 1931, *Too Young to Marry,* Loretta Young, Grant Withers, O. P. Heggie, Emma Dunn; 1936, *Love Begins at 20,* Patricia Ellis, Warren Hull, Hugh Herbert; 1940, *Calling all Husbands,* Ernest Truex, Florence Bates, George Tobias, George Reeves.

Broken Journey (6/23/42, Henry Miller, 23)

War correspondent returns home, becomes involved in romantic triangle. ". . . talks itself to death" (*World-Telegram*). C: Warner Anderson, Zita Johann, Edith Atwater, Phyllis Povah, Tom Powers. A: Andrew Rosenthal. P: Martin Burton. D: Arthur Hopkins.

Broken Wing, The (11/29/20, 48th Street, 248)

Aviator crashes through roof of Mexican house, develops amnesia, outwits bandits, falls in love with beautiful Mexican senorita, escapes with her to Argentina. Billed as a comedy-drama, this melodramatic exhibit of 1920 was long on plot, short on sense. C: Charles Trowbridge, George Abbott, Joseph Calleia, Inez Plummer, Louis Wolheim. A: Paul Dickey (D) and Charles W. Goddard.
SV: Par, 1932, Melvyn Douglas, Lupe Velez, Leo Carrillo.

Brooklyn Biarritz (2/27/41, Royale, 4)

Nondescript cast in slice-of-life comedy-melodrama about Coney Island. Much was made of the fact that the stage of the theatre was filled with real sand. Unfortunately, it was also filled with unreal characters. "The authors tried for a slice of life and drew a slice of hamburger—with onion" *(News)*. A: Beatrice Alliot and Howard Newman. P: Taylor and Elkins. D: J. B. Daniels. SD: Frederick Fox.

Brooklyn, U.S.A. (12/21/41, Forrest, 57)

Tough, documentary-style melodrama about the notorious "Murder, Inc." crime syndicate. The play started off in high gear, but ran out of gas by the middle of Act Two. *Brooklyn, U.S.A.* was co-authored by screenwriter John Bright *(Public Enemy)* and crime reporter Asa Bordages. It was co-produced by Bern Bernard and actor Lionel Stander. C: Eddie Nugent, Julie Stevens, Martin Wolfson, Sidney Lumet, Adelaide Klein, Tom Pedi, Byron McGrath, Robert H. Harris. D: Lem Ward. SD: Howard Bay.

Brother Cain (9/12/41, Golden, 19)

Sibling rivalry in a family of Polish coal miners. ". . . all of piece—bad play, bad acting and bad production" *(Herald Tribune)*. A: Michael Kallesser and Richard Norcross. P: American Civic Theatre. D: Charles Davenport.

Brother Rat (12/16/36, Biltmore, 575)

The comic misadventures of three Virginia Military Institute buddies (Eddie Albert, Jose Ferrer, Frank Albertson). As a hapless, secretly married cadet, Eddie Albert ran away with the acting honors in this hit comedy written by two V. M. I. graduates, John Monks, Jr. and Fred F. Finklehoffe. C: Ezra Stone, James Monks, Robert Griffith. P/D: George Abbott.
SV: WB, 1938, Wayne Morris, Eddie Albert, Ronald Reagan, Priscilla Lane, Jane Wyman, Jane Bryan; 1952, *About Face*, Gordon MacRae, Eddie Bracken, Dick Wesson, Joel Grey, Phyllis Kirk.

Brothers (12/25/28, 48th Street, 255)

Twin brothers—one poor but upright, the other wealthy and degenerate—meet after many years and swap places. Ridiculous heredity-versus-environment melodrama, with Bert Lytell in a dual role as the identical twins. A: Herbert Ashton, Jr. P: John Henry Mears. D: Arthur Hurley.
SV: Col, 1930, Bert Lytell, Dorothy Sebastian, William Morris.

Brouhaha (4/26/60, East Broadway, 2)

To raise some cash, and loosen purse strings in Washington and Moscow, the impoverished ruler of a Middle Eastern kingdom fabricates a revolution. This resolutely unfunny O/B satirical comedy was written by Anglo-American (Budapest-born) author George Tabori. It originally was presented in London in 1958 with Peter Sellers in the leading role. The New York production was drastically revised by Tabori to make the principal male role suitable for Viveca Lindfors (Mrs. Tabori). C: David Hurst, Russell Nype. P: Stratton Productions and Liska March. D: Tad Danielewski.

BURLEQUE 69

Brown Danube (5/17/39, Lyceum, 21)

Austrian beauty (Jessie Royce Landis) escapes marriage to a Nazi brute (Dean Jagger) by threatening to reveal his Jewish parentage. Lacklustre 1939 melodrama by Burnet Hershey. C: George Macready, Ernest Lawford, Eduard Franz, Edgar Stehli, Damian O'Flynn. P: Helen Bonfils and George Somnes (D).

Brown of Harvard (2/26/06, Princess, 101)

Tom Brown, Harvard's star athlete, wins the big race, the big football game and the hand of a professor's daughter. Rah-rah college comedy was a potpourri of roughhouse comedy and maudlin sentiment. C: Henry Woodruff, Howard Estabrook, Laura Hope Crews. A: Rida Johnson Young. P/D: Henry Miller.

Brown Sugar (12/2/37, Biltmore, 4)

Heavily plotted and heavy-handed melodrama with a Harlem locale and an all-black cast Diminutive, squeaky-voiced Butterfly McQueen made her Broadway debut in this George Abbott (P/D) offering which closed after four performances. C: Juano Hernandez, Christola Williams, Canada Lee, Georgette Harvey, Haven Johnson, Ruby Elzy, Alvin Childress, Beulah Edmonds, Richard Huey. A: Bernie Angus.

Bruno and Sidney (5/3/49, New Stages, 6)

A scholar (Billy Redfield), living in a remodeled Manhattan tenement, pursues a mouse named Bruno because he believes the rodent is scientifically valuable. Far-out but unfunny O/B farce. A: Edward Caulfield. P: New Stages. D: Philip Loeb.

Buccaneer, The (10/2/25, Plymouth, 20)

Stilted Maxwell Anderson-Laurence Stallings swashbuckler dealing with seventeenth-century British buccaneer Captain Henry Morgan (William Farnum) and his courtship of a beauteous widow (Estelle Winwood). P/D: Arthur Hopkins.

Buckaroo (3/16/29, Erlanger, 9)

Cowgirl (Nydia Westman) succeeds in putting her brand on a girl-shy bronco buster (James Bell) during a Chicago rodeo. 20's comedy turned out to be a bum steer. A: A. and E. Barker and Charles Beahan. P/D: Hamilton MacFadden.

Budget, The (9/20/32, Hudson, 7)

Poor comedy about the problems of a young homeowner during the Depression. C: Lynne Overman, Mary Lawlor, Raymond Walburn. A: Robert Middlemass. P: Harry Askin and Hugh Ford (D).

Buffalo Skinner, The (2/19/59, Theatre Marquee, 28)

An Oklahoma youth takes off for the boxcars and bordellos in an effort to find the meaning of life. Picaresque, semiautobiographical O/B drama written and directed by actor Lonny Chapman. C: Lou Antonio, Will Kuluva, Crahan Denton, Nancy Franklin. P: Frierson, Gold and White.

Bullfight (1/12/54, de Lys, 56)

The corrupt and domineering son (Hurd Hatfield) of a famed Mexican bullfighter destroys everyone—including his adoring younger brother—who falls under his evil spell. "... in the first rank of off-Broadway theatre work ... has depth and feeling" (*New York Times*). C: Mario Alcalde, Vivian Nathan, Tamara Daykarhanova, Loretta Leversee, Milton Selzer. A: Leslie Stevens. P: Modern American Theatre. D: Joseph Anthony.

Burlesque (9/1/27, Plymouth, 372)

The ups and downs of an inebriated hoofer (Hal Skelly), his soubrette wife (Barbara Stanwyck), and their best friend

Burlesque. **Hal Skelly and Barbara Stanwyck (September 1, 1927).** *Courtesy Museum of the City of New York Theatre and Music Collection.*

(Oscar Levant); sentimental backstage melodrama spawned a host of similar laugh-clown-laugh plays and films. Barbara Stanwyck catapulted to attention as Bonnie, the loyal wife, in *Burlesque*. She won the approval of her peers by refusing a screen test, stating that she would rather devote her talents to the legitimate theatre. "I had great plans for her," recalled Arthur Hopkins (P/D), "but the Hollywood offers kept coming. There was no competing with them. As a result, one of the theatre's great potential actresses was embalmed in celluloid." A: George Manker Watters and Arthur Hopkins.
R: (12/25/46, Belasco, 439) by Jean Dalrymple. C: Bert Lahr, Jean Parker. D: Arthur Hopkins.
SV: Par, 1929, *The Dance of Life*, Nancy Carroll, Hal Skelly, Oscar Levant; 1937, *Swing High, Swing Low*, Carole Lombard, Fred MacMurray, Dorothy Lamour, Charles Butterworth; Fox, 1948, *When My Baby Smiles at Me*, Betty Grable, Dan Dailey, Jack Oakie, June Havoc, James Gleason.

Burning Bright (10/18/50, Broadhurst, 13)

Symbolic drama by John Steinbeck b/o his novel of the same name. The plot deals with a sterile husband whose wife turns to a younger man to give her a child, and of her eventual reconciliation with her husband when he discovers the truth. In an effort to give the play a sense of universality, Steinbeck's characters appear in various scenes under different names and circumstances, but remain basically the same people. "*Burning Bright* does not have much eloquence in the theatre. . . . The play is cramped, literal and elementary" (*New York Times*). C: Barbara Bel Geddes, Kent Smith, Martin Brooks, Howard da Silva. P: Rodgers and Hammerstein. D: Guthrie McClintic. CD: Aline Bernstein. SD: Jo Mielziner.

Burning Deck, The (3/1/40, Maxine Elliott's, 3)

A group of jaded sophisticates try to straighten out their tangled lives on the Côte d'Azur. "Fourteen characters in search of a plot . . ." (*News*). C: Onslow Stevens, Zita Johann, Gregory Gaye, Vera Allen, Russell Hardie, Edith King. A: Andrew Rosenthal. P: Jack Small. D: Robert Milton.

Bus Stop (3/2/55, Music Box, 478)

A severe snowstorm brings an interstate bus to a halt in a small Kansas town in the middle of the night. Into a dingy roadside diner stagger the assorted passengers, chief among them Cherie, a brassy saloon singer, and Bo, a rambunctious, lovesick cowboy intent on shanghaiing Cherie and carrying her off like a roped steer to his Montana ranch. Cherie has a mind of her own, however, and refuses to be bullied into matrimony. Before the evening ends, Bo has learned to temper his caveman approach with humility and tenderness, and Cherie is now willing and eager to marry him. This warmly appealing 1955 comedy-drama, an expert blend of pathos and humor, was written by William Inge and staged by Harold Clurman. The play was splendidly acted by Kim Stanley as the soiled "chantoosie," Albert Salmi as the naïve, tough-talking cowboy, and Elaine Stritch as the hard-boiled café owner. C: Anthony Ross, Phyllis Love, Lou Polan, Crahan Denton, Patrick McVey. P: Robert Whitehead and Roger L. Stevens. CD: Paul Morrison. SD: Boris Aronson.

SV: Fox, 1956, Marilyn Monroe, Don Murray, Betty Field, Arthur O'Connell, Eileen Heckart (directed by Joshua Logan).

Business Before Pleasure (8/15/17, Eltinge, 357)

Another in the *Potash and Perlmutter* (1913) series of harum-scarum business farces in Jewish dialect. C: Barney Bernard, Alexander Carr. A: Montague Glass and Jules Eckert Goodman. P: A. H. Woods. D: George Marion.

But for the Grace of God (1/12/37, Guild, 42)

Unemployed father (James Bell) is forced to rely on the meager support of his two sons; one son goes to prison, the other dies of tuberculosis. Disjointed, unrelievedly lachrymose drama by Leopold Atlas, author of *Wednesday's Child* (1934). P: The Theatre Guild i.a.w. Sidney Harmon. D: Benno Schneider.

But for Whom Charlie (3/12/64, ANTA, 47)

S. N. Behrman's last play, a "serious comedy" about contemporary morals, the American literary scene, and cultural foundations, wherein a gentle philanthropist (Jason Robards, Jr.) finally triumphs over an opportunistic colleague (Ralph Meeker) who has been exploiting him for years. Poorly cast and poorly directed (by Elia Kazan), *But for Whom Charlie* was not a success. C: David Wayne, Faye Dunaway, Salome Jens, Clinton Kimbrough, Michael Strong, Patricia Roe, Barbara Loden. P: Repertory Theatre of Lincoln Center. SD: Jo Mielziner. M: David Amram.

But Not for Love (11/26/34, Empire, 8)

Mediocre 30's drama about a smalltown wife and her faithless husband. C: Hortense Alden, Walter Greaza, Effie Shannon. A: Geraldine Emerson. P/D: Shepard Traube.

—But Not Goodbye (4/11/44, 48th Street, 23)

Metaphysical whimsy by George Seaton* in which an elderly shipbuilder (Harry Carey) and his father (J. Pat O'Malley) return from the beyond to straighten out some tangled family affairs. (Since the father was killed in a tavern brawl at age thirty-six, he is considerably younger than his son;. ". . . a sparse and feeble comedy . . . containing homey reminders of the peach-jam era of American drama" *(Sun)*. "A comic fantasy which inspires affection" *(News)*. C: Elizabeth Patterson, Wendell Corey, Sylvia Field. D/SD: Richard Whorf. —*But Not Goodbye* was produced by John Golden i.a.w. film producer Harry Joe Brown. The latter, i.a.w. movie director Ralph Murphy, had tested an earlier version of the comedy in San Francisco in 1940 under the title *About Tomorrow,* with Frank Craven, J. M. Kerrigan, and Sally Eilers heading the cast.

SV: MGM, 1946, *The Cockeyed Miracle,* Frank Morgan, Keenan Wynn, Cecil Kellaway, Audrey Totter.

---

*George Seaton's screenplays range from the Marx Brothers' *A Day at the Races* to *The Song of Bernadette*. His writer-director credits include *Miracle on 34th Street, The Country Girl,* and *Airport*. —*But Not Goodbye* was his only Broadway play.

But, Seriously . . . (2/27/69, Henry Miller, 4)

Character study of a successful but spineless screenwriter. Sluggish comedy-drama by Hollywood scripter Julius J. Epstein (*Casablanca, Arsenic and Old Lace, Pete 'n' Tillie,* etc.). C: Tom Poston, Bethel Leslie, Richard Dreyfuss (deb.), Sally Gracie, Dick Van Patten, Steven Gravers. P: Oestreicher/Kipness/Leventhal. D: John Allen.

Butter and Egg Man, The (9/23/25, Longacre, 241)

A hayseed comes to New York, invests in show business, and beats the smart Broadway boys at their own game. Rollicking 1925 comedy hit by George S. Kaufman, "The Great Collaborators' " only solo playwriting effort. C: Gregory Kelly, Sylvia Field, Lucille (Webster) Gleason, Eloise Stream. P: Crosby Gaige. D: James Gleason.

R: (10/17/66, Cherry Lane, 32) by Theatre 1967. C: David Christmas, Vicki Cummings, Tyne Daly. D: Burt Shevelove.

SV: WB, 1932, *The Tenderfoot,* Joe E. Brown, Ginger Rogers, Lew Cody; 1937, *Dance Charlie Dance,* Stuart Erwin, Jean Muir, Glenda Farrell, Allen Jenkins; 1940, *An Angel from Texas,* Eddie Albert, Ronald Reagan, Rosemary Lane, Wayne Morris, Jane Wyman; 1953, *Three Sailors and a Girl,* Gordon MacRae, Jane Powell, Gene Nelson, Sam Levene.

Note: A silent version of *The Butter and Egg Man* (WB, 1928) starred Jack Mulhall and was directed by Richard Wallace.

Butterflies Are Free (10/21/69, Booth, 1,128)

An unpretentious comedy that ultimately placed in the fifty longest running shows in Broadway history. The story is a deft combination of wit and sentiment. A young blind man (Keir Dullea) seeks independence from his overly protective mother (Eileen Heckart). To that end, he takes a New York apartment, leaving mother behind in Scarsdale. But not for long. She soon appears, almost catching him *flagrante delicto* with the affectionate, slightly zany girl next door (Blythe Danner). The ensuing tug-of-war between mother and girl friend, and the struggle between mother and son manage to be simultaneously funny and moving. If the happy ending is predictable, it is also exactly what the audience wants. The freshness and durability of *Butterflies Are Free* lie in the unhackneyed quality of the characters. The blind hero is not only devoid of self-pity but disarmingly indifferent to his handicap. The girl may remark that she'd planned to go to UCLA but couldn't find a parking place, yet she's neither fool nor freak and grows with the play into a delightful, sympathetic woman. Nor is the mother the stereotyped horror so often encountered. She has dignity and wry humor, and accepts defeat at the end in a graceful, beautifully written scene. ". . . a darling play, a lovely play" (John Chapman, *New York Daily News*). ". . . humorous, winning, and quietly moving" (Richard Watts, *New York Post*). Blythe Danner won the Tony Award as Best Featured Actress, a category she shared with fellow nominee Eileen Heckart. As in other hits running for years, numerous cast changes occurred. Perhaps the most unexpected was the unique presence of Gloria Swanson in the mother's role. (The play's title is a quotation from Dickens' novel *Bleak House.*) A: Leonard Gershe. C: Keir Dullea, Blythe Danner, Eileen Heckart, Michael Glaser. D: Milton Katselas. P: Arthur Whitelaw, Max Brown, Byron Goldman. SD: Richard Seger.

SV: Columbia, 1972, Goldie Hawn, Edward Albert, Eileen Heckart, Mike Warren (directed by Milton Katselas from Gershe's adaptation of his play).

The Butter and Egg Man. **George Kelly, Lucille Webster, Sylvia Field (1925–26).**
Courtesy Museum of the City of New York Theatre and Music Collection.

Button, Button (10/23/29, Bijou, 5)
Muddled farce poking fun at insanity. A five-performance washout. C: Lynne Overman, Alison Skipworth, Ann Shoemaker, John Westley. A: Maurice Clark. P: Herman Shumlin i.a.w. H. C. Potter (D) and George Haight.

Buy, Buy, Baby (10/7/26, Princess, 12)
Wealthy eccentric (Alison Skipworth) offers a cool million to the first relative who becomes a parent. Inane farce with a good cast: Shirley Booth, Laura Hope Crews, Verree Teasdale, Thurston Hall. A: Russell Medcraft and Norma Mitchell (based on a play by Francis R. Bellamy and Lawton Mackall). P/D: Bertram Harrison.

Buy Me Blue Ribbons (10/17/51, Empire, 13)
A former Hollywood child star buys a swashbuckling verse play in which to make a Broadway comeback. He is so bad in the part that he is forced out of his own production. Stock farce, written to order by Sumner Locke Elliott for producer Jay Robinson, whose performance in the leading role prompted Walter Kerr (*Herald Tribune*) to remark: "He is suffering from delusions of adequacy." C: Audrey Christie, Vicki Cummings, Enid Markey, Gavin Gordon. D: Cyril Ritchard. CD/SD: Jack Landau.

By Request (9/27/28, Hudson, 28)
Meandering comedy about the reluctant infidelity of a newlywed husband. C: Elliott Nugent, J. C. Nugent, Verree

Teasdale. A/D: Elliott and J. C. Nugent. P: George M. Cohan.

By Your Leave (1/24/34, Morosco, 37)

Middle-aged couple (Howard Lindsay and Dorothy Gish) agree to go their separate ways in search of one last romantic fling. Slapdash comedy had its moments. C: Josephine Hull, Esther Dale, Kenneth MacKenna, Ernest Glendinning. A: Gladys Hurlbut and Emma Wells. P: Richard Aldrich and Alfred de Liagre, Jr. (D). SD: Jo Mielziner.

SV: RKO, 1934, Frank Morgan, Genevieve Tobin, Betty Grable.

C

Cactus Flower (12/8/65, Royale, 1,234)
A swinging Park Avenue dentist (Barry Nelson) decides to marry his kooky mistress (Brenda Vaccaro). Since she has been led to believe he has a wife and children, he persuades his prim receptionist (Lauren Bacall) to pose as his wife and convince the girl their marriage is on the rocks. The receptionist blossoms into a sophisticated beauty and the bachelor-dentist falls for her instead. This glossy smash hit comedy was hailed by the *New York Post* as "steadily entertaining." C: Burt Brinckerhoff, Robert Moore, Arny Freeman. A/D: Abe Burrows, b/o a play by Barillet and Gredy. P: David Merrick. Produced in London (1966) with Margaret Leighton and Tony Britton in the leading roles.
SV: Col, 1969, Ingrid Bergman, Walter Matthau, Goldie Hawn, Jack Weston (directed by Gene Saks from a screenplay by I. A. L. Diamond).

Café (8/28/30, Ritz, 4)
Faltering comedy-drama by Marya Mannes, set in the Latin Quarter of Paris, and dealing with a handsome, quixotic artist whom women find irresistible. "... lacks a point of view.... Such plays as *Café* are harmful to transatlantic travel" *(New York Times)*. C: Rollo Peters, Frances Fuller, Georgia Caine, Marjorie Gateson, King Calder, Sam Byrd. P: William A. Brady i.a.w. John Tuerk. D: Jose Ruben.

Café Crown (1/23/42, Cort, 141)
An aging star (Morris Carnovsky) of the Yiddish theatre tries to persuade a prosperous, middle-aged busboy (Sam Jaffe) to back his new production of *King Lear*. The Café Royal, a famous theatrical restaurant catering to members of New York's once-legendary Jewish theatre, provided the setting for this engaging comedy written by H. S. Kraft and directed by Elia Kazan. C: Sam Wanamaker (deb.), Whit Bissell, Eduard Franz, Paula Miller, Mitzi Hajos. SD: Boris Aronson.
Musicalized by H. S. Kraft, Albert Hague, and Marty Brill (1964) with Sam Levene, Theodore Bikel, Alan Alda, Tommy Rall, and Brenda Lewis.

Cage, The (6/18/70, Playhouse, 126)
O/B prison drama. A young man struggles to adjust to the rigors of life in prison. The play was not more meaningful for having been written by an ex-inmate of San Quentin, on parole from a life sentence, but the grit of realism was undeniably present, as well as considerable dramatic tension. Audience response supported a four-month run for this unusual personal memoir. A: Rick Cluchey. C: Rick Cluchey, Robert Poole, Ernie Allen, Randolph Dobbs, Henry Everhart, Gene Ackley. D: Kenneth Kitch. P: David Carroll in the Barbwire Theater Production. SD: Jonathan Stuart.

Caine Mutiny Court Martial, The (1/20/54, Plymouth, 405)

Herman Wouk's dramatization of the latter sequences from his Pulitzer Prize novel, *The Caine Mutiny*. The play concentrates on the courtroom proceedings against Lieutenant Maryk (John Hodiak), accused of forcibly relieving Captain Queeg (Lloyd Nolan) of command during a typhoon in the Pacific. The odds and naval tradition are against Maryk. But as his reluctant defense attorney, Lt. Barney Greenwald (Henry Fonda), proceeds to expose the captain's petty tyrannies and incompetence, the weakness in Queeg's character is gradually revealed in a devastating portrait of mental disintegration, and Maryk is acquitted. In a final scene, Greenwald, conscience-ridden and drunk, deplores that he had to break Captain Queeg, a once-meritorious career officer, and argues that discipline in the Navy should be respected and cherished at any cost. Walter Kerr (*Herald Tribune*) summed up the prevailing critical opinion of the time when he hailed the play as a "shrewd and shattering . . . theatrical adventure." Presented by Paul Gregory with a minimum of scenery and props, the production was expertly staged by Charles Laughton (who replaced Dick Powell as director after the first two weeks of rehearsal). Superbly acted by an all-male cast, *Caine* enjoyed the distinction of running simultaneously as a play and a film (see below) while still fresh from its triumphal tenure as a 3,500,000-copy best-seller-list blockbuster. Among the bit players in the Broadway production was a young actor by the name of James Baumgarner. In the final months of the show he replaced the late John Hodiak as Lt. Maryk. Then he went to Hollywood, was given a contract with Warner Brothers, was rechristened James Garner, and rose to stardom in the TV series *Maverick*.

Note: The Caine Mutiny was filmed (1954) by Columbia with a cast headed by Humphrey Bogart, Jose Ferrer, Van Johnson, Fred MacMurray, Robert Francis, Tom Tully, E. G. Marshall, and Lee Marvin. The picture was directed by Edward Dmytryk.

Calculated Risk (10/31/62, Ambassador, 221)

Which member of a New England textile firm's board of directors is secretly betraying his company to an unscrupulous stock manipulator? Reasonably engrossing melodrama by Joseph Hayes, author of *The Desperate Hours* (1955); b/o a play by Ross and Singer. C: Joseph Cotten, Patricia Medina (deb.), Gerald O'Loughlin, Frank Conroy, Roland Winters, Russell Collins, John Beal, Gene Blakely, Alexander Clark. P: Erskine, Stevens, Hayes i.a.w. Lyn Austin. D: Robert Montgomery.

Calico Wedding (3/7/45, National, 5)

To make her husband jealous, a wife flirts with a handsome young explorer. ". . . feeble and hopeless . . . a silly and lightweight comedy" *(Sun)*. *Calico Wedding* was written and directed by screenwriter Sheridan Gibney (*I Am a Fugitive From a Chain Gang, The Story of Louis Pasteur, Anthony Adverse*, etc.). C: Louis Jean Heydt, William Post, Grete Mosheim, Forrest Orr. P: Meyer and Myers.

Call Me By My Rightful Name (1/31/61, Sheridan Square, 127)

O/B comedy-drama about a Columbia University student who discovers that his black roommate has had a love affair with the girl he intends to marry. "The best off-Broadway play of the year" *(Newsday)*. C: Robert Duvall, Joan Hackett, Alvin Ailey. A: Michael Shurtleff b/o a novel by S. F. Pfoutz. D: Milton Katselas.

Call Me Ziggy (2/12/37, Longacre, 3)

Michael Todd (P) made his Broadway bow with this 1937 fiasco about a shoestring producer (Joseph Buloff) and his assorted problems. *Call Me Ziggy* called it quits after three performances. A: Dan Goldberg. D: Gregory Deane.

Call on Kuprin, A (5/25/61, Broadhurst, 12)

Reasonably lively suspense melodrama revolving around the cloak-and-dagger efforts of an American reporter in Moscow to help a Soviet scientist escape to the United States. C: Jeffrey Lynn, George Voskovec, Eugenie Leontovich. A: Jerome Lawrence and Robert E. Lee b/o the novel by Maurice Edelman. P: Griffith and Prince. D: George Abbott. SD: Donald Oenslager.

Call the Doctor (8/31/20, Empire, 129)

Shaky little David Belasco (P/D) comedy about a "Doctor of Domestic Difficulties" who dispenses advice to the lovelorn until she herself is smitten by the love bug. C: Janet Beecher, Philip Merivale, Charlotte Walker, Fania Marinoff, William Morris. A: Jean Archibald.

Cameo Kirby (12/20/09, Hackett, 24)

The romance and adventures of a riverboat gambler in the Old South. Meandering Booth Tarkington-Harry Leon Wilson comedy-drama. C: Dustin Farnum, Conway Tearle, Emmett Corrigan. P: Liebler and Company. D: Hugh Ford.

SV: Fox, 1930, J. Harold Murray, Norma Terris, Myrna Loy, Stepin Fetchit.

Call the Doctor. Fania Marinoff, Janet Beecher, William Morris, Charlotte Walker, and Philip Merivale (August 31, 1920). *Courtesy Museum of the City of New York Theatre and Music Collection.*

Camino Real (3/19/53, National, 60)

An apocalyptic vision of the contemporary world, Tennessee Williams' surrealist fantasy disregards all boundaries of time or space. The setting is a walled city in a tropical police state from which the characters try to escape without success. These include some of the great romantics of history: Lord Byron, Casanova, Marguerite Gautier, and Kilroy, the quintessential American dreamer "with a heart as big as a baby." It is through Kilroy's eyes that we view these dispossessed victims of circumstance, trapped "like caged birds" on a terminal road that leads from nowhere to nowhere, frantically searching for some shred of meaning to the riddle of existence. Vividly staged by Elia Kazan, with action spilling across the footlights, down the aisles, and sometimes into the balconies, this 1953 production elicited strongly negative reactions from many first-string critics: "Obscure and maddeningly self-conscious . . . an enigmatic bore" (Richard Watts, Jr.) ". . . as uncontrolled as a nightmare, and as uncoordinated as a scrapbook" (Louis Kronenberger). "The worst play yet written by the best playwright of his generation" (Walter Kerr). Though *Camino Real* was "a mutilated play," said Williams some years later, it contained his "best writing." "But there were things in it that didn't seem quite rational, even in terms of the wildness of the play," admitted the author. C: Eli Wallach, Jo Van Fleet, Hurd Hatfield, Joseph Anthony, Barbara Baxley, Jennie Goldstein, Frank Silvera, David J. Stewart, Henry Silva, Martin Balsam, Vivian Nathan, Nehemiah Persoff, Fred Sadoff, Salem Ludwig, Michael Gazzo, Guy Thomajan. P: Cheryl Crawford and Ethel Reiner i.a.w. Walter P. Chrysler, Jr. CD/SD: Lemuel Ayers. M: Bernardo Segall.

R: (5/16/60, St. Marks, 89). C: Clinton Kimbrough, Collin Wilcox, Nan Martin, Lester Rawlins. D: Jose Quintero.

R: (1/8/70, Lincoln Center, 52). C: Al Pacino, Jessica Tandy, Jean-Pierre Aumont, Sylvia Syms, Susan Tyrrell, Victor Buono. D: Milton Katselas.

Canary Dutch (9/8/25, Lyceum, 39)

Hack melodrama about an elderly counterfeiter who murders a fellow ex-con to protect the reputation of his long-lost daughter. C: Willard Mack (A), Sidney Toler, Catherine Dale Owen. P/D: David Belasco.

Candle in the Wind (10/22/41, Shubert, 95)

Maxwell Anderson drama, directed by Alfred Lunt, dealing with the efforts of an American actress (Helen Hayes) in occupied Paris to get her French lover out of a Nazi concentration camp. "Pedestrian in its writing, its thinking and its emotions" *(Herald Tribune)*. C: Evelyn Varden, Lotte Lenya, Louis Borell, Tonio Selwart, John Wengraf, Joseph Wiseman. P: The Theatre Guild and The Playwrights' Company. SD: Jo Mielziner.

Candyapple, The (11/23/70, Edison, 1)

A comedy that professes to show the changing attitudes of Roman Catholics toward their religion. On the eve of Frank McGrath's wedding, his priest-brother, Larry, arrives to perform the ceremony. Disconcertingly, he is accompanied by his wife, and announces he is giving up the Church. When the news is broken to the boys' father (veteran actor John Beal), he reacts in commendably modern fashion by applauding the decision and confesses his own faith has been a case of duty rather than belief. ("Candyapple" is a description of Roman Catholicism that occurs in the play.) "The Catholic Church has weathered many a harsh blow in its long history, but I doubt if it has ever been subject to a sillier contemplation than it received in *The Candyapple*"

(Richard Watts, *New York Post*). A: John Grissmer. C: John Beal, Arlen Dean Snyder, Joy Garrett, Ray Edelstein, Raymond Singer, Noel Conlon, Irene Bunde. P: William F. DeSeta. D: Stuart Bishop. SD: David R. Ballou.

Cantilevered Terrace, The (1/17/62, 41st Street, 39)

The decline and fall of a wealthy American family as seen, chiefly, through the eyes of its inbred, aristocratic mother (Mildred Dunnock). Offbeat, frequently engrossing O/B comedy-drama by William Archibald (A/D), author of *The Innocents* (1950). CD/SD: Paul Morrison.

Cape Smoke (2/16/25, Martin Beck, 105)

Voodoo in South Africa, a witch doctor's curse, and other assorted thriller shenanigans. Pretty silly stuff. C: James Rennie, Ruth Shepley, Percy Waram. A: Walter Archer Frost. P: Charles K. Gordon. D: A. E. Anson.
SV: Released with synchronized sound effects by Fox (1929) as *Black Magic* with Josephine Dunn, Earle Foxe, Henry B. Walthall.

Caponsacchi (10/26/26, Hampden's, 271)

Rococo costume melodrama with mellifluous-voiced Walter Hampden (P/D) as a priest accused of murder and pardoned at the last moment by the Pope. Adapted by Arthur Goodrich and Rose A. Palmer from Robert Browning's *The Ring and the Book*.

Cappy Ricks (1/13/19, Morosco, 128)

A surly old sea dog objects to the romance of his daughter and his first mate. Breezy comedy by Edward E. Rose (D), based on the stories of Peter B. Kyne. C: William Courtenay, Thomas A. Wise, Marion Coakley. P: Oliver Morosco.
SV: Republic, 1935, *Cappy Ricks Returns*, Robert McWade; 1937, *The Affairs of Cappy Ricks*, Walter Brennan, Mary Brian; WB, 1937, *The Go-Getter*, Charles Winninger, George Brent, Anita Louise (directed by Busby Berkeley).

Caprice (12/31/28, Guild, 178)

Stylish boudoir comedy with the Lunts at the peak of their comedic form. The illegitimate son (Douglass Montgomery) of a middle-aged Viennese lawyer (Alfred Lunt) arrives for a visit and promptly falls in love with a fascinating houseguest (Lynn Fontanne). When she confesses that she is his father's mistress, he and his mother (Lily Cahill) depart in a huff, leaving the wily mistress once again in command of the situation. A: Philip Moeller (D) b/o play by Sil-Vara. P: The Theatre Guild.

Captain Applejack (12/30/21, Cort, 366)

Blasé young man longs for adventure, finds it by dreaming he is a piratical ancestor. Lively melodramatic farce by Walter Hackett (A/D). C: Wallace Eddinger, Phoebe Foster, Ferdinand Gottschalk, Mary Nash, Hamilton Revelle. P: Sam H. Harris.
SV: WB, 1930, John Halliday, Mary Brian.

Captain Jinks of the Horse Marines (2/4/01, Garrick, 168)

Ethel Barrymore's first starring role on Broadway as Madame Trentoni, an opera singer who encounters social prejudice because of her profession. The Clyde Fitch (A/D) comedy was thin to the point of emaciation, but the radiant, twenty-two-year-old Miss Barrymore's performance was so captivating that the play, originally scheduled for a two-week engagement, played to packed houses for seven months. P: Charles Frohman. Musicalized by Gensler and Jones as *Captain Jinks* (1925) with Louise Brown, Joe E. Brown, J. Harold Murray, Marion Sunshine.

Captain Jinks of the Horse Marines. **Ethel Barrymore.** *Courtesy Museum of the City of New York Theatre and Music Collection.*

Captains and the Kings, The (1/2/62, Playhouse, 7)

Admiral Hyman Rickover, here called Richard Kohner (Dana Andrews), encounters anti-semitism and the opposition of his hidebound superiors in his struggle to launch the Navy's first nuclear-powered submarine. "A vigorous and entertaining drama [despite] some unconvincing theatrical excesses" (*Post*). ". . . pasteboard playmaking" (*Herald Tribune*). C: Charlie Ruggles, Peter Graves,* Lee Grant, Conrad Nagel, Joseph Campanella,* Gavin MacLeod.* A: Leo Lieberman. P: The Theatre Guild and Joel Schenker. D: Joseph Anthony.

---

*Broadway debuts.

Captain Kidd, Jr. (11/13/16, Cohan and Harris, 128)

A bookseller, his granddaughter, and a budding novelist who works in the shop leave their musty bookshop to search for buried treasure in Cape Cod. They return disconsolately to New York, poorer than when they left. But, as in all farces of this sort, there is, of course, a happy ending. "*Captain Kidd, Jr.* would probably have grown into a musical comedy if song numbers could have been crowded between the laughs. It is of the same irresponsible stuff that librettos are made" (*New York Times*). C: Otto Kruger, Edith Taliaferro, Adele Rowland, Zelda Sears. A: Rida Johnson Young. P: Cohan and Harris. D: Sam Forrest.

Captive, The (9/29/26, Empire, 160)

Irene (Helen Menken) is in love with another woman. Jacques (Basil Rathbone) hopes marriage will cure his beloved of her "abnormal erotic passion." It doesn't, and Irene eventually leaves her husband to return to her female love. "An unprecedented play [written] with infinite tact and reticence" (Alexander Woollcott, *World*). C: Norman Trevor, Ann Andrews, Arthur Wontner. A: Adapted by Arthur Hornblow, Jr.* from a play by Edouard Bourdet. P: Charles Frohman, Inc. D: Gilbert Miller. This classic study of homosexual love, one of the most internationally discussed plays of its time, had the misfortune to open on Broadway at a bad time. A rash of wretchedly smutty plays had found their way to the boards that season (1926), and moralists were up in arms. *The Captive* was cited as "an indecent display of lesbianism" and forced to close. Incidentally, the accent the play placed on violets as a symbol of the third sex ruined the violet business at florists for many years thereafter. A story of the time, probably apocryphal, had Sam Goldwyn expressing a desire to purchase film rights to *The Captive*. "You can't film that," he was cautioned, "it deals with lesbians." "So all right," countered Goldwyn, "where they got lesbians, we'll use Austrians."

---

*Noted Hollywood producer *(Ruggles of Red Gap, The Asphalt Jungle, Oklahoma!*, etc.).

Caravan (8/29/28, Klaw, 21)

Tangled love affairs and murder in a gypsy caravan traveling through France. "A placid melodrama . . . dull and uninteresting" *(New York Times)*. C: Virginia Pemberton, Robert Hyman, Elsa Shelley. A: Clifford Pember and Ralph Cullinan. P: Richard Herndon. D: Rollo Lloyd.

Career (4/30/57, **Seventh Avenue South**, 232)

Engrossing O/B drama about an actor's struggle to win theatrical success. At the end, after twenty-five rootless, miserable years, he finally achieves stardom on Broadway. Was it worth it? According to author James Lee, there is only one answer for an actor. ". . . this joyless chronicle of life in the New York theatre is fundamentally knowledgeable and discerning" *(New York Times)*. C: Charles Aidman, Nancy Rennick, Norman Rose, Norma Crane, Mary James, Larry Hagman. P: James Preston and Charles Olsen (D).

SV: Par, 1959, Anthony Franciosa, Dean Martin, Shirley MacLaine, Carolyn Jones, Joan Blackman (directed by Joseph Anthony).

Career Angel (5/23/44, National, 22)

A guardian angel helps a kindly cleric resolve assorted problems in a financially troubled Catholic orphanage. "The whimsical idea behind it is agreeable enough . . . but most of *Career Angel* is forced and tenuous" *(PM)*. C: Glenn Anders, Whitford Kane, Carleton Carpenter. A: Gerald M. Murray. P: Billings and Dicks i.a.w. David Shay. D: Don Appell.

Note: Career Angel originally was produced O/B (11/18/43) by the Blackfriars' Guild. The semiprofessional production was well received by press and public.

Carefree Tree, The (10/11/55, Phoenix, 24)

The Romeo and Juliet story told in the stylized form of a Chinese legend. "More tedious, theatre-wise, than all the long centuries of the many Chinese dynasties" *(News)*. C: Farley Granger (deb.), Janice Rule, Larry Gates, Edith Meiser, Sorrell Booke, Blanche Yurka, Frederic Warriner, Thayer David, Jerry Stiller, Sada Thompson, Alvin Ailey, Michael Higgins, Frances Sternhagen. A: Aldyth Morris. P: Phoenix Theatre. D/SD: Jack Landau. CD: Alvin Colt.

Carnival (12/24/19, 44th Street, 13)

A jealous actor (Godfrey Tearle) tries to

strangle his actress-wife when she plays Desdemona to his Othello. Unconvincing melodrama with a plot that has done yeoman service, most notably in the Ruth Gordon-Garson Kanin 1948 screenplay, *A Double Life*. A: Matheson Lang and H.C.M. Hardinge, from a play by Pordes-Milo. P: Tearle, MacLeod, and Ephraim. D: Godfrey Tearle.

Carnival (4/24/29, Forrest, 20)

When an innocent lad proposes marriage, a carnival "cooch" dancer tries to disillusion him about her past life. All else failing, she kills herself. Clumsy and lugubrious 20's drama. C: Norman Foster, Anne Forrest. A: William R. Doyle. P: Irving Lande.

Carry Me Back to Morningside Heights (2/27/68, Golden, 7)

Sidney Poitier returned to Broadway to direct this flimsy one-joke charade about a masochistic Jewish youth (David Steinberg) who, to expiate his guilt feelings, becomes the personal slave of a young Negro student (Louis Gossett). C: Cicely Tyson, Diane Ladd,* Johnny Brown. A: Robert Alan Aurthur. P: Saint-Subber i.a.w. Harold Loeb.

---

*Broadway debut.

Carry Nation (10/29/32, Biltmore, 31)

Multiscened biographical drama of the notorious temperance agitator (Esther Dale) who, convinced of her divine mission, destroyed countless Kansas saloons with her trusty hatchet. Joshua Logan, Myron McCormick, Mildred Natwick, and James Stewart made their Broadway acting debuts in this ponderous 1932 opus. Also in the cast: Byron McGrath, Frieda Altman, Barbara O'Neil, Katherine Emery. A: Frank McGrath. P: Arthur J. Beckhard. D: Blanche Yurka.

Carry On (1/23/28, Masque, 8)

Businessman dominates his family with tragic results. Feeble drama by Owen Davis. C: Berton Churchill, Elizabeth Patterson. P: Carl Reed. D: Clifford Brooke.

Casanova (9/26/23, Empire, 78)

Casanova (Lowell Sherman) falls in love with an ardent beauty (Katharine Cornell) but fate forces them to part. Twenty years later he meets their daughter but cannot make himself known to her, and dies. Plodding costume piece by Sidney Howard, based on a play by Lorenzo de Azertis. C: Ernest Cossart, Mary Ellis. P: A. H. Woods and Gilbert Miller. M: Deems Taylor.

Case of Becky, The (10/1/12, Belasco, 95)

A girl (Frances Starr) with a dual personality problem is cured through hypnosis. Shoddy, unconvincing 1912 melodrama. A: Edward Locke. P/D: David Belasco.

Case of Libel, A (10/10/63, Longacre, 242)

Dramatization of the libel suit by war correspondent Quentin Reynolds, here called Dennis Corcoran (John Randolph), against ultrareactionary columnist Westbrook Pegler, here called Boyd Bendix (Larry Gates). Reynolds brought suit to stop Pegler's distorted and unjust attacks on his patriotism and personal life. The courtroom action in the play centered around the attempts of the prosecuting attorney (Van Heflin) to expose the dangers of extremism, and the efforts of the opposition attorney (Sidney Blackmer) to (unsuccessfully) defend his fanatically right-wing client. ". . . compulsively interesting" (*Herald Tribune*). A: Henry Denker b/o the book *My Life in Court* by Louis Nizer. P: Roger L. Stevens and Joel Schenker. D: Sam Wanamaker. SD: Donald Oenslager.

Case of Clyde Griffiths (3/13/36, Barrymore, 19)

Lee Strasberg directed this "modernized" version of *An American Tragedy* which sought, unsuccessfully, to interpret Theodore Dreiser's story in terms of the class struggle. The large cast included Alexander Kirkland, Margaret Barker, Phoebe Brand, Morris Carnovsky, Luther Adler, Art Smith, Roman Bohnen, Sanford Meisner. In bit parts: Jules (John) Garfield, Robert Lewis, Elia Kazan, Anthony Ross, Whitney Bourne. A: Erwin Piscator and Lena Goldschmidt. P: The Group Theatre and Milton Shubert. SD: Watson Barratt.
See *An American Tragedy*.

Case of Youth, A (3/23/40, National, 5)

Comedy about a Swiss miss who saves her stockbroker-father from jail. "A case of arrested theatre development" *(News)*. ". . . three acts as unsmiling as . . . a collection of Bela Lugosi's passport photographs" *(Post)*. C: Arthur Margetson, Valerie Cossart, Ellen Schwanneke. A: Wesley Towner b/o a play by Ludwig Hirschfeld and Eugene Wolf. P: Courtney Burr. D: Arthur Sircom.

Casey Jones (2/19/38, Fulton, 25)

Saga of a railroad engineer (Charles Bickford) afflicted with failing vision and retired to a whistle-stop station. In the end, Casey Jones quits his soulless job and takes to the open road in search of a better life. C: Van Heflin, Peggy Conklin, Charles Dingle, Frances Williams, Robert Strauss (deb.), Howard Da Silva, Joseph Sawyer. This Group Theatre production was notable on several counts: it gave Elia Kazan his first major Broadway directorial assignment; it won acclaim for Mordecai Gorelik (SD), whose design of a railroad locomotive was the hit of the show; and, finally, despite its weaknesses, the play offered evidence of considerable talent by author Robert Ardrey. *Casey Jones* was the second Ardrey script to be produced on Broadway within a fortnight. (*How to Get Tough About It* opened ten days earlier.) Both plays were box-office failures.

Castro Complex, The (11/18/70, Stairway, 7)

Weak comedy of a young New York woman with a strange obsession. Before she can derive any pleasure or satisfaction from her fiancé's love-making, he must dress up like Fidel Castro. She has a crush on him, and her hapless young man must impersonate the Cuban dictator in order to arouse her. An able cast could do nothing to save the play, which suffered the fate of all one-joke comedies: bored audiences. A: Mel Arrighi. C: Marian Hailey, Raul Julia, Terry Kiser. D: James Burrows. P: Jeff Britton. SD: Kert Lundell.

Cat and the Canary, The (2/7/22, National, 349)

One of the most popular mystery-comedies of the 1920's and the prototype of a vast number of subsequent "let's-scare-the-heroine-to-death" chillers. A young heiress (Florence Eldridge) is forced to spend the night in a gloomy old mansion with the proviso that she be of sound mind in order to retain her inheritance. The girl—despite sliding panels, clutching hands, disappearing bodies, voodoo incantations, and all sorts of other nervewracking occurrences—manages to keep her sanity with the help of the timid soul hero (Henry Hull) who falls in love with her. C: John Willard, Blanche Friderici. A: John Willard. P: Kilbourn Gordon.
R: (1/4/65, Stage 73, 143) by The Whodunit Company. C: Adale O'Brien, Tom Wheatley. D: Ammon Kabatchnik.
SV: U, 1930, *The Cat Creeps,* Helen Twelvetrees, Neil Hamilton, Raymond Hackett, Lilyan Tashman; Par, 1939, *The Cat and*

The Canary, Bob Hope, Paulette Goddard, Gale Sondergaard, Douglass Montgomery.

Note: The cast of the highly popular silent film version (U, 1927) included Laura La Plante, Tully Marshall, Flora Finch, Gertrude Astor, Creighton Hale, and Lucien Littlefield.

Cat-Bird, The (2/16/20, Maxine Elliott's, 33)

An entomologist (John Drew) renews a romance with a middle-aged widow (Janet Beecher). Very mild comedy by Rupert Hughes. P/D: Arthur Hopkins.

Cat Screams, The (6/16/42, Martin Beck, 7)

Quarantined in a Mexican pension, a group of American tourists find themselves enveloped in a wave of suicides. "It is easy to keep the plot's secret, for it is not worth giving away" *(Journal-American).* C: Mildred Dunnock, Gordon Oliver, Doris Nolan, Herbert Yost, Lloyd Gough, Lea Penman, Martin Wolfson. A: Basil Beyea b/o a novel by Todd Downing. P: Martha Hodge. D: Arthur Pierson.

Catch Me if You Can (3/9/65, Morosco, 96)

Mystery revolving around the disappearance of a bride on her honeymoon. Diverting comedy-whodunit with a truly startling surprise ending. Written by Jack Weinstock and Willie Gilbert;* b/o a play by Robert Thomas. C: Dan Dailey, Bethel Leslie, Tom Bosley, George Mathews, Eli Mintz, Patrick McVey, Jo Tract. P: Guber, Ford and Gross. D: Vincent J. Donehue. SD: George Jenkins.

---

*Coauthors of the 1961 Pulitzer Prize musical, *How to Succeed in Business Without Really Trying*.

Catherine Was Great (8/2/44, Shubert, 191)

Spectacular costume drama by and with Mae West. Dealing with the public and private career of Catherine of Russia, the play dwelt primarily on the celebrated empress' carnal conquests. Highlight: Miss West's brief but memorable curtain speech: "Catherine had 300 lovers. I did the best I could in a couple of hours." Song: "He Must be Strong, Solid and Sensational" (sung by the star in a black wig and a peasant's costume). "Mae West returned to Broadway last night, decked out like a battleship in a swimming pool. . . . The new show at the Shubert is ornamental, expensive and awful" *(Herald Tribune).* ". . . so far as Catherine of Russia is concerned, East is East and West is West and never the twain shall meet" (George Jean Nathan). Opulently produced by Michael Todd, *Catherine Was Great* premiered to an audience that had bought four million dollars worth of war bonds in order to purchase tickets. Despite a critical drubbing, the play ran 191 performances on Broadway and then embarked upon a long and profitable cross-country tour. C: Joel Ashley, Philip Huston, Gene Barry, Robert Strauss, Ray Bourbon, Dayton Lummis, Robert Morse (deb.). D: Roy Hargrave. CD: Mary Percy Schenck and Ernest Schrapps. SD: Howard Bay.

Caught in the Rain (12/31/06, Garrick, 161)

In order to save an older friend from ruin, an alleged woman-hater (William Collier) agrees sight unseen to marry the fellow's daughter. Shortly thereafter, however, he falls in love with a pretty young girl and tries vainly to extricate himself from his marital agreement. Guess who the young girl turns out to be. "A merry little affair from beginning to end . . . ingenious and funny" *(New York Times).* C: George Nash, Wallace Eddinger, Nanette Comstock. A: William Collier and Grant Stewart. P: Charles Frohman. Musicalized by William B. Friedlander as *Pitter Patter* (1920).

Caught Wet (11/4/31, Golden, 13)

During a society houseparty, a valuable pearl necklace is stolen. Who done it? Dull mystery-comedy by Rachel Crothers (A/D). C: Sylvia Field, Gertrude Michael. P: John Golden.

Caukey (2/17/44, Blackfriars', 22)

Intriguing reversal of the black vs. white problem in which the Negroes are rich and powerful, while the "Caukeys" (Caucasians) are the underprivileged minority. ". . . searingly sardonic and ironical arraignment of race prejudice" *(World-Telegram)*. "The Negro problem is much too serious to play tricks with, no matter with what good intentions" *(PM)*. This O/B comedy-drama was written by Rev. Thomas McGlynn, son of actor Frank McGlynn. P: Blackfriars' Guild. D: Dennis Gurney.

Cave Dwellers, The (10/19/57, Bijou, 97)

William Saroyan's rueful, essentially storyless fable about a group of penniless has-beens who find shelter from the outside world in an abandoned New York theatre. "The most winning play Mr. Saroyan has written in eighteen years" *(New York Times)*. C: Wayne Morris,* Barry Jones, Eugenie Leontovich, Susan Harrison,* Gerald Hiken, John Alderman,* Clifton James,* Ivan Dixon.* P: Carmen Capalbo (D) and Stanley Chase. CD: Ruth Morley. SD: William Pitkin. M: Bernardo Segall.
R: (10/16/61, Greenwich Mews, 6). C: Geraldine Fitzgerald, Anthony Zerbe. D: Michael Lindsay-Hogg.

---

*Broadway debuts.

Ceiling Zero (4/10/35, Music Box, 102)

Action-filled melodrama about the aeronautic (and romantic) problems of a veteran pilot. Written by Commander Frank Wead of the Naval Air Force, Ceiling Zero proved to be a fast-paced, highly professional thriller. C: Osgood Perkins, John Litel, Nedda Harrigan, Margaret Perry, John Boruff, Walter Greaza. P: Brock Pemberton. D: Antoinette Perry.
SV: WB, 1936, James Cagney, Pat O'Brien, June Travis, Stuart Erwin, Barton MacLane (directed by Howard Hawks); 1941, *International Squadron,* Ronald Reagan, James Stephenson, Julie Bishop, Cliff Edwards, Reginald Denny, Olympe Bradna, William Lundigan.
Note: Illinois-born playwright-scenarist Frank "Spig" Wead first gained fame as the holder of five world's records for flying. Starting as a barnstormer, he ended up a war hero. A back injury put a halt to Wead's aviation career. To make a living, he turned to writing Hollywood screenplays *(Hell Divers, West Point of the Air, China Clipper,* etc.). In 1957 his life story was filmed by MGM as *The Wings of Eagles* with John Wayne portraying the spunky hero under John Ford's direction.

Celebrity (12/26/27, Lyceum, 24)

Wobbly comedy about the prizefight racket; Herman Shumlin's Broadway debut as a producer. C: Gavin Gordon, Crane Wilbur. A: Willard Keefe. D: Edward Goodman.

Cellar and the Well, The (12/10/50, ANTA, 9)

Glum study of Irish-American life in the slum quarters of Chicago. "A random, amateurish drama that has been staged with no perceptible skill, and can be set down as notably incompetent theatre work" *(New York Times)*. C: Eda Heinemann, Dorothy Sands, Henderson Forsythe (D). A: Phillip Pruneau. P: George Freedley and Roger L. Stevens. SD: Paul Morrison.

Censored (2/26/38, 46th Street, 9)

Young playwright (Frank Lovejoy) runs afoul of the censors when his maiden opus is produced on Broadway. Foolish 30s farce-melodrama. A: Conrad Seiler and Max Marcin (D). P: A. H. Woods.

Ceremonies in Dark Old Men (2/4/69, St. Marks, 40)

Highly acclaimed O/B drama about black ghetto life. Set in Harlem in 1958, the play deals with a family who aspire to better things but go about it in the wrong way. Leading characters: the father, an unsuccessful barber who clings to memories of his tapdancing vaudeville days; his sons, both street-smart, unemployed, and out to make a fast buck; and his daughter, the family realist and provider who believes their apartment "was built for us to die in." About playwright Lonne Elder III's work, which was first presented for a limited engagement by the Negro Ensemble Company, the *New York Post* drama critic wrote: "This is a drama of power and importance. The best new American play of the season." "*Ceremonies*," wrote the *New Yorker* critic, "is the first play by Elder to be done professionally, and if any American has written a finer one I can't think what it is." C: Douglas Turner, David Downing, William Jay, Rosalind Cash, Samual Blue Jr., Judyann Jonsson, Arthur French. D: Edmund Cambridge.

Revived O/B by Michael Ellis (4/28/69, Pocket, 320) with a cast headed by Richard Ward, Billy Dee Williams, Richard Mason, Bette Howard, Denise Nicholas, Carl Lee, Arnold Johnson, under the direction once again of Edmund Cambridge.

Ceremony of Innocence, The (1/1/68, American Place, 14)

Historical drama (11th-century England) dealing with the efforts of Britain's King Ethelred, a benevolent and peace-loving man, to defend his throne not only against the invading Danes, but also against the hawkish members of his own court. "... glows with craftsmanship and dramatic imagination" (*Variety*). Presented O/B by The American Place Theater under the direction of Arthur A. Seidelman. C: Donald Madden, Sandy Duncan, David Birney, Olive Deering, Nancy R. Pollock, William Devane, Ralph Clanton, Dolph Sweet.

Chains (9/19/23, Playhouse, 131)

A liberated flapper (Helen Gahagan) refuses to marry her ex-lover (Paul Kelly) despite parental pressure. Routine drama by Jules Eckert Goodman. C: Gilbert Emery, Katherine Alexander, William Morris. P: William A. Brady. D: William A. Brady, Jr.

Chalked Out (3/25/37, Morosco, 12)

Innocent man (Frank Lovejoy) is railroaded to prison; stale melodrama was written by Lewis Lawes (warden of Sing Sing prison) and Jonathan Finn. C: Tom Tully, Otto Hulett, Harry Bellaver. P: Brock Pemberton. D: Antoinette Perry.
SV: WB, 1939, *You Can't Get Away with Murder*, Humphrey Bogart, John Litel, Billy Halop, Gale Page, Henry Travers.

Challenge, The (8/5/19, Selwyn, 72)

Young socialist (Alan Dinehart) falls in love with the daughter of a conservative (Holbrook Blinn), learns to appreciate the free enterprise system. Talky, naïve political problem play by Eugene Walter. P: The Selwyns.

Champagne Complex, The (4/12/55, Cort, 23)

A pretty girl (Polly Bergen) has an uncontrollable urge to disrobe whenever she drinks champagne. To cure this complex, her stuffy fiancé (John Dall) introduces the lass to his dashing psychiatrist-uncle

(Donald Cook). Predictably, the girl and the analyst discover they were meant for each other. This transparently slim three-character farce was written by Leslie Stevens. P: Gayle Stine. D: Michael Gordon. SD: Charles Elson. M: Jerry Stevens.

Champion, The (1/3/21, Longacre, 176)

The farcical problems and conflicts of a boxing champ and his snobbish British father. Featherweight comedy by A. E. Thomas and Thomas Louden. C: Grant Mitchell, Arthur Elliott, Ann Andrews. P: Sam H. Harris. D: Sam Forrest.

Changelings, The (9/17/23, Henry Miller, 139)

A book publisher and a novelist, friends for twenty years, decide to exchange wives. Bright comedy with an excellent cast: Henry Miller, Blanche Bates, Laura Hope Crews, Ruth Chatterton, Geoffrey Kerr, Reginald Mason, Felix Krembs. A: Lee Wilson Dodd. P/D: Henry Miller.

Channel Road, The (10/17/29, Plymouth, 60)

Alexander Woollcott-George S. Kaufman drama b/o de Maupassant's novelette *Boule de Suif*. In Normandy, 1870, during the Franco-Prussian war, a harlot with a heart of gold saves a party of French aristocrats by giving her favors to a German brute. Turgid costume piece; a semifiasco. "We got mixed notices," Kaufman recalled. "They were good and rotten." C: Siegfried Rumann, Anne Forrest, Edith Van Cleve, Edgar Stehli. P/D: Arthur Hopkins.

Chaparral (9/9/58, Sheridan Square, 14)

Soporific saga of a degenerate Texas family, and of a drunken lecher with incestuous desires toward his pretty sister. Presented O/B with a cast headed by Rip Torn, Janet Ward, Gene Hackman, Ruth White. A/D: Valgene Massey. P: Wolsk and Livingston. SD: Will Steven Armstrong.

Charm School, The (8/2/20, Bijou, 88)

Young fellow inherits a girls' boarding school, falls in love with one of the pupils. Frothy comedy by Alice Duer Miller and Robert Milton. C: Sam Hardy, James Gleason, Minnie Dupree, Morgan Farley, Margaret Dale, Blyth Daly. P/D: Robert Milton. Musicalized by J. Fred Coots as *June Days* (1925) with Roy Royston, Elizabeth Hines, Jay C. Flippen.
SV: Par, 1936, *Collegiate*, Jack Oakie, Joe Penner, Ned Sparks, Frances Langford, Betty Grable.

Chase, The (4/15/52, Playhouse, 31)

Wordy melodrama about a small-town sheriff agonizing over the plight of an escaped mad-dog convict who has threatened to kill him. ". . . sluggish, emotionally flat . . . like a watered-down western with moral commercials" (*Herald Tribune*). C: John Hodiak (deb.), Kim Hunter, Kim Stanley, Murray Hamilton, Lonny Chapman, Sam Byrd, G. Albert Smith, Nan McFarland. A: Horton Foote. P/D: Jose Ferrer. SD: Albert Johnson.
SV: Col, 1966, Marlon Brando, Robert Redford, Jane Fonda, E. G. Marshall, Angie Dickinson, Miriam Hopkins, Janice Rule, Martha Hyer, Robert Duvall, Henry Hull, James Fox, Diana Hyland, Jocelyn Brando (directed by Arthur Penn from a screenplay by Lillian Hellman).

Cheaper to Marry (4/15/24, 49th Street, 87)

A businessman (Robert Warwick) robs his partner (Alan Dinehart) to keep his mistress (Florence Eldridge) in luxury. Hack melodrama with a good cast including Berton Churchill, Ruth Donnelly, Claiborne Foster, Horace Braham. A: Samuel Shipman. P: Richard Herndon.

Cheating Cheaters (8/9/16, Eltinge, 286)

The glamorous mastermind (Marjorie Rambeau) of a gang of crooks turns out to be a detective. Highly contrived melodrama moved at a fast clip. A: Max Marcin. P: A. H. Woods. D: Franklyn Underwood.

SV: U, 1934, Fay Wray, Cesar Romero.

Cheri (10/12/59, Morosco, 56)

Aimless tale of an aging Parisian cocotte who loses her petulant nineteen-year-old lover to a younger woman. Spanning almost two decades (1911–29), this dramatization by Anita Loos of two novels by Colette was characterized by the *New York Post* as "a startlingly dull, prosaic and . . . foolish piece of theatrical claptrap." C: Kim Stanley, Horst Buchholz (deb.), Lili Darvas, Edith King. P: The Playwrights Company and Robert Lewis (D). CD: Miles White. SD: Oliver Smith.

Chicago (12/30/26, Music Box, 173)

Roxie Hart (Francine Larrimore) shoots a lover to death as he is buttoning his pants. With the aid of a cynical reporter named Jake (Charles Bickford), a venal lawyer named Billy Flynn (Edward Ellis), and a tremulous sob-sister named Mary Sunshine (Eda Heinemann), the gum-chewing heroine manages to turn her murder trial into a three-ring circus. This bawdy, hilariously funny courtroom satire was written by Maurine Watkins. A Radcliffe graduate and a student of George Pierce Baker at Yale University, the well-bred authoress knew her play needed strong language. In her script she left a number of blank spaces for the injection of such swear words as might be deemed necessary. Producer Sam H. Harris and director George Abbott were only too happy to supply the requisite amount of profanity. For the role of Roxie Hart, the hard-boiled man-killer, Harris and Abbott shied away from type-casting and engaged the winsome Francine Larrimore. It was her biggest hit, but she hated the part. C: Robert Barrat, Dorothy Stickney, Juliette Crosby.

Projected: Musical version (1974) by Kander and Ebb, with Gwen Verdon and Chita Rivera in leading roles.

SV: Fox, 1942, *Roxie Hart,* Ginger Rogers, Adolphe Menjou, George Montgomery, Lynne Overman, Phil Silvers, Nigel Bruce, Spring Byington, Sara Allgood, Jeff Corey.

Note: A silent version (Pathé, 1928) featured Phyllis Haver, Victor Varconi, Eugene Pallette, May Robson.

Chicken Every Sunday (4/5/44, Henry Miller, 317)

Period comedy (1916) about a get-rich-quick schemer and his patient wife who run a raffish boarding house in Tucson, Arizona. "Raucous and diffuse" *(Sun). Chicken Every Sunday* was adapted by Julius and Philip Epstein from a book by Rosemary Taylor. C: Mary Philips, Rhys Williams, Hope Emerson, Ann Thomas, Guy Stockwell. P: Edward Gross. D: Lester Vail. CD: Rose Bogdanoff. SD: Howard Bay.

SV: Fox, 1948, Dan Dailey, Celeste Holm, Alan Young, Natalie Wood.

Note: The brothers Epstein, two of Hollywood's highest-salaried scenarists during the lush days of the 1940's and 50's, adapted many stage successes to the screen *(The Man Who Came to Dinner, The Male Animal, Arsenic and Old Lace,* etc.). They also wrote the Academy Award-winning script for *Casablanca* with Howard Koch.

Chicken Feed (9/24/23, Little, 146)

A trio of wives go on strike and demand wages for their services. Typical John

Golden (P) offering, modestly amusing. C: Roberta Arnold, Arthur Aylsworth. A: Guy Bolton. D: Winchell Smith.

Child Buyer, The (12/21/64, Garrick, 32)

Superior O/B sci-fi drama in which a giant corporation proposes to brainwash young prodigies and then reeducate them electronically in the pure sciences. "A species of science fiction with a vigorous, intelligent viewpoint about the materialism and corruption of our age" (*New York Times*). C: Charles Durning, Marian Reardon, Brian Chapin, Lester Rawlins, Alan Mixon, Paul McGrath, Alan Bunce, John C. Becher, Dee Victor, Wyman Pendleton. A: Paul Shyre b/o the novel by John Hersey. P: The Theatre Guild. D: Richard Altman. SD: Eldon Elder.

Child of Fortune (11/13/56, Royale, 23)

An impoverished journalist is persuaded by his sweetheart to wed a doomed American heiress and thereby, upon her death, ensure their own futures. Knowledge of the deception kills the heiress, but the lovers are prevented from marrying by their troubled consciences. This Edwardian romance was adapted by Anglo-American author Guy Bolton from Henry James' novel *Wings of the Dove*. ". . . decorous, attenuated and old maidish . . . a routine romance" (*New York Times*). C: Edmund Purdom (deb.), Betsy von Furstenberg, Martyn Green, Pippa Scott, Mildred Dunnock, Norah Howard. P/D: Jed Harris.

Note: The James novel was musicalized as an opera (1961) by Douglas Moore, with John Reardon and Martha Lipton prominent in the cast.

Child of Manhattan (3/1/32, Fulton, 86)

Preston Sturges' amusing "romantic comedy" dealing with a saucy dance-hall hostess (Dorothy Hall) who becomes the mistress of a wealthy roué (Reginald Owen). Illicit pregnancy, marriage, and divorce complicate their relationship, but the affair ends happily as the odd couple resume their original penthouse arrangement. C: Douglas Dumbrille, Jessie Ralph. P: Peggy Fears. D: Howard Lindsay.

SV: Col, 1933, Nancy Carroll, John Boles, Buck Jones, Jane Darwell.

Children! Children! (3/7/72, Ritz, 1)

A thriller spoiled by the lack of a satisfying climax. Gwen Verdon, more usually seen in musicals (*Can-Can, Damn Yankees,* etc.), is here a baby-sitter just recovered from a nervous breakdown. She takes on a New Year's Eve assignment to look after three children in a fancy duplex, but she'd have been better advised to celebrate with a few drinks at the corner bar. The children, two boys and a girl, lose no time showing they are precociously and insatiably evil. Having murdered one sitter by pushing her down stairs, it is evident they plan the same fate for Ms. Verdon, though not before they've had their fill of sadistic attacks on her nervous system. When the parents return they don't believe her accusations against the tots, and reveal in themselves the viciousness that infects their children. "Miss Verdon is a fine actress and her portrayal of a trapped woman is believable and appealing. Shawn Campbell and Johnny Doran are credibly menacing boys and little Ariane Munker is at once lovely and abominable as the awful girl" (Richard Watts, *New York Post*). A: Jack Horrigan. C: Gwen Verdon, Shawn Campbell, Johnny Doran, Ariane Munker, Dennis Patrick, Elizabeth Hubbard, Elaine Hyman, Josef Sommer. P: Arthur Whitelaw, Seth Harrison i.a.w. Ben Gerard. D: Joseph Hardy. SD: Jo Mielziner.

Children from Their Games (4/11/63, Morosco, 4)

World-weary iconoclast tries to persuade a wartime buddy to kill him and thereby end his futile existence. Irwin Shaw's black comedy had flashes of strikingly ironic humor, but was "strangely intermittent in its effectiveness" (*Post*). C: Martin Gabel, John McMartin, Gene Hackman, Brenda Vaccaro, Peggy Cass, Bernie West, Ralph Purdum. P: Roger L. Stevens and Sam Wanamaker (D) i.a.w. Austin and Samrock. SD: Oliver Smith.

Children of Darkness (1/7/30, Biltmore, 79)

Newgate Prison in eighteenth-century London was the setting of this acrid, literate, diamond-sharp comedy by Edwin Justus Mayer (A/D). A conniving jailkeeper presides over a raffish gallery of rogues and debtors. His buxom daughter falls in love with one of the debtors, an impoverished count, and schemes to keep him her prisoner for life. In the end, leaving the jailer's wench pregnant, the philosophic count commits suicide. C: Basil Sydney, Mary Ellis, Eugene Powers, Charles Dalton, Walter Kingsford. Despite generally laudatory reviews, *Children of Darkness* lasted only ten weeks on Broadway. It was "too esoteric . . . caviar to the general," said Joseph Verner Reed who co-produced the play with Kenneth Macgowan. In 1958 the tragi-comedy was revived O/B (2/28/58, Circle in the Square, 30l) by Jose Quintero (P/D) with George C. Scott and Colleen Dewhurst in the leading roles. The revival scored a great success with both press and public.

Children of Earth (1/12/15, Booth, 39)

A $10,000-prize play written by a New Hampshire housewife, *Children of Earth* dramatized the problems of a female alcoholic. Selected from more than fifteen hundred manuscripts submitted by United States writers, the play was moderately well received by the press but was a box-office failure. C: Effie Shannon, Herbert Kelcey, Gilda Varesi, A. E. Anson, Reginald Barlow, Theodore von Eltz. A: Alice Brown. P/D: Winthrop Ames.

Children of the Moon (8/17/23, Comedy, 109)

The Atherton family of San Francisco suffers from inherited lunacy, a form of moon madness that has compelled the son to crash his plane in the path of the moon. In an effort to escape her malevolent mother with her Cassandra-like warnings of impending doom, the daughter of the family flies off with her aviator lover and, presumably, also dies in the moonlit night. Gripping, offbeat, uniquely original drama by Martin Flavin. C: Henrietta Crosman, Beatrice Terry, Florence Johns, Whitford Kane. P: Jacob Weiser i.a.w. Jones and Green.

Children of the Wind (10/24/73, Belasco, 6)

A dismal period piece about an alcoholic actor and his family. In a theatrical rooming house in the '30's, the bibulous thespian, his long-suffering wife and vulnerable young son, and their acidulous landlady play out a turgid drama of minimal impact. Playwright Jerry Devine had no better luck with this serious study of alcoholism than with his earlier comic treatment of the subject, *Never Live Over a Pretzel Factory*. Veteran director Shepard Traube, despite a career of distinction, (*Angel Street, The Patriots,* etc.) could not save *Children of the Wind* from the shortest straight-play run of the Broadway season. C: James Callahan, Sarah Hardy, Barry Goss, Ann Thomas. P: Shepard Traube and Buff Cobb.

Children's Hour, The (11/20/34, Maxine Elliott's, 691)

Lillian Hellman's first play, a vivid and

powerful psychological melodrama that emphasized the evil implicit in a lie and the dangers of character assassination. Dealing with a malicious child who destroyed her school and ruined the lives of two teachers by whispering they were lesbians, *The Children's Hour* struck Broadway like a thunderbolt. "Will make your eyes start from their sockets as its agitating tale unfolds," wrote Percy Hammond in the *New York Herald Tribune*. ". . . it spellbound the first audience with its incessant tenseness," said Walter Winchell in the *Daily Mirror*. The play was based on a famous scandal case fought through the Scottish courts in the early nineteenth century. It took Miss Hellman, a thirty-five-dollar-a-week script reader for MGM, "a year and a half of stumbling stubbornness" to write *The Children's Hour*. The play ran 691 performances. Critical consensus was that the Hellman drama should have won the Pulitzer Prize. Instead, the award went to Zoe Akins' sentimental chronicle play, *The Old Maid*. Outraged by the decision, the New York drama critics formed their own organization (the Drama Critics Circle) to bestow their own prize each year for the best play of the season. Their first selection (1935) was Maxwell Anderson's *Winterset*. C: Anne Revere, Katherine Emery, Robert Keith, Florence McGee, Katherine Emmet, Eugenia Rawls. P/D: Herman Shumlin. CD/SD: Aline Bernstein and Syrjala.

R: (12/18/52, Coronet, 189) by Kermit Bloomgarden. C: Patricia Neal, Kim Hunter, Robert Pastene, Iris Mann, Katherine Emmet. D: Lillian Hellman.

SV: UA, 1936, *These Three*, Miriam Hopkins, Merle Oberon, Joel McCrea, Bonita Granville, Catherine Doucet, Marcia Mae Jones, Alma Kruger; UA, 1962, Audrey Hepburn, Shirley MacLaine, James Garner, Miriam Hopkins, Fay Bainter, Veronica Cartwright.

Note: The lesbian theme was excised from the 1936 film version in favor of a conventional triangle story. This was done to conform to the dictates of the Hays Office which further ruled that not even the play's title could be used in making or publicizing the Samuel Goldwyn production. The 1962 movie was far more explicit but, surprisingly, less effective. Both screen versions were directed by William Wyler.

Child's Play (2/17/70, Royale, 342)

Thriller of mysterious evil in a Roman Catholic boys' school. Against a gothic stage set of the faculty room, somber with dark wood and tall, mullioned windows, the students begin to turn on each other in inexplicable acts of mounting violence, the victims mute and eerily unprotesting. At first unaware, the faculty is ultimately enfolded in tragic manner. The dramatic focus is on three lay teachers: a neurotic classics instructor (Fritz Weaver), a fatherly English professor (Pat Hingle), and a young sports coach (Ken Howard). The interaction of these three with each other and the boys brings the play to a chilling conclusion. After the manner of melodrama in the '70's, the ending leaves much to the audience's imagination, but this did not deter enthusiastic first-nighters from calling for the author at play's end. "A gripping theatrical experience . . . high-voltage theater" (Douglas Watt, *New York Daily News*). ". . . genuine Grand Guignol horror" (Clive Barnes, *New York Times*). ". . . instead of building to a suspenseful breaking point, runs disastrously downhill . . . a conclusion that attempts to be profound and is virtually meaningless" (John J. O'Connor, *Wall Street Journal*). "A second rate horror movie" (Joseph Mazo, *Women's Wear Daily*). Divided about the play, the critics praised the performers and the production, an estimate later echoed at the Tony Awards ceremony. In the Straight Play category, Fritz Weaver won for Best Actor, Ken Howard for Best Supporting Actor, Joseph Hardy for Best Director, and Jo Mielziner, Best Scenery and Lighting. A: Robert Marasco. C: Fritz Weaver, Pat Hingle, Ken Howard, David Rounds, Peter MacLean, Michael McGuire, Lloyd Kramer, Christopher Deane, Bryant Fraser, Robbie Reed, Patrick Shea, John Handy, Mark Hall, Frank Fiore, Ron Martin. P: David Merrick. D: Joseph Hardy. SD: Jo Mielziner.

SV: Paramount, 1972, James Mason, Robert Preston, Beau Bridges, David Rounds (directed by Sidney Lumet).

Chivalry (12/15/25, Wallack's, 23)

Flamboyant attorney gets murderess acquitted, then tells the jury how they've been duped. So-so courtroom melodrama. C: Edmund Breese, Violet Heming, Doris Rankin. A: William Hurlbut. P: Joseph Shea. D: James Durkin.

Chorus Lady, The (9/1/06, Savoy, 315)

Trashy backstage piffle about a tough, breezy showgirl.(Rose Stahl) who struggles to keep her sister's virtue intact. A/D: James Forbes. P: Henry B. Harris.

Christian Pilgrim, The (11/11/07, Liberty, 14)

Turgid allegorical drama based on John Bunyan's "Pilgrim's Progress," tracing the journey of Pilgrim from conversion to death and salvation. C: Henrietta Crosman, Tyrone Power, Sr. A: James MacArthur. P: Henry B. Harris and Maurice Campbell (D).

Christmas Eve (12/27/39, Henry Miller, 6)

The sensitive daughter in a family of swaggering eccentrics is embarrassed by her mother's pregnancy. Forced to assist at the delivery, she is exposed to the miracle of motherhood and, presumably, cured of her pathological fastidiousness.

Highlight: the onstage birth of a child to the accompaniment of harrowing screams of anguish from the mother. "Whew, what a play!" *(New York Times)*. *Christmas Eve* was written by Dr. Gustav Eckstein, noted zoologist, physiologist, and devoted friend of Alexander Woollcott and the Lunts. C: Katherine Locke, Beth Merrill, Kent Smith, Sidney Lumet, Mildred Natwick, James Rennie, Robert Ross, Vincent Donehue. P/D: Guthrie McClintic.

Christopher Blake (11/30/46, Music Box, 114)

Forced to choose between his divorcing parents, a twelve-year-old boy escapes into dream reveries in an effort to understand what is happening to him. This 1940's drama was written and directed by Moss Hart. "A curiously unsatisfying combination of fantasy and realism . . . gravely handicapped by its elaborately cumbersome production" *(Post)*. C: Richard Tyler, Shepperd Strudwick, Martha Sleeper. P: Joseph M. Hyman and Bernard Hart. SD: Harry Horner.

SV: WB, 1948, *The Decision of Christopher Blake*, Ted Donaldson, Alexis Smith, Robert Douglas.

Chrysalis (11/15/32, Martin Beck, 23)

Pampered debutante (Margaret Sullavan) and her devil-may-care lover (Humphrey Bogart) learn the meaning of devotion from a small-time criminal named Honey Rogers (Elisha Cook, Jr.) and his adoring gun moll (June Walker). Murky, ridiculously plotted melodrama with a stellar cast: Osgood Perkins, Lily Cahill, Elia Kazan (deb.), Kathleen Comegys, Mary Orr, Thurston Hall. A: Rose Albert Porter. P: Martin Beck i.a.w. Lawrence Langner and Theresa Helburn (D). SD: Cleon Throckmorton.

SV: Par, 1934, *All of Me*, Fredric March Miriam Hopkins, George Raft, Helen Mack, Blanche Frederici, Gilbert Emery, Kitty Kelly.

Cinderella Man, The (1/17/16, Hudson, 192)

A struggling young poet is rescued from his garret by a millionaire's daughter. Cute variant on the Cinderella theme by Edward Childs Carpenter. C: Shelly Hull, Phoebe Foster, Frank Bacon, Lucille La Verne, Reginald Mason, Berton Churchill. P: Oliver Morosco. D: Robert Milton.

City, The (12/21/09, Lyric, 190)

Clyde Fitch's last play, produced posthumously, and dramatizing the corrupting influence of urban life on country folk. A shrill, sensationalistic melodrama involving incest, illegitimacy, and drug addiction, the premiere of *The City* was probably the most dramatic opening night in Broadway history. When Fitch's dope fiend screamed "You're a goddam liar!" across the footlights, pandemonium broke out. It was the first time such an epithet had ever been heard in a New York theatre. "A mixture of horror at the forbidden word, excitement over the pungent play, and mourning over the playwright's death drove the audience toward mass hysteria," said one writer. Several members of the audience fainted, among them the drama critic for the *New York Sun*. "It was the most tense, the most hysterical of first nights," actress Lucile Watson recalled years later. "I never experienced anything remotely like it before or since." C: Walter Hampden, Mary Nash, Lucile Watson, Tully Marshall. P: Messrs. Shubert. D: John Emerson.

Civilian Clothes (9/12/19, Morosco, 150)

Snobbish southern belle (Olive Tell) has kept her marriage to an army captain a secret. Her husband (Thurston Hall) takes a job as butler in her home to teach her a lesson—and does. Typical 1919 comedy. A: Thompson Buchanan. P: Oliver Morosco. D: Frank Underwood.

Clair De Lune (4/18/21, Empire, 64)

A degenerate duchess (Ethel Barrymore) is fascinated by the hideously disfigured face of a charlatan-clown (John Barrymore). No good comes of this unholy affinity, and the play ends in murder, suicide, and general misery for all concerned. *Clair De Lune* was adapted from Victor Hugo's novel, *The Man Who Laughed* (1869), by John Barrymore's second wife, poetess Michael Strange. The critics severely castigated the play and hinted that sheer nepotism was responsible for its having reached the stage. In fact, one critic (James Whitaker, *Chicago Tribune*) headlined his review: "For the Love of Mike!" Alexander Woollcott summed up the prevailing mood by dismissing the exhibit as "a shambling and laboriously macabre piece." All in all, *Clair De Lune* proved a dismal mistake for the Barrymores and producer Charles Frohman. C: Dennis

The City by Clyde Fitch (1909–10). *Courtesy Museum of the City of New York Theatre and Music Collection.*

King (deb.), Henry Daniell (deb.), Violet Kemble Cooper, Jane Cooper. D: E. Lyall Swete.

Clandestine on the Morning Line (10/30/61, Actors Playhouse, 24)

An unlettered middle-aged optimist and her bachelor brother reunite a pregnant young woman and her lover. Amusing O/B comedy-drama with several attractive and original characters. C: Rosetta LeNoire and James Earl Jones. A: Josh Greenfield. D: Allen Davis.

Clansman, The (1/8/06, Liberty, 51)

Painting the Ku Klux Klan as knights in shining armor, this viciously anti-Negro tract by Baptist clergyman Thomas Dixon was, happily, a failure on Broadway. A decade later, *The Clansman* became D. W. Griffith's epochal silent film, *The Birth of a Nation* (1915), the first of the gigantic screen epics for which Hollywood later became famous. P: George H. Brennan. D: Frank Hatch.

Clarence (9/20/19, Hudson, 300)

The comedy that made Alfred Lunt a star and typed Helen Hayes as a cute "flapper" for several seasons thereafter. A timorous, bumbling ex-doughboy (Alfred Lunt) straightens out the tangled affairs of an irresponsible family, encourages the romantic escapades of a pair of adolescent brats (Helen Hayes and Glenn Hunter), calms the flighty stepmother (Mary Boland) out of her incipient tantrums, and finally marries the family's pretty governess (Elsie Mackay). "Thoroughly delightful" (Alexander Woollcott, *New York Times*). "*Clarence* is the best light comedy which has been written by an American" (Heywood Broun, *Tribune*). A: Booth Tarkington. P: George C. Tyler. D: Frederick Stanhope.
SV: Par, 1937, Roscoe Karns, Charlotte Winters.

Clarice (10/16/06, Garrick, 79)

A South Carolina doctor (William Gillette) falls in love with his ward, but masks his true feelings believing the girl cares for a younger man. Old-hat story, smoothly handled. C: Marie Doro, Lucille La Verne. A/D: William Gillette. P: Charles Frohman.

Clash by Night (12/27/41, Belasco, 49)

Produced by Billy Rose and directed by Lee Strasberg, this Clifford Odets drama cast Tallulah Bankhead as a slatternly Staten Island housewife who falls in love with an egotistical motion-picture projectionist (Joseph Schildkraut). When her slow-witted husband (Lee J. Cobb) finally learns the truth, he strangles his dapper rival. A pointless subplot centered around the romance of a neurotic neighbor and her unemployed sweetheart. These roles were played by Katherine Locke and Robert Ryan (deb.). *Clash by Night* was severely trounced by the reviewers. (*Trash by Night* was the headline used in one of the more charitable notices.) Castigated by the critics he had hoped to impress, Billy Rose's exposure to "art" left him sadly disenchanted—and many thousands of dollars poorer.
SV: RKO, 1952, Barbara Stanwyck, Paul Douglas, Robert Ryan, Marilyn Monroe, Keith Andes.

Classmates (8/29/07, Hudson, 102)

The life of budding officers at West Point from the day they enter the academy to the day they graduate. Flag-waving yarn was frayed with age even in 1907. C: Robert Edeson, Frank McIntyre, Wallace Eddinger. A: William C. de Mille and Margaret Turnbull. P: Henry B. Harris. D: George W. Barnum.

Claudia (2/12/41, Booth, 453)

Comedy-drama about the coming of age of a childlike bride with a mother fixation.

Despite the efforts of her patient husband (Donald Cook), Claudia (Dorothy McGuire) remains ingenuous and unpredictable. It takes the impending death of her beloved mother (Frances Starr) to shock Claudia into independence and maturity. "A charming play . . . there is much quiet delight in it" (*Sun*). Written and directed by Rose Franken, author of *Another Language* (1932), *Claudia* was one of producer John Golden's biggest successes. In a letter to this editor, Golden volunteered that, of the more than one hundred plays he had presented on Broadway, *Claudia* was his favorite. Her performance in the title role made hitherto unknown Dorothy McGuire an overnight star. C: Olga Baclanova, John Williams.

SV: Fox, 1943, Dorothy McGuire, Robert Young, Ina Claire, Reginald Gardiner, Olga Baclanova.

Clear All Wires (9/14/32, Times Square, 91)

American newspaperman (Thomas Mitchell) in Russia gets into trouble when he fakes an attempted assassination story. Breezy comedy by Bella and Samuel Spewack, produced and directed by Herman Shumlin. Musicalized by Cole Porter and the Spewacks as *Leave It to Me* (1938) with Victor Moore, William Gaxton, Sophie Tucker, Tamara, Mary Martin, Gene Kelly, Van Johnson.

SV: MGM, 1933, Lee Tracy, Una Merkel, Benita Hume, James Gleason.

Clearing in the Woods, A (1/10/57, Belasco, 36)

A neurotic career girl delves back into her past—into troubled memories of herself and the men in her life—in an effort to come to terms with her perfectionist nature. In this psychological fantasy by Arthur Laurents, the heroine's alter egos (the central character at earlier stages of her life) were portrayed by three different actresses who resembled leading lady Kim Stanley. "A labored and curiously unstimulating drama" (*Post*). C: Pernell Roberts, Robert Culp, Onslow Stevens, Lin McCarthy, Joan Lorring, Anne Pearson, Barbara Myers. P: Roger L. Stevens and Oliver Smith (SD). D: Joseph Anthony. CD: Lucinda Ballard.

R: (2/12/59, Sheridan Square, 102). C: Nancy Wickwire, Gene Lyons, Barbara Lord (succeeded by Joan Hackett). D: Jack Ragotzy.

Climate of Eden, The (11/6/52, Martin Beck, 20)

Into a jungle paradise inhabited by a highly unorthodox minister and his uninhibited brood comes a bitterly cynical, mentally unstable young man from the cities. How he is saved from his neurotic terrors by the missionary's two daughters provides the crux of this "striking, original and absorbing drama" (*Post*). *The Climate of Eden* was adapted from Edgar Mittelholzer's novel *Shadows Move Among Them*, by Moss Hart (A/D) who called it "by far the most interesting piece of work I have ever done for the theatre." The production lasted little more than two weeks on Broadway. Its failure so dispirited Hart that he swore he would never write another play as long as he lived. Instead he started keeping a diary. From this evolved *Act One* (Random House, 1959), one of the finest theatre autobiographies ever published. C: John Cromwell, Isobel Elsom, Rosemary Harris,* Penelope Munday, Lee Montague,* Ray Stricklyn,* Ken Walken,* Earle Hyman, Jane White. P: Joseph M. Hyman and Bernard Hart. SD: Frederick Fox.

---

*Broadway debuts.

Climax, The (4/12/09, Weber's, 240)

An evil opera physician with mesmeric powers convinces the beautiful Adelina, a golden-voiced soprano, that she will never sing again unless she bends to his

The Climax. **Leona Watson and Hubert Wilke (1909).** *Courtesy Museum of the City of New York Theatre and Music Collection.*

will Puerile but popular four-character melodrama in the *Svengali* tradition. C: Leona Watson, Effingham A. Pinto, Albert Bruning, William Lewers. A: Edward Locke. P/D: Joseph Weber.

SV: U, 1928, Jean Hersholt, Kathryn Crawford; 1944, Boris Karloff, Susanna Foster, Turhan Bey, Gale Sondergaard.

Climbers, The (1/21/01, Bijou, 163)

Clyde Fitch (A/D) play satirizing turn-of-the-century social climbers in Little Old New York. Broadway applauded Fitch's audacious comedy-drama; London audiences were revolted by the author's gallery of shallow, venal snobs. C: Amelia Bingham, Clara Bloodgood, Robert Edeson, Frank Worthing, Ferdinand Gottschalk, Madge Carr Cook, Minnie Dupree, Annie Irish. P: Amelia Bingham.

Close Harmony (12/1/24, Gaiety, 24)

Comedy by Dorothy Parker and Elmer Rice. A henpecked suburbanite finds solace in the companionship of the lady next door, a spirited and attractive ex-chorus girl married to an alcoholic. They decide to leave their respective mates and elope together, but habit and convention are too strong, and the spark flickers out. Despite generally good reviews, *Close Harmony* died at the box office. One of the problems perhaps was that the play opened the same evening (December 1,

1924) as Irving Berlin's *Music Box Revue* (Fanny Brice, Grace Moore, Clark and McCullough) and George and Ira Gershwin's *Lady, Be Good!* (Fred & Adele Astaire, Cliff Edwards, Walter Catlett). Both of these musical shows were smash hits and reviews of same garnered most of the space in next day's newspapers. In any event, *Close Harmony* closed on Broadway after a brief three-week run. C: James Spottswood, Wanda Lyon. P: Arthur Hopkins (D) and Philip Goodman.

Closing Door, The (12/1/49, Empire, 22)

Creaking melodrama by and with Canadian-American actor-author Alexander Knox in which a psychopath, nurturing a lifelong hatred for his successful brother, almost kills his own son before being carted off to a mental institution. "A straggling thriller . . . and not too believable . . ." (*Sun*). C: Doris Nolan,* Richard Derr, Jo Van Fleet, Eva Condon, Ronald Alexander, Lonny Chapman (deb.). P: Cheryl Crawford. D: Lee Strasberg.

---

*Mrs. Alexander Knox.

Clothes (9/11/06, Manhattan, 113)

Young woman (Grace George) with limited income tries to keep up appearances, encounters all sorts of complications resulting from her extravagance in dress. "A comedy-drama of a familiar type . . . mainly conventional [but] theatrically appealing" (*New York Times*). C: Frank Worthing, Robert T. Haines, Douglas Fairbanks, Louise Closser Hale. A: Avery Hopwood and Channing Pollock. P: William A. Brady i.a.w. Wagenhals and Kemper.

Cloud 7 (2/14/58, Golden, 11)

Suburbanite shocks his neighbors when he quits an excellent job in the city to practice togetherness with his wife and daughter. Tepid, short-lived domestic comedy. C: Ralph Meeker, Martha Scott, John McGiver. A: Max Wilk. P: Baron and Earl. D: Jed Horner. SD: Albert Johnson.

Cloudy with Showers (9/1/31, Morosco, 63)

Shy English professor (Thomas Mitchell) gets involved with gangsters and girls. Disappointing comedy by Floyd Dell and Thomas Mitchell (D), co-authors of *Little Accident* (1928). P: Patterson McNutt.

Clutching Claw, The (2/14/28, Forrest, 23)

Inane haunted house yarn. C: Ralph Morgan, Minnie Dupree. A: Ralph Thomas Kettering. P: Barbour and Bryant. D: Rollo Lloyd.

Coastwise (11/30/31, Provincetown, 37)

Tough riverboat floozy (Shirley Booth) meets proper English gentleman (Richard Stevenson) who tries to turn her into a lady. Trite variation on the Pygmalion theme; originally produced O/B by Ed Gardner (Miss Booth's husband and, later, "Archie" of *Duffy's Tavern* fame), the play was subsequently transferred to Broadway for a brief and unprofitable run. A: H. A. Archibald and Don Mullally (D).

Cobra (4/22/24, Hudson, 240)

Should a man (Louis Calhern) tell his best friend (Ralph Morgan) that his friend's wife (Judith Anderson) tried to seduce him? The hero is spared making this decision when the wife conveniently dies in a fire. Some good actors were squandered on this popular but totally meretricious drama. A: Martin Brown. P: L. Lawrence Weber.

Cock Robin (1/12/28, 48th Street, 100)

Implausible, gimmicky whodunit by Philip Barry and Elmer Rice. An actor is murdered on stage during an amateur production. Nine players are suspects, and suspicion falls in turn on each of them before the culprit is revealed. C: Edward Ellis, Beulah Bondi, Beatrice Herford, Muriel Kirkland, Howard Freeman, James Todd, Moffat Johnston, Richard Stevenson. P/D: Guthrie McClintic. SD: Jo Mielziner.

Cold Wind and the Warm, The (12/8/58, Morosco, 120)

S. N. Behrman's semiautobiographical period piece dealing with Jewish neighborhood life in Worcester, Massachusetts, in 1908, and the coming of age of a sensitive youth whose best friend and mentor commits suicide. "An affectionate, frequently humorous but oddly unresolved play" *(News)*. C: Eli Wallach, Maureen Stapleton, Morris Carnovsky, Timmy Everett, Suzanne Pleshette, Sig Arno, Sanford Meisner, Vincent Gardenia, Sidney Armus, Carol Grace. P: Producers Theatre. D: Harold Clurman. CD: Motley. SD: Boris Aronson.

Colette (5/6/70, Ellen Stewart, 101)

A biography of French writer Sidonie Gabrielle Claudine Colette (1873–1954), more comfortably known by her pen name: Colette. As most of her long life is covered, the play is necessarily episodic, though the transitions are skillfully managed. Her career and her several marriages are explored through a combination of stage techniques including monologues and flashbacks. While informative, the narrative is not arresting. Colette's life, save for the imprisonment of her Jewish husband by the Nazis, was seldom dramatic. She was a healthy, spirited woman, not afflicted by the storms and traumas so often suffered by great artists, and passed the majority of her years contentedly. The play is affectionate tribute, not passionate theatre. Zoe Caldwell as Colette, and Mildred Dunnock as her mother won critical praise, as did Keene Curtis and Barry Bostwick, who played multiple parts. A: Elinor Jones b/o Colette's autobiographical writings. C: Zoe Caldwell, Mildred Dunnock, Keene Curtis, Charles Siebert, Barry Bostwick, Holland Taylor. D: Gerald Freedman. P: Cheryl Crawford i.a.w. Mary W. John. SD: David Mitchell. CD: Theoni V. Aldredge.

Collector's Item (2/8/52, Booth, 3)

"Heavy-handed and thoroughly witless farce" *(Herald Tribune)* about a family of international rogues who deal in antiques. C: Allyn Joslyn, James Gregory, Erik Rhodes, Louis Sorin, Florida Friebus. A: Lillian Day and Alfred Golden. P: Roger Clark i.a.w. Lloyd Isler. D: Golden and Clark.

College Widow, The (9/20/04, Garden, 278)

To snare a promising football recruit, a college coach asks his girl to show interest in the boy. She does, with resultant complications. Mirthful farce by George Ade. C: Frederick Truesdell, Dorothy Tennant. P: Henry W. Savage. D: George Marion.

Musicalized by Jerome Kern as *Leave It To Jane* (1917).

SV: WB, 1930, *Maybe It's Love*, Joe E. Brown, Joan Bennett; 1936, *Freshman Love*, Frank McHugh, Patricia Ellis, Warren Hull.

Note: A silent version (WB, 1927) starred Dolores Costello.

Colonel Satan (1/10/31, Fulton, 17)

Meandering, highly fictionalized comedy-melodrama by Booth Tarkington dealing with the exploits of expatriate Aaron Burr in Paris, 1811. C: McKay Morris, Jessie Royce Landis, Arthur Treacher. P: George C. Tyler. D: Stanley Logan.

Come Angel Band (2/18/36, 46th Street, 2)

This play by noted screenwriter Dudley Nichols* and Stuart Anthony was a disappointing effort on almost every count. The convoluted plot dealt with a country boy (Elisha Cook, Jr.) who abducts his teenage sweetheart on her wedding night, murders her elderly bridegroom, and is condemned to hang for his crime. *Come Angel Band* closed after its second performance. C: Eleanor Lynn, Curtis Cooksey. P: Eugene Walter. D: Melville Burke.

---

*Screenplay credits include *The Informer, Stagecoach, The Long Voyage Home,* etc.

Come Back, Little Sheba (2/15/50, Booth, 190)

Produced in 1950, William Inge's first Broadway play dealt with the unhappy marriage of a slatternly housewife and her alcoholic husband. An emotionally searing drama, splendidly acted and staged, *Come Back, Little Sheba* received sharply divided notices. According to its author, "some of the reviews showed an almost violent repugnance to the play." Moreover, the production did good business for only a few weeks and then, in Inge's words, "houses began to dwindle to the size of tea parties." Because of its relatively low operating cost, the play managed to hang on for a six-month run. In the leading roles, Shirley Booth and Sidney Blackmer gave the best performances of their respective careers. In addition to numerous other awards, Miss Booth won the Oscar in the subsequent 1952 screen version. C: Joan Lorring, Lonny Chapman, Daniel Reed, John Randolph, Robert Cunningham, Olga Fabian, Wilson Brooks, Paul Krauss, Arnold Schulman. P: The Theatre Guild. D: Daniel Mann. SD: Howard Bay.
SV: Par, 1952, Burt Lancaster, Shirley Booth, Terry Moore, Richard Jaeckel (directed by Daniel Mann).

Come Blow Your Horn (2/22/61, Atkinson, 677)

Neil Simon's first Broadway play, a machine-stitched comedy highlighting the problems of an exasperated Jewish businessman and his two rebellious playboy sons. ". . . fabricated and often strained. . . . but I'll be surprised if it doesn't find a large and gratified public" (*Post*). C: Hal March,* Lou Jacobi, Pert Kelton, Warren Berlinger, Sarah Marshall, Arlene Golonka, Carolyn Brenner. P: William Hammerstein and Michael Ellis. D: Stanley Prager. SD: Ralph Alswang.
SV: Par, 1963, Frank Sinatra, Lee J. Cobb, Molly Picon, Barbara Rush, Tony Bill, Jill St. John (directed by Bud Yorkin).
Note: "I began *Come Blow Your Horn* as an exercise," said Neil Simon. "It was eight weeks in the writing, three years in the rewriting, and it had at least eight producers before I ever saw it on a stage. . . . Had I known I'd go through all this, I probably never would have started writing plays."

---

*Broadway debut.

Come Live With Me (1/26/67, Billy Rose, 4)

Leaden farce about the romantic entanglements of an American screenwriter (Soupy Sales) in London. A: Lee Minoff and Stanley Price. P: Helen Bonfils and Morton Gottlieb. D: Joshua Shelley.

Come Marching Home (5/18/46, Blackfriars', 19)

Robert Anderson's* first play, *Come Marching Home* dealt with a Navy veteran who is persuaded to run for state senator and encounters bitter opposition from the local corrupt political machine. Though faced by certain defeat, he vows to remain in politics until he has awakened the public to the need for clean government. "Nowhere in Times Square will one find more honesty of purpose . . ." *(New York Times)*. Presented O/B by the Blackfriars' Guild with a nondescript cast; capable direction by Dennis Gurney.

**Tea and Sympathy* (1953) was Mr. Anderson's first Broadway success. His screenplay credits include *Until They Sail, The Nun's Story,* etc.

Come on Strong (10/4/62, Morosco, 36)

A pair of show business aspirants (Van Johnson and Carroll Baker) finally come to terms with themselves and acknowledge their need for each other. Hackneyed comedy-drama by Garson Kanin (A/D). P: Hillard Elkins and Al Goldin. SD: Oliver Smith.

Come Out of the Kitchen (10/23/16, Cohan, 224)

In order to rent their mansion to a rich Yankee, an impoverished southern family pass themselves off as their own servants. Agreeable fluff by A. E. Thomas, based on a story by Alice Duer Miller. C: Ruth Chatterton, Walter Connolly, Bruce McRae, Robert Ames, Charles Trowbridge, William Boyd. P/D: Henry Miller.

Musicalized by Harold Levey as *The Magnolia Lady* (1924) with Ruth Chatterton, Ralph Forbes, Skeets Gallagher, Minor Watson.
SV: Par, 1930, *Honey,* Nancy Carroll, Lillian Roth, Mitzi Green, Skeets Gallagher, Harry Green.

Come Seven (7/19/20, Broadhurst, 72)

Incredibly tasteless comedy dealing with the misadventures of a group of light-fingered, crap-shooting Uncle Tom's and Aunt Jemima's. Acted by an all-white cast in blackface. An abomination. C: Earle Foxe, Lucille La Verne. A: Octavus Roy Cohen, based on his "Florian Slappey" stories. P: George Broadhurst. D: Lillian Trimble Bradley.

Come What May (5/15/34, Plymouth, 24)

Thirty hectic years in the lives of a middle-class couple. Plot-heavy, essentially pointless chronicle drama. C: Hal Skelly (P), Mary Philips. A: Richard F. Flournoy. D: Leo Bulgakov.

Comedian, The (3/13/23, Lyceum, 87)

Middle-aged matinee idol (Lionel Atwill) falls in love with incompetent young would-be actress, is forced to choose between love and art, and chooses art. Bowdlerized David Belasco (A/P/D) version of boulevard comedy by Sacha Guitry. C: Elsie Mackay, A. P. Kaye.

Comes a Day (11/6/58, Ambassador, 28)

A financially ambitious mother (Judith Anderson) schemes to marry her only daughter to a wealthy sadist (George C. Scott) in order to recoup the family fortunes. Making his Broadway debut, Mr. Scott gave "one of the great bravura, flamboyant performances in recent memory" *(Journal-American),* but the play was dismissed as a "baffling, uneven . . . and fumbling narrative." C: Arthur O'Connell, Brandon de Wilde, Diana van der Vlis, Larry Hagman,* Michael J. Pollard.* A: Speed Lamkin. P: Cheryl Crawford and Alan Pakula. D: Robert Mulligan. CD: Noel Taylor. SD: Sam Leve.

---

*Broadway debuts.

Comes the Revelation (5/26/42, Jolson, 2)

Nineteenth-century charlatan (Wendell Corey) convinces his disciples that the American Indian was descended from the children of Israel. Complications follow. ". . . it is very, very bad indeed" *(World-Telegram).* A: Louis Vittes. P: Chanin and Karlan. D: Herman Rosten.

Comet, The (12/30/07, Bijou, 56)

El Comet (Nazimova), a glamorous, world-weary *femme fatale*, falls in love with the son of the man who betrayed her years before. When the impressionable youth discovers his father's relations with his beloved, he shoots himself. "It is long drawn out, it is tedious, and it is vague" *(New York Times)*. This glum, pseudo-Ibsenesque drama was the first play written by Owen Johnson, American novelist famous for his cheerful, homespun Lawrenceville school stories. C: Dodson Mitchell, Brandon Tynan.

Comic Artist, The (4/19/33, Morosco, 21)

Tepid comedy-drama about a pair of possessive women who almost succeed in wrecking the lives of a cartoonist and his older brother. C: Blanche Yurka, Lora Baxter, Robert Allen, Richard Hale, Lea Penman. A: Susan Glaspell and Norman Matson. D: Arthur Beckhard.

Comic Strip (5/14/58, Barbizon Plaza, 156)

Zany O/B farce about the misadventures of a young boy in New York City during the days when Fiorello H. LaGuardia was mayor of the city. "Well-named, well-played, basically mad and altogether enjoyable" *(New York Times)*. C: Michael Constantine, Anna Appel, Tom Pedi, Cliff Norton, Gary Morgan. A: George Panetta b/o his novel, *Jimmy Potts Gets a Haircut*. P: Norman Forman. D: Ruth Rawson.
Musicalized as *King of the Whole Damn World* (1962) by George Panetta and Robert Larimer; presented O/B by Mr. Forman and staged by Jack Ragotzy.

Command Decision (10/1/47, Fulton, 409)

Taut World War II drama dealing with the moral agony of a flight commander forced to send his men on suicide missions over Nazi Germany. Standouts in an all-male cast were Paul Kelly as the intrepid commander and James Whitmore (deb.) as his loyal and outspoken technical sergeant. Reversing the usual procedure of adapting a play from a novel, Air Force veteran William Wister Haines first wrote *Command Decision* as a drama and subsequently, at the suggestion of his publisher, converted it into a novel. C: Jay Fassett, Paul McGrath, Paul Ford, Stephen Elliott, Lewis Martin, Edward Binns, Edmon Ryan, Arthur Franz. P: Kermit Bloomgarden. D: John O'Shaughnessy.
SV: MGM, 1948, Clark Gable, Walter Pidgeon, Van Johnson, Brian Donlevy, Charles Bickford, John Hodiak, Edward Arnold (directed by Sam Wood).

Commodore Marries, The (9/4/29, Plymouth, 37)

Walter Huston had an actor's field day (albeit briefly) in this offbeat comedy b/o Smollett's *Adventures of Peregrine Pickle* (1751). Virtually plotless, the play dealt with an eccentric old sea dog who insists, loudly and profanely, on running his home as he once ran his ship. A: Kate Parsons. P/D: Arthur Hopkins.

Common Clay (8/26/15, Republic, 316)

A pretty housemaid (Jane Cowl) is seduced by the scion (Orme Caldara) of the house. Abandoned, she sues for child support, learns she is the illegitimate daughter of the presiding judge (John Mason), goes to New York, becomes an opera singer, and finally is reunited with the scion-seducer who now wishes to give his child a name. This ridiculously plotted tearjerker, larded with heavy dollops of feminine martyrdom, was a positive wow with 1915 audiences. A: Cleves Kinkead. P: A. H. Woods. D: Byron Ongley.
SV: Fox, 1930, Constance Bennett, Lew Ayres; 1936, *Private Number*, Loretta Young, Robert Taylor,

Basil Rathbone, Patsy Kelly, Joe E. Lewis.

Common Ground (4/25/45, Fulton, 69)

Captured by the Nazis, a U.S.O. unit is given a choice of spreading anti-American propaganda or being shot. After some debate, the entertainers choose death rather than dishonor. ". . . fails to sustain its early promise and excitement" *(Sun)*. C: Luther Adler, Paul McGrath, Philip Loeb, Mary Healy, Donald Murphy, Nancy Noland, Joseph Vitale. A: Edward Chodorov. P: Edward Choate. D: Edward Chodorov and Jerome Robbins. SD: George Jenkins.

Common Sin, The (10/15/28, Forrest, 24)

Mistress tricks wife into confessing she murdered her husband. Poor 20's melodrama by Willard Mack (A/P/D). C: Lee Patrick, Thurston Hall, Millicent Hanley, Frederic Worlock.

Commuters, The (8/15/10, Criterion, 160)

Farcical comedy about the complications that result when a well-meaning but interfering bachelor (Taylor Holmes) takes up residence in a suburban community of happily married couples. "Much of the writing is clever, but the piece is out of focus [and] lacks definite central interest" *(New York Times)*. A/D: James Forbes. P: Henry B. Harris.

Company's Coming (4/20/31, Lyceum, 8)

A tennis nut (Lynne Overman) and his wife (Frieda Inescort) pawn a championship cup, spend the next two acts trying to retrieve it. Rosalind Russell had a small role in this woefully thin 1931 farce. "A thick stew of random laughs and indigestible dullness" *(New York Times)*. A: Alma Wilson. P: Stanley Sharpe. D: Zeke Colvan.

Complex, The (3/3/25, Booth, 47)

A girl undergoes psychoanalysis and is cured of her father fixation. Flimsy Freudian study. C: Dorothy Hall (deb.), Robert Montgomery. A: Louis E. Bisch. P: The Reed Producers, Inc. D: Percy Haswell.

Compulsion (10/24/57, Ambassador, 140)

Multi-scened, documentary-styled drama b/o the 1920's Leopold-Loeb "crime of the century," presenting first the psychological drama of the two spoiled rich men's sons (Roddy McDowall and Dean Stockwell) who murder a younger boy and, second, the courtroom trial that followed their arrest. "Not so much a play as a parade of clinical shocks and harrowing blasts at the emotions. . . . Among its shortcomings are its great length and lack of suspense" *(World-Telegram)*. C: Michael Constantine, Howard da Silva, Frank Conroy, Lloyd Gough, Ina Balin (deb.), Barbara Loden (deb.), Suzanne Pleshette (deb.), Ben Astar, Roger de Koven, Reynolds Evans, John Marley, Elliott Sullivan, Bernard Lenrow. A: Meyer Levin b/o his novel. P: Michael Myerberg i.a.w. L. S. Gruenberg. D: Alex Segal. SD: Peter Larkin.
SV: Fox, 1959, Orson Welles, Dean Stockwell, Bradford Dillman, E. G. Marshall, Martin Milner (directed by Richard Fleischer).

Conflict (3/6/29, Fulton, 52)

A lowly clerk (Spencer Tracy) returns from World War I a much-decorated flight commander, marries his former employer's niece, finally divorces her because of differences in their social positions. Meandering 20's drama with a fine performance by Tracy. C: Edward Arnold, Frank McHugh, Albert Dekker, George Meeker, Peggy Allenby, Dennie Moore, Clifford Odets (understudy to Spencer Tracy). A: Warren F. Lawrence.

P: Spad Producing Co., Inc. D: Edward Clarke Lilley.

Congai (11/27/28, Harris, 137)

Lurid South Seas melodrama about a man-hating half-caste (Helen Menken) who delights in driving men mad with passion. A: Harry Hervey and Carleton Hildreth b/o the Hervey novel. P: Sam H. Harris. D: Rouben Mamoulian.

Congratulations (4/30/29, National, 39)

Ham actor runs for mayor, cleans up the town. Labored 20's comedy. C: Henry Hull, Preston Foster. A: Morgan Wallace. P: Lawrence Shubert Lawrence. D: Edward Clarke Lilley.

Connection, The (7/15/59, Living Theatre, 768)

Offbeat, powerful theatre piece dealing with a group of drug-addicted derelicts awaiting the arrival of their heroin supplier, and the temporary peace that follows their injections. Described by its author, Jack Gelber, as a series of prearranged "verbal improvisations"; presented with a no-name cast by the O/B Living Theatre under the direction of Judith Malina. "The most original piece of new American playwriting in a long, long time" (Henry Hewes, *Saturday Review*). "The most exciting new American play that off-Broadway has produced since the war" (Kenneth Tynan, *The New Yorker*).

Connie Goes Home (9/6/23, 49th Street, 19)

So that she may travel by train at half-fare, an enterprising young woman disguises herself as a child. Amusing notion was here developed in heavy-handed slapstick fashion. C: Sylvia Field, Aline MacMahon, Fred Irving Lewis, Donald Foster, Berton Churchill. A: Edward Childs Carpenter, based on a story by Fannie Kilbourn. P: Kilbourn Gordon. D: Frederick Stanhope.

SV: Par, 1942, *The Major and the Minor*, Ginger Rogers, Ray Milland, Robert Benchley, Diana Lynn, Rita Johnson; 1955, *You're Never Too Young*, Dean Martin, Jerry Lewis, Raymond Burr, Nina Foch.

Conquest (2/18/33, Plymouth, 10)

A retelling of the *Hamlet* story with the principal characters and setting transferred to twentieth-century Connecticut. Hamlet, here called Frederick (Raymond Hackett), returns home after two years in Germany, suspecting that his stepfather (Hugh Buckler) had been the paramour of his mother (Judith Anderson) and the murderer of his father (Henry O'Neill). The introspective youth avenges his father's death and, with the help of his moonstruck childhood sweetheart (Jane Wyatt), dedicates his life to rebuilding the family honor. *Conquest* was a *succes d'estime*, but a box-office failure. It was written, produced and directed by Arthur Hopkins.

Note: Elmer Rice also went to *Hamlet* for the characters and plot of *Cue for Passion* (1958).

Conscience (9/11/24, Belmont, 132)

Learning that his wife has become a prostitute in his absence, a man murders her, is tormented by his conscience, and dies fleeing the law in the frozen Yukon. Contrived and predictable flashback melodrama. C: Ray Collins, Lillian Foster. A: Don Mullally. P: A. H. Woods.

Constant Sinner, The (9/14/31, Royale, 64)

Babe Gordon (Mae West), the bejewelled and restless mistress of a black racketeer, is "the kind of woman every man wants to meet—at least once." As indicated by the play's title, Babe is a constant sinner. Hence, it isn't long before this blowsy damozel is attracted to a couple of other magnetic males—a department store magnate ("the handsomest man in New York") and a prizefighter-stud charged with murder. This 1931 comedy-melodrama was described by one reviewer as "a triumph of Mae over matter." It was during the run of the play that Paramount Pictures offered Miss West five thousand dollars a week to make her film debut in a fairly small (fourth-billed) role in *Night after Night*. George Raft, star of the picture, said later of Mae's screen debut: "She stole everything but the cameras." C: Russell Hardie, George Givot, Walter Glass (Ray Walker). A/D: Mae West. P: Constant Productions, Inc. (Messrs. Shubert).

Conversation at Midnight (11/12/64, Billy Rose, 4)

Posthumously produced drama by Edna St. Vincent Millay in which a group of men, representing varying shades of opinion, discuss controversial social, political, and aesthetic issues of the time. "Talk that sings and soars. . . . But essentially it is talk, not drama" *(New York Times)*. ". . .more soporific than Illuminating . . . a luckless tribute to the memory of a distinguished American poet" *(Post)*. C: Eduard Franz, Larry Gates, Al Freeman, Jr., James Patterson, John Randolph. P: Worley Thorne i.a.w. Susan Davis. D: Robert Gist.

Note: Edna St. Vincent Millay (1892–1950) completed *Conversation at Midnight*, her only full-length play, in 1936, but the manuscript was destroyed in a fire. Miss Millay rewrote the play from memory. It was published in 1937, but did not receive a Broadway production until 1964.

Cook for Mr. General, A (10/19/61, Playhouse, 28)

Shenanigans in an army rehabilitation center in the wartime Pacific. Uneven, occasionally extremely funny knock-about farce with an all-male cast that included Bill Travers,* Roland Winters, John McGiver, Gerald O'Loughlin, Thomas Carlin, Alan Bunce, Otis Bigelow, Roberts Blossom,* Richard X. Slattery,* George Furth,* Dustin Hoffman.* A: Steven Gethers. P: Darrid, Saidenberg and Ruskin. D: Fielder Cook. SD: Will Steven Armstrong.

---

*Broadway debuts.

Cool World, The (2/22/60, O'Neill, 2)

Episodic melodrama about the rise and fall of a Negro youth in the gang jungles of Harlem. ". . . keyhole realism . . . an illustrated social sermon rather than an imaginative play of real character and depth" *(New York Times)*. C: Billy Dee Williams, Roscoe Lee Browne, Calvin Lockhart, Hilda Simms, Cicely Tyson, Alice Childress, Raymond St. Jacques, James Earl Jones, Alease Whittington, Lynn Hamilton. A: Warren Miller and Robert Rossen (D)* b/o the novel by Mr. Miller. P: Lester Osterman. SD: Howard Bay.

---

*Hollywood writer-producer-director (*Body and Soul, All the King's Men, The Hustler*, etc.).

Coop, The (3/1/66, Actors Playhouse, 24)

Life on murderer's row in a state prison. Grim O/B entry with effective performances by Clifton James and William LeMassena as two of the inmates. A: Ralph S. Arzoomanian. D: Martin Fried.

Copperhead, The (2/18/18, Shubert, 120)

Milt Shanks (Lionel Barrymore) is suspected of being a Confederate spy and of having given information to the South that caused the death not only of some of his friends but of his own son. Many years later, when the happiness of his granddaughter is at stake, the reviled and ostracized old man produces a letter from Abraham Lincoln justifying Shanks' long silence, exonerating him as a traitor, and

The Copperhead. **Lionel Barrymore (1918).** *Courtesy Museum of the City of New York Theatre and Music Collection.*

saluting him as a patriot. This Augustus Thomas A/D) drama (based on a story by Frederick Landis) built slowly to a tremendous final scene, a scene in which, according to the *New York Sun,* the little-known Lionel Barrymore "gave such an exhibition of feeling and technical finish as the contemporary stage rarely witnesses. The effect of his acting was to arouse the audience to the highest pitch of enthusiasm." Barrymore received fifteen solo curtain calls on that historic opening night of *The Copperhead.* Brother John and sister Ethel were present to bask in his triumph. C: Chester Morris, Raymond Hackett, Doris Rankin (Mrs. Lionel Barrymore). P: John D. Williams.

Coquette (11/8/27, Maxine Elliott's, 366)

Unable to marry the boy she loves, a flirtatious southern belle kills herself. This 1927 tearjerker was redeemed by a memorable Helen Hayes performance in the title role (her first strong dramatic part on Broadway). "In the last act, when reality burns low, the playwrights are caught red-handed in the heartless procedure of wringing tears for the sheer delight of torture without regard for either necessity or logic. . . . In Helen Hayes' Norma *Coquette* takes on a real importance. It is by far the best performance of her career. . ." *(Theatre Arts).* C: Eliot Cabot, Charles Waldron, Una Merkel. A: George Abbott (D) and Ann Preston Bridgers.

SV: UA, 1929, Mary Pickford, Johnny Mack Brown, Louise Beavers.

Note: During the run of *Coquette,* Helen Hayes (Mrs. Charles MacArthur) became pregnant, and was forced to leave the show. Because of the ensuing highly publicized lawsuit instituted by producer Jed Harris, Miss Hayes' child, Mary, became known throughout the world as "the Act of God" baby. Thereafter, theatrical contracts generally included an "Act of God" clause.

Coquette. **Helen Hayes and Eliot Cabot (1927).** *Courtesy Museum of the City of New York Theatre and Music Collection.*

Co-respondent Unknown (2/11/36, Ritz, 121)

A divorce-seeking husband becomes enamored of the pretty young co-respondent engaged to provide evidence of adultery. Saucy sex comedy, nicely acted and skillfully produced. C: James Rennie, Ilka Chase, Phyllis Povah, Peggy Conklin, Richard Sterling, Martin Wolfson. A: Mildred Harris and Harold Goldman. P: MacKenna, Mayer and Mielziner. D: Kenneth MacKenna. SD: Jo Mielziner.

Cornered (12/8/20, Astor, 141)

Madge Kennedy as twin sisters, one good and one not so good. The play was not so good, either. A: Dodson Mitchell. P: Henry W. Savage. D: John McKee.

SV: WB, 1931, *The Road to Paradise,* Loretta Young, Jack Mulhall.

Note: A silent version of *Cornered* (WB, 1924) starred Marie Prevost.

Counsellor-at-Law (11/6/31, Plymouth, 397)

The meteoric career of an aggressive Jewish lawyer (Paul Muni) is threatened when an early breach of ethics catches up with him. On the verge of disbarment, his faithless gentile wife and fair-weather friends desert him. He attempts suicide, but is saved by his loving and devoted Jewish secretary. Absorbing, shrewdly atmospheric drama was a resounding success. "The play wrote itself easily, almost effortlessly, in five or six weeks," said Elmer Rice (A/P/D). "In three weeks it paid off its production cost—which was less than eleven thousand dollars!" When Muni was summoned back to Hollywood for picture commitments, Otto Kruger (who had headed the Chicago company) took over the leading role in New York. C: Anna Kostant, Louise Prussing, Constance McKay, John Qualen, Jennie Moscowitz, Victor Wolfson, Gladys Feldman.

R: (11/24/42, Royale, 258) by John Golden. C: Paul Muni, Olive Deering, Joan Wetmore, Jennie Moscowitz, Joseph Pevney. D: Elmer Rice.

SV: *Counsellor-at-Law* (U, 1933) was William Wyler's first major directorial assignment. When Paul Muni refused to recreate his stage success on screen, John Barrymore was signed to appear in his stead. Bebe Daniels, Thelma Todd, and Melvyn Douglas rounded out the cast. The screenplay was written by Elmer Rice.

Counterattack (2/3/43, Windsor, 84)

Two Red Army soldiers hold a group of Nazi prisoners at bay in a shelled basement on the Eastern front. ". . . well-intentioned and splendidly mounted [but] lean on theatrical substance" *(Herald Tribune).* Adapted and extensively revised by Janet and Philip Stevenson from a play by Vershinin and Ruderman. C: Morris Carnosky, Sam Wanamaker, Barbara O'Neil, John ireland, Richard Basehart (deb.), Karl Malden, Harold Stone, Martin Wolfson, Bert Freed, Orin Jannings. P: Lee Sabinson. D: Margaret Webster. SD: John Root.

SV: Col, 1945, Paul Muni, Larry Parks, Marguerite Chapman, George Macready (directed by Zoltan Korda from a screenplay by John Howard Lawson.)

Country Boy, The (8/30/10, Liberty, 143)

Small-town fellow bids farewell to his girlfriend and leaves for New York to win his fortune. The heartless big town beats him down. He is saved from suicide by a dyspeptic newspaper man who advises him to return home which, happily, he does. This banal comedy-drama by Edgar Selwyn (A/D) was not one of 1910's dramatic triumphs. It did, however, manage to achieve a respectable run of 143 performances. C: Forrest Winant,

Robert McWade, Jr., Willette Kershaw. P: Henry B. Harris.

Country Cousin, The (9/3/17, Gaiety, 128)

Small-town girl comes to New York, triumphs over big-city sophisticates, wins the hand of the handsome and wealthy George Tewksberry Reynolds III. Middling comedy by Booth Tarkington and Julian Street. C: Alexandra Carlisle, Eugene O'Brien, Grace Elliston, Donald Gallaher, Marion Coakley. P: Tyler, Klaw & Erlanger. D: Robert Milton.

Country Girl, The (11/10/50, Lyceum, 235)

Clifford Odets' (A/D) backstage drama about a has-been actor, whose alcoholism and self-pity have ruined his career, and who is helped in his comeback fight by the loyalty of his long-suffering, much-misunderstood wife. ". . . a vivid and stinging play about theatre people" *(New York Times)*. C: Paul Kelly, Uta Hagen, Steven Hill, Phyllis Love.* P: Dwight Deere Wiman. SD: Boris Aronson.

Note: The national touring company starred Robert Young, Nancy Kelly, and Dane Clark.
R: (9/29/66, City Center, 22). C: Joseph Anthony, Jennifer Jones, Rip Torn, Robin Strasser, Richard Beymer. D: Martin Fried.
R: (3/12/68, Greenwich Mews, 15) as *Winter Journey*. This O/B production was directed and co-produced by Mitchell Nestor. Walter Allen and Barbara Loden were among those in the cast.
R: (3/15/72, Billy Rose, 61). C: Jason Robards, Maureen Stapleton, George Grizzard, Roland Winters. D: John Houseman.
SV: Par, 1954, Bing Crosby, Grace Kelly, William Holden, Anthony Ross (written and directed by George Seaton).

---
*Broadway debut.

County Chairman, The (11/24/03, Wallack's, 222)

Jingoistic, satirical study of small-town Hoosier politics, c. 1880. A contest for political control of the town is complicated by the fact that one of the contestants is in love with his rival's daughter. Maclyn Arbuckle scored a personal hit as the blustering but amiable county chairman, playing the role from 1903 to 1907. A: George Ade. P: Henry W. Savage. D: George Marion.
R: (5/25/36, National, 8) by The Players. C: Charles Coburn, Alexander Kirkland, Dorothy Stickney, Rose Hobart, Jackie Kelk, James Kirkwood, Linda Watkins. D: Sam Forrest.
SV: Fox, 1935, Will Rogers, Mickey Rooney, Berton Churchill.

Courage (10/8/28, Ritz, 263)

Problems of a self-sacrificing widow with seven children. "So cloyingly sentimental it makes *Mrs. Wiggs of the Cabbage Patch* seem like *What Price Glory?* by comparison" *(Broadway Reporter)*. C: Janet Beecher, Junior Durkin, Charlotte Henry. A: Tom Barry. P: Lew Cantor. D: Priestly Morrison.
SV: WB, 1930, Belle Bennett, Rex Bell, Marian Nixon, Leon Janney; 1938, *My Bill*, Kay Francis, John Litel, Bonita Granville, Dickie Moore, Anita Louise, Bobby Jordan.

Cradle Snatchers (9/7/25, Music Box, 485)

To arouse their husbands' jealousy, three middle-aged wives (Mary Boland, Edna May Oliver, Margaret Dale) hire a trio of callow college youths (Humphrey Bogart,* Raymond Guion,** Raymond Hackett) to make love to them. Highly amusing farce, the comedy hit of 1925. A: Russell Medcraft and Norma Mitchell. P:

Sam H. Harris. D: Sam Forrest. Musicalized by Cole Porter and Herbert and Dorothy Fields as *Let's Face it* (1941) with Danny Kaye, Nanette Fabray, Mary Jane Walsh, Eve Arden, Vivian Vance, Edith Meiser, Benny Baker.

SV: Par, 1943, *Let's Face It*, Bob Hope, Betty Hutton, Eve Arden, ZaSu Pitts.

Note: A silent version of *Cradle Snatchers* (Fox, 1927) was directed by Howard Hawks. Louise Fazenda and Arthur Lake headed the cast.

---

*Bogart played the most amorous of the three youths, a hot-blooded Latin charmer named Jose Vallejo. He wowed the ladies. One reviewer (female) wrote: "Humphrey Bogart created a furor....He is as young and handsome as Valentino...and as graceful as any of our best romantic actors."

**This performer changed his name to Gene Raymond when he entered talking pictures (1931).

Craig's Wife (10/12/25, Morosco, 360)

Pulitzer Prize play by George Kelly (A/D). Classic study of a selfish, compulsively dominating bitch-wife who worships her home above all else. In the end, the disagreeable Mrs. Craig is in complete control of her house, but she is also completely alone. C: Chrystal Herne, Charles Trowbridge, Josephine Hull. P: Rosalie Stewart.

R: (2/12/47, Playhouse, 69) by Gant Gaither. C: Judith Evelyn, Philip Ober. D: George Kelly.

SV: Col, 1936, Rosalind Russell, John Boles, Billie Burke, Thomas Mitchell, Jane Darwell; 1950, *Harriet Craig*, Joan Crawford, Wendell Corey, Lucile Watson, Allyn Joslyn.

Note: A silent version (Pathé, 1928) featured Irene Rich, Warner Baxter, and Lilyan Tashman.

Crashing Through (10/29/28, Republic, 40)

Dowager is scandalized when her daughter refuses to marry the brawny riveter whose child she is expecting. Clichéd comedy-drama. C: Henrietta Crosman, Rose Hobart, Gavin Gordon. A: Saxon Kling. P/D: Oliver D. Bailey.

Cream in the Well, The (1/20/41, Booth, 24)

Dour drama about the incestuous love of a neurotic farm girl for her seafaring brother. "... a sadly ineffectual work" *(Herald Tribune)*. "... balderdash of a curdling sort" *(Post)*. *The Cream in the Well* was written by Lynn Riggs, author of *Green Grow the Lilacs* (1931) upon which the musical play, *Oklahoma!* was based. C: Leif Erickson, Martha Sleeper, Myron McCormick, Mary Morris. P: Carly Wharton and Martin Gabel (D). SD: Jo Mielziner.

Creation of the World and Other Business, The (11/30/72, Sam S. Shubert, 20)

Arthur Miller struggles with an age-old question: "Since God made everything and God is good—why did He make Lucifer?" It is the first of three ambitious questions in this comedy-drama. None are resolved. Miller sets his story in the Garden of Eden. Unsurprisingly, the principal characters are Adam (Bob Dishy), Eve (Zoe Caldwell), the Lord (Stephen Elliott), and Lucifer (George Grizzard). The play follows the Book of Genesis through the murder of Abel and concludes with Adam vainly crying after the departing Cain, who is presumably on his way eastward from Eden. The writing combines the flippant and the serious in an uneasy melding that pleased neither audiences nor critics. The jokes needed more wit and the attempts at profundity greater clarity. "... has provided us with a lethargic evening by toying with myth" (Douglas Watt, *New York Daily News*). "... deserves no comment or any attempt to unravel its stupefyingly boring muddleheadedness" (Jack Kroll, *Newsweek*). "... an unexpected vein of humor . . . a good first act" (Richard Watts, *New York Post*). Miller subsequently reworked the play into a musical comedy called *Up From Creation*. A: Arthur Miller. C: George Grizzard, Zoe Caldwell, Bob Dishy, Stephen Elliott, Barry Primus, Mark Lamos, Lou Gilbert, Dennis Cooley, Lou Polan. D: Gerald Freedman. P: Robert Whitehead. SD: Boris Aronson.

Creeping Fire (1/16/35, Vanderbilt, 23)

After falling in love with his stepmother, a disturbed teenager becomes involved in arson and murder. Sputtering, low-voltage melodrama by Marie Baumer. C: Ted Fetter, Eric Dressler, Marjorie Peterson, Bernard Gorcey. P: Glen McNaughton and John Cameron (D).

Creoles (9/22/27, Klaw, 28)

Penniless mother hopes to sell innocent daughter to lecherous landowner, but the silly child prefers a no-'count pirate. Ridiculous costume piece set in old New Orleans and written in a kind of pidgin English patois. C: Princess Matchabelli, Helen Chandler, Alan Dinehart, George Nash, Natacha Rambova. A: Samuel Shipman and Kenneth Perkins. P: Richard Herndon. D: Benrimo.

Musicalized by Green, Berton, Carlo and Sanders as *Louisiana Lady* (1947) with Edith Fellows, Monica Moore, Charles Judels.

Crime (2/22/27, Eltinge, 186)

A dewy-eyed salesgirl (Sylvia Sidney) and a naïve young elevator operator (Douglass Montgomery) become involved with a criminal mastermind (James Rennie). Conventional underworld melodrama with a good cast: Chester Morris, Jack LaRue, Kay Johnson, Katherine (Kay) Francis, Irving Rapper. A: Samuel Shipman and John B. Hymer. P: A. H. Woods. D: A. H. Van Buren.
SV: RKO, 1938, *Law of the Underworld,* Chester Morris, Anne Shirley, Eduardo Ciannelli, Walter Abel, Lee Patrick, Paul Guilfoyle, Jack Carson.

Crime in the Whistler Room, The (10/12/24, Provincetown, 23)

This O/B drama by Edmund Wilson, one of America's foremost authors and literary critics, was severely trounced by the critics. Superficially the play dealt with the conflict that arises when a liberal but inhibited social worker takes a street waif into her home with a view toward reclaiming her for society. This *Pygmalion* theme, however, was frequently blunted by the author's Marxist viewpoint and his scatter-shot approach to sociological issues of the day. C: Mary Morris, Mary Blair, Walter Abel, Edgar Stehli, E. J. Ballantine. P: Provincetown Players. D: Harold McGee.

Crime Marches On (10/23/35, Morosco, 46)

Tennessee poet (Elisha Cook, Jr.) comes to New York, gets mixed up in a murder case. Denouement: it was all just a bad dream. Mary Rogers (Will Rogers' daughter) played the object of Cook's affection in this witless 30's farce. A: Bertrand Robinson and Maxwell Hawkins. P: Bushar and Tuerk. D: Edward Clarke Lilley.

Criminal Code, The (10/2/29, National, 174)

The criminal code compels a model prisoner to remain silent concerning the identity of a fellow inmate-murderer. Stripped of all privileges and locked in his cell, he finally kills a brutal officer and is sentenced to life imprisonment. Hard-hitting, grimly effective 20's melodrama. C: Arthur Byron, Russell Hardie, Walter Kingsford, Ethel Griffies, Thomas Findlay. A: Martin Flavin. P/D: William Harris, Jr.
SV: Col, 1931, Walter Huston, Constance Cummings, Phillips Holmes.

Critic's Choice (12/14/60, **Barrymore**, 189)

Patchwork comedy about the dilemma faced by a New York drama critic (Henry Fonda) when he is forced to review his wife's disastrously bad play. ". . . choice hilarity on occasion, but the occasions are too few and far between" *(Mirror)*. C: Georgann Johnson, Mildred Natwick, Murray Hamilton, Virginia Gilmore, Eddie Hodges, Billie Allen. A: Ira Levin. P/D: Otto Preminger. CD: Oleg Cassini. SD: George Jenkins.
SV: WB, 1963, Bob Hope, Lucille Ball, Rip Torn, Marilyn Maxwell, Jessie Royce Landis, Jim Backus, John Dehner.
Note: Walter Kerr, himself a critic with a playwright-wife (Jean Kerr), reputedly served as the prototype for the play's central character.

Cross Roads (11/11/29, Morosco, 28)

When a demure college girl learns that her medical student boyfriend has had an affair with a waitress, she finds it hard to forgive him, but eventually does. Unpretentious study of college life, 1920's style, with a good cast: Sylvia Sidney, Eric Dressler, Franchot Tone, Irene Purcell, Peggy Shannon, Mary Morris, Dennie Moore, Oscar Polk. A: Martin Flavin. P: Lewis E. Gensler. D: Guthrie McClintic.
SV: RKO, 1932, *The Age of Consent*, Richard Cromwell, Eric Linden, Dorothy Wilson, Arline Judge, John Halliday, Aileen Pringle.
Note: San Francisco-born Martin Flavin switched careers at the age of forty from successful businessman to successful dramatist. In 1929 three of his plays—*Cross Roads* among them—opened on Broadway within the space of six weeks. The other two plays were *The Criminal Code,* a big hit, and *Broken Dishes,* in which Bette Davis made her Broadway debut. All three plays were filmed by Hollywood.

Cross-Town (3/17/37, 48th Street, 5)

Unbelievably bad comedy about a would-be author (Joseph Downing); written by Joseph Kesselring, author of *Arsenic and Old Lace* (1941). P: John Dietz. D: William B. Friedlander.

Crowded Hour The (11/22/18, Selwyn, 139)

Incredible, plot-heavy soap opera that proved much to the liking of World War I (1918) American audiences. Peggy Lawrence (Jane Cowl), telephone operator, makes a hit on Broadway. When war is declared, pretty Peggy enlists as a "Y" worker to entertain our boys overseas. There she meets the married man she loved back in the states, risks her life to send a telephone message that saves the lives of a thousand men, is temporarily blinded, but finds happiness at last in sending her married lover back to his adoring wife. C: Orme Caldara, Christine Norman, Henry Stephenson. A: Edgar Selwyn (P/D) and Channing Pollock.

Crown Prince, The (3/23/27, Forrest, 45)

Retelling of the Mayerling tragedy wherein Crown Prince Rudolph of Austria and his mistress met death together in the royal hunting lodge. "A fine moving romantic tragedy . . . makes its dramatic points with vigorous precision" *(New York Times)*. C: Basil Sydney, Mary Ellis, Kay Strozzi, Henry Stephenson, Ferdinand Gottschalk, Jerome Lawler. A: Zoe Akins b/o play by Ernest Vajda. P: L. Lawrence Weber. D: Lawrence Marston.

Crucible (9/4/33, Forrest, 8)

Poor cops and robbers melodrama played by a no-name cast. A/P: D. Hubert Connelly. D: Guy Bragdon.

Crucible, The (1/22/53, Martin Beck, 197)

Set in Salem, Massachusetts, Arthur Miller's drama explores the infamous witch hunts that ravaged the Puritan community during the last decade of the seventeenth century. The central characters are John and Elizabeth Proctor, an outspoken farm couple innocently drawn into the Salem frenzy by a vindictive accuser. Attempting to clear his wife, Proctor implicates himself. He is offered his life for a confession of witchcraft, but refuses and goes to his death. *The Crucible* was written and produced during the early 1950's, a time when hysterical fear of communism took on some of the dimensions of the Salem witch hunts. The play received respectful but generally tepid reviews, due in large part to a ponderous production. The two decades since its first performance have brought the play's wider applications and deeper meanings into clearer focus, revealing *The Crucible* as a drama of considerable impact and emotional power. C: Arthur Kennedy, Beatrice Straight, Walter Hampden, E. G. Marshall, Madeleine Sherwood, Jenny Egan, Fred Stewart, Philip Coolidge, Jean Adair, Joseph Sweeney. P: Kermit Bloomgarden. D: Jed Harris. CD: Edith Lutyens. SD: Boris Aronson.

R: (3/11/58, Martinique, 633). C: Michael Higgins, Barbara Barrie. D: Word Baker.

R: (4/6/64, Belasco, 16). C: Farley Granger, Anne Meacham. D: Jack Sydow.

R: (4/27/72, Lincoln Center, 44). C: Robert Foxworth, Martha Henry. D: John Berry.

Musicalized as an opera (1961) by Robert Ward and Bernard Stambler. The Miller play was produced in London during the season of 1964–65 with a cast headed by Colin Blakely, Sarah Miles, and Joyce Redman.

Note: *The Crucible* was filmed (1958) by Raymond Rouleau from a screenplay by Jean-Paul Sartre. The players included Simone Signoret, Yves Montand, Mylene Demongeot, and Raymond Rouleau. The movie was made in France because the prizewinning author was blacklisted in America at the time.

Cry of Players, A (11/14/68, Lincoln Center, 72)

Fictionalized account of Shakespeare's life as a young man in 1850's Stratford. The budding poet (Frank Langella) is portrayed as a high-spirited, irresponsible youth who deserts his possessive wife, Anne (Anne Bancroft), once he hears the siren call of the stage. ". . . written with charm, grace and eloquence" (*Post*). A Cry of Players was authored by William Gibson (*Two For the Seesaw, The Miracle Worker,* etc.), and presented in repertory with *King Lear*. C: Stephen Elliott, Rene Auberjonois, Robert Symonds, Rosetta LeNoire, Susan Tyrrell, Kristoffer Tabori. D: Gene Frankel. CD: Patricia Stuart. SD: David Hays. M: Richard Peaslee.

Cuban Thing, The (9/24/68, Henry Miller, 1)

A middle-class Cuban family switches its allegiance from Batista to Castro. Wearisome political drama by Jack Gelber (A/D) closed after one performance. C: Rip Torn, Jane White, Michael Wager, Conrad Bain. P: Ivor David Balding.

Cuckoos on the Hearth (9/16/41, Morosco, 129)

To a lonely Maine farmhouse at the height of a blizzard comes a rotund and acidulous mystery writer, followed shortly thereafter by a phony clergyman, a Nazi agent, and various and sundry other menacing characters. One of these wayfarers is an escaped homicidal maniac. But which one? Before the evening ends, author Parker Fennelly* provides not one but two alternate denouements, together with a generous sampling of ideas and situations from such shows as *Arsenic and Old Lace, Our Town,* and *The Man Who Came to Dinner.* "Mr. Fennelly's 'shudder comedy' is a kind of Omnibus of the American Theater, but with all the pages inserted in the wrong order" *(PM).* C: Percy Kilbride, Howard Freeman, Frederic Tozere, Margaret Callahan, George Mathews, Howard St. John, Henry Levin. P: Brock Pemberton. D: Antoinette Perry.

---

*Parker Fennelly is best remembered as Titus ("Howdy, Bub") Moody on Fred Allen's radio show.

Cue for Passion (12/19/40, Royale, 12)

Disagreeable columnist (Gale Sondergaard) conspires to make the murder of her equally unpleasant author-husband (George Coulouris) appear a suicide. Well-acted, moderately diverting whodunit. (The two central characters reputedly were patterned after Dorothy Thompson and Sinclair Lewis.) C: Doris Nolan, Oscar Karlweis (deb.), Claire Niesen (deb.), Whit Bissell, Mel Ferrer, Clay Clement, Lili Valenty, Ralphe Locke. A: Edward Chodorov and H. S. Kraft. P: Aldrich and Myers. D: Otto Preminger.

Cue for Passion (11/25/58, Henry Miller's, 39)

Elmer Rice's (A/D) retelling of the Hamlet legend transplanted to contemporary Southern California. "An absorbing psychological drama" *(Journal-American).* "Elmer Rice has been quoted as saying he'd fooled around with this one a quarter of a century. It's worth the wait" *(World-Telegram and Sun).* C: John Kerr, Diana Wynyard, Robert Lansing, Anne Revere, Lloyd Gough, Joanna Brown, Russell Gaige, P: The Playwrights Company and Franchot Productions. CD: Dorothy Jenkins. SD: George Jenkins.

Cup of Trembling, The (4/20/48, Music Box, 31)

Wordy, unconvincing drama about the reclamation of an alcoholic (Elisabeth Bergner). C: Arlene Francis, Millard Mitchell, John Carradine, Anthony Ross, Martin Wolfson, Louis Hector, Hope Emerson, Philip Tonge, Beverly Bayne, Iris Mann. A: Louis Paul b/o his novel, *Breakdown.* P: Paul Czinner (D) and C. P. Jaeger.

Cure for Curables, A (2/25/18, 39th Street, 112)

One of those helter-skelter farce-comedies set in motion by the *deus ex machina* of a stage will. In this variation, a group of hypochondriacs idle away their days at a fashionable "rest cure" sanitarium. To fulfill the terms of an eccentric's will, a doctor (William Hodge) must cure these malingerers within thirty days and, moreover, make them sign an affidavit stating that they indeed are "cured." "There is the shadow of an idea in the play and the gleam of an uplift.... It is a typical Hodge vehicle, in short" *(New York Times).* A/D: Earl Derr Biggers and Lawrence Whitman (based on a story by Cora Harris). P: Lee Shubert.

Curious Savage, The (10/24/50, Martin Beck, 31)

Because of her penchant for giving away large sums of money, an elderly millionairess (Lillian Gish) is committed to a private sanitarium by her greedy stepchildren. Gaining strength of spirit from her fellow inmates, she manages to turn the tables on her unpleasant family. Produced by The Theatre Guild and Lewis and Young, this 1950 comedy received generally unfavorable notices and closed after thirty-one performances. Author John Patrick attributed the play's failure to Peter Glenville's direction. "It was staged like an English music hall production," complained Patrick. Though a Broadway flop, the play proved an enormous hit in stock and community theatres. The author is reported to have earned in excess of $400,000 from the amateur rights.

Curtain Call (4/22/37, Golden, 4)

Poorly written drama about the ill-fated romance of actress Eleonora Duse and poet-playwright Gabriele D'Annunzio. C: Ara Gerald, Guido Nadzo, Selena Royle. A: Le Roy Bailey. P: Quigley and Schachtel. D: Dickson Morgan.

Curtain Rises, The (10/19/33, Vanderbilt, 61)

Spinster (Jean Arthur) engages an actor (Donald Foster) to make love to her. Contrived frou-frou set in romantic Vienna. A: Benjamin Kaye. P: Green and McCoy. D: Ernest Truex.

Cut of the Axe (2/1/60, Ambassador, 2)

Crooked politician tries to frame two innocent vagrants for a local murder. "An exceptionally foolish blood-and-thunder tale . . . confusing to the point of sheer chaos" *(Post)*. C: Thomas Mitchell, James Westerfield, Robert Lansing, Milo Boulton. A: Sheppard Kerman b/o the novel by Delmar Jackson. P: Allen and Cassel. D: John O'Shaughnessy. SD: Howard Bay.

Czarina, The (1/31/22, Empire, 136)

The affairs of Catherine the Great (Doris Keane) treated in satiric fashion, pointing up the havoc wrought on her faithful retainers when the empress casts her roving eye on a dashing soldier (Basil Rathbone) only to have her romantic interests diverted by the arrival of the handsome French ambassador (Ian Keith). Droll boudoir comedy, extensively revised and adapted for American audiences by Edward Sheldon from a play by Lengyel and Biro. Basil Rathbone made his Broadway debut in this 1922 comedy. P: Charles Frohman, Inc. D: Gilbert Miller.

SV: Fox, 1945, *A Royal Scandal,* Tallulah Bankhead, William Eythe, Charles Coburn, Vincent Price, Anne Baxter, Mischa Auer (directed by Ernst Lubitsch and Otto Preminger).

D

Daddies (9/5/18. Belasco, 340)

Mawkish World War I comedy about a group of fuddy-duddy bachelors who agree to adopt some French war orphans. Jeanne Eagels was one of the orphans and George Abbott was the bachelor who got stuck with triplets. A: John L. Hobble. P/D: David Belasco.

Daddy Long-Legs (9/28/14, Gaiety, 264)

Wealthy playboy (Charles Waldron) anonymously sponsors the education of an orphanage drudge (Ruth Chatterton). She blossoms into a beautiful young lady, they fall in love, and live happily ever after. This sentimental Cinderella yarn was one of 1914's biggest hits. A: Jean Webster. P/D: Henry Miller.

SV: Fox, 1931, Janet Gaynor, Warner Baxter; 1935, *Curly Top,* Shirley Temple, John Boles; 1955, Leslie Caron, Fred Astaire.

Note: A silent version (WB, 1919) starred Mary Pickford and Mahlon Hamilton.

Daddy's Gone A-Hunting (8/31/21, Plymouth, 129)

When their little daughter dies, a wife (Marjorie Rambeau) decides to leave her irresponsible artist-husband (Frank Conroy). Sentimental, inconclusive drama by Zoe Akins. P/D: Arthur Hopkins.

SV: Par, 1931, *Women Love Once,* Paul Lukas, Eleanor Boardman.

Daisy Mayme (10/25/26, Playhouse, 113)

A shrewd, fortyish spinster shows a middle-aged bachelor how to handle his parasitic relatives, and then marries him, substituting her own brand of breezy tyranny for theirs. Mordant, well-written George Kelly (A/D) comedy-drama of middle-class life. C: Jessie Busley, Josephine Hull, Madge Evans, Alma Kruger, Carlton Brickert. P: Rosalie Stewart.

Damask Cheek, The (10/22/42, Playhouse, 93)

A plain-looking Englishwoman (Flora Robson) visits New York in 1909 and falls in love with her second cousin (Myron McCormick). How the resourceful spinster wins him away from his gold-digging fiancée (Celeste Holm) provided the plot of this leisurely, witty period comedy. ". . . charm, literate writing and beguiling characterizations . . . an amusing evening's entertainment" *(Herald Tribune). The Damask Cheek* was co-written by Anglo-American author John Van Druten (D) and Columbia University professor-critic Lloyd Morris. C: Margaret Douglass, Joan Tetzel, Peter Fernandez, Zachary Scott (deb.). P: Dwight Deere Wiman. CD/SD: Raymond Sovey.

Dame Nature (9/26/38, Booth, 48)

Tender comedy-drama about a love affair between adolescents (Montgomery Clift and Lois Hall) and the reactions of the boy's obtuse parents to news of the girl's pregnancy. Ad. and extensively revised by actress Patricia Collinge from a play by Andre Birabeau, *Dame Nature* had the misfortune to open on September 26, 1938. As the premiere audience entered the theatre, the news broke that Hitler had invaded Czechoslovakia. In the words of one Theatre Guild (P) executive, "our insubstantial comedy died in front of our eyes." C: Jessie Royce Landis, Onslow Stevens. D: Worthington Miner. SD: Norris Houghton.

Damn the Tears (1/21/27, Garrick, 11)

Glum, pointless drama about a baseball player (Ralph Morgan) who becomes a bum, sinks lower and lower, and is finally jailed as a vagrant. A: William Gaston. P: Alexander McKaig. D: Sigourney Thayer.

Damn Your Honor (12/30/29, Cosmopolitan, 8)

Composer Vincent Youmans produced this elaborate costume romp about a nineteenth-century buccaneer (John Halliday) who seduces the governor's beautiful wife (Jessie Royce Landis). A fiasco. A/D: Bayard Veiller and Becky Gardiner.

Dance Night (10/14/38, Belasco, 3)

Lifeless melodrama about a gang of young New Jersey hoodlums. Directed by Lee Strasberg; written by Kenyon Nicholson, author of *The Barker* (1927), *Sailor, Beware!* (1933), etc. C: Lyle Bettger, Mary Folfe, Bert Conway, David Wayne, Perry Bruskin, Mary Servoss. P: Robert Rockmore.

Dancer, The (9/29/19, Harris, 61)

Straitlaced in-laws try every means in their power to break up the marriage of a showgirl to their social register son. It took three authors (Edward Locke, Max Marcin, and Louis K. Anspacher) to concoct this soppy soaper. C: John Halliday, Isabelle Lowe, Renee Adoree, Jose Ruben. P: Messrs. Shubert.

Dancer, The (6/5/46, Biltmore, 5)

Living in Paris with his homosexual "patron" (Colin Keith-Johnston), a once-famous ballet dancer (Anton Dolin) devotes himself to murdering local prostitutes until the law catches up with him. "The show strives desperately to be an esoteric bit of grand guignol only to wind up an unpleasant bore" *(Herald Tribune)*. A: Milton Lewis and Julian Funt. P: George Abbott. D: Everett Sloane. CD/SD: Motley. M: Paul Bowles.

Note: During the pre-Broadway tour, Mr. Dolin replaced Leon Fokine in the role of the deranged dancer. The play was suggested by episodes in the life of Nijinsky, the great Russian ballet dancer whose career was cut short (1919) by insanity.

Dance With Your Gods (10/6/34, Mansfield, 9)

Skeptic invokes ancient voodoo curse. Sixteen-year-old Lena Horne (deb.) had a small role in this murky spook sonata set in New Orleans. C: Rex Ingram, Ben Smith, Charles Waldron, Georgette Harvey. A: Kenneth Perkins. P: Laurence Schwab. D: Robert B. Sinclair. SD: Donald Oenslager.

Dancing Mothers (8/11/24, Booth, 311)

Puerile but popular jazz-age look at the New Morality. Learning that her husband, Hugh (Henry Stephenson), is a notorious philanderer and that her hard-drinking daughter, Kittens (Helen Hayes), has been seeing man-about-town Gerald Naughton (John Halliday), a mother (Mary Young) decides to do some stepping out herself. She arranges a romantic tryst with Gerald and announces to her shocked family that "Times have changed...I have become a woman of today. I have become a dancing mother." With that, leaving husband, daughter, lover (and audience) wide-eyed and envious, Mother dances off to Europe alone. A: Edmund Goulding and Edgar Selwyn (P/D).

Dancing Partner (8/5/30, Belasco, 119)

Brash young man wagers he can seduce any woman he chooses within thirty days, but he falls in love and loses the bet. Mildly risqué David Belasco (P/D) froufrou. C: Lynne Overman, Irene Purcell, Henry Stephenson, Charlotte Granville, Claudia Morgan. A: Frederic and Fanny Hatton b/o play by Engel and Grunwald.

SV: MGM, 1931, *Just a Gigolo*, William Haines, Irene Purcell.

Daphne in Cottage D (10/15/67, Longacre, 49)

A neurotic young widow (Sandy Dennis) and a married doctor (William Daniels) enter into a relationship founded on their mutual unhappiness. Anemic two-character comedy-drama; nice performance by Mr. Daniels. A: Stephen Levi. P: Leder/Michael Productions. D: Martin Fried.

Dark, The (2/1/27, Lyceum, 13)

Scarred and blinded in an accident, a man (Louis Calhern) shields his face from his wife (Ann Andrews) with a mask. Then, one night, he removes the mask. Ten-twent'-thirt' melodrama; directed by George Cukor. A: Martin Brown. P: William A. Brady, Jr. and Dwight Deere Wiman.

Dark at the Top of the Stairs, The (12/5/57, Music Box, 468)

A small-town 1920's Oklahoma family—a blustering traveling salesman (Pat Hingle), his long-suffering spouse (Teresa Wright), her rowdy sister (Eileen Heckart)—as seen through the eyes of an introverted preteenage son who helps them put an end to their quarrels when they discover how small their differences are. Staged by Elia Kazan, *The Dark at the Top of the Stairs* was William Inge's fourth Broadway hit in a row. The three earlier plays were *Come Back, Little Sheba* (1950), *Picnic* (1953), and *Bus Stop* (1955). Reviews of this 1957 production ranged from Richard Watts' "A moving, perceptive and effective drama" to Louis Kronenberger's "Somewhat ploppy . . . dramatically a little commonplace." C: Charles Saari, Timmy Everett, Judith Robinson, Evans Evans, Frank Overton. P: Saint Subber and Elia Kazan. CD: Lucinda Ballard. SD: Ben Edwards.

SV: WB, 1960, Robert Preston, Dorothy McGuire, Angela Lansbury, Eve Arden, Shirley Knight (directed by Delbert Mann).

Note: This semiautobiographical drama was a revision of William Inge's first play, *Farther Off from Heaven*, which Margo Jones presented at her Dallas, Texas, theatre in 1947. The script was brought to Miss Jones' attention by Tennessee Williams.

Dark Hammock (12/11/44, Forrest, 2)

Lady scientist turns sleuth to trap a murderess. "Long-winded and dull" *(PM)*. C: Elissa Landi, Mary Wickes, Mary Orr. A: Mary Orr and Reginald Denham (D). P: Meyer Davis and Sam H. Grisman.

Dark Hours, The (11/14/32, New Amsterdam, 8)

Spectacular but lethargic dramatization of the Christ story; written (and backed) by humorist Don Marquis of *archy and mehitabel* fame. While the play was in rehearsal, Marquis was temporarily stricken blind. *The Dark Hours* was a dire failure. C: Herbert Ranson, Hugh Miller, Charles Bryant. P: Lodewick Vroom. D: Marjorie Marquis. SD: Cleon Throckmorton.

Dark of the Moon (3/14/45, 46th Street, 318)

Eerie fantasy about a witch-boy who is permitted to assume human form and wed the beautiful Barbara Allen on condition that she remain faithful to him for one year. In the frenzy of a religious revival, Barbara is led to betray her husband, resulting in her death and his return to the world of the mountain witches. Set in the Great Smokies of North Carolina, this free adaptation of the famous Barbara Allen ballad proved surprisingly successful on Broadway, despite the fact that the play's virtues were frequently obscured by miscasting, inexpert direction, and a generally defective production. C: Richard Hart, Carol Stone, Roy Fant, Gar Moore, John Gerstad. A: Howard Richardson and William Berney. P: Messrs. Shubert. D: Robert E. Perry. SD: George Jenkins.

R: (2/26/58, Carnegie Hall Playhouse, 85). C: John Brachita, Ann Hillary, Conrad Bain. D: Norman Roland.

R: (4/3/70, Arena Theatre, 86). C: Chandler Hill, Margaret Howell. D: Kent Broadhurst.

Dark Tower, The (11/25/33, Morosco, 57)

Murder melodrama written and directed by Alexander Woollcott and George S. Kaufman. A Svengali-like husband, supposedly dead, returns unexpectedly to once again entangle his actress-wife in his sinister clutches. Her career and sanity are saved by a mysterious European producer who stabs the vicious husband to death and then conveniently disappears. Denouement: the mysterious stranger turns out to be the heroine's devoted brother in disguise. "As skilled and entertaining an exhibit as you will find in the town. And I wish to God that were higher praise" (Dorothy Parker, *Vanity Fair*). C: Basil Sydney, Margalo Gillmore, William Harrigan, Margaret Hamilton, Leona Maricle, Margaret Dale, Ernest Milton, Porter Hall. P: Sam H. Harris. SD: Jo Mielziner. (*Note:* The London cast was headed by Basil Sydney, Edna Best, Martita Hunt, Francis L. Sullivan, and Frith Banbury). Prior to the New York opening, star Basil Sydney (doomed by his dual role to enlarge himself with padding) complained loudly during the dress rehearsal: "I hate like blazes to walk out on that stage opening night with a big paunch." There was a moment of embarrassed silence. George S. Kaufman stole a look at his chubby coauthor and then said gravely: "You have grossly insulted Alexander Woollcott." Woollcott was both startled and touched. "And for that," continued Kaufman, after the ghost of a pause, "you will receive a gold medal." A gloomy and somewhat loosely woven mystery, *The Dark Tower* closed after seven weeks of middling business. "It was a tremendous success," quipped Woollcott, "except for the minor detail that people wouldn't come to see it."

SV: WB, 1934, *The Man With Two Faces*, Edward G. Robinson, Mary Astor, Louis Calhern, Ricardo Cortez, Mae Clarke.

Dark Victory (11/7/34, Plymouth, 55)

Judith Traherne* (Tallulah Bankhead), suffering from a brain tumor that will ultimately prove fatal, attempts to crowd a lifetime of happiness into a few stolen months. "After fifteen minutes it does not seem to matter in the least what happens to Judith Traherne.... And when you do not fight with her, for her life, there is no play" (*Theatre Arts*). C: Earle Larimore, Ann Andrews, Dwight Fiske. A: George Brewer and Bertram Bloch. P: Alexander McKaig. D: Robert Milton. SD: Robert Edmond Jones.

SV: WB, 1939, Bette Davis, George Brent, Humphrey Bogart, Geraldine Fitzgerald, Ronald Reagan, Cora Witherspoon, Henry Travers (directed by Edmund Goulding);

UA, 1963, *Stolen Hours*, Susan Hayward, Michael Craig, Diane Baker (directed by Daniel Petrie).

---

*Katharine Hepburn originally was slated to play this role. When leading man Stanley Ridges withdrew from the cast shortly before the tryout premiere, the production was cancelled.

Darkness at Noon (1/13/51, Alvin, 186)

Jailed for having opposed the party line through "counter-revolutionary tactics," a Soviet commissar (Claude Rains) recalls via flashbacks the events that led to his imprisonment. In the end, rather than compromise himself by signing a trumped-up confession, he goes stoically to his execution. *Darkness at Noon*, adapted from Arthur Koestler's novel by Sidney Kingsley (A/D), won the Drama Critics Circle award as best play of the year. "Brilliant anti-Communist propaganda" (*Herald Tribune*). "A complicated melodrama . . . somewhere between the novel and the theatre the intellectual distinction has gone out of the work" (*New York Times*). C: Kim Hunter, Jack Palance, Alexander Scourby, Philip Coolidge, Lois Nettleton, Will Kuluva, Geoffrey Barr, Richard Seff. P: The Playwrights Company. SD: Frederick Fox.

Note: Edward G. Robinson starred in the national touring company production.

Darling of the Gods, The (12/3/02, Belasco, 182)

Colorful, exotic David Belasco (P/D) fantasy-melodrama set in Japan. Princess Yo-San (Blanche Bates) is tricked by her cruel war minister (George Arliss) into revealing the hiding place of her rebel-lover, Prince Kara (Robert T. Haines). For her betrayal, Yo-San must wander one thousand years in hell, but Kara

The Darling of the Gods. **Blanche Bates and George Arliss (1902).** *Courtesy Museum of the City of New York Theatre and Music Collection.*

promises to wait for her. In the final scene, the thousand years have elapsed; Kara and Yo-San meet in the first Celestial Heaven and ascend to the next step toward eternity together. *The Darling of the Gods* was one of the most lavish and successful of Belasco productions. A: Belasco and John Luther Long.

Date With April, A (4/15/53, Royale, 13)

Constance Bennett made her Broadway bow in this featherweight bit of fluff about the on-again, off-again romance of a concert pianist and a Hemingwayesque novelist. ". . . one long tissue of misunderstandings, the most serious of which is author George Batson's notion that he has written a comedy. . . . I guess April is still the cruelest month of all" *(Herald Tribune)*. C: Edmon Ryan, Evelyn Varden. P: Kenneth Banghart and Diana Green. D: Reginald Denham.

Daughter of Silence (11/30/61, Music Box, 36)

Moral problems multiply rapidly in a small Italian town when a lawyer undertakes the defense of a teenage girl accused of killing the town mayor. Frequently absorbing courtroom melodrama by Morris L. West b/o his novel of the same name. C: Emlyn Williams, Rip Torn, Janet Margolin (deb.), Joanne Linville (deb.), Geoffrey Lumb, Frederic Tozere, William Hansen, Vincent Gardenia, Joe De Santis. P: Richard Halliday. D: Vincent J. Donehue. SD: Oliver Smith.

Daughters of Atreus (10/14/36, 44th Street, 13)

A handsomely produced, frequently eloquent paraphrase of the Agamemnon legend, with a cast headed by Eleonora Mendelssohn, Maria Ouspenskaya, and Joanna Roos. The play was written over a period of fifteen years by Tennessee-born author Robert Turner. Dame Sybil Thorndike read the script, liked it, and brought it to the attention of Delos Chappell (P). *Daughters of Atreus* was a distinguished failure. Praised by the critics but shunned by the public, the production was forced to close after thirteen performances. C: Gale Gordon, Edmond O'Brien, Cornel Wilde, Tom Neal, Eric Wollencott, Edgar Stehli, John Boruff, Olive Deering, Edward Trevor. D: Frederic McConnell. CD: James Reynolds. SD: Jo Mielziner.

David Harum (10/1/00, Garrick, 148)

Folksy fable about a shrewd country banker (William H. Crane) who plays cupid. A: R. and M. Hitchcock from the novel by Edward Westcott. P: Charles Frohman. D: Edward E. Rose.

SV: Fox, 1934, Will Rogers, Evelyn Venable, Kent Taylor, Louise Dresser, Noah Beery, Stepin Fetchit.

Dawn of a Tomorrow, The (1/25/09, Lyceum, 152)

A girl called Glad reforms some burglars, cures an old man's amnesia, and sets an example of cheer in the more dismal precincts of London town. Extravagantly mawkish yarn by Frances Hodgson Burnett. C: Eleanor Robson, Aubrey Boucicault, Allan Pollock, Fuller Mellish P: Liebler and Co. D: Hugh Ford.

Day in the Sun (5/16/39, Biltmore, 6)

Ne'er-do-well (Taylor Holmes) saves innocent man from the electric chair. Threadbare 30's comedy. A: Edward Sammis and Ernest Heyn. P: Forbes Dawson. D: Arthur Sircom.

Day the Money Stopped, The (2/20/58, Belasco, 4)

Excessively talky drama revolving around a squabble between two brothers (Richard Basehart and Kevin McCarthy) over their late father's will. C: Mildred Natwick, Collin Wilcox (deb.), William Hansen. A: Maxwell Anderson and Brendan Gill b/o the novel by Mr. Gill. P:

Stanley Gilkey and Producers Theatre. D: Harold Clurman.

Daybreak (8/14/17, Harris, 71)

Unhappy wife seeks to conceal her motherhood from sadistic husband. Lachrymose drama by Jane Cowl and Jane Murfin. C: Blanche Yurka, Reginald Mason, Margaret Dale. P: Selwyn and Company. D: Jane Cowl and Wilfred North.

Days and Nights of Beebee Fenstermaker, The (9/17/62, Sheridan Square, 304)

Wry, perceptive O/B drama about a sensitive smalltown girl who comes to the big city to be a writer, and of the disillusionment that reality brings to her dreams of success. C: Rose Gregorio, Robert Duvall. A: William Snyder. P: Judy Marechal and Ulu Grosbard (D).

Days to Come (12/15/36, Vanderbilt, 7)

Shrill, confused, poorly acted drama by Lillian Hellman. The play dramatized the effects of a strike upon a tradition-bound manufacturing family that has ruled a small midwestern town for generations. In the end, both capital and labor suffer grievously as a result of the class warfare. *Days to Come* was an ignominious failure for Miss Hellman and for producer-director Herman Shumlin. The play opened to uniformly bad reviews and closed after seven performances. C: Florence Eldridge, William Harrigan, Charles Dingle, Frieda Altman, Ben Smith, Joseph Sweeney.

Days Without End (1/8/34, Henry Miller, 57)

Eugene O'Neill's "modern miracle play" in which the hero's split personality becomes whole again through a return to the Catholicism of his childhood. Novelist John Loving, O'Neill's protagonist, is played by two actors, John representing religious faith, Loving his cynical alter ego. When his wife contracts pneumonia and faces death, John prostrates himself before the cross. His sin (adultery) is forgiven, his wife recovers, and his baser self dies. "Holy hokum" (*Journal-American*). "The story-telling is sophomoric; the writing is no match for the theme" (*New York Times*). *Days Without End* was neither a critical nor popular success. Bitterly disappointed with the play's reception, O'Neill retreated into a twelve-year silence that lasted until the Broadway premiere of *The Iceman Cometh* (1946). C: Earle Larimore, Stanley Ridges, Selena Royle, Ilka Chase, Robert Loraine. P: The Theatre Guild. D: Philip Moeller. SD: Lee Simonson.

Note: When *Days Without End* was produced in London (1935) with Henry Daniell as John and Neil Porter as Loving, the play was warmly received by the critics. The *Daily Telegraph* called it "enthralling." The *Times* declared: "*Days Without End* is made valuable by the author's special insight into a truth—which the stage ordinarily fails to recognize—that we poor mortals are not Dr. Jekyll and Mr. Hyde by turns but simultaneously, and that conflicting desires do not necessarily succeed one another, but may be active within us at the same time."

De Lancey (9/4/05, Empire, 68)

Playboy (John Drew) falls in love with the wrong girl, but it takes the entire evening—plus a fall from a horse and a broken leg—to make him see the light. Trivial froth by Augustus Thomas, author of *Alabama* (1894), *Arizona* (1900), *Colorado* (1901), etc. "Mr. Thomas was at one time content to get his inspiration from a map of the United States, but the dust is gathering on his geography" (*New York Times*). C: Margaret Dale, Doris Keane. P: Charles Frohman.

De Luxe (3/5/35, Booth, 15)

Sluggish drama by Louis Bromfield and John Gearon about a kept man (Melvyn Douglas), his aging "patroness" (Cora Witherspoon), and a variety of other unhappy and unpleasant American expatriates in Paris. C: Violet Heming, Claudia Morgan, Alan Bunce, Clyde Fillmore, Elsa Maxwell, Blanche Ring, Ann Andrews, Tom Ewell. P/D: Chester Erskine. SD: Jo Mielziner.

De Luxe Annie (9/4/17, Booth, 119)

A detective closes in on a pair of clever swindlers who gain the confidence of their victims by posing as de luxe-edition book agents. "Exciting and well-knit mystery . . . skillfully contrived and executed" *(New York Times)*. C: Jane Grey, Vincent Serrano. A: Edward Clark. P/D: Arthur Hammerstein.

Dead End (10/28/35, Belasco, 684)

A harsh indictment of the urban environment, Sidney Kingsley's saga of the slums was played out against a striking setting of a New York tenement street dead-ending into the East River. The play's parallel plots concern a young woman trying to save her kid brother from a life of crime, a crippled architect struggling for recognition, a gangster returning home to see his mother and meeting his death. Expertly staged by its author, and produced with meticulous realism by Norman Bel Geddes (P/SD), this 1935 drama was an unqualified success from the rising of its first curtain. *Dead End* was also the genesis of that phenomenon known variously as the Dead End Kids, the Bowery Boys, and the East Side Kids. Well into middle-age, many of *Dead End's* original juvenile delinquents played increasingly comical counterparts of their grim stage roles in a series of low-budget feature films. C: Billy Halop, Gabriel Dell, Huntz Hall, Bobby Jordan, Leo Gorcey, David Gorcey, Sidney Lumet, Theodore Newton, Joseph Downing, Marjorie Main, Dan Duryea, Elspeth Eric, Carroll Ashburn, Sheila Trent, Philip Bourneuf, Marc Daniels, Bernard Punsley, Bernard Zaneville (Dane Clark).

SV: UA, 1937, Joel McCrea, Sylvia Sidney, Humphrey Bogart, Claire Trevor, Wendy Barrie, Marjorie Main, Huntz Hall, Leo Gorcey, Billy Halop, Gabriel Dell, Bernard Punsley, Ward Bond, Allen Jenkins (directed by William Wyler from a screenplay by Lillian Hellman).

Dead Pigeon (12/23/53, Vanderbilt, 21)

A material witness in a gangland murder is decoyed to a seaside hotel where her "suicide" can conveniently be arranged by a pair of crooked cops ostensibly assigned to guard her life. This three-character melodrama had some diverting moments, but lacked tension and sustained suspense. C: Lloyd Bridges, James Gregory, Joan Lorring. A: Lenard Kantor. P: Harald Bromley (D) and Haila Stoddard.

SV: Col, 1955, *Tight Spot,* Edward G. Robinson, Ginger Rogers, Brian Keith, Lorne Greene.

Deadfall (10/27/55, Holiday, 20)

Vengeful widow sets out to frame her husband's murderer. Soporific courtroom melodrama with Hollywood's John Ireland and Joanne Dru (deb.) in leading roles. C: Clarence Derwent, Jay Jostyn, Sheila Bond, Harold Vermilyea. A: Leonard Lee. P: Martin Goodman i.a.w. J. M. Gordon. D: Michael Gordon.

Deadly Game, The (2/2/60, Longacre, 39)

Philosophic melodrama about three retired Swiss gentlemen—all men of law—who amuse themselves by holding mock trials of unwary visitors to their remote chateau. Sure of his innocence, a loud-mouthed American salesman agrees to humor his eccentric hosts by standing trial for murder. Before the evening is over, the blustering salesman is forced to admit that he was responsible for his boss's death—and must thereupon suffer the consequences of his guilt. "A steadily engrossing evening . . . coldly haunting" (*Post*). ". . . only intermittently gripping" (*Mirror*). C: Pat Hingle, Claude Dauphin, Max Adrian, Ludwig Donath, Frank Campanella. A: James Yaffe b/o the novel *Trapps* by Friedrich Duerrenmatt. P: Wilkes and Manchester i.a.w. Emil Coleman. D: William Gaskill. SD: Wolfgang Roth.

Revived O/B (2/13/66, Provincetown, 105) under the direction of Alton Wilkes.

Dear Barbarians (2/21/52, Royale, 4)

Comedy about the squabbling of an aspiring songwriter (Donald Murphy) and his matrimonial-minded mistress (Cloris Leachman). ". . . a trivial and tiresome script" (*Herald Tribune*). C: Betsy von Furstenberg, Nicholas Joy, Violet Heming. A: Lex Richards. P/D: Gant Gaither. CD/SD: Jack Landau. M: Cy Coleman.

Dear Charles (9/15/54, Morosco, 155)

In order to legitimatize her children, an unwed mother (Tallulah Bankhead) sends for her three old beaux, introduces them to their respective progeny, and tries to decide which one she should now marry. "Miss Bankhead, as the doting but errant mother, acts with devastating authority. Her performance reminds one of a Heifetz or a Horowitz bestowing his genius on a pop trifle" (*Mirror*). C: Robert Coote, Werner Klemperer, Hugh Reilly, Alice Pearce, Fred Keating, Norah Howard. P: Aldrich and Myers i.a.w. Julius Fleischmann. D: Edmund Baylies. SD: Donald Oenslager. *Dear Charles* was b/o *Slightly Scandalous* (1944), a flop comedy by Frederick Jackson that was translated into French by Marc-Gilbert Sauvajon and retranslated back into English by Alan Melville.

Dear Jane (11/14/32, Civic, 12)

The romance of Jane Austen (Josephine Hutchinson) and the foppish Sir John Evelyn (Joseph Schildkraut) ends when young Jane realizes his lordship opposes her literary career. Fairly entertaining costume comedy, produced O/B in rep. C: Eva Le Gallienne, Leona Roberts, Richard Waring, Howard da Silva, Robert H. Gordon, Joseph Kramm. A: Eleanor Holmes Hinkley. P/D: Eva Le Gallienne.

Dear Judas (10/5/47, Mansfield, 16)

Biblical drama, based on Robinson Jeffers' poem, in which Judas betrays Jesus not to punish but to save Him. ". . . singularly awkward and unimpressive" (*Sun*). C: Roy Hargrave, Ferdi Hoffman, Margaret Wycherly, Harry Irvine. A/P/D: Michael Myerberg.

Dear Me (1/17/21, Republic, 144)

A group of literary and artistic failures is regenerated by a go-getting, positive-thinking young man. Unpretentious, amusing light comedy by Luther Reed and Hale Hamilton. C: Hale Hamilton, Grace La Rue. P: John Golden. D: Winchell Smith.

Dear Me, The Sky Is Falling (3/2/63, Music Box, 145)

A Jewish matriarch (Gertrude Berg) learns to control her rebellious family through Freudian psychology. ". . . an unpretentious play that makes its points with a goodly measure of wit and wisdom" (*Mirror*). C: William Daniels, Howard da Silva, Jill Kraft, Minerva Pious, Ron Leibman, Tresa Hughes. A: Leonard Spigelgass b/o a story by Gertrude Berg and James Yaffe. P: The Theatre Guild. D: Herman Shumlin.

Dear Old Darling (3/2/36, Alvin, 16)

Retired businessman (George M. Cohan) becomes involved with a young gold digger and her calculating mother. Weak Cohan (A/P) comedy. C: Marian Shockley, Ruth Shepley. D: Sam Forrest.

Dear Ruth (12/13/44, Henry Miller, 683)

A teenager writes love letters to a soldier in her older sister's name. When the soldier eventually appears to claim his hypothetical admirer, the complications begin. This wartime comedy, written by Norman Krasna and directed by Moss Hart, was a smash hit. ". . . slight but eminently satisfying" (*Herald Tribune*). C: Virginia Gilmore, John Dall, Howard Smith, Phyllis Povah, Lenore Lonergan, Bartlett Robinson. P: Joseph M. Hyman and Bernard Hart.
SV: Par, 1947, William Holden, Joan Caulfield, Mona Freeman, Edward Arnold, Billy DeWolfe.

Death of a Salesman (2/10/49, Morosco, 742)

Two days in the life of Willy Loman, an aging traveling salesman "riding on a smile and a shoeshine" in futile pursuit of the American Dream of success. After thirty-six years of struggle and worry, Willy is coming up empty. Unbidden memories—ranging over years of self-deception and despair—return to haunt him as his energies wane and his mind begins to crack. Moving relentlessly to its inevitable conclusion, the play ends with the suicide of this back-slapping mediocrity. In the elegiac final scene, Willy's wife underscores the tragedy implicit in the destruction of this seemingly unimportant little man. "A play to make history" (*Herald Tribune*). "A poignant, shattering and devastating drama . . . a triumph in writing, in acting and in stage-

Death of a Salesman. Cameron Mitchell, Lee J. Cobb, Thomas Chalmers, and Arthur Kennedy (1948–49). *Courtesy Museum of the City of New York Theatre and Music Collection.*

craft" (*Sun*). C: Lee J. Cobb, Mildred Dunnock, Arthur Kennedy, Cameron Mitchell, Howard Smith, Thomas Chalmers, Alan Hewitt, Tom Pedi, Constance Ford (deb.). P: Kermit Bloomgarden and Walter Fried. D: Elia Kazan. M: Alex North. SD: Jo Mielziner. *Death of a Salesman* was given a superlative production, and Lee J. Cobb's performance in the leading role received high praise. Willy Loman has also been portrayed by Thomas Mitchell (Chicago), Paul Muni (London), and Fredric March (screen version). Arthur Miller's play, winner of many honors including the Pulitzer Prize and Critics Circle Award, has earned a secure place in the permanent repertory of the American theatre.

SV: Col, 1951, Fredric March, Mildred Dunnock, Kevin McCarthy, Cameron Mitchell (directed by Laslo Benedek).

Death Takes a Holiday (12/26/29, Barrymore, 181)

Death enters the human world to learn why mortals fear him, and falls in love with the gentle Grazia. When it comes time for "His Serene Highness" to leave, Grazia begs to accompany him, and Death takes her. Beautifully conceived, strikingly poetic fantasy by Walter Ferris b/o a play by Alberto Cassella. The reproduction of *Death Takes a Holiday* surmounted a variety of casting problems. John Barrymore was interested in portraying Death, but could not break free from his Hollywood commitments, so Philip Merivale inherited the part. Katharine Hepburn was signed for the role of Grazia, but was fired during the Philadelphia tryout and replaced by Rose Hobart. Helen Vinson later took over this role in the return engagement (2/16/31, Ambassador, 32). P: Lee Shubert. D: Lawrence Marston.

SV: Par, 1934, Fredric March, Evelyn Venable, Guy Standing, Gail Patrick, Helen Westley, Katherine Alexander, Kent Taylor, Henry Travers, Edward Van Sloan (directed by Mitchell Leisen from a screenplay by Maxwell Anderson).

Debut (2/22/56, Holiday, 5)

Comedy about a southern belle who falls in love with a Yankee journalist. "One more play like *Debut* and the North will secede" (*New York Times*). C: Inger Stevens (deb.), Tom Helmore, G. Albert Smith. A: Mary Drayton b/o a novel by Isabel Dunn. P: Horner and Sturm. D: John Gerstad.

Decision (5/27/29, 49th Street, 56)

Scheming relatives try to defraud a woman (Margaret Barnstead) of her suddenly acquired wealth and part her from her adopted children. Drab 20's soap opera. A: Carl Henkle. P: Robert Sterling.

Decision (2/2/44, Belasco, 158)

An incorruptible high-school principal alerts his town to the dirty tricks being employed by a reactionary senator. When the principal is framed on a rape charge and lynched, his son vows to carry on the fight against home-front fascism. "The best-written, best-acted and best-directed play I have seen this season" (*News*). ". . . an immensely timely play and a very telling one. . . . It is good theater" (*PM*). *Decision* was written and directed by Edward Chodorov.* When no Broadway producer would take a chance on the play, the author—i.a.w. Edward Choate (P)—backed the production himself. C: Raymond Greenleaf, Larry Hugo, Gwen Anderson, Jean Casto, Merle Maddern, Georgia Burke, Howard Smith, Matt Crowley, Paul Ford.

---

*Plays include *Kind Lady* (1935), *Oh, Men! Oh, Women!* (1953), etc. Among Mr. Chodorov's many screenplays are *The Story of Louis Pasteur, The Hucksters,* and *Road House*.

Declassee (10/6/19, Empire, 257)

Infidelity and the consequences of divorce among the titled rich; one of Ethel Barrymore's most popular vehicles. Lady Helen Haden (Ethel Barrymore) gives up home and husband for an unrequited love. She loses her social position, suffers much travail, meets with a fatal automobile accident, and expires gracefully. "If, during my theatre-going lifetime, there has been any other performance so perfect as the one she [Miss Barrymore] gives . . . I can only say that I had the hideous ill luck to miss it" (Dorothy Parker, *Vanity Fair*). A: Zoe Akins. P: Charles Frohman.

SV: WB, 1929, *Her Private Life*, Billie Dove, Walter Pidgeon, Roland Young, Thelma Todd, ZaSu Pitts (directed by Alexander Korda).

Note: A silent version of *Declassee* (WB, 1925) starred Corinne Griffith.

Deep Are the Roots (9/26/45, Fulton, 477)

Returning to his home in the deep South, a black war hero is beaten, jailed and accused of stealing a watch by his former employer, an unreconstructed southern senator. An interracial romance with the senator's liberal-minded daughter further complicates matters in this popular but highly contrived and melodramatic 1945 problem play. C: Gordon Heath, Barbara Bel Geddes, Charles Waldron, Carol Goodner, Lloyd Gough, Harold Vermilyea, Evelyn Ellis, Helen Martin. A: Arnaud d'Usseau and James Gow. P: Kermit Bloomgarden and George Heller. D: Elia Kazan.

Deep Mrs. Sykes, The (3/19/45, Booth, 72)

A domineering wife begins to suspect her husband of infidelity. Even when her suspicions are proven totally unfounded, the overbearing Mrs. Sykes stubbornly refuses to concede any flaw in her much-vaunted "woman's intuition," thus bringing dissension and unhappiness to all around her. "An adult play for adult minds" (*World-Telegram*), *The Deep Mrs. Sykes* etched a corrosive portrait of one of the most malicious, stupid, and poisonously egotistical women in dramatic literature. This 1945 comedy-drama was written and directed by George Kelly,* author of *The Show-Off* (1924), *Craig's Wife* (1925), etc. C: Catherine Willard, Neil Hamilton, Jean Dixon, Romney Brent. P: Gilkey and Payne.

---

*Uncle of actress Grace Kelly.

Deep Purple, The (1/9/11, Lyric, 152)

Crude but lively badger game melodrama from the playwriting factory of Paul Armstrong and Wilson Mizner. Mizner, one of the wits of his time ("To my embarrassment, I was born in bed with a lady"), defined playwriting as "the art of telling lies at two dollars a head." When the irascible Armstrong took *The Deep Purple* away from producer Thedore Liebler after a fight and wired his collaborator: "Are You With Me?", Mizner wired back, "I'm With You If You Win." C: Richard Bennett, Emmett Corrigan, Catherine Calvert. D: Hugh Ford.

Deep Tangled Wildwood, The 11/5/23, Frazee, 16)

George S. Kaufman-Marc Connelly satirical comedy. A playwright (James Gleason) visits his old home town in search of the simple virtures only to find that his small-town friends have become fast-stepping sophisticates. Disillusioned, he returns to Manhattan for some peace and quiet. Minor-league entry from the great Kaufman-Connelly team. P: George C. Tyler and Hugh Ford (D).

Deer Park, The (2/1/67, de Lys, 128)

Norman Mailer's surprisingly flaccid (and surprisingly conventional) exploration of sin-and-salvation at a posh southern

California resort peopled by both movie studio bigwigs and Hollywood has-beens. Presented O/B with a cast that included Rip Torn, Hugh Marlowe, Marsha Mason, Beverly Bentley, and Will Lee. P: Garen/Mailer/Walsh. D: Leo Garen.

Delicate Balance, A (9/22/66, Martin Beck, 132)

Edward Albee's Pulitzer Prize play, a highly structured, elusively plotted drama dealing with the responsibilities of love and friendship. In the play, a sense of vague menace hangs over a well-to-do, middle-aged New England couple (Hume Cronyn and Jessica Tandy). The threat deepens when two close friends arrive seeking refuge, having been driven from their home by some sudden, undefined, overwhelming fear. Their presence generates a series of uneasy confrontations. They force the family—the weak-willed husband, domineering wife, their emotionally crippled daughter, and the wife's alcoholic sister—to face the fact that they have all lost the capacity to love, and indeed have reached that delicate balance between sanity and madness. ". . . probing, tantalizing . . . filled with humor and compassion and touched with poetry" *(News)*. C: Rosemary Murphy, Marian Seldes, Carmen Mathews, Henderson Forsythe. P: Barr/Wilder. D: Alan Schneider. SD: William Ritman.

SV: American Film Theater, 1973, Katharine Hepburn, Paul Scofield, Lee Remick, Kate Reid, Joseph Cotten, Betsy Blair (directed by Tony Richardson).

Demi-Virgin, The (10/18/21, Times Square, 268)

A pair of temperamental Hollywood personalities marry, separate, and reunite during the shooting of a silent film. Frothy farce, helped along at the box office by clever publicity campaign. C: Hazel Dawn, Glenn Anders, Charles Ruggles. A: Avery Hopwood. P: A. H. Woods. D: Bertram Harrison and Charles Mather.

Desert Incident, A (3/24/59, Golden, 7)

Pearl Buck's first work for the theatre, a triangle drama concerned chiefly with a Polish girl romantically torn between two equally dull atomic scientists. "There has seldom been such an unhappy combination of banal writing and inept direction. Even the casting was bizarre, to put it mildly" *(Journal-American)*. C: Shepperd Strudwick, Paul Roebling, Sylvia Daneel, Cameron Prud'homme. P: Tad Danielewski (D) i.a.w. Morris Feld. SD: Howard Bay.

Design for a Stained Glass Window (1/23/50, Mansfield, 8)

A sixteenth-century English woman goes to her death rather than renounce Catholicism. "An earnest, well-intentioned and hopelessly inept play" *(Post)*. Martha Scott played the martyred heroine and Charlton Heston her doleful husband in this plodding historical drama by William Berney and Howard Richardson, authors of *Dark of the Moon* (1945). P: Jack Segasture. D: Ella Gerber. CD/SD: Stewart Chaney.

Desire Under the Elms (11/11/24, Greenwich Village, 208)

Eugene O'Neill's masterful tragedy set on a New England farm, c. 1850. Unyielding ("God is hard") old Ephraim Cabot (Walter Huston) takes a young third wife (Mary Morris) only to have her seduce his son, Eben (Charles Ellis), have a child by him, and then strangle the baby to prove to Eben that her love is greater than her greed for the farm. This gnarled and probing drama is indisputably one of the masterpieces of the American theatre. Critical reaction to the play was on the tepid side, though all reviewers had nothing but praise for 40-year-old Walter Huston in the demanding role of 75-year-old Ephraim Cabot. Huston was equally enamored of this once-in-a-lifetime part. In a letter to this editor some years ago, the actor eulogized the play's

Desire Under the Elms. **Part II, Scene II (1924–25).** *Courtesy Museum of the City of New York Theatre and Music Collection.*

"brutal realism, its honesty, its sincerity—from all of which there comes a poetic beauty. Although it is American to the core, so to speak, it is as universal as marital relations. Although it is laid in 1850, it is as timeless as a play can be. . . . In my estimation, it is far and away the best play I know of by a contemporary playwright." Eugene O'Neill said that Huston was the only actor who had brought one of his characters "completely to life" and added, "He made the character live in a way that an author usually sees only in hopeful dreams." The play shocked certain segments of the public; efforts were made by the police to close the production, and the issue was taken to court. Common sense prevailed and the drama was permitted to resume its run without further interruption. The play later was transferred uptown. C: Walter Abel, Macklin Marrow, Donald Oenslager. D/SD: Robert Edmond Jones.

R: (1/16/52, ANTA, 47) by ANTA. C: Karl Malden, Carol Stone, Douglas Watson, Colleen Dewhurst (as a neighbor). D: Harold Clurman.

R: (1/8/63, Circle in the Square, 384). C: George C. Scott, Colleen Dewhurst, Rip Torn. D: Jose Quintero.

SV: Par, 1958, Burl Ives, Sophia Loren, Anthony Perkins.

Desk Set, The (10/24/55, Broadhurst, 296)

Love and automation clash when an efficiency expert installs a computer in a broadcasting company's research department. This featherweight comedy by William Marchant provided a slender but serviceable showcase for star Shirley Booth. C: Byron Sanders, Elizabeth Wilson, Joyce Van Patten, Frank Milan, Mary Gildea, Louis Gossett. P: Fryer and Carr. D: Joseph Fields. SD: George Jenkins.

SV: Fox, 1957, Katharine Hepburn, Spencer Tracy, Gig Young, Joan Blondell, Dina Merrill (directed by Walter Lang).

Desperate Hours, The (2/10/55, Barrymore, 212)

A helpless suburbanite (Karl Malden) confronts three escaped convicts (Paul Newman, George Grizzard, George Mathews) who take over his home and threaten himself and his family while awaiting getaway money. "An almost perfect melodrama—fast, tight, logical, combining sentiment with gunfire in exactly the right proportions" (*The New Yorker*). C: Nancy Coleman, James Gregory, Kendall Clark. A: Joseph Hayes b/o his novel of the same name. P: Howard Erskine and Joseph Hayes. D: Robert Montgomery. SD: Howard Bay.

SV: Par, 1955, Humphrey Bogart, Fredric March, Arthur Kennedy, Martha Scott, Gig Young, Dewey Martin, Robert Middleton (directed by William Wyler).

Detective Story (3/23/49, Hudson, 581)

Vigorous melodrama by Sidney Kingsley

(A/D) set in the squad room of a metropolitan police station. The central character is a fiercely conscientious detective named James McLeod (Ralph Bellamy). A fanatically intolerant man, McLeod's personal code has become as twisted as that of the criminals with whom he deals each day. While crusading against a wily abortionist, the detective uncovers certain ugly truths about his own loving wife. McLeod is destroyed by the news and dies in a hail of gunfire, begging forgiveness for his sins. "An exciting and jangling melodrama, sharply written and played" (*Sun*). Filled with fascinating minor characters—racketeers, murderers, shyster lawyers, bums, shoplifters—*Detective Story* was written and staged with almost clinical realism. Extraordinarily well-acted by Ralph Bellamy and a fine supporting cast, the play was one of the major successes of the late 1940's. C: Meg Mundy, James Westerfield, Lee Grant, Joseph Wiseman, Michael Strong, Horace McMahon, Alexander Scourby, Maureen Stapleton, Edward Binns, Robert Strauss, Lou Gilbert, Jean Adair, Warren Stevens, Joan Copeland, Les Tremayne, Harry Worth. P: Lindsay and Crouse. SD: Boris Aronson.

SV: Par, 1951, Kirk Douglas, Eleanor Parker, William Bendix, Lee Grant, Michael Strong, Horace MacMahon, Joseph Wiseman (directed by William Wyler).

Detour, The (8/23/21, Astor, 48)

A farm mother patiently saves one thousand dollars so that her daughter may escape the farm and study art. When she learns that the girl has no artistic talent, the mother decides to save her money—and her illusions—for her grandchildren. Interesting rural character study by Owen Davis, written two years before his Pulitzer Prize drama, *Icebound* (1923). C: Effie Shannon, Augustin Duncan, Willard Robertson. P: Messrs. Shubert. D: Augustin Duncan.

Devil in the Cheese (12/29/26, Hopkins, 165)

An archaeologist digs up a piece of cheese, eats it, and thereby is enabled to explore the inside of his lovesick daughter's head. Tedious and nonsensical "fantastic comedy," written, acted and directed in comic-strip terms. ". . . a routine bib-and-tucker show, written for the nurseries" (*Herald-Tribune*). C: Robert McWade, Linda Watkins, Fredric March,* Bela Lugosi, Dwight Frye, Catherine Doucet. A: Tom Cushing. P/D: Charles Hopkins.

---

*Fredric March's last Broadway appearance until *Yr. Obedient Husband* (1938), twelve years later.

Devils (3/17/26, Maxine Elliott's, 29)

Fire-and-brimstone preacher accuses a country girl of witchcraft and drives her to commit suicide. Uneven but frequently engrossing 20's drama. C: John Cromwell (D). A: Daniel N. Rubin. P: William A. Brady, Jr. and Dwight Deere Wiman.

Devil's Advocate, The (3/9/61, Billy Rose, 116)

A dying priest is sent to the Italian countryside to investigate the possible canonization of a reputedly Christlike political activist. Was the man a saint or a sinner? In a series of cinematic-styled flashbacks, it turns out he was a bit of both. "A powerful, absorbing drama . . . restores one's belief in the potentialities of the Broadway theatre" (*New York Times*). C: Leo Genn, Sam Levene, Edward Mulhare, Eduardo Ciannelli, Olive Deering, Tresa Hughes, Michael Kane, Boris Tumarin. A/P/D: Dore Schary b/o the novel by Morris L. West. SD: Jo Mielziner.

Devils Galore (9/12/45, Royale, 5)

A couple of Satan's henchmen (Ernest Cossart and Rex O'Malley) visit Manhattan, and are shocked by its inhabitants' immorality. "... as crumby as a piece of streusel cake." *(Herald Tribune).* A: Eugene Vale. P: William Cahn. D: Robert Perry.

Diamond Lil (4/9/28, Royale, 323)

The quintessential Mae West. In this classic Gay 90's spoof, the buxom queen of a Bowery saloon finds herself attracted by a stalwart Salvation Army captain. Can this red-blooded male resist the opulent charms of the undulating Diamond Lil? He can and he does—until moments before the final curtain when it transpires that he's really a detective in disguise, sent to get the goods on the Tenderloin's thriving white-slave traffic. "Pure trash, or rather impure trash though it is, I wouldn't miss *Diamond Lil* if I were you" (Charles Brackett, *The New Yorker*). C: Curtis Cooksey, Jack La Rue, Rafaella Ottiano. A/D: Mae West. P: Jack Linder. R: (2/5/49, Coronet, 181) by Rosen and Freezer. C: Mae West, Richard Coogan, Steve Cochran, Jeff Morrow, Sylvia Syms, Billy Van. D: Charles K. Freeman.

SV: Par, 1933, *She Done Him Wrong*, Mae West, Cary Grant, Gilbert Roland, Noah Beery, Rochelle Hudson, Rafaella Ottiano.

Note: This is the film credited with having saved Paramount Pictures from bankruptcy.

Diamond Orchid (2/10/65, Henry Miller, 5)

Thinly disguised tale of the life of Eva Peron, from obscure radio actress to First Lady of Argentina. Intriguing biographical drama marred by miscasting and an ungainly production. C: Jennifer West, Mario Alcalde, Finlay Currie, Bruce Gordon, Leonardo Cimino, Margery Maude, Helen Craig. A: Jerome Lawrence and Robert E. Lee.* P: Gilbert Miller i.a.w. Stevens Productions. D: Jose Quintero. CD: Donald Brooks. SD: David Hays.

―――
*Co-authors of *Inherit the Wind* (1955), *Auntie Mame* (1956), etc.

Diana (12/9/29, Longacre, 8)

Florid chronicle play based on the life and loves of Isadora Duncan, here called Diana Bolton. C: Mary Nash, Charles Quigley, Jefferson De Angelis, Ludmilla Toretzka. A: Irving Kaye Davis. P: L. Lawrence Weber i.a.w. Hugh Ford (D).

Diary of Anne Frank, The (10/5/55, Cort, 717)

The true-life chronicle of a thirteen-year-old Jewish girl hiding with her family and friends from the Nazis in an Amsterdam garret during World War II. Their struggles to survive together in cramped intimacy over a two-year period are recreated in graphic, understated fashion, with the various episodes bridged by Anne's narration of brief passages from her diary. Shortly before the Allied liberation, the Gestapo finally ferrets the group out, and Anne Frank and the others are put to death in concentration camps. Impeccably acted, directed, and mounted, this profoundly moving drama won the Pulitzer Prize, the Critics Circle Award, and virtually every other coveted theatre prize of the year. C: Susan Strasberg,* Joseph Schildkraut, Gusti Huber, Jack Gilford, Lou Jacobi,* Dennie Moore, Clinton Sundberg, David Levin,* Eva Rubinstein, Gloria Jones.* A: Frances Goodrich and Albert Hackett b/o the book, *Anne Frank: The Diary of a Young Girl*. P: Kermit Bloomgarden. D: Garson Kanin. SD: Boris Aronson.

SV: Fox, 1959, Millie Perkins, Joseph Schildkraut, Lou Jacobi, Ed Wynn, Shelley Winters, Richard Beymer, Diane Baker (directed by George Stevens).

―――
*Broadway debuts.

Dictator, The (4/4/04, Criterion, 64)

Mistaken identity, revolution, counter-revolution, a military *coup d'état*—these were some of the plot ingredients in this harum-scarum farce laid in a Central American banana republic. *The Dictator* was written by war correspondent-novelist-soldier of fortune Richard Harding Davis, one of the most colorful figures of America's Gilded Age. C: William Collier, John Barrymore, George Nash, Lucile Watson, Thomas Meighan. P: Charles Frohman.

Musicalized by Silvio Hein and Frank Craven as *The Girl From Home* (1920) with Frank Craven, Jed Prouty, and Gladys Caldwell.

Diff'rent (12/27/20, Provincetown, 74)

Early Eugene O'Neill tragedy of sexual frustration. A New England girl breaks her engagement to a sea captain because of his infidelity to her. Thirty years later she has become a shrill, neurotic spinster who tries to seduce the captain's young nephew. Heartbroken, the captain hangs himself. "Stands out as an event in the dramatic year" (Alexander Woollcott, *New York Times*). Most critics did not share Woollcott's enthusiasm for O'Neill's Strindbergian melodrama, finding it shakily constructed and awkwardly written. C: Mary Blair, James Light, Charles Ellis. P: Provincetown Players. D: Charles O'Brien Kennedy. SD: Cleon Throckmorton.

R: (10/17/61, Mermaid, 88). C: Marian Seldes, Michael Higgins, Robert Drivas. D: Paul Shyre.

Dinner at Eight (10/22/32, Music Box, 243)

Multiscened George S. Kaufman (D) and Edna Ferber comedy-drama, expertly cast and skillfully staged. A series of deftly written vignettes exposes the deception and hypocrisy underlying contemporary (1932) New York society. A fashionable dinner party thrown by a shallow hostess serves as the catalyst whereby a variety of social-climbing characters reveal themselves: a vulgar businessman and his sluttish wife, a down-on-his-luck matinee idol who finally commits suicide, a society doctor with a weakness for his female patients, a once-famous *grande dame* of the stage. Kaufman and Ferber peppered their play with various dramatic and amusing behind-the-scenes crises involving the hired help. *Dinner at Eight* was a solid hit with the press and public. It was produced by Sam H. Harris. C: Ann Andrews, Gregory Gaye, Marguerite Churchill,* Cesar Romero, Margaret Dale, Constance Collier, Paul Harvey, Judith Wood, Austin Fairman, Conway Tearle, Sam Levene, Olive Wyndham. The successful West Coast production of *Dinner at Eight* was headed by Louis Calhern, Hedda Hopper, Alice White, Jobyna Howland, Martha Sleeper, and Don Alvardo.

R: (9/27/66, Alvin, 127) by Martin, Osterman, King and Hyman. C: June Havoc, Walter Pidgeon, Ruth Ford, Arlene Francis, Robert Burr, Pamela Tiffin, Jeffrey Lynn, Darren McGavin, Phil Leeds, Mindy Carson, Blanche Yurka. D: Tyrone Guthrie.

SV. MGM, 1933, Marie Dressler, John Barrymore, Lionel Barrymore, Jean Harlow, Wallace Beery, Lee Tracy, Edmund Lowe, Billie Burke, Madge Evans, Jean Hersholt, Karen Morley, Louise Closser Hale, Phillips Holmes, May Robson, Grant Mitchell (directed by George Cukor).

---

*Succeeded by Margaret Sullavan and later by Jane Wyatt.

Dinny and the Witches (12/9/59, Cherry Lane, 29)

Leaden O/B fantasy by William Gibson* in which the leading character defies death by assuming control of a timeless world. C: Bill Heyer, Kay Doubleday, Renee Taylor, Julie Bovasso, Avril Gentles. P: Jess Kimmel (D) and Alfred Stern.

---

*Author of *Two for the Seesaw* (1958), *The Miracle Worker* (1959), etc.

Dinosaur Wharf (11/8/51, National, 4)

Melodrama about union racketeering and violence on the New York City waterfront. ". . . taut, tough and timely" (*News*). ". . . dreary, pretentious and interminable" (*Herald Tribune*). C: James Gregory, Lois Wheeler, Harrison Dowd, Leo Penn, Sal Mineo, Barnard Hughes, John Marley, Sally Gracie, William Darrid (deb.). A: Joel Wyman. P/D: Terese Hayden. SD: Samuel Leve.

Disenchanted, The (12/3/58, Coronet, 189)

Episodic, flashback-styled account of the decline and fall of F. Scott Fitzgerald, here called Manley Halliday (Jason Robards, Jr.). To raise some urgently needed money, the weary, disillusioned novelist attempts (unsuccessfully) to collaborate with a younger writer (George Grizzard) on a hack screenplay. Subjected to terrible pressures by his unstable wife (Rosemary Harris) and others, Halliday untimately learns "a second chance, that's our delusion; a first chance, that's all we have," but by then it is too late for him to profit by the knowledge. "A little unwieldy and a little overwritten. . . . But there is nothing cheap or glib about [the play]" (*New York Times*). C: Whitfield Connor, Jason Robards, Sr., Salome Jens, Jon Cypher,* Nancy Kovack.* A: Budd Schulberg and Harvey Breit, b/o the novel by Mr. Schulberg. P: Darrid and Saidenberg. D: David Pressman. CD: Ann Roth. SD: Ben Edwards.

---
*Broadway debuts.

Dishonored Lady (2/4/30, Empire, 127)

Beautiful woman (Katharine Cornell) with unsavory past poisons her ex-lover when she finds true love at last. Shoddy melodrama by Margaret Ayer Barnes and Edward Sheldon. C: Francis Lister, Fortunio Bonanova, Paul Harvey, Harvey Stephens. P: Gilbert Miller and Guthrie McClintic (D).

SV: UA, 1947, Hedy Lamarr, Dennis O'Keefe, John Loder, William Lundigan, Paul Cavanaugh, Natalie Schafer.

Distaff Side, The (9/25/34, Booth, 178)

Leisurely look at the marital and romantic problems of a quintet of women in a middle-class English household. Written by Anglo-American author John Van Druten, *The Distaff Side* was a skillfully drawn study of domestic life in the author's quietest vein of naturalism. C: Sybil Thorndike, Mildred Natwick, Viola Roache, Estelle Winwood, Viola Keats, Bretaigne Windust. P: Dwight Deere Wiman and Auriol Lee (D).

Distant Bell, A (1/13/60, O'Neill, 5)

Period play (1930's New England) about a widow who comes back after ten years in a mental institution to find that her ruthless relatives have turned her three neurotic daughters against her. In the end, the unhappy mother chooses to return to the sanitarium. ". . . a touching creation . . . excellent theatre" (*World-Telegram and Sun*). ". . . fatuous and pointless" (*Post*). C: Martha Scott, Andrew Prine, Phyllis Love, Evans Evans, Patricia Roe, Nydia Westman, Frieda Altman, Mabel Cochran. A: Katherine Morrill. P/D: Norman Twain. SD: Mordecai Gorelik.

Distant City, The (9/22/41, Longacre, 2)

A seventy-year-old strumpet (Gladys George) finds God. ". . . distinctly repulsive. . . . The whole evening is something to forget about, if anybody can" (*PM*). A: Edwin B. Self. P: John Tuerk. D: Edward Byron.

Distant Drum, A (1/20/28, Hudson, 11)

An opportunistic fortune hunter (Louis Calhern) finally gets his just deserts. Acid character study of a thoroughgoing rotter. A: Vincent Lawrence. P/D: William Harris, Jr.

Distant Drums (1/18/32, Belasco, 40)

Well-written historical drama by Dan Totheroh concerning various hardships endured by members of a covered wagon expedition over the Oregon trail in 1848. C: Pauline Lord, Arthur Hohl, Edward Pawley, Beulah Bondi, Edward Ellis, Thomas Findlay, Eda Heinemann. P/D: Guthrie McClintic.

Distant Shore, The (2/21/35, Morosco, 12)

After murdering his shrewish wife, a mild-mannered British dentist (Roland Young) sets sail for Canada with his lovesick secretary, but is apprehended by the authorities and sentenced to be hanged. Monotonous, heavy-handed melodrama was based on the Dr. Crippen (here called Dr. Bond) murder case that rocked 1910 London to its foundations. C: Jeanne Casselle, Sylvia Field, Harry Green. A: Donald Blackwell and Theodore St. John. P: Dwight Deere Wiman. D: Robert Ross.

Diversion (1/11/28, 49th Street, 61)

Betrayed by a wanton actress (Cathleen Nesbitt), an impressionable young man (Richard Bird) strangles her, then convinces his surgeon-father (Guy Standing) to give him poison with which to commit suicide. *Diversion* was a hack job, written to order and, in the words of Anglo-American author John Van Druten, "a good deal more melodramatic and a good deal less sound" than he had hoped it might be. C: Leo G. Carroll, Rose Hobart, Harry Green. P: Adolph Klauber. D: Jane Cowl.
SV: WB, 1929, *The Careless Age,* Douglas Fairbanks, Jr., Loretta Young, Carmel Myers.

Divided by Three (10/2/34, Barrymore, 31)

Crushed by the revelation that his mother (Judith Anderson) is an adulteress, a son (James Stewart) leaves home. The unhappy mother toys with the idea of divorce but, instead, elects to remain with her emotionally shattered and financially bankrupt husband. He needs her. This chic drawing-room drama was co-authored by Beatrice (Mrs. George S.) Kaufman and Margaret Leech (wife of publisher Ralph Pulitzer). *Divided by Three* received divided notices and had a brief Broadway run of four weeks. C. Hedda Hopper, James Rennie. P/D: Guthrie McClintic. SD: Donald Oenslager.

Note: Margaret Leech Pulitzer twice won the literary prize established by her father-in-law. She won her first prize in 1942 with *Reveille in Washington,* a portrait of the nation's capital during the Civil War; in 1960 she received her second Pulitzer prize in history for *In the Days of McKinley.* She died in New York City in 1974 at the age of eighty.

Divine Drudge, A (10/26/33, Royale, 12)

Industrialist falls in love with simple *hausfrau,* but she elects to remain with her small-town husband. This saccharine saga, written by Vicki Baum and John Golden (P/D), marked the Broadway debut of noted Viennese actress Mady Christians. C: Walter Abel, Tamara Geva, Minor Watson, Josephine Hull. SD: Jo Mielziner.

Divine Moment, A (1/6/34, Vanderbilt, 9)

Restless wife indulges in brief romantic fling with younger man. Hokum. C: Peggy Fears (P), William Ingersoll, Charlotte Granville. A: Robert Hare Powel. D: Rowland Leigh.

Do Not Pass Go (4/19/65, Cherry Lane, 16)

Demented youth taunts (and ultimately murders) elderly supermarket coworker. Suspenseful O/B two-character drama; excellently acted by Charles Nolte (A) and Roberts Blossom. P: Theatre 1965. D: Alan Schneider. SD: William Ritman.

Doctor Monica (11/6/33, Playhouse, 16)

Emotional conflicts and crises in the life of a woman doctor. Turgid three-character drama by actress Laura Walker, b/o on a play by Marja M. Szczepkowska. C: Nazimova, Gale Sondergaard, Beatrice de Neergaard. D: Dmitri Ostrov.

SV: WB, 1934, Kay Francis, Warren William, Jean Muir, Verree Teasdale, Emma Dunn, Ann Shoemaker.

Doctor Social (2/11/48), Booth, 5)

Plastic surgeon renounces his fancy practice in favor of cancer research. ". . . a compounded soporific." (*New York Times*). C: Dean Jagger, Haila Stoddard, Al Shean, Mae Questel, Eda Heinemann, Ronald Alexander. A: Joseph Estry (pseud. for Dr. Maxwell Maltz). P: Harold Barnard. D: Don Appell.

Doctor X (2/9/31, Hudson, 80)

Murder stalks the scientific laboratory of Dr. Xavier (Howard Lang) as a full-moon strangler strikes and strikes again. Horrific mystery melodrama used cannibalism, dismemberment, and necrophilia to get its shock effects, and get them it did. A: Howard Warren Comstock and Allen C. Miller. P: William and Harry Brandt. D: Josephine Victor.

SV: WB, 1932, Lionel Atwill, Fay Wray, Lee Tracy, Preston Foster, Robert Warwick, Mae Busch, John Wray, Harry Beresford.

Doctors Disagree (12/28/43, Bijou, 23)

Can a successful woman surgeon find happiness—or must she forswear love? Terribly sudsy soap opera by Rose Franken (A/D), author of *Another Language* (1932), *Claudia* (1941), etc. C: Barbara O'Neil, Philip Ober, Dolly Haas, Eda Heinemann, Ann Thomas, John Ireland.

P: William Brown Meloney i.a.w. Armitage and Davis.

Dodsworth (2/24/34, Shubert, 317)

Samuel Dodsworth (Walter Huston), wealthy automobile manufacturer, retires and goes to Europe with his frivolous wife Fran (Fay Bainter). Fran becomes involved in several love affairs with European adventurers. Lonely and unhappy, Dodsworth ends by leaving his wife for the more mature companionship of Edith Cortright (Nan Sunderland).* Skillfully adapted by Sidney Howard from Sinclair Lewis' novel, and brilliantly acted by its leading players, *Dodsworth* was a dramatic hit of the first caliber. C: Maria Ouspenskaya, John Williams, Frederic Worlock, Kent Smith, Hal K. Dawson, Harlan Briggs, Ethel Jackson. P: Max Gordon. D: Robert Sinclair. SD: Jo Mielziner.

SV: UA, 1936, Walter Huston, Ruth Chatterton, Mary Astor, Paul Lukas, David Niven, Maria Ouspenskaya, Gregory Gaye, John Payne, Odette Myrtil, Spring Byington, Harlan Briggs (directed by William Wyler).

---

*(Mrs. Walter Huston).

Does a Tiger Wear a Necktie? (2/25/69, Belasco, 39)

A dedicated English teacher strives to communicate with a class of drug-addicted teenagers in a correctional institution. Compelling drama; brilliant performances by Hal Holbrook as the teacher and Al Pacino (Broadway debut) as his most incorrigible student. C: Lauren Jones, Roger Robinson, Jose Perez, Lazaro Perez, David Opatoshu, Jon Richards. A: Don Petersen. P: Philip Rose and Huntington Hartford i.a.w. Jay Weston. D: Michael Schultz. SD: Edward Burbridge.

Don Q., Jr. (1/27/26, 49th Street, 14)

Woefully amateurish 1926 curio designed to showcase the talents of tennis star Bill Tilden. The plot had something or other to do with the efforts of a good-hearted social worker (William T. Tilden, 2nd) to help free a troubled kid from reform school. A: Bernard S. Schubert. D: Arthur Hurley.

Note: After fourteen performances, *Don Q., Jr.* changed its name to *That Smith Boy* and reopened at the Mayfair Theatre on 2/20/26. It ran an additional twenty performances even though the production was rumored to average a mere twenty-six dollars a performance. *Variety* dubbed it: "The Lemon of the Year."

Donovan Affair, The (8/30/26, Fulton, 128)

The much-disliked host of a fashionable dinner party is murdered. Run-of-the-mill whodunit by Owen Davis. C: Ray Collins, Phoebe Foster, Paul Harvey, Robert T. Haines. P: Albert Lewis (D) i.a.w. Donald Davis.

SV: Columbia, 1929, Jack Holt (directed by Frank Capra).

Don't Bother Mother (2/3/25, Little, 3)

Trite comedy about an aging actress who tries to keep her grown children a secret from the public. C: Mary Hall, Jay Fassett. A: E. B. Dewing and Courtenay Savage. P: Bender and Storm.

Don't Drink the Water (11/17/66, Morosco, 598)

Woody Allen's farce about a family of American tourists mistaken for spies and held prisoner in a communist country. "Filled with funny lines . . . bright and humorous dialogue" (*Post*). C: Lou Jacobi, Kay Medford, Anthony Roberts, Anita Gillette. P: David Merrick i.a.w. Rollins and Joffe. D: Stanley Prager. CD: Motley. SD: Jo Mielziner.

SV: Embassy, 1969, Jackie Gleason, Estelle Parsons.

Don't Look Now (11/2/36, Bayes, 16)

Movie mogul (Joseph Buloff) pursues runaway actress. Dismal comedy from the Gustav Blum (P/D) factory. A: John Crump.

Double Door (9/21/33, Ritz, 138)

A tyrannical, fanatically proud *grande dame* rules her family with an iron hand. When her younger brother marries beneath his station, she tries every means in her power to break up the match. Finally, she locks the bride in a secret room with the object of accomplishing her death. A last-minute rescue is effected, and the thwarted, maniacal creature has an epileptic stroke which leaves her gibbering insanely at the curtain's fall. *Double Door* was a compelling, expertly crafted horror play. The leading role was acted by Mary Morris in America and by Sybil Thorndike in England. C: Anne Revere, Richard Kendrick. A: Elizabeth McFadden. P: H. C. Potter (D) and George Haight.

SV: Par, 1934, Mary Morris, Anne Revere, Evelyn Venable, Kent Taylor.

Double Dummy (11/11/36, Golden, 21)

Paroled convict organizes a contract bridge tournament, gets involved with gangsters. Slapdash 30's farce was produced by columnist Mark Hellinger and James Ullman, and directed by Edith Meiser. It marked the Broadway debut of Paul Douglas in the role of a radio announcer. C: Hanley Stafford, Charles D. Brown, Martha Sleeper, Dudley Clements, John McGovern, Adelaide Klein. A: Doty Hobart and Tom McKnight.

Double in Hearts (10/16/56, Golden, 7)

Substandard sex farce about a straying husband who moves in with a philandering actor-friend to escape the clutches of his domineering wife. C: William Redfield, Julia Meade, Neva Patterson, Laurence Hugo. A: Paul Nathan. P: Straus, Vroom and Karns. D: John Gerstad.

Doughgirls, The (12/30/42, Lyceum, 671)

Rowdy comedy success about three young gold diggers on the prowl in overcrowded wartime Washington. The hit of the evening was scored by Arlene Francis as Natalia Chodorov, a Russian sniper who moves in on the daffy trio, struggles to learn American ways, and takes brisk walks to Baltimore and back for exercise. Thanks largely to the George S. Kaufman (D) touch, *The Doughgirls* turned out to be good fun. The play was written by Joseph Field, coauthor (with Jerome Chodorov) of *My Sister Eileen* (1940) and *Junior Miss* (1941). C: Virginia Field, Doris Nolan, Arleen Whelan, Natalie Schafer. P: Max Gordon.

SV: WB, 1944, Ann Sheridan, Alexis Smith, Jane Wyman, Eve Arden, Jack Carson, Irene Manning, Charlie Ruggles, Alan Mowbray, John Alexander, Craig Stevens, Donald MacBride.

Dove, The (2/11/25, Empire, 159)

Don Jose (Holbrook Blinn), a mustache-twirling south-of-the-border bandit, is mad for the charms of Dolores Romero (Judith Anderson), sultry cabaret singer in the Purple Pigeon café down the road a piece. Dolores, however, only has eyes for two-fisted *Americano* Johnny Powell (William Harrigan), which leads to assorted complications. This fourth-rate David Belasco (P/D) claptrap was acted to perfection by a first-rate company and wowed 1925 audiences with its steamy melodramatics and comic strip convolutions. A: Willard Mack, based on a story by Gerald Beaumont.

SV: RKO, 1932, *Girl of the Rio,* Dolores Del Rio, Leo Carrillo, Norman Foster; 1939, *The Girl and the Gambler,* Leo Carrillo, Steffi Duna, Tim Holt.

Note: A silent version (UA, 1928) featured a cast headed by Noah Beery, Norma Talmadge, and Gilbert Roland.

Down to Miami (9/11/44, Ambassador, 8)

Gentile banker and Jewish merchant scheme to prevent the marriage of their respective son and daughter. ". . . makes the somewhat similar *Abie's Irish Rose* seem like the Pulitzer Prize winner. . ." *(New York Times).* ". . . inconceivably bad in every respect. . . . Even the intermissions were interminable, as though the play were written from act to act" *(PM).* A: Conrad Westervelt. P: Edgar MacGregor. D: J. B. Daniels.

Dozens, The (3/13/69, Booth, 4)

Slender fable of a Harlem show business couple's involvement in the political upheaval of an emerging African nation. C: Al Freeman, Jr., Paula Kelly, Morgan Freeman. A: Laird Koenig. P: Hale Matthews. D: Edward Parone.

Dr. Cook's Garden (9/25/67, Belasco, 8)

A venerable physician (Burl Ives) in an idyllic New England community has for years been systematically poisoning his "undesirable" patients (those who are crippled, or ugly, or just plain nasty). When his protégé (Keir Dullea) stumbles upon the truth, his life, too, is threatened. Unconvincing, badly miscast melodrama by novelist Ira Levin *(A Kiss Before Dying, Rosemary's Baby);* staged by Mr. Levin when George C. Scott withdrew as director midway through rehearsals. P: Saint-Subber. SD: David Hays.

Dracula (10/5/27, Fulton, 265)

A visitor from Transylvania (Bela Lugosi)

comes to Broadway in search of new blood. Good, workmanlike dramatization of the Bram Stoker classic, played out in the obligatory three settings: library, boudoir, musty vault. C: Dorothy Peterson, Edward Van Sloan, Nedda Harrigan, Terrence Neill. A: John Balderston and Hamilton Deane. P: Horace Liveright. D: Ira Hards.

SV: U, 1931, Bela Lugosi, David Manners, Helen Chandler, Dwight Frye, Edward Van Sloan.

Dream Child (9/27/34, Vanderbilt, 24)

Father (J. C. Nugent) encourages dullard son (Alan Bunce) to have a romantic fling before settling down. Wispy comedy-drama lacked punch or point. A: J. C. Nugent. P: Albert Ingalls, Jr. D: Julius Evans.

Dream Girl (12/14/45, Coronet, 348)

Georgina Allerton (Betty Field) runs an unsuccessful bookstore, writes unpublishable novels, and daydreams incessantly. In Georgina's imagination, the people of her everyday life become heroes and villains while she herself, of course, is always the heroine of these gaudily romantic flights of fancy. The play examines a day in the life of this likable ninny, from her awakening at eight A.M. in her virginal bed, to her retirement at three A.M. with an extrovert newspaperman (Wendell Corey) who has eloped with Georgina and, presumably, will wean her away from chronic daydreaming. "In *Dream Girl* Elmer Rice has written a captivating comedy, and in it his wife, Betty Field, gives an enchanting performance" *(News)*. Georgina ("a part that pales Hamlet's into polite insignificance" said one reviewer) is one of the most demanding roles ever written. There are innumerable costume changes, six-hundred cues, and there are only sixty seconds in each act when the character is not on stage. As Georgina, Miss Field distinguished herself with an immensely skillful and versatile *tour de force* characterization. Also applauded was Jo Mielziner's ingenious triple-track scenery. C: Evelyn Varden, William A. Lee, Sonya Stokowski, Edmon Ryan, Kevin O'Shea, James Gregory. P: The Playwrights' Company. D: Elmer Rice. CD: Mainbocher.

R: (5/9/51, City Center, 15). C: Judy Holliday, Don DeFore, Ann Shoemaker, Edmon Ryan, Marian Winters, William A. Lee. D: Morton Da Costa.

Musicalized by James Van Heusen, Sammy Cahn and Peter Stone as *Skyscraper* (1965) with Julie Harris, Peter Marshall, Charles Nelson Reilly.

SV: Par, 1948, Betty Hutton, Macdonald Carey, Peggy Wood, Walter Abel, Patric Knowles, Virginia Field (directed by Mitchell Leisen).

Drifting (1/2/22, Playhouse, 63)

A deacon's daughter (Alice Brady), stranded in China, is saved from a life of sin by a vagrant soldier named Badlands McKinney (Robert Warwick). Humphrey Bogart made his Broadway debut in this pulp-fiction melodrama, playing two small speaking roles. Commented critic Alexander Woollcott: "The young man [Bogart] is what is usually and mercifully known as inadequate." A: John Colton and D. H. Andrews. P: William A. Brady. D: John Cromwell.

SV: U, 1929, *Shanghai Lady,* Mary Nolan, James Murray.

Drink to Me Only (10/8/58, Adelphi, 77)

To defend a bibulous client, a young lawyer (Tom Poston) drinks two quarts of whisky in twelve hours, thereby destroying the prosecution's contention that such a dose would be lethal. This George Abbott (D) farce tried to stretch a one-joke situation into a full evening of theatre. It had its comic points, but not enough of them. C: John McGiver, Paul Hartman, Jack Gilford, Cameron Prud'homme, Royal Beal, Sherry Britton, Leona Powers, Georgann Johnson.

A: Abram S. Ginnes and Ira Wallach. P: George Ross i.a.w. John Robert Lloyd (SD).

Druid Circle, The (10/22/47, Morosco, 69)

Embittered professor (Leo G. Carroll) almost wrecks the lives of two young students. Languid, intermittently effective drama by John Van Druten (A/D); Ethel Griffies scored a personal triumph in the role of the professor's venerable, crochety mother. P: Alfred de Liagre, Jr.

Drums Begin, The (11/24/33, Shubert, 11)

George Abbott was the director and Judith Anderson the star of this muddled mixture of melodrama, symbolism, and pacifist preachment. French actress Valerie Latour (Judith Anderson), engaged in making an anti-war film in Europe, falls in love with her leading man (Walter Abel). Their affair ends when he discovers that Valerie was a German spy during World War I. C: Lionel Stander, Moffat Johnston, Jose Ruben, Kent Smith. A: Howard Irving Young. P: George Abbott and Philip Dunning.

Du Barry (12/25/01, Criterion, 165)

Lavish, ornate, highly fictionalized account of the rise and fall of the guttersnipe milliner (Mrs. Leslie Carter) who became the mistress of Louis XV. ". . . contains a plenitude of needless talk" (William Winter, *Tribune*). C: Hamilton Revelle, Claude Gillingwater, Ruth St. Denis. A/P/D: David Belasco.

SV: UA, 1930, *Du Barry, Woman of Passion*, Norma Talmadge, William Farnum.

Dulcy (8/13/21, Frazee, 246)

George S. Kaufman's and Marc Connelly's first Broadway success, and the comedy that elevated Lynn Fontanne to stardom. Dulcy is a bromidic, meddlesome birdbrain with a passion for interfering and a genius for blundering. By some miracle, however, her bungling saves her husband's business career from disaster. "Admirable . . . gay and reasonably subtle" (Percy Hammond, *Chicago Tribune*). "As Dulcinea, she [Lynn Fontanne] is brilliant—no less. . . . She can do great things and perhaps she will" (Alexander Woollcott, *New York Times*). Also sharing in the acting honors was Howard Lindsay as Vincent Leach, an effeminate silent screenwriter. C: Elliott Nugent, John Westley, Gregory Kelly, Wallis Clark. P: George C. Tyler and H. H. Frazee. D: Howard Lindsay. *Dulcy* was planned, outlined, and written in less than four weeks. Kaufman and Connelly based their hit comedy on Dulcinea, a character invented by columnist and cliché-collector Franklin P. Adams. During the early 1920's, *Dulcyisms* became as famous and widely repeated as malapropisms.

SV: MGM, 1930, *Not So Dumb*, Marion Davies, Elliott Nugent, Raymond Hackett, Donald Ogden Stewart, Franklin Pangborn; 1940, Ann Sothern, Ian Hunter, Roland Young, Billie Burke, Reginald Gardiner, Dan Dailey.

Note: A silent version (WB, 1923) starred Constance Talmadge (directed by Sidney Franklin).

Dummy, The (4/13/14, Hudson, 200)

A pert, curly-haired child actress named Joyce Fair (who grew up to become Clare Boothe Luce) helped boy detective Ernest Truex to solve a kidnapping and rout bad guy Edward Ellis in this entertaining comedy-melodrama. A: Harvey J. O'Higgins and Harriet Ford. P: Play Producing Co. D: T. D. Frawley.

SV: Par, 1929, Ruth Chatterton, Fredric March, ZaSu Pitts, Jack Oakie.

Dunce Boy, The (4/1/25, Daly's, 43)

Mountain woman tries to shield retarded son from the harsh realities of life. She fails, and the play ends with the boy's

The Dummy. **Ernest Truex and Joseph Brennan (April 13, 1914).** *Courtesy Museum of the City of New York Theatre and Music Collection.*

suicide. Grim tragedy by Lula Vollmer. C: Antoinette Perry, Gareth Hughes, Donald Cameron. P: Art Theatre. D: Henry Stillman.

Dunnigan's Daughter (12/26/45, Golden, 38)

Produced by the Theatre Guild, and directed by Elia Kazan, this loquacious conversation piece by S. N. Behrman dealt with a megalomaniacal tycoon (Dennis King) in Mexico whose second wife (June Havoc) eventually leaves him for a young and forthright State Department employee (Richard Widmark). "Grisly tedium" (George Jean Nathan). ". . . dull, unwieldy and artificial . . ." *(Sun)*. C: Jan Sterling, Luther Adler. SD: Stewart Chaney.

Dylan (1/18/64, Plymouth, 273)

The final four years in the life of the brilliant, tormented, self-destructive Welsh poet Dylan Thomas (Alec Guinness), beloved husband of Caitlin Thomas (Kate Reid)—and beloved of many other women—who drank himself to a premature death and died in New York City in 1953 at age thirty-nine. "A sensitive, sympathetic and compelling depiction of a painful event in recent literary history; an absorbing study in human disintegration" *(Post)*. ". . . the play only reports . . . it provides no new insights" *(World-Telegram and Sun)*. A: Sidney Michaels. P: George and Granat. D: Peter Glenville. SD: Oliver Smith.

Revived OB (2/7/72, Mercer O'Casey, 48) with a cast headed by Will Hare, Rue McClanahan, and Carleton Carpenter, under the direction of Lee D. Sankowich.

Dynamo (2/11/29, Martin Beck, 66)

Eugene O'Neill on America's deification of the machine. The son (Glenn Anders) of a minister rebels against the fundamentalist teachings of his childhood and becomes convinced that electricity is the only god. Driven mad by his lust for a seductive atheist (Claudette Colbert), he murders the girl, flings himself upon the dynamo, and is executed. "Sour and incoherent and extraordinarily dismal" (St. John Ervine, *World*). Rife with Freudian implications, *Dynamo* employed the *Strange Interlude* device of spoken thoughts, or asides, but to little effect since the characters remained abstractions. Originally announced as the first of a trilogy, *Dynamo* was a resounding failure. More than one Theatre Guild (P) subscriber wrote that he would renew his subscription only on condition that the remaining plays of the trilogy not be presented. O'Neill was said to resent the fact that the critics paid more attention to Claudette Colbert's legs than they did to the real meaning of his drama. "Henceforth," he wrote George Jean Nathan, "I myself cast not only actresses, but legs!" Upon rereading the script after the play closed, O'Neill admitted that he was "appalled by its raggedness. . . . It was in no shape for production." C: Dudley Digges, Helen Westley, George Gaul, Catherine Doucet. D: Philip Moeller. SD: Lee Simonson.

E

Earl of Pawtucket, The (3/23/03, Manhattan, 191)

Popular farce of its time in which an English lord (Lawrence D'Orsay), desiring to remain anonymous while visiting America, takes a Yankee's name with resultant comic complications. A/D: Augustus Thomas. P: Kirke La Shelle.

Earth Between, The (3/5/29, Provincetown, 39)

Bette Davis made her O/B debut in this pedestrian drama of Nebraska farm life. The story dealt with the conflict between a possessive father (Carl Ashburn) and his only child, Floy Jennings (Bette Davis). The father discourages the attentions to his daughter of every farmhand in the neighborhood. In the end, he succeeds in his plan: the girl will remain a spinster for life and tend to him in his old age. The critics were not overly impressed by the play, but they were by Miss Davis. The *New York Times* reviewer described her as "an interesting creature who plays in a soft, inassertive style." Another critic wrote: "The performances are good, particularly that of newcomer Bette Davis, playing a wraith of a child with true emotional insight." Bette Davis recalls the opening night of this O/B production as "the greatest night" in her life. "Nothing," she has written, "will ever equal the emotion I knew that night. I was a success in my first New York play." A: Virgil Geddes. D: James Light.

Earth Journey (4/27/44, Blackfriars', 16)

American version of a Chinese fantasy wherein an idol is brought to life by a princess. "A little too quaint and poetical for these rough and robust days" (*Brooklyn Eagle*). Produced O/B by that prestigious and enterprising semiprofessional group, the Blackfriars' Guild. A: Sheldon Davis. D: Dennis Gurney.

Easiest Way, The (1/19/09, Belasco Stuyvesant, 157)

The dramatic thunderbolt of its time, Eugene Walter's melodrama about a kept woman who falls in love, attempts to "go

The Easiest Way. **Frances Starr and Joseph Kilgour (January 19, 1909).** *Courtesy Museum of the City of New York Theatre and Music Collection.*

straight," but ends by taking "the easiest way," shocked audiences and critics alike. The *Evening World* reviewer called it "an evening of good acting and bad morals." Another critic asked: "Is it indecent, vile, corrupt, lascivious?" and proceeded to answer all four questions in the affirmative. The play's impact was heightened by the casting of pretty, ladylike Frances Starr in the role of the mistress, by the naturalistic stagecraft of David Belasco (P/D), and by the downbeat "true to life" ending with its sensational curtain line—"I'm going to Rector's to make a hit, and to hell with the rest"—which constituted a milestone of sorts in the American theatre. In 1921 the play was revived by Belasco with Miss Starr once again in the lead, and the production ran for 63 performances.

SV: MGM, 1931, Constance Bennett, Robert Montgomery, Adolphe Menjou, Anita Page, Marjorie Rambeau, Clark Gable.

East Is West (12/25/18, Astor, 680)

The *Madame Butterfly* plot with a happy ending tacked on when little Ming Toy (Fay Bainter) turns out to be white a few moments before the final curtain. An enormous success with theatregoers but, in the words of critic Heywood Broun, "a velly lotten play." C: Hassard Short, George Nash, Forrest Winant. A: Samuel Shipman and John B. Hymer. P: William Harris, Jr. D: Clifford Brooke.

SV: U, 1930, Lupe Velez, Edward G. Robinson, Lew Ayres.

Eastward in Eden (11/18/47, Royale, 15)

Still another theatre piece about the strange, frustrated life of Emily Dickinson. First there was *Alison's House* (1930) with Eva Le Gallienne; followed by *Brittle Heaven* (1934) with Dorothy Gish as the New England poetess; then Martha Graham's dance-drama, *Letter to the World* (1940); and finally this dramatization by Dorothy Gardner with Beatrice Straight and Onslow Stevens in the leading roles. A literate, tasteful, but undramatic evening in the theatre. P: Nancy Stern. D: Ellen Van Volkenburg.

Easy Come, Easy Go (10/26/25, Cohan, 180)

A "cheating cheaters" farce by Owen Davis in which a pair of likable crooks (Victor Moore and Otto Kruger) succeed in fleecing their more respectable brethren in the worlds of high society and high finance. C: Edward Arnold, Nan Sunderland, Vaughn DeLeath, Betty Garde. P: Lewis and Gordon i.a.w. Sam H. Harris. D: Priestly Morrison.

Musicalized by Joseph Meyer and Edward Eliscu as *Lady Fingers* (1929) with Eddie Buzzell, Marjorie White, John Price Jones, Esther Muir.

SV: Par, 1930, *Only Saps Work,* Leon Errol, Stuart Erwin.

Easy Mark, The (8/26/24, 39th Street, 104)

Town rube (Walter Huston) gets the better of some phony oil men. Typical formula comedy, thoroughly routine despite the fine acting of Mr. Huston. A: Jack Larrie. P: Independent Theatre, Inc.

Easy Street (8/14/24, 39th Street, 12)

Jealous husband (Ralph Kellard) suspects wife (Mary Newcomb) of earning extra money as a prostitute. Pernicious junk. A/P/D: Ralph Thomas Kettering.

Ebb Tide (6/8/31, New Yorker, 16)

Rambunctious widow (Marjorie Main) and her illegitimate offspring get in a heap o' trouble with dope peddlers. Future film producer-director William Castle had a supporting role in this painfully corny 1931 melodrama. A: Harry Chapman Ford. P: Artmart Productions. D: J. Kent Thurber.

Edgar Allan Poe (10/5/25, Liberty, 8)

An abortive attempt by *Harper's Bazaar* editor Catherine Chisholm Cushing to dramatize the generally wretched lives of Poe (James Kirkwood) and his unhappy wife (Lila Lee). "Nevermore, quoth this raven!" *(Broadway Reporter)*. P/D: Arthur Hurley.

Edmund Burke (10/2/05, Majestic, 28)

Rickety stage piece about the British statesman who was sympathetic toward the American colonies and the Irish Catholics. C: Chauncey Olcott, Gladys Smith (Mary Pickford). A: Theodore Burt Sayre. P: Augustus Pitou.

Edwin Booth (11/24/58, 46th Street, 24)

Episodic, highly embroidered biography of the noted Shakespearean actor (Jose Ferrer) as recalled by William Winter (Lorne Greene), reigning drama critic of the time. "A quiet evening of set munching" (John McClain, *Journal-American*). "... if anyone ever writes a play about the Marx Brothers, Mr. Ferrer will be my first choice for all three" (Kenneth Tynan, *The New Yorker*). C: Richard Waring, Ian Keith, Lois Smith. A: Milton Geiger. P/D: Jose Ferrer. CD: Edith Head. SD: Zvi Geyra. M: Paul Bowles.

Effect of Gamma Rays on Man-in-the-Moon Marigolds, The (4/7/70, Mercer-O'Casey, 819)

That the flowering of a new growth can occur in the most devastated soil is the theme of this Pulitzer Prize-winning drama. A bitter woman (Sada Thompson), defeated by life and living in squalor, rules her two teenaged daughters with a whim of iron. She inflicts on them whatever emotion she happens to feel, from outright cruelty (in the murder of a pet rabbit), to a rare display of maternal affection (tending her older girl during an epileptic fit). The younger daughter, a vulnerable yet valiant child, is conducting a school experiment having to do with the exposure of marigold seeds to radioactive material. When the project puts her in the finals of the school science contest, it would seem that a victory may be at hand. However, despite her win, only sadness and continuing struggle are the result. The mother's final words, "I hate the world" are juxtaposed with the daughter's hopeful whisper, "Atom. Atom. What a beautiful word." "... a great human drama" (Lee Silver, *New York Daily News*). "See this play—it has a compassion all its own" (Clive Barnes, *New York Times*). "Sada Thompson calls clear attention to the fact that she is one of the American theater's finest actresses" (Walter Kerr, *New York Times*). The play was produced at Houston's Alley Theater in 1965, then appeared in a TV adaptation starring Eileen Heckart in 1966 prior to its O/B triumph in 1970. In addition to the Pulitzer Prize, the New York Drama Critics' Circle named *Marigolds* the Best American Play of the year. A: Paul Zindel. C: Sada Thompson, Pamela Payton-Wright, Amy Levitt, Judith Lowry, Swoosie Kurtz. D: Melvin Bernhardt. P: Orin Lehman.

SD: Fred Voelpel.
SV: Fox, 1972, Joanne Woodward, Nell Potts, Roberta Wallach (directed and produced by Paul Newman from Alvin Sargent's screenplay).

Egghead, The (10/9/57, Barrymore, 21)

A liberal teacher (Karl Malden) unwittingly champions the Communist partyline in the cause of academic freedom. Earnest but heavy-handed problem play by Molly (Mrs. Elia) Kazan. C: Lloyd Richards, Phyllis Love, Biff McGuire, Eduard Franz. P: Hope Abelson. D: Hume Cronyn.

Egotist, The (12/25/22, 39th Street, 49)

Ben Hecht's first play. High-flown but promising study of a jealous, egomaniacal man of the theatre (Leo Ditrichstein) who finally is deserted both by his wife and mistress. P: Lee Shubert. D: Ditrichstein.

Eight O'Clock Tuesday (1/6/41, Henry Miller, 16)

Who stabbed and killed a much-hated domestic tyrant? Unstimulating flashback mystery by Robert Wallsten and Mignon G. Eberhart b/o the latter's novel, *Fair Warning*. C: Pauline Lord, Celeste Holm, McKay Morris, Bramwell Fletcher, Cecil Humphreys, Herbert Rudley, Philip Tonge, Margaret Douglas. P: Luther Greene (D) and James Struthers. SD: Lemuel Ayers.

Elevating a Husband (1/22/12, Liberty, 120)

Silly marital mixup comedy, coauthored by Lipman and Shipman. C: Louis Mann, Conway Tearle, Edward Everett Horton, Emily Ann Wellman. P: Werba and Luescher. D: Gustav Von Seyfferitz.

Elizabeth the Queen (11/3/30, Guild, 145)

Maxwell Anderson's drama dealing with "those lovers whom a kingdom kept apart," the aging, imperious Tudor wench (Lynn Fontanne) and the young, dashing Earl of Essex (Alfred Lunt). Written in alternate scenes of blank verse and pseudo-poetic prose, this historical romance evoked one of the most thunderous opening night ovations in New York theatre history. C: Percy Waram (Raleigh), Morris Carnovsky (Bacon), Whitford Kane (Burbage). P: The Theatre Guild. D: Philip Moeller. CD/SD: Lee Simonson.
R: (11/13/66, City Center, 14) for a limited engagement with Judith Anderson and Donald Davis in the leading roles.
SV: WB, 1939, *The Private Lives of Elizabeth and Essex,* Bette Davis, Errol Flynn, Olivia de Havilland, Donald Crisp, Vincent Price, Nanette Fabray, Henry Daniell, Leo G. Carroll.
Note: A long excerpt from *Elizabeth the Queen* was used as the opening scene in MGM's 1931 film version of Molnar's *The Guardsman*—the Lunts' only costarred screen appearance.

Elmer Gantry (8/9/28, Playhouse, 44)

Wobbly dramatization of Sinclair Lewis's 1927 novel about an ex-divinity student and con man supreme who makes a fiery entry into the revival movement. C: Edward Pawley, Vera Allen, Lumsden Hare (D). A: Patrick Kearney. P: Joseph Shea.
Musicalized by Bellwood-Lebowsky-Tobias as *Gantry* (1970) with Robert Shaw, Rita Moreno.
SV: The Lewis novel was filmed by United Artists (1960) in a multi-Oscar-winning production with Burt Lancaster, Jean Simmons, Shirley Jones, Arthur Kennedy, Dean Jagger, Patti Page and Edward Andrews.

Elmer the Great (9/24/28, Lyceum, 40)

A not-too-bright baseball pitcher (Walter Huston) is tempted to throw the big game in order to clear himself with his sweetheart. This Ring Lardner comedy came on strong, but struck out before the last inning. C: Nan Sunderland (Mrs. Walter Huston), Katherine (Kay) Francis, Fred de Cordova. P: George M. Cohan. D: Sam Forrest.
SV: Par, 1929, *Fast Company,* Jack Oakie, Evelyn Brent, Skeets Gallagher; WB, 1933, Joe E. Brown, Frank McHugh, Patricia Ellis, Preston Foster, Claire Dodd; 1939, *Cowboy Quarterback,* Bert Wheeler, Marie Wilson, Eddie Foy, Jr., William Demarest, DeWolf Hopper, Gloria Dickson.

Embezzled Heaven (10/31/44, National, 52)

A poor peasant (Ethel Barrymore) attempts to bribe her way into God's grace by supporting a dissolute priest-nephew. Stately, slow-moving dramatization by L.

Bush-Fekete and Mary Helen Fay of the Franz Werfel novel. C: Albert Basserman (deb.), Eduard Franz, Bettina Cerf, Sanford Meisner, Martin Blaine. P: The Theatre Guild. D: B. Iden Payne. SD: Stewart Chaney.

Emperor Jones, The (11/1/20, Provincetown, 192)

Eugene O'Neill's classic study of man's reversion to primitive fear. Brutus Jones, a lordly American Negro, rules a small island in the West Indies. When his subjects rebel against his tyranny, he escapes to the jungle where—to the steadily accelerating beat of the native tom-toms—he is tortured by terror of the supernatural, and finally captured. A landmark in the growth and development of the American drama, with a superlative performance in the title role by Charles S. Gilpin. Also in the cast (as Smithers, the Cockney trader) was Jasper Deeter. P: Provincetown Players. D: George Cram Cook.

The most notable revivals were in 1925 (Paul Robeson as Jones, Cecil Clovely as Smithers, 28 perfs.) and 1926 (Gilpin as Jones, Moss Hart as Smithers, 61 perfs.) Musicalized as an opera (1932) by Louis Gruenberg with Lawrence Tibbett in the title role.

SV: UA, 1933, Paul Robeson and Dudley Digges in DuBose Heyward's screen adaptation.

Emperor's Clothes, The (2/9/53, Barrymore, 16)

In Budapest, 1930, a blacklisted schoolteacher (Lee J. Cobb) ekes out a living by translating trashy American fiction while loudly denouncing the police-state society of the times. His actions fire the imagination of his young son (Brandon de Wilde), but tend to bewilder his conventionally minded wife (Maureen Stapleton). The father is forced to destroy his son's faith by a calculated act of compromise, but redeems himself in the end. Intriguing but ultimately ponderous and verbose drama by Anglo-American (Budapest-born) author George Tabori. C: Anthony Ross, Esmond Knight (deb), Nydia Westman, Tamara Daykarhanova, Mike Kellin, Michael Strong. P: Robert Whitehead i.a.w. The Playwrights Company. D: Harold Clurman. CD: Ben Edwards. SD: Lester Polakov.

Empress of Destiny (3/9/38, St. James, 5)

Lavish but soporific spectacle-drama dealing with Catherine the Great (Elissa Landi) and her marriage to the impotent, half-witted Prince Peter (Glenn Hunter). C: Mary Morris, Dennis Hoey, Damian O'Flynn, Ben Starkie, Stiano Braggiotti. A: Jessica Lee and Joseph Lee Walsh. P: Frederick Ayer i.a.w. Ilya Mottyleff (D).

Enchanted April, The (8/24/25, Morosco, 32)

Four women (Helen Gahagan, Alison Skipworth, Elizabeth Risdon, Merle Maddern) rent an Italian villa in an effort to shut themselves off from the complications of the outside world, especially those concerned with the opposite sex. Frail but entertaining whimsy, adapted by Kane Campbell from the novel by "Elizabeth." P: Rosalie Stewart. D: John Hayden.

SV: RKO, 1935, Ann Harding, Frank Morgan.

End as a Man (9/15/53, Theatre de Lys, 137)

Harrowing portrait of paranoia in a southern military academy. As sadistic upper classman Jocko de Paris, Ben Gazzara scored a great success in his New York stage debut. Also applauded were cadets Pat Hingle (deb.), Anthony Franciosa, Albert Salmi, Mark Richman (deb.), Arthur Storch (deb.), Paul Richards, William Smithers, and Harry Guardino (deb.). Calder Willingham's adaptation of his novel was originally produced O/B for thirty-two performances, and then transferred uptown to the Vanderbilt Theatre. P: Claire Heller. D: Jack Garfein.

SV: Col, 1957, *The Strange One*, Ben Gazzara, George Peppard, Pat Hingle, Mark Richman, Geoffrey Horne, Julie London (directed by Jack Garfein).

End of Summer (2/17/36, Guild, 152)

Having narrowly escaped financial exploitation by a self-aggrandizing psychiatrist, a charming but rather empty-headed millionairess (Ina Claire) takes up with a ruthless young radical who plans to use her money for the sake of "the cause." Her love affair, she comes to realize, is the end of summer not only for herself but for her class as well. Also in the cast of S. N. Behrman's witty and provocative comedy of manners: Osgood Perkins, Van Heflin, Mildred Natwick, Shepperd Strudwick, Minor Watson, Tom Powers, Doris Dudley. P: The Theatre Guild. D: Philip Moeller. SD: Lee Simonson.

Endecott and the Red Cross (5/7/68, American Place, 15)

A dramatization by poet-playwright Robert Lowell of two Nathaniel Hawthorne stories dealing with the conflict between early American puritanism and cheerful nonconformity. Governor Endecott (Kenneth Haigh) comes to Merry Mount, Massachusetts, in 1630 and leads the assault of the grim Puritans upon Thomas Morton's happy-go-lucky, hedonistic colony of maypole dancers. Esoteric but engrossing drama, directed by John Hancock and produced O/B by the American Place Theater.

Enemy, The (10/20/25, Times Square, 202)

World War I—its causes and effects—as seen through the eyes of a Viennese family. Press agent, drama critic, and theatrical jack-of-all-trades Channing Pollock wrote this pacifist preachment ("Hate is The Enemy of Mankind"), which was greeted warmly by playgoers of the time. C: Fay Bainter, Walter Abel. P: Crosby Gaige. D: Robert Milton.

Enemy Is Dead, The (1/14/73, Bijou, 1)

A message play. Anti-Semitism is still alive in America and must be confronted and rooted out. Throughout the first act, a Protestant husband and his Jewish wife, vacationing in a mountain cabin, alternately amuse and antagonize each other with jokes, games, and fantasies. Reality intrudes in Act II. A neighbor comes calling. Initially pleasant, he turns out to be head of the rural fascists, and intent on war with the Jewish-communist conspiracy that controls the nation. Outraged, the husband abandons his fantasizing. Intimidating the bigot with an unloaded rifle, he peppers the man's soul with a few choice words and sends him packing. This comedy-drama was poorly received. The critics praised the three actors in the play for their efforts, but felt those efforts were not worth making. A: Don Petersen. C: Linda Lavin, Arthur Storch, Addison Powell. P: Lee Schumer and Morton Wolkowitz. D: Arthur Sherman. SD: Kert Lundell.

Engagement Baby, The (5/21/70, Helen Hayes, 4)

Modest comedy by screenwriter Stanley Shapiro (*Pillow Talk, That Touch of Mink*). A successful Jewish advertising man discovers he has an eighteen-year-old illegitimate son (an engagement baby). Moreover, he is black, and forthwith, the ad man's career and marriage start down the drain, though it all comes right at the end. In between, there have been sporadic moments of wit and wisdom. Though the play did not please reviewers, Barry Nelson and Clifton Davis, as father and son, won critical praise. A: Stanley Shapiro. C: Barry Nelson, Clifton Davis, Constance Towers, Tom Aldredge. D: Gene Frankel. P: Edgar Lansbury, J. I. Rodale i.a.w. Nan Pearlman. SD: Robin Wagner.

Enter Laughing (3/13/63, Henry Miller, 419)

Based on Carl Reiner's autobiographical novel, this comedy dealt with a stagestruck delivery boy from the Bronx who decides to become an actor. Since the delivery boy happened to be played by Alan Arkin, the evening turned out to be "marvelously funny . . . side-splitting . . . uproarious" (*New York Times*). Gene Saks made his Broadway directorial debut with this successful 1963 comedy. Starred in the production were Sylvia Sidney, Vivian Blaine, Alan Mowbray, and Irving Jacobson (deb.). Also prominent in the cast: Michael J. Pollard, Barbara Dana, Meg Myles. A: Joseph Stein. P: Morton Gottlieb. SD: Ed Wittstein.

SV: Col, 1967, Jose Ferrer, Elaine May, Reni Santoni, Shelley Winters, Jack Gilford, Michael J. Pollard, David Opatoshu, Don Rickles, Janet Margolin, Richard Deacon, Rob Reiner (directed by Carl Reiner).

Enter Madame (8/16/20, Garrick, 366)

Brittle, amusing comedy about a capricious prima donna (Gilda Varesi) whose alternating tenderness and tantrums serve to estrange her bewildered spouse. Written by Miss Varesi (whose mother, Mme. Elena Varesi, was a famous European diva) in collaboration with Dolly Byrne. P/D: Brock Pemberton.

SV: Par, 1935, Elissa Landi, Cary Grant, Lynne Overman, Richard Bonnelli.

Entertain a Ghost (4/9/62, Actors Playhouse, 8)

Marital difficulties of playwright and his actress-wife. Uneven but frequently intriguing O/B comedy-drama by Louis Peterson, author of *Take a Giant Step* (1953). C: Stuart Damon, Carol Rossen, Loretta Leversee. P/D: Ira Cirker.

Episode (2/4/25, Bijou, 21)

Infidelity in the New York social set. Tame comedy-drama, produced by Lee Shubert. C: Gilbert Emery (A), William Courtleigh, Eugene Powers. D: Melville Burke.

Errant Lady (9/17/34, Fulton, 40)

Domineering mother (Leona Powers) gets her comeuppance. Frail comedy by theatrical press agent Nat N. Dorfman. P: Harry Albert. D: Priestly Morrison.

Erstwhile Susan (1/18/16, Gaiety, 167)

A flamboyant actress (Mrs. Fiske) descends on a Pennsylvania Dutch community, revolutionizes the home life of one rustic, rescues his drudge of a daughter from her status as a nonpaid servant, and departs in style at the end on the arm of the governor of Pennsylvania. "An odd, sometimes faltering, rather desultory little comedy [acted by] the most brilliant comedienne of the American stage" (*New York Times*). A: Marian de Forest, based on a novel by Helen R. Martin. P: Corey-Williams-Riter, Inc. D: Harrison Grey Fiske.

Escape This Night (4/22/38, 44th Street, 11)

A pair of frightened refugees seek sanctuary from Nazi agents in the Braille room of the New York Public Library. Spy melodrama had little in its favor except an intriguing (if implausible) setting. C: Arnold Korff, Ellen Hall, Walter Coy, Francesca Bruning, Hume Cronyn, George Mathews, David Wayne (deb.). A: Robert Steiner (D) and Harry Horner (SD). P: Robinson Smith.

Eternal Road, The (1/7/37, Manhattan Opera, 152)

One of the costliest failures in Broadway history, Max Reinhardt's morality pageant has perhaps never been equalled for sheer scenic splendor. Oscar Hammerstein's huge opera house was literally dismantled and then rebuilt to disclose a multileveled mountain stretching to "the very portals of Heaven itself." A pageant of Jewish history in Old Testament style, the biblical spectacle boasted magnificent Norman Bel Geddes settings, lighting, and costumes (1,172 of them); a richly evocative Kurt Weill score; and a cast of Cecil B. De Mille proportions that included Sam Jaffe, Lotte Lenya, Sidney Lumet, Kurt Kasznar, and a small army of *supers*. Epic in conception, *The Eternal Road* unfortunately turned out to be static and ponderous in execution. C: Thomas Chalmers, Rosamond Pinchot, Olive Deering, Herbert Rudley, Dickie Van Patten, Harold Johnsrud, Abner Biberman, Earl Weatherford, Katherine Carrington. A: Ad. from the Franz Werfel text by Ludwig Lewisohn and William A. Drake. P: Crosby Gaige and Meyer W. Weisgal. D: Max Reinhardt.

Ethan Frome (1/21/36, National, 119)

Faithful, incisive dramatization of Edith Wharton's chronicle of frustration and tragedy on a bleak New England farm, with the author's devastatingly ironic ending left intact. Saddled with a hateful invalid spouse (Pauline Lord), Ethan Frome (Raymond Massey) turns to his wife's homeless young cousin (Ruth Gordon) for warmth and affection. They agree to put an end to things, but their suicide attempt fails, leaving them both hopeless cripples. "One of the finest of American plays" (*Sun*). "Mrs. Wharton would be grateful for the splendid gifts the theatre has laid at the feet of her masterpiece" (*New York Times*). "The American theatre at its absolute best" (*American*). C: Charles Henderson, Tom Ewell. A: Owen and Donald Davis. P: Max Gordon. D: Guthrie McClintic. SD: Jo Mielziner.

Eugenia (1/30/57, Ambassador, 12)

The third attempt in as many seasons to transfer a Henry James novel to the stage. (See *Child of Fortune* and *Portrait of a Lady*.) This time it was that subtle study in contrasting cultures, *The Europeans*, adapted by Randolph Carter as a vehicle for the irrepressible Tallulah Bankhead. "There can be no question whatever that Miss Tallulah Bankhead is an irresistible force, but in *Eugenia* she has flatly, finally and irrevocably met an immovable object" (*Herald Tribune*). "Only Mae West as Snow White could have seemed more unsuited to a part" (Louis Kronenberger). "Why will these playwrights insist on disturbing Henry's shade? Why don't they go after Ouida, or Gene Stratton Porter, or Elinor Glyn?" (*World-Telegram*). P: John C. Wilson. D: Herbert Machiz. CD: Miles White. SD: Oliver Smith.

Eva the Fifth (8/28/28, Little, 63)

Mild satire on the *Uncle Tom* road shows of a bygone era. Two sisters, both child performers, scheme to outwit each other for the coveted role of Little Eva. A kind of forerunner of, and comic variation on, the *What Ever Happened to Baby Jane?* plot. C: Claiborne Foster, Lois Shore, William Wadsworth, Nila Mack. A: John Golden and Kenyon Nicholson. P: John Golden (D) and Edgar Selwyn.
SV: MGM, 1930, *The Girl in the Show*, Bessie Love, Raymond Hackett.

Evangeline (10/4/13, Park, 17)

Lachrymose dramatization by Thomas W. Broadhurst of Longfellow's classic tale of the Nova Scotia lass (Edna Goodrich) who, parted from her lover, becomes a Sister of Mercy. According to Arthur Hopkins (P/D), the play was "smothered beneath an avalanche of ridicule and abuse." Hopkins launched a

bitter attack on the critics for their "venomous and unenlightened" reviews of *Evangeline*, which he called "the most significant theatrical production of the past decade." The noted producer-director concluded his signed statement to the press with these words: "The tragedy of it all! When will it end—when will newspaper owners decide that the theatre is a great influence that deserves their help? When will they awaken to the fact that the American theatre is years behind the theatres of Europe? When will they realize that its greatest handicap is silly-witted, venomous, and cringing dramatic criticism?"
SV: UA, 1929, Dolores Del Rio.

Eve of St. Mark, The (10/7/42, Cort, 306)

After Pearl Harbor is attacked, a farm boy leaves his mother and girl to keep a rendezvous with death on an island in the Philippines. Maxwell Anderson's unabashedly sentimental war drama—a far cry from the romantic iconoclasm of his World War I classic, *What Price Glory?*—turned out to be his greatest popular and critical success in many seasons. ". . . written straight from the heart . . . a war drama of emotional tension, humor and poetic splendor" (*Herald Tribune*). C: William Prince, Aline MacMahon, Mary Rolfe, James Monks, Eddie (Michael) O'Shea, George Mathews, Martin Ritt, Matt Crowley. P: The Playwrights Company. D: Lem Ward. SD: Howard Bay.
SV: Fox, 1944, William Eythe, Anne Baxter, Vincent Price, Michael O'Shea, Dickie Moore.

Every Man for Himself (12/9/40, Guild, 3)

Alcoholic screenwriter (Lee Tracy) can't recall the plot idea he sold a film producer during a four-day binge. "Foolish, frantic and fatuous" (*Herald Tribune*). A: Milton Lazarus. P: Arthur Hutchinson and Arthur Ripley (D).

Every Thursday (5/10/34, Royale, 60)

Family maid (Queenie Smith) instructs her employer's seventeen-year-old son (Leon Janney) in the facts of life. Single entendre comedy lacked wit, taste, or point. A: Doty Hobart. P: Wee and Leventhal. D: Theodore Vichman.

Everybody Loves Opal (10/11/61, Longacre, 21)

Comedy about a cheerful frump (Eileen Heckart) and the three improbable villains (Stubby Kaye, Donald Harron, Brenda Vaccaro)* who plot—unsuccessfully, of course—to murder her for a ten-thousand-dollar insurance policy. "Goofy, extravagant and enjoyable" (*News*). ". . .a grimly whimsical little effort" (*New York Times*). C: James Coco, John Napier. A: John Patrick. P: Roger L. Stevens i.a.w Seven Arts Productions. D: Cyril Ritchard. SD: Jo Mielziner.

---
*Broadway debut.

Everyday (11/16/21, Bijou, 30)

A 19-year-old Missouri girl (Tallulah Bankhead) rebels against her domineering father and insists on wedding the idealistic lad (Henry Hull) she loves, poor though he may be. Tepid drama by Rachel Crothers (A/D). C: Lucile Watson, Frank Sheridan, Minnie Dupree. P: Mary Kirkpatrick.

Everything in the Garden (11/29/67, Plymouth, 84)

A group of bored suburban housewives become part-time prostitutes in order to afford the luxuries they crave. This black comedy by Edward Albee (based on a play by Giles Cooper) started off promisingly enough as an indictment of contemporary hedonism and conformity, but swerved abruptly into emotional melodramatics and absurdist excesses. C: Barbara Bel Geddes, Barry Nelson, Beatrice Straight, Robert Moore, Richard

Thomas, Whitfield Connor. P: Barr and Wilder. D: Peter Glenville. CD/SD: William Ritman.

Everything's Jake (1/16/30, Assembly, 76)

Witty but uneven comedy by Don *(archy and mehitabel)* Marquis about a wealthy bootlegger, whooping it up in Paris of the 20's, who learns that the market crash has wiped him out. C: Thurston Hall, Jean Adair, Catherine Willard and, in the role of a chef, critic and theatre historian George Freedley. P: Theatre Assembly. D: Walter Greenough.

Everywhere I Roam (12/29/38, National, 13)

Johnny Appleseed (Norman Lloyd) watches The Man (Dean Jagger) and The Wife (Katherine Emery) forsake the soil for high living in the big city. Garbled, all but unintelligible allegorical fable co-produced by Marc Connelly (D) and Bela Blau. C: Joan Wetmore, Annamary Dickey, Robert Porterfield, Robert Breen. A: Arnold Sundgaard and Marc Connelly. CD/SD: Robert Edmond Jones. CH: Felicia Sorel. M: Lehman Engel.

Eve's Leaves (3/26/25, Wallack's, 12)

Extravagant wife with a limited income becomes involved with a crafty couturier. Humdrum comedy-drama. C: Ray Collins (P), Elwyn Harvey. A: Harry Chapman Ford.

Excess Baggage (12/26/27, Ritz, 216)

A pair of small-time vaudevillians (Miriam Hopkins and Eric Dressler) try to make the big time, fail, and then succeed in this agreeable, reasonably unhackneyed show-business comedy-drama. C: Frank McHugh, Morton Downey, Frances Goodrich. A: John McGowan. P: Barbour, Crimmins, and Bryant. D: Melville Burke.

Note: Of the eleven plays—an all-time record—that opened on Broadway the night of December 26, 1927, *Excess Baggage* was the only production among them to find favor with playgoers.

SV: Tower, 1934, *Big Time or Bust,* Regis Toomey, Gloria Shea.

Exciters, The (9/22/22, Times Square, 35)

"Rufus" Rand (Tallulah Bankhead), a blasé, teen-age flapper, enters into a marriage of convenience with a glib, fast-talking burglar (Alan Dinehart). Flamboyant, generally unbelievable comedy. C: Chester Morris, Aline MacMahon, Enid Markey, Thais Lawton. A: Martin Brown. P: The Selwyns. D: Edgar Selwyn.

Excursion (4/9/37, Vanderbilt, 114)

On the final cruise of a Coney Island steamer, the captain decides to head his tub for a magic island where his passengers may find a new and better life for themselves. Gently persuasive fantasy of charm and originality. C: Whitford Kane, Shirley Booth, Anthony Ross, Frances Fuller, Connie Gilchrist, Jennie Moscowitz, Fred Stewart, Marilyn Erskine, Robert Williams, Joseph Olney, John O'Shaughnessy, Billy (William) Redfield. A: Victor Wolfson. P: John C. Wilson. D: Worthington Miner. SD: G. E. Calthrop.

Note: Two decades after its original production, a musical version called *A Month of Sundays,* written by Burt Shevelove, tried out in Boston with Nancy Walker and Gene Lockhart heading the cast, but never reached Broadway.

Excuse Me (2/13/11, Gaiety, 160)

The misadventures of a wide-eyed ingenue (Ann Murdock) aboard the pullman car of a train. Predictable farce-comedy by Rupert Hughes. P: Henry W. Savage. D: George Marion.

Musicalized by Jerome Kern as *Toot-*

Toot! (1918) with Louise Groody and Greek Evans.

Exercise, The (4/24/68, Golden, 5)

Two actors on a bare stage search for "truth" through a series of "improvisations." Lackluster conversation piece by Lewis John Carlino. A: Anne Jackson, Stephen Joyce. P: Austin/Smith/Cohen/Stark. D: Alfred Ryder.

Experience (10/27/14, Booth, 255)

Youth (William Elliott) leaves Mother and Love when Ambition calls him to the Great City. There he neglects Opportunity for Pleasure, Excitement, Intoxication, and Temptation and then finds himself reduced to the company of Poverty, Delusion, and Crime. This simple-minded morality play by George V. Hobart (A/D) was much in favor with 1914 audiences and ran for 255 performances on Broadway. P: William Elliott.

Expressing Willie (4/16/24, 48th Street, 293)

A shrewd mother exposes her son's bohemian friends for the frauds and parasites they really are. Bright and cheerful comedy that was a great hit with matinee audiences. C: Chrystal Herne, Louise Closser Hale, Richard Sterling, Warren William, Merle Maddern. A/D: Rachel Crothers. P: Equity Players.

Extra (1/23/23, Longacre, 23)

Son (Chester Morris) takes over newspaper business while Dad's away, turns the paper into a liberal publication and a booming success. Tedious comedy by Jack Alicoate. P: Alicoate and William Collier, Jr. D: Walter Wilson.

Musicalized by Tom Johnstone as *When You Smile* (1925) with Jack Whiting, Wynne Gibson, Imogene Coca.

Eye on the Sparrow (5/3/38, Vanderbilt, 6)

Flighty socialite-mother can't adjust to straitened circumstances. Eighteen-year-old Montgomery Clift made a nice impression as the son in this otherwise dreary 1938 comedy. C: Catherine Doucet, Philip Ober, Edgar Stehli, Katherine Deane. A: Maxwell Selser. P: Girvan Higginson. D: Antoinette Perry.

Eyes of Youth (8/22/17, Maxine Elliott's, 414)

A young woman imagines her future along three of the four paths presently open to her, and finally chooses the one path she hasn't investigated. At least she knows it couldn't be any worse than the other three. Elaborate mumbo-jumbo, laced with thick gobs of sentiment, and served up as a multiple-role vehicle for Marjorie Rambeau. One of the big hits of 1917, especially with the ladies. A: Max Marcin and Charles Guernon. P: A. H. Woods and Messrs. Shubert. D: Lawrence Marston.

F

Fabulous Invalid, The (10/8/38, Broadhurst, 65)

George S. Kaufman (D) and Moss Hart's elaborate valentine to the American theatre, a cavalcade of scenes from notable plays and musicals, 1900–1930. To carry their story, the authors fabricated the tale of three ghosts who haunt the stage of the Alexandria Theatre from its illustrious opening night through its decline to a cheap burlesque house. "The first part of the play is labored and sentimental. Not until the second part . . . does the show come to life" *(Theatre Arts)*. C: Doris Dalton, Stephen Courtleigh, Jack Norworth, Ernest Lawford, Charles King, Iris Adrian, Sid Stone, Mona Moray, Ferdi Hoffman, Grace Valentine, Alan Handley, Meg Mundy. P: Sam H. Harris. SD: Donald Oenslager.

Face of a Hero (10/20/60, O'Neill, 36)

An idealistic lawyer (Jack Lemmon) in a corrupt southern community becomes so hypnotized by his role as "town hero" that he prosecutes a vicious young idler (George Grizzard) for a crime he knows he did not commit. Murky, ambiguous melodrama with a fine cast: C: James Donald, Albert Dekker, Frank Conroy, Betsy Blair, Edward Asner, Sandy Dennis, Russell Collins, Roy Poole, Ellen Holly, Kip McArdle, Lynn Hamilton, Edwin Sherin. Staged by film director Alexander Mackendrick *(The Man in the White Suit, Sweet Smell of Success*, etc.). A: Robert L. Joseph b/o the novel by Pierre Boulle. P: Lester Osterman. SD: Ben Edwards. CD: Ann Roth.

Fair and Warmer (11/6/15, Eltinge, 377)

Inconsequential, lighter-than-air farcical comedy by Avery Hopwood, author of *The Gold Diggers* (1919), *The Bat* (1920), and similar trivial but highly successful theatrical fare. C: Madge Kennedy, Ralph Morgan, Janet Beecher, Hamilton Revelle. P: Selwyn and Company. D: Robert Milton.

Fair Game (11/2/57, Longacre, 217)

Breezy comedy about the efforts of an attractive model to fend off the improper advances of various garment center wolves. Ellen Burstyn (billed as Ellen McRae) made her Broadway debut as the decorative dress model, while Sam Levene garnered most of the evening's laughs as a lecherous Seventh Avenue garment manufacturer. C: Robert Webber, Hugh Reilly, Sally Gracie. A: Sam Locke. P: Joseph M. Hyman. D: Paul Roberts. SD: Frederick Fox.

Fair Game for Lovers (2/10/64, Cort, 8)

Comedy about an antifeminist widower and his nubile daughter. ". . . stubbornly lacking in hilarity" *(Post)*. C: Leo Genn, Forrest Tucker, Alan Alda, Maggie Hayes, Pegeen Lawrence. A: Richard Dougherty. P: Herbert Swope, Jr. i.a.w. Bufman and Seiden. D: Paul Shyre. CD/SD: Ralph Alswang.

Faith Healer, The (1/19/10, Savoy, 6)

A religious prophet wanders into a midwestern community, but loses his "divine healing mission" when he succumbs to love. Intriguing drama by William Vaughn Moody, author of *The Great Divide* (1906). C: Henry Miller, Laura Hope Crews, Jessie Bonstelle, Robert McWade. P/D: Henry Miller.

Faithfully Yours (10/18/51, Coronet, 68)

Deciding that her husband's fidelity is abnormal, an empty-headed wife (Ann Sothern) tries to persuade her spouse (Robert Cummings) to be unfaithful. "A singularly witless and out-of-date farce" (*Herald Tribune*). A: L. Bush-Fekete and Mary Helen Fay b/o a play by Jean Bernard-Luc. P: Richard W. Krakeur. D: Richard Whorf. CD: Adrian. SD: Paul Morrison.

Fall and Rise of Susan Lenox (6/9/20, 44th Street, 26)

An unhappy heroine (Alma Tell) of many amours finally finds true love. Turgid claptrap. A: George V. Hobart, based on a novel by David Graham Phillips. P: Messrs. Shubert.
SV: MGM, 1931, *Susan Lenox, Her Fall and Rise*, Greta Garbo, Clark Gable, Jean Hersholt, Alan Hale, John Miljan.

Fall Guy, The (3/10/25, Eltinge, 177)

A gullible young man (Ernest Truex) becomes the patsy for a gang of bootleggers and dope pushers. This popular comedy by James Gleason and George Abbott marked Mr. Abbott's debut as a Broadway director. P: Messrs. Shubert i.a.w. G. B. McLellan.
SV: RKO, 1930, Jack Mulhall, Ned Sparks, Mae Clarke.

Fall of Eve, The (8/31/25, Booth, 48)

A young wife (Ruth Gordon) almost loses her husband because of her suspicious nature. Mild comedy by John Emerson (P/D) and Anita Loos. C: Reginald Mason, Cora Witherspoon.
SV: Col, 1929, Patsy Ruth Miller, Ford Sterling.

False Dreams, Farewell (1/15/34, Little, 25)

Disaster at sea as an ocean liner sinks on her maiden voyage. Muddled, multi-scened melodrama with a large cast. C: Clarence Derwent, Clyde Fillmore, Frieda Inescort, Glenn Anders, Claudia Morgan, Blaine Cordner, Millard Mitchell, Harry Green, Charles Quigley, Royal Dana, Lora Baxter. A: Hugh Stange. P/D: Frank Merlin.

Fame (11/18/74, John Golden, 1)

Weak comedy about a sexy actress who seems to be based on the character of the late Marilyn Monroe. Originally presented off-off-Broadway. ". . . limp rag of a comedy . . . . It withered a long, slow death" (Clive Barnes, *New York Times*). A: Anthony J. Ingrassia. C: Ellen Barber, Ruth Hornish, Jeremy Stevens, Christine Lavren, Lawrie Driscoll, Bibi Besch, Robert Miano, Nancy Reardon. D: Anthony J. Ingrassia. P: James J. C. Andrews and Tony Zanetta for Mainman. SD: Douglas W. Schmidt.

Family, The (3/30/43, Windsor, 7)

Unwieldy adaptation of Nina Federova's best-selling novel dealing with a family of exiled White Russians leading a "valiant but threadbare existence" in Tientsin, China, prior to the Japanese invasion of 1937. "An uneven and curiously jumbled play . . ." (*Sun*). C: Lucile Watson, Carol Goodner, Evelyn Varden, Nicholas (Richard) Conte, Elisabeth Fraser, Arnold Korff, Boris Tumarin. A: Victor Wolfson. P: Oscar Serlin. D: Bretaigne Windust. SD: Boris Aronson.

Family Affair, A (11/27/46, Playhouse, 6)

When an aspiring playwright writes a comedy about his family, his parents start behaving like the characters in his play. ". . . inoffensive and routine" (*News*). C: John Williams, Ann Mason, Joel Marston. A: Henry R. Misrock. P: Long and Hart. D: Alexander Kirkland.

Family Affairs (12/10/29, Maxine Elliott's, 7)

Neglected wife (Billie Burke) schemes to win back her straying husband. Mediocre 20's comedy. A: Earle Crooker and Lowell Brentano. P: Arthur Hopkins (D) and L. Lawrence Weber.

Family Cupboard, The (8/21/13, Playhouse, 140)

When a henpecked husband decides to return to his wife, his vindictive mistress vows to get even by seducing his son. "Melodramatic excesses . . . punctuated by a few really tense scenes [and] lightened by a considerable amount of humor in character and lines" (*New York Times*). C: William Morris, Alice Brady, Irene Fenwick, Olive Harper Thorne, Forrest Winant, Franklyn Ardell. A: Owen Davis. P: William A. Brady. D: John Cromwell.

Family Portrait (3/8/39, Morosco, 111)

The life of Jesus as seen through the eyes of his family. Christ does not appear in the play, but his character is shown through the reactions of his disbelieving brothers and sisters. Only Mary (Judith Anderson) never loses faith in her son. "One of the most moving expressions of truth and beauty I have ever seen in the theatre . . ." (*World-Telegram*). C: Evelyn Varden, Margaret Webster (D), Philip Coolidge, Tom Ewell. A: Lenore Coffee and William Joyce Cowen. P: Cheryl Crawford i.a.w. Tuttle and Skinner. CD/SD: Harry Horner. M: Lehman Engel.

Family Upstairs, The (8/17/25, Gaiety, 72)

Interfering mother keeps ruining her daughter's marital chances. Formula domestic comedy. C: Clare Woodbury, Ruth Nugent, Walter Wilson, Sidney Salkow. A: Harry Delf. P: Sam H. Harris i.a.w. Lewis and Gordon. D: Sam Forrest.

SV: Fox, 1930, *Harmony at Home*, Marguerite Churchill, Rex Bell; 1939, *Stop, Look and Love*, William Frawley, Minna Gombell, Jean Rogers.

Family Way, The (1/13/65, Lyceum, 5)

Second-rate comedy about a widowed actress (Collin Wilcox) who becomes innocently involved with several men, ends by marrying her agent (Jack Kelly). A: Ben Starr. P: Leonard Sillman, Sandy Farber, Eddie White i.a.w. Ann Rork. D: Michael Gordon. SD: Ben Edwards.

Famous Mrs. Fair, The (12/22/19, Henry Miller, 343)

An ambitious feminist (Blanche Bates) returns after four years of war work overseas to find her rebellious daughter (Margalo Gillmore) involved with a fortune hunter, and her husband (Henry Miller) being consoled by the lady next door. Fame, fortune, and a career are all very well, she concludes, but a woman's place is in the home. This play by James Forbes was one of the leading successes of 1919. ". . . hailed on all sides as practically the ultimate achievement in American comedy [but] it is almost impossible to discern just what all the raving is about" (Dorothy Parker, *Vanity Fair*). P: A. L. Erlanger.

Fancy Meeting You Again (1/14/52, Royale, 8)

Comedy about reincarnation in which a determined lass (Leueen MacGrath) pursues the same man (Walter Matthau) for five thousand years. In flashbacks we see the object of her affections as a stone age caveman, an Egyptian playboy, and a Roman shepherd. In his present incarnation (as an acidulous art critic), the reluctant hero finally offers marriage and a happy ending for the play. Written by George S. Kaufman (D) and Leueen MacGrath (Mrs. Kaufman), *Fancy Meeting You Again* had several very funny lines and situations, but not enough of them. It closed after one week. C: Glenn Langan, Ruth McDevitt, Margaret Hamilton, Reynolds Evans, Earl Jones. P: Cowles and Segal. SD: Albert Johnson.

Fanny (9/21/26, Lyceum, 63)

Fanny Brice braved Broadway in this heavy-breathing, unintentionally funny melodrama called, with singular lack of imagination, *Fanny*. The Willard Mack opus had been trumpeted in the press as "a semi-serious play containing emotional possibilities for Miss Brice" but, instead, turned out to be a clichéd horse-opera of gold on the ranch and dirty work in the bunkhouse. Warren William was cast as the good guy, John Cromwell was the bad guy, and Fanny was a tender-hearted Miss Fixit who vamps the villain and saves the day. "Oy, it was just a terrible play," said Miss Brice. When the show closed after a brief eight-week run, Fanny went back to vaudeville and never again ventured into drama. P/D: David Belasco.

Fanshastics (1/16/24, Henry Miller, 96)

Environment-versus-heredity comedy contrasting the lives of two sisters (Grace George and Laura Hope Crews) separated at birth. One grows up in the lap of luxury, the other is raised in Shantytown poverty. Their paths cross as adults but they never discover their true relationship. Implausible (and imprudently titled) opus; later rechristened *Merry Wives of Gotham*. C: Berton Churchill, Arthur Sinclair, Mary Ellis. A: Laurence Eyre. P/D: Henry Miller.

Far Country, A (4/4/61, Music Box, 271)

Dramatization of one of the earliest and most famous recorded cases of Sigmund Freud (Steven Hill). This psychological case history traced the halting but ultimately successful efforts of the young Viennese neurologist to cure a pain-ridden paralytic (Kim Stanley) by forcing her to face suppressed memories of guilt hidden in her unconscious mind. A compelling play with a bravura performance by Miss Stanley; written by Henry Denker, author of *Time Limit!* (1956), *A Case of Libel* (1963), etc. C: Sam Wanamaker, Salome Jens, Lili Darvas, Patrick O'Neal. P: Roger L. Stevens and Joel Schenker i.a.w. Lyn Austin. D: Alfred Ryder. SD: Donald Oenslager.

Farewell Summer (3/29/37, Fulton, 8)

Dismal comedy-drama about a biology student (Lois Wilson) who falls in love with her teacher (Walter Gilbert). "*Farewell Summer . . . farewell!*" (*New York Times*). A: North Bigbee and Walter Holbrook. P: Walter Franklin. D: B. F. Kamsler.

Farewell to Arms, A (9/22/30, National, 24)

Static adaptation of the Hemingway novel dealing with the ill-fated romance of an American ambulance driver and an English nurse in Italy during World War I. C: Glenn Anders, Elissa Landi, Crane Wilbur, Jack La Rue, Harold Huber. A: Laurence Stallings. P: A. H. Woods. D: Rouben Mamoulian.

SV: Par, 1932, Gary Cooper, Helen Hayes, Adolphe Menjou; WB, 1951, *Force of Arms*, William Holden, Nancy Olson, Frank Lovejoy; Fox, 1957, Rock Hudson, Jennifer Jones, Vittorio de Sica, Mercedes McCambridge, Elaine Stritch, Alberto Sordi, Oscar Homolka, Kurt Kasznar.

Farmer Takes a Wife, The (10/30/34, 46th Street, 104)

Ex-chorus boy Henry Fonda *(New Faces of 1934)* in the role that made him a star. A sentimental, occasionally salty comedy of Erie Canal life in the 1800's, *The Farmer Takes a Wife* dealt with the love affair between a virtuous farm boy (Fonda) and a daughter (June Walker) of riverboat folk, or "canawlers" as they were then called. Their romance is briefly threatened by the girl's mean-tempered former boyfriend, but all ends happily, of course, in this leisurely period comedy. "Henry Fonda, who has his first big opportunity here, gives a manly, modest performance in a style of captivating simplicity" *(New York Times)*. C: Herb Williams, Margaret Hamilton, Gibbs Penrose, Robert Ross, Kate Mayhew, Joseph Sweeney. A: Frank B. Elser and Marc Connelly (D) b/o the novel *Rome Haul* by Walter D. Edmonds. P: Max Gordon. SD: Donald Oenslager.

SV: Fox, 1935, Henry Fonda, Janet Gaynor, Charles Bickford, Slim Summerville, Andy Devine, Margaret Hamilton, Jane Withers, Siegfried Rumann, John Qualen; 1953, Betty Grable, Dale Robertson, Thelma Ritter, John Carroll, Eddie Foy, Jr.

Fast Life (9/26/28, Ambassador, 20)

To save the life of his best friend, the governor's son confesses to a murder. Trite 20's melodrama. C: Chester Morris, Claudette Colbert, Crane Wilbur, Donald Dillaway, Donald McClelland. A: Samuel Shipman and John B. Hymer. P: A. H. Woods. D: A. H. Van Buren.

SV: WB, 1929, Douglas Fairbanks, Jr., Loretta Young, Chester Morris.

Fatal Weakness, The (11/19/46, Royale, 119)

Learning of her husband's infidelity, an incurably romantic matron (Ina Claire) gives him his freedom and, in the final scene, sets out to attend his wedding to the other woman. "A comedy of very mixed values . . ." *(New York Times)*. C: Howard St. John, Margaret Douglass, Mary Gildea. A/D: George Kelly. P: The Theatre Guild. CD: Bianca Stroock. SD: Donald Oenslager.

Father and the Boys (3/2/08, Empire, 88)

Businessman (William H. Crane) sets out to prove to his sons that he can be as "modern" in his thinking as they. Amiable George Ade comedy. P: Charles Frohman. D: William Seymour.

SV: Fox, 1931, *Young as You Feel*, Will Rogers, Fifi D'Orsay.

Father Uxbridge Wants To Marry (10/28/67, American Place, 11)

Provocative O/B allegorical drama dealing with the musings and memories of an elevator operator whose job will soon be terminated through automation. C: Gene Roche, Ken Kercheval, John Coe, Olympia Dukakis, Carol Carpenter. A: Frank Gagliano. P: American Place Theater. D: Melvin Bernhardt.

Father's Day (3/16/71, John Golden, 1)

Wonderfully funny comedy of three divorcées, and their feelings about themselves, each other, and the married state. Friendly neighbors in a Manhattan highrise, they've invited their ex-husbands for drinks on Father's Day. As the play weaves its frequently hilarious course, the interaction of the characters reveals absorbing and enlightening truths about the relationship of each couple. The three women are interestingly contrasted: a brittle, cynical actress with an acid wit and nasty mouth, a ladylike liberal who seems to float above the fray, and a vulnerable young innocent. The ladies have the stage to themselves through Act I, providing as sustained an exercise in virtuoso bitch-wit as has been heard since Clare Luce's *The Women*. When the men appear in Act II, a leavening sobriety is added to the frothy amusement and the thoughtful aspects of *Father's Day* come to the fore. There is no conventional happy ending. *Father's Day* is unsentimental and very funny. Though subsequent productions were successful in Washington, D.C., and San Francisco, the play was a one-performance flop in New York. On reading Clive Barnes' uncompromisingly negative review in the *New York Times* the producers immediately closed down. The play had no chance to find its audience. ". . . genuinely amusing, written with sharp wit as well as grace" (Richard Watts, *New York Post*). " . . . takes a strong hold . . . you stay hooked" (Douglas Watt, *New York Daily News*). A: Oliver Hailey. C: Brenda Vaccaro, Marian Seldes, Jennifer Salt, Ken Kercheval, Donald Moffat, Biff McGuire. D: Donald Moffat. P: Joseph Kipness and Lawrence Kasha. SD: Jo Mielziner. CD: Ann Roth.

Faun, The (1/16/11, Daly's, 48)

Mild satirical fantasy about a mythical creature (William Faversham) who invades the home of a sedate country squire. A: Edward Knoblock. P/D: Faversham.

Fear Market, The (1/26/16, Booth, 118)

Plucky heroine sets out to break up a society blackmail racket only to find that her father is at the head of it. Mediocre melodrama by Amelie Rives (Princess Troubetzkoy). C: Lucile Watson, Merle Maddern, Sydney Shields, Edmund Breese, Edwin Nicander. P: Harrison Grey Fiske (D) and George Mooser.

Feathers in a Gale (12/21/43, Music Box, 7)

This period comedy dealt with the plight of three impecunious New England widows, about to be sold as domestics, and of their efforts to snare husbands before it is too late. "*Feathers in a Gale* is very windy stuff . . . quaint but soporific" *(Post)*. C: Peggy Conklin, Norman McKay, Paula Trueman, Harry Ellerbe. A: Pauline Jamerson and Reginald Lawrence. P: Arthur Hopkins (D) and Martin Burton. CD: Aline Bernstein. SD: Raymond Sovey.

Note: In Cape Cod, in the early nineteenth century, it was the custom to auction off indigent women to the highest bidders. (Three dollars was considered a fair price.)

Federal Theatre Project

Founded in 1935 to help combat unemployment in the performing arts, the W. P. A. Federal Theatre Project was America's only attempt to set up a low-priced, nationally sponsored theatre. Under the overall direction of Hallie Flanagan, director of drama at Vassar College, theatre units were formed throughout the country. Fifteen thousand men and women were employed at an average wage of twenty dollars a week. Thousands of productions—classics, variety shows, experimental works—were mounted with varying degrees of success. Notable were such Orson Welles-John Houseman productions as: *Dr. Faustus,* the Negro *Macbeth,* and Marc Blitzstein's musical *The Cradle Will Rock.* Other Federal Theatre Project successes included T. S. Eliot's *Murder in the Cathedral, The Swing Mikado,* and the children's play *Pinocchio.* Outstanding among the new plays presented were *Prologue to Glory* by E. P. Conkle, dealing with Lincoln's early years; *It Can't Happen Here* by Sinclair Lewis and John C. Moffitt, dealing with fascism in America, and produced simultaneously in twenty-one theatres across the country; and *One-Third of a Nation* by Arthur Arent, dealing with substandard housing conditions in New York. This last-named play was an example of Living Newspaper technique. Pioneered by the Federal Theatre, Living Newspaper presentations dramatized a variety of contemporary social and economic problems in quasi-documentary fashion. After four years of low-cost entertainment, seen by thirty million people in two hundred theatres and auditoriums across the nation, the Federal Theatre Project was accused of communist infiltration and was killed by an act of Congress in mid-1939.

Festival (1/18/55, Longacre, 23)

A celebrated pianist is led to believe that a child prodigy is his illegitimate son. ". . . more labored than mirthful . . . more frenetic than festive" *(New York Times)*. C: Paul Henreid, Betty Field, Pat Hingle, Luba Malina, George Voskovec. A: Sam and Bella Spewack. P: Walter Fried i.a.w. Felix Brentano. D: Albert Marre.

Field God, The (4/21/27, Greenwich Village, 45)

Paul Green's play about the tribulations of a poor white farmer and his invalid wife. ". . . sheer excess of invention . . . obviously overwritten" *(New York Times)*. Presented O/B by Edwin Wolfe (P/D). C: Fritz Leiber, Adelaide Fitz-Allen, Ruth Mason.

Fields Beyond, The (3/6/36, Mansfield, 3)

College professor is falsely accused of homosexuality. Bold in subject matter (for 1936), but sketchily developed domestic drama. C: Reed Brown, Jr., Merle Maddern, Helen Claire. A: Francis Bosworth. P: Raymond Hewitt. D: Milton Smith.

Fiesta (9/17/29, Garrick, 39)

Two Mexican brothers (Jack La Rue and Carl Benton Reid) almost kill each other for love of a fifteen-year-old girl (Virginia Venable). To radical playwright Michael Gold, the girl symbolized the spirit of Mexico "torn asunder by warring factions." Plodding O/B drama, badly miscast. P: Experimental Theatre, Inc. D: James Light.

Fifth Column, The (3/6/40, Alvin, 87)

Written under fire in shell-wracked Madrid, Ernest Hemingway's saga of the Spanish civil war reached Broadway after innumerable delays, revisions, and tryout headaches. As an American newspaperman plunged into a web of espionage, Franchot Tone contributed the most striking performance of his career. Lee J. Cobb as an anti-fascist German and Lenore Ulric as a sultry Moorish trollop were also a great help, as was Lee Strasberg's forceful direction and Howard Bay's impressive setting of Madrid's battered, war-torn Hotel Florida. "Mr. Hemingway's initial fling at the stage is a most auspicious one" *(World-Telegram)*. C: Katherine Locke, Arnold Moss. P: The Theatre Guild (with substantial backing from Billy Rose).

Note: Long before the New York premiere of his first and only play, Hemingway washed his hands of the entire project and retired to his home in Cuba. Benjamin Glazer was called in, with Hemingway's blessing, to write additional dialogue and tighten the script.

Fifth Season, The (1/23/53, Cort, 654)

Yiddish theatre veteran Menasha Skulnik made his Broadway debut in this farce about the financial and romantic problems of two garment-trade partners. Critics applauded Skulnik's "marvelously endearing comedic talents," but dubbed his vehicle "shoddy merchandise." Despite generally negative reviews, *The Fifth Season* prospered on Broadway for more than a year and a half. C: Richard Whorf, Phyllis Hill, Nita Talbot, Lois Wheeler, Dick Kallman, A: Sylvia Regan. P: George Kondolf. D: Gregory Ratoff.

Fighting Hope, The (9/22/08, Stuyvesant, 231)

A devoted wife (Blanche Bates) manages to destroy evidence of her embezzler-husband's guilt, then suddenly becomes aware that he is indeed guilty as charged. "A false and clumsy and woefully artificial play" (Walter Prichard Eaton, *Sun*). This melodrama by William J. Hurlbut had a profitable run on Broadway due to the popularity of Miss Bates, the play's star. P/D: David Belasco.

Finishing Touches (2/8/73, Plymouth, 164)

In *Finishing Touches*, author Jean Kerr *(Mary, Mary, Poor Richard)* is warmly engaging, but her comedic vision seems oddly dated, more attuned to the sexually conventional '50's than the liberated '70's. Here she poses the problems of a college professor with a middle-aged, roving eye, and his loyal wife who briefly considers retaliation with her husband's best friend. As wholesomely played by Robert Lansing and Barbara Bel Geddes, it's a certainty that nothing shocking will come of their temptations. A secondary plot line concerns the eldest of the couple's three sons, a Harvard senior who brings his mistress home for a visit. Predictably dismayed, the parents decree separate bedrooms for the young pair. Throughout, everyone is glibly witty and behaves in that civilized manner that is a hallmark of light comedy. All ends happily in an agreeable glow of triumphant middle-class virtue. ". . . mildly entertaining comedy with occasional bright lines" (Douglas Watt, *New York Daily News*). "It is funny, it is wise, and it is believable in characterizations and story" (Richard Watts, *New York Post*). A: Jean Kerr. C: Barbara Bel Geddes, Robert Lansing, Gene Rupert, James Woods, Pamela Bellwood, Scott Firestone, Oliver Conant, Denise Galik. D: Joseph Anthony. SD: Ben Edwards. P: Robert Whitehead and Roger L. Stevens.

Fire! (1/28/69, Longacre, 6)

Complex allegorical drama concerned with "the devolution of humanity." Promethean performance in the leading role by Rene Auberjonois, but the play was too "belligerently obscure" *(Broadway Reporter)* to survive for long on the main stem. A: John Roc. P: David Black i.a.w. Jonathan Burrows. D: Charles Moore.

Firebrand, The (10/15/24, Morosco, 287)

Deft, stylish boudoir comedy dealing with the amours of that swashbuckling sculptor and Renaissance rogue, Benvenuto Cellini (Joseph Schildkraut). Cellini's infatuation for a regal duchess (Nana Bryant) is complicated by the antics of her nitwit husband the duke (Frank Morgan) who, in turn, much desires the favors of the lovely but naïve Angela (Florence Mason). After any number of comic machinations and misunderstandings, Angela returns to her duke and Cellini to his duchess. C: Edward G. Robinson, Allyn Joslyn, Hortense Alden. A: Edwin Justus Mayer. P: Schwab, Liveright & Mandel.
Musicalized by Kurt Weill and Ira Gershwin as *The Firebrand of Florence* (1945) with Earl Wrightson, Lotte Lenya, Melville Cooper, Beverly Tyler.
SV: UA, 1934, *The Affairs of Cellini*, Fredric March, Constance Bennett, Frank Morgan, Fay Wray, Louis Calhern (directed by Gregory La Cava from a screenplay by Bess Meredyth).

First American Dictator (3/14/39, Bayes, 9)

The rise and fall of Louisiana's Governor Huey P. Long. Poorly written, produced and directed, with a nondescript cast. A: Nathan Sherman and Jacob Weiser. P: George Lewis. D: Humphrey Davis.

First Apple, The (12/27/33, Booth, 52)

Girl, living with her parents in New Jersey, has trouble deciding between two suitors. Modest little comedy by screenwriter Lynn Starling (*Private Worlds, Piccadilly Jim*, etc.). C: Irene

Purcell, Conrad Nagel, Albert Dekker, Spring Byington, Nana Bryant. P: Lee Shubert. D: Bela Blau.

First Crocus, The (1/2/42, Longacre, 5)

Uneventful comedy-drama about a Minnesota farm family ruled by an overbearing mother. C: Martha Hedman, Edwin Philips, Hugo Haas, Jocelyn Brando. A: Arnold Sundgaard. P: T. Edward Hambleton. D: Halsted Welles.

First Fifty Years, The (3/13/22, Princess, 48)

A half-century of married life viewed during significant wedding anniversary milestones. Tedious two-character play. C: Tom Powers, Clare Eames. A: Henry Myers. P: Lorenz Hart and Irving Strouse.

First Flight (9/17/25, Plymouth, 11)

Soporific costume drama by Maxwell Anderson and Laurence Stallings dealing with a romantic episode in the life of young Captain Andrew Jackson. C: Rudolph Cameron, Helen Chandler, Blaine Cordner. P/D: Arthur Hopkins.

First Is Last (9/17/19, Maxine Elliott's, 62)

A reunion of college chums (among them Richard Dix, Edward G. Robinson, Hassard Short) reveals that all but one—the class poet—are utter failures. Interesting but tame comedy-drama. C: Phoebe Foster, Robert Strange, Kathleen Comegys. A: Samuel Shipman and Percival Wilde. P/D: William Harris, Jr.

First Lady (11/26/35, Music Box, 244)

Diverting comedy by Katharine Dayton and George S. Kaufman (D) dealing with the rivalry between two Washington hostesses (Jane Cowl and Lily Cahill), each of whom would like to reside in the White House. "Although the story is improbable it is not impossible, for Washington is the capital of improbability" (*New York Times*). During the run of *First Lady,* George S. Kaufman went to Florida on a vacation. When he returned, he found that Jane Cowl, a playwright herself, had changed a number of his lines. He promptly sent her a wire saying, "Your performance is better than ever and improving daily. Sorry I can't say the same for your lines." C: Stanley Ridges, Judson Laire, Thomas Findlay, Don Beddoe. P: Sam H. Harris. SD: Donald Oenslager.

R: (5/28/52, City Center, 16). C: Helen Gahagan, Edna Best, Peggy Ann Garner, Ona Munson, Scott McKay, Ruth McDevitt, Addison Richards, Frederic Tozere. D: David Alexander.

SV: WB, 1937, Kay Francis, Verree Teasdale, Preston Foster, Walter Connolly, Anita Louise, Victor Jory, Marjorie Rambeau, Louise Fazenda, Sara Haden, Harry Davenport, Grant Mitchell, Gregory Gaye.

First Legion, The (10/1/34, 46th Street, 112)

A priest's faith is renewed when a crippled boy is cured of infantile paralysis thanks to his unquestioning belief in an alleged miracle. "Stageworthy drama.... The theme is treated with appealing realism and candor" (*The Stage*). *The First Legion* was set in a Jesuit seminary and enacted by an all-male cast. Though it had only a moderate Broadway run, the play was a great success on tour and subsequently throughout Europe. C: Bert Lytell, Charles Coburn, Frankie Thomas, Whitford Kane, William Ingersoll, John Litel, Pedro de Cordoba, Thomas Findlay, Tom Ewell. A: Emmet Lavery. P: Bert Lytell and Phil Green. D: Anthony Brown.

SV: UA, 1951, Charles Boyer, William Demarest, Lyle Bettger.

First Love (12/25/61, Morosco, 24)

Episodic comedy-drama chronicling the lifelong devotion between French author-diplomat Romain Gary and his fanatically devoted mother. Hugh O'Brian (deb.) played the adult Romain in ingratiating fashion, and Lili Darvas (replacing Elisabeth Bergner shortly before the Broadway premiere) gave an arresting performance as the gallant, indomitable mother. ". . . wonderfully well-mounted and performed, but regrettably unimpressive in dramatic fulfillment" (*Journal-American*). A: Samuel Taylor b/o the memoir *Promise at Dawn* by Romain Gary. P: Roger Stevens and Frederick Brisson i.a.w. Mr. Taylor. D: Alfred Lunt. CD: Theoni V. Aldredge. SD: Donald Oenslager.

SV: Embassy, 1971, *Promise at Dawn*, Melina Mercouri, Assaf Dayan, Fernand Gravet (written and directed by Jules Dassin).

First Man, The (3/4/22, Neighborhood Playhouse, 27)

Unsuccessful Eugene O'Neill drama dealing with the eternal war between the sexes. An anthropologist (Augustin Duncan) feels betrayed when his wife (Margaret Mower) becomes pregnant. Both had forsworn children to lead a life of total dedication to each other. The wife dies in agonizing childbirth; the father finally makes peace with his motherless son. "Prolix, circuitously reiterative and clumsy" (Alexander Woollcott, *New York Times*). P/D: Augustin Duncan.

First Million, The (4/28/43, Ritz, 5)

Raffish family of Ozark bank robbers scheme to get their first million before retiring. ". . . crude and feeble hillbilly comedy . . . a hopeless little number" (*Sun*). Produced (at a cost of twenty thousand dollars) by an eighteen-year-old actor named Jimmy Elliott; closed after five performances. C: Dorrit Kelton, Harlan Briggs, Russell Collins, Wendell Corey. A: Irving Elman. D: John Kennedy.

First Mortgage (10/10/29, Broadhurst, 4)

Unhappy suburbanite tries to escape the deadly routine of his life by having an affair with a neighbor. Glum 20's drama by Louis Weitzenkorn, author of *Five Star Final* (1930). C: Walter Abel, Leona Maricle, Sara Haden. P: Farnsworth and Hayman. D: Jose Ruben.

First One Asleep, Whistle (2/26/66, Belasco, 1)

Problems of an unwed mother and her preteenage daughter. Unsuccessful comedy-drama by Oliver Hailey, author of the much underrated *Father's Day* (1971), which likewise closed after a single Broadway performance. C: Salome Jens, Frank Converse. P: Edgar and Bruce Lansbury. D: John Berry.

First Stop to Heaven (1/5/41, Windsor, 8)

Rooming house manager tries to save her building from being torn down. "Aimless, plotless, witless" (*News*). C: Alison Skipworth, Taylor Holmes, James Bell, Eduard Franz. A: Norman Rosten. P: Margaret Hewes. D: Robert Henderson.

First Year, The (10/20/20, Little, 725)

Husband (Frank Craven) and small-town wife (Roberta Arnold) struggle to adjust to the first year of married life. Amusing, highly successful domestic comedy by Frank Craven. P: John Golden. D: Winchell Smith.

SV: Fox, 1932, Janet Gaynor, Charles Farrell.

Five Alarm Waltz (3/13/41, Playhouse, 4)

All about what might have happened had William Saroyan married Clare Boothe Luce. Elia Kazan played the cocky Saroyanesque hero with style and vigor, but the Lucille S. Prumbs comedy was "too often merely noisy and tiresome.... I await with interest Mr. Saroyan's play about Miss Prumbs" (*PM*). C: Louise Platt, Howard Freeman, Roman Bohnen, Ann Thomas. P: Everett Wile. D: Robert Lewis.

Five Star Final (12/30/30, Cort, 176)

Absorbing melodrama about a ruthless newspaper publisher whose probing of a long-forgotten scandal drives two people to suicide. This stinging attack on muckraking journalism was written by Louis Weitzenkorn, editor of the *Graphic*, a leading New York tabloid of the time. The play was skillfully staged by Worthington Miner in a multiple three-part set. C: Arthur Byron, Berton Churchill, Allen Jenkins, Frances Fuller, Merle Maddern, King Calder. P: A. H. Woods.

SV: WB, 1931, Edward G. Robinson, H. B. Warner, Marian Marsh, George E. Stone, Frances Starr, Boris Karloff, Ona Munson, Aline MacMahon, Gladys Lloyd; 1936, *Two Against the World*, Humphrey Bogart, Beverly Roberts, Henry O'Neill, Claire Dodd.

Flag is Born, A (9/5/46, Alvin, 120)

Tevya (Paul Muni), a wandering Jew; Zelda (Celia Adler), his dying wife; and David (Marlon Brando), an embittered young refugee, seek rest in a graveyard on their way to the Holy Land. Visions of the great biblical heroes from their racial past appear to the three homeless travelers. As the play ends, the old couple die, but the young Jew is on his way to the Promised Land to help found the new state of Israel. This well-intended but soporific pageant, written by Ben Hecht, was put on by the American League for a Free Palestine to raise money for the transportation of homeless European Jews to Israel. "The cause of the Jews ... deserves a finer script ..." (*New York Times*). "The production as a whole is slipshod and rather wearisome" (*Herald Tribune*). C: Quentin Reynolds (narrator), John Baragrey, Jonathan Harris, Steve Hill, Mario Berini, Tom Emlyn Williams. M: Kurt Weill.

Note: Despite mixed reviews, *A Flag is Born* netted the Irgun nearly a million dollars. When Paul Muni left the cast, Luther Adler (D) took over the chief role. Because he believed in the play, Marlon Brando worked at a salary of thirty dollars a week. The following year (1947) Brando made theatre history with his dynamic portrayal of Stanley Kowalski in Tennessee Williams' *A Streetcar Named Desire*.

Flame, The (9/4/16, Lyric, 96)

Stranded Americans in the Yucatan jungles witness native rites, ritualistic sacrifice, etc. Ridiculous mishmash. C: William Courtleigh, Violet Heming, Peggy O'Neil. A/P/D: Richard Walton Tully.

Flamingo Road (3/19/46, Belasco, 7)

Tough carnival dancer tangles with corrupt Florida sheriff. "A tawdry, ungainly and cluttered melodrama ... inexpert and meretricious ..." (*Sun*). C: Francis J. ("Happy") Felton, Judith Parrish, Will Geer, Philip Bourneuf, Paul Ford. A: Robert and Sally Wilder. P: Rowland Stebbins. D: Jose Ruben.

SV: WB, 1949, Joan Crawford, Sydney Greenstreet, Zachary Scott, Gladys George, David Brian, Fred Clark, Gertrude Michael, Alice White.

Fledgling (11/27/40, Hudson, 13)

Unrelievedly glum drama about a distraught daughter who kills her incurably ill mother and then proceeds to take her own life. "*Fledgling*, fly away from my door!" (*World Telegram*). C: Ralph Morgan, Tom Powers, Sylvia Weld, Norma Chambers, John Hoysradt, Lora Baxter, Walter Coy. A: Ad. by Philip Lewis and Eleanor Chilton from Miss

Chilton's novel, *Follow the Furies*. P: Otis Chatfield-Taylor. D: Heinrich Schnitzler. SD: Richard Whorf.

Flight (2/18/29, Longacre, 41)

Humdrum comedy-drama about a society girl (Miriam Hopkins) who has trouble deciding between a playboy and an aviator. A: Susan Meriwether and Victor Victor. P: Laura D. Wilck. D: Lemist Esler.

Flight Into Egypt (3/18/52, Music Box, 46)

Bedeviled by diplomatic red tape, a courageous family of Viennese refugees patiently wait in Cairo for visas to America. When the war-crippled father learns that his ill health bars the granting of the visa, he kills himself. ". . . effective enough theatrically . . . but rarely captures the deeply harrowing emotional power that its theme calls for" (*Post*). Written by Anglo-American (Budapest-born) author George Tabori; staged by Elia Kazan. C: Paul Lukas, Gusti Huber (deb.), Zero Mostel, Jo Van Fleet, Joseph Anthony, David Opatoshu, Paul Mann, Don Keefer, Fred Stewart. P: Irene Mayer Selznick. CD: Anna Hill Johnstone. SD: Jo Mielziner.

Flight to the West (12/30/40, Guild, 136)

Passengers of different nationalities and political beliefs are on a Pan-American clipper flying from wartime Lisbon to New York. This cross-section of humanity includes a young American Jew (Hugh Marlowe) and his gentile wife (Betty Field),* a Nazi agent (Paul Henreid), a German refugee (Eleonora Mendelssohn), an oil man (James Seeley) all in favor of appeasement, and the two chief crew members (Karl Malden and Kevin McCarthy). The climax of the play arrives when the Nazi spy is discovered and detained in Bermuda. Well-acted, ably directed by author Elmer Rice, and aided by an ingenious Jo Mielziner setting, this *Grand Hotel* of the airways had no trouble winning the approval of the press. "The most absorbing American drama of the season" (*New York Times*).

*Miss Field married Elmer Rice in 1942. They were divorced in 1955.

Flowering Peach, The (12/28/54, Belasco, 135)

The story of Noah and the ark retold in terms of a Jewish family comedy. Freely adapted from the Book of Genesis, and written in colloquial language, the simple tale tells how Noah persuades his squabbling family that God has given all of them a mission; how God helps them solve their problems in the face of catastrophic adversity; and how Noah finally learns the virtue of humility with the coming of the flood. The allegorical fable (with its obvious contemporary parallels) ends with the grounding of the ark, and the departure of the family to replenish and repopulate the earth. *The Flowering Peach*, Clifford Odets' (A/D) last Broadway play, received mostly lukewarm notices. However, Brooks Atkinson (*New York Times*) praised it as Odets' finest work for the theatre, while Eric Bentley (*New Republic*) called it: "The best American play I have ever reviewed in these columns." C: Menasha Skulnik, Berta Gersten, Mario Alcalde, Martin Ritt, Janice Rule, Barbara Baxley, Leon Janney. P: Robert Whitehead. SD: Mordecai Gorlik. Musicalized by Richard Rodgers, Martin Charnin and Peter Stone as *Two by Two* (1970) with Danny Kaye, Joan Copeland, Madeline Kahn.

Flowers of the Forest (4/8/35, Martin Beck, 40)

With the help of a young mystic (Burgess Meredith), an unhappy wife (Katharine Cornell) exorcises the ghost of her lover (Hugh Williams), a poet killed in the Great War. Lachrymose, disjointed antiwar drama by Anglo-American author John Van Druten. C: Margalo Gillmore, John Emery, Charles Waldron, Moffat Johnston, Brenda Forbes. P: Katharine Cornell. D: Guthrie McClintic. SD: Jo Mielziner.

Flowers of Virtue, The (2/5/42, Royale, 4)

Vacationing businessman foils fascist takeover in rural Mexico. Written and staged by Marc Connelly, author of *The Green Pastures* (1930). "A discursive little drama that [lacks] theatrical vitality" *(New York Times)*. C: Frank Craven, Vladimir Sokoloff, Isobel Elsom, Thomas Gomez, Kathryn Givney, Jess Barker, Leon Belasco. P: Cheryl Crawford. SD: Donald Oenslager.

Fly Away Home (1/15/35, 48th Street, 202)

Returning home after twelve years, an errant father (Thomas Mitchell) sets out to regain the love of his four children, and halt the impending remarriage of his ex-wife (Ann Mason) to an ultra-liberal professor (Albert Dekker). Montgomery Clift made his Broadway debut as Thomas Mitchell's son in this entertaining, well-acted comedy-drama. Also in the cast: Sheldon Leonard, Clare Woodbury. A: Dorothy Bennett and Irving White. P: Theron Bamberger. D: Thomas Mitchell.

SV: WB, 1939, *Daughters Courageous,* Claude Rains, John Garfield, Fay Bainter, Jeffrey Lynn, The Lane Sisters (Priscilla, Lola, Rosemary), Gale Page, Donald Crisp, May Robson, Frank McHugh; 1942, *Always in My Heart,* Walter Huston, Kay Francis, Gloria Warren, Sidney Blackmer.

Fly by Night (6/2/33, Belmont, 4)

Romance and murder in a traveling tent show. Grade B comedy-melodrama by screenwriter Richard Flournoy. C: Paul Guilfoyle, Alan Bunce, Ruth Nugent, Anthony Ross. P: Charles Sullivan. D: Murray Phillips.

Flying Gerardos, The (12/29/40, Playhouse, 24)

Comedy about a bookworm who becomes involved with a family of trapeze artists. ". . . hackneyed in theme and dull in execution" *(World-Telegram)*. C: Florence Reed, Harlan Briggs, William Wentworth, Lyle Bettger, Lois Hall. A: Kenyon Nicholson (D) and Charles Robinson. P: Edward Choate.

Fog (2/7/27, National, 97)

Sinister doings aboard a mystery yacht. Contrived melodrama by John Willard, author of *The Cat and the Canary* (1922). C: Robert Keith, Vivienne Osborne, Frank McHugh, Hugh O'Connell. P: Lorton Productions, Inc. D: Arthur Hurley.
SV: World-Wide, 1929, *Black Waters,* James Kirkwood, Mary Brian.

Fog-Bound (4/1/27, Belmont, 27)

Woman (Nance O'Neil) remains with cruel husband for the sake of her daughter. Dull dishpan drama by Hugh Stanislaus Stange. P: Richard Herndon. D: Alfred Hickman.

Fool, The (10/23/22, Times Square, 272)

"What would happen to a man in this day and age who tried to live as Christ did?" A young minister sets out to answer this question and, in so doing, loses everything but gains his immortal soul. Sincere but platitudinous dramatic sermon became a substantial success largely through the determined drum-beating efforts of its author, Channing Pollock. C: James Kirkwood, Lowell Sherman, Henry Stephenson. P/D: Frank Reicher.

Fool There Was, A (3/24/09, Liberty, 93)

The rapid descent and downfall of a

once-virtuous family man at the hands of an evil *femme fatale*. Heavy-breathing melodrama provided the basis for the silent film (Fox, 1914) that swept Theda Bara to stardom. C: Robert Hilliard, William Courtleigh, Katherine Kaelred. A: Porter Emerson Browne. P: Frederic Thompson. D: George Marion.

Foolish Notion (3/13/45, Martin Beck, 103)

On the eve of her remarriage, a tempestuous actress (Tallulah Bankhead) learns that her supposedly dead soldier-husband is very much alive and, in fact, is on his way home to her. The rest of the play is concerned with a series of dream scenes in which the actress, and various members of her household, each imagine how they will react to the situation about to confront them. ". . . a series of charades, occasionally effective, sometimes humorous, but on the whole empty and tediously repetitious" *(Post)*. "So smart, so brilliant, so clever that I haven't the slightest idea what it is about and I was bored stiff by it" *(World-Telegram)*. This fanciful comedy by Philip Barry was staged by John C. Wilson and produced by The Theatre Guild. C: Donald Cook, Henry Hull, Mildred Dunnock, Aubrey Mather, Barbara Kent, Joan Shepard, Maria Manton.* CD: Mainbocher. SD: Jo Mielziner.

---

*Daughter of Marlene Dietrich.

Foolscap (1/11/33, Times Square, 13)

George Bernard Shaw and Luigi Pirandello stage a play for their fellow inmates in a sanitarium for the well-to-do insane. Tedious theatre-of-the-absurd comedy. C: Frederic Worlock, Eduardo Ciannelli, Geoffrey Kerr (D), Henry O'Neill, Alan Marshal (deb.), Richard Whorf. A: Gennaro Curci and Eduardo Ciannelli. P: Sheppard and Buchanan.

Footloose (5/10/20, Greenwich Village, 162)

While in Rome, an unscrupulous social climber (Emily Stevens) blackmails her way into an elegant home, is finally routed only by threat of exposure of her shady past. Muddled and synthetic drama by Zoe Akins, adapted from a play by Merivale and Grove. C: Elisabeth Risdon, Norman Trevor, O. P. Heggie, Tallulah Bankhead. P: George C. Tyler. D: O. P. Heggie.

For All of Us (10/15/23, 49th Street, 216)

A ditch-digger (William Hodge) cures a banker's paralysis through Christian Science. Sincere but stultifying tract-drama. A/D: William Hodge. P: Lee Shubert.

For Heaven's Sake, Mother! (11/16/48, Belasco, 7)

Actress (Nancy Carroll) discovers she is to become a mother and a grandmother simultaneously. A friendly neighbor (Molly Picon) is on hand to give advice. Highlights: Miss Picon's interpolated vaudeville routines, Miss Carroll's rendition of "A Precious Little Thing Called Love" from her movie hit, *Shopworn Angel*. "A witless whimsy . . . a hopeless enterprise" *(Herald Tribune)*. A/D: Julie Berns. P: David Kay.

For Keeps (6/14/44, Henry Miller, 29)

F. Hugh Herbert comedy about a neglected child of divorced parents who pines to be sophisticated and pretends to be older than she is. ". . . superficial, artificial and meretricious" *(PM)*. The fifteen-year-old heroine of *For Keeps* was played by Patricia Kirkland, daughter of actress Nancy Carroll and playwright Jack Kirkland. Also in the cast: Frank Conroy, Julie Warren, Donald Murphy. P/D: Gilbert Miller.

For Love or Money (11/4/47, Henry Miller, 263)

Young girl sets her cap for dashing older man, and wins him. June Lockhart (deb.) won plaudits as the heroine of this formula comedy by F. Hugh Herbert. C: John Loder, Vicki Cummings. P: Barnard Straus. D: Harry Ellerbe.

SV: U, 1958, *This Happy Feeling*, Debbie Reynolds, Curt Jurgens, John Saxon, Alexis Smith, Mary Astor, Estelle Winwood, Troy Donahue, Gloria Holden, Joe Flynn.

For the Defense (12/19/19, Playhouse, 77)

A district attorney (Richard Bennett) defends his girlfriend (Winifred Lenihan) when she is charged with the murder of a nefarious hypnotist. Stagey, overwrought melodrama by Elmer Rice, once again using the flashback technique he pioneered in *On Trial* (1914), this time considerably less successfully. P: John D. Williams.

For Valor (11/18/35, Empire, 8)

Ex-soldier is mistaken for a great war hero. Frail 30's comedy. C: Frank Craven (D), June Walker. A: Martha Hedman and Henry Arthur House. P: George C. Tyler.

Foreign Affairs (4/13/32, Avon, 21)

Screen star Jean Arthur made her Broadway debut in this comedy about a naïve scullery maid who becomes romantically involved with a jaded diplomat (Henry Hull) in the Italian Tyrol. Miss Arthur's performance was applauded by the press, but *Foreign Affairs* was dismissed as "a fallen soufflé." C: Dorothy Gish, Osgood Perkins, J. Edward Bromberg, Carl Benton Reid. A: Paul Hervey Fox and George Tilton. P: B. Franklin Kamsler and Lester Fuller (D).

Forever After (9/9/18, Central, 312)

Poor boy (Conrad Nagel) loves rich girl (Alice Brady). He proves himself worthy of her when he is sent overseas, is wounded, and becomes something of a World War 1 hero. Syrupy, lachrymose play by Owen Davis. P: William A. Brady. D: Frank Hatch.

Forsaking All Others (3/1/33, Times Square, 101)

Tallulah Bankhead returned to Broadway (after ten years as the darling of the London stage) in this comedy about the tribulations of a bride jilted at the altar. In the end, the put-upon heroine realizes it is faithful friend Jefferson Tingle (Fred Keating) she really loved all the while. Arch Selwyn was billed as nominal producer of this rickety stage vehicle, but it was Miss Bankhead who backed the production to the tune of a forty thousand dollar loss. Three directors were called in to whip the show into shape during its pre-Broadway tryout; directorial credit was finally given to Thomas Mitchell. C: Ilka Chase, Barbara O'Neil, Anderson Lawler, Cora Witherspoon, Harlan Briggs, Donald MacDonald, Roger Sterns, Nancy Ryan, Millicent Hanley. A: Edward Roberts and Frank Cavett.

SV: MGM, 1934, Joan Crawford, Clark Gable, Robert Montgomery, Charles Butterworth, Billie Burke, Rosalind Russell.

Fortune and Men's Eyes (2/23/67, Actors Playhouse, 382)

Searing account of the corruption of an innocent young farm boy (Terry Kiser) when he is thrown into contact with sexual deviates in a Canadian prison. Grim, profoundly disturbing O/B drama by John Herbert. P: David Rothenberg and Mitchell Nestor (D).

Revived O/B (10/22/69, Stage 73, 231) with Mark Shannon and Michael Greer heading a cast directed by Sal Mineo.

SV: MGM, 1971, Wendell Burton, Michael Greer, Zooey Hall (directed by Harvey Hart).

Fortune Hunter, The (9/4/09, Gaiety, 345)

John Barrymore became Broadway's reigning matinee idol in this snappy 1909 farce-comedy about a handsome city slicker who sets out to win the richest girl in town, but instead falls in love with a druggist's daughter. C: Hale Hamilton, Mary Ryan. A/D: Winchell Smith. P: Cohan and Harris. Musicalized by Jerome Kern as *The City Chap* (1925) with Skeets Gallagher, Phyllis Cleveland, Irene Dunne, George Raft, Betty Compton.

Forty Carats (12/26/68, Morosco, 780)

Breezy smash-hit comedy about the romance that develops between a forty-year-old New York divorcée and an attractive youth of twenty-two. "Sparkling from start to finish" (*Hollywood Reporter*). C: Julie Harris, Marco St. John, Glenda Farrell, Murray Hamilton, Polly Rowles, Gretchen Corbett, Nancy Marchand, John Cecil Holm. A: Jay Allen* b/o a play by Barillet and Gredy. P: David Merrick. D: Abe Burrows.

SV: Col, 1973, Liv Ullman, Edward Albert, Gene Kelly, Binnie Barnes, Nancy Walker (directed by Milton Katselas).

---

*Author of *The Prime of Miss Jean Brodie* (1968).

49th Cousin, The (10/27/60, Ambassador, 100)

The reformation of an intolerant, cantankerous German Jew (Menasha Skulnik) in turn-of-the-century Syracuse, New York. Wobbly comedy and, in the words of *New York Post* critic Richard Watts, Jr., "far from worthy of its brilliant and lovable comic star." C: Martha Scott, Marian Winters, Evans Evans, Gerald Hiken, Eli Mintz. A: Florence Lowe and Caroline Francke. P: The Theatre Guild and George Kondolf. D: Jack Smight. SD: Stewart Chaney.

42 Seconds From Broadway (3/11/73, Playhouse, 1)

A mild comedy of a Catholic boy and Jewish girl who yearn for acting careers and become platonic roommates in a flat just off The Great White Way. Stardom eludes them, but by play's end, determined girl has netted nervously backward boy amidst fairly diverting situations. The cast was generally lauded for its efforts, in particular Regina Baff and Henry Winkler as the young couple. Winkler was termed "an adroit laugh-getter" by Douglas Watt in the *New York Daily News*, undoubtedly no surprise to television buffs. In addition to his stage work in regional and New York theatre, films such as *Katherine* and *The Lords of Flatbush*, Winkler was by the mid-seventies enjoying magazine cover popularity as a leading player in the TV series "Happy Days." A: Louis Del Grande. C: Regina Baff, Henry Winkler, Antonia Rey, Michael Vale, Billy Longo, Edward Kovens, James Tolkan, Anthony Spina, Martin Garner, Bob Dermer, John Branon, Judith Cohen, Susan Peretz, Patti Costa. D: Arthur Storch. P: Arthur Cantor.

Forward the Heart (1/28/49, 48th Street, 19)

Blinded war vet falls in love with his mother's Negro maid. "Very slight, very inexpert and very weak" (*Sun*). C: William Prince, Mildred Joanne Smith, Natalie Schafer, Harry Bannister. A: Bernard Reines. P: Theatre Enterprises, Inc. and Leon J. Bronesky. D: Peter Frye.

Fountain, The (12/10/25, Greenwich Village, 24)

Eugene O'Neill's romantic fantasy dealing with the quest of Ponce de Leon (Walter Huston) for eternal youth.

Ambushed by Indians and severely wounded, de Leon dies convinced that he has found the answer to the riddle of life ("All things dissolve, flow on eternally!"). This short-lived poetic drama, rewritten many times over a four-year period, was an artistic as well as commercial failure. Walter Huston was badly miscast as the heroic Ponce de Leon, but it is doubtful if any actor could have injected sufficient theatrical vitality into O'Neill's fanciful experiment in romantic symbolism. C: Henry O'Neill, Crane Wilbur, Rosalinde Fuller, Curtis Cooksey, Edgar Stehli, Egon Brecher, Morris Ankrum. P: Kenneth Macgowan, Robert Edmond Jones (D/SD), Eugene O'Neill. M: Macklin Morrow.

Four Twelves Are 48 (1/17/51, 48th Street, 2)

Vulgar, tedious comedy about the sex life of some Osage Indians. Directed in heavy-handed fashion by Otto Preminger; written by Joseph Kesselring, author of *Arsenic and Old Lace* (1941). C: Anne Revere, Ernest Truex, Hiram Sherman, Doro Merande, Pat Crowley, Joshua Shelley, Ludwig Donath, Royal Dano, Rosetta Le Noire. P: Aldrich and Myers, Fleischmann and Preminger.

Four Walls (9/19/27, Golden, 144)

Ex-con Benny Horowitz tries to go straight, becomes implicated in an accidental murder, and gives himself up to the law. Engrossing George Abbott (D) thriller with an excellent performance in the leading role by newcomer Muni Weisenfreund (Paul Muni). C: Lee Strasberg, Sanford Meisner, Clara Langsner, Bella Finkel (Mrs. Paul Muni). A: Dana Burnet and George Abbott. P: John Golden. *Four Walls* was Muni's first Broadway hit. It was also the first time in his career that he had played anything but old men or character parts. "I was as embarrassed as if I lost my clothes," Muni recalled years later. "All of a sudden I was naked. I didn't have any beard or wigs."
SV: MGM, 1934, *Straight Is the Way*, Franchot Tone, Gladys George, May Robson, Karen Morley, Nat Pendleton, Jack La Rue.
Note: A silent version (MGM, 1928) starred John Gilbert and Joan Crawford.

Four Winds (9/25/57, Cort, 21)

Highfalutin' soap opera about a thrice-wed poor little rich girl and the bounder who schemes to become husband number four. C: Ann Todd (deb.), Peter Cookson, Conrad Nagel, Luella Gear, Carl Esmond, James Rennie. A: Thomas W. Phipps. P: Worthington Miner and Kenneth Wagg. D: Guthrie McClintic. SD: Donald Oenslager.

Fourth Estate, The (10/6/09, Wallack's, 93)

When a managing editor loses his battle against big city corruption, he kills himself. Vigorous but implausible 1909 melodrama; the first play to expose "the venal tabloid press." C: Charles Waldron, Pauline Frederick. A: Joseph Medill Patterson and Harriet Ford. P: Liebler and Company. D: Hugh Ford.

Foxhole in the Parlor (5/23/45, Booth, 45)

A psychoneurotic soldier (Montgomery Clift) struggles to adjust to civilian life. He is helped in his efforts to achieve emotional well-being by some sympathetic Greenwich Village friends, hindered by his totally insensitive sister (Grace Coppin), who threatens to have him institutionalized. Clift gave an expert performance as the tortured hero, but the play by Elsa Shelley emerged as languid, murky, and diffuse. P: Harry Bloomfield. D: John Haggott. SD: Lee Simonson.

Fragile Fox (10/12/54, Belasco, 55)

Trapped in Belgium during World War II,

an embattled American unit suffers severe casualties due to the drunken incompetence of its combat captain. The play's climax occurs when one of his subordinates finally shoots the detestible captain to protect the lives of the remaining men. This wartime melodrama with an all-male cast was characterized by Richard Watts, Jr. *(Post)* as "lacking in point and dramatic forcefulness." C: Andrew Duggan, Dane Clark, Don Taylor, James Gregory, Crahan Denton, Addison Powell, Lionel Wilson. A: Norman A. Brooks. P: Paul Vroom i.a.w. Barnard Straus. D: Herbert Swope, Jr. SD: Ralph Alswang.

SV: UA, 1956, *Attack!*, Jack Palance, Eddie Albert, Lee Marvin, Robert Strauss (directed by Robert Aldrich).

Frankie and Johnnie (9/25/30, Republic, 61)

Prostitute falls in love with riverboat gambler until a shameless hussy named Nellie Bly comes between them. Crude retelling of the old story offended the moralists, was closed by the police. C: Anne Forrest, Frank McGlynn, Jr., Roberta Beatty, Jerome Cowan. A/P: Jack Kirkland. D: Lee Elmore.

SV: RKO, 1935, Helen Morgan, Chester Morris, Lilyan Tashman, Florence Reed (screenplay by Moss Hart).

Free Soul, A (1/12/28, Playhouse, 100)

George Cukor directed this mediocre melodrama about a spoiled girl who falls in love with a criminal client of her inebriate attorney-father. Later, when this free-souled creature becomes involved in a murder, it is dear old dad who comes to the rescue with his courtroom pyrotechnics. C: Kay Johnson, Melvyn Douglas (deb.), Lester Lonergan, George Baxter, James Bell. The Willard Mack script was based on the relationship of writer Adela Rogers St. John and her father, famed criminal lawyer Earl Rogers. Veteran producer William A. Brady assumed the role of the alcoholic barrister midway in the run, and gave an engagingly flamboyant performance in the part.

SV: MGM, 1931, Norma Shearer, Lionel Barrymore, Leslie Howard, Clark Gable, James Gleason; 1953, *The Girl Who Had Everything*, Elizabeth Taylor, William Powell, Gig Young, Fernando Lamas.

French Doll, The (2/20/22, Lyceum, 120)

Saucy Georgine (Irene Bordoni) sets her cap for wealthy T. Wellington Wick (Thurston Hall) until she spies a handsome younger lad (Don Burroughs). Trifling 20's farce, with interpolated songs, set in ultra-chic Palm Beach. Highlight: Miss Bordoni's crooning of the delightfully suggestive George Gershwin-B.G. DeSylva song, "Do It Again." A: A. E. Thomas, based on a play by Armont and Gerbidon. P: E. Ray Goetz. D: W. H. Gilmore.

French Touch, The (12/8/45, Cort, 33)

Flimsy farce, badly miscast, about the efforts of a celebrated French actor-manager (Brian Aherne) to outwit the Nazis during the German occupation of Paris. Written by Joseph Fields and Jerome Chodorov; staged by noted film director René Clair. C: Arlene Francis, John Wengraf. P: Herbert H. Harris. SD: George Jenkins.

Friendly Enemies (7/22/18, Hudson, 440)

When war breaks out between the United States and Germany, conflicts erupt between lifelong German-American friends. Pat patriotic comedy-drama; one of the big stage hits of World War I. C: Louis Mann, Sam Bernard. A: Samuel Shipman and Aaron Hoffman. P: A. H. Woods. D: Robert Milton.

SV: UA, 1942, Charles Winninger, Charlie Ruggles, Nancy Kelly, James Craig.

Friendship (8/31/31, Fulton, 24)

Romance between a young night club hostess (Lee Patrick) and a sympathetic older man (George M. Cohan). "Mr. Cohan is infinitely more ingratiating as an actor than as a playwright" *(Sun)*. C: Minor Watson, Helen F. Cohan. A/P/D: George M. Cohan.

Frogs of Spring, The (10/20/53, Broadhurst, 15)

Loosely woven comedy about two middle-aged Manhattan neighbors whose Rover Boy antics prove something of a trial to their wives and offspring. ". . . a vignette rather than a play . . . . Too much froth and too little substance" *(Mirror)*. C: Hiram Sherman, Anthony Ross, Barbara Baxley, Haila Stoddard, Jerome Kilty, Fred Gwynne. A: Nathaniel Benchley. P: Austin and Noyes i.a.w. Radnitz and Sagalyn. D: Burgess Meredith. SD: Boris Aronson.

Front Page, The (8/14/28, Times Square, 281)

Brilliantly constructed, enormously entertaining comedy-melodrama by Ben Hecht and Charles MacArthur set in Chicago's brash and raucous newspaper world of the 1920's. A battle of wits unfolds between hardheaded editor Walter Burns (Osgood Perkins) and star reporter Hildy Johnson (Lee Tracy). Burns' ruthless efforts to keep Hildy from quitting are played out in a Chicago press room while rival newspapers try to scoop them on a pending execution and an upcoming mayoral election. In the end, to keep his ace reporter from leaving town with his bride-to-be, Burns phones the police with instructions to arrest Hildy and bring him back. His reason: "The son-of-a-bitch stole my watch!" *The Front Page* hit Broadway like a thunderbolt in the 1928-29 season. Its cynicism, profanity and gutter language scandalized many people. It remains, in the words of Tennessee Williams, "the play that uncorseted the American theatre." C: Dorothy Stickney, George Barbier, Frances Fuller, Allen Jenkins, Joseph Calleia, Willard Robertson, Eduardo Ciannelli. P: Jed Harris. D: George S. Kaufman.

R: (9/4/46, Royale, 79) by Stromberg, Jr. and Spengler. C: Arnold Moss, Lew Parker, Olive Deering, Cora Witherspoon, Ray Walston, Benny Baker, Pat Harrington, Bruce MacFarlane, Joe De Santis, William Lynn. D: Charles MacArthur.

R: (5/10/69, Barrymore, 222) by Theatre 1969. C: Robert Ryan, Bert Convy, Peggy Cass, John McGiver, Katharine Houghton, Julia Meade, Doro Merande, Arnold Stang, Don Porter, Conrad Janis, Harold J. Kennedy (D). Cast replacements during the return engagement of this revival included Helen Hayes, Dody Goodman, Molly Picon, Butterfly McQueen, James Flavin, Maureen O'Sullivan, Paul Ford, Jules Munshin, Robert Alda, Jan Sterling, Jesse White.

SV: UA, 1931, Adolphe Menjou, Pat O'Brien, Edward Everett Horton (directed by Lewis Milestone); Col, 1940, *His Girl Friday,* Cary Grant, Rosalind Russell, Ralph Bellamy, Gene Lockhart, Porter Hall, John Qualen (directed by Howard Hawks).

Projected: Upcoming remake with Jack Lemmon, Walter Matthau, Carol Burnett, with Billy Wilder slated to direct.

Full Circle (11/7/73, ANTA, 21)

If talented names could ensure success, *Full Circle* would have been a hit. It was directed by Otto Preminger *(Margin for Error, The Moon is Blue),* based on the only play of novelist Erich Maria Remarque, and adapted for the American stage by the versatile Peter Stone, writer for stage *(1776, Two by Two)* and screen

(*Charade, Father Goose, Mirage*). The scene is Berlin at the end of World War II, with Hitler dead and the Russians rapidly closing on the ravaged city. An anti-nazi German (Leonard Nimoy), having escaped a concentration camp, takes refuge with an apolitical young widow (Bibi Andersson). When the Russians invade and take control, he is accused of Hitlerism by a gestapo officer trying to pass himself off as a Jew. Though the ploy doesn't work, the hero's fate is ironic. He will not accept communism any more readily than fascism, so has escaped one tyranny only to fall victim to another. Despite the power of its melodrama, *Full Circle* came full circle in less than three weeks. The critics were notably divided. ". . . theatrically effective. Mr. Preminger's direction is skillful" (Richard Watts, *New York Post*). "Preminger's work is a disgrace to the professional theater" (Martin Gottfried, *Women's Wear Daily*). ". . . a script that might have served for a B-movie thriller in the late '40's" (Douglas Watt, *New York Daily News*). In such doubtful circumstances, Swedish actress Bibi Andersson, a member of filmmaker Ingmar Bergman's stock company, made her American stage debut. P: Otto Preminger. C: Leonard Nimoy, Bibi Andersson, Josef Sommer, Max Brandt, James Tolkan, Linda Carlson, Stan Wiklin, Peter Weller, David Ackroyd. SD: Robin Wagner.

Full House, A (5/10/15, Longacre, 112)

When a thief and a lawyer inadvertently exchange traveling bags, the shifty attorney comes into possession of a valuable stolen necklace, while the thief gets his hands on some incriminating letters. "Amusing farce compounded of cheerful nonsense and played at full speed" (*New York Times*). C: Ralph Morgan, Herbert Corthell, May Vokes, Claiborne Foster. A: Fred Jackson. P: H. H. Frazee. D: Edgar MacGregor.

Fulton of Oak Falls (2/10/37, Morosco, 37)

Problems of a small-town father (George M. Cohan) and his adolescent daughter. Homey little comedy served (briefly) to reunite the famous producing team of Cohan and (Sam H.) Harris. C: Jessamine Newcombe, Doro Merande, Rita Johnson, Harold Vermilyea. A: George M. Cohan b/o a story by Parker Fennelly. D: Sam Forrest.

Fun City (1/2/72, Morosco, 9)

A frenzied farce purporting to show that no matter how awful it is to live in New York City, New Yorkers will never leave it. Unfortunately, this theme has been more cleverly explored by others, notably Neil Simon. The authors of *Fun City* can do no better than tack a succession of jokes onto an ill-constructed plot about a young woman who wants to save New York by having it secede from the Union and become the fifty-first state. The cast is talented and some of the gags are good, but the play starts at such high speed that it can only slow down. And does. A: Lester Colodny, Joan Rivers, Edgar Rosenberg. C: Joan Rivers (deb.), Gabriel Dell, Paul Ford, Rose Marie, Renee Lippin, Pierre Epstein, Victor Arnold, Louis Zorich, Howard Storm, J. J. Barry, Noel Young. P: Alexander H. Cohen and Rocky H. Aoki. D: Jerry Adler. SD: Ralph Alswang.

Fun Couple, The (10/26/62, Lyceum, 3)

Good cast—Jane Fonda, Dyan Cannon (deb.), Bradford Dillman, Ben Piazza—in an aimless comedy about a pair of newlyweds who defer facing reality by clinging to their childlike passion for fun-and-games. ". . . incredible nonsense" *(New York Times)*. ". . . an epic bore" *(Post)*. *The Fun Couple* closed after its third performance. It was written by Neil Jansen (nom de plume for producer Jay Julien) and John Haase, b/o Mr. Haase's novel. P: Jay Julien i.a.w. Andre

Goulston and Eldon Elder (SD). D: Andreas Voutsinas. M: Albert Hague.

Furies, The (3/7/28, Shubert, 41)

When the young husband (Alan Campbell) of an attractive society matron (Laurette Taylor) is found murdered, everyone seems to have a motive. It turns out his insane attorney killed him. Miss Taylor gave a brilliant performance in this florid but otherwise conventional whodunit written by Zoe Akins and directed by George Cukor. It was tragic that the greatest of all American actresses squandered her genius on plays unworthy of her gifts, doubly tragic in this case since—except for a short-lived revival (1932) of a James Barrie play—*The Furies* marked Miss Taylor's last Broadway appearance for more than a decade. C: Estelle Winwood, A. E. Anson, Frederic Worlock. P: John Tuerk.

SV: WB, 1930, Lois Wilson, H. B. Warner, Montagu Love.

Futz! (6/13/68, de Lys, 233)

Provocative, highly imaginative O/B play about a farmer (John Bakos) whose love affair with his pig totally demoralizes his rustic neighbors. Written by Rochelle Owens, directed by Tom O'Horgan.

G

Gabrielle (3/25/41, Maxine Elliott's, 2)

A tubercular patient in a Swiss sanitarium is driven to her death by the Svengali-like tactics of a malicious novelist. This murky drama, b/o Thomas Mann's *Tristan,* closed after its second performance. C: Eleanor Lynn, John Cromwell, Harold Vermilyea, Frederic Tozere, Whit Bissell, Byron McGrath, Frieda Altman, Martin Wolfson. A: Leonardo Bercovici. P: Rowland Leigh. D: Randolph Carter.

Note: Tristan, a short story written in 1902, furnished the basic source material for Thomas Mann's masterpiece, *The Magic Mountain* (1924).

Gamblers, The (10/31/10, Maxine Elliott's, 192)

Shrill 1910 melodrama about the venal world of high finance. C: George Nash, Jane Cowl. A/P: Charles Klein.

SV: WB, 1929, H. B. Warner, Jason Robards, Sr.

Gambling (8/26/29, Fulton, 155)

The father (George M. Cohan) of a murdered girl plays his gambler's hunches in tracking down the murderer. Loosely written melodrama, expertly underplayed by Cohan (A/P). "From the first minutes to the last he [Cohan] fills a false play with integrity by the sheer credibility of his acting" (Percy Hammond, *Herald Tribune*). "Somebody should create a foundation which would endow all stage aspirants with tickets for the new Cohan play. They will not find a more likely master" (Heywood Broun, *World-Telegram*). D: Sam Forrest.

SV: Fox, 1935, George M. Cohan, Dorothy Burgess, Wynne Gibson.

Gang War (8/20/28, Morosco, 77)

Rival gang leaders plot each other's demise with machine guns, bombs from the air, and assorted triple-cross tactics. Noisy shoot-'em-up stuff by veteran melodramatist Willard Mack (A/P/D).

SV: FBO (Film Booking Office), 1928, Jack Pickford, Olive Borden.

Gang's All Here, The (10/1/59, Ambassador, 132)

Semifictionalized account of the 1920's Teapot Dome scandal of Warren G. Harding's administration in which amiable, easygoing Harding (here called Griffith P. Hastings) discovers too late that his Cabinet member cronies are all crooks, and dies a disillusioned man. "Effective drama with a conscience . . . extraordinarily interesting" (*New York Times*). C: Melvyn Douglas, E. G. Marshall, Arthur Hill, Howard Smith, Jean Dixon, Paul McGrath, Bert Wheeler (dramatic stage debut), Victor Kilian, Fred Stewart, Bernard Lenrow. A: Jerome Lawrence and Robert E. Lee. P: Kermit Bloomgarden i.a.w. Sylvia Drulie. D: George Roy Hill. CD: Patricia Zipprodt. SD: Jo Mielziner.

Garden of Eden, The (9/27/27, Selwyn, 23)

Headstrong lass (Miriam Hopkins), tutored in the ways of the world by a broken-down baroness (Alison Skipworth), spurns the love of a penniless youth (Douglass Montgomery) and marries a seventy-five-year-old prince instead. Not nearly as amusing as it should have been, but nicely acted, handsomely produced. C: Russ Whytal, Harlan Briggs, T. Wigney Percyval, Doris Rankin, Ivan Simpson. A: Avery Hopwood b/o play by Bernauer and Oesterreicher. P: Arch Selwyn. D: Edwin H. Knopf*

---

*Longtime Hollywood producer (*The Valley of Decision, Lili,* etc.).

Garden of Paradise, The (11/28/14, Park, 17)

A mermaid rescues a king from a watery grave and barters her life for a brief season of love and an immortal soul. Lyrical adaptation by Edward Sheldon of Hans Christian Andersen's fairy tale, "The Little Mermaid," harmed by overly ornate, unwieldy scenic design. C: Emily Stevens, Frank Conroy. P: Liebler and Company. D: O. P. Heggie. SD: Joseph Urban.

Garden of Sweets, The (10/31/61, ANTA, 1)

Turmoil and trauma in a Greek-American family. "An evening of almost inexpressible dreariness" (*Post*). C: Katina Paxinou, Lou Antonio, Madeleine Sherwood, Martine Bartlett. A: Waldemar Hansen. P: Frye and Squires. D: Milton Katselas. SD: Boris Aronson.

Gayden (5/10/49, Plymouth, 7)

Melodrama about a wealthy psychopath (Jay Robinson) of supposedly irresistible fascination. Gayden's greatest joy in life is to attract and then destroy all who come into contact with him. By the end of the play, his doting mother (Fay Bainter) finally realizes that her charming and affable son is a cold-blooded sadist. "A pedestrian thriller about a singularly un-

pleasant young man" (*New York Times*). A: Mignon and Robert McLaughlin. P: Gant Gaither. D: Lex Richards. CD: Emeline Roche. SD: Willis Knighton.

Gazebo, The (12/12/58, Lyceum, 218)

Macabre comedy about a blackmailed TV writer (Walter Slezak) who plots a real murder with surprising results. "A consistently amusing crime escapade" (*New York Times*). "A frail suspense-chuckler . . ." (*Mirror*). C: Jayne Meadows, Edward Andrews, Leon Janney. Written by Anglo-American author-screenwriter Alec Coppel (*The Captain's Paradise, Vertigo,* etc.); b/o a story by Myra and Alec Coppel. P: The Playwrights Company and Frederick Brisson. D: Jerome Chodorov. SD: Jo Mielziner.

SV: MGM, 1959, Glenn Ford, Debbie Reynolds, Carl Reiner, John McGiver, Doro Merande, Mabel Albertson (directed by George Marshall).

General Seeger (2/28/62, Lyceum, 2)

Unconvincing drama about a fifty-seven-year-old martinet-general (George C. Scott)* who discovers that he was responsible for driving his sensitive son to suicide. C: Dolores Sutton, Ann Harding, Paul Stevens, Roscoe Lee Browne, Lonny Chapman, Tim O'Connor. A: Ira Levin. P: George C. Scott (D) and Theodore Mann.

---

*Mr. Scott stepped into the title role when William Bendix withdrew during the preBroadway tryout.

Generation (10/6/65, Morosco, 299)

A straitlaced adman is disturbed by news of his daughter's recent anti-establishment marriage, and infuriated by the plans of his beatnik son-in-law to deliver their soon-to-arrive baby himself. Lightweight comedy owed its Broadway success chiefly to Henry Fonda's engaging performance in the role of the well-meaning, ulcer-ridden father. C: Richard Jordan, Holly Turner, A. Larry Haines, Sandy Baron, Don Fellows. A: William Goodhart. P: Frederick Brisson. D: Gene Saks. SD: George Jenkins. M: Jerry Bock.

SV: Embassy, 1969, David Janssen, Kim Darby, Peter Duel, Carl Reiner, James Coco, Sam Waterston, Andrew Prine (directed by George Schaefer).

Genius and the Goddess, The (12/10/57, Henry Miller, 7)

The wife (Nancy Kelly) of a middle-aged scientist (Alan Webb) has a fling with her husband's youthful assistant (Michael Tolan). Presumably the extramarital affair strengthens the shaky marriage. The play ends with husband and wife reconciled, and the youth taking off for a teaching job in California. ". . . contrived situations, pat characterizations and lacklustre ideology . . . pretty pitiable stuff" *(Journal-American)*. A: Aldous Huxley, Beth Wendel and Alec Coppel, b/o Mr. Huxley's novel. P: Courtney Burr i.a.w. Liska March. D/SD: Richard Whorf.

Gentle Grafters (10/27/26, Music Box, 13)

Man-hating gold digger falls in love, but her best friend manages to nip the romance in the bud. Interesting Owen Davis drama with a weak third act. C: Katherine Alexander, Robert Keith, Charlotte Granville. P: Sam H. Harris. D: Sam Forrest.

Gentle People, The (1/5/39, Belasco, 141)

Victimized by a Brooklyn mobster, two kindly old men contrive to take justice into their own hands and kill their oppressor. This anti-fascist parable by Irwin Shaw was one of the Group Theatre's most successful productions. It was splendidly acted by a first-rate cast headed by Franchot Tone, Sylvia Sidney, Sam Jaffe, Roman Bohnen, Elia Kazan, Karl Malden, and, notably, Lee J. Cobb as a bankrupt businessman. Highlight: a mordant, frequently hilarious scene in a Turkish bath where the gangster's murder is planned. *The Gentle People* was described by its author as "a fairy tale with a moral." "In it," wrote Irwin Shaw, "justice triumphs and the meek prove victorious over arrogant and violent men. The author does not pretend that this is the case in real life." D: Harold Clurman. SD: Boris Aronson.

SV: WB, 1941, *Out of the Fog,* John Garfield, Ida Lupino, Thomas Mitchell, Eddie Albert, George Tobias, John Qualen, Leo Gorcey, Aline MacMahon, Jerome Cowan.

Gentleman from Athens, The (12/9/47, Mansfield, 7)

Anthony Quinn made his Broadway debut in this 40's comedy about a roughneck junior congressman who uses strong-arm tactics to promote his World Government bill. ". . . the very worst sort of hack writing" *(PM)*. C: Edith Atwater, Alan Hewitt, Feodor Chaliapin, Lou Polan, Gavin Gordon. P: Martin Gosch i.a.w. Eunice Healy. D: Sam Wanamaker.

Note: Lela Rogers, Ginger Rogers's outspoken, ultra right-wing mother, caused quite a stir in the press by branding this play subversive. As it turned out, the only thing red about this innocuous and short-lived exhibit was the red side of the producer's ledger. The Emmet Lavery comedy closed after seven performances. Quipped one critic: "I wonder if Ginger Rogers's mother wouldn't make a more interesting study than Mr. Lavery's plot."

Gentleman from Mississippi, A (9/29/08, Bijou, 407)

A genial southern senator (Thomas A. Wise) and his breezy young protégé-secretary (Douglas Fairbanks) manage to get the better of some corrupt congressmen on Capitol Hill. "A series of rapid-fire laughs from curtain to curtain" *(New York Times)*. A: Harrison Rhodes and Thomas A. Wise. P: William A. Brady and Joseph R. Grismer.

Gentleman of France, A (12/30/01, Wallack's, 120)

Fanciful swashbuckler set in the troubled times when Henry of Navarre aspired to the French throne. C: Kyrle Bellew, Eleanor Robson, Charlotte Walker, Edgar Selwyn. A: Harriet Ford, founded on the story by Stanley J. Weyman. P: Liebler and Co. D: Kyrle Bellew and E.D. Lyons.

Gentlemen of the Press (8/27/28, Henry Miller, 128)

The struggles of an underpaid rewrite man to break out of the daily newspaper grind and into the big money of public relations. Pleasant comedy-drama by critic-columnist Ward Morehouse that had the misfortune to open on Broadway two weeks after another newspaper play, Hecht and MacArthur's blockbuster hit, *The Front Page*. C: John Cromwell, Hugh O'Connell, Millard Mitchell, and Russel Crouse (future coauthor of *Life with Father, State of the Union,* etc.). P: H. S. Kraft and T. E. Jackson. D: George Abbott.

SV: Par, 1929, Walter Huston, Kay Francis, Charlie Ruggles, Betty Lawford, Norman Foster.

Gentlemen Prefer Blondes (9/28/26, Times Square, 201)

Anita Loos' comic novel of the flapper era transformed into a raffishly amusing stage cartoon. Lorelei Lee (June Walker) is a blonde mantrap with an almost grim instinct for security in the form of jewelry. Together with her wisecracking friend Dorothy (Edna Hibbard), Lorelei is sent to Europe to broaden her mind. On the ocean liner, she meets the rich and eligible Henry Spoffard (Frank Morgan). The two girls have many gold-digging adventures in London, Paris, and New York, but it is Dorothy who winds up at the altar with Henry. A: Anita Loos and John Emerson. P/D: Edgar Selwyn. Musicalized (1949) by Joseph Fields, Anita Loos, Jule Styne and Leo Robin with Carol Channing, Yvonne Adair, Jack McCauley, George S. Irving and Eric Brotherson heading the cast; revived as *Lorelei* (1974) with the book of the musical slightly revised by Solms and Parent and some new songs by Styne, Comden and Green. C: Carol Channing, Tamara Long, Peter Palmer.

SV: Fox, 1953, Marilyn Monroe, Jane Russell, Charles Coburn (directed by Howard Hawks). A silent version (Paramount, 1928) featured Ruth Taylor and Alice White (directed by Mal St. Clair).

Note: Lorelei Lee made her first appearance in a series of sketches in 1925 in *Harper's Bazaar* and by the third installment the magazine tripled its newsstand sales. The following year Lorelei came out in book form and was translated into thirteen languages.

Gentlewoman (3/22/34, Cort, 12)

Bourgeois neurotic (Stella Adler) falls in love with radical poet (Lloyd Nolan) incapable of sustaining a lasting relationship. Their affair is doomed from the outset, and so was this play by John Howard Lawson. The Communist party bitterly attacked the author as "politically confused." Contritely, Lawson underwent an intensive reevaluation of his work in terms of marxist orthodoxy and then fled to Hollywood where his screenwriting talents found expression in such films as *Algiers, Blockade, Five Came Back*, etc. C: Morris Carnovsky, Russell Collins, Claudia Morgan, Frances Williams, Roman Bohnen. P: The Group Theatre i.a.w. D. A. Doran, Jr. D: Lee Strasberg. SD: Mordecai Gorelik.

George Washington (3/1/20, Lyric, 16)

Stagey "ballad drama" chronicling events in the life of Washington (Walter Hampden) from 1750 to 1778. A: Percy MacKaye. P/D: Hampden.

George Washington Slept Here (10/18/40, Lyceum, 173)

Bucolic farce by George S. Kaufman (D) and Moss Hart (their last collaborative effort) about a misguided city couple who buy a converted Pennsylvania farmhouse and try to make the place habitable. "Slightly less than fair-to-middling" *(Post)*. *George Washington Slept Here* had only a moderate Broadway run, but was a substantial success with summer stock companies. C: Ernest Truex, Jean Dixon, Dudley Digges, Percy Kilbride, Mabel Taliaferro, Ruth Weston, Bobby Readick. P: Sam H. Harris.

SV: WB, 1942, Jack Benny, Ann Sheridan, Charles Coburn, Percy Kilbride, Hattie McDaniel, John Emery, Franklin Pangborn.

Geraniums in My Window (10/26/34, Longacre, 27)

Waitress discovers her dishwasher-husband is actually a wealthy playboy in disguise. Painfully arch comedy by Samuel Ornitz and Vera Caspary (author of *Laura*), staged by Hollywood "B" director Sidney Salkow, produced by comedian Phil Baker and Laura D. Wilck. C: Audrey Christie, Bruce MacFarlane, Eda Heinemann, Tom Ewell.

Gertie (11/15/26, Bayes, 248)

Ambitious working girl toys with the "easy life" but finally settles for a garage mechanic. Innocuous 20's comedy. C: Pat O'Brien, Constance McKay, Elisha Cook, Jr. A: Tadema Bussiere. P/D: Gustav Blum.

Get Away Old Man (11/24/43, Cort, 13)

William Saroyan's comedy about the conflict between an obnoxious movie mogul (Ed Begley) and an arrogant young writer (Richard Widmark), a self-styled genius who prefers hobnobbing with strays and drunks to scripting the producer's pet story, *Ave Maria*. In the end, the writer defies the ruthless producer, and decamps for San Francisco to repossess his soul. "A weak and ineffectual comedy that includes some enormously funny incidental material" *(Sun)*. C: Glenn Anders, Beatrice Pearson, Edwin Hodge, Hilda Vaughn, Joyce Mathews. P/D: George Abbott. *Get Away Old Man* was inspired by its author's brief fling at screenwriting with Metro-Goldwyn-Mayer. Studio head Louis B. Mayer was impressed by Saroyan and wanted to groom him for an important producer-director job with the company. (Saroyan's starting salary was $1,500 a week. In addition, he was paid $60,000 for his short story *The Human Comedy*, which Metro filmed with Mickey Rooney in the leading role.) Louis B. Mayer's enthusiasm for the writer was short-lived. Within three months, Saroyan had left the studio. Shortly thereafter he wrote *Get Away Old Man*. In his book, *Hollywood Rajah*, Mayer's biographer Bosley Crowther pointed out that "everybody recognized" the play's central character as an acid-etched portrait of Mayer. "It drew a devastating picture of a vicious egoist," wrote Crowther. "Considering the enthusiasm and high hopes that Mayer had for Saroyan at the start, this must have been extremely mortifying for [Mayer]."

Get Me in the Movies (5/21/28, Earl Carroll, 32)

Village simp (Sterling Holloway) becomes Hollywood screenwriter, tries hard to remain faithful to his small-town sweetheart. Listless farce-comedy by Charlton Andrews and Philip Dunning. P: Laura D. Wilck. D: Ralph Murphy.

Get-Rich-Quick Wallingford (9/19/10, Gaiety, 424)

George M. Cohan farce about the reformation of a glib, success-at-any-price con man. The comedy hit of 1910. C: Hale Hamilton, Grant Mitchell, Edward Ellis, Frances Ring. A: Cohan, from George R. Chester's novel. P: Cohan and Harris. D: Sam Forrest.

SV: MGM, 1931, *The New Adventures of Get-Rich-Quick Wallingford,* William Haines, Jimmy Durante, Leila Hyams.

Getting Gertie's Garter (8/1/21, Republic, 120)

Successful bedroom-hayloft farce revolving around attempts to retrieve a diamond-studded garter. "*Up In Mabel's Room* done again in a duller way. . . .There is no more interest in a garter as a naughty thing than there is in a virgin's wimple" (Percy Hammond). C: Hazel Dawn, Donald MacDonald, Adele Rowland. A: Wilson Collison and Avery Hopwood. P: A. H. Woods. D: Bertram Harrison.

SV: UA, 1945, Dennis O'Keefe, Marie McDonald, Barry Sullivan, Binnie Barnes.

Ghost Between, The (3/22/21, 39th Street, 128)

A woman is faithful to her husband's memory until a handsome doctor proposes a trial marriage. Muddled mixture of tragedy and farce. C: Laura Walker, Arthur Byron, Glenn Anders. A: Vincent Lawrence. D: W. H. Gilmore.

The Ghost Breaker. **Margaret Boland and Katherine Emmett (Lyceum Theatre, March 3, 1913).** *Courtesy Museum of the City of New York Theatre and Music Collection.*

Ghost Breaker, The (3/3/13, Lyceum, 72)

Spooky doings in a haunted castle. Amusing nonsense with H. B. Warner as the stalwart hero and Katherine Emmett as the frightened heroine. A: Paul Dickey and Charles W. Goddard. P/D: Maurice Campbell.

SV: Par, 1940, *The Ghost Breakers,* Bob Hope, Paulette Goddard, Richard Carlson, Paul Lukas, Anthony Quinn; 1953, *Scared Stiff,* Dean Martin, Jerry Lewis, Lizabeth Scott, Carmen Miranda, Dorothy Malone.

Ghost of Yankee Doodle, The (11/22/37, Guild, 48)

War-mongering publisher (Dudley Digges) woos liberal matriarch (Ethel Barrymore). Badly bungled 1937 pacifist drama by Sidney Howard, set "eighteen months after the next world war," had little popular appeal, and closed after a brief six-week run. C: Frank Conroy, Richard Carlson, Russell Hardie, Marilyn Erskine, Lloyd Gough, George Nash, Kathleen Comegys, Eliot Cabot, John Drew Devereaux. P: The Theatre Guild. D: John Cromwell.

Ghost Writer, The (6/19/33, Masque, 24)

Wobbly 30's drama about the travails of a freelance author adrift in Manhattan. Written by Martin Mooney, former publicist-crime reporter who faced prison rather than divulge his news sources, and later parlayed this bit of exotica into a screenwriting and producing career. C: Hal Skelly, Peggy Conklin, William Frawley. P: Hopkins and Heyer. D: Jo Graham.

Giants, Sons of Giants (1/6/62, Alvin, 9)

Internist struggles to establish a private clinic in a small American town. Written and directed by Joseph Kramm, author of *The Shrike* (1952). "A desperately sick play" *(New York Times)*. ". . .downright dismal" *(Post)*. C: Claude Dauphin, Nancy Kelly, Paul McGrath, Eda Heinemann. P: Totero and Cioffi. SD: Peter Larkin.

Gideon (11/9/61, Plymouth, 236)

Paddy Chayefsky's dramatization of the Old Testament story of Gideon (Douglas Campbell) and the angel of God (Fredric March).* As in the biblical tale, the Israelites are about to be overwhelmed by the Midianites. Because Jehovah talks to him man-to-man, and convinces him that he has been appointed the redeemer of his people, Gideon—a modest dolt of a fellow—is able to lead his army to victory against Israel's enemy. "Combines bold imagination, intensity. . .and a delightful vein of humor" *(Post)*. C: Eric Berry, Alan Manson, Mark Lenard, Victor Kilian, Mitchell Jason, George Segal.** P: Fred Coe and Arthur Cantor. D: Tyrone Guthrie. SD: David Hays.

---

*Mr. March's last Broadway appearance.
**Broadway debut.

Gift of Time, A (2/22/62, Barrymore, 92)

Unrelievedly grim study of a man (Henry Fonda) dying of cancer. The climax finds him slashing his wrists with the razor his loving and compassionate wife (Olivia de Havilland) has brought him. ". . .one of the most depressing plays ever written. . .an emotional experience of unrelenting candor" *(Post)*. Arguably Mr. Fonda's finest performance, but *A Gift of Time* was too harrowing for most theatregoers and closed after a relatively short run. C: Joseph Campanella, Marian Seldes, Guy Sorel, Philip Huston. A/D: Garson Kanin b/o the book *Death of a Man* by Lael Tucker Wertenbaker. P: William Hammerstein i.a.w. Shaber and Snyder. CD: Edith Lutyens Bel Geddes. SD: Boris Aronson.

Gigi (11/24/51, Fulton, 217)

Wryly impudent comedy by Anita Loos b/o the novel by Colette. Set in Paris at the turn of the century, the story tells of a pert, high-spirited creature of sixteen brought up in a highly unconventional way. Since the women of her family specialize in being courtesans, they have selected a wealthy playboy to be Gigi's "protector." But the effervescent heroine double-crosses her relatives by going respectable, and so enchants her would-be protector that he ends by making Gigi his bride instead of his mistress. "A gay little trinket" *(Herald Tribune)*. ". . . very trivial and old-fashioned" *(New York Times)*. *Gigi* made an overnight star of then-unknown Audrey Hepburn (deb.). She was appearing in a minor Franco-British film, *Monte Carlo Baby* and, while filming in a hotel lobby, was spotted by famed authoress Colette. "I could not take my eyes away," said Colette. "There, I said to myself incredulously, is Gigi. That afternoon I offered her the part in the Broadway play." In virtually one leap, the 21-year-old actress went from obscurity to fame. Shortly after the Broadway opening, producer Gilbert Miller elevated Miss Hepburn to stardom, with her name emblazoned above the play's title. The basic story of *Gigi* (including the happy ending) was based on a true-life incident related to Colette in the mid-1920's. The novel appeared in 1944 when the French authoress was 71 years old, and it was a tremendous success. It was the last of Colette's novels, though she lived on until the age of 81. C: Cathleen Nesbitt, Doris Patson, Josephine Brown, Bertha Belmore, Michael Evans, Francis Compton. D: Raymond Rouleau. SD: Raymond Sovey.

Musicalized by Lerner and Loewe (1973) with Karin Wolfe, Alfred Drake, Daniel Massey. Agnes Moorehead, Maria Karnilova.

SV; MGM, 1958, Leslie Caron, Maurice Chevalier, Louis Jourdan, Hermione Gingold, Isabel Jeans, Eva Gabor, Jacques Bergerac (directed by Vincente Minnelli).

Note: Gigi was filmed as a French (non-musical) picture in 1948. The star was Daniele Delorme.

Ginger Man, The (11/21/63, Orpheum, 52)

Intriguing but uneven O/B comedy-drama about the problems of an irresponsible American law student in present-day Dublin. C: Patrick O'Neal, Margaret Phillips, Marian Seldes, Stefan Gierasch. A: J. P. Donleavy. P: Ivor David Balding and Leo Garen (D).

Gingerbread Lady, The (12/13/70, Plymouth, 193)

A mordant comedy by Neil Simon. After ten weeks in a sanitarium, alcoholic singer Evy Meara returns to her New York brownstone determined to stay dry. It's a tough job. Her closest friends are a homosexual actor doomed to mediocrity and a girl friend who thinks of nothing but her looks. All middle-aged, lacking the resilience of youth, they flounder about, helping and hindering each other. Unsurprisingly, Evy goes off the wagon. Adding to her woes is an ex-lover who treats her brutally. Her only ally is the staunchly loyal young daughter who battles to keep her mother sober. Unlikely material for comedy, but if the plot is somber, the dialogue is as funny, the jokes as bright and inventive as in any of Simon's less demanding plays. A saving wit leavens the self-pity of this sad company of losers. The uncomplicated sunniness of *Barefoot in the Park* is nowhere present; *Gingerbread Lady* has an ambiance more complexly colored. The critics expressed uncertainty as to how successfully the disparate elements of the play had been melded, but there was unanimity in their appraisal of the leading lady's performance. "Maureen Stapleton at the top of her form . . . a joy . . . too marvelous to be missed" (Douglas Watt, *New York Daily News*). "Maureen Stapleton's blowsy, carousing, bravura performance . . ." (Walter Kerr, *New York Times*). For her efforts Ms. Stapleton came away with the season's Tony Award for Best Actress. A: Neil Simon. C: Maureen Stapleton, Betsy von Furstenberg, Michael Lombard, Ann Ruymen (deb.), Charles Siebert, Alex Colon. D: Robert Moore. P: Saint-Subber. SD: David Hays. CD: Frank Thompson.

Gingham Dog, The (4/23/69, Golden, 5)

Compelling study of the disintegrating interracial marriage between a Southern liberal (George Grizzard) and a Harlem negress (Diana Sands). First Broadway play by Lanford Wilson, author of *The Hot l Baltimore* (1973). P: Stoddard/

Wright/Wilder/Scott. D: Alan Schneider.

Gioconda Smile, The (10/7/50, Lyceum, 41)

A British bounder is framed by a vengeful old maid for the murder of his invalid wife—a crime actually committed by the jealous spinster herself. This psychological melodrama by Anglo-American author Aldous Huxley was adapted from his 1922 short story and subsequent (1947) Hollywood film. "Diffuse and banal . . . a cluttered drama that alternates between hokum and pretentiousness" (*New York Times*). C: Basil Rathbone, Valerie Taylor, George Relph. P/D: Shepard Traube. SD: Feder.

SV: U, 1947, *A Woman's Vengeance*, Charles Boyer, Jessica Tandy, Ann Blyth, Mildred Natwick, Cedric Hardwicke.

Gipsy Trail, The (12/4/17, Plymouth, 111)

A mousy Sir Galahad (Roland Young) insists on observing all the social proprieties. Finding that the lady of his heart would like him better if he were more romantic, he decides to abduct her. However, he is careful to gain her father's consent in advance and have his grandmother along on the trip as chaperon. In the end, the girl runs off with her dashing chauffeur leaving her befuddled swain behind to muse on the inconstancy of womankind. "Excellent light comedy . . . a deserved success" (*New York Times*). C: Phoebe Foster, Ernest Glendinning, Effie Ellsler, Katherine Emmett. A: Robert Housum. P/D: Arthur Hopkins.

Girl and the Judge, The (12/4/01, Lyceum, 125)

A wife (Annie Russell) tries to conceal her kleptomania from her family. Overheated Clyde Fitch (A/D) drama. P: Charles Frohman.

Girl Can Tell, A (10/29/53, Royale, 60)

Coquettish belle has trouble deciding which of six suitors to marry. This period comedy (1930's Manhattan) was written and staged by F. Hugh Herbert, author of *Kiss and Tell* (1943) and *The Moon Is Blue* (1951). ". . . monumentally uninteresting" (*New York Times*). C: Janet Blair (deb.), Paul McGrath, Lulu Mae Hubbard, Tod Andrews, Marshall Thompson, Dean Harens, Joan Wetmore, Donald Symington, Jack Whiting, William Kester, William Windom. P: Aldrich and Myers i.a.w. Julius Fleischmann.

Girl Could Get Lucky, A (9/20/64, Cort, 8)

Two-character comedy about the romance and subsequent adjustment to marriage of a thirtyish secretary (Betty Garrett) and a roughneck cabdriver (Pat Hingle). ". . . virtually devoid of story . . . flat and unexhilarating" (*Post*). A/D: Don Appell. P: Oestreicher and Feldman.

Girl in the Freudian Slip, The (5/18/67, Booth, 4)

Sluggish farce about a psychiatrist who develops a yen for a former patient. C: Alan Young, Marjorie Lord, Susan Brown, Russell Nype. A: William F. Brown. P: Ellis/Hale/McKenzie. D: Marc Daniels.

Girl in the Limousine, The (10/6/19, Eltinge, 137)

Lover invades girlfriend's bedchamber, is mistaken for her husband, with resultant complications. "The most densely populated bed in town . . . Someone is either in or under it, or both, during the entire evening. . . . Undeniably very funny" (Dorothy Parker, *Vanity Fair*). C: Charles Ruggles, Doris Kenyon, Zelda Sears, John Cumberland, Claiborne Foster, Barnett Parker. A: Wilson Collison and Avery Hopwood. P: A. H. Woods.

The Girl of the Golden West, **Act I. (Left to right in front of bar) Frank Keenan, Blanche Bates, Robert Hilliard, and J. W. Cope (1905).** *Courtesy Museum of the City of New York Theatre and Music Collection.*

Girl of the Golden West, The (11/14/05, Belasco, 224)

Rip-roaring David Belasco (A/P/D) melodrama about a virtuous barmaid (Blanche Bates), coveted by a villainous sheriff (Frank Keenan), and her love for a noble outlaw (Robert Hilliard). Highlight: drops of blood staining the sheriff's white handkerchief and revealing the presence of the wounded outlaw in the loft above.

SV: WB, 1930, Ann Harding, James Rennie, Harry Bannister; MGM, 1938, Jeanette MacDonald, Nelson Eddy, Walter Pidgeon, Leo Carrillo, Buddy Ebsen, Cliff Edwards.

Note: Puccini's opera based on the Belasco melodrama premiered at New York's Metropolitan in 1910. The leading roles were sung by Emmy Destinn, Enrico Caruso, and Pasquale Amato.

Girl on the Via Flaminia, The (2/9/54, Circle in the Square, 111)

In occupied Rome, 1944, a poor Italian girl (Betty Miller) finds herself stigmatized by the police and populace when she enters into an ill-fated love affair with an American soldier (Leo Penn). ". . . provocative and incisive" *(Journal-American)*. ". . . curiously lacking in emotional appeal" *(Post)*. A: Alfred Hayes b/o his novel of the same name. P/D: Jose Quintero.

SV: UA, 1953, *Act of Love,* Kirk Douglas, Dany Robin (directed by Anatole Litvak).

Girl Trouble (10/25/28, Belmont, 22)

Dominated son finally breaks free of his mother's apron strings. Mediocre farce-comedy by Barry Conners, author of *Applesauce* (1925), *The Patsy* (1925), etc. C: Alan Dinehart (D), Dorothy Hall, Lucia Moore, Sara Haden. P: Richard Herndon.

Girl with the Green Eyes, The (12/25/02, Savoy, 108)

A woman almost destroys her life, and the lives of those around her, because of her demonic jealousy and suspicion. Glib, popular Clyde Fitch (A/D) drama. C: Clara Bloodgood, Edith Taliaferro, Lucile Watson, Robert Drouet. P: Charles Frohman.

Girls in 509, The (10/15/58, Belasco, 117)

Satirical farce about a pair of rock-ribbed Republicans (Imogene Coca and Peggy Wood) who went into complete seclusion when FDR was elected president in 1932. Now, twenty-five years later, they are suddenly forced into contact with the outside world when their New York hotel is demolished. By the end of the play, both ladies conclude that there's not much difference nowadays between the two major political parties. ". . . funny only at intervals . . . ultimately tedious" *(New York Times)*. C: Robert Emhardt, King Donovan, Fred Stewart. A: Howard Teichmann. P: Alfred de Liagre, Jr. D: Bretaigne Windust. CD: Lucinda Ballard. SD: Donald Oenslager.

Girls of Summer (11/19/56, Longacre, 56)

A drama rife with pent-up neuroses and psychoses as a thirtyish spinster (Shelley Winters) tries to break up the summer romance of her younger sister and a

The Girl with the Green Eyes, **wedding scene. At center, Robert Drouet and Clara Bloodgood (1903).** *Courtesy Museum of the City of New York Theatre and Music Collection.*

bullheaded construction foreman (Pat Hingle). ". . . a flat and unexhilarating investigation into the bypaths of sex and frustration" *(Post).* ". . . as though Tennessee Williams had rewritten *The Voice of the Turtle" (Herald Tribune).* C: George Peppard (deb.), Lenka Peterson, Arthur Storch. A: N. Richard Nash. P: Cheryl Crawford. D: Jack Garfein. SD: Boris Aronson. M: Stephen Sondheim.

Give and Take (1/15/23, 49th Street, 188)

The conflicts between a successful California fruit canner and his college-educated, radically oriented son whose progressive ideas almost run the factory into bankruptcy. Fairly amusing slapdash farce-comedy by Aaron Hoffman. C: Louis Mann, George Sidney, Vivian Tobin. P: Max Marcin. D: W. H. Gilmore. R: (9/29/43, Bijou, 85) by A. L. Berman as *All For All.* C: Jack Pearl, Harry Green, Lyle Bettger, Loring Smith. D: Harry Green.

Give Us This Day (10/27/33, Booth, 3)

An inheritance divides and destroys members of a greedy New York City family. Drab, unconvincing drama by future screenwriter Howard Koch *(The Letter, Casablanca,* etc.). C: Paul Guilfoyle, Linda Watkins, Harlan Briggs. P: Curtis and Myers. D: Arthur Sircom.

Glad of It (12/28/03, Savoy, 32)

John Barrymore made his Broadway debut in a small role in this flaccid, essentially plotless Clyde Fitch (A/D) opus, written largely in lower East Side "dese-dem-dose" vernacular. C: Lucile Watson, Zelda Sears, Millie James, Grant Mitchell, Thomas Meighan, Hassard Short, Robert Warwick. P: Charles Frohman.

Glad Tidings (10/11/51, Lyceum, 100)

Literate, well-written romantic comedy about a middle-aged bachelor who discovers he is the father of a nineteen-year-old daughter. C: Melvyn Douglas (D), Signe Hasso, Haila Stoddard. A: Edward Mabley. P: Harald Bromley.

Glamour Preferred (11/15/40, Booth, 11)

Wife of a Hollywood glamour boy vanquishes the other woman in her husband's life. Creaky filmland comedy had little to recommend it. "Joke after joke is laboriously lifted from its sarcophagus and spun out of its winding sheet, until the stage is crowded with verbal mummies" *(Post).* C: Glenn Langan, Betty Lawford, Loring Smith, Flora Campbell, Louis Sorin, Stefan Schnabel, James Gregory, Elaine Perry, Henry Levin. A: Florence Ryerson and Colin Clements. P: Brock Pemberton. D: Antoinette Perry.

Glass Menagerie, The (3/31/45, Playhouse, 561)

Set in a shabby St. Louis tenement of the 1930's, Tennessee Williams' famous "memory play" explored the frustrated lives of three disparate characters: Amanda Wingfield (Laurette Taylor), a faded Southern belle clinging to memories of a more genteel past; Laura (Julie Haydon), her painfully shy and crippled daughter; and Tom (Eddie Dowling), the rebellious son who desperately wants to escape from his dull job and burdensome family. Concerned because Laura has no suitors, Amanda nags Tom into bringing home a friend (Anthony Ross) from work who, it turns out, is already engaged to be married. The play ends with Laura retreating to her dream world and her collection of glass figurines, while Tom finally flees home, as his father did before him. This poignant, semiautobiographical drama almost didn't make it to New York. In its opening week in Chicago, the play took in less than 3,500 dollars at the box office, and there was talk of closing the production then and there. Fortunately, business improved in subsequent weeks as

The Glass Menagerie. **Julie Haydon and Laurette Taylor (1945).** *Courtesy Museum of the City of New York Theatre and Music Collection.*

Chicago critics and columnists repeatedly urged their readers to attend the play. By the time *The Glass Menagerie* was ready to open in New York, news of its excellence preceded it. In addition, Laurette Taylor's return to the footlights in the Williams drama, after an absence of many years, stirred great expectations. America's first actress had led a tortured life (including recurrent bouts with alcoholism) since the death of her playwright-husband, Hartley Manners, in 1928. In the role of Amanda, Miss Taylor made the most triumphant comeback in the annals of the American stage. "The pure distilled essence of great acting," said one critic. "I never hope to see again, in the theatre, anything as perfect," said another. Amanda Wingfield proved to be Laurette Taylor's last part. She died the following year (1946) at age sixty-two. P: Eddie Dowling and Louis J. Singer. D: Eddie Dowling, Margo Jones, Laurette Taylor. M: Paul Bowles. SD: Jo Mielziner.

R: (11/21/56, City Center, 15). C: Helen Hayes, James Daly, Lois Smith, Lonny Chapman. D: Alan Schneider.

R: (5/4/65, Atkinson, 175). C: Maureen Stapleton, George Grizzard, Piper Laurie, Pat Hingle. D: George Keathley.

SV: WB, 1950, Gertrude Lawrence, Jane Wyman, Kirk Douglas, Arthur Kennedy (directed by Irving Rapper).

Note: The Glass Menagerie was Tennessee Williams' first Broadway play. Originally titled *The Gentleman Caller,* it was written while the author was under contract to Metro-Goldwyn-Mayer. Williams dutifully submitted the script to the studio, but they rejected it. Following the play's Broadway success, MGM reputedly bid $425,000 for the screen rights.

Gloria and Esperanza (2/4/70, ANTA, 13)

The off-off Broadway theatre group known as La Mama Experimental Theater Club came to Broadway as a guest of the American National Theater and Academy (ANTA). The play selected for this prestigious showcasing was a farce-fantasy about the maturation of a poet, Julius Esperanza. The playwright, Julie Bovasso, acted the part of his girl friend, Gloria. The play is an odyssey of self-discovery for Esperanza, placing him in locales as varied as a madhouse and a TV studio, peopled with crazy psychiatrists, villainous midgets, girl basketball-player dancers, and Oriental guerrillas. Circus music, pop tunes, and pageants with masks and extravagant costumes added to the anarchic tone of the production. The writing ranged from wild burlesque to lofty sentiment and the resultant mix elicited critical reactions ranging from delight to disdain. "... represents La Mama both at its most adventurous and its most self-indulgent... You do not have to understand Miss Bovasso's play to enjoy it" (Clive Barnes, *New York Times*). "A fantasy of excruciating length ... permissive, semi-professional" (Douglas Watt, *New York Daily News*). A: Julie Bovasso. C: Kevin O'Connor, Julie Bovasso, Herve Villechaize, Daffi, Dan Durning, Leonard Hicks, Alex Beall, Reigh Hagen, Maury Cooper, Ted Henning, John Bacher, Dennis Sokal, Wes Williams, Sara Dolley, Deirdre Simone, Marie D'Elia, Ella Luxembourg, Tom Rosica, Louis Ramos, Jane Sanford. D: Julie Bovasso. P: ANTA.

Gloriana (11/25/38, Little, 5)

Poorly written and produced comedy-drama about Queen Elizabeth (Blanche Yurka) and her love for the young Earl of Essex (Boyd Crawford). C: Tom Powers (D), Leslie Denison, Harold Vermilyea, Robert Breen, Celeste Holm (deb.). A: Ferdinand Bruckner. P: Theatre House, Inc.

Glorious Betsy (9/7/08, Lyric, 24)

Winsome French lass (Mary Mannering) falls in love with Napoleon's brother. Painfully arch comedy. A: Rida Johnson Young. P: Messrs. Shubert i.a.w. James K. Hackett. D: J. C. Huffman.

SV: WB, 1936, *Hearts Divided*, Marion Davies, Dick Powell, Claude Rains, Charlie Ruggles, Edward Everett Horton, Arthur Treacher.

Glory Hallelujah (4/6/26, Broadhurst, 15)

In the lobby of a seedy New York City hotel, various residents react to news of the end of the world in different ways. Intriguing but uneven comedy-drama by Thomas Mitchell and Bertram Bloch. C: Charles Bickford, June Walker, Lee Tracy, Allen Jenkins, Morris Ankrum, Hilda Vaughn. P/D: Guthrie McClintic.

God Loves Us (10/18/26, Maxine Elliott's 32)

Middle-aged greeting card writer is fired from his job, tries to make a new life for himself. Bleak drama by humorist J. P. McEvoy; retitled *The Go-Getters*. C: J. C. Nugent, Helen Lowell, Douglass Montgomery, Dorothy Peterson. P: Actors' Theatre. D: Kenneth Macgowan.

Goddess of Reason, The (2/15/09, Daly's, 48)

The adventures of a peasant girl (Julia Marlowe) during the French Revolution. Ambitious verse pageant by Mary Johnston, spectacular but lethargic. C: Sydney Greenstreet, Laurence Eyre. P: Messrs. Shubert. D: J. C. Huffman.

God's Favorite (12/11/74, Eugene O'Neill, 119)

A Neil Simon work that relates the story of Job. For laughs. The well-known sufferer of the Bible is here transplanted to affluent Long Island, and has become a cardboard box manufacturer (Vincent Gardenia). When a burglar alarm signals a prowler on the premises, it proves to be a messenger from God (Charles Nelson Reilly) announcing disaster on the way. The unique and unfailing Simon wit and marvelous playing by Gardenia and Reilly help disguise the flaws in this imaginative play. ". . . not one of his better works. Not only is the opening slow, but also the ending is anticlimactic . . . the cast is a Biblical delight" (Clive Barnes, *New York Times*). "The curtain rises on Act Two with devastation quite complete: strands of crystal from the vanished chandelier drooping forlornly over half a sofa, still smoking; the caryatids broken-backed, the towering rear window shriveled to matchsticks. The response out front is spontaneous creeping hilarity" (Walter Kerr, *New York Times*). A: Neil Simon. C: Vincent Gardenia, Charles Nelson Reilly, Terry Kiser, Maria Karnilova, Nick LaTour, Rosetta LeNoire, Laura Esterman, Lawrence John Moss. D: Michael Bennett. P: Emanuel Azenberg and Eugene V. Wolsk. SD: William Ritman. CD: Joseph G. Aulisi.

Gods of the Lightning (10/24/28, Little, 29)

Powerful indictment of the Sacco-Vanzetti case by Maxwell Anderson and Harold Hickerson—a theme Anderson successfully returned to seven years later in *Winterset* (1935). When a payroll messenger in a mining town is murdered, a bold labor organizer (Charles Bickford) and a timid anarchist (Horace Braham) are arrested and jailed. Their trial is blatantly rigged, the laborite's fiancée (Sylvia Sidney) is threatened, witnesses are bribed, and, finally, the two workmen are executed. *Gods of the Lightning* was a short-lived but highly effective journalistic melodrama, splendidly acted and produced. C: Barton MacLane, Morris Ankrum, Leo Bulgakov. P/D: Hamilton MacFadden.

Go-Getters, The

See *God Loves Us.*

Goin' Home (8/23/28, Hudson, 77)

Interesting but badly muddled 20's drama about the marriage of a black foreign legionnaire to a French lass shortly after the end of World War I. Fireworks erupt when a white officer (his former master on the old plantation) happens along. In the end, the soldier and the officer return to the states together, leaving the French girl to fend for herself. C: Richard Hale, Russell Hicks, Barbara Bulgakov. A: Ransom Rideout. P: Brock Pemberton. D: Brock Pemberton and Antoinette Perry.

Going Gay (8/3/33, Morosco, 24)

Trite comedy about an unconventional actress who almost wrecks her daughter's marriage to a society swell. C: Edith King, Walter Kingsford, Rita Vale, Thais Lawton, Barnett Parker, Alan Marshal. A: William Miles and Donald Blackwell (D). P: Messrs. Shubert.

Gold (6/1/21, Frazee, 13)

Eugene O'Neill's tragedy in four acts was an extension and elaboration of his early one-act play, *Where the Cross Is Made*. Obsessed by lust for buried treasure, a sea captain (Willard Mack) broods guiltily over the murder of two of his former shipmates. They were slain to prevent them revealing the hiding place of the treasure. The captain's growing insanity triggers the death of his wife and the madness of his son. When he dies, the prized treasure turns out to be a chest full of worthless trinkets. ". . . youthful romantic melodrama . . . a feeble play" (J. Ranken Towse, *Post*). *Gold* was one of O'Neill's least effective efforts. Years later he dismissed the play as "painfully bungled." P: John D. Williams. D: Homer Saint-Gaudens.

Gold Diggers, The (9/30/19, Lyceum, 720)

Highly successful comedy concerning a trio of money-chasing chorus girls out to land some "rich millionaires." As the leader of the girls, Ina Claire gave an especially deft and winning performance. C: Bruce McRae, H. Reeves-Smith, Horace Braham, Jobyna Howland, Luella Gear, Lilyan Tashman. A: Avery Hopwood. P/D: David Belasco.

SV: WB, 1929, *The Gold Diggers of Broadway*, Winnie Lightner, Nick Lucas, Ann Pennington, Nancy Welford, Lilyan Tashman, Conway Tearle; 1933, *Gold Diggers of 1933*, Ruby Keeler, Dick Powell, Joan Blondell, Warren William, Aline MacMahon, Ginger Rogers, Guy Kibbee, Ned Sparks; 1951, *Painting the Clouds with Sunshine*, Virginia Mayo, Dennis Morgan, Gene Nelson, Tom Conway.

Note: A silent version (WB, 1923) starred Hope Hampton.

Gold Eagle Guy (11/28/34, Morosco, 66)

The rise and fall of a ruthless San Francisco shipping magnate (J. Edward Bromberg) who meets a well-deserved death in the 1906 earthquake. Lavish costume drama failed to enthuse critics or public. C: Stella Adler, Luther Adler, Morris Carnovsky, Elia Kazan, Jules (John) Garfield, Clifford Odets, Alan Baxter, Roman Bohnen, Sanford Meisner, Robert Lewis, Art Smith, Russell Collins, Alexander Kirkland, Margaret Barker. A: Melvin Levy. P: The Group Theatre i.a.w. D. A. Doran, Jr. D: Lee Strasberg. CH: Helen Tamiris. SD: Donald Oenslager.

Golden Boy (11/4/37, Belasco, 248)

Clifford Odets' story of a moody Italian boy, Joe Bonaparte, who is torn between dreams of being a violinist or winning fame and fortune as a prizefighter. He opts for the prizefight racket and becomes surprisingly good at it. Caught in a whirlpool called "success," Joe is pulled irresistibly toward the center with a dizzying speed that can end only in his death. "For the most part it is a pithy and thoroughly absorbing drama that restores to the theatre a pungent theatrical talent" *(New York Times)*. *Golden Boy* was the most successful production in the history of The Group Theatre (P). It was also Clifford Odets' most popular play. Some critics saw parallels between the story of Joe Bonaparte—a frustrated man following a career for which he has a secret loathing—and Odets' desertion of Broadway for Hollywood. C: Luther Adler, Frances Farmer, Morris Carnovsky, Roman Bohnen, Art Smith, Jules (John) Garfield, Lee J. Cobb, Elia Kazan, Phoebe Brand, Robert Lewis, Howard da Silva, Martin Ritt, Karl Malden (deb.). D: Harold Clurman. SD: Mordecai Gorelik. *Note:* The national touring company cast was headed by Francis Lederer, Louis Calhern, Lee J. Cobb, and Betty Furness, and was directed by Stella Adler. R: (3/12/52, ANTA, 55) by ANTA. C: John Garfield, Lee J. Cobb, Art Smith, Bette Grayson, Joseph Wiseman, Arthur O'Connell, Jack Klugman. D: Clifford Odets. Musicalized (1964) by Clifford Odets, William Gibson, Charles Strouse, and Lee Adams with a cast headed by Sammy Davis, Paula Wayne, Lola Falana, and Billy Daniels.

SV: Col, 1939, William Holden, Barbara Stanwyck, Adolphe Menjou, Lee J. Cobb, Joseph Calleia, Sam Levene (directed by Rouben Mamoulian).

Note: Odets had promised the title role in

Golden Boy to twenty-four-year-old John Garfield. Instead, the Group Theatre relegated the actor to a minor comedy-relief part in the production. Thoroughly disgruntled by this decision, Garfield fled to Hollywood shortly thereafter. He returned to Broadway in 1952 to star in the revival of *Golden Boy*. He died May 21, 1952 at the age of thirty-nine.

Golden Days (11/1/21, Gaiety, 40)

Small-town gal (Helen Hayes) makes boyfriend jealous by flirtin' with another feller. Mawkish, super-sugary comedy by Marion Short and Sidney Toler (D). (Toler later gained a measure of screen fame as inscrutable Oriental detective Charlie Chan). C: Donald Gallaher, Selena Royle. P: Tyler and Erlanger.

Golden Fleecing (10/15/59, Henry Miller, 84)

Breezy farce about a naval officer's scheme to use his ship's electronic computer to beat the roulette wheel at a Venice casino. C: Tom Poston, Suzanne Pleshette, Constance Ford, Robert Elston, Robert Carraway, Mickey Deems, Richard Kendrick. A: Lorenzo Semple, Jr. P: Courtney Burr and Gilbert Miller. D: Abe Burrows. SD: Frederick Fox. M: Dana Suesse.
SV: MGM, 1961, *The Honeymoon Machine,* Steve McQueen, Jim Hutton, Paula Prentiss, Dean Jagger, Jack Weston (directed by Richard Thorpe).

Golden Journey, The (9/15/36, Booth, 23)

Three impoverished writers, sharing a flat in Manhattan's East Fifties, spend most of their time chasing wealthy women. Would-be chic comedy failed to ring the bell. C: Alan Bunce, Hugh Rennie, Alan Hewitt, Eleanor Lynn, Leona Powers. A: Edwin Gilbert. P: Messrs. Shubert. D: Harry Wagstaff Gribble.

Golden Six, The (10/25/58, York, 16)

A cycle of intrigue, corruption, and violence results when Augustus Caesar is forced to choose one of his six grandsons as his successor. This intricately plotted account of the decline and fall of the Roman Empire was Maxwell Anderson's last play. Presented O/B by Warner LeRoy (D) and Norman Twain, the 1958 production failed to impress the critics and ran little more than two weeks. C: Viveca Lindfors, Paul Mann, Alvin Epstein, Thayer David, Roger Evan Boxill.

Golden State, The (11/25/50, Fulton, 25)

Machine-stitched comedy about the get-rich-quick schemes of some scatter-brained southern California nitwits. C: Josephine Hull, Ernest Truex, Polly Rowles, Jocelyn Brando, John Randolph. A/D: Samuel Spewack. P: Bella Spewack.

Goldfish, The (4/17/22, Maxine Elliott's, 169)

Ambitious divorcée (Marjorie Rambeau) keeps marrying (and divorcing) until she achieves financial security. True confessions hokum, very popular with the ladies. C: Wilton Lackaye, Lucille La Verne, Robert T. Haines, Norma Mitchell. A: Gladys Unger, from a play by Armont and Gerbidon. P: Messrs. Shubert. D: Stuart Walker.

Good, The (10/5/38, Windsor, 9)

Frigid wife drives her husband into the arms of another woman and her son into the arms of another man. Awkwardly handled 30's drama was a quick failure. C: Frances Starr, Robert Keith, Leona Powers, Harry Bannister. A/D: Chester Erskine. P: Norman and Irvin Pincus.

Good as Gold (3/7/57, Belasco, 4)

A young botanist (Roddy McDowall) stumbles upon a magic formula to grow giant-size vegetables at high speed. He envisions his discovery as a boon to mankind that will end starvation, but it isn't long before he is being investigated by dimwitted congressmen and hounded as a subversive by the FBI. ". . . generates a fair number of chuckles . . . but it falls apart long before the final curtain" *(World-Telegram)*. ". . . a disappointingly feeble and haphazard cartoon. . . . The use of the Federal Bureau of Investigation as a satirical butt, by the way, appears to have aroused such shocked indignation in certain out-of-town critical minds that the kidding was toned down by the alarmed management. It is very mild now, which is one of the comedy's weaknesses" *(Post)*. This 1957 satirical comedy was adapted from a novel by Alfred Toombs by John Patrick, author of *The Hasty Heart* (1945) and *The Teahouse of the August Moon* (1953). C: Zero Mostel, Paul Ford, Robert Emhardt, Dana Elcar, Loretta Leversee. P: Cheryl Crawford i.a.w. William Myers. D: Albert Marre. SD: Peter Larkin.

Good Bad Woman, A (2/9/25, Comedy, 17)

Trashy melodrama about a heartless harlot who seduces her employer's young son. C: Helen MacKellar, Robert Strange, Edith King. A: William J. McNally. P: William A. Brady and A. H. Woods.

Good Earth, The (10/17/32, Guild, 56)

Ambitious adaptation of Pearl Buck's popular novel detailing the rise of Wang Lung (Claude Rains), a Chinese peasant, from poverty to riches. Though greed and vanity almost destroy Wang, his vigor, fortitude, and enduring love of the soil see him through such adversities as famine, revolution, pestilence, and the death of his patient and loving wife O-Lan (Alla Nazimova). Well acted by its principal players—including Henry Travers as Wang's father, Sydney Greenstreet as his uncle, and Jessie Ralph as his aunt—*The Good Earth* proved a competent but uninspired dramatization of Miss Buck's Pulitzer Prize novel. A: Owen and Donald Davis. P: The Theatre Guild. D: Phillip Moeller. SD: Lee Simonson.
SV: MGM, 1937, Paul Muni, Luise Rainer, Walter Connolly, Jessie Ralph, Charley Grapewin, Tilly Losch, Keye Luke.

Good Fellow, The (10/5/26, Playhouse, 8)

George S. Kaufman-Herman J. Mankiewicz comedy about a small-town backslapper (John E. Hazzard) whose misguided loyalty to a fraternal organization jeopardizes his family's financial security. The play, a resounding box-office failure, contained some neat satirical jabs at Rotarian-type "joiners." P: Crosby Gaige. D: George S. Kaufman and Howard Lindsay.
SV: Par, 1943, *The Good Fellows,* Cecil Kellaway, Mabel Paige, Helen Walker, James Brown, Rod Cameron.

Good Gracious Annabelle (10/31/16, Republic, 111)

Complications ensue when some temporarily impecunious society characters hire themselves out as servants on a posh Long Island estate. Delightfully witty 1916 comedy by Clare Kummer. The excellent cast was headed by Roland Young, Walter Hampden, Lola Fisher, Edwin Nicander and May Vokes. P/D: Arthur Hopkins. SD: Robert Edmond Jones.
SV: Fox, 1931, *Annabelle's Affairs,* Jeanette MacDonald, Victor McLaglen, Roland Young.

Good Hunting (11/21/38, Hudson, 2)

A fatuous British general sends his troops

to almost certain death behind enemy lines. Overstated but frequently incisive satire on the military mentality—a witty black comedy years ahead of its time. *Good Hunting* was written by Nathanael West and Joseph Schrank. Schrank was chief sketchwriter of the hit musical revue, *Pins and Needles,* and co-author of *Page Miss Glory* (1934). West is best remembered for his novels, *The Day of the Locust* and *Miss Lonelyhearts.* He married Eileen McKenney, the heroine of *My Sister Eileen;* they were killed in an automobile accident in 1940. *Good Hunting* was Nathanael West's only play. It closed after two performances. C: Aubrey Mather, Nicholas Joy, Estelle Winwood, George Tobias. P: Jerome Mayer (D) and Leonard Field, SD: Norris Houghton.

Good Little Devil, A (1/8/13, Republic, 133)

Mary Pickford as a little blind girl whose sight is restored by a band of fairies. Fine cast in a saccharine saga written by Austin Strong, author of *Three Wise Fools* (1918) and *Seventh Heaven* (1922); based on a play by Rosemond Gerard and Maurice Rostand. C: Lillian Gish, Ernest Truex, Norman Taurog, Ernest Lawford, Etienne Girardot, Regina Wallace, William Norris, Wilda Bennett. P/D: David Belasco.

Good Men and True (10/25/35, Biltmore, 11)

Hackneyed melodrama about a group of jurors debating a midwestern murder trial. C: Martha Sleeper, Donald Foster,

A Good Little Devil. Scene with Lillian Gish, Wilda Bennett, Claire Burke, Mary Pickford, Regina Wallace, Georgia Fursman, and Edan Griffen (1913). *Courtesy Museum of the City of New York Theatre and Music Collection.*

Weldon Heyburn. A: Brian Marlow and Frank Merlin (P). D: Louis M. Simon.

Good Morning Corporal (8/8/44, Playhouse, 13)

Patriotic ninny marries a soldier, sailor, and marine at the same time. ". . . a libel on the arts of playwriting and directing" *(World-Telegram)*. C: Charita Bauer, Joel Marston, Russell Hardie, Lionel Wilson. A: Milton Herbert Gropper and Joseph Shalleck. P/D: William B. Friedlander.

Good Neighbor (10/21/41, Windsor, 1)

Warmhearted Jewish matriarch (Anna Appel) hides German youth in her Baltimore home, and is shot and killed for her pains. Nobel Prize novelist Sinclair Lewis made his Broadway debut as director (and principal backer) of this awkward tolerance preachment. The play closed after one performance. A: Jack Levin. P: Sam Byrd.

Good Soup, The (3/2/60, Plymouth, 21)

The life of a calculating cocotte as she goes from man to man, from rags to riches, and from youth to middle age. Told in a series of flashbacks, with the central character portrayed by two actresses (Ruth Gordon as the middle-aged whore, Diane Cilento as her younger self). ". . . commonplace, repetitious . . . a monotonous tale" *(New York Times)*. C: Mildred Natwick, Sam Levene, Ernest Truex, Jules Munshin, George S. Irving, Lou Antonio, Pat Harrington. A: Garson Kanin (D) b/o a play by Felicien Marceau. P: David Merrick.

Goodbye Again (12/28/32, Masque, 212)

The love life of a novelist on a midwestern lecture tour is complicated by the appearance of an old flame. "A humorously observant fable . . . told with a saucy eye to authentic character" (George Jean Nathan, *Judge*). Osgood Perkins played the amorous novelist and Sally Bates was his witty, oh-so-wise secretary. The surprise hit of the eyening was scored by twenty-four-year-old James Stewart in the brief, two-line role of a chauffeur. His slowly drawled exit line ("Mrs. Mainwaring's going to be sore as hell") never failed to bring down the house. C: Myron McCormick, Katherine Squire, Hugh Rennie, Jackie Kelk. A: Allan Scott and George Haight. P/D: Arthur J. Beckhard.

SV: WB, 1933, Warren William, Joan Blondell, Genevieve Tobin, Hugh Herbert, Ruth Donnelly, Wallace Ford; 1941, *Honeymoon for Three*, George Brent, Ann Sheridan, Osa Massen, Charles Ruggles, Jane Wyman, Lee Patrick, Walter Catlett, Johnny Downs.

Goodbye Charlie (12/16/59, Lyceum, 109)

Farce about a murdered Hollywood lecher who returns to earth as a sexy female (Lauren Bacall) with predatory male traits and libido intact. "A one-joke play [that] quickly dwindles into monotony and dullness. . . . *Goodbye Charlie* gives no indication that sex change is a good comic plot conception" *(Post)*. C: Sydney Chaplin, Sarah Marshall. A/D: George Axelrod. P: Leland Hayward. SD: Oliver Smith.

SV: Fox, 1964, Debbie Reynolds, Tony Curtis, Walter Matthau, Pat Boone, Joanna Barnes, Martin Gabel (directed by Vincente Minnelli).

Goodbye in the Night (3/18/40, Biltmore, 8)

An escaped lunatic goes on a murder rampage to settle an old grudge. This confusing, badly botched mystery drama was produced and directed by George Abbott. To add to the general confusion, the actors' names were printed in the program without specifying which parts they played. "The involutions of its plot would doubtless evade Philo Vance, Einstein, Sherlock Holmes, J. Edgar

Hoover . . ." *(Post).* C: James Bell, Millard Mitchell, Natalie Schafer, Mary Mason, Paul Ballantyne, Ruth McDevitt, Marilyn Erskine, Jean Adair, Edith Van Cleve. A: Jerome Mayer.

Goodbye, My Fancy (11/17/48), Morosco, 446)

When liberal congresswoman Agatha Reed (Madeleine Carroll) returns to her old school to receive an honorary degree, she finds academic freedom being curtailed by the spineless college president (Conrad Nagel) whom she had once loved. Her disenchantment drives Agatha into the arms of a *Life* photographer (Sam Wanamaker). "A tremendously likable comedy . . . a thoroughly engaging play" *(Sun).* No film star in years received better notices in a Broadway debut performance than Madeleine Carroll in *Goodbye, My Fancy.* Also sharing in the critical plaudits was Shirley Booth in the role of the heroine's wisecracking secretary. A: Fay Kanin. P: Michael Kanin i.a.w. Aldrich and Myers. D: Sam Wanamaker. CD: Emeline Roche. SD: Donald Oenslager.

SV: WB, 1951, Joan Crawford, Robert Young, Frank Lovejoy, Eve Arden, Janice Rule, Lurene Tuttle, Howard St. John.

Goodbye People, The (12/3/68, Barrymore, 7)

Frequently touching character study of the problems of an elderly Coney Island concessionaire. In the leading role, Milton Berle gave a surprisingly sensitive, understated performance. *The Goodbye People* was written and directed by Herb Gardner, author of *A Thousand Clowns* (1962). C: Brenda Vaccaro, Bob Dishy, Tony Lo Bianco. P: Feuer and Martin.

Good-bye Please (10/24/34, Ritz, 2)

Romantic problems of a sophisticated New York couple. Dreary 30's comedy. C: Selena Royle, Robert Keith, Eric Dressler, Percy Kilbride. A: Burt Clifton. P/D: Edward Mendelssohn.

Goose for the Gander, A (1/23/45, Playhouse, 15)

Neglected wife (Gloria Swanson) invites a trio of admirers for a weekend visit in order to make her husband (Conrad Nagel) jealous. Miss Swanson made her Broadway debut in this wobbly 40's comedy. ". . . a dismaying trifle, an error for all concerned" *(Sun).* A: Harold J. Kennedy. P: Leventhal and McCoy. D: Tommy Ward. CD: Valentina. SD: Frederick Fox.

Goose Hangs High, The (1/29/24, Bijou, 186)

The efforts of a well-to-do family—especially the irresponsible younger generation—to adjust themselves to sudden financial reverses. Entertaining, cleverly written comedy-drama by Lewis Beach. C: Norman Trevor, Katherine Grey, Eric Dressler, Mrs. Thomas Whiffen. P: Dramatists' Theatre. D: James Forbes.

SV: Par, 1932, *This Reckless Age,* Buddy Rogers, Peggy Shannon, Charles Ruggles, Richard Bennett, Frances Starr.

Gorilla, The (4/28/25, Selwyn, 257)

"Out go the lights! Into the mystery-mansion stalks *The Gorilla*—the mind of a master criminal with the lust-cravings of a beast. Enter Mulligan and Garrity, two blundering detectives who see all, hear all, and know nothing. . . ." Thus ran the ads for this 1925 spoof of the shriek-and-shudder *genre.* Clever, suspenseful, highly comical mystery-comedy. C: Clifford Dempsey, Frank McCormack, Robert Strange. A: Ralph Spence. P: Donald Gallaher. D: Walter Scott.

SV: WB, 1931, Lila Lee, Joe Frisco, Harry Gribbon, Walter Pidgeon; Fox, 1939, The Ritz Brothers, Lionel Atwill, Bela Lugosi, Joseph

Calleia, Anita Louise, Edward Norris, Patsy Kelly, Wally Vernon, Paul Harvey.

Gorilla Queen (4/24/67, Martinique, 64)

Homosexually slanted satire on the Maria Montez-Sabu-Turhan Bey screenland epics of the 1940's. An O/B curio with a no-name cast; incidental music and lyrics by Al Carmines. A: Ronald Tavel. P: Paul Libin. D: Lawrence Kornfeld.

Gossipy Sex, The (4/19/27, Mansfield, 23)

Unfunny portrait of a loudmouth troublemaker. C: Lynne Overman, Una Merkel, Thomas W. Ross. A: Lawrence Grattan. P: John Golden. D: Sam Forrest.

Governor's Lady, The (9/10/12, Republic, 135)

Wife fears losing her husband to a younger woman. Third-rate triangle drama. Highlight: a scene in Childs' Restaurant, transferred to the stage with photographic fidelity, complete even to sizzling wheatcakes. C: Gladys Hanson, Emma Dunn, Emmett Corrigan, Stuart Walker, Milton Sills. A: Alice Bradley. P: David Belasco and William Elliott. D: Belasco.

Gramercy Ghost (4/26/51, Morosco, 100)

A revolutionary war ghost falls in love with a mortal. ". . . a harmless but oddly tedious little play . . . offers scant fun" (*Post*). C: Sarah Churchill (deb.), Richard Waring, Robert Sterling (deb.), Mabel Paige, Harry Townes, John Marley. A: John Cecil Holm. P: Roger Clark i.a.w. E. M. Frankel. D: Reginald Denham.

Grand Army Man, A (10/16/07, Stuyvesant, 149)

Soggy David Warfield vehicle about the travails of a kindly Civil War veteran and his dishonest foster son. C: Taylor Holmes, William Elliott, Jane Cowl, Antoinette Perry. A: David Belasco, Pauline Phelps, Marion Short. P/D: Belasco.

Grand Duke, The (11/1/21, Lyceum, 131)

When a Russian roué (Lionel Atwill) discovers he has an illegitimate son (Morgan Farley) in Paris, he secretly stage manages the youth's romantic escapades. Sophisticated, adroitly written David Belasco (P/D) comedy by Achmed Abdullah, extensively revised from a play by Sacha Guitry. A few seasons after *The Grand Duke* closed on tour, author Abdullah, in collaboration with Faith Baldwin, penned a thinly disguised portrait of Belasco and his amours in a sensationalistic novel entitled *Broadway Interlude*. The aging producer was painted as a lecherous tyrant who would go to any lengths to impose his iron will.

The Governor's Lady. **Emmett Corrigan and Emma Dunn (September 10, 1912).** *Courtesy Museum of the City of New York Theatre and Music Collection.*

Broadway Interlude was subsequently dramatized for the stage (1934).

Grand Hotel (11/13/30, National, 444)

A bored ballerina, a public stenographer, a dying bookkeeper, and a crooked industrialist find their paths cross within the walls of a luxurious Berlin hotel during an eventful thirty-six hour period. Written by Vicki Baum (Austrian novelist, later a naturalized American), this fascinating and panoramic play was the talk of the town in 1930. The all-star film version won the Academy Award as best picture of the year. C: Eugenie Leontovich, Henry Hull, Sam Jaffe, Siegfried Rumann, Hortense Alden, Rafaella Ottiano, Walter Vonnegut, Joseph Calleia. Ad.: William A. Drake. P/D: Herman Shumlin.

SV: MGM, 1932, Greta Garbo, John Barrymore, Joan Crawford, Wallace Beery, Lionel Barrymore, Lewis Stone, Jean Hersholt, Rafaella Ottiano (directed by Edmund Goulding); 1945, *Weekend at the Waldorf,* Ginger Rogers, Lana Turner, Walter Pidgeon, Van Johnson, Edward Arnold, Robert Benchley, Phyllis Thaxter, Keenan Wynn (directed by Robert Z. Leonard).

Note: *At the Grand,* a musical version of *Grand Hotel* starring Paul Muni, was produced on the West Coast in 1958, but never reached Broadway.

Grand Prize, The (1/26/55, Plymouth, 21)

During a TV quiz show, a romantically inclined secretary wins the chance to become her boss's boss for twenty-four hours. ". . . an intermittent and mechanical little antic" *(Post).* Betsy Palmer (deb.) made an attractive heroine; John Newland as the supposedly irresistibly handsome boss was considerably less effective in the leading male role. Also in the cast: Tom Poston, June Lockhart, William Windom, Nancy Wickwire. A: Ronald Alexander. P/D: Shepard Traube.

Grand Tour, The (12/10/51, Martin Beck, 8)

Slight tale of a spinster schoolteacher on a European holiday and of the young bank embezzler with whom she falls in love. "Not substantial or convincing enough—or absorbing enough—to be compelling theatre" *(News).* C: Beatrice Straight, Richard Derr. A/D: Elmer Rice. P: The Playwrights Company. CD: Motley. SD: Howard Bay. "*The Grand Tour* opened and closed in a week," said Elmer Rice. "It was far from a total loss, however, for it has had numerous foreign productions, and more radio and television performances both here and abroad than any other play of mine."

Grandma's Diary (9/22/48, Henry Miller, 6)

Radio writer gets her plots from her grandmother's diary; one of the most witless and amateurish plays ever presented on Broadway. "I know that there were three acts because I was one of the few spectators foolhardy enough to sit through them. . . . It is truly the laughless comedy" *(Post).* A/P/D: Albert Wineman Barker.

Grass Harp, The (3/27/52, Martin Beck, 36)

An oddly assorted quartet find sanctuary from the evils of the world in a forest tree house, until they are ousted from their arboreal retreat by their fellow townspeople. Opinions as to the merits of this whimsical fable by Truman Capote were mixed. The play failed on Broadway, but was successfully revived O/B (4/27/53), under Jose Quintero's direction, at the arena-styled Circle in the Square Theatre in Greenwich Village. The Broadway cast of *The Grass Harp* was headed by Mildred Natwick, Russell

Collins, Georgia Burke, Johnny Stewart, Lenka Peterson, Alice Pearce, Ruth Nelson, Jonathan Harris, Sterling Holloway, and Val Dufour. P: Saint Subber i.a.w. Rita Allen. D: Robert Lewis. CD/SD: Cecil Beaton. M: Virgil Thomson. Musicalized (1971) by Kenward Elmslie and Claibe Richardson with Barbara Cook, Carol Brice, Ruth Ford, Russ Thacker, Karen Morrow, John Baragrey, Max Showalter.

Great Barrington, The (2/19/31, Avon, 15)

Tedious comedy about a ghost (Otto Kruger) who returns to set matters right for his snobbish descendants. C: Anne Revere (deb.), Natalie Schafer, Charles Dalton. A: Franklin L. Russell. P: Oliver Bailey.

Great Big Doorstep, The (11/26/42, Morosco, 28)

The efforts of a Cajun family in Louisiana to move out of their tumbledown shack and into a proper home. Modest folk comedy, well-acted by Louis Calhern and Dorothy Gish. A: Frances Goodrich and Albert Hackett b/o a novel by E. P. O'Donnell. P/D: Herman Shumlin. SD: Howard Bay.

Great Day in the Morning (3/28/62, Henry Miller, 13)

Will a boozing, brawling, good-hearted divorcée (Colleen Dewhurst) return to the Roman Catholic church after an absence of twenty years? This was the central situation in this nostalgic period comedy about a group of roistering Irish-Americans in the St. Louis of 1928. "A ramshackle vehicle for some wonderfully warm and completely believable characters" (Post). C: J. D. Cannon, Peggy Burke, Frances Sternhagen, Clifton James, David Canary, Thomas Carlin, Lou Frizzell, Eulabelle Moore. A: Alice Cannon.* P: Theodore Mann and George C. Scott. D: Jose Quintero. CD: Noel Taylor. SD: Lester Polakov.

---

*Wife of actor J. D. Cannon.

Great Divide, The (10/3/06, Princess, 238)

A straitlaced New England heroine (Margaret Anglin) promises to marry a rough-hewn Westerner (Henry Miller) if he will save her from the clutches of three Arizona desperados. Thereafter, the play's interest lies in the efforts of the two leading characters to bridge the gap between the puritanism of the East and the easygoing tolerance of the West. Considered a landmark production, hailed as The Great American Drama of its time, *The Great Divide* seems contrived and melodramatic today. It did, however, blaze the way for subsequent plays of originality and literary merit. C: Henry B. Walthall, Mrs. Thomas Whiffen, Laura Hope Crews. A: William Vaughn Moody. P/D: Henry Miller.

SV: WB, 1930, Dorothy Mackaill, Ian Keith, Myrna Loy; 1931, *Woman Hungry,* Sidney Blackmer, Lila Lee.

Great Gatsby, The (2/2/26, Ambassador, 113)

Reasonably faithful transcription of F. Scott Fitzgerald's 1925 novel about racketeer Jay Gatsby who buys a fabulous Long Island estate to be near the woman he loved and lost. ". . . retains most of the novel's peculiar glamour" *(New York Times)*. Well-acted, especially by James Rennie as Gatsby and Florence Eldridge as Daisy, and smoothly staged by George Cukor, *The Great Gatsby* provided an engrossing evening in the theatre. C: Eliot Cabot, Carol Goodner, Porter Hall, Catherine Willard. A: Owen Davis. P: William A. Brady.

SV: Par, 1949, Alan Ladd, Betty Field, Macdonald Carey, Barry Sullivan, Ruth Hussey, Howard da Silva,

Shelley Winters; 1974, Robert Redford, Mia Farrow, Bruce Dern, Karen Black, Scott Wilson, Sam Waterston, Lois Chiles, Howard da Silva.

Note: A silent version (Par, 1926) featured a cast that included Warner Baxter, Lois Wilson, Neil Hamilton, Georgia Hale, William Powell, Hale Hamilton, and Eric Blore.

Great God Brown, The (1/23/26, Greenwich Village, 271)

Symbolic drama by Eugene O'Neill in which the leading characters wear dual personality masks representing the faces they present to the world. The protagonists, self-confident businessman William Brown and sensitive artist Dion Anthony, are physically two but psychically one. When Anthony dies, Brown takes his mask. Anthony's wife accepts Brown as her husband, for she has known and loved only Dion's mask, not his true self. C: Robert Keith, William Harrigan, Leona Hogarth, Ann Shoemaker. When no commercial manager would back his "mystical mystery play," O'Neill produced it himself in partnership with Kenneth Macgowan and Robert Edmond Jones (D/SD). Despite an ambiguous third act ("the last scenes approach chaos" said one reviewer), *The Great God Brown* was a critical and popular success. A few weeks after its O/B opening, the production was transferred uptown for an eight-month run. *The Great God Brown* was said to be its author's personal favorite of all his plays.

R: (10/6/59, Coronet, 32) by Theatre Incorporated. C: Fritz Weaver, Robert Lansing, Nan Martin, Gerry Jedd, J. D. Cannon. D: Stuart Vaughan.

R: (12/10/72, Lyceum, 19) by New Phoenix Company. C: John McMartin, John Glover, Katherine Helmond, Marilyn Sokol. D: Harold Prince.

The Great God Brown. **Leona Hogart and William Harrigan (Greenwich Village Theatre, 1926).** *Courtesy Museum of the City of New York Theatre and Music Collection.*

Great Indoors, The (2/1/66, O'Neill, 7)

Muddled opus about multiracial problems in the deep South. C: Geraldine Page, Curt Jurgens (deb.), Clarence Williams III. A: Irene Kamp. P: George and Granat. D: George Schaefer.

Great Lover, The (11/10/15, Longacre, 245)

Temperamental opera star (Leo Ditrichstein) loses his sweetheart to younger rival. Frothy sex comedy by Ditrichstein and Frederic and Fanny Hatton. The play ran for two years in London. P: Cohan and Harris. D: Sam Forrest.

R: (10/11/32, Waldorf, 23) by Wee and Leventhal. C: Lou Tellegen. D: Gustave Bowhan.

Great Magoo, The (12/2/32, Selwyn, 11)

Comedy-drama by Ben Hecht and Gene Fowler about the torrid romance of a flagpole sitter and a Coney Island trollop. Described by its authors as "something like *Romeo and Juliet*," this bawdy opus was blackjacked by the critics. The show was produced by Billy Rose and directed by George Abbott. C: Paul Kelly, Claire Carleton, Harry Green, Millard Mitchell, Percy Kilbride, Dennie Moore, Charlotte Granville, Victor Kilian.

SV: Par, 1934, *Shoot the Works,* Jack Oakie, Dorothy Dell, Arline Judge, Alison Skipworth, Roscoe Karns, William Frawley, Lew Cody, Ben Bernie; 1939, *Some Like it Hot,* Bob Hope, Shirley Ross, Una Merkel, Gene Krupa.

Great Necker, The (3/6/28, Ambassador, 39)

Foolish farce about a would-be movie magnate who tries to charm a bevy of well-to-do belles. C: Taylor Holmes, Raymond Walburn, Marjorie Gateson, Irene Purcell, Blanche Ring. A: Elmer Harris. P: Chamberlain Brown. D: J. Fred Butler.

Great Scott (9/2/29, 49th Street, 16)

First play by screenwriter *(Casablanca, The Letter, Letter from an Unknown Woman, The Thirteenth Letter)* Howard Koch, co-author of *In Time to Come* (1941). *Great Scott* dealt with a young college graduate who revitalizes a paternalistically run company town by putting his labor-management theories into practice. Slowly paced, shrilly written, it wasn't much of a play. C: Ray Harper, Millard Mitchell. P: L. A. Safian. D: Albert Bannister.

Great Sebastians, The (1/4/56, ANTA, 174)

A vaudeville mind-reading act (Alfred Lunt and Lynn Fontanne) become embroiled in a political conspiracy behind the Iron Curtain. Threatened with imprisonment unless they collaborate with the Communists, the self-centered but lovable frauds escape across the border in the nick of time. This "melodramatic comedy" was written and produced by Howard Lindsay and Russel Crouse, authors of *Life with Father* (1939), *State of the Union* (1945), etc. ". . . a rather flimsy charade . . . *The Great Sebastians* really ought to be better; but the Lunts couldn't be" *(Journal-American).* C: Simon Oakland, Ben Astar, Eugenia Rawls. D: Bretaigne Windust. CD: Mainbocher. SD: Raymond Sovey.

Great White Hope, The (10/3/68, Alvin, 556)

Epic drama dealing with the rise and fall of Jack Johnson (here called Jack Jefferson), the world's first black heavyweight champion (1908–15). The play depicts Johnson in collision with society as he tries to ignore the outrage over his white mistress and battle the racist forces seeking to remove his crown. In the end, plunged into poverty and despair, he is subjected to the ultimate degradation: being forced to throw a championship fight to a white opponent whom he could easily have beaten. *The Great White Hope,* which marked the Broadway debut of author Howard Sackler, won the Pulitzer, Critics, and Tony Awards as best play of the year. The production was splendidly directed and acted, especially by James Earl Jones in the leading role—a virtuoso performance that made theatre history. C: Jane Alexander,* Lou Gilbert, Marlene Warfield,* Jimmy Pelham,* Peter Masterson, Eugene R. Wood, Marshall Efron, George Mathews. P: Herman Levin. CD: David Toser. SD: Robin Wagner.

SV: Fox, 1970, James Earl Jones, Jane Alexander, Lou Gilbert, Joel Fluellen, Chester Morris, Robert Webber, Marlene Warfield, Hal Holbrook, Beah Richards, R. G.

Armstrong, Moses Gunn (directed by Martin Ritt).

---

*Broadway debuts.

Greatest Man Alive!, The (5/8/57, Barrymore, 5)

Meandering comedy about the unsuccessful efforts of a seventy-two-year-old windbag (Dennis King) to commit suicide. A: Tony Webster. P: Frederick Fox (SD) i.a.w. Elliott Nugent (D).

Greatest Show on Earth, The (1/5/38, Playhouse, 29)

Offbeat tale dealing with the love life of circus animals. Acting honors went to Frank Lovejoy and Anthony Ross as a pair of noble lions, Margaret Perry as a young lioness, and Edgar Stehli as the villain of the piece—a sneaky, troublemaking snake named Slimy. This fantastic 1938 comedy-drama at least had the virtue of novelty. A: Vincent Duffey and Irene Alexander. P: Helen Bonfils and George Somnes (D). CD: Frank Bevan. SD: John Root.

Greeks Had a Word for It, The (9/25/30, Harris, 224)

Sophisticated comedy of three gold-digging females pooling their resources to trap eligible bachelors. C: Dorothy Hall, Muriel Kirkland, Verree Teasdale, Hardie Albright, Frederic Worlock, Ernest Glendinning. A: Zoe Akins. P/D: William Harris, Jr.

SV: UA, 1932, Ina Claire, Joan Blondell, Madge Evans; Fox 1953, *How to Marry a Millionaire,* Marilyn Monroe, Betty Grable, Lauren Bacall, William Powell, David Wayne, Rory Calhoun, Cameron Mitchell.

Green Grow the Lilacs (1/26/31, Guild, 64)

Earthy, colorful folk-comedy of pioneer life on which the musical play *Oklahoma!* was based. The love affair between Curly (Franchot Tone), a jaunty cowhand, and Laurey (June Walker), a pretty farm girl, is threatened by a lecherous hired hand (Richard Hale). On their wedding night, Curly is finally forced to kill the sinister ranch hand, thus leaving the young couple free to face the future together. Lilting cowboy ballads, interpolated at key moments throughout the play, added to the atmospheric charm of this Theatre Guild production directed by Herbert J. Biberman. Despite generally favorable reviews, the play ran a mere sixty-four performances on Broadway. C: Helen Westley (Aunt Eller), Lee Strasberg (Peddler), Ruth Chorpenning (Ado Annie).

Musicalized by Rodgers and Hammerstein as *Oklahoma!* (1943) with Alfred Drake, Joan Roberts, Betty Garde, Joseph Buloff, Lee Dixon, Howard da Silva, Celeste Holm, Joan McCracken, Bambi Linn, Marc Platt.

SV: Magna Pictures, 1955, *Oklahoma!,* Gordon MacRae, Shirley Jones, Charlotte Greenwood, Eddie Albert, Gloria Grahame, Rod Steiger, James Whitmore, Gene Nelson.

Green Pastures, The (2/26/30, Mansfield, 640)

Pulitzer Prize-winning drama by Marc Connelly (A/D); one of the classics of the American theatre. *The Green Pastures* set out to dramatize Roark Bradford's stories of the Bible as imagined by Negro children in a small southern Sunday school. Beginning with its famous fish fry in heaven, highlighted by the unforgettable entrance cue of "Gangway for de Lawd God Jehovah!" the play depicted the Negro's idea of creation, the flood, and the history of the world up to the coming of Christ and his crucifixion ("Oh, look at him! Oh, look, dey goin' to make him carry it up dat high hill! Dey goin' to nail him to it! Oh, dat's a terrible burden for one man to carry!"). Critic

Heywood Broun *(Telegram)* wrote that the play was "more stirring than anything I have seen in the theatre." Brooks Atkinson *(New York Times)* called it "The divine comedy of the modern theatre." In the role of The Lord, Richard B. Harrison gave a superlative performance. A former pullman porter who had never acted before, Harrison became one of the heroes of his race. He played the part for eighty weeks on Broadway and for four seasons on tour. Others in the all-Negro cast included: Wesley Hill, Charles H. Moore, and the Hall Johnson Choir. P: Laurence Rivers (Rowland Stebbins). M: Hall Johnson. SD: Robert Edmond Jones.

R: (3/15/51, Broadway, 44) by Wigreen Company i.a.w. Harry Fromkes. C: William Marshall, Ossie Davis, Avon Long, John Marriott, Alonzo Bosan, Hall Johnson Choir. D: Marc Connelly.

SV: WB, 1936, Rex Ingram, Oscar Polk, Eddie ("Rochester") Anderson, Frank Wilson (directed by William Keighley and Marc Connelly).

Grey-Eyed People, The (12/17/52, Martin Beck, 5)

Wisecracking comedy about an advertising executive (Walter Matthau) torn between loyalty to a politically blackmailed friend and his own survival in a Redbaiting industry. ". . . a curiously indigestible compound of message and ordinary monkeyshines" *(Herald Tribune)*. A: John D. Hess. P: Albert Selden. D: Morton Da Costa. SD: Eldon Elder.

Greyhound, The (2/29/12, Astor, 108)

A clever detective stalks a gang of crooks aboard a luxury liner. Trite melodrama had the advantage of a (then) novel setting. C: Henry Kolker, Robert McWade, Elita Proctor. A: Paul Armstrong and Wilson Mizner. P: Wagenhals and Kemper. Attending the gala opening night of *The Greyhound* was the father of co-author and noted wit Wilson Mizner.

"This is a very remarkable play," a theatregoer said to the old man as the final curtain fell. "It is indeed," answered Mizner's father, "and the most remarkable thing about it is that it took two men to write it."

Grounds for Divorce (9/23/24, Empire, 130)

To teach her successful lawyer-husband (Philip Merivale) a lesson, a neglected wife (Ina Claire) files for divorce, but the squabbling couple reconcile by the final curtain. Gay Paris locale comedy by Guy Bolton, extensively revised from a play by Ernest Vajda. P/D: Henry Miller.

Growing Pains (11/23/33, Ambassador, 28)

Coquettish teenager drives all the boys wild. Fairly cute little comedy by Aurania Rouverol. C: Junior Durkin, Johnny Downs, Eddie Acuff, Joan Wheeler, Leona Hogarth. P/D: Arthur Lubin.

Guest in the House (2/24/42, Plymouth, 153)

An invalid almost destroys a suburban household with her pathological mischief-making. ". . . a lurid and overextended piece of trash" *(PM)*. A shrewd advertising campaign helped *Guest in the House* achieve a moderately successful Broadway run. The play was written by veteran screenwriters Hagar Wilde and Dale Eunson. C: Mary Anderson, Leon Ames, Pert Kelton, Louise Campbell, William Prince. P: Stephen and Paul Ames. D: Reginald Denham.

SV: UA, 1944, Anne Baxter, Ralph Bellamy, Aline MacMahon, Ruth Warrick, Margaret Hamilton, Jerome Cowan, Marie McDonald.

Guide, The (3/6/68, Hudson, 5)

An enterprising confidence man disrupts a poverty-stricken Indian village when he attempts to pass himself off as a saint. Dignified but dull dramatization of the novel by R. K. Narayan. C: Zia Mohyeddin, Titos Vandis, Michael Kermoyan. A: Harvey Breit and Patricia Rinehart. P: Noel Weiss. D: George L. Sherman.

Guinea Pig, The (1/7/29, President, 64)

First play by Preston Sturges, author of *Strictly Dishonorable* (1929), and writer-director of many classic film comedies. *The Guinea Pig* was an amiable but undistinguished comedy about a lady playwright who is told to have an affair in the interests of better dramaturgy. She proceeds forthwith to take this advice and, of course, falls in love with her male "guinea pig" subject. P: Preston Sturges. D: Walter Greenough.

Guns (8/6/28, Wallack's, 48)

Lots of atmosphere but not much logic in this tale of Chicago beer runners during the prohibition era. Written by James Hagan, author of *One Sunday Afternoon* (1933). P/D: Jack Kingsberry.

Gypsy (1/14/29, Klaw, 64)

George Cukor directed this clinical study of an emotionally unstable, sexually promiscuous female. Written by Maxwell Anderson, *Gypsy* dealt with a Greenwich Village bohemian who rebels against her marriage ties. She leaves her husband, has an abortion, drifts from one affair to another ("I fail everybody in the end"), and finally commits suicide. Frequently interesting but utlimately unsatisfying 20's drama. C: Claiborne Foster, Louis Calhern, Wallace Ford, Lester Vail. P: Richard Herndon.

Gypsy Jim (1/14/24, 49th Street, 48)

Comedy-drama by Oscar Hammerstein II and Milton Herbert Gropper. An eccentric millionaire (Leo Carrillo) pretends to have supernatural powers in order to effectively disperse practical charity. Verdict:

"Oscar Hammerstein II and Milton Gropper
    Wrote a comedy that came an awful cropper."
       (Alexander Woollcott, *World*)

C: Wallace Ford, Elizabeth Patterson. P: Arthur Hammerstein. D: Clifford Brooke. M: Herbert Stothart.

H

Habitual Husband, The (12/24/24, 48th Street, 11)

When a husband elopes with a woman who "understands" him, his wife insists on accompanying them as chaperon. Feeble, unfunny comedy by Dana Burnet. C: Grant Mitchell, Margalo Gillmore, Clarence Derwent. P: The Actors' Theatre, Inc. D: Dudley Digges and Josephine Hull.

Hairy Ape, The (3/9/22, Provincetown, 120)

Eugene O'Neill's famous expressionistic drama dealing with the futility of brute strength in a mechanistic society. Yank (Louis Wolheim), a lusty, primitive coal stoker on an ocean liner, is sustained by his belief that the man who works with his hands for a living somehow "belongs." When a spoiled society girl faints at the sight of him, this modern-day "hairy ape" begins to question the worth of his existence. He finally dies in a gorilla's cage, asking: "Where do I get off at? Where do I fit in?" "A bitter, brutal, wildly fantastic play of nightmare hue and nightmare distortion" (Alexander Woollcott, *New York Times*). O'Neill's "comedy of ancient and modern life" proved surprisingly popular not only in America, but throughout Europe, Russia and the Orient. It was interpreted by many as a work of revolutionary propaganda. Not so, declared the author. The

The Hairy Ape. Scene in IWW office (1922). *Courtesy Museum of the City of New York Theatre and Music Collection.*

Hairy Ape was merely "a symbol of Man, who has lost his old harmony with nature." When Arthur Hopkins (P/D) transferred the off-Broadway production to Broadway's Plymouth Theatre, he replaced Mary Blair in the role of the neurotic society girl with a beautiful but little-known actress named Carlotta Monterey. "The first time I met O'Neill," the actress recalled, "I thought him the rudest man I'd ever seen. And he had no use for me." In July 1929, Carlotta Monterey married Eugene O'Neill. They remained together until the dramatist's death twenty-four years later.

SV: UA, 1944, William Bendix, Susan Hayward, John Loder, Alan Napier, Dorothy Comingore.

Half-Caste, The (3/29/26, National, 63)

Cruising his palatial yacht off the Samoan islands, a dissolute playboy (Fredric March) seduces a native girl only to learn that she is his half-sister. Horrified, the rich brat sets sail for America. The girl? She kills herself. ". . . a brazen and half-conscious caricature. . . . Fredric March, a good-looking and temperamental youngster, impersonated the unlucky debauchee as well as possible" *(Herald Tribune)*. A: Jack McClellan. D: Edgar MacGregor.

Half Gods (12/21/29, Plymouth, 17)

A man and wife undergo analysis in hopes of saving their shakey marriage. Weak satirical jab at the new "psychoanalysis fad" by Sidney Howard. C: Donn (Donald) Cook, Mayo Methot, Siegfried Rumann, Dorothy Sands. P/D: Arthur Hopkins.

SV: U, 1930, *Free Love,* Conrad Nagel, Genevieve Tobin.

Half Naked Truth, The (6/7/26, Mayfair, 41)

Stale sex comedy about an unemployed man (John Litel) who agrees to pose in the nude for an attractive sculptress. A: N. Brewster Morse. P. Mabel Ryan. D: Douglas Wood.

Halfway to Hell (1/2/34, Fulton, 7)

Murder in a spooky lighthouse; intolerably boring pulp melodrama by Crane Wilbur (A/D). "When Mr. Wilbur calls his play *Halfway to Hell,* he underestimates the distance" *(New York Times).* P: Elizabeth Miele i.a.w. M. Van R. Schuyler.

Hallams, The (3/4/48, Booth, 12)

Domestic drama dealing with the efforts of an autocratic matriarch to run the lives of her middle-aged sons and daughters-in-law. ". . . loose-jointed and uneven . . . a play of little substance" *(Sun).* C: Ethel Griffies, Katharine Bard, June Walker, Mildred Dunnock, Alan Baxter, Mildred Wall, Royal Beal, Matt Briggs, Dean Norton. *The Hallams* was written by Rose Franken (A/D) as a sequel to her successful 1932 comedy-drama, *Another Language.* The play was produced by Miss Franken's husband, William Brown Meloney.

Hallowe'en (2/20/36, Vanderbilt, 12)

Demonology in modern-day New England, with a priest and a rabbi joining forces to exorcise the devil. Some shuddery moments in this intermittently effective Grand Guignol exhibit. C: Robert T. Haines, Zamah Cunningham, Ian MacLaren, Edith King. A: Henry Myers. P/D: William de Mille.

Hamilton (9/17/17, Knickerbocker, 80)

His political enemies maneuver Alexander Hamilton (George Arliss) into a compromising position involving the young and beautiful Mrs. Reynolds (Jeanne Eagels). Hamilton nimbly sidesteps the potential scandal by sacrificing his personal happiness. Interesting biographical drama by Mary Hamlin and George Arliss. P: Tyler, Klaw and Erlanger. D:

Dudley Digges.
SV: WB, 1931, *Alexander Hamilton*, George Arliss, Dudley Digges, Doris Kenyon, Alan Mowbray, June Collyer, Montagu Love.

Hand in Glove (12/4/44, Playhouse, 40)

Atmospheric thriller about a psychopathic cockney whose impotence drives him to seek sexual relief in murder. In order to divert suspicion, the young man tries to pin his crimes on a local half-wit, but eventually is trapped by a Scotland Yard detective. This variant on the Jack the Ripper story was written by Anglo-American authors Charles K. Freeman and Gerald Savory, and b/o Mr. Savory's novel, *Hughie Roddis*. The play was staged by film director James Whale.* "... a horror play with no horror in it ... *(World-Telegram)*. "... despite all its faults, it is the best thing of its kind that Broadway has offered in some time" *(PM)*. C: Aubrey Mather, Isobel Elsom, Viola Roache, George Lloyd. P: Arthur Edison. SD: Sam Leve.

---

*Mr. Whale directed such horror classics as *Frankenstein*, *The Bride of Frankenstein*, and *The Invisible Man*.

Hand of the Potter, The (12/5/21, Provincetown, 21)

Tragedy in four acts by Theodore Dreiser. A sexually depraved young Russian Jew, a victim of impulses he cannot control, rapes and murders an eleven-year-old girl, is tried for his crime before a grand jury, but commits suicide before society can extract its vengeance. *The Hand of the Potter* was an attempt by Dreiser to dramatize his favorite theme—the inscrutability of life. Working at fever pitch, he finished the play in three weeks and sent it to his friend and mentor, H. L. Mencken. With typical candor, Mencken replied that he found the drama "hopeless," that the subject of sexual perversion was "impossible on the stage," and, finally, that Dreiser's treatment was totally lacking in dramatic effectiveness. "The whole thing is loose, elephantine and devoid of sting. It has no more dramatic structure than a jellyfish. The play is a piece of pish," Mencken concluded. "I have more respect for my own judgment in this matter than I have for yours," snapped Dreiser, and proceeded to circulate the script to leading New York managers. Arthur Hopkins and Charles Coburn were among those who purchased the play, but allowed their options to lapse. When the play finally was presented off-Broadway, it received almost unanimously condemnatory reviews ("Conspicuously offensive . . . repulsive . . . an unbelievably bad pathological drama") and lasted a mere 21 performances. Dreiser blamed the production, direction, acting, and "puritanical attitude" of the critics for the play's failure. He simply was unable to accept the fact that it was a poorly conceived and poorly written drama. C: J. Paul Jones, Lutha (Luther) Adler, Nathaniel Freyer. P: Provincetown Players. D: George Cram Cook.

Handful of Fire (10/1/58, Martin Beck, 5)

Passions erupt down Mexico way when a pure-in-heart peon (Roddy McDowall) and a dastardly gambling czar (James Daly) clash over the favors of a village innocent (Joan Copeland). "... ambitiously poetic and symbolical ... an arty bore" *(Mirror)*. C: Kay Medford, Leonardo Cimino, Thelma Pelish, Mark Rydell. A: N. Richard Nash. P: David Susskind and The Playwrights Company. D: Robert Lewis. CD: Lucinda Ballard. SD: Jo Mielziner.

Hangman's House (12/16/26, Forrest, 4)

Conflict between an Irish father and his rebellious daughter. Old hat and poorly written. C: Katherine Alexander, Walter Abel, Joseph Kilgour, Percy Waram, Katherine Emmet. A: Willard Mack, based on a novel by Donn Byrne. P: William A. Brady, Jr. (D) and Dwight Deere Wiman.

Hangman's Whip (2/24/33, St. James, 11)

"The natives are restless tonight" dialogue characterized this jungle melodrama about a sadistic Congo ruler, his pretty wife, and the handsome hero who would rescue her from her brutish husband. This rubbishy fable was written by future Hollywood scenarists Norman Reilly Raine and Frank Butler. Raine went to Warner Brothers, where he collaborated on such screenplays as *The Adventures of Robin Hood* and the Oscar-winning *The Life of Emile Zola*. Butler signed with Paramount Pictures, where he wrote several popular Bing Crosby vehicles, notably *Going My Way,* for which he, too, was honored with an Academy Award. As for *Hangman's Whip,* it expired after eleven performances. C: Montagu Love, Ian Keith, Barton MacLane, Helen Flint. P: Kondolf and Taylor i.a.w. William A. Brady, Jr. D: Robert Bell.
SV: Par, 1933, *White Woman,* Charles Laughton, Carole Lombard, Charles Bickford, Kent Taylor.

Happiest Days, The (4/11/39, Vanderbilt, 7)

A love affair between two teenagers ends in suicide and murder. Lugubrious drama by Charlotte Armstrong, future queen of the American suspense novel, was a 1939 Broadway failure. C: Uta Hagen, John Craven, Jimmy Lydon, William Harrigan, Kathryn Givney, Russell Collins. P: Courtney Burr. D: Marc Connelly.

Happiest Millionaire, The (11/20/56, Lyceum, 271)

Intermittently amusing period comedy (Philadelphia, 1916) dealing mainly with the efforts of eccentric millionaire Anthony J. Drexel Biddle (Walter Pidgeon) to prevent the marriage of his daughter (Diana van der Vlis) to tobacco heir Angier Duke (George Grizzard). A: Kyle Crichton b/o the book *My Philadelphia Father* by Cordelia Drexel Biddle and Mr. Crichton. P/D: Howard Erskine and Joseph Hayes. SD: George Jenkins.
SV: BV, 1967, Fred MacMurray, Greer Garson, Geraldine Page, Tommy Steele, Gladys Cooper, Hermione Baddeley, Lesley Ann Warren, John Davidson, Eddie Hodges.

Happiest Years, The (4/25/49, Lyceum, 8)

Hackneyed comedy about a meddlesome mother who suspects her college-student son-in-law of cheating on his wife. C: Peggy Wood, June Walker, Loring Smith, Douglas Watson, Judy Parrish. A: Thomas Coley and William Roerick. P: Gertrude Macy. D: James Neilson.

Happily Ever After (3/15/45, Biltmore, 12)

A marrying parson (Gene Lockhart) turns out to be unordained. "A little comedy that's horribly old-fashioned, incredibly corny, and monstrously dull" *(PM)*. *Happily Ever After* was written by drama critics Donald Kirkley and Howard Burman. P: Klawans and Payne-Jennings. D: Crane Wilbur.

Happily Never After (3/10/66, O'Neill, 4)

Aimless comedy about tangled sexual relations among the Long Island summertime commuter set. C: Gerald S. O'Loughlin, Barbara Barrie, Karen Black, Ken Kercheval, Rochelle Oliver. A: J. A. Ross. P: George and Granat. D: Joseph Anthony.

Happiness (12/31/17, Criterion, 136)

A poor Brooklyn girl (Laurette Taylor) delivers a frock to a bored Park Avenue debutante and remains to teach her the meaning of happiness. Sentimental fable by J. Hartley Manners (A/D) pleased escapist-minded World War I audiences. C: Lynn Fontanne, Violet Kemble Cooper, O. P. Heggie, J. M. Kerrigan, Hubert Druce. P: Tyler, Klaw, and Erlanger.

Happiness Is Just a Little Thing Called a Rolls Royce (5/11/68, Barrymore, 1)

Flabby sex comedy about the misunderstandings between a young lawyer and his pushy wife. C: Pat Harrington, Hildy Brooks, John McGiver, Alexandra Berlin. A: Arthur Alsberg and Robert Fisher. P: Anamark Productions. D: David Alexander.

Happy Birthday (10/31/46, Broadhurst, 564)

The usually demure Helen Hayes sang, danced and kicked up her heels in this Cinderella yarn by Anita Loos, author of *Gentlemen Prefer Blondes* (1926). Miss Hayes played a mousy little librarian named Addie Bemis. Secretly enamored of a bank teller, she pursues the young man into a Newark honky-tonk, takes the first drink of her life, and promptly embarks on a marathon binge of pink ladies, creme de menthe, scotch, and champagne. As Addie discovers the joys of alcohol, life takes on a beautiful glow. Bottles light up and talk to her, tables and bar stools rise in the air, and the saloon becomes an iridescent wonderland. Before the evening is over, the drab librarian has blossomed into a siren, has routed her hussy of a rival, and has won her young man. "An ingenious and charming comedy...." *(Sun).* "Sentimental rubbish" *(Time).* C: Louis Jean Heydt, Enid Markey, Grace Valentine, Robert Burton, Lorraine Miller. P: Richard Rodgers and Oscar Hammerstein. D: Joshua Logan. CD: Lucinda Ballard. SD: Jo Mielziner. Song: "I Haven't Got a Worry in the World" by Richard Rodgers and Oscar Hammerstein.

Happy Birthday, Wanda June (10/7/70, Theater de Lys and Edison, 190)

Novelist Kurt Vonnegut, Jr. *(Slaughterhouse Five, Cat's Cradle)* with a comedy self-described as "a simple-minded play about men who enjoy killing." The author's distinctive imagination molds a farcical tale of a big game hunter, a parody of Hemingwayism, who returns to civilization after eight lost years in the jungle. He finds his wife, whom he left a carhop and is now an educated sophisticate, being wooed by a doctor and a vacuum cleaner salesman. Though the characters adopt those attitudes that aid Vonnegut in ridiculing overbearing masculinity, a generous sympathy for the benighted hero is artfully conveyed as well. Largely plotless, the conflict between the characters lies in their varying attitudes toward war and peace. If the message is obvious, the expression is inimitable. The doorbells of the hero's home are animal voices; his best buddy dropped an atomic bomb on Nagasaki, the vacuum cleaner salesman makes more money than the doctor; and of course there is Wanda June, a ten-year-old girl run over on her birthday, who appears as a ghost and has nothing to do with the main course of the action. Humor, thoughtfulness, and compassion abound in Vonnegut's unique version of humanity. *Happy Birthday, Wanda June* opened O/B and closed after 47 performances due to a strike by Actors' Equity. It reopened on Broadway 12/22/70 for an additional 143 performances. ". . . listen to Mr. Vonnegut's small, quiet voice of inspired idiocy" (Clive Barnes, *New York Times*). ". . . a disappointing beginning for a brilliant novelist as dramatist" (James Davis, *New York Daily News*). A: Kurt Vonnegut, Jr. C: Kevin McCarthy, Marsha Mason (deb.), William Hickey, Keith Charles, Nicolas Coster, Steven Paul, Ariane Munker, Louis Turenne, Pamela Saunders. D: Michael J. Kane. P: Lester M. Goldsmith. SD: Ed Wittstein.

Happy Days, The (5/13/41, Henry Miller, 23)
Aviator becomes romantically involved with a quintet of French-Canadian youngsters. "... gentle and rather flimsy ..." *(Journal-American)*. Adapted and extensively revised by Zoe Akins from a play by Claude-Andre Puget. C: Diana Barrymore, Joan Tetzel, Edward Ashley. P: Raphael and Robert Hakim. D: Arthur Ripley.

Happy Landing (3/26/32, 46th Street, 25)
Daredevil aviator (Russell Hardie) is separated from his sweetheart (Margaret Sullavan) by headline-hunting promoters. Relentlessly routine comedy-drama. C: Catherine Dale Owen, Harry Davenport. A: John B. Hymer and William E. Barry. P: Messrs. Shubert. D: Lawrence Marston.
SV: Monogram, 1934, Ray Walker, Jacqueline Wells.

Happy Time, The (1/24/50, Plymouth, 614)
Comedy about a raffish, uninhibited French-Canadian family in the 1920's, and the first stirrings of adolescence and sexual curiosity in the twelve-year-old boy of the household. "... tender, funny and moving" *(Herald Tribune)*. C: Claude Dauphin, Leora Dana, Kurt Kasznar, Richard Hart, Eva Gabor (deb.), Johnny Stewart, Edgar Stehli. A: Samuel Taylor b/o the book by Robert Fontaine. P: Rodgers and Hammerstein. D: Robert Lewis. CD/SD: Aline Bernstein. Musicalized (1968) by N. Richard Nash, John Kander and Fred Ebb, with Robert Goulet and David Wayne heading the cast.
SV: Col, 1952, Charles Boyer, Louis Jourdan, Marsha Hunt, Linda Christian, Bobby Driscoll (directed by Richard Fleischer).

Harbor Lights (10/4/56, Playhouse, 4)
Linda Darnell (deb.) as a Staten Island housewife torn between her first and second husbands. Poorly produced, directed, and written, this 1956 soap opera perished after its fourth performance. C: Robert Alda, Paul Langton, Pat Harrington. A: Norman Vane. P: Anthony Parella. D: Guy Thomajan.

Harem, The (12/2/24, Belasco, 183)
A wife (Lenore Ulric) disguises herself as a veiled Turkish princess, vamps her own husband (William Courtenay) to test his fidelity, and finally drags her unsuspecting mate off to a hotel room. This leering, heavy-handed sex comedy was mauled by the reviewers, embraced by sensation-hungry playgoers. Produced and directed by the "The Priest of the Playhouse," David Belasco, *The Harem* ran through the spring despite protests from the anti-vice crusaders and rumblings from the district attorney's office. A: Avery Hopwood, extensively revised from a play by Ernest Vajda.

Harlem (2/20/29, Apollo, 94)
The rapid downfall and disintegration of a once-proud southern family of blacks when they move to a squalid railroad flat in Harlem. Cheap 20's exploitation piece that did its bit to foster the myth of Negro inferiority. The no-name cast of sixty performers included fifty-nine blacks and one white. The play was written by William J. Rapp (white) and Wallace Thurman (black). P: Edward A. Blatt. D: Chester Erskine.

Harold (11/29/62, Cort, 20)
Three Bronx buddies form a syndicate to launch a gawky, unsophisticated neighborhood kid (Anthony Perkins) into high society. Tepid comedic variation on the Pygmalion theme. C: Don Adams (deb.), Nathaniel Frey, John Fiedler, Rochelle Oliver, Sudie Bond, Joe E. Marks, Sidney Armus, Stephen Cheng.

A: Herman Raucher. P: Saint Subber i.a.w. Ben Edwards (SD). D: Larry Blyden.

Harp of Life, The (11/27/16, Globe, 136)

A mother (Laurette Taylor) maintains that sexual ignorance will cause problems for her 19-year-old son and his fiancée, and indeed it does. Lynn Fontanne made her Broadway debut as the shy fiancée and scored an overnight sensation in the role. As for the play, most reviewers found it artificial and Victorian in its approach to what was then called "sex hygiene." C: Philip Merivale, Gail Kane, Frank Kemble Cooper, Dion Titheradge. A/D: J. Hartley Manners. P: Tyler, Klaw, and Erlanger.

Harriet (3/3/43, Henry Miller, 377)

Three decades in the life of "the little woman who made the great war," abolitionist Harriet Beecher Stowe (Helen Hayes). The play traced its heroine's marriage to an absent-minded widower (Rhys Williams); her relationship with other members of the crusading Beecher clan; and the monumental impact of her anti-slavery novel, *Uncle Tom's Cabin*, that helped change the course of American history. ". . . a great actress at work [in] an episodic, leisurely and loosely written piece" *(Sun)*. *Harriet* was directed by Elia Kazan and written by the husband-and-wife team of Florence Ryerson and Colin Clements. Coincidentally, Robert E. Sherwood was working on a play about Mrs. Stowe (also intended as a vehicle for Miss Hayes) when *Harriet* was tried out in Syracuse, New York. Gilbert Miller (P) persuaded the star to cast her lot with the Ryerson-Clements script rather than wait for Sherwood's version of the same story. She agreed and, consequently, the Sherwood play was never completed. Despite generally tepid reviews, *Harriet* proved to be one of Helen Hayes' biggest popular successes. C: Jane Seymour, Joan Tetzel, Carmen Mathews. CD: Aline Bernstein. SD: Lemuel Ayers.

Harry, Noon and Night (5/5/65, Pocket, 6)

The homosexual liaison between Harry (Robert Blake), an angry-at-the-world American writer living in Munich, and his masochistic German lover (Jordan Charney), is terminated when the American lad's older brother (Gerald S. O'Loughlin) arrives on the scene, intent on taking Harry back home with him to Ohio. ". . . rises to wild, exciting heights, but becomes inchoate under the impact of its confusing drives" *(New York Times)*. This short-lived black comedy by Ronald Ribman was presented O/B in 1965 with a cast that included David Huddleston, Lynn Bernay, and Bruce Glover. D: Davie Eliscu.

Harvest (9/19/25, Belmont, 17)

A city boy (Fredric March) spends the summer with some Michigan farm folk, makes love to their daughter, and then goes on his way. ". . . dull and uninteresting" *(News)*. C: Louise Closser Hale, Augustin Duncan. A: Kate Horton. P: Messrs. Shubert i.a.w. John Cromwell (D).

Harvest of Years (1/12/48, Hudson, 16)

Domestic problems of a Swedish-American farm family in northern California. "Diffuse to the point of pointlessness" *(News)*. Written by screenwriter DeWitt Bodeen (*The Seventh Victim, The Curse of the Cat People, I Remember Mama*, etc.). C: Esther Dale, Russell Hardie, Leona Maricle, Lenka Peterson, Philip Abbott (deb.). P/D: Arthur J. Beckhard.

Harvey (11/1/44, 48th Street, 1,775)

Mary Chase's Pulitzer Prize play about a gentle tippler whose best friend is a six-foot-one-and-a-half-inch rabbit. Elwood P. Dowd (Frank Fay) first meets

Harvey leaning against a lamp post and addressing Dowd by name. "Didn't you think that rather peculiar?" inquires a psychiatrist. "No," says Dowd, "you know how it is in a small town; everybody knows everybody else." Most of the other characters in the play are unable to see Harvey; hence, any number of cockeyed complications ensue thanks to the imaginary rabbit. On the other hand, perhaps Harvey is real. The question is debatable. ". . . a full-bodied and irresistible comedy which no theatre-lover can afford to miss" *(Herald Tribune)*. ". . . the most delightful, droll, endearing, funny and touching piece of stage whimsey I ever saw. . ." *(News)*. Denver newspaperwoman Mary Chase did eighteen drafts of *Harvey* over a two-year period. The play tried out in Boston with Harvey played by an actor in a $600 rabbit costume. The whole comedy fell flat when the gigantic rabbit became visible. At the next performance, Harvey was made "imaginary" and immediately became "real" to everyone. Vaudevillian Frank Fay was paged for the role of Elwood P. Dowd only after several other actors (Jack Haley, Edward Everett Horton, Robert Benchley, Harold Lloyd) had turned down the part. Fay gave a consummate performance as the amiably bibulous hero. Memorable, too, was Josephine Hull as his distraught widowed sister, Veta, who is mistakenly locked up by "white slavers" when she takes her brother to a rest home. *Harvey* racked up 1,775 performances to become the fourth longest-running play in Broadway history. Other actors who played Elwood P. Dowd included James Stewart (who also starred in the 1970 revival), Joe E. Brown, Bert Wheeler, Jack Buchanan, James Dunn, and Brock Pemberton who produced the show. The comedy was directed by Antoinette Perry.

R: (2/24/70, ANTA, 79) by ANTA. C: James Stewart, Helen Hayes, Jesse White, Henderson Forsythe. D: Stephen Porter.
SV: U, 1950, James Stewart, Josephine Hull, Cecil Kellaway, Jesse White (directed by Henry Koster).

Hasty Heart, The (1/3/45, Hudson, 204)

The John Patrick play about a lonely and embittered Scot soldier who discovers he has only a few weeks to live, and of the friendships he finally makes with the other men in his convalescent ward. Set in a British general hospital on the Burma front, this soundly crafted "comedy about a tragedy" was one of the most popular plays of the World War II years. C: Richard Basehart, John Lund, Anne Burr, Earl Jones. P: Howard Lindsay and Russel Crouse. D: Bretaigne Windust.
SV: WB, 1949, Richard Todd, Patricia Neal, Ronald Reagan.
Note: John Patrick's screenwriting credits range from the Charlie Chan and Mr. Moto series in the 1930's to *High Society* and *Les Girls* in the 1950's. His most successful play was *The Teahouse of the August Moon* (1953).

Hat, a Coat, a Glove, A (1/31/34, Selwyn, 14)

Trying to defend his wife's lover in a murder case, a lawyer throws suspicion on himself. Wildly implausible courtroom melodrama; adapted and extensively revised by William A. Drake from a play by Wilhelm Speyer. C: A. E. Matthews, Nedda Harrigan, Lester Vail. P: Crosby Gaige and D. K. Weiskopf. D: Crosby Gaige and Robert C. Fischer.
SV: RKO, 1934, *Hat, Coat and Glove*, Richardo Cortez, John Beal; 1944, *A Night of Adventure*, Tom Conway, Jean Brooks, Nancy Gates.

Hatful of Rain, A (11/9/55, Lyceum, 398)

Helped by his sympathetic brother (Anthony Franciosa), a junkie (Ben Gazzara) tries to conceal his drug addiction from his pregnant wife (Shelley Winters) and thick-headed father (Frank Silvera). Uneven, overwrought melodrama by Michael V. Gazzo generated considerable impact in its best moments, particularly those involving a trio of nefarious dope pushers (Henry Silva, Harry Guardino, Paul Richards). Very well acted by a uniformly fine cast; impressively staged by Frank Corsaro. P: Jay Julien. SD: Mordecai Gorelik.

SV: Fox, 1957, Don Murray, Eva Marie Saint, Anthony Franciosa, Lloyd Nolan, Henry Silva (directed by Fred Zinnemann).

Note: Steve McQueen (deb.) replaced Ben Gazzara during the Broadway run. Harry Guardino also made his Broadway debut in this 1955 production.

Haunted House, The (9/2/24, George M. Cohan, 103)

Mystery writer (Wallace Eddinger) solves murder in spooky summer cottage. Formula mystery-farce by Owen Davis. P: Lewis and Gordon. D: Howard Lindsay.

Have I Got a Girl for You! (12/2/63, Music Box, 1)

Bronx matriarch schemes to get the right girl for her bachelor son. "Marvelously unfunny" *(News)*. C: Nancy R. Pollock, Simon Oakland, Paula Laurence, Dick Van Patten, Michael Gorrin, Patricia Benoit. A: Irving Cooper. P: Joseph Kipness and Richard W. Krakeur i.a.w. David Kaufman. D: Don Richardson.

Having Wonderful Time (2/20/37, Lyceum, 310)

Amusing and at times touching comedy about a group of New York office toilers on a two-week summer vacation. The setting is one of those adult camps where the pursuit of happiness is relentless and around the clock. The principal character, a Bronx stenographer (Katherine Locke), falls in love with one of the camp waiters (John Garfield), an unemployed lawyer. He feels too poor to ask her to wed, but when an unscrupulous "wolf" (Sheldon Leonard) tries to seduce the pretty stenographer, she and the would-be attorney decide to get married after all. Written by Arthur Kober* with humor, warmth, and a keen ear for the nuances of Bronx dialect, *Having Wonderful Time* was a substantial Broadway hit. When Hollywood filmed the play (see below), the Jewish patois was completely excised. The result was a mild, innocuous comedy that lacked both flavor and point. C: Kay Loring, Philip Van Zandt, Cornel Wilde, Ann Thomas, Irving Israel. P: Marc Connelly (D) i.a.w. Bela Blau. Musicalized by Arthur Kober, Joshua Logan, and Harold Rome as *Wish You Were Here* (1952) with Jack Cassidy, Patricia Marand, Sheila Bond, Paul Valentine, Sidney Armus, Larry Blyden, Florence Henderson, Frank Aletter, Harry Clark, Tom Tryon, Phyllis Newman.

SV: RKO, 1938, Ginger Rogers, Douglas Fairbanks, Jr., Lucille Ball, Peggy Conklin, Eve Arden, Lee Bowman, Red Skelton.

---

*Among Mr. Kober's screenplay collaborations are *Up Pops the Devil*, *Big Broadcast of 1937*, and *The Little Foxes*, the latter adapted from the play by his ex-wife, Lillian Hellman.

Hawk Island (9/16/29, Longacre, 24)

To enliven a houseparty, a practical joker (Clark Gable) fakes a murder, then is hoised with his own petard when a murder actually occurs. Gable gave a good account of himself as the rugged hero, but this 20's melodrama was on the flimsy side. A/D: Howard Irving Young. P: Thomas Kilpatrick.

SV: RKO, 1930, *Midnight Mystery*, Hugh Trevor, Betty Compson, Lowell Sherman.

Headquarters (12/4/29, Forrest, 13)

Police inspector (William Farnum) investigates murder of film star. William Gargan and Sam Levene had bit roles in this plodding whodunit. A: Hugh Stange. P: Wilmer, Vincent and Aarons. D: Jo Graham.

Heads or Tails (5/2/47, Cort, 35)

Insurance agents scheme to prevent a threatened suicide. "It probably is the World's Worst Play" *(News)*. C: Les Tremayne, Jed Prouty, Audra Lindley, Werner Klemperer. A: H. J. Lengsfelder and Ervin Drake. P: Your Theatre, Inc. D: Edward F. Cline.*

---

*W. C. Field's favorite director; film credits include *Million Dollar Legs, My Little Chickadee, The Bank Dick,* and many others.

Hear That Trumpet (10/7/46, Playhouse, 8)

Melodramatic tale dealing with the ups and downs of a struggling Chicago jazz band. "... 'a hackneyed, rather trashy plot ..." *(PM)*. C: Bobby Sherwood, Sidney Bechet, Ray Mayer, Frank Conroy, Audra Lindley, Marty Marsala, Bart Edwards. A: Orin Jannings. P/D: Arthur Hopkins.

Heart of Wetona, The (2/29/16, Lyceum, 95)

Pretty Indian maiden (Lenore Ulric) suffers at the hands of deceitful white men. Banal melodrama set on an Oklahoma reservation. C: Lowell Sherman, William Courtleigh, Curtis Cooksey, Chief Deer. A: George Scarborough. P: Charles Frohman and David Belasco. D: Belasco.

Heat Lightning (9/15/33, Booth, 43)

A jailbird invades an Arizona autocamp run by a good-hearted drudge. When he repays her kindness by robbing her safe, she shoots him. Mediocre melodrama from the George Abbott play factory. C: Jean Dixon, Robert Gleckler, Eddie Acuff. A: Leon Abrams and George Abbott (D). P: Abbott-Dunning, Inc.

SV: WB, 1934, Aline MacMahon, Preston Foster, Ann Dvorak, Glenda Farrell, Lyle Talbot, Frank McHugh, Ruth Donnelly, Jane Darwell, Edgar Kennedy; 1941, *Highway West,* Brenda Marshall, Arthur Kennedy, Olympe Bradna, William Lundigan, Slim Summerville.

Heaven Tappers, The (3/8/27, Forrest, 9)

Moonshining in the Blue Ridge Mountains. An empty still. C: Charles Waldron, Margaret Lawrence. A: George Scarborough and Annette Westbay. P: Lee Shubert i.a.w. Edwin Carewe (D).

Heavenly Express (4/18/40, National, 20)

The Overland Kid (John Garfield), a puckish, mandolin-strumming angel of death, returns to earth. His mission: to escort Granny Graham (Aline MacMahon), patroness of hoboes, to the hobo paradise where bees buzz in the cigarette trees and streams of whiskey flow from cool rocks. (The Almighty Vagabond, it seems, decided the boys up there needed mothering.) As the supernatural streamliner arrives to take Granny to heaven, the play ends. "A vague, hollow and curiously aimless work. Mr. Garfield ... seems far from happy in his Peter Pannish role ..." *(Herald Tribune)*. *Heavenly Express* was given a fine production and a first-rate cast. The play, which had a brief three-week run, marked the producing debut of Kermit Bloomgarden *(Death of a Salesman, The Diary of Anne Frank, Look Homeward, Angel,* etc.). C: Harry Carey, Art Smith, Curt Conway, Burl Ives, Nicholas (Richard) Conte, Philip Loeb, Russell Collins. A: Albert Bein. D: Robert Lewis. M: Lehman Engel. SD: Boris Aronson.

Heavy Traffic (9/5/28, Empire, 61)

Cuckold finds more evidence than he bargained for when he seeks proof of his wife's adultery. Unpleasant comedy by Arthur Richman. C: Mary Boland, Reginald Mason, Jean Dixon, Leo G. Carroll, A. E. Matthews, Edward Crandall, Kay Strozzi, Robert Strange. P: Charles Frohman, Inc. D: Bertram Harrison.

Heigh-Ho, Everybody (5/25/32, Fulton, 5)

Lamentable comedy about the misadventures of a Rudy Vallee-type crooner (Joseph Santley). A: Herbert Polesie and John McGowan. P: John T. Adams i.a.w. Arthur Hurley (D).

Heiress, The (9/29/47, Biltmore, 410)

Dramatization of Henry James' novel, *Washington Square*. Set in 1850 New York, the play concerns a spinster driven to disillusionment and cruelty by a guileful suitor and an unloving father. Catherine Sloper (Wendy Hiller), the graceless daughter of a well-to-do surgeon (Basil Rathbone), is courted by fortune hunter Morris Townsend (Peter Cookson). When he learns that Catherine will be disinherited if she weds him, Townsend jilts her. Later, after her father's death, Catherine secures her revenge by encouraging the attentions of the now penitent Townsend and then renouncing him. "...a good and forthright play, given theatrical distinction by exceptional acting and direction" *(Post)*. C: Patricia Collinge, Betty Linley. A: Ruth and Augustus Goetz. P: Fred F. Finklehoffe. D: Jed Harris. SD: Raymond Sovey.

R: (2/8/50, City Center, 16). C: Margaret Phillips, Basil Rathbone, John Dall, Edna Best, Betty Linley. D: George Schaefer.

SV: Par, 1949, Olivia de Havilland, Ralph Richardson, Montgomery Clift, Miriam Hopkins, Vanessa Brown (directed by William Wyler).

Hell Freezes Over (12/28/35, Ritz, 25)

First play by John Patrick, author of *The Hasty Heart* (1945), *The Teahouse of the August Moon* (1953), etc. Dealing with a dirigible crash in the Arctic wastes and the excruciating deaths, one by one, of the seven male survivors, *Hell Freezes Over* proved a bit too frigid and depressing for Broadway's taste. The play marked Joshua Logan's directorial debut, and offered some stalwart trouping on the part of Louis Calhern, Myron McCormick, John Litel, George Tobias and Lee Baker, but the show never caught fire at the box office. After three weeks of chilly business, *Hell Freezes Over* melted away. P: George Kondolf. SD: John Root.

Hell-Bent Fer Heaven (1/4/24, Klaw, 128)

Pulitzer Prize drama by Professor Hatcher Hughes of Columbia University. In the Blue Ridge Mountains, a lying, hypocritical religious fanatic lusts after a mountain girl and tries to kill her lover. The mountain folk finally become aware of his false piety and drive the fanatic from the community. Effective but highly melodramatic portrait of hillbilly life and camp-meeting religion. C: Glenn Anders, George Abbott, John F. Hamilton, Augustin Duncan, Margaret Borough. P: Marc Klaw. D: Augustin Duncan.

Hell's Bells (1/26/25, Wallack's, 139)

A couple of Arizona con men try to palm off some mine stock in rural Connecticut. Pat formula comedy, notable for the pairing of a dandified juvenile named Humphrey Bogart and a pretty ingenue named Shirley Booth (deb.). A: Barry Conners. P: Herman Gantvoort. D: John Hayden.

Help Wanted (2/11/14, Maxine Elliott's, 92)

Dime-novel "exposé" of the perils faced by innocent stenographers in the lecherous business world of 1914. Written by Chicago newshound (and future N.Y.

Daily Mirror editor) Jack Lait. C: Charles Ruggles, Charles Richman, Katherine Emmett, Lois Meredith, Jessie Ralph. P: Oliver Morosco. D: T. D. Frawley.

Henry Behave (8/23/26, Bayes, 96)

Limp comedy by Lawrence Langner about a Long Island martinet and his long-suffering family. C: John Cumberland, Edward G. Robinson, Pat O'Brien, Gladys Lloyd.* P/D: Gustav Blum.

---

*Became Mrs. Edward G. Robinson on January 21, 1927.

Her First Affaire (8/22/27, Bayes, 138)

Flapper vamps happily married man. Wearisome 20's comedy. C: Aline MacMahon, Grace Voss, Stanley Logan, Anderson Lawler, Ethel Wilson. A: Merrill Rogers. P: Gustav Blum.

Her Friend the King (10/7/29, Longacre, 24)

An exiled monarch becomes romantically involved with a wealthy American widow. "A mild and meager little comedy" *(New York Times)*. C: William Faversham, Hugh Sinclair, Ara Gerald. A: A. E. Thomas and Harrison Rhodes. P: L. Lawrence Weber. D: F. G. Bell.

Her Great Match (9/4/05, Criterion, 93)

The love of an American girl (Maxine Elliott) and a suave German prince (Charles Cherry) triumphs over differences in their social positions. Mediocre Clyde Fitch (A/D) comedy-drama. P: Charles Dillingham.

Her Man of Wax (10/11/33, Shubert, 14)

A statue of Napoleon comes to life—which was more than could be said of the play. C: Lenore Ulric, Lloyd Corrigan, Carl Benton Reid. A: Julian Thompson b/o a play by Walter Hasenclever. P: Lee Shubert. D: Arthur Lubin.

Her Master's Voice (10/23/33, Plymouth, 220)

Complications ensue when a jobless husband (Roland Young) is mistaken for a servant by his wife's wealthy aunt (Laura Hope Crews). Amusing, splendidly acted farce-comedy by Clare Kummer (mother-in-law of star Roland Young). C: Elizabeth Patterson, Frances Fuller, Frederick Perry. P: Max Gordon. D: Worthington Miner.

SV: Par, 1936, Edward Everett Horton, Laura Hope Crews, Elizabeth Patterson, Peggy Conklin.

Her Own Way (9/28/03, Garrick, 107)

A millionaire (Arthur Byron) sets out to financially ruin a society family in order to force their beautiful daughter (Maxine Elliott) to marry him. Old-hat nineteenth-century plot in chic twentieth-century setting. A/D: Clyde Fitch. P: Charles Dillingham.

Her Unborn Child (3/5/28, Eltinge, 76)

Anti-abortion tract; nondescript cast, terrible script. A: Howard McKent Barnes and Grace Hayward; revised by Melville Burke (D). P: Majestic Productions.

SV: Windsor, 1933, Adele Romson, Doris Rankin.

Her Way Out (6/23/24, Gaiety, 24)

Washington society arbiter (Beatrice Terry) is exposed as a former bordello madam but a liberal senator (Edward Arnold) wants to marry her anyway. Putrid pulp-fiction stuff. A: Edwin Milton Royle. P: Associated Players. D: Walter Wilson.

Here Come the Clowns (12/7/38, Booth, 88)

A deranged stagehand searches for God in the *Café des Artistes*, a hangout for theatre people and assorted misfits (a transvestite, a dwarf, a lesbian, a homosexual, etc.). The lives of these baffled, tortured characters are shaken by the arrival of Max Pabst, a malevolent illusionist. Under his baleful influence, the assorted vaudevillians relive key moments from their separate tragedies. Fatally wounded by a bullet destined for Pabst, the stagehand recognizes God in the free will of man. This confusing but frequently fascinating allegorical fable so intrigued the critics that many of them paid it a second visit and reviewed the play a second time. *Here Come the Clowns* was adapted by Philip Barry from his 1938 novel, *War in Heaven*. C: Eddie Dowling (P), Madge Evans, Leo Chalzel, Russell Collins, Doris Dudley, Ralph Bunker, James Hagan, A. H. Van Buren, Hortense Alden. D: Robert Milton. SD: John Koenig.

Here Today (9/6/32, Barrymore, 39)

A noted writer (Ruth Gordon) sets out to win back her ex-husband, and does. "Funny . . . witty . . . sometimes greatly gleeful" *(American)*. The authoress in *Here Today* was clearly patterned after Dorothy Parker. Despite a spirited performance by Ruth Gordon, and first-rate staging by George S. Kaufman, this play by George Oppenheimer lasted only five weeks on Broadway. Dorothy Parker turned up again as the leading character in Ruth Gordon's comedy *Over 21* (1944), in which Miss Gordon once again starred under George Kaufman's direction. When someone asked Miss Parker why she didn't write her autobiography, she replied: "Because George Oppenheimer and Ruth Gordon would sue me for plagiarism." C: Donald MacDonald, Paul McGrath, Charles D. Brown, Charlotte Granville. P: Sam H. Harris.

Hero, The (3/14/21, Longacre, 4)

A war hero reveals himself to be a liar, seducer, and thief when he moves into the quiet suburban home of his kindly insurance-clerk brother. Skillful, compactly written drama by Gilbert Emery. Originally presented by Sam H. Harris for four special matinee performances with Grant Mitchell, Jetta Goudal, and Robert Ames heading the cast under the direction of Sam Forrest.
R: (9/5/21, Belmont, 80). C: Richard Bennett, Fania Marinoff, Robert Ames.

Heroine, The (2/19/63, Lyceum, 23)

In order to restore her husband's waning confidence, a wife employs an attractive call girl to pose as an innocent and seduce her middle-aged spouse. The scheme works so well that the husband's self esteem becomes insufferable. ". . . a cheerful item" *(New York Times)*. ". . . a mild little fabrication . . ." *(Post)*. C: Kay Medford, Joe Silver, Murray Hamilton, Beverly Bentley, Doris Belack. A: Frank Tarloff. P: Philip Rose. D: Lawrence Arrick.

Hey You, Light Man! (3/1/63, Mayfair, 52)

Illusion-versus-reality in a deserted New York theatre. Provocative, frequently intriguing O/B comedy-drama; first play by Oliver Hailey, author of *Father's Day* (1971). C: Alfred Ryder (D), Madeleine Sherwood.

Hickory Stick (5/8/44, Mansfield, 8)

Problems of an idealistic teacher (Steve Cochran) in a tough vocational school in the New York slums. ". . . a singularly bad play" *(Herald Tribune)*. C: Lawrence Fletcher, Richard Basehart. A: Frederick Stephani and Murray Burnett. P: Ewing and Elkins. D: J. B. Daniels.

Hidden (10/4/27, Lyceum, 80)

Freudian farrago wherein a guilt-ridden spinster seduces her brother-in-law, then takes her own life. C: Beth Merrill, Philip Merivale, Mary Morris, Marjorie Gateson. A: William Hurlbut. P/D: David Belasco.

Hidden River, The (1/23/57, Playhouse, 61)

Intricately plotted philosophical melodrama concerned with the efforts of a closely knit French family to identify the betrayer of their son, a World War II resistance leader. Generally affirmative reviews greeted this 1957 offering, but the play was not a box-office success. C: Robert Preston, Dennis King, Lili Darvas, Peter Brandon, Gaby Rodgers, Jack Bittner, David King-Wood, Tonio Selwart. A: Ruth and Augustus Goetz b/o the novel by Storm Jameson. P: Martin Gabel and Henry Margolis. D: Robert Lewis. CD: Anna Hill Johnstone. SD: Stewart Chaney.

Hidden Stranger (1/8/63, Longacre, 7)

Plastic surgeon (Torin Thatcher) and his problems in Florence, Italy. Ludicrously inept "psychological melodrama" by Dr. Maxwell Maltz. "Plastic surgeon who write bad play, lose face" (*World-Telegram*). P: Pygmalion Productions. D: Peter Cotes.

High Gear (10/6/27 Wallacks, 20)

Pitiable farce about a dumb Dora (Shirley Booth) who schemes to stay in the graces of her wealthy uncle. A: Larry E. Johnson. D: Roy Walling.

High Hatters, The (5/10/28, Klaw, 10)

High jinks in a mental institution. Leaden farce by columnist Louis Sobol. C: Gilbert Douglas, Robert Montgomery. P: Louis Isquith, Inc. D: Ralph Murphy.

High Road, The (11/19/12, Hudson, 71)

A woman (Mrs. Fiske) finds fulfillment when she becomes self-supporting. Slow-moving drama, billed as "a pilgrimage in five parts," written by Edward Sheldon. C: Arthur Byron, Charles Waldron, Frederick Perry, Barrett Clark. P/D: Harrison Grey Fiske.

High Stakes (9/9/24, Hudson, 120)

Alcoholic writer (Lowell Sherman) exposes conniving wife (Phoebe Foster) of his older brother (Wilton Lackaye) for the blackmailing floozy she is. Odious melodrama by Willard Mack. P: A. H. Woods.
SV: RKO, 1931, Lowell Sherman, Mae Murray.

High Tor (1/9/37, Martin Beck, 171)

Van Dorn (Burgess Meredith), a young romantic with a scornful view of civilization, finds refuge from the modern world on a lofty Hudson River mountain top—a property much desired by a firm of hard-fisted land developers. That night, during a storm that engulfs the mountain, Van meets a ghostly crew of long-dead sailors, and falls in love with their ward, a beautiful Dutch girl. (The poetic idealism of these seventeenth-century wanderers is in sharp contrast to the harsh materialism of the play's twentieth-century characters.) In the morning, when the phantoms have gone, Van Dorn faces reality and realizes he will be forced to sell his mountain. This charming fantasy by Maxwell Anderson had many virtues, not the least of which was a rich vein of rare humor. *High Tor* won the New York Drama Critics Circle award as best play of the year. C: Peggy Ashcroft (deb.), Harold Moffet, Thomas W. Ross, Mab Maynard, Harry Irvine, Byron McGrath, John Philliber, Charles D. Brown, Hume Cronyn. P/D: Guthrie McClintic. SD: Jo Mielziner.

Highest Tree, The (11/4/59, Longacre, 21)

Stricken with leukemia, a noted physicist decides to devote his remaining days to working with his geneticist-son in a worldwide effort to abolish further nuclear bomb tests. "An editorial rather than a play. . . . The writing is stiff as cardboard, and the direction stained-glassy" (*Mirror*). After twenty years as MGM's story editor, Kenneth MacKenna returned to the stage in the role of the dying physicist in this short-lived drama by Dore Schary (A/D). Robert Redford made his Broadway debut in this 1959 play as "Buzz," the callow son of Howard St. John and Natalie Schafer. Others in the cast included Richard Anderson, Larry Gates, William Prince, Frank Milan, Diana Douglas (deb.), Miriam Goldina, Joe De Santis. P: The Theatre Guild and Mr. Schary. SD: Donald Oenslager.

Highland Fling, A (4/28/44, Plymouth, 27)

Comedy-fantasy dealing with the efforts of a long-deceased Scottish ghost to reform a mortal sinner and thereby gain admittance to heaven. ". . . broadly whimsical . . . but often quite good fun" (*World-Telegram*). C: Ralph Forbes, John Ireland, Frances Reid, Karl Swenson, Margaret Curtis (A). P/D: George Abbott. CD: Motley. SD: John Root.

Hilda Crane (11/1/50, Coronet, 70)

Can a woman with a past still find happiness? Apparently not, according to this 1950 study of a two-time divorcée (Jessica Tandy) who, unable to decide between a safe if loveless third marriage and passionate romance, ends by committing suicide. ". . . frail and wavering . . . a play which talks a great deal about agony but captures very little of it in dramatic form" (*Herald Tribune*). C: Beulah Bondi, Evelyn Varden, John Alexander, Frank Sundstrom, Eileen Heckart. A: Samson Raphaelson. P: Arthur Schwartz. D: Hume Cronyn. SD: Howard Bay.
- SV: Fox, 1956, Jean Simmons, Guy Madison, Jean-Pierre Aumont, Judith Evelyn, Evelyn Varden (directed by Philip Dunne).

Hill Between, The (3/11/38, Little, 11)

Complications ensue when a young doctor returns with his socialite wife to visit his mountain kinfolk. Interesting regional drama by Lula Vollmer. C: Philip Ober, Dorothy Patten, Sara Haden, Mildred Dunnock. P: Robert Porterfield. D: Elizabeth Hull.

him (4/18/28, Provincetown, 21)

E. E. Cummings' surrealistic fantasy in which him (William S. Johnstone) and his girlfriend me (Erin O'Brien-Moore) struggle with the questions of identity and reality through a bewildering maze of metaphysical abstractions and interpolated vaudeville turns. ". . . a facetious cerebration . . . the irony and satire are more mannered than apposite" (*New York Times*). Lionel Stander, playing a mincing homosexual, made his New York debut as the First Fairy in *him*. This O/B play was staged by James Light.

Hipper's Holiday (10/18/34, Maxine Elliott's, 4)

Penniless youth (Burgess Meredith) becomes involved in a holdup. Hume Cronyn made his Broadway debut in this short-lived comedy playing the role of a janitor and understudying leading man Meredith. A: John Crump. P: Marian T. Carter. D: Alan Williams.

His and Hers (1/7/54, 48th Street, 76)

A plagiarism suit brings a pair of divorced playwrights (Robert Preston and Celeste Holm) back together again. Drowsy comedy by the husband-and-wife team of Fay and Michael Kanin. C: Elizabeth Patterson, George Voskovec, Howard St. John. P: Albert Selden and Morton Gottlieb. D: Michael Gordon.

His Bridal Night (8/16/16, Republic, 77)

The Dolly Sisters, those look-alike Hungarian music hall entertainers, made their legitimate theatre debut in this made-to-order farce. The plot, such as it was, dealt with the efforts of a bewildered bridegroom to figure out which of the two feminine Dromios he has married. "*His*

Bridal Night is not only no play for the graduating class at Miss Minchin's Academy; it is no play for the fastidious. . . . As for acting, they [the Dolly Sisters] do quite well [but] their speaking voices are a bit trying, and occasionally give something of the shock you experience when a beauty in the Follies at whom you have been gazing suddenly speaks. You wish she hadn't. When the two Dollys and Lucile Watson all talk at once the effect is dazing. . . . The floral offerings that went down the aisle and over the footlights after the second act were so large and so many that it would have saved no end of inconvenience and expense if the premiere had simply been held at the Botanical Gardens" *(New York Times).* C: John Westley, Pedro de Cordoba, Lucile Watson, Jessie Ralph. A: Lawrence Rising ("revised and elaborated" by Margaret Mayo). P: A. H. Woods. D: Bertram Harrision.

His Honor, Abe Potash (10/14/19, Bijou, 215)

Abe (Barney Bernard) is the political machine candidate for mayor of the town. Once he's elected, however, honest Abe turns the tables on the bosses and insists on fair play for everyone. Good-natured, unpretentious comedy by Montague Glass and Jules Eckert Goodman. P: A. H. Woods.

His Majesty Bunker Bean (10/2/16, Astor, 72)

Convinced by a fake mystic that he is a reincarnation of Napoleon and an Egyptian monarch of the pre-dynastic era, a credulous youth overcomes his mouselike complex. Reasonably entertaining farce with Taylor Holmes, based on stories by Harry Leon Wilson. "Buoyant and boisterous and youthful" *(Telegram).* "A refreshingly American comedy, full of American spirit" *(World).* A: Lee Wilson Dodd. P: Joseph Brooks. D: Robert Milton.

SV: RKO, 1936, *Bunker Bean,* Owen Davis, Jr., Louise Latimer, Lucille Ball, Hedda Hopper, Berton Churchill.

His Majesty's Car (10/23/30, Ethel Barrymore, 12)

A pretty commoner (Miriam Hopkins) is mistaken for the king's latest favorite. The fairy tale comes true when she meets the monarch and promptly sweeps him off his royal feet. Tedious mythical kingdom fluff, adapted and extensively revised by Fanny and Frederic Hatton from a play by Attila Von Orbok. C: Anthony Kemble-Cooper, Edward Crandall, James Dunn, Peggy Conklin, Theodore St. John, Wells Richardson, Emile Littler. P: Messrs. Shubert. D: Stanley Logan.

His Queen (5/11/25, Hudson, 11)

Shopgirl learns she's the queen of a mythical kingdom, is killed by revolutionists. Abysmal. C: Francine Larrimore, Robert Warwick, Edward Emery, Minnie Dupree, Lumsden Hare. A: John Hastings Turner. P/D: Oliver Morosco.

Hitch Your Wagon (4/8/37, 48th Street, 28)

Twenty-five-year-old Garson Kanin made his directorial bow with this short-lived farce, suggested by the well-publicized John Barrymore-Elaine Barrie romance that made tabloid headlines during the 30's. In the play (as in real life), an alcoholic actor flees a sanitarium and takes refuge in the home of a would-be actress (here called Camille Schwartz) and her ambitious mother. In the play, the actor willingly returns to the sanitarium to escape the publicity-seeking duo. In real life, Barrymore married the girl, thirty years his junior, much to the delight of gossip columnists of the time. As for *Hitch Your Wagon,* it was mauled by the critics and ran less than a month on

Broadway. C: George Curzon, Dennie Moore, Dora Weissman, Frank Munn, Joseph Sweeney, Millicent Green, William Tracy, Mary Wickes, Keenan Wynn, Jim Backus. A: Bernard C. Schoenfeld. P: Pearson and Baruch.

Hit-the-Trail-Holliday (9/13/15, Astor, 336)

Amusing George M. Cohan (A/P/D) farce based on the career of evangelist Billy Sunday (here called Billy Holliday). The play was written by Cohan from an idea by George Middleton and Guy Bolton as a vehicle for Cohan's brother-in-law, Fred Niblo. Niblo later became one of the leading directors of the silent screen with such pictures to his credit as *The Mark of Zorro, Blood and Sand, Ben Hur,* etc.

Hobo (2/11/31, Morosco, 5)

Clichéd odyssey of a rebellious youth (Paul Kelly) and his adventures "on the road." A/D: Frank Merlin. P: James Elliott.

Hogan's Goat (11/11/65, American Place, 607)

Splendid O/B verse drama about a heated mayoralty contest in 1890 Brooklyn between arrogant Irish-American political newcomer Matt Stanton (Ralph Waite) and the incumbent mayor (Tom Ahearne), who is backed by the machine and is a ruthless campaigner. Stanton subordinates everything to his consuming ambition, which is thwarted only after he causes the death of his loving wife (Faye Dunaway). *Hogan's Goat,* a first play by Harvard Professor William Alfred, proved to be one of the greatest successes in off-Broadway history. C: Cliff Gorman, Barnard Hughes, Tresa Hughes, Conrad Bain, Roland Wood. P: American Place Theater. D: Frederick Rolf. CD/SD: Kert Lundell.

Musicalized by Alfred/Marre/Leigh/Robinson as *Cry for Us All* (1970) with Steve Arlen, Joan Diener, Robert Weede, Tommy Rall, Helen Gallagher, William Griffis, Dolores Wilson.

Hole in the Head, A (2/28/57, Plymouth, 156)

Comedy-drama about the efforts of an improvident Jewish widower (Paul Douglas) to (a) bring up his small son and (b) save his shoddy Miami Beach hotel from bankruptcy. His older brother (David Burns) and sister-in-law (Kay Medford) arrange a match with a lonely young widow (Lee Grant). When this falls through, they try to whisk the boy back to New York where he can be looked after properly. Instead, the boy chooses to stay with his ne'er-do-well dad, and the father manages to hang on to his shoestring Shangri-La. ". . . often hilarious and frequently touching" *(Journal-American).* ". . . it took alternate spells of boring me and irritating me most of the evening" *(News).* Arnold Schulman's play was originally written for television and aired in 1955 under the title *The Heart Is a Forgotten Hotel.* C: Tommy White, Joyce Van Patten, Tom Pedi. P: Robert Whitehead. D: Garson Kanin. SD: Boris Aronson.

Musicalized by Ernest Kinoy and Walter Marks as *Golden Rainbow* (1968) with Steve Lawrence, Eydie Gorme, and Scott Jacoby.

SV: UA, 1959, Frank Sinatra, Edward G. Robinson, Eleanor Parker, Thelma Ritter, Carolyn Jones, Eddie Hodges, Keenan Wynn (directed by Frank Capra).

Hole in the Wall, The (3/26/20, Punch & Judy, 73)

A band of crooks work their skulduggery disguised as spiritualistic mediums. Low-grade thriller. C: John Halliday, Martha Hedman. A: Fred Jackson. P: Aarons and Seitz. D: Ira Hards.

SV: Par, 1929, Edward G. Robinson, Claudette Colbert, Donald Meek.

Holiday (11/26/28, Plymouth, 230)

Johnny Case, a cheerful nonconformist, becomes engaged to the socially prominent daughter of a millionaire. Neither she nor her businessman-father share his philosophy that life is a holiday to be enjoyed while young, but her unconventional sister, Linda, is a kindred spirit and falls hopelessly in love with the young man. Before the play is over, Linda has found the courage to break away from her oppressively gilded existence and join Johnny on his holiday. This delightful comedy by Philip Barry was one of the major hits of the 1928–29 season. C: Hope Williams,* Ben Smith, Donald Ogden Stewart, Dorothy Tree, Monroe Owsley. P/D: Arthur Hopkins.

The play was revived in December, 1973, by the New Phoenix Repertory Company. C: John Glover, Charlotte Moore, Robin Pearson Rose, Thomas A. Stewart. D: Michael Montel.

SV: RKO-Pathé, 1930. Ann Harding, Mary Astor, Robert Ames, Edward Everett Horton, Hedda Hopper; Col, 1938, Katharine Hepburn, Cary Grant, Lew Ayres, Doris Nolan, Edward Everett Horton, Jean Dixon, Binnie Barnes, Henry Kolker, Henry Daniell (directed by George Cukor from a screenplay by Donald Ogden Stewart).

---

*Katharine Hepburn, Hope Williams' understudy, was never given the opportunity to go on in the role of Linda Seton. She finally got to play the part ten years later, however, in the successful second screen version of *Holiday*.

Holiday for Lovers (2/14/57, Longacre, 100)

Don Ameche made his Broadway debut in this comedy about an American businessman's efforts to shield his nubile daughters from romance while touring Europe. Mr. Ameche was personable and ingratiating, but the play was pure hokum. C: Carmen Mathews, Audrey Christie, George Mathews, Sandra Church (deb.), Ann Flood, Thomas Carlin. A: Ronald Alexander. P/D: Shepard Traube. CD: Helene Pons. SD: John Robert Lloyd.

SV: Fox, 1959, Clifton Webb, Jane Wyman, Jill St. John, Carol Lynley, Paul Henreid, Gary Crosby, Jose Greco.

Holmeses of Baker Street, The (12/9/36, Masque, 54)

Sherlock Holmes, according to the authors of this 30's oddity, had a daughter named Shirley. Like her father, Shirley Holmes possesses such brilliant analytical faculties that, before the evening is over, she manages to outwit the notorious White X gang and put Scotland Yard to shame. This melodramatic comedy was neither sufficiently exciting nor amusing enough to tarry more than a few weeks in New York. The play was adapted by William Jourdan Rapp and Leonardo Bercovici from a script by Basil Mitchell. C: Helen Chandler, Cyril Scott, Conway Wingfield, Cecilia Loftus, Don Dillaway. P: Elizabeth Miele. D: Reginald Bach.

Holy Terror, A (9/28/25, George M. Cohan, 32)

Small-town sheriff (George Abbott) is framed for murder. Run-of-the-mine melodrama by Winchell Smith (D) and George Abbott, based on an unproduced play by Abbott and Maxwell Anderson entitled *The Feud*. C: Leona Hogarth, Richard Carlyle, Millard Mitchell. P: John Golden.

Home of the Brave (12/27/45, Belasco, 69)

1940's drama dealing with anti-semitism and men at war. A Jewish GI who has lost his memory and the ability to walk is in the care of an army psychiatrist as the play opens. Using narcosynthesis, the doctor encourages the soldier to relive the events leading up to his collapse. These are dramatized in a series of flashbacks.

In the end, the GI's guilt complex and paralysis are cured, and he regains the confidence to return to civilian life with a disabled buddy. This hard-hitting drama with an all-male cast was weakened by an uncertain, unconvincing third act. *Home of the Brave* was written by former nightclub entertainer and radio scriptwriter Arthur Laurents.* It was his first Broadway play. The Stanley Kramer screen version (see below) changed the leading character from a Jew to a Negro. C: Joseph Pevney, Eduard Franz, Russell Hardie, Alan Baxter, Henry Barnard, Kendall Clark. P: Lee Sabinson i.a.w. William Katzell. D: Michael Gordon. SD: Ralph Alswang.

SV: UA, 1949, James Edwards, Douglas Dick, Jeff Corey, Steve Brodie, Lloyd Bridges (directed by Mark Robson).

―――――
*Author of *The Time of the Cuckoo* (1952) and such musical plays as *West Side Story, Gypsy,* etc.

Home Towners, The (8/23/26, Hudson, 64)

Cynical small-towner visits New York and almost breaks up his best friend's impending marriage. Fairly entertaining George M. Cohan (A/P) comedy-drama. C: Robert McWade, William Elliott, Chester Morris, Georgia Caine. D: John Meehan.

SV: WB, 1936, *Times Square Playboy*, Warren William, Gene Lockhart, Barton MacLane, June Travis.

Honest Liars (7/19/26, Sam H. Harris, 97)

Robert Woolsey (of Wheeler and Woolsey) in a rickety farce set in a private sanitarium. A: Robert Weenolsen and Sherrill Webb. P: George MacFarlane. D: Frank Smithson.

Honeymoon (12/23/32, Little, 73)

Two young couples play marital musical chairs in Paris. Humdrum comedy by music critic Samuel Chotzinoff and George Backer. C: Thomas Mitchell (D), Katherine Alexander, Ross Alexander, Rachel Hartzell, Joseph Calleia. P: Harold Stone.

Honeys, The (4/28/55, Longacre, 36)

Macabre farce by Roald Dahl* about two long-suffering wives (Jessica Tandy and Dorothy Stickney) who decide to murder their husbands, a pair of despotic twin brothers (Hume Cronyn in a dual role). "... riotously funny ... irresistibly zany" (*Mirror*). "... not sufficiently demented ... the quips are infrequently hilarious." (*New York Times*). C: Mary Finney, Dana Elcar. P: Cheryl Crawford. D: Frank Corsaro. CD: Motley. SD: Ben Edwards.

―――――
*Anglo-American novelist and short-story writer; husband of actress Patricia Neal.

Hook 'N Ladder (4/29/52, Royale, 1)

An "incredibly melancholy antic" (*Post*) about a trio of double-dealing fire-engine salesmen. "It's plays like *Hook 'N Ladder* that give failures a bad name" (*Herald Tribune*). A: Charles Horner and Henry Miles. P/D: Al Moritz.

Hook-Up, The (5/7/35, Cort, 21)

To save an advertising account, a timid radio actor is bamboozled into a real-life on-the-air wedding ceremony. Spotty farce-comedy, enlivened by the antics of Ernest Truex in the role of the harried broadcaster. C: Edith Taliaferro, Helen Lynd, Georgette Harvey, Patricia Peardon. A: Jack Lait and Stephen Gross. P: Leslie J. Spiller. D: Frank Merlin. SD: Nat Karson.

Hope for a Harvest (11/26/41, Guild, 38)

A woman (Florence Eldridge) tries to persuade her embittered cousin (Fredric March) to make peace with his Italian neighbors and cultivate her broken-down ranch. "Unpersuasive and undramatic. . . ." (*Herald Tribune*). Written by Sophie Treadwell, author of *Machinal* (1928). C: Alan Reed, Doro Merande, Arthur Franz, Edith King. P: The Theatre Guild. D: Lester Vail.

Hope for the Best (2/7/45, Fulton, 117)

Journalist (Franchot Tone) is encouraged by a pretty girl (Jane Wyatt) to use his syndicated column as a forum for the promotion of liberal ideas. ". . . more debate than dramaturgy" *(News)*. A: William McCleery. P: Jean Dalrymple and Marc Connelly (D). SD: Motley.

Horse Fever (11/23/40, Mansfield, 25)

A young man smuggles a racehorse into his hotel room. Dismal farce tried to combine the plots of *Three Men on a Horse* and *Room Service* without success. "If *Horse Fever* can achieve a Broadway production, anything can" (*Herald Tribune*). C: Ezra Stone, Millard Mitchell, Joseph Pevney. A: Eugene Conrad, Zac and Ruby Gabel. P: Alex Yokel. D: Milton Stiefel.

Horses in Midstream (4/2/53, Royale, 4)

A French authoress and a New England banker, living contentedly in sin for thirty years, find their idyllic existence complicated by the sudden arrival of the banker's runaway granddaughter. Placid romantic comedy by Andrew Rosenthal. C: Cedric Hardwicke (D), Lili Darvas, Diana Lynn, Scott Forbes (deb.), Carol Goodner, Ludmilla Toretzka. P: Gilbert Miller and Donald Oenslager (SD).

Hot Corner, The (1/25/56, Golden, 5)

Skimpy farce about a hot-tempered baseball manager and his efforts to make a comeback in the major leagues. "Richly unhumorous" *(Post)*. C: Sam Levene (D), Don Murray, Vicki Cummings, Eric Brotherson. A: Allen Boretz and Ruby Sully, P: Eleanore Saidenberg. SD: Ralph Alswang.

Hot Ice (2/7/74, Evergreen, 94)

Mad, anarchic O/B comedy in which the Marx Bros. would feel beautifully at home. The "hot ice" of the title is not stolen jewelry. Instead, the plot is about cryogenics, putting dead bodies on ice till time for thawing and renewed life in some more peaceable era than the present. The problem is that the cryogenics folks are so enthusiastic about their mission that they don't draw the line at people already deceased. They are apt to snatch and freeze anyone they can get their hands on. The nemesis of the group is Buck Armstrong (Charles Ludlam), who infiltrates the organization by claiming a degree in air-conditioning. Assisting him is a lovely widow who poses agreeably as a corpse. A zany farce, sometimes chaotic, but always hilarious. ". . . a manic collection of gags, wordplays and horseplay, with enough sense beneath the nonsense to make the evening frozen food for thought" (Mel Gussow, *New York Times*). A/D: Charles Ludlam. C: Charles Ludlam, Lola Pashalinski, Bill Vehr, Black-Eyed Susan, Richard Irish, Jack Mallory, Stephen Sterne, Georg Osterman, John D. Brockmeyer, Robert Beers, Susan Kapilow, Endust, Randy Hunt. P: The Ridiculous Theater Company. SD/CD: Edward Avedisian.

Hot l Baltimore, The (3/22/73, Circle in the Square, 1,166)

Slice-of-life comedy-drama set in the lobby of an old hotel. Soon to be torn down, the Hotel Baltimore (the "e" in Hotel is missing from the marquee, thus the title) is home to an engaging group of eccentrics and losers, threatened with destruction as surely as the hotel. Through three acts, no perceptible plot emerges. The characters simply talk and interact, but so appealingly they become persons to care about, who linger in the memory after the final curtain. There are no strident dramatics, no "big finish." *The Hot l Baltimore* ends with a quietly valiant dance performed by two of the tenants. The characters are nicely varied: cheery April and volatile Suzy who are prostitutes; Mr. Morse, a senile old checkers-player; a young hooker known only as Girl because she can't settle on a name for herself; tough, out-of-work Jackie and the simple-minded brother she protects; nice guy Bill, the hotel night clerk; Millie, an elderly waitress. All these and others are alive with vibrant humanity. *The Hot l Baltimore* opened in a loft theater off-off Broadway on 1/27/73 for 17 performances as a production of the Circle Repertory Theater Company. Public approval enabled it to move O/B on 3/22/73 for a long run. The critical reception was as enthusiastic as the public's. ". . . both funny and sad . . . and the combination is an unbeatable winner" (Clive Barnes, *New York Times*). The New York Drama Critics Circle named it Best American Play of the season. In 1975, it became a short-lived situation comedy on ABC-TV with Conchata Ferrell repeating her stage role of April. A: Lanford Wilson C: Conchata Ferrell, Judd Hirsch, Mari Gorman, Stephanie Gordon, Jonathan Hogan, Trish Hawkins, Helen Stenborg, Henrietta Bagley, Rob Thirkield, Zane Lasky, Antony Tenuta, Burke Pearson, Louise Clay, Peter Tripp, Marcial Gonzales. D: Marshall W. Mason. P: Kermit Bloomgarden and Roger Ailes. i.a.w. Circle Repertory Theater Company. SD: Ronald Radice.

Hot Money (11/7/31, Cohan, 9)

Foolish farce about a high-pressure promoter and his problems. C: Leo Donnelly, Peggy Conklin, Hobart Cavanaugh. A: Aben Kandel. P: James W. Elliott. D: Bertram Harrison.

SV: WB, 1932, *High Pressure,* William Powell, Evelyn Brent, George Sidney, Guy Kibbee, Evelyn Knapp, Frank McHugh, Alison Skipworth; 1936, Ross Alexander, Beverly Roberts, Joseph Cawthorn, Anne Nagel.

Hotbed (11/8/28, Klaw, 19)

Bigotry, repression, and clandestine sex at a coeducational college. Earnest but overheated problem tract; first play by Paul Osborn, author of many subsequent Broadway successes including *On Borrowed Time* (1938), *A Bell for Adano* (1944), *Point of No Return* (1951). C: William Ingersoll, Josephine Hull, Preston Sturges. P: Brock Pemberton. D: Brock Pemberton and Antoinette Perry.

Hotel Universe (4/14/30, Martin Beck, 81)

A sextet of unhappy and frustrated people assemble on a terrace in the south of France. All are sick with nerves for they have recently witnessed a suicide that reminds them of their own contemplated self-destruction. By inducing his guests to reenact key moments from their respective pasts, a noted physicist helps to liberate them from their suicidal impulses. Interesting Freudian-metaphysical drama by Philip Barry; a two-hour play presented without intermission or the fall of a curtain. Extremely well acted, especially by Ruth Gordon as Lily Malone, a Dorothy Parker-type character. Also in the cast: Franchot Tone, Glenn Anders, Morris Carnovsky, Katherine Alexander, Earle Larimore, Phyllis Povah. P: The Theatre Guild. D: Philip Moeller.

Hottentot, The (3/1/20, George M. Cohan, 113)

A timid soul with a great fear of horses is mistaken for a famous jockey and compelled to ride in a steeplechase. Lively farce nonsense. C: William Collier, Ann Andrews, Frances Carson, Donald Meek. A: Victor Mapes and William Collier. P: Sam H. Harris.

SV: WB, 1929, Edward Everett Horton, Patsy Ruth Miller; 1939, *Going Places,* Dick Powell, Anita Louise, Ronald Reagan, Allen Jenkins, Walter Catlett, Louis Armstrong, Maxine Sullivan.

House Beautiful, The (3/12/31, Apollo, 108)

Allegorical fable of a New Jersey housewife who envisions her salesman-husband as a modern-day Sir Galahad, venturing forth each morning to battle the forces of wickedness and graft in the big city. "*The House Beautiful* is the play lousy" (Dorothy Parker, *New Yorker*). C: James Bell, Mary Philips, Raymond Walburn, Lionel Stander. A: Channing Pollock. P: Crosby Gaige. D: Worthington Miner.

House in Paris, The (3/20/44, Fulton, 16)

Expatriates work out their destinies in a Parisian salon presided over by a fanatically possessive matriarch (Ludmilla Pitoeff). Four authors—Mawby Green, Edward Feilbert, Caroline Francke, and Arthur Richman—had a hand in this fusty dramatization of Elizabeth Bowen's novel. ". . . clumsy, confused and dated. . ." (*Post*). P: H. Clay Blaney. D: Clarence Derwent. SD: Stewart Chaney.

House in the Country, A (1/11/37, Vanderbilt, 32)

Gangster uses Pennsylvania farmhouse as a hideout. Unsatisfactory mixture of comedy, farce, and melodrama; written by Melvin Levy, author of *Gold Eagle Guy* (1934). C: Tom Powers, Will Geer, Leon Ames, Louise Campbell. P: Murray Queen. D: Melville Burke.
SV: RKO, 1937, *Hideaway*, Fred Stone, J. Carrol Naish, Emma Dunn.

House of Blue Leaves, The (2/10/71, Truck & Warehouse, 337)

O/B black comedy about an eccentric New York family at the time of Pope Paul's 1965 visit to the U.S. Artie Shaughnessy (Harold Gould) is a middle-aged zookeeper who dreams of becoming a Hollywood songwriter. The excitement of the Pope's appearance not only heightens his desire for this new life but seems to aggravate the manias of those around him as well. They are numerous. Artie is burdened by a mentally disordered wife named Bananas—at one point she mistakes Brillo pads for hamburgers—while downstairs lives his girl friend, Bunny (Anne Meara), who equates suffering with a story culled from *Modern Screen* about Sandra Dee's search for some missing hair curlers. His soldier son, Ronnie (William Atherton), has gone AWOL in order to blow up the Pope, and there are the peripheral figures of a deaf sexpot, a zany Hollywood producer, and a trio of nuns, one of whom casts off her habit announcing that once a bride of Christ, she is now a young divorcée. The bomb plot fails when the sexpot and two of the nuns are blown up accidentally, Bunny and the producer go off together, the MPs capture Ronnie, and at final curtain, Artie strangles Bananas. A play full of excruciatingly funny lines, *The House of Blue Leaves* was named Best American Play of the season by the New York Drama Critics Circle. A: John Guare. C: Harold Gould, Anne Meara, Katherine Helmond, William Atherton, Frank Converse, Margaret Linn, Alix Elias, Rita Karin, Kay Michaels, Thomas F. Flynn, Bruce Cobb. D: Mel Shapiro. P: Warren Lyons and Betty Ann Besch. SD: Karl Eigsti. CD: Jane Greenwood.

House of Connelly, The (9/28/31, Martin Beck, 83)

Pseudo-realistic folk drama by Paul Green, author of *In Abraham's Bosom* (1926), dealing with the conflict between "the old and new South"; first production of The Group Theatre, for ten years (1931–41) a vital force in the American theatre. The central character in the play is young Will Connelly (Franchot Tone), the good-natured but weak scion of a once-proud Southern family. Instead of marrying a wealthy aristocrat who would save the family from poverty, Will elects to wed the daughter of a "poor white"

The House of Connelly. Franchot Tone, Morris Carnovsky, and Margaret Barker (a Group Theatre production, 1931). *Courtesy Museum of the City of New York Theatre and Music Collection.*

tenant farmer. Despite vicious family opposition to the match, it is she who inspires Will to bury the dead past and bring prosperity back to the house of Connelly. "Between Mr. Green's prose poem and the Group Theatre's performance, it is not too much to hope that something fine and true has been started in the American theatre" *(New York Times).* C: Morris Carnovsky, Art Smith, Mary Morris, Stella Adler, Margaret Barker, Rose McClendon, J. Edward Bromberg, Robert Lewis, Clifford Odets. D: Lee Strasberg and Cheryl Crawford.
SV: Fox, 1934, *Carolina,* Janet Gaynor, Lionel Barrymore, Robert Young, Richard Cromwell.

House of Doom, The (1/25/32, Masque, 8)

Mad doctor invents a soul-transformation machine. Wretched melodrama; nondescript cast. A: Charles Champlin. P: J. J. White, D: George Graves.

House of Fear, The (10/7/29, Republic, 48)

A magician and a psychic join forces to trap a murderer. "Another burlesque-mystery play . . . a childish hodgepodge . . ." *(New York Times).* C: Effie Shannon, Clay Clement, Frank Thomas, Lea Penman. A: Wall Spence. P: Ray Productions. D: Elmer Brown.

House of Glass, The (9/1/15, Candler, 245)

A woman awaits the day when her stern businessman-husband discovers that she is an ex-convict. That day arrives when a detective is hired to prosecute one of her husband's employees caught stealing from the company. "Tense and engrossing melodrama . . . a substantial evening's entertainment" *(New York Times).* C: Mary Ryan, Frank M. Thomas, Frederick Bart, Thomas Findlay. A: Max Marcin. P: Cohan and Harris. D: Sam Forrest.

House of Mirth, The (10/22/06, Savoy, 14)

Unsuccessful dramatization of Edith Wharton's novel of a modern-day Becky Sharp and her travels through "the shoddy, self-seeking world of high society." C: Fay Davis, Grant Mitchell. A: Edith Wharton and Clyde Fitch (D). P: Charles Frohman.

House of Shadows (4/21/27, Longacre, 29)

Haunted-house yarn replete with sliding panels, subterranean passageways, stalwart hero (Tom Powers), frightened heroine (Marguerite Churchill). Junk. A: Leigh Hutty. P: William A. Brady, Jr. and Dwight Deere Wiman i.a.w. J. H. Del Bondio. SD: Livingston Platt.

House of Women, The (10/3/27, Maxine Elliott's 40)

The conflict between a proud matriarch, her two neurotic daughters, and their respective suitors. Lugubrious family life chronicle by Louis Bromfield b/o his first novel, *The Green Bay Tree*. C: Nance O'Neil, Elsie Ferguson, Helen Freeman, Walter Abel, Curtis Cooksey. P/D: Arthur Hopkins.

Houseboat on the Styx (12/25/28, Liberty, 103)

It seems that a bunch of the boys (Nero, Napoleon, Sherlock Holmes, P. T. Barnum, et al) were whooping it up down below when a few of the girls (Cleopatra, Sapho, Salome, Delilah, Queen Elizabeth, Lucretia Borgia) decided to crash the satanic stag party. Campy 20's mishmash, fairly diverting in a wild-eyed sort of way. C: Hal Forde, Blanche Ring, John E. Hazzard. A: Kenneth Webb and John E. Hazzard. P: Ned Jakobs. D: Oscar Eagle.

Houseparty (9/9/29, Knickerbocker, 178)

College boy (Roy Hargrave) accidentally kills the town whore during a fraternity party,* agonizes lest her body be found. It is, but he is exonerated of the crime. Curious mixture of melodrama and comedy achieved considerable suspense in its better moments. A: Kenneth Britton and Roy Hargrave. P: Tyler and Erlanger. D: Harry Wagstaff Gribble.

*Songwriters Johnny Mercer and Everett Miller played two of the fraternity brothers at the party.

Houses of Sand (2/17/25, Hudson, 31)

Arthur (Paul Kelly) confides to his buddy Schuyler (Charles Bickford) that he's strangely drawn to all things oriental, especially to the pretty Miss Golden Fragrance (Vivienne Osborne). In Act Three, young Arthur learns that he is part Japanese himself and, therefore, can wed Miss G. F. with a clear conscience. Curtain. This soppy romantic drama might well have been titled *Monsieur Butterfly*. A: G. Marion Burton. P: Michael Mindlin. D: Daniel V. Arthur and Clifford Brooke.

Housewarming (4/7/32, Hopkins, 4)

A silly marital tiff ends with the bride setting fire to the entire house. *Housewarming* might better have been entitled *Much Ado About Nothing*. C: Katherine Wilson, Louis Jean Heydt. A: Gilbert Emery. P: Ann Ayers. D: Pauline Frederick.

How Beautiful With Shoes (11/28/35, Booth, 8)

Escaped lunatic (Myron McCormick) abducts country girl on her wedding day. Murky 30's drama by Wilbur Daniel Steele and Anthony Brown (D). P: Anthony Laudati.

How Come, Lawd? (9/30/37, 49th Street, 2)

Clumsy "Negro folk-drama" about the conflict between a naïve Alabama farm hand (Rex Ingram) and a would-be union organizer (Leigh Whipper). A: Donald Heywood. P: Negro Theatre Guild. D: Charles Adler.

How I Wonder (9/30/47, Hudson, 63)

Confused fantasy about the musings of an astronomy professor (Raymond Massey) searching for a way to prevent earth's annihilation in an atomic war. An attempt at whimsy was made by introducing characters representing the professor's mind (Everett Sloane) and a dream woman (Meg Mundy) from another planet. "A very dismal evening...." *(Sun)*. "How I wonder how *How I Wonder* ever got to Broadway" *(Journal-American)*. C: Carol Goodner, Bethel Leslie, Henry Jones, John Marriott. The play was written by dramatist-screenwriter Donald Ogden Stewart. P:

Ruth Gordon and Garson Kanin (D) i.a.w. Victor Samrock and William Fields. CD: Helene Pons. SD: Donald Oenslager.

How Long Till Summer (12/27/49, Playhouse, 7)

Ambitious black lawyer becomes involved with corrupt political machine. ". . . hackneyed and diffuse. . . ."*(New York Times)*. C: Josh White, Josh White, Jr., Frank Wilson, Ida James, Leigh Whipper, Arthur O'Connell, Peter Capell, Fredi Washington, Sam Gilman. A: Sarett and Herbert Rudley (D). P: Bronsky and Gilbert. SD: Ralph Alswang.

How to Get Tough About It (2/8/38, Martin Beck, 23)

Waitress (Katherine Locke), forced to choose between a cynical labor organizer (Kent Smith) and an idealistic boatbuilder (Myron McCormick), chooses the idealist. Well-characterized but loosely plotted comedy-drama by Robert Ardrey. C: Jose Ferrer, Karl Malden, Millard Mitchell, George Nash, Connie Gilchrist. P/D: Guthrie McClintic. SD: Norris Houghton.

How to Make a Man (2/2/61, Atkinson, 12)

Futuristic comedy about a robot (Peter Marshall), constructed by a do-it-yourself enthusiast (Tommy Noonan), who decides that being human isn't much fun after all. "A play suitable for people who read only comic books" *(New York Times)*. ". . . monumental disaster . . . with no semblance of humor, taste or ingenuity" *(Journal-American)*. C: Barbara Britton, Vicki Cummings, Erik Rhodes, Michael Dunn, Monica May. A: William Welch b/o a story by Clifford Simak. P: Dick Randall. D: Eddie Bracken. SD: Harry Horner.

Howdy, King (12/13/26, Morosco, 48)

Texan (Minor Watson) discovers he is the ruler of a mythical kingdom. Grade-C *Graustarkiana*. A: Mark Swan. P: Anne Nichols. D: Clifford Brooke.

Howdy Stranger (1/14/37, Longacre, 77)

To land a motion picture contract, an animal-shy radio crooner (Frank Parker) must pretend he's a cowhand. Silly 30's farce. A: Robert Sloane and Louis Pelletier, Jr. P: Hammerstein and Du-For. D: Carl Hunt.

SV: WB, 1938, *Cowboy from Brooklyn*, Dick Powell, Pat O'Brien, Priscilla Lane, Ann Sheridan, Dick Foran, Ronald Reagan, James Stephenson, Jeffrey Lynn; 1948, *Two Guys from Texas*, Dennis Morgan, Jack Carson, Dorothy Malone, Forrest Tucker, Fred Clark.

Howie (9/17/58, 46th Street, 5)

Innocuous comedy about a brash young know-it-all who finally finds his niche as a TV quiz contestant. C: Albert Salmi, Leon Ames, Peggy Conklin, Patricia Smith, Patricia Bosworth, Gene Saks, John Fiedler. A: Phoebe Ephron. P: The Playwrights Company, James Slevin and John Gerstad (D).

How's Your Health? (11/26/29, Vanderbilt, 46)

Hypochondriac forgets his ailments when he starts drinking. 1929 farce by Booth Tarkington and Harry Leon Wilson contained several very funny scenes. ". . . entertainment for those who wish to laugh long and loud" *(New York Times)*. C: Roy Atwell, Donald Brian, Herbert Corthell. P: Lyle Andrews and R. H. Burnside (D). SD: Cirker and Robbins.

Humbug, The (11/27/29, Ambassador, 13)

Trite melodrama about an unscrupulous

hypnotist (John Halliday) who preys upon susceptible females. A/P/D: Max Marcin.

Humoresque (2/27/23, Vanderbilt, 31)

Laurette Taylor and Luther Adler in Fannie Hurst's tearful tale of a Jewish mama's sacrifices for her violinist-son. "A performance [Miss Taylor's] that is astounding . . . we have never admired her or wondered at her more. . . ." (Alexander Woollcott, *New York Times*). Though Laurette Taylor scored a personal triumph as the wise and loving Sarah Kantor in *Humoresque,* the public would have none of it. As critic Burns Mantle later commented: "The Jews did not think she was Jewish and the Irish did not admire her for trying to be." P/D: J. Hartley Manners.
SV: WB, 1946, Joan Crawford, John Garfield, Oscar Levant, Ruth Nelson, Craig Stevens, J. Carrol Naish.

Hurricane (12/25/23, Frolic, 125)

Everything happens to poor Ilka (Olga Petrova). She runs away from a Texas ranch to escape her dastardly stepfather, gets mixed up in the flourishing white slave traffic in Kansas City, becomes a high-priced call girl in Miami, and ends up a successful interior decorator in New York. Dreadful. A: Olga Petrova. P: Richard Herndon.

Huui, Huui (11/16/68, Public, 51)

Incisive character study of an indigent writer in alienation from society. Produced O/B by Joseph Papp (D) with a cast that included Barry Primus, David Congdon, and Charles Durning. A: Anne Burr.

I

I Am a Camera (11/28/51, Empire, 262)

Giddy, amoral Sally Bowles captured Broadway in the person of Julie Harris, whose performance delighted the critics and elicited the adjective "stunning" from three major reviewers *(New York Times, Herald Tribune, Post)*. Her vibrancy was effectively pitted against the moody introspection of the young Christopher Isherwood (William Prince), who serves as narrator and hero of this autobiographical story set in Berlin, 1930. Meeting in a sleazy rooming house, the oddly matched pair develop a platonic relationship born of their individual needs. A romantic subplot touches on the Nazi persecution of Jews, but less effectively so according to George Jean Nathan, who thought this part of the play was "soapbox rhetoric." Despite seeming weaknesses in construction, *I Am a Camera* was received with general enthusiasm and won the New York Drama Critics Circle Award for 1951. C: Marian Winters, Olga Fabian, Martin Brooks, Edward Andrews, Catherine Willard. A/D: John Van Druten, b/o *Berlin Stories* by Christopher Isherwood. P: Gertrude Macy i.a.w. Walter Starcke. SD: Boris Aronson.

Musicalized by John Kander, Fred Ebb and Joe Masteroff as *Cabaret* (1966) with Jill Haworth, Bert Convy, Joel Grey, Lotte Lenya, Jack Gilford.

SV: British, 1955, Julie Harris, Laurence Harvey, Shelley Winters, Ron Randell (directed by Henry Cornelius); AA, 1972, *Cabaret*, Liza Minnelli, Michael York, Joel Grey, Helmut Griem, Marisa Berenson (directed by Bob Fosse).

I Am My Youth (3/7/38, Playhouse, 8)

Turgid biography of William Godwin, socialist author-philosopher, whose daughters became romantically involved with Byron and Shelley. C: Charles Waldron, Frank Lawton, Viola Roache, Linda Watkins, Sylvia Weld. A: Ernest Pascal and Edwin Blum. P/D: Alfred de Liagre, Jr. CD/SD: Donald Oenslager.

Note: Godwin's daughter, Mary, eloped with Percy Bysshe Shelley when she was seventeen. The following year she wrote the famous novel of terror, *Frankenstein* (1818).

I Gotta Get Out (9/25/47, Cort, 4)

Trio of bookies use a dowager's kitchen as a base of operations. ". . . scattered, fabricated and stale-humored" *(World-Telegram)*. C: David Burns, Edith Meiser. A: Joseph Fields (D) and Ben Sher. P: Harris and Meyer.

I Killed the Count (8/31/42, Cort, 29)

Scotland Yard is baffled when four suspects confess to the same murder. ". . . more ingenious than entertaining" *(Journal-American)*. Written by Anglo-American author Alec Coppel. C: Louis Hector, Clarence Derwent, Doris Dalton. P: Messrs. Shubert. D: Frank Carrington and Agnes Morgan.

I Know My Love (11/2/49, Shubert, 246)

Episodic comedy dealing with fifty years in the lives of a Boston industrialist (Alfred Lunt) and his understanding wife (Lynn Fontanne). This sentimental vehicle gave the Lunts the opportunity to run the gamut from old age to youth. "Untidy in construction, cluttered with clichés and. . . . deficient in wit" *(New York Times)*. C: Geoffrey Kerr, Katharine Bard, Hugh Franklin, Anne Sargent, Mary Fickett, Betty Caulfield. A: S. N. Behrman b/o a play by Marcel Achard. P: The Theatre Guild and John C. Wilson. D: Alfred Lunt. SD: Stewart Chaney.

I Know What I Like (11/24/39, Hudson, 11)

Wealthy girl falls in love with struggling artist. Feeble 30's comedy. C: John Beal, Helen Claire, Haila Stoddard. A: Justin Sturm. P: Hambleton and Skinner. D: Auriol Lee.

I Like It Here (3/27/46, Golden, 52)

A Mr. Fixit refugee sets a troubled American household to rights. "A dull, shaky and completely hopeless little comedy" *(Sun)*. C: Oscar Karlweis, Bert Lytell, Beverly Bayne, William Terry, Seth Arnold. A: A. B. Shiffrin. P: William Cahn. D: Charles K. Freeman.

I Loved You Wednesday (10/11/32, Harris, 63)

Architect (Humphrey Bogart) is torn between his wealthy wife (Rose Hobart) and the pretty girl (Frances Fuller) he had known and loved during his student days in Paris. Henry Fonda had a small role in this slick but empty 1932 romantic comedy-drama. Also in the cast: Henry O'Neill, Jane Seymour. A: Molly Ricardel and William Du Bois. P: Crosby Gaige. D: Worthington Miner.
SV: Fox, 1933, Warner Baxter, Elissa Landi, Victor Jory, Laura Hope Crews.

I Must Love Someone (2/7/39, Longacre, 191)

Glossy, highly fictionalized period piece about the lives and loves of the *Florodora* sextet. (In real life, all six chorus girls in this famous musical show married millionaires.) Highlight: a recreation of the famous "Tell Me, Pretty Maiden" number as staged in the original production of *Florodora* (1900). The play was coauthored by Leyla Georgie and Jack Kirkland (P), author of *Tobacco Road* (1933). During the run, Nancy Carroll (the former Mrs. Kirkland) replaced Martha Sleeper in the leading role. With Miss Carroll's name in lights, business boomed and *I Must Love Someone* managed a healthy run of 191 performances. D: Frank Merlin.

I, Myself (5/9/34, Mansfield, 7)

Ghost (Charles Trowbridge) returns to shield his widow from a false murder charge. Grade-C comedy-drama. A: Adelyn Bushnell. P: Pearson and Baruch. D: Charles Hopkins.
SV: Fox, 1937, *Laughing at Trouble*, Jane Darwell, Margaret Hamilton.

I Never Sang for My Father (1/25/68, Longacre, 124)

Character study of a forty-year-old son who tries—and fails—to establish a loving relationship with his elderly, cantankerous father. Perceptive, deeply moving drama by Robert Anderson. C: Hal Holbrook, Alan Webb, Teresa Wright, Lillian Gish. P: Gilbert Cates i.a.w. Doris Vidor. D: Alan Schneider. SD: Jo Mielziner.
SV: Col, 1970, Gene Hackman, Melvyn Douglas, Estelle Parsons, Dorothy Stickney (directed by Gilbert Cates).

I Remember Mama (10/19/44, Music Box, 714)

A Norwegian family with a gallant, indomitable mother establishes a modest home on San Francisco's Steiner Street in this period comedy (1910) by John Van Druten (A/D). To give her children a sense of security, Mama (Mady Christians) pretends they have a flourishing bank account. By the end of the play, Mama has gotten her children educated and one of them, Katrin (Joan Tetzel), is on her way toward becoming a successful writer. "A family chronicle—picturesque, sentimental, humorous, warm and faintly exotic—to which everyone can respond in some degree and which a great many people will take to their hearts" *(PM)*. Marlon Brando made his Broadway debut in *I Remember Mama* as Nels, the dutiful fifteen-year-old son who shocks his family by puffing his first cigarette quite openly in public."Of such trivia a masterpiece is made," observed Robert Garland *(Journal-American)* and added: "The Nels of Marlon Brando is, if he doesn't mind me saying so, charming." The play was based on Kathryn Forbes' best-selling book, *Mama's Bank Account*, in which she told of her San Francisco childhood and of her parents, aunts, and uncles who had come to America from Norway. This 1944 comedy launched the phenomenally successful producing team of (Richard) Rodgers and (Oscar) Hammerstein. The play, an unqualified hit, ran 714 performances. C: Oscar Homolka, Adrienne Gessner, Frances Heflin, Carolyn Hummel, Richard Bishop. CD: Lucinda Ballard. SD: George Jenkins.

SV: RKO, 1948. Irene Dunne, Barbara Bel Geddes, Oscar Homolka, Philip Dorn, Ellen Corby, Cedric Hardwicke, Edgar Bergen, Rudy Vallee, Florence Bates (directed by George Stevens from a screenplay by DeWitt Bodeen).

Note: The national touring company starred Charlotte Greenwood as "Mama" with Kurt Katch featured as Uncle Chris.

I Want a Policeman (1/14/36, Lyceum, 47)

Young second wife is accused of wealthy husband's murder. Run-of-the-mill whodunit. C: Sylvia Field, Estelle Winwood, Barry Sullivan (deb.), Eric Wollencott, Weldon Heyburn, Clinton Sundberg. A: Rufus King and Milton Lazarus. P: Curtis and Myers. D: Arthur Sircom.

I Was Dancing (11/8/64, Lyceum, 16)

An old vaudevillian (Burgess Meredith) comes home after a lifetime away to find that his son (Orson Bean) is a stranger—and determined to pack him off to an old folks' home. Ruefully humorous, thinly plotted comedy by Edwin O'Connor b/o his novel of the same name. C: Pert Kelton, Eli Mintz, David Doyle, Barnard Hughes. P: David Merrick. D: Garson Kanin.

I Was Waiting for You (11/13/33, Booth, 8)

Artist discards his aging mistress for a younger model. Feeble boulevard comedy with a company of American actors struggling unsuccessfully to portray denizens of France. C: Bretaigne Windust, Glenn Anders, Vera Allen, Myron McCormick, Helen Brooks, Joshua Logan. A: Melville Baker b/o play by Jacques Natanson. P: Edward Choate. D: Arthur J. Beckhard. SD: Jo Mielziner.

Icebound (2/10/23, Sam H. Harris, 170)

Pulitzer Prize drama by Owen Davis. A family of greedy New Englanders impatiently await their mother's death so that they can get their hands on her money. Instead, she leaves her money to the drudge who has faithfully tended her, with the proviso that it is to be held in trust for the black sheep of the family whom the drudge loves. Bleakly realistic regional drama, soundly constructed, compactly written. C: Phyllis Povah,

The Iceman Cometh (1946–47). *Courtesy Museum of the City of New York Theatre and Music Collection.*

Robert Ames, Edna May Oliver, John Westley, Willard Robertson. P: Sam H. Harris. D: Sam Forrest.

Iceman Cometh, The (10/9/46, Martin Beck, 136)

Eugene O'Neill returned to the theatre after a twelve-year absence with this four-act morality play set in a Hell's Kitchen barroom in the year 1912. The bums, misfits, and social outcasts of Harry Hope's moldy saloon-flophouse are given to boozy self-pity and pipe dreams of a better tomorrow. ("The lie of a pipe dream," says one of them, "is what gives life to the whole misbegotten mad lot of us, drunk or sober.") Hickey, a gladhanding traveling salesman and reformed drunk, arrives on the scene and endeavors to regenerate his derelict friends. They are to test their pipe dreams in the outside world and come to terms with themselves. "Just stop lying about yourself and kidding yourself about tomorrows," advises Hickey. The experiment is a disaster. When Hickey turns out to be insane, and is apprehended for the murder of his wife, the down-and-outers cheerfully return to their whiskey-sodden illusions. Verbose, repetitive, and slowly paced, *The Iceman Cometh* made no concessions to popular taste. A kind of Americanized *Lower Depths*, the play was called "a superb drama of splendid and imposing stature" by Richard Watts, Jr. in the *New York Post*. Written in 1939, but not produced until 1946, *Iceman* was the last O'Neill play presented during the author's lifetime. The Broadway production featured a fine portrayal by Dudley Digges as Harry Hope, a less than adequate one by James Barton in the pivotal role of Hickey. Competently but unimaginatively staged by Eddie Dowling, *The Iceman Cometh* closed after only 136 performances. Revived O/B a decade later (5/8/56, Circle in the Square, 565) under Jose Quintero's direction, the play seemed far more lively, moving and effective. A huge success with press and public, the 1956 revival thrust into prominence a trio of unknowns: Jason Robards, Jr. (outstanding as Hickey), Conrad Bain (Larry), and Peter Falk (Rocky). A subsequent 1973 revival at Manhattan's

Joseph E. Levine-Circle in the Square theatre cast James Earl Jones as Hickey in "a production not conspicuously endowed with strength or cohesiveness" (*Time Magazine*). The 1946 Broadway cast included: Carl Benton Reid, Nicholas Joy, Tom Pedi, Paul Crabtree, E. G. Marshall, John Marriott, Morton L. Stevens, Al McGranary, Russell Collins, Leo Chalzel, Frank Tweddell, Jeanne Cagney, Ruth Gilbert, Marcella Markham. P: The Theatre Guild. SD: Robert Edmond Jones.

SV: AFT (American Film Theater), 1973, Lee Marvin, Fredric March, Robert Ryan, Jeff Bridges, Bradford Dillman, Martyn Green, Tom Pedi, Moses Gunn, George Voskovec (directed by John Frankenheimer).

Idiot's Delight (3/24/36, Shubert, 299)

Pulitzer Prize comedy-drama by Robert E. Sherwood in which a dozen guests of various nationalities find themselves marooned in a Swiss hotel on the eve of World War II. Above the frightened banter, the author's voice can be heard damning the munitions makers, the world's indifference to fascism, and the stupidity of war. Among the guests in the hotel are a glib American song-and-dance man (Alfred Lunt)* and a fake Russian countess (Lynn Fontanne) he had casually bedded years before in Nebraska. In the end, only these two likable charlatans elect to remain behind, laughing, singing, and drinking champagne as the holocaust begins. *Idiot's Delight* was one of the American theatre's earliest reactions to the war clouds looming over Europe. It opened in New York two days after Italy had invaded Ethiopia. The London production (with Raymond Massey and Tamara Geva in the leading roles) premiered less than a week after Hitler's army had marched into Austria. The Sherwood comedy was a great popular success. The public responded strongly to its pacifist theme and stern anti-fascist preachments. Moreover, the two starring roles were made to order for the Lunts, who played them with customary perfection. C: Sydney Greenstreet, Richard Whorf, Francis Compton, Bretaigne Windust (D), Barry Thomson, Thomas Gomez, Edgar Barrier. P: The Theatre Guild. SD: Lee Simonson.

SV: MGM, 1939, Clark Gable, Norma Shearer, Edward Arnold, Burgess Meredith, Charles Coburn, Laura Hope Crews, Joseph Schildkraut, Virginia Grey.

---

*Alfred Lunt admitted patterning his characterization of the brash hoofer-comic after Milton Berle and Harry Richman, both of whom Lunt studied during several night club excursions prior to the start of rehearsals.

If a Body (4/30/35, Biltmore, 46)

A young man becomes involved with crooked gamblers while under hypnosis. Flimsy farce with a no-name cast. A: Edward Knoblock and George Rosener (D). P: Pierre de Reeder.

If Booth Had Missed (2/4/32, Maxine Elliott's, 20)

Poorly handled but intriguing historical conjecture: what would have happened had Lincoln escaped assassination and lived through the Reconstruction years? According to the author, he would have been impeached, acquitted by a single vote, and shot as he rose in the senate to give thanks. "*If Booth Had Missed* missed so completely that even the ushers failed to show up on the third night" (George Jean Nathan, *Judge*). C: Daniel Poole, Charlotte Walker, Royal Dana. A: Arthur Goodman. P: Walter Hartwig i.a.w. William A. Brady. D: Milton Smith.

If I Was Rich (9/2/26, Mansfield, 92)

Henpecked failure is goaded by his wife into passing himself off as wealthy and successful. Engaging little comedy-

Idiot's Delight. **Alfred Lunt at piano (1936).** *Courtesy Museum of the City of New York Theatre and Music Collection.*

drama by William Anthony McGuire (A/P/D). C: Joe Laurie, Jr., Ruth Donnelly, Raymond Walburn, Mildred McLeod.

If I Were You (1/24/38, Mansfield, 8)

Through the supernatural powers of an Irish maid (Betty Field), a husband (Bernard Lee) and wife (Constance Cummings) are able to change sexes, with resultant comic confusion. So-so risqué farce, adapted from the Thorne Smith novel, *Turnabout*, by Paul Hervey Fox (P) and Benn W. Levy (D).

SV: UA, 1940, *Turnabout*, Carole Landis, John Hubbard, Mary Astor, Adolphe Menjou, Verree Teasdale, William Gargan, Joyce Compton, Donald Meek, Franklin Pangborn, Marjorie Main.

If Love Were All (11/13/31, Booth, 11)

Learning that her mother (Aline MacMahon) is having an affair with a married man (Hugh Buckler), a precocious young girl (Margaret Sullavan) tries to keep the clandestine romance a secret from her psychologist-father (Walter Kingsford). An ingratiating performance by ingenue Sullavan was the main plus factor in this muddled comedy-drama. A: Cutler Hatch. P: Actor-Managers, Inc. D: Agnes Morgan.

If This Be Treason (9/23/35, Music Box, 40)

Interesting 1935 drama about a pacifist president who journeys to Japan in hopes of averting war between the two countries. *If This Be Treason* received mixed reviews and closed after five weeks. C: McKay Morris, Armina Marshall, Tom

Powers, Arthur Hughes. A: (Reverend) John Haynes Holmes and Reginald Lawrence. P: The Theatre Guild. D: Harry Wagstaff Gribble.

I'll Take the High Road (11/9/43, Ritz, 7)

Defense plant employee (Jeanne Cagney) exposes her boss as a pro-Nazi traitor. "... inexpert and feckless.... As for me, I'll take the low road" *(PM)*. A: Lucille Prumbs. P: Clifford Hayman and Milton Berle. D: Sanford Meisner.

Immoral Isabella? (10/27/27, Bijou, 60)

Queen Isabella doesn't care a fig about the *Nina, Pinta,* and *Santa Maria*. What she really wants is to get that handsome Christopher Columbus to bed with her. Jejune jape. C: Frances Starr, Reginald Mason, Eugene Powers. A: Lawton Campbell. P: Chamberlain Brown. D: Mabel Brownell.

Immoralist, The (2/8/54, Royale, 104)

Dramatization of André Gide's autobiographical novel about a young homosexual (Louis Jourdan) who marries a shy neighborhood girl (Geraldine Page) and takes her with him to North Africa in hopes that she will save him from himself. The rest of the play depicts the gradual disintegration of their marriage as the husband is tempted by a corrupt houseboy (James Dean), and the wife retreats into alcoholism and despair. "An admirable piece of work ... austere, crushing and genuine" *(New York Times)*. "... very little emotion ... an almost somnambulistic air of detachment. ... an interesting but arid play" *(Herald Tribune)*. *The Immoralist* was written by Ruth and Augustus Goetz, authors of *The Heiress* (1947), which they adapted from Henry James' novel *Washington Square*. C: Charles Dingle, David J. Stewart, John Heldabrand, Paul Huber, Adelaide Klein. P: Billy Rose. D: Daniel Mann. CD: Motley. SD: George Jenkins.

R: (11/7/63, Bouwerie Lane, 210). C: Frank Langella, Marcie Hubert. D: George Keathley.

Immortal Thief, The (10/2/26, Hampden's, 26)

Stodgy costume drama about one of the two thieves who was crucified beside Jesus on the cross. C: Walter Hampden, Mabel Moore, Edith Barrett, Thomas Gomez. A: Tom Barry. P/D: Walter Hampden.

Impossible Years, The (10/13/65, Playhouse, 670)

Cheapjack farce about a psychiatrist trying to cope with his nubile daughter's sex life. This 1965 offering owed its Broadway success to Alan King's ingratiating performance in the leading role. A: Bob Fisher and Arthur Marx. P: Black and Hyman. D: Arthur Storch.

SV: MGM, 1968, David Niven, Lola Albright, Chad Everett, Ozzie Nelson (directed by Michael Gordon).

In Abraham's Bosom (12/30/26, Provincetown, 277)

Paul Green's Pulitzer Prize folk-tragedy of negro life in the deep South. Abraham (Jules Bledsoe) wants to teach his people. His white father, Colonel McCranie, finally persuades the school board to let Abe teach, but the Negroes are reluctant pupils. Abe's own son turns against his father, and the school closes when the old colonel dies. Frustrated, taunted, beaten by white men when he tries to reopen his school, Abe kills his shiftless white half-brother in a frenzy, and is lynched. "So well-written and so well-played that even the near-Southerners who applaud *Dixie* the loudest may be urged to sympathy" *(Herald-Tribune)*. C: Frank Wilson,[*] Rose McClendon. P: Provincetown Players. D: Jasper Deeter.

---

[*]Mr. Wilson took over the role of Abraham when the play resumed its O/B run on 9/6/27.

In a Garden (11/16/25, Plymouth, 73)

Lissa (Laurette Taylor) is married to Adrian Terry (Frank Conroy), a playwright who believes he can control the lives of human beings as skillfully as he controls the destinies of his fictional characters. To test his theories, the playwright contrives to effect a liaison between his wife and a handsome diplomat (Louis Calhern), who had been her first love years ago. Lissa discovers the plot and, disillusioned, leaves both husband and lover for a life of her own. Written by Philip Barry as a vehicle for Katharine Cornell, *In a Garden* was dismissed by the critics as "murky" and "self-consciously theatrical." A tribute to the play, and to Laurette Taylor's artistry, was the fact that first nighters returned *en masse* for the final performance. P/D: Arthur Hopkins.

In Any Language (10/7/52, Cort, 45)

Labored farce about a fading Hollywood star (Uta Hagen) who goes to Rome to revitalize her career under the guidance of an Italian movie genius, learns that she is not up to the demands of the role, and settles instead for a reconciliation with her estranged husband (Walter Matthau). In minor supporting roles: silent screen siren Nita Naldi and nightclub pianist Louis ("Goldie") Hawkins. C: Joe De Santis, Eileen Heckart, Gloria Marlowe. A: Edmund Beloin and Henry Garson. P: Jule Styne and George Abbott (D). CD/SD: Raoul Pene du Bois.

In Bed We Cry (11/14/44, Belasco, 47)

Ultra-chic beautician (Ilka Chase) can't decide between three men. "It made me Ilka" *(Hollywood Reporter)*. ". . . sheer drivel" *(Post)*. C: Paul McGrath, Frederic Tozere, Francis DeSales, Ruth Matteson. A: Ilka Chase b/o her novel of the same name. P/D: John C. Wilson. SD: Joseph B. Platt. CD: Adrian.

In Clover (10/13/37, Vanderbilt, 3)

Feeble comedy about the tribulations (weekend guests, quarrelsome neighbors, etc.) of a city couple who rent a dilapidated country home. (Kaufman and Hart made use of the same basic plot and situations in their 1940 comedy, *George Washington Slept Here*.) *In Clover* was written by Allan Scott, author of *Goodbye Again* (1932). C: Myron McCormick, Claudia Morgan, Jose Ferrer, Louise Platt, Joseph Sweeney, Dennie Moore. P: J. and J. Krimsky. D: Bretaigne Windust. SD: Norris Houghton.

In His Arms (10/13/24, Fulton, 40)

Papier-mâché puppy-love triangle comedy with a nice cast: Margaret Lawrence, Geoffrey Kerr, Effie Shannon, Vernon Steele, Edna May Oliver, Eliot Cabot, Cornelia Otis Skinner. A: Lynn Starling. P: Sam H. Harris.

In Love With Love (8/6/23, Ritz, 122)

A flirtatious beauty (Lynn Fontanne) keeps two young suitors dangling. Trivial comedy by Vincent Lawrence. C: Henry Hull, Ralph Morgan, Robert Strange, Berton Churchill. P: William Harris, Jr. D: Robert Milton.

SV: Fox, 1930, *Crazy That Way,* Joan Bennett, Regis Toomey, Kenneth MacKenna, Jason Robards, Sr.

In the Bar of a Tokyo Hotel (5/11/69, Eastside, 25)

Tennessee Williams' drama about the conflict between a once famous, now failing painter and his grasping, wildly promiscuous wife. A slowly paced, only occasionally affecting study of two neurotics locked in mortal combat. Presented O/B with a cast headed by Donald Madden, Anne Meacham, and Lester Rawlins. P: Marks/Jaffe. D: Herbert Machiz.

In the Best of Families (2/2/31, Bijou, 141)

Misunderstandings and recriminations mount when an abandoned baby is left on the doorstep of a suburban family. Frenetic farce had little to recommend it. C: Charles Richman, Florence Edney. A: Anita Hart and Maurice Braddell. P: Thomas Kilpatrick. D: Jo Graham.

In the Counting House (12/13/62, Biltmore, 4)

Stereotyped drama about father-son conflicts in the business world. C: Howard da Silva, Sydney Chaplin, Kay Medford, Nancy Pollock, Paul Richards, Robert Pastene. A: Leslie Weiner. P: David J. Cogan. D: Arthur Penn.

In the Next Room (11/27/23, Vanderbilt, 164)

A priceless Boule cabinet from the Louvre falls into the hands of an American collector and brings sudden death in its wake. Pleasantly shivery thriller by Harriet Ford and socialite Eleanor (Mrs. August Belmont) Robson, based on Burton Stevenson's mystery novel, *The Boule Cabinet*. C: Morris Ankrum, Mary Kennedy, Merle Maddern, Wright Kramer. P: Winthrop Ames and Guthrie McClintic (D).

SV: WB, 1930, Jack Mulhall, Alice Day; 1941, *The Case of the Black Parrot*, William Lundigan, Maris Wrixon, Eddie Foy, Jr.

In the Palace of the King (12/31/00, Republic, 138)

To be near her lover, a plucky heroine (Viola Allen) disguises herself as her blind sister and makes her way to the court of King Philip II of Madrid. Undistinguished costume melodrama based on the novel by F. Marion Crawford. C: Robert T. Haines, William Norris. A: Lorimer Stoddard. P: Liebler and Company. D: William Seymour.

In the Summer House (12/29/53, Playhouse, 55)

Tragicomic study of a group of maladjusted southern Californians and their fumbling efforts to escape reality. The two central characters are a domineering mother (Judith Anderson) who bullies her timid daughter into submission, and a loving and rejected mother (Mildred Dunnock) who finds solace in alcohol. In the end, the possessive mother is deserted by her offspring, while her alcoholic rival at least finds comfort in her illusions. Highlight: Judith Anderson's opening monologue, a ten-minute soliloquy that brilliantly established the self-deluding, ferociously selfish nature of the character. Playing a harried waitress, Jean Stapleton (of TV's "All in the Family") won critical praise in her Broadway debut performance. A: Jane Bowles. P: Oliver Smith (SD) and The Playwrights Company. D: Jose Quintero. M: Paul Bowles. CD: Noel Taylor.

R: (3/25/64, Little Fox, 15). Heading the cast of this O/B revival, directed by Alfred Ryder, were: Estelle Parsons, Leora Dana, and James Farentino.

In Time to Come (12/28/41, Mansfield, 40)

Drama by Howard Koch and John Huston dealing with Woodrow Wilson's fight for world peace during the final years of his presidency. "A dignified, arresting and remarkably convincing historical document" *(Herald Tribune)*. "An uncommonly provocative evening in the theatre" *(Post)*. Produced and directed by Otto Preminger, this 1941 offering was respectfully received by the critics. A public still stunned by the attack on Pearl Harbor and America's entry into World War II was in no mood, however, for a piece mourning the fate of the League of Nations. *In Time to Come* eked out a scant forty performances. C: Richard Gaines, Nedda Harrigan, Russell Collins, William Harrigan, Arnold Korff, House

Jameson, James Gregory, Philip Coolidge, Harold J. Kennedy.

Note: Authors Koch and Huston co-scripted such screenplays as *Sergeant York* and *Three Strangers*. Howard Koch won an Academy Award for *Casablanca;* Huston went on to become one of Hollywood's most successful directors (*The Maltese Falcon, The Treasure of the Sierra Madre, The African Queen,* etc.)

In Times Square (11/23/31, Longacre, 8)

Unexceptional mystery-comedy set in a Broadway theatre during rehearsals of a new play. Tame stuff and pretty silly, too. C: Reginald Mason, Walter Greaza, Thelma Ritter. A: Dodson L. Mitchell and Clyde North (D). P: Macollum and Greet.

Incomparable Max, The (10/19/71, Royale, 23)

A pair of dramatized stories by English essayist-critic Max Beerbohm (1872–1956) hooked together by the continuing presence of Sir Max himself, who strolls in and out of the action making typically caustic comments. The first story is of the poet Enoch Soames, unacknowledged in his own time, who sells his soul to the Devil in order that he may read what posterity has to say of him. Longing for recognition, he discovers instead that he is nothing but a creation of Max Beerbohm. The second tale is of A. V. Laider, a man of prophesy, but regrettably weak of will. When he sees a train wreck written in the palms of his traveling companions, he can do nothing to avert tragedy. Despite translation into another medium, Beerbohm's unique style and manner survive beautifully in both stories. The device of having the great man himself take part was questioned by several critics, but Clive Revill impersonated him with urbanity. As Soames and Laider, Richard Kiley was superb. The rest of the cast, most of whom played multiple parts, was generally praised. A: Jerome Lawrence and Robert E. Lee. C: Richard Kiley, Clive Revill, Martyn Green, Louis Turenne, Rex Thompson, Fionnuala Flanagan, Christina Gillespie, Michael Egan, John Fitzgibbon, Claude Horton, Constance Carpenter, Betty Sinclair, Donald Marye. D: Gerald Freedman. P: Michael Abbott, Rocky H. Aoki, and Jerry Hammer. SD: David Mitchell.

Indian Summer (10/27/13, Criterion, 24)

Middle-aged artist woos and wins younger girl. Drowsy drama by Augustus Thomas (A/D). C: John Mason, Martha Hedman. P: Charles Frohman.

Indians (10/13/69, Brooks Atkinson, 96)

Superficially an extravaganza, *Indians* is an assault on the conscience of the audience: we must not forget the West was won by destruction of the Indian and the buffalo. The message is laid on without subtlety, but flashes by in entertaining style. The play opens with Buffalo Bill (Stacy Keach) about to begin one of his famous Wild West shows. Cantering downstage center on a marvelously fake horse, it is only a moment before he falters in his introduction and lurches instead into a rationale of the cruelty done to the Indians. His continuing apologia is the framework for the play, but the intent is to shift the blame from the shoulders of Bill and his contemporaries to the audience. The guilt must be shared. In and out of historical context, through fast-paced scenes full of ingenious stagecraft, we are introduced to Sitting Bull, Geronimo, Wild Bill Hickok, Ned Buntline, and assorted beleaguered Indians and unsympathetic whites. Depending on the prejudices of the viewer, *Indians* is compelling or unaffecting, but its final line deserves comment. It is spoken by Chief Joseph of the Nez Percé tribe: "Hear me, my chiefs. I am tired. My heart is sick and sad. From where the sun now stands, I will fight no more, forever." The words are not the playwright's but those of Joseph himself at the time of his surrender. Would that *Indians* could have attained such eloquence. Premiered in 1968 by the Royal Shakespeare Company in London, Americans saw the play at the Arena Stage in Washington, D.C., prior to its Broadway opening as a lavish, quarter-million-dollar production with a cast of nearly fifty players. ". . . wonderfully pictorial . . . makes our theater come alive again" (John Chapman, *New York Daily News*). ". . . one of those penitential exercises in which nothing can be heard but the beating of breasts for past guilts" (Walter Kerr, *New York Times*). Robert Altman's 1976 film, *Buffalo Bill and the Indians,* is not a screen version of *Indians.* Credits for the film state it was "suggested" by Kopit's play. A: Arthur Kopit. C: Stacy Keach, Manu Tupou, Charles Durning, Sam Waterston, Raul Julia, Barton Heyman. D: Gene Frankel. P: Lyn Austin, Oliver Smith, Joel Schenker, Roger Stevens. SD: Oliver Smith CD: Marjorie Slaiman.

Information Please (10/2/18, Selwyn, 46)

Mild shipboard comedy-romance about a flighty wife (Jane Cowl) who keeps her virtue intact by locking herself in her stateroom. This play, written by Miss Cowl and Jane Murfin, was the first attraction to play the Selwyn Theatre. C: Orme Caldara, Blanche Yurka, Henry Stephenson. P: Selwyn and Company. D: Bertram Harrison.

Inherit the Wind (4/21/55, National, 806)

Semidocumentary reenactment of the historic Scopes "monkey trial" of 1925 in which a Tennessee school teacher was arrested and put in the dock for acquainting his students with Darwin's evolutionary theories. The principal characters are molded on William Jennings Bryan, bombastic, silver-tongued orator and three-time Presidential candidate who prosecuted the case, and Clarence Darrow, famed criminal lawyer who defended the young teacher and pleaded the cause of reason and freedom of thought. A bitter courtroom clash between Fundamentalism and Darwinism ensues, with Darrow skillfully undermining Bryan's credibility and driving him to collapse in the witness chair—much to the delight of visiting newspaperman-iconoclast H. L. Mencken. Despite a hostile atmosphere and a prejudiced court, Darrow wins the landmark case. As for Bryan, the great orator succumbs literally to derision; outraged by the court verdict, he suffers a fatal heart attack, and dies. "One of the most exciting dramas of the last decade" *(News).* "A tidal wave of a drama . . . a triumphant production" *(World-Telegram).* After several years of retirement in California, Paul Muni returned to the stage to play the leading role of Clarence Darrow in *Inherit the Wind,* and garnered the finest reviews of his career for his dazzling, tour de force performance. It was Muni's last Broadway appearance. (He became ill during the run and was replaced by Melvyn Douglas.) Ed Begley (as Bryan) and Tony Randall (as Mencken) were also applauded, but it was Muni's show all the way. C: Bethel Leslie, Karl Light, Muriel Kirkland, Staats Cotsworth, Louis Hector, Salem Ludwig, William Darrid, Michael Constantine. A: Jerome Lawrence and Robert E. Lee. P: Herman Shumlin (D) i.a.w. Margo Jones. SD: Peter Larkin.
SV: UA, 1960, Spencer Tracy, Fredric March, Gene Kelly, Florence Eldridge, Dick York, Donna Anderson, Harry Morgan, Elliott Reid, Philip Coolidge, Claude Akins, Paul Hartman, Noah Beery, Jr., Norman Fell (directed by Stanley Kramer).

Inheritors (3/21/21, Provincetown, 26)

Susan Glaspell's chronicle play dramatized the predominantly conservative views of succeeding generations toward the administration of a Midwestern college founded by a liberal ancestor. Miss Glaspell's contribution to the literature of radicalism was dismissed by Alexander Woollcott (*New York Times*) as "painfully dull, pulseless and desultory." Nineteen-year-old Ann Harding made her New York debut in this O/B production and won excellent reviews for her leading role performance. The play later (3/7/27, Civic, 21) became a staple of Eva Le Gallienne's Civic Repertory Theatre, with a cast that included Josephine Hutchinson, Robert Ross, J. Edward Bromberg, Eva Le Gallienne (D), Egon Brecher, and John Eldridge.

Ink (11/1/27, Biltmore, 15)

Contrived "satirical melodrama" about a double-dealing newspaper publisher who becomes implicated in a front-page scandal. Written by Dana Watterson Greeley (pseud. for William J. McNally)*. C: Charles Richman, William Harrigan, Dwight Frye, Kay Strozzi. P: Charles L. Wagner. D: T. Daniel Frawley.

---

*Overseas correspondent for the *Minneapolis Tribune*; author of *A Good Bad Woman* (1925) and *Prelude to Exile* (1936).

Innkeepers, The (2/2/56, Golden, 4)

Torpid drama about a security risk (Darren McGavin) and his wife (Geraldine Page) trying to make a new life for themselves in Mexico. A: Theodore Apstein. P: Gordon Pollock i.a.w. Cook and Flournoy. D: Jose Quintero. SD: David Hays.

Innocent Voyage, The (11/15/43, Belasco, 40)

Richard Hughes' famous novel, *A High Wind in Jamaica*, provided the source material for this Paul Osborn (A/D) play in which a group of English children of the last century find themselves aboard a pirate ship, much to the discomfiture of the captain and crew. As in the novel, the youngsters' "innocence" is something with which the pirates cannot cope; they are, in effect, taken captive by the children. Sharply divided reviews greeted this Theatre Guild production, which attempted to blend piquant comedy, tragedy, and melodrama in approximately equal proportions. "A dramatic triumph . . . distinguished in every way" (*World-Telegram*). ". . . very tiresome, confusing and sometimes downright distasteful. . . ." (*Post*). C: Oscar Homolka, Herbert Berghof, Dean Stockwell, Guy Stockwell, Abby Bonime, Lois Wheeler, Clarence Derwent.

SV: British, 1965, *A High Wind in Jamaica*, Anthony Quinn, James Coburn, Nigel Davenport, Dennis Price, Gert Frobe, Lila Kedrova.

Innocents, The (2/1/50, Playhouse, 141)

Flawless dramatization of Henry James' ghost story, "The Turn of the Screw." Set in a Victorian country house, the celebrated tale deals with a pair of motherless children haunted by the ghosts of two former servants. Are the demons real, or merely figments of the children's governess's imagination? The play's ending remains as chillingly ambiguous as in the James original. "In a lifetime of constant playgoing, I do not recall a single theatre-piece which held me as spellbound" (*Journal-American*). C: Beatrice Straight, Isobel Elsom, Iris Mann, David Cole. A: William Archibald. P: Peter Cookson. D: Peter Glenville. CD: Motley. SD: Jo Mielziner. M: Alex North.

SV: British, 1961, Deborah Kerr, Michael Redgrave, Peter Wyngarde, Megs Jenkins, Pamela Franklin, Martin Stephens (directed by Jack Clayton from a screenplay by William Archibald and Truman Capote).

Inquest (4/23/70, Music Box, 28)

In 1951 two American Jews, Julius and

Ethel Rosenberg, were convicted of conspiracy to commit espionage. In 1953 they were executed. *Inquest* is a dramatization of their trial, interlaced with flashbacks to prior events. The play purports to be factual, the program stating that all dialogue is from documented quotations or reconstructions of actual happenings. Also stated is that the reconstructions are "inventions in the service of truth rather than facts." The "truth" is the author's, and results in an unobjective treatment. The play has found the defendants innocent before the trial starts and makes its case for them with loaded dice. The hapless couple and those who side with them are honest, righteous souls while the prosecution is uniformly despicable. Thus, the plain-appearing Rosenbergs are played by Anne Jackson and George Grizzard, two vital and attractive personalities who immediately enlist audience sympathy. By contrast, principal prosecution witness David Greenglass (Jack Hollander) is a transparent villain, slovenly, fat, and untrustworthy. The judge is prejudiced, the prosecutor a bully. The play raises points of legitimate controversy, but dulls their impact by theatrical overkill, such as rear-screen projections of Hiroshima victims, Eisenhower at golf, and scowling Joe McCarthy. *Inquest* is an argument for the Rosenbergs' innocence that will convert only those already in agreement. The critics tended to dismiss the play as propaganda. A: Donald Freed b/o *Invitation to an Inquest* by Walter and Miriam Schneir. C: Anne Jackson, George Grizzard, James Whitmore, Mason Adams, Mike Bursten, Michael Lipton, Jack Hollander, Phil Leeds, Sylvie Straus, Sylvia Gassel, Hildy Brooks. P: Lee Guber and Shelly Gross. D: Alan Schneider. SD: Karl Eigsti.

Inside Story, The (2/22/32, National, 24)

Louis Corotto (Louis Calhern), tough-as-nails Chicago ganglord, frames an innocent lad on a murder charge. Run-of-the-mill 30's melodrama. C: Marguerite Churchill, Stanley Ridges, Roy Roberts, Edward Ellis, William Courtenay, Brian Donlevy. A: George Bryant and Francis M. Verdi. P: A. H. Woods. D: A. H. Van Buren.

Inside the Lines (2/9/15, Longacre, 103)

British agent (Lewis Stone) poses as a German spy. Serviceable blood-and-thunder hokum by Earl Derr Biggers. C: Carroll McComas, Henry Stephenson, Robert McWade. Also in the cast: William Keighley, future film director (*Green Pastures, The Man Who Came to Dinner,* etc.). P: Zimmermann and Harris. D: Felix Edwards.
SV: RKO, 1930, Ralph Forbes, Betty Compson.

Interlock (2/6/58, ANTA, 4)

A ruthlessly possessive invalid takes over the life of an aspiring pianist. Clumsy psychological melodrama by Ira Levin, author of *No Time for Sergeants* (1955), etc. C: Celeste Holm, Maximilian Schell (deb.), Rosemary Harris. P: Myers, Fleischmann and Trenerry. D: Philip Burton. SD: Howard Bay.

International, The (1/12/28, New Playwrights, 27)

When thousands of innocent workers throughout the world are slaughtered, Wall Street turns out to be the villain. Impassioned but dramatically unconvincing attack on the capitalist system by John Howard Lawson (A/D). The communist press was dismayed by the author's bourgeois "love conquers all" ending to the play. C: Franchot Tone, George Tobias, George N. Price, Herbert T. Bergman, Eduard Franz. P: New Playwrights.

International Incident, An (4/2/40, Barrymore, 15)

Comedy by journalist-historian Vincent

Sheean (his only play) about a lady lecturer (Ethel Barrymore) whose eyes are opened to the facts of industrial strife in Detroit. "A very minor incident indeed. . . . Mr. Sheean's script is all words and no play" *(Post)*. C: Kent Smith, Arthur Kennedy, Cecil Humphreys, Josephine Hull, Eda Heinemann, Lea Penman. P/D: Guthrie McClintic.

Intimate Relations (3/28/32, Ambassador, 24)

Comedy about a merry widow (Blanche Ring) who takes her husband's illegitimate son under her wing. ". . . an infirm trifle . . . surpassingly dull" *(New York Times)*. A: Earle Crooker. P: Forbes and Lawren. D: Edward Hartford.

Intimate Strangers, The (11/7/21, Henry Miller, 91)

Kittenish spinster (Billie Burke) falls in love with young lawyer (Alfred Lunt). To test his devotion, she introduces him to her niece (Frances Howard*), but the affable bachelor prefers the charming spinster to the sophisticated flapper. Droll but dated (even for 1921) Booth Tarkington comedy. C: Glenn Hunter, Elizabeth Patterson. P: Florenz Ziegfeld, A. L. Erlanger, Charles Dillingham. D: Ira Hards.

---

*Frances Howard married producer Samuel Goldwyn in 1925.

Intruder, The (7/25/28, Biltmore, 5)

Complications ensue when a married doctor seduces a pretty patient. Dismal soap opera with a no-name cast. A: Paul Eldridge. P/D: Edward Sargent Brown.

Invisible Foe, The (12/30/18, Harris, 112)

An uncle returns from the grave to see justice meted out to his nefarious nephew. "Never was a soaring, soul-stirring idea treated in a more pedestrian manner than in *The Invisible Foe*. . . . The real foe [is] the author" *(New York Times)*. A: Walter Hackett. P/D: Thomas Dixon.

Invitation to a Beheading (3/8/69, Public, 67)

Generally praiseworthy O/B adaptation of Vladimir Nabokov's novel about the nightmarish reveries of a man awaiting execution for an unspecified (and possibly nonexistent) crime. C: Charles Durning, John Heffernan, Susan Tyrrell, Joseph Bova. A: Russell McGrath. P: Joseph Papp. D: Gerald Freedman. SD: Ming Cho Lee. M: John Morris.

Invitation to a March (10/29/60, Music Box, 113)

Arthur Laurents' (A/D) satirical fantasy about individualism vs. conformity—a humdrum, status-conscious, drinks-at-seven, dinner-at-eight existence that's always putting a bored bride-to-be (Jane Fonda) to sleep. Enter the hero: a handsome Prince Charming (James MacArthur in his New York stage debut) who awakens the heroine to the joys of a free-spirited, unfettered life. Mr. Laurents' adult fairy tale crackled with deft wisecracks, amusing lines, and novel theatrical devices (characters talked almost as much to the audience as to one another), but *Invitation to a March* ultimately sank under the weight of its own whimsy. C: Celeste Holm,* Eileen Heckart, Madeleine Sherwood, Richard Derr, Tom Hatcher, Jeffrey Rowland. P: The Theatre Guild. CD: Lucinda Ballard. SD: William Pitkin. M: Stephen Sondheim.

---

*In the role abandoned by Shelley Winters during the pre-Broadway tryout.

Invitation to a Murder (5/17/34, Masque, 52)

Gale Sondergaard, Humphrey Bogart, and Walter Abel were the leading players in this predictable, creaking-door type melodrama set in a centuries-old estate off the coast of southern California. The plot revolved around the matriarch of the family being buried alive. She escapes her deathtrap in the nick of time and thereupon proceeds to wreak vengeance upon her grasping relatives. A: Rufus King. P: Ben Stein. D: A. H. Van Buren.

SV: WB, 1942, *The Hidden Hand,* Craig Stevens, Julie Bishop, Cecil Cunningham, Elisabeth Fraser, Willie Best, Ruth Ford.

Iron Men (10/19/36, Longacre, 16)

Scenically impressive but dramatically meager tale of skyscraper construction workers. Written by Francis Gallagher (former secretary to playwright Philip Barry); produced by famed designer Norman Bel Geddes (D/SD). C: William Haade, Harold Moffet, Gloria Blondell, Eddie Bracken, Harry Horner.

Is Zat So? (1/5/25, 39th Street, 634)

Funny lowbrow farce about a dimwit prizefighter and his hyperthyroid trainer masquerading as butler and footman in a snazzy Fifth Avenue mansion. C: James Gleason, Robert Armstrong, Tom Brown. P: Earle Boothe. When no producer would take a chance with *Is Zat So?*, authors James Gleason and Richard Taylor formed a syndicate and sold enough "stock" to finance their own production. The comedy, an overnight hit, ran 634 performances.

SV: Par, 1935, *Two Fisted,* Lee Tracy, Roscoe Karns, Grace Bradley, Kent Taylor, Gail Patrick.

Note: A silent version (Fox, 1927) featured George O'Brien, Edmund Lowe, and Douglas Fairbanks, Jr.

Isle of Children (3/16/62, Cort, 11)

Doleful drama about a dying thirteen-year-old girl. Patty Duke gave an accomplished performance as the doomed heroine, but the play proved to be "extremely tedious" *(Journal-American).* Staged by film director Jules Dassin *(Never on Sunday, Rififi,* etc.). C: Noel Willman, Norma Crane, Louise Latham, Bonnie Bedelia, Stefan Gierasch, James Aubrey. A: Robert L. Joseph. P:Lester Osterman i.a.w. Shirley Bernstein. SD: Howard Bay.

It All Depends (8/10/25, Vanderbilt, 16)

When her father becomes romantically involved with her best friend, "a thrill-seeking flapper" decides to reform. Wordy 20's comedy-drama. C: Katherine Alexander, Norman Trevor, Lee Patrick. A: Kate McLaurin. P: John Cromwell (D) and William Brady, Jr. SD: Livingston Platt.

It Happened Tomorrow (5/5/33, Ritz, 11)

In an effort to prevent future wars, the kingdom of Mythica attempts to prohibit the birth of male infants. Unbelievably inept comedy with a no-name cast. A/P: Leo Levy and Frank Marcus (D).

It Is the Law (11/29/22, Ritz, 121)

Mediocre Elmer Rice melodrama (based on an unpublished novel by Hayden Talbot) dealing with the legal doctrine of double jeopardy. A man plots the perfect crime and pins it on his supposed best friend, but his mania for revenge proves his undoing. C: Arthur Hohl, William Ingersoll, Alma Tell. P: Samuel Wallach.

It Is to Laugh (12/26/27, Eltinge, 37)

Problems of the Goldfish family when they move from the Bronx to Manhattan's West End Avenue. Seesaw mixture of tears and laughter by Fannie Hurst. C: John Davidson, Edna Hibbard. P: Barbour, Crimmins and Bryant. D: Rollo Lloyd.

SV: Col, 1929, *Younger Generation,* Jean Hersholt, Ricardo Cortez, Lena Basquette.

It Never Rains (11/19/29, Republic, 178)

Shady real estate deal threatens the romance of a young girl (Sidney Fox). Another bolt of homespun from Aurania Rouverol, author of *Skidding* (1928), the launching pad for the *Andy Hardy* film series. P: Hyman Productions. D: Paul Martin.

It Pays to Advertise (9/8/14, Cohan, 399)

Bustling farce about the rivalry between a young soap magnate and his Doubting Thomas father. The boyish hero learns the dollar value of intensive advertising ("13 Soap—Unhealthy For Dirt!"), eventually sells out to the old man, makes a million, and marries the girl. C: Grant Mitchell, Ruth Shepley, John Cope. A: Roi Cooper Megrue. P: Cohan and Harris. D: Sam Forrest.

SV: Par, 1931, Carole Lombard, Norman Foster.

It Takes Two (2/3/47, Biltmore, 8)

The postwar housing shortage forces a young Reno-bound couple to remain together under the same roof until the inevitable third-act reconciliation occurs. "A thin and shaky comedy" *(Sun)*. C: Martha Scott, Hugh Marlowe, John Forsythe, Vivian Vance, Anthony Ross, Temple Texas, Reta Shaw. A: Virginia Faulkner and Dana Suesse. P: George Abbott (D) and Richard Aldrich.

It's a Grand Life (2/10/30, Cort, 25)

Content with her lot in life, a society matron (Mrs. Fiske) refuses to acknowledge the failings of her husband and children. Wearisome comedy by Hatcher Hughes and Alan Williams. P: Erlanger and Tyler. D: Harrison Grey Fiske.

It's a Wise Child (8/6/29, Belasco, 378)

In order to break off her engagement to an older man (Harlan Briggs) and marry a younger fellow (Humphrey Bogart), a bachelor girl (Mildred McCoy) pretends she is about to become a mother. Cute 20's comedy, considered quite daring in its day. C: Minor Watson, Sidney Toler, Porter Hall, Helen Lowell. A: Laurence E. Johnson. P/D: David Belasco.

SV: MGM, 1931, Marion Davies, Sidney Blackmer, James Gleason, Lester Vail.

I've Got Sixpence (12/2/52, Barrymore, 23)

Murky drama by John Van Druten (A/D) dealing with the lugubrious love affair of a cynical ex-Communist and an idealistic young woman in search of a new faith. C: Edmond O'Brien, Viveca Lindfors (deb.), Patricia Collinge, Vicki Cummings. P: Macy and Starcke. SD: Boris Aronson.

Ivy Green, The (5/5/49, Lyceum, 7)

Creaky historical drama (London, 1836–70) dealing with the life and loves of Charles Dickens (Dan O'Herlihy). "A plodding and lifeless drama" *(Sun)*. C: Judith Evelyn, Hurd Hatfield, Neva Patterson, Ernest Cossart, Ruth White, Carmen Mathews, June Dayton. A: Mervyn Nelson. P: Hall Shelton. D: Roy Hargrave and Richard Barr. CD/SD: Stewart Chaney.

J

J.B. (12/11/58, ANTA, 364)

Archibald MacLeish's verse drama about the necessity of man's reconciling himself to the injustices of the universe. J.B. (Pat Hingle) is a successful, much-envied American businessman whose blessings are taken from him one by one: his fortune is lost, his home is destroyed, his five children are killed, his body festers, his wife leaves him. Despite these humbling tragedies, J.B. (like his biblical counterpart, Job) refuses to curse God and eventually is restored, in mind and body, through the healing power of love. The morality tale is played out against the background of a traveling circus wherein a balloon-seller (Raymond Massey) and a popcorn-peddler (Christopher Plummer) impersonate God and Satan, respectively. First produced at Yale University in a more poetic, more austere version, J.B. has since been played in most European countries and translated into many languages. Under Elia Kazan's high-pressure direction, the script was considerably revised for Broadway. Though it won the Pulitzer Prize as best play of the year, and gained respectful attention from many reviewers, there were some critics who found J.B. sorely wanting on both philosophic and dramatic terms. Chief among its detractors was *The New Yorker*'s Kenneth Tynan: "*J.B.* is the Book of Job, that greatest of hard-luck stories, retold in the form of a morality play. The characters are modern, but speak in bumpy alliterative verse, and the narrative technique is similarly medieval. . . . Although his misfortunes are clearly explicable in human terms, J.B. insists on ascribing them to God, who periodically thunders at him over the public-address system. At the end, capriciously, the author turns about and asserts that there is no divine judge upstairs; there is simply conjugal love on earth. Since holocausts are inevitable, all we can do is try to get on better with our wives. . . . Long before the final curtain I was bored to exasperation by the lack of any recognizable human response to calamity." C: Nan Martin, James Olson, Clifton James. P: Alfred de Liagre, Jr. SD: Boris Aronson

Jack in the Pulpit (1/6/25, Princess, 7)

Crook is redeemed when he discovers religion. Stale comedy. C: Robert Ames, Marion Coakley, Eda Heinemann. A: Gordon Morris. P: Ames and Bostwick.

Jacobowsky and the Colonel (3/14/44, Martin Beck, 415)

During the invasion of France, a Jewish refugee (Oscar Karlweis) and an antisemitic Polish colonel (Louis Calhern) join forces and flee Paris together. Their flight from the Nazis is complicated by the colonel's insistence on taking along his beautiful French mistress (Annabella). The play is chiefly concerned with the efforts of this ill-assorted trio to reconcile their viewpoints. The arrogant, feudalistic colonel ("one of the finest minds of the fifteenth century") gets them into one scrape after another. The little Jew, a professional in the art of survival, wins the mistress's admiration by saving their skins with his quick-witted resourcefulness. In the end, having proven his worth again and again, it is he and not the girl whom the colonel takes with him to England. This uneven but frequently touching and entertaining comedy was adapted by S. N. Behrman from a play by Franz Werfel. (Clifford Odets had worked on an earlier version of the script with the accent on drama rather than comedy). Behrman drastically revamped the play, which turned out to be a substantial hit of the 1944-45 season. Oscar Karlweis walked off with the evening's acting honors as Jacobowsky, the rueful, practical-minded refugee. Elia Kazan's skillful staging was also a decisive factor in the production's success. C: J. Edward Bromberg, E. G. Marshall, Harold Vermilyea, Hilda Vaughn, Herbert Yost, Jane Marbury, Philip Coolidge. P: The Theatre Guild i.a.w. film producer Jack Skirball (*Saboteur, Shadow of a Doubt,* etc.). M: Paul Bowles. SD: Stewart Chaney.

SV: Col, 1958, *Me and the Colonel,* Danny Kaye, Curt Jurgens, Nicole Maurey, Francoise Rosay (directed by Peter Glenville).

Note: Critic Burton Rascoe (*New York World-Telegram*) told his readers that Annabella's "incredibly talentless" performance in this play had made him "spiritually ill." The next day the chic French actress sent Rascoe a bottle of castor oil.

Jane (2/1/52, Coronet, 100)

To the consternation of her relatives, a wealthy but dowdy Liverpool widow marries a penniless architect twenty years her junior, moves to London and—because of her disarming candor—soon becomes a success in high society. Tiring of the social whirl, she gives her young husband his freedom and settles instead for a newspaper tycoon of her own vintage. "A civilized comedy that has been written with wit, grace, taste and intelligence . . ." (*New York Times*). C: Edna Best, Basil Rathbone, Howard St. John, Irene Browne, Philip Friend, Adrienne Corri (deb.), William Whitman, Sarah Marshall. A: S. N. Behrman b/o a story by W. Somerset Maugham. P: The Theatre Guild. D: Cyril Ritchard.

Jane Eyre (5/1/58, Belasco, 52)

Expensively mounted dramatization of Charlotte Brontë's novel (1847) about a demure governess who falls in love with Edward Rochester, moody master of Thornfield, and of the catastrophe that eventually hurls them into one another's arms; written and backed (at an estimated loss of $600,000) by A & P food-chain heir Huntington Hartford. ". . . pretty archaic in both subject matter and style" (*Post*). C: Eric Portman, Jan Brooks, Blanche Yurka, Francis Compton, Frank Silvera, Norah Howard, Jane White. P: Courtney Burr i.a.w. Sterling Productions. D: Demetrios Vilan. SD: Ben Edwards.

SV: Monogram, 1934, Colin Clive, Virginia Bruce; Fox, 1944, Orson Welles, Joan Fontaine, Margaret O'Brien, Elizabeth Taylor, Peggy Ann Garner; British, 1971, George C. Scott, Susannah York (released directly to television in the United States).

Note: Earlier adaptations of *Jane Eyre* toured the country with Katharine Hepburn (1936) and Sylvia Sidney (1943) in the title role, but neither production reached Broadway. Errol Flynn signed to play Mr. Rochester in the above-noted Huntington Hartford version of the Brontë classic. He appeared in the out-of-town tryout for two weeks and was suspended by Equity: the reason for Flynn's departure from the cast (and Equity censure) was that he failed to memorize his lines. He was replaced in the part by British star Eric Portman.

Janice Meredith (12/10/00, Wallack's, 92)

Creaky costume drama about the love of patriotic Janice Meredith (Mary Mannering) for an indentured servant of her Tory father. A: Adapted from Paul Ford's novel by Ford and Edward E. Rose. P: Frank McKee. D: R. A. Roberts.

Janie (9/10/42, Henry Miller, 642)

Paper-thin wartime comedy about a small-town junior miss and her flirtations with the boys of a nearby army camp; helped to long-run popularity by a microscopic payroll and a two-for-one ticket campaign. C: Gwen Anderson, Howard St. John, Linda Watkins. A: Josephine Bentham and Herschel Williams. P: Brock Pemberton. D: Antoinette Perry.
SV: WB, 1944, Joyce Reynolds, Robert Hutton, Edward Arnold, Ann Harding, Robert Benchley, Alan Hale.

January Thaw (2/4/46, Golden, 48)

City slickers are forced to share a Connecticut farmhouse with some country bumpkins. "An empty-headed, hyperthyroid little farce...." *(PM)*. C: Robert Keith, Charles Middleton, Helen Carew, Henry Jones. A: William Roos b/o a novel by Bellamy Partridge. P: Michael Todd. D: Ezra Stone.

Janus (11/24/55, Plymouth, 251)

Two months out of every year, a wife (Margaret Sullavan) slips away from home and family to collaborate (in more ways than one) with a Frenchman (Claude Dauphin) on sexy novels. When the wife's unsuspecting husband (Robert Preston) bursts inadvertently upon the scene, complications ensue. Mildly amusing farce had its moments, but the laughs were intermittent. C: Robert Emhardt, Mary Finney. A: Carolyn Green. P: Alfred de Liagre, Jr. D: Reginald Denham. SD: Donald Oenslager.

Note: In the play, Janus is the pen name adopted by the best-selling authors. In Roman mythology, Janus was the god having two faces; hence to be Janus-faced is to be two-faced and deceiving.

Jarnegan (9/24/28, Longacre, 138)

The friendship between a cynical motion-picture director and a naïve starlet ends when she is seduced by a rival mogul and dies following an abortion. Savage indictment of Hollywood, so vitriolic that most other filmland fables pale by comparison. C: Richard Bennett, Joan Bennett (deb.), Wynne Gibson, James Bell, Robert Cain, Henry O'Neill, Dennie Moore, Beatrice Kay. (Walk-ons during the climactic Hollywood party scene included Sam Levene, Frank Ross, and Lionel Stander). A: Charles Beahan and Garrett Fort b/o Jim Tully's novel. P: C. K. Gordon and Paul Streger. D: Richard Bennett.

Note: Rumor had it that George Abbott did considerable play-doctoring of this script.

Jason (1/21/42, Hudson, 125)

A flamboyant playwright tries to seduce the pretty wife of a fastidious drama critic. Knowing of the attempted seduction, the critic is torn between praising and damning the author's new opus. "... painfully artificial and literary" *(PM)*. Highlight: the performance of E. G. Marshall (deb.) as a blasé seaman who's been everywhere, done everything, and found none of it interesting. C: Alexander Knox, Nicholas (Richard) Conte, Helen Walker, Tom Tully, Raymond Greenleaf. A/D: Samson Raphaelson. P: George Abbott.

Note: Alexander Knox, playing the urbane drama critic of the title, was succeeded in the part by Lee J. Cobb, Charles Bickford, and George Macready.

Jayhawker (11/5/34, Cort, 24)

A swaggering Kansas congressman (Fred Stone) of the Civil War era tries to arrange a truce between the armies of Grant and Lee. This "drama of American politics" by novelist Sinclair Lewis and drama critic Lloyd Lewis (no relation) introduced musical comedy star Fred Stone in his legitimate play debut. Stone was fine, but after a pungent first act, "*Jayhawker* petered out through a weak second act and spineless third, for no other reason than lack of playwriting skill" *(Theatre Arts)*. *Jayhawker* also marked the Broadway debut (in a much smaller role) of Milburn Stone, the cranky, contentious Doc Adams of TV's "Gunsmoke" series. The play was directed by Joseph Losey and produced by Henry Hammond. C: Walter C. Kelly, Carol Stone, Paul Guilfoyle, Ludmilla Toretzka, Edward McNamara, Eddie Acuff, O. Z. Whitehead.

Jazz Singer, The (9/14/25, Fulton, 315)

A cantor's son (George Jessel) prefers show business to the synagogue, but eventually returns to his father's calling. Sentimental but effective comedy-drama by Samson Raphaelson. C: Howard Lang, Sam Jaffe. P: Albert Lewis (D) and Max Gordon i.a.w. Sam H. Harris.
SV: WB, 1927, Al Jolson, Warner Oland, May McAvoy.
Note: This legendary "first talkie" was actually a silent film with a few snippets of dialogue and songs. It was only after George Jessel refused to do the movie version of his hit play that Al Jolson, a screen unknown, was paged for the part. The film earned over three million dollars, an astronomical sum in those days. *The Jazz Singer* was remade by Warners in 1953 with Danny Thomas, Peggy Lee, Mildred Dunnock, and Eduard Franz.

Jealous Moon, The (11/20/28, Majestic, 72)

A group of lifesize marionettes become romantically unstrung. Wooden fantasy. C: Jane Cowl, Philip Merivale, Joyce Carey, Harry Davenport, Guy Standing, Hale Norcross. A: Theodore Charles and Jane Cowl. P: William A. Brady, Jr. and Dwight Deere Wiman. D: Priestly Morrison.

Jealousy (10/22/28, Maxine Elliott's, 136)

The obsessive suspicion of a bridegroom leads to the murder of his wife's ex-lover. Tedious two-character melodrama by Eugene Walter b/o play by Louis Verneuil. C: John Halliday, Fay Bainter. P: A. H. Woods. D: Guthrie McClintic. R: (10/1/46, Plymouth, 31) as *Obsession* by Homer Curran i.a.w. Lewis and Young. C: Basil Rathbone, Eugenie Leontovich. A: Jane Hinton (new adaptation). D: Reginald Denham.
SV: Par, 1929, Fredric March, Jeanne Eagels, Henry Daniell, Halliwell Hobbes; WB, 1946, *Deception*, Bette Davis, Claude Rains, Paul Henreid, John Abbott.

Jeb (2/21/46, Martin Beck, 9)

A black war hero returns to his home in the South to find that the town won't let him hold a decent job. Disillusioned, Jeb flees to the North, but eventually decides to go back home and fight again in the cause of civil liberties. ". . . neither a good play nor sufficiently sustained theater" *(PM)*. C: Ossie Davis (deb.), Ruby Dee (deb.), Santos Ortega. A: Robert Ardrey. P/D: Herman Shumlin. SD: Jo Mielziner.

Jenny (10/8/29, Booth, 111)

Stodgy corporation lawyer (Guy Standing) falls in love with a glamorous actress (Jane Cowl). Innocuous, mildly pleasant comedy by Margaret Ayer Barnes and

Edward Sheldon. C: Joyce Carey, Katherine Emmet. P: William A. Brady, Jr. and Dwight Deere Wiman. P: Frederick Stanhope.

Jenny Kissed Me (12/23/48, Hudson, 20)

This first play by Jean Kerr, author of *Mary, Mary* (1961), *Poor Richard* (1964), etc., gave little evidence of its author's considerable talent for witty dialogue and shrewd character drawing. Jenny, an eighteen-year-old Ugly Duckling, comes to live in the household of a gruff and crotchety priest. The cleric's clumsy efforts to make his ward attractive to the boys constitutes the plot of this 40's comedy. "... a well-intentioned bore ... makes goodness alarmingly dull" *(Post)*. C: Leo G. Carroll, Pamela Rivers, Alan Baxter, Frances Bavier. P: James Russo (D), Michael Ellis, Alexander H. Cohen i.a.w. C. M. Shapiro.

Jerry (3/28/14, Lyceum, 41)

Pretty, iron-willed lass named Jerry (Billie Burke) resolves to marry her aunt's middle-aged fiancée. Cloying comedy by Catherine Chisholm Cushing, author of *Pollyanna* (1916). C: Allan Pollock, Shelly Hull, Gladys Hanson. P: Charles Frohman.

Note: It was during the run of *Jerry* (between the Saturday matinee and evening performances) that Billie Burke married Florenz Ziegfeld.

Jest, The (4/9/19, Plymouth, 256)

The Barrymore brothers in superb fettle in a lurid, colorful four-act melodrama of passion and revenge in the days of Lorenzo the Magnificent. Because of his effeminate ways, the poet Giannetto (John Barrymore) has been the butt of brutal and ferocious attacks by Neri (Lionel Barrymore), a ruthless bully and drunken mercenary. Weaving a Machiavellian web of revenge, Giannetto eventually drives his antagonist to fratricide and madness. The play ends with Neri a raving lunatic and Giannetto praying for his soul. "The final curtain falls on *The Jest* at a quarter to twelve.... Every member of the audience is still in his seat, clamoring for more at the end of the last act. There can be no greater tribute" (Dorothy Parker, *Vanity Fair*). "To the future of such actors, it is impossible to set any limits. Some day we shall see them, perhaps, as Othello and Iago" (John Corbin, *New York Times*). This expectation never materialized. *The Jest* (extensively revised by American author Edward Sheldon) was the last play in which the Barrymores acted together. C: Gilda Varesi. Also, in a walk-on role, Louis Wolheim, the future star of *The Hairy Ape* (1922) and *What Price Glory?* (1924). A: Sem Benelli. P/D: Arthur Hopkins. SD: Robert Edmond Jones.

R: (2/4/26, Plymouth, 78). C: Basil Sidney, Alphonz Ethier, Maria Ouspenskaya, Violet Heming.

Jewel Robbery (1/13/32, Booth, 53)

Debonair jewel thief finds romance with his latest victim. Chic comedy by Bertram Block b/o play by Laszlo Fodor. C: Basil Sydney, Mary Ellis, Clarence Derwent, Cora Witherspoon, Eugene Powers. P/D: Paul Streger.

SV: WB, 1932, William Powell, Kay Francis, Helen Vinson, Ruth Donnelly, Alan Mowbray, Hardie Albright, C. Henry Gordon, Herman Bing.

Jezebel (12/19/33, Barrymore, 32)

In pre-Civil War Louisiana, a proud, willful Southern belle (Miriam Hopkins) seeks revenge when her lover marries a Northern girl. A yellow fever epidemic conveniently solves most of the problems of the principal characters. "A lovely show to look at but, unfortunately, not so good to listen to" *(Theatre Arts)*. Tallulah Bankhead was rehearsing the leading role in *Jezebel* when she fell ill of a peritoneal infection. Miriam Hopkins took over on short notice for the ailing Miss Bankhead, but to little avail. *Jezebel* was a short-lived and costly Broadway casualty. Bette Davis' later played the Southern hussy on the screen and won an Academy Award for her pains. C: Joseph Cotten, Reed Brown, Jr., Owen Davis, Jr., Cora Witherspoon, Frederic Worlock, Lew Payton, Gage Clarke, Helen Claire. A: Owen Davis. P: Katharine Cornell and Guthrie McClintic (D). SD: Donald Oenslager.

SV: WB, 1938, Bette Davis, Henry Fonda, George Brent, Fay Bainter, Margaret Lindsay, Donald Crisp, Spring Byington, Richard Cromwell (directed by William Wyler).

Jigsaw (4/30/34, Barrymore, 49)

Daughter discovers that her divorced mother (Spring Byington) has been having an affair with a married man (Ernest Truex). Witty but awkwardly plotted comedy by Dawn Powell. C: Helen Westley, Eliot Cabot, Shepperd Strudwick, Gertrude Flynn, Cora Witherspoon, Charles Richman. P: The Theatre Guild. D: Philip Moeller.

Jimmie's Women (9/26/27, Biltmore, 217)

Rickety 20's farce about a playboy who keeps his marriage a secret. C: Robert Williams, Minna Gombell, Beatrice Terry. A/D: Myron C. Fagan. P: B. F. Witbeck.

Jimmy Shine (12/5/68, Atkinson, 153)

Dustin Hoffman* played the title role in this episodic comedy about the reveries of an unsuccessful Greenwich Village artist who maintains his essentially sunny disposition despite life's vicissitudes. "... a funny, lovely, painfully gentle play..." *(Women's Wear Daily)*. Written by Murray Schisgal, author of *Luv* (1964); incidental music and lyrics by John Sebastian. C: Rose Gregorio, Pamela Payton-Wright, Rue McClanahan, Cleavon Little, Eli Mintz. P: Nichtern/Bufman. D: Donald Driver.

---

*Broadway debut.

Joan of Lorraine (11/18/46, Alvin, 199)

Maxwell Anderson's version of the Joan of Arc story presented in the form of a play rehearsal that finds the leading actress (Ingrid Bergman) and the director (Sam Wanamaker) at odds over the proper interpretation of Joan's faith. "... a stimulating play in which Ingrid Bergman is giving a magnificent performance" *(New York Times)*. "*Joan of Lorraine* neither adds to nor decreases the dramatic stature of Maxwell Anderson, but it should make us all appreciate Miss Bergman" *(Post)*. C: Romney Brent, Kevin McCarthy, Berry Kroeger, Lewis Martin, Harry Irvine, Joseph Wiseman. P: The Playwrights Company. D: Margo Jones, Sam Wanamaker, Alan Anderson. CD/SD: Lee Simonson.

SV: RKO, 1948, *Joan of Arc,* Ingrid Bergman, Jose Ferrer, Francis L. Sullivan, J. Carrol Naish, Ward Bond, Shepperd Strudwick, Cecil Kellaway (directed by Victor Fleming from a screenplay by Maxwell Anderson and Andrew Solt).

Note: This was a straightforward historical treatment of Joan's girlhood, trial, and martyrdom. The intriguing play-within-a-play framework of the Maxwell Anderson drama was completely discarded in the film version.

John (11/2/27, Klaw, 11)

Philip Barry's biblical drama recounting episodes in the life of John the Baptist. Through a brave attempt at lyric tragedy, *John* was written in a disconcertingly colloquial style. In addition, it was badly miscast. Yiddish actor Jacob Ben-Ami as

Joan of Lorraine (1946–47). *Courtesy Museum of the City of New York Theatre and Music Collection.*

John could scarcely be understood, British actress Constance Collier was totally unbelievable as Herodias. P: The Actor's Theatre. D: Guthrie McClintic. SD: Norman Bel Geddes.

John Loves Mary (2/4/47, Booth, 423)

When he agrees to wed a British girl only to get her safely to America, a GI runs into complications with his fiancée and her family. Slickly fabricated farce-comedy by Norman Krasna; expertly acted, especially by Tom Ewell, Nina Foch (deb.), and Lyle Bettger. C: William Prince, Loring Smith, Ann Mason, Harry Bannister, Max Showalter, Pamela Gordon.* P: Rodgers and Hammerstein i.a.w. Joshua Logan (D). CD: Lucinda Ballard. SD: Frederick Fox.
SV: WB, 1949, Ronald Reagan, Patricia Neal, Jack Carson, Wayne Morris, Edward Arnold, Virginia Field, Katherine Alexander, Paul Harvey, Ernest Cossart.

---

*Daughter of Gertrude Lawrence.

Johnny 2 × 4 (3/16/42, Longacre, 65)

Rambling melodrama about the rise and fall of a Greenwich Village speakeasy from 1926 to the repeal of prohibition in 1933. ". . . a sort of maudlin crying jag about the swell fellows, the wonderful girls and the charming killers of the period" (*Herald Tribune*). Eighteen-year-old Lauren Bacall (billed as Betty Perske) made her Broadway debut as a walk-on in *Johnny 2 × 4*. C: Jack Arthur, Evelyn Wyckoff, Isabel Jewell, Bert

Frohman, Barry Sullivan, Harry Bellaver, Monica Lewis, Leonard Sues, The Yacht Club Boys. A/P: Rowland Brown. D: Anthony Brown. SD: Howard Bay.

Johnny Belinda (9/18/40, Belasco, 321)

Nova Scotia deaf-mute (Helen Craig), raped by the town bully (Willard Parker), shoots him when he tries to take her baby from her. Acquitted of murder, she gains speech upon being reunited with her child, and is paroled in the custody of the young doctor (Horace McNally) who loved her all the time. ". . . a Cook's tour of the clichés and ineptitudes of hokum theatre" (*New York Times*). A: Elmer Harris. P/D: Harry Wagstaff Gribble.
SV: WB, 1948, Jane Wyman, Lew Ayres, Charles Bickford, Stephen McNally,* Agnes Moorehead, Jan Sterling.

---

*Stephen McNally was cast as the villain-seducer in the screen version of *Johnny Belinda*. On Broadway (billed as Horace McNally), he had originated the role of the stalwart doctor-hero.

Johnny No-Trump (10/8/67, Cort, 1)

With the help of an understanding uncle, a sensitive sixteen-year-old youth manages to break away from the ultraconformist influence of his mother. Absorbing, vividly written play by Mary Mercier received mixed reviews and closed after one performance. C: Pat Hingle, Sada Thompson, Don Scardino, Bernadette Peters,* James Broderick, Barbara Lester. P: Barr/Wilder/Woodward. D: Joseph Hardy.

---

*Broadway debut.

Johnny on a Spot (1/8/42, Plymouth, 4)

Rawcous farce about the frantic election-eve efforts of a political campaign manager (Keenan Wynn) to conceal the news of his boss's sudden death in a bordello. Written by Charles MacArthur (A/D), co-author of *The Front Page* (1928), *20th Century* (1932), etc. "Has all the elements of a good farce except one. It isn't funny" (*Post*). C: Edith Atwater, Will Geer, Dennie Moore, Joseph Sweeney. P: John Shubert.

Jolly's Progress (12/5/59, Longacre, 9)

Small-town Southerner (Wendell Corey) is misunderstood when he undertakes the education of a resentful Negro waif (Eartha Kitt). "The humor is obvious, the sentiment mawkish. The result is a well-meaning but rather primitive work" (*Mirror*). C: Anne Revere, Ellis Rabb, Vinnette Carroll. A: Lonnie Coleman b/o his novel *Adam's Way*. P: The Theatre Guild and Arthur Loew. D: Alex Segal. SD: George Jenkins.

Jonah (2/15/66, St. Clements, 13)

Slowly paced O/B version of the story of Jonah (Sorrell Booke) who disregards Jehovah's instructions and is punished for his dereliction. A: Paul Goodman. P: American Place Theater. D: Lawrence Kornfeld.

Jonah! (9/21/67, Stage 73, 22)

Witty O/B variation on the Old Testament tale of the biblical prophet (Laurens Moore) who—accompanied by the Greek warrior Ulysses (Joseph Warren)—enjoys an instructive sojourn in the belly of the whale. A: T. J. Spencer. P/D: Hal Thompson.

Jonesy (4/9/29, Bijou, 96)

College boy (Gene Raymond) shocks his small-town parents (Spring Byington and Donald Meek) by announcing that he intends to marry an actress. Typical 20's domestic comedy. C: Nydia Westman, Helen Brooks. A: Anne Morrison and John Peter Toohey. P/D: Earle Boothe.

Joseph (2/12/30, Liberty, 13)

George Jessel as the stalwart biblical hero who is sold into slavery, imprisoned, and eventually released to become governor of Egypt. "Thin to the point of transparency . . . a comedy that is not fully sustained" (*New York Times*). Directed by George S. Kaufman, produced by John Golden, written by Bertram Bloch, *Joseph* was a thirteen performance casualty of the 1930 season. Trapped in the cast: Douglas Dumbrille (as Pharaoh), Ferdinand Gottschalk (as Potiphar).

Journey by Night, A (4/16/35, Shubert, 7)

Dismal drama about a Viennese bank clerk (James Stewart) who turns embezzler-murderer for love of a whore. "He is as Viennese as a hamburger," said one critic of Stewart's performance. *A Journey by Night* was adapted and extensively revised by Arthur Goodrich from a play by Leo Perutz. Pola Negri had signed with the Messrs. Shubert (P) to appear as the whore in an earlier version of this clichéd *Sturm und Drang* opus, but the production closed out of town. C: Albert Dekker, Greta Maren, Eduardo Ciannelli, Nicholas Joy, Kate Mayhew. D: Robert Sinclair.

Journey of the Fifth Horse, The (4/21/66, St. Clements, 11)

In 19th-century Russia, a timid, introspective reader in a publishing house (Dustin Hoffman) is given a diary to take home, study, and report back on the following day. The assignment sets three worlds spinning: the reader's dream world, the real world of the moment, and the world of the diarist, all interlocked and interacting. Excellently written and acted O/B experimental drama by Ronald Ribman, based in part on a story by Ivan Turgenev. P: American Place Theater. D: Larry Arrick.

Journey to Jerusalem (10/5/40, National, 17)

Mary (Arlene Francis), Joseph (Horace Braham), and their twelve-year-old son Jesus (Sidney Lumet) set forth on a Passover pilgrimage. By the time they reach the temple in Jerusalem, both Jesus and His parents realize that His mission on earth will lead inevitably to torment, death, and a crown of thorns. ". . . doesn't quite succeed in its difficult mission" (*Herald Tribune*). C: Arnold Moss, Frederic Tozere, Karl Malden, Joseph Wiseman, Joe De Santis, James Gregory, Joseph Kramm. A: Maxwell Anderson. P: The Playwrights' Company. D: Elmer Rice. SD: Jo Mielziner.

Journey to the Day (11/11/63, Theatre de Lys, 29)

Engrossing O/B drama dealing with various mental patients in group therapy at a state hospital, and their mutual journey toward the day of recovery. C: Shirley Knight, Paul Sand, Michael Baseleon, Robert Pastene, Flora Campbell, Rose Gregorio, Peter de Vise, Jack Hollander, Harold Herbstman, Kay Mitchell. A: Roger O. Hirson. D: Fred Coe.

Journeyman (1/29/38, Fulton, 41)

A con man (Will Geer) poses as a preacher, fleeces some gullible Georgia farm folk, then proceeds blithely on his way. Awkward dramatization of the Erskine Caldwell novel by poet-novelist Alfred Hayes and Leon Alexander. P: Sam Byrd. D: Erskine Caldwell and J. E. Shugrue. SD: Nat Karson.

Joy Forever, A (1/7/46, Biltmore, 16)

Rambling comedy about an impoverished painter (Guy Kibbee) who is suddenly rediscovered by the art world. C: Dorothy Sands, Nicholas Joy, Loring Smith, Natalie Schafer. A: Vincent McConnor. P: Davis and Thomson. D: Reginald Denham.

Joy to the World (3/18/48, Plymouth, 124)

Movie producer, encouraged by a pretty

research assistant, battles Hollywood censorship in his efforts to film the life of labor leader Samuel Gompers. Alfred Drake played the crusading young producer and Marsha Hunt (deb.) the comely researcher in this briskly staged, handsomely produced satirical comedy. "The gayest and most substantial commentary on Hollywood doings that the stage has yet effected . . ." (*Herald Tribune*). "Grade B stuff . . . below the level of *Once in a Lifetime*" (*New York Times*). *Joy to the World* was staged by film director Jules Dassin, and written by Allan Scott, whose screenplay credits include *Top Hat, Roberta,* and *Follow the Fleet.* C: Myron McCormick, Morris Carnovsky, Kurt Kasznar (deb.), Clay Clement, Theodore Newton, Mary Welch, Hugh Rennie, Bert Freed. P: John Houseman and William R. Katzell. SD: Harry Horner.

Joyous Season, The (1/29/34, Belasco, 16)

A Mother Superior (Lillian Gish) pauses briefly at the fashionable home of her troubled Boston kinfolk, and helps resolve various family problems before continuing on her way. The theme of Philip Barry's comedy-drama (originally titled *State of Grace*) was the effect of religious faith on worldly life. The play had been written as a vehicle for Maude Adams. When Miss Adams decided not to return to the stage, Lillian Gish inherited the leading role and gave a subtle and perceptive performance in the part. *The Joyous Season* received mixed reviews. Arthur Hopkins (P/D) withdrew the production after sixteen performances. Twelve years later (1946) Hopkins revived the play with Ethel Barrymore heading the cast. It played a successful ten-week engagement in Chicago, but did not venture into New York. C: Jane Wyatt, Mary Kennedy, Eric Dressler, Jerome Lawler, Alan Campbell, John Eldredge, Florence Williams, Moffat Johnston, Kate Mayhew. SD: Robert Edmond Jones.

Judas (1/24/29, Longacre, 12)

Judas Iscariot (Basil Rathbone) depicted as a wise and loyal friend to Jesus, and the most grievously misunderstood of the twelve apostles. Bloodless costume drama by Walter Ferris and Basil Rathbone. ". . . both the play and Mr. Rathbone's acting of the part are, to this chronicler, presumptuous" (*New York Times*). P: William A. Brady, Jr. and Dwight Deere Wiman. D: Richard Boleslawski.

Judgment Day (9/12/34, Belasco, 94)

Scorching courtroom melodrama by Elmer Rice (A/P/D), based on the infamous Nazi Reichstag fire trial, with the locale switched to an unspecified Balkan country. The plot revolved around the attempted assassination of a fascist leader and the prosecution—or, more accurately, persecution—of a trio of anti-Nazis falsely accused of the crime. "Swift . . . melodramatic . . . uses the theatre effectively to reflect current issues, pillory a wrong and proclaim a burning indignation" (*Theatre Arts*). In 1934, *Judgment Day* seemed theatricalized and overstated to isolationist United States audiences. As Burns Mantle, *New York Daily News* critic, pointed out, audiences refused to believe it possible for "so vicious and brazen a travesty of justice to have taken place in any civilized state." Time, of course, proved that if anything Elmer Rice *understated* the case against Hitler. C: Walter Greaza, Josephine Victor, Eric Wollencott, Vincent Sherman, Fania Marinoff, St. John Terrell, House Jameson (as Hitler, here called Vesnic). SD: Aline Bernstein.

Note: Hitler accused the Communists of setting fire to the Reichstag building in Berlin, 1933. It is almost certain that the fire was actually instigated by the Nazis, a stratagem that accelerated Hitler's accession to power.

Judge's Husband, The (9/27/26, 49th Street, 112)

Middling comedy about a woman judge and her stay-at-home husband. C: William Hodge (A), Gladys Hanson. P: Lee Shubert. D: Thomas Coffin Cook.

Judith of Bethulia (12/5/04, Daly's, 16)

Dignified dramatization of the legendary Jewish heroine (Nance O'Neil) who saved her people by gaining the favor of invading general Holofernes (Charles Dalton) and then murdering him. C: Lowell Sherman (deb.). A: Thomas Bailey Aldrich. P: John Schoeffel. D: McKee Rankin.

Julia, Jake and Uncle Joe (1/28/61, Booth, 1)

Comedy about *New York Times'* drama critic Brooks Atkinson, here called Jake Ryan (Myles Eason), who becomes a Moscow correspondent for his newspaper, is arrested as a spy while engaged in bird-watching, and released only when his chic wife (Claudette Colbert) appeals to Stalin's (Boris Marshalov) grim sense of humor. "I'm afraid this one is for the bird-watchers" (*Herald Tribune*). *Julia, Jake and Uncle Joe* was a one-performance fiasco. A: Howard Teichmann b/o a book by Oriana (Mrs. Brooks) Atkinson. P: Roger L. Stevens and John Shubert i.a.w. Sherman S. Krellberg. D: Richard Whorf. CD/SD: Frederick Fox.

Julie (5/9/27, Lyceum, 8)

Bankrupt beldam (Alison Skipworth) tries to sell her nubile foster-daughter (Betty Pierce) to a lecherous old bootlegger (Edward Arnold). Dreadful. A: Corning White. P: Homeric Productions, Inc. D: Arthur Hurley.

June Moon (10/9/29, Broadhurst, 272)

Funny spoof of Tin Pan Alley by Ring Lardner and George S. Kaufman (D), b/o Lardner's story, *Some Like 'Em Cold*. A dumb oaf from Schenectady comes to New York to make his mark as a songwriter ("Not the music part; just the words. Lyrics, they're called"). By a fluke, a song of his becomes a hit. With success comes disillusionment. His ideals are shattered, and his pockets picked clean by a two-timing gold digger. But a happy ending is provided by a little homebody who has stood by faithfully all the while. C: Norman Foster, Linda Watkins, Jean Dixon, Harry Rosenthal, Lee Patrick, Florence Rice (deb.), Philip Loeb. P: Sam H. Harris.
SV: Par, 1931, Jack Oakie, Frances Dee, Harry Akst.

Junior Miss (11/18/41, Lyceum, 710)

Light-hearted look at the problems besetting a thirteen-year-old subdeb with a movie-fed imagination. Believing her father a philanderer and her uncle a jailbird, she plunges her family into a variety of scrapes, all of which are satisfactorily resolved by the final curtain. ". . . a steadily amusing comedy" (*Journal-American*). C: Patricia Peardon, Philip Ober, Barbara Robbins, Alexander Kirkland, Paula Laurence, Matt Briggs, Francesca Bruning, Billy (William) Redfield. A: Jerome Chodorov and Joseph Fields b/o Sally Benson's *New Yorker* stories. P: Max Gordon. D: Moss Hart. SD: Frederick Fox.
SV: Fox, 1945, Peggy Ann Garner, Barbara Whiting, Allyn Joslyn, Mona Freeman, Sylvia Field.

Junk (1/5/27, Garrick, 9)

Aptly titled melodrama about a kindly junk man (Sydney Greenstreet) who tries to play Mr. Fixit and becomes involved in a murder. C: Emma Dunn, Jay Fassett.

A: Edwin B. Self. P: Shesgreen and Vroom. D: Charles Coburn.

Just A Woman (1/17/16, 48th Street, 136)

Loyal wife strives to elevate workingman husband. When he does strike it rich, she learns that money begets nothing but misery. Low-grade melodramatic piffle from the pen of Eugene Walter, author of *Paid in Full* (1908), *The Easiest Way* (1909), etc. C: Walter Hampden, Josephine Victor, Albert Hackett. P: Messrs. Shubert. D: J. C. Huffman.

SV: RKO, 1933, *No Other Woman,* Irene Dunne, Charles Bickford, Eric Linden.

Just Life (9/14/26, Henry Miller, 80)

Glamorous opera star (Marjorie Rambeau) tries to adjust to domesticity and a philandering husband. Hokey 20's drama. C: Clyde Fillmore, Norman Foster, Vivian Tobin. A: John Bowie. P: Jacob Oppenheimer. D: Oscar Eagle.

Just Married (4/26/21, Comedy, 307)

Complications ensue when a lady (Vivian Martin) awakens in her stateroom to find her adjoining bed occupied by an inebriated young man (Lynne Overman). Fairly amusing farce by Anne Nichols and Adelaide Matthews. P: Jules Hurtig i.a.w. Messrs. Shubert. D: Huffman and Stork.

Just Out of College (9/27/05, Lyceum, 61)

Breezy George Ade comedy satirizing the value of a college education in the business world. An impecunious young man borrows $20,000 from his prospective father-in-law (known in the trade as "the pickle king"), successfully launches a rival pickle factory, and thus is free to marry the pickle king's daughter. P: Charles Frohman. D: William Seymour.

Just Suppose (11/1/20, Henry Miller, 88)

The Prince of Wales (Geoffrey Kerr) visits America incognito and falls in love with a clever and fashionable southern girl (Patricia Collinge). His Royal Highness to be puts duty before love, however, and reluctantly returns to Great Britain, leaving his tearful American sweetheart behind. Leslie Howard made his Broadway debut as the prince's pal in this wispy but uncannily prophetic comedy—though no one could have forseen back in 1920 how the real Prince of Wales would later rewrite the script to suit himself. C: Mrs. Thomas Whiffen, William J. Keighley. A: A. E. Thomas.

Musicalized by Meyer, Charig and Robin as *Just Fancy* (1927) with Joseph Santley, Ivy Sawyer, Eric Blore, Raymond Hitchcock, H. Reeves-Smith, Mrs. Thomas Whiffen.

Just to Remind You (9/7/31, Broadhurst, 16)

Young businessman (Paul Kelly) battles protection racketeers. Overwritten Owen Davis melodrama. C: Sylvia Field, Jerome Cowan, Edward H. Robins, Gladys Hurlbut. P: Sam H. Harris. D: Melville Burke.

K

Kataki (4/9/59, Ambassador, 20)

A callow American GI (Ben Piazza) and a mature Japanese soldier (Sessue Hayakawa) confront each other on an otherwise deserted Pacific island during World War II. Intermittently effective two-character play suffered from wordiness, lack of dramatic action. A: Shimon Wincelberg. P: Garon and Sokoler. D: Alan Schneider. SD: Peter Dohanos.

- SV: Cinerama Releasing, 1969, *Hell in the Pacific,* Lee Marvin, Toshiro Mifune (directed by John Boorman).

Keep Her Smiling (8/5/18, Astor, 104)

When a humble clerk (Sidney Drew*) is made the dummy director of a corporation, and given one share of stock, his empty-headed and extravagant wife (Mrs. Sidney Drew) spins a dream of social and financial glory that almost ruins him. In the end, however, the world takes the little man at his wife's valuation. "Breezy and high spirited . . . very cleverly staged and acted" (*New York Times*). A: John Hunter Booth, based on Edgar Franklin's *Saturday Evening Post* stories. P/D: Richard Walton Tully.

---

*Sidney Drew, a blithe and engaging comedian, was the uncle of Ethel, John, and Lionel Barrymore.

Keeper of the Keys (10/18/33, Fulton, 24)

Charlie Chan (William Harrigan) solves a couple of murders at Lake Tahoe, Nevada. The villain was easy to spot in this weak dramatization of an Earl Derr Biggers' novel. C: Howard St. John, Roberta Beatty, Roy Roberts, Dwight Frye. A: Valentine Davies. P/D: Sigourney Thayer.

Keeping Expenses Down (10/20/32, National, 12)

Hollywood composer Dmitri Tiomkin produced this comic-strip-level comedy about the misadventures of a pair of bumbling realtors. A twelve-performance washout. C: Louis Sorin, Bernard Gorcey. A: Montague Glass and Dan Jarrett (D).

Kempy (5/15/22, Belmont, 212)

Within the space of twenty-four hours, a young plumber (Elliott Nugent) meets and marries a headstrong miss and then discovers that he's really in love with her sister. Engaging comedy, the surprise hit of 1922. C: Ruth Nugent, J. C. Nugent, Grant Mitchell, Lotus Robb. A: J. C. and Elliott Nugent (with extensive, though uncredited, revisions by Howard Lindsay). P: Richard G. Herndon. D: Augustin Duncan.

- SV: MGM, 1930, *Wise Girls,* Elliott Nugent, J. C. Nugent, Roland Young.

Key Largo (11/27/39, Barrymore, 105)

To atone for his desertion under fire during the Spanish civil war, King

McCloud (Paul Muni) seeks out the family of one of his dead companions. He finds them wholly in the power of a ruthless gangster. Tempted to play deserter again, McCloud finally understands that "a man must die for what he believes." He shoots the gangster and is himself killed. "It comes across as an honorable intention rather than a good play" (*Post*). C: Jose Ferrer, Uta Hagen, Frederic Tozere, Karl Malden, James Gregory (deb.). A: Maxwell Anderson. P: The Playwrights' Company. D: Guthrie McClintic. SD: Jo Mielziner.

SV: WB, 1948, Humphrey Bogart, Edward G. Robinson, Lauren Bacall, Lionel Barrymore, Claire Trevor, Thomas Gomez (directed by John Huston; coscripted by Huston and Richard Brooks).

Kibitzer (2/18/29, Royale, 127)

Amusing comedy with Edward G. Robinson in fine form as Izzy Lazarus, busybody proprietor of a cigar store on Manhattan's Amsterdam Avenue. When Lazarus unexpectedly comes into some money, his predilection for kibitzing—a word this play helped popularize—almost brings about his downfall. Written by Robinson and Jo Swerling, coauthor of *Guys and Dolls* (1950), *Kibitzer* offered conclusive proof of what *Theatre Arts Monthly* called "Edward G. Robinson's astonishing talent as a character actor." P/D: Patterson McNutt.

SV: Par, 1929, Harry Green, Mary Brian.

Kick In (10/15/14, Longacre, 188)

"Chick" Hewes (John Barrymore), a brash, tough-talking ex-convict, tries to get an honest job and reform, but the law won't let him. Hackneyed underworld melodrama by Willard Mack. Prominent in the supporting cast were Jane Grey, Forrest Winant, and Katherine Harris (Mrs. John Barrymore). P: A. H. Woods. D: Byron Ongley.

SV: Par, 1931, Clara Bow, Regis Toomey, Donald Crisp.

Kicking the Castle Down (1/18/67, Gramercy Arts, 23)

Meandering O/B drama exploring the conflicts and misunderstandings between a despondent young man and his family on New Year's Eve. C: Peter Simon, Gale Sondergaard, Trish Van Devere. A: Robert Kornfeld. P: Tricorn Productions. D: David Young.

Kiki (11/29/21, Belasco, 580)

Saucy comedy about a Parisian chorus girl (Lenore Ulric), living platonically (but hopefully) in the apartment of a revue producer. At the final curtain, Kiki gets her man. Strenuously edited, revised, and laundered for American audiences by David Belasco (Ad./P/D) from the French of André Picard. C: Sam B. Hardy, Thomas Mitchell, Thomas Findlay, Sidney Toler, Max Figman.

SV: UA, 1931, Mary Pickford, Reginald Denny, Joseph Cawthorn.

Note: A silent version (WB, 1926) starred Norma Talmadge and Ronald Colman (directed by Clarence Brown).

Kill That Story (8/29/34, Booth, 119)

Reporter gets the goods on his crooked publisher and, in so doing, wins back his ex-wife. Lively comedy-melodrama, directed by George Abbott. Song: "Two Cigarettes in the Dark" (sung by Gloria Grafton). C: James Bell, Matt Briggs. A: Harry Madden and Philip Dunning. P: Abbott-Dunning.

Killdeer, The (3/12/74, Newman, 48)

O/B domestic drama. According to the program notes: The killdeer is a monogamous family bird. *The Killdeer* is a well-meaning but ineffectual family man struggling against the myriad tensions of contemporary life in suburbia.

He drinks too much and is always poised on the edge of failure. His wife is staunchly loyal, but he's lost contact with his two sons. They don't understand him. Despite strong performances by Barbara Barrie and Ralph Waite, *The Killdeer* packs minimal dramatic punch. As the portrait of a self-deceiving loser, the play is a salesman's death minus Arthur Miller. ". . . typical of the slick mediocrity that has given the Broadway theater a bad name" (Clive Barnes, *The New York Times*). A: Jay Broad. C: Ralph Waite, Barbara Barrie, George Voskovec, Franklin Cover, William Bogert, Jack Ramage, Timothy Nissen, Dolores Kenan, Michael-Raymond O'Keefe. D: Melvin Bernhardt. P: Joseph Papp, New York Shakespeare Festival Public Theater. SD: Marjorie Kellogg.

Kind Lady (4/23/35, Booth, 99)

First-class melodrama about a wealthy spinster (Grace George) whose home is gradually taken over by a sadistic pauper (Henry Daniell) and his sinister clan. In pursuit of the lady's fortune, this gang of cutthroats manage to alienate the kindly aristocrat from her family and friends, and almost convince her that she is insane. Only at the very last moment does the beleaguered heroine succeed in conveying word of her plight to the outside world. Skillfully adapted by Edward Chodorov from Hugh Walpole's story, *The Silver Mask,* and splendidly acted by its two leading players, *Kind Lady* provided an uncommonly suspenseful evening in the theatre. C: Alan Bunce, Thomas Chalmers, Elfrida Derwent. P: Potter and Haight. D: H. C. Potter. SD: Jo Mielziner.

R: (9/3/40, Playhouse, 107) by William A. Brady. C: Grace George, Stiano Braggiotti, Elfrida Derwent, Clarence Derwent, Dorothy McGuire, Melchor (Mel) Ferrer, Joan Wetmore. D: Felix Jacoves.

SV: MGM, 1935, Aline MacMahon, Basil Rathbone; 1951, Ethel Barrymore, Maurice Evans, Angela Lansbury, Keenan Wynn, Betsy Blair.

Kind Sir (11/4/53, Alvin, 166)

Feeble antic about a glamorous actress (Mary Martin) who sets her cap for a suave banker (Charles Boyer) and finally wins him. "What a waste of talent!" *(New York Times)*. C: Dorothy Stickney, Margalo Gillmore, Frank Conroy, Robert Ross. A: Norman Krasna. P/D: Joshua Logan. CD: Mainbocher. SD: Jo Mielziner.

SV: WB, 1958, *Indiscreet,* Cary Grant, Ingrid Bergman, Cecil Parker, Phyllis Calvert (directed by Stanley Donen).

Kindling (12/5/11, Daly's, 39)

Sincere, frequently moving drama of the slums and the misery precipitated by a bitter labor strike. C: Margaret Illington, Byron Beasley. A: Charles Kenyon. P: Edward Bowes. D: J. C. Huffman.

King Can Do No Wrong, The (11/16/27, Masque, 13)

Murder-espionage yarn set in a mythical kingdom. Lionel Atwill was the principal actor trapped in this frenetic foolishness. A/D: Frank Merlin. P: James W. Elliott.

King of Hearts (4/1/54, Lyceum, 268)

Hired by an egocentric cartoonist (Donald Cook) to "ghost" a famous comic strip, a young artist (Jackie Cooper) falls for the cartoonist's pretty fiancée (Cloris Leachman) and succeeds in winning her away from his arrogant boss. Bright, bubbly comedy; deftly directed by drama critic Walter Kerr, whose wife, Jean Kerr, coauthored the play with Eleanor Brooke. P: Elaine Perry. SD: Frederick Fox.

SV: Par, 1956, *That Certain Feeling,* Bob Hope, Eva Marie Saint, George Sanders, Pearl Bailey (directed by Norman Panama and Melvin Frank).

Kismet (12/25/11, Knickerbocker, 184)

An adventurous beggar (Otis Skinner) with the soul of a poet kills his enemy, drowns the evil wazir, and marries his beauteous daughter to the handsome Caliph of Baghdad—all in the space of one day. Gaudily resplendent Arabian Nights' tale was Otis Skinner's greatest popular success. C: Rita Jolivet, Merle Maddern, Hamilton Revelle, Gregory Kelly. A: Edward Knoblock. P: Charles Frohman, Klaw and Erlanger. D: Harrison Grey Fiske and Lawrence Marston.

Musicalized by Wright and Forrest (adapted from Borodin's music) in 1953, with Alfred Drake, Richard Kiley, Doretta Morrow, Joan Diener, Beatrice Kraft.

SV: WB, 1930, Otis Skinner, Loretta Young, David Manners, Montagu Love; MGM, 1944, Ronald Colman, Marlene Dietrich, Edward Arnold, James Craig; 1955, Howard Keel, Ann Blyth, Dolores Gray, Monty Woolley, Vic Damone, Sebastian Cabot.

Kiss and Tell (3/17/43, Biltmore, 962)

Smash hit George Abbot (P/D) comedy in which fifteen-year-old Corliss Archer (Joan Caulfield) is forced to pretend she is pregnant in order to shield her secretly married brother (Richard Widmark). "... a comic delight ... exceedingly attractive ..." (*Herald Tribune*). Radio actor Widmark first attracted wide attention in this frothy F. Hugh Herbert opus. When Widmark left the cast, his role was taken by another then-unknown performer, Kirk Douglas. C: Jessie Royce Landis, Robert Keith, Paula Trueman, Judith Parrish, Frances Bavier.

SV: Col, 1945, Shirley Temple, Walter Abel, Robert Benchley, Jerome Courtland, Katherine Alexander, Porter Hall.

Kiss in a Taxi, The (8/25/25, Ritz, 103)

A Parisian *cocotte* (Claudette Colbert) is legally adopted by the wife (Janet Beecher) of her current sugar daddy (Arthur Byron). Breezy fluff, adapted by Clifford Grey from a play by Hennequin and Veber. C: John Williams, Lee Patrick. P: A. H. Woods. D: Bertram Harrison.

Kiss Mama (10/1/64, Actors Playhouse, 142)

Jewish girl marries into closely knit Italian-American family. Amusing O/B comedy by George Panetta. C: Julius La Rosa, Rose Gregorio, Peggy Pope, Augusta Ciolli, Rudolf Weiss, Tom Pedi, Francine Beers, Val Bisoglio. D: Ruth Rawson.

Kiss the Boys Good-bye (9/28/38, Henry Miller, 286)

Clare Boothe's satire on Hollywood's frantic search for an actress to play Scarlett O'Hara in *Gone With the Wind*. In Miss Boothe's comedy, a naive Southern belle, victimized by various filmland sophisticates, turns on her antagonists and walks off with the acting plum of the decade. Though reviewers (and audiences) characterized *Kiss the Boys Good-bye* as a light evening's entertainment, authoress Clare Boothe insisted that her play aspired to greater heights—that it was, in fact, "a political allegory about fascism in America." C: Helen Claire, Philip Ober, Sheldon Leonard, Benay Venuta, Hugh Marlowe, Millard Mitchell, John Alexander. P: Brock Pemberton. D: Antoinette Perry.

SV: Par, 1941, Mary Martin, Don Ameche, Oscar Levant, Connee Boswell, Elizabeth Patterson.

Kiss Them For Me (3/20/45, Belasco, 110)

A trio of naval heroes arrive in San Francisco for some rest and relaxation, with the accent on the latter. After four days of being hustled by civilians and exploited by the paper navy, the boys are only too glad to return to combat action. Highlight: the performance of Judy Holliday (deb.) as a patriotic floozy who is willing to help the Navy any way she can. "... confused, rambling and disjointed ..." *(Post)*. C: Richard Widmark, Dennis King, Jr., Richard Davis, Jayne Cotter, George Mathews, Daniel Petrie. A: Luther Davis b/o the novel *Shore Leave* by Frederic Wakeman. P: Moses and Hanna. D: Herman Shumlin.

SV: Fox, 1957, Cary Grant, Jayne Mansfield, Leif Erickson, Larry Blyden, Ray Walston, Suzy Parker.

Kitty Mackay (1/7/14, Comedy, 278)

Poor Scottish lass falls in love with a Berkeley Square swell who turns out to be her half-brother; complications successfully unraveled by the final curtain. Soppy comedy by Catherine Chisholm Cushing. C: Molly McIntyre, Eugene O'Brien, Henry Stephenson. P/D: William Elliott.

Musicalized by Hugo Felix as *Lassie* (1920) with Tessa Kosta.

Knock on Wood (5/28/35, Cort, 11)

The sordid wheelings and dealings of a couple of tough, sharp-witted talent agents in the Hollywood jungle of the thirties. Unpalatable, unfunny comedy by screenwriter Allen Rivkin (*Dancing Lady, The Farmer's Daughter,* etc.). C: Albert Dekker, James Rennie, Bruce MacFarlane, Lee Patrick, Sallie Phipps, Horace MacMahon. P: Elias Weinstock. D: John Hayden. SD: Watson Barratt.

Kongo (3/30/26, Biltmore, 135)

"Deadleg" Flint (Walter Huston), sadistic ruler of a black empire in the Belgian Congo, seethes with revenge against the white man who broke his back and paralyzed him for life. He finally gains the revenge he seeks by driving his enemy to suicide. No literary classic this, but vastly entertaining in its dime-novel fashion. A/P/D: Chester DeVonde and Kilbourn Gordon.

SV: MGM, 1932, Walter Huston, Conrad Nagel, Lupe Velez, Virginia Bruce, C. Henry Gordon.

Note: The silent version (MGM, 1929) was entitled *West Of Zanzibar*. The cast was headed by Lon Chaney and Lionel Barrymore.

L

La Gringa (2/1/28, Little, 21)

Mexican girl (Claudette Colbert) leaves convent, messes up the lives of a couple of men, then returns to the convent. Murky 20's drama. A: Tom Cushing. P/D: Hamilton MacFadden.

La Turista (3/4/67, St. Clement's, 29)

Grimly amusing allegorical O/B entry in which a patient (Sam Waterston) finds the medical profession powerless to cope with a primitive disease. A: Sam Shepard. P: American Place Theater. D: Jacques Levy.

Ladder, The (10/22/26, Mansfield, 794)

One of the most unusual productions in the history of the American theatre, *The Ladder* was an incredibly bad play by J. Frank Davis dealing with reincarnation. Edgar B. Davis, millionaire oil man and no relation to the author, financed the production. Anxious for the public to hear the play's message, he invited audiences to attend free. Few came. *The Ladder* played 794 performances and ran up a total deficit of close to one million dollars. The whole thing had simply been the whim of the fabulously wealthy Edgar B. Davis, whose oil wells brought him profits of $100,000 a week. C: Antoinette Perry, Irene Purcell, Vernon Steele, Hugh Buckler, Ross Alexander, Edgar Stehli, Edward J. McNamara. P/D: Brock Pemberton.

Ladies and Gentlemen (10/17/39, Martin Beck, 105)

A juror (Helen Hayes) in a murder trial falls in love with the foreman (Philip Merivale) of the jury; one of Miss Hayes' weakest vehicles. ". . . as tedious as a probate action in surrogate's court" *(World-Telegram)*. C: Robert Keith, Evelyn Varden, Connie Gilchrist, Joseph Sweeney, Pat Harrington, William Lynn. A: Charles MacArthur and Ben Hecht b/o a play by L. Bush-Fekete. P: Gilbert Miller. D: Charles MacArthur and Lewis Allen. SD: Boris Aronson.

SV: WB, 1950, *Perfect Strangers*, Ginger Rogers, Dennis Morgan, Thelma Ritter, Margalo Gillmore, Anthony Ross, Paul Ford.

Note: Herbert Marshall costarred with Miss Hayes in the tryout, but left the production prior to the New York opening.

Ladies Leave (10/1/29, Hopkins, 15)

Frustrated wife (Blyth Daly) leaves dull husband (Walter Connolly) for equally dull lover (Henry Hull), finally flees to Vienna, presumably to be psychoanalyzed. Dull comedy by Sophie Treadwell, author of *Machinal* (1928). C: Catherine Doucet, Charles Trowbridge. P/D: Charles Hopkins.

Ladies' Money (11/1/34, Barrymore, 36)

A couple of gangsters hide out in a New York rooming house. Slapdash George Abbott (A/D) melodrama b/o a play by Lawrence Hazard and Richard Flournoy. C: Eric Linden, Jerome Cowan, Hal K. Dawson. Also in the cast as "Red," one of the gunmen, was twenty-two-year-old Garson Kanin, who had dyed his hair red to get the part. "He was so bright and so imaginative that I took to him immediately," said Abbott. After *Ladies' Money* ended its brief run, Kanin became George Abbott's production assistant and right-hand man, a post he continued to hold for several years thereafter. P: Courtney Burr.

Ladies' Night (8/9/20, Eltinge, 375)

Painfully shy young man is forced to take refuge in a ladies' Turkish bath. Female impersonation, "laffs" out of Joe Miller's jokebook, and considerable slapstick comedy in this sophomoric farcical comedy by Avery Hopwood and Charlton Andrews. C: Charles Ruggles, John Cumberland, Claiborne Foster, Adele Rowland. P: A. H. Woods. D: Bertram Harrison.
R: (1/17/45, Royale, 78) by Lang and Rosen as *Good Night, Ladies.* C: Skeets Gallagher, James Ellison. D: Edward Clarke Lilley.
Note: This hoary revival shattered Chicago's long-run record by playing to packed houses for 100 weeks.
SV: WB, 1928, *Ladies' Night in a Turkish Bath,* Dorothy Mackaill, Jack Mulhall.

Ladies of Creation (9/8/31, Cort, 71)

Ambitious career woman fires her down-to-earth business manager, discovers she needs and loves him. Humdrum comedy by Gladys Unger. C: Chrystal Herne, John Litel, Spring Byington, Charles Trowbridge, Paula Trueman. P: Raymond Moore. D: George Somnes.

Ladies of the Corridor, The (10/21/53, Longacre, 45)

The Dorothy Parker-Arnaud d'Usseau play about a group of lonely widows and divorcées in a New York residential hotel. A series of dramatic vignettes rather than a cohesive drama, *The Ladies of the Corridor* focused primarily on three characters: an elderly invalid (Frances Starr) who keeps her son (Shepperd Strudwick) in line by threatening to expose a homosexual incident in his past; a gallant type (Edna Best) who loses her young lover (Walter Matthau) because of her possessiveness; a cast-off wife (Betty Field) who resolves matters by jumping out the hotel window. ". . . a loosely contrived play with more stock ideas in it than you would expect from Miss Parker and Mr. d'Usseau" *(New York Times).* C: June Walker, Vera Allen, Margaret Barker, Lonny Chapman. P: Walter Fried. D: Harold Clurman. CD: Noel Taylor. SD: Ralph Alswang.

Ladies of the Evening (12/23/24, Lyceum, 159)

Sleazy and sensationalistic drama about "a poor little painted doll" (Beth Merrill) who finds redemption in the love of a good man (James Kirkwood). A: Milton Herbert Gropper. P/D: David Belasco.
SV: Col, 1930, *Ladies of Leisure,* Barbara Stanwyck, Lowell Sherman, Marie Prevost, Nance O'Neil.

Ladies of the Jury (10/21/29, Erlanger's, 80)

A charming eccentric (Mrs. Fiske) casts the only "not guilty" vote in a murder trial, schemes to bring the judge (Wilton Lackaye) and the other jurors around to her way of thinking, and does. Pleasant light comedy; one of the last New York appearances of distinguished American actress Minnie Maddern Fiske. "This great planet among the stars. She is Mrs. Fiske and there can never be another. She is incalculable and altogether peerless" *(Burns Mantle, News).* A: Fred Ballard. P: Erlanger and Tyler. D: Harrison Grey Fiske.

SV: RKO, 1932, Edna May Oliver, Ken Murray; 1937, *We're on the Jury,* Helen Broderick, Victor Moore.

Lady, The (12/4/23, Empire, 85)

Lady cabaret owner tries to support her child and stay pure at the same time. Ten percent melodrama, ninety percent soap opera. C: Mary Nash, Austin Fairman, Elizabeth Risdon, Ludmilla Toretzka, Junior Durkin. A: Martin Brown. P: A. H. Woods.
SV: MGM, 1933, *The Secret of Madame Blanche,* Irene Dunne, Lionel Atwill, Phillips Holmes, Una Merkel.

Lady Alone (1/20/27, Forrest, 45)

Literate but lacklustre drama about an impoverished sophisticate (Alice Brady) who commits suicide when her wealthy lover refuses to wed her. A: Laetitia McDonald. P: L. Lawrence Weber i.a.w. David Wallace (D).

Lady, Behave (11/16/43, Cort, 23)

Dimwit poses as a psychiatrist, treats a variety of assorted morons. "... starts off be being incredibly dull and gradually adds vulgarity to its tedium" *(Herald Tribune).* C: Pert Kelton, Jack Sheehan, Carol Stone. A/D: Alfred Golden. P: High Bennett.

Lady Dedlock (12/31/28, Ambassador, 50)

Fustian romantic melodrama based on Dickens' *Bleak House.* Bleak indeed. C: Margaret Anglin (D), Ethel Griffies, Hubert Druce, Francis Compton. A: Paul Kester. P: Phillips and Leventhal.

Lady Detained, A (1/9/35, Ambassador, 13)

Socialite is kidnapped by bootleggers. Dismal comedy-melodrama. C: Claudia Morgan, Oscar Shaw, Clifford Brooke (D). A: Samuel Shipman and John B. Hymer. P: S. L. Latham.

Lady Has a Heart, The (9/25/37, Longacre, 90)

The prime minister's valet leads a double life as a Socialist member of parliament. Vincent Price played the politically ambitious gentleman's gentleman, and Elissa Landi was the object of his affections in this tired mythical kingdom comedy. A: Edward Roberts b/o a play by L. Bush-Fekete. P: Rufus Phillips (D) and Watson Barratt (SD).
SV: Fox, 1938, *The Baroness and the Butler,* William Powell, Annabella, Helen Westley, Joseph Schildkraut, Henry Stephenson, J. Edward Bromberg.

Lady in Love, A (2/21/27, Lyceum, 17)

Intermittently amusing costume romp set in seventeenth-century England wherein the heroine, married to a jealous old scoundrel, eventually finds happiness with a fellow her own age. C: Peggy Wood, Sydney Greenstreet, Gavin Gordon, Rollo Lloyd (D), Allyn Joslyn, Dennie Moore. A: Dorrance Davis. P: A. and R. Riskin.

Lady Lies, The (11/26/28, Little, 24)

When a mistress loses her lover's support after seven devoted years, his children intercede in her behalf. Mawkish and embarrassing 20's soap opera. C: William Boyd, Nan Sunderland, Betty Lawford. A: John Meehan. P: Santley, Barter and McGowan. D: David Burton.
SV: Par, 1929, Claudette Colbert, Walter Huston.

Lady of Letters (3/28/35, Mansfield, 20)

College professor's wife is mistaken for best-selling authoress. Vapid 30's comedy. C: Muriel Kirkland, Shepperd Strudwick. A: Turner Bullock. P/D: Dmitri Ostrov.

Lady of the Lamp, The (8/17/20, Republic, 111)

Under the influence of opium, an American (George Gaul) dreams he is a Chinese emperor. When he awakens, he meets the girl of his dreams. Primitive fantasy-melodrama by Earl Carroll (A/P/D).

Lady of the Orchids, The (12/13/28, Henry Miller, 20)

The soignee, much-married Peggy Hopkins Joyce braved Broadway (though not for long) in this inept triangle drama. Poor Peggy. A/P: E. Ray Goetz b/o play by J. Nathanson. D: William H. Gilmore.

Lady of the Rose (5/19/25, 49th Street, 8)

Playwright is thwarted in his efforts to find the perfect dream-heroine. Stagey, Pirandello-esque drama by Martin Flavin. C: Henry Herbert, Margaret Mower. P/D: Jacob A. Weiser.

Lady Who Came to Stay, The (1/2/41, Maxine Elliott's, 4)

Three weird sisters (Mildred Natwick, Evelyn Varden, Mady Christians) drive their brother's penniless widow (Beth Merrill) to her grave. When the eldest sister also dies, the two ghosts return to haunt the gloomy Victorian mansion as symbols of love and hate. A spectacular fire resolves the supernatural conflict. "... an extremely high-pitched and incoherent melodrama, never convincing, never exciting, and often just preposterous" (*PM*). A: Kenneth White b/o a novel by R. E. Spencer. P/D: Guthrie McClintic. SD: Donald Oenslager.

Lady's Virtue, A (11/23/25, Bijou, 147)

Bored wife practically pushes her husband into the arms of a glamorous opera star. Unconvincing romantic drama by Rachel Crothers (A/D). Heading the cast: Florence Nash, Mary Nash, Robert Warwick, George Barbier and Guido Nadzo, the last-named actor immortalized when George S. Kaufman quipped in print: "Guido Nadzo was nadso guido." P: Messrs. Shubert.

Laff That Off (11/2/25, Wallack's, 390)

Girl (Shirley Booth) shares bachelor apartment (platonically) with three boys—until she falls in love with one of the fellows (Alan Bunce). Typical, mildly diverting 20's comedy. A: Don Mullally. P: Earl Carroll. D: Roy Walling.

Lamp at Midnight (12/21/47, New Stages, 51)

O/B drama dealing with the historic conflict between Galileo and the Roman Catholic Church. Denounced for propounding heretical views, the founder of modern science is summoned to Rome, tried by the Inquisition, and forced to abjure belief that the sun is the central body around which earth and the planets revolve. "A play of surging and inspiring beauty" (*World-Telegram*). "... deeply moving with a passionate theme and a resolute point of view" (*New York Times*). C: Peter Capell, Kathryn Eames, Frederic De Wilde, Martin Balsam, Leon Janney, Paul Mann, Karl Weber. A: Barrie Stavis. P: New Stages. D: Boris Tumarin.

Land Is Bright, The (10/28/41, Music Box, 79)

Elaborate, plot-heavy chronicle play by George S. Kaufman (D) and Edna Ferber dealing with three generations of a robber baron family from the 1890's to the Second World War. "... claptrap melodrama [but] very entertaining" (*Post*). C: Leon Ames, Phyllis Povah, Hugh Marlowe, Diana Barrymore, Arnold Moss, Martha Sleeper, K. T. Stevens, Ralph Theadore, Lili Valenty. P: Max Gordon. SD: Jo Mielziner. CD: Irene Sharaff.

Land of Fame (9/21/43, Belasco, 6)

Greek guerrillas try to outwit and outfight the Nazi invaders. ". . . fumbling and cluttered . . . written with great sincerity, but with no distinction" (*Sun*). C: Stefan Schnabel, Norman Rose, Whitford Kane, Beatrice Straight, Richard Basehart, Ed Begley (deb.). Albert and Mary Bein. P: Albert Bein (D) and Frederick Fox (SD).

Land's End (12/11/46, Playhouse, 5)

Young fisherman (Walter Coy) kills himself after betraying his fiancée (Helen Craig) with her best friend (Shirley Booth). This retelling of the Tristan and Isolde legend was adapted by Thomas Job from the Mary Ellen Chase novel, *Dawn in Lyonesse*. "A self-conscious little charade which seems to mistake literary allusion for dramatic illusion" (*News*). C: Minnie Dupree, Merle Maddern, Theodore Newton, Frieda Altman, Fred Stewart. P: Paul Feigay i.a.w. George Somnes. D: Robert Lewis.

Last Analysis, The (10/1/64, Belasco, 28)

Attempting to conduct his own psychoanalysis, a once-famous Jewish comedian (Sam Levene) relives the events of his early life in an effort to regain his "lost self." Novelist Saul Bellow's first play—a richly textured, structurally untidy farce with an underlying streak of dark pessimism—suffered from miscasting and an ungainly Broadway production. ". . . if you welcome the rush of an overflowing, sportive, serious mind, you will forgive the faults of Mr. Bellow's first venture into the theater and rejoice at its unbuttoned gusto and comic invention, which are like a strong, fresh breeze" (*New York Times*). C: Tresa Hughes, Ann Wedgeworth, Anthony Roberts, Leon Janney, Charles Boaz, Alix Elias, Will Lee, Minerva Pious. P: Stevens-Bonfils-Seawell-Oppenheim. D: Joseph Anthony. Revived O/B (6/23/71, Circle in the Square, 46) with Joseph Wiseman in the leading role, in a production directed by Theodore Mann.

Last Mile, The (2/13/30, Harris, 285)

Powerful melodrama dealing with an attempted jail break by the death-row occupants of an Oklahoma prison. "Killer" Mears (Spencer Tracy) engineers the break, but walks out into machine-gun fire when he realizes he and the men are trapped. This hard-hitting argument against capital punishment by John Wexley was the first Broadway success of noted producer-director Herman Shumlin (P). Spencer Tracy's tough-as-nails portrayal of "Killer" Mears made him a Broadway name. John Ford saw him in the play and insisted that Fox Pictures sign him to play the lead in Ford's upcoming film of prison life, *Up the River*. The success of this gangster movie typed Tracy as one of the screen's tough guys for many years thereafter. *The Last Mile* was also a boon to Clark Gable's career. He played Mears in the West Coast production. During the Los Angeles run, Lionel Barrymore arranged a screen test for him at MGM. The rest is history. *The Last Mile* ran 285 performances on Broadway. Also in the cast were: James Bell, Joseph Calleia, Henry O'Neill, Howard Phillips, Bruce MacFarlane, Hale Norcross. The play was directed by Chester Erskine.

SV: World-Wide, 1932, Preston Foster; UA, 1959, Mickey Rooney.

Last of Mrs. Lincoln, The (12/12/72, ANTA, 63)

A study of the widowhood of Mary Todd Lincoln, her impecunious habits, her struggle with Congress for a pension, the tragic death of her son, Tad, and her own ticklish position as a Southerner rumored to be a Confederate sympathizer. The potential for dynamic theatre was present, but an overly respectful attitude to history dulled the drama. This second of three Lincoln plays during the '72–73 season, coming after *The Lincoln Mask* and preceding *Look Away,* was considered as drab as the others. The play's distinction was the performance of Julie Harris in the title role. She enacted the neurotic, controversial lady with a vivid range of emotion that was engrossing and moving. Leora Dana played her sister to good effect, and as Robert Lincoln, the son who regretfully committed his mother to an asylum, David Rounds was singled out for superior work. The large cast was beautifully costumed, and kept in continual motion by two turntables that revealed a succession of handsome sets. Unfortunately, *The Last of Mrs. Lincoln* demonstrated that history is not dramatic when burdened by a stifled imagination. For their performances, Ms. Harris and Ms. Dana won Tonys for Best Actress and Best Supporting Actress, respectively. A: James Prideaux. C: Julie Harris, Leora Dana, David Rounds, Ralph Clanton, Richard Woods, Tobias Haller, Maureen Anderman, Brian Farrell, Kate Wilkinson, Dorothi Fox, George Connolly, Dennis Cooney, Macon McCalman, Joseph Attles, Marc Jefferson, Louis Schaefer. P: Richard Barr, Charles Woodward, and the American National Theater and Academy. D: George Schaefer. SD: William Ritman. CD: Noel Taylor.

Last of the Red Hot Lovers (12/28/69, Eugene O'Neill, 706)

Neil Simon's comedy of a middle-aged man's attempts at infidelity. In three acts, with three women, they all fail, all amusingly and with a full measure of the Simon charm. Barney Cashman (James Coco) is a fish house proprietor who's been twenty-three years faithfully married to his high school sweetheart. Now forty-seven, he has thoughts of his mortality and the passing parade, and yearns for one sweet moment of exciting, illicit romance. Since his mother's apartment is conveniently empty during the day, he attempts a series of afternoon seductions, first with a bold, brittle sophisticate, then with a crazy, would-be actress. finally with his wife's best friend. All are zany disasters. At play's end, Barney is phoning his wife, trying to wheedle her into an assignation. Though wit and jokes abound, there is a touching quality to the humor. Simon told *Newsweek* he deliberately cut laughs to "protect the serious moments in my plays." The serious moments in *Last of the Red Hot Lovers* are what make the play memorable. ". . . extraordinarily funny and yet also endearing" (Clive Barnes, *New York Times*). ". . . delightfully hilarious and witty, as well as filled with the wisdom about human nature characteristic of all his work" (Richard Watts, *New York Post*). A: Neil Simon. C: James Coco, Linda Lavin, Marcia Rodd, Doris Roberts. P: Saint-Subber. D: Robert Moore. SD: Oliver Smith. CD: Donald Brooks.

SV: Paramount, 1972, Alan Arkin, Sally Kellerman, Paula Prentiss, Renee Taylor (directed by Gene Saks from Neil Simon's screenplay).

Last Stop (9/5/44, Barrymore, 23)

Inmates of an old ladies' home go on strike, solve a murder and, presumably, live happily ever after. ". . . a little horror" (*New York Times*). C: Catherine Doucet, Minnie Dupree, Enid Markey, Eda Heinemann, Effie Afton. A: Irving Kaye Davis. P: Victor Hugo-Vidal. D: Erwin Piscator.

Last Warning, The (10/24/22, Klaw, 236)

Murder mystery set in a supposedly haunted theatre, solved by a drama buff detective. Lively thriller by Thomas F. Fallon, based on a novel by Wadsworth Camp. C: William Courtleigh, Ann Mason, Clarence Derwent, Charles Trowbridge. P: Mindlin and Goldreyer.

SV: U, 1939, *House of Fear,* William Gargan, Irene Hervey, Alan Dinehart, Robert Coote, El Brendel.

Late Christopher Bean, The (10/31/32, Henry Miller, 211)

After his death, the late Christopher Bean is suddenly acclaimed a great artist. Abby, the family servant, holds Bean's grasping relatives in her power for it is she who has custody of his most highly prized masterpiece. Moreover, it turns out that she was secretly married to the artist. *The Late Christopher Bean* was a perceptive and amusing portrait of provincial New England life. It was adapted and extensively revised by Sidney Howard from a play by Rene Fauchois. C: Pauline Lord, Walter Connolly, Beulah Bondi, George Coulouris, Ernest Lawford, Clarence Derwent. P/D: Gilbert Miller. The successful London production (adapted by Emlyn Williams) costarred Edith Evans and Cedric Hardwicke.
SV: MGM, 1933, *Christopher Bean*, Marie Dressler, Lionel Barrymore, Jean Hersholt, Beulah Bondi, Russell Hardie, Helen Mack.

Late George Apley, The (11/23/44, Lyceum, 384)

Sly lampooning of a stuffy, blue-blooded Bostonian and his family; adapted by John P. Marquand and George S. Kaufman (D) from Mr. Marquand's Pulitzer Prize novel. Using only a few key episodes from the book, the play concentrated on gently satirizing the tradition-bound, intensely respectable Back Bay world of 1912 from which the Apley son and daughter endeavor to escape. A pleasant if somewhat slowly paced comedy of manners, *The Late George Apley* was a hit with both press and public. Leo G. Carroll contributed a distinguished performance in the title role. C: Janet Beecher, Percy Waram, Margaret Dale, Margaret Phillips, David McKay, Joan Chandler, Reynolds Evans, Howard St. John. P: Max Gordon. CD/SD: Stewart Chaney.
Chaney.
SV: Fox, 1947, Ronald Colman, Peggy Cummins, Vanessa Brown, Edna Best, Percy Waram, Richard Ney, Richard Haydn, Mildred Natwick (directed by Joseph L. Mankiewicz).
Note: The Late George Apley was Mr. Marquand's only play.

Late Love (10/13/53, National, 95)

Engaged to paint the portrait of a stodgy novelist (Neil Hamilton), an outspoken lady artist (Arlene Francis) plays Miss Fixit and frees the writer's family from his overfastidious tyranny. This flimsy comedy marked the Broadway debuts, in important subsidiary roles, of Cliff Robertson and Elizabeth Montgomery. Also in the cast: Lucile Watson, Frank Albertson, Ann Dere. A: Rosemary Casey. P: Michael Abbott. D: John C. Wilson.

Laugh, Clown, Laugh! (11/28/23, Belasco, 136)

The Pagliacci story with some additional David Belasco (A/P/D) flourishes. A melancholy clown (Lionel Barrymore) is in love with his young ward (Irene Fenwick). Misconstruing her devotion for pity, and not wishing to stand in the way of her future happiness, he commits suicide. Lionel Barrymore's fine performance was the big plus factor in this lachrymose fable, written by Belasco and Tom Cushing from a play by Faurto Martini. C: Ian Keith, Sidney Toler, Henry Herbert, Vaughn De Leath.

Launcelot and Elaine (9/12/21, Greenwich Village, 32)

Interesting, fairly successful poetic drama by Edwin Milton Royle, based on Tennyson's "Idylls of the King," with Selena Royle as Queen Guinevere; Josephine Royle as Elaine, the lily maid of Astolot; and Pedro de Cordoba as Sir Lancelot. P: Playwright and Players Company. D: Edward Elsner.

Laundry, The (2/13/63, Gate, 30)

Hideously deformed son of a French laundress is sold to a circus side show, revered as a saint, and then murdered. O/B version of the ancient Minotaur myth was hailed by *Newsweek* as "a haunting mixture of melodrama and mythology." A: Howard Richardson b/o a play by David Guerdon. D: Nicolas Bataille.

Laura (6/26/47, Cort, 44)

Stage version of the classic mystery film about a detective's infatuation for a (supposedly) murdered career girl. "... much more skillfully managed by Hollywood ... a wan and woebegone affair" *(Post)*. C: Otto Kruger, Hugh Marlowe, K. T. Stevens. A: Vera Caspary and George Sklar. P: H. Clay Blaney i.a.w. S. and R. Steckler. D: Clarence Derwent.

SV: The Vera Caspary novel was filmed (Fox, 1944) with a cast headed by Gene Tierney, Dana Andrews, Clifton Webb, Judith Anderson, Vincent Price (directed by Otto Preminger).

Law and the Man, The (12/20/06, Manhattan, 54)

Pedestrian dramatization of Victor Hugo's *Les Miserables* (1862) wherein minor culprit Jean Valjean (Wilton Lackaye) is relentlessly pursued by the forces of nineteenth-century French law. A/D: Wilton Lackaye. P: William A. Brady.

SV: Fox, 1935, *Les Miserables,* Fredric March, Charles Laughton, Cedric Hardwicke, Rochelle Hudson, Florence Eldridge, John Beal; 1952, Michael Rennie, Robert Newton, Sylvia Sidney, Edmund Gwenn, Elsa Lanchester, Cameron Mitchell, Florence Bates.

Law Breaker, The (2/1/22, Booth, 90)

A banker's daughter sets out to reform a crook and, after the requisite amount of melodramatics and misunderstandings, succeeds. Thoroughly conventional melodrama with a good cast: Blanche Yurka, William Courtenay, Frederick Bickel (Fredric March), Clifford Dempsey, John Cromwell (D). A: Jules Eckert Goodman. P: William A. Brady.

Law of the Land, The (9/30/14, 48th Street, 221)

A wife murders her brute of a husband, is shielded from the police investigation by sympathetic friends and servants. Implausible George Broadhurst (A/P/D) melodrama. C: Julia Dean, Milton Sills, George Fawcett.

Lawful Larceny (1/2/22, Republic, 225)

Wife seeks revenge against husband's mistress by stealing her money and jewels. Paltry melodrama. C: Margaret Lawrence, Alan Dinehart, Lowell Sherman, Gail Kane, Sara Haden. A: Samuel Shipman. P: A. H. Woods. D: Bertram Harrison.

SV: RKO, 1930, Bebe Daniels, Lowell Sherman.

Lazybones (9/22/24, Vanderbilt, 72)

Shiftless ne'er-do-well (George Abbott) finds an abandoned baby girl in a market basket. Eighteen years later he proposes marriage to the girl and she accepts. Claptrap. C: Beth Merrill, Elizabeth Patterson, Willard Robertson, Martha Bryan-Allen, Leona Hogarth. A: Owen Davis. P: Sam H. Harris. D: Guthrie McClintic.

Leading Lady, The (10/18/48, National, 8)

A popular turn-of-the-century actress (Ruth Gordon) is unable to pursue her career when her tyrannical actor-husband dies. "A hollow evocation of a vanished era ... as lifeless as a yellowed playbill" *(Herald Tribune)*. C: Ian Keith, John Carradine, Mildred Dunnock, Ethel

Griffies, Wesley Addy, James MacColl (as playwright Clyde Fitch), Ossie Davis. Douglas Watson. A: Ruth Gordon. P: Samrock and Fields. D: Garson Kanin. CD: Mainbocher. SD: Donald Oenslager.

Leaf and Bough (1/21/49, Cort, 3)

Overwritten, ostentatiously directed (by Rouben Mamoulian), this 40's drama told of the unhappy love affair between an embittered young bank clerk (Richard Hart) and an idealistic farm girl (Coleen Gray). When the boy's disagreeable brother (Charlton Heston) convinces the hero that his sweetheart is just another village tart, the boy rapes her atop a mountain. Somehow or other, the death of the girl's grandfather serves to reunite the now-remorseful swain and his slightly tarnished ladylove, and they decide to brave life's complexities together. ". . . intolerably solemn and pretentious . . . a bad imitation of Tennessee Williams" *(New York Times)*. *Leaf and Bough* marked the playwriting debut of Joseph Hayes, author of *The Desperate Hours* (1955), *Calculated Risk* (1962), etc. C: Anthony Ross, Alice Reinheart, David White. P: Charles P. Heidt. SD: Carl Kent.

Leah Kleschna (12/12/04, Manhattan, 131)

A thief (Mrs. Fiske) is regenerated when she falls in love with an amateur criminologist (John Mason). Enjoyable hokum. C: George Arliss, Emily Stevens, Etienne Girardot. A: C. M. S. McLellan. P/D: The Fiskes.
R: (4/21/24, Lyric, 32) by William A. Brady. C: Helen Gahagan, William Faversham, Arnold Daly, Lowell Sherman, Katherine Alexander, Jose Ruben, Arnold Korff.

Leave Her to Heaven (2/27/40, Longacre, 15)

John Van Druten melodrama about a restless wife (Ruth Chatterton) who so inflames her jealous chauffeur-lover (Edmond O'Brien) that he murders her aged husband (Reynolds Denniston) and is sentenced to hang for the crime. The play ends with the guilt-ridden *femme fatale* taking her own life. "Commonplace and unrelievedly sordid" *(Herald Tribune)*. P: Dwight Deere Wiman. D: Auriol Lee.

Ledge, A (11/18/29, Assembly, 16)

Accused of theft, a young businessman is forced by his partners to "walk the plank"—the top floor ledge of a skyscraper office building. Melodramatic hodgepodge, written by Paul Osborn and b/o a short story by Henry Holt. P: Theatre Assembly.

Left Bank, The (10/5/31, Little, 241)

An expatriate writer in Paris flatly refuses to return to "the spiritual vacuum" which is America. In the end, his wife chooses to go back to the land where she has her roots, leaving her self-centered husband behind. Amusing, shrewdly written comedy-drama by Elmer Rice (A/P/D). C: Katherine Alexander, Horace Braham, Merle Maddern, Donald MacDonald.

Legal Murder (2/15/34, President, 7)

Threadbare O/B melodrama based on the Scottsboro case. A: Dennis Donoghue. P: A. J. Allen. D: S. Jay Kaufman.
See *They Shall Not Die*.

Legend of Lizzie, The (2/9/59, Adelphia, 2)

Murky retelling of the Lizzie Borden murder case in Fall River, Mass. in 1892. ". . . diffuse and pretentious . . . has no coherent point of view" *(New York Times)*. C: Anne Meacham, Douglass Montgomery, Muriel Kirkland, Frank M. Thomas, William Daniels, Lee Richardson. A: Reginald Lawrence. P: Hartney

Arthur (D) and Nat Stevens. CD/SD: Ballou.

Legend of Sarah (10/11/50, Fulton, 29)

Dawdling farce about an ancestor-worshiping miss. Written by James Gow and Arnaud d'Usseau, authors of *Tomorrow the World* (1943) and *Deep Are the Roots* (1945). C: Marsha Hunt, Tom Helmore, Ethel Griffies, Edmon Ryan, Philip Coolidge, Joseph Sweeney, Judith Parrish. P: Kermit Bloomgarden. D: Benn W. Levy. CD: Ben Edwards. SD: Ralph Alswang.

Lend Me Your Ears! (10/5/36, Mansfield, 8)

Foolish comedy about a small-town politician (Walter C. Kelly) who arouses his constituents' ire when he invites a nudist convention to town. A: Philip Wood and Stewart Beach. P: Peters, Field and Weenolsen. D: Leo Bulgakov.

Note: Vaudeville monologist Walter C. Kelly was the brother of playwright George Kelly and the uncle of actress Grace Kelly.

Les Blancs (11/15/70, Longacre, 40)

A drama that explores the evil of colonialism in Africa. This was the final work of Lorraine Hansberry, the distinguished American playwright who died January 12, 1965. Unfinished at her death, the text as presented was credited both to her and to her husband, Robert Nemiroff. The result drew qualified endorsements from the critics, it being pointed out that in the five years since Ms. Hansberry's death, much of the play had become dated. Nevertheless, it was considered often powerful, sometimes moving—if almost always overly didactic. The central character, Matoseh, is a black African who returns from Europe to the village of his birth for his father's funeral. The country is in turmoil as it struggles toward independence, but Matoseh has a white wife in London, and is now torn in his loyalties. Around him swirl the predictable arguments of stereotypical characters: the foolish, well-meaning white liberal; the British officer who believes only in violent repression; his black counterpart intent on spilling blood; the wise, old doctor who says all the right things about the white man's guilt. The play surges inexorably to a bloody denouement. "... it is forceful and provocative" (Richard Watts, *New York Post*). "Too much of it sounds like political propaganda" (Clive Barnes, *New York Times*). A: Lorraine Hansberry; final text adapted by Robert Nemiroff. C: James Earl Jones, Cameron Mitchell, Ralph Purdum, Earle Hyman, Lili Darvas, Harold Scott, Humbert Allen Astredo, Marie Andrews, Clebert Ford, Charles Moore, Joan Derby. D: John Berry. P: Konrad Matthaei. SD: Peter Larkin. CD: Jane Greenwood.

Let Freedom Ring (11/6/35, Broadhurst, 109)

A mill foreman is torn between loyalty to the company and devotion to his own clan when a strike threatens. Powerful, well-acted drama by Albert Bein b/o a novel by Grace Lumpkin. C: Shepperd Strudwick, Will Geer, Robert Porterfield, Robert Williams, Tom Ewell, Charles Dingle. P: Albert Bein and Jack Goldsmith. D: Worthington Miner.

Let Me Hear You Smile (1/16/73, Biltmore, 1)

At the core of *Let Me Hear You Smile* is a valid theme: the universal desire to escape the pain and problems that plague human beings at every age from birth to death. Unfortunately, in exploring this theme, the play is no more than pallidly likable, neither very funny nor very moving. It is divided into three episodes, showing its players at three stages of their lives. In Act I, a housewife nearing forty mourns her departing youth and feels that to escape her family will somehow slow the inexorably ticking clock. She does not leave, however, and in the second act, she and the man who will be her husband are shown at the age of six, worrying over school and wondering if they should run away from home. The last act finds the couple at retirement age. The husband has sold his business, but dreading senescence, devises a plan for them to go to New Zealand where life will begin anew. The couple are played by Sandy Dennis and James Broderick. Ms. Dennis brings on her familiar arsenal of mannerisms but her stage presence is undeniably effective. Broderick, too often cast in wishy-washy film roles, displays an engaging warmth and incisiveness. The third member of the cast is Paul B. Price, agreeable as the heroine's brother. A: Leonora Thuna and Harry Cauley. P: Michael and Barclay Macrae. D: Harry Cauley. SD: Peter Larkin.

Let Us Be Gay (2/19/29, Little, 132)

At a weekend houseparty, a divorcée is asked to rescue the twenty-year-old granddaughter of the house from the attentions of a debonair older man who turns out to be the divorcée's exhusband. After some boudoir badinage, a reconciliation between the two is effected. Entertaining, deftly written Rachel Crothers (A/D) comedy. C: Francine Larrimore, Warren William, Charlotte Granville, Rita Vale, Ross Alexander. P: John Golden.
SV: MGM, 1930, Norma Shearer, Marie Dressler, Hedda Hopper, Rod La Rocque.

Letters to Lucerne (12/23/41, Cort, 23)

Placid drama showing the effects of World War II on various girls of different nationalities in a fashionable Swiss boarding school. ". . . its narrative is better suited to the novelette than to the stage" (*Herald Tribune*). *Letters to Lucerne* brought out a celebrity-studded first-night audience. Reason: the leading roles were enacted by the daughters of such famous men as conductor Leopold Stokowski, author Stephen Morehouse Avery, impressario Dwight Deere Wiman (P), and actors Richard Barthelmess and Clive Brook. (Best performance, according to the critics, was the one given by Sonya Stokowski.) C: Grete Mosheim, Katherine Alexander, Lilia Skala, Nancy Wiman, Mary Barthelmess, Phyllis Avery, Faith Brook. A: Fritz Rotter and Allen Vincent. D: John Baird.

Liberty Jones (2/5/41, Shubert, 22)

Liberty Jones, dying from indifference and neglect in her red, white and blue boudoir, is rescued from an uncertain fate by a young American liberal. Philip Barry's anti-fascist allegory, handsomely produced by The Theatre Guild, was blasted by the critics as being both obscure and simplistic. The majority opinion was summed up by Louis Kronenberger in the New York newspaper *PM*: "I think it's a fine idea to say 'Go blast Fascism to hell and not back.' But I think it's a frightful idea to say it in baby talk." C: Nancy Coleman, John Beal, Tom Ewell, Howard Freeman, William Lynn, Martha Hodge, Norman Lloyd, Joseph Anthony, William Castle, Lew Christensen (CH), Constance Dowling. D: John Houseman. CD/SD: Raoul Pene du Bois. M: Paul Bowles.

Life (10/24/14, Manhattan Opera House, 161)

Innocent man condemned to death in New York escapes at the eleventh hour and flees to Mexico where he and the villain have a face-to-face confrontation in the stockade of a Mexican mine. This motheaten melodrama by Thompson Buchanan was produced on a gargantuan Drury Lane scale at New York's Manhattan Opera House with an enormous cast headed by Walter Hampden, John Bowers, Dion Titheradge, Effingham Pinto, and Eugene Powers. P: William A.

Brady. D: John Cromwell, Frank Hatch, and William A. Brady.

Life Begins (3/28/32, Selwyn, 8)

Heart throbs galore in the maternity ward of a city hospital. "It is amusing, moving and wholesome, and yet much too general in its point of view to leave any definite impression" *(New York Times)*. C: Joanna Roos, Alan Bunce, Glenda Farrell, Mildred Dunnock (deb.). A: Mary Macdougal Axelson. P/D: Joseph Santley (codirected by Robert Sinclair.)

SV: WB, 1932, Loretta Young, Eric Linden, Aline MacMahon, Glenda Farrell, Preston Foster, Frank McHugh, Vivienne Osborne, Elizabeth Patterson, Gilbert Roland; 1940, *A Child is Born*, Geraldine Fitzgerald, Jeffrey Lynn, Gladys George, Spring Byington, Gale Page, Eve Arden.

Life of Reilly, The (4/29/42, Broadhurst, 5)

Baseball pitcher falls under the spell of a fortune teller. "... an utterly implausible and generally dull farce" *(News)*. C: Loring Smith, Glenda Farrell, Howard Smith, Peter Hobbs, Polly Walters, George Mathews. A: William Roos. P: Tuttle and Bromley. D: Roy Hargrave.

Life with Father (11/8/39, Empire, 3,224)

The most successful play in the history of the American theatre (3,224 performances), this period comedy was adapted by Howard Lindsay and Russel Crouse from Clarence Day's *New Yorker* sketches, with Lindsay in the role of irascible but warm-hearted Father Day and Dorothy Stickney (Mrs. Lindsay) as Vinnie, his strong-willed but muddle-headed wife. The play has little plot, other than Vinnie's single-minded campaign to have Father baptized. Its humor stems from its depiction of late-Victorian manners and mores in the "absolutely conventional world" of New York family life in the 1880's. "Sooner or later every one will have to see *Life With Father*, which opened at the Empire last evening . . . it is overpoweringly funny . . . enchanting . . . a darlin' play" (Brooks Atkinson, *New York Times*). Produced for the modest sum of thirty-five thousand dollars, *Life With Father* made millions for its backers, authors, and its neophyte producer, Oscar Serlin. A sequel, *Life With Mother*, dealt with further adventures and domestic contretemps of the red-headed Day clan. Produced in 1948, it ran 265 performances. C: Teresa Wright (deb.), John Drew Devereaux, Richard Simon. D: Bretaigne Windust. CD/SD: Stewart Chaney. Chaney.

R: (10/19/67, City Center, 22). C: Leon Ames, Dorothy Stickney, Sandy Duncan, Rusty Thacker, Gary Enck. D: Gus Schirmer.

SV: WB, 1947, William Powell, Irene Dunne, Elizabeth Taylor, Edmund Gwenn, ZaSu Pitts, Jimmy Lydon, Martin Milner (directed by Michael Curtiz from a screenplay by Donald Ogden Stewart).

Life with Mother (10/20/48, Empire, 265)

Sequel to *Life With Father* (1939) dealing mainly with Mother Day's determination to make Father give her a long-overdue engagement ring. Despite uniformly favorable reviews, *Life With Mother* was not a financial success on Broadway. It ended its comparatively brief run with a loss of forty thousand dollars. C: Howard Lindsay, Dorothy Stickney, Robert Emhardt, Gladys Hurlbut, Ruth Hammond, John Drew Devereaux. A: Howard Lindsay and Russel Crouse b/o the stories of Clarence Day. P: Oscar Serlin. D: Guthrie McClintic. SD: Donald Oenslager and Stewart Chaney.

Life's Too Short (9/20/35, Broadhurst, 11)

A husband's jealousy drives his wife into

the arms of her ex-lover—her husband's boss. Jed Harris produced and directed this 1935 comedy-drama. Everything about the production was uninspired. C: John Litel, Evelyn Varden, Doris Dalton, Lea Penman. A: John Whedon and Arthur Caplan.

Light of Asia, The (10/9/28, Hampden's, 23)

Dramatization of the life of Buddha, here called Siddartha (Walter Hampden), set in India during the sixth century B.C. Siddartha renounces a life of luxury, undergoes long and severe penance, and emerges after many years as the wise and noble holy man who "cast away the world to save the world." Soporific spectacle; suggested by Sir Edwin Arnold's classic poem. A: Georgina Jones Walton. P/D: Walter Hampden. CH: Ruth St. Denis.

Light Up the Sky (11/18/48, Royale, 214)

Comedy about a group of temperamental theatre people gathered in Boston to try out a new play. Savage wrangling ensues when the production appears to be a flop; when the play turns out to be a hit, comradeship and good will reign supreme. "A loud, broad, tempestuous comedy that is acted at top speed by a wonderful cast" *(New York Times)*. C: Glenn Anders, Virginia Field, Sam Levene, Audrey Christie, Phyllis Povah, Barry Nelson, Philip Ober, Bartlett Robinson, Jane Middleton, Donald McClelland, Ronald Alexander, Simon Oakland (deb.), John Seymour. P: Joseph M. Hyman and Bernard Hart. Originally intended as a serious play with comic undertones. *Light Up the Sky* was extensively rewritten by Moss Hart (A/D) during its Boston tryout and converted into a gaily malicious farce. The leading characters—a tearful director, an effusive star, an arrogant producer and his brassy wife—allegedly were based on show business notables Guthrie McClintic, Gertrude Lawrence, Billy Rose, and Eleanor Holm. A highly acclaimed 1949 west coast production of the play featured a cast that included Gregory Peck, Jean Parker, Florence Bates, Fred Clark, Tom Powers, and Hayden Rorke, with Nancy Kelly and Guy Madison later taking over the roles played by Parker and Peck.

Lightnin' (8/26/18, Gaiety, 1,291)

This cheery, sentimental saga was the first play in American stage history to pass the 1,000 mark, achieving the then unprecedented run of 1,291 performances. The story dealt with Lightnin' Bill Jones (Frank Bacon), an oldster with a fondness for the bottle and a weakness for tall stories. This beguiling loafer is the sometime host at his wife's Calivada Hotel on the California-Nevada state line at Lake Tahoe. In the course of the play, Lightnin' outwits some rascally lawyers, reunites a pair of young lovers, and is reconciled with his long-suffering spouse. C: Harry Davenport, Ralph Morgan, Jessie Pringle. A: Frank Bacon and Winchell Smith. P/D: Winchell Smith and John Golden. The star and coauthor of *Lightnin'* was an undiscovered actor and an old man when his play opened on Broadway. When Bacon died in 1922, he had acted the leading role more than two thousand times. His son. Lloyd Bacon, became a prominent Hollywood director *(Forty-Second Street, Footlight Parade, A Slight Case of Murder,* etc.).

R: (9/15/38, Golden, 54) by John Golden (P/D) with Fred Stone in the title role.

SV: Fox, 1930, Will Rogers, Louise Dresser, Joel McCrea.

Lights Out (8/14/22, Vanderbilt, 12)

Egbert Winslow (Robert Ames), a young, would-be screenwriter, gets involved with a gang of Runyonesque crooks. Potentially funny comedy emerged as labored whimsy, due in part to miscasting and flat direction. C: William Ingersoll, C. Henry Gordon, Felix Krembs. A: Paul Dickey and Mann Page. P: Mrs. Henry B.

Harris. D: Walter Wilson.

SV: RKO, 1938, *Crashing Hollywood*, Lee Tracy, Joan Woodbury.

Lilac Time (2/6/17, Republic, 176)

Sentimental World War I romance of a French girl (Jane Cowl) and an English aviator (Orme Caldara). A: Jane Cowl and Jane Murfin. P: Selwyn and Company. D: George Platt.

SV: A notable silent version (with synchronized sound effects) of *Lilac Time* was produced by First National (WB, 1928) starring Colleen Moore and Gary Cooper.

Lilies of the Field (10/4/21, Klaw, 169)

Wronged wife joins the oldest profession, suffers the pangs of mother love, finally gains custody of her daughter. Bathos supreme in this unrelievedly lachrymose drama by William Hurlbut. C: Marie Doro, Norman Trevor, Mary Phillips, Alison Skipworth, Cora Witherspoon. P: Garrick Productions. D: H. M. Webster.

SV: WB, 1930, Corinne Griffith, John Loder, Ralph Forbes.

Lilly Turner (9/19/32, Morosco, 24)

The ups and downs of a cooch dancer with a traveling medicine show. Drab and sordid yarn. C: Dorothy Hall, John Litel, James Bell, Robert Barrat, Granville Bates, Joseph Crehan, Percy Kilbride. A/P/D: Philip Dunning and George Abbott.

SV: WB, 1933, Ruth Chatterton, George Brent, Frank McHugh, Guy Kibbee, Ruth Donnelly, Mayo Methot, Marjorie Gateson, Robert Barrat.

Lily of the Valley (1/26/42, Windsor, 8)

Somber Ben Hecht (A/D) fantasy about a missionary meeting in the county morgue attended by the shades of recently deceased derelicts. Each of these unfortunates tells his life story to the preacher conducting the service—the one human to whom the ghostly outcasts are visible. Reviews of *Lily of the Valley* were sharply divided: ". . . strangely haunting . . . an unusual theatre adventure" (*Herald Tribune*). ". . . just about the slowest, dullest, talkiest, most wavering piece of mysticism you could possibly conceive" (*PM*). ". . . strangely absorbing and sometimes almost unbearably poignant" (*Post*). ". . . a collaboration by Hecht and Macabre . . . only the ghost of a show" (*Journal-American*). After digesting the reviews, Mr. Hecht vented his spleen by composing an open letter to the drama editors in which he described the critics thusly: "A group of aesthetically exhausted old men with literary nerve centers worn out from too much slapdash service in the theatre . . . a fungus-egoed coterie of fretful and wearied scribblers. . . ." *Lily of the Valley* closed after eight performances. C: Siegfried Rumann, Myron McCormick, Minnie Dupree, Alison Skipworth, Clay Clement, Joseph Pevney. P: Gilbert Miller. SD: Harry Horner.

Lily Sue (11/16/26, Lyceum, 47)

Incredibly corny Western dealing with the tribulations of "a right purty ranch gal" (Beth Merrill) from Sweet Grass, Montana. Sample dialogue: "Maw, I know we ain't a prayin' family, but if you never asked God for nothin', git down on yore knees an' tell Him to git me to Sweet Grass afore that gang hangs Duke Adams." A: Willard Mack. P/D: David Belasco.

Lincoln Mask, The (10/30/72, Plymouth, 8)

Opening with Lincoln's arrival at Ford's Theater for that fateful performance of *Our American Cousin*, *The Lincoln Mask* then reviews his life and career in eight flashbacks ranging over twenty-five years. With the unstable Mary Todd at his side, Lincoln is here presented as something of a neurotic seer, given to brooding visions of national turmoil in the far future and a more immediate unhappy fate for himself. He is more concerned with the abolition of slavery than with secession, and fights the Civil War primarily to free the blacks. With the players from *Our American Cousin* appearing at intervals to remind the audience of the ultimate end, there is so much foreshadowing of events that dramatic impact is blunted. "No play about the Great Emancipator can be totally without interest, but *The Lincoln Mask* comes dangerously close . . ." (Richard Watts, *New York Post*). ". . . we'd all have been better off with *Our American Cousin*" (Douglas Watt, *New York Daily News*). A: V. J. Longhi. C: Fred Gwynne, Eva Marie Saint, Tom Rosqui, Joseph Warren, Eric Tavaris, Jean Bruno, W. B. Brydon, Alek Primrose, Tanny McDonald, Albert Henderson, Thomas Barbour, Ray Stewart, Patricia Cope, Ronnie Claire Edwards, Earl Hindman. P: Albert W. Selden and Jerome Minskoff. D: Gene Frankel.

Lion and the Mouse, The (11/20/05, Lyceum, 686)

The baleful influence of big business on Washington politics was the theme of this very successful 1905 melodrama by Charles Klein. The leading characters were patterned after John D. Rockefeller (the villain) and muckraking journalist Ida Tarbell (the heroine). The play, contrived but theatrically effective, ran to packed houses for two years on Broadway, with four companies touring the country. C: Grace Elliston, Richard Bennett, Edmund Breese. P: Henry B. Harris. D: William Harris and R. A. Roberts.
SV: WB, 1928, Lionel Barrymore, May McAvoy.

Lion in Winter, The (3/3/66, Ambassador, 92)

In 1183, Henry II (Robert Preston) summons his imprisoned wife, Eleanor of Aquitaine (Rosemary Harris), and three sons to his castle at Chinon in France. Torn apart by fierce political ambitions, the twelfth-century royal couple spend the Christmas holidays squabbling and plotting in an attempt to settle the thorny question of the succession to the throne on Henry's death, a succession that affects the fate of both England and France. "A work of intelligence, astringent wit, and much theatrical skill" (*New York Times*). According to author James Goldman, "the fabric of the play was cut for laughter." Consequently, this semihistorical comedy-drama abounds in deliberate anachronisms. Brilliantly written, directed and acted, *The Lion in Winter* failed to win box-office support and closed after a Broadway run of less than three months. C: Suzanne Grossmann, Christopher Walken, Dennis Cooney, James Rado, Bruce Scott. P: Wolsk/Hyman/King/Azenberg. D: Noel Willman. CD/SD: Will Steven Armstrong. M: Thomas Wagner.
SV: Avco-Embassy, 1968, Peter O'Toole, Katharine Hepburn, Jane Merrow, Anthony Hopkins, John Castle, Timothy Dalton, Nigel Terry (directed by Anthony Harvey).

Listen, Professor! (12/22/43, Forrest, 29)

Elderly, reclusive scholar (Dudley Digges) is revitalized when his fifteen-year-old granddaughter comes to live with him. Slight but frequently engaging comedy-drama, adapted and extensively revised by press agent Peggy Phillips; based on a Soviet play by Alexander Afinogenov, who was killed during a Nazi bombing. P: Milton Baron i.a.w. Jean Muir and Toni Ward. D: Sanford Meisner. CD: Lucinda Ballard. SD: Howard Bay.

Little A (1/15/47, Henry Miller, 21)

Trapped in a loveless marriage, a meek businessman (Otto Kruger) comes to suspect that his coddled son is not really his, and that his avaricious wife (Jessie

Royce Landis) had been his father's mistress. These suspicions being confirmed, the timid soul plots revenge, but the plan backfires and results in gratuitous violence. "Sheer tripe" (*Herald Tribune*). A: Hugh White. P: Sam Nasser i.a.w. Harry Lambert. D: Melville Burke.

Little Accident (10/9/28, Morosco, 304)

A bachelor (Thomas Mitchell) discovers he has just become the father of a child. When he learns that the mother (Katherine Alexander) plans to offer the infant for adoption, he kidnaps the baby. Cozy comedy written by novelist Floyd Dell and Thomas Mitchell. P: Crosby Gaige. D: Graham and Hurley.

SV: U, 1930, Douglas Fairbanks, Jr., Anita Page, ZaSu Pitts; 1939, Richard Carlson, Hugh Herbert, Ernest Truex; RKO, 1944, *Casanova Brown*, Gary Cooper, Teresa Wright, Frank Morgan, Anita Louise.

Little Blue Light, The (4/29/51, ANTA, 16)

Literary critic Edmund Wilson's only Broadway play, a gloomy and discursive conversation piece dealing with the political and social future of the United States. A disorderly dramatic grab bag of metaphysics, mysticism, and allegory, *The Little Blue Light* dramatized the efforts of a crusading publisher (Melvyn Douglas) to defend himself against powerful pressure groups of both left and right to a totalitarian world "of the not-remote future." According to Robert Coleman in the *New York Daily Mirror*, the play was "a muddled mish-mash of philosophy, romance, melodrama, sex and symbolism." C: Burgess Meredith, Arlene Francis, Martin Gabel, Peter Cookson. P: Quintus Productions. D: Albert Marre. SD: Lester Polakov.

Little Brother, The (11/25/18, Belmont, 120)

Stilted problem play dealing with the conflicts arising from the marriage of a rabbi's daughter and a priest's ward. "An attempt to shed a new light upon an old and vexing problem. . . . The play is deficient structurally in that its dramatic peak occurs at the end of the first act, and that the pace of the piece slackens visibly from then onward" (*New York Times*). C: Walker Whiteside, Tyrone Power, Sr., Richard Dix. A: Milton Goldsmith and Benedict James. P/D: Walter Hast.

Little Brown Jug (3/6/46, Martin Beck, 5)

Sadistic derelict (Percy Kilbride)* blackmails his way into the home of a mother and daughter, and almost destroys both their lives before his stranglehold on them is broken. ". . . a very mild thriller" (*Sun*). C: Katharine Alexander, Arthur Margetson, Marjorie Lord, Arthur Franz, Ronald Alexander. A: Marie Baumer. P: Courtney Burr. D: Gerald Savory.

---

*Character actor Percy Kilbride was best known for his portrayal of Pa Kettle in the *Ma and Pa Kettle* film series.

Little Dark Horse (11/16/41, Golden, 9)

Bachelor uncle (Walter Slezak) discovers that his illegitimate nephew is black. ". . . reeks of bad taste" (*World-Telegram*). A: Theresa Helburn b/o a play by Andre Birabeau. P: Blackwell and Curtis. D: Melville Burke.

Little Darling (10/27/42, Biltmore, 23)

Daughter (Barbara Bel Geddes) encourages an affair between her widowed father (Leon Ames) and her best friend (Phyllis Avery). "A brittle farce which . . . becomes exceedingly tenuous" (*Herald Tribune*). C: Karen Morley, Arthur Franz. P: Tom Weatherly. D: Alfred de Liagre, Jr. *Little Darling* was written by novelist-scenarist (*My Man Godfrey*) Eric Hatch.

Little Foxes, The (2/15/39, National, 410)

Lillian Hellman's superbly crafted melodrama about the hateful and rapacious Hubbard family, plotting and plundering their way to wealth and power in the deep South at the turn of the century. Regina (Tallulah Bankhead), the most ruthlessly acquisitive of the lot, blackmails her two brothers, sacrifices her daughter's happiness, and coolly drives her invalid husband to his death by refusing him the medicine that would save his life. It is she who emerges as the triumphant member of this gang of predators, but it is a hollow victory. Regina is deserted by her daughter, and ridden with guilt, as the final curtain falls. "An important and distinguished play" (*Herald Tribune*). "Tallulah Bankhead at last has her glistening teeth in a role that meets her histrionic talent" (*World-Telegram*). *The Little Foxes* was, in effect, a stinging attack on the capitalist system. Splendidly acted and directed, it gave Tallulah Bankhead the most rewarding role of her career, but the engagement was an unhappy one. There were constant battles between Miss Bankhead, producer-director Herman Shumlin, and author Lillian Hellman. Seven years later Miss Hellman returned to the Hubbard family in *Another Part of the Forest* (1946), which showed the ruthless clan at an earlier stage of their lives. C: Patricia Collinge, Frank Conroy, Charles Dingle, Carl Benton Reid, Dan Duryea, Florence Williams, Lee Baker. SD: Howard Bay.

R: (10/26/67, Lincoln Center, 100). C: Anne Bancroft, George C. Scott, Margaret Leighton. E. G. Marshall, Richard A. Dysart, Austin Pendleton, Maria Tucci, William Prince. D: Mike Nichols. Musicalized by Marc Blitzstein as *Regina* (1949) with Jane Pickens, Brenda Lewis, William Wilderman, Priscilla Gilette, Russell Nype, William Warfield, David Thomas and George Lipton.

SV: RKO, 1941, Bette Davis, Herbert Marshall, Patricia Collinge, Teresa Wright, Richard Carlson, Dan Duryea, Charles Dingle, Carl Benton Reid (directed by William Wyler).

Little Journey, A (12/26/18, Little, 252)

A train wreck teaches a girl (Estelle Winwood) the meaning of service to others. Saccharine Rachel Crothers (A/D) comedy-drama. C: Cyril Keightley, Jobyna Howland, Gilda Varesi, Vera Fuller Mellish. P: Messrs. Shubert.

Little Miss Bluebeard (8/28/23, Lyceum, 175)

"I Won't Say I Will (But I Won't Say I Won't)" sings the capricious Colette (Irene Bordoni) to her composer-boyfriend—which pretty much sums up the plot of this mildly risqué boudoir farce. Aside from the interpolated George Gershwin-B.G. DeSylva tune noted above, Miss Bordoni also crooned the lovely ballad, "So This Is Love" by her husband, E. Ray Goetz, in this production. C: Bruce McRae, Eric Blore. A: Avery Hopwood. P: Charles Frohman, Inc. i.a.w. E. Ray Goetz. D: W. H. Gilmore.

SV: Par, 1930, *Her Wedding Night*, Clara Bow, Ralph Forbes, Charlie Ruggles, Skeets Gallagher.

Little Moon of Alban (12/1/60, Longacre, 20)

This period drama, set during the 1920's at the time of the Black and Tan troubles, dealt with a volunteer nurse (Julie Harris) who discovers that one of her patients is the English lieutenant (John Justin in his Broadway debut) who shot and killed her fiancé (Robert Redford). Torn between her vows as a Sister of Charity and her desire for vengeance, the heroine finds her dilemma heightened when the handsome lieutenant falls in love with her. "A placid drama [and] a very talkative one" *(News)*. A: James Costigan. P: Mildred Freed Alberg. D: Herman Shumlin.

Little Murders (4/25/67, Broadhurst, 7)

A mild-mannered pacifist (Elliott Gould) becomes romantically involved with a kooky optimist (Barbara Cook) and her outrageous family—matriarchal mother, milquetoast father, and homosexual brother. Jules Feiffer's first Broadway play—a savage, ironic, devastatingly funny comment on family relationships, the terrors of violence-ridden urban life, and the forces that turn the average citizen from apathy to militancy—was a quick failure. Partially rewritten by the author, and restaged by Alan Arkin, the play was revived off-Broadway two years later with great success, playing to packed houses for one solid year. The cast of the Broadway production included David Steinberg, Ruth White, Heywood Hale Broun, Richard Schaal, and Phil Leeds. P: Alexander H. Cohen. D: George L. Sherman. SD: Ming Cho Lee.

R: (1/5/69, Circle in the Square, 400). C: Fred Willard, Linda Lavin, Vincent Gardenia, Elizabeth Wilson, Jon Korkes. D: Alan Arkin.

SV: Fox, 1971, Elliott Gould, Marcia Rodd, Vincent Gardenia, Elizabeth Wilson, Jon Korkes, Donald Sutherland, Lou Jacobi, Alan Arkin (directed by Alan Arkin).

Little Ol' Boy (4/24/33, Playhouse, 11)

Juvenile delinquent (Burgess Meredith) and his buddy plot their escape from reform school, are captured, and sent to jail. Actor Meredith scored his first Broadway success in this vigorous social-minded melodrama. The play also marked the directorial debut of Joseph Losey. C: Edwin Philips, Frank M. Thomas, Jr., Garson Kanin, John Drew Colt, Lionel Stander, William Lynn. A: Albert Bein. P: Henry Hammond, Inc. SD: Mordecai Gorelik.

Little Old New York (9/8/20, Plymouth, 311)

Immigrant colleen masquerades as a boy to claim an inheritance. Popular period comedy set in New York, 1810, with Vanderbilt, Astor, and Washington Irving among the characters. C: Genevieve Tobin, Ernest Glendinning, Donald Meek. A: Rida Johnson Young. P: Sam H. Harris. D: Sam Forrest.

SV: Fox, 1940, Alice Faye, Fred MacMurray, Richard Greene.

Little Princess, The (1/14/03, Criterion, 34)

Cloying tale of Victorian waif (Millie James) seeking her long-lost father. A: Frances Hodgson Burnett. P: Charles B. Dillingham. D: Francis Neilson.

SV: Fox, 1939, Shirley Temple, Richard Greene, Anita Louise, Ian Hunter, Cesar Romero, Arthur Treacher.

Little Shot (1/17/35, Playhouse, 4)

Man hires a gangster to kill him, changes his mind, but is unable to contact his executioner to call off the deal in time. Trite comedy-melodrama burdened with one of the oldest and most shopworn of plots. C: Donald MacDonald, Lillian Bond. A: Percival Wilde. P: Pearson and Baruch. D: Bretaigne Windust.

Little Spitfire, The (8/16/26, Cort, 201)

Playboy marries chorus girl; his family objects. So-so 20's comedy. C: Sylvia Field, Raymond Van Sickle, A. H. Van Buren (D). A: Myron C. Fagan. P: B. F. Witbeck.

Little Teacher, The (2/4/18, Playhouse, 128)

Vermont schoolmarm gets into trouble when she befriends and protects two cruelly mistreated children. "As effective as it is veracious and simple" (*New York Times*). C: Mary Ryan, Curtis Cooksey, Edward G. Robinson (who stole the acting honors of the evening playing a Canuck friend of the hero). A: Harry James Smith. P: Cohan and Harris. D: Sam Forrest.

Little Women (10/14/12, Playhouse, 184)

Louisa M. Alcott's March family transferred to the stage with most of the story's familiar high spots retained in toto. Standouts in the cast were Alice Brady (Meg), Marie Pavey (Jo), Howard Estabrook (Laurie), and John Cromwell (John Brook). A: Marian de Forest. P: William A. Brady. D: Jessie Bonstelle and Bertram Harrison.
Musicalized by William Dyer as *Jo* (1964).
SV: RKO, 1933, Katharine Hepburn, Joan Bennett, Frances Dee, Jean Parker, Edna May Oliver, Spring Byington, Douglass Montgomery, Paul Lukas (directed by George Cukor); MGM, 1949, June Allyson, Margaret O'Brien, Elizabeth Taylor, Janet Leigh, Mary Astor, Peter Lawford (directed by Mervyn LeRoy).

Littlest Rebel, The (11/14/11, Liberty, 55)

Curly-haired moppet saves her Confederate soldier-daddy from imprisonment by visiting President Lincoln. Simpering saga of Civil War days pleased the family trade. C: Mary Miles Minter, Dustin Farnum, William Farnum. A: Edward Peple. P: A. H. Woods. D: Edgar MacGregor.
SV: Fox, 1935, Shirley Temple, John Boles, Jack Holt, Karen Morley, Bill Robinson.

Live Life Again (9/29/45, Belasco, 2)

The Hamlet story transferred to turn-of-the-century Nebraska. ". . . not only an imaginative and moving drama, but a fascinating theatrical exercise . . ." (*Post*). "A shocking piece of blank-verse mumbo-jumbo. . . . Methinks it should have died a-borning" (*Herald Tribune*). C: Donald Buka, Thomas Chalmers, Beatrice de Neergaard, Parker Fennelly, Mary Rolfe. A: Dan Totheroh. P: S. S. Krellberg. D: Sawyer Falk. SD: Albert Johnson.

Live Wire, The (8/17/50, Playhouse, 28)

Garson Kanin (A/D) comedy about a group of indigent actors living together in peace and harmony until a conniving schemer moves in on them and becomes the serpent in their cooperative Garden of Eden. ". . . repetitious and random . . . *The Live Wire* blows a fuse" (*Herald Tribune*). C: Scott McKay, Sheila Bond, Jack Gilford, Peggy Cass, Pat Harrington, Peter Turgeon, Murvyn Vye, Elliott Reid, Rex Williams. P: Michael Todd. SD: Donald Oenslager.

Lo and Behold! (12/12/51, Booth, 38)

A waspish author (Leo G. Carroll) returns from the hereafter to preside over the romance of two young lovers (Lee Grant and Jeffrey Lynn). According to critic John Chapman (*News*), this comedy ghost story by John Patrick had "funny lines, good performances, wobbly plot." C: Cloris Leachman, Doro Merande, Paul Crabtree. P: The Theatre Guild. D: Burgess Meredith. CD/SD: Stewart Chaney.

Locked Room, The (12/25/33, Ambassador, 8)

A murder case is solved by a cynical insurance investigator (Walter Gilbert). Skimpy 30's mystery. A: Herbert Ashton, Jr. P: M. S. Schlesinger and William B. Friedlander (D).

Loco (10/16/46, Biltmore, 37)

Philandering businessman is restored to

his family by a model with a heart of gold. ". . . garishly trivial" (*Herald Tribune*). C: Jean Parker (deb.), Jay Fassett, Beverly Bayne, Elaine Stritch (deb.), Parker Fennelly, Morgan Wallace. A: Dale Eunson and Katherine Albert. P/D: Jed Harris.

Lombardi, Ltd. (9/24/17, Morosco, 296)

A dressmaker (Leo Carrillo) is captivated by a gold-digging mannequin who shows her true colors by ditching him for a wealthy broker. Modest comedy by Frederic and Fanny Hatton enjoyed a long and profitable run. C: Warner Baxter, Grace Valentine, Janet Dunbar. P: Oliver Morosco. D: Clifford Brooke.

Long Days, The (4/20/51, Empire, 3)

Badly miscast, poorly directed drama about the domination of a New England family by an iron-willed matriarch. ". . . wordy, shallow and inconclusive" (*Herald Tribune*). C: Frances Starr, Jeffrey Lynn, Katharine Bard, Neva Patterson. A: Davis Snow. P: Tait-Buell. D: Edward Ludlum.

Long Day's Journey Into Night (11/7/56, Hayes, 390)

Eugene O'Neill's four-act autobiographical drama; considered by many critics the finest play ever written by an American. A work, in O'Neill's words, "of old sorrow, written in tears and blood," the play is set in 1912 Connecticut and depicts one day in the life of the ill-starred Tyrone family: James, the father, a miserly matinee idol embittered by the dissipation of his talent; his wife, Mary, hopelessly addicted to morphine; Jamie, the older son, an alcoholic wastrel; and Edmund (the young Eugene O'Neill), a fledgling writer suffering from tuberculosis. The tensions build slowly but inexorably as events of the past are brought out into the open and the recriminations escalate to a shattering, uncompromising, and unforgettable climax. "A masterpiece of understanding, compassion and dark, tormented beauty" (*Post*). "Apart from its power, honesty, wisdom, passion and compassion, the play is a notable example of how an act of personal exorcism—'to face my dead,' as O'Neill put it—can emerge as an enduring work of art" (*Time Magazine*). O'Neill began work on *Long Day's Journey Into Night* in the early summer of 1939, at the age of fifty. He finished it the following year, and placed the manuscript in his publisher's vault with instructions that it not be produced until at least twenty-five years after his death (1953). However, Carlotta Monterey O'Neill, the author's widow, relented and sanctioned the Broadway production in 1956, sixteen years after the play's completion. Superlatively acted, directed, and produced, the four-hour-long drama won both the Pulitzer Prize and the Drama Critics Circle Award as best play of the year. C: Fredric March, Florence Eldridge, Jason Robards, Jr.* Bradford Dillman,* Katharine Ross.* P: Leigh Connell, Theodore Mann, and Jose Quintero (D). CD: Motley. SD: David Hays.

R: (4/21/71, Promenade, 121). C: Robert Ryan, Geraldine Fitzgerald, Stacy Keach, James Naughton, Paddy Craft. D: Arvin Brown.

Note: A London production (1972) featured a cast headed by Laurence Olivier, Constance Cummings, Dennis Quilley and Ronald Pickup.

SV: Embassy, 1962, Katharine Hepburn, Ralph Richardson, Jason Robards, Jr., Dean Stockwell, Jeanne Barr (directed by Sidney Lumet).

---

*Broadway debuts.

Long Dream, The (2/17/60, Ambassador, 5)

Wanting a better life for his boy, a Mississippi black gets mixed up in local graft with corrupt white men. Undistinguished problem play by Ketti Frings* b/o the novel by Richard Wright. C: Lawrence Winters, Al Freeman, Jr., Arthur Storch, R. G. Armstrong, Isabelle Cooley, Clifton James, Barbara Loden, Clarence Williams III, Helen Martin. P: Cheryl Crawford and Joel Schenker i.a.w. October Productions. D: Lloyd Richards.

---

*Novelist-screenwriter (*Hold Back the Dawn, Come Back, Little Sheba, The Shrike*); author of the Pulitzer Prize play *Look Homeward, Angel* (1957).

Long Watch, The (3/20/52, Lyceum, 12)

Comedy-melodrama about wartime WAVES and their problems with a tough lady lieutenant. "A very minor little effort" (*Post*). "The plot is straight Twentieth Century Fox" (*Herald Tribune*). C: Walter Abel, Sonia Sorel, Christine White, Anne Meacham, Carl Betz, Patricia Englund. A: Captain Harvey Haislip and Morrie Ryskind (Mr. Ryskind withdrew his name as coauthor before the Broadway opening). P: Anthony B. Farrell and Charles Coburn. D: John Larson.

Long Way from Home, A (2/8/48, Maxine Elliott's, 6)

Gorki's *The Lower Depths* transferred to the deep South and enacted by an all-black cast; produced by the Experimental Theatre for a limited engagement of six performances. ". . . has about the same daring experimental value as pouring ketchup on beans" (George Jean Nathan). C: William Marshall, Josh White, Ruby Dee, Fredi Washington, Mildred Smith, Maurice Ellis, Harry Bolden, Alonzo Bosan. A: Randolph Goodman and Walter Carroll. D: Alan Schneider.

Look Away (1/7/73, Playhouse, 1)

One of three plays during the '72–73 season about Abraham Lincoln's widow, *Look Away* is a two-character conversation piece between Mary Todd Lincoln and her confidante/companion, Elizabeth Keckley. It is the final night of Mrs. Lincoln's confinement in a mental institution. Awaiting release, she and her friend talk of the past and future, act out bits from scenes they have lived through previously, and occasionally address the audience. The material of the play is largely derived from actual documents: letters, newspapers, and books. The author, Jerome Kilty, using this method in 1960, had greater success adapting the correspondence between George Bernard Shaw and Mrs. Patrick Campbell into the play *Dear Liar*. With *Look Away*, the skill of the players provides the appeal. Aside from informational bits about the President and his lady, there is little that is theatrically effective. A: Jerome Kilty, b/o *Mary Todd Lincoln: Her Life and Letters* by Justin and Linda Turner. C: Geraldine Page, Maya Angelou. P: Charles B. Bloch i.a.w. Burry Fredrik. D: Rip Torn. SD: Ben Edwards. CD: Jane Greenwood.

Look Homeward, Angel (11/28/57, Barrymore, 564)

Splendid adaptation of Thomas Wolfe's epic novel of a North Carolina family dominated by a grasping, narrow-minded, materialistic mother who drives her tormented husband to drink, one son to a premature death, and another son (the prototype of young Thomas Wolfe) to leave her so that he may be "unbeaten and beloved." "One of the finest plays in American dramatic literature" (*Post*). *Look Homeward, Angel* was dramatized by screenwriter Ketti Frings (*Hold Back the Dawn, The Shrike, Come Back, Little Sheba*, etc.), and won both the Pulitzer Prize and the Drama Critics Circle Award as best play of the year. C: Jo Van Fleet, Anthony Perkins, Arthur Hill, Hugh Griffith, Bibi Osterwald, Rosemary Murphy (deb.), Frances Hyland, Arthur

Storch, Florence Sundstrom, Victor Kilian. P: Kermit Bloomgarden and Theatre 200. D: George Roy Hill. CD: Motley. SD: Jo Mielziner.

Look: We've Come Through (10/25/61, Hudson, 5)

Comedy-drama about the sexual coming of age of a plain, shy New York girl and an equally vulnerable lad with a homosexual past. Sensitively staged by Jose Quintero; beautifully acted by Collin Wilcox as the mousy and myopic heroine; Ralph Williams (deb.) as the boy unsure of his masculinity; Burt Reynolds as an ambiguously manly sailor who seduces the boy; Zohra Lampert as the heroine's cynical roommate; Clinton Kimbrough as a would-be cowboy star; and Zack Matalon as a conniving bisexual theatrical agent. "... a quiet and unhurried play ... unfailingly touching, humorous and real" *(Post)*. *Look: We've Come Through* was written by Hugh Wheeler, author of *Big Fish, Little Fish* (1961), and such musicals as *A Little Night Music* and the revised version of *Candide*. P: Saint Subber and Frank Prince i.a.w. David Black. SD: David Hays.

Loose Ankles (8/16/26, Biltmore, 161)

Gigolo answers a marriage ad and falls in love with the pretty heiress who placed the "Object Matrimony" advertisement. Amusing Brock Pemberton (P/D) 20's comedy. C: Harold Vermilyea, Kathleen Comegys, Osgood Perkins, George Barbier. A: Sam Janney.
SV: WB, 1930, Loretta Young, Douglas Fairbanks, Jr., Louise Fazenda.

Loose Moments (2/4/35, Vanderbilt, 8)

Romantic misunderstandings and comic entanglements in a southern mansion where tourists are accommodated. "Interminable" *(New York Times)*. C: Joseph Cotten, Elizabeth Love, Doro Merande. A: Courtenay Savage and Bertram Hobbs. P/D: Walter Hartwig.

Lord Blesses the Bishop, The (11/27/34, Adelphi, 7)

The husband of a busy career woman hires a practical-minded miss to become the mother of his child. Lamentable, clumsily written comedy-drama by Pulitzer Prize-winning author Hatcher Hughes (A/D). C: Claudia Morgan, Wilton Graff, Hugh Rennie. P: Glen McNaughton.

Lord Pengo (11/19/62, Royale, 175)

Comedy-drama about the life and times of 1930's art dealer Sir Joseph Duveen, here called Lord Pengo (Charles Boyer), who finds fame and fortune by selling celebrated paintings to millionaires. "... civilized, graceful, expertly played and almost totally undramatic" *(Post)*. C: Agnes Moorehead, Brian Bedford, Henry Daniell, Ruth White, Reynolds Evans, Lee Richardson, Edmon Ryan, Cliff Hall. A: S. N. Behrman b/o his *New Yorker* series, *The Days of Duveen*. P: Paul Gregory and Amy Lynn i.a.w. Friedlander and Parver. D: Vincent J. Donehue. CD: Lucinda Ballard. SD: Oliver Smith.

Lorenzo (2/14/63, Plymouth, 4)

While touring Italy, a group of strolling players become involved in a minor Renaissance war. "... burns with honest eloquence" *(Post)*. "... a superfluity of rhetoric ... and a modicum of drama" *(New York Times)*. Written by Jack Richardson, author of *The Prodigal* (1960). C: Alfred Drake, Fritz Weaver, David Opatoshu, Carmen Mathews, Robert Drivas, Louise Sorel, William Hansen, Ivor Francis, Herb Edelman. P: Alexander H. Cohen. D: Arthur Penn. CD. Motley. SD: David Hays.

Los Angeles (12/19/27, Hudson, 16)

Broadway gold digger turns a Hollywood studio upside down with her blackmailing tactics. Satire on silent film days never came off. C: Frances Dale, Helen Vinson, Alison Skipworth, Jack LaRue, Harold

Vermilyea. Louis Sorin. A: Max Marcin and Donald Ogden Stewart.* P: George M. Cohan. D: Sam Forrest.

---

*Author of *Rebound* (1930); many film scripts including *The Philadelphia Story*, *Keeper of the Flame*, etc.

Loss of Roses, A (11/28/59, O'Neill, 25)

William Inge's fifth Broadway play and first failure, a period piece set in small-town Missouri in 1933, about the ill-fated affair between a stranded show girl and the twenty-one-year-old son of her best friend. Warren Beatty (deb.) gave an excellent performance as the petulant, unstable son with an unnatural attachment toward his mother (Betty Field in the role vacated by Shirley Booth during the play's pre-New York tryout); Carol Haney (in her dramatic stage debut) played the blowsy, tank town actress who tumbles into the hay with young Mr. Beatty. "A very bad play . . . completely ineffectual" *(Post)*. C: Robert Webber, Michael J. Pollard, Margaret Braidwood, Joan Morgan, James O'Rear. P: Saint Subber and Lester Osterman. D: Daniel Mann. CD: Lucinda Ballard. SD: Boris Aronson. M: Robert Emmett Dolan.
SV: Fox, 1963, *The Stripper*, Joanne Woodward, Richard Beymer, Claire Trevor, Carol Lynley, Robert Webber, Michael J. Pollard, Louis Nye, Gypsy Rose Lee (directed by Franklin Schaffner).

Lost Boy (1/5/32, Mansfield, 15)

Caught in the crossfire between a sympathetic psychiatrist and a bullying superintendent, a reform school inmate (Elisha Cook, Jr.) is goaded into murder and suicide. Glum 1932 melodrama, capably performed by a cast that included Edgar Barrier, Ann Thomas and Jules (John) Garfield. A: T. C. Upham. P: Burton Harfod. D: James Light.

Lost Horizons (10/15/34, St. James, 56)

Provocative fantasy about a young actress (Jane Wyatt) who commits suicide only to learn in the next world that her life held much promise; had she gone on living, she would have been instrumental in helping many individuals whose paths had not yet crossed hers. C: Walter Gilbert, Forrest Orr, Mabel Paige, John Gallaudet, Kathleen Comegys, Kathryn Givney, Arthur Pierson, Vernon Crane. A: Harry Segall, extensively revised by John Hayden (D). P: Rowland Stebbins.

Lottery Man, The (12/6/09, Bijou, 200)

Handsome young fellow offers himself as husband to any woman who holds the lucky number in a lottery. Harum-scarum comedy was highly popular with audiences in 1909. C: Cyril Scott, Janet Beecher, Helen Lowell. A: Rida Johnson Young. P: Messrs. Shubert. D: Edith Ellis.

Loud Red Patrick, The (10/3/56, Ambassador, 93)

Period comedy (Cleveland, 1912) about an overbearing Irish-American widower faced with the problem of raising four daughters, and his attempts to prevent the oldest girl from marrying a lad of whom he does not approve. "Life with O'Father . . . a heart-warming frolic" *(Mirror)*. ". . . . thin as spun candy and just as old-fashioned" *(Herald Tribune)*. C: Arthur Kennedy, David Wayne, James Congdon. A: John Boruff b/o the book by Ruth McKenney. P: Richard W. Krakeur, Robert Douglas (D) and David Wayne. CD/SD: Paul Morrison.

Loud Speaker (3/7/27, 52nd Street, 29)

John Howard Lawson's radical cartoon farce satirizing American politics from the communist point of view. A windbag running for governor of New York gets drunk and tells a nationwide radio audience what he really thinks of them. "A pretentious and humorless piece" (Franklin P. Adams, *The Diary of Our Own Samuel Pepys*). C: Porter Hall, Romney Brent, Margaret Douglass, Leonard Sillman. P: New Playwrights Theatre. D: Harry Wagstaff Gribble.

Louder, Please (11/12/31, Masque, 68)

Fairly diverting comedy about a Hollywood press agent (Lee Tracy) who fakes a lost-at-sea yarn about one of his filmland clients (Louise Brooks). *Louder, Please* was the first play written by young (twenty-two-year-old) Norman Krasna, future Hollywood screenwriter-director and author of such Broadway hits as *Dear Ruth* (1944), *John Loves Mary* (1947), etc. C: Millard Mitchell, Percy Kilbride. P: A. L. Jones. D: George Abbott.

Love and Kisses (12/18/63, Music Box, 13)

Comedy about the domestic problems of teenage newlyweds. "Relentlessly commonplace" *(Post)*. C: Larry Parks, Mary Fickett, Dennis Cooncy, Alberta Grant, Bert Convy, Susan Browning. A: Anita Rowe Block. P: Dore Schary (D) i.a.w. Walter Reilly.

Love 'Em and Leave 'Em (2/3/26, Sam H. Harris, 152)

Two sisters, both working as department store clerks, are rivals for the affections of the same man. In the end, the older girl wins out over the selfish younger one. Sentimental, wisecracking comedy by George Abbott (D) and John V. A. Weaver. C: Florence Johns, Katherine Wilson, Donald MacDonald. Donald Meek, Eda Heinemann. P: Jed Harris.
SV: Par, 1929, *The Saturday Night Kid*, Clara Bow, Jean Arthur, James Hall, Edna May Oliver.
Note: A silent version (Paramount, 1926) featured Evelyn Brent, Louise Brooks, Lawrence Gray, and Osgood Perkins.

Love Goes to Press (1/1/47, Biltmore, 5)

Adventures of a pair of women war correspondents on the Italian front in 1944. "A feeble bedroom comedy without the bedroom" (George Jean Nathan). Written by Martha Gellhorn (the former Mrs. Ernest Hemingway) and Virginia Cowles; enacted in stock company fashion by a generally nondescript cast. P: Munsell and Bernstein. D: Wallace Douglas.

Love, Honor and Betray (3/12/30, Eltinge, 45)

Good cast—Alice Brady, Clark Gable, Wilton Lackaye, George Brent (deb.), Glenda Farrell—in a murky tale set in a cemetery haunted by the ghosts of three men driven to their graves by the same woman. A: Fanny and Frederic Hatton b/o a play by A. Antoine. P: A. H. Woods. D: Don Mullally.

Love in a Mist (4/12/26, Gaiety, 120)

Love among the socialite set in the Blue Ridge Mountains of Virginia. Light triangle piece by Amelie Rives and Gilbert Emery (D). C: Madge Kennedy, Sidney Blackmer, Frieda Inescort, Tom Powers. P: Charles L. Wagner.

Musicalized by Calvin Brown as *Say When* (1928) with Dorothy Fitzgibbons, Bartlett Simmons, Alison Skipworth, Raymond Guion (Gene Raymond).

Love in E-Flat (2/13/67, Atkinson, 24)

A pair of lovers decide to "bug" each other's apartments. Unpleasant comedy by Norman Krasna. C: Hal Buckley, Kathleen Nolan. P: Alfred de Liagre, Jr. D: George Seaton. SD: Donald Oenslager.

Love Is a Time of Day (12/22/69, Music Box, 8)

Wispy romantic comedy of a boy, a girl, and an appealing mongrel dog. The boy and girl are college students. She's a virgin who wants to become a missionary; he is simply on the make. In this two-character exercise in young love, they talk a great deal about sex. She bemoans his lack of genuine feeling, and it is only when he cries over the accidental death of the dog, thus proving his sensitivity, that she falls into his arms. ". . . a moderately decent commercial vehicle . . . Sandy Duncan has a giggle as infectious as the common cold" (Clive Barnes, *New York Times*). ". . . unfunny, uninventive, inaccurate, out-of-date, and stubborn about all of these things" (Walter Kerr, *New York Times*). A: John Patrick.* C: Sandy Duncan, Tom Ligon. D: Bernard Thomas. P: Shepherd Productions. SD/CD: Lloyd Burlingame.

---

*Veteran writer John Patrick has been active in radio, films, and the stage. His plays include *The Curious Savage*, *The Hasty Heart*, and most notably *Teahouse of the August Moon*, for which he won the Pulitzer Prize, the New York Drama Critics Circle Award, and the Tony Award. Among his screenplays are *Love Is a Many Splendored Thing* and *Some Came Running*.

Love Is Like That (4/18/27, Cort, 24)

A Russian prince (Basil Rathbone) becomes involved with a social-climbing widow and a *nouveau riche* New Yorker. Labored comedy by S. N. Behrman and Kenyon Nicholson. ". . . dreary entertainment . . . . Pooling their talents in this light collaboration, these two new dramatists, one suspects, have been of little service to each other" (*New York Times*). C: Catherine Willard, Lucile Watson, Ann Davis, Charles Richman. P: Jones and Green. D: Dudley Digges.

Love Me Little (4/15/58, Hayes, 8)

Tedious comedy about a guileless ingenue and her novelist-father. C: Donald Cook, Joan Bennett, Susan Kohner (deb.), Meg Mundy, Joan Hovis. A: John G. Fuller b/o the novel by Amanda Vail. P: Alexander H. Cohen. D: Alfred Drake. CD: Motley. SD: Ralph Alswang.

Love Me Long (11/7/49, 48th Street, 16)

Divorced couple, about to wed younger mates, rediscover each other. "A five-and-ten-cent replica of *Private Lives*" (*New York Times*). C: Shirley Booth, Anne Jackson, Russell Hardie, George Keane, Harry Bannister, Heywood Hale Broun, Daniel Reed. A: Doris Frankel. P: Brock Pemberton. D: Margaret Perry and Brock Pemberton.

Love Nest, The (12/22/27, Comedy, 25)

A movie magnate's wife, forced to play the perfect homebody, gets drunk, tells the Hollywood crowd what she thinks of them, and runs off with the butler. Surprisingly banal, humorless Robert E. Sherwood comedy b/o Ring Lardner's story of the same name. C: June Walker, Clyde Fillmore, Otto Hulett, Albert Carroll, Paula Trueman. P: Actor-Managers, Inc. i.a.w. Sidney Ross. D: Agnes Morgan.

Love on Leave (6/20/44, Hudson, 7)

Farce about a child psychologist (Millard Mitchell) and his sexually precocious teenage daughter. "The worst play I have ever seen" (*Journal-American*). A: A. B. Shiffrin. P: Stewart and Goodman. D: Eugene S. Bryden.

Lovely Lady (10/14/25, Belmont, 21)

Flirtatious widow tries to break up a happy marriage. Literate comedy-drama by Jesse Lynch Williams. C: Elizabeth Risdon, Lily Cahill, Miriam Hopkins, Bruce McRae. P: Wagenhals and Kemper. D: Collin Kemper.

Lovely Me (12/25/46, Adelphi, 37)

The first and (to date) only play by best-selling novelist Jacqueline Susann. Written in collaboration with actress Beatrice Cole, this 40's comedy dealt with the efforts of a temperamental Russian singer (Luba Malina) to marry the supposedly wealthy manager of a dog-lovers' club, and thus resolve her financial difficulties. The reappearance of two of the lady's former spouses—a flagpole sitter (Mischa Auer) and a theatrical press agent (Millard Mitchell)—temporarily complicate the prima donna's matrimonial plans. ". . . a catalogue of worn jokes, depressing situations and minor obscenities" (*News*). "On excellent authority Jacqueline Susann and Beatrice Cole are said to have gone off to the country and written *Lovely Me* in two weeks' time. At the Adelphi Saturday night I was wondering what on earth they could have done to fill out that fortnight!" (*Journal-American*). P: David Lowe. D: Jessie Royce Landis.

Note: This play was tried out by producer Vinton Freedley under the title, *The Temporary Mrs. Smith*, with Francine Larrimore as star. Freedley abandoned the production in Philadelphia. Recast and retitled, the show braved Broadway a few weeks later as *Lovely Me*. It closed after a month's run.

Lovers, The (5/10/56, Martin Beck, 4)

Darren McGavin and Joanne Woodward (deb.) played leading roles in this lavishly produced costume melodrama revolving around the "droit du seigneur," the medieval custom that permitted the lord of the manor to sleep with the bride of any of his vassals on her wedding night. When the lord refuses to renounce the girl, the peasants revolt. In the ensuing violence, the bride, husband, and lord are killed, and are denied religious burial until a compassionate monk defies his superiors to perform the rites. "An impressive work of art" (*New York Times*). ". . . confused, dramatically ineffectual and given to an unintentional air of pretentiousness" (*Post*). C: Hurd Hatfield, Vivian Nathan, Morris Carnovsky, Mario Alcalde, Bramwell Fletcher, Pernell Roberts, Robert Lansing, Gerald Hiken, Robert Burr. A: Leslie Stevens. P: The Playwrights Company and Gayle Stine. D: Michael Gordon. CD: John Boyt. SD: Charles Elson.

SV: U, 1965, *The War Lord*, Charlton Heston, Richard Boone, Maurice Evans, Rosemary Forsyth, Guy Stockwell, James Farentino (directed by Franklin Schaffner from a screenplay by John Collier and Millard Kaufman).

Lovers' Lane (2/6/01, Manhattan, 127)

A young minister is victimized by his shallow, small-town congregation. Pedestrian comedy-drama by Clyde Fitch (A/D). P: William A. Brady.

Love's Call (9/10/25, 39th Street, 20)

American tourists in Mexico are detained at gunpoint by a villainous bandit. "The masterpiece of bad plays" (Brooks Atkinson). This dramaturgical tortilla was written, produced, and directed by one Joe Byron Totten. To protect the innocent, the actors (all unknowns) will not be listed here.

Love's Old Sweet Song (5/2/40, Plymouth, 44)

William Saroyan's fable about the chance meeting between a smooth-talking con man (Walter Huston) and a befuddled spinster (Jessie Royce Landis). Their subsequent romance is threatened when the Yearlings, a family of sixteen Okies, take possession of the spinster's home, but love triumphs in the end. Crowded with frequently beguiling but irrelevant characters and incidents, this 1940 comedy lasted but briefly on Broadway. "A series of fragments from a torn surrealistic valentine . . ." (John Mason Brown, *Post*). ". . . the most delightfully contagious theatre evening that I have spent in a long time" (Stark Young, *New Republic*). C: Arthur Hunnicutt, Doro Merande, Peter Fernandez, Howard Freeman, Alan Reed, Alan Hewitt, Beatrice Newport, Lloyd Gough, James S.

Elliott. P: The Theatre Guild i.a.w. Eddie Dowling. D: William Saroyan and Eddie Dowling. M: Paul Bowles. SD: Watson Barratt.

Note: In a letter to this editor, William Saroyan noted that *Love's Old Sweet Song* was his favorite play. When asked why, he replied simply: "I like it most."

Low Bridge (2/9/33, 57th Street, 3)

Leisurely, seriocomic account of life in the 1800's along the Erie Canal. This experimental production with a no-name cast was adapted by Frank B. Elser from Walter D. Edmonds' novel, *Rome Haul*. Following its brief three-performance O/B run, Marc Connelly was called in as coauthor to doctor the script and restructure the play which premiered on Broadway the following year (1934) as *The Farmer Takes a Wife*. It was a hit and, in the leading role, Henry Fonda scored his first success on stage and, subsequently, on screen in the film version. P: The Players Theatre. D: William J. O'Neill.

Lower North (8/25/44, Belasco, 11)

Aimless comedy-drama about life in a naval training station. ". . . painfully trite" *(PM)*. C: Arthur Hunnicutt, Dort Clark, Rusty Lane, Paul Ford. A: Martin Bidwell. P: Max Jelin. D: David Burton.

Lucky Break, A (8/11/25, Cort, 23)

To test the loyalty of his friends, a millionaire (George MacFarlane) feigns bankruptcy. "A mild little comedy" *(New York Times)*. C: Lucille Sears, Louise Galloway. A: Zelda Sears. P: American Producing Company.

Musicalized by DeLeon, Levey and Murphy as *Rainbow Rose* (1926) with Jack Whiting, Jack Squire and Louise Galloway.

Lucky Sam McCarver (10/21/25, Playhouse, 30)

An ambitious speakeasy owner uses people callously in his climb to the top. His self-indulgent socialite wife leaves him only to die of a heart attack shortly thereafter. Talky 20's fable written and directed by Sidney Howard. C: John Cromwell, Clare Eames, Rose Hobart, James Bell. P: William A. Brady, Jr. and Dwight Deere Wiman i.a.w. John Cromwell.

Lullaby (2/3/54, Lyceum, 45)

When a thirty-eight-year-old mama's boy (Jack Warden) suddenly elopes with a cigarette girl (Kay Medford), his doting mother (Mary Boland) does everything in her power to break up the match. "The comedy tends to run downhill after a brawling first act [but] the acting is wonderful" *(New York Times)*. A: Don Appell. P: Jerome Mayer (D) and Irl Mowery i.a.w. Toby Ruby.

Lullaby, The (9/17/23, Knickerbocker, 148)

The sin of Madelon Claudet (Florence Reed) was to bear a child out of wedlock. From there it was downhill all the way until poor Madelon became a painted harlot walking the dingy sidestreets of Paris. This hoary fable pulled out all the emotional stops in unabashed tearjerker fashion; matinee audiences sniffed appreciatively and, a few years later, the film version (see below) won an Academy Award for Helen Hayes in her screen debut. C: Frank Morgan, Rose Hobart, Charles Trowbridge. A: Edward Knoblock. P: Charles Dillingham. D: Fred Latham.

SV: MGM, 1931, *The Sin of Madelon Claudet*, Helen Hayes, Lewis Stone, Robert Young, Jean Hersholt, Karen Morley, Neil Hamilton, Charles Winninger, Cliff Edwards, Marie Prevost, Alan Hale, Halliwell Hobbes, Frankie Darro.

Lulu Belle (2/9/26, Belasco, 461)

A tempestuous Harlem harlot (Lenore

Lulu Belle. **Street scene (February 9, 1926).** *Courtesy Museum of the City of New York Theatre and Music Collection.*

Ulric in sepia makeup) claws her way to the top of the oldest profession only to be choked to death by a jealous ex-lover (Henry Hull). Lurid, *Carmen*-like melodrama, written by Edward Sheldon and Charles MacArthur, and staged in gaudy, picture-book fashion by David Belasco (P/D). Its steamy subject matter, vivid settings, and enormous cast (nineteen whites, ninety-three blacks) helped make *Lulu Belle* a solid hit with sensation-seeking playgoers. The Negro community was outraged, however, and called the production a libel on the black race. Which it was.

SV: Col, 1948, Dorothy Lamour, George Montgomery, Otto Kruger, Glenda Farrell, Albert Dekker.

Lunatics and Lovers (12/13/54, Broadhurst, 336)

Buddy Hackett made his Broadway debut in this raffish farce written, directed, and coproduced by Pulitzer Prize playwright Sidney Kingsley, author of *Men in White* (1933), *Dead End* (1935), *Detective Story* (1949), etc. Hackett played Dan Cupid, a shady Broadway character who works hard at turning a dishonest dollar. With the law breathing down his neck, and in need of legal advice, Cupid invites an alcoholic judge (Dennis King) to a wild party in his fleabag hotel room. Before the evening is over, a drunken brawl has broken out, a philandering husband has been reconciled with his estranged wife, and Dan Cupid finds himself engaged to a well-heeled call girl, and his troubles with the cops resolved—at least for the moment. "A rowdy and dynamic sex farce [but] too much of it is pretty laborious" (*Post*). C: Sheila Bond, Mary Anderson, Arthur O'Connell, Vicki Cummings, Nat Cantor. P: M. Kirshner. SD: Frederick Fox.

Lure, The (8/14/13, Maxine Elliott's 132)

Lurid white slavery epic set in a palatial bordello. Strictly dime-novel stuff. C: Mary Nash, Vincent Serrano. A: George

Scarborough. P: Messrs. Shubert. D: J. C. Huffman.

Luv (11/11/64, Booth, 901)

Seeking to end his miserable existence, Harry Berlin (Alan Arkin) prepares to jump off a bridge. Milt Manville (Eli Wallach), an old friend and former classmate, intervenes. But Milt, prosperous and assured though he seems, has his own problems: his wife Ellen (Anne Jackson) won't divorce him so that he can marry the woman he loves. Milt's plan for ending everyone's frustration is to spruce Ellen up, palm her off on Harry, and then wed the girl of his dreams. The plan works only too well. A few months later, however, Milt and Ellen want to shed their respective second mates and return to their original conjugal state. Having once saved Harry from suicide, Milt must now try to murder him. "Continuously uproarious . . . indescribably funny" (*Post*). This zany spoof of the romantic triangle play also satirized a wide variety of themes—alienation, despair, tangled sexual relationships—dear to the heart of avant-garde writers. Staged with great comic flair and inventiveness by Mike Nichols, and acted to perfection by its trio of stars, *Luv* won unstinting praise from all the New York critics. This three-character comedy hit marked the Broadway debut of dramatist Murray Schisgal. P: Claire Nichtern. CD: Theoni V. Aldredge. SD: Oliver Smith.

SV: Col, 1967, Jack Lemmon, Peter Falk, Elaine May, Eddie Mayehoff, Paul Hartman (directed by Clive Donner).

M

MacBird! (2/22/67, Village Gate, 386)

Controversial O/B updating of Shakespeare's *Macbeth,* focusing on the violent conflict between Lyndon B. Johnson and Robert Kennedy following John F. Kennedy's assassination. ". . . brutally provocative . . . grimly amusing" (*New York Times*). C: Stacy Keach, William Devane, Rue McClanahan, Cleavon Little (deb.). A: Barbara Garson. P: John Curtis. D: Roy Levine. CD: Jeanne Button. SD: Clarke Dunham.

Machinal (9/7/28, Plymouth, 93)

A young woman (Zita Johann) meets a man (Clark Gable) in a speakeasy, kills her businessman-husband for the sake of her new love, and is tried and executed for her sin. Suggested by the sensational Snyder-Gray murder trial, author Sophie Treadwell offered the case as an example of how a machine-dominated society can corrupt and ultimately destroy the individual. Written in terse, staccato dialogue, with impressionistic settings by Robert Edmond Jones, *Machinal* captured the image of a drab, mechanistic nightmare world with stunning effectiveness. The play provided then-unknown Clark Gable with his best legitimate theatre role. (His salary was seventy-five dollars a week.) Arthur Hopkins (P/D) on Gable: "He had played in stock companies and had tried unsuccessfully to get into the movies. He had decided to try New York. I gave him the lead opposite Miss Johann. He played it beautifully."

Machinal was revived (4/7/60) for 79 performances at the Gate Theatre. The two leading roles were excellently enacted by Dolores Sutton and Vincent Gardenia. Gene Frankel directed the O/B production.

Mackerel Skies (1/23/34, Playhouse, 23)

Synthetic tale of a jealous socialite-mother who tries to thwart her daughter's operatic career. C: Violet Kemble Cooper, Carol Stone, Tom Powers, Cora Witherspoon. A: John Haggart. P: George Bushar i.a.w. John Tuerk. D: John Roche.

Mad Hopes, The (12/1/32, Broadhurst, 12)

Story of a feather-brained matron and her irresponsible, impecunious children. Daffy comedy was written by actor Romney Brent as a vehicle for Billie Burke, who relinquished the leading role after the west coast tryout. C: Violet Kemble Cooper, Jane Wyatt, Rex O'Malley, Harry Ellerbe. P/D: Bela Blau.

Madam, Will You Walk (12/1/53, Phoenix, 48)

Sidney Howard's posthumous comedy on the Faust theme in which the Prince of Darkness (Hume Cronyn) is portrayed as an amiable fellow who sets out to bring a touch of romance into the life of a shy and lonely heiress (Jessica Tandy). In the process, he finds that he has made her "unreasonably irresistible" to himself. The girl, however, prefers to settle down with a mortal, and the mysterious stranger goes on his way. "... a gay, ironic, inventive fantasy ..." (*New York Times*). C: Norman Lloyd, Robert Emmett, Leon Janney, Susan Steell, Edwin Jerome, John Randolph. P: Phoenix Theatre. D: Cronyn and Lloyd. SD: Donald Oenslager.

Note: This was the first production of New York's Phoenix Theatre, founded by Norris Houghton and T. Edward Hambleton. The play had originally been produced in the fall of 1939 with George M. Cohan, Arthur Kennedy, Peggy Conklin, Sara Allgood, and Keenan Wynn in the cast. The production—directed by Margaret Webster with settings by Robert Edmond Jones and music by Kurt Weill—was withdrawn after brief tryouts in Baltimore and Washington. *Madam, Will You Walk* was the last play written by Sidney Howard, one of America's foremost playwrights (*They Knew What They Wanted, The Silver Cord, Yellow Jack, Dodsworth,* etc.). Howard's major Hollywood contribution was the script of *Gone With The Wind*. He died in an accident on his farm during the summer of 1939.

Madame Butterfly (3/5/00, Herald Square, 24)

Skillful dramatization by David Belasco (Ad./P/D) of John Luther Long's short story of the tragic love of Cho-Cho-San (Blanche Bates) for Lieut. Pinkerton (Frank Worthing). Giacomo Puccini was present at the London first night of *Madame Butterfly* and immediately realized its operatic possibilities. The first performance at La Scala was a fiasco. Revised by the composer, the opera scored a triumph on its second hearing. Within two years *Madame Butterfly* was in the standard repertory of every opera house in the world.

SV: Belasco's play (minus the Puccini score) was filmed by Paramount (1932) with Sylvia Sidney, Cary Grant, Charles Ruggles.

Madame Capet (10/25/38, Cort, 7)

Poorly produced, badly miscast biographical drama dealing with the life—and death—of Marie Antoinette (Eva Le Gallienne). The producer ran out of funds. Consequently, the closing notice was posted at the final dress rehearsal before the New York opening. C: George Coulouris, William Post, Jr., Anne Baxter, Merle Maddern, Staats Cotsworth, Blanche Ring, Frederic Tozere. A: George Middleton b/o a play by Marcelle Maurette. P: Eddie Dowling. D: Jose Ruben.

Madame Sand (11/19/17, Criterion, 64)

Romantic comedy-drama dealing with the tempestuous George Sand (Mrs. Fiske), her love affairs with Chopin and de Musset, her friendship with Liszt and Heine, and her fervent belief in equal rights for women. A witty and literate play, splendidly acted by Mrs. Fiske. C: Ferdinand Gottschalk, Jose Ruben, Walter Kingsford. A: Philip Moeller. P: Tyler, Klaw, and Erlanger. D: Arthur Hopkins.

Made in Heaven! (10/24/46, Henry Miller, 92)

Marital misunderstandings in suburbia. "A hobbling and flagging comedy" (*Sun*). C: Donald Cook, Carmen Mathews, Katharine Bard, Lawrence Fletcher, Ann Thomas. A: Hagar Wilde. P: John Golden. D: Martin Manulis.

Madeleine and the Movies (3/6/22, Gaiety, 80)

Weak George M. Cohan (A/P/D) melodramatic farce about a naïve girl (Georgette Cohan) who falls in love with a handsome screen idol (James Rennie).

Maggie Pepper (8/31/11, Harris, 147)

A department store clerk (Rose Stahl) mistakes the youthful proprietor of the store for a salesman, shows him how to run the store more efficiently, wins a coveted position and a new career. Pleasant comedy by Charles Klein.
Musicalized by Werner Janssen as *Letty Pepper* (1922) with Charlotte Greenwood.

Maggie the Magnificent (10/21/29, Cort, 32)

The performances of James Cagney and Joan Blondell, two then-unknowns, were the chief plus-factors in this humdrum tragi-comedy by George Kelly (A/D). The story dealt with a vulgar mother who makes life impossible for her sensitive daughter (Shirley Warde). Eventually, the girl leaves home for more congenial surroundings. *Maggie the Magnificent* closed after a brief four-week run in New York. P: Laurence Rivers, Inc.

Magic and the Loss, The (4/9/54, Booth, 27)

Problems of a Madison Avenue divorcée trying to compete as an equal in a man's world and, at the same time, fulfill her duties as a mother. In the end, the career woman loses both her son and her lover, but wins a promotion in her advertising agency. Generally tepid reviews greeted this quietly understated domestic drama. However, the cast—Uta Hagen as the unhappy heroine, Robert Preston as her ex-husband, Lee Bowman as her sleekly opportunistic lover—won praise for their performances. A: Julian Funt. P: Alexander H. Cohen and Ralph Alswang (SD). D: Michael Gordon.

Magic Touch, The (9/3/47, International, 12)

Forties comedy about a young married couple struggling to get by on $28.50 a week. "Without a germ of merit in any department" (George Jean Nathan). C: William Terry, Sara Anderson, Howard Smith, Hope Emerson, Carleton Carpenter. A: Charles Raddock and Charles Sherman. P: John Morris Chanin. D: Herman Rotsten.

Magnificent Yankee, The (1/22/46, Royale, 160)

Three decades in the lives of Justice Oliver Wendell Holmes (Louis Calhern) and his devoted wife (Dorothy Gish), from Holmes' arrival in Washington at the age of sixty-one to his retirement from the Supreme Court at age ninety-two. This leisurely, episodic biographical drama spanned the period from Theodore Roosevelt's presidency to Franklin D. Roosevelt's inauguration, and included among its characters Henry Adams, Owen Wister, and Justice Louis Brandeis. A: Emmet Lavery. P/D: Arthur Hopkins.
SV: MGM, 1950, Louis Calhern, Ann Harding, Eduard Franz.

Magnolia (8/27/23, Liberty, 40)

In pre-Civil War days, a young Southerner (Leo Carrillo) is considered a coward because he refuses to fight a duel. Eventually he gains a "killing" reputation at gambling and returns a hero to the old plantation. Languorous comedy by Booth Tarkington based on his novel, *The Fighting Coward*. C: Malcolm Williams, Elizabeth Patterson. P: Alfred E. Aarons. D: Ira Hards.
SV: Par, 1929, *River of Romance*, Buddy Rogers, Wallace Beery, Mary Brian; 1935, *Mississippi*, Bing Crosby, W. C. Fields, Joan Bennett.

Magnolia Alley (4/18/49, Mansfield, 8)

Romantic complications in a southern boarding house. Tawdry, sniggering sex comedy with a good cast: Jessie Royce Landis, Julie Harris, Jackie Cooper (deb.), Anne Jackson, Bibi Osterwald, Fred Stewart Frances Bavier, Hildy

Parks. A: George Batson. P: Lester Cutler. D: Carl Shain.

Mahogany Hall (1/17/34, Bijou, 22)

Pianist in a house of prostitution spurns the advances of the madam for whom he tickles the ivories each night. Bottom-of-the-barrel exhibit. C: Eduardo Ciannelli (D), Olga Baclanova. A: Charles Robinson. P: John R. Sheppard, Jr.

Maid in the Ozarks (7/15/46, Belasco, 103)

Billed as "the worst play in the world," this hillbilly farce played 86 weeks in Los Angeles and 62 weeks in Chicago before it reached Broadway. Thirteen straggling weeks (at cut-rate prices) was all the exhibit could muster in New York, and then it took to the hills. To recount the half-wit plot, or list the names of cast members trapped in this odoriferous curio, would constitute a waste of the typesetter's (and reader's) valuable time. A: Claire Parrish. P/D: Jules Pfeiffer.

Main Street (10/5/21, National, 86)

Problems of a small town doctor's wife. Competent but uninspired dramatization of Sinclair Lewis' novel. C: Alma Tell, McKay Morris. A: Harvey O'Higgins and Harriet Ford. P: Messrs. Shubert.
SV: WB, 1936, *I Married a Doctor,* Pat O'Brien, Josephine Hutchinson, Guy Kibbee, Ross Alexander.
Note: A silent version of *Main Street* (WB, 1923) starred Florence Vidor.

Major Andre (11/11/03, Savoy, 12)

Sympathetic study of the British soldier who negotiated with Benedict Arnold for the betrayal of West Point and was hanged as a spy. *Major Andre* was a departure in style for "drawing-room dramatist" Clyde Fitch (A/D), one of the most prolific and successful playwrights of his time. At one point in his career, Fitch had five plays running simultaneously on Broadway—a feat no other playwright has ever matched. Fitch's stage royalties averaged $250,000 a year in an era of no taxes. *Major Andre* was a failure; it remained Clyde Fitch's favorite of all his plays. C: Arnold Daly, Arthur Byron, Guy Bates Post, Dodson Mitchell, Ernest Lawford, Thomas Meighan, Frank McIntyre, Wallace Eddinger, Chrystal Herne, Mrs. Thomas Whiffen. P: Frank McKee.

Major Pendennis (10/26/16, Criterion, 76)

A worldly uncle (John Drew) presides over the love affairs of his callow nephew. Skillful dramatization by Langdon Mitchell of Thackeray's novel set in Victorian England. C: Brandon Tynan, Alison Skipworth, Helen Menken, Helen MacKellar, Walter Kingsford, Lester Lonergan. P: John D. Williams. D: B. Iden Payne.

Majority of One, A (2/16/59, Shubert, 556)

When a Jewish matron (Gertrude Berg) falls in love with a Japanese widower (Cedric Hardwicke), her daughter (Ina Balin) and disapproving son-in-law (Michael Tolan) almost succeed in wrecking the affair. ". . . a splendidly cornfed comedy . . . it's delicious" (*Herald Tribune*). C: Mae Questel, Barnard Hughes. A: Leonard Spigelgass. P: The Theatre Guild and Dore Schary (D). CD: Motley. SD: Donald Oenslager.
SV: WB, 1961, Rosalind Russell, Alec Guinness, Ray Danton, Madlyn Rhue, Mae Questel (directed by Mervyn LeRoy).

Make a Million (10/23/58, Playhouse, 308)

Formula farce about the problems of a harried TV quiz show producer (Sam Levene) when he discovers that his prize contestant is pregnant without benefit of clergy. A: Norman Barasch and Carroll Moore. P: Spector and Harris. D: Jerome Chodorov.

Make Way for Lucia (12/22/48, Cort, 29)

Mild comedy of manners about the battle between two women for social supremacy in a small English town in 1912. C: Isabel Jeans, Catherine Willard, Cyril Ritchard, Philip Tonge, Kurt Kasznar, Viola Roache. A/D: John Van Druten, b/o the *Lucia* novels of E. F. Benson. P: The Theatre Guild. CD/SD: Lucinda Ballard.

Make Yourself at Home (9/13/45, Barrymore, 4)

Fading film star tries for Broadway comeback. "... vintage sheepdip...." *(PM)*. C: Bernadene Hayes, Philip Houston. A: Vera Mathews. P: Albert Chapereau and Johnnie Walker (D).

Malcolm (1/11/66, Shubert, 7)

Edward Albee's black comedy about the death of innocence in contemporary society. Adapted from James Purdy's novel, this bizarre allegorical fable deals with the misadventures of a pure-in-heart teenager who sets out to explore life, is corrupted by everyone he meets, and ultimately degraded and destroyed by the wickedness of the world. *Malcolm* was attacked by the critics as "feverishly disorganized [and] virulently anti-feminist," and closed after seven performances. Song: "Hot in the Rocker" by William Flanagan and Edward Albee. C: Estelle Parsons, Ruth White, Matthew Cowles, Henderson Forsythe, John Heffernan, Wyman Pendleton. P: Barr and Wilder. D: Alan Schneider. SD: William Ritman.

Male Animal, The (1/9/40, Cort, 243)

James Thurber and Elliott Nugent, two Ohio State alumni (class of 1920), wrote this uproarious 1940 comedy dealing with campus politics, academic freedom, and the eternal battle of the sexes. The play reached its high-water mark in Act Two when the mild-mannered English professor (played by coauthor Nugent) finally turns on his tormentors who are shouting "Red!" because he wants to read a letter to his class written by Vanzetti, while an ex-football hero threatens his domestic tranquility. Fortifying his courage with alcohol, he launches into a wonderfully disjointed account of the ferocity of penguins, swans, and bull elephants defending their mates. Result: one of the funniest drunk scenes ever written. "It dismisses you from the theatre in a state of dazed hilarity" *(New York Times)*. C: Elliott Nugent, Leon Ames, Ruth Matteson, Don DeFore, Gene Tierney, Matt Briggs, Ivan Simpson, Amanda Randolph. P/D: Herman Shumlin. SD: Aline Bernstein. (The west coast tryout of *The Male Animal* featured a cast headed by Myron McCormick, Mary Astor, Leon Ames and J. C. Nugent).

R: (4/30/52, City Center, 313) by John Golden. C: Elliott Nugent, Martha Scott, Robert Preston, John Gerstad, Matt Briggs, Halliwell Hobbes, Eulabelle Moore. D: Michael Gordon.

SV: WB, 1942, Henry Fonda, Olivia de Havilland, Jack Carson, Joan Leslie, Don DeFore, Eugene Pallette; 1952, *She's Working Her Way Through College*, Ronald Reagan, Virginia Mayo, Gene Nelson, Don DeFore, Phyllis Thaxter.

Note: James Thurber was pleased by the acclaim accorded his first playwriting effort, but admitted that he found the whole experience more than a little unnerving: "After you have worked on nothing but dialogue for five months, you wonder if you can ever learn to write straight English prose again, the kind that comes in paragraphs and looks so nice...."

Mamba's Daughters (1/3/39, Empire, 162)

Ethel Waters made an auspicious acting debut as Hagar, a vengeful illiterate, in this melodramatic tale of three generations of Charleston Negroes. The climax of the play comes when an evil gambler rapes her daughter. Hagar kills him and then herself. The play also traces the misadventures of "Saint" Wentworth (Jose Ferrer), member of a moribund patrician family, and Mamba (Georgette Harvey), Hagar's mother, an amiable negress attached to the Wentworths. *Mamba's Daughters* was adapted by Dorothy and DuBose Heyward from Mr. Heyward's novel of the same name. Song: "Lonesome Walls" by Jerome Kern (lyrics by DuBose Heyward). C: Canada Lee, Anne Brown, Helen Dowdy, Georgia Burke, J. Rosamond Johnson, Willie Bryant, Alberta Hunter, Fredi Washington, Reginald Beane. P/D: Guthrie McClintic.

Mamma's Affair (1/19/20, Little, 98)

A hypochondriacal mother (Effie Shannon) tries to marry her neurasthenic daughter to the son of her best friend, but the girl chooses a doctor instead. Typical 20's domestic comedy. A: Rachel Barton Butler. P: Oliver Morosco.

Man, The (1/19/50, Fulton, 92)

A psychopathic handyman terrifies a lonely widow. "A superior thriller" (*Herald Tribune*). ". . . reminiscent of *Kind Lady* with *Night Must Fall* overtones, but not nearly so good as either of those thrillers" (*Mirror*). C: Dorothy Gish, Don Hanmer, Peggy Ann Garner, Richard Boone, Robert Emhardt. A: Mel Dinelli. P: Kermit Bloomgarden. D: Martin Ritt. SD: Jo Mielziner.
SV: RKO, 1952, *Beware, My Lovely*, Ida Lupino, Robert Ryan, Taylor Holmes (directed by Harry Horner).

Man Bites Dog (4/25/33, Lyceum, 7)

Assorted shenanigans in the newsroom of *The Daily Tab*. Silly newspaper farce. C: Leo Donnelly, Dennie Moore, Raymond Walburn, Millard Mitchell, Martin Gabel (deb.), Horace MacMahon, Don Beddoe, Victor Kilian. A: Don Lochbiler and Arthur Barton (D). P: Bamberger and Klawans.

Man from Cairo, The (5/4/38, Broadhurst, 21)

Clerk poses as boulevardier. Lethargic 30's comedy produced by Michael Todd. C: Joseph Buloff, Helen Chandler, Viola Roache. A: Dan Goldberg b/o a play by Yvan Noe. D: Harry Wagstaff Gribble.

Man from Home, The (8/17/08, Astor, 496)

A homespun Hoosier lawyer (William Hodge) travels to Sorrento to save his ward from marriage to a fortune-hunting aristocrat. Jingoistic, flag-waving, enormously popular Booth Tarkington-Harry Leon Wilson comedy. P: Liebler and Company. D: Hugh Ford.

Man in the Dog Suit, The (10/30/58, Coronet, 36)

An ineffectual bank clerk discovers he can assert himself only while wearing a masquerade party dog costume. "A pallid fable" (*World-Telegram*). C: Hume Cronyn, Jessica Tandy, Carmen Mathews, Clinton Sundberg, Kathleen Comegys, John McGovern, Tom Carlin. A: Albert Beich and William H. Wright b/o a novel by Edwin Corle. P: The Producers Theatre. D: Ralph Nelson. SD: Donald Oenslager.

Man Inside, The (11/11/13, Criterion, 63)

Well-intentioned but tedious David Belasco (P/D) prison reform drama. Written by Roland Burnham Molineux, a convicted murderer awaiting execution on death row in Sing Sing prison. C: Milton Sills, Charles Dalton, Byron Beasley, A. E. Anson, Helen Freeman.

Man of the Hour, The (12/4/06, Savoy, 479)

Idealistic New York City mayor successfully bucks corrupt political machine. Lively George Broadhurst melodrama. C: George Fawcett, Douglas Fairbanks, Frederick Perry. P: William A. Brady and Joseph R. Grismer.

Man of the People, A (9/7/20, Bijou, 15)

The final year in the life of Abraham Lincoln (Howard Hall). Poor biographical drama by Baptist clergyman Thomas Dixon (A/P), author of *The Clansman* (1906), upon which D. W. Griffith based his epochal silent film, *The Birth of a Nation*. D: Augustin Duncan.

Man on Stilts, The (9/9/31, Plymouth, 6)

Construction worker embarks upon a cross-country walking tour, is turned into a nationally publicized character by an alcoholic reporter. Slapdash satirical farce produced and directed by Arthur Hopkins. C: Hobart Cavanaugh, Harry Ellerbe, Eda Heinemann, Harold Kennedy, Jack Daniels, Lillian Emerson. A: Edwin and Albert Barker.

Man Who Came Back, The (9/2/16, Playhouse, 457)

The spoiled son of a New York millionaire falls in love with a San Francisco cabaret singer, is shanghaied on a vessel bound for China, and, after the requisite amount of *Sturm und Drang*, finally proves himself a man. This highly popular melodrama of romance and regeneration was written by Jules Eckert Goodman, co-author of the *Potash and Perlmutter* (1913) comedy series, *Many Mansions* (1937), etc. C: Henry Hull, Mary Nash, Ernest Lawford, Charlotte Granville. P: William A. Brady. D: John Cromwell. SV: Fox, 1931, Janet Gaynor, Charles Farrell.

Man Who Came to Dinner, The (10/16/39, Music Box, 739)

International literary celebrity Sheridan Whiteside (Monty Woolley) slips on some ice on an Ohio family's doorstep and becomes an unwilling and unwelcome invalid guest, with the entire household at his viper-tongued mercy. "The comedy of insult reaches a high peak of merriment" *(Herald Tribune)*. Moss Hart and George S. Kaufman (D) based this 1939 comedy hit on the well-publicized eccentricities of their friend and boon companion, Alexander Woollcott, raconteur, essayist, and critic. It was even dedicated to him by the authors, "For reasons that are nobody's business." When Woollcott refused to play the leading role on Broadway (a decision he later admitted regretting), former Yale professor Monty Woolley was engaged to impersonate Whiteside, one of the longest and most demanding character roles ever written. After a somewhat shaky start on opening night, the hitherto unknown actor hit his stride and gave, in the words of *World-Telegram* critic Sidney B. Whipple, "one of the truly great comic performances of our times." *The Man Who Came to Dinner* was successfully performed by Clifton Webb, Robert Morley, and Alexander Woollcott (who changed his mind after the Broadway opening and decided that he couldn't wait to play himself onstage), but the role of Sheridan Whiteside belongs, indisputably and forever, to Monty Woolley. C: Edith Atwater, Carol Goodner, John Hoysradt, David Burns, Mary Wickes, Ruth Vivian, Theodore Newton, Mrs. Priestly Morrison. P: Sam H. Harris. SD: Donald Oenslager. Song: "What Am I to Do?" by Cole Porter. Musicalized by James Lipton and Laurence Rosenthal as *Sherry!* (1967) with Clive Revill, Dolores Gray,

Elizabeth Allen, Jon Cypher, Paula Trueman.
Note: The Man Who Came to Dinner was a phenomenal summer stock money-maker. An especially interesting production was that offered at the Bucks County Playhouse in the summer of 1940. George S. Kaufman played the role of Sheridan Whiteside, while Moss Hart took the part of Beverly Carlton, the Noel Coward-like playwright. They were supported by Harpo Marx—speaking lines for the first time in twenty-five years—as the frenetic and happily demented Banjo.
SV: WB, 1942, Monty Woolley, Bette Davis, Ann Sheridan, Jimmy Durante, Billie Burke, Reginald Gardiner, Laura Hope Crews, Grant Mitchell, Richard Travis, Elisabeth Fraser, George Barbier, Mary Wickes.

Man Who Had All the Luck, The (11/23/44, Forrest, 4)

This first play by twenty-nine-year-old Arthur Miller was a disastrous four-performance failure; no major American dramatist has had a less promising Broadway baptism. The diffuse and cluttered plot of this 1944 comedy-drama centers around a small-town garage mechanic upon whom fate never fails to smile. Everything he does turns out right. Convinced that it's only a matter of time before his luck runs out, he starts worrying about retribution. In the end, the title character finally realizes that his continued good fortune is merely the result of lifelong diligence, foresight, and hard work—the moral being that a man's luck is what he makes it. ". . . incredibly turbid in its writing and stuttering in its execution" *(Herald Tribune)*. "If the play held me in my seat for three interminable acts, it was largely out of incredulity" *(The New Yorker)*. C: Karl Swenson, Herbert Berghof, Dudley Sadler, Lawrence Fletcher, Eugenia Rawls, Forrest Orr. P: Herbert H. Harris. D: Joseph Fields.

Man Who Killed Lincoln, The (1/17/40, Longacre, 5)

Atrociously acted, ineptly written historical drama about the life and times of John Wilkes Booth. ". . . reduces Booth to the status of a man who was even worse as an actor than he was misguided as a conspirator. Had the real Booth been given to such attitudinizings, cape-swingings, leg-twirlings, lock-pullings, eye-rollings, and space-clutchings he would no doubt have been mercifully barred admittance to Ford's Theatre" *(Post)*. C: Richard Waring, Sam Byrd, Whitford Kane, Charles Keane, Joseph Kramm, Horace (Stephen) McNally. A: Elmer Harris b/o a book by Philip Van Doren Stern. P: Joseph M. Gaites. D: Felix Brentano.

Man Who Never Died, The (11/21/58, Jan Hus, 125)

O/B drama dealing with Joe Hill (Mark Gordon), the celebrated I.W.W. labor leader who was executed in 1915 for a murder he did not commit. ". . . a naïve and maudlin . . . rabble-rousing labor play" *(New York Times)*. A: Barrie Stavis. P: Irving Strouse. D: Robert Mayberry. SD: John Robert Lloyd.

Man Who Reclaimed His Head, The (9/8/32, Broadhurst, 28)

A pacifist (Claude Rains) is driven mad by his faithless wife (Jean Arthur), who becomes the mistress of a war-profiteering publisher. When the publisher betrays his hopes for peace on the eve of World War I, the pacifist murders him. Murky drama; a virtuoso performance by Rains. A: Jean Bart. P: Hammerstein and Weber. D: Herbert Biberman.
SV: U, 1935, Claude Rains, Joan Bennett, Lionel Atwill.

Man with Blond Hair, The (11/4/41, Belasco, 7)

Norman Krasna (A/D) melodrama about an escaped Nazi aviator trapped in a Jewish tenement flat in Manhattan. "A farrago of incompetence, tastelessness and absurdity" (PM). "The Rover Boys Play Hitler" *(Journal-American)*. C: Rex Williams, Eleanor Lynn, Dora Weissman, Alfred Ryder, James Gregory. P: Frank Ross. SD: Howard Bay.

Mandingo (5/22/61, Lyceum, 8)

Lurid melodrama of miscegenation and incest on a slave-breeding Alabama plantation in 1832. C: Franchot Tone, Dennis Hopper (deb.), Brooke Hayward (deb.), Coley Wallace (deb.), Georgia Burke. A: Jack Kirkland* b/o the novel by Kyle Onstott. P: Baxter and Friedman. D: Louis MacMillan. SD: Frederick Fox.

---

*Author of the play *Tobacco Road* (1933).

SV: Par, 1975, James Mason, Susan George, Perry King (directed by Richard Fleischer from a screenplay by Norman Wexler).

Manhattan (8/15/22, Playhouse, 89)

Middle-aged writer falls in love with his young secretary. Pallid comedy by Henry Hull and Leighton Osmun. (*Accent On Youth*, 1934, later made use of much the same plot). C: Norman Trevor, Marguerite Maxwell, Helen Gahagan (deb.), Raymond Walburn, Hilda Spong. P/D: John Cromwell.

Manhattan Nocturne (10/26/43, Forrest, 23)

Woebegone, middle-aged novelist (Eddie Dowling) falls in love with a call girl in a cheap New York hotel. Terry Holmes (deb.) was acclaimed for her performance as the wistful young prostitute, but the play was "barnacled with clichés and bad writing" *(PM)*. C: Wendell Corey, Howard Smith. A: Roy Walling. P: Drey and Brandt. D: Stella Adler.

Manon Lescaut (3/19/01, Wallack's, 15)

Dreary retelling of the Abbé Prevost novel (1731) of the luxury-loving courtesan. Sans the Puccini or Massenet score, Manon proved a deadly bore. C: Effie Shannon, Herbert Kelcey, Guy Bates Post, Frederick Perry. A: Theodore Burt Sayre. D: Max Freeman.

Man's Estate (4/1/29, Biltmore, 55)

A would-be architect gives up his dreams of success to marry the girl he loves. Mild comedy-drama by *Ladies' Home Journal* editors Bruce Gould and Beatrice Blackmar. C: Earle Larimore, Margalo Gillmore, Dudley Digges (D), Elizabeth Patterson, Armina Marshall. P: The Theatre Guild.

Man's Man, A (10/13/25, 52nd Street, 120)

Trying to better themselves economically, an ineffectual clerk (Dwight Frye) and his scatterbrained wife (Josephine Hutchinson) almost wreck their marriage. Graphic, unsentimentalized portrait of middle-class life. A: Patrick Kearney. P: The Stagers. D: Edward Goodman.

SV: MGM, 1929, William Haines, Josephine Dunn.

Man's World, A (2/8/10, Comedy, 71)

A woman (Mary Mannering) discovers that the man she loves is the father of her adopted child. Early Rachel Crothers (A/D) drama examined the double standard in deft and literate fashion. P: Messrs. Shuberts.

Many a Slip (2/3/30, Little, 56)

Innocuous comedy-drama by Edith Fitzgerald and Robert Riskin (D) in which a Boston girl (Sylvia Sidney) traps a

Greenwich Village boy (Douglass Montgomery) into marriage by feigning pregnancy. C: Dorothy Sands, Tom Brown, Elisha Cook, Jr. P: Lew Cantor.

Note: During the Broadway run of *Many a Slip*, coauthors Fitzgerald and Riskin were paged by Hollywood. She joined MGM's writing stable and turned out glossy vehicles for Garbo, Crawford, Marion Davies, et al; he became one of America's most distinguished screenwriters (*It Happened One Night, Mr. Deeds Goes to Town, Lost Horizon,* etc.).

SV: WB, 1931, *Illicit*, Barbara Stanwyck, Ricardo Cortez, James Rennie, Joan Blondell, Charles Butterworth; 1933, *Ex-Lady*, Bette Davis, Gene Raymond, Frank McHugh, Monroe Owsley, Claire Dodd, Kay Strozzi.

Many Happy Returns (1/5/45, Playhouse, 3)

A father sets out to rescue his son from an adventuress, only to become romantically involved with the *femme fatale* himself. Mary Astor made her Broadway debut in this 40's comedy and received excellent notices for her performance as the middle-aged mantrap. The play, however, was trounced by the critics and vanished after three performances. Author Clare Kummer lodged a protest with the Dramatists' Guild over script changes made by the management without her approval, but lost the case in court. C: Neil Hamilton, Rex O'Malley. P: Harry Bloomfield. D: Peter Berneis (pseud.).

Many Mansions (10/27/37, Biltmore, 157)

A young theology student comes into conflict with the forces of orthodox Christianity, but vows to continue his work for an enlightened church. Lee Strasberg directed this earnest but uninspired 1937 drama by the father-and-son team of Jules Eckert Goodman and Eckert Goodman. C: Alexander Kirkland, Flora Campbell, Seth Arnold, William Post, Gage Clarke, Ted Fetter, Walter Coy, Dan Duryea.

Marathon (1/27/33, Mansfield, 11)

Problems of a marathon dance contestant. Atmospheric but clichéd Depression era saga. C: Isabel Dawn, Robert Strange, Frank Rowan, Paul Guilfoyle, Jerome Cowan, Millard Mitchell. A: Isabel Dawn and Boyce de Gaw. P: Joseph Bernard. D: Clyde North.

Marathon '33 (12/22/63, ANTA, 48)

A down-on-her-luck youngster (Julie Harris) enters a dance marathon, and battles grueling fatigue and the trickery of her competitors in an effort to win the contest. June Havoc's (A/D) autobiographical account of this seamy, Depression-era phenomenon was more documentary than drama, but the production itself was "a tour de force of theatricality" (*New York Times*). Enacted by a sizable contingent of Actors Studio (P) personnel; notable performance by Lee Allen (deb.) as Miss Harris' clownish dancing partner. C: Lonny Chapman, Olive Deering, Conrad Janis, Tim Everett, Iggie Wolfington, Lane Bradbury, Joe Don Baker, Gabriel Dell, Don Fellows, Ralph Waite, Robert Heller, Adelaide Klein. CD: Noel Taylor. SD: Peter Larkin. M: Conrad Janis.

Marching Song (2/17/37, Bayes, 61)

To protest the firing of a blacklisted worker, a strike is called. Strikebreakers try to sabotage the walkout with guns, tear gas, and bombs, but the workers are ultimately victorious. A vigorous melodrama, *Marching Song* was the last Broadway play by Marxist author John Howard Lawson. Lawson deserted the theatre in 1937 and became a Hollywood screenwriter (*Algiers, Sahara, Action in the North Atlantic*, etc.). He was one of the "Hollywood Ten" who became embroiled with the House Un-American Activities Committee in 1947, and served a one-year sentence for contempt of Congress. *Marching Song* was also the final production mounted by The Theatre Union (P), a nonprofit, socially conscious organization dedicated to proletarian drama. C: Grover Burgess, Frieda Altman, Rex Ingram, Frances Bavier, Martin Wolfson. D: Anthony Brown.

Marco's Millions (1/9/28, Guild, 102)

Eugene O'Neill's satiric study of that thirteenth-century hustler, Marco Polo (Alfred Lunt). The arch-trader amasses a fortune in the Orient, but his crude materialism disgusts the great Kublai Khan (Baliol Holloway) and breaks the heart of the Khan's granddaughter, Princes Kukachin (Margalo Gillmore). "The sourest and most magnificent poke in the jaw that American business and the American businessman have ever got" (George Jean Nathan). Despite a sumptuous Theatre Guild production, O'Neill's East versus West satire emerged as something of a humorless bore and was only moderately successful. C: Dudley Digges, Henry Travers, Ernest Cossart, Albert Dekker, Morris Carnovsky. D: Rouben Mamoulian. SD: Lee Simonson.
R: (3/3/30, Liberty, 8). C: Earle Larimore (Marco), Sydney Greenstreet (Khan), Sylvia Field (Kukachin), Henry Travers (Chu-Yin).
R: (2/20/64, ANTA, 38) by Lincoln Center Rep. C: Hal Holbrook (Marco), David Wayne (Khan), Zohra Lampert (Kukachin), Joseph Wiseman (Chu-Yin). D: Jose Quintero.

Margin for Error (11/3/39, Plymouth, 264)

Clare Boothe's satirical melodrama about a Jewish cop (Sam Levene) assigned to guard the German consul (Otto Preminger) in New York. When the much-hated Nazi is not only shot, but stabbed and poisoned as well, it behooves Patrolman Finkelstein to find out who done it. ". . . as full of holes as a sieve [but] taut and tricky enough to be entertaining" (*News*). C: Bramwell Fletcher, Bert Lytell, Leif Erickson, Matt Briggs, Elspeth Eric, Edward McNamara. P: Aldrich and Myers. D: Otto Preminger. *Note:* Lionel Stander and Fay Wray were featured in the West Coast production.
SV: Fox, 1943, Milton Berle, Otto Preminger, Joan Bennett.

Marie Antoinette (11/22/21, Playhouse, 16)

Familiar tale of the frivolous Austrian princess (Grace George) who became queen of France, and her love for the handsome Count Axel Fersen (Pedro de Cordoba). Unable to stem the tide of revolution, the queen is sentenced and sent to the guillotine. ". . . a pretentiously produced play that was exposed to merciless view . . . about two weeks before a cautious management would have deemed it fit for the encounter" (Alexander Woollcott, *New York Times*). A: "Edymar" (pseud.). D: Grace George and John Cromwell.
SV: MGM, 1938, Norma Shearer, Tyrone Power, John Barrymore, Robert Morley, Joseph Schildkraut, Gladys George, Anita Louise, Reginald Gardiner.

Marie-Odile (1/26/15, Belasco, 119)

A young nun (Frances Starr) believes that babies are gifts from angels in Heaven. Thus, when she meets a handsome German soldier (Jerome Patrick) and nine months later gives birth to an infant son, poor Marie-Odile is banished from the convent. "Lacking in cumulative force, in human appeal, in every essential of dramatic quality" (Samuel Hoffenstein, *New York Sun*). Hoffenstein's review of Edward Knoblock's drama infuriated David Belasco (P/D) to such an extent that he personally visited the *Sun's* man-

Marriage Bed, The (1/7/29, Booth, 72)

Marital infidelity among the young married set. Fair 20's comedy-drama. C: Alan Dinehart, Ann Davis, Helen Flint, Elizabeth Patterson, Helen Chandler, Edward Emery. A: Ernest Pascal b/o his novel. P: Sam H. Harris. D: Robert Milton.
SV: Par, 1932, *Husband's Holiday*, Clive Brook, Charles Ruggles, Vivienne Osborne.

Marriage for Three (11/11/31, Bijou, 5)

Wife discovers mistress is bearing her husband's child. Tasteless, third-rate triangle comedy. C: Jessie Royce Landis, Verree Teasdale, Claudia Morgan, Frederick Perry. A: Elmer Harris. P: Lee Shubert. D: Stanley Logan.

Marriage Is for Single People (11/21/45, Cort, 6)

Comedy about a small-town lass who comes to New York, becomes a big city heartbreaker. ". . . unforgivably inept" (*Sun*). C: Gertrude Beach, Nana Bryant, Joel Marston, Anne Francine. A: Stanley Richards. P: Holden and Kronberg. D: Stanley Logan.

Marriage-Go-Round, The (10/29/58, Plymouth, 431)

A statuesque Swedish beauty triggers a domestic crisis when she selects a happily married professor of cultural anthropology to father her child. ". . . a charade played by experts . . . a triumph of theatrical skills" (*New York Times*). ". . . considerably handicapped by a curious coyness in its approach . . . not more than intermittently entertaining" (*Post*). C: Charles Boyer, Claudette Colbert, Julie Newmar, Edmon Ryan. A: Leslie Stevens. P: Paul Gregory. D: Joseph Anthony. CD: Lanvin-Castillo. SD: Donald Oenslager.
SV: Fox, 1960, James Mason, Susan Hayward, Julie Newmar, Robert Paige.

Marseilles (11/17/30, Henry Miller, 16)

Sidney Howard's adaptation of Marcel Pagnol's *Marius, Fanny,* and *Cesar* trilogy captured little of the rueful, bittersweet quality of the original. In the Howard version, Fanny (Frances Torchiana) is deserted and left with child by the adventure-loving Marius (Alexander Kirkland). At the urging of Marius' father, Cesar (Dudley Digges), she marries the middle-aged merchant, Panisse (Guy Kibbee), and learns to love him. C: Alison Skipworth, Hubert Druce, Ted Fetter. P/D: Gilbert Miller.

The Pagnol trilogy was musicalized by S. N. Behrman, Joshua Logan, and Harold Rome as *Fanny* (1954) with Ezio Pinza, Walter Slezak, Florence Henderson, and William Tabbert.
SV: MGM, 1938, *Port of Seven Seas*, Wallace Beery, Frank Morgan, Maureen O'Sullivan, John Beal (directed by James Whale from a screenplay by Preston Sturges); WB, 1961, *Fanny*, Maurice Chevalier, Charles Boyer, Leslie Caron, Horst Buchholz (directed by Joshua Logan from a screenplay by Julius Epstein).

Mary Jane's Pa (12/3/08, Garden, 89)

Wandering husband (Henry E. Dixey) returns home. Soggy small-town-life saga. A: Edith Ellis. P: Henry W. Savage.
SV: WB, 1935, Guy Kibbee, Aline MacMahon, Nan Grey, Tom Brown.

Mary, Mary (3/8/61, Hayes, 1,572)

Jean Kerr's smash hit comedy* about a book publisher who, on the eve of his divorce, discovers he still loves his wife, a beautiful girl with a devastatingly critical sense of humor. A movie idol and a health-food faddist complicate matters but, by the end of Act Three, the forthright heroine has learned to stifle her too-ready wit long enough to recapture her husband. "... very diverting and amusing" (Judith Crist, *Herald Tribune*). "... urbane, witty and sophisticated" (Thomas Dash, *Women's Wear Daily*). C: Barbara Bel Geddes, Barry Nelson, Michael Rennie (deb.), John Cromwell, Betsy von Furstenberg. P: Roger L. Stevens i.a.w. Lyn Austin. D: Joseph Anthony. SD: Oliver Smith.

SV: WB, 1963, Debbie Reynolds, Barry Nelson, Michael Rennie, Diane McBain, Hiram Sherman (directed by Mervyn LeRoy).

---

*Sixth longest-running (nonmusical) production in Broadway history.

Mary of Scotland (11/27/33, Alvin, 236)

Mary Stuart's return to Scotland from France in 1561 sparks Elizabeth Tudor's fear of a Stuart claim to the English throne, and so begins one of history's most famous feuds as the two ladies vie and maneuver for the crown of England. For two acts the scene shifts from Scotland to London and back again as Elizabeth sets her traps and Mary struggles to escape them until she is finally captured and placed in custody. In Act Three the queens meet face to face—a dramatic liberty since, in reality, they never met. In the confrontation scene that ends the play, Mary—despite persecution, imprisonment, and, ultimately, death at the scaffold—wins a kind of victory by refusing to abdicate the Scottish throne. "... the best historical drama that has ever been written by an American..." (John Mason Brown, *Post*). An excellent cast—Helen Hayes as a small but splendidly regal Mary, Helen Menken as the spiteful Elizabeth, and Philip Merivale as a bold and dashing Bothwell—helped to make Maxwell Anderson's poetic drama a great popular and critical success. C: Moroni Olsen, Ernest Cossart, Ernest Lawford, Anthony Kemble-Cooper, George Coulouris, Stanley Ridges, Charles Dalton, Wilton Graff, Edgar Barrier, Cecil Holm. P: The Theatre Guild. D: Theresa Helburn. SD: Robert Edmond Jones.

SV: RKO, 1936, Katharine Hepburn, Fredric March, Florence Eldridge, John Carradine, Robert Barrat, Moroni Olsen, Ian Keith, Ralph Forbes, Donald Crisp, Alan Mowbray, Frieda Inescort, Douglas Walton (directed by John Ford from a screenplay by Dudley Nichols).

Note: In *Elizabeth the Queen* (1930), Maxwell Anderson painted a sympathetic portrait of the British monarch. In *Mary of Scotland,* Anderson cast her as a villainess.

Mary the Third (2/5/23, 39th Street, 163)

A sophisticated flapper vows to "live in sin" rather than submit to the hypocrisies of marriage, but changes her mind when her squabbling parents are reconciled. In the end, romantic love triumphs: Mary dismisses questions of economics and eugenics and chooses her mate because she thinks he needs her. Popular Rachel Crothers (A/D) comedy-drama contrasted the courtship habits of three generations (daughter, mother, grandmother). C: Louise Huff, Ben Lyon, Morgan Farley, Beatrice Terry. P: Lee Shubert.

Masque of Kings, The (2/8/37, Shubert, 89)

Maxwell Anderson's version of the Mayerling tragedy that ended in the double suicide of Crown Prince Rudolph (Henry Hull) and his mistress, Baroness Marie Vetsera (Margo). In the play, Rudolph is an idealistic liberal who joins a revolt led by Count Hoyos (Leo G. Carroll) against the tyranny of Rudolph's father, the wily Emperor Franz Joseph (Dudley Digges). When the heir to the Hapsburg throne realizes that corruption is necessary to maintain political power, he takes his life. The critics found Anderson's poetic drama turgid and unconvincing. C: Pauline Frederick, Glenn Anders, John Hoysradt, Claudia Morgan, Alan Hewitt. P: The Theatre Guild. D: Philip Moeller. CD/SD: Lee Simonson.

Masque of Venice, The (3/2/26, Mansfield, 15)

Members of the literati set gather in the grand salon of a Venetian palace and exchange bon mots. One of the main troubles with the play was that the *mots* weren't especially *bon*. C: Arnold Daly, Antoinette Perry, Osgood Perkins, Selena Royle, Kenneth MacKenna. A: George Dunning Gribble. P: Brock Pemberton (D), William A. Brady, Jr., Dwight Deere Wiman.

Masquerade (3/16/59, Golden, 1)

Inept psychological study of a frigid wife (Cloris Leachman) and what made her that way. ". . . a banal typhoon . . . a hopeless theatrical fiasco" (*Journal-American*). C: Donald Cook, Glenda Farrell, Gene Lyons, Mark Richman. A: Sigmund Miller. P: Richard W. Krakeur i.a.w. Louis d'Almeida. D: Jed Horner. CD: Robert Mackintosh. SD: Paul Morrison.

Masquerader, The (9/3/17, Lyric, 160)

Journalist switches places with look-alike politician. Diverting trifle with Guy Bates Post in a dual role. A: John Hunter Booth, adapted from Katherine Cecil Thurston's novel. P/D: Richard Walton Tully. SV: UA, 1933, Ronald Colman, Elissa Landi.

Master Mind, The (2/17/13, Harris, 128)

The district attorney's butler (Edmund

The Master Mind. Elliott Dexter, Katherine LaSalle, and Edmund Breese (Harris Theatre, February 17, 1913). *Courtesy Museum of the City of New York Theatre and Music Collection.*

Breese) turns out to be the criminal genius who has been threatening his life. "Certainly no more far-fetched story has ever found its way into yellow covers or to the stage" (*New York Times*). A: Daniel D. Carter. P: Werba and Luescher. D: Robert Milton.

Master of the Inn, The (12/21/25, Little, 41)

A self-sacrificing mystic goes about mending broken souls. Unbearably mawkish stuff. C: Robert Loraine, Ian Keith, Verree Teasdale, Vincent Sardi, Jr. A: Catherine Chisholm Cushing (suggested by Robert Herrick's book of the same title). P: Hubert Druce (D) and William Streett.

Matchmaker, The (12/5/55, Royale, 486)

Thornton Wilder's period comedy (1880's New York) detailing the adventures of Mrs. Levi (Ruth Gordon), a scheming matchmaker who sets her cap for wealthy Horace Vandergelder (Loring Smith), a cantankerous merchant enamored of one Mrs. Molloy (Eileen Herlie),* who, in turn, becomes infatuated with the merchant's young clerk, Cornelius Hackl (Arthur Hill).* When the principals accidentally meet at an expensive restaurant, all sorts of madcap complications ensue. "Loud, slapdash and uproarious . . . extraordinarily original and funny" *(New York Times)*. *The Matchmaker* was a revised version of Wilder's *The Merchant of Yonkers,* a 1938 flop b/o an old Viennese farce. *The Merchant* failed to amuse the public and was withdrawn after five weeks. It was Garson Kanin, Ruth Gordon's husband, who insisted the play be given a second chance. Thanks in large measure to Tyrone Guthrie's brilliant direction, the reworking worked amazingly well. C: Robert Morse,* Rosamund Greenwood,* Phil Leeds. P: The Theatre Guild and David Merrick. CD/SD: Tanya Moiseiwitsch.

Musicalized by Michael Stewart and Jerry Herman as *Hello, Dolly!* (1964) with Carol Channing, David Burns, Eileen Brennan, Charles Nelson Reilly, Sondra Lee, and David Hartman.

SV: Par, 1958, Shirley Booth, Shirley MacLaine, Anthony Perkins, Paul Ford, Robert Morse (directed by Joseph Anthony); Fox, 1969, *Hello, Dolly!* Barbra Streisand, Walter Matthau, Michael Crawford, E. J. Peaker, Louis Armstrong (directed by Gene Kelly).

Note: *Hello, Dolly!,* the second longest-running musical in Broadway history (2,844 performances) earned a profit of $9 million on a $350,000 investment. Producer David Merrick's slice of that was $4.5 million. After Carol Channing left the show, six other stars played the title role in New York. They were: Ginger Rogers, Martha Raye, Betty Grable, Pearl Bailey, Phyllis Diller, and Ethel Merman.

---

*Broadway debuts.

Mating Dance (11/3/65, O'Neill, 1)

The love affair of a successful publisher (Van Johnson) and a young miss is complicated by the reluctance of the man's wife—a lady Senator—to grant him a divorce. Frenetic farce closed after its opening night performance. C: Marian Winters, Marian Hailey, J. D. Cannon, Richard Mulligan, Paul Sorvino. A: Eleanor Harris Howard and Helen McAvity. P: Elliot Martin. D: Ronny Graham.

Matrimony Pfd. (11/12/36, Playhouse, 61)

Chic fluff about a giddy matron (Grace George), her illegitimate son (Rex O'Malley), and the reluctant groom (A. E. Matthews) she is edging toward the altar. Adapted by Miss George and James Forbes from a comedy by Louis Verneuil. C: Sylvia Field, Jose Ruben (D), Rosemary Ames. P: William A. Brady.

Matty and the Moron and Madonna (3/29/65, Orpheum, 33)

Conflict between a saintlike child of the slums and his crazed mother. Grimly effective O/B drama by Herbert Lieberman; staged by Jose Quintero. C: Betty Miller, Glenn Scimonelli, Felice Orlandi, Katharine Ross. CD: Noel Taylor. SD: David Hays.

Maybe Tuesday (1/29/58, Playhouse, 5)

Comedy about a group of working girls sharing a New York City apartment while husband-hunting in the big city. ". . . highly obvious humor of a labored and mechanical manufacture" *(Post)*. C: Patricia Smith, Alice Ghostley, Zohra Lampert, Richard Derr, Barry Newman. A: Mel Tolkin and Lucille Kallen. P: Reiner and Lawrence. D: Elliot Silverstein.

Me (11/23/25, Princess, 32)

A tramp (Jerome Lawler) kills a recluse and assumes his identity. Implausible melodrama by Henry Myers, produced by Arthur Kober, directed by Edward Clarke Lilley.

Me and Molly (2/26/48, Belasco, 156)

Life with the Goldbergs of radio-TV fame, dealing primarily with the efforts of the Bronx family to establish their own dress business. ". . . simple and homely, with a few tears and a lot of laughs" (*World-Telegram*). C: Gertrude Berg (deb.), Philip Loeb, Eli Mintz, David Opatoshu. A: Gertrude Berg. P: Smith, Feigay and Kenwith. D: Ezra Stone. Musicalized by Adelson, Garfinkle, Livingston, and David as *Molly* (1973) with Kaye Ballard.

SV: Par, 1950, *Molly*, Gertrude Berg, Philip Loeb, Eli Mintz, David Opatoshu.

Me and Thee (12/7/65, Golden, 1)

Complications ensue when an ultraconservative couple decide to liberalize their life-styles. Predictable comedy lasted one night on Broadway. C: Durward Kirby (deb.), Barbara Britton. A: Charles Horine. P: Delancey Productions. D: Perry Bruskin.

Me, Candido! (10/15/56, Greenwich Mews, 159)

Entertaining O/B comedy-drama about the complications that ensue when a New York Puerto Rican family attempt to adopt a homeless eleven-year-old shoeshine boy. ". . . absorbing, solid, vigorous, fresh" (*New York Times*). C: Jose Perez, Jerry Jarrett, Anna Appel, Carlos Montalban, Miriam Colon. A: Walt Anderson. P/D: Sidney Walters.

Meanest Man In The World, The (10/12/20, Hudson, 204)

Kind-hearted lawyer who decides success will come only if he's tough and nasty meets an idealistic career girl who converts him back to his former good-natured ways. Thin comedy by Augustin MacHugh; originally an Alan Dinehart vaudeville sketch. C: Frank M. Thomas, Marion Coakley, Ruth Donnelly. P: George M. Cohan. D: John Meehan.

SV: Fox, 1943, Jack Benny, Priscilla Lane, Edmund Gwenn, Anne Revere, Eddie "Rochester" Anderson.

Medicine Show (4/12/40, New Yorker, 35)

The American Medical Association was the villain of this documentary-styled argument for socialized medicine. This 1940 play made out a strong case for a national health plan. "The argument is sober and logical; the drama sober and unimaginative. . . . *Medicine Show* is all tract" (*Sun*). Jules Dassin, future film director (*Rififi, Never on Sunday*, etc.), made his directorial debut with *Medicine Show*. C: Martin Gabel, Dorothy McGuire, Alfred Ryder, Norman Lloyd, Philip Bourneuf, Olive Deering, Perry Bruskin, John Randolph, Leigh Whipper. A: Oscar Saul and H. R. Hays. P: Carly Wharton and Martin Gabel.

Meet a Body (10/16/44, Forrest, 24)

Multiple murders in a Manhattan mortuary. Ramshackle thriller, ponderously staged by horror-film specialist, William Castle. ". . . a comedy-melodrama which garners few laughs and fewer shudders" (*News*). C: Whitford Kane, Al Shean, Forrest Orr, Harry Gribbon, Ruth McDevitt, Le Roi Operti. A: Jane Hinton. P: H. Clay Blaney.

Meet the Wife (11/26/23, Klaw, 261)

Humphrey Bogart (as Gregory Brown) and Clifton Webb (as Victor Staunton) were the frisky "Tennis, anyone?" juveniles in this amusing comedy about a celebrity-chasing suburbanite (Mary Boland) who discovers to her mingled delight and horror that she is a bigamist. C: Charles Dalton, Ernest Lawford, Eleanor

Griffin. A: Lynn Starling. P: Stewart and French.
SV: Col, 1931, Laura La Plante, Lew Cody.

Melody Man, The (5/13/24, Ritz, 61)
Comedy by "Herbert Richard Lorenz" (pseudonym for Herbert Fields-Richard Rodgers-Lorenz Hart) satirizing popular songwriting methods and the music publishing business on Tin Pan Alley. An Austrian composer (Lew Fields) is both bewildered and heartbroken to find his ambitious Dresden Sonata revamped as a pop hit. However, when his pretty daughter marries a jazz publisher, the father is financially enabled to return to the writing of classical music. Reviews of *The Melody Man* were sharply divided. Percy Hammond *(Herald Tribune)* found the show "feeble, immature and meandering." However, Quinn Martin *(World)* hailed it as "tremendously funny" while Alexander Woollcott *(Sun)* saluted its "enormously comic interludes." Two Rodgers and Hart numbers were incorporated into the plot as parodies of typical Tin Pan Alley songs. They were "Moonlight Mama" and "I'd Like To Poison Ivy (Before She Poisons Me)." In the cast of *The Melody Man* were Betty Weston, Donald Gallaher, Eva Puck, Sammy White, and, as a student violinist, an unknown juvenile named Fredric March. P: Lew Fields. D: Lawrence Marston and Alexander Leftwich.
SV: Col, 1930, John St. Polis, Alice Day, William Collier, Jr.

Melody of Youth, The (2/15/16, Fulton, 111)
Eva Le Gallienne was the ingenue and William Harrigan the juvenile in this mild comedy of romantic entanglements in a belligerently Irish family. C: James O'Neill, Brandon Tynan, Lily Cahill, Florine Arnold. A/D: Brandon Tynan. P: Hackett and Tyler.

Member of the Wedding, The (1/5/50, Empire, 501)
Carson McCullers' character sketch of a lonely southern tomboy named Frankie Addams who longs for companionship, but must settle for the company of the family cook and her cousin, John Henry, a bespectacled young man of seven. In her frustration Frankie decides to accompany her older brother and his bride on their honeymoon and is heartbroken when they leave without her. By the end of the play, John Henry has died, while Frankie has found a boyfriend and is verging on the threshold of maturity. "A sensitive, unusual and touching play of genuine individuality" *(Post)*. Superbly directed and memorably acted by twenty-five-year-old Julie Harris as the twelve-year-old ugly duckling heroine, Ethel Waters as the sympathetic cook, Brandon de Wilde (deb.) as John Henry—*The Member of the Wedding* surprised the Broadway wiseacres by becoming a commercial as well as artistic success. It won the Drama Critics Award as best play of the year, ran 501 performances, and was filmed by Hollywood. It was Tennessee Williams who urged Carson McCullers to try her hand at playwriting. The first draft of the play was written during the summer of 1946 in Williams' cottage on Nantucket Island. Mrs. McCullers and Williams spent their mornings at opposite ends of a long table, she working on *The Member of the Wedding* and he on *A Streetcar Named Desire*. In adapting her novel of the same name to the stage, Mrs. McCullers rejected established patterns of dramatic construction. "It is an inward play," she wrote, "and the conflicts are inward conflicts. . . . It is concerned with the weight of time, the hazard of human existence, bolts of chance." P: Whitehead, Rea and Martineau. D: Harold Clurman. CD/SD: Lester Polakov.

Musicalized by Carson McCullers, G.

Wood and Theodore Mann as *F. Jasmine Addams* (1971).

SV: Col, 1952, Julie Harris, Ethel Waters, Brandon de Wilde, Arthur Franz, Nancy Gates, James Edwards (directed by Fred Zinnemann).

Men of Distinction (4/30/53, 48th Street, 4)

Unsavory farce by novelist Richard Condon *(The Manchurian Candidate)* about a conniving Manhattan publicist (Robert Preston) and his equally unscrupulous clients. ". . . tasteless and witless. . ." *(News)*. C: Orson Bean, David Burns, Martin Ritt, Chandler Cowles. P: Chandler Cowles and Martin Gabel (D). CD/SD: David Ffolkes.

Men in White (9/26/33, Broadhurst, 357)

Pulitzer Prize play by Sidney Kingsley about a young intern in a great hospital. Torn between a wealthy society girl and the selfless example set by an idealistic old doctor, the intern ends by choosing medicine, and leaves for Vienna to study surgery. "It is a good brave play and is just the play to summon all the latent idealism from the young players of the Group Theatre" *(New York Times)*. Viewed by today's standards, *Men in White* seems hackneyed, perhaps because its basic plot has since been reprised so often. In 1933 it was hailed as practically the ultimate in social message melodrama. Its effectiveness lay in its painstakingly detailed reproduction of operating room procedures, in the masterful settings by Mordecai Gorelik, the ensemble acting of a large and dedicated company, and the fluid staging of director Lee Strasberg. *Men in White* was the first popular and financial success of The Group Theatre. C: Alexander Kirkland, J. Edward Bromberg, Morris Carnovsky, Margaret Barker, Luther Adler, Alan Baxter, Robert Lewis, Sanford Meisner, Phoebe Brand, Clifford Odets, Elia Kazan. P: The Group Theatre, Sidney Harmon and James R. Ullman.

SV: MGM, 1934, Clark Gable, Myrna Loy, Jean Hersholt, Otto Kruger, Elizabeth Allan, Wallace Ford.

Men Must Fight (10/14/32, Lyceum, 35)

A pacifist secretary of state comes to realize that America has no alternative but to go to war against expansionist-minded Japan. Interesting 1932 drama set (prophetically) in the year 1940. C: Gilbert Emery, Janet Beecher, Douglass Montgomery, Erin O'Brien-Moore, Alma Kruger, Kent Smith (deb.), Edgar Barrier. A: Reginald Lawrence and S. K. Lauren. P: Joseph P. Bickerton, Jr. D: Arthur Sircom.

SV: MGM, 1933, Lewis Stone, Diana Wynyard, Phillips Holmes.

Men to the Sea (10/3/44, National, 23)

Play by newspaperman Herbert Kubly dealing with the assorted problems of sailors' wives in a Brooklyn rooming house. ". . . a clutter of disorganized scenes, mystical nonsense and sentimental asides" *(Herald Tribune)*. C: Toni Gilman, Michael Strong, Maurice Ellis, Mildred Smith, Tom Noonan, Joyce Mathews, Paul Crabtree. P: Dave Wolper. D: Eddie Dowling.

Men We Marry, The (1/16/48, Mansfield, 3)

A materialistic mother (Shirley Booth), egged on by some catty friends, tries to discourage her daughter's romance with a penniless medical student. "Anything longer-winded or shorter-witted . . . would be difficult to conceive" *(PM)*. C: John Williams, Neil Hamilton, Margaret Hamilton, Doris Dalton. A: Elisabeth Cobb and Herschel Williams. P: Edgar Luckenbach. D: Martin Manulis.

Mendel, Inc. (11/25/29, Harris, 216)

Papa would rather stay home and invent

things than go to work. Flavorous Jewish family life comedy, filled with belly laughs. Written by David Freedman, legendary gag-writer of the 20's and 30's whose revue sketches for Fanny Brice, Bert Lahr, Beatrice Lillie, and other stars were in a class by themselves. C: Alexander Carr, Joe Smith, Charles Dale. P/D: Lew Cantor.

SV: WB, 1930, *The Heart of New York*, George Sidney, Smith and Dale, Aline MacMahon, Anna Appel.

Merchant of Yonkers, The (12/28/38, Guild, 39)

Thornton Wilder's 1938 comedy relating the adventures of Mrs. Levi (Jane Cowl), a meddling busybody who sets her cap for wealthy Horace Vandergelder (Percy Waram), a tight-fisted merchant enamored of one Mrs. Molloy (June Walker) who, in turn, becomes infatuated with the merchant's young clerk, Cornelius Hackl (Tom Ewell). When the principals accidentally meet at an expensive restaurant, all sorts of roguish complications ensue. (If the plot sounds familiar, it is. Reworked by the author as *The Matchmaker* (1955), the period comedy was successfully brought back to Broadway seventeen years later with Ruth Gordon in the leading role. It was then filmed by Hollywood with Shirley Booth as the wily Mrs. Levi. Finally, Carol Channing got to play the scheming heroine in the triumphant musical version, *Hello, Dolly!* (1964), a role later interpreted onscreen by Barbra Streisand.) As for *The Merchant of Yonkers* (which Thornton Wilder adapted from an old Viennese farce), it failed to amuse the public and was withdrawn after five weeks. The show was produced by Herman Shumlin and directed (in heavy-handed fashion) by Max Reinhardt. C: Bartlett Robinson, Nydia Westman, John Call, Philip Coolidge, Joseph Sweeney. SD: Boris Aronson.

Merely Murder (12/3/37, Playhouse, 3)

When their hated stepbrother is murdered, an irresponsible young man and his sister both confess to the crime. Witless mystery-comedy by A. E. Thomas b/o a novel by Georgette Heyer. C: Rex O'Malley, Claudia Morgan, George Macready. P: Laurence Rivers (Rowland Stebbins). D: Miriam Doyle.

Mermaids Singing, The (11/28/45, Empire, 53)

Impressionable miss offers herself to middle-aged, married playwright. Being a scrupulous fellow, he spurns the offer of illicit sex, and sends the girl back to her callow fiancé. ". . . forced and tedious" *(New York, Times)*. This 40's comedy was written by Anglo-American author John Van Druten (A/D). The Prufrockian title is from a T. S. Eliot poem. C: Walter Abel, Beatrice Pearson, Frieda Inescort, Lois Wilson, Walter Starkey, Dina Merrill (deb.). P: Alfred de Liagre, Jr. SD: Raymond Sovey.

Merrily We Roll Along (9/29/34, Music Box, 155)

Multi-scened drama by George S. Kaufman (D) and Moss Hart dealing with the moral disintegration of a successful playwright haunted by the betrayal of his talent. In this, their most serious play, Kaufman and Hart used a retrogressive method of storytelling, tracing the career of their disillusioned hero backward step by step from the cynicism of middle age to the idealism of youth. *Merrily We Roll Along* was the second collaboration of Kaufman and Hart, following their immensely successful farce-comedy, *Once in a Lifetime* (1930). The play garnered mixed reviews. To some critics, it was an inspiring tragedy. Others dubbed it a "stunt play" which attempted, unsuccessfully, to defy all traditional laws of dramaturgy. *Merrily We Roll Along* was a *succés d'estime*, but was otherwise disappointing to its authors. Attempts were made to analyze the reason for the play's failure. According to George S. Kaufman, the best diagnosis of the trouble was made by Herman Mankiewicz, who said: "Here we have this young man, a successful playwright, wealthy, honored, loved by beautiful women, the owner of yachts, sought out by everyone, and the problem the play poses is, how the hell did the poor son-of-a-bitch ever get himself into such a jam!" C: Kenneth MacKenna, Mary Philips, Walter Abel, Jessie Royce Landis. In bit roles: Hollywood starlet Eleanore Whitney, screenwriter Henry Ephron, actor John (later Arthur) Kennedy (deb.). P: Sam H. Harris. SD: Jo Mielziner.

Merry Andrew (1/21/29, Henry Miller, 24)

Pleasant comedy about a small town druggist (Walter Connolly) who kicks over the traces when faced with retirement. C: Effie Shannon, Nedda Harrigan, Joseph Crehan. A: Lewis Beach. P: Laurence Rivers, Inc. D: John Hayden.
SV: Fox, 1934, *Handy Andy*, Will Rogers, Peggy Wood, Mary Carlisle, Robert Taylor.

Merry Wives of Gotham

See *Fanshastics*.

Merry-Go-Round (4/22/32, Provincetown, 56)

Bellboy (Elisha Cook, Jr.) witnesses a murder, is threatened by the politically influential gangland boss (Harold Huber) who committed the crime, and is finally killed by the scapegoat-hunting policemen assigned to guard him. A scathing exposé of municipal corruption, *Merry-Go-Round* created a minor sensation when it was produced O/B in the spring of 1932. "The play attracted enough attention to warrant a transfer to an uptown theatre," wrote Burns Mantle, "but when the move was suggested as many political barriers as possible were put in the way. When these were finally hurdled the play was given a chance at the Avon Theatre, but died of its own extravagances in five weeks." A: Albert Maltz and George Sklar. P: Michael Blankfort and Walter Hart (D).
SV: U, 1932, *Afraid to Talk,* Eric Linden, Louis Calhern, Sydney Fox, Edward Arnold, Tully Marshall, Berton Churchill.

Merton of the Movies (11/13/22, Cort, 398)

George S. Kaufman-Marc Connelly satirical comedy about a naïve, movie-struck grocery clerk (Glenn Hunter) who inadvertently becomes a successful comic in two-reel Western travesties. Based on the story of the same name by Harry Leon Wilson. "A delight in every way" (John Corbin, *New York Times*). C: Florence Nash, Gladys Feldman. P: George C. Tyler. D: Hugh Ford.
SV: Par, 1932, *Make Me A Star,* Stuart Erwin, Joan Blondell, ZaSu Pitts, Ben Turpin; MGM, 1947, Red Skelton, Virginia O'Brien, Gloria Grahame, Leon Ames, Alan Mowbray, Hugo Haas.
Note: The 1932 Paramount version featured guest star appearances by such luminaries as Tallulah Bankhead, Maurice Chevalier, Fredric March, Claudette Colbert, Gary Cooper, Jack Oakie, Clive Brook, Sylvia Sidney, and Charlie Ruggles.

Message from Mars, A (10/7/01, Garrick, 184)

A Martian (Henry Stephenson) visits a Scroogelike astronomer (Charles Hawtrey) in his laboratory, reveals to him the misery and despair of the poor, finally awakens compassion in the heart of the cynic and, mission accomplished, returns to Mars. "It is a really novel, simple, unaffected, and attractive sort of play, and as it was acted last night ought to please even hardened theatregoers" (*New York Times*). *A Message from Mars* marked the Broadway debuts of both Mr. Hawtrey, one of England's most popular character comedians, and Mr. Stephenson, who went on to become one of Hollywood's busiest and most reliable character actors. Written by Richard Ganthony, an American, the play was even more successful in London (where it ran two years) than in New York.

Meteor (12/23/29, Guild, 92)

A ruthless, egomaniacal financier (Alfred Lunt) triumphs over his rivals but, in the process, loses his wife (Lynn Fontanne). "A brilliant, provocative, and original character study set down in a frail play" (*Herald Tribune*). C: Douglass Montgomery, Edward Emery. A: S. N. Behrman. P: The Theatre Guild. D: Philip Moeller. Moeller.

Metropole (12/6/49, Lyceum, 2)

Harum-scarum farce about Harold Ross (here called Frederick M. Hill), volatile and bellicose editor of *The New Yorker* magazine for many years, and his problems with writers, deadlines, interoffice skulduggery, and ex-wives. "A raucous and hollow comedy" (*Sun*). ". . . a poor, contrived play but . . . nevertheless rebelliously comical and occasionally hilarious" (George Jean Nathan). C: Lee Tracy, Arlene Francis, Edith Atwater, Jane Seymour, Reynolds Evans, Henry Jones, Gavin Gordon, Royal Dano, Reed Brown, Jr. A: William Walden. P: Max Gordon. D: George S. Kaufman. SD: Edward Gilbert.

Michael Drops In (12/27/38, Golden, 8)

Blasé publisher (Onslow Stevens) is smitten by the charms of a small-town authoress (Arlene Francis). Flimsy 30's comedy by William Du Bois. P: Marie Louise Elkins and Edward Massey (D).

Middle of the Night (2/8/56, ANTA, 477)

Paddy Chayefsky's first stage play, the story of a fifty-three-year-old widower's problems when he falls in love with a twenty-four-year-old girl. Edward G. Robinson returned to Broadway after a twenty-five-year absence to play the gentle Jewish widower and won critical acclaim for his quietly understated performance. As to the merits of the play itself, however, reviews were divided: "A touching and interesting drama" (*Post*). ". . . a soap opera . . . a testimonial to the hopeless ordinariness of Chayefsky's resources as a dramatist" (*News*). *Middle of the Night* was expanded from the author's 1954 television play that starred E. G. Marshall and Eva Marie Saint. C: Gena Rowlands (deb.), June Walker, Martin Balsam, Anne Jackson, Lee Philips, Nancy R. Pollock, Effie Afton. P/D: Joshua Logan. CD: Motley. M: Lehman Engel. SD: Jo Mielziner.

SV: Col, 1959, Fredric March, Kim Novak, Glenda Farrell, Lee Grant, Martin Balsam, Effie Afton (directed by Delbert Mann).

Midgie Purvis (2/1/61, Martin Beck, 21)

Tallulah Bankhead in Mary Chase's whimsical farce about a prankish society matron who masquerades as a doddering crone. Miss Bankhead's best performance in years, but the play emerged as "a spotty and ramshackle comedy" (*Post*). C: William Redfield, Clinton Sundberg, Alice Pearce, Nydia Westman, Russell Hardie, John Cecil Holm, Kip McArdle, Jane Van Duser. P: Whitehead and Stevens i.a.w. A. R. Glancy, Jr. D: Burgess Meredith. CD: Guy Kent. SD: Ben Edwards. M: Saul Kaplan.

Midnight (12/29/30, Guild, 48)

Capital punishment advocate faces a dilemma when his daughter murders her lover. Shrill, socially conscious melodrama produced by The Theatre Guild. C:

Linda Watkins, Glenn Anders, Clifford Odets, Josephine Hull, Jack La Rue, Frederick Perry, Harold Vermilyea, Royal Dana. A: Claire and Paul Sifton. D: Philip Moeller.
SV: U, 1934, Henry Hull, Sidney Fox, Humphrey Bogart, O. P. Heggie.

Mid-Summer (1/21/53, Vanderbilt, 109)

Sentimental period piece (New York City, 1907) dealing with the efforts of an uneducated wife to persuade her teacher-husband to give up his dreams of a show business career and return to the classroom. Reviews of this Vina Delmar play were mixed, but there was unanimous praise for Geraldine Page (Broadway debut) as the warmhearted, illiterate wife and mother. Also making their debuts in *Mid-Summer* were Mark Stevens as the ambitious husband and Jenny Hecht (Ben Hecht's daughter) as the couple's precocious nine-year-old child. C: Vicki Cummings, Howard Smith, Edgar Stehli, Robert Emmett. P: Paul Crabtree (D) and Frank J. Hale. CD: Motley. SD: Howard Bay.

Mid-West (1/7/36, Booth, 22)

Returning to his father's drought-stricken Kansas farm, a young radical (Van Heflin) tries to organize the neighboring farmers, is lynched for his pains. Lacklustre 30's drama by James Hagan, author of the successful comedy, *One Sunday Afternoon* (1933). C: Curtis Cooksey, Jean Adair, John Alexander. P: Messrs. Shubert. D: Melville Burke.

Mighty Man Is He, A (1/6/60, Cort, 5)

The wife and the mistress of a theatrical producer (whose bedroom prowess is responsible for the play's title) join forces to vanquish a little chippy who has been threatening their prerogatives. "An obsolete farce in a hackneyed literary style" (*New York Times*). C: Nancy Kelly, Polly Rowles, Diana van der Vlis, Claude Allister, John Cecil Holm. A: Arthur Kober and George Oppenheimer. P: Joy and Green. D: Reginald Denham.

Mike Downstairs (4/18/68, Hudson, 4)

Spotty, overwritten comedy-drama about the travails of an anti-establishment Italian-American (Dane Clark). A: George Panetta. P: Bufman/Margolies/Franck. D: Donald Driver.

Milk Train Doesn't Stop Here Anymore, The (1/16/63, Morosco, 69)

At a villa on Italy's Divine Coast, a coarse, dying millionairess forms an alliance with a pallid poet known as the Angel of Death. The elderly harridan woos him with the pleasures of the senses, he pleads with her to recognize God. Eventually, the old woman comes to realize that the Christlike stranger is not for sale, that he merely wishes to comfort her at the time of her death. This Tennessee Williams tragicomedy—a curious mixture of macabre humor and impending doom—lacked dramatic focus. Despite flashes of wit and dark poetry, the play was as meandering as its title. C: Hermione Baddeley, Paul Roebling, Mildred Dunnock, Ann Williams. P: Roger L. Stevens i.a.w. Austin and Samrock. D: Herbert Machiz. M: Paul Bowles. SD: Jo Mielziner.
R: (1/1/64, Atkinson, 5) by David Merrick i.a.w. Neil Hartley. C: Tallulah Bankhead, Tab Hunter, Ruth Ford, Marian Seldes. D: Tony Richardson.
SV: British, 1968, *Boom!*, Elizabeth Taylor, Richard Burton, Noel Coward, Joanna Shimkus, Michael Dunn (directed by Joseph Losey).

Milky Way, The (5/8/34, Cort, 63)

Rowdy farce about a mild-mannered milkman who accidentally becomes middleweight champion of the world. C: Hugh O'Connell, Brian Donlevy, Gladys George, Leo Donnelly. A: Lynn Root and

Harry Clork. P: Harmon and Ullman. D: William W. Schorr.

SV: Par, 1936, Harold Lloyd, Adolphe Menjou, Verree Teasdale, Lionel Stander, Milburn Stone; RKO, 1946, *The Kid from Brooklyn,* Danny Kaye, Virginia Mayo, Steve Cochran, Vera-Ellen, Lionel Stander, Fay Bainter, Walter Abel.

Mima (12/12/28, Belasco, 180)

Fantastic David Belasco (Ad./P/D) theatrical curio; a melange of modernistic machinery and medieval morality play, with a plot simple-minded beyond belief. The Devil's efficiency expert (A. E. Anson) invents a "psycho-corrupter," a machine so powerful that it can corrupt a human soul beyond redemption. To demonstrate this awesome tangle of machinery, a virtuous forester (Sidney Blackmer) is snatched from earth and thrust into the machine with a sexy mannikin named Mima (Lenore Ulric). Under her influence, the forester commits every sin in the book, but he forgives Mima. This is too much for the machine. It sputters, wheezes, and collapses in a blinding white light, and the forester returns to earth unharmed. "All night those of us who were seated on the right aisle had been embarrassed by the intrusions of devils as they leaped from the auditorium to the stage and back again, but now we were positively endangered. I blanched as a fiend almost landed on Gilbert Gabriel's stomach. I trembled for Stark Young as an imp floundered toward him. I saw fear in the eyes of George Jean Nathan as one large, hairy and very abdominous devil ran screaming toward him. Then in a flash, I understood what the purpose of the whole performance was. Mr. Belasco had devilish designs upon the critics" (St. John Ervine, *New York World*). To recreate Hell, seventy-five-year-old David Belasco spared no expense. He virtually dismantled the proscenium arch, sheathed the theatre's boxes and balconies in metal, and converted the interior of his playhouse into the equivalent of a battleship boiler-room. The reviewers were impressed by the metallic *mise-en-scéne*, but not by the absurd script that had been adapted and extensively revised by Belasco from a play by Ferenc Molnar. *Mima* lost a quarter-of-a-million dollars. Thereafter, Belasco confined his producing activities to light comedies.

Minick (9/24/24, Booth, 154)

George S. Kaufman-Edna Ferber comedy-drama. To the discomfort of all concerned, an old man (O. P. Heggie) comes to live with his son and daughter-in-law on Chicago's South Side. He finally decides that the Old Men's Home is a more congenial place for him to end his days. *Minick,* adapted from a short story by Miss Ferber, proved an uneasy blend of pathos and satire. C: Phyllis Povah, Frederic Burt, Antoinette Perry. P/D: Winthrop Ames.

SV: WB, 1932, *The Expert,* "Chic" Sale, Lois Wilson, Walter Catlett, Dickie Moore; 1939, *No Place to Go,* Fred Stone, Dennis Morgan, Gloria Dickson, Frank Faylen.

Minor Miracle (10/7/65, Henry Miller's, 4)

Minor comedy about the problems of an easygoing, down-to-earth Catholic priest (Lee Tracy) in the Yorkville section of Manhattan. Written by novelist Al Morgan (*The Great Man, Cast of Characters,* etc.). C: Dennis King, Pert Kelton, Robert H. Harris. P: Zev Bufman and Howard Erskine (D).

Miracle Man, The (9/21/14, Astor, 97)

George M. Cohan drama dealing with the influence exerted on a community by a faith healer. The relative failure of the play was a bitter disappointment to Cohan. C: George Nash, Frank Bacon, Gail Kane. A/D: Cohan. P: Cohan and Harris.

SV: Par, 1932, Chester Morris, Sylvia

Sidney, Hobart Bosworth, Ned Sparks.

Note: Lon Chaney's performance as a deformed cripple in Paramount's silent version of *The Miracle Man* (1920) made his reputation.

Miracle Worker, The (10/19/59, Playhouse, 719)

William Gibson's dramatization of an early chapter in the life of Helen Keller, and the struggle of her indomitable teacher Annie Sullivan to break through the barriers that surrounded the deaf, dumb, and blind child. Despite some unwieldy theatrical devices, the play generated considerable emotional power in its key scenes. Highlight: the fight-for-authority sequence in which the determined Irish tutor finally succeeds in triumphing over the savage, recalcitrant youngster. C: Anne Bancroft, Patty Duke (deb.), Patricia Neal, Torin Thatcher, James Congdon, Kathleen Comegys, Beah Richards, Michael Constantine. P: Fred Coe. D: Arthur Penn.

SV: UA, 1962, Anne Bancroft, Patty Duke, Inga Swenson, Victor Jory, Andrew Prine, Kathleen Comegys (directed by Arthur Penn).

Mirage, The (9/30/20, Times Square, 190)

Small-town girl (Florence Reed) achieves the luxury she craves as a rich man's plaything, engineers "a noble deception" to keep from hurting her ex-boyfriend. Lugubrious melodrama by Edgar Selwyn (A/P/D). C: Alan Dinehart, Florence Nash, Reginald Mason.

SV: MGM, 1931, *Possessed,* Joan Crawford, Clark Gable, Wallace Ford, John Miljan, Skeets Gallagher.

Miranda of the Balcony (9/4/01, Manhattan, 62)

After seven years of pretending to mourn a husband she loathed, a widow (Mrs. Fiske) learns the scoundrel is still alive. His murder, in the last act of the play, paves the way for a happy ending. Synthetic, stilted drama on the *Enoch Arden* theme, adapted by Anne Crawford Flexner from a novel by A. E. W. Mason. C: Robert T. Haines, Max Figman, Etienne Girardot, Annie Irish, J. E. Dodson, Emily Stevens. P/D: Harrison Grey Fiske.

Note: It was at the opening night of *Miranda of the Balcony* that theatre programs as we know them were first handed to an audience.

Mirrors (1/18/28, Forrest, 13)

Wife-swapping, 1920's style. Rancid fare. C: Sylvia Sidney, Raymond Guion (Gene Raymond), Hale Hamilton, Albert Hackett. A: Milton Herbert Gropper. P/D: Albert Lewis.

Mis' Nelly of N'Orleans (2/4/19, Henry Miller, 127)

A middle-aged woman seeking romance tries to mend a broken love affair. Engaging comedy-drama with a blithe performance in the leading role by Mrs. Fiske. A: Laurence Eyre. P: Cohan and Harris. D: Harrison Grey Fiske.

Misleading Lady, The (11/25/13, Fulton, 183)

To gain some newspaper headlines, a would-be actress (Inez Buck) throws herself at a misogynistic, world-famous explorer (Lewis Stone) and is kidnapped for her pains. Frothy screwball comedy with an impossibly tangled plot. George Abbott, making his Broadway debut as an actor, had a small role in this Charles Goddard-Paul Dickey play. P: William Harris, Jr. D: Holbrook Blinn.

SV: Par, 1932, Claudette Colbert, Edmund Lowe, Stuart Erwin.

Miss Lonelyhearts (10/3/57, Music Box, 12)

Assigned by his browbeating editor (Pat O'Brien) to write an advice-to-the-lovelorn column, a young reporter (Fritz Weaver) makes the mistake of becoming personally involved in his clients' tragedies, and pays for his compassion with his life. "A pretentious and unrewarding experience in the theatre" *(Journal-American)*. C: Ruth Warrick, Irene Dailey, Henderson Forsythe, Janet Ward, Maurice Ellis, Pippa Scott, Dan Morgan, Marian Reardon, William Hickey, Anne Meara, Jo Anna March. A: Howard Teichmann b/o the novel by Nathanael West. P: Osterman and Glancy i.a.w. Diana Green. D: Alan Schneider. CD: Patricia Zipprodt. SD: Jo Mielziner. M: Jule Styne.
SV: UA, 1933, *Advice to the Lovelorn*, Lee Tracy, Sterling Holloway, Sally Blane, Jean Adair, Paul Harvey (directed by Alfred Werker); 1958, *Lonelyhearts*, Montgomery Clift, Robert Ryan, Myrna Loy, Maureen Stapleton, Dolores Hart (directed by Vincent J. Donehue).

Miss Lulu Bett (12/27/20, Belmont, 201)

Pulitzer Prize drama about a good-hearted family drudge who leaves her small-minded sister and domineering brother-in-law to marry a bigamist. Shrewdly-written, observant drama of midwestern family life, adapted by Zona Gale from her best-selling novel. C: Carroll McComas, Louise Closser Hale, Willard Robertson, Catherine Doucet. P/D: Brock Pemberton.

Miss Quis (4/7/37, Henry Miller, 37)

A charwoman comes into an inheritance. Mildly pleasant comedy-drama was co-authored by Peggy Wood (who played the Cinderella-heroine of the title) and critic-columnist Ward Morehouse, author of *Gentlemen of the Press* (1928). C: Jessie Royce Landis, James Rennie, Eda Heinemann. P: Vinton Freedley. D: Bertram Harrison. SD: Donald Oenslager.

Miss Swan Expects (2/20/39, Cort, 8)

Weak satire on the publishing business; comedy by the usually reliable Bella and Samuel Spewack (D) was not up to snuff. C: Peggy Conklin, John Beal, George Nash, William Bendix, Eduard Franz, John Williams, Ann Andrews, Joyce Arling, O. Z. Whitehead. P: William Harris, Jr.

Missouri Legend (9/19/38, Empire, 48)

The last week in the life of Jesse James (Dean Jagger), here presented as a pious, God-fearing family man who robs banks and trains only to help the poor, and to keep his wife (Dorothy Gish) in reasonable comfort. The play ends with fellow-outlaw Billy Gashade (Jose Ferrer) eulogizing his friend in song after "dirty little coward" Bob Ford (Dan Duryea) shot Jesse in the back. ". . . romantically humorous . . . the best of it is shrewd theatre" *(New York Times). Missouri Legend* was written by Elizabeth B. Ginty, longtime secretary to producer David Belasco.
C: Mildred Natwick, Russell Collins, Karl Malden, James Craig, Richard Bishop, Joseph Sweeney, John Philliber. P: Guthrie McClintic (D) i.a.w. Max Gordon.

Mister Antonio (9/18/16, Lyceum, 48)

Mild Booth Tarkington comedy contrasting a simple, life-loving Italian organ-grinder (Otis Skinner) with various ultra-conventional Pennsylvania village folk. P: Charles Frohman. D: Gustav Von Seyffertitz.
SV: Tiffany, 1929, Leo Carrillo.

Mister Johnson (3/29/56, Martin Beck, 44)

Comedy-drama about a childlike West African Negro clerk whose enthusiasm

Mister Antonio, **by Booth Tarkington. Scene with Otis Skinner (September 18, 1916).**
Courtesy Museum of the City of New York Theatre and Music Collection.

for the white man's civilization leads to tragedy. Caught between two cultures, he is hopelessly doomed. Despite an enormously skillful performance by Earle Hyman in the title role, Mister Johnson seemed "attenuated, sprawling . . . and lacking in cumulative dramatic power." C: Josephine Premice, Gaby Rodgers, William Sylvester, Thayer David, Earl Jones, Lawrence Fletcher, Rosetta Le Noire. A: Norman Rosten b/o the novel by Joyce Cary. P: Cheryl Crawford and Robert Lewis (D). CD/SD: William and Jean Eckart.

Mister Roberts (2/18/48, Alvin, 1,157)

Celebrated World War II comedy-drama dealing with the men of a drab navy cargo vessel sailing "from Apathy to Tedium" in the backwaters of the Pacific. Lieutenant Roberts (Henry Fonda) acts as buffer between the cantankerous captain and the long-suffering crew. After waging many battles on behalf of the men, Roberts finally wins a transfer to combat duty, and is killed by a Japanese suicide plane. ". . . one of the most uproarious, heartwarming, and yet touching evenings Broadway has yielded in many a long year" (John Mason Brown, *Saturday Review of Literature*). A few critics argued that this rowdily sentimental comedy by Thomas Heggen* and Joshua Logan (D) took a Rover Boy's attitude toward the war, but no reviewer could fault the production's high level of excellence. Henry Fonda gave one of his finest performances in the title role, and was admirably supported by David Wayne as Ensign Pulver, William Harrigan as The Captain, and Robert Keith as Doc. Jocelyn Brando (sister of Marlon Brando) had the lone feminine role in an otherwise all-male company. C: Ralph Meeker, Harvey Lembeck, Rusty Lane, Steven Hill, Murray Hamilton, Marshall Jamison. P: Leland Hayward. SD: Jo Mielziner.

R: (12/5/56, City Center, 15). C: Charlton Heston, Orson Bean, William Harrigan, Fred Clark, Frank Campanella, Nancy Berg, Dick Button, Clinton Kimbrough, Joe Hardy, Burt Reynolds (deb.). D: John Forsythe.

SV: WB, 1955, Henry Fonda, James Cagney, Jack Lemmon, William Powell, Betsy Palmer, Ward Bond, Nick Adams (directed by John Ford and Mervyn LeRoy from a screenplay by Frank Nugent and Joshua Logan).

---

*Novelist-playwright Thomas Heggen committed suicide in May, 1949, for reasons never disclosed. He was twenty-nine years old.

Note: The London production of *Mr. Roberts* (1950), starring Tyrone Power and Jackie Cooper, was a dire failure.

Mister Romeo (9/5/27, Wallack's, 16)

Middle-aged philanderer becomes involved with a couple of burlesque queens. Lamentable exhibit. C: J. C. Nugent, Thais Lawton. A: Harry Wagstaff Gribble and Wallace A. Manheimer. P: Murray Phillips. D: Edward Eliscu.

Mistress Nell (10/9/00, Bijou, 104)

Sprightly costume piece about Nell Gwynne (Henrietta Crosman), the orange vendor who became the mistress of Charles II (Aubrey Boucicault). In this variation by George C. Hazelton, Jr., Nell is given papers signed by the king to be delivered to France. She succeeds in her mission by disguising herself as a boy.

Moby Dick (11/28/62, Barrymore, 13)

Orson Welles' stage adaptation of Herman Melville's epic tale of the cruise of the *Pequod* and its destruction in the far reaches of the Pacific by the mammoth White Whale. To establish the proceedings in proper period and locale, Welles used a play-within-a-play technique, with a group of 19th-century American actors preparing a production of *Moby Dick* on a bare stage. "A whale of a try [but] there is more Welles than Melville, more pretension than sensitivity, in this ambitious attempt" *(Mirror)*. "The rigging is more impressive than the recitation. . . . Mr. Welles has not dramatized the text, he has only shredded it . . ." *(Herald Tribune)*. C: Rod Steiger, Roy Poole, Max Helpmann, Bruno Gerussi, Frances Hyland. P: Adler and Liff. D: Douglas Campbell.

SV: The Melville novel has been filmed three times by Warner Brothers: in 1926 as a silent film entitled *The Sea Beast* with John Barrymore as Captain Ahab; in 1930 as an early talking picture with Barrymore again cast in the leading role; in 1956 with a cast headed by Gregory Peck, Richard Basehart, Leo Genn, and Orson Welles, and with John Huston directing from a screenplay by Ray Bradbury.

Modern Virgin, A (5/20/31, Booth, 45)

A seventeen-year-old girl (Margaret Sullavan) learns about life and love from a married man (Roger Pryor). Trifling sex comedy; Miss Sullavan made an auspicious Broadway debut as the wide-eyed ingenue of the title. C: George Houston, Claudia Morgan, Nicholas Joy, Fred Irving Lewis. A: Elmer Harris. P: Messrs. Shubert. D: Stanley Logan.

Molière (3/17/19, Liberty, 64)

Interesting biographical drama of the great French dramatist (Henry Miller) highlighting Molière's friendship with his benefactor, Louis XIV (Holbrook Blinn); the unrequited passion of the king's mistress (Blanche Bates) for the defiant young playwright; Molière's unfortunate marriage to the frivolous Armande (Estelle Winwood); and, finally, the death of Molière following his performance in the title role of his last play, *The Imaginary Invalid* (1673). A/P/D: Philip Moeller. P/D: Henry Miller.

Money Business (1/20/26, National, 13)

Delicatessen owner invests his life savings in the stock market, gets rich quick, then loses everything. Poverty-stricken comedy. C: Lew Fields, Luther Adler. A/P: Oscar M. Carter. D: Lawrence Marston.

Money Mad

See *Bet Your Life*.

Monique (10/22/57, Golden, 63)

A woman doctor and her married lover conspire to do away with the man's shrewish wife. Rambling mystery-melodrama with an ingenious trick ending. C: Patricia Jessel, Denholm Elliott, Percy Waram. A: Dorothy and Michael Blankfort b/o a novel by Pierre Boileau and Thomas Narcejac and the 1955 French film *Diabolique*. P: Shepard Traube (D) i.a.w. S. W. Sharmat.

Monkey (2/11/32, Mansfield, 29)

Police inspector (Richard Whorf) solves a New York murder case. Tepid mystery-comedy. A: Sam Janney. P/D: Robert Sparks.

Monster, The (8/9/22, 39th Street, 112)

Dr. Gustave Ziska, a sinister surgeon attended by a legless servant named Caliban, lives in an eerie mansion equipped with enough trap doors, sliding panels, and bogus scientific gadgetry to give even the great Dr. Frankenstein pause. Into this veritable chamber of horrors stumble a beautiful girl and a handsome, inquisitive newspaper reporter. "Will the sadistic fiend have his way with these two, or will they manage to escape in time?" This was the question posed in lurid ads publicizing *The Monster,* one of the livelier shriek-and-shudder shows of the decade, which kept audiences on the edge of their seats for 112 performances. C: Wilton Lackaye, McKay Morris, Marguerite Risser. A: Crane Wilbur. P: Joseph M. Gaites. D: Lawrence Marston. R: (2/10/33 Waldorf, 38) by Wee and Leventhal with De Wolf Hopper as the sadistic Dr. Ziska. D: Frank McCormack.

Montserrat (10/29/49, Fulton, 65)

Six innocent hostages—two women and four men—face execution at the hands of a sadistic inquisitor unless they can persuade the young Spanish officer, Montserrat, to reveal the whereabouts of revolutionist Simón Bolivar. Montserrat refuses to betray the patriot, and so the hostages are shot, one by one. As word comes that Bolivar has fled to safety, Montserrat goes willingly to his death. ". . . intellectually arresting, but rarely is it deeply moving" *(Post)*. Emlyn Williams played the inquisitor and William Redfield (miscast) had the title role in this period melodrama (1812) laid during the Spanish occupation of Venezuela. The play was adapted by Lillian Hellman (A/D) from a drama by Emmanuel Robles. C: Julie Harris, John Abbott, Reinhold Schunzel, William Hansen, Vivian Nathan, George Bartenieff, Francis Compton, Kurt Kasznar, Nehemiah Persoff. P: Kermit Bloomgarden and Gilbert Miller. CD: Irene Sharaff. SD: Howard Bay.
R: (1/8/61, Gate, 49). C: Leonardo Cimino, John Heldabrand. D: Boris Tumarin.

Moon Besieged, The (12/5/62, Lyceum, 1)

Somberly pretentious historical drama

about the martyrdom of abolitionist John Brown (Charles Tyner). "Bloodless, flat and ineffective" *(Post)*. A: Seyril Schochen. P: Lorin Price i.a.w. Louise Arnold. D: Lloyd Richards. CD: Robert Fletcher. SD: Ming Cho Lee.

Moon Is a Gong, The (3/12/26, Cherry Lane, 19)

John Dos Passos' expressionistic play satirizing various aspects of jazz-age America, with particular emphasis on the prevailing standardization of business and culture. ". . . from the general cacophony of this loose and structureless extravaganza, one suspects that he [Dos Passos] has looked upon America and found it wanting. . . . As an exhibition and an experiment . . . it is novel and arresting" *(New York Times)*. C: Allyn Joslyn, Helen Chandler, Harold Kennedy, Leona Maricle. P: J. B. Rublee. D: Edward Massey. SD: Mordecai Gorelik.

Moon Is Blue, The (3/8/51, Henry Miller, 924)

F. Hugh Herbert's frothy comedy hit about a naïve young actress (Barbara Bel Geddes) caught in a compromising situation between a boyish Manhattan architect (Barry Nelson) and his fiancée's debonair father (Donald Cook). "Jaunty as a fine Easter bonnet" *(News)*. P: Aldrich and Myers i.a.w. Julius Fleischmann. D: Otto Preminger. SD: Stewart Chaney.

SV: UA, 1953, William Holden, David Niven, Maggie McNamara, Tom Tully (directed by Otto Preminger).

Moon Is Down, The (4/7/42, Martin Beck, 71)

John Steinbeck's drama of the Nazi invasion of Norway, and how the people of a small Norwegian town prefer to die rather than yield their liberties. In the end, the mayor of the village goes gallantly to his death as a hostage, secure in the knowledge that "herd men win battles, but free men win wars." The play, adapted by Steinbeck from his best-selling novel, proved only intermittently effective on stage. Uninspired casting and direction obscured the script's virtues. Another problem was that the invading Nazis were portrayed as good-natured, kindly, boy scout types. "These Germans are too nice for comfort or belief," said John Mason Brown in the *New York World-Telegram*. "By making his invaders more sinned against than sinning, Mr. Steinbeck has dissipated his drama," echoed Richard Lockridge in the *New York Sun*. C: Otto Kruger, Ralph Morgan, Whitford Kane, Joseph Sweeney, Jane Seymour, William Eythe (deb.), Lyle Bettger, Russell Collins, E. J. Ballantine, Alan Hewitt, Leona Powers. P: Oscar Serlin. D: Chester Erskine.

SV: Fox, 1943, Cedric Hardwicke, Henry Travers, Lee J. Cobb, Margaret Wycherly.

Moon Over Mulberry Street (9/4/35, Lyceum, 300)

Italian-American youth (Cornel Wilde) becomes enamored of Park Avenue socialite, finally realizes his true love is the simple Italian girl next door. Homely folk comedy, set in New York's Little Italy, had a lengthy run via cut-rate tickets. C: Gladys Shelley, Olga Druce. A: Nicholas Cosentino. P: O'Neill and de Maria. D: William Muir.

Moon Vine, The (2/11/43, Morosco, 21)

Southern belle falls in love with penniless actor, much to the horror of her ultra-proper family. "A synthetic comedy that never seems even faintly real" *(Post)*. Yul Brynner (billed as Youl Bryner) had a minor role in this 1943 opus set in turn-of-the-century Louisiana. C: Haila Stoddard, Arthur Franz, Will Geer, Vera Allen, Philip Bourneuf. A: Patricia Coleman. P: Jack Kirkland. D: John Cromwell. CD/SD: Lucinda Ballard.

Moonchildren (2/21/72, Royale, 16)

An ingratiating comedy, *Moonchildren* chronicles the coming-of-age of eight college students during the fall semester of 1965. Rooming together communal style, they are funny and appealing as they pursue "relevance," the need to "relate," and more half-heartedly, education. Not drug oriented nor more than fashionably radical, they are casually promiscuous and enamored of the humorous put-on. What little plot there is tends to grimness. The mother of one student dies of cancer, a romance goes sour, and the final curtain is an unhappy one. Though poignant, it's unsatisfying. The crew of students have been too enjoyable companions, from the delightful opening where three of them preside over the birth of kittens on a darkened stage, to a zany self-immolation aborted with watered gasoline. These are intelligent, likable individuals: Bob, groping for entity and the means to communicate; Kathy, his girl, waiting for a commitment; Shelly, an original who likes to sit under tables; studious Norman and ladies' man Dick; placid Ruth; and Mike and Cootie who pretend to be brothers. Well directed, the actors won general praise and Cara Duff-MacCormick as Shelly was nominated for a Tony as Best Supporting Actress. Commissioned by London's Royal Court Theater, the play was produced there as *Cancer*. At Arena Stage in Washington, D.C., and retitled *Moonchildren* it ran forty performances before moving to Broadway with the same cast of principals. Though it stayed briefly, the play was not dead. On 11/4/73, with a new cast directed by John Pasquin, *Moonchildren* was revived O/B for a rousing 394 performances. A: Michael Weller. C: James Woods, Jill Eikenberry, Cara Duff-MacCormick, Christopher Guest, Stephen Collins, Maureen Anderman, Kevin Conway, Edward Herrmann. P: David Merrick i.a.w. Byron Goldman, Max Brown by arrangement with Martin Rosen and Arena Stage Productions. D: Alan Schneider. SD: William Ritman.

Moon-Flower, The (2/25/24, Astor, 48)

A lowly clerk (Sidney Blackmer) meets and romances a beautiful woman (Elsie Ferguson) in glamorous Monte Carlo, but she leaves him for a wealthy duke (Frederic Worlock). Tedious twaddle. A: Zoe Akins, from a play by Lajos Biro. P: Charles L. Wagner.

Moonlight and Honeysuckle (9/29/19, Henry Miller, 97)

Demure young girl (Ruth Chatterton) fabricates a disreputable past to test the love of her three suitors. Predictable comedy by George Scarborough, similar in plot to Middleton and Bolton's *Polly With A Past* (1917). C: Lucile Watson, James Rennie, Charles Trowbridge, Katherine Emmett. P/D: Henry Miller.

Moor Born (4/3/34, Playhouse, 63)

This play by Dan Totheroh dealt with three crucial years (1845–48) in the lives of the tragic Brontë family, and the sacrifices made by Emily (Helen Gahagan), Charlotte (Frances Starr), and Anne (Edith Barrett) on behalf of their dissolute brother, Branwell (Glenn Anders). The publication in 1847 of *Agnes Grey, Jane Eyre,* and *Wuthering Heights* alerted discerning critics to the literary genius of the three sisters. The play ended the following year (1848) with the deaths of Emily and Branwell. Skillfully directed by Melvyn Douglas, *Moor Born* proved a sensitively written, frequently absorbing biographical drama. P: Bushar and Tuerk.

SV: The Brontë sisters were ill-served by a florid pseudobiography entitled *Devotion* (WB, 1947) scripted by Keith Winter and directed by Curtis Bernhardt. The cast was headed by Ida Lupino (Emily), Olivia de Havilland (Charlotte), Nancy Coleman (Anne), Arthur Kennedy (Branwell), Paul Henreid (Rev. Nichols), and Sydney Greenstreet (Thackeray).

More Stately Mansions (10/31/67, Broadhurst, 142)

An eagerly awaited theatre event—Ingrid Bergman's return to the stage, after 21 years, in the American premiere of Eugene O'Neill's last play—turned out to be a major disappointment. The critics characterized the evening as "murky . . . slow-moving . . . soporific," and the star's performance was thought to leave "much to be desired." Set in 1830's New England, the play tells how an unyielding matriarch (Miss Bergman) battles for control of her introverted and idealistic son, Simon (Arthur Hill), against his equally determined wife, Sara (Colleen Dewhurst). As he watches the two women in his life join forces to dominate him, Simon becomes increasingly deranged, a spell broken only when his mother finally retreats into her own fantasy world. At the end—as the drama shifts abruptly from naturalism to symbolism—we are left to infer that Simon will eventually regain both his sanity and his lost idealism. *More Stately Mansions*, left unrevised at O'Neill's death, was cut and edited by Jose Quintero (D) from the playwright's notes. The drama was intended to form part of a projected nine-play cycle, a family history spanning many years in American life. Only four of the plays were written, and only two survive: *More Stately Mansions* and the play that leads up to it, *A Touch of the Poet*. P: Elliot Martin. CD: Jane Greenwood. SD: Ben Edwards.

More the Merrier, The (9/15/41, Cort, 16)

The Colorado castle of a millionaire newspaper tycoon is mistaken for a hotel by a group of snowbound tourists. Highlight: the frantic transfer from one room to another of a corpse on roller skates. This slapstick melodrama, directed by Otto Preminger, was dismissed by reviewer Howard Barnes (*Herald Tribune*) as "frenetically boring . . . a dull and witless burlesque." C: Frank Albertson, Keenan Wynn, Millard Mitchell, Teddy Hart, Grace McDonald, Doro Merande, J. C. Nugent, Louis Hector, Will Geer, Saint Subber. A: Frank Gabrielson and Irvin Pincus. P: Otto Preminger and Norman Pincus.

Morning Star (4/16/40, Longacre, 63)

Molly Picon, darling of the Yiddish theatre, made her Broadway debut in this sentimental chronicle of Jewish family life. The comedy dealt with day-to-day crises of a widowed mother and her brood living on the lower East Side of Manhattan, 1910–1931. "A friendly and likable little play" (*Herald Tribune*). C: Joseph Buloff, Harold J. Stone, Sidney Lumet, Ross Harvey, David Morris, Georgette Harvey. A: Sylvia Regan. P: George Kondolf. D: Charles K. Freeman.

Morning's at Seven (11/30/39, Longacre, 44)

Rueful, frequently enchanting comedy about the placid lives of two neighboring midwestern families in their late sixties and early seventies. Youth is represented by a forty-year-old son named Homer, who is finally (perhaps) going to marry his thirty-nine-year-old sweetheart. (They have been engaged a mere seven years.) The disclosure that Homer's fiancée is pregnant triggers a series of seriocomic crises in both families. "Warmingly funny . . . gently delightful . . . a minor triumph" (*Sun*). *Morning's at Seven* was directed by Joshua Logan with the accent on farce. Though the original Broadway production lasted only forty-four performances, the comedy's reputation has grown through the years. C: Dorothy Gish, Russell Collins, John Alexander, Enid Markey, Effie Shannon, Thomas Chalmers, Jean Adair, Herbert Yost, Kate McComb. A: Paul Osborn. P: Dwight Deere Wiman. SD: Jo Mielziner.

R: (6/22/55, Cherry Lane, 125). C: Kate Harrington, Harrison Dowd, June Walker, Dorrit Kelton, Walter Klavun, Martha Morton, Tom Bosley, Gubi Mann. D: Warren Enters.

Most Immoral Lady, A (11/26/28, Cort, 160)

Undistinguished comedy about a lady blackmailer (Alice Brady) who attempts to reform. A/D: Townsend Martin. P: William A. Brady, Jr. and Dwight Deere Wiman.
SV: WB, 1929, Leatrice Joy, Walter Pidgeon, Sidney Blackmer.

Most of the Game (10/1/35, Cort, 23)

Breezy American newspaperman straightens out a British writer's tangled love life. Wispy comedy by Anglo-American author John Van Druten. C: James Bell, Robert Douglas and, in a bit role, Joshua Logan. P: Dwight Deere Wiman and Auriol Lee (D).

Mother Carey's Chickens (9/25/17, Cort, 39)

Sentimental tearjerker with Edith Taliaferro about a wise, compassionate mother and her brood of young ones. Adapted from Kate Douglas Wiggin's novel by Miss Wiggin and Rachel Crothers. P: John Cort. D: R. F. Cummings.
SV: RKO, 1938, Fay Bainter, Ruby Keeler, Anne Shirley, Walter Brennan, Virginia Weidler, Ralph Morgan; BV, 1962, *Summer Magic,* Dorothy McGuire, Hayley Mills, Burl Ives, Una Merkel, Michael J. Pollard.

Mother Lode (12/22/34, Cort, 9)

Melvyn Douglas (D) and his wife Helen Gahagan costarred in this sprawling historical drama set in early (1860's) San Francisco. The hero buys an interest in the Comstock Lode, helps build San Francisco into the west coast's most beautiful city, loses his fortune, but regains his visionary faith in the future when he is reunited with his loyal sweetheart. *Mother Lode* was withdrawn after nine performances. C: Beulah Bondi, Tex Ritter, Lester Lonergan, Barbara O'Neil. A: Dan Totheroh and George O'Neil. P: Bushar and Tuerk.
SV: RKO, 1936, *Yellow Dust,* Richard Dix, Leila Hyams.

Mother Sings (11/12/35, 58th Street, 7)

Drab Freudian melodrama about a possessive mother who poisons her son's mind against women and turns him into a psychotic murderer. C: Mary Morris, Wendell Phillips, Bernardine Hayes. A/D: Hugh Stange. P: William Crosby.

Mountain Man, The (12/12/21, Maxine Elliott's, 163)

Proud Virginia mountaineer tries to curb a trigger temper. World War I helps calm him down a mite as does returning a hero from the war and winning the girl he loves. Atmospheric comedy-drama by Clare Kummer, greatly aided by Sidney Blackmer's performance in the leading role. C: Catherine Dale Owen, Chester Morris. P: Charles L. Wagner. D: Clare Kummer and Edward Elsner.

Mourning Becomes Electra (10/26/31, Guild, 158)

Taking the Orestes legend from Greek drama, Eugene O'Neill transposed it to post-Civil War New England and treated the theme of revenge in Freudian terms. Instead of being hounded by the Fates, O'Neill's New Englanders are obsessed by incestuous desires. As in the Greek fable, a returning warrior is slain by his faithless wife and her lover. His murder—avenged by his daughter, Lavinia—triggers further homicide and death. When the killing ends, Lavinia locks herself in the ancestral mansion to expiate the family curse in solitary,

Mourning Becomes Electra. **Alla Nazimova (standing) and Alice Brady (1931–32).** *Courtesy Museum of the City of New York Theatre and Music Collection.*

lifelong penance. "It may turn out to be the only permanent contribution yet made by the twentieth century to dramatic literature" (Joseph Wood Krutch, *The Nation*). Eugene O'Neill intended his fourteen-act trilogy to be performed on three successive nights. Later, it was decided that it would have to be done as one long play that would run, with a dinner intermission, from five P.M. to nearly midnight. Superbly acted by Alice Brady and Alla Nazimova, *Mourning Becomes Electra* was one of the memorable events in the history of the American theatre. Many critics consider the play O'Neill's masterpiece. C: Earle Larimore, Thomas Chalmers, Lee Baker, Arthur Hughes, Erskine Sanford. P: The Theatre Guild. D: Philip Moeller. SD: Robert Edmond Jones.

R: (5/9/32, Alvin, 12). C: Judith Anderson, Florence Reed, Walter Abel, Crane Wilbur.

(*Note:* This was a limited New York engagement of the touring company production).

R: (11/15/72, Circle in the Square-Joseph E. Levine Theatre, 55). C: Colleen Dewhurst, Pamela Payton-Wright, Donald Davis, Stephen McHattie, Alan Mixon, William Hickey, Jocelyn Brando. D: Theodore Mann.

SV: RKO, 1947, Rosalind Russell, Michael Redgrave, Katina Paxinou, Raymond Massey, Leo Genn, Kirk Douglas, Nancy Coleman (written, produced and directed by Dudley Nichols).

Move On, Sister (10/24/33, Playhouse, 7)

Millionaire leaves his money to a prostitute (Fay Bainter); greedy relatives try to swindle the poor soul out of her rightful inheritance. unsavory 30's drama, as tawdry as its title. C: Harry Davenport, Ernest Glendinning, Moffat Johnston. A: Daniel N. Rubin. P: A. H. Woods. D: A. H. Van Buren.

Mr. Adam (5/25/49, Royale, 5)

Sniggering sex comedy about the last man in the world not rendered sterile by an atomic explosion; adapted by Jack Kirkland (A/P/D) from the novel by Pat Frank. "A little atrocity . . . banal and tasteless and offensive . . ."(*Sun*). ". . . more suited to production behind a barn than in a theatre" (George Jean Nathan). C: James Dobson, Elisabeth Fraser, Frank Albertson, Howard Freeman.

Mr. and Mrs. North (1/12/41, Belasco, 163)

A pleasant young couple return to their Greenwich Village apartment to find a cadaver in the closet and a second murder in the offing. At the last moment, the scatterbrained wife solves the crimes with the aid of a cooking recipe. Absolved of suspicion, the Norths plan to move to another apartment where there will be less closet space. This diverting mystery-comedy opened on Broadway two nights after the premiere of another murder play. *Mr. and Mrs. North* had a moderately successful run, but suffered by comparison with its phenomenally successful rival, *Arsenic and Old Lace*. C: Peggy Conklin, Albert Hackett, Millard Mitchell, Philip Ober. A: Owen Davis b/o the novel, *The Norths Meet Murder*, by Frances and Richard Lockridge.* P/D: Alfred de Liagre, Jr. SD: Jo Mielziner.

SV: MGM, 1941, Gracie Allen, William Post, Jr., Paul Kelly, Rose Hobart, Tom Conway.

---

*Mystery novelist Richard Lockridge was drama critic of the *New York Sun* for many years.

Mr. Barnum (9/9/18, Criterion, 24)

Quaint, leisurely character comedy of circus life in the mid-eighteenth century with jovial pioneer showman P. T. Barnum (Thomas A. Wise) shepherding his flock of freaks from one stand to another, presiding over the marriage of General Tom Thumb, preaching the gospel of humbuggery, and discovering the great American doctrine that it pays to advertise. C: Carlotta Monterey, Richard Gordon, Phoebe Foster. A: Harrison Rhodes and Thomas A. Wise. P: Charles Dillingham.

Note: The life of this master showman was brought to the screen in *The Mighty Barnum* (UA, 1934). The screenplay by Gene Fowler and Bess Meredyth was a fanciful, highly fictionalized affair. The cast was headed by Wallace Beery (Barnum), Adolphe Menjou, Virginia Bruce, Janet Beecher, Rochelle Hudson, Lucille La Verne, and Herman Bing.

Mr. Barry's Etchings (1/31/50, 48th Street, 31)

Innocuous comedy about an amiable counterfeiter (Lee Tracy) who uses his talents to help those in need. A: Walter Bullock and Daniel Archer. P: Brock Pemberton. D: Pemberton and Margaret Perry.

Mr. Big (9/30/41, Lyceum, 7)

George S. Kaufman made his producing debut with this mystery-comedy misfire. The plot dealt with a murder taking place during the premiere performance of a Broadway play. The district attorney and police commissioner (both of whom are in the opening night audience) take over the investigation and uncover the culprit. "... a badly botched evening" *(Journal-American)*. C: Hume Cronyn, Fay Wray, Betty Furness, Barry Sullivan, Harry Gribbon, Oscar Polk, Mitzi Hajos, Robert Whitehead. A: Arthur Sheekman and Margaret Shane. P/D: George S. Kaufman.

Mr. Gilhooley (9/30/30, Broadhurst, 31)

Helen Hayes (grievously miscast) as a tough-talking Irish prostitute who finally is strangled to death by her jealous lover. Drab, sketchily written play by Frank B. Elser b/o the novel by Liam O'Flaherty; a dire failure. (Ben Hecht dubbed it "Uncle Vanya in Dublin"). C: Arthur Sinclair, Maire O'Neill. P/D: Jed Harris.

Mr. Moneypenny (10/17/28, Liberty, 62)

A timid clerk (Donald Meek) sells his soul in return for limitless wealth, learns to rue the bargain. Artless allegorical fable by Channing Pollock (A/P). Making his Broadway debut as Donald Meek's son was eighteen-year-old Evan (later Van) Heflin. Also in the cast: Margaret Wycherly, Hale Hamilton, Ruth Nugent, Catherine Dale Owen. D: Richard Boleslawski.

Mr. Peebles and Mr. Hooker (10/10/46, Music Box, 4)

God and the Devil battle for the souls of some Tennessee valley folks. ". . . remarkably tasteless and tedious . . . a real sow's ear" *(Herald Tribune)*. C: Rhys Williams, Howard Smith, Jeff Morrow, Paul Huber, Arthur Hunnicutt. A: Edward E. Paramore b/o novel by Charles Givens. P: Joseph M. Hyman.

Note: Film director Martin Ritt made his Broadway directorial debut with this short-lived morality play. Ritt subsequently directed such features as *The Long Hot Summer, Sounder, Pete 'n' Tillie,* etc.

Mr. Pickwick (9/17/52, Plymouth, 61)

Episodic comedy "freely drawn from incidents in Charles Dickens' *The Pickwick Papers.*" Taking ample liberties with the original, adapter Stanley Young centered his play around Pickwick's ordeal at the hands of his misguided landlady, culminating in the famous breach-of-promise trial. ". . . thoroughly delightful" *(New York Times)*. ". . . extremely mild fun" *(Post)*. C: George Howe, Clive Revill, Estelle Winwood, Nydia Westman, Phillippa Bevans, Louis Hector, Basil Howes, Nigel Green, Jacques Aubuchon, Sarah Marshall. P: The Playwrights Company. D: John Burrell.

Mr. Pitt (1/22/24, 39th Street, 87)

An ineffectual paper hanger (Walter Huston), married to a mean-spirited shrew (Minna Gombell) is idolized (and idealized) by a gentle spinster (Antoinette Perry). Nothing goes right in Mr. Pitt's life. When his wife runs off with a jazz trombonist, Mr. Pitt takes off for the Klondike. Twenty years later he returns to find his wife dead and his college-educated son as ashamed of him as his wife had been. This interesting but overly placid character study of a shy, good-hearted "average man" was adapted by Zona Gale from her novel, *Birth.* Other cast members included Parker Fennelly, C. Henry Gordon, and Borden Harriman. P/D: Brock Pemberton.

Mr. Sycamore (11/13/42, Guild, 19)

Whimsical fable about a postman (Stuart Erwin) who decides it would be nice to turn into a tree, and does. "The play stops growing long before the tree does" *(PM)*. *Mr. Sycamore*, adapted from a story by Robert Ayre, was written by screenwriter Ketti Frings (*Hold Back the Dawn, Come Back, Little Sheba*, etc.). Miss Frings later won the Pulitzer Prize for her dramatization of Thomas Wolfe's *Look Homeward, Angel* (1957). C: Lillian Gish, Russell Collins, Enid Markey, Otto Hulett, John Philliber, Harry Townes, Leona Powers. P: The Theatre Guild. D: Lester Vail. SD: Samuel Leve.

Mrs. Boltay's Daughters (10/23/15, Comedy, 17)

Sixteen-year-old Eva Le Gallienne (in blackface) made her Broadway debut as a Negro maid in this flimsy comedy-drama by Marion Fairfax. A puerile theatrical mistake. C: Rita Jolivet, Merle Maddern, Forrest Winant. P: Fiske and Mooser. D: Harrison Grey Fiske.

Mrs. Bumpstead-Leigh (4/3/11, Lyceum, 64)

An ambitious social climber changes her name and nationality in an endeavor to conquer high society. Her campaign is complicated, however, when she is recognized by a former Iowa boyfriend who knew her when she was plain Della Sales. Highly amusing satirical comedy by Houghton Mifflin editor Harry James Smith who was killed in 1918 on a mission for the Red Cross. C: Mrs. Fiske, Henry E. Dixey, Florine Arnold. P/D: Harrison Grey Fiske.

R: (4/1/29, Klaw, 72) by George C. Tyler. C: Mrs. Fiske, Sidney Toler, Stella Mayhew.

Mrs. Gibbons' Boys (5/4/49, Music Box, 5)

George Abbott (P/D) farce about a doting mother and her three hoodlum sons. ". . . outrageous rubbish . . . about as coarse and as absurd as a play can get to be" (*Sun*). *Mrs. Gibbons' Boys* was coauthored by Will Glickman and Joseph Stein who went on to write the books for such musicals as *Plain and Fancy* and *Mr. Wonderful*. Joseph Stein also wrote the long-run musical hit, *Fiddler on the Roof*. C: Glenda Farrell, Ray Walston, Lois Bolton, Royal Dano, Francis Compton, Edward Andrews.

SV: British, 1962, Kathleen Harrison, Lionel Jeffries, Diana Dors, Milo O'Shea.

Mrs. January and Mr. X (3/31/44, Belasco, 43)

An ex-president (Frank Craven) of the United States meets and falls in love with a flibbertigibbet widow (Billie Burke) who fancies herself a radical. Convinced that a communist revolution is coming, she converts the rock-bound Republican to more liberal ways with the result that the G.O.P. drafts him to run for the presidency again. ". . . a flimsy whimsy" (*Herald Tribune*). C: Barbara Bel Geddes, Nicholas Joy. A: Zoe Akins. P: Richard Myers. D: Elliott Nugent and Arthur Sircom. CD: Adrian. SD: Paul Morrison.

Mrs. Kimball Presents (2/29/44, 48th Street, 7)

Lady producer develops a yen for her leading man. ". . . the only favorable comment we can make is that it began late and was over early" (*Post*). C: Arthur Margetson, Vicki Cummings, Jesse White, Michael Ames. A/P: Alonzo Price. P: Gerken and Chandler.

Mrs. Leffingwell's Boots (1/11/05, Savoy, 123)

Mrs. Leffingwell's boots are discovered in the bedroom of a handsome young bachelor. Horrors! What will her friends and neighbors think? More important, what will her jealous husband think? Eventually, of course, how the innocent quilted-silk footwear found their way to the bachelor's quarters is satisfactorily explained, and the farce ends with husband and wife in each other's arms. "Very funny in spots . . . narrowly misses being one of the best [comedies] of the season" (*New York Times*). C: Margaret Illington, William Courtenay, Vincent Serrano, Ernest Lawford. A/D: Augustus Thomas. P: Charles Frohman.

Mrs. McThing (2/20/52, ANTA, 350)

Mrs. Howard V. Larue II (Helen Hayes) incurs the wrath of a vengeful witch who substitutes a prissy little boy (Brandon de Wilde) for her roughneck son (also played by Master de Wilde), and spirits the real lad off to a life of crime with a trio of incompetent burglars. When the mother sets out to reclaim her nine-year-old mobster, she is bewitched and transformed into a scrubwoman in the gangsters' Shantyland Pool Hall Lunchroom. In the end, the haughty Mrs. Larue is taught to see some good in everyone, is delighted to take the boy back on his own terms, and adopts the witch's little girl in the bargain. "A delectably imaginative fable" (*Herald Tribune*). ". . . rather too heavily antic and too studiously whimsical [but] does have flights of real imagination and humor" (*Post*). It took Mary Chase, author of *Harvey* (1944), five years to complete the script of this "play for children of all ages." *Mrs. McThing* was expected to play two weeks as a limited-run offering by ANTA (American National Theatre and Academy), but the comic fantasy became a surprise Broadway hit, and the fortnight's engagement was indefinitely extended. C: Jules Munshin,* Irwin Corey,* Fred Gwynne,* Ernest Borgnine,* Iggie Wolfington,* Enid Markey, Lydia Reed. D: Joseph

Buloff. CD: Lucinda Ballard. SD: Lester Polakov.

---

*Broadway (dramatic stage) debuts.

Mrs. O'Brien Entertains (2/8/39, Lyceum, 37)

Hackneyed George Abbott (P/D) comedy about the Americanization of some shanty Irish in the New York of 1848. C: Margaret Mullen, Harry Shannon, Gene Tierney (deb.). A: Harry Madden. CD/SD: Jo Mielziner.

Mrs. Partridge Presents (1/5/25, Belmont, 146)

The younger generation rebels against the domination of their well-meaning mother. Charming comedy by Mary (Mrs. Deems Taylor) Kennedy and Ruth Hawthorne. Belasco star Blanche Bates played the mother adroitly, but it was ingenue Ruth Gordon who stole the show. C: Edward (later John) Emery (deb.), Sylvia Field, Eliot Cabot, Charles Waldron. P/D: Guthrie McClintic.

Mrs. Patterson (12/1/54, National, 101)

Earthbound fantasy about the grandiose daydreams of a fifteen-year-old southern lass (Eartha Kitt) who longs to be "a rich white woman." Eventually the girl is forced to renounce her daydreams, and face the realities of her poverty-stricken life. C: Enid Markey, Avon Long, Ruth Attaway, Estelle Hemsley, Helen Dowdy. A: Charles Sebree and Greer Johnson. L/M: James Shelton. P: Leonard Sillman. D: Guthrie McClintic. CD/SD: Raoul Pene du Bois.

Mrs. Wiggs of the Cabbage Patch (9/3/04, Savoy, 150)

Plucky, shanty-town widow and her large brood of children face adversity with fortitude and unquenchable optimism. Pleasant, sentimental comedy-drama adapted from Alice Hegan Rice's novel.

C: Madge Carr Cook, Thurston Hall, William Hodge, Mabel Taliaferro, Helen Lowell. A: Anne Crawford Flexner. P: Liebler and Company. D: Oscar Eagle.
SV: Par, 1934, Pauline Lord, W. C. Fields, ZaSu Pitts, Donald Meek, Virginia Weidler; 1940, Fay Bainter, Hugh Herbert, Vera Vague.

Mud Turtle, The (8/20/25, Bijou, 52)

Waitress marries farm boy, tries to convince his family she's not a wanton. Routine and predictable. C: Helen MacKellar, Buford Armitage. A: Elliott Lester. P: A. and R. Riskin. D: Willard Mack.
SV: Fox, 1930, *City Girl*, Charles Farrell, Mary Duncan.

· **Mulatto (10/24/35, Vanderbilt, 373)**

Langston Hughes' grim tale of a Georgia plantation owner who is the father of several children by his Negro housekeeper. In the end, the haughty landowner is strangled to death by the most defiant of his half-caste sons. The boy then takes his own life, thereby thwarting the vengeance of a lynch mob. The plight of the mulatto—spurned by the whites, resented by the blacks—was captured in vivid fashion in this harrowing melodrama. C: Stuart Beebe, Rose McClendon, Hurst Amyx, Connie Gilchrist. P/D: Martin Jones. Musicalized by Langston Hughes and Jan Meyerowitz as *The Barrier* (1950) with Lawrence Tibbett and Muriel Rahn.

Mulberry Bush, The (10/26/27, Republic, 29)

The divorce plans of a young couple (Claudette Colbert and James Rennie) are altered when they find themselves locked overnight in the same bedroom. Weak 20's farce by Edward Knoblock. C: Isobel Elsom, Edwin Nicander. P: Charles Dillingham and A. H. Woods. D: Clifford Brooke.

The Music Master. David Warfield and Jane Cooper (Knickerbocker Theatre, 1906). *Courtesy Museum of the City of New York Theatre and Music Collection.*

Music Master, The (9/26/04, Belasco, 540)

Hugely successful tearjerker about a gentle German musician (David Warfield) who comes to America to search for his beloved duaghter. C: Jane Cowl, Minnie Dupree. A: Charles Klein. P/D: David Belasco. One of the towering hits of the 1900-1910 era, *The Music Master* surpassed the five hundred performance mark at a time when one hundred performances was considered a substantial run. So great was David Warfield's success in this masterpiece of hokum that he played no other role until 1907. In 1924 at the age of fifty-eight, the popular character comedian announced his decision to retire. He spurned all inducements to return to show business, including one for a million dollars to make a film of *The Music Master.* When asked why, he said: "I'd rather have people ask me why did you stop acting than why don't you stop acting?"

My Daughter, Your Son (5/13/69, Booth, 47)

Cheerful situation-comedy revolving around the marriage plans of a screenwriter's daughter and a dentist's son. C: Robert Alda, Vivian Vance, Bill McCutcheon, Dody Goodman, Don Scardino, Lee Lawson, Gene Lindsey. A: Phoebe and Henry Ephron. P: Hocker/Warren. D: Larry Arrick.

My Dear Children (1/31/40, Belasco, 117)

After seventeen years in Hollywood, John Barrymore returned to Broadway in this leisurely farce about an aging romantic actor and the problems visited upon him by the sudden appearance of his three grown daughters. The swankiest firstnight audience of the season assembled in hopes that the star would indulge in some of the scandalous monkeyshines and outrageous ad-libs with which he regaled theatregoers during the pre-Broadway tryout of the play. Barrymore obliged by imitating brother Lionel, by giving a doleful reading of *The Owl and the Pussycat,* and—at one point in the evening—by hushing a tittering audience with Hamlet's "To be or not to be" soliloquy. For the most part, however, he stuck to the script with a kind of grim, weary determination. In the words of one critic: "A superbly gifted actor on a tired holiday." And, from George Jean Nathan: "I always said that I'd like Barrymore's acting 'till the cows came home. Well, ladies and gentlemen, last night the cows came home." C: Doris Dudley, Philip Reed, Tala Birell, Otto Hulett, Arnold Korff, Leo Chalzel. A: Catherine Turney and Jerry Horwin. P: Aldrich and Myers. D: Otto Preminger.

My Fair Ladies (3/23/41, Hudson, 32)

Two American showgirls (Betty Furness and Celeste Holm) masquerade as titled English refugees. ". . . the work of two American gentlemen masquerading as playwrights. It is a sensationally dreary effort" *(PM)*. Future best-selling authoress Jacqueline Susann had a minor role (as a Miss Grumley) in this 1941 comedy. C: Russell Hardie, Otto Hulett, Vincent Donehue. A: Arthur L. Jarrett and Marcel Klauber. P: Albert Lewis (D) and Max Siegel.

My Girl Friday (2/12/29, Republic, 253)

Trio of conniving chorus girls outsmart their would-be seducers. Odious 20's farce. C: Esther Muir, Nat Pendleton. A/D: William A. Grew. P: Schnebbe-Bacon, Inc.

My Heart's in the Highlands (4/13/39, Guild, 44)

William Saroyan's first play, a poignant mood piece set in Fresno, California in 1914. To the home of an improvident poet (Philip Loeb) and his nine-year-old son (Sidney Lumet) comes an aged Shakespearean actor who plays the bugle so sweetly that the neighbors bring gifts of food as a tribute. The old actor dies, and the poet and his family are evicted from their home for nonpayment of rent. The boy ends the play by turning to his father and saying: "I'm not mentioning any names, Pa, but something's wrong somewhere." Reviews of *My Heart's in the Highlands* were sharply divided. Brooks Atkinson in the *New York Times* hailed it as "an amusing, tender, whimsical poem." Wolcott Gibbs in *The New Yorker* wrote: "This collision between the most completely undisciplined talent in American letters and the actors of the Group Theatre bored me nearly to distraction and I would advise you to stay away from it unless you are especially fond of being badgered in the name of experimental drama." Robert Lewis made his directorial debut with this production and was praised for his "responsive and inventive" staging. C: Art Smith, William Hansen, Hester Sondergaard, Nicholas (Richard) Conte. CD/SD: Herbert Andrews. M: Paul Bowles.

My Lady Friends (12/3/19, Comedy, 214)

The farce-comedy upon which the musical *No, No, Nanette* was based dealt with a wealthy Bible publisher with a weakness for helping pretty young girls in trouble. It made use of such stock farce elements as mistaken identity, a jealous wife, a wily lawyer, an innocent ingenue, and a philandering husband, and offered this familiar pastiche in energetic, reasonably sprightly fashion. C: Frank Morgan, June Walker, Clifton Crawford, Edith King. A: Frank Mandel and Emil Nyitray. P: H. H. Frazee.

My Lady's Dress (10/10/14, Playhouse, 57)

Ponderous, multi-scene drama tracing the design and manufacture of a fashionable dress for a fashionable lady (Mary Boland). A: Edward Knoblock. P: Joseph Brooks. D: Frank Vernon.

My Mother, My Father and Me (3/23/63, Plymouth, 17)

Lillian Hellman's satirical travesty of American middle-class life in which a New York Jewish family—dominant mother (Ruth Gordon), submissive father (Walter Matthau), senile grandmother (Lili Darvas), and beatnik son (Anthony Holland)—are plagued by their own greed, stupidity, and lack of moral values. ". . . often immensely funny . . . relentlessly bitter [but] its central story lacks focus . . ." *(Post)*. C: Dorothy Greener, Tom Pedi, Helen Martin, Leona Powers, Eda Heinemann, Joe E. Marks, Sudie Bond, Barbara Mostel, Heywood Hale Broun, Mark Lenard, Milo Boulton, Henry Gibson. A: Lillian Hellman b/o the novel, *How Much?* by Burt Blechman. P: Kermit Bloomgarden. D: Gower Champion (with an uncredited assist from Arthur Penn). SD: Howard Bay.

My Name is Aquilon (2/9/49, Lyceum, 31)

Handsome confidence man seeks employment as personal secretary to a black-market profiteer, ends by running off with his employer's nubile daughter. "A threadbare little comedy" *(Sun)*. Jean-Pierre Aumont, Lilli Palmer, and Phyllis Kirk made their Broadway debuts in this 40's Theatre Guild production. C: Arlene Francis, Lawrence Fletcher, Doe Avedon. A: Philip Barry b/o a play by Jean Pierre Aumont. D: Robert B. Sinclair. CD: Valentina and Castillo. SD: Stewart Chaney.

My Sister Eileen (12/26/40, Biltmore, 866)

Rollicking farce about two Ohio sisters trying to survive in a nutty Greenwich Village apartment while seeking fame, fortune and romance in New York. "Side-splitting . . . the giddiest delight to be seen here-abouts since *You Can't Take It With You*" *(Post)*. In true "show must go on" tradition, the opening night performance of *My Sister Eileen* was performed with humor and grace by a company that had only recently been informed of the tragic death of Eileen McKenney, heroine of the play's title. She and her author-husband, Nathanael West, were killed in an automobile accident shortly before the Broadway premiere. C: Shirley Booth, Jo Ann Sayers, Morris Carnovsky, William Post, Jr., Richard Quine, Bruce MacFarlane, Gordon Jones, Effie Afton, Eda Heinemann. A: Joseph Fields and Jerome Chodorov b/o Ruth McKenney's autobiographical *New Yorker* stories. P: Max Gordon. D: George S. Kaufman. SD: Donald Oenslager.
Musicalized by Fields, Chodorov, Leonard Bernstein, Betty Comden and Adolph Green as *Wonderful Town* (1953) with Rosalind Russell, Edith Adams, George Gaynes, Chris Alexander, Dody Goodman.

SV: Col, 1942, Rosalind Russell, Janet Blair, Brian Aherne, George Tobias, Allyn Joslyn, June Havoc, Elizabeth Patterson, Richard Quine (directed by Alexander Hall); 1955, Betty Garrett, Janet Leigh, Jack Lemmon, Kurt Kasznar, Dick York, Bob Fosse, Tommy Rall (directed by Richard Quine).

My Sweet Charlie (12/6/66, Longacre, 31)

Forced by circumstances to hide out together in an abandoned Gulf coast cottage, a southern white girl (Bonnie Bedelia) and a northern black man (Louis Gossett) learn to overcome their mutual hostility and prejudices. ". . . deeply and honestly touching . . . remarkably poignant" *(Post)*. A: David Westheimer b/o his novel. P: Bob Banner Associates. D: Howard Da Silva. SD: Jo Mielziner.

My Three Angels (3/11/53, Morosco, 344)

A trio of escaped convicts take refuge with a French family besieged by conniving relatives. Before proceeding on their way, the three obliging scoundrels arrange a couple of convenient murders and thus set matters right for their grateful hosts. ". . . an engaging and pleasantly preposterous comedy" *(News)*. C: Walter Slezak, Darren McGavin, Jerome Cowan, Henry Daniell, Carmen Mathews, Will Kuluva, Robert Carroll, Eric Fleming, Joan Chandler, Nan McFarland. A: Sam and Bella Spewack b/o a play by Albert Husson. P: Saint Subber, Rita Allen and Archie Thomson. D: Jose Ferrer. CD: Lucinda Ballard. SD: Boris Aronson.

SV: Par, 1955, *We're No Angels*, Humphrey Bogart, Peter Ustinov, Aldo Ray, Joan Bennett, Basil Rathbone, Leo G. Carroll (directed by Michael Curtiz).

Mystery Man, The (1/26/28, Bayes, 100)

Bachelor finds a murdered man on his living room sofa. Second-rate whodunit, produced and directed by that indefatigable cut-rate ticket entrepreneur, Gustav Blum. C: Weldon Heyburn, Allyn Joslyn. A: Morris Ankrum and Vincent Duffey.

Mystery Ship, The (3/14/27, Garrick, 121)

Low-grade whodunit with no-name cast, bargain basement production. A: Edgar Schoenberg and Milton Silver. P/D: Gustav Blum.

Mystery Square (4/4/29, Longacre, 44)

The adventurous Prince Florizel (Gavin Muir) joins London's Suicide Club, comes within an ace of losing his royal life. Languid melodrama based, in part, on Robert Louis Stevenson's celebrated short story, *The Suicide Club*. ". . . an unhappy amalgram of literature and Broadway tricks . . . stiltedly rhetorical and self-consciously ornate" *(New York Times)*. A: Hugh Anderson and George Bamman. P/D: Murray Phillips. SD: Cleon Throckmorton.

SV: MGM, 1936, *Trouble for Two*, Robert Montgomery, Rosalind Russell, Frank Morgan, Louis Hayward, Reginald Owen, David Holt, Virginia Weidler.

Note: Prince Florizel was supposed to be a counterpart of the Prince of Wales, who later became King Edward VII.

N

Naked Genius, The (10/21/43, Plymouth, 36)

Semi-autobiographical comedy by Gypsy Rose Lee about the weird home life of Honey Bee Carroll (Joan Blondell), a strip-tease artiste with literary ambitions and a yen for culture. Honey Bee agrees to wed a socially prominent book publisher, but, at the last moment, settles instead for her burlesque manager (Millard Mitchell). "... the whole thing is an appalling mess, a silly and vulgar and embarrassing hodge-podge..." *(PM)*. Despite bad reviews, *The Naked Genius* was a smash hit in its pre-Broadway tryout. Both Gypsy Rose Lee and George S. Kaufman (D) begged Michael Todd (P) to close the show out of town. "Take it off," they implored, anticipating a Broadway debacle. Todd turned a deaf ear to their pleas. Reason: the screen rights had been sold on a percentage arrangement. Consequently, the showman was determined to drag the exhibit to New York and keep it running a stipulated three weeks in order to collect $350,000 from 20th Century-Fox. After its 36th performance, the show was carted to the warehouse. Quipped Miss Lee: "For the sake of the legitimate theatre, I have just tossed my typewriter out the window." C: Phyllis Povah, Rex O'Malley, Doro Merande, Bertha Belmore, Georgia Sothern.
SV: Fox, 1946, *Doll Face*, Vivian Blaine, Dennis O'Keefe, Perry Como, Carmen Miranda.

Nancy's Private Affair (1/13/30, Vanderbilt, 136)

Divorcée wins back her ex-husband by turning herself into a glamour girl. Familiar comedy from an old stencil. C: Minna Gombell, Lester Vail, Stanley Ridges. A/P/D: Myron C. Fagan.
SV: RKO, 1931, *Smart Woman*, Mary Astor, Robert Ames, Edward Everett Horton, John Halliday, Ruth Weston.

Napoleon (3/8/28, Empire, 12)

The last six years in the life of the little emperor (Lionel Atwill) highlighting his escape from Elba; his love for the Polish countess Maria Walewska (Selena Royle); the Waterloo campaign; and Napoleon's death from cancer on St. Helena. Dreary historical drama written in picture-book captions; hammy performance by Atwill in the title role. A: B. Harrison Orkow. P: James W. Elliott. D: Robert Milton and Frank Merlin.

Nathan Weinstein, Mystic, Connecticut (2/25/66, Atkinson, 3)

Labored comedy about the conflict between a retired civil servant (Sam Levene) and his neurotic daughter (Zohra Lampert). A: David Rayfiel. P: Philip Rose, Herschel Bernardi, and Jeanne Otto. D: Peter Kass.

National Anthem, The (1/23/22, Henry Miller, 114)

A play about a pair of jazz-age alcoholics, written by J. Hartley Manners as a vehicle for his wife, Laurette Taylor. A young bride (Laurette Taylor) believes she can reform her hard-drinking husband (Ralph Morgan). Instead, she, too, becomes a hopeless dipsomaniac. "An acrid sermon in four acts [featuring] a superb performance by a great actress" (Alexander Woollcott, *New York Times*). The lukewarm reception to her husband's tract on the evils of drink prompted this comment from Laurette; "There is no profit in being a prophet." P: George C. Tyler. D: J. Hartley Manners.

Native Son (3/24/41, St. James, 114)

Black chauffeur Bigger Thomas accidentally kills his wealthy employer's neurotic daughter and becomes a hunted man. While police and reporters search for the missing girl, he burns her body in the furnace of the house in which he works. Captured, tried, and convicted, Bigger goes to his death defiantly. Through an unintentional act of murder, he has struck a blow against the sanctity and security of the white man's world. Vividly staged by Orson Welles, *Native Son* generated terrific emotional impact. "Stark melodrama, touched by the hand of genius" was the way one reviewer described the production. In the role of sullen, tortured Bigger Thomas, Canada Lee gave an excellent performance. The play was performed in ten scenes without intermission. Based on Richard Wright's novel, *Native Son* was adapted for the stage by Mr. Wright and Paul Green. C: Ray Collins, Everett Sloane, Anne Burr, Erskine Sanford, Nell Harrison, Paul Stewart, Philip Bourneuf, Rena Mitchell, Evelyn Ellis, Helen Martin, Joseph Pevney, Frances Bavier, John Berry. P: Orson Welles and John Houseman i.a.w. Bern Bernard. SD: James Morcom.

SV: Classic, 1950, Richard Wright, Jean Wallace.

Natural Affection (1/31/63, Booth, 36)

A teenage delinquent returns home from reform school and threatens the relationship of his mother (Kim Stanley) and her loud-mouthed lover (Harry Guardino). William Inge's inquiry into sexual depravity (adultery, incest, homosexuality, nymphomania) concludes in lurid melodrama when the embittered lad avenges himself on his mom's sex by murdering a girl. ". . . revels in degradation . . . a great misfortune" *(Post)*. ". . . perfectly wretched . . . a monstrous chimera . . ." *(The New Republic)*. C: Gregory Rozakis (deb.), Tom Bosley, Monica May. P: Oliver Smith (SD) i.a.w. Manuel Seff. D: Tony Richardson. CD: Ann Roth. M: John Lewis.

Natural Look, The (3/11/67, Longacre, 1)

Good cast—Gene Hackman, Brenda Vaccaro, Jerry Orbach, Zohra Lampert, Ethel Griffies—trapped in a trite, marriage-versus-career comedy-drama. A: Lee Thuna. P: Black/Price/Slade/Harvey. D: Martin Fried.

Nature's Way (10/16/57, Coronet, 61)

A homosexual tries to separate a handsome young playwright from his pregnant wife. This was only one of many plot ingredients in this satirical farce by Herman Wouk. Among the other subjects Mr. Wouk took pot shots at in *Nature's Way* were "tranquilizer drugs, fashionable obstetricians, interior decorators, television producers, penthouses, the income tax and Tennessee Williams. . . . I must confess that I didn't find it very funny. . . . *Nature's Way* is far from one of Mr. Wouk's triumphs" *(Post)*. C: Orson Bean, Betsy von Furstenberg, Scott McKay, Beatrice Arthur, Audrey Christie, Robert Emhardt, Edmon Ryan, Joe Silver, Barry Newman,* Godfrey Cambridge,* Sorrell Booke. P/D: Alfred de Liagre, Jr. SD: Donald Oenslager.

---

*Broadway debuts.

Naughty Anthony (1/8/00, Herald Square, 90)

Romantic entanglements jeopardize the career of a straitlaced professor of morality. Feeble farce by David Belasco (A/P/D). C: Blanche Bates, Frank Worthing, Albert Bruning, Claude Gillingwater, Brandon Tynan.

Naughty Cinderella (11/9/25, Lyceum, 121)

Frothy bedroom comedy in which a flirtatious French secretary (Irene Bordoni) pretends to be *trés risqué*, but she's really a good girl, folks. C: Henry Kendall, Nat Pendleton. A: Avery Hopwood b/o a play by Peter and Falk. P: Charles Frohman. D: W. H. Gilmore.

SV: Par, 1932, *This is the Night*, Cary Grant, Lili Damita, Roland Young, Charles Ruggles.

Note: Born in Cleveland, Ohio, Avery Hopwood was hailed by one critic as "the only living man who could write French farce better than a Frenchman." His successes included *Seven Days* (1907), *Fair and Warmer* (1915), *The Gold Diggers* (1919), and *The Bat* (1920). He was drowned in the surf at Nice in 1928 at the age of forty-six.

Nearly Married (9/5/13, Gaiety, 123)

Marital mixups and legal complications almost ruin a second honeymoon. "Extremely amusing farce . . . heartily recommended" *(New York Times)*. C: Bruce McRae, Jane Grey, John Westley. A/D: Edgar Selwyn. P: Cohan and Harris.

Ned McCobb's Daughter (11/29/26, John Golden, 144)

A shrewd and indomitable Yankee (Clare Eames) copes with her worthless husband (Earle Larimore), comforts her unsuccessful father (Albert Perry), and outsmarts her flashy bootlegger brother-in-law (Alfred Lunt). Lively melodramatic comedy-drama by Sidney Howard.

Nearly Married. **Jane Grey and Bruce McRae (Gaiety Theatre, September 5, 1913).** *Courtesy Museum of the City of New York Theatre and Music Collection.*

"Nowhere have I ever seen anything better than Mr. Alfred Lunt's acting as Babe Callahan, bootlegger" (Franklin P. Adams, *The Diary Of Our Own Samuel Pepys*). C: Edward G. Robinson, Margalo Gillmore, Philip Loeb, Morris Carnovsky. P: The Theatre Guild. D: Philip Moeller.

SV: A silent version (Pathé, 1928) featured Irene Rich, Robert Armstrong, and Carole Lombard.

Nemesis (4/4/21, Hudson, 56)

Jealous husband kills faithless wife and pins the murder on her lover. Murky melodrama by Augustus Thomas. C: Emmett Corrigan, Olive Tell, Pedro de Cordoba. P: George M. Cohan. D: John Meehan.

Nerves (9/1/24, Comedy, 16)

Lugubrious World War I drama by Stephen Vincent Benet and editor-publisher John Farrar (Farrar and Rinehart). Two daredevil fliers (Kenneth

MacKenna and Paul Kelly) are in love with the same girl (Winifred Lenihan). One of the daredevils loses his nerve (and his legs) and nobly steps aside so that his sweetheart and best pal can find happiness together. P/D: William A. Brady, Jr. Humphrey Bogart had a small but prominent role in *Nerves* as the heroine's brother, Bob Thatch. Also prominent in the supporting cast was Mary Phillips, whom Bogart married in 1928. After their divorce in 1937, Miss Phillips married Kenneth MacKenna who played the legless hero in *Nerves* and who later (1939) became MGM's story editor, a post he held for many years thereafter.

Nervous Wreck, The (10/9/23, Sam H. Harris, 271)

A timid-soul hypochondriac (Otto Kruger) goes to Arizona for rest and quiet, becomes a hero in spite of himself. Extremely funny farce-comedy by Owen Davis. C: June Walker, Edward Arnold, Hobart Cavanaugh, Albert Hackett. P: Lewis and Gordon. D: Addison Pitt.

Musicalized by Walter Donaldson and Gus Kahn as *Whoopee* (1928) with Eddie Cantor, Ruth Etting, Paul Gregory, Ethel Shutta, Gladys Glad, Tamara Geva, Albert Hackett, Buddy Ebsen.

SV: UA, 1930, *Whoopee,* Eddie Cantor, Paul Gregory, Ethel Shutta; RKO, 1944, *Up In Arms,* Danny Kaye, Dinah Shore, Dana Andrews, Louis Calhern, Margaret Dumont.

Never Live Over a Pretzel Factory (3/28/64, O'Neill, 9)

Foolish farce about a bibulous movie star (Dennis O'Keefe) who becomes involved with a trio of youthful filmmakers in Manhattan. Making their Broadway debuts in this short-lived 1964 offering were Martin Sheen, Lawrence Pressman, Gino Conforti, Nancy Franklin, Gloria Bleezarde. A: Jerry Devine. P: Paul Vroom, Buff Cobb, Albert Marre (D). SD: Howard Bay. M: Mitch Leigh.

Never No More (1/7/32, Hudson, 16)

A Southern plantation is the scene of rape, murder, and an old-style lynching. Strident melodramatic tragedy with an all-black cast that included Rose McClendon, Lew Payton, and Leigh Whipper. A: James Knox Millen. P/D: Robert Sparks.

Never Say Die (11/12/12, 48th St., 141)

Hypochondriac (William Collier) gets married thinking he has only a short time to live. Nimble farce-comedy by Collier (D) and W. H. Post. P: Lew Fields.

Musicalized by Walter Donaldson and Joseph Meyer as *Sweetheart Time* (1926) with Eddie Buzzell as the nervous-wreck bridegroom.

SV: Par, 1939, Bob Hope, Martha Raye, Alan Mowbray, Monty Woolley, Gale Sondergaard, Andy Devine.

Never Say Never (11/20/51, Booth, 7)

Comedic problems of a young couple living together without benefit of clergy. "... flat, stale and unprofitable" (*Post*). C: Anne Jackson, Hugh Reilly, Nita Talbot, Don Briggs. A: Carl Leo. P: Rosen and Meyer. D: Robert B. Sinclair. SD: Frederick Fox.

Never Too Late (11/27/62, Playhouse, 1,007)

Long-run comedy hit about the reactions of a middle-aged husband (Paul Ford) when he learns he is about to become a father again. "A good old-fashioned domestic farce" (*News*). C: Maureen O'Sullivan (deb.), Orson Bean, John Alexander, Fran Sharon, House Jameson, Leona Maricle. A: Sumner Arthur Long. P: Martin and Hollywood. D: George Abbott. SD: William and Jean Eckart. M: Jerry Bock, Sheldon Harnick, John Kander. *Note:* The London production starred Fred Clark and Joan Bennett in the leading roles.

SV: WB, 1965, Paul Ford, Maureen O'Sullivan, Connie Stevens, Jim

Hutton, Jane Wyatt, Lloyd Nolan, Henry Jones (directed by Bud Yorkin).

New Life, A (9/15/43, Royale, 69)

Nightclub singer battles wealthy in-laws for custody of her newborn child. Highlight: a harrowingly realistic childbirth scene, well-acted by leading lady Betty Field (wife of the play's author-director, Elmer Rice). ". . . a curiously hollow play—talky and heavy-handed" *(Sun)*. C: Ann Thomas, John Ireland, George Lambert. P: The Playwrights' Company.

New Toys (2/18/24, Fulton, 25)

A bored wife tries the stage, fails, and returns chastened to husband and child. "Plain buncombe through and through" (John Corbin, *New York Times*). "Stuff and nonsense" (Heywood Broun, *World*). C: Vivienne Osborne, Ernest Truex, Louise Closser Hale, Robert McWade. A: Oscar Hammerstein II and Milton Herbert Gropper. P: Sam H. Harris. D: Sam Forrest.

New York Exchange (12/30/26, Klaw, 82)

A mixed-up gigolo, played by Donn (later Donald) Cook, is kept in pampered luxury by a middle-aged "patroness" (Alison Skipworth). He finally finds the strength of character to leave her and strike out on his own. Surprisingly frank (for its time) study of bisexuality and Manhattan gay life. A: Peter Glenny. P: Ivan L. Wright. D: Clarke Silvernail.

New York Idea, The (11/19/06, Lyric, 66)

"Marry for whim and leave the rest to the divorce court—that's the New York idea of marriage." This was the theme of Langdon Mitchell's play in which the heroine (Mrs. Fiske) finally leaves her second husband to return to her first. A play of wit and substance, one of the outstanding high comedies of the American theatre. C: George Arliss, John Mason, Emily Stevens, Dudley Digges. P/D: Harrison Grey Fiske. R: (9/28/15, Playhouse) in repertory by Grace George. C: Grace George, Conway Tearle, John Cromwell, Ernest Lawford, Mary Nash, Guthrie McClintic.

Next Half Hour, The (10/29/45, Empire, 8)

Lugubrious melodrama by Mary Chase, author of *Harvey* (1944), in which a superstitious Irish-American (Fay Bainter) learns eventually that, for all her trust in banshees, prophecies, and premonitions, God has His own way of ordaining fate. "A long-winded tragedy [that] never succeeds in establishing the eerie mood of Celtic fantasy and lyricism at which it so obviously aims" *(Post)*. C: Jean Adair, Thelma Schnee, Art Smith, Conrad Janis, Francis Compton. P: Max Gordon. D: George S. Kaufman.

Nice People (3/2/21, Klaw, 247)

Tallulah Bankhead, Katharine Cornell, and Francine Larrimore as a trio of fast-stepping flappers of the post World War I set. Francine, the most brazen of the hussies, is redeemed (in a totally unconvincing ending) by the love of a good man, but Tallulah and Kit go on smoking and drinking and heaven only knows what else. Rachel Crothers (A/D) wrote this 20's saga of flaming youth, and Sam H. Harris was the producer. C: Robert Ames, Frederick Perry, Merle Maddern.

Nice Women (6/10/29, Longacre, 64)

Young girl (Sylvia Sidney) falls in love with older man (Robert Warwick). So-so 20's comedy. C: Verree Teasdale, George Barbier. A: William A. Grew. P: L. Lawrence Weber. D: William B. Friedlander.
SV: U, 1932, Sidney Fox, Frances Dee, Alan Mowbray.

Nice People. **Katharine Cornell, Francine Larrimore, and Tallulah Bankhead (1920–21).** *Courtesy Museum of the City of New York Theatre and Music Collection.*

Nigger, The (12/4/09, New, in repertory)

Sensationalistic 1909 melodrama about a southern governor, elected on a white supremacy platform, who discovers he has Negro blood. At the end of the play, he prepares to reveal his secret to his constituents. Produced in repertory by the short-lived New Theatre (backed by such millionaire drama lovers as the Astors, Morgans, and Vanderbilts), *The Nigger* was a boldly controversial play for its time. C: Guy Bates Post, Annie Russell, Lee Baker, Pedro de Cordoba. A: Edward Sheldon.

Nigger Rich (9/20/29, Royale, 11)

A young man (Eric Dressler) with an enviable war record turns out to be a rotter. 20's melodrama was as tasteless as its title; notable only in that it gave Spencer Tracy, as a friend of the "hero," his first starring role in the theatre. A/D: John McGowan. P: Lee Shubert.

Night Before Christmas, The (4/10/41, Morosco, 22)

Slapdash farce by Laura and S. J. Perelman about a gang of crooks who buy a rundown luggage shop and use it to tunnel into an adjoining bank vault. "For a play that never seemed to get started I thought it would never end" *(Journal-American).* C: George Mathews, Ruth Weston, Forrest Orr, Phyllis Brooks, Harry Bratsburg, Louis Sorin, Shelley Winters (deb.). P: Courtney Burr. D: Romney Brent. SD: Boris Aronson.

SV: WB, 1942, *Larceny, Inc.*, Edward G. Robinson, Broderick Crawford, Jane Wyman, Jack Carson, Anthony Quinn, Harry Davenport, Jackie Gleason.

Night Circus, The (12/2/58, Golden, 7)

The ill-fated romance of an irresponsible poor little rich girl (Janice Rule) and an embittered seaman (Ben Gazzara). ". . . pretentiously solemn. . . . The complications of this misalliance are sordid and endless, and are probed by some of the fanciest dialogue of the season" *(New York Times)*. C: Shepperd Strudwick, Arlene Golonka, Al Lewis, Arthur Storch. A: Michael V. Gazzo. P: Jay Julien. D: Frank Corsaro. SD: David Hays.

Night Duel, The (2/15/26, Mansfield, 17)

Lured to a man's bedroom, a virtuous wife (Marjorie Rambeau) retains her honor at gunpoint. Trash. A/P/D: Daniel Rubin and Edgar MacGregor.

Night Hawk (2/24/25, Bijou, 120)

Tough, fortyish streetwalker (Mary Newcomb) is pumped full of monkey glands, sheds twenty years in the twinkling of an eye, and promptly makes a play for the doctor's kid brother. Odious rubbish. A: Roland Oliver. P: Mulligan and Trebitsch. D: Arthur Hurley.

R: (12/25/26, Frolic, 144) by Lepane Amusement Company, with Carroll McComas as the prostitute *extraordinaire*.

Night Hostess (9/12/28, Martin Beck, 119)

Murder in a Manhattan gambling den. Passable 20's melodrama whose claim to fame is that it introduced nineteen-year-old Katharine Hepburn (billed as Katherine Burns) in her first Broadway appearance. Miss Hepburn was one of the nightclub hostesses and had little to do except stand around and look exotic. C: Norman Foster, Ruth Lyons, Porter Hall. A: Philip Dunning. P: John Golden. D: Winchell Smith.

SV: MGM, 1930, *Woman Racket*, Blanche Sweet, Tom Moore.

Night Life (10/23/62, Atkinson, 63)

Sidney Kingsley's (A/P/D) variation on the *Grand Hotel* theme in which a motley group of individuals gather in a New York after-hours spot and—to the accompaniment of old songs played and sung by the club's pianist (Bobby Short) and resident torch singer (Carol Lawrence)—work out their separate destinies. Kingsley used the key club setting as a microcosm of the contemporary world, but his symbolic melodrama failed to fuse into a successful drama. C: Neville Brand (deb.), Walter Abel, Carmen Mathews, Jack Kelly, Salome Jens, Jessica Walter, Paula Wayne, Murray Roman, Leonardo Cimino, Raymond St. Jacques, Barry Newman, Victor Thorley. SD: Albert Johnson.

Night Music (2/22/40, Broadhurst, 20)

A benevolent detective (Morris Carnovsky) presides over the love affair between a cocky messenger boy (Elia Kazan) and a forlorn young actress (Jane Wyatt), all three struggling to survive amidst the monumental indifference of New York City. Clifford Odets' Chekhovian-styled comedy-drama was described by critic John Gassner as "a fugue with variations that went off in too many directions. It proved to be more bewildering than enlightening." In the words of Brooks Atkinson *(New York Times)*, Night Music was "a foolish play by a man of great talent. It is time—high time—for him to awake and sing." C: Tom Tully, Roman Bohnen, Sanford Meisner, Philip Loeb, David Opatoshu, Art Smith, Walter Coy, Nicholas (Richard) Conte, Bette Grayson, Fred Stewart. P: The Group Theatre. D: Harold Clurman. SD: Mordecai Gorelik.

R: (4/8/51, ANTA, 9) by E. L. T. C: Rod Steiger, Leonard Barry, Bette Grayson. D: Peter Kass.

Night of January 16th, The (9/16/35, Ambassador, 232)

Threadbare little courtroom melodrama

by Ayn Rand in which the "jury" was selected from the audience. There were two endings depending on the verdict rendered. The play managed to run seven months on gimmicks. Opening night, producer Al Woods put boxing champ Jack Dempsey in the jury to create excitement. Another performance played to an audience that was totally blind, with Helen Keller as the foreman of the jury. C: Doris Nolan, Walter Pidgeon. D: John Hayden.

R: (2/22/73, McAlpin, 30) as *Penthouse Legend*. The cast of this O/B revival was headed by Kay Gillian and Harvey Solin. D: Philip J. Smith.

SV: Par, 1941, Robert Preston, Ellen Drew, Nils Asther, Alice White, Rod Cameron, Cecil Kellaway.

Night of the Auk (12/3/56, Playhouse, 8)

Claude Rains, Christopher Plummer, Wendell Corey, Dick York, and Martin Brooks return to earth in a rocket ship after a successful landing on the moon. A dismal and doomed lot they are, for according to dramatist Arch Oboler's 1956 play, atomic war has broken out on earth and mankind will soon be as extinct as the dodo. "A pessimistic, soap-boxy editorial..." *(Mirror)*. P: Kermit Bloomgarden. D: Sidney Lumet. SD: Howard Bay.

Night of the Dunce (12/28/66, Cherry Lane, 47)

A courageous librarian (Anne Revere) tries to prevent a band of hoodlums from wantonly destroying her library. Well-written, suspenseful O/B thriller. C: Tony Musante, Robert Salvio, Terry Kiser, Salem Ludwig. A: Frank Gagliano. P: Barr/Wilder/Albee. D: Joseph Hardy. SD: William Ritman.

Night of the Iguana, The (12/28/61, Royale, 316)

A group of lost and lonely people "who live on the fantastic level but who have got to operate on the realistic level" work out their assorted destinies at a ramshackle inn on the west coast of Mexico in the year 1940. Principal characters: the brash, nymphomaniacal proprietress (Bette Davis) of the hotel; a defrocked clergyman (Patrick O'Neal) bent on destruction; a gentle spinster (Margaret Leighton) and her aged poet-grandfather (Alan Webb), who live by their wits. This Tennessee Williams play builds to an extremely moving tragi-ironic conclusion as these four bedeviled misfits touch one another's lives. From their conflicts comes the realization that life must be endured, and that one must find a way—any way—to survive. "... one of Tennessee Williams' finest dramas ... searching, mystic, poetic ... a beautiful play" *(News)*. C: Patricia Roe, Lane Bradbury, James Farentino (deb.), Christopher Jones (deb.). P: Charles Bowden i.a.w. Violla Rubber. D: Frank Corsaro. CD: Noel Taylor. SD: Oliver Smith.

SV: MGM, 1964, Richard Burton, Deborah Kerr, Ava Gardner, Sue Lyon, Grayson Hall (directed by John Huston).

Note: Originally written with Katharine Hepburn in mind, and based partially on his short story of the same name, *The Night of the Iguana* was described by its author as one of his "non-black" plays. "Bestiality still exists," he said, "but I don't want to write about it any more. From now on I want to be concerned with the kinder aspects of life." Bette Davis rejected the role of the gentle maiden lady in this 1961 production in favor of a smaller part—the coarse, slatternly owner of the Mexican hotel. When the play opened out of town, it looked like an almost certain failure. On the basis of the Chicago tryout, *Time Magazine* characterized the show as "a massive turkey." Restaged and extensively rewritten, *The Night of the*

Iguana went on to win the New York Drama Critics Circle Award as best play of the year.

Night Over Taos (3/9/32, 48th Street, 13)

A Spanish grandee (J. Edward Bromberg) tries to lead a revolt against the rapacious American land-grabbers in Taos, New Mexico, in 1847. Betrayed by his own son (Franchot Tone), he takes poison rather than accept defeat. Turgid, absurdly miscast poetic drama by Maxwell Anderson, poorly directed by Lee Strasberg. C: Sanford Meisner, Luther Adler, Walter Coy, Mary Morris, Paula Miller, Morris Carnovsky, Stella Adler, Ruth Nelson, Phoebe Brand, Art Smith, Clifford Odets, Grover Burgess. P: The Group Theatre. SD: Robert Edmond Jones.

Night Remembers, The (11/27/34, Playhouse, 23)

A chance meeting with a damsel in distress leads a young Brooklynite (Van Heflin) to believe his life is threatened by malevolent supernatural forces. Confused but intriguing 30's melodrama. C: Mary Holsman, Brandon Tynan, Sheldon Leonard, Philip Bourneuf. A: Martha Madison. P: Peters and Spiller. D: Leo Bulgakov.

Night Watch (2/28/72, Morosco, 121)

A neurotic heiress still broods over the death of her first husband and his mistress. Her solicitous second husband suggests rest in a Swiss sanitarium. It's a good idea. The bad dreams she's been having abruptly become waking nightmares. Frantically, she insists there's a man's bloody corpse in the window of the house next door. No one else sees anything. Later, she claims there's a woman's body in the same place. The skeptical police find nothing and respond no further to her calls. She grows ever more hysterical. Her beautiful best friend offers sympathy. The husband calls in a psychiatrist. Is the poor woman crazy? The audience knows better, of course. Though the plot elements of *Night Watch* are familiar, they are woven into a thriller that steadily builds suspense and is replete with ingenious surprises. Best of all, the play doesn't fall apart at the end. The climax is solidly effective. As the tormented heroine, Joan Hackett gave a virtuoso performance, with efficient backing by the supporting players. ". . . a most superior thriller" (Clive Barnes, *New York Times*). ". . . an evening of satisfying menace and mystification" (Richard Watts, *New York Post*). ". . . an impeccably structured psychological thriller" (Kevin Sanders, WABC-TV). *Night Watch* was author Lucille Fletcher's first Broadway play. She is best known for her thirty-minute exercise in suspense, *Sorry, Wrong Number,* performed unforgettably by Agnes Moorehead in its original radio form, and later by Barbara Stanwyck in the less satisfying motion picture version. P: George W. George and Barnard S. Straus. C: Joan Hackett, Len Cariou, Elaine Kerr, Keene Curtis, Barbara Cason, Jeanne Hepple, Martin Shakar, William Kiehl, Rudy Bond. D: Fred Coe. SD: George Jenkins. CD: Donald Brooks. Lighting: Tharon Musser.

SV: Avco-Embassy, 1973. C: Elizabeth Taylor, Laurence Harvey, Billie Whitelaw. D: Brian Hutton.

Nightstick (11/10/27, Selwyn, 85)

Melodramatic triangle piece about a policeman and a convict in love with the same woman. The cop kills the con, and gets the girl. It took four writers—John Wray, Elliott Nugent, J. C. Nugent, and future soap opera queen Elaine Carrington—to concoct this Hollywood-slanted yarn. Hollywood, ultimately, is where their scenario ended up as one of the very first all-talking gangster films. C: Thomas Mitchell, Lee Patrick, John Wray, Raymond Hackett, Kathryn Givney, Victor Kilian. P/D: Crosby Gaige.

SV: UA, 1929, *Alibi,* Chester Morris.

Nighty-Night (9/9/19, Princess, 154)

Husband pursues runaway bride. Farcical fluff. C: Francis Byrne, Suzanne Willa. A: Martha Stanley and Adelaide Matthews. P: Adolph Klauber.

Nina (12/5/51, Royale, 45)

Gloria Swanson (tenacious wife), David Niven (debonair lover), and Alan Webb (mousy husband) were the marquee attractions in this "old-fashioned boudoir farce staged with singular maladroitness by Gregory Ratoff" *(News)*. According to another reviewer, this triangle comedy was "as out of tune as an attic harpsichord." Miss Swanson did everything in her power to quit *Nina* before it opened on Broadway, but to no avail. The producers (John C. Wilson and H. M. Tennent, Ltd.) insisted on holding the cinema queen to her run-of-the-play contract. *Nina* was adapted and extensively revised by Samuel Taylor from a play by Andre Roussin.

Nine Girls (1/13/43, Longacre, 5)

College girl turns sleuth to find the killer of a sorority sister. Skimpy murder melodrama with an all-female cast. C: Barbara Bel Geddes, K. T. Stevens, Marilyn Erskine, Irene Dailey, Adele Longmire. A: Wilfred H. Pettitt. P: A. H. Woods. D: Reginald Denham.
  SV: Col, 1944, Ann Harding, Evelyn Keyes, Anita Louise, Jinx Falkenburg, Nina Foch, Jeff Donnell, Marcia Mae Jones.

Nine Pine Street (4/27/33, Longacre, 29)

Pallid melodrama based on the famed 1892 murder case involving Lizzie Borden, here called Effie Holden (Lillian Gish), the New England spinster accused (later acquitted) of killing her father and stepmother. C: Raymond Hackett, Roberta Beatty, William Ingersoll. A: John Colton and Carleton Miles b/o a play by William Miles and Donald Blackwell. P: Margaret Hewes. D: A. H. Van Buren. SD: Robert Edmond Jones.

1931— (12/10/31, Mansfield, 12)

The problems of an unemployed young laborer (Franchot Tone) during the depths of the Depression. In the end, the hero and his girl head for Union Square to join the communist sympathizers. "Seldom has a bad play stunned an audience quite so completely as *1931–*" (*New York Times*). Reviews of this early Group Theatre production were mostly unfavorable and the play—a searingly bitter anticapitalist tract—was taken off after twelve performances. C: Morris Carnovsky, J. Edward Bromberg, Phoebe Brand, Mary Morris, Art Smith, Clifford Odets, Stella Adler, Ruth Nelson. A: Claire and Paul Sifton. D: Lee Strasberg.

Nineteenth Hole, The (10/11/27, Cohan, 119)

Cheerful little comedy about a writer (Frank Craven) who neglects his wife, friends, and work when he becomes a golf addict. A: Frank Craven. P: A. L. Erlanger. D: Sam Forrest.

Ninety-Day Mistress, The (11/6/67, Biltmore, 24)

Fearful of a permanent relationship with any man, an emancipated miss (Dyan Cannon) imposes a time limit on her love affairs—until she meets and falls in love with a young detective (Martin Milner).* Wispy sex comedy by J. J. Coyle, a former dancer with Jose Limon and Pearl Lang. C: Walter Abel, Ruth Ford, Tony Lo Bianco. P: Rose/Wilde/Nederlander/Steinbrenner. D: Philip Rose.

---
*Broadway debut.

Ninth Guest, The (8/25/30, Eltinge, 72)

Eight people are invited to a dinner party and informed that death is the ninth guest and that, one by one, each will be killed before the evening is over. In the end, only a pair of young lovers escape the revenge meted out by their madman-host. Ingenious mystery-melodrama by Owen Davis (A/D). C: Alan Dinehart, Berton Churchill, Thais Lawton, William Courtleigh, Owen Davis, Jr. P: A. H. Woods.

SV: Col, 1934, Donald Cook, Genevieve Tobin.

Nirvana (3/3/26, Greenwich Village, 5)

John Howard Lawson's expressionistic fantasy about a search for a new, worldwide religion. ". . . quite sophomoric . . . never far this side of preposterous . . ." (*New York Times*). C: Crane Wilbur, Earle Larimore, Juliette Crosby, Ludmilla Toretzka. P: Noble-Ryan-Livy. D: Robert Noble. SD: Mordecai Gorelik.

No Hard Feelings (4/8/73, Martin Beck, 1)

Despite the star names of Eddie Albert and Nanette Fabray, *No Hard Feelings* didn't last more than one performance. Written by the authors of *Norman, Is That You?*, the play was an unswallowable mix of social criticism and comedy. The target was middle-class values, but the romantic triangle plot, played for farce, was a misdirected arrow that missed the bull's-eye of incisive comment. A: Sam Bobrick and Ron Clark. C: Eddie Albert, Nanette Fabray, Conrad Janis, A. Larry Haines, Stockard Channing, David Marlow, Beverly Dixon, Dino Narizzano, Alan Manson. P: Orin Lehman, Joseph Kipness, Lawrence Kasha. D: Abe Burrows SD: Robert Randolph.

No More Frontier (10/22/31, Provincetown, 28)

Interesting O/B drama chronicling "the search for new horizons" by four generations of a pioneer family. The play ranged in time from 1875 to interplanetary travel in "the world of the future." Written by future screenwriter Talbot Jennings (*Mutiny on the Bounty, The Good Earth, Northwest Passage*). C: Cameron King, Ruth Gillmore, John Beal (deb.), Jackie Kelk, William Castle, Charles Walters. P: Shepard Traube (D) and Max Sonino.

No More Ladies (1/23/34, Booth, 162)

A sophisticated wife saves her marriage by flirting with another man. Bright romantic comedy; deftly acted, especially by Melvyn Douglas as the philandering husband of the heroine and Lucile Watson as her racy grandmother. C: Ruth Weston, Rex O'Malley. A: A. E. Thomas. P: Lee Shubert. D: Harry Wagstaff Gribble.

SV: MGM, 1935, Joan Crawford, Robert Montgomery, Franchot Tone, Edna May Oliver, Charles Ruggles, Gail Patrick, Arthur Treacher, Joan Burfield (Joan Fontaine).

No More Women (8/3/26, Ambassador, 7)

Romantic problems of a two-fisted lumberjack (Charles Bickford). Wooden comedy. A: Samuel Shipman and Neil Twomey. P: Schwab and Mandel. D: Edgar MacGregor.

No Place To Be Somebody (5/4/69, Public, 250)

Powerful character study of a contemporary "Little Caesar," a ruthlessly ambitious black man who tends and owns a bar in a neighborhood controlled by white hoodlums. When he tries to muscle in on the neighborhood rackets, he incurs the enmity of the Mafia, and is killed. "A rock-'em-sock-'em 'black-black comedy' bursting with life and fact and laughter and anger and it held me in high tension for a good three hours. . . . A turbulence of living language" (*Post*). *No Place To Be Somebody,* the first playwriting effort of actor-director Charles Gordone, won the Pulitzer Prize as best play of the year—the first time the prize was awarded to a black dramatist. C: Nathan George, Ron O'Neal, Ronnie Thompson, Walter Jones, Laurie Crews. Presented O/B by Joseph Papp for the New York Shakespeare Festival Public Theater; directed by Ted Cornell.

Subsequently revived O/B (1/20/70, Promenade, 312) with substantially the same cast that appeared in the 1969 production.

No Questions Asked (2/5/34, Masque, 16)

Alcoholic playboy finds redemption when he weds pregnant waif. Hackneyed comedy-drama cut from an all too familiar stencil. C: Ross Alexander, Barbara Robbins, Spring Byington, Brian Donlevy, Milo Boulton. A: Anne Morrison Chapin. P: John Golden. D: John Golden and Edward Goodman.

No Time for Comedy (4/17/39, Barrymore, 185)

A successful playwright (Laurence Olivier) decides that his comedies are too frivolous for the times (the eve of World War II). Under the influence of an addled, love-struck patroness, he writes a perfectly terrible play about death and dishonor. His actress-wife (Katharine Cornell) saves their marriage (and, presumably, her husband's career) by persuading him to return to his *métier* of comedy. "Translucent merrymaking . . . a trifle that has been wrought with distinction" (*New York Times*). It was generally conceded that Katharine Cornell was miscast in a role that cried out for the comedic talents of a Gertrude Lawrence, a Lynn Fontanne, or an Ina Claire. Consequently, Laurence Olivier walked off with the evening's acting honors as the boyish playwright. C: Margalo Gillmore, John Williams, Robert Flemyng. A: S. N. Behrman. P: The Playwrights Company. D: Guthrie McClintic. SD: Jo Mielziner.
SV: WB, 1940, James Stewart, Rosalind Russell, Genevieve Tobin, Charles Ruggles, Allyn Joslyn.

No Time for Sergeants (10/20/55, Alvin, 796)

Vastly amusing comic-strip hokum about a Georgia hayseed who gets drafted into the Air Force and, because of his inherent honesty and innocence, creates havoc for his colleagues and superiors. Andy Griffith (deb.) came through with a powerhouse performance in the leading role of Will Stockdale, ably abetted by Roddy McDowall as his loyal buddy and Myron McCormick as his long-suffering sergeant. This long-run comedy hit was adapted from Mac Hyman's novel by Ira Levin, author of *Rosemary's Baby* and such plays as *Critic's Choice* (1960), *Dr. Cook's Garden* (1967), etc. C: Howard Freeman, Royal Beal, Robert Webber, Earle Hyman, Don Knotts (deb.), James Millholin, Bill Hinnant. P: Maurice Evans i.a.w. Emmett Rogers. D: Morton Da Costa. SD: Peter Larkin.
SV: WB, 1958, Andy Griffith, Myron McCormick, Nick Adams, Murray Hamilton, Howard Smith, Don Knotts, Will Hutchins (directed by Mervyn LeRoy).

No Trespassing (9/7/26, Sam H. Harris, 23)

Trite comedy-drama about a jaded society girl who tries to seduce an idealistic young minister. C: Kay Johnson, Russell Hicks, Nicholas Joy. A: John Hunter Booth. P/D: Hassard Short.

No Way Out (10/30/44, Cort, 8)

Woman doctor (Irene Hervey) exposes unscrupulous physician (Robert Keith). ". . . a lethargic thriller" (*Herald Tribune*). A: Owen Davis. P: Robert Keith. D: Davis and Keith.

Nobody Loves an Albatross (12/19/63, Lyceum, 188)

Hard-boiled comedy about a fast-talking, no-talent television writer-producer (Robert Preston) who plagiarizes an old Shirley Temple movie script. Though he loses his job, his girl, and his reputation, his instinct for self-preservation is such that he cons his way into an even-better-paying position with another studio. "A hilarious comedy with a slashing satirical edge" (*New York Times*). C: Carol Rossen, Constance Ford, Marian Winters, Phil Leeds, Jack Bittner, Barnard Hughes, Leon Janney, Richard Mulligan, Frank Campanella, Marie Wallace. A: Ronald Alexander. P: Elliot Martin and Philip Rose. D: Gene Saks. SD: Will Steven Armstrong.

Nobody's Widow (11/15/10, Hudson, 215)

Plotless, puerile farce by Avery Hopwood. Blanche Bates' last appearance under the management of David Belasco (P/D).

Nocturne (2/16/25, Punch and Judy, 12)

Superficial dramatization of Frank Swinnerton's gentle, ironic novel about two middle-class sisters, and the unrequited passion of one of them for a ne'er-do-well sailor (Warren William). A/P/D: Henry Stillman.

Nona (10/4/32, Avon, 31)

Socialite woos and wins hot-tempered dancer. Dreary "romantic farce" had little to recommend it. C: Lenore Ulric, Arthur Margetson, Russell Hicks, Patricia Calvert, Millard Mitchell, Harlan Briggs, Oscar Polk. A: Gladys Unger. P: Peggy Fears. D: Burk Symon.

Noose, The (10/20/26, Hudson, 197)

To keep his parentage a secret, a young man murders a hoodlum and is sentenced to be hanged for the crime. Stereotyped mother-love saga and gangster melodrama was notable for marking the Broadway dramatic debut of Barbara Stanwyck in a small but pivotal role. C: Rex Cherryman, Mae Clarke, Ann Shoemaker, George Nash, Lester Lonergan. A/D: Willard Mack. P: Mrs. Henry B. Harris.

SV: Par, 1936, *I'd Give My Life,* Sir Guy Standing, Frances Drake, Tom Brown, Janet Beecher.

Norman, Is That You? (2/19/70, Lyceum, 12)

Comedy of homosexuality and the generation gap. A dry cleaner from Ohio (Lou Jacobi) disconsolate because his wife has left him, comes to New York to visit his son, Norman. Norman is no comfort. He's become a window dresser and shares an apartment with a male lover. Father, predictably horrified, tries to convert his fallen boy, his ploys ranging from heated debate through weary sarcasm to a prostitute hired for therapeutic purposes. When the dry cleaner's wife appears, she utters the play's title in amazement. As spoken by Maureen Stapleton, it is very funny. The ending finds the couple reunited, Norman drafted, and the lover going home with what must be considered his in-laws. The critics dismissed the play as hackwork. They were quick to point out it was the creation of television writers, and reserved their praise for old pros Jacobi and Stapleton. Though a failure, *Norman, Is That You?* was far from through. It enjoyed great success in England and Europe, and was a long-run hit as staged in Los Angeles with a black cast headed by Billy Daniels. A: Ron Clark and Sam Bobrick. C: Lou Jacobi, Maureen Stapleton, Martin Huston, Walter Willison, Dorothy Emmerson. D: George Abbott. P: Harold D. Cohen. SD: William & Jean Eckart.

SV: MGM, 1976, Redd Foxx, Pearl Bailey, Michael Warren (directed by George Schlatter).

Not for Children (2/13/51, Coronet, 7)

Satire on the problems of the legitimate theatre. Elmer Rice (A/D) employed blackouts, vaudeville skits, a pair of interlocutors (Betty Field and Elliott Nugent), and a generally confusing "play-within-a-play-within-a-play" technique to hammer home his points. "A baffling piece of theatrical hocus-pocus . . . it misses very widely and very definitely" (*Herald Tribune*). P: The Playwrights Company. CD: Mainbocher. SD: John Root. M: Robert Emmett Dolan.

Note: Not for Children was originally written in 1934, but did not reach Broadway until 1951.

Not Herbert (1/26/26, 52nd Street, 145)

A jewel thief (Clarke Silvernail) poses as a timid soul. Frenetic four-act farce; moderate fun. A: Howard Irving Young. P: The Playshop. D: Edwin Maxwell.

Not So Fast (5/22/23, Morosco, 102)

Dreary comedy-drama about the rivalry between two family guardians played by Taylor Holmes and Leon Gordon. A: Conrad Westervelt. P: John Henry Mears. D: Leon Gordon.

Not So Long Ago (5/4/20, Booth, 137)

In the New York of the 1870's, a poor seamstress (Eva Le Gallienne) invents a romance with an aristocratic young man (Sidney Blackmer). Whimsical, pleasant period comedy by Arthur Richman. C: Thomas Mitchell, Mary Kennedy. P: Messrs. Shubert. D: Edward Elsner.

Nothing But Lies (10/8/18, Longacre, 135)

Another farce in the same general mold as *Nothing But the Truth* (1916). To avoid incriminating himself and his firm in the presence of a muckraking journalist, a glib advertising man (William Collier) is forced to tell nothing but lies all evening long. In so doing, of course, he bewilders and infuriates his partners, friends, and sweetheart. "Every one on the stage is miserable and, thanks to the amiable logic of farce, this makes the audience quite happy [and] yields an abundance of new laughs" (*New York Times*). A: Aaron Hoffman. P: Anderson and Weber.

Nothing But the Truth (9/14/16, Longacre, 332)

Young man (William Collier) wagers he can tell nothing but the absolute, unvarnished truth for twenty-four hours. Sprightly farce by James Montgomery, based on a story by Frederick Isham. P: H. H. Frazee. D: Collier.

Musicalized by Charig, Jerome, and Caesar as *Yes, Yes, Yvette* (1927) with Jack Whiting, Jeanette MacDonald, Charles Winninger; and by Waller and Tunbridge as *Tell Her the Truth* (1932) with John Sheehan, Jr., Lillian Emerson, Andrew Tombes, Margaret Dumont, William Frawley, Raymond Walburn, Hobart Cavanaugh.

SV: Par, 1929, Richard Dix, Helen Kane, Ned Sparks, Wynne Gibson, Berton Churchill; 1941, Bob Hope, Paulette Goddard, Edward Arnold, Leif Erickson, Glenn Anders, Rose Hobart.

Now I Lay Me Down to Sleep (3/2/50, Broadhurst, 44)

The problems of an eccentric South American general (Fredric March) and a spinster with a suicide complex (Florence Eldridge) are solved when they find themselves trapped in an Ecuadorean earthquake. "Self-conscious, arty and pretentious" (*Journal-American*). C: Rick Jason, Milton Parsons, Lili Valenty, Stefan Schnabel, Henry Lascoe, Charles Chaplin, Jr., Roy Poole. A: Elaine Ryan b/o the novel by Ludwig Bemelmans. P: Stern and Nichols. D: Hume Cronyn.

Now You've Done It (3/5/37, Henry Miller, 43)

Bumbling politician's career is saved by his maid, a former whorehouse employee who knows all the town's secrets. This tasteless, short-lived comedy was written by Denver newspaperwoman Mary Chase, produced by Brock Pemberton, and staged by Antoinette Perry. Seven years later this trio was reunited for one of the most beloved comedies of the American theatre, Mary Chase's Pulitzer Prizewinning *Harvey* (1944). C: Walter Greaza, Evelyn Varden, Richard Carlson, Margaret Perry.

Now-a-days (8/5/29, Forrest, 8)

Alcoholic playboy (Melvyn Douglas) is accused of murdering a bootlegger, but "a no good dame" (Mayo Methot) finally confesses to the crime. Trite 20's melodrama. A: Arthur F. Brash. P: William A. Brady. D: Jessie Bonstelle.

Number, The (10/30/51, Biltmore, 87)

A young woman becomes involved with numbers racketeers. Synthetic melodrama crammed with clichés. C: Martha Scott, Dane Clark, Murvyn Vye, Louise Larabee. A: Arthur Carter. P: Vroom and Cooper. D: George Abbott.

Nut Farm, The (10/14/29, Biltmore, 41)

Brother (Wallace Ford) and sister (Natalie Schafer) mortgage their nut farm to get into the movies. Low-grade farce. A: John C. Brownell. P: John Henry Mears. D: Harry MacFayden.

SV: Monogram, 1935, Wallace Ford, Joan Gale.

O

O, Evening Star! (1/8/36, Empire, 5)

Unsuccessful but frequently fascinating comedy-drama about the Hollywood comeback of down-and-out character actress Marie Dressler (here called Amy Bellaire), and of her subsequent death from cancer in 1934 at the height of her film career. C: Jobyna Howland, James Todd, Frank Conroy, Merle Maddern, Eddie Albert (deb.), Ezra Stone (deb.), O. Z. Whitehead, Whitney Bourne. A: Zoe Akins. P: Harry Moses. D: Leontine Sagan.

O, Nightingale (4/15/25, 49th Street, 29)

Lecherous marquis tries to educate small-town girl to the facts of big city life. Undistinguished comedy by Sophie Treadwell (P), author of *Machinal* (1928). C: Ernest Lawford, Martha-Bryan Allen. D: John Kirkpatrick.

Odd Couple, The (3/10/65, Plymouth, 964)

Neil Simon's smash hit comedy about mismatched roommates, a fussy neatnik (Art Carney) and a slob of a sportswriter (Walter Matthau), who take up housekeeping together in New York—and drive each other crazy. "Wildly, irresistibly, incredibly and continuously funny" (*News*). C: Nathaniel Frey, Paul Dooley, Sidney Armus, John Fiedler, Carole Shelley, Monica Evans. P: Saint Subber. D: Mike Nichols. SD: Oliver Smith. *Note: The Odd Couple* was produced in London with Jack Klugman and Victor Spinetti in the roles originated by Messrs. Matthau and Carney.

SV: Par, 1968, Jack Lemmon, Walter Matthau, John Fiedler, Herb Edelman, Larry Haines, David Sheiner, Carole Shelley, Monica Evans, Iris Adrian (directed by Gene Saks).

Odds on Mrs. Oakley, The (10/2/44, Cort, 24)

Divorced couple become involved with gamblers when they share custody of a racehorse. "A silly and utterly incompetent farce" (*Sun*). C: Joy Hodges, John Archer (deb.). A: Harry Segall. P: Robert Reud. D: Arthur Sircom.

Of Love Remembered (2/18/67, ANTA, 9)

Half-a-century in the lives of a Norwegian-American family. Torpid drama by Arnold Sundgaard. C: Ingrid Thulin (deb.), James Olson, Janet Ward, George Gaynes. P: Cantor and Vanoff. D: Burgess Meredith.

Of Mice and Men (11/23/37, Music Box, 207)

John Steinbeck's tragic drama of need and devotion between an unlikely pair of itinerant farmhands: Lennie (Broderick Crawford), a childlike giant, and George (Wallace Ford), his lonely, intelligent protector. When Lennie accidentally strangles a rancher's sluttish wife (Claire Luce), an anguished George chooses to spare his friend the bewildering impersonality of the law by killing him himself. ". . . infinitely moving, somberly beautiful . . . a masterpiece" (*New York Times*). C: Sam Byrd, Will Geer, John F.

Hamilton, Thomas Findlay, Leigh Whipper. P: Sam H. Harris. D: George S. Kaufman. SD: Donald Oenslager.

Musicalized (1958) by Ira Bilowit, Wilson Lehr and Alfred Brooks, with a cast headed by Art Lund, Leo Penn, Jo Sullivan and John F. Hamilton.

SV: UA, 1939, Lon Chaney, Jr., Burgess Meredith, Betty Field, Charles Bickford, Bob Steele, Noah Berry, Jr. (directed by Lewis Milestone).

Off to Buffalo (2/21/39, Barrymore, 7)

Vaudeville headliner (Joe Cook) and his cronies take over the home of a staid Brooklynite (Hume Cronyn) prior to putting on the big show. Slapdash farce had some amusing moments. It was written by Max Liebman and Allen Boretz. P: Albert Lewis. D: Melville Burke.

Officer 666 (1/29/12, Gaiety, 192)

Zany mistaken identity farce involving a bogus policeman and a burglarious art expert. "Many surprises . . . humorous situations and considerable bright dialogue" (*New York Times*). C: Wallace Eddinger, George Nash, Vivian Martin. A: Augustin MacHugh (with extensive though uncredited revisions by Winchell Smith). P: George M. Cohan and Sam H. Harris. D: Sam Forrest.

Off-Key (2/8/27, Belmont, 15)

Aptly titled soap opera wherein a devoted wife (Florence Eldridge) makes the mistake of telling her novelist-husband (McKay Morris) about a premarital affair. C: Lucile Watson, Kenneth Hunter, Margaret Douglas, Albert Hackett. A: Arthur Caesar. P: R. V. Newman.

Officer 666 (**January 29, 1912**). *Courtesy Museum of the City of New York Theatre and Music Collection.*

Oh Dad, Poor Dad (2/26/62, Phoenix, 454)

Oh Dad, Poor Dad, Mamma's Hung You in the Closet and I'm Feelin' So Sad—to give its full nonstop title—was the avant-garde sensation of the 1962 O/B theatre season. Labeled "A Pseudoclassical Tragifarce in a Bastard French Tradition," this absurdist satire conjured up a surrealist world populated by man-eating plants, man-eating fish, and man-eating women. Principal character: Madame Rosepettle, a devouring female who kicks sand in the faces of loving couples on the beach, keeps the stuffed body of her late husband in the closet, and instills complexes in her seventeen-year-old son, Jonathan, that Oedipus might have envied. Into Madame's Carribbean hotel suite comes an iron-willed ingenue who sets out to seduce the stammering, unworldly Jonathan, and pays with her life for this act of folly. The play ends with Madame Rosepettle voicing the question asked by members of the audience all evening: "What is the meaning of this?" "Funny, weird, stageworthy and nonsensical" (*New York Times*). This nightmarish black comedy was written by twenty-five-year-old Arthur Kopit while he was an undergraduate at Harvard. The production was staged in highly effective comic-strip fashion by Jerome Robbins. C: Jo Van Fleet, Austin Pendleton (deb.), Barbara Harris, Sandor Szabo, Tony Lo Bianco. P: Producers Theatre, Inc. i.a.w. Roger L. Stevens. CD: Patricia Zipprodt. SD: William and Jean Eckart. M: Robert Prince.

R: (8/27/63, Morosco, 47). C: Hermione Gingold, Sam Waterston, Alix Elias, Sandor Szabo, John Hallow.

Note: A 1961 London production featured Stella Adler and Andrew Ray in leading roles.

SV: Par, 1967, Rosalind Russell, Robert Morse, Barbara Harris, Jonathan Winters, Hugh Griffith, Lionel Jeffries (directed by Richard Quine and Alexander Mackendrick).

Oh, Mama (8/19/25, Playhouse, 70)

Giddy stepmother (Alice Brady) divorces her husband and sets up housekeeping with her handsome young stepson. Sniggering farce-comedy, adapted by Wilton Lackaye and Harry Wagstaff Gribble (D) from a farce by Louis Verneuil. C: Kenneth MacKenna, John Cromwell, Edwin Nicander, Paul Porcasi.

Oh, Men! Oh, Women! (12/17/53, Henry Miller, 382)

On the eve of his marriage, a fashionable psychoanalyst (Franchot Tone) discovers that his supposedly guileless bride-to-be has had a fairly extensive amorous life. From then on, it's a question of "Physician, heal thyself" as the increasingly distraught analyst struggles to get a grip on his own emotions. "Witty, intelligent, satirical and just plain downright funny" (*News*). C: Betsy von Furstenberg, Anne Jackson, Gig Young (deb.), Larry Blyden. A/D: Edward Chodorov. P: Cheryl Crawford i.a.w. Anderson Lawler. SD: William and Jean Eckart.

SV: Fox, 1957, David Niven, Ginger Rogers, Tony Randall, Dan Dailey, Barbara Rush (directed by Nunnally Johnson).

Oh, Mr. Meadowbrook! (12/26/48, Golden, 40)

Mousy bachelor learns facts of life from three predatory females. "A witless, poverty-stricken show [that] is no more sophisticated than ten-cent store perfume" (*Herald Tribune*). C: Ernest Truex, Vicki Cummings, Sylvia Field, Harry Ellerbe (D). A: Ronald Telfer and Pauline Jamerson. P: John Yorke.

Oh, Promise Me (11/24/30, Morosco, 135)

Publicity-hungry lawyer (Lee Tracy) frames and subsequently wins a case on perjured testimony. Rowdy farce written and staged by Howard Lindsay and Bertrand Robinson. C: Donald Meek, Mary Philips. P: Sam H. Harris.

SV: U, 1933, *Love, Honor and Oh, Baby!,* Slim Summerville, ZaSu Pitts, George Barbier, Verree Teasdale, Lucile Gleason.

Old Acquaintance (12/23/40, Morosco, 170)

The professional and personal rivalry of two women authors, one (Jane Cowl) a serious artist, and the other (Peggy Wood) a writer of shallow successes. A tangled romantic situation threatens to jeopardize the ladies' lifelong friendship, but serves instead to cement it. "Human, likable and almost consistently interesting" (*Herald Tribune*). "Scarcely worth the trouble every one has taken with it" (*New York Times*). C: Kent Smith, Adele Longmire. A: John Van Druten. P: Dwight Deere Wiman. D: Auriol Lee. SD: Richard Whorf.

SV: WB, 1943, Bette Davis, Miriam Hopkins, Gig Young, John Loder, Anne Revere.

Old Lady 31 (10/30/16, 39th Street, 160)

By dressing up in women's clothes, an elderly sea captain connives to join his wife at the old ladies' home. Sentimental, appealing comedy-drama by Rachel Crothers (D), based on a novel by Louise Forsslund. C: Emma Dunn, Reginald Barlow. P: Lee Kugel.

SV: MGM, 1940, *The Captain Is a Lady,* Charles Coburn, Beulah Bondi, Billie Burke, Helen Broderick, Marjorie Main, Dan Dailey, Virginia Grey.

Old Maid, The (1/7/35, Empire, 298)

Charlotte (Helen Menken) allows her illegitimate daughter to be raised by her cousin, Delia (Judith Anderson). As the years pass, Charlotte must stand by and watch her child fall in love, marry, and never guess that the prim and dour old maid of the family is really her mother. This sentimental chronicle of maternal love surprised everyone by winning the Pulitzer Prize as the best play of American authorship of the 1934–35 season. Dissatisfied with the award, the New York drama critics formed an organization (the Drama Critics Circle) to bestow their own award each year. Their first selection (1935) was Maxwell Anderson's *Winterset.* C: John Cromwell, George Nash, Margaret Dale. A: Zoe Akins b/o a novelette by Edith Wharton. P: Harry Moses. D: Guthrie McClintic. SD: Stewart Chaney.

SV: WB, 1939, Bette Davis, Miriam Hopkins, George Brent, Donald Crisp, James Stephenson, William Lundigan, Jane Bryan, Louise Fazenda, Jerome Cowan, Cecilia Loftus.

Old Man Murphy (5/18/31, Royale, 64)

Irish tippler comes to America, straightens out the political and marital affairs of his expatriate son. Pleasant comedy by Patrick Kearney and Harry Wagstaff Gribble (D). C: Arthur Sinclair, Henry O'Neill, Maire O'Neill, Peggy Conklin. P: Robert V. Newman.

SV: RKO, 1935, *His Family Tree,* James Barton, Maureen Delany.

Old Rascal, The (3/24/30, Bijou, 72)

A western judge, in New York on a spree, is threatened by blackmailers. Haphazard comedy-melodrama written, produced and starring William Hodge. D: Maurice Barrett.

Old Soak, The (8/22/22, Plymouth, 325)

Bibulous but kindly Clem Hawley takes the blame for his son's misdeeds, suffers the martyrdom of his patient wife, finally brings happiness to everyone in town except the villain of the piece, an abstemious deacon. Affectionate study of an amiable, middle-aged lush, nicely written by Don Marquis, best known for his poetry-spouting cockroach in *archy and mehitable*. C: Harry Beresford, Minnie Dupree, Robert McWade, Mary Philips. P/D: Arthur Hopkins.

SV: MGM, 1937, *The Good Old Soak*, Wallace Berry, Una Merkel, Betty Furness, Eric Linden, Janet Beecher, Ted Healy, Margaret Hamilton.

Note: Don Marquis brought back the character of "The Old Soak" in a comedy called *Everything's Jake* (1930). The show failed and Marquis fled to Hollywood. His fine talent was frittered away scripting Shirley Temple movies.

Oliver Goldsmith (3/19/00, 5th Avenue, 33)

Atmospheric but dawdling Augustus Thomas comedy-drama dealing with the eighteenth-century writer (Stuart Robson); Goldsmith's friendship with Garrick (Henry E. Dixey), Boswell (Beaumont Smith), and Dr. Johnson (H. A. Weaver); and the production of his celebrated comedy, *She Stoops to Conquer*.

Oliver Oliver (1/5/34, Playhouse, 11)

Penniless socialite tries to promote the marriage of her spineless son, Oliver Oliver, to a wealthy debutante. Wispy comedy by Paul Osborn. C: Bretaigne Windust, Ann Andrews, Helen Brooks. P: Dwight Deere Wiman. D: Auriol Lee.

Olympia (10/16/28, Empire, 47)

A proud princess (Fay Compton) meets a haughty hussar (Ian Hunter) who persists in courting her to the dismay of her royal relatives (Laura Hope Crews, Cora Witherspoon, Arnold Korff). Sidney Howard adapted (and extensively revised) this minor Ferenc Molnar comedy set in fashionable turn-of-the-century Vienna. P/D: Gilbert Miller.

SV: MGM, 1929, *His Glorious Night*, John Gilbert, Catherine Dale Owen, Nance O'Neil; Par, 1960, *A Breath of Scandal*, Sophia Loren, John Gavin, Maurice Chevalier, Angela Lansbury, Isabel Jeans.

Omar, the Tentmaker (1/13/14, Lyric, 103)

Fanciful, melodramatic hodgepodge "based on the life, times and Rubaiyat of Omar Khayyam." The Fitzgerald lines were declaimed by Guy Bates Post as the youthful Omar. "A mongrel mixture of old-fashioned blood-and-thunder melodrama, with treachery, and poisoned foods, prison walls, clanking chains, and stolen keys . . ." (*New York Times*). A/P/D: Richard Walton Tully.

On an Open Roof (1/28/63, Cort, 1)

Cliché-laden drama about the professional and domestic problems of a Puerto Rican lawyer (Don Gordon) and his wife (Diana van der Vlis). A: Avraham Inlender. P: Ridgely Bullock, Milton Katselas (D) and Current Productions i.a.w. W. Clement Stone.

On Borrowed Time (2/3/38, Longacre, 321)

Warmly engaging comedy-fantasy about an old man and his grandson who chase Death (personified as Mr. Brink) up an apple tree and, by means of a charm, keep him there. In the end, Mr. Brink tricks the boy into climbing the tree and fatally injuring himself. In order not to be separated from his grandson, the old man renounces his strange power over Death, and he and the boy are happily reunited in the next world. *On Borrowed Time* was one of the great popular successes of the 1930's. C: Dudley Digges, Frank Conroy, Dorothy Stickney, Jean Adair, Peter Miner. A: Paul Osborn b/o the novel by Lawrence Edward Watkin. P: Dwight Deere Wiman. D: Joshua Logan. SD: Jo Mielziner.

R: (2/10/53, 48th Street, 78) by Krakeur and Hale. C: Victor Moore, Leo G. Carroll, Beulah Bondi, David John Stollery, Kay Hammond, Melinda Markey. D: Marshall Jamison.
SV: MGM, 1939, Lionel Barrymore, Cedric Hardwicke, Beulah Bondi, Una Merkel, Bobs Watson, Henry Travers, Nat Pendleton.
Note: A successful 1946 West Coast revival featured Boris Karloff, Ralph Morgan, Beulah Bondi, Margaret Hamilton and Joseph Crehan.

On Stage (10/29/35, Mansfield, 47)

Playwright finds he can no longer control his characters' destinies—nor, for that matter, his own. Mild *Pirandelloesque* comedy. C: Osgood Perkins, Selena Royle, Alan Marshall, Claudia Morgan, Donald MacDonald, Frederic Worlock, Louis Hector. A: B. M. Kaye. P: Laurence Rivers (Rowland Stebbins). D: Robert Ross.

On the Hiring Line (10/20/19, Criterion, 48)

Complications ensue when a wealthy businessman hires a pair of detectives to pose as cook and butler in his home. Labored comedy with a competent cast: Cyril Scott, Laura Hope Crews, Minna Gombell, Sidney Toler, Robert Hudson, Vivian Tobin, Donald Gallaher, John Blair. A: Harvey O'Higgins and Harriet Ford. P/D: George C. Tyler.
SV: WB, 1944, *Make Your Own Bed,* Jack Carson, Jane Wyman, Alan Hale, George Tobias, Irene Manning, Ricardo Cortez, Tala Birell, Kurt Katch.

On the Quiet (2/11/01, Madison Square, 160)

Yale man tries to conceal his secret marriage. Amusing William Collier farce vehicle. A: Augustus Thomas. P: Smyth and Perley.

On the Stairs (9/25/22, Playhouse, 72)

An unscrupulous Hindu fakir (Arnold Daly) woos a frightened heiress (Margaret Dale) in a house haunted by the ghost of her father. Judith Anderson (billed as Frances Anderson) made her Broadway debut as Mrs. Belmore in this gimcrack spook melodrama by William Hurlbut. P: Joseph E. Shea. D: Edgar MacGregor.

On to Fortune (2/4/35, Fulton, 8)

Socialist-minded son steals a million dollars in bonds from his father's bank. Satirical comedy by Lawrence Langner and Armina Marshall missed by a mile. C: Myron McCormick, Ilka Chase, Glenn Anders, Roy Atwell, Josephine Hull, Worthington Miner (D), Robert T. Haines, Hugh Rennie. P: Gaige and Heidt.

On Trial (8/19/14, Chandler, 365)

The first play by twenty-two-year-old law student Elmer L. Reizenstein (Elmer Rice), author of *The Adding Machine* (1923), *Street Scene* (1929), *Dream Girl* (1945), etc. A cleverly crafted courtroom melodrama, *On Trial* dramatized the prosecution and defense of a man charged with murder in the first degree. It was the first play to use the "flashback" technique of the cinema, with the testimony of the witnesses visualized, with each flashback carrying the story forward. The play was hailed as "a triumph of dramatic construction." Another reviewer (Louis Sherwin, *Globe*) called it: "The most striking novelty that has been seen for years. Undoubtedly it will bring about important changes in the technique of the theatre." Though he later dismissed it as "a shrewd piece of stage carpentry," *On Trail* made Rice's reputation overnight. It also earned him well over $100,000 in royalties. C: Frederick Perry, Mary Ryan, Frederick Truesdell. P: Cohan and Harris i.a.w. Arthur Hopkins. D: Sam Forrest.

On Trial. **Frederick Truesdell, Hans Robert, and Helene Lackaye (October 1914).**
Courtesy Museum of the City of New York Theatre and Music Collection.

SV: WB, 1929, Pauline Frederick, Bert Lytell, Lois Wilson, Jason Robards, Sr.; 1939, Margaret Lindsay, John Litel, James Stephenson, Edward Norris. Jan Sterling, Scott McKay, Russell Nype, Ralph Dunn, Leona Powers. A: Owen G. Arno. P: Burgin and di Cosmi. D: Reginald Denham. CD: Audré. SD: Feder.

On Whitman Avenue (5/8/46, Cort, 150)

Community frictions are precipitated when a black veteran and his wife move into a white neighborhood. "... an awkward and straggling drama [that] sags and drags" (*Sun*). C: Canada Lee, Perry Wilson, Will Geer. A: Maxine Wood. P: Canada Lee and Mark Marvin i.a.w. George McLain. D: Margo Jones.

Once for the Asking (11/20/63, Booth, 1)

Leaden whimsy about a fairy godmother who, with the aid of musk dust and mustard seed, makes wishes come true. "Abysmal" (*Post*). C: Dorothy Sands,

Once in a Lifetime (9/24/30, Music Box, 401)

Uproarious Hollywood satire by Moss Hart and George S. Kaufman (D). A third-rate vaudeville trio decide to go west and try their luck with the newly invented talkies. The most stupid of the three is made a director. He works from the wrong script, neglects to turn on the lights, and absent-mindedly cracks nuts throughout the shooting. The film is hailed as an artistic triumph, and the bumbling ex-trouper is deified by the industry. C: Hugh O'Connell, Jean Dixon, Grant Mills, Spring Byington, George S. Kaufman, Leona Maricle, Charles Halton, Oscar Polk. P: Sam H.

Harris. On opening night, George S. Kaufman made a curtain speech in which he told the audience that "eighty per cent of this play is Moss Hart." Strictly speaking, this was not Hart's first Broadway play. A few months earlier he had been represented as coauthor (with Dorothy Heyward) of a short-lived musical-comedy entitled *Jonica* (4/7/30, Craig, 40). *Once in a Lifetime* was a smash hit of enormous proportions. Shortly after it opened, Jesse Lasky (head of Paramount Pictures) wired Kaufman: "Offer $40,000 for screen rights." Kaufman wired back: "Offer $40,000 for Paramount company." Followed an hour later by: "Disregard my offer. Have changed my mind."

R: *Once in a Lifetime* had a disastrous one-performance O/B revival (1/28/64, York, 1) under the auspices of Peter Bogdanovich (P/D). The cast included Sandy Baron, Eve Roberts, and Lionel Wilson.

SV: U, 1932, Jack Oakie, Aline MacMahon, Sidney Fox, ZaSu Pitts, Louise Fazenda, Russell Hopton, Gregory Ratoff, Onslow Stevens.

Once More, With Feeling (10/21/58, National, 263)

A temperamental symphony conductor (Joseph Cotten) discovers he doesn't want his estranged wife (Arlene Francis) to divorce him after all. Highlight: Walter Matthau's performance as the conductor's long-suffering agent. Harry Kurnitz' satire on the music world had its share of funny lines but "not enough of them to conceal its familiar plot and regulation characters" (*Post*). C: Paul Richards, Leon Belasco, Frank Milan, Rex Williams, Ralph Bunker. P: Martin Gabel and Henry Margolis. D: George Axelrod. SD: George Jenkins.

SV: Col, 1960, Yul Brynner, Kay Kendall, Mervyn Johns (directed by Stanley Donen).

Once There Was a Russian (2/18/61, Music Box, 1)

Catherine the Great (Francoise Rosay in her Broadway debut) engages bumbling do-gooder John Paul Jones (Albert Salmi) to help Prince Potemkin (Walter Matthau) wage war against the Turks in 1787. Labored satirical costume comedy by Sam Spewack; a one-performance disaster. C: Julie Newmar, Sig Ruman, Carol Grace, Eric Christmas. P: Key, Segal, Schwartz, Howard and Randall i.a.w. Justin Sturm. D: Gene Frankel. CD/SD: Tony Walton.

Musicalized by Frank Loesser, Sam Spewack, and Bob Fosse (director-choreographer) as *Pleasures and Palaces* (1965) with Jack Cassidy, John McMartin, Phyllis Newman, Leon Janney, Mort Marshall, and Eric Brotherson in the cast. The show closed during its pre-Broadway tryout.

Once Upon a Tailor (5/23/55, Cort, 8)

Mild folk comedy (1880's Austria) about a village tailor (Oscar Karlweis) who turns matchmaker. Written by Baruch Lumet, father of director Sidney Lumet; ad. by Henry Sherman. P: The Playwrights Company and George Boroff. D: Joseph Anthony. SD: Boris Aronson.

One (9/14/20, Belasco, 111)

Twin sisters (both portrayed by Frances Starr) have but one soul between them. Such a situation is bound to cause problems, and it does, until one of the twins furnishes the other with a whole soul by killing herself. Weird psychic mumbo-jumbo melodrama by Edward Knoblock, served up with his customary *panache* by David Belasco (P/D).

One Bright Day (3/19/52, Royale, 29)

A pharmaceutical executive learns that his plant is manufacturing a potentially hazardous drug. Should he recall the product and face bankruptcy, or trust to

One. **Frances Starr, Marie Burke, and Philip Desborough (September 14, 1920).** *Courtesy Museum of the City of New York Theatre and Music Collection.*

luck that no one will die from using the drug? In the end, he decides to do the honorable thing and disclose the facts to the public. Howard Lindsay, Walter Matthau, and Glenn Anders played the leading roles in this contrived (but often compelling) 1952 problem play. A: Sigmund Miller. P: Howard Lindsay and Russel Crouse. D: Michael Gordon.

One By One (12/1/64, Belasco, 7)

The romance of a courageous crippled girl and a bitter young paraplegic. Dore Schary (A/P/D) play lacked impact; a heartbreaking story was reduced to conventional formula. C: Donald Madden, Sharon Laughlin (deb.), Donald Woods, Richard McMurray. SD: Donald Oenslager.

One Eye Closed (11/24/54, Bijou, 3)

Feeble jape about an escaped convict who hides out in the household of his former flame. C: John Baragrey, Haila Stoddard (P), Tom Helmore, George Mathews, Iggie Wolfington, John Fiedler, Harry Ellerbe. A: Justin Sturm. D: Romney Brent.

One Flew Over the Cuckoo's Nest (11/13/63, Cort, 82)

Randle P. McMurphy, a free spirit who has conned his way out of a prison work farm and into a state mental institution, there encounters a sadistic head nurse who demands complete conformity and submission to her will. Attempting to bring a little of the outside world to the other inmates, McMurphy defies her authority, and pays for his rebellion with his life. This 1963 comedy-drama by Dale Wasserman was b/o Ken Kesey's allegorical novel of the same name. Hindered by an exceedingly arch performance by Kirk Douglas in the leading role, this production received generally negative reviews and closed after a relatively brief run. Partially rewritten by Mr. Wasserman, the play surfaced a few years later to become an O/B success, not only in New York, but in many other parts of the world as well. A San Francisco production of the play is now in its sixth consecutive year, the longest-running dramatic presentation in that city's theatrical history. The screen version, directed by Milos Foreman, starred Jack Nicholson as McMurphy. C: Joan Tetzel, Gene Wilder, William Daniels, Ed Ames,* Gerald S. O'Loughlin, Malcolm Atterbury,* Arlene Golonka, K. C. Townsend. P: David Merrick and Edward Lewis i.a.w. Seven Arts and Eric Productions. D: Alex Segal. SD: Will Steven Armstrong.

R: O/B (3/23/71, Mercer-Hansberry, 1,025) with William Devane as McMurphy under the direction of Lee D. Sankowich.

Note: Says author Dale Wasserman: "In 1963, I thought the play was cremated and buried forever after the failure of the Broadway production starring Kirk Douglas. But lo and behold, it rose from the dead. . . . Douglas was only interested in being The Star and endearing himself to the audience. That attitude castrated the Broadway production. . . . Another factor in the show's resurgence is how much times and audiences have changed. People are now ready to accept the metaphor of an insane asylum as the society in which we live."

---

*Broadway debuts.

One Good Year (11/27/35, Lyceum, 223)

Would-be mother chooses a prospective father for her unborn child on the basis of eugenics. Tiresome, heavy-handed sex comedy. A: Stephen Gross and Lin S. Root. P: Al Rosen. D: George Rosener.

One Night in Rome (12/2/19, Criterion, 107)

An English girl (Laurette Taylor), masquerading as a sultry Italian fortune-teller, fascinates a young admirer (Philip Merivale) with her unorthodox views on life and love. "A poor uncertain little comedy" (Alexander Woollcott, *New York Times*). A/D: J. Hartley Manners. P: George C. Tyler.

One of the Family (12/21/25, 49th Street, 230)

A timid soul is bedeviled by his hidebound New England family for marrying a girl not of their choosing. Agreeable light comedy of "the worm turns" school. C: Grant Mitchell, Kay Johnson, Beulah Bondi, Louise Closser Hale, Mary Phillips, Raymond Van Sickle. A: Kenneth Webb. P: John Tuerk.

One of Us (9/9/18, Bijou, 24)

To get evidence against a gang of clever thieves, a man pretends to be an ex-convict and burglar. Brisk but totally predictable melodrama written by Jack Lait (future editor of the *New York Daily Mirror*) and Jo Swerling. Swerling, credited as coauthor of *Guys and Dolls* (1950), was a leading Hollywood scriptwriter. He authored or coauthored screenplays for such films as *Platinum Blonde, A Man's Castle, The Whole Town's Talking, Made For Each Other, Lifeboat*, etc. P/D: Oliver Morosco.

One Sunday Afternoon (2/15/33, Little, 338)

Small-town dentist Biff Grimes (Lloyd Nolan) is framed and sent to jail by a politically ambitious contractor—who also walks off with Biff's sweetheart. The dentist nurses his revenge and is rewarded years later when the chiselling contractor appears for emergency dentistry. Biff plans to murder his rival but, at the last moment, decides that he is the luckier man of the two and merely extracts the bully's tooth—without gas. This simple but appealing comedy-drama was framed in a present-day prologue and epilogue. The core of the play was set thirty years earlier in turn-of-the-century America. On the opening night of *One Sunday Afternoon,* an assassination attempt was made on the life of President Franklin D. Roosevelt. The following day, strikes were called, the banks closed, and the play shut down. A week later a financial "angel" came to the show's rescue. It reopened in a blaze of publicity, ran 338 performances, toured the country successfully, and turned its penniless author into a reasonably wealthy young man. Well-acted (especially by newcomer Lloyd Nolan) and expertly directed by Moscow Art Theatre alumnus Leo Bulgakov, *One Sunday Afternoon* came within one vote of winning the Pulitzer Prize. (The award that year went instead to Maxwell Anderson's *Both Your Houses*). C: Francesca Bruning, Rankin Mansfield, Mary Holsman. A: James Hagan. P: Peters and Spiller.

SV: Par, 1933, Gary Cooper, Fay Wray, Neil Hamilton, Frances Fuller; WB, 1941, *The Strawberry Blonde,* James Cagney, Olivia de Havilland, Rita Hayworth, Jack Carson, Alan Hale, George Tobias, Una O'Connor, George Reeves; 1948, Dennis Morgan, Janis Paige, Dorothy Malone, Don DeFore, Ben Blue.

One Thing After Another (12/28/37, Fulton, 15)

Dimwitted heiress (Ann Mason) becomes involved with gangsters. Inept comedy-melodrama. A: Sheldon Noble. P/D: Walter Craig.

One-Man Show (2/8/45, Barrymore, 36)

Triangle drama with a difference—the trio in this case involving a daughter with a pathological attachment to her possessive father, and the young man who finally succeeds in freeing the girl from this quasi-incestuous relationship. First play by Ruth and Augustus Goetz, authors of *The Heiress* (1947), *The Immoralist* (1954), etc. "A skillful production of an interesting play" (*Sun*). C: Constance Cummings, Frank Conroy, John Archer. P/D: Jed Harris. SD: Stewart Chaney.

Only Game in Town, The (5/20/68, Broadhurst, 16)

A Las Vegas showgirl falls in love with a compulsive gambler. Warm, witty, much underrated comedy-drama by Frank D. Gilroy, author of *The Subject Was Roses* (1964). *The Only Game in Town* was produced by Edgar Lansbury with Tammy Grimes, Barry Nelson (D) and Leo Genn in the leading roles. Under Daniel Petrie's direction, the play originally was tried out with a cast headed by Carolan Daniels, Richard Mulligan, and Albert Paulsen, but the production closed out of town before reaching Broadway.

SV: Fox, 1970, Elizabeth Taylor, Warren Beatty (directed by George Stevens).

Only in America (11/19/59, Cort, 28)

Homespun comedy-drama about Jewish writer Harry Golden (Nehemiah Persoff) who went to North Carolina to set up a now-and-then journal called *The Carolina Israelite,* and found the Christian community rallying to his defense when it was learned that he had once served a five-year prison sentence. ". . . a veritable Niagara of false emotions and stretched-out jokes" (*Herald Tribune*). C: Shepperd Strudwick, Ludwig Donath, Enid Markey, Lynn Hamilton, Alan Alda (deb.), Vincent Gardenia, Flora Campbell, Shannon Bolin, Don Fellows, Josh White, Jr. A: Jerome Lawrence and Robert E. Lee b/o the book by Harry Golden. P/D: Herman Shumlin. SD: Peter Larkin.

Only the Heart (4/4/44, Bijou, 47)

An embittered Texas mother destroys the

lives of her husband and children. "... a dreary domestic tragedy" (*Herald Tribune*). C: June Walker, Mildred Dunnock, Will Hare. P: American Actors Theatre. D: Mary Hunter. CD/SD: Frederick Fox. Written by Horton Foote, *Only the Heart* was originally produced O/B at the Provincetown Playhouse (12/5/42) for a limited run. Heading the cast were Hilda Vaughn, Richard Hart, and Constance Dowling.

Note: Texas-born Horton Foote, one of the pioneer playwrights of television, was represented on Broadway by *The Chase* (1952), *The Trip to Bountiful* (1953), and *The Traveling Lady* (1954).

Open House (12/14/25, Daly's, 73)

To clinch a business deal, a wife (Helen MacKellar) makes a play for one of her husband's clients (Bela Lugosi). Puerile comedy by Samuel Ruskin Golding (P) D: Stillman and Lawrence.

Open House (6/3/47, Cort, 7)

The home of a flighty widow (Mary Boland) is mistaken for a house of prostitution. "... dull, silly, rickety, inept little comedy..." (*PM*). A: Harry Young. P: Rex Carlton. D: Coby Ruskin.

Opportunity (7/30/20, 48th Street, 138)

Silent film star Nita Naldi, Hollywood's "Queen of the Vampires," inflames a young stockbroker with unrequited passion, propels him into a nervous breakdown and back into the arms of his loving wife in this potboiler by Owen Davis. C: James L. Crane, Lily Cahill, Kenneth MacKenna, Clifford Dempsey. P: William A. Brady. D: Frank Hatch.

Order Please (10/9/34, Playhouse, 23)

Cowboy becomes involved with a disappearing corpse in a New York hotel. Frenetic but resolutely unfunny mystery-comedy. C: James Bell, Vivienne Osborne, Tala Birell, Clifford Dempsey, William Hopper (deb.). A/D: Edward Childs Carpenter b/o a play by Walter Hackett. P: Bushar and Tuerk.

SV: MGM, 1935, *One New York Night*, Franchot Tone, Una Merkel.

Ordinary Man, An (9/9/68, Cherry Lane, 24)

In the not-too-distant future, when America has become a virtual dictatorship and all black citizens have been herded into concentration camps, a white man (Michael Baseleon) stands trial for genocide. Absorbing O/B thesis-drama. A: Mel Arrighi. P: Margaret Hayes. D: Harold Stone.

Orpheus Descending (3/21/57, Martin Beck, 68)

In attempting to bring salvation to a sex-starved southern storekeeper (Maureen Stapleton) whose elderly husband is dying of cancer, a wandering troubadour (Cliff Robertson) ensures their joint destruction. In a shrilly melodramatic finale, the husband shoots his wife and sets fire to the store, and the guileless troubadour is torn to bits by the sheriff's bloodhounds. This Tennessee Williams drama attempted to transfer the Orpheus legend to small-town Mississippi. Most critics found the play overwritten, discursive, and structurally weak. *Orpheus Descending* was a reworking of *Battle of Angels* (1940), Mr. Williams' first produced play, which expired in Boston after becoming something of a *cause célèbre* in that city. Boston first-nighters were stunned by the bluntness and candor of its dialogue. The young, unknown playwright didn't mince his words. Neither did Boston's City Councillor. He labeled the exhibit "putrid" and demanded it be closed immediately, adding: "The police should arrest the persons responsible for bringing shows of this type to Boston." (Meaning the Theatre Guild, director Margaret Webster and star Miriam Hopkins. "It's not a dirty show," countered

Miss Hopkins. "I haven't got to the point where I have to appear in dirty shows.") "The play was more of a disappointment to us than to you," the Guild admitted in an unprecedented letter to its Boston subscribers. The show turned out badly, the letter concluded, "but who knows whether the next one by the same author may not prove a success?" (That "next one" was The *Glass Menagerie,* one of the finest plays of the American theatre, produced in New York in the Spring of 1945.) Despite its dire failure in 1940, Tennessee Williams was deeply attached to *Battle of Angels* and kept working on the script, off and on, for a period of seventeen years. When the revised version finally reached Broadway in 1957 as *Orpheus Descending,* it shuttered after a brief run of 68 performances. C: Lois Smith, Crahan Denton, Joanna Roos, Robert Webber. P: Robert Whitehead. D: Harold Clurman. CD: Lucinda Ballard. SD: Boris Aronson.

R: (10/5/59, Gramercy Arts, 230). C: Ann Hamilton, John Ramondetta, Diane Ladd. D: Adrian Hall.

SV: UA, 1960, *The Fugitive Kind,* Marlon Brando, Anna Magnani, Joanne Woodward, Maureen Stapleton, Victor Jory (directed by Sidney Lumet from a screenplay by Tennessee Williams and Meade Roberts).

Ostriches (3/30/25, Comedy, 8)

Tasteless tripe about the rivalry between a mother (Janet Beecher) and daughter (Katherine Alexander) for the affections of the mother's lover. A: Edward Wilbraham. P: William A. Brady, Jr. and Dwight Deere Wiman.

Other Girl, The (12/29/03, Criterion, 160)

Society girl is saved from potentially disastrous marriage by clever tactics of girlhood chum. Far-fetched, frothy comedy with a good cast including Lionel Barrymore, Richard Bennett, and Elsie de Wolfe (who became Lady Mendl and the darling of the international set). A/D: Augustus Thomas. P: Charles Frohman.

Other Men's Wives (11/12/29, Times Square, 23)

Labored mistaken identity farce set in a seaside hotel in France. C: Claiborne Foster, Hugh Sinclair, Dorothy Hall, Harvey Stephens. A: Walter Hackett. P/D: Edgar Selwyn.

SV: WB, 1930, *Sweethearts and Wives,* Clive Brook, Billie Dove, Sidney Blackmer, Leila Hyams.

Other One, The (10/3/32, Biltmore, 16)

A woman who committed suicide takes over the mind and body of her twin sister (Helen Ford). Slow-paced supernatural drama lacked suspense. A: Henry Myers. P: Thomas Kilpatrick. D: Harold Winston.

Other Rose, The (12/20/23, Morosco, 84)

Headstrong youth (Henry Hull), living with his mother (Effie Shannon) in Maine, falls in love with two girls (Fay Bainter and Carlotta Monterey) both named Rose. Very mild comedy-drama by George Middleton, adapted from a play by Edouard Bourdet. P/D: David Belasco.

Ouija Board, The (3/29/20, Bijou, 64)

A fake spiritualist meets his downfall when he calls upon unsuspected supernatural forces. Effective chiller by Crane Wilbur. C: William Ingersoll, George Gaul, Edward Ellis, Crane Wilbur. P: A. H. Woods. D: W. H. Gilmore.

Our Lan' (9/27/47, Royale, 41)

On an island off the Georgia coast at the close of the Civil War, a band of freed slaves attempt to cultivate land given them by General Sherman. When President Andrew Johnson rescinds Sherman's decree, a tragic conflict ensues that ends in the wholesale slaughter of the blacks. "A tedious historical work" (*Herald Tribune*). Originally produced O/B (4/18/47, Henry Street, 12), where it won considerable critical acclaim, *Our Lan'* lasted only 41 performances uptown. It was written by black playwright Theodore Ward, author of *Big White Fog* (1940). C: William Veasey, Julie Haydon, Muriel Smith, Louis Peterson. P: Eddie Dowling (D) and Louis J. Singer.

Our Mrs. McChesney (10/19/15, Lyceum, 151)

A traveling saleswoman (Ethel Barrymore) in the petticoat line becomes a successful business woman. Popular light comedy based on Edna Ferber's short stories. C: William Boyd, Lola Fisher. A: George V. Hobart (D) and Edna Ferber. P: Charles Frohman.

Our Town (2/4/38, Henry Miller, 336)

Thornton Wilder's Pulitzer Prize drama of life, love, and death in a New England village at the turn of the century; notable for its novelty of form, *Our Town* was performed without scenery on a bare, curtainless stage, with the "stage manager" serving as narrator. Virtually plotless, the real protagonist of the play is the town itself and its influence upon George Gibbs and Emily Webb as they share childhood and school, fall in love, and marry. Emily dies in childbirth but, in one of the most poignant scenes ever written, is permitted to revisit earth for one day. By abandoning almost all the conventions of the stage, and by employing the most moving and universal of themes, Thornton Wilder fashioned a play that has claimed a secure place in the standard repertory of the American theatre. "... profoundly moving.... I came away from the theatre exalted.... In the deepest sense of the word, *Our Town* is a religious play" (Brooks Atkinson, *New York Times*). C: Frank Craven, John Craven, Martha Scott (deb.), Jay Fassett, Evelyn Varden, Thomas W. Ross, Helen Carew, Doro Merande, Philip Coolidge, Marilyn Erskine, Billy (William) Redfield, Thomas Coley, Alfred Ryder, Jean (Louise) Platt, Charles Walters. P/D: Jed Harris.

R: (1/10/44, City Center, 24). C: Marc Connelly, Montgomery Clift, Martha Scott, Curtis Cooksey, Evelyn Varden, Parker Fennelly, Doro Merande. D: Wesley McKee.

R: (3/23/59, Circle in the Square, 385). C: John Beal, Clinton Kimbrough, Jane McArthur, Dana Elcar, Michael Pollard, George Segal. D: Jose Quintero.

R: (11/27/69, ANTA, 36). C: Henry Fonda, Ed Begley, Harvey Evans, Elizabeth Hartman, Mildred Natwick, Irene Tedrow, John Randolph, John Beal, Margaret Hamilton, Thomas Coley. D: Donald Driver.

SV: UA, 1940, William Holden, Martha Scott, Frank Craven, Fay Bainter, Beulah Bondi, Thomas Mitchell, Guy Kibbee.

Note: Generally forgotten perhaps is the fact that *Our Town* came perilously close to never reaching Broadway. The Boston tryout was critically and financially a disaster. Jed Harris had decided to abandon the production. Playwright Marc Connelly, in Boston at the time, said, "Jed, you're crazy. This play is going to win the Pulitzer Prize." Harris took Connelly's advice and brought the play to New York.

Our Wife (3/2/33, Booth, 20)

Dreary 30's comedy about a clinging wife (June Walker) who pursues her runaway husband (Humphrey Bogart) and his new love (Rose Hobart) from New York to Paris to Naples. A: Lyon Mearson and Lillian Day. P: Brotherton and Halle. D: Edward C. Lilley.

SV: Col, 1941, Melvyn Douglas, Ruth Hussey, Ellen Drew, Charles Coburn, John Hubbard.

Ourselves (11/12/13, Lyric, 29)

Society woman tries to rehabilitate reform school girl by taking her into her home. Dreary Rachel Crothers (A/D) drama. C: Jobyna Howland, Grace Elliston. P: Messrs. Shubert.

Out Cry (3/1/73, Lyceum, 12)

Tennessee Williams being unsatisfyingly enigmatic. A two-character play about a brother and sister who act out a two-character play. They are trapped in a deserted theatre, or perhaps an insane asylum, giving voice to ill-defined torments in every register from quiet monologues to ranting hysterics. Their dilemma, whatever it may be exactly, has no resolution. At the end they have not triumphed, only survived. For the viewer they remain phantom figures in an unreal landscape. *Out Cry* is a reworking of Williams' earlier *The Two-Character Play*, produced in regional theatre in the United States. In 1967, a London production with Peter Wyngarde and Mary Ure ran twenty-four performances. The original was not well received. Nor was the rewrite. The tenor of criticism expressed sad dismay at Williams' lack of discipline and loss of power. ". . . in every respect a disaster . . . stale Pirandellicatessen" (Jack Kroll, *Newsweek*). ". . . an extremely mystifying evening of theater" (Douglas Watt, *New York Daily News*). ". . . shapeless, aimless, self-indulgent script" (Martin Gottfried, *Women's Wear Daily*). C: Michael York, Cara Duff-MacCormick. P: David Merrick Arts Foundation and Kennedy Center Productions, Inc. D: Peter Glenville. SD: Jo Mielziner.

Out from Under (5/4/40, Biltmore, 9)

Small-town editor pens scandalous bestseller. ". . . one of the emptiest comedies of modern times" (*New York Times*). C: John Alexander, Ruth Weston, Vivian Vance, Margaret Douglas, Philip Ober. A: John Walter Kelly. P: Brock Pemberton. D: Antoinette Perry.

Out of Step (1/29/25, Hudson, 21)

Thin comedy about a would-be band leader and his conventional Ohio family. C: Eric Dressler, Marcia Byron, Rose Hobart, Sara Haden, Muriel Kirkland. A: A. A. Kline. P: Dramatists' Theatre. D: James Forbes.

Out of the Frying Pan (2/11/41, Windsor, 104)

Silly but frequently funny farce about a group of stage hopefuls who entice a theatrical producer to their communal apartment and try to trap the poor fellow into giving them jobs. C: Alfred Drake, Barbara Bel Geddes (deb.), Florence MacMichael, Mabel Paige, Reynolds Evans, George Mathews. A: Francis Swann. P: William Deering and Alexander Kirkland (D).

SV: UA, 1943, *Young and Willing*, William Holden, Susan Hayward, Eddie Bracken, Robert Benchley, Barbara Britton.

Out of the Sea (12/5/27, Eltinge, 16)

A married woman falls in love with a poet and, when their love is thwarted, drowns herself in the sea. Bleak drama by humorist Don *(archie and mehitabel)* Marquis, set in Cornwall, England. C: Beatrix Thomson, Rollo Peters, Claude Rains, Lyn Harding, O. P. Heggie, Reginald Barlow. P: George C. Tyler. D: Walter Hampden.

Out There (3/27/17, Globe, 80)

A gin-soaked cockney scrub (Laurette Taylor) is redeemed when she enlists as a Red Cross nurse and becomes the Jeanne d'Arc of a wartorn hospital ward. This loosely sketched drama by J. Hartley Manners (A/D) was essentially a series of character studies of World War I volunteers and their varying reactions to 'Aunted Annie, the little cockney nurse who longs only to do her "bit" for her country. C: Lynn Fontanne, J. M. Kerrigan, Colin Campbell, Frank Kemble Cooper,

Hubert Druce. P: Tyler, Klaw & Erlanger. Ten days after the opening of *Out There*, the United States declared war on Germany. The play's arrival on Broadway could not have been more fortuitous. Its blending of pathos and patriotism, its moralistic fury at the atrocities of the Hun, moved audiences to cheers and bravos. New York's Mayor John Mitchell requested pictures of 'Aunted Annie to be used as enlistment posters. Annie's ardent, oft-repeated phrase to those who seemed hesitant to serve their country, "If I go, will you go?," became the enthusiastic rallying cry at innumerable recruiting centers. The play was revived (5/17/18, Century, 8) for a limited engagement under the sponsorship of the American Red Cross, taking its one and only fling in Broadway show business. The extraordinary all-star cast included: Laurette Taylor, George M. Cohan, George Arliss, H. B. Warner, O. P. Heggie, James K. Hackett, Chauncey Olcott, James T. Powers, Helen Ware, Beryl Mercer, George MacFarlane, and Julia Arthur. All players contributed their services. The week's engagement on Broadway, and subsequent three-week tour, netted the Red Cross almost three-quarters of a million dollars.

Out West of Eighth (9/20/51, Barrymore, 4)

Raucous farce about cowhands on the loose in Manhattan. "A rootin', tootin' bore" *(Mirror)*. C: Robert Keith, Jr., Richard Carlyle, Barbara Baxley, Irene Cowan, Dennis Weaver (deb.). A: Kenyon Nicholson. P: Courtney Burr and Malcolm Pearson. D: Marc Connelly and Burgess Meredith (both gentlemen declining directorial credit in the printed program).

Outcast (11/2/14, Lyceum, 168)

Girl (Elsie Ferguson) from the slums crashes society by marrying a drunken playboy (Charles Cherry). Trite, glum, and soapy. A/D: Hubert Henry Davies. P: Charles Frohman, Klaw, and Erlanger.

SV: WB, 1935, *The Girl From Tenth Avenue*, Bette Davis, Ian Hunter, Colin Clive, Alison Skipworth.

Outrageous Fortune (11/3/43, 48th Street, 77)

Into the home of a wealthy, maladjusted Jewish family comes a wise and understanding woman of the world (Elsie Ferguson) who attempts to shed some light on their assorted problems, anxieties, and neuroses. These include: homosexuality, bisexuality, infidelity, mother complexes, racial discrimination, and fear of illness, aging, and death. ". . . enough subject matter for seven or eight plays . . ." *(Post)*. ". . . pretentious when it means to be thoughtful, uncertain when it means to be precise" *(New York Times)*. Though confused and unresolved, *Outrageous Fortune* was also literate, provocative, and steadily interesting. George Jean Nathan called it "the best play of the season." It was written by Rose Franken (A/D), author of *Another Language* (1932) and *Claudia* (1941). C: Margalo Gillmore, Frederic Tozere, Maria Ouspenskaya, Margaret Hamilton, Eduard Franz, Brent Sargent, Dean Norton, Adele Longmire, Margaret Williams, Mabel Taylor. P: William Brown Meloney. SD: Raymond Sovey.

Outside Looking In (9/7/25, Greenwich Village, 113)

A gang of hoboes led by a swaggering bully named Oklahoma Red (Charles Bickford) convene in a boxcar to pass judgment on a young tramp named Little Red (James Cagney) for being a "sissy." This colorful social satire by Maxwell Anderson (based on Jim Tully's autobiography *Beggars of Life*) burlesqued the injustices of society's trial by jury and effectively dramatized the hoboes' contempt for authority. ". . . the most honest acting now to be seen in New York. I believe that Mr. Barrymore's effective performance of Hamlet would be a mere feat of elocution if compared to the characterizations of either Mr. Bickford or Mr. Cagney, both of whom are unknown" (Burns Mantle, *News*). This production was transferred to Broadway a few weeks after its O/B opening, and ran a total of 113 performances. P: Macgowan, Jones and O'Neill. D: Augustin Duncan. SD: Cleon Throckmorton.

SV: Par, 1928, *Beggars of Life,* a part-talking release with Wallace Beery and Louise Brooks.

Over Night (1/2/11, Hackett, 160)

A timid soul and his militant suffragette wife, and a blustering bully and his clinging-vine spouse, prepare to depart on their respective honeymoons aboard the good ship S. S. *Hendrik Hudson.* Through a last-minute blunder, the bully and suffragette are left ashore. The boat starts up the river with the newlywed couples thus rearranged. Extremely funny 1911 farce was an overnight hit for its young, fresh-out-of-college author, Philip H. Bartholomae. C: Margaret Lawrence, Herbert A. Yost, Robert Kelly, Jean Newcombe. P: William A. Brady.

Over 21 (1/3/44, Music Box, 221)

Wartime comedy by and with Ruth Gordon. The thinnish plot told of a sophisticated writer who stands by her middle-aged husband through the rigors of officers' candidate school in Miami Beach. "As a first try at playwriting, it betrays some ragged edges, but it builds into a merry evening . . ." *(Herald Tribune).* C: Harvey Stephens, Loring Smith, Philip Loeb, Dennie Moore, Beatrice Pearson. P: Max Gordon. D: George S. Kaufman. SD: Raymond Sovey.

SV: Col, 1945, Irene Dunne, Alexander Knox, Charles Coburn.

Note: Dorothy Parker was said to have been the model for the madcap authoress played by Miss Gordon.

Overtons, The (2/6/45, Booth, 175)

Cora Overton (Arlene Francis) suspects her husband, Jack (Jack Whiting), of having an affair with a predatory actress (Glenda Farrell), but the Overtons are reunited by the end of the play. Written by Vincent Lawrence as a sequel to his 1926 comedy-drama, *Sour Grapes.* "An inept and scrambled play, badly acted and directed" *(Sun).* P: Paul Czinner. D: Elisabeth Bergner. CD: Hattie Carnegie. SD: Edward Gilbert.

Owl and the Pussycat, The (11/18/64, ANTA, 427)

The romance of an introverted would-be writer (Alan Alda) and a barely literate prostitute (Diana Sands) who moves into his San Francisco apartment and takes over his life. Beguiling two-character comedy, written and played with verve and charm. A: Bill Manhoff. P: Philip Rose, Pat Fowler, Seven Arts. D: Arthur Storch. SD: Jo Mielziner.

SV: Col, 1970, Barbra Streisand, George Segal, Robert Klein (directed by Herbert Ross).

P

P.S. I Love You (11/19/64, Henry Miller, 12)

Romantic misunderstandings among married members of the international set. Tiresome comedy by Lawrence Roman, author of *Under the Yum-Yum Tree* (1960); b/o a play by Andre Roussin. C: Geraldine Page, Lee Patterson, Gilles Pelletier. P: Morton Gottlieb and Helen Bonfils. D: Henry Kaplan. CD/SD: Raoul Pene du Bois.

P.S. 193 (10/30/62, Writers Stage, 48)

Excellent O/B drama dealing with the murderous conflict between a disturbed war veteran (James Earl Jones) and a mild-mannered philosophy professor (Severn Darden). A: David Rayfiel. D: Andre Gregory.

Paganini (9/11/16, Criterion, 48)

Unconvincing, highly fictionalized portrait of the Italian violinist (George Arliss) whose virtuosity became a legend. C: Dudley Digges, Mrs. George Arliss. A: Edward Knoblock. P: Tyler, Klaw, and Erlanger. D: Frederick Stanhope.

Pagan Lady (10/20/30, 48th Street, 153)

Minister's son (Franchot Tone) is seduced by a harlot. A sleazy piece of goods. C: Lenore Ulric, Russell Hardie, Thomas Findlay. A: William Du Bois. P: Green and Gensler. D: John D. Williams. SV: Col, 1931, Charles Bickford, Evelyn Brent, Conrad Nagel, Roland Young.

Page Miss Glory (11/27/34, Mansfield, 63)

A couple of down-and-outers (James Stewart and Charles D. Brown) enter a national beauty contest by submitting a faked photograph made up of the best features of several movie stars. When their composite photo wins the twenty-five-hundred-dollar first prize, the hustling promoters are then faced with the problem of producing their nonexistent candidate. Helter-skelter George Abbott (D) farce, quite funny at times. C: Dorothy Hall, Peggy Shannon, Bruce MacFarlane, Betty Field (deb.). A: Joseph Schrank and Philip Dunning. P: Laurence Schwab and Philip Dunning. SV: WB, 1935, Marion Davies, Dick Powell, Pat O'Brien, Mary Astor, Frank McHugh, Lyle Talbot, Patsy Kelly, Allen Jenkins, Barton MacLane, Berton Churchill, Hobart Cavanaugh, Al Shean, Lionel Stander.

Paid in Full (2/25/08, Astor, 167)

Embezzler persuades his young wife to visit his employer and bargain for his freedom with her physical charms. Seamy melodrama by Eugene Walter. C: Tully Marshall, Lillian Albertson. P: Wagenhals and Kemper. D: Collin Kemper.

Pair of Sixes, A (3/17/14, Longacre, 207)

Two partners in the ladies' garter business quarrel and decide to settle their differences via a game of poker—the

A Pair of Sixes. **Hale Hamilton and Maude Eburne (March 17, 1914).** *Courtesy Museum of the City of New York Theatre and Music Collection.*

winner to become the boss and the loser to serve as his butler for a year. Rollicking farce of 1914 had more than its share of laughs. C: Hale Hamilton, Ann Murdock, Maude Eburne. A: Edward Peple. P: H. H. Frazee. D: Edgar MacGregor.

Musicalized by Gensler, Schwab, and DeSylva as *Queen High* (1926) with Charles Ruggles, Frank McIntyre, Mary Lawlor, Luella Gear.

SV: Par, 1930, *Queen High,* Charles Ruggles, Frank Morgan, Ginger Rogers, Stanley Smith.

Paisley Convertible, The (2/11/67, Henry Miller, 9)

Lightweight fluff about a pair of newlyweds bedeviled by ex-lovers and in-law problems. C: Bill Bixby, Joyce Bulifant, Marsha Hunt, Betsy von Furstenberg, Jed Allan. A: Harry Cauley. P: Michael Ellis. D: James Hammerstein.

Pajama Tops (5/31/63, Winter Garden, 52)

Infidelity, mistaken identity, homosexuality, and heterosexuality in a Deauville villa. Unabashed sex farce successfully toured the country for almost a decade; on Broadway it expired after little more than six weeks. A: Mawby Green and Ed Feilbert b/o a play by Jean De La Traz. P: Seiden and Bufman. D: Richard Vath.

Palm Tree in a Rose Garden, A (11/26/57, Cricket, 84)

The efforts of a career-frustrated widow and former beauty contest winner to achieve through a protegée the filmland fame that eluded her. Set in a Hollywood boardinghouse tenanted by young movie colony hopefuls, this absorbing O/B tragicomedy was well written, well produced, and well acted by a cast headed by Vicki Cummings, Barbara Baxley, and Laurinda Barrett. P: O'Brien and Cone. D: Warren Enters.

Pals First (2/26/17, Fulton, 152)

A college-educated, down-on-his-luck tramp impersonates a missing heir. "A rough-hewn play [with] a scarcely astonishing 'surprise finish' . . . compounded of some highly popular materials" (*New York Times*). C: William Courtenay, Thomas A. Wise, Auriol Lee. A: Lee Wilson Dodd, based on a novel by Francis Perry Elliott. P: J. F. Zimmerman, Jr. D: Ira Hards.

Panic (3/14/35, Imperial, 3)

In an effort to prevent the stock market collapse, a leading financier (Orson Welles) tries to persuade his fellow bankers to pool their resources. He fails and is himself destroyed in the crash. This experimental verse-drama by Archibald MacLeish gave nineteen-year-old Orson Welles his first major Broadway role. The play received generally unsympathetic reviews and was withdrawn after its third performance. C: Zita Johann, Richard

Whorf, Joanna Roos, George Glass, Russell Collins, Rose McClendon, Bernard Zanville (Dane Clark), Wesley Addy, Albert Lewis, John O'Shaughnessy, Abner Biberman. P: Phoenix Theatre, Inc. (John Houseman). D: James Light. CH: Martha Graham. SD: Jo Mielziner.

Papa Is All (1/6/42, Guild, 63)

Tyrannical Pennsylvania Dutch father finally gets his comeuppance. "Patterson Greene's patricidal comedy . . . suffers from malnutrition . . . like a tureen of bouillon made from two cubes" (*World-Telegram*). C: Jessie Royce Landis, Carl Benton Reid, Celeste Holm, Emmett Rogers, Dorothy Sands, Royal Beal. P: The Theatre Guild. D: Carrington and Morgan.

Papp (4/17/69, American Place, 39)

Obscure O/B allegory, set in some future Dark Age, illustrating the thesis that if there were no God, man would have to invent Him. C: Albert Paulsen, Rudy Bond, Arnold Soboloff, Barbara Hayes. A: Kenneth Cameron. P: American Place Theater. D: Martin Fried.

Paradise (12/26/27, 48th Street, 8)

Lonely spinster invents fictitious husband. Treacle. C: Lillian Foster, Warren William, Elizabeth Patterson, Minnie Dupree, Selena Royle, Eloise Stream, Tom Brown. A: William Hurlbut. P/D: Robert Milton.

Paradise Lost (12/9/35, Longacre, 72)

Written in 1935, with the country in the grip of the Depression, Clifford Odets' drama explored the lives of the Gordons, a middle-class New York family struggling to survive amid rapidly changing values. Crowded with confusing symbols and irrelevant incidents, the play attempted to dramatize the collapse of American liberalism, and its hope of redemption through a new social system. *Paradise Lost* met with a lukewarm reception and closed after seventy-two performances. Its failure was a bitter blow to Odets. He vowed to renounce the Broadway theatre and promptly signed a Hollywood contract. His first screenwriting assignment was Paramount's *The General Died at Dawn,* a successful melodrama that co-starred Gary Cooper and Madeleine Carroll. C: Morris Carnovsky, Stella Adler, Luther Adler, Frieda Altman, Sanford Meisner, Walter Coy, Elia Kazan, Roman Bohnen, Robert Lewis, Vincent Sherman. P: The Group Theatre. D: Harold Clurman. SD: Boris Aronson.

Paris Bound (12/27/27, Music Box, 234)

Philip Barry's successful comedy about infidelity and divorce. A young wife learns that her husband has been unfaithful. Contemplating divorce, she discovers to her surprise that her own friendship with a composer could easily develop into an affair, and she accepts her husband's casual adultery philosophically. C: Madge Kennedy, Donn (Donald) Cook, Hope Williams, Gilbert Emery. P/D: Arthur Hopkins. SD: Robert Edmond Jones. M: Frank Harling.

SV: Pathé, 1929, Ann Harding, Fredric March, Ilka Chase, Leslie Fenton.

Parlor, Bedroom and Bath (12/24/17, Republic, 232)

Unprepossessing young man is converted into a Lothario. Amusing bedroom farce. C: John Cumberland, Florence Moore, Francine Larrimore, Helen Menken. A: C. W. Bell and Mark Swan. P: A. H. Woods. D: Bertram Harrison.

SV: MGM, 1931, Buster Keaton, Charlotte Greenwood, Reginald Denny.

Parlor Story (3/4/47, Biltmore, 23)

Journalism professor becomes politically entangled with reactionary newspaper publisher. ". . . a discursive and frequently tedious comedy" (*Sun*). C: Walter Abel, Edith Atwater, Royal Beal. A: William McCleery. P: Paul Streger. D: Bretaigne Windust.

Parnell (11/11/35, Barrymore, 98)

The ill-fated love of the Irish Nationalist leader for Mrs. Katie O'Shea was the subject of this absorbing historical drama. Named corespondent in a widely publicized divorce suit brought by Mrs. O'Shea's estranged husband, Parnell is stripped of his political power by the scandal, and dies a broken man. *Parnell* was written by Elsie Schauffler, a forty-seven-year-old Kansas housewife. The authoress died shortly before the Broadway premiere of her much-acclaimed biographical drama. C: George Curzon, Margaret Rawlings, John Emery, Effie Shannon, Ruth Matteson. P: Smith and Ayer. D: Guthrie McClintic. SD: Stewart Chaney.

R: (5/4/36, 48th Street, 32) with Dennis King and Edith Barrett in the leading roles.

SV: MGM, 1937, Clark Gable, Myrna Loy, Edna May Oliver, Billie Burke, Donald Crisp. Alan Marshal (directed by John Stahl from a screenplay by John Van Druten and S. N. Behrman).

Partners Again (5/1/22, Selwyn, 250)

Jewish dialect business farce in the *Potash and Perlmutter* (1913) series. Comic-book-level slapstick material, but audiences of the time liked it. C: Alexander Carr, Barney Bernard. A: Montague Glass and Jules Eckert Goodman. P: The Selwyns i.a.w. A. H. Woods. D: Bertram Harrison.

Party's Over, The (3/27/33, Vanderbilt, 48)

Good-natured son finally rebels against his parasitic family. Capable cast in so-so comedy. C: Harvey Stephens, Katherine Alexander, Claire Trevor, Effie Shannon, Peggy Conklin, Ross Alexander, Georgette Harvey. A/P: Daniel Kusell. D: Howard Lindsay.

SV: Col, 1934, Stuart Erwin, Ann Sothern.

Passenger to Bali, A (3/14/40, Barrymore, 4)

Walter Huston (directed by son John Huston) came to Broadway in this allegorical melodrama about a sinister derelict ("a dictator in search of a country") who boards a tramp steamer in the guise of a missionary and remains to become an incubus. A raging typhoon ends this mysterious stranger's troublemaking when he meets his death on the sinking vessel. "*A Passenger to Bali* is obscure and often faulty, but it is provocative" (*Herald Tribune*). C: Colin Keith-Johnston, William Harrigan, Cecil Humphreys, Edgar Stehli. A: Ellis St. Joseph. P: Montgomery Ford. SD: Lawrence Goldwasser.

Passing Present, The (12/7/31, Barrymore, 16)

The disintegration of a once-proud New York family, with the plot hinging on the efforts of the daughter of the house to shield her embezzler-brother from the consequences of his actions. Interesting but confused domestic drama written by Gretchen Damrosch, daughter of conductor Walter Damrosch. C: Hope Williams, Morgan Farley, Maria Ouspenskaya, E. J. Ballantine. P/D: Arthur Hopkins.

Passion of Josef D, The (2/11/64, Barrymore, 15)

Paddy Chayefsky's (A/D) Brechtian-styled chronicle-drama of the Russian Revolution, focusing primarily on the rise of the ruthless young Joseph Stalin (Peter Falk), from the day in 1917 when he was released from prison to the moment, seven years later, when he took over the reins of power at the coffin of his dead leader Lenin (Luther Adler). The play was a hodgepodge of many different styles, veering sharply between tragedy, melodrama, and music-hall farce. Particularly criticized was Chayefsky's portrait of Trotsky (Alvin Epstein) as a comic popinjay. "... flamboyant and theatrical rather than dramatic. As a canvas of revolution, it is vastly oversimplified" (*New York Times*). C: Milt Kamen, Elizabeth Hubbard, Ramon Bieri. P: Cantor, Fogelson, and Lawrence. CD: Domingo A. Rodriguez. SD: Will Steven Armstrong. M: David Amram.

Note: Paddy Chayefsky on the play's Broadway failure: "I wrote it out of pique. I was sick of being reduced to being judged a realistic writer. I thought if I directed it in an imitation of Tyrone Guthrie I could get away with it, but that was a mistake, and I couldn't spend as much time as was essential in the rewriting. I'll never direct again."

Passionate Pilgrim, The (10/19/32, 48th Street, 5)

Poorly written and produced saga of the life and times of Will Shakespeare (Albert Dekker). C: Beverly Roberts. George Macready. A: Margaret Crosby Munn. P/D: Howard Inches.

Pastoral (11/1/39, Henry Miller, 14)

Drowsy comedy about a middle-aged European couple trying to start a chicken farm in the Catskills. C: John Banner, Ruth Weston, Cornel Wilde, Georgette Harvey. A: Victor Wolfson. P: Helen Bonfils and George Somnes (D).

Paths of Glory (9/26/35, Plymouth, 24)

Members of a World War I French army division are condemned to death in battle to satisfy the ruthless ambition of their commanding general. Cluttered, multi-scened dramatization by Sidney Howard of Humphrey Cobb's shattering antiwar novel. *Paths of Glory,* a twenty-four-performance Broadway failure, later became a highly acclaimed motion picture. C: Jack Roseleigh, Cyril Scott, William Harrigan, Myron McCormick, Lee Baker, Edgar Barrier, Jerome Cowan, Leonard Penn, George Tobias, Dick Purcell, Milo Boulton, E. J. Ballantine, Jack Daniels. P/D: Arthur Hopkins.

SV: UA, 1957, Kirk Douglas, Adolphe Menjou, George Macready, Ralph Meeker, Wayne Morris (directed by Stanley Kubrick).

Patriots, The (1/29/43, National, 172)

Sidney Kingsley's play dealing with the conflict between Jefferson and Hamilton during the early days of the republic. ". . . thoughtful, provocative and pertinent" (*Journal-American*). C: Raymond Edward Johnson, Madge Evans, House Jameson, Cecil Humphreys, Juano Hernandez, Hope Lange (deb.). P: The Playwrights Company and Rowland Stebbins. D: Shepard Traube. SD: Howard Bay.

R: (12/20/43, City Center, 8). C: Walter Hampden, Julie Haydon, Guy Sorel, Cecil Humphreys.

Patsy, The (12/23/25, Booth, 242)

Cute comedy about an enterprising youngster (Claiborne Foster) who finally turns the tables on her domineering older sister. A: Barry Conners. P: Richard Herndon. D: Alan Dinehart.

SV: A silent version of this play was filmed by MGM in 1928 with Marion Davies and Marie Dressler in the leading roles. The picture was directed by King Vidor.

Peace on Earth (11/29/33, Civic, 142)

Idealistic professor seals his doom when he becomes involved in a munitions strike and is framed for murder. Vigorous antiwar drama by George Sklar and Albert Maltz. C: Robert Keith, Victor Kilian, John Boruff, Jules (John) Garfield (deb.). P: The Theatre Union. D: Robert B. Sinclair. SD: Cleon Throckmorton.

Pearl of Great Price, The (11/1/26, Century, 33)

Pilgrim (Claudette Colbert), a wide-eyed, virtuous lass, guards her chastity zealously. When her dear old mother (Effie Shannon) dies, little Pilgrim is left alone in the world. In her journey through life, she crosses "The Street of Indecision," visits "The Auction Room of Shame," and finally reaches "The Trysting Place of Happiness" where she finds "True Love" at last. This heavy-handed morality play was both simplistic and smutty. It was produced by the Messrs. Shubert. A: Robert McLaughlin. D: J. C. Huffman.

Peepshow (2/3/44, Fulton, 28)

A philanderer is dogged by his conscience. The role of the cad's alter ego—who dresses identically, communicates largely in pantomime, and speaks only when he and the hero-heel are alone—was engagingly portrayed by David Wayne. John Emery played the cad, and Tamara Geva and Joan Tetzel were two of the ladies with whom he dallied. ". . . tedious and tasteless charade" (*Herald Tribune*). ". . . negligible comedy, a tricky piece, more of a notion than a play" *(Sun)*. *Peepshow* was written by Anglo-American author Ernest Pascal, whose screenplay credits include *Lloyds of London* and *Hound of the Baskervilles*. The comedy was co-produced by Mr. Pascal i.a.w. film producer Samuel Bronston. D: David Burton. SD: Lemuel Ayers.

Peg O' My Heart (12/20/12, Cort, 603)

An untutored Irish girl (Laurette Taylor) inherits a fortune and goes to London to live with her aristocratic English relatives. Life is difficult for Peg in this frigid, ultra-proper atmosphere. All ends well, however, when she succeeds in saving her catty cousin from a scandal and "Jerry" (H. Reeves-Smith), a young British nobleman, falls in love with her. "To see a new star who had a right to be a star was so astonishing that we all lost our senses last night and roared at Laurette Taylor! She proved that she is now the best comedienne on the American stage. In 10 minutes she gave us more acting than we have been accustomed to seeing in 10 months. No wonder we were amazed" (Louis Sherwin, *Globe*). *Peg O' My Heart*, the first attraction to play the Cort Theatre, was written by J. Hartley Manners (A/D) as a vehicle for his wife, Laurette Taylor. This sentimental comedy was Miss Taylor's most conspicuous success until her triumphant return to Broadway more than thirty years later as the star of Tennessee Williams' *The Glass Menagerie* (1945). After *Peg* had run for a year to capacity houses, six road companies were sent out to tour the hinterlands. From these companies alone, the lucky author netted ten thousand dollars a week. Since each road company poster carried Laurette Taylor's name above that of the company star, and in larger type (as the creator of "Peg"), countless numbers of people who never saw Miss Taylor in the part thought that they had. C: Hassard Short, Reginald Mason, Christine Norman. P: Oliver Morosco.

R: (2/14/21, Cort, 88) by A. L. Erlanger. C: Laurette Taylor, A. E. Matthews.

Musicalized by Hugo Felix as *Peg-O'-My-Dreams* (1924) with Suzanne Keener, Roy Royston, G. P. Huntley, Chester Hale.

SV: MGM, 1933, Marion Davies, Onslow Stevens, Alan Mowbray.

Note: The silent version (Metro, 1923) starred Laurette Taylor and was directed by King Vidor.

Penny Arcade (3/10/30, Fulton, 24)

The romance of a carnival barker and the daughter of a penny arcade proprietress is complicated when the boy is framed for the murder of a racketeer. The girl clears the barker by revealing the guilty party—her cowardly brother. Sleazy melodrama contained some good performances, notably those of James Cagney (in his farewell Broadway appearance) as the weakling brother, and Joan Blondell as a wisecracking photographer's assistant. C: Eric Dressler, Lenita

Lane, George Barbier, Millard Mitchell, Paul Guilfoyle. A: Marie Baumer. P: William Keighley (D) and W. P. Tanner.
SV: WB, 1930, *Sinner's Holiday*, Grant Withers, Evelyn Knapp, James Cagney, Joan Blondell, Lucille La Verne.
Note: Al Jolson bought the screen rights to *Penny Arcade* and sold the property to Warner Brothers with the stipulation that Cagney and Blondell reprise their roles in the film version. The picture marked their screen debuts. William Keighley later directed such James Cagney films as *G-Men, The Fighting 69th, Torrid Zone,* and *The Bride Came C.O.D.*

Penny Wars, The (10/15/69, Royale, 5)

Flawed drama of a youth maturing in upstate New York, 1939. Set against him is his stepfather, a Jewish refugee from Hitler's Germany. Each is trying to find himself, the youth through the familiar avenues of sex and political awareness, the older man by defensive arrogance and purposeful alienation from the society that has saved his life. Their conflict ends tragically with the stepfather's suicide. Adapted from his novel of the same name, Elliott Baker's dramatization reflects the problems in translating one medium to another. The material remains stubbornly novelistic with too few scenes that are theatrically effective. ". . . too much of the time it is a bore" (Clive Barnes, *New York Times*). Actress Barbara Harris made her directorial debut with *The Penny Wars,* and her handling of the large cast won general approval. In particular, Kristoffer Tabori as the young protagonist, Kim Hunter as his mother, and George Voskovec as the refugee were praised. A: Elliott Baker. C: Kristoffer Tabori, Kim Hunter, George Voskovec, Dolph Sweet, Catherine Bacon, Jeffrey Hamilton, John Korkes, Rita Karin, Jack Valente, Ben Kapen, Brooks Morton, Lois Holmes, Martha Galphin, Judy Nugent, John Anania, John Gerstad, Lou Tiano, Joe Alfasa, James Doolan, Mel Winkler, Robert Delbert, Kathryn Baumann, Avis McArther. D: Barbara Harris. P: David Merrick Arts Foundation. SD: William Ritman. CD: Jane Greenwood.

Penny Wise (4/19/37, Morosco, 64)

Inconsequential 30's comedy about a philandering playwright and his understanding wife. C: Kenneth MacKenna, Linda Watkins, Irene Purcell. A: Jean Ferguson Black. P: Juliana Morgan. D: Arthur Sircom.

Penrod (9/2/18, Globe, 48)

Booth Tarkington's adolescent hero and his gang of "detecatifs" capture a criminal. Beguiling little comedy with a topnotch cast: Helen Hayes, Paul Kelly, Lillian Roth, Helen Chandler, Ben Grauer, Robert Vaughn, Katherine Emmett, and Andrew Lawlor, Jr. as Penrod. A: Edward E. Rose. P: Tyler, Klaw and Erlanger. D: Dudley Digges and Edward E. Rose.
SV: WB, 1951, *On Moonlight Bay,* Doris Day, Gordon MacRae.
Note: A silent version (WB, 1922) starred Wesley Barry. Warner Brothers subsequently turned Tarkington's *Penrod* stories into a series of low-budget features (1937-38) for The Mauch Twins.

People Don't Do Such Things (11/23/27, 48th Street, 13)

A man, his wife, and his mistress decide to live together. It doesn't work out. Dim 20's farce. C: Lynne Overman, Isobel Elsom, Millicent Hanley. A: Lyon Mearson and Edgar M. Schoenberg. P: Jones and Green.

People vs. Ranchman, The (10/27/68, Fortune, 41)

Angry citizens confront a convicted (but

unrepentant) rapist (William Devane). Innovative O/B drama, written and directed in avant-garde fashion. A: Megan Terry. P: Otto/Johnson/Hobard. D: Robert Greenwald.

Perfect Marriage, The (11/16/32, Bijou, 14)

At a golden wedding anniversary, it is disclosed that the marriage endured because both partners were free to engage in separate romantic liaisons. Tiresome flashback comedy-drama by Arthur Goodrich. C: Fay Bainter, George Gaul, Edith Barrett, George Baxter, Jackie Kelk. P: William Caryl. D: Melville Burke.

Perfect Marriage, The (10/26/44, Barrymore, 92)

Wordy skirmish between a well-to-do husband (Victor Jory) and his chic wife (Miriam Hopkins) who discover, after ten years of supposed wedded bliss, that they can't stand each other. ". . . trivial and dreary . . . as pretentious as it is dull" (*Herald Tribune*). A/D: Samson Raphaelson. P: Cheryl Crawford. CD: Valentina. SD: Oliver Smith.
SV: Par, 1946, David Niven, Loretta Young, Eddie Albert, Charles Ruggles, ZaSu Pitts, Virginia Field, Rita Johnson.

Perfect Setup, The (10/24/62, Cort, 5)

Public relations counsel is torn between his wife and mistress. Hackneyed three-character triangle comedy by screenwriter-director Jack Sher (*Four Girls in Town, The Three Worlds of Gulliver,* etc.). C: Gene Barry, Angie Dickinson (deb.), Jan Sterling. P: Martin Melcher i.a.w. Selma Tamber. D: Lamont Johnson.

Perfectly Scandalous (5/13/31, Hudson, 5)

Did young Oliver Drake sleep with his glamorous aunt or didn't he? Perfectly dreadful. "*Perfectly Scandalous* was one of those plays in which all of the actors, unfortunately, enunciated very clearly" (Robert Benchley, *The New Yorker*). C: Natalie Schafer, Grant Gordon. A: Hutcheson Boyd. P: Ray Gallo. D: Robert Lawrence.

Period of Adjustment (11/10/60, Hayes, 132)

Tennessee Williams' "serious comedy" detailing the "period of adjustment" in the relationships of two couples—a pair of bumbling newlyweds (Barbara Baxley and Robert Webber)—and a longer-married twosome (Rosemary Murphy and James Daly) on the verge of breaking up. As the final curtain falls, both couples are reassuringly tucked into separate beds—in the right combinations. "A serious comedy that is neither especially serious nor notably comic" (*New York Times*). "An affectionate and rather charming little domestic comedy" (*News*). "A turbid stew . . ." (*The New Yorker*). P: Cheryl Crawford. D: George Roy Hill. SD: Jo Mielziner.
SV: MGM, 1962, Jane Fonda, Anthony Franciosa, Jim Hutton, Lois Nettleton, John McGiver, Jack Albertson, Mabel Albertson (directed by George Roy Hill from a screenplay by Isobel Lennart).
Note: For a while, Tennessee Williams thought of directing the Broadway production of *Period of Adjustment* himself. Halfway through rehearsals, he relinquished the reins to George Roy Hill and admitted sadly: "I can't direct my way out of a paper bag."

Personal Appearance (10/17/34, Henry Miller, 501)

Amusingly risqué comedy about a tempestuous screen star (Gladys George) who can't keep her hands off good-looking young men. While promoting

Drifting Lady, her latest film epic, the movie queen takes a fancy to a husky young gas station attendant (Philip Ober) and arranges to take the boy back to Hollywood with her. At the last moment, her wily press agent (Otto Hulett) effectively sabotages this scheme. *Personal Appearance* was a smash hit. A: Lawrence Riley. P: Brock Pemberton. D: Antoinette Perry and Brock Pemberton.

SV: Par, 1936, *Go West, Young Man,* Mae West, Randolph Scott, Warren William, Alice Brady, Elizabeth Patterson, Lyle Talbot, Isabel Jewell.

Peter Ibbetson (4/17/17, Republic, 71)

This fanciful tale, based on the novel by George Du Maurier, was adapted by John Raphael and Constance Collier and extensively revised and rewritten for American audiences by Edward Sheldon. It was one of John and Lionel Barrymore's greatest successes. The story tells of two lovers (John Barrymore and Constance Collier) who become separated but can meet in their dreams. The hero spends the better part of his life in jail for murdering his evil uncle (Lionel Barrymore). He bears his fate happily because he can spend part of each day in perfect spiritual communion with his beloved. "An interesting and ingenious play that catches something of the . . . strange elation of one of the happiest stories ever told" (*New York Times*). C: Laura Hope Crews, Wallis Clark, Madge Evans. P: Messrs. Shubert. D: Clifford Brooke. The complicated lighting effects for the play were supervised by Maude Adams. Florenz Ziegfeld furnished the lighting equipment. R: (4/8/31, Shubert, 21). C: Dennis King, Jessie Royce Landis, George Nash, Valerie Taylor, Wallis Clark. D: Constance Collier. Musicalized by Deems Taylor as an opera (1931) with Lucrezia Bori as the Duchess of Towers.

SV: Par, 1935, Gary Cooper, Ann Harding, Ida Lupino, John Halliday, Douglas Dumbrille.

Peterpat (1/6/65, Longacre, 21)

Marital ups and downs of a mystery writer (Dick Shawn) and his wife (Joan Hackett). Tenuous two-character comedy with some bright lines and situations. A: Enid Rudd. P: Twain and Katz. D: Joe Layton. SD: David Hays. M: Walter Marks.

Petrified Forest, The (1/7/35, Broadhurst, 194)

Robert E. Sherwood's "philosophical melodrama" about a disillusioned idealist who meets both his love and his death in a bleak roadside restaurant in the Arizona desert. Out of the desert comes Alan Squier (Leslie Howard), on his way to the Petrified Forest, i.e., to self-destruction, the only answer he can find to a meaningless existence in which nature is "taking the world away from the intellectuals and giving it back to the apes." Duke Mantee (Humphrey Bogart), a fleeing gangster, later grants the hero his boon of extinction. Having deeded his life insurance policy to a kindred soul (Peggy Conklin), Squier is glad to die to ensure her escape from the "Petrified Forest." "Downright enjoyable . . . a stimulating play . . . a lusty show" (*New York Times*). P: Gilbert Miller and Leslie Howard i.a.w. Arthur Hopkins (D). SD: Raymond Sovey.

SV: WB, 1936, Leslie Howard, Bette Davis, Humphrey Bogart, Genevieve Tobin, Dick Foran, Porter Hall, Charley Grapewin; 1945, *Escape in the Desert,* Helmut Dantine, Philip Dorn, Alan Hale, Irene Manning, Jean Sullivan.

Note: Wanting a big name for the gangster role, Warner Brothers was eager to give contract player Edward G. Robinson the Duke Mantee part in their screen version of *The Petrified Forest* (1936). Leslie Howard flatly refused to do the film unless the studio signed Bogart as well. Warners reluctantly capitulated to Howard's demands. Bogart accompanied Howard to Hollywood and never again returned to the Broadway stage.

Petticoat Fever (3/4/35, Ritz, 137)

Giddy farce about the efforts of a sex-starved radio operator in Labrador to bed a glamorous woman pilot. "Keeps the audience laughing steadily" (*Theatre Arts*). C: Dennis King, Doris Dalton, Leo G. Carroll, Ona Munson. A: Mark Reed. P: Richard Aldrich and Alfred de Liagre, Jr. (D).

SV: MGM, 1936, Robert Montgomery, Myrna Loy, Reginald Owen.

Philadelphia Story, The (3/28/39, Shubert, 417)

Tracy Lord (Katharine Hepburn) is a willful Philadelphia socialite with a set of impossibly high moral standards. On the eve of her second marriage to a priggish snob (Frank Fenton), Tracy's ex-husband (Joseph Cotten) makes an appearance. The wedding plans are further complicated by the presence of a reporter (Van Heflin) and wisecracking photographer (Shirley Booth) from a national gossip magazine. In the space of twenty-four hours, events conspire to teach this self-righteous aristocrat the meaning of tolerance, and the play ends as Tracy is reunited with her former husband. This sparkling comedy by Philip Barry was a perfect example of the right play at the right time. In a role especially tailored for her talents, Katharine Hepburn returned to Broadway in triumph. The play re-established its author's fading reputation as a writer of drawing-room comedy, and resolved the precarious financial plight of The Theatre Guild. (Barry, Miss Hepburn, and Howard Hughes put up seventy-five percent of the play's production cost. The Theatre Guild owned twenty-five percent of the hit show. The profits were substantial enough to rescue the Guild from the threat of insolvency.)

C: Nicholas Joy, Forrest Orr, Vera Allen, Lenore Lonergan, Dan Tobin. D: Robert B. Sinclair. SD: Robert Edmond Jones.

SV: MGM, 1940, Katharine Hepburn, Cary Grant, James Stewart, Ruth Hussey, John Howard, Roland Young, John Halliday, Virginia Weidler, Mary Nash, Henry Daniell (directed by George Cukor from a screenplay by Donald Ogden Stewart); 1956, *High Society,* Grace Kelly, Bing Crosby, Frank Sinatra, Celeste Holm, John Lund, Louis Calhern, Louis Armstrong (directed by Charles Walters from a screenplay by John Patrick).

Philip Goes Forth (1/12/31, Biltmore, 98)

Would-be playwright discovers he lacks talent, effects a reconciliation with his businessman-father. Minor George Kelly (A/D) satirical comedy. C: Harry Ellerbe, Madge Evans, Thurston Hall, Dorothy Stickney, Cora Witherspoon, Thais Lawton. P: Laurence Rivers, Inc. (Rowland Stebbins).

Pick-Up Girl (5/3/44, 48th Street, 197)

A juvenile court was the setting for this frequently absorbing 1944 case history of a fifteen-year-old prostitute. ". . . a fine production . . . a candid and sincere play," (*Sun*). *Pick-Up Girl* was written by actress Elsa Shelley (Juliet to Walter Hampden's Romeo). The play was produced by Michael Todd's staff. (Todd was inducted into the navy shortly before the script went into rehearsal). C: Pamela Rivers, William Harrigan, Doro Merande. D: Roy Hargrave. SD: Watson Barratt.

Picnic (5/2/34, National, 2)

Communist learns about life and love from a Wall Street capitalist. Dreary drama by Gretchen Damrosch, daughter of composer-conductor Walter Damrosch. C: Percy Waram, Joanna Roos, Esther Dale, Jean Adair, Hugh Rennie, Millard Mitchell, Frieda Altman. P: Arthur J. Beckhard. D: Kaye Lowe.

Picnic (2/19/53, Music Box, 477)

Dozing under a hot sun on a Labor Day morning, a sleepy Kansas town is awakened by the impact of a swaggering, muscle-flexing vagrant (Ralph Meeker) on the lives of its sexually frustrated womenfolk. By the time he leaves next day, he has succeeded in nearly breaking the heart of a tomboy ugly duckling (Kim Stanley), has stimulated a schoolteacher (Eileen Heckart) to drive her reluctant boyfriend (Arthur O'Connell) to the altar, and, finally, has inspired a proud beauty (Janice Rule)* to leave her well-to-do fiancé (Paul Newman)* and run away with him. This slice of small-town Americana won both the Pulitzer Prize and the New York Drama Critics Circle Award as best play of the year. *Picnic* (originally titled *The Front Porch*) was written by William Inge. Several critics grumbled that Joshua Logan's high-pressure staging tended to distort the author's innately honest characterization and quietly understated dialogue. All major reviewers praised the acting of a uniformly fine cast and Jo Mielziner's setting and lighting. C: Peggy Conklin, Elizabeth Wilson,* Reta Shaw, Ruth McDevitt, Morris Miller. P: The Theatre Guild and Joshua Logan.
SV: Col, 1955, William Holden, Kim Novak, Rosalind Russell, Betty Field, Cliff Robertson, Susan Strasberg, Arthur O'Connell, Nick Adams, Phyllis Newman, Verna Felton (directed by Joshua Logan).

---

*Broadway debuts.

Pie in the Sky (12/22/41, Playhouse, 6)

Bankrupt bluebloods scheme to marry off their nitwit son to a blowsy oil heiress. "A farce by intention, a grim tragedy in execution" (*World-Telegram*). C: Luella Gear, Oscar Shaw, Enid Markey, Leona Powers, Herbert Corthell. A: Bernadine Angus. P: Edgar MacGregor (D) and Lyn Logan.

Pierre of the Plains (10/12/08, Hudson, 32)

Minor western adventure-romance, adapted by Edgar Selwyn (A/D) from Gilbert Parker's novel, *Pierre and his People*. C: Edgar Selwyn, Elsie Ferguson. P: Henry B. Harris.
SV: MGM, 1942, John Carroll, Ruth Hussey, Bruce Cabot, Reginald Owen, Henry Travers.

Pigeons and People (1/16/33, Harris, 66)

A reformer invites a stranger to his home only to find he can't get rid of him. When the unwelcome house guest finally leaves, the audience remains uncertain whether he was merely a philosophic tramp, a crook, or a lunatic. "It is a rare piece of hocus-pocus which begins without a beginning, continues without a theme and stops without having arrived at a conclusion" (*New York Times*). This odd but intriguing George M. Cohan (A/P) charade was staged for two hours without an intermission. C: George M. Cohan, Walter Gilbert, Paul McGrath, Olive Reeves-Smith, Reynolds Denniston. D: Sam Forrest.

Pigs (9/1/24, Little 347)

With the help of his girlfriend (Nydia Westman), an enterprising lad (Wallace Ford) raises the money to buy sick pigs and cure them at a profit. Innocuous homespun comedy pleased the family crowd back in 1924. A: Anne Morrison and Patterson McNutt. P: John Golden.

Piker, The (1/15/25, Eltinge, 43)

Bernie Kaplan (Lionel Barrymore), a young Jewish bank messenger, falls in love with gold-digging chorus girl June

Knight (Irene Fenwick).* Before he knows what's happening to him, poor Bernie has become involved in embezzlement and blackmail, and ends by winding up in a mental institution. Maudlin melodrama by Anglo-American writer Leon Gordon, author of *White Cargo* (1923). P: A. H. Woods. D: Priestly Morrison.

―――――
*Irene Fenwick was Mrs. Lionel Barrymore.

Pillar to Post (12/10/43, Playhouse, 27)

In order to get a room in an overcrowded tourist camp, a salesgirl persuades a soldier to pose as her husband. "It is a harmless, naïve, clumsy little play that has happened to stop off here on its way to Hollywood" *(Post)*. C: Perry Wilson, Carl Gose, Richard Hart. A: Rose Simon Kohn. P: Brock Pemberton. D: Antoinette Perry.

- SV: WB, 1946, *Pillow to Post*, Ida Lupino, Sydney Greenstreet, William Prince, Stuart Erwin, Ruth Donnelly, Louis Armstrong.

Pink Elephant, The (4/22/53, Playhouse, 5)

Sluggish farce about a mild-mannered ghost writer (Steve Allen) who finally exposes the dirty tricks campaign of his Republican bigwig boss. C: Howard Smith, David White, Patricia Barry, Jean Casto, Bruce Gordon, Heywood Hale Broun. A: John G. Fuller. P: Paul, Kaufman and Walliser. D: Harry Ellerbe.

Piper Paid (12/25/34, Ritz, 15)

Expatriate socialite can't decide between three men. Turbid, hopelessly bungled 30's drama. C: Edith Barrett, Raymond Hackett, Spring Byington, Harry Green. A: Sarah B. Smith and Viola Brothers Shore. P: Harold K. Berg. D: Clifford Brooke.

Pirate, The (11/25/42, Martin Beck, 176)

Manuela (Lynn Fontanne), wife of the mayor of a small West Indies village, mistakes a strolling player (Alfred Lunt) for a notorious buccaneer. He in turn recognizes the mayor as the real pirate and, consequently, is in fair danger of hanging. In the end, the debonair mountebank wins Manuela, while the unwanted husband is exposed and carted off to jail. ". . . an audacious theatrical gesture that does not come off" *(Post)*. This minor costume frolic by S. N. Behrman was "suggested" by *The Sea Robber*, a play by German dramatist Ludwig Fulda. C: Estelle Winwood, Alan Reed, Clarence Derwent, Lea Penman, Muriel Rahn, Juanita Hall, Maurice Ellis, Walter Mosby, Robert Emhardt, Inez Matthews, William Le Massena. P: The Playwrights Company and The Theatre Guild. D: Alfred Lunt and John C. Wilson. CD: Miles White. CH; Felicia Sorel. M: Herbert Kingsley. SD: Lemuel Ayers.

- SV: MGM, 1948, Judy Garland, Gene Kelly, Walter Slezak, Gladys Cooper, Reginald Owen (directed by Vincente Minnelli).

Pit, The (2/10/04, Lyric, 77)

Hard-hitting study of the "ravening wolves" of the business world and the struggle between two rival groups of speculators to manipulate the wheat market. Adapted from Frank Norris' novel by Channing Pollock, the play opened on Pollock's twenty-first birthday and earned a half-million dollars before it closed. This was in pre-Dramatists Guild days, however, and Pollock received only one thousand dollars (in twenty weekly payments of fifty dollars each) for his scripting services. C: Wilton Lackaye, Douglas Fairbanks, Hale Hamilton. P: William A. Brady.

Place for Polly, A (4/18/70, Ethel Barrymore, 1)

Comedy of an unscrupulous New York

publisher who intends to print his sexy sister-in-law's plagiarized novel. His wife, Polly, is a bit of a dimwit—she's part of a drive to tear down Lincoln Center—but she knows right from wrong. Various questions of ethics and morality are posed, but remain undeveloped in a fitfully amusing script that resolves both plot and theme in a simplistic, unsatisfying manner. "Everything is fundamentally false . . ." (Clive Barnes, *New York Times*). ". . . most of the writing ranges from lackluster to tasteless" (Douglas Watt, *New York Daily News*). A: Lonnie Coleman. C: Marian Mercer, Konrad Matthaei, Cathryn Damon, Robert Moberly, Alan Manson, Evelyn Russell, William Mooney, Daniel Keyes, Dortha Duckworth. D: Ronny Graham. SD: Clarke Dunham. CD: Frank Thompson.

Place of Our Own, A (4/2/45, Royale, 8)

Period comedy-drama (Ohio, 1919) about the conflict between an idealistic editor and his isolationist father-in-law. ". . . cumbersome and lifeless" *(Sun)*. C: Robert Keith, J. C. Nugent, John Archer, Jeanne Cagney, Mercedes McCambridge (deb.). A/D: Elliott Nugent. P: John Golden i.a.w. Elliott Nugent and Robert Montgomery.

Places, Please! (11/12/37, Golden, 3)

Back Bay Bostonians refuse to accept an actress (Lillian Emerson) as their future daughter-in-law. Trite 30's comedy. A: Aurania Rouverol. P: Jack Curtis.

Plan M (2/20/42, Belasco, 6)

Incredible spy melodrama in which the Nazi High Command substitutes one of its own men (Len Doyle) for the head of the London war office. *Plan M* was written by John Wayne's favorite screenwriter, James Edward Grant.* "Mr. Grant's Mother Goose plot yields one of the most useless dramas of the season" *(New York Times)*. ". . . such far-fetched and unconvincing hokum that it leaves you quite . . . bored" *(PM)*. P: Aldrich and Myers. D: Marion Gering. SD: Lemuel Ayers.

---

*Credits include *Sands of Iwo Jima, Hondo, The Alamo, McLintock!*, etc.

Play, Genius, Play! (10/30/35, St. James, 6)

Violin virtuoso kicks over the traces, injures his hand in a night club brawl, returns penitent and chastened to his ivory tower existence. Wearisome 30's comedy. C: Hardie Albright, Ferdinand Gottschalk, Theresa Maxwell Conover, Clarence Derwent. A: Judith Kandel. P: Lew Cantor. D: Jo Graham.

Play It Again, Sam (2/12/69, Broadhurst, 453)

Woody Allen's hit comedy about a timid film buff (with a Bogart complex), and his fumbling attempts to find romance after his wife leaves him. "A hilarious evening . . . a cheerful romp" *(New York Times)*. C: Diane Keaton, Anthony Roberts, Sheila Sullivan, Jerry Lacy. P: David Merrick i.a.w. Rollins and Joffe. D: Joseph Hardy.

SV: Par, 1972, Woody Allen, Diane Keaton, Tony Roberts, Jerry Lacy, Susan Anspach, Viva (directed by Herbert Ross).

Play Without a Name, A (11/26/28, Booth, 48)

Flaccid comedy-drama highlighting various problems of a struggling young married couple (Peggy Wood and Kenneth MacKenna). A/D: Austin Strong. P: Frank C. Reilly.

Playroom, The (12/5/65, Atkinson, 33)

Teenagers kidnap a little girl for spite and end by murdering the tot to escape punishment. Horrific shocker proved too grisly to win support at the box office. C: Karen Black, Richard Thomas, Bonnie Bedelia, Peter Kastner, Tom Helmore,

Augusta Dabney. A: Mary Drayton. P: Kermit Bloomgarden and Trude Heller i.a.w. Youngstein and Karr. D: Joseph Anthony. SD: Jo Mielziner.

Please, Mrs. Garibaldi (3/16/39, Belmont, 4)

The only play written (to date) by critic-essayist-novelist (*The Company She Keeps, The Group*) Mary McCarthy. *Please, Mrs. Garibaldi* proved to be a machine-stitched comedy about a nonconformist Italian lass who, despite her parents' pleas, refuses to marry her seducer. "The play is weak . . . and the acting is substandard merchandise" (*New York Times*). C: Giuseppe Sterni, Dorothy Emery. P/D: Hall Shelton.

Pleasure Man (10/1/28, Biltmore, 3)

Mae West (A/D) turns her attention to homosexuality, murder, and revenge by castration during a gay party attended by a couple of dozen female impersonators. This 20's curio was produced by Carl Reed with a large cast that included Alan Brooks, Edgar Barrier, and Chuck Connors II. The show tried out in the Bronx, a not uncommon practice in those days. "Oh, my dear, you must throw on a shawl and run over to see Mae West's *Pleasure Man*," declared *Variety's* tongue-in-cheek reviewer. "It's the queerest show you've ever seen. All of the Queens are in it. . . . They all do specialties and make whoopee until the tragedy occurs. And, dearie, it's *some* tragedy. . . . That West girl knows her box office, and this one is in right now. It can't miss, and if you think it can, hope you get henna in your tooth brush. But don't miss it. . . . And go early, for some of the lines can't last." Neither did *Pleasure Man*. Opening night on Broadway, the police rushed onstage during a tense moment in the third act and hauled the entire cast and crew off in paddy wagons. With the play "closed indefinitely," the two hundred thousand dollar advance ticket sale had to be refunded. Mae was furious. Her play, she said, had been dealt "a blow below the belt."

Pleasure of His Company, The (10/22/58, Longacre, 474)

After a fifteen-year absence, a debonair charmer returns to his aristocratic San Francisco household and proceeds to disrupt his daughter's "sensible" wedding to a hopelessly prosaic young rancher. "An enormously satisfactory comedy . . . filled with heart and humor" (*Journal-American*). C: Cyril Ritchard (D), Cornelia Otis Skinner, Dolores Hart (deb.), George Peppard, Charlie Ruggles, Walter Abel. A: Samuel Taylor and Cornelia Otis Skinner. P: Frederick Brisson and The Playwrights Company. CD: Edith Head. SD: Donald Oenslager.

SV: Par, 1961, Fred Astaire, Lilli Palmer, Debbie Reynolds, Tab Hunter, Charlie Ruggles, Gary Merrill (directed by George Seaton).

Plumes in the Dust (11/6/36, 46th Street, 11)

Unpersuasive chronicle drama dealing with the tormented life of Edgar Allan Poe (Henry Hull) from the age of seventeen to his death from alcoholism in 1849 at the age of forty. The play was written by Sophie Treadwell, author of *Machinal* (1928) and *Hope for a Harvest* (1941). P/D: Arthur Hopkins.

Plutocrat, The (2/20/30, Vanderbilt, 100)

American businessman (Charles Coburn) becomes involved with a Parisian charmer on a Mediterranean cruise, returns chastened to home and family. Sedate comedy by Arthur Goodrich b/o the novel by Booth Tarkington. P: Mr. and Mrs. Charles Coburn. D: Coburn and Goodrich.

SV: Fox, 1932, *Business and Pleasure*,

Will Rogers, Joel McCrea, Jetta Goudal.

Pocket Watch, The (1/5/66, Actors Playhouse, 725)

Tender O/B comedy-drama concerning the socioeconomic problems of a poverty-stricken Jewish family in suburban Massachusetts. A: Alvin Aronson. P: New Playwrights. D: Sherwood Arthur.

Point of Honor, A (2/11/37, Fulton, 4)

Benedict Arnold betrays West Point to Major André of the British army. However, Arnold's sister reveals the conspiracy in the nick of time, and the American cause is saved. Straggling historical drama lacked dramatic conviction. C: Wilfrid Lawson, Florence Reed, Lloyd Gough, Lillian Emerson. A: Jo Eisinger and Stephen Van Gluck. P/D: Luther Greene.

Point of No Return (12/13/51, Alvin, 364)

Now that he is within reach of the vice-presidency of a large Manhattan bank, Charles Gray (Henry Fonda) discovers that economic and social success isn't really what he wanted after all. To find out what sent him into the rat race to begin with, he embarks on a spiritual pilgrimage into his own past. By reliving the scenes and events of his youth (c. 1929) in small-town New England, Charles is able to recover his integrity and self-respect. "Intelligent, literate, witty and well-made" *(News)*. This multi-scened 1951 production reached New York after the usual tryout pangs in Philadelphia and Boston. ("It was just about perfect at the Boston opening, less perfect a few nights later when everybody began tinkering," sniped Boston critic Elliot Norton.) *Point of No Return*, adapted by Paul Osborn from the novel by John P. Marquand, was a huge success. Faultlessly acted and skillfully staged, it kept Henry Fonda and a large company gainfully employed on Broadway for a solid year. C: Leora Dana, Frank Conroy, John Cromwell, Robert Ross, Bartlett Robinson, Patricia Smith (deb.), Madeleine Clive, Colin Keith-Johnston, Phil Arthur, Frances Bavier. P: Leland Hayward. D: H. C. Potter (with an uncredited assist from Elia Kazan). CD: Mainbocher. SD: Jo Mielziner.

Poldekin (9/9/20, Park, 44)

A young Bolshevist (George Arliss) comes to the United States and learns the virtues of capitalism. Feeble comedy-drama by Booth Tarkington. C: Edward G. Robinson, Sidney Toler, Elsie Mackay, Julia Dean. P: George C. Tyler.

Polly of the Circus (12/23/07, Liberty, 160)

Pretty acrobat (Mabel Taliaferro) falls in love with handsome minister (Malcolm Williams). Colorful hokum. A: Margaret Mayo. P: Frederic Thompson. D: Winchell Smith.

SV: MGM, 1932, Marion Davies, Clark Gable, C. Aubrey Smith, Ray Milland.

Polly Preferred (1/11/23, Little, 202)

High-pressure salesman transforms chorus girl Polly Brown into a movie star by incorporating her and selling shares in her filmland future. Cute comedy, nicely acted by Genevieve Tobin, William Harrigan, David Burns (deb.). A: Guy Bolton. P: F. Ray Comstock and Morris Gest. D: Winchell Smith.

Polly With a Past (9/6/17, Belasco, 315)

To make herself more desirable and interesting, a girl (Ina Claire) manufactures a picturesque past. Diverting comedy by George Middleton and Guy Bolton launched Ina Claire's career as a star of the legitimate stage. P/D: David Belasco. Musicalized by Stothart, Charig, and

Polly with a Past. **Ina Claire, Bruce McRae, and Stanley Logan (Belasco Theatre, September 1917).** *Courtesy Museum of the City of New York Theatre and Music Collection.*

Caesar as *Polly* (1929) with Fred Allen, Lucy Monroe, and "June."

Pollyanna (9/18/16, Hudson, 112)

Gooey tale of an insufferably cheerful waif (Patricia Collinge) who brings sweetness and light to the home of her stern maiden aunt, straightens out the love affairs of her elders, and teaches her "Glad Game" (if you break an arm, be glad it wasn't your leg) to the entire neighborhood. Based on the million-copy bestseller by Eleanor Porter, the name *Pollyanna* became a synonym for fatuous optimism. C: Effie Shannon, Philip Merivale. A: Catherine Chisholm Cushing. P: Tyler, Klaw, and Erlanger. D: Frederick Stanhope.
SV: BV, 1960, Hayley Mills, Jane Wyman, Richard Egan, Karl Malden, Adolphe Menjou, Agnes Moorehead.

Polygamy (12/1/14, Playhouse, 159)

Blistering attack on the Mormon religion. A happily married man is forced by the church to take a widow as his second wife. A gratuitous happy ending is arranged only when the reluctant bridegroom packs his bags and leaves Utah for good. C: Ramsey Wallace, Chrystal Herne, Katherine Emmett. A: Harvey O'Higgins and Harriet Ford. P: Modern Play Co. D: Gustav Von Seyfferitz.

Pomeroy's Past (4/19/26, Longacre, 88)

When a shy bachelor adopts an illegitimate child, all sorts of misunderstandings ensue. Tenuous comedy by Clare Kummer. C: Ernest Truex (D), Laura Hope Crews, Helen Chandler, Osgood Perkins, Dorothy Peterson. P: Boothe, Gleason, and Truex.

Ponder Heart, The (2/16/56, Music Box, 149)

Whimsical comedy, b/o the short story by Eudora Welty, about a guileless southern eccentric (David Wayne) suspected of murdering his childlike young bride. Highlight: an outlandishly comic third-act trial scene wherein the defendant's shining innocence makes a mockery of courtroom procedure. "... original, charming and funny" *(New York Times)*. C: Una Merkel, Sarah Marshall, Will Geer, Don Hanmer, Juanita Hall, Ruth White, John McGovern, John Marriott. A: Joseph Fields and Jerome Chodorov. P: The Playwrights Company. D: Robert Douglas. SD: Ben Edwards.

Poor Little Rich Girl, The (1/21/13, Hudson, 160)

A lonely child (Viola Dana) is given an accidental overdose of sleeping medication. The rest of the play is a dramatization of her delirium. Charming, highly imaginative fantasy; first stage offering of noted producer-director Arthur Hopkins. A: Eleanor Gates. P: Arthur Hopkins. D: Richard Walton Tully.

Note: A silent version of *Poor Little Rich Girl* was filmed (Artcraft, 1917) with Mary Pickford in the leading role. A 1936 version (20th Century-Fox) with Shirley Temple, Alice Faye, and Jack Haley, retained the title, but completely revamped the plot of this famous juvenile story.

Poor Nut, The (4/27/25, Henry Miller, 300)

A shy botany student (Elliott Nugent) conquers his inferiority complex when he falls in love with a charming co-ed, wins a track meet, and becomes a big man on campus. Entertaining comedy by J. C. and Elliott Nugent, briskly staged by Howard Lindsay. P: Patterson McNutt.

SV: WB, 1931, *Local Boy Makes Good*, Joe E. Brown, Dorothy Lee.

Note: A silent version of *The Poor Nut* (WB, 1927) featured Jack Mulhall, Jean Arthur, and Charlie Murray.

Poor Richard (12/2/64, Hayes, 118)

Jean Kerr's romantic comedy-drama centered around a triangle consisting of a raffishly charming British poet (Alan Bates), his American publisher (Gene Hackman), and the publisher's pert and pretty secretary (Joanna Pettet), who has been secretly in love with the poet since she was fifteen. "... thoroughly delightful" *(Post)*. "... too thin in plot and character to remain airborne ..." *(New York Times)*. P: Stevens Productions. D: Peter Wood. SD: Oliver Smith.

Poppa (12/24/28, Biltmore, 98)

Pincus Schwitzky (Sam Jaffe) is a well-meaning busybody on New York's lower East Side. His meddling eventually lands Pincus in jail, but everything works out all right in the end. Lightweight comedy by Bella and Samuel Spewack, extensively revised by George Abbott (D). P: H. S. Kraft.

Popsy (2/10/41, Playhouse, 4)

Horrendously inept comedy about an elderly mathematics professor (Al Shean) whose retirement plans are jeopardized by his three skittish daughters. "... one of the worst plays ever written" *(New York Times)*. "If anything worse than *Popsy* appears, please let us close the theatres ..." *(PM)*. A: Fred Herendeen. P: Hammerstein and Du-For. D: Rowland Edwards.

Porgy (10/10/27, Guild, 367)

Classic folk drama of Negro life in

Charleston's Catfish Row; dramatized by Dorothy and Du Bose Heyward from the latter's novel, and subsequently musicalized (1935) by George and Ira Gershwin as *Porgy and Bess*. The story deals with the love of the crippled peddler Porgy (Frank Wilson) for the beautiful but weak-willed Bess (Evelyn Ellis), and his murder of the evil longshoreman, Crown (Jack Carter). When Sportin' Life (Percy Verwayne) tempts Bess with "happy dust" and persuades her to go with him to New York, Porgy patiently sets out after Bess in his goat cart. The Theatre Guild production, with its striking use of Negro spirituals, was vividly staged by Rouben Mamoulian in picturesque settings by Cleon Throckmorton. Despite its occasionally patronizing portrayal of the black man as a lovable primitive, *Porgy* provided a memorable and affecting evening in the theatre. C: Rose MacLendon, Georgette Harvey, Richard Huey, Leigh Whipper.

Portrait in Black (5/14/47, Booth, 62)

A wealthy San Francisco widow and the doctor-lover who helped kill her invalid husband believe they have committed the perfect murder. Then an anonymous letter informs the guilty pair their crime is known. To protect themselves, they must murder again. Shortly thereafter, a second letter arrives revealing that they have killed the wrong man. At the last moment, the psychopathic widow is disclosed as the letter-writing culprit. ". . . too low-pitched and draggy . . . chilly without being chilling" *(PM)*. C: Claire Luce, Donald Cook, Sidney Blackmer. A: Ivan Goff and Ben Roberts. P: Lowe and Luckenbach. D: Reginald Denham. CD: Helene Pons. SD: Donald Oenslager.

SV: U, 1960, Lana Turner, Anthony Quinn, Sandra Dee, John Saxon, Richard Basehart, Lloyd Nolan, Anna May Wong, Ray Walston.

Portrait of a Lady (12/21/54, ANTA, 7)

Jennifer Jones made an inauspicious Broadway debut in this adaptation of Henry James' 1881 novel about a high-spirited American girl who journeys to Europe in search of "culture and sophistication." Admired by many men, she makes the mistake of marrying a petulant and penniless American expatriate (Robert Flemyng), thereby losing forever the consumptive young cousin (Douglas Watson) who might have made her happy. "A talky and steadily unexciting stage version of a creaky piece of Victorian inaction . . ." *(News)*. The play was written by William Archibald, who had great success in adapting Henry James' *The Turn of the Screw* into a Broadway hit, *The Innocents* (1950). *Portrait of a Lady*, which marked the opening of the ANTA Theatre, closed after seven performances. C: Cathleen Nesbitt, Barbara O'Neil, Eric Fleming, Jan Farrand, Kathleen Comegys, Halliwell Hobbes. P: Austin, Noyes and Producers Theatre. D: Jose Quintero. CD: Cecil Beaton. SD: William and Jean Eckart.

Possession (10/2/28, Booth, 37)

Wife wins back her errant husband. Frail 20's comedy by Edgar Selwyn (A/P/D). C: Walter Connolly, Margaret Lawrence, Roberta Beatty, Edna Hibbard, Robert Montgomery.

Post Road (12/4/34, Masque, 210)

Clever Connecticut spinster (Lucile Watson) foils a gang of kidnappers. "A shrewd and exciting melodrama" *(Sun)*. C: Edward Fielding, Percy Kilbride, Edmon Ryan. A: Wilbur Daniel Steele and Norma Mitchell. P: Potter and Haight. D: H. C. Potter.

Note: Charlotte Greenwood starred in a popular adaptation of *Post Road* entitled *Leaning on Letty* which toured (1936-38) the United States and Australia with great success. Movie czar Will Hays refused to

Potash and Perlmutter. **Louise Dresser, Alexander Carr, and Barney Bernard (Cohan Theatre, August 16, 1913).** *Courtesy Museum of the City of New York Theatre and Music Collection.*

allow Hollywood to film *Post Road*. His reason: the Lindbergh kidnapping case was still too fresh in the public mind.

Postman Always Rings Twice, The (2/25/36, Lyceum, 71)

Film star Richard Barthelmess came to Broadway in this moderately effective dramatization by James M. Cain of his best-selling novel. The restless wife of a California lunchroom proprietor seduces a wandering ne'er-do-well, and induces him to murder her husband. The lovers subsequently are involved in an automobile accident that results, ironically, in both their deaths. C: Mary Philips, Joseph Greenwald, Joseph Cotten. P: Jack Curtis. D: Robert Sinclair. SD: Jo Mielziner.

SV: MGM, 1946, Lana Turner, John Garfield, Cecil Kellaway, Hume Cronyn, Leon Ames, Audrey Totter.

Postmark Zero (11/1/65, Atkinson, 8)

Slow, uninspired semidocumentary dramatization of the Battle of Stalingrad as seen through the eyes of various German soldiers. C: Hardy Kruger, John Heffernan, Alvin Epstein, Viveca Lindfors. A: Robert Nemiroff. P: D'Lugoff, Nemiroff and Fried i.a.w. Triangle Productions. D: Peter Kass.

Potash and Perlmutter (8/16/13, Cohan, 441)

Long-run Jewish dialect farce about a couple of feuding business partners (Barney Bernard and Alexander Carr) who hire a Russian refugee bookkeeper. A: Montague Glass. P: A. H. Woods. D: Hugh Ford.

Potash and Perlmutter in Society (10/21/15, Lyric, 196)

Slapdash Jewish dialect farce (also known as *Abe and Mawruss);* a sequel to

Potash and Perlmutter (1913). This time the squabbling business partners crash high society with comically disastrous results. C: Barney Bernard, Julius Tannen, Mathilde Cottrelly, Claiborne Foster, Lee Kohlmar, Louise Dresser, Edwin Maxwell. A: Roi Cooper Megrue (D) and Montague Glass. P: A. H. Woods.

Potters, The (12/8/23, Plymouth, 245)

J. P. McEvoy comedy dealing mainly with the efforts of Pa Potter (Donald Meek) to get rich quick and thus stifle the constant nagging of Ma Potter (Catherine Calhoun Doucet). Loosely sketched cartoon had more than its share of laughs. C: Raymond Guion (Gene Raymond), Mary Carroll, Helen Chandler. P: Richard Herndon.

Precedent (4/14/31, Provincetown, 184)

In 1916, labor organizer Thomas J. Mooney was convicted of a bomb killing and sentenced to death. Mooney's case aroused world interest because of widespread belief in his innocence; his sentence was subsequently commuted to life imprisonment.* From the facts of this landmark case, lawyer I. J. Golden wrote *Precedent*. With Royal Dana in the role of Mooney (here called Delaney), this 1931 O/B production proved a stirring and frequently eloquent melodrama. A surprise hit, *Precedent* was later transferred uptown to Broadway for a successful run. P: Sidney Harmon. D: Walter Hart.

---

*Tom Mooney was paroled and released from prison in 1939.

Precious (1/14/29, Royale, 24)

Older man marries designing gold digger, schemes to pair her off with a younger man, thereby correcting his marital error. Frail comedy by James Forbes. C: John Cumberland, Dorothy Hall, Cora Witherspoon, Hale Hamilton, Verree Teasdale. P: Rosalie Stewart. D: Melville Burke.

Pre-Honeymoon (4/30/36, Lyceum, 253)

While his fiancée is away, a senator amuses himself with a bubble dancer. Sophomoric 30's farce by Alford Van Ronkel and Anne Nichols (P/D). C: Jessie Royce Landis, Louis Jean Heydt, Clyde Fillmore, Sylvia Field, Roy Roberts, Georgette Harvey.

Prelude to Exile (11/30/36, Guild, 48)

That irascible genius Richard Wagner (Wilfrid Lawson) falls desperately in love with the wife (Eva Le Gallienne) of his wealthy patron (Leo G. Carroll). Their love is not to be, but from it the composer gains the inspiration for *Tristan und Isolde*. Produced by The Theatre Guild, this dawdling biographical drama by newspaperman William J. McNally had a brief Broadway run. C: Lucile Watson, Evelyn Varden, Henry Levin. D: Philip Moeller. CD/SD: Lee Simonson.

Prescott Proposals, The (12/16/53, Broadhurst, 125)

A United Nations delegate (Katharine Cornell) is involved in a potential scandal—not to mention a threat to world peace—when her former lover, now a member of the Czech delegation, disobligingly drops dead in her bedroom. Miss Cornell played the idealistic heroine with charm and conviction, but Lorne Greene seemed acutely uncomfortable in the leading male role. (The romantic scenes between Miss Cornell and Mr. Greene were described by one reviewer as "the most antiseptic love affair since Pelleas went for Melisande.") *The Prescott Proposals* was written by Howard Lindsay (D) and Russel Crouse and produced by Leland Hayward. ". . . a well-meaning but confused melodrama" *(Mirror)*. ". . . markedly lightweight [but] often good fun" *(Herald Tribune)*. C: Felix Aylmer, Roger Dann, Boris Tumarin, Bartlett Robinson, Ben Astar, Minoo Daver, Robert Culp (deb.), Joe Masteroff. CD: Mainbocher. SD: Donald Oenslager.

Pretty Little Parlor (4/17/44, National, 8)

Ruthless stepmother ruins the lives of all around her. "... empty of all but words" *(New York Times)*. This painfully inept period melodrama (1905), written by actress Claiborne Foster, closed after eight performances. C: Stella Adler, Sidney Blackmer, Joan Tetzel, Ed Begley, Marilyn Erskine. P: John Moses and Ralph Bellamy (D). CD: Paul DuPont. SD: Stewart Chaney.

Price, The (11/1/11, Hudson, 77)

A vengeful widow tries to pin the guilt for her husband's death on "the other woman." Moderately effective George Broadhurst melodrama. C: Helen Ware, Warner Oland, Jessie Ralph, Harrison Hunter. P: Henry B. Harris. D: Frank Reicher.

Price, The (2/7/68, Morosco, 429)

After an absence of more than twelve years, Arthur Miller returned to the Broadway theatre with this absorbing morality play. The central conflict revolves around the bitter antagonism between two long-estranged brothers who meet again after many years to dispose of their late father's belongings. One of the brothers is a policeman (Pat Hingle) who sacrificed his career and financial security to care for his invalid father; the other (Arthur Kennedy) is an eminent surgeon who walked out on his family responsibilities to concentrate on personal success. The jealousy and resentment each feels toward the other flares into outright hostility—thereby revealing both men's true characters to themselves and to the audience—in a final scene of stinging power and abrasiveness. "... one of the most engrossing and entertaining plays that Miller has ever written. It is superbly, even flamboyantly theatrical..." *(New York Times)*. C: Kate Reid, Harold Gary. P: Robert Whitehead i.a.w. Robert W. Dowling. D: Ulu Grosbard. CD/SD: Boris Aronson.

Pride and Prejudice (11/5/35, Music Box, 219)

Excellent adaptation of Jane Austen's classic tale of the husband-hunting Bennet sisters, of their scheming mother and unmettlesome father, and of the men they are to marry. The dramatization captured the frivolous absurdities of eighteenth-century middle-class English society where "to be a wife is to be a success." The chief liberty taken with the Austen text was to reduce the number of Bennet girls from five to three. *Pride and Prejudice* is a good example of a great work of literature transferred to the stage with charm, taste, and wit unimpaired. C: Adrianne Allen, Colin Keith-Johnston, Lucile Watson, Percy Waram, Helen Chandler, Joan Tompkins, Brenda Forbes, Nancy Hamilton, Alma Kruger, Viola Roache. A: Helen Jerome. P: Max Gordon. D: Robert Sinclair. SD: Jo Mielziner.

Musicalized by Abe Burrows, and Goldman, Paxton, and Weiss as *First Impressions* (1959), with Polly Bergen, Farley Granger, Hermione Gingold, Phyllis Newman, James Mitchell.

SV: MGM, 1940, Greer Garson, Laurence Olivier, Mary Boland, Edna May Oliver, Edmund Gwenn, Maureen O'Sullivan, Karen Morley, Ann Rutherford, Marsha Hunt (directed by Robert Z. Leonard from a screenplay by Aldous Huxley).

Pride of Jennico, The (3/6/00, Criterion, 111)

A madcap princess and her maid exchange places. Contrived, melodramatic romantic pastiche, set in Bohemia, nicely acted by its two leading players, James K. Hackett and Bertha Galland. A: Abby Sage Richardson and Grace L. Furniss based in part on a novel by Agnes and

Edgerton Castle. P: Charles Frohman. D: Edward E. Rose.

Pride's Crossing (11/20/50, Biltmore, 8)

Dismal melodrama about the conflict between a New England widow and her late husband's avaricious mistress. "Incredible, confusing and cumbersome" (*Journal-American*). C: Mildred Dunnock, Tamara Geva, John Baragrey. A: Victor Wolfson. P: T. Edward Hambleton. D: Martin Manulis.

Prime of Miss Jean Brodie, The (1/16/68, Hayes, 378)

A "liberated" schoolmistress in 1930's Edinburgh mesmerizes her students with naïve notions about art and politics, and awes her charges by boasting of her love affairs. When one of her favorite pupils discloses Miss Brodie's misguided allegiance to fascism, her career is terminated. Complex portrait of a self-deluded, irrepressible, unwittingly cruel woman; memorable performance by Zoe Caldwell in the title role. "Endearing, hilarious, utterly splendid . . ." (*News*). A: Jay Allen b/o the novella by Muriel Spark. P: Robert Whitehead i.a.w. Robert W. Dowling. D: Michael Langham. Originally presented in London during the season of 1965–66 with Vanessa Redgrave as Miss Brodie.
SV: Fox, 1969, Maggie Smith, Robert Stephens, Pamela Franklin, Celia Johnson (directed by Ronald Neame).

Primer for Lovers, A (11/18/29, Longacre, 24)

Romantic mixups and entanglements at a weekend house party. Tiresome screwball farce. C: Alison Skipworth, Robert Warwick, Rose Hobart. A: William Hurlbut. P: Herman Gantvoort. D: William P. Adams.

Primrose Path, The (1/4/39, Biltmore, 166)

Racy, funny, beautifully acted tale of the happy-go-lucky life of three generations of prostitutes, and of the pretty black sheep (Betty Field) of the family who prefers marriage to the primrose path of dalliance. C: Helen Westley, Marilyn Erskine, Betty Garde, Russell Hardie, Florida Friebus, Clyde Fillmore. A: Robert Buckner and Walter Hart, b/o the novel, *February Hill* by Victoria Lincoln. P/D: George Abbott.
SV: RKO, 1940, Ginger Rogers, Joel McCrea, Marjorie Rambeau, Henry Travers, John Carroll, Miles Mander, Queenie Vassar.

Prince and the Pauper, The (11/1/20, Booth, 158)

Trim, straightforward retelling of Mark Twain's classic tale of the lookalike beggar boy who changes place with a prince in sixteenth-century London. C: William Faversham, Ruth Findlay, Clare Eames. A: Amelie Rives. P: Messrs. Shubert. D: William Faversham.
SV: WB, 1937, Errol Flynn, Billy and Bobby Mauch, Claude Rains, Eric Portman, Alan Hale.

Prince Chap, The (9/4/05, Madison Square, 106)

Lightweight comedy-drama founded on one of the oldest plots in dramatic literature. A baby girl is left in the care of a young bachelor. Misunderstanding the situation, his sweetheart jilts him. Years later, the bachelor realizes it is his ward, now grown to womanhood, whom he really loves. "Ably written . . . succeeds in pleasing" (*New York Times*). C: Cyril Scott, Cecil B. De Mille, Thomas A. Wise. A: Edward Peple.

Prince Consort, The (3/6/05, New Amsterdam, 32)

The queen's consort tries to retain his masculinity even after being pronounced "wife and man." Frothy trivia. C: Henry E. Dixey, Ellis Jeffreys, Ben Webster. A: Boosey and Lennox from a play by Xanrof and Chancel. P: Liebler and Company. D: Arnold Daly.

SV: Par, 1929, *The Love Parade,* Maurice Chevalier, Jeanette MacDonald, Lillian Roth, Lupino Lane, Eugene Pallette, Ben Turpin, Virginia Bruce.

Prince of India, The (9/24/06, Broadway, 73)

The Wandering Jew (William Farnum) legend transferred to Constantinople. Archaic even for 1906. A: J. I. C. Clarke, based on the novel by General Lew Wallace. P: Klaw and Erlanger. D: Herbert Gresham and Lawrence Marston.

Prince There Was, A (12/24/18, Cohan, 159)

The wealthy but bored "Mr. Prince" (George M. Cohan) decides to explore the seamy side of life in a cheap boarding house, where he finds love and happiness. Moderately engaging comedy-drama, acted with gusto and charm by the jaunty "Crown Prince of the American Theatre." C: Ruth Donnelly, Jessie Ralph. A: Cohan, from Dorrough Aldrich's story. D: Frederick Stanhope.

Prisoner of Second Avenue, The (11/11/71, O'Neill, 780)

Neil Simon's ninth straight Broadway success had an unlikely comedic premise: a highly paid executive, agonized by the grating, unrelenting irritants of big-city living, is driven to a nervous breakdown when he loses his job. That a play with such a plot could emerge as "full of humor and intelligence . . . fine fun" (*Post*) is tribute to Simon's gift for witty lines and warm characterizations. Mike Nichols directed Peter Falk, the executive, and Lee Grant, his harried, faithful wife, so effectively that he won for himself the Tony Award, and for Vincent Gardenia, the hero's loving brother, both the Tony Award and the Variety Poll of New York Drama Critics as best supporting actor. The subsequent replacement of Falk and Grant by Art Carney and Barbara Barrie did not diminish the play's appeal, and these players and others after them, sentenced the *Prisoner* to nearly two years on Broadway. C: Florence Stanley, Dena Dietrich, Tresa Hughes. P: Saint-Subber.

SV: WB, 1975, Jack Lemmon, Anne Bancroft, Gene Saks, Elizabeth Wilson (directed by Melvin Frank).

Privilege Car (3/3/31, 48th Street, 48)

Conflicts and romantic rivalries of some circus roustabouts. Mild melodrama. C: Alan Bunce, Paul Guilfoyle, Elisha Cook, Jr., Lee Patrick. A: Edward Foran and Willard Keefe. P: Abraham and Fields. D: Melville Burke.

Processional (1/12/25, Garrick, 105)

Proletarian hero Dynamite Jim (George Abbott) is attacked and blinded by anti-Marxist forces in a West Virginia mining town; then the striking workers finally revolt and win their battle for better working conditions. Set in a variety show framework, John Howard Lawson's "jazz symphony of American life" created quite a stir. The author's satirical targets ranged from motherhood and apple pie to the fascist leanings of the American government. (At one point, the leader of the Ku Klux Klan proudly reveals that every member of the U.S. Congress has just joined the Klan.) This frequently amusing semivaudeville show was actually a deadly serious political document advocating class warfare. *Processional* was probably the most innovative and skillful proletarian drama of the 1920's. C: June Walker, Philip Loeb, Blanche Frederici, Ben Grauer, Donald Macdonald, Lee Strasberg, Sanford Meisner, Arthur Sircom, Alvah Bessie. P: The Theatre Guild. D: Philip Moeller. SD: Mordecai Gorelik.

R: (10/13/37, Maxine Elliott's, 81) by the WPA Federal Theatre. C: George Mathews, Ruth Gilbert. D: Lem Ward. M: Earl Robinson.

Prodigal, The (2/11/60, Downtown, 164)

Modern retelling of the Orestes (Dino Narizzano) legend dealing with political opportunism and vengeance. Produced O/B in the winter of 1960, the play's existentialist, antiheroic attitude, and its attack on the senselessness of war, captivated the critics: "An exceptionally fine first play" (*Post*). "The season's best new playwright" (*Time*). ". . . fresh, fascinating, and filled with a lively psychology" (*Herald Tribune*). A: Jack Richardson. P: William Landis. D: Rhodelle Heller.

Proof Through the Night (12/25/42, Morosco, 11)

Shrill melodrama about a group of volunteer nurses in the dying days of Bataan. Best performance: Carol Channing as a confused lesbian named Steve. ". . . only intermittently satisfying" (*Herald Tribune*). C: Ann Shoemaker, Katherine Emery, Florence MacMichael, Florence Rice, Thelma Schnee, Katherine Locke, Julie Stevens. A/D: Allan R. Kenward. P: Lee Shubert. SD: Albert Johnson.

SV: MGM, 1943, *Cry Havoc,* Margaret Sullavan, Ann Sothern, Joan Blondell, Fay Bainter, Marsha Hunt, Ella Raines.

Protective Custody (12/28/56, Ambassador, 3)

Synthetic and implausible melodrama about a glamorous foreign correspondent who is kidnaped and brainwashed by the Soviets. ". . . bored the bejaspers out of me" (*News*). C: Faye Emerson, Fritz Weaver, Thayer David. A: Howard Richardson and William Berney. P: Anderson Lawler i.a.w. Will Lester. D: Herbert Berghof. CD/SD: Peter Larkin.

Proud Woman, A (11/15/26, Maxine Elliott's, 8)

Snobbish woman almost breaks up her sister's impending marriage. Flimsy, uncertain comedy-drama by Arthur Richman. C: Elizabeth Risdon, Florence Eldridge, Margaret Wycherly. P: Edgar Selwyn. D: John Hayden.

Public Relations (4/6/44, Mansfield, 28)

Comedy about the weekend reunion of a royal family of Hollywood in which the aging stars, both remarried, discover they still care for one another. The leading characters supposedly were patterned after Mary Pickford and Douglas Fairbanks, Sr. ". . . as dissonant and unimaginative as a Bronx cheer" (*Herald Tribune*). ". . . silly and unpleasant and stupefyingly dull" (*PM*). C: Philip Merivale, Ann Andrews, Betty Blythe, Michael Ames, James Russo. A: Dale Eunson. P: Robert Blake. D: Edward Childs Carpenter. SD: Stewart Chaney.

Puppets (3/9/25, Selwyn, 57)

White slavery in New York's Little Italy with heroine Miriam Hopkins saved from a fate worse than death by marionette owner C. Henry Gordon. ". . . very small potatoes and if all the speaking parts could be cut out and the marionettes substituted, it would be rather nice" (*American*). C: Fredric March, Dwight Frye, Remo Bufano, Elizabeth Taylor. A: Frances Lightner. P/D: Brock Pemberton.

Puppy Love (1/27/26, 48th Street, 112)

Boy masquerades as a chauffeur to be near his girl. Low-level comedy with a high-level saccharine content. C: William Hanley, Vivian Martin, Spring Byington. A: Adelaide Matthews and Martha Stanley. P: Anne Nichols. D: Clifford Brooke.

Pure in Heart, The (3/20/34, Longacre, 7)

Would-be actress finds true love with an

escaped convict. In the end, both are murdered by the police. Muddled Marxist fable by John Howard Lawson. C: Dorothy Hall, James Bell, Tom Powers, Frances Langford, Peter Donald. P: Richard Aldrich and Alfred de Liagre, Jr. D: Edward Massey. CH: Albertina Rasch. M: Richard Myers. SD: Jo Mielziner.

Puritan, The (1/23/36, Belmont, 4)

Aware that his baser instincts have led him to kill a prostitute, a religious fanatic (Denis O'Dea) commits suicide. Uninspired dramatization of Liam O'Flaherty's powerful novel of the Dublin slums. A/P/D: Chester Erskine.

Purlie Victorious (9/28/61, Cort, 261)

Ossie Davis' satiric farce about a self-ordained minister who returns to the cotton plantation country of the Old South to open an integrated church. A bright spoof of all the clichés about the supposed devotion of white masters to their black slaves; as such, often delightfully funny. C: Ossie Davis, Ruby Dee, Sorrell Booke, Godfrey Cambridge, Alan Alda, Beah Richards, Helen Martin. P: Philip Rose. D: Howard Da Silva. SD: Ben Edwards.

Musicalized by Ossie Davis, Philip Rose, Peter Udell, and Gary Geld as *Purlie* (1970) with Cleavon Little, Melba Moore, Helen Martin, John Heffernan, and Sherman Hemsley.

SV: Trans-Lux, 1963, *Gone Are The Days* (filmed with substantially the same cast as appeared in the stage production); directed by Nicholas Webster.

Purple Mask, The (1/5/20, Booth, 139)

The dashing Count de Trevieres (Leo Ditrichstein) baffles Napoleon's gendarmes with his feats of derring-do. To cap his triumphs, he rescues the lovely Laurette de Chateaubriand (Lily Cahill) from a fate worse than death. Roguish costume melodrama in the best swashbuckling tradition. A: Matheson Lang, based on a play by Armont and Manoussi. P: Lee Shubert. D: Ditrichstein.

SV: U, 1955, Tony Curtis, Gene Barry, Angela Lansbury, Colleen Miller, Dan O'Herlihy.

Pursuit of Happiness, The (10/9/33, Avon, 248)

A Hessian soldier falls in love with a headstrong colonial lass. Delightful period (American Revolution) comedy. Highlight: the bundling scene—the quaint old American custom that permitted a young couple to keep warm by going to bed together with their clothes on, with a saw-toothed bundling board between them. C: Tonio Selwart, Peggy Conklin, Raymond Walburn, Charles Waldron, Dennie Moore, Oscar Polk. A: Lawrence Langner and Armina Marshall. P: Laurence Rivers (Rowland Stebbins). D: Miriam Doyle. Musicalized by Herbert and Dorothy Fields, Rouben Mamoulian, and Morton Gould as *Arms and the Girl* (1950) with Nanette Fabray, George Guetary, Pearl Bailey, John Conte, Eda Heinemann.

SV: Par, 1934, Francis Lederer, Joan Bennett, Charles Ruggles, Mary Boland, Minor Watson.

Pyramids (7/19/26, Cohan, 32)

When her husband's lecherous boss is murdered, an extravagant wife is the prime suspect. Weak 20's whodunit. C: Charles Waldron, Carroll McComas. A: Samuel Ruskin Golding. P: Wallace and Martins. D: Priestly Morrison.

Q

Queen Bee (11/12/29, Belmont, 22)

A woman's need to dominate the lives of all around her leads to tragedy. Mediocre 20's drama. C: Gertrude Bryan, Ian Keith, Brian Donlevy. A: Louise Fox Connell and Ruth Hawthorne. P: Joseph B. Glick. D: Alan Dinehart.

Queen Victoria (11/15/23, 48th Street, 44)

Lethargic chronicle play dealing with the life of Victoria (Beryl Mercer) from 1837 to her diamond jubilee in 1897. Written by David Carb and critic-theatre historian Walter Prichard Eaton, one of America's most knowledgeable and erudite drama scholars. C: Ulrich Haupt (Prince Albert), Clarence Derwent (Disraeli), William Ingersoll (Lord Palmerston), George Farren (Gladstone), Frances Goodrich (Lady Gay Hawthorne). P: Equity Players, Inc. D: Priestly Morrison.

Queen's Husband, The (1/25/28, Playhouse, 125)

Fairly diverting Robert E. Sherwood mythical kingdom comedy, with Roland Young as a royal worm who turns when his domineering wife is away, quells a revolution in her absence, and marries his daughter to the handsome commoner she loves. "George Barr McCutcheon in a beard" (Charles Brackett, *The New Yorker*). C: Katherine Alexander, Gladys Hanson, Reginald Barlow, Dwight Frye. P: William A. Brady, Jr. and Dwight Deere Wiman. D: John Cromwell.

SV: RKO, 1931, *The Royal Bed,* Lowell Sherman, Mary Astor, Nance O'Neil, Robert Warwick, Gilbert Emery, J. Carrol Naish.

Note: Queen Marie of Rumania paid a highly-publicized visit to the United States in 1926. The visit was reportedly the inspiration for Sherwood's *The Queen's Husband,* and also for the Gershwin-Romberg musical, *Rosalie,* that same season.

Queer People (2/15/34, National, 13)

The seamy exploits of a dim-witted Hollywood press agent and his success-at-any-price movieland clients. Disjointed, multiscened comedy-farce-melodrama; a queer mixture indeed. Howard Hughes purchased the screen rights to *Queer People,* but never filmed the play. C: Hal Skelly, Gladys George, Nita Naldi, Helen Claire, Flavia Arcaro, Dwight Frye, Frank de Silva. A: John Floyd b/o a novel by Carroll and Garrett Graham. P: Galen Bogue. D: Melville Burke.

Quiet Please (11/8/40, Guild, 16)

To teach her philandering husband a lesson, a screen star has an affair with a handsome gas station attendant. "Clumsily and feebly written" (*Herald Tribune*). This labored Hollywood satire marked the playwriting debut of F. Hugh Herbert, author of such hit comedies as *Kiss and Tell* (1943), *The Moon is Blue* (1951), etc. The comedy (coauthored by

Hans Kraly) was presented by Henry Duffy, veteran west coast impressario, and Jesse L. Lasky, pioneer film producer. It was staged by Russell Fillmore. C: Jane Wyatt, Donald Woods, Fred Niblo, Ann Mason, Gordon Jones, Bruce MacFarlane, Anthony Kemble Cooper.

Quo Vadis (4/9/00, New York, 96)

Lavish spectacle dealing with the plight of Christian martyrs during the reign of Emperor Nero. On the above date (April 9, 1900), two different adaptations of Henry Sienkiewicz's epic novel opened on the same night. The dramatization by Stanislaus Stange was the more popular and ran ninety-six performances. The adaptation by Jeannette L. Gilder lasted thirty-six performances. P: F. C. Whitney. D: Max Freeman.

SV: MGM, 1951, Robert Taylor, Deborah Kerr, Peter Ustinov.

R

Race of Hairy Men! A (4/29/65, Henry Miller's, 4)

Undistinguished comedy about two Manhattan couples who attempt (unsuccessfully) to experiment with mate-swapping. Written by novelist Evan Hunter (*The Blackboard Jungle*, etc.). C: Brandon de Wilde, April Shawhan, Martin Huston, Joan McCall. P: Elaine Perry (D) and Ben Edwards (SD).

Racket, The (11/22/27, Ambassador, 120)

Taut melodrama linking crime and big-city politics, with the action taking place in a Chicago police station during a thirty-six-hour period. Leading characters: an honest cop (John Cromwell), an enterprising newspaper reporter (Norman Foster), and a ruthless Italian racketeer (Edward G. Robinson). Robinson walked off with the evening's principal honors for his portrayal of Joe Scarsi, the sinister, Capone-like henchman. *Theatre Magazine* hailed his performance as "a masterly creation of character." It was the only gangster role Robinson ever played on the stage. The play was a big New York hit, but Chicago wouldn't allow the production to open in that city. It was too true to life to suit the city fathers. C: Willard Robertson, Marion Coakley, Hugh O'Connell, Edward Eliscu. A: Bartlett Cormack. P: Alexander McKaig. D: John Cromwell.
SV: RKO, 1951, Robert Mitchum, Robert Ryan, Lizabeth Scott, William Talman (directed by John Cromwell).
Note: A silent version (Paramount, 1928) featured Louis Wolheim, Thomas Meighan, Marie Prevost, Mary Astor and John Cromwell. It was directed by Lewis Milestone.

Ragged Army (2/26/34, Selwyn, 2)

Capital versus labor conflicts in a small New England town. Badly organized and poorly written propaganda play. C: Lloyd Nolan, Thomas Chalmers, Johnny Downs, Lee Baker. A: Beulah Marie Dix and Bertram Millhauser. P/D: Crosby Gaige.

Rain (11/7/22, Maxine Elliott's, 648)

In the rain-drenched port of Pago Pago, a missionary (Robert Kelly) strives to save the soul of prostitute Sadie Thompson (Jeanne Eagels), but finds his evangelical zeal giving way to lust. Tortured by guilt, he slits his throat; the disillusioned Sadie, her blatant, raucous self once again, leaves the island with a handsome marine. "A drama of altogether extraordinary grip and significance" (John Corbin, *New York Times*). Adapted from a W. S. Maugham story by American writer Clemence Randolph and Anglo-American author John Colton, *Rain* was one of the theatre's most thunderous hits. Jeanne Eagels scored a tremendous personal success as the vulgar, hard-boiled San Francisco tart in this Sam H. Harris production, directed by John D. Williams. Critic Percy Hammond said that of the thousands of first nights he had covered, "the one I most enjoyed was the premiere of *Rain*." Critic-columnist Ward Morehouse said the premiere brought forth "an emotional demonstration never exceeded in the theatre of this country and century. First nighters stood and screamed . . . they were as wild as spectators at a football game." Tallulah Bankhead was signed for the part of Sadie Thompson in the London production, but after a week's rehearsal was fired by Somerset Maugham and replaced by Olga Lindo. Maugham later confessed that his "greatest professional mistake" was not letting Bankhead play *Rain*. She eventually did play the role in New York in a short-lived 1935 revival (2/12/35, Music Box, 47).

Musicalized by Vernon Duke-Howard Dietz-Rouben Mamoulian as *Sadie Thompson* (1944) with June Havoc and Lansing Hatfield.

SV: UA, 1932, Joan Crawford, Walter Huston, William Gargan, Beulah Bondi, Guy Kibbee, Walter Catlett; Col, 1953, *Miss Sadie Thompson,* Rita Hayworth, Jose Ferrer, Aldo Ray.

Note: A silent version (UA, 1928), entitled *Sadie Thompson,* cast Gloria Swanson, Lionel Barrymore, and Raoul Walsh in the leading roles.

Rain From Heaven (12/24/34, Golden, 99)

At a houseparty in her home near London, the charming and warm-hearted Lady Wyngate (Jane Cowl) tries to mediate clashes of opinion among five diverse guests: a German-Jewish music critic, a Russian pianist, a scholarly Soviet emigré, a reactionary American businessman, and his idealistic younger brother. Political and romantic complications ensue. In the end, Lady Wyngate decides that she can not risk marriage to the young American idealist, nor can she stand in the way of the German Jew's return to his native land to continue the fight for liberalism despite almost certain death. One of the earliest anti-Nazi plays by an American author, this provocative comedy-drama by S. N. Behrman suffered by virtue of intellectual largesse. The play attempted to deal with too many problems at the same time. C: John Halliday, Jose Ruben, Thurston Hall, Lily Cahill, Ben Smith. P: The Theatre Guild. D: Philip Moeller. SD: Lee Simonson.

Rainbow, The (3/11/12, Liberty, 104)

A daughter sets out to reunite her father (Henry Miller) and mother (Laura Hope Crews). Pleasant comedy by A. E. Thomas with a charming performance by ingenue Ruth Chatterton as the daughter. P/D: Henry Miller.

Rainmaker, The (10/28/54, Cort, 125)

Into the life of a lonely southwesterner (Geraldine Page) comes a brash young con artist (Darren McGavin) who not only boasts that he can bring rain to the drought-plagued area, but also transforms the Dust Bowl spinster into a woman ready for love. "A lusty antic in a popular comedy vein" *(New York Times)*. C: Cameron Prud'homme, Richard Coogan, Albert Salmi. A: N. Richard Nash. P: Ethel Linder Reiner i.a.w. Hope Abelson. D: Joseph Anthony. SD: Ralph Alswang.

Musicalized by Nash, Schmidt, and Jones as *110 in the Shade* (1963) with Inga Swenson, Robert Horton, Stephen Douglass, Will Geer.

SV: Par, 1956, Katharine Hepburn, Burt Lancaster, Wendell Corey, Lloyd Bridges, Earl Holliman, Cameron Prud'homme, Wallace Ford (directed by Joseph Anthony).

Rainy Day in Newark, A (10/22/63, Belasco, 7)

A labor leader (Eddie Mayehoff) inherits

a New Jersey factory and finds himself hamstrung by the very conditions he had insisted upon imposing as a union official. Splendid satiric idea sidetracked by uninventive plotting, predictable wisecracks. C: Zachary Scott, Gene Hackman, John McMartin, Dody Goodman, Mary McCarty, Tom Ahearne, Ivor Francis. A: Howard Teichmann. P: Stevens Productions. D: Albert Marre. SD: Ed Wittstein.

Raisin in the Sun, A (3/11/59, Barrymore, 530)

Touching, beautifully acted comedy-drama about a hard-working Negro family and their attempts to move out of their cramped, sunless Chicago flat and into an all-white neighborhood. The son (Sidney Poitier) takes the insurance money entrusted to him by his widowed mother (Claudia McNeil) and unwisely invests it in a liquor store, only to have his partner abscond with the funds. Consequently, the other members of the family see their dreams of a better life shattered, but decide to move to the new neighborhood anyway. In losing its fortune, the family gains something greater—its pride. *A Raisin in the Sun*—a phrase from a poem by Langston Hughes—was the first play written by twenty-nine-year-old Lorraine Hansberry, the first woman of her race ever to have a play produced on Broadway. The gifted black authoress died of cancer in 1965 at age thirty-five. *A Raisin in the Sun* won the Drama Critics Circle Award as best play of the year. C: Ruby Dee, Diana Sands (Broadway debut), Louis Gossett, Ivan Dixon, John Fiedler, Glynn Turman. P: Philip Rose and David Cogan. D: Lloyd Richards. SD: Ralph Alswang.

Musicalized by Nemiroff, Zaltzberg, Woldin, and Brittan as *Raisin* (1973) with Virginia Capers, Joe Morton, and Ralph Carter.

SV: Released by Columbia (1961) with substantially the same cast as appeared in the Broadway production. The film was directed by Daniel Petrie.

Ramshackle Inn (1/5/44, Royale, 216)

An old-maid librarian outfoxes a gang of cutthroats in a spooky New England inn. ZaSu Pitts, of the fluttery hands and outlandish millinery, made her Broadway debut in this melodramatic farce. "... a tedious bit of balderdash. ... That the star moves triumphantly through the skullduggery and nonsense of the plot is a genuine tribute to her acting skill" *(Herald Tribune)*. A: George Batson. P: Robert Reud. D: Arthur Sircom.

Rashomon (1/27/59, Music Box, 159)

A thousand years ago in Kyoto, Japan, the wife of a samurai officer is raped and her husband killed by a roving bandit. Three conflicting versions of what happened are given at the bandit's trial. Each version is true in its fashion, and it is clear that the play (like the celebrated Japanese film from which it was adapted) is concerned with the elusive nature of "truth" and how it changes in the eye of the beholder. "An inviting theatrical experiment" *(Herald Tribune)*. "... a pretentious bore" *(News)*. C: Rod Steiger, Claire Bloom, Akim Tamiroff, Oscar Homolka, Noel Willman. A: Fay and Michael Kanin. P: David Susskind and Hardy Smith. D: Peter Glenville. CD/SD: Oliver Messel. M: Laurence Rosenthal.

SV: The Japanese film, *Rashomon* (1951), featured Toshiro Mifune in the leading role, and was directed by Akira Kurosawa. The Hollywood version was retitled *The Outrage* (MGM, 1964) with a cast headed by Paul Newman, Claire Bloom, Edward G. Robinson, Laurence Harvey, William Shatner, and Howard da Silva. The film was directed by Martin Ritt.

Rat Race, The (12/22/49, Barrymore, 84)

Comedy-drama by Garson Kanin (A/D) dealing with the love affair between a dancehall hostess (Betty Field) and a naïve jazz musician (Barry Nelson). "Although Mr. Kanin has great talent for dialogue, people and parts, *The Rat Race* is sketchy to the point of limpness" *(New York Times)*. C: Ray Walston, Doro Merande, Joseph Sweeney, Dennie Moore, Pat Harrington, Rex Williams, Joe Bushkin. P: Leland Hayward.

SV: Par, 1960, Debbie Reynolds, Tony Curtis, Jack Oakie, Kay Medford,

Ready Money (8/19/12, Maxine Elliott's, 128)

A counterfeiter forces a small fortune in bogus thousand-dollar bills into the hands of a destitute young man (William Courtenay). The virtuous hero soon learns that "You don't have to have money to make it. All you have to do is to make people think you have it." "Most amusing ... its popularity is assured" *(New York Times)*. A: James Montgomery. P: H. H. Frazee. D: Robert Milton.

Ready Money. **Ben Johnson and Joseph Kilgour (Maxine Elliott Theatre, August 19, 1912).** *Courtesy Museum of the City of New York Theatre and Music Collection.*

Musicalized by Harry Carroll as *Oh, Look!* (1918) with Harry Fox, George Sidney, Genevieve Tobin, Clarence Nordstrom.

SV: Par, 1943, *Riding High,* Dick Powell, Dorothy Lamour, Victor Moore, Cass Daley, Rod Cameron, Gil Lamb, Marie McDonald.

Ready When You Are, C.B! (12/7/64, Atkinson, 80)

Insecure actress (Julie Harris) is regenerated by an affair with a Hollywood idol (Lou Antonio). ". . . a painfully slender and unstimulating comedy" *(Post)*. C: Estelle Parsons, Arlene Golonka, Betty Walker. A: Susan Slade, P: David Black. D: Joshua Logan. SD: Will Steven Armstrong.

Rebecca of Sunnybrook Farm (10/3/10, Republic, 216)

The adventures of a ten-year-old waif who comes to live with her two old maid aunts. Sentimental fiction (a million copy bestseller) brought to the stage with its homespun homilies and tearfully happy ending intact. C: Edith Taliaferro, Ernest Truex, Ralph Kellard. A: Kate Douglas Wiggin and Charlotte Thompson. P: Klaw and Erlanger. D: Lawrence Marston.

SV: Fox, 1932, Marian Nixon, Ralph Bellamy (with screenplay by S. N. Behrman).

Note: A 1938 Shirley Temple vehicle from 20th Century-Fox retained the title, but completely revamped the plot of this famous juvenile story.

Rebound (2/3/30, Plymouth, 124)

Two members of the smart set marry on the rebound, discover to their mutual surprise that the marriage works, and that they have fallen in love with each other. Entertaining, brightly written comedy by Donald Ogden Stewart. C: Hope Williams, Donn (Donald) Cook, Donald

Ogden Stewart. P/D: Arthur Hopkins.
SV: Pathé, 1931, Ina Claire, Robert Ames, Myrna Loy.

Recapture (1/29/30, Eltinge, 23)

Comedy-drama by Preston Sturges set in the Bellevue-Superbe-Palace Hotel at Vichy, France. In this ultrachic setting, a divorced man about Europe (Melvyn Douglas) is having a weekend fling with a chorus girl (Glenda Farrell). Meeting his ex-wife (Ann Andrews) in the hotel lobby, he finds himself falling in love with her all over again. The passion is one-sided, however, and the romantic encounter ends tragically. "Mr. Sturges' insane sense of humor still holds good . . . What *Recapture* lacks is the fulfillment of its central idea" *(New York Times)*. C: Hugh Sinclair, Cecilia Loftus, Mullally.

Reclining Figure (10/7/54, Lyceum, 116)

A budding young art dealer (newscaster Mike Wallace in his Broadway debut) sells a Renoir nude to an eccentric collector (Percy Waram), only to discover that the painting is a brilliant fake perpetrated by his double-dealing mentor (Martin Gabel). This satire on the charlatans of the art world had witty lines and funny gags, but its plot narrative was laboriously established and its story-line predictable. *Reclining Figure* was a first play by novelist-screenwriter Harry Kurnitz, whose Hollywood credits include *The Man Between, Witness for the Prosecution, How To Steal a Million,* etc. C: Georgann Johnson, David Opatoshu, Berry Kroeger, Nehemiah Persoff. P: Martin Gabel and Henry M. Margolis i.a.w. Peter Cusick. D: Abe Burrows. SD: Frederick Fox.

Red Cat, The (9/19/34, Broadhurst, 14)

Entertainer impersonates lookalike nobleman. Dated comedy with old-hat plot and threadbare situations. C: Francis Lister, Ruth Weston, Tamara Geva, Rex O'Malley, Porter Hall, Barnett Parker. A: Jessie Ernst b/o a play by Lothar and Adler. P: A. H. Woods. D: Bertram Harrison.
SV: UA, 1935, *Folies Bergére*, Maurice Chevalier, Merle Oberon, Ann Sothern, Ann Dvorak, Eric Blore; Fox, 1941, *That Night in Rio,* Don Ameche, Alice Faye, Carmen Miranda; 1951, *On the Riviera,* Danny Kaye, Gene Tierney, Corinne Calvet.

Red Dust (1/2/28, Daly's, 8)

Superintendent of an Indochina rubber plantation has an affair with his chief engineer's unfaithful wife, but eventually realizes that a voluptuous prostitute, on the run from the police, is the woman for him. Steamy tropical fiction stuff; an eight-performance disaster. C: Curtis Cooksey, Sydney Shields. A: Wilson Collison. P: Hugo W. Romberg. D: Ira Hards.
SV: MGM, 1932, Clark Gable, Jean Harlow, Mary Astor, Gene Raymond, Donald Crisp, Tully Marshall; 1940, *Congo Maisie,* Ann Sothern, John Carroll, Rita Johnson, Shepperd Strudwick, E. E. Clive; 1953, *Mogambo,* Clark Gable, Ava Gardner, Grace Kelly, Laurence Naismith, Donald Sinden.

Red Eye of Love (6/12/61, Living Theatre, 169)

Satirical exposé of the American success myth. Lively, highly original O/B comedy by Arnold Weinstein. D/SD: John Wulp.

Red Harvest (3/30/37, National, 15)

Frequently engrossing melodrama about the adventures of a Red Cross unit in the Great War. C: Leona Powers, Frederic Tozere, John Alexander, Carl Benton

Reid, Lloyd Gough, Elizabeth Love, Chester Stratton, Doro Merande, Martha Hodge. A: Walter Charles Roberts. P: Brock Pemberton. D: Antoinette Perry.

Red Light Annie (8/21/23, Morosco, 89)

Naïve small-town couple come to the big city and fall under the influence of dope peddlers. The husband becomes a jailbird and the wife a snowbird. In the end, Red Light Annie (as the free-with-her-favors wife is now known) shoots the villain of the piece dead while a sympathetic detective looks the other way. "Patent reversible melodrama . . . [typical] mid-Victorian popular fiction" (John Corbin, *New York Times*). C: Mary Ryan, Frank M. Thomas, Edward Ellis. A: Norman Houston and Sam Forrest (D). P: A. H. Woods i.a.w. Sam H. Harris.

Red Planet (12/17/32, Cort, 7)

Elaborately produced, awkwardly written sci-fi melodrama of husband-and-wife scientists deciphering messages from Mars. C: Bramwell Fletcher, Valerie Taylor, Eugene Powers, Richard Whorf, Henry Herbert, Wilfrid Seagram, Louis Hector. A: John Balderston and J. E. Hoare. P: Laurence Rivers (Rowland Stebbins). D: Burk Symon and Chester Erskine. SD: Lee Simonson.
SV: UA, 1952, *Red Planet Mars*, Peter Graves, Andrea King, Herbert Berghof.

Red Rainbow, A (9/14/53, Royale, 16)

Anti-communist melodrama about the murder of an unprincipled newspaper columnist. "Hopelessly incompetent" (*Post*). ". . . inconceivably dreadful . . ." (*News*). C: Howard Smith, Robert Middleton, Effie Afton. A/P/D: Myron C. Fagan.

Re-Echo (1/10/34, Forrest, 5)

Selfish banker gets his comeuppance. Dismal drama. C: Thurston Hall, Phyllis Povah, Harry Davenport. A: I. J. Golden. P/D: Carol Sax.

Reflected Glory (9/21/36, Morosco, 127)

Muriel Flood (Tallulah Bankhead), an actress at the peak of her fame, debates leaving the stage to become a wife and mother. Given the opportunity to carry out her threat, however, the tempestuous star elects to devote her life to her career. Undistinguished comedy-drama by George Kelly (A/D), bolstered by Miss Bankhead's box-office appeal. C: Philip Reed, Ann Andrews, Alden Chase, Clay Clement. P: Lee Shubert i.a.w. Curran and Gaites.

Relations (8/20/28, Masque, 105)

Flimsy comedy-drama about a Jewish businessman (Horace Braham) who discovers that his relations are robbing him blind. A/P/D: Edward Clark.

Remains To Be Seen (10/3/51, Morosco, 198)

A brassy band vocalist and a timid apartment house manager become involved in a murder mystery. Moderately entertaining comedy-melodrama by Howard Lindsay and Russel Crouse. C: Janis Paige (deb.), Jackie Cooper, Howard Lindsay, Warner Anderson, Karl Lucas, Hugh Rennie, Ossie Davis, Frank Campanella. P: Leland Hayward. D: Bretaigne Windust. SD: Raymond Sovey.
SV: MGM, 1953, June Allyson, Van Johnson, Angela Lansbury, Louis Calhern, Dorothy Dandridge.

Remarkable Mr. Pennypacker, The (12/30/53, Coronet, 221)

A freethinking family man turns out to be a bigamist and the father of seventeen children. How Mr. Pennypacker finds a solution to his two-family dilemma provides the climax to this cheerful comedy set in 1890's Delaware. C: Burgess Meredith, Martha Scott, Glenn

Anders, Una Merkel, Michael Wager, Phyllis Love, Thomas Chalmers. A: Liam O'Brien. P: Robert Whitehead and Roger Stevens. D: Alan Schneider. CD/SD: Ben Edwards.

SV: Fox, 1959, Clifton Webb, Dorothy McGuire, Charles Coburn, Jill St. John, Ray Stricklyn, Dorothy Stickney, Ron Ely, David Nelson.

Remember the Day (9/25/35, National, 120)

Pleasant nostalgic tale of a compassionate schoolteacher's life, her unhappy romance, and her guidance of one outstanding pupil. C: Francesca Bruning, Russell Hardie, Frankie Thomas, Jane Seymour, Keenan Wynn (deb.). A: Philip Dunning (P) and Philo Higley. D: Melville Burke.

SV: Fox, 1941, Claudette Colbert, John Payne, Anne Revere.

Remote Control (9/10/29, 48th Street, 79)

Breezy 20's whodunit set in a radio studio. C: Frank Beaston, Edward Van Sloan, Patricia Barclay, Hobart Cavanaugh, Larry Funk's WPH Nut Crackers. A: Clyde North (D), Albert C. Fuller, and Jack T. Nelson. P: Jones and Green.

SV: MGM, 1930, William Haines, Charles King.

Rendezvous (10/12/32, Broadhurst, 21)

Disillusioned veteran becomes a racketeer, sacrifices his life in a noble cause. Warner Brothers "tough guy" Barton MacLane played the leading role in this unsuccessful melodrama of his own authorship. C: Jerome Cowan, E. J. Ballantine, John Monks, Jr. P/D: Arthur Hopkins.

Reprise (5/1/35, Vanderbilt, 1)

A would-be suicide repays the good samaritan who saved his life by stealing his business. Poor script, nondescript cast, bargain basement production. A one-performance fiasco. A: W. D. Bristol. P: Frederick Mailey. D: George Somnes.

Requiem for a Nun (1/30/59, Golden, 43)

William Faulkner's only play, a somber tale of sin and atonement set in the fictional town of Jefferson, Mississippi, and dealing, principally, with the events and motives that precipitated a murder. The murderess is a black servant named Nancy Mannigoe. The victim: the infant child of a tormented southern belle named Temple Drake, in whose secret past lies the key to the tragedy. Originally written as a novel in 1951 and conceived as a sequel to *Sanctuary* (1931), the play was co-adapted for the stage by leading lady Ruth Ford. "A calculated, somewhat overwritten, but wholly valid experiment" (*Herald Tribune*). ". . . episodic and repetitious" (*Mirror*). C: Ruth Ford, Zachary Scott, Scott McKay, Bertice Reading (deb.). P: The Theatre Guild and Myers and Fleischmann. D: Tony Richardson. SD: Motley.

Note. Though *Requiem for a Nun* has not as yet been filmed, its counterpart, *Sanctuary,* has twice been adapted to the screen: Paramount, 1933, *The Story of Temple Drake,* Miriam Hopkins, Jack LaRue, William Gargan, Florence Eldridge, Elizabeth Patterson (directed by Stephen Roberts); Fox, 1961, Lee Remick, Yves Montand, Bradford Dillman, Odetta (directed by Tony Richardson).

Retreat to Pleasure (12/17/40, Belasco, 23)

Irwin Shaw's comedy about three suitors—a socialist (Leif Erickson), capitalist (Hume Cronyn), and playboy (John Emery)—who pursue an attractive young woman (Edith Atwater) from Manhattan to Miami. The play ends with the lady deciding to remain a spinster. "A zephyr in a teacup" *(Sun)*. *Retreat to Pleasure* was the final production of the Group Theatre. The settings were designed by Donald Oenslager, and the direction was by Harold Clurman.

Return Engagement (11/1/40, Golden, 8)

Passé actor (Bert Lytell) and actress (Mady Christians), who were once married to each other, rekindle the spark during a summer theatre engagement. "[It] plays like a first draft" *(Sun)*. Written by Lawrence Riley, author of *Personal Appearance* (1934). C: Evelyn Varden, Audrey Christie, Leona Powers, Alex Nicol. P: Schmidlapp and Gaites. D: Frank Merlin and Rowland Leigh.

Return of Peter Grimm, The (10/17/11, Belasco, 231)

A gentle Dutchman (David Warfield) returns from death to visit his family and ensure the happiness of his beloved ward. Tender and affecting David Belasco (P/D) fantasy. Authorship of the play, claimed by Belasco, has since been attributed to Cecil B. De Mille.

SV: RKO, 1935, Lionel Barrymore, Helen Mack, Edward Ellis, Donald Meek.

Return of the Vagabond, The (5/17/40, National, 7)

A jaunty stranger (George M. Cohan) spends a melodramatic night in a New England inn breaking up a gang of bank robbers. A sequel to *The Tavern* (1920), *The Return of the Vagabond* marked the last stage appearance of Cohan (A/P). ". . . a jest that has grown stale" *(Herald Tribune)*. C: Celeste Holm, McKay Morris, Edward McNamara. D: Sam Forrest.

Reunion in Vienna (11/16/31, Martin Beck, 280)

One of the Lunts' greatest successes, Robert E. Sherwood's comedy told of the return of the wild Hapsburgian crown prince Rudolph (Alfred Lunt), now a taxi driver, to the scene of his remembered glories, and of his efforts to recapture the affection of his former mistress (Lynn Fontanne), now the wife of Vienna's leading psychoanalyst (Minor Watson). "Such gay and exciting entertainment . . . that you must go, budget or no budget" *(The New Yorker)*. Highlight: the performance of the incomparable Helen Westley as Frau Lucher (read Frau Sacher of hotel fame), the lusty, cigar-smoking panderer to the wishes of the Hapsburgs. Footnote: the Lunts were offered leading roles in *Mourning Becomes Electra,* but turned down the O'Neill drama to appear in the Sherwood comedy. C: Henry Travers, Lloyd Nolan, Eduardo Ciannelli. P: The Theatre Guild. D: Worthington Miner.

SV: MGM, 1933, John Barrymore, Diana Wynyard, Frank Morgan, May Robson, Una Merkel, Henry Travers, Eduardo Ciannelli.

Note: Some years ago when this editor asked Billy Rose to name his favorite play, he chose *Reunion in Vienna,* adding: "I can think of half a dozen other plays in my generation more distinguished in content. But you asked for my favorite play."

Revelry (9/12/27, Masque, 49)

Samuel Hopkins Adams' novel about the Harding administration scandals dramatized in workmanlike, uninspired fashion by Maurine Watkins, author of *Chicago* (1926). C: Berton Churchill, George MacFarlane, Eleanor Woodruff, Rose Hobart, William B. Mack, Harry Bannister, James Crane. P/D: Robert Milton.

Revolt (10/31/28, Vanderbilt, 29)

Battling the forces of liberalism in both home and parish, a stern fundamentalist parson cracks under the strain and proceeds to kill himself. Grim and pointless drama by Harry Wagstaff Gribble (A/D). C: Hugh Buckler, Elizabeth Allen, Paul Guilfoyle. P: William Powell.

Rhapsody, The (9/15/30, Cort, 16)

Austrian composer finally conquers his obsessive hatred of a German officer who humiliated him during the war. Sketchy, Freudian-slanted drama never came to grips with its subject. C: Louis Calhern, Natalie Schafer, Julia Hoyt. A: Louis K. Anspacher. P: George M. Cohan. D: Sam Forrest.

Rich Full Life, The (11/9/45, Golden, 27)

A visit from the most popular boy in high school helps cure a sickly girl of her sneezes and sniffles. ". . . the first dramatization of the common cold" *(Journal-American)*. This syrupy soap opera was to have marked Elizabeth Taylor's stage debut. MGM had purchased rights to the play as a Broadway vehicle for their thirteen-year-old star. For one reason or another, Miss Taylor withdrew from the assignment at the last moment. Virginia Weidler replaced her, and gave a good account of herself in a trying role. Judith Evelyn had the equally thankless part of the girl's doting mother. C: Frederic Tozere, Ann Shoemaker, Frank M. Thomas, Edith Meiser. A: Vina Delmar. P/D: Gilbert Miller.
SV: MGM, 1947, *Cynthia,* Elizabeth Taylor, Mary Astor, George Murphy, S. Z. Sakall, Gene Lockhart, Spring Byington, Jimmy Lydon.

Richard Carvel (9/11/00, Empire, 128)

Entertaining dramatization of Winston Churchill's swashbuckler novel of the American Revolution. The hero (John Drew) incurs his uncle's enmity. Before he can claim his inheritance, young Richard Carvel suffers kidnapping by pirates, incarceration in debtor's prison, and battle wounds while serving with John Paul Jones. Eventually, Richard triumphs over his evil uncle and is re- united with the girl he loves. C: Arthur Byron, Dodson Mitchell, Ida Conquest. A: Edward E. Rose. P: Charles Frohman.

Richard Savage (2/4/01, Lyceum, 26)

Glum biographical drama of the English poet (Henry Miller) whose stormy life was recounted in Dr. Johnson's biography, and who died in debtor's prison in 1743. A: Madeleine Ryley. P: Wagenhals and Kemper. D: Henry Miller.

Riddle Me This (2/25/32, Golden, 100)

A hard-drinking reporter and a tough police captain join forces to solve a murder. Entertaining comedy. C: Thomas Mitchell, Frank Craven (D), Erin O'Brien-Moore. A: Daniel N. Rubin. P: John Golden.
SV: Par, 1932, *Guilty as Hell,* Victor McLaglen, Edmund Lowe.

Riddle: Woman, The (10/23/18, Harris, 165)

A despicable blackmailer who preys on women finally gets his comeuppance. Trite and pretentious melodrama. C: Bertha Kalich, Robert Edeson, Albert Bruning, A. E. Anson, Chrystal Herne. A: Charlotte E. Wells and Dorothy Donnelly. P: George Mooser. D: W. H. Gilmore.

Right Next to Broadway (2/21/44, Bijou, 15)

Problems of a Seventh Avenue dress designer. ". . . incredibly childish and completely unamusing . . ." *(PM)*. C: Jeannette C. Chinley, John Baragrey, Jonathan Harris. A/P: Paul K. Paley. D: William B. Friedlander.

Rimers of Eldritch, The (2/20/67, Cherry Lane, 32)

A murder in a bible belt community exposes the bigotry and hypocrisy underlying small-town life. Stageworthy, imaginatively written O/B drama by Lanford Wilson, author of *The Hot l Baltimore* (1973). P: Barr/Wilder/Albee. D: Michael Kahn.

Ring Around Elizabeth (11/17/41, Playhouse, 10)

Harassed mother (Jane Cowl) feigns amnesia to escape her obnoxious family. Dawdling comedy by mystery novelist Charl (later Charlotte) Armstrong. C: McKay Morris, Barry Sullivan, Marilyn Erskine. P: Allen Boretz and William Schorr (d) i.a.w. Alfred Bloomingdale.

Ring Round the Bathtub (4/29/72, Martin Beck, 1)

Comedy of an Irish-American family during Depression days in Chicago. Father is the central character, a bullying bore as tiresome to the audience as he is to his long-suffering family. They include his wife, two daughters, and mother. All deserve better. The author tries for nostalgia in this autobiographically inspired play, but the ultimate effect is unconvincing. A: Jane Trahey. C: Richard Mulligan, Elizabeth Ashley, Carmen Mathews, Carol Kane, Eileen Kearney, Kathleen Maguire, Louis Turenne, Margaret Linn, Alek Primrose, James Greene, Kate Wilkinson, John Cannon. D: Harold Stone. SD: Ed Wittstein. P: Jacqueline Babbin and Jay Wolf.

Ring Two (11/22/39, Henry Miller, 5)

Domestic crises in the home life of a retired actress. Feeble George Abbott (P/D) comedy. C: June Walker, Paul McGrath, Gene Tierney, Tom Powers, Betty Field, Edith Van Cleve. A: Gladys Hurlbut.

Ringside (8/29/28, Broadhurst, 37)

George Abbott (D) lent his talents to this story of a boxer who slugs his way to the championship. Lightweight drama, not in the contender class. C: Richard Taber, John Meehan, Brian Donlevy. A: Edward E. Paramore, Jr., Hyatt Daab, George Abbott. P: Gene Buck.

SV: RKO, 1929, *Night Parade*, Hugh Trevor, Aileen Pringle, Ann Pennington.

Ringside Seat (11/22/38, Guild, 7)

Weak comedy-melodrama about a small-towner (Grant Mitchell) who becomes involved with gangsters. A: Leonard Ide. P/D: Rufus Phillips.

Riot Act, The (3/7/63, Cort, 44)

Skimpy comedy about a strong-willed Irish-American mother (Dorothy Stickney) who keeps her three strapping policemen sons tied to her apron strings. C: Ruth Donnelly, Mark Dawson, Sylvia Miles, Linda Lavin, Adam Kennedy, Thomas Connolly. A: Will Greene. P: Emmett Rogers and Stanley Gordon i.a.w. W. Clement Stone. D: Jack Landau.

Rise of Silas Lapham, The (11/25/19, Garrick, 47)

William Dean Howells' novel transferred to the stage in pedestrian fashion. Wealthy but plebian Silas Lapham turns into a social climber when he moves with his family to Boston. The loss of his entire fortune leads to Silas' regeneration and his return to the simple life in Vermont. Former matinee idol James K. Hackett, badly miscast, portrayed Silas. Also in the cast: Helen Westley, Henry Travers, Erskine Sanford. A: Lillian Sabine. P: The Theatre Guild. D: Philip Moeller. SD: Lee Simonson.

Ritzy (2/10/30, Longacre, 32)

The promise of sudden riches corrupts a young married couple (Miriam Hopkins and Ernest Truex). Drab comedy by Viva Tattersall and Sidney Toler (D). P: L. Lawrence Weber.

Rivalry, The (2/7/59, Bijou, 81)

Dramatization of the Abraham Lincoln (Richard Boone)-Stephen Douglas (Martin Gabel) debates when the two men were campaigning for the senatorship from Illinois. Douglas, fighting for states' rights, won the election, but it was this campaign tour that brought Lincoln to national prominence and gave him the Presidency three years later (1861). In addition to highlighting the political issues, this play by Norman Corwin (A/D) utilized Mrs. Douglas (Nancy Kelly), who accompanied her husband on the tour, as both performer and narrator. ". . . timely and absorbing" (*Mirror*). ". . . belongs on the book shelf, not the stage" (*World-Telegram and Sun*). P: Cheryl Crawford and Joel Schenker. CD: Motley. SD: David Hays. M: David Amram.

River Niger, The (3/27/73, Brooks Atkinson, 280)

Memorable tale of a black family in contemporary Harlem. Forcefully written, peopled with three-dimensional characters, its dialogue totally convincing whether roiling in the gutter or spiraling upward in poetic flights, the play is strong enough to survive a melodramatic subplot involving black militants and a bloody finale. The central figure is Johnny Williams (Douglas Turner Ward), a sixtyish house painter, a failed man who is a loving husband and father. He is also a noble man and a poet. Proudly, he welcomes home his Air Force officer son (Les Roberts) only to discover the young man has no use for the rare status of black military officer. Instead, he plans to study law. The anguished Johnny walks out on the boy's homecoming party, but the bender he goes on is not unproductive. When he returns, he has completed a poem that's been long in work. Titled "The River Niger," it ties together the Niger, Mississippi, and Hudson Rivers as wellsprings of the black experience. The poem is stunning, and Johnny's recitation of it is highly moving. He also comes to agree with his son that life for all blacks is a case of finding the most effective battlefield. He goes forth to his own battlefield and his doom. *The River Niger* may wear the pejorative tag "message play," but it is beautifully eloquent. ". . . a complex and deep-depth drama" (Jerry Tallmer, *New York Post*). ". . . strikes at the gut, and with considerable power" (Edwin Wilson, *Wall Street Journal*). The play opened O/B 12/5/72 and played 120 performances before transferring to Broadway with the same cast for a further 280 performances. It won the Tony Award for Best Play. A: Joseph A. Walker. C: Douglas Turner Ward, Roxie Roker, Les Roberts, Frances Foster, Graham Brown, Grenna Whitaker, Lennal Wainwright, Neville Richen, Saundra McClain, Charles Weldon, Dean Irby. D: Douglas Turner Ward. P: Negro Ensemble Company, Inc. SD: Gary James Wheeler.

SV: CNA, 1976, James Earl Jones, Cicely Tyson, Lou Gossett, Glynn Turman, Jonelle Allen (directed by Krishna Shah from Joseph A. Walker's adaptation of his play).

Road to Rome, The (1/31/27, Playhouse, 392)

An attractive Roman matron (Jane Cowl) saves her city from Hannibal (Philip Merivale) by the not reluctant sacrifice of her virtue. This witty, pseudo-historical satire offered as good a reason as any for Hannibal's historic retreat after crossing the Alps, when Rome seemed within his grasp. "A hymn of hate against militarism—disguised, ever so gaily, as a love song" (Charles Brackett, *The New Yorker*). Robert E. Sherwood, film critic for the old *Life* magazine, wrote *The Road to Rome* in three weeks, working afternoons and weekends. It was his first play. The script was turned down by the Theatre Guild, the Shuberts, and Gilbert

Miller. Miller's rejection note read: "I don't even like *first-rate* Shaw." Philip Merivale wrote this editor some years back that Hannibal was the best role of his career: "As for the play: It had many master strokes in it: tenderness, wit, and fun—and always at the author's call the rhythms of the masters in English dramatic prose. And finally all these gifts were so well appreciated by the public, that in spite of its excellence, the play ran a year on Broadway and another year on the road." C: Barry Jones, Joyce Carey, Jessie Ralph. P: William A. Brady, Jr. and Dwight Deere Wiman. D: Lester Lonergan.

SV: MGM, 1955, *Jupiter's Darling*, Esther Williams, Howard Keel, George Sanders, Marge and Gower Champion.

Road to Yesterday, The (12/31/06, Herald Square, 216)

This popular comedy-drama treated the subject of reincarnation in elaborate, heavy-handed fashion. A girl (Minnie Dupree) imagines what some of her friends and acquaintances were like in Elizabethan times. In this previous incarnation, the virtuous minister turns out to be an heroic adventurer, the supercilious villain of the piece was a mere varlet in a taproom, etc. Awakened from her reverie, the girl is delighted to return to the present. A: Beulah Marie Dix and E. G. Sutherland. P: Lee Shubert. D: J. C. Huffman.

Road Together, The (1/17/24, Frazee, 1)

This one performance curio dealt with a woman (Marjorie Rambeau) who sacrifices everything to help her husband win the office of district attorney, only to discover in the end that he is a liar, cheat, and philanderer. From Alexander Woollcott's review in the *N. Y. Herald:* "Instead of being a play, *The Road Together* last night turned into something suggesting a tug of war. . . . The star of the occasion . . . was apparently laboring under some mental strain." From a front page story in the *New York Times:* "A. H. Woods closed *The Road Together* at the Frazee Theatre last night at the request of George Middleton, the author. . . . The occasion marked the first time that a play having an established star has closed after a single performance in New York. . . . The closing of the show was not altogether unexpected by the first-night audience which noted something was decidedly amiss." Miss Rambeau's opening night performance was tragically inept. The actress later explained that during the performance she had sprained a previously broken ankle and had been in severe pain. After the play closed, she suffered a nervous collapse and later sailed for Europe to escape newspaper reporters and bad publicity. A physician in Paris, maintaining that gangrene had set in, advised amputation of her leg. Shortly thereafter, Miss Rambeau attempted suicide. Her friend John McCormack, the noted tenor, found her unconscious and took the necessary steps to save her life. Eventually surgeons in Brussels treated the actress's leg and she soon was back treading the boards as brilliantly as ever.

Roads of Destiny (11/27/18, Republic, 101)

"Suggested" by O. Henry's short story of a young shepherd-poet (Edmund Lowe) who heads for Paris in search of romance and adventure, this Channing Pollock dramatization retained little of the original source material and emerged as a routine, thoroughly unexceptional drama. C: Florence Reed, Alma Kruger. P: A. H. Woods. D: W. H. Gilmore.

Roadside (9/26/30, Longacre, 11)

A roistering, freedom-loving young maverick named Texas (Ralph Bellamy) roams the prairies, taking romance where he finds it, until a pretty girl tames his spirit and persuades him that it's time to marry and settle down. Written with great gusto and charm, *Roadside* was shabbily treated by the critics, and closed after eleven performances. This colorful period comedy, set in 1905, was the work of Lynn Riggs, author of *Green Grow the Lilacs* (1931) which was musicalized (1943) as *Oklahoma!* P/D: Arthur Hopkins.

Robin Landing (11/18/37, 46th Street, 12)

Thinking him dead, a man (Louis Calhern) marries the wife (Nan Sunderland) of his brother (Ian Keith); the Enoch Arden story transferred to the Kentucky wilderness of 1770. Colorful verse drama was well-characterized, well-acted. C: Whitford Kane, Thomas Gomez, Fred Stewart. A: Stanley Young. P: Harmon and Hambleton. D: Halsted Welles. SD: Donald Oenslager.

Rock Me, Julie (2/3/31, Royale, 7)

Steven (Paul Muni) loves Charlotte (Helen Menken), but when he finds her pregnant by another man, he refuses to adopt her illegitimate child. Dismal soap opera wasted the talents of a first-rate cast. C: Dorothy Sands, Jean Adair, Otto Hulett. A: Kenneth Raisbeck. P: Green and Gensler. D: James Light.

Rocket to the Moon (11/24/38, Belasco, 131)

A middle-aged dentist falls in love with his secretary. The affair is doomed and, in the end, the dentist returns to his nagging wife. After an excellent first act, this play by Clifford Odets ran steadily downhill. *Rocket to the Moon* had been intended as a vehicle for Odets' wife, Luise Rainer, but film commitments prevented the actress from appearing in the play. C: Morris Carnovsky, Eleanor Lynn, Luther Adler, Art Smith, Ruth Nelson, Leif Erickson, Sanford Meisner, William Challee. P: The Group Theatre. D: Harold Clurman. SD: Mordecai Gorelik.

Roger Bloomer (3/1/23, 48th Street, 50)

A vivid and effective satire on bourgeois manners and morals; John Howard Lawson's first play. Roger Bloomer (Henry Hull) is a baffled adolescent who comes to New York to find self-knowledge and free himself from the conventions of his midwestern childhood. Poverty and increasing maladjustment are his lot in a business-dominated society. When his girl friend is killed under peculiar circumstances (attempted suicide), Roger is thrown into prison as a material witness. The final scene is an expressionistic nightmare montage during the course of which Roger finally finds a way of life that is right for him. Throughout the play, stream-of-consciousness monologues, visions, dreams, and dance sequences are intermingled. C: Mary Fowler, Louis Calhern. P: Equity Players, Inc.

Roll, Sweet Chariot (10/2/34, Cort, 7)

A southern shanty town is invaded by a steamroller gang, intent on building a new road that threatens the isolation of the community. "A great production. . . . Melodrama in the grand manner of the theatre" (*Theatre Arts*). Despite generally favorable reviews, Paul Green's "symphonic play of the Negro people" was a quick Broadway failure. C: Frank Wilson, Rose McClendon. P: Margaret Hewes. D: Hewes, Basshe and Pratt. M: Dolphe Martin.

Rollo's Wild Oat (11/23/20, Punch and Judy, 234)

Befuddled, totally talentless would-be thespian (Roland Young) decides to present *Hamlet* with himself in the title role. Frequently hilarious satirical farce by Clare Kummer. D: W. L. Gilmore.

Roman Candle (2/3/60, Cort, 5)

Pretty psychic (Inger Stevens) pursues handsome scientist (Robert Sterling). Sputtering farce by Hollywood writer-director Sidney Sheldon (*The Bachelor and the Bobbysoxer, Dream Wife,* etc.). C: Julia Meade, Walter Greaza, Lloyd Gough, Eddie Firestone. P: Ethel Linder Reiner. D: David Pressman. SD: David Hays.

Romance (2/10/13, Maxine Elliott's, 160)

Romance was one of the most popular dramas of the decade, a conspicuous success not only in America but throughout the world. It recounted the unhappy love affair of a New York clergyman (William Courtenay) and a tempestuous Italian prima donna (Doris Keane) with a shady past. In the end, the minister loses the opera star but gains her moral reformation. Doris Keane played the role of the glamorous Mme. Cavallini for two years in this country and then went to London where she had a record-breaking run of four years. C: A. E. Anson, Gilda Varesi, Claiborne Foster. A: Edward Sheldon. Musicalized by Sigmund Romberg as *My Romance* (1948) with Anne Jeffreys and Lawrence Brooks.

SV: MGM, 1930, Greta Garbo, Lewis Stone, Elliott Nugent, Gavin Gordon, Louise Seymour (directed by Clarence Brown from a screenplay by Edwin Justus Mayer and Bess Meredyth).

Romance and Arabella (10/17/17, Harris, 29)

Alfred Lunt made his Broadway debut in this trifling comedy playing Claude Estabrook, a young Greenwich Village poet who makes passionate love to the flighty, merry widow heroine (Laura Hope Crews). A: William Hurlbut. P: Joseph Riter. D: George Platt.

Romancin' Round (10/3/27, Little, 24)

Petty officer falls in love with virtuous waitress. As bad as its title. C: Ralph Morgan, Helen MacKellar. A: Conrad Westervelt. P: L. Lawrence Weber. D: C. T. Davis.

Romantic Mr. Dickens, The (12/2/40, Playhouse, 8)

Nineteen-year-old Diana Barrymore made her Broadway debut in this dull biographical drama concerned with the extracurricular love life of the great English novelist, Charles Dickens (Robert Keith). "Miss Barrymore is a vibrant young lady with an excellent speaking voice. . . . This is the best Barrymore debut for some time" *(New York Times).* A: H. H. and Marguerite Harper. P: John Tuerk. D: Arthur Sircom. SD: Watson Barratt.

Room in Red and White, A (1/18/36, 46th Street, 25)

Deranged husband is murdered by his wife and son. Lugubrious melodrama with a clever twist ending. C: Chrystal Herne,* Richard Kendrick, Leslie

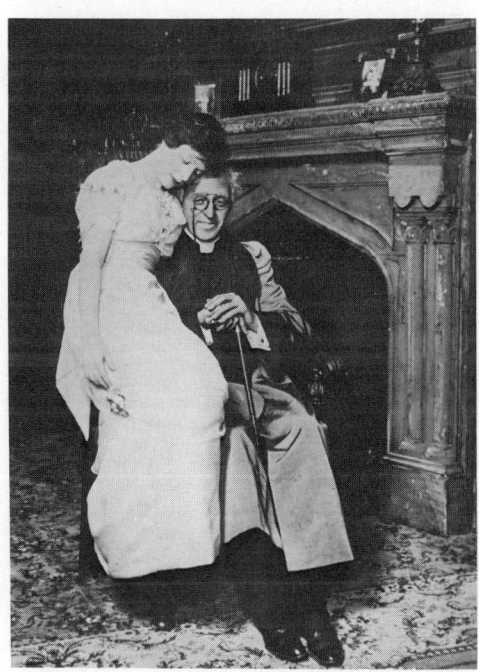

Romance. **Louise Seymour and William Courtenay (Maxine Elliott Theatre, February 10, 1913).** *Courtesy Museum of the City of New York Theatre and Music Collection.*

Adams, Louise Platt, Joshua Logan. A/D: Roy Hargrave. P: Wiman and Kondolf. SD: Jo Mielziner.

---

*Miss Herne's last Broadway appearance.

Room Service (5/19/37, Cort, 500)

Uproarious George Abbott (P/D) farce about a theatrical troupe stranded without cash in a smart New York hotel; one of the great comedy successes of the 1930's. It was his production assistant, Garson Kanin, who persuaded Abbott to take over *Room Service* after another producer (Sam H. Harris) had abandoned the production in Philadelphia. Abbott rewrote the script with the authors, John Murray and Allen Boretz, and recast the play with his own "stock company" of actors. Standouts in the company were Sam Levene as the shoestring producer, Eddie Albert (later succeeded by Hume Cronyn) as the naïve playwright from the sticks, and Donald MacBride as the frantic hotel manager. Others in the cast included Philip Loeb, Teddy Hart, Margaret Mullen, and Betty Field. RKO set a new high for film rights to stage hits by paying $255,000 for *Room Service* as a vehicle for the Marx Brothers. *Room Servce* was George Abbott's fourth smash hit comedy in two years. (The others were *Three Men on a Horse, Boy Meets Girl,* and *Brother Rat.*)

R: (4/6/53, Playhouse, 16) by Hart and Hershey. C: Jack Lemmon (deb.), Everett Sloane, John Randolph, Stanley Prager. D: Mortimer Offner. Revived O/B (5/12/70, Edison, 71) with a cast headed by Ron Liebman under the direction of Harold Stone.

SV: RKO, 1938, The Marx Bros., Lucille Ball, Ann Miller, Frank Albertson, Donald MacBride; 1944, *Step Lively,* Frank Sinatra, Adolphe Menjou, George Murphy, Gloria De Haven, Eugene Pallette, Anne Jeffreys.

Roomful of Roses, A (10/17/55, Playhouse, 88)

Sudsy comedy-drama about a remarried mother (Patricia Neal) who tries to win back the love and respect of her resentful teenage daughter. C: Betty Lou Keim, David White, Alice Frost. A: Edith Sommer. P: Guthrie McClintic (D) and Stanley Gilkey. SD: Donald Oenslager.

SV: Fox, 1956, *Teenage Rebel,* Ginger Rogers, Michael Rennie, Betty Lou Keim, Mildred Natwick (directed by Edmund Goulding).

Roosty (2/14/38, Lyceum, 8)

Gangster tries to instruct his teenage son in the ways of crime, but the boy opts to remain with a kindly farmer and trod the path of virtue. Banal melodrama directed by Lee Strasberg. C: William Harrigan, Russell Hardie, Abner Biberman, Mary Morris, Katherine Emery, James McCallion. A: Martin Berkeley. P: Albert Lewis.

Rope (2/22/28, Biltmore, 32)

Lurid sex-versus-religion story set in a small Tennessee town. C: Crane Wilbur, Elizabeth Patterson, Willard Robertson. A: David Wallace and T. S. Stribling b/o novel by Stribling. P: James W. Elliott. D: Frank Merlin.

Rope Dancers, The (11/20/57, Cort, 189)

Grim tale of an Irish-American couple in turn-of-the-century New York whose daughter has been born with six fingers on her left hand. The puritanical, guilt-ridden mother views the child's plight as a punishment from God, and blames her shiftless husband for the deformity that keeps their daughter a pariah. After the daughter's death, the mother is able to absolve her guilt, and she and her husband are reunited. "Only in rare moments does the drama take on the quality of emotional enrichment that transforms the clinical into the tragic" *(Post)*. C: Siobhan McKenna, Art Carney (deb.),

Joan Blondell, Theodore Bikel, Beverly Lunsford (deb.). A: Morton Wishengrad. P: The Playwrights Company and Gilbert Miller. D: Peter Hall. SD: Boris Aronson.

Rose Briar (12/25/22, Empire, 89)

A cabaret singer (Billie Burke) becomes a corespondent in a divorce case, effects a reconciliation between the Reno-bound wife and husband (Julia Hoyt and Frank Conroy), and winds up at the altar with the dashing fellow (Alan Dinehart) she's had her eye on all along. Wispy Booth Tarkington comedy, sumptuously produced by Florenz Ziegfeld, proved a mildly diverting vehicle for the vivacious young Billie Burke. Highlight: Miss Burke's singing of the Jerome Kern-Booth Tarkington ballad, "Love and the Moon."

Rose of the Rancho, The (11/27/06, Belasco, 240)

Pictorially splendid but dramatically threadbare tale of the settlement of California and the displacement of the Spanish land owners by predatory Americans. C: Frances Starr, Hamilton Revelle, Charles Richmond, Jane Cowl, J. Harry Benrimo. A: David Belasco and Richard Walton Tully. P/D: Belasco.

SV: Par, 1936, Gladys Swarthout, John Boles, Charles Bickford, Willie Howard.

Rose Tattoo, The (2/3/51, Martin Beck, 306)

Serafina delle Rose (Maureen Stapleton), a hot-blooded Sicilian-born widow, gives herself to an itinerant truck driver (Eli Wallach) when she discovers that her late, supposedly devoted husband actually had feet of clay. Casting aside all thoughts of religious devotion and peasant superstition, Serafina takes up living again with a grand flourish. Under the spell of renewed love, she even relents sufficiently to give her blessing to the budding affair between her fifteen-year-old daughter (Phyllis Love) and a virginal sailor (Don Murray).*Set in a clannish Sicilian community along the American Gulf Coast, this 1951 comedy-drama by Tennessee Williams was marred by excessive symbolism of the most heavy-handed sort. Reviews of the play and production were sharply divided: "Original, imaginative and tender..." *(New York Times)*. "Thin, frequently offensive and never sufficiently provocative" *(Journal-American)*. "It is a warmer and happier play than anything I've written," countered the author, and proceeded to make extensive script revisions after the Broadway opening. *The Rose Tattoo* had been designed to showcase the talents of Anna Magnani. She hesitated to appear on Broadway, fearing her English wasn't up to the task, and then-unknown Maureen Stapleton was given the pivotal role of Serafina in her stead. In 1955, Magnani agreed to do the movie version. Her English proved adequate and her performance won both the Academy Award and the New York Film Critics "best actress" citation. C: Ludmilla Toretzka, Sonia Sorel, Robert Carricart, Andrew Duggan,* Sal Mineo,* Vivian Nathan, Martin Balsam, David Stewart. P: Cheryl Crawford. D: Daniel Mann. CD: Rose Bogdanoff. SD: Boris Aronson. M: David Diamond.

R: (10/20/66, City Center, 76). C: Maureen Stapleton, Harry Guardino, Maria Tucci, Christopher Walken. D: Milton Katselas.

Projected: A musical version, to be titled *Serafina*, by Tennessee Williams, Jule Styne and Leslie Bricusse.

SV: Par, 1955, Anna Magnani, Burt Lancaster, Marisa Pavan, Ben Cooper, Jo Van Fleet (directed by Daniel Mann).

---

*Broadway debuts.

with fly-by-night actor. "... vulgarity runs a race with tedium that ends up in a photo-finish" *(PM).* C: June Walker, Sidney Blackmer, Eddie Nugent, Phyllis Brooks, Patricia Kirkland, Edith Meiser. A: Mary Orr and Reginald Denham (D). P: Clifford Hayman.

Round Up, The (8/26/07, New Amsterdam, 155)

Trite western melodrama set in Apache territory, with the United States Artillery riding to the rescue at 10:30 P.M. and resolving all difficulties, romantic and otherwise. C: Maclyn Arbuckle, Julia Dean, Orme Caldara. A: Edmund Day. P: Klaw and Erlanger. D: Brooks, Gresham, and Marston.

R: (3/7/32, Majestic, 8) by Reed and Wichfeld. C: Tex Ritter, Gertrude Michael.
SV: Par, 1941, Richard Dix, Preston Foster, Patricia Morison, Don Wilson, Ruth Donnelly.

Royal Family, A (9/5/00, Lyceum, 175)

The king and the queen try to force the beautiful Princess Angela into a politically advantageous marriage. Typical mythical kingdom comedy. C: Annie Russell, Lawrence D'Orsay, Richard Bennett. A: Robert Marshall. P: Charles Frohman. D: Joseph Humphreys. Musicalized by Alberta Nichols as *Angela* (1928) with Jeanette MacDonald, Eric Blore, Alison Skipworth.

Royal Family, The (12/28/27, Selwyn, 343)

George S. Kaufman-Edna Ferber play dealing with three generations of a famous theatrical family (the Barrymores) for whom the call of the stage is the only consideration. A delightful comedy. C: Haidee Wright, Otto Kruger, Ann Andrews, Sylvia Field, Roger Pryor, Catherine Doucet, Jefferson De Angelis. P: Jed Harris. D: David Burton.

R: (1/10/51, City Center, 16). C: Ethel Griffies, John Emery, Ruth Hussey, Peggy Ann Garner, J. Edward Bromberg, Robert Webber, Ossie Davis, Evelyn Ellis, Theodore Newton. D: Richard Whorf.
SV: Par, 1930, *The Royal Family of Broadway,* Fredric March, Ina Claire, Henrietta Crosman, Mary Brian, Charles Starrett, Frank Conroy, Arnold Korff (directed by George Cukor from a screenplay by Herman Mankiewicz and Gertrude Purcell).
Note: When *The Royal Family* was presented in London in 1934, its title was changed (for obvious reasons) to *Theatre Royal.* Noel Coward was producer-director, and the stellar cast was headed by Laurence Olivier, Marie Tempest, Madge Titheradge, W. Graham-Brown and George Zucco.

Royal Fandango, A (11/12/23, Plymouth, 24)

Foolish satirical comedy about a lovelorn princess (Ethel Barrymore) and her romantic escapades in Biarritz. A: Zoe Akins. P/D: Arthur Hopkins. Appearing in the play in small supporting roles were Edward G. Robinson and Spencer Tracy. Tracy, in fact (cast as a newspaper photographer), had only one line, but waiting for his entrance opening night was a bundle of nerves. Suddenly Miss Barrymore stopped beside him and said quietly: "Relax. That's all you have to do—just relax." "I've been capitalizing on that advice ever since," the actor confessed some years later.

Royal Virgin, The (3/17/30, Booth, 8)

Straightforward, uninspired retelling of the Elizabeth and Essex story. C: Thais Lawton, Hugh Buckler, Verree Teasdale, Vivienne Osborne, Wilfrid Seagram.

A/D: Harry Wagstaff Gribble. P: W. P. Tanner.

Rugged Path, The (11/10/45, Plymouth, 81)

Spencer Tracy returned to Broadway after a fifteen-year absence in this 1940's war play by Robert E. Sherwood. More tract than drama, *The Rugged Path* dealt with a liberal newspaper editor who joins the Navy, becomes a cook on a destroyer, and meets his death with gallantry and heroism on a remote Pacific island. ". . . a series of animated editorials . . . self-conscious, wordy and disappointing . . ." (*Herald Tribune*). "The hero is sometimes protagonist, sometimes symbol, sometimes Robert E. Sherwood. . . . the play as a whole is a tangled Sherwood Forest of Ideas" (*Time*). Rugged indeed were the problems faced by this production during its out-of-town tryout tour. Nervous about appearing on the stage and unhappy with his role, Spencer Tracy dreaded facing the New York critics. During the Boston run, he walked out on the show. Though persuaded to return, the actor's instincts concerning the fate of the Sherwood play proved correct. Despite the star's personal popularity, *The Rugged Path* lasted less than three months on Broadway. When the show closed, Tracy went back to Hollywood and vowed never again to appear on a legitimate theatre stage, a promise he kept until his death in 1967. C: Martha Sleeper, Clinton Sundberg, Clay Clement, Jan Sterling, Lawrence Fletcher. P: The Playwrights Company. D: Garson Kanin. SD: Jo Mielziner.

Ruggles of Red Gap (12/25/15, Fulton, 33)

Feeble adaptation of Harry Leon Wilson's rollicking tale of the English butler who suddenly finds himself in the wild American West. Sigmund Romberg furnished incidental music for this Messrs. Shubert production. C: Ralph Herz, Louise Closser Hale, Jobyna Howland, Jessie Ralph, Philip Dunning. A: Harrison Rhodes. D: J. H. Benrimo.

SV: Par, 1935, Charles Laughton, Charles Ruggles, Mary Boland, Roland Young, ZaSu Pitts; 1950, *Fancy Pants,* Bob Hope, Lucille Ball, Bruce Cabot, Eric Blore.

Ruint (4/7/25, Provincetown, 30)

A family of Carolina mountaineers try to force a philandering city slicker into marrying their daughter. John Huston and Sam Jaffe had supporting roles in this O/B comedy by Hatcher Hughes, author of *Hell-Bent fer Heaven* (1923). ". . . very engaging [but] needs . . . a more defined point of view" (Stark Young, *New York Times*). C: Jane Burby, Caroline Newcombe, David Landau, William Leonard. D: James Light.

Run, Little Chillun! (3/1/33, Lyric, 130)

Negro folk drama dealing with a soul-saving contest in a small southern town. Skimpy plot; magnificent choral work by the famed Hall Johnson Choir. C: Harry Bolden, Fredi Washington, Alston Burleigh, Edna Thomas. A: Hall Johnson. P: Robert Rockmore. D: Frank Merlin.

R: (8/11/43, Hudson, 16) by Lew Cooper i.a.w. Meyer Davis and George Jessel. D: Clarence Muse.

Run Sheep Run (11/3/38, Windsor, 12)

Undistinguished comedy-drama about a big city columnist who returns to the small town of his birth and learns, in the words of Thomas Wolfe, that "you can't go home again." C: Hugh O'Connell, Beatrice Herford, Ruth Weston, Alan Bunce, Enid Markey, Dickie Van Patten, William Bendix (deb.). A: Raymond Knight. P: Donald Blackwell (D) and Raymond Curtis.

Russet Mantle (1/16/36, Masque, 116)

A wandering poet seeks employment on a Santa Fe ranch. There he meets and falls in love with a banker's daughter who turns out to be even more of a social rebel than he. "A comedy of superlative quality" (Robert Benchley, *The New Yorker*). C: John Beal, Martha Sleeper, Margaret Douglass, Evelyn Varden, Jay Fassett, Helen Craig, Harry Bellaver. A: Lynn Riggs. P: Mayer and Queen. D: Robert Ross. SD: Donald Oenslager.

Russian People, The (12/29/42, Guild, 39)

Sluggish, contrived tribute to the courage and heroism of the beleaguered Russian people in their fight against the Nazi invader. ". . . melodrama of the vintage of the gaslit era" (*World-Telegram*). C: Leon Ames, Luther Adler, Herbert Berghof, Elisabeth Fraser, Eduard Franz, Eleonora Mendelssohn, Robert Simon, Victor Varconi. A: Clifford Odets b/o a play by Konstantin Simonov. P: The Theatre Guild. D: Harold Clurman. SD: Boris Aronson.

Ryan Girl, The (9/24/45, Plymouth, 48)

To save her illegitimate son's reputation, a former "Follies" girl (June Havoc) shoots the boy's no-good gangster-father (Edmund Lowe) dead. *The Ryan Girl* was written and directed by longtime Hollywood director Edmund Goulding (*Grand Hotel, Dark Victory, The Razor's Edge,* etc.). ". . . a tawdry melodrama, and a very bad one" (*Sun*). C: Una O'Connor, Doris Dalton, Curtis Cooksey. P: Messrs. Shubert i.a.w. Albert de Courville.

S

Sabrina Fair (11/11/53, National, 318)

Samuel Taylor's Cinderella fable about a lowly chauffeur's daughter (Margaret Sullavan) romanced by a misanthropic millionaire (Joseph Cotten) to keep her from marrying his playboy brother (Scott McKay). "A humorous romantic comedy that is acted with style and taste..." (*New York Times*). C: John Cromwell, Russell Collins, Cathleen Nesbitt, Luella Gear. P: The Playwrights Company. D: H. C. Potter. SD: Donald Oenslager.

SV: Par, 1954, *Sabrina*, Humphrey Bogart, Audrey Hepburn, William Holden, John Williams, Martha Hyer (directed by Billy Wilder).

Sag Harbor (9/27/00, Republic, 76)

Pleasant rural comedy-drama by James A. Herne contrasting the love of two brothers for the same woman. *Sag Harbor* was the first attraction to play the Republic Theatre. Lionel Barrymore made his Broadway debut at the age of twenty-two in this play. According to Barrymore, the critics were "unanimously inattentive" to his acting. He was dismissed from the cast after a few performances. C: James A. Herne, William Hodge, Lionel Barrymore, Chrystal Herne, Julia Herne.

Sailor, Beware! (9/28/33, Lyceum, 500)

Dynamite Jones, a sailor famed for his easy conquests, is pitted against Stonewall Jackson, a Canal Zone hostess equally famed for keeping suitors at bay. Gobs and hostesses alike lay bets as to which of the two will be the first to surrender. Upon this slender thread of virtue hangs the whole play—one of the breeziest, bawdiest comedies of the Depression era, and the surprise hit of the 1933 season. A one-set show with a low-salaried cast, *Sailor, Beware!* proved to be a bonanza for its neophyte producer, Courtney Burr. The attraction consistently sold out, eight performances a week. Minor footnote: the gamy farce so shocked a visiting Minneapolis attorney that he sued the producer for four dollars—and expenses. It was never disclosed whether he won or lost the case. C: Bruce MacFarlane, Audrey Christie, Horace MacMahon. A: Kenyon Nicholson (D) and Charles Robinson.

R: (5/3/35, Lafayette, 16) by the Harlem Players. C: Juano Hernandez, Christola Williams, Canada Lee, Juanita Hall. D: Shepard Traube and Mack Hilliard.

SV: Par, 1942, *The Fleet's In*, William Holden, Dorothy Lamour, Betty Hutton, Eddie Bracken; 1951, Dean Martin, Jerry Lewis, Corinne Calvet, Marion Marshall, Leif Erickson. (*Note:* The 1951 Paramount version of *Sailor, Beware!* was almost completely revamped and rewritten, and converted into a typical Martin and Lewis screen vehicle.)

Saint, The (10/11/24, Greenwich Village, 17)

Unsuccessful but interesting O/B drama

by one of America's foremost drama critics, Stark Young. An idealistic student (Leo Carrillo) deserts the seminary for the random life of a traveling variety show, touring Mexico. Deserted by the showgirl he loves, the student wanders back to his seminary to find the answer to the riddle of life. But "life never goes backward, the wheel keeps on turning," and the final curtain finds him setting off down the road again, intent on whatever the world may hold for him. "A play of lofty aim, written with great delicacy and possessing many moments of beauty.... And yet, primarily because play and performance do not quite merge, the effect of the whole is blurred and uncertain..." (*New York Times*). Maria Ouspenskaya made her New York English-speaking debut in *The Saint* playing a character called Paris Pigeons, one of the more colorful and exotic members of the variety troupe. Also in the cast were C. Henry Gordon, Helen Freeman, and Charles Ellis. D: Richard Boleslawski. SD: Robert Edmond Jones. M: Macklin Marrow.

Saint Wench (1/2/33, Lyceum, 12)

The life of a seventeenth-century peasant girl from sinner to saint. Tasteless, unconvincing comedy-drama by John Colton. C: Helen Menken (P), Russell Hardie, Edward Leiter. D: Charles Hopkins.

Sakura (12/25/28, Belmont, 7)

Mediocre 20's melodrama in which a Japanese prince (Walker Whiteside) foils a secret agent plot at the American embassy in Tokyo. A: Atherton Brownell. P/D: Walker Whiteside.

Salomy Jane (1/19/07, Liberty, 122)

Vigorous tale of feuds, fights, and friendships in the Old West and a heroine's faith in happy endings. C: Eleanor Robson, H. B. Warner, Holbrook Blinn. A: Paul Armstrong, from a story by Bret Harte. P: Liebler and Company. D: Hugh Ford.

SV: Fox, 1932, *Wild Girl*, Joan Bennett, Charles Farrell.

Salt Water (11/26/29, Golden, 87)

Sea captain longs for adventure, but his wife wants him to pilot a ferry boat. "... affable comedy in ... the familiar vein" (*New York Times*). C: Frank Craven, Una Merkel. A: Dan Jarrett and John Golden (P/D).

SV: U, 1933, *Her First Mate*, Slim Summerville, ZaSu Pitts (directed by William Wyler).

Salvation (1/31/28, Empire, 31)

Evangelist (Pauline Lord) with an eye to the dollar finally gets religion herself and walks out on her exploiters. Shrill, unconvincing Sidney Howard-Charles MacArthur drama, suggested by the life and career of Aimee Semple McPherson. C: George MacFarlane, Osgood Perkins, Donald Gallaher, Helen Ware, Marjorie Main. P/D: Arthur Hopkins.

Salvation Nell (11/17/08, Hackett, 71)

A Salvation Army officer (Mrs. Fiske) finally effects the reformation of her jailbird-lover (Holbrook Blinn). "The most daring play New York has ever seen. It not only dramatizes the Salvation Army, but it serves up Hell's Kitchen piping hot" (Ashton Stevens). Peopled with derelicts, drunks, and whores, *Salvation Nell* was acclaimed for its honesty and "unblinking realism." It was the first play written by twenty-one-year-old Edward Sheldon, author of *The Nigger* (1909), *The Boss* (1911), *Romance* (1913), and many other successful dramas. Bedridden and blind for years, Sheldon continued writing until 1930, and kept up his interest in the theatre until his death in 1946. P/D: Harrison Grey Fiske.

SV: Tiffany, 1931, Helen Chandler, Ralph Graves.

Sandalwood (9/22/26, Gaiety, 39)

Lugubrious tale of a dying man (William Harrigan) and the wife (Pauline Lord) who has never understood or appreciated him. A: Owen Davis and Fulton Oursler. P/D: Robert Milton.

Sandro Botticelli (3/26/23, Provincetown, 24)

An infatuated young girl (Eva Le Gallienne) meets Botticelli (Basil Sydney) at a party given by Lorenzo the Magnificent (Allyn Joslyn) and agrees to pose for the artist in the nude as Venus. She dies of a cold before Botticelli can complete his masterpiece. "There were many beautiful and poetical passages in the play," recalled Miss Le Gallienne some years later, "but it did not stand up under performance. . . . The venture was a dismal failure." A: Mercedes de Acosta. P: Players Company, Inc.

Sap, The (12/15/24, Apollo, 35)

Small-town scatterbrain (Raymond Hitchcock) takes the blame for his brother-in-law's embezzlement of bank funds. Heavy-handed farce never rang the bell. A: William A. Grew. P: Nicolai and Welch. D: Arthur Hurley.
SV: WB, 1930, Edward Everett Horton, Alan Hale, Patsy Ruth Miller.

Sap from Syracuse (1/8/30, Harris, 25)

Good-natured boob masquerades as a famous mining engineer, wins the hand of a beautiful countess. Humdrum farce; also known as *So Was Napoleon*. C: Hugh O'Connell, Elsa Ersi, Ruth Donnelly. A: Jack O'Donnell and John Wray. P: Newman and Johnson. D: John Hayden.
SV: Par, 1930, Jack Oakie, Ginger Rogers, George Barbier.

Sap Runs High, The (2/4/36, Bijou, 24)

Relieved of his savings by a crooked broker, a henpecked family man (James Bell) manages to recoup his losses. Feeble 30's comedy. A: H. T. Porter and Alfred White. P: Milton Kroopf. D: Theodore J. Hammerstein.

Sapho (2/5/00, Wallack's, 84)

Audiences of 1900 were shocked by this Clyde Fitch dramatization of Alphonse Daudet's novel detailing the adventures of a French courtesan (Olga Nethersole). Said William Randolph Hearst (*New York Journal*): "We think there exists in this country a respect for decent women and for young girls. We expect the police to forbid on the stage what they would forbid in streets and low resorts." These and similar editorials in other papers brought about the arrest of Miss Nethersole, a highly dramatic courtroom trial, reams of front page publicity, and finally a not-guilty verdict. *Sapho* reopened on Broadway in a blaze of box office glory. For the record, it was a very bad play.
SV: MGM, 1931, *Inspiration*, Greta Garbo, Robert Montgomery, Lewis Stone, Marjorie Rambeau, John Miljan, Beryl Mercer.

Saturday Night, A (2/28/33, Playhouse, 39)

Domestic crises on the night of a birthday party. Synthetic comedy-drama by Owen Davis. C: Peggy Wood, Hugh O'Connell, Arthur Margetson. P: William A. Brady. D: Melville Burke.

Saturday Night (2/25/68, Sheridan Square, 66)

A lonely Bronx librarian (Zina Jasper) seeks escape in fantasy from the drabness of her life. *Variety* characterized this touching O/B comedy-drama by Jerome Kass as "colorful . . . perceptive . . . meaningful" The play was skillfully staged by Burt Brinckerhoff.

Saturday Night Kid, The (5/15/58, Provincetown, 14)

A lecherous Manhattan cab driver

threatens the romance of a pair of star-crossed lovers. Talky, high-flown three-character comedy-drama; presented O/B with Martin Brooks, Nan Martin, and Joseph Sullivan in the lead roles. A: Jack Dunphy. P: Carr and Cohn. D: Leonard Barry.

Saturday's Children (1/26/27, Booth, 310)

Maxwell Anderson's simple but beguiling saga of white-collar marriage on forty dollars a week. Egged on by her older sister, a secretary traps her sweetheart into matrimony only to find the institution not all it was cracked up to be. Ruth Gordon was the girl and Roger Pryor (succeeded by Humphrey Bogart) was the boy. Also in the cast: Beulah Bondi, Frederick Perry, Ruth Hammond. P: The Actor's Theatre, Inc. D: Guthrie McClintic.

SV: WB, 1929, Corinne Griffith, Grant Withers; 1935, *Maybe It's Love*, Gloria Stuart, Ross Alexander, Ruth Donnelly, Henry Travers, Frank McHugh; 1940, John Garfield, Anne Shirley, Claude Rains, Lee Patrick, George Tobias.

Savages Under the Skin (3/24/27, Greenwich Village, 28)

All about the tyrannical white ruler (Louis Calhern) of Saba Saba, a black colony in the South Seas. Trash. A: Harry Foster and Wynn Proctor. P: Carl Reed. D: John D. Williams. SD: Livingston Platt.

Save Me the Waltz (2/28/38, Martin Beck, 8)

Mythical kingdom comedy by Katharine Dayton, co-author of *First Lady* (1935). "Hackneyed hokum" *(New York Times)*. Produced with a lavish hand, enacted by a stellar cast, *Save Me the Waltz* was a box-office disaster. C: John Emery, Jane Wyatt, Leo G. Carroll, Mady Christians, Laura Hope Crews, George Macready, Brenda Forbes, Leslie Barrie, Arnold Korff, Martha Sleeper, Hayden Rorke, Molly Pearson, Reginald Bach. P: Max Gordon i.a.w. Sam H. Harris. D: Robert B. Sinclair. SD: Jo Mielziner.

Scarecrow, The (1/17/11, Garrick, 23)

In seventeenth-century Massachusetts, a vengeful woman blacksmith and the yankee equivalent of Mephistopheles bring a scarecrow to life. Learning he is only an animated creature, and inspired by his encounters with humanity, the scarecrow nobly turns against his evil creators and destroys himself. At that moment, his mirrored reflection reveals him to be a true man. This "tragedy of the ludicrous" by Percy MacKaye, based on a tale by Nathaniel Hawthorne, remains one of the most imaginative and theatrically effective fantasies written by an American dramatist. It is a superb blend of dark-hued melodrama and poetic symbolism. C: Edmund Breese, Frank Reicher, Alice Fisher. P: Henry B. Harris. D: Edgar Selwyn.

R. *The Scarecrow* was revived for a limited engagement at Off-Broadway's Theatre de Lys on 6/16/53. Heading the cast were Patricia Neal, Eli Wallach, and Douglas Watson.

Scarlet Fox, The (3/27/28, Masque, 79)

Canadian mounty (Willard Mack) gets his man. Old-fashioned blood and thunder melodrama. A/D: Willard Mack. P: James W. Elliott.

Scarlet Pages (9/9/29, Morosco, 78)

A noted criminal lawyer (Elsie Ferguson) defends a girl (Claire Luce) on a murder charge. The girl turns out to be her daughter. "*Madame X* comes to General Sessions" *(The Broadway Reporter)*. A: Samuel Shipman and John B. Hymer. P: A. H. Woods. D: Ira Hards.

SV: WB, 1930, Elsie Ferguson, John Halliday, Marian Nixon.

Scarlet Sister Mary (11/25/30, Ethel Barrymore, 23)

Ethel Barrymore in blackface as an ignorant South Carolina negress who loves not wisely but too well. "It is difficult to understand what attracted Miss Barrymore to such a trifling narrative" *(New York Times)*. C: Estelle Winwood, Horace Braham, Marjorie Main, Beatrice Terry, Walter Gilbert, Ethel Barrymore Colt (deb.), Charles Quigley, Ted De Corsia, Alan Campbell. A: Daniel Reed b/o the Pulitzer Prize novel by Julia Peterkin. P: Lee Shubert. D: E. M. Blyth (Ethel Barrymore).

Scene of the Crime, The (3/28/40, Fulton, 12)

The effects of a crime upon a murderer's saintly family. Unbearably saccharine soap opera. C: Chester Stratton, David Wayne, Louis Sorin. A: Frank Gould. P: Harry Howard. D: Frank Merlin.

Schemers (9/15/24, Bayes, 24)

Four drama critics named Alan Olcott, Alexander Gale, Percy Ammond, and A. Wood Brown (obviously patterned after Alexander Woollcott, Alan Dale, Percy Hammond and Heywood Broun) are tricked into viewing a new opus being rehearsed by a theatrical producer (William Harrigan). The critics wisely turn thumbs down on the deplorable offering. Pitiably inept play-within-a-play comedy by one Dr. William Irving Sirovich. P: Herman Timberg.

School for Brides (8/1/44, Royale, 375)

Leering sex farce inspired by the marital adventures of playboy Tommy Manville. A much-married millionaire backs a school for brides with the proviso that he may claim the valedictorian as his seventh spouse. ". . . vulgar without being funny" *(Journal-American)*. C: Roscoe Karns, Bernadene Hayes, Yolande Donlan (deb.). A: Frank Gill, Jr. and George Carleton Brown. P: Howard Lang. D: Harold Morton.

Schoolhouse on the Lot (3/22/38, Ritz, 55)

First play by Joseph Fields and Jerome Chodorov, authors of *My Sister Eileen* (1940), *Junior Miss* (1941), *The Ponder Heart* (1956), etc. A spoof of Hollywood and the (child) star system, *Schoolhouse on the Lot* caused no great stir, and departed after a seven-week run. C: Onslow Stevens, Mary Mason, Sidney Lumet, Eda Heinemann. P: Philip Dunning (D) i.a.w. Lee Shubert and George Jessel.

Scratch (5/6/71, St. James, 4)

Stephen Vincent Benet's short story *The Devil and Daniel Webster* as dramatized by Pulitzer Prize-winning poet Archibald MacLeish. Talky and tedious, the play recounts the tale of Jabez Stone, who sells his soul to the Devil, otherwise known as Scratch, in return for seven years of material riches. When the term of the contract is up, Stone desperately appeals to his friend, Daniel Webster (Patrick Magee), to save him. The climax of the play is a trial, with Scratch and Webster contesting for the body and soul of Stone before a jury of villains including Aaron Burr and Captain Kidd. Despite this ruffian jury, Webster's eloquence wins the day and saves Stone. As befits a famous work, *The Devil and Daniel Webster* has seen dramatic life in several media: as an opera with music by Douglas Moore and lyrics and libretto by Benet, on film under the title *All That Money Can Buy* with Walter Huston as Scratch, and as the MacLeish play. A certain amount of critical controversy has attended all the story's manifestations. When the play was in its pre-Broadway run in Boston, it received a negative review from the *Boston Globe*. Promptly, the paper's editorial page rebuked its own critic for lese majesty toward MacLeish.

Fortunately, this sort of artistic Big Brother-ism is rare. ". . . moments of brilliance . . . veteran Will Geer portrays Satan with relish" (Richard Watts, *New York Post*). "MacLeish has turned a charming and beautifully scaled story into an inflated and disastrously abstract play" (Jack Kroll, *Newsweek*). A: Archibald MacLeish, b/o Stephen Vincent Benet's *The Devil and Daniel Webster*. C: Will Geer, Patrick Magee, Will Mackenzie, Joanne Nail, Rex Robbins, Roy Poole, Thomas Barbour, Daniel Keyes, Mary Loane. D: Peter Hunt. P: Stuart Ostrow. SD: John Conklin.

Scuba Duba (10/10/67, New, 692)

Novelist Bruce Jay Friedman's smash-hit O/B comedy about a young American liberal, vacationing in the south of France, who discovers that his wife has run off with a black skin diver. ". . . side-splitting . . . a genuine original, a zany charade . . ." *(New York Times)*. C: Jerry Orbach, Jennifer Warren, Cleavon Little, Brenda Smiley, Conrad Bain, Rudy Challenger, Christine Norden, Judd Hirsch. P: Ivor David Balding i.a.w. Ferleger and Crowe. D: Jacques Levy. CD: Willa Kim. SD: Peter Larkin.

Sea Horse, The (4/15/74, Westside, 128)

O/B romance. A poignant love story of two lonely people, a fat, cynical lady saloon-keeper and a merchant seaman. The Sea Horse is a waterfront bar, owned and operated by Gertrude Blum (Conchata Ferrell), whose occasional boyfriend, Harry Bales (Edward J. Moore), has decided it's time they end the tentative quality of their relationship and make the firm commitment of marriage. Gertrude is harshly fearful and refuses, but Harry is a persistent suitor. Through a long night he gradually breaks down her resistance, though not without inflicting emotional wounds on both of them. Despite its single plot element, the play is never tedious. The writing is compassionate and unsentimental, and the characters emerge in multidimensions, becoming the sort of persons for whom a happy ending is not only logical, but heartily desired by audiences. ". . . an extended two-character sketch, but the two characters never wear out their welcome . . . Marshall W. Mason's direction is impeccable and the performances by Conchata Ferrell and Edward J. Moore are among the finest to be seen on any stage this season" (Mel Gussow, *New York Times*). *The Sea Horse* was first produced off-off-Broadway by the Circle Repertory Theater Company on 3/3/74, before moving off-Broadway for its successful run. A: Edward J. Moore. C: Conchata Ferrell, Edward J. Moore. D: Marshall W. Mason. P: Kermit Bloomgarden, Max Allentuck, and Orin Lehman in The Circle Repertory Theater Company production. SD: David Potts.

Sea Woman, The (8/24/25, Little, 32)

The tribulations of a good woman (Blanche Yurka) beset by a wicked foster-daughter. Willard Robertson wrote this melodramatic mishmash; Paul Kelly and Roger Pryor were the juveniles in the cast. P: L. L. Weber. D: William B. Friedlander.

Searching for the Sun (2/19/36, 58th Street, 5)

Sensitively written but sketchily developed drama about life in a hobo jungle, with boy and girl outcasts trying to make a go of things during the great Depression. C: Edwin Philips, Olive Deering, Whitford Kane, Vernon Crane. A: Dan Totheroh. P: Albert Ingalls, Jr. D: Evans and Hathaway.

Searching Wind, The (4/12/44, Fulton, 326)

Lillian Hellman's drama about a career diplomat (Dennis King) who has never taken a firm stand on anything. Flashbacks to the 1920's and 30's reveal this appeasement-minded U. S. ambassador encountering fascism in Rome, nazism in Berlin, and the peace-at-any-price philosophy of the French in the grim autumn of 1938. Highlight: a final scene in which the diplomat's soldier-son (Montgomery Clift), who has lost a leg in battle, tells his well-bred family why he is ashamed of them. ". . . a drama of sincerity and stature . . ." *(Sun)*. ". . . a pretentious, well-meaning drama that always seems on the verge of saying something of tremendous import, but never does. It is windy, but not often searching" *(Post)*. C: Cornelia Otis Skinner, Dudley Digges, Barbara O'Neil, Arnold Korff, Joe De Santis. P/D: Herman Shumlin. CD: Aline Bernstein. SD: Howard Bay.

SV: Par, 1946, Robert Young, Sylvia Sidney, Ann Richards, Dudley Digges, Douglas Dick, Albert Basserman (directed by William Dieterle).

Season Changes, The (12/23/35, Booth, 8)

Dullish comedy concerning the on-again, off-again romance of a liberated young female and her married lover. C: Doris Dudley, Eliot Cabot. A: Arthur Richman. P/D: Robert Milton.

Season in the Sun (9/28/50, Cort, 367)

A successful journalist attempts to write a serious novel in the idyllic environment of Fire Island. It isn't long, however, before his summer cottage is invaded by assorted Long Island bores, screwballs, and dipsomaniacs. His peace and privacy shattered, the writer and his family flee back to the relative tranquility of Manhattan. This comedy by Wolcott Gibbs, associate editor and long-time drama critic of *The New Yorker* magazine, received highly flattering reviews and enjoyed a substantial Broadway run. C: Richard Whorf, Nancy Kelly, Eddie Mayehoff, Anthony Ross, Joan Diener, Paula Laurence, King Calder, Jack Weston, George Ives. P: Courtney Burr and Malcolm Pearson. D: Burgess Meredith. SD: Boris Aronson.

Season of Choice (4/13/59, Barbizon Plaza, 7)

The life of a southern aristocrat is blighted when he weds a girl of lower social status. "Honey, it is not much like Tennessee Williams" *(New York Times)*. Presented O/B with a cast headed by Douglas Watson, Betsy von Furstenberg, Collin Wilcox, Keir Dullea (deb.), Ethel Smith, Dorrit Kelton, John Marriott. A: Nathaniel Banks. P: Bowden, Barr, and Bullock. D: Charles Bowden. SD: Will Steven Armstrong.

Second Best Bed (6/3/46, Barrymore, 8)

Learning that Anne Hathaway plans to divorce him, Will Shakespeare returns to Stratford-on-Avon determined to break up her marriage to a local clod. "An untidy dramatic jumble . . . woefully bad, in both writing and execution" *(Herald Tribune)*. This 1946 period comedy was the first Broadway play written by N. Richard Nash, author of *The Rainmaker* (1954) etc. The play's title comes from Shakespeare's will, in which he left only his "second best bed" to Ms. Hathaway. C: Ruth Chatterton,* Barry Thomson, Ralph Forbes, Richard Dyer-Bennet. CD/SD: Motley.

---

*Miss Chatterton coproduced *Second Best Bed* (with John Huntington) and codirected the comedy (with Mr. Nash).

Second Man, The (4/11/27, Guild, 178)

Realizing that the "second man" within him is an opportunist, a self-indulgent novelist (Alfred Lunt) returns to his wealthy mistress (Lynn Fontanne). She will allow him to be what he has always wanted to be—a prosperous dilettante. Shimmering, epigrammatic study of a man's dual nature; one of the finest examples of American high comedy. *The Second Man*, S. N. Behrman's first play, took more than a decade to reach the stage; its success brought Behrman immediate celebrity. C: Margalo Gillmore, Earle Larimore. P: The Theatre Guild. D: Philip Moeller.

SV: RKO, 1930, *He Knew Women*, Lowell Sherman, Alice Joyce.

Second Threshold (1/2/51, Morosco, 126)

A middle-aged career man plans to terminate a life that has gone flat and stale, until a last-minute reconciliation with his daughter makes him realize that he wants to go on living. Philip Barry's posthumous comedy-drama, with revisions by Robert E. Sherwood, received mixed reviews and had a moderate Broadway run. Barry had worked on *Second Threshold,* off and on, over a period of eleven years. He died before completing the script to his satisfaction. C: Clive Brook (deb.), Margaret Phillips, Betsy von Furstenberg (deb.). P/D: Alfred de Liagre, Jr. SD: Donald Oenslager.

Secret Affairs of Mildred Wild, The (11/14/72, Ambassador, 23)

Comedy of a troubled matron who retreats for solace into a make-believe world gleaned from the movies. Despite workable gags and generally amusing dialogue, the play is obscure, never fully limning the heroine's character, nor explicating her need for "secret affairs." These zany fantasies involve her with *Gone With the Wind* and Rhett Butler, King Kong, Tarzan, and a lively fling as Shirley Temple leading a song and dance number. The redoubtable Maureen Stapleton does her best as Mildred but can't save the show, a disappointment from the author of *The Effect of Gamma Rays on Man-in-the-Moon Marigolds.* A: Paul Zindel. C: Maureen Stapleton, Lee Wallace, Elizabeth Wilson, Florence Stanley, Neil Flanagan, Joan Pape, Doris Roberts, Bill McIntyre, Pat Corley, Paul De Witt. D: Jeff Bleckner. P: James B. McKenzie and Spofford J. Beadle. SD: Santo Loquasto. CD: Carrie F. Robbins. The incidental music that enlivened Mildred's secret affairs included contributions from Irving Berlin, Cole Porter, Mack Gordon and Harry Revel, and Max Steiner.

Secret Room, The (11/7/45, Royale, 21)

Leda Ferroni (Eleonora Mendelssohn), a victim of Nazi persecution, is offered refuge in the home of an American psychiatrist. Seeking emotional recompense for her frustrated maternal instincts, Leda alienates the psychiatrist's children from their mother (Frances Dee). Before she is led away to the insane asylum, Leda commits one murder and attempts a second. ". . . frequently preposterous . . . a thriller that doesn't come off" *(Sun).* This Freudian melodrama, directed by Moss Hart, was written by Robert Turney, author of *Daughters of Atreus* (1936). The play was produced by Joseph M. Hyman and Bernard Hart i.a.w. Haila Stoddard.

See My Lawyer (9/27/39, Biltmore, 224)

Milton Berle* made his legitimate acting debut in this George Abbott (P) farce, and contributed a surprisingly understated, skillful, and engaging performance in the leading role. The plot revolved around the tribulations of three struggling lawyers (Milton Berle, Gary Merrill, Millard Mitchell) when they suddenly acquire a nitwit millionaire playboy as their only client. "*See My Lawyer* works terribly hard and shamelessly for its humor, but in its madcap way it achieves quite a bit of it" *(Herald Tribune).* C: Eddie Nugent, Teddy Hart, Mary Rolfe, Robert Griffith. A: Richard Maibaum and Harry Clork. D: Ezra Stone.

SV: U, 1945, Olsen and Johnson, Grace McDonald.

---

*In the role originally intended for then-unknown Danny Kaye.

See Naples and Die (9/24/29, Vanderbilt, 62)

In 1929, the same year his grim tenement drama *Street Scene* was produced, Elmer Rice (A/D) wrote a giddy farce set in ultrachic Sorrento. *See Naples and Die* dealt with the romance of an American heiress (Claudette Colbert) who pursues her lover (Roger Pryor) to the Bay of Naples even though she has just married a fortune-hunting Russian prince (Pedro de Cordoba). After a couple of revolutionists conveniently shoot the heiress's blackmailing husband, true love triumphs. "For months Elmer Rice worked to win the Pulitzer Prize on one side of the street, and now he goes and loses it on the other" (Kelcey Allen, *Women's Wear Daily*). P: Lewis Gensler.
SV: WB, 1930, *Oh, Sailor Behave!*, Olsen and Johnson, Irene Delroy, Charles King, Noah Beery.

See the Jaguar (12/3/52, Cort, 5)

James Dean made his Broadway debut in this badly muddled symbolic melodrama by N. Richard Nash, author of *The Rainmaker* (1954). Dean played the village simpleton, an innocent boy of seventeen in a mountain district community ruled by a loutish storekeeper with a passion for caging the things around him. Stalked by this brutish varmint (for reasons too complicated to summarize in the space allotted this entry), the boy is captured and imprisoned in a cage originally intended for a jaguar. At the final curtain he is set free by a gentle schoolteacher (Arthur Kennedy) who is shot and killed for his pains. ". . . wildly ineffectual . . . full of sound and fury, signifying nothing" *(Post)*. C: Cameron Prud'homme, Constance Ford, Roy Fant, Margaret Barker, George Tyne. P: Lemuel Ayers (SD) i.a.w. Helen Jacobson. D: Michael Gordon. M: Alec Wilder.

Seed of the Brute (11/1/26, Little, 72)

Overblown drama about a blustering politician, his aristocratic wife, and sensitive son. C: Robert Ames, Doris Rankin, Donn (Donald) Cook, Jane Seymour, Hilda Vaughn. A/D: Knowles Entrikin. P: William A. Brady, Jr. and Dwight Deere Wiman.

Seeds in the Wind (5/25/48, Empire, 7)

The homeless orphan survivors of Lidice band together, in the Carpathian mountains of Czechoslovakia, to wrest the world from the grown-ups. ". . . a paltry theatrical celebration of a terrible event" (*Herald Tribune*). C: Sidney Lumet, Tonio Selwart, Abby Bonime. A: Arthur Goodman. P: Healy and Bromley. D: Paul Tripp.

Seeing Things (6/17/20, Playhouse, 103)

Scatterbrained wife fakes suicide, returns as a ghost to spy on her husband. Inane farce. C: Dorothy Mackaye, John Westley, Frank McIntyre. A/D: Margaret Mayo and Aubrey Kennedy. P: Wagenhals and Kemper.

Seen But Not Heard (9/17/36, Henry Miller, 60)

Three precocious teenagers investigate the murder of an aunt and find the trail leading to their favorite uncle. Thirteen-year-old Anne Baxter, granddaughter of architect Frank Lloyd Wright, made her Broadway debut in this moderately diverting 1936 mystery-comedy. C: Frankie Thomas, Raymond Roe, Kent Smith, Paul McGrath. A: Marie Baumer and Martin Berkeley. P: D. A. Doran. D: Arthur Sircom.

Seidman and Son (10/15/62, Belasco, 216)

Predictable comedy about the troubles of a dress manufacturer (Sam Levene) at home and office. C: Nancy Wickwire, Vincent Gardenia, Stewart Moss, Morgan Sterne, Diana Muldaur, Frances Chaney. A: Elick Moll b/o his novel. P:

The Theatre Guild, Joel Schenker and Michael Kanin i.a.w. Elliot Martin. D: Carmen Capalbo.

Sellout, The (9/6/33, Cort, 5)

Widow (Minnie Dupree) gets involved with gangsters. Hopelessly inept comedy. A: Albert G. Miller. P: Drama Craftsmen. D: Ashley Miller.

Send Me No Flowers (12/5/60, Atkinson, 40)

Believing he has only a short time to live, a hypochondriac (David Wayne) sets out to procure a new husband for his wife (Nancy Olson). ". . . a desultory comedy . . . slender, machine-made and only intermittently entertaining" (*Post*). A: Norman Barasch and Carroll Moore. P: Burr and Specter. D: James Dyas.

SV: U, 1964, Rock Hudson, Doris Day, Tony Randall, Clint Walker, Paul Lynde (directed by Norman Jewison).

Separate Rooms (3/23/40, Maxine Elliott's, 613)

By threatening to reveal the lady's shady past, a Broadway columnist (Alan Dinehart) blackmails the frigid wife (Glenda Farrell) of his younger brother (Lyle Talbot) into becoming a dutiful spouse. It took four authors to concoct this rudimentary farce; cut-rate tickets and a sex-oriented publicity/advertising campaign helped the production to prosper for 613 performances. C: Jack Smart, Mozelle Britton, Austin Fairman. A: Joseph Carole, Alan Dinehart, Alex Gottlieb, Edmund Joseph. P: Bobby Crawford. D: William B. Friedlander.

Serena Blandish (1/23/29, Morosco, 94)

A "fabulous comedy" (so read the playbill) by S. N. Behrman b/o the novel by Enid Bagnold. Serena (Ruth Gordon) is a wide-eyed charmer, honest to a fault, cursed with a sense of humor, a sense of the fantastic, and an inability to say no. Chaperoned through the glittering world of Mayfair society by a worldly countess (Constance Collier), Serena loses her chance of marriage to wealthy Lord Ivor Cream (Henry Daniell) because she has not learned how to be sufficiently calculating or heartless. Characteristically, when she falls in love, it is with the penniless illegitimate son (Hugh Sinclair) of a butler (A. E. Matthews). "An insecure play, thin at times to the point of transparence [yet] it engenders moments of the rarest beauty" (*New York Times*). C: Clarence Derwent, Julia Hoyt. P: Jed Harris. SD: Robert Edmond Jones.

Serpent's Tooth, A (8/24/22, Little, 36)

Wastrel son is finally rejected by his once-devoted mother. Two fine actors, Marie Tempest and Leslie Howard, gave accomplished performances as the doting matriarch and her spineless offspring, but the play itself was so haphazard and tepid that Alexander Woollcott dubbed it "A Tempest in a teapot." A: Arthur Richman. P: John Golden. D: Robert Milton. Milton.

Servant in the House, The (3/23/08, Savoy, 80)

A Christlike figure (Walter Hampden) solves the problems of a modern household. Popular religious tract-drama by Anglo-American author Charles Rann Kennedy. P/D: Henry Miller.

Set a Thief— (2/21/27, Empire, 80)

Unknown murderer signs his death notes "S. Q. V."—an inscription that baffles the police and, presumably, the audience. Fairly diverting melodrama set in a spooky library. C: Margaret Wycherly, Calvin Thomas, Gladys Feldman, Natacha Rambova.* A: Edward E. Paramore. D: Alexander Leftwich.

---

*Mrs. Rudolph Valentino.

Set My People Free (11/3/48, Hudson, 29)

Historical drama (South Carolina, 1810–1822) in which former slave Denmark Vesey (Juano Hernandez) organizes a black rebellion against the Charleston whites. Betrayed by one of his followers (Canada Lee), Vesey's uprising fails to come off. ". . . a diffuse and episodic play but one of considerable power and eloquence" (*Sun*). C: Mildred Joanne Smith, Frank Wilson, Leigh Whipper, Blaine Cordner, William Marshall, William Warfield, Alonzo Bosan. A: Dorothy Heyward. P: The Theatre Guild. D: Martin Ritt. SD: Ralph Alswang.

Seven (12/27/29, Republic, 34)

Virtually plotless tale of a squad of World War I American aviators who go to their deaths one by one. ". . . spoken narrative rather than a play" (*New York Times*). C: Robert Strange, Preston Foster, Millard Mitchell, Tom Douglas. A: Frank J. Collins. P: James Cooper. D: Lionel Atwill.

Seven Chances (8/8/16, Cohan, 151)

Unprepossessing young fellow (Frank Craven) will inherit twelve million dollars if he can find someone to marry within twenty-four hours. Machine-made David Belasco (P/D) farce. C: Otto Kruger, Helen MacKellar, Carroll McComas. A: Roi Cooper Megrue.

Seven Days (11/10/09, Astor, 397)

When a house is quarantined, nobody—including a clownish burglar, an officious policeman, a flighty aunt, etc.—is permitted to leave the premises. Slapdash farce by Mary Roberts Rinehart and Avery Hopwood was the comedy hit of 1909. C: Florence Reed, Lucille La Verne, Alan Pollock, Herbert Corthell. P: Wagenhals and Kemper.

Seven Descents of Myrtle, The (3/27/68, Barrymore, 29)

A dying transvestite homosexual (Brian Bedford) marries an addle-brained burlesque stripper (Estelle Parsons) in order to deprive his brawny half-brother (Harry Guardino) of their mother's estate. One of Tennessee Williams' most unprepossessing works, a luridly melodramatic (almost parodistic) study of degradation and depravity in the deep South. P: David Merrick. D: Jose Quintero. CD: Jane Greenwood. SD: Jo Mielziner.

SV: WB, 1970, *Last of the Mobile Hot-Shots*, James Coburn, Lynn Redgrave, Robert Hooks (directed by Sidney Lumet from a screenplay by Gore Vidal).

Seven Keys to Baldpate (9/22/13, Astor, 320)

Classic mystery-farce by George M. Cohan (based on a story by Earl Derr Biggers); perhaps the trickiest of all trick-ending plays. An author (Wallace Eddinger) wagers he can write a novel in twenty-four hours if he has absolute quiet. Accordingly, he goes to a deserted summer resort in the dead of winter. However, Baldpate Inn has become a rendezvous for thieves, and the hero's life is soon in danger. In the epilogue, we discover the harrassed author at his typewriter: everything portrayed has been his story! One of the most ingenious and entertaining melodramas of the American theatre. P: Cohan and Harris. D: Cohan. R: (5/27/35, National, 8) by The Players for a limited engagement. C: George M. Cohan, Walter Hampden, Otis Skinner, Josephine Hull, Irene Rich, Zita Johann, James Kirkwood, James T. Powers, Ruth Weston, Edward McNamara, Ernest Glendinning. D: Sam Forrest.

SV: RKO, 1929, Richard Dix; 1935, Gene Raymond; 1947, Philip Terry.

Seven Year Itch, The (11/20/52, Fulton, 1,141)

George Axelrod's comedy hit about a publishing executive (Tom Ewell) who starts thinking like a bachelor when his wife goes on a summer vacation. Before the evening ends, this Walter Mitty-like daydreamer almost succumbs to the charms of a sexy neighbor—until he contemplates the possible consequences of infidelity. ". . . delightful nonsense" (*News*). C: Vanessa Brown, Neva Patterson, Robert Emhardt. P: Courtney Burr and Elliott Nugent. D: John Gerstad. M: Dana Suesse. SD: Frederick Fox.

SV: Fox, 1955, Marilyn Monroe, Tom Ewell, Evelyn Keyes, Sonny Tufts, Victor Moore, Oscar Homolka, Carolyn Jones, Doro Merande (directed by Billy Wilder).

Seventeen (1/22/18, Booth, 225)

Smitten by the charms of baby-talking Lola Pratt (Ruth Gordon), Willie Baxter (Gregory Kelly) "borrows" his father's dress suit to impress his teenage lady love and gets into more trouble than he bargained for. Quaintly amusing puppy love comedy with Miss Gordon uproarious as the heartless flirt who drives all the boys wild. C: Paul Kelly, Lillian Roth, Morgan Farley, George Gaul. A: Adapted from Booth Tarkington's novel by Hugh Stanislaus Stange and Stannard Mears. P/D: Stuart Walker. Musicalized by William Kernell as *Hello, Lola* (1926) with Edythe Baker, Richard Keene, Elisha Cook, Jr., Jay C. Flippen; musicalized by Walter Kent as *Seventeen* (1951) with Kenneth Nelson, Ann Crowley, Frank Albertson, Doris Dalton, Dick Kallman.

SV: Par, 1940, Jackie Cooper, Betty Field, Peter Lind Hayes, Otto Kruger, Ann Shoemaker.

Seventh Heaven (10/30/22, Booth, 683)

An itinerant sewer cleaner named Chico rescues a timorous street waif named Diane from the clutches of her absinthe-soaked harpy of a sister. Diane waits patiently for Chico to return from the war so that their marriage may be consummated. When he finally does return, he is both blinded and shell-shocked. At the final curtain, the young lovers are tearfully reunited. This maudlin melodrama laid in Paris was one of the biggest hits of the 1920's, chalking up a run of 683 Broadway performances before it took to the road. Most showmen concurred that the script didn't stand a chance. Among the producers, directors, and stars who originally spurned this soggy saga were Arthur Hopkins, Edgar Selwyn, Earl Carroll, Winchell Smith, Robert Milton, Thomas Meighan, William Gillette, Douglas Fairbanks, and Lionel Barrymore. C: Helen Menken, George Gaul, Frank Morgan. A: Austin Strong. P/D: John Golden.

Musicalized by Victor Young (1955) with Gloria DeHaven, Ricardo Montalban, Beatrice Arthur, Kurt Kasznar, Robert Clary, Scott Merrill, Chita Rivera.

SV: Fox, 1937, Simone Simon, James Stewart, Gale Sondergaard, Jean Hersholt, Gregory Ratoff.

Note: Like many other remakes, this 1937 production was deemed far inferior to Fox's 1927 Janet Gaynor-Charles Farrell silent screen version.

Sex (4/26/26, Daly's, 375)

Margie LaMont (Mae West), a torrid trollop who follows the fleet, finally wins the navy lieutenant of her choice. This 1920's example of *dramaticus erotica* was penned by Miss West under the pseudonym of "Jane Mast." The show dismayed critics, outraged bluenoses, and delighted ticket scalpers. Well-heeled civilians paid as much as fifty dollars apiece for orchestra seats, while raftloads of cheering sailors packed the galleries. Many newspapers would not accept ads for the production, so placards and posters with the one word "SEX" flooded New York. Inevitably, the play was raided and Miss West sentenced to ten days in the workhouse. Having sampled the heady wine of dramaturgy, however, it wasn't long before the high priestess of Eros was busy plotting new theatrical epics with which to conquer Broadway. P: C. W. Morganstern. D: Edward Elsner.

Sh! the Octopus (2/21/28, Royale, 47)

Murder in a deserted lighthouse. Low-grade mystery-farce. C: Clifford Dempsey, Harry Kelly. A: Ralph Murphy and Donald Gallaher (P/D).
SV: WB, 1937, Hugh Herbert, Allen Jenkins.

Shadow of Heroes (12/5/61, York, 20)

Provocative O/B drama dealing with the 1956 Hungarian revolt against the totalitarian people's republic. Written by Robert Ardrey, author of *Thunder Rock* (1939), *Jeb* (1946), etc. C: Muni Seroff, George Gaynes, Salome Jens, Frieda Altman, Peter Boyle. D: Warner Le Roy.
Note: Originally produced in London in 1958 with Emlyn Williams, Peggy Ashcroft, and Alan Webb in the leading roles.

Shadow of My Enemy, A (12/11/57, ANTA, 5)

Documentary-styled account of the Alger Hiss-Whittaker Chambers courtroom case. ". . . restates the obvious without adding to it anything of much significance" (*New York Times*). ". . . too flatly dramatized to make for a play with any creative dramatic distinction" (*Post*). C: Ed Begley, Gene Raymond, William Harrigan, John McGovern, Leon Janney. A: Sol Stein. P: Nick Mayo. D: Daniel Petrie. SD: Donald Oenslager.

Shame Woman, The (10/16/23, Greenwich Village, 295)

Mountain woman kills a philanderer to protect the reputation of her adopted daughter, then calmly goes to the gallows for her crime. Interesting O/B production of regional drama by Lula Vollmer. C: Florence Rittenhouse, Minnie Dupree. P: The Independent Theatre, Inc.

Shanghai Gesture, The (2/1/26, Martin Beck, 331)

Mother Goddam, wealthy owner of a Chinese whorehouse, is obsessed with a desire for revenge against Sir Guy Charteris, the white man who wronged her most grievously some twenty years earlier. She invites Charteris to dinner and then forces him to witness the sale of their illegitimate daughter into prostitution. Learning that the girl has become a dope fiend, nymphomaniac, and degenerate, the Oriental tigress solves matters by strangling her to death. "A pâté of box-office drivel" (George Jean Nathan). C: McKay Morris, Mary Duncan, C. Henry Gordon, Cyril Keightley. P: A. H. Woods. This lurid tale of vice in the Orient was probably the definitive 20's *camp* melodrama. It was written by John Colton, co-author of *Rain* (1922), as a comeback vehicle for Belasco star, Mrs. Leslie Carter. Following the disastrous Newark and Atlantic City tryouts, director Guthrie McClintic insisted on replacing the red-headed sixty-four-year-old actress, and Florence Reed was summoned to play what was to become her most famous role. Miss Reed's celebrated second act "I survived" speech remains to this day one of the great stage moments of twentieth-century theatregoing.
SV: UA, 1941, Walter Huston, Gene Tierney, Victor Mature, Ona Munson, Maria Ouspenskaya, Albert Basserman, Eric Blore, Phyllis Brooks, Leonid Kinsky, Marcel Dalio (directed by Josef von Sternberg.)

Shannons of Broadway, The (9/26/27, Martin Beck, 288)

Amiable 20's comedy about two troupers, played by James Gleason (A) and Lucille Webster (Mrs. Gleason), who opt for the bucolic life in New England. P: Gaige and Boothe. D: Paul Dickey.

SV: U, 1929, James and Lucile Gleason; U, 1938, *Goodbye, Broadway,* Charles Winninger, Alice Brady, Tom Brown.

Shavings (2/16/20, Knickerbocker, 122)

The tranquil life of a bachelor (Harry Beresford) is shattered when a widow (Clara Moores) and her young daughter (Lillian Roth) rent a nearby summer cottage. Humdrum comedy based on Joseph C. Lincoln's novel. A: Pauline Phelps and Marion Short. P: Henry W. Savage.

She Couldn't Say No (8/31/26, Booth, 72)

Go-getting secretary successfully pleads breach-of-promise suit for her lawyer-boss. Anemic 20's farce. C: Florence Moore, Ralph Kellard. A: B. M. Kaye. P: A. and R. Riskin. D: Rollo Lloyd.

SV: WB, 1930, Winnie Lightner, Chester Morris, Sally Eilers; 1940, Eve Arden, Roger Pryor, Cliff Edwards.

She Got What She Wanted (3/4/29, Wallack's, 118)

Amorous landlady has designs on her male boarders. Leering sex comedy with a no-name cast. A: George Rosener. P: George Wintz. D: Edward Elsner.

She Had to Know (2/2/25, Times Square, 81)

After ten years of marriage, a neglected wife (Grace George) tests her wiles on a couple of her husband's friends. Frothy bedroom comedy, adapted by Miss George from a play by Paul Geraldy. D: John Cromwell.

She Loves Me Not (11/20/33, 46th Street, 367)

A couple of Princeton youths (Burgess Meredith and John Beal) gallantly try to conceal a scantily clad, gangster-fleeing chorus girl (Polly Walters) in their dormitory room. Rollicking 30's farce benefitted from a robust comedic performance by Burgess Meredith, a clever double-deck setting designed by Raymond Sovey, and a lively satirical script by Howard Lindsay (D) b/o a novel by Edward Hope. Also on the plus side were a couple of pleasant incidental musical numbers ("After All, You're All I'm After" and the title song) by Arthur Schwartz and Edward Heyman, agreeably crooned (and subsequently recorded) by leading man John Beal. C: Philip Ober, Florence Rice. P: Wiman and Weatherly.

SV: Par, 1934, Bing Crosby, Miriam Hopkins, Kitty Carlisle, Henry Stephenson; 1942, *True to the Army,* Allan Jones, Ann Miller, Judy Canova, Jerry Colonna; Fox, 1955, *How to Be Very, Very Popular,* Betty Grable, Robert Cummings, Charles Coburn, Sheree North, Fred Clark, Orson Bean.

She Means Business (1/26/31, Ritz, 8)

Enterprising wife saves her philandering husband's business. Banal farce-comedy by Samuel Shipman. C: Ann Davis, Ernest Glendinning, Wallis Clark, Ruth Donnelly. P: James Elliott. D: Frederick Stanhope.

SV: WB, 1932, *Manhattan Parade,* Winnie Lightner, Charles Butterworth, Smith and Dale.

Sheep on the Runway (1/31/70, Helen Hayes, 105)

Columnist Art Buchwald's first play is a satirical farce about American foreign policy going awry in a mythical asian country. A Red-hunting Washington journalist, the harassed, idiotic American ambassador, and the plumply amiable prince of the country tangle with bombs, palace revolutions, Pentagon intrusions, and rumored Communist invasions. All concerned are targets for the playwright's mordant insights and mocking humor. Though the critics had reservations about the play's construction, it was generally liked, and Martin Gabel as the hawkish newspaperman, David Burns as the ambassador, and Richard Castellano as the prince were applauded. Special praise went to Barnard Hughes as an absurd Pentagon general. A: Art Buchwald. C: David Burns, Elizabeth Wilson, Martin Gabel, Richard Castellano, Barnard Hughes, Remak Ramsay, Will Mackenzie, Neil Flanagan, Jeremiah Morris, Margaret Ladd, Kurt Garfield, Henry Proach. P: Rogert L. Stevens, Robert Whitehead and Robert W. Dowling. D: Gene Saks. SD: Peter Larkin. CD: Jane Greenwood.

Shelf, The (9/27/26, Morosco, 32)

Tiresome comedy-drama about a middle-aged woman who decides to have one last fling. C: Frances Starr, Arthur Byron, Thelma Ritter (deb.), Donald Meek, Lee Patrick, Jessie Ralph. A: Dorrance Davis. P/D: William B. Friedlander.

Sherlock Holmes (10/30/53, Century, 3)

Unwieldy pastiche of various Conan Doyle stories, with Basil Rathbone as the celebrated Baker Street sleuth and Thomas Gomez as his archenemy. Professor Moriarty. "Cumbersome and uneven . . . both the play and the performance lack a point of view" *(New York Times).* C: Jarmila Novotna, Jack Raine, Terence Kilburn, Chester Stratton, Eileen Peel, Elwyn Harvey, Mary Orr. A: Ouida (Mrs. Basil) Rathbone. P: Bill Doll. D: Reginald Denham. CD/SD: Stewart Chaney.

Ship Comes In, A (9/19/34, Morosco, 37)

Psychologist (Jacob Ben-Ami) turns out to be more neurotic than any of his patients. Flat Freudian fable written by noted psychiatrist Joseph Anthony. P: Richard Herndon i.a.w. J. C. Mayer. D: Augustin Duncan.

Shooting Star (6/12/33, Selwyn, 16)

The rise and fall of a tempestuous, alcoholic, drug-addicted actress. Elaborate but lethargic backstage drama, suggested by the life of Jeanne Eagels. C: Francine Larrimore, George Houston, Lee Patrick, Cora Witherspoon. A: Noel Pierce and Bernard C. Schoenfeld. P: Gaige and Nash. D: Bela Blau.

Shore Leave (8/8/22, Lyceum, 152)

A shy New England spinster (Frances Starr) sets her cap for Bilge Smith (James Rennie), a salty, woman-chasing gob. By the end of the play, she tames him and hooks him. Fairly entertaining David Belasco (P/D) comedy. A: Hubert Osborne. Musicalized by Vincent Youmans as *Hit the Deck* (1927) with Charles King, Louise Groody, Brian Donlevy.

SV: *Shore Leave* has seen yeoman service on the screen in several different incarnations. The best screen version was RKO's *Follow the Fleet* (1936) with an Irving Berlin score and a cast which included Fred Astaire, Ginger Rogers, Randolph Scott, Harriet Hilliard, Astrid Allwyn, Betty Grable, Lucille Ball, and Tony Martin. *Hit the Deck* by Youmans has been filmed twice, by RKO (1930) with Jack Oakie and Polly Walker, and by MGM (1955) with Tony Martin, Jane Powell, Debbie Reynolds, Vic Damone, Walter Pidgeon, Ann Miller, Gene Raymond, Russ Tamblyn, Kay Armen, J. Carrol Naish, Richard Anderson, and Jane Darwell.

Shot in the Dark, A (10/18/61, Booth, 389)

A saucy Parisian parlor maid (Julie Harris) is accused of killing her lover. The police examiner (William Shatner) is so impressed by the girl's candor concerning her affairs—not only with her lover, but also with her formidably aristocratic employer (Walter Matthau)*—that he decides she is not the guilty party. When the examiner uncovers the real murderer, the grateful gamine offers herself to him as a reward for saving her life. "A droll, dry and engaging murder mystery" *(Herald Tribune)*. C: Gene Saks, Diana van der Vlis, Louise Troy, Hugh Franklin, Pierre Epstein. A: Harry Kurnitz b/o a play by Marcel Achard. P: Leland Hayward. D: Harold Clurman. SD: Ben Edwards.

SV: UA, 1964, Peter Sellers, Elke Sommer, George Sanders, Herbert Lom (directed by Blake Edwards from a screenplay by Mr. Edwards and William Peter Blatty).

---

*Mr. Matthau replaced Donald Cook, who died during the pre-Broadway tryout of this 1961 comedy-mystery.

The Show Shop. **Douglas Fairbanks and George Sidney (December 31, 1914).** *Courtesy Museum of the City of New York Theatre and Music Collection.*

Shout From the Rooftops (10/28/64, Renata, 15)

Freudian-slanted O/B drama centering on the problems of a frigid wife. Absorbing, well-written play by novelist Jess Gregg. C: Grayson Hall, Susan Towers, Jerome Guardino. P/D: Tom Millott.

Show Shop, The (12/31/14, Hudson, 156)

Stage-struck girl agrees to marry boy if her show fails. Unfortunately, "Dora's Dilemma," a sure flop, turns out to be a big Broadway hit. Highly amusing backstage comedy by James Forbes (A/D). C: Douglas Fairbanks, Patricia Collinge, Ned Sparks, Zelda Sears, George Sidney. P: Selwyn and Company.

Show-Off, The (2/5/24, Playhouse, 571)

Though he is only a humble freight clerk, braggart Aubrey Piper is one of the world's worst show-offs. Bent on acquiring easy wealth, Aubrey makes many blunders but always manages to rationalize them, much to the disgust of his sharpspoken mother-in-law. In the end, through a fluke, Aubrey becomes the hero of the hour. Despite his obnoxious traits, he finally enlists our sympathy. We have become fascinated by the egoism and nerve of this brash, middle-class opportunist. "The best comedy which has yet been written by an American" (Heywood Broun, *World*). C: Louis John Bartels, Helen Lowell, Juliette Crosby, Lee Tracy, Regina Wallace. A/D: George Kelly. P: Stewart and French. *The Show-Off* was voted best play of the year by the Pulitzer Prize jury, but Columbia University's trustees diverted the award to Professor Hatcher Hughes' *Hell-Bent fer Heaven,* whereupon, according to critic Burns Mantle, "there was threatened rioting in the streets and several of the more emotional drama critics grew hysterical in protest." Author

George Kelly did win the Pulitzer Prize (1925–26), however, with his next play, *Craig's Wife* (1925). *The Show-Off* has been frequently revived. Following are the most notable N.Y. revivals:

R: (12/12/32, Hudson, 103) by Leventhal and Wee. C: Raymond Walburn (D), Jean Adair. R: (5/31/50, Arena, 6) by Heilweil and Thomas. C: Lee Tracy, Jane Seymour. D: Martin Manulis. R: (12/5/67, Lyceum, 69) by APA Repertory. C: Clayton Corzatte, Helen Hayes.

SV: Par, 1929, *Men Are Like That,* Hal Skelly; MGM, 1934, Spencer Tracy, Madge Evans; MGM, 1946, Red Skelton, Marilyn Maxwell.

Shrike, The (1/15/52, Cort, 161)

Despondent over his inability to get a job in the theatre, Jim Downs takes an overdose of sleeping pills and lands in the psychiatric ward of a public hospital. He soon discovers that his estranged wife is taking advantage of her legal status to keep him institutionalized. As the price of his release from the hospital she demands his return to her. Caught helpless in her snare, Jim is forced to renounce the girl he really loves and allow himself to be "paroled" in the custody of his predatory spouse. "A relentless, bitter and clinical piece of stage work" *(Herald Tribune).* This psychological melodrama, splendidly acted by Jose Ferrer (P/D) as the hounded husband and Judith Evelyn as the evil wife, was awarded the Pulitzer Prize as the best play of the year. *The Shrike* was written by Joseph Kramm; the set design was by Howard Bay.

SV: U, 1955, Jose Ferrer, June Allyson (directed by Jose Ferrer).

Note: The shrike is a predatory bird that murders other birds wantonly and impales its prey on thorns.

Sick-A-Bed (2/25/18, Gaiety, 80)

To avoid the witness chair in a divorce suit, a man feigns illness. Before you can say "A Farce in Three Acts," the malingerer's bedroom is crowded with quack physicians, attractive nurses, maids and valets, lawyers, friends and relatives. "Rather obvious but . . . highly laughable [with] a number of hilarious moments" *(New York Times).* C: Mary Boland, Edwin Nicander. A: Ethel Watts Mumford. P: Klaw and Erlanger. D: Edgar MacGregor.

Siege (12/8/37, Longacre, 6)

Unsuccessful Irwin Shaw melodrama about a group of Loyalists trapped in an ancient mountain fortress during the early days of the Spanish Civil War. ". . . has no form, no style and no point of view" *(New York Times). Siege* closed after six performances. C: Sheldon Leonard, Rose Hobart, Abner Biberman. P/SD: Norman Bel Geddes. D: Chester Erskine.

Sign in Sidney Brustein's Window, The (10/15/64, Longacre, 101)

The efforts of an idealistic Greenwich Village intellectual to save his faltering marriage, and also to do battle against the establishment and get a reform candidate elected to office. This eagerly awaited second play by Lorraine Hansberry* received mixed notices from the critics. Richard Watts, Jr. *(Post)* summed up the majority opinion: ". . . has scenes of power and insight, and it is written with forthright integrity, but it suffers seriously from . . . its cluttered top-heaviness of approach." C: Gabriel Dell, Rita Moreno, Alice Ghostley, Dolph Sweet. P: D'Lugoff, Nemiroff, and Jahre. D: Peter Kass.

---

*Miss Hansberry wrote *A Raisin in the Sun* (1959), which won the New York Drama Critics Circle Award as best play of the year. The gifted black authoress died of cancer in 1965 at age thirty-five.

Sign on the Door, The (12/19/19, Republic, 187)

Husband accidentally kills wife's

paramour; she is accused of the crime. Passable melodrama by Channing Pollock. C: Lowell Sherman, Mary Ryan, Lee Baker. P: A. H. Woods.

SV: UA, 1930, *The Locked Door,* Barbara Stanwyck, Rod La Rocque, Betty Bronson.

Signature! (2/14/45, Forrest, 2)

A crafty judge is unmasked as a murderer. Period melodrama (Virginia, 1856) was written by Elizabeth McFadden, author of *Double Door* (1933). ". . . diffuse and old-fashioned" *(Sun).* C: Frederic Tozere, Donald Murphy, Marjorie Lord, Anne Jackson (deb.). P: Skinner and Willard. D: Roy Hargrave.

Silence (11/12/24, National, 199)

An accused murderer (H. B. Warner) remains silent in an attempt to save his daughter from blackmail and scandal. His silence almost leads him to the electric chair. Effective melodrama by Max Marcin (A/D). P: Crosby Gaige.

SV: Par, 1931, Clive Brook, Marjorie Rambeau.

Silent Night, Lonely Night (12/3/59, Morosco, 124)

Drama by Robert Anderson, author of *Tea and Sympathy* (1953), about two lonely people (Henry Fonda and Barbara Bel Geddes) who find love in a New England inn on Christmas Eve. One reviewer described the play as "uneventful and excessively verbose," while another dubbed the offering *Tea and Apathy.* C: Lois Nettleton, Bill Berger, Eda Heinemann, Peter de Vise. P: The Playwrights Company. D: Peter Glenville. SD: Jo Mielziner.

Silver Cord, The (12/20/26, John Golden, 130)

Sidney Howard's classic psychological study of inverted mother love. A poisonously possessive matriarch (Laura Hope Crews) totally dominates the lives of her two sons, subverts the engagement of one, and nearly wrecks the marriage of the other. "A notable play" (Stark Young, *The New Republic*). "One of the most satisfactory evenings I have ever spent in a theatre" (Percy Hammond, *Herald Tribune*). C: Margalo Gillmore, Earle Larimore, Eliot Cabot, Elizabeth Risdon. P: The Theatre Guild. D: John Cromwell.

SV: RKO, 1933, Irene Dunne, Joel McCrea, Laura Hope Crews.

Silver Whistle, The (11/24/48, Biltmore, 219)

A jaunty hobo (Jose Ferrer) invades an old folks home and gives the inmates a new zest for life. "An engaging fable about a modern Cyrano . . . an amusing, disarming and oddly endearing little comedy . . . Mr. Ferrer makes it live and sing" *(Post).* C: Doro Merande, William Lynn, Frances Brandt, George Mathews, Robert Carroll, Eleanor Wilson, Kathleen Comegys, Burton Mallory, Jane Marbury. A: Robert McEnroe. P: The Theatre Guild. D: Paul Crabtree (with an uncredited assist from Joshua Logan). SD: Herbert Brodkin.

SV: Fox, 1951, *Mr. Belvedere Rings the Bell,* Clifton Webb, Zero Mostel, Joanne Dru, Hugh Marlowe, Doro Merande, William Lynn.

Sin of Pat Muldoon, The (3/13/57, Cort, 5)

Lugubrious tale of an Irish-American family's efforts to bring their dying father back into the Church. ". . . an excessively sentimental and appallingly disjointed fabrication" *(News).* C: James Barton, Elaine Stritch, James Olson. A: John McLiam. P: Richard Adler and Roger L. Stevens. D: Jack Garfein. SD: Mordecai Gorelik.

Sing High, Sing Low (11/12/31, Harris, 70)

Frothy satire on backstage snipings and scandals in the opera world. Fair production values, nondescript cast. A: Murdock Pemberton and David Boehm. P: Walker Towne. D: Clarence Derwent.

Sing Me No Lullaby (10/14/54, Phoenix, 30)

Persecuted because of his former leftist leanings, a blacklisted mathematician decides to flee to Russia. Though he now despises communism, the moral climate of America has left him no other choice, he feels, but to seek sanctuary in the USSR. This 1954 problem play, set within the framework of a college reunion, was written by Robert Ardrey. "Some of the fuzziest rhetoric and least lifelike characters in recent socio-dramatic history.... The trouble with *Sing Me No Lullaby* is that it is a serious comic strip, and there is no such thing" (*Herald Tribune*). C: Jack Warden, Richard Kiley, Jessie Royce Landis, Beatrice Straight, Larry Gates, John Marley, Marian Winters, John Fiedler, Michael Lipton. P: Phoenix Theatre. D: Paul Stewart.

Sing Till Tomorrow (12/28/53, Royale, 8)

Incoherent saga about a Philadelphia druggist whose second wife falls in love with his son. "Solemn gibberish" (*New York Times*). "A new low in contemporary drama" (*World-Telegram*). A: Jean Lowenthal. P: Dorothy Natter. D: Basil Langton.

Singapore (11/14/32, 48th Street, 24)

Evil spouse employs trained cobras to kill her unsuspecting husband. Wild-eyed melodrama by actor Robert Keith. C: Donald Woods, Louise Prussing, Frank De Silva. P: John Henry Mears. D: Lee Elmore.

Singing Jailbirds (12/6/28, Provincetown, 79)

Upton Sinclair's expressionistic drama dealing with the fate of an I.W.W. organizer in solitary confinement. Shut up in a black hole, and fed on bread and water to break his spirit, this militant migrant suffers hallucinations, loses his reason, and finally dies. "... primarily propaganda and not play" (*New York Times*). C: Grover Burgess, Lionel Stander. D: Em Jo Basshe.

Note: Socialist author Upton Sinclair is best known for his novel, *The Jungle* (1906), and his "Lanny Budd" political adventure stories.

Sinner (2/7/27, Klaw, 129)

Anemic variation on *The Taming of the Shrew;* wispy comedy tried hard to be sophisticated, didn't make it. C: Alan Dinehart (D), Claiborne Foster, Raymond Walburn, Merle Maddern, Vera Allen. A: Thompson Buchanan. P: Richard Herndon.

Sinners (1/7/15, Playhouse, 220)

Pretty girl (Alice Brady) returns to New Hampshire from the wicked city, tries to keep the details of her sordid past from her invalid mother (Emma Dunn). "An old-fashioned, unblushingly sentimental melodrama by the indefatigable Owen Davis" (*New York Times*). C: Florence Nash, John Cromwell, Robert Edeson, Charles Richman. P: William A. Brady. D: John Cromwell.

6 Rms Riv Vu (10/17/72, Helen Hayes, 247)

A warm and charming comedy about two strangers (Jerry Orbach, Jane Alexander) accidentally locked in a vacant apartment each is considering renting. Past first youth, both have well-established marriages. He's a copywriter, she's the wife of an architect. Neither is unhappy, yet neither is beyond a mild flirtation. But morally conservative, products of a less permissive era, they tiptoe around the mutual attraction engendered by their forced confinement. When they surrender to each other it is not passion but the spirit of gentle adventure that motivates them. The second act introduces their respective mates (Jennifer Warren and Ron Harper). They prove such likable people that when the lovers decide they won't see each other again, the decision is far from tragic. A pregnant woman gets the apartment, everyone goes home with his own spouse, and all ends happily. There is no more plot than that, and no more is needed. A moment in the lives of mature, ingratiating people has been observed with humor and understanding, a signal achievement for author Bob Randall, whose first full-length play this was. His accomplishment was enhanced by a polished production, director and principals winning praise, and Jennifer Warren receiving a Theater World Award for most promising new performer. (The play's title is ad jargon for "six rooms, river view.") A: Bob Randall. C: Jerry Orbach, Jane Alexander, Ron Harper, Jennifer Warren, Jose Ocasio, Francine Beers, Anna Shaler, F. Murray Abraham. P: Alexander H. Cohen and Bernard Delfont. D: Edwin Sherin. SD: William Ritman.

Six-Cylinder Love (8/25/21, Sam H. Harris, 430)

A pair of newlywed suburbanites live beyond their means because of the wife's passion for automobiles. Amiable farce-comedy by William Anthony McGuire. C: Ernest Truex, June Walker, Berton Churchill, Hedda Hopper, Donald Meek. P: Sam H. Harris. D: Sam Forrest.
SV: Fox, 1931, Spencer Tracy, Una Merkel, Sidney Fox, Edward Everett Horton, William Collier, El Brendel, Florence Eldridge; 1939, *The Honeymoon's Over,* Stuart Erwin, Marjorie Weaver, Jack Carson.

Sixth Finger in a Five Finger Glove (10/8/56, Longacre, 2)

Comedy about a "swap shop" proprietor who discovers he owns title to the town where he lives and works. ". . . all thumbs . . . stupefyingly naive . . ." (*New York Times*). C: Jimmie Komack, Salome Jens, Frank Campanella, Conrad Bain. A: Scott Michel. P: Caplin and Fingar. D: John Holden. SD: Paul Morrison. M: Charles Strouse.

Skidding (5/21/28, Bijou, 469)

Judge Hardy and his "typical American family" involved in various domestic problems in the fictitious town of Carvel, Idaho. This 1928 comedy provided the basis for the popular *Andy Hardy* film series. "Just passable is the highest rating it deserves" (*New York Times*). C: Carleton Macy, Charles Eaton, Marguerite Churchill, Walter Abel, Clara Blandick, Louise Carter. A: Aurania Rouverol. P: Hyman Adler and Marion Gering (D).
SV: MGM, 1937, *A Family Affair,* Lionel Barrymore, Mickey Rooney, Spring Byington, Cecilia Parker, Julie Haydon, Eric Linden, Sara Haden, Charley Grapewin.
Note: This was the first of fifteen Hardy family films made by MGM during a ten-year period (1937–1947). Commencing with the second film in the series, *You're Only Young Once* (1938), Lewis Stone and Fay Holden replaced Lionel Barrymore and Spring Byington as Judge Hardy and wife.

Skin Deep (10/17/27, Liberty, 8)

Strained comedy about a wife (Chrystal Herne) who cures her husband (Reginald Owen) of philandering by encouraging his flirtations. C: Spring Byington, Frances Goodrich, Guido Nadzo. A: Lynn Starling. P: M. J. Nicholas. D: Bertram Harrison.

The Skin of Our Teeth. **Florence Eldridge, Frances Heflin, Fredric March, and Tallulah Bankhead (1942–43).** *Courtesy Museum of the City of New York Theatre and Music Collection.*

Skin of Our Teeth, The (11/18/42, Plymouth, 355)

Thornton Wilder's seriocomic tribute to the indestructibility of the human race. The play traces the lives of Mr. and Mrs. Antrobus (Fredric March and Florence Eldridge), their son (Montgomery Clift), daughter (Frances Heflin), and servant Sabina (Tallulah Bankhead) from the dawn of history to the present. A New Jersey couple, Mr. and Mrs. Antrobus have been married five thousand years. Through pestilence, flood, and war, these durable optimists manage again and again to survive by the skin of their teeth. Jumbling time and space, this Pulitzer Prize-winning comedy abounds in deliberate anachronisms. (At one point a baby dinosaur seeks shelter from the Ice Age in the Antrobus living room while a Western Union messenger delivers a singing telegram.) These and other such nonrealistic touches disconcerted the literal-minded, but delighted the cognoscenti. Alexander Woollcott, for example, thought *The Skin of Our Teeth* was the finest play ever written by an American. Other reviewers dubbed it "a wacky extravaganza," "a zany mixture of *Hellzapoppin* and *Finnegans Wake,*" "a comically mad allegory." A spectacular Broadway success, *The Skin of Our Teeth* benefitted from inspired casting and acting, notably by Tallulah Bankhead as the eternal temptress, Sabina. It also had the advantage of novel, imaginative staging by Elia Kazan in his first major directorial assignment. Kazan would later direct such notable plays as *A Streetcar Named Desire* and *Death of a Salesman,* but *The*

Skin of Our Teeth was the production that opened the door for him. C: Florence Reed, E. G. Marshall, Lizabeth Scott (deb.), Dickie Van Patten, Remo Bufano, Stanley Prager, Morton Da Costa. P: Michael Myerberg. CD: Mary Percy Schenck. SD: Albert Johnson.

R: (8/17/55, ANTA, 22) by Robert Whitehead. C: Helen Hayes, Mary Martin, George Abbott, Florence Reed, Don Murray, Heller Halliday, Frank Silvera. D: Alan Schneider.

Note: It was Helen Hayes who suggested that Tallulah Bankhead play Sabina. (Thornton Wilder had envisioned Miss Hayes, Ruth Gordon, or Fanny Brice in the part.) Miss Bankhead was later succeeded in the role by Miriam Hopkins and Gladys George.

Skydrift (11/13/45, Belasco, 7)

Paratroopers killed in action return to Earth to seek communion with their loved ones. ". . . as great a bore as it is a botch" (*PM*). C: Alfred Ryder, Olive Deering, Eli Wallach, Paul Crabtree. A: Harry Kleiner. P: Rita Hassan. D: Roy Hargrave.

Skylark (10/11/39, Morosco, 256)

On her tenth wedding anniversary, a neglected wife (Gertrude Lawrence) toys with the idea of leaving her husband (Donald Cook) for a fling with a family friend (Glenn Anders). ". . . an unoriginal and highly mechanical work. . . . Few plays of recent seasons have owed more to their star" (*Herald Tribune*). George S. Kaufman's opinion: "A bad play saved by a bad performance." C: Vivian Vance, Robert Burton, Walter Gilbert. A/D: Samson Raphaelson. P: John Golden.

SV: Par, 1941, Claudette Colbert, Ray Milland, Brian Aherne, Binnie Barnes, Walter Abel, Ernest Cossart, Grant Mitchell.

Skyrocket (1/11/29, Lyceum, 11)

A conceited young businessman-inventor (Humphrey Bogart) strikes it rich with unhappy consequences. Only when he loses his fortune does he come to appreciate his loyal wife (Mary Philips)* and down-to-earth father (J. C. Nugent). Tepid comedy-drama by Mark Reed. P: Gilbert Miller i.a.w. Guthrie McClintic (D).

---

*Married Bogart in 1928. The marriage lasted nine years.

Sky's the Limit, The (12/17/34, Fulton, 24)

(Joe) Smith and (Charles) Dale in a spoof of the advertising and broadcasting business. Few laughs despite the strenuous efforts of the two vaudeville headliners. C: Don Beddoe, Ruth Altman, Martin Gabel. A: Pierce Johns and Hendrik Booraem. P: Raymond Golden. D: Sidney Salkow.

Sleep, My Pretty One (11/2/44, Playhouse, 4)

A paralytic mother (Pauline Lord) resorts to murder to keep her bachelor son (Harry Ellerbe) from marrying. ". . . lacking in credibility, excitement and suspense" (*Sun*). A: Charlcie and Oliver Garrett.* P: Richard W. Krakeur i.a.w. Roger Clark. D: Roy Hargrave.

---

*Oliver Garrett's screenplays include *Manhattan Melodrama, Night Flight,* and *The Man I Married.*

Sleep No More (8/31/44, Cort, 7)

Promoter (Robert Armstrong) acquires a pill that makes sleep unnecessary. Dreary farce, full of yawns. A: Lee Loeb and Arthur Strawn. P: Clyde Elliott. D: Cledge Roberts.

Sleepless Night, A (2/18/19, Bijou, 71)

Flimsy mistaken identity farce with an

interesting cast: Peggy Hopkins Joyce, Lucile Watson, Ernest Glendinning, Carlotta Monterey, William Morris, Donald Gallaher. A: Jack Larrie and Gustav Blum. P: Messrs. Shubert. D: Oscar Eagle.

Slight Case of Murder, A (9/11/35, 48th Street, 70)

Just when he plans to turn "legitimate," ex-racketeer Remy Marco returns to his Saratoga home to find the bullet-riddled bodies of four gangsters on his premises. How Remy and his henchmen dispose of the corpses—and then round them up again to collect a reward—furnished most of the fun in this daffy comedy by Damon Runyon and Howard Lindsay (P/D). Jose Ferrer made his Broadway debut in this raffish 1935 offering. He played a young cop and he had one line: "What's going on here?" C: John Harrington, Georgia Caine, Phyllis Welch, Joseph Sweeney.
SV: WB, 1938, Edward G. Robinson, Allen Jenkins, Ruth Donnelly, Jane Bryan, Willard Parker, John Litel, Edward Brophy, Harold Huber, Bobby Jordan, Margaret Hamilton; 1953, *Stop, You're Killing Me*, Broderick Crawford, Claire Trevor, Sheldon Leonard, Margaret Dumont.

Slightly Married (10/25/43, Cort, 8)

Fortyish mother pretends it is she who is going to have her unwed daughter's baby. ". . . not only humorless, mechanical, improbable and dull but also, essentially, revolting" (*World-Telegram*). C: Leona Maricle, Leon Ames, Mona Barrie, Scotty Beckett. A: Aleen Leslie. P/D: Melville Burke.

Slightly Scandalous (6/13/44, National, 7)

Now that her children (each illegitimately sired of a different father) are grown and seeking respectable marriages, a mother (Janet Beecher) decides she had best get married herself. With this in mind, she invites the three fathers for a visit. However, when the children can't agree which father to select, mother decides to continue pretending they are the offspring of a fictitious parent. ". . . a feeble theatrical jape" (*Herald Tribune*). P: Charles Leonard i.a.w. Thomas McQuillan. Frederick Jackson (A/D) based *Slightly Scandalous* on a play by Roland Bottomley (also starring Miss Beecher) that never got to Broadway. Eventually, after being translated into French and retranslated back into English, this durable trifle turned up again on Broadway as *Dear Charles* (1954). With Tallulah Bankhead in the leading role this time, *Dear Charles* chalked up a healthy run of 157 performances.

Slow Dance on the Killing Ground (11/30/64, Plymouth, 88)

A troubled girl and a black youth on the run from the law seek refuge from the world in a neighborhood candy store run by a refugee from Nazi Germany. Before the evening is over, the three oddly mismatched characters have exposed their inner fears, their self-deceptions, and their need for understanding and compassion. ". . . forceful and steadily arresting" (*Post*). "What begins as a melodrama eventually becomes a disquisitory debate, a sex comedy, and a soap opera; each of the three acts seems totally independent of the other two" (*New Republic*). This three-character play marked the Broadway debut of dramatist William Hanley. C: George Rose, Clarence Williams III, Carolan Daniels. P: Cronyn-Allen-Hodgdon-Stevens-Bonfils-Seawell. D: Joseph Anthony. SD: Oliver Smith.

Small Craft Warnings (4/2/72, Truck and Warehouse Theater, 200)

O/B drama of a group of losers gathered together in a second-rate bar. Hardly original, but in the hands of Tennessee

Williams poetic, compassionate, and insightful. There is little plot. The characters are examined with tender respect by the author: strident, vulnerable Leona; her lover, Bill, a fading stud; an alcoholic doctor who's lost his license to practice medicine; two mismatched homosexuals; a pathetic hooker; and the bar proprietor. Each has his moment with a monologue that exposes the turmoil of the soul in Williams' unique language. The play rises to no dramatic heights. It is a series of character studies touched with genius. ". . . proof that the distinguished playwright hasn't lost his touch . . . his version of William Saroyan's *The Time of Your Life*" (Richard Watts, *New York Post*). ". . . warmed-over Williams . . . little or no conviction" (Douglas Watt, *New York Daily News*). Midway through the New York run, Tennessee Williams played the boozing doctor for two performances. A subsequent London production starring Elaine Stritch and Edward Judd was well received. A: Tennessee Williams. C: Helena Carroll, Brad Sullivan, David Hooks, Alan Mixon, David Huffman, Cherry Davis, Gene Fanning, William Hickey, John David Kees. D: Richard Altman. P: Ecco Productions.

Small Hours, The (2/15/51, National, 20)

Problems of a mousy wife who becomes convinced that her successful publisher-husband no longer needs her. ". . . random and artificial . . . a scattered and indecisive play" (*Herald Tribune*). This elaborately produced, multiscened drama by George S. Kaufman (D) and Leueen MacGrath was a quick Broadway failure. C: Dorothy Stickney, Paul McGrath, Polly Rowles, Joan Wetmore, Michael Wager. P: Max Gordon. SD: Donald Oenslager.

Small Miracle (9/26/34, Golden, 118)

Engrossing melodrama by Norman Krasna set in the lounge of a Broadway theatre during the performance of a play. Among the leading characters: an unfaithful wife (Ilka Chase), her lover (Edward Crandall), a convict (Joseph Calleia), an usher (Elspeth Eric), and the coatroom boy (Myron McCormick) who has gotten the pretty usher "in trouble" and must marry her—or else. Before the performance upstairs is over, the convict makes a break for freedom and is killed. The problems of the other characters are more tidily resolved. P: Courtney Burr. D: George Abbott.

SV: Par, 1935, *Four Hours to Kill*, Richard Barthelmess, Helen Mack, Joe Morrison, Ray Milland, Henry Travers.

Small Timers, The (1/27/25, Punch and Judy, 47)

Formula comedy about the problems of a pair of teenage vaudeville performers. C: Leslie John Cooley, Julie Barnard, Parker Fennelly. A: Knowles Entrikin. P: Art Theatre. D: Henry Stillman.

Small War on Murray Hill (1/3/57, Barrymore, 12)

Lord Howe (Leo Genn), commander of the British forces, fritters away his military advantage after the battle of Brooklyn Heights by dallying with Mrs. Mary Murray (Jan Sterling) on her husband's Manhattan farm, thereby allowing Generals Isaac Putnam and George Washington to escape almost certain defeat. Robert E. Sherwood's posthumous comedy, founded on a legendary American revolutionary war anecdote, received negative reviews and closed after a run of little more than a week. ". . . too reflective for light comedy, yet not nearly stimulating enough for a comedy of ideas" (*Time Magazine*). C: Daniel Massey (deb.), Stefan Schnabel, Nicholas Joy, Michael Lewis, Joseph Holland, Francis Compton, Patricia Bosworth, Jonelle Allen, Vinnette Carroll. P: The Playwrights Company. D: Garson Kanin. CD: Irene Sharaff. SD: Boris Aronson.

Smile of the World, The (1/12/49, Lyceum, 5)

Triangle drama by Garson Kanin (A/D) about a reactionary Supreme Court justice (Otto Kruger), his disillusioned wife (Ruth Gordon), and the idealistic young law clerk (Warren Stevens) with whom the wife falls in love. ". . . pretentious and static" (*New York Times*). C: Laura Pierpont, Ossie Davis, Ruby Dee. P: The Playwrights Company. SD: Donald Oenslager.

Smilin' Through (12/30/19, Broadhurst, 175)

A girl (Jane Cowl) falls in love with the son of a murderer. The ghost of her grandmother (also played by Miss Cowl) tries to interfere with this ill-starred romance. "The work treats of what a perfectly corking institution death is, anyway; according to the author, there is practically nothing to it—the idea is that we'd all go smilin' through the years, if we only knew what was coming to us in the end. . . . If all ghosts could only look like Miss Cowl, not a woman in the audience but would gladly pass on immediately" (Dorothy Parker, *Vanity Fair*). C: Orme Caldara, Henry Stephenson, Charlotte Granville, Philip Tonge. A: Allan Langdon Martin (pseud. for Jane Cowl and Jane Murfin). P: The Selwyns. D: Priestly Morrison.
Musicalized by Vincent Youmans as *Through the Years* (1932) with Natalie Hall, Michael Bartlett, Charles Winninger, Reginald Owen.
- SV: MGM, 1932, Norma Shearer, Fredric March, Leslie Howard; 1941, Jeanette MacDonald, Gene Raymond, Brian Aherne.
- Note: A silent version (WB, 1922) starred Norma Talmadge.

Snafu (10/25/44, Hudson, 156)

Reactions of a typical American family when their teenage son comes home from the war a hardened soldier; excellent performance by Billy (later William) Redfield in the leading role. "Snafu" (military slang meaning, in polite language, situation normal—all fouled up) proved a loosely constructed but amusing George Abbott (P/D) comedy. C: Russell Hardie, Enid Markey, Bethel Leslie, Patricia Kirkland. A: Louis Solomon and Harold Buchman.
- SV: Col, 1946, Robert Benchley, Vera Vague, Conrad Janis.

Snark Was a Boojum, The (9/1/43, 48th Street, 5)

Three expectant mothers huddled together in an old New England homestead, a raging blizzard, an eccentric's will, an escaped maniac prowling the premises—these were some of the stock ingredients of this wacky but witless mystery-comedy. The title, together with an interminable number of quotations, came from *Alice in Wonderland*. "Lousy with whimsy . . ." (*News*). C: Frank Lovejoy, Catherine Willard, Mervyn Nelson, Florence MacMichael. A: Owen Davis b/o a novel by Richard Shattuck. P: Alex Yokel i.a.w. Jay Faggen. D: Alexander Kirkland.

Snookie (6/3/41, Golden, 15)

Comic strip artist is suspected of being a test-tube father. "Hits an ultimate low in adult entertainment . . ." (*World-Telegram*). C: Eddie Nugent, Lawrence Weber, J. C. Nugent, Julie Stevens, William Harrigan. A: Thomas A. Johnstone. P: Olsen and Johnson. D: William B. Friedlander.

So Many Paths (12/6/34, Ritz, 28)

Hokey tale of a would-be opera star (Norma Terris) who sacrifices everything in pursuit of her career. C: George Blackwood, Matt Briggs, Natalie Schafer, Lea Penman. A: Irving Kaye Davis. P: Cohn and Scanlon. D: Priestly Morrison.

So Proudly We Hail (9/22/36, 46th Street, 14)

Vigorous drama about the hazing and systematic brutalization of a new cadet (Richard Cromwell) at a military school. Written by an unknown author, Joseph M. Viertel, and staged by an unknown director, Anton Bundsmann (Anthony Mann),* *So Proudly We Hail* generated considerable dramatic punch and vitality even though its Broadway run was a brief one. C: Eddie Bracken, Edward Andrews (deb.), Charles Walters, Edwin Philips, Ethel Jackson, Charles Dingle, Vernon Crane. P: James R. Ullman.

---

*Anthony Mann later directed such Hollywood films as *Winchester 73*, *God's Little Acre*, *The Fall of the Roman Empire*, etc.

So This Is London (8/30/22, Hudson, 357)

American lad falls in love with English girl; both sets of parents strenuously object. Pleasant light comedy by Arthur Goodrich with some nice satirical touches. C: Edmund Breese, Lily Cahill, Donald Gallaher, Marie Carroll, Lawrence D'Orsay. P: George M. Cohan. D: John Meehan.
SV: Fox, 1930, Will Rogers, Irene Rich.

So This Is Politics (6/16/24, Henry Miller, 144)

Women's Lib advocate (Marjorie Gateson) runs for mayor of the town and wins. Fairly spry comedy by Barry Conners. C: William Courtleigh, Glenn Anders, Dwight Frye. P: Carl Reed. Later retitled *Strange Bedfellows*.

So Was Napoleon

See *Sap from Syracuse*.

Social Register, The (11/9/31, Fulton, 97)

Society playboy (Sidney Blackmer) falls in love with musical comedy soubrette (Lenore Ulric). Some bright lines in this otherwise conventional 30's comedy; written and directed by Anita Loos and John Emerson. P: Erlanger Productions.
SV: Col, 1934, Colleen Moore, Alexander Kirkland, Charles Winninger, Robert Benchley, Pauline Frederick.

Society Girl (12/30/31, Booth, 22)

Prizefighter tames society playgirl. Banal comedy had little to recommend it. C: Claire Luce, Russell Hardie, Brian Donlevy. A: John Larkin, Jr. P: William Brandt. D: Stanley Logan.
SV: Fox, 1932, James Dunn, Spencer Tracy, Peggy Shannon.

Soldiers and Women (9/2/29, Ritz, 64)

Tangled love affairs in a British military outpost in India. Clichéd melodrama. C: Violet Heming, A. E. Anson, Verree Teasdale. A: Paul Hervey Fox and George Tilton. P: Lew Cantor. D: Joseph H. Graham.
SV: Col, 1930, Aileen Pringle, Grant Withers.

Soldier's Wife (10/4/44, Golden, 255)

Domestic comedy-drama about an army officer's readjustment to civilian life. "It is light, and it is empty. Dramaturgically, it adds up to nothing because it tosses in everything" *(PM)*. C: Myron McCormick, Martha Scott, Glenn Anders, Frieda Inescort, Lili Darvas (deb.). A/D: Rose Franken. P: William Brown Meloney.

Solid Gold Cadillac, The (11/5/53, Belasco, 526)

A minor stockholder (Josephine Hull) in a huge corporation attends a stockholders' meeting, asks some embarrassing questions, and is promptly given a job to keep her quiet. Instead of remaining silent, however, the lady foils the wicked board of directors, seizes control of the corporation, and, by the final curtain, is riding around town in "a solid gold Cadillac driven by a solid gold chauffeur." This *Cinderellaesque* satire on big business, written by Howard Teichmann and George S. Kaufman (D), was hailed as "an occasion of great rejoicing . . . a howling hit" by William Hawkins (*World-Telegram*). Other reviews were less laudatory, but *The Solid Gold Cadillac* went on to become a solid hit with playgoers. A very funny offstage narrative (voiced by Fred Allen) was a great help to the production. C: Loring Smith, Henry Jones. P: Max Gordon. *Note:* The London production (1964) featured Margaret Rutherford and Sidney James in the leading roles.

SV: Col, 1956, Judy Holliday, Paul Douglas, Fred Clark, John Williams, Arthur O'Connell, with narration voiced by George Burns (directed by Richard Quine from a screenplay by Abe Burrows).

Solid South (10/14/30, Lyceum, 23)

Bette Davis scored a personal success in this short-lived satirical comedy directed by Rouben Mamoulian. The story dealt with the complications that ensue when the widowed daughter-in-law (Jessie Royce Landis) and granddaughter (Bette Davis) of a dyed-in-the-wool southerner (Richard Bennett) are wooed by a couple of damn yankees from Pittsburgh, Pennsylvania. "As broad farce . . . it is indecorously funny . . . [but] neither the play nor the performance has been perfectly shaken together" (*New York Times*). C: Elizabeth Patterson, Owen Davis, Jr., Moffat Johnston, Lew Payton, Georgette Harvey, Richard Huey. A: Lawton Campbell. P: Alexander McKaig.

Soliloquy (11/28/38, Empire, 2)

Pretentious folderol about a bookkeeper (John Beal) who murders his nagging wife, flees the police (and his conscience), and is finally apprehended and executed. The hero's unspoken thoughts were conveyed to the audience by means of recordings, but this gimmick did nothing to help the play. Glenn Ford (billed as Gwyllyn Ford) made his Broadway debut in this short-lived melodrama. A: Victor Victor. P: Henry Weissman. D: Eugene Schulz-Breiden.

Solitaire (1/27/42, Plymouth, 23)

John Van Druten comedy-drama about the friendship between a poor little rich girl (Pat Hitchcock)* and a middle-aged hobo (Victor Kilian). ". . . frail and tenuous" (*Journal-American*). A: Ad. from a novel by Edwin Corle. P: Dwight Deere Wiman. D: Dudley Digges. SD: Jo Mielziner.

---

*Twelve-year-old daughter of Alfred Hitchcock.

Some One in the House (9/9/18, Knickerbocker, 32)

George S. Kaufman's first play, a melodramatic comedy in four acts by Larry Evans and Walter Percival, rewritten by Kaufman to suit the talents of an ingenue in the cast named Lynn Fontanne. *Some One in the House* ("There wasn't," the playwright later confessed gloomily) was a rickety crook melodrama with a twist ending. It expired after four weeks of dismal business. However, Kaufman was so pleased by the Lynn Fontanne impersonation of a lovely but dim-witted young matron that he began thinking of an entire play written about a similar character— and that is how the successful comedy *Dulcy* (1921) was born, which elevated Miss Fontanne to stardom. C: Dudley Digges, Sidney Toler, Hassard Short, Robert Barrat, Robert Hudson, William B. Mack. P: George C. Tyler. C: Frederick Stanhope.

Something About a Soldier (1/4/62, Ambassador, 12)

A compassionate commanding officer (Kevin McCarthy) saves an extraordinarily bright and sensitive Jewish soldier (Sal Mineo) from dangerous combat duty by railroading him into a psycho ward. Bland comedy-drama by Ernest Kinoy b/o the novel by Mark Harris. C: Ralph Meeker, Ken Kercheval, David Doyle, Gretchen Walther, Anthony Roberts, John Crowther, Jeb Schary. P: The Theatre Guild and Dore Schary (D).

Something Different (11/28/67, Cort, 103)

Carl Reiner's (A/D) farce about a dramatist's increasingly frenzied efforts to recreate, within his plush Tudor-styled suburban home, the atmosphere of lower middle-class poverty in which he wrote his first (and only) successful play. Wildly funny situations and sight gags, but the author's story line was far too thin to sustain a full evening in the theatre. C: Bob Dishy, Gabriel Dell, Linda Lavin, Maureen Arthur, Claudia McNeil. P: King/Hyman/Wolsk/Azenberg.

Something Gay (4/29/35, Morosco, 72)

When a sophisticated New Yorker (Tallulah Bankhead) finds her husband (Walter Pidgeon) romancing another woman, she retaliates by flirting with a suave British playwright (Hugh Sinclair). Old-hat triangle comedy which not even the redoubtable Miss Bankhead could save. Song: "You Are So Lovely and I'm So Lonely" by Rodgers and Hart. A: Adelaide Heilbron. P: Messrs. Shubert. D: Thomas Mitchell. SD: Donald Oenslager.

Something for Nothing (12/9/37, Windsor, 2)

Contest winner, pursued by crooks, seeks shelter with screwball family. Unadulterated trash. C: Ben Lackland, Sylvia Field, Millard Mitchell, Lulu McConnell. A: Harry Essex and Sid Schwartz. P: Stuart Drake. D: Harry Wagstaff Gribble.

Something to Brag About (8/13/25, Booth, 4)

Timid soul turns tough guy in an effort to retrieve some money that he thinks was stolen from him. Labored farce by Edgar Selwyn (P/D) and William Le Baron.* C: Richard Sterling, Sylvia Field, Enid Markey.

SV: MGM, 1935, *Baby Face Harrington*, Charles Butterworth, Una Merkel.

---

*Longtime Hollywood producer (*Cimarron, Rio Rita, She Done Him Wrong*, etc.).

Son-Daughter, The (11/19/19, Belasco, 223)

In the redlight district of New York's Chinatown, the almond-eyed daughter (Lenore Ulric) of Dong Tong (Thomas Findlay) is parted from her handsome Chinese lover (Edmund Lowe) and sold to a wealthy merchant. The money, her father gravely informs her, will help finance the revolution in China. She doesn't like the idea and gets even by strangling her bridegroom on the marriage bed. "Last season in the exuberance of youth, I used to think that no play along the same lines [as *East Is West*] could possibly be worse; that was before the dying year brought *The Son-Daughter*" (Dorothy Parker, *Vanity Fair*). A: George Scarborough and David Belasco (P/D).

SV: MGM, 1932, Helen Hayes, Ramon Novarro, Lewis Stone, Warner Oland, H. B. Warner, Ralph Morgan.

Song and Dance Man, The (12/31/23, Hudson, 96)

A down-and-out trouper (George M. Cohan*) gets involved in a robbery, is

pardoned, and goes back to being "the best song and dance man in the profession." "A moderately amusing play has become somehow good with this delightful comedian at large in it" (Alexander Woollcott, *New York Times*). C: Mayo Methot, Louis Calhern, Frederick Perry, John Meehan. A/P/D: Cohan.
- SV: Fox, 1936, Paul Kelly, Claire Trevor, Michael Whalen, Ruth Donnelly.

---

*In the role originally intended for Lynne Overman.

Song of Bernadette, The (3/26/46, Belasco, 3)

Dramatization by Jean and Walter Kerr (D) of Franz Werfel's novel about the peasant girl (Elizabeth Ross) of Lourdes who incurred local wrath because of her visions of the Virgin Mary, but who eventually won over the skeptics and was accepted as a saint. ". . . doesn't hold together as drama or as narrative . . . it is very unimpressive as stage fare" (*Sun*). P: Victor Payne-Jennings and Frank McCoy.
- SV: The Werfel novel was filmed (Fox, 1943) with a cast headed by Jennifer Jones, William Eythe, Charles Bickford, Vincent Price, Lee J. Cobb, Gladys Cooper, and Anne Revere.

Song of Songs, The (12/22/14, Eltinge, 191)

Trite Americanized version of Sudermann's novel. A naïve girl marries a predatory senator, and subsequently becomes involved with many men, until she finally finds the "song of songs" (true love). C: Irene Fenwick, Dorothy Donnelly, Ernest Glendinning, Forrest Winant, Cyril Keightley, John Mason, Thomas A. Wise. A: Edward Sheldon. P: A. H. Woods. D: Byron Ongley.
- SV: Par, 1933, Marlene Dietrich, Brian Aherne, Lionel Atwill, Alison Skipworth.

Song Writer, The (8/13/28, 48th Street, 54)

When a socially prominent gentile girl weds a Jewish tunesmith, both their families strenuously object. Pat and predictable tale, suggested by the highly publicized marriage of Irving Berlin to Postal Telegraph heiress Ellin Mackay. C: Mayo Methot, Georgie Price, Jennie Moscowitz, Robert Sinclair, Hugh Huntley. A: Crane Wilbur. P: Alex Yokel. D: Alexander Leftwich.
- SV: MGM, 1930, *Children of Pleasure,* Lawrence Gray, Wynne Gibson.

Sons and Soldiers (5/4/43, Morosco, 22)

Max Reinhardt directed this Irwin Shaw fantasy in which a pregnant young wife (Geraldine Fitzgerald) debates whether to have her baby at some risk to her life. In a series of elaborately staged dream sequences, she imagines what the world has in store for her unborn child (Gregory Peck) twenty years hence. In the end, she faces the danger of dying to affirm the importance of life. ". . . a scanty play—loose, faltering, talky and immature" (*Sun*). C: Stella Adler, Herbert Rudley, Leonard Sues, Karl Malden, Millard Mitchell, Jesse White, Ted Donaldson, Phyllis Hill. P: Max Reinhardt, Norman Bel Geddes (SD) and Richard Myers.

Sophie (12/25/44, Playhouse, 9)

Aimless comedy-drama about a Czech widow (Katina Paxinou) and her family trying to make a go of things in a Connecticut town. *Sophie* was written by George Ross and Rose C. Feld, b/o the latter's *New Yorker* magazine stories. P: Meyer Davis and George Ross. D: Michael Gordon.

Sound of Hunting, A (11/20/45, Lyceum, 23)

On the day a squad of GI's are to be relieved of duty, they discover that one of their men is trapped under fire. They refuse to leave until their comrade, whom none of them especially liked, is rescued. When the missing man is found dead, the squad proceeds on its way to Naples. "... an extended sketch, full of promise, but lean on theatrical compulsion" (*Herald Tribune*). "Probably the best American war play since *What Price Glory?*" (George Jean Nathan). The all-male cast of *A Sound of Hunting* included Sam Levene, Frank Lovejoy and Burton (Burt) Lancaster (deb.). It was written by poet-novelist-screenwriter (*A Walk in the Sun, A Place in the Sun,* etc.) Harry Brown. Despite generally laudatory reviews, the play was withdrawn after 23 performances. P: Irving L. Jacobs. D: Anthony Brown. SD: Samuel Leve.

SV: Col, 1958, *Eight Iron Men,* Lee Marvin, Richard Kiley, Arthur Franz.

Sound of Silence, A (3/8/65, Maidman, 88)

Psychological conflicts ensue when a black clergyman visits the home of a white southerner. Generally effective O/B drama by Harold Willis; staged by John Sillings.

Sour Grapes (9/6/26, Longacre, 40)

With romance gone out of their marriage, Alice (Alice Brady) and John Overton (John Halliday) try various stratagems, none successful, in an effort to rekindle the spark. Fairly diverting comedy-drama by Vincent Lawrence. P/D: William Harris, Jr.

SV: RKO, 1934, *Let's Try Again,* Clive Brook, Diana Wynyard.

See *The Overtons*.

South Pacific (12/29/43, Cort, 5)

Cast up on a small Japanese-held island in the Pacific, a rebellious black seaman (Canada Lee) decides that he no longer cares who wins World War II. It is only when a native island boy is callously shot by the Japanese that the seaman realizes he, too, has a stake in the outcome of the war. As the curtain falls, he exits, gun in hand, to do battle. "... never comes to grips with its rather fascinating thesis" (*Herald Tribune*). A: Howard Rigsby and Dorothy Heyward. P: David Lowe. D: Lee Strasberg. M: Paul Bowles. SD: Boris Aronson.

Southern Exposure (9/26/50, Biltmore, 23)

Scandal-mongering author visits Mississippi, falls under the spell of a local belle, and reforms. Tedious farce filled with stock characters and situations. C: Cameron Mitchell, Pat Crowley, Betty Greene Little. A: Owen Crump. P: Margo Jones (D), Tad Adoue, and Manning Gurian.

Southwest Corner, The (2/3/55, Holiday, 36)

Moderately interesting domestic drama about the conflict between an elderly Vermont widow and the grasping, insensitive female companion who takes over her home and her life. C: Eva LeGallienne, Enid Markey, Parker Fennelly. A: John Cecil Holm b/o the novel by Mildred Walker. P: John Huntington. D: George Schaefer. SD: Ralph Alswang.

Spanish Love (8/17/20, Maxine Elliott's, 308)

Two hot-blooded young Spaniards (William Powell and James Rennie) fall in love with the same girl and become bitter enemies. The death of one paves the way for a happy ending. Gaudy but glum drama by Avery Hopwood and Mary Roberts Rinehart. P: Wagenhals and Kemper.

Speak Easy (9/26/27, Mansfield, 57)

Banal melodrama about a country girl who gets involved with prizefighters, bootleggers, and other "interestin' riffraff" while visiting a Hell's Kitchen speakeasy. C: Dorothy Hall, Edward Woods, Arthur Vinton, Ann Shoemaker, Leo G. Carroll. A: Edward Knoblock and George Rosener. P/D: William B. Friedlander.

SV: Fox, 1929, Lola Lane, Paul Page.

Speaking of Murder (12/19/56, Royale, 37)

Fair-to-middling melodrama about a nasty secretary-governess (Brenda de Banzie in her Broadway debut) who murders any rivals foolhardy enough to marry her handsome employer (Lorne Greene). Highlight: Estelle Winwood's performance as a bibulous blackmailing biddy. C: Neva Patterson, Billy Quinn. A: Audrey and William Toos. P: Courtney Burr and Burgess Meredith. D: Delbert Mann. SD: Frederick Fox.

Spider, The (3/22/27, 46th Street, 100)

During a vaudeville show featuring Chartrand the Great, a magician of extraordinary ability and charm, a shot rings out and a member of the audience falls over dead. From that point on, the action spills over the footlights and into the aisles. Officers are posted at every exit to prevent escape. House lights go on and off. The magician slips in and out of his handcuffs with amazing dexterity. At the last moment, the murderer is discovered in the audience and apprehended. Delightful, highly effective whodunit, well-written, well-acted, and well-produced. C: John Halliday, Roy Hargrave, Thomas Findlay. A: Fulton Oursler and Lowell Brentano. P: Albert Lewis (D) and Sam H. Harris.

SV: Fox, 1931, Edmund Lowe, Lois Moran, El Brendel, Warren Hymer; 1945, Richard Conte, Faye Marlowe, Kurt Kreuger, Martin Kosleck.

Spite Corner (9/25/22, Little, 124)

Long-standing family feud temporarily blocks the marriage of two young lovers. Leisurely small-town comedy-drama by Frank Craven. C: Madge Kennedy, Jason Robards, Sr. P: John Golden.

Spofford (12/14/67, ANTA, 202)

When his niece (Barbara Britton) is spurned by the son of a local nouveau riche family, a retired Connecticut chicken farmer (Melvyn Douglas) decides to find out about his wealthy neighbors and, in the process, turns the town upside down. Meandering comedy by Herman Shumlin (A/D) based on Peter DeVries' novel *Reuben, Reuben*. Splendid performance by Mr. Douglas and, in a key supporting role, by character actress-comedienne Pert Kelton. P: Zev Bufman i.a.w. James Riley. SD: Donald Oenslager.

Spoilers, The (3/11/07, New York, 16)

Stagey adaptation of Rex Beach's two-fisted tale of Yukon gold fever and the love of two rugged prospectors for the same girl. A: Rex Beach and James MacArthur. P: Daniel Frohman.

SV: Par, 1930, Gary Cooper, William Boyd; U, 1942, John Wayne, Marlene Dietrich, Randolph Scott, Richard Barthelmess, Harry Carey, Margaret Lindsay; U, 1955, Jeff Chandler, Anne Baxter, Rory Calhoun.

Note: The classic version of *The Spoilers* starred William Farnum (1914) and featured what was probably the most realistic fight scene ever staged for the cameras. A subsequent silent version (1920) pitted Noah Beery against Milton Sills.

Spread Eagle (4/4/27, Martin Beck, 80)

To protect his Mexican mining interests, an American billionaire secretly finances General de Castro's revolution. Upshot: a bloody war between the United States and Mexico. Incisively staged by George

Spread Eagle. Allen Vincent, Aline McMahon, and Donald Meek (April 4, 1927). *Courtesy Museum of the City of New York Theatre and Music Collection.*

Abbott and handsomely produced by Jed Harris, *Spread Eagle* packed quite a wallop. The play was written by veteran newspapermen George S. Brooks and Walter B. Lister. C: Osgood Perkins, Aline MacMahon, Fritz Williams, Felix Krembs, Allen Vincent, Donald Meek, Charles D. Brown.

P/D: Guthrie McClintic. SD: Donald Oenslager.

Note: Twenty-one-year-old Kirk Douglas (billed as George Spelvin, Jr.) made his Broadway debut as a singing Western Union messenger boy in this 1941 comedy.

Spring Again (11/10/41, Henry Miller, 241)

Wife (Grace George) squares accounts with her ancestor-worshipping husband (C. Aubrey Smith) by penning a successful radio serial that shakes the branches of his family tree. "A mechanical comedy [with] some funny lines and amusing situations" (*Post*). C: Joseph Buloff, Ann Andrews, William Talman, Robert Keith. A: Isabel Leighton and Bertram Bloch.

Spring Dance (8/25/36, Empire, 23)

When a plain girl is jilted by a Yale man, her college chums join forces to badger the hapless male into matrimony. A New England woman's college was the setting for this Cinderella yarn by Philip Barry b/o a play by Eleanor Golden and Eloise Barrangon. With Imogene Coca as the wallflower-heroine, *Spring Dance* looked like an almost certain Jed Harris (P/D) success in its tryout production. When the play reached Broadway, Miss Coca had been replaced by Louise Platt. The play was "circused," according to its author, and most of its charm was lost. After twenty-three performances, *Spring Dance* wafted away. The critics, however, were unstinting in their praise of one performer—twenty-four-year-old Jose Ferrer in the role of The Lippincot, the hero's oddly-named sidekick, who knows everything about women "except how to get along without them." C: Ruth Matteson, Martha Hodge, Mary Wickes, Richard Kendrick, Tom Neal, Philip Ober.

SV: MGM, 1938, *Spring Madness*, Maureen O'Sullivan, Lew Ayres, Burgess Meredith, Ruth Hussey, Frank Albertson.

Spring Fever (8/3/25, Maxine Elliott's, 56)

A shipping clerk joins a fashionable golf club and is mistaken for a millionaire. Fairly amusing comedy by Vincent Lawrence. C: James Rennie, Marion Coakley. P: A. H. Woods. D: Bertram Harrison.

SV: MGM, 1930, *Love in the Rough*, Robert Montgomery, Dorothy Jordan.

Note: A silent version (MGM, 1927) featured William Haines and Joan Crawford.

Spring Freshet (10/4/34, Plymouth, 12)

Hackneyed character study of an iron-willed Maine matriarch. C: Esther Dale, Elizabeth Patterson, Thurston Hall, Richard Whorf, Francesca Bruning, Viola Frayne. A/D: Owen Davis. P: Lee Shubert.

Spring Song (10/1/34, Morosco, 40)

Jewish girl seduces her sister's fiancé, pays for her sin by dying in childbirth. Lugubrious drama, set on New York's lower East Side, and written by Bella and Samuel Spewack, authors of such comedy hits as *Boy Meets Girl* (1935), etc. C: Francine Larrimore, Norman Stuart, Sam Levene, Garson Kanin, Frieda Altman. P: Max Gordon. D: Eddie Sobol.

Spring Thaw (3/21/38, Martin Beck, 8)

Tolerant husband (Roland Young) tries to ignore his young wife's infidelities. Strained comedy by Clare Kummer. P: Max Gordon. D: Arthur Hopkins. SD: Donald Oenslager.

Springboard, The (10/12/27, Mansfield, 37)

Listless comedy-drama by Alice Duer Miller about a philandering husband and his forgiving wife. C: Madge Kennedy, Sidney Blackmer, Walter Connolly, Elizabeth Risdon. P: Charles L. Wagner. D: T. Daniel Frawley.

Springtime Folly (2/26/51, Golden, 2)

Squabbling and double-dealing of partners in the maternity dress business. "The most dismal theatre event of the season" (*New York Times*). "This comedy should be preserved—in formaldehyde" (*News*). C: Jack Whiting, Irene Dailey, Mabel Taliaferro, Philip Abbott. A: Schulman, Lieberson and Lieberson. P: United Producers. D: Leon Michel.

Squab Farm, The (3/13/18, Bijou, 45)

Tallulah Bankhead made her Broadway debut (in a nonspeaking role) as a Hollywood starlet in this satire on silent pictures. "A garish travesty on life in the movies, all in bad taste" (*New York Times*). C: Alma Tell, Lowell Sherman, Harry Davenport. A: Frederic and Fanny Hatton. P: Messrs. Shubert. D: J. C. Huffman.

Squall, The (11/11/26, 48th Street, 262)

One of those plays that was so bad it was almost good. A gypsy waif named Nubi invades the home of a sex-starved Spanish family and proceeds to seduce every male in sight including father, son, and hired hand. During one of the more supercharged scenes on opening night, little Nubi kept muttering: "Me Nubi. Nubi good girl. Nubi stay." At which point critic Robert Benchley beat a hasty retreat up the aisle, announcing to the audience: "Me Benchley. Benchley bad boy. Benchley go." Trumpeted the show's press agent, Richard Maney: "The Play That Made a Street-Walker of Robert Benchley." Maney also labeled the exhibit "A Passionate Drama of the Sexes" and boasted: "The implication that there were more than two sexes was a taunt the curious could not withstand." Thanks to such stratagems, and with the aid of cut-rate tickets, *The Squall* managed to hang around for 262 performances. Making her Broadway debut in the production was Dorothy Stickney. (She was succeeded by Sylvia Sidney, likewise making her Broadway bow.) Others in the cast: Blanche Yurka, Romney Brent, Horace Braham, Henry O'Neill, Lee Baker. A: Jean Bart. P: Jones and Green. D: Lionel Atwill.

SV: WB, 1930, Myrna Loy, Loretta Young, Alice Joyce, Richard Tucker, ZaSu Pitts.

Square Crooks (3/1/26, Daly's, 144)

Jittery ex-thief (Russell Mack) tries to go straight, but everything conspires to send him back to jail. "A moderately entertaining crook melodrama . . ." (*New York Times*). A: James P. Judge. P: Bannister and Powell. D: Albert Bannister.

Square in the Eye (5/19/65, de Lys, 31)

Avant-garde O/B opus detailing the interminable squabbling between a would-be artist and his dying wife. ". . . capricious, circuitous and boring . . ." (*New York Times*). C: Philip Bruns, Carol Rossen, Conrad Bain. A: Jack Gelber. D: Ben Shaktman.

Square Peg, A (1/27/23, Punch and Judy, 41)

Nagging wife destroys the lives of everyone in her family. Soundly written, extremely depressing domestic drama by Lewis Beach. C: Beverly Sitgreaves, Leona Hogarth, Walter Abel. P/D: Guthrie McClintic.

Square Root of Wonderful, The (10/30/57, National, 45)

Carson McCullers' comedy-drama about the efforts of a young divorcée (Anne Baxter) to break away from her emotionally unstable ex-husband and domineering mother-in-law, and find happiness with an understanding architect. "After *The Member of the Wedding* Carson McCullers' second play seems commonplace . . . frail, delicate . . . listless" (*New York Times*). C: Jean Dixon, Philip Abbott, William Smithers, Martine Bartlett. P: Saint Subber and Figaro, Inc. D: George Keathley. SD: Jo Mielziner.

Squaw Man, The (10/23/05, Wallack's, 222)

Highly successful romantic melodrama by Edwin Milton Royle. An English soldier (William Faversham) must choose between Nat-u-ritch (Mabel Morrison), the Indian squaw he married, and the girl and the earldom awaiting him in England. The dilemma is resolved when Nat-u-ritch, not wishing to stand in the way of her husband's happiness, shoots herself. P: Liebler and Company. D: Royle and Faversham.

R: (1/9/11, Broadway, 8). C: Dustin Farnum, William S. Hart, Dudley Digges, Theodore Roberts, George Fawcett, Chrystal Herne. D: Addison Pitt.

R: (1/26/21, Astor, 50) by Lee Shubert. C: William Faversham, Josephine Royle, Willard Robertson. D: Faversham.

Musicalized by Rudolph Friml as

The White Eagle (1927) with Allan Prior, Marion Keeler, Lawrence D'Orsay.

SV: MGM, 1930, Warner Baxter, Lupe Velez, Charles Bickford. *Note:* A silent version of *The Squaw Man* (1913) with Dustin Farnum as the renegade Englishman was notable as the first film made by Samuel Goldwyn, Jesse Lasky, and Cecil B. De Mille (who directed and co-produced). The film made a substantial hit.

Squealer, The (11/12/28, Forrest, 66)

Dope peddling and white slavery in wicked old San Francisco, with the earthquake thrown in for good measure. Low-grade melodramatic piffle with Peaches Browning, of tabloid fame, in an otherwise no-name cast. A: Mark Linder. P: Jack Linder. D: Clarke Silvernail.

Stage Door (10/22/36, Music Box, 169)

A theatrical boarding house for aspiring actresses was the setting of this pleasant but unexceptional George S. Kaufman-Edna Ferber comedy-drama. The play recorded the progress of a typical young ingenue* (Margaret Sullavan) from hardship and disappointment to final success on Broadway. Despite many discouragements, this stage-struck damsel remains true to the legitimate theatre, and refuses to be lured into an "easier and more profitable career" in motion pictures. C: Frances Fuller, Phyllis Brooks, Mary Wickes, Onslow Stevens, Richard Kendrick, Tom Ewell, Lee Patrick, Leona Roberts. P: Sam H. Harris. D: George S. Kaufman. SD: Donald Oenslager.

SV: RKO, 1937, Katharine Hepburn, Ginger Rogers, Adolphe Menjou, Gail Patrick, Constance Collier, Andrea Leeds, Lucille Ball, Eve Arden, Franklin Pangborn, Jack Carson, Ann Miller, Katherine Alexander, Ralph Forbes (directed by Gregory La Cava from a screenplay by Morrie Ryskind and Anthony Veiller).

Note: "Now and again Hollywood produces a version of a play that is superior to the parent work," observed the film critic for the *New York Times*. Considerably changed and rewritten, *Stage Door* onscreen was a vast improvement upon its stage original.

---

*Joan Bennett played this role on tour.

Stalag 17 (5/8/51, 48th Street, 472)

Comedy-melodrama set in a German POW camp where a group of American enlisted men are confined behind barbed wire fences. They gripe about the food, yearn for letters from home, and prepare to celebrate a skimpy Christmas. But underlying all the horseplay is a life-and-death struggle to expose a German agent who has been planted in the barracks and is betraying their escape plans to the Nazis. "Lively and theatrical . . . a boisterous thriller" (*Herald Tribune*). C: John Ericson (deb.), Robert Strauss, Harvey Lembeck, Laurence Hugo, Frank Maxwell, Garry Davis, Frank Campanella, Richard Poston (deb.), Eric Fleming. A: Donald Bevan and Edmund Trzcinski. P/D: Jose Ferrer. SD: John Robert Lloyd.

SV: Par, 1953, William Holden, Otto Preminger, Don Taylor, Robert Strauss, Peter Graves, Sig Ruman (directed by Billy Wilder).

Star Spangled (3/10/36, Golden, 23)

Three Polish-American brothers—a politician (Garson Kanin), a ball player (Millard Mitchell), and an escaped convict (George Tobias)—are reunited during a hectic weekend in the Chicago home of their widowed mother (Natasha Boleslavsky). Hard-boiled satirical comedy by Robert Ardrey (his first play) had several amusing scenes, but the narrative structure was weak. *Star Spangled* was withdrawn by Arthur Hopkins (P/D) after a brief three-week run.

Star Spangled Family (4/10/45, Biltmore, 5)

Conflict between a young widow and her resentful mother-in-law. ". . . a hunk of junk" (*News*). C: Frances Reid, Jean Adair, Edward Nugent, Dennie Moore. A: B. Harrison Orkow. P: Philip Waxman and Joseph Kipness. D: William Castle.

Starlight (3/3/25, Broadhurst, 71)

The life and loves of Sarah Bernhardt (here called Aurelie) as portrayed by Doris Keane in her last New York appearance. Widely heralded out of town, *Starlight* flickered fitfully on Broadway. A: Gladys Unger, based on a work by Abel Hermant. P: Frank Egan i.a.w. Charles Frohman, Inc. D: Edith Ellis.

- SV: A silent version of this play (MGM, 1928, *The Divine Woman*) starred Greta Garbo. The supporting cast included Lars Hanson, Lowell Sherman, John Mack Brown, and Polly Moran.

Star-Spangled Girl, The (12/21/66, Plymouth, 261)

Two left-wing San Francisco lads fall in love with a right-wing beauty. Neil Simon's weakest comedy, a three-character contrivance that seldom generated anything heartier than an occasional chuckle. C: Anthony Perkins, Richard Benjamin, Connie Stevens. P: Saint Subber. D: George Axelrod.

- SV: Par, 1971, Sandy Duncan, Tony Roberts.

Star-Wagon, The (9/29/37, Empire, 221)

Maxwell Anderson's variant on the "time machine" plot in which a middle-aged couple (Burgess Meredith and Lillian Gish) are transported back to their youth (Ohio, 1902) and given a second chance at marrying for money instead of for love. Returned to the present, they realize they made the right choice the first time. ". . . the play is richer in period comedy than in metaphysics. It is entertaining and quite harmless" (Mary McCarthy, *Partisan Review*). C: Russell Collins, Kent Smith, Edmond O'Brien, Howard Freeman, Whit Bissell, Mildred Natwick, John Philliber, Alan Anderson. P/D: Guthrie McClintic. SD: Jo Mielziner.

State of the Union (11/14/45, Hudson, 765)

Pulitzer Prize comedy by Howard Lindsay and Russel Crouse about a wealthy businessman whom the Republican party's top brass attempt to groom for the presidency. When he discovers the compromises he will be forced to make, the idealistic industrialist retires from the race, to the consternation of his crooked supporters and the delight of his staunch wife. Bristling with satirical jabs at voter apathy and fraudulent campaign practices in both parties, *State of the Union* met with a highly favorable press and enjoyed a long and profitable Broadway run. The play (purportedly suggested by Wendell Wilkie's 1940 presidential bid) retained its topicality by the injection each night of new lines pertaining to current events of the day. Ralph Bellamy received excellent notices as the businessman-hero who would rather be right than president. Making her Broadway debut, Ruth Hussey scored a comparable success as his quick-witted, courageous spouse.* C: Myron McCormick, Minor Watson, Kay Johnson. P: Leland Hayward. D: Bretaigne Windust.

- SV: MGM, 1948, Spencer Tracy, Katharine Hepburn, Van Johnson, Angela Lansbury, Adolphe Menjou, Lewis Stone, Howard Smith, Raymond Walburn, Charles Dingle, Margaret Hamilton (directed by Frank Capra).

---

*Helen Hayes (for whom the play was originally written) turned down this role; so did Katharine Hepburn and Margaret Sullavan.

Status Quo Vadis (2/18/73, Brooks Atkinson, 1)

A satire that pummels American society in heavy-handed fashion. The characters wear numbers from One to Five to indicate their class status, and the targets of the play are by the numbers as well: big business, sexual customs, organized religion. The plot is no fresher than the message. A blue collar factory worker falls in love with his boss' daughter. He is a Number Five, at the bottom of the heap. She, of course, is a Number One. The hero's upwardly mobile course is strewn with obstacles and in the end, the system wins. He loses his love to a Dartmouth man, and settles for a pretty, but plebeian, secretary. The play had been earlier produced in Chicago with much the same cast seen in the New York performance. A/D: Donald Driver. C: Bruce Boxleitner, Gail Strickland (deb.), Rebecca Taylor, Ted Danson, Robert E. Thompson, Geraldine Kay, Roberts Blossom, Lee Zara, Don Marston, Charles Welch. P: George Keathley and Jack Lenny. SD: Edward Burbridge. CD: David Toser.

Steambath (6/30/70, Truck and Warehouse, 128)

Blackly funny O/B comedy about a young man (Anthony Perkins) puzzled to find himself in a steamroom. Coming to the realization that he's dead, as are all the others in the room, he's miffed at the untimeliness of it. He'd just gotten a divorce, quit the Police Academy, is writing a novel about Charlemagne, and doing charity work among brain-damaged welders. His sense of the fitness of things is further outraged when God turns out to be the bath attendant (Hector Elizondo), a Puerto Rican who talks slang and is anything but majestic. The hero's entreaties to return to all the important activities of his life fall on deaf ears. It becomes clear at the final curtain that his life was, in fact, empty and useless. A stinging wit permeates the writing of *Steambath* and Perkins and Elizondo take full advantage of it. Author Friedman earlier wrote the 1967 success *Scuba Duba*. A: Bruce Jay Friedman. C: Anthony Perkins, Hector Elizondo, Conrad Bain, Marvin Lichterman, Jere Admire, Annie Rachel, Teno Pollick, Gabor Morea, Mitchell Jason, Jack Knight, Eileen Dietz, Alfred Hinckley, William Walsh. D: Anthony Perkins. P: Ivor David Balding. SD: David Mitchell. CD: Joseph G. Aulisi.

Steel (11/17/31, Times Square, 14)

Steelworker-organizer is almost murdered when he takes a stand against unjust working conditions. Frequently engrossing social protest drama by John Wexley (A/D), author of *The Last Mile* (1930) and *They Shall Not Die* (1934). C: Paul Guilfoyle, Egon Brecher, Barton MacLane, Edgar Stehli, Royal Dana. P: Richard Geist.

Steel (12/19/39, Provincetown, 9)

A laborer (Don DeFore), convinced that steel is the only god, ends his life by jumping into a vat of molten metal. Badly muddled O/B drama; thematically similar to Eugene O'Neill's *Dynamo* (1929). A: Harold Igo. P: Producers Theatre. D: Ad Karns.

Step on a Crack (10/17/62, Barrymore, 1)

Tormented son plots death of his father's paramour. Rita Hayworth was to have made her Broadway debut in this "ridiculous, overblown and downright embarrassing melodrama" (*World-Telegram*), but was replaced by Pauline Flanagan prior to the New York opening. C: Gary Merrill, Donald Madden, Maggie McNamara, Margaret Hayes, William Hickey. A: Bernard Evslin. P: Roger L. Stevens and Herbert Swope, Jr. (D). SD: George Jenkins. M: Bobby Scott.

Stepdaughters of War (10/6/30, Empire, 24)

Lugubrious look at the lives and loves of lady ambulance drivers in France during the Great War. C: Katherine Alexander, Warren William, Ethel Griffies, Eda Heinemann. A: Kenyon Nicholson b/o the novel by Helen Zenna Smith. P: Charles Frohman, Inc. D: Chester Erskine.

Stepping Out (5/20/29, Fulton, 24)

A couple of old goats try to seduce a pair of Hollywood gold diggers. Then their wives return. Competent cast trapped in a tasteless farce. C: Walter Connolly, Herbert Corthell, Grace La Rue, Jobyna Howland, Martha Sleeper, Hale Hamilton, Lillian Bond. A: Elmer Harris. P: Charles Dillingham i.a.w. Eddie Dowling and Edgar MacGregor (D).
- SV: MGM, 1931, Charlotte Greenwood, Cliff Edwards.

Stepping Sisters (4/22/30, Belmont, 327)

Frothy farce about three ex-burlesque queens trying to crash high society. C: Theresa Maxwell Conover, Helen Raymond, Grace Huff, Frederic Tozere, William Lynn. A: Howard Warren Comstock. P/D: Albert Bannister.
- SV: Fox, 1932, Minna Gombell, Louise Dresser, William Collier.

Stevedore (4/18/34, Civic, 110)

Lonnie, a black New Orleans stevedore, is framed on a false charge of rape. He escapes not only the police, but also a gang of white hoodlums in the pay of his anti-union company. When the gang threatens to burn down the Negro quarter of the city, Lonnie persuades his companions to defend themselves. Reinforced by sympathetic white union men, the blacks win the pitched battle that ensues, though Lonnie himself is killed. Effective, frequently stirring 1934 propaganda play was both a protest against racial discrimination in the South and a plea for closer cooperation between white and black workers. C: Jack Carter, Harry Bolden, Rex Ingram, Leigh Whipper, Georgette Harvey, Frank Gabrielson. A: Paul Peters and George Sklar. P: The Theatre Union. D: Michael Blankfort and Irving Gordon.

Stick-in-the-Mud (11/26/35, 48th Street, 9)

Drowsy comedy about life on a grounded Missouri steamboat. C: Thomas Mitchell (D), Sylvia Field, Bruce MacFarlane, Rex Ingram, Doris Dudley, Jose Ferrer. A: Frederick Hazlitt Brennan. P: Curtis and Hoagland.

Sticks and Bones (3/1/72, John Golden, 245)

Drama of a returned Vietnam war veteran. Written in a style bordering the surreal, the play introduces us to Ozzie and Harriet, complacent middle-class American parents, and Rick, their vacuous guitar-playing younger son. Home from battle comes their older boy, David, blinded but possessed of a harsh vision of truth his family will not accept. He is accompanied by a Vietnamese girl whom only he can see. She follows him about silently, a wordless Greek chorus. David's concept of reality, molded by war, is played against the television-insulated witlessness of the family to harrowing effect. Rick's repetitive "Hi, Mom, Hi, Dad" as he bounces into the house becomes as wracking as fingernails on a blackboard. The family's resistance to facing reality ends with their urging David to stop his misery and theirs by committing suicide. Rick loans him his razor and aids him in cutting his wrists. "... searing and strikingly original antiwar play ... a powerful human document" (Douglas Watt, *New York Daily News*). "... a sophomoric piece of drivel" (Rex Reed, *New York Sunday News*). *Sticks and Bones* opened 11/7/71 at the O/B Anspacher Theater, part of Joseph Papp's New York Shakespeare Festival's Public Theater complex. There were 121 performances before the play moved to Broadway for 245 more. The cast remained the same, excepting David Selby, who was replaced as David by Drew Snyder. Besides a special citation from the New York Drama Critics' Circle, *Sticks and Bones* received the Tony Award for Best Play and Elizabeth Wilson as Harriet won for Best Supporting Actress. A: David Rabe. C: Tom Aldredge, Elizabeth Wilson, Drew Snyder, Cliff DeYoung, Hector Elias, Charles Siebert, Asa Ginn. D: Jeff Bleckner. P: Joseph Papp. SD: Santo Loquasto.

Still Waters (3/1/26, Henry Miller, 16)

To win his party's nomination, a windbag senator (Thurston Hall) with a fondness for the bottle votes for Prohibition. Weak comedy-drama by Augustus Thomas (A/P/D).

Stop Thief (12/25/12, Gaiety, 149)

Two likable jewel thieves crash a society wedding. Funny mistaken identity farce. C: Richard Bennett, Vivian Martin, Mary Ryan, William Boyd, Frank Bacon. A: Carlyle Moore. P: Cohan and Harris. D: Sam Forrest.

Stop-Over (1/11/38, Lyceum, 23)

Trigger-happy criminal hides out in the country home of a reclusive, world-weary actor. Intriguing melodrama had a brief Broadway run. Written by magazine writer Matt Taylor and his brother Sam Taylor, Hollywood writer-director of silent screen fame. C: Arthur Byron, Sidney Blackmer, Muriel Kirkland, Staats Cotsworth, Billy (William) Redfield. P: Chase Productions. D: Worthington Miner. SD: Norris Houghton.

Stork, The (1/26/25, Cort, 8)

To keep the premier of France home nights, his wife plots his political demise. Turgid comedy adapted by Ben Hecht from a play by Laszlo Fodor. C: Geoffrey Kerr, Katherine Alexander, Ferdinand Gottschalk. P: Schwab and Mandel. D: Frederick Stanhope.

Stork Mad (9/30/36, Ambassador, 5)

Stupid farce about a pair of feuding hillbilly families and their offspring. Co-authored by scenarist Lynn Root and actor Frank Fenton. C: Percy Kilbride, Ann Thomas, Lynn Root. P: James R. Ullman. D: William Schorr. SD: S. Syrjala.

Storm, The (10/2/19, 48th Street, 282)

Virtuous orphan lass is trapped all winter in a remote cabin with two men. Heavy-breathing melodrama was hot stuff back in 1919. C: Helen MacKellar, Edward Arnold, Robert Rendel. A: Langdon McCormick. P/D: George Broadhurst.
SV: U, 1930, Lupe Velez, William Boyd, Paul Cavanaugh (directed by William Wyler).

Storm Operation (1/11/44, Belasco, 23)

Maxwell Anderson's drama of the North African invasion, tied to a trite triangle scenario concerning the rivalry between an American sergeant and an English captain for the love of an Australian nurse. Highlight: the performance of radio writer (and future TV-film producer) Cy Howard (deb.) as a breezy, double-talking Signal Corps noncom. ". . . an extremely bad play . . . staggeringly dull" *(PM)*. C: Myron McCormick, Bramwell Fletcher, Gertrude Musgrove, Millard Mitchell, Alan Schneider. P: The Playwrights Company. D: Michael Gordon.

Story for a Sunday Evening, A (11/17/50, Playhouse, 11)

Mild backstage triangle comedy presented in a play-within-a-play

framework. C: Paul Crabtree (A/P/D), Cloris Leachman, Nan Martin, Henry Jones.
R: (1/16/62, Cherry Lane, 8) as *A Stage Affair*. The cast of this O/B revival, under Mr. Crabtree's direction, included Carleton Carpenter, Tom Pedi, and Louise King.

Story for Strangers, A (9/21/48, Royale, 7)

A talking horse reforms the larcenous citizens of a Michigan town. This whimsical parable-play was written and directed by Marc Connelly, author of *The Wisdom Tooth* (1926), *The Green Pastures* (1930), etc. ". . . a dawdling and feeble fantasy" *(Sun)*. C: James Dobson, Joseph Sweeney, Joan Gray. P: Dwight Deere Wiman.

Story of Mary Surratt, The (2/8/47, Henry Miller, 11)

Mary Surratt (Dorothy Gish) kept the Washington boardinghouse where John Wilkes Booth and his fellow conspirators hatched their unsuccessful plot to abduct Abraham Lincoln. During the national period of hysteria that followed Lincoln's assassination, Mrs. Surratt was condemned to death by a hostile military court. It now seems certain she was innocent of complicity in the crime, and her hanging a gross miscarriage of justice. This interesting historical drama by John Patrick (A/D) received mixed reviews and was withdrawn after eleven performances. C: Kent Smith, James Monks, Elizabeth Ross, Harlan Briggs. P: Lewis and Young.

Strange Bedfellows (1924)

See *So This Is Politics*.

Strange Bedfellows (1/14/48, Morosco, 229)

Period comedy (San Francisco, 1896) about the battle of the sexes that results when an anti-suffragette politician tangles with his equal-rights-for-women daughter-in-law. "Synthetic but amusing" *(Post)*. The play was written by the wife-and-husband team of Florence Ryerson and Colin Clements, authors of *Harriet* (1943). (Mr. Clements died shortly after the Broadway premiere of *Strange Bedfellows*.) C: Joan Tetzel, John Archer, Carl Benton Reid, Nydia Westman. P: Philip A. Waxman. D: Benno Schneider. SD: Ralph Alswang.

Strange Fruit (11/29/45, Royale, 60)

A weak-willed southerner (Mel Ferrer) falls in love with a beautiful black girl (Jane White). When she becomes pregnant, however, he turns against her, thus setting into motion a train of events culminating in his own murder, and the lynching of his innocent black houseboy for the crime. ". . . sprawling, talkative and confused" *(Journal-American)*. Miss White, Ralph Meeker, and Murray Hamilton made their Broadway debuts in *Strange Fruit*. Also in the cast: Juano Hernandez, Vera Allen, Eugenia Rawls, Earl Jones, Ralph Theadore. A: Lillian and Esther Smith, b/o the former's novel. P/D: Jose Ferrer. SD: George Jenkins.

Strange Gods (4/15/33, Ritz, 9)

When a scientist dies, his wife's lover is suspected of foul play. Drab 30's melodrama. C: John Litel, Vera Allen. A: Jessica Ball. P: Samuel Wallach. D: Priestly Morrison.

Strange Interlude (1/30/28, Golden, 426)

Eugene O'Neill's prodigious, convention-shattering nine-act drama, replete with soliloquies and asides to express the inner thoughts of his characters. The case history of introspective, neurotic Nina Leeds (Lynn Fontanne) from girlhood to middle age: *Strange Interlude* showed how her castrating possessiveness and insatiable sexual appetite

Strange Interlude. Glenn Anders, Lynn Fontanne, Tom Powers, Earle Larimore (1928). *Courtesy Museum of the City of New York Theatre and Music Collection.*

destroyed five men—her husband, son, father, and two lovers. "Not only a great American play but the great American novel as well" (Dudley Nichols, *World*). "An interesting stunt carried about four acts too far" (Robert Benchley, *The New Yorker*). Despite mixed reviews, *Strange Interlude* was the talk of the town from its first showing. Performances began at 5:15, adjourned for a dinner recess, then resumed at 8:30. There were six performances a week (no matinees), with nearby restaurants doing a thriving business. The unsympathetic role of Nina Leeds was rejected by several stellar actresses including Katharine Cornell and Alice Brady. After Lynn Fontanne left the cast, Nina was played respectively by Judith Anderson, Gale Sondergaard, and Pauline Lord. Mary Ellis essayed the part in London but the play was not a great success there. *Strange Interlude* won the Pulitzer Prize for 1927–1928. C: Glenn Anders, Earle Larimore, Tom Powers, Helen Westley, Charles Walters. P: The Theatre Guild. D: Philip Moeller. SD: Jo Mielziner.

R: (3/11/63, Hudson, 104) by The Actors Studio. C: Geraldine Page, Ben Gazzara, Franchot Tone, Betty Field, Pat Hingle, William Prince, Jane Fonda, Richard Thomas, Geoffrey Horne. D: Jose Quintero.

SV: MGM, 1932, Norma Shearer, Clark Gable, Robert Young, Ralph Morgan, May Robson, Maureen O'Sullivan, Alexander Kirkland.

Strange Play, A (6/1/44, Mansfield, 4)

Strange indeed was this triangle "comedy" in which one of the characters (an ex-playwright who describes himself as "a waterfall gone dry") attempts to concoct a drama before the eyes of the audience. This four-performance curio was written by radio vocalist Patti Spears. "Simply godawful" (*News*). ". . . the worst play I ever saw" (*Journal-American*). P/D: Eugene Endrey.

Strange Woman, The (11/17/13, Lyceum, 88)

A woman of the world (Elsie Ferguson) shocks the inhabitants of an Iowa town with her emancipated views. Interesting portrait of small-town hypocrisy. A: William Hurlbut. P: Klaw and Erlanger.

Strangler Fig, The (5/6/40, Lyceum, 8)

Impossibly complicated mystery, written by actress Edith Meiser, and set on an island off the Florida coast where a plant goes about strangling people it doesn't like. Miss Meiser's play was b/o a novel by John Stephen Strange. C: Eddie Nugent, Madeleine Clive, Dooley Wilson, Edith Meiser. P: William Herz. D: Frank Coletti.

Straw, The (11/10/21, Greenwich Village, 20)

Minor Eugene O'Neill drama set in a tuberculosis sanitarium in Connecticut. A jilted girl (Margalo Gillmore) falls in love with a fellow patient (Otto Kruger). When the young man is cured and leaves, the girl loses all desire to live. However, the ex-patient returns, professes his love for her, and together they face the uncertain future a bit more hopefully. ". . . interesting and moving" (Alexander Woollcott, *New York Times*). "The most depressing play that could possibly be encountered within theatre walls" (Louis De Foe, *World*). P/D: George C. Tyler.

A Streetcar Named Desire. **Marlon Brando and Jessica Tandy (1947–48).** *Courtesy Museum of the City of New York Theatre and Music Collection.*

Street Scene (1/10/29, Playhouse, 601)

Elmer Rice's Pulitzer Prize-winning, grimly realistic drama of New York tenement life. A stagehand, whose wife has been having a sordid affair with the milkman, returns unexpectedly and kills them both. The incident serves chiefly to crystallize the reactions of a large number of representative character types, and to capture the varying moods of daily life in a heedless, impersonal city. ". . . builds engrossing trivialities into a drama that is rich and compelling" (*World*). C: Beulah Bondi, Erin O'Brien-Moore, Horace Braham, John Qualen, Mary Servoss, Leo Bulgakov, Robert Kelly, Astrid Alwynn. SD: Jo Mielziner. *Street Scene* was rejected by almost every manager in New York. Finally it was accepted by veteran old-timer William A. Brady (with Lee Shubert as a silent partner). Numerous actors declined roles in this "sure flop." Director George Cukor walked out after the third day of rehearsals; George

S. Kaufman, George Abbott, and Rouben Mamoulian flatly refused the staging assignment, thus forcing inexperienced Elmer Rice to take over as director. The play opened without benefit of a pre-Broadway tryout after only two invitation previews. *Street Scene* premiered to a wildly enthusiastic audience and to unanimously favorable reviews, stayed around for 601 performances, trouped the country, was a success in London and throughout Europe, was converted by Samuel Goldwyn into a successful motion picture, and turned up a few years later (1/9/47, Adelphi, 148) as an ambitious mini-opera by Kurt Weill and Langston Hughes.

SV: UA, 1931, Sylvia Sidney, Beulah Bondi, Estelle Taylor, William Collier, Jr., John Qualen (directed by King Vidor).

Streetcar Named Desire, A (12/3/47, Barrymore, 855)

Blanche DuBois, delicate, neurasthenic, and empty of purse, seeks refuge in the shabby New Orleans home of her married sister. Stanley Kowalski, her brutish brother-in-law, proves to be Blanche's nemesis. When he exposes her promiscuous past, thereby thwarting her efforts to establish a new life, Blanche retreats into psychosis and is committed to a mental institution. This drama of a woman's gradual disintegration brought thirty-six-year-old Tennessee Williams the Pulitzer Prize, the New York Drama Critics Circle Award, and international renown. Originally titled *The Poker Night*, the play was written with Tallulah Bankhead and John Garfield in mind as Blanche and Stanley. Jessica Tandy and the virtually unknown Marlon Brando eventually inherited these roles, with Kim Hunter (deb.) and Karl Malden lending staunch support under Elia Kazan's potent direction. *A Streetcar Named Desire* was produced with taste and distinction by a newcomer from Hollywood, Irene M. Selznick, daughter of Louis B. Mayer and former wife of David O. Selznick. One of the few critics who disliked the Tennessee Williams drama was George Jean Nathan. He dubbed it *The Glands Menagerie* and said the play suggested "a wayward bus occupied by John Steinbeck, William Faulkner and James Cain all tipsy and all telling stories simultaneously." Williams, on the other hand, considers *Streetcar* his masterpiece, and most critics and theatre historians (including this editor) agree with him. CD: Lucinda Ballard. SD: Jo Mielziner. M: Lehman Engel.

R: (5/23/50, City Center, 24). C: Uta Hagen, Anthony Quinn. D: Elia Kazan.

R: (2/15/56, City Center, 15). C: Tallulah Bankhead, Gerald O'Loughlin. D: Herbert Machiz.

R: (4/26/73, Lincoln Center, 130). C: Rosemary Harris, James Farentino (succeeded by Lois Nettleton and Robert Forster). D: Ellis Rabb.

SV: WB, 1951, Vivien Leigh, Marlon Brando, Kim Hunter, Karl Malden (directed by Elia Kazan).

Note: A *Streetcar Named Desire*, the play that established Marlon Brando as an important actor, marked his last Broadway appearance. Jack Palance was Brando's understudy during the New York run.

Streets Are Guarded, The (11/20/44, Henry Miller, 24)

Stranded with a few companions on a remote island in the Pacific, an old seaman imagines that a mysterious marine is the Saviour. ". . . a generally baffling and curiously unsatisfying drama" *(Post)*. C: Phil Brown, George Mathews, Jeanne Cagney. A: Laurence Stallings. P: John C. Wilson. D: John Haggott. SD: Lee Simonson.

Street Scene, **by Elmer Rice (1929).** *Courtesy Museum of the City of New York Theatre and Music Collection.*

Strictly Dishonorable (9/18/29, Avon, 563)

Preston Sturges' delectable comedy set in a New York speakeasy. An impressionable young thing from Mississippi meets an Italian opera singer and agrees to spend the night with him even though he warns her his intentions are "strictly dishonorable." However, the sophisticate finds that southern innocence is too much for him. Instead of seducing the girl, he ends by proposing marriage. "Quick, witty and delicately risque" (*Sun*). C: Tullio Carminati, Muriel Kirkland, Louis Jean Heydt, Carl Anthony, and Edward J. McNamara (an ex-cop from New Jersey who stole the evening's acting honors with his portrayal of a cynical New York cop). P: Brock Pemberton. D: Antoinette Perry and Brock Pemberton.

SV: U, 1931, Paul Lukas, Lewis Stone, Sidney Fox, George Meeker; MGM, 1951, Ezio Pinza, Janet Leigh, Millard Mitchell.

Strip for Action (9/30/42, National, 109)

Giddy farce about the complications that ensue when a burlesque troupe descends on a Maryland army camp to put on a show. Written by Howard Lindsay and Russel Crouse, co-authors of *Life with Father* (1939), *State of the Union* (1945), etc. "A cockeyed delight" (*Journal-American*). "I can't remember when I've had a better time in the theater" (*PM*). C: Keenan Wynn, Joey Faye, Billy Koud, Wendell Corey, Eleanor Lynn, Jack Albertson, Jean Carter, Harry Bannister. P: Oscar Serlin, Lindsay and Crouse. D: Bretaigne Windust.

Strip Girl (10/19/35, Longacre, 33)

The bumpy life of a strip-tease artiste (Mayo Methot) with a heart of gold.

Pernicious junk. A: Henry Rosendahl. P: L. Lawrence Weber. D: Jose Ruben.

Stripped (10/21/29, Ambassador, 24)

Who stole the crown jewels and where are they hidden? Tedious melodramatic folderol written by Jane Murfin, longtime Hollywood scenarist (*Alice Adams, Come and Get It, Pride and Prejudice*, etc.), and wife of actor Donald Crisp. C: Lionel Atwill (D), Jessie Royce Landis.

Subject was Roses, The (5/25/64, Royale, 832)

Frank D. Gilroy's prize-winning three-character play. Set in a middle-class Bronx apartment at the close of World War II, the drama examines the conflicts that arise when a young veteran returns to the home of his quarrelsome Irish-American parents. His boisterous, uneducated father and frigid, overpossessive mother resent his new maturity. The struggle between the parents for their son's love, and the failure of all three to communicate with one another, ultimately forces the young lad to leave home forever. "An honest and touching work [written] with simplicity, humor and integrity" (*New York Times*). C: Martin Sheen, Jack Albertson, Irene Dailey. P/SD: Edgar Lansbury. D: Ulu Grosbard.
SV: MGM, 1968, Patricia Neal, Jack Albertson, Martin Sheen (directed by Ulu Grosbard).
Note: This 1964 drama turned out to be the sleeper of the decade. A script that was turned down by at least fifteen Broadway producers and, when it did make a shaky start, was not given more than a few weeks to run, went on to win the Pulitzer, Critics Circle, and Tony prizes as best play of the year. It opened on Broadway with a producer who had never produced a Broadway play, a director who had never directed one, a scenic artist who had never designed one, and with three actors who were not well known. Mr. Gilroy's first Broadway play, *The Subject was Roses* had its premiere late in the season, which is considered by many experienced producers as unwise. It was unheralded and unsung. Its advance sale totaled $162. Despite enthusiastic notices, the producer had to borrow $10,000 after the opening to keep the show running. After an uncertain start, the production began to operate in the black, and showed an estimated half-million dollar profit by the time it closed.

Substitute for Murder (10/22/35, Barrymore, 15)

Psychologist has trouble coping with his stepchildren. Ineptly scripted, ridiculously titled comedy. C: Jessie Royce Landis, Myron McCormick, Francis Lister. A: William Jourdan Rapp and Leonardo Bercovici. P/D: William Harris, Jr.

Subway, The (1/25/29, Cherry Lane, 35)

Expressionistic drama by Elmer Rice about a young filing clerk (Jane Hamilton), bewildered by metropolitan existence and unhappy in love, who ends by throwing herself under the wheels of a subway train. ". . . like some of the local trains of its namesake, it manages to get nowhere in particular . . ." (*New York Times*). Presented O/B by the Lenox Hill Players under the direction of Adele Nathan.

Subway Express (9/24/29, Liberty, 270)

Nifty, skillfully crafted 20's whodunit with the action confined to a single car during a round trip subway express ride. Standouts in a cast of fifty were Edward Ellis as a harried police inspector, Dorothy Peterson as the terrified heroine and, in bit roles, Barton MacLane as a beady-eyed cop and Helen Mack as a flirtatious flapper. A: Eva Kay Flint and Martha Madison. P: Edward A. Blatt. D: Chester Erskine.

SV: Col, 1931, Jack Holt, Aileen Pringle, Jason Robards, Sr.

Success Story (9/26/32, Maxine Elliott's, 120)

An ambitious young Jew claws his way to the top of a prestigious gentile advertising agency and, in the process, loses his soul. "Moving and interesting" (Heywood Broun, *World*). "For the first time this season Broadway has seen a play about which audiences may disagree with some point and passion" (Joseph Wood Krutch, *The Nation*). This early Group Theatre production, written by Marxist playwright John Howard Lawson, did not please most left-wing reviewers. They criticized the author for being more interested in an individual rather than a class struggle. C: Luther Adler, Franchot Tone, Stella Adler, Morris Carnovsky, Art Smith, Ruth Nelson, Russell Collins (deb.). D: Lee Strasberg. SD: Mordecai Gorelik.

SV: RKO, 1934, *Success at Any Price*, Douglas Fairbanks, Jr., Colleen Moore, Frank Morgan, Genevieve Tobin, Edward Everett Horton.

Successful Calamity, A (2/5/17, Booth, 144)

Millionaire (William Gillette) feigns bankruptcy in order to bring his spendthrift family into line. Diverting light comedy by Clare Kummer. C: Roland Young, Estelle Winwood, Katherine Alexander. P/D: Arthur Hopkins.

SV: WB, 1930, George Arliss, Mary Astor, Grant Mitchell, Evelyn Knapp, Hale Hamilton, Randolph Scott, Tom Brown.

Such a Little Queen (8/31/09, Hackett, 103)

The exiled king and queen of Herzegovina struggle bravely to adjust to the ways of the New World. Finally, in order that he may regain his rightful throne, the little queen sends her beloved monarch back to his own land without her. "A pretty little fairy story, delicately told" (*New York Times*). C: Elsie Ferguson, Frank Gilmore, Jessie Ralph. A: Channing Pollock. P: Henry B. Harris. D: Frank Keenan.

Musicalized by Reginald De Koven as *Her Little Highness* (1913) with Mitzi Hajos, Allan Pollock, Mae Murray.

Sudden and Accidental Re-education of Horse Johnson, The (12/18/68, Belasco, 5)

Talky comedy about a "rough diamond" (Jack Klugman) who quits his blue-collar job to find the meaning of life. A: Douglas Taylor. P: Persson/Lehman/Harnick/Carr. D: George Morrison.

Suds in Your Eye (1/12/44, Cort, 37)

Three raffish, beer-drinking biddies strive to keep a San Diego junkyard from going under the hammer. ". . . crude, aimless, atmospheric and frequently funny . . ." (*Sun*). C: Jane Darwell, Brenda Forbes, Kasia Orzazewski. A/D: Jack Kirland, b/o on the novel by Mary Lasswell. P: Brown and Del Bondio.

Summer and Smoke (10/6/48, Music Box, 102)

Tennessee Williams' ironic fable about an inhibited southern spinster who, in reclaiming a cynical wastrel's soul, loses her own. Alma Winemiller (Margaret Phillips), daughter of a smalltown minister, is idealistically in love with the boy next door, a lecherous young medical student named John Buchanan (Tod Andrews). She attemps to uplift him morally; he tries to teach her about life and sex. Both succeed too well in their lessons. By the end of the play, John is more interested in spirituality than seduction, while Alma is preparing to embark on a career as the town prostitute. Reviews of this somber allegorical drama were generally unsympathetic. "Definitely one of Tennessee Williams' lesser achievements" said one critic. Four years later, *Summer and Smoke* returned to New York, under Jose Quintero's direction, to become the most sensationally acclaimed O/B production of the year (4/24/52, Circle in the Square, 356). The same critics who had scorned the Broadway version now heaped superlatives upon the play and players, especially newcomer Geraldine Page in the pivotal role of Alma. As for the 1948 Broadway production, it closed after a modest run of 102 performances. C: Anne Jackson, Ray Walston, Monica Boyer, Earl Montgomery, Marga Ann Deighton, Raymond Van Sickle. P/D: Margo Jones. M: Paul Bowles. SD: Jo Mielziner.

SV: Par, 1961, Geraldine Page, Laurence Harvey, Rita Moreno, Una Merkel, Earl Holliman, Pamela Tiffin (directed by Peter Glenville).

Summer Night (11/2/39, St. James, 4)

Unconvincing melodrama set against the background of a marathon dance contest. C: Louis Calhern, Violet Heming, Wesley Addy, Boyd Crawford, Susan Fox, Lyle Bettger, Howard da Silva, Lionel Stander, Helen Flint, Gage Clarke. A: Vicki Baum and Benjamin Glazer. P: Lewis E. Gensler. D: Lee Strasberg. SD: Robert Edmond Jones.

Summer of Daisy Miller, The (5/27/63, Phoenix, 17)

Static O/B adaptation of Henry James' novella about an unsophisticated American girl (Bryarly Lee) who runs athwart European conventions with tragic results. A: Bertram Greene. P: Stewart Chaney (SD) and Theatre 12. D: Denis Vaughan.

Note: The Henry James story was filmed by Paramount (1974) with a cast headed by Cybill Shepherd, Barry Brown, Cloris Leachman, Mildred Natwick, and Eileen Brennan. The production was directed by Peter Bogdanovich from a screenplay by Frederic Raphael.

Summertree (3/3/68, Forum, 127)

Poignant O/B drama about the reveries of a twenty-year-old youth as he surveys his life just prior to his death as a Vietnam war casualty. C: David Birney, Blythe Danner, Philip Sterling, Priscilla Pointer. A: Ron Cowen. P: Repertory Theater of Lincoln Center. D: David Pressman.

Revived O/B (12/9/69, Players, 184) with Lenny Baker in the leading role; directed by Stephen Glassman.

SV: Col, 1971, Michael Douglas, Brenda Vaccaro, Jack Warden, Barbara Bel Geddes, Kirk Callaway, Rob Reiner (directed by Anthony Newley).

Sun and I, The (3/20/49, New Stages, 23)

The biblical story of Joseph, treated in stilted, quasi-satirical fashion. Richard Kiley made his New York stage debut in this O/B production. C: Karl Weber, Nancy R. Pollock. A: Barrie Stavis. P: New Stages. D: Boris Tumarin.

Sun Field, The (12/9/42, Biltmore, 5)

Ballplayer marries Vassar graduate who betters his mind, but wrecks his batting average. *The Sun Field* was based on a novel of the same name by Heywood Broun. ". . . a genuine bore" *(Herald Tribune)*. C: Joel Ashley, Claudia Morgan, Tom Tully, Karl Malden, Betty Kean. A: Milton Lazarus. P: Howard Lang. D: Edward Clarke Lilley.

Sun Kissed (3/10/37, Little, 53)

Befuddled proprietor (Charles Coburn) of Los Angeles boardinghouse becomes involved in the romantic entanglements of his guests. Drowsy 30's comedy. C: Russell Hardie, Francesca Bruning, Jean Adair. A: Raymond Van Sickle. P: Helen Bonfils and George Somnes (D).

Sunday (11/15/04, Hudson, 79)

A beautiful foundling (Ethel Barrymore) is left in the care of four illiterate miners. Vapid comedy-drama, notable only for introducing a line of dialogue: "That's all there is; there isn't any more." Interpolated by Miss Barrymore into the script, this catch–phrase swept the country. A: "Thomas Raceward" (pseud. for T.Q. Percyval, Horace Hodges, and Edward Irwin). P: Charles Frohman. D: William Seymour.

Sunday Breakfast (5/28/52, Coronet, 16)

Domestic problems of a wrangling Connecticut family. ". . . a mournful dirge . . . harrowing, unrewarding and pointless . . ." (*Mirror*). C: Anthony Ross, Cloris Leachman, Douglas Watson. A: Emery Rubio and Miriam Balf. P: ANTA. D: Stella Adler. CD/SD: Ben Edwards.

Sunday in New York (11/29/61, Cort, 188)

Should a twenty-two-year-old virgin (Pat Stanley) allow herself to be seduced by an attractive stranger (Robert Redford)? Frothy farce by Norman Krasna, author of *Dear Ruth* (1944), *John Loves Mary* (1947), etc. C: Conrad Janis, Ron Nicholas, Pat Harrington, Sondra Lee. P: David Merrick. D: Garson Kanin. SD: David Hays.
SV: MGM, 1963, Jane Fonda, Cliff Robertson, Rod Taylor, Robert Culp, Jim Backus.

Sundown Beach (9/7/48, Belasco, 7)

Psychiatric problems of war veterans and their wives and sweethearts; first Broadway production of The Actors Studio. "Earnest and overwritten. . . . a cluttered and congested drama [that] remains singularly lifeless all evening" (*Sun*). *Sundown Beach* was directed by Elia Kazan and written by novelist Bessie Breuer (wife of artist Henry Varnum Poor). C: Julie Harris, Steven Hill, Cloris Leachman, Phyllis Thaxter, Warren Stevens, Nehemiah Persoff, Edward Binns, Anne Hegira, Lenka Peterson, Martin Balsam, Don Hanmer, Jennifer Howard, Alex Nicol. P: Louis J. Singer. SD: Ben Edwards.

Sunrise at Campobello (1/30/58, Cort, 556)

Dore Schary's* inspiring story of Franklin D. Roosevelt's early years from 1921, when he was stricken by polio at his summer home in Campobello, Canada, to 1924 when he walked with steel-braced legs to the rostrum in Madison Square Garden to nominate Al Smith for President of the United States. "Superb . . . an enormously moving and gratifying experience in the theatre" (*Journal-American*). Ralph Bellamy scored a personal triumph in this play with his extraordinarily effective impersonation of FDR. C: Mary Fickett, Henry Jones, Alan Bunce, Anne Seymour, Mary Welch, James Earl Jones, William Fort. P: The Theatre Guild and Dore Schary. D: Vincent J. Donehue.
SV: WB, 1960, Ralph Bellamy, Greer Garson, Hume Cronyn, Jean Hagen, Ann Shoemaker, Alan Bunce, Tim Considine (directed by Vincent J. Donehue).

---

*Screenwriter-producer and longtime MGM production head (1948–56).

Sunshine (8/17/26, Lyric, 15)

Sugary comedy-drama about a warm-hearted country lawyer (O. P. Heggie) who brings a ray of sunshine into everyone's life. A: Henry C. White. P: Paul M. Trebitsch. D: Victor Morley.

Sunshine Boys, The (12/20/72, Broadhurst, 538)

A warm and funny tale of two ancient vaudeville comics, and an affectionate tribute to a vanished art form. Billed for 43 years as "The Sunshine Boys," Al

Lewis and Willie Clark (Sam Levene and Jack Albertson) have split up acrimoniously and gone separate ways eleven years before the action of the play begins. Clark is a pajama-clad curmudgeon, living alone in a New York hotel room, his greatest pleasure scanning the obituary column of weekly *Variety*. Lewis, slightly more reasonable, lives with a married daughter in New Jersey. The catalyst that reunites them is CBS. The network plans a history-of-comedy special and wants Lewis and Clark to do a skit for the show. The task of getting the old men together, and keeping them together, falls to Clark's long-suffering nephew, a theatrical agent. The armed truce he arranges, and the trials of the elderly comics at each other's hands, makes for brilliant and moving comedy. Play's end finds them tacitly accepting the good and bad of unbreakable bonds that a half-century association has forged. ". . . a surprisingly gentle comedy. . . . Jack Albertson and Sam Levene are absolutely perfect in it" (Douglas Watt, *New York Daily News*). ". . . a cripplingly funny show" (T. E. Kalem, *Time*). A: Neil Simon. C: Sam Levene, Jack Albertson, Lewis J. Stadlen, Joe Young, John Batiste, Minnie Gentry, Leo Meredith. D: Alan Arkin. P: Emanuel Azenberg and Eugene V. Wolsk. SD: Kert Lundell.

SV: MGM, 1975, Walter Matthau, George Burns, Richard Benjamin (directed by Herbert Ross from Neil Simon's adaptation of his play). Though it is not the prime purpose of this volume to offer anecdotal material about screen versions, it is worth noting that the role of Willie Clark was to have marked the motion picture return (after a 30-year absence) of one of America's supreme comic artists, Jack Benny. When asked how he and costar Matthau could both be made to appear 70 years old when Matthau was just 54 and Benny 80, Benny replied, "Simple. They'll just make us both look older." Jack Benny died of cancer on 12/26/74.

Sun-Up (5/25/23, Provincetown, 361)

Popular folk-play by Lula Vollmer dramatizing the effects of World War I on a group of Carolina mountaineers. The Widow Cagle (Lucille La Verne) gives shelter to a young war deserter and learns that his father was the revenuer who killed her own husband. She is about to kill the young man when she hears the voice of her dead son urging clemency, and she resolves hereafter to live in peace. P: Players Company, Inc. i.a.w. Lee Kugel. D: Henry Stillman and Benjamin Kauser. Lee Shubert took an interest in *Sun-Up* and moved the production from the Provincetown to Broadway's Princess Theatre. Graced with a fine performance by Lucille La Verne as the embittered, illiterate Widow Cagle, and studded with considerable hillbilly humor and local color, *Sun-Up* had the advantage of novelty when it first appeared. Viewed by today's standards, the script seems simplistic and melodramatic.

R: (10/22/28, La Verne, 137) with Miss La Verne (P/D) again in the leading role.

Sunup to Sundown (2/1/38, Hudson, 7)

Grim 30's drama about the plight of child laborers on a tobacco plantation. Well staged by Joseph Losey; capably acted by a large cast that included Sidney Lumet, Jimmy Lydon, Florence McGee, Eugene Gericke, Percy Kilbride, Carl Benton Reid, Walter Greaza, and Ludmilla Toretzka. A: Francis Edwards Faragoh. P: D. A. Doran. SD: Howard Bay.

Sure Fire (10/20/26, Waldorf, 37)

A playwright (Robert Armstrong) shuns melodramatic hokum until he himself is involved with a mustache-twirling villain and a damsel in distress. Amusing idea ineptly handled. C: Gene Lockhart, Norman Foster, Hugh O'Connell. A:

Ralph Murphy. P: Boothe, Gleason, and Truex. D: Rollo Lloyd.

Survivors, The (1/19/48, Playhouse, 8)

Philosophical melodrama by Peter Viertel and Irwin Shaw demonstrating the futility of war in terms of a frontier feud. Set in post-Civil War Missouri, the story tells of two decent men driven to destroy each other by the violent spirit of the time. In the end, both men are killed, thereby settling nothing at all—which is precisely the play's point. ". . . curiously jumbled . . . uncertain and haphazard" (*Sun*). "A movie horse opera without a horse" (George Jean Nathan). C: Louis Calhern, Richard Basehart, Kevin McCarthy, Hume Cronyn, Anthony Ross, E. G. Marshall, Marc Lawrence, Russell Collins, Neil Fitzgerald, Marianne Stewart, Jane Seymour, Ray Walston. P: Bernard Hart and Martin Gabel (D). SD: Boris Aronson.

Susan and God (10/7/37, Plymouth, 287)

Flighty, insensitive Susan Trexel (Gertrude Lawrence) returns from Europe agog over a religious movement based on a fancy variety of do-goodism. Her alcoholic husband (Paul McGrath) and neglected daughter (Nancy Kelly) want to be included in Susan's campaign to save the world. Hence, Susan must stop being a gushing social butterfly and put her newfound religion into practice. In reclaiming her family, Susan reclaims her own soul and finds her God. This smart, neatly satirical Rachel Crothers (A/D) comedy-drama was one of Gertrude Lawrence's greatest stage successes, and in it she gave one of her finest performances according to most critics. (One of the few nay-sayers was Louis Kronenberger who wrote: "There are moments when Miss Lawrence seems to be playing Susan *and* God at the same time.") Leading man Osgood Perkins (Anthony Perkins' father) died of a heart attack following the first tryout performance in Washington, D. C. Understudy Paul McGrath stepped into the role of the dipsomaniac husband and played it throughout the Broadway run. C: Edith Atwater, Vera Allen, Eleanor Audley. P: John Golden. SD: Jo Mielziner. Miss Lawrence agreed to a limited return engagement revival of *Susan and God* (12/13/43, City Center, 8). It was the first drama to play the cavernous, newly-christened City Center. The supporting company included Conrad Nagel, Eleanor Audley, Doris Day, and Francis Compton. With seats scaled from 55 cents to $1.65 top, New Yorkers stormed the playhouse for tickets, and Mayor Fiorello LaGuardia's long-cherished dream of a popular-priced theatre became a reality.

SV: MGM, 1940, Joan Crawford, Fredric March, Ruth Hussey, Rita Hayworth, John Carroll, Nigel Bruce, Bruce Cabot, Rita Quigley, Rose Hobart, Constance Collier, Gloria De Haven, Marjorie Main (directed by George Cukor from a screenplay by Anita Loos).

Susan Slept Here (7/11/61, 41st Street, 16)

Arch little O/B comedy b/o the 1954 movie about a middle-aged Hollywood writer (Alan Dale) who finds himself falling in love with a seventeen-year-old delinquent (Joy Harmon). Written by screenwriters-producers Steve Fisher (*Tokyo Joe, Dead Reckoning, I Wake Up Screaming*) and Alex Gottlieb (*Blue Gardenia, Marry Me Again*). D: Matt Cimber.

SV: RKO, 1954, Dick Powell, Debbie Reynolds, Anne Francis, Glenda Farrell.

Suzanna and the Elders (10/29/40, Morosco, 30)

Leering look at the practice of plural marriage in one of the many socialistic communities that flourished throughout America in the nineteenth century. Written by Lawrence Langner and Armina Marshall, authors of *The Pursuit of Happiness* (1933). C: Haila Stoddard, Morris Carnovsky, Paul Ballantyne, Philip Coolidge, Lloyd Bridges, Tom Ewell, Howard Freeman, Theodore Newton. P: Jack Kirkland. D: Worthington Miner. CD/SD: Stewart Chaney.

Swan Song (5/15/46, Booth, 158)

Melodrama by the illustrious team* of Ben Hecht and Charles MacArthur about a psychotic young pianist who plots the death of a twelve-year-old keyboard rival. "An unmitigated bore" (*Herald Tribune*). C: Jacqueline Horner, Scott McKay, David Ellin, Marianne Stewart. P: John Clein. D: Joseph Pevney.

---

*Coauthors of *The Front Page* (1928), *20th Century* (1932), etc. Based on a script by Ramon Romero and Harriett Hinsdale, *Swan Song* was aptly titled. It was the last collaborative effort of Hecht and MacArthur.

Sweet Bird of Youth (3/10/59, Martin Beck, 375)

Tennessee Williams' study of an ambitious hustler (Paul Newman), a faded movie queen (Geraldine Page), and their fateful stopover in a Gulf Coast resort. Chance Wayne, the professional gigolo, has lured Hollywood has-been Alexandra Del Lago to his Florida home town in order to see the girl he loved and left behind. The girl, it transpires, has been infected by Chance with venereal disease, and her politically powerful demagogue-father (Sidney Blackmer) and brother (Rip Torn)* plan to castrate the man responsible. In the end, the avengers close in on the remorseful gigolo who has been deserted by his actress-paramour and, far worse, by his youth. Despite some second-act melodramatic confusion, this 1959 drama (staged in semi-stylized fashion by Elia Kazan) was hailed by the critics as "enormously exciting . . . magnificently theatrical . . . corrosively powerful" Highlight: Geraldine Page's stunning performance as the tempestuous, frowsy, hashish-addicted film star. C: Diana Hyland,* Martine Bartlett, Bruce Dern, Madeleine Sherwood, Logan Ramsey, Charles Tyner. P: Cheryl Crawford. CD: Anna Hill Johnstone. SD: Jo Mielziner. M: Paul Bowles.

SV: MGM, 1962, Paul Newman, Geraldine Page, Ed Begley, Shirley Knight, Madeleine Sherwood, Rip Torn, Mildred Dunnock (written and directed by Richard Brooks).

---

*Broadway debuts.

Sweet Chariot (10/23/30, Ambassador, 3)

Black go-getter strives unsuccessfully to promote an African homeland for his race. Muddled comedy-drama on a vital theme. C: Frank Wilson, Fredi Washington. A: Robert Wilder. P/D: Michael Mindlin.

Sweet Charity (12/28/42, Mansfield, 8)

Mild George Abbott (D) farce lampooning women's clubs. Highlight: three of the Helen Hokinson-type girls mistake reefers for cigarettes and go on a smoking spree that renders them completely dippy. Written by screenwriters Irving Brecher (*The Marx Brothers At the Circus, Meet Me in St. Louis,* etc.) and Manual Seff (*Footlight Parade, Gold Diggers of 1935,* etc.). C: Viola Roache, Enid Markey, Augusta Dabney, Philip Loeb, Jane Seymour, Whit Bissell. P: Alfred Bloomingdale.

Sweet Kitty Bellairs (12/9/03, Belasco, 206)

Good-hearted Irish lass (Henrietta Crosman) intrigues her way to fame, fortune, and respectability in eighteenth-century Merrie England. Pleasant David Belasco (A/P/D) gambol based on *The Bath Comedy,* a novel by Edgerton and Agnes

Sweet Kitty Bellairs. **Henrietta Crosman, Louise Moodie, Edwin Stevens (1903).** *Courtesy Museum of the City of New York Theatre and Music Collection.*

Castle. Jane Cowl made her Broadway debut in this play.

Musicalized by Rudolph Friml as *Kitty Darlin'* (1917).

SV: WB, 1930, Claudia Dell, Walter Pidgeon, Ernest Torrence.

Sweet Mystery of Life (10/11/35, Shubert, 11)

Insurance agent schemes to keep five-million–dollar policy-holder alive and kicking. Frenetic 30's farce produced and directed by Herman Shumlin. C: Gene Lockhart, Hobart Cavanaugh, Broderick Crawford. A: Richard Maibaum, Michael Wallach and George Haight.

SV: WB, 1936, *Gold Diggers of 1937*, Dick Powell, Joan Blondell, Victor Moore, Glenda Farrell, Osgood Perkins, Lee Dixon, Jane Wyman.

Sweet Nell of Old Drury (12/31/00, Knickerbocker, 18)

Ada Rehan as the golden-haired orange vendor, Nell Gwyn, who became Charles II's mistress and bore him two sons. Contrived claptrap by Paul Kester. D: Ben Teal.

R: (5/16/23, Forty-Eighth Street, 51) by the Equity Players. C: Laurette Taylor, Alfred Lunt, Lynn Fontanne, Howard Lindsay. D: J. Hartley Manners.

Sweet River (10/28/36, 51st Street, 5)

George Abbott (A/P/D) came a cropper with this modernized version of Harriet Beecher Stowe's *Uncle Tom's Cabin*. Sentimental and slow moving, the costly production was sent to the storehouse after its fifth performance. C: Matt

Briggs, Juano Hernandez, Margaret Mullen, Charles Dingle. M: Juanita Hall. SD: Donald Oenslager.

Sweet Stranger (10/21/30, Cort, 32)

Girl decides she would rather be a rich man's plaything than a married drudge, changes her mind when she meets an eligible young businessman. Meager comedy marked the Broadway debut of Lloyd Nolan in a supporting role. C: Ralph Morgan, Linda Watkins, Viola Roache, Clyde Fillmore, Mel Efird.* A: Frank Mitchell Dazey and Agnes Christine Johnston. P: Paul Streger. D: Worthington Miner.

---

*Married Lloyd Nolan in 1933.

Swing Your Lady! (10/18/36, Booth, 101)

Rowdy farce about a dimwitted wrestler (John Alexander) whose manager (Joe Laurie, Jr.) matches him in the ring against a lady blacksmith (Hope Emerson). Complications arise when the two fighters fall in love. C: Dennie Moore, Billy (William) Redfield (deb.). A: Kenyon Nicholson and Charles Robinson. P: Milton Shubert. D: Bertram Harrison.
SV: WB, 1938, Humphrey Bogart, Frank McHugh, Nat Pendleton, Louise Fazenda, Penny Singleton, *Note:* Humphrey Bogart on the subject of *Swing Your Lady:* "If you want to know the worst picture I ever made, go and get them to screen that one for you."

Swords (9/1/21, National, 36)

Ambitious, uneven blank verse melodrama set in medieval times; Sidney Howard's first play. A pure and noble wife (Clare Eames), held captive in the castle of a wicked German, murders her tormentor and is acclaimed by all for her "act of spiritual courage." *Swords* marked the opening of the National Theatre (now the Billy Rose Theatre). Shortly after the play completed its brief run, author Howard married leading lady Eames. C: Charles Waldron, Jose Ruben, Jane Darwell. P/D: Brock Pemberton. SD: Robert Edmond Jones.

Symphony (4/25/35, Cort, 3)

Glum 30's piece about an impoverished writer who commits suicide when he finds that he can't support his bride. C: Fred de Cordova, Edith Barrett, Shirling Oliver, Ruth Matteson. A: Charles March. P: Michael Myerberg. D: Felix Weissberger.

T

Tailor Made Man, A (8/27/17, Cohan and Harris, 398)

A lowly tailor decides to prove his theory that clothes make the man. Borrowing an elegant dress suit and one-hundred dollars, he sets out to conquer the world of high society—and does. Engaging comedy by Harry James Smith. C: Grant Mitchell, Helen MacKellar, William Hodges. P: Cohan and Harris. D: Sam Forrest.

SV: MGM, 1931, William Haines, Dorothy Jordan.

Take a Giant Step (9/24/53, Lyceum, 76)

Louis Peterson's poignant comedy-drama about the coming of age of a middle-class Negro lad in a white-dominated northern town. Sensing the growing estrangement of his schoolmates, he sets out to explore the adult world with generally unhappy results. Sobered, the teenage youth squares himself off with family and friends and settles down to his schoolbooks. "Genuinely moving and amusing . . . it brings humor and warmth to the stage" *(Mirror)*. C: Louis Gossett (deb.), Estelle Hemsley, Frederick O'Neal, Jane White, Estelle Evans, Warren Berlinger, Frank Wilson. P: Austin and Noyes. D: John Stix.

R: (9/25/56, Jan Hus, 264). C: Bill Gunn, Beah Richards, Godfrey Cambridge, Rosetta LeNoire. D: Ira Cirker.

SV: UA, 1959, Johnny Nash, Ruby Dee, Estelle Hemsley, Frederick O'Neal, Beah Richards, Ellen Holly.

Take Her, She's Mine (12/21/61, Biltmore, 404)

Formula comedy about the difficulties of a doting father (Art Carney) in adjusting to the sexual coming-of-age of his college-bound daughter. C: Elizabeth Ashley, Phyllis Thaxter, June Harding. A: Phoebe and Henry Ephron. P: Harold S. Prince. D: George Abbott. SD: William and Jean Eckart.

SV: Fox, 1963, James Stewart, Sandra Dee, Audrey Meadows, Robert Morley, John McGiver.

Take It As It Comes (2/10/44, 48th Street, 16)

Sudden wealth almost wrecks a small-town family. ". . . a mechanical and tedious little banality" *(World-Telegram)*. C: Frank Wilcox, Louise Lorimer, Richard Basehart. A: E. B. Morris. P: A. L. Robinson. D: Anthony Brown.

Take My Advice (11/1/27, Belmont, 47)

Professional optimist straightens out the tangled affairs of a typical suburban family. So-so 20's comedy. C: Ralph Morgan, Raymond Guion (Gene Raymond), Vivian Tobin, Raymond Walburn. A: Elliott Lester. P/D: William Caryl.

Take My Tip (4/11/32, 48th Street, 24)

Small time investor (Donald Meek) goes broke in the Wall Street crash. Frail comedy by theatrical press agent Nat Dorfman. P: Mack Hilliard. D: Frank Merlin.

Talker, The (1/8/12, Harris, 144)

Women's Lib advocate turns out to be just a tease with the men. The play, too, was all talk, no action. C: Lillian Albertson, Tully Marshall, Pauline Lord, Warren Munsell. A/D: Marion Fairfax. P: Henry B. Harris.

Tall Story (1/29/59, Belasco, 108)

Bribed to throw the Big Game, a star basketball player deliberately flunks his exams, thereby rendering himself ineligible to play. Stridently youthful farce by Howard Lindsay and Russel Crouse b/o a novel by Howard Nemerov. C: Robert Elston, Nina Wilcox, Marc Connelly, Hans Conried, Marian Winters, John Astin, Robert Wright, Mason Adams. P: Rogers and Weiner. D: Herman Shumlin. CD: Noel Taylor. SD: George Jenkins.
SV: WB, 1960, Anthony Perkins, Jane Fonda, Marc Connelly, Ray Walston, Anne Jackson, Murray Hamilton, Robert Wright (directed by Joshua Logan).

Talley Method, The (2/24/41, Henry Miller, 56)

The son and daughter of a cold and intolerant surgeon (Philip Merivale) view their father's forthcoming marriage to a poetess (Ina Claire) with apprehension and disapproval. In the end, the fiancée breaks off her engagement and leaves the discontented household pretty much as she found it. Mixed reviews greeted this uneven, cerebral comedy-drama by S. N. Behrman. Highlight: Hiram Sherman's portrayal of a middle-aged Columbia University student who aims to prove that St. Thomas Aquinas was a Marxist P: The Playwrights Company. D: Elmer Rice. SD: Jo Mielziner.

Tangletoes (2/17/25, 39th Street, 23)

Chorus girl can't adjust to married life in suburbia. Trite domestic comedy-drama. C: Mildred MacLeod, Morgan Farley. A: Gertrude Purcell. P: Edmund Plohn. D: Edwin Maxwell and Hubert Druce.

Tante (10/28/13, Empire, 79)

Madame Okraska (Ethel Barrymore), a jealous, egomaniacal musical genius, almost succeeds in destroying the life of her young ward. Fusty theatrics with the lovely Miss Barrymore cast in a totally unsympathetic role for a change. The play was adapted from a novel by the distinguished American writer Anne Douglas Sedgwick, who lived mostly in Paris and "thought out her stories in French." *Tante* was not a success. C: Charles Cherry, William Ingersoll, Haidee Wright. A/D: C. Haddon Chambers. P: Charles Frohman.

Tapestry in Gray (12/27/35, Shubert, 24)

Murky psychological drama, elaborately produced by motion picture mogul B. P. Schulberg (father of novelist Budd Schulberg). *Tapestry in Gray* recounted, in a series of flashbacks, how a castrating female (Elissa Landi) ruined the lives and careers of two dedicated physicians (Melvyn Douglas and Minor Watson) by her overwhelming possessiveness. The play was written, cinematic fashion, in forty-six scenes. C: Arnold Korff, Jack Lescoulie. A: Martin Flavin. D: Marion Gering. SD: Donald Oenslager.

Tarnish (10/1/23, Belmont, 255)

A perfectionist (Ann Harding) learns to relax her rigid moral code a trifle, and to forgive the failings of others. For, as her shrewd Irish landlady tells her: "The men are a poor lot . . . but the thing is, darlin', to get one that cleans easy." Unpretentious, well-written domestic drama by Gilbert Emery. C: Tom Powers, Fania Marinoff. P/D: John Cromwell.

Tarzan of the Apes (9/7/21, Broadhurst, 14)

Edgar Rice Burroughs' King of the Jungle story was transplanted to Broadway with two of the acts set in Greystoke Castle, England—which reveals better than anything else the lack of imagination in this ludicrously stage-bound dramatization. Ronald Adair was the brawny hero, lost in Africa as a child and raised among the apes, and Ethel Dwyer played Jane. A/P: George Broadhurst, based on a play by Woodgate & Gibbons. D: Mrs. Trimble Bradley.

SV: A silent film version of *Tarzan of the Apes* (WB, 1918) starred Elmo Lincoln and Enid Markey. The first sound version—and perhaps the best in the series—was *Tarzan, the Ape Man* (MGM, 1932) with Johnny Weissmuller and Maureen O'Sullivan, remade (MGM, 1959) with Dennis Miller and Joanna Barnes. Dialogue for the 1932 version was written by Britain's urbane Ivor Novello.

Tavern, The (9/27/20, Cohan, 252)

A motley crew of characters, including a mysterious vagabond (Arnold Daly), seek shelter in an old country inn on a dark and stormy night. Suspense and farcical complications abound until the final curtain when it is learned that the vagabond is really an escaped lunatic. Written as a serious romantic melodrama by one Cora Dick Gantt, rewritten by George M. Cohan (P) as an uproarious travesty, the forerunner of many similar satires. D: John Meehan.

R: (5/19/30, Fulton, 32). C: George M. Cohan, Mary Philips. The APA revived the play in repertory for a limited engagement on 3/3/62 with George Grizzard and Rosemary Harris, and on 3/5/64 with Ellis Rabb and Nancy Marchand in the cast.

Note: In 1940, George M. Cohan wrote, produced, and starred in a companion piece to *The Tavern* called *The Return of the Vagabond* with Celeste Holm and McKay Morris in the cast. It lasted 7 performances.

Tchin-Tchin (10/25/62, Plymouth, 222)

The title means "hello and goodbye" in Chinese. A haughty Englishwoman (Margaret Leighton) and a crude Italian construction worker (Anthony Quinn) are drawn to each other when their respective spouses run off together. This bittersweet farce proceeds to tell how the jilted pair find company in misery, renounce all connection with their conventional pasts, and engage in a humorous but ultimately disastrous love affair of their own. "Outrageously comic and tenderly rueful" *(New York Times)*. C: Charles Grodin (deb.), Sandy Baron, Jean Barker. A: Sidney Michaels b/o a play by Francois Billetdoux. P: David Merrick i.a.w. Warner LeRoy. D: Peter Glenville. SD: Will Steven Armstrong. *Note:* Six months after *Tchin-Tchin* opened on Broadway, Miss Leighton and Mr. Quinn left the company. Their roles were taken over by Arlene Francis and Jack Klugman.

Tea and Sympathy (9/30/53, Barrymore, 712)

Falsely accused of homosexuality, a sensitive youth is brought to manhood by a schoolmaster's sympathetic wife. "... effective sentimental drama of unquestionable box-office magnetism" *(Post)*. Directed by Elia Kazan, Robert Anderson's first Broadway play teamed Deborah Kerr (deb.) and John Kerr (no relation) as the understanding schoolmistress and the confused schoolboy. Joan Fontaine and Anthony Perkins later took

over these roles in this long-run Broadway hit. C: Leif Erickson, Dick York, Alan Sues, Florida Friebus, John McGovern. P: The Playwrights Company i.a.w. Mary K. Frank. CD: Anna Hill Johnstone. SD: Jo Mielziner.
SV: MGM, 1956, Deborah Kerr, John Kerr, Leif Erickson, Edward Andrews, Darryl Hickman, Dean Jones (directed by Vincente Minnelli).

Tea for Three (9/19/18, Maxine Elliott's, 300)

A man decides that the best way to cure his best friend's unreasoning jealousy is to flirt with the friend's attractive wife. Margaret Lawrence was the Wife, Frederick Perry the Husband, and Arthur Byron the Friend in this reasonably diverting triangle comedy by Roi Cooper Megrue (A/D). P: Selwyn and Company.

Teahouse of the August Moon, The (10/15/53, Martin Beck, 1,027)

The misadventures of an Army captain (John Forsythe) assigned to bring U.S. democracy and efficiency to a postwar Okinawan village. Aided by Sakini (David Wayne), his affable, intensely practical interpreter (and the play's interlocutor), the captain outwits his bumbling military superiors and succeeds in giving the islanders the teahouse of their dreams. "Completely captivating" *(New York Times)*. "An enchanting play, filled with the most extraordinary good sense about human and international relations" *(World-Telegram)*. Splendidly cast and performed, impeccably staged by Robert Lewis, *The Teahouse of the August Moon* became one of the most successful comedies of the American theatre. In addition, it won the Pulitzer Prize and the Drama Critics Circle Award as best play of the year. C: Paul Ford, Larry Gates, Mariko Niki, William Hansen. A: John Patrick b/o the novel by Vern Sneider. P: Maurice Evans i.a.w. George Schaefer. CD: Noel Taylor. SD: Peter Larkin. M: Dai-Keong Lee.
R: (11/8/56, City Center, 14). C: Gig Young, Rosita Diaz, John Alexander, Michi Kobi, Barnard Hughes. D: Billy Matthews.

Musicalized by Patrick, Freeman and Underwood as *Lovely Ladies, Kind Gentlemen* (1970) with Kenneth Nelson, Ron Husmann, David Burns, Eleanor Calbes.
SV: MGM, 1956, Marlon Brando, Glenn Ford, Paul Ford, Eddie Albert (directed by Daniel Mann).

Teaspoon Every Four Hours, A (6/14/69, ANTA Theater, 1)

A weak attempt to capitalize on the humor supposedly intrinsic in the trials and tribulations of a Jewish father (not mother for a change.) TV and night club comedian Jackie Mason made his Broadway debut as the harassed dad, but was not well served by the vehicle he coauthored with Mike Mortman. As widower Nat Weiss, Mason must not only fend off matchmakers at every turn, but deal with the problem of his grown son, who has put a black, gentile girl in the family way. For all its failings, the play was notable in one respect: it achieved a Broadway record of ninety-seven preview performances prior to its opening (and closing) day. "Mr. Mason . . . is a rather attractive performer. But if he wants to become legitimate, possibly he should be warned that even Sir Laurence Olivier, Sir Michael Redgrave, and Sir John Gielgud . . . do not feel it incumbent upon them to write their own scripts" (Clive Barnes, *New York Times*). C: Barry Pearl, Lee Wallace, Lee Meredith, Roger Morgan, Marilyn Cooper, Bernie West, Billie Allen, Vera Moore. P: Bernard M. Weber. D: Jeremy Stevens. SD: Robert Randolph.

Tell Me, Pretty Maiden (12/16/37, Mansfield, 28)

As a famous actress (Doris Nolan) tells her life story to a reporter, the play flashes back to what really happened. Mildly entertaining comedy-melodrama. A: Dorothy Day Wendell. P: Bushar and Tuerk. D: Arthur Sircom.

Temper the Wind (12/27/46, Playhouse, 35)

Provocative, frequently compelling postwar drama dealing with the efforts of an American occupational force colonel to denazify a Bavarian manufacturing town, still in the grip of its old warmongering rulers. ". . . the most forceful and absorbing topical drama of the season" (*New York Times*). C: Blanche Yurka, Reinhold Schunzel, Herbert Berghof, Tonio Selwart, Walter Greaza, Thomas Beck, George Mathews, Paul Tripp. A: Edward Mabley and Leonard Mins. P: Straus and Haas. D: Reginald Denham.

Temporary Island, A (3/14/48, Maxine Elliott's, 6)

When he falls in love with a beautiful equestrienne, a teacher runs off and joins a circus. Ponderous, high-flown period comedy (New England, 1881) by college professor Halsted Welles (A/D); produced by the Experimental Theatre for a limited run of six performances. C: Vera Zorina, Philip Bourneuf, Ernest Truex, Rita Gam (deb.), Walter (Jack) Palance.

Ten Million Ghosts (10/23/36, St. James, 1)

Orson Welles had the leading role in this ill-fated antiwar play by Sidney Kingsley (A/P/D), author of *Men in White* (1933), *Dead End* (1935), *Detective Story* (1949), etc. The drama dealt with the conflict between an idealistic French poet (Welles) and a coldly cynical armaments salesman (George Coulouris). Both men are suitors for the hand of the same girl (Barbara O'Neil). The triangle is resolved when the poet is killed in the war, and the merchant of death claims his bride. The opening night of *Ten Million Ghosts* (which turned out to be the closing night as well) was a fiasco. In the munitions factory scenes, the play's pacifist message was drowned out by the blasting of machines. The sound level was pitched so high that the actors were all but inaudible. When the final curtain fell, there was prolonged booing from the gallery. The costly production, which the author had financed with his own money, closed after a single performance. C: Martin Gabel, Dodson Mitchell, Lee Baker, Otto Hulett, Meg Mundy, J. Carroll Ashburn, Philip Bourneuf. SD: Donald Oenslager.

Tender Trap, The (10/13/54, Longacre, 101)

Contrived but fairly amusing farce about a footloose Manhattan bachelor who finally is trapped into marriage by a determined young miss. C: Ronny Graham, Robert Preston, Kim Hunter, Janet Riley, Julia Meade, Joey Faye, Jack Manning, Parker McCormick. A: Max Shulman and Robert Paul Smith. P: Clinton Wilder. D: Michael Gordon.

SV: MGM, 1955, Frank Sinatra, Debbie Reynolds, David Wayne, Celeste Holm, Carolyn Jones (directed by Charles Walters).

Tenth Avenue (8/15/27, Eltinge, 88)

Two small-time chiselers try to hustle their rent money; one gets murdered, the other winds up marrying his landlady. Rowdy, sentimental melodrama with a nice cast: Frank Morgan, William Boyd, Frank McHugh, Gregory Ratoff, Edna Hibbard. A: John McGowan and Lloyd Griscom. P: Lexington Productions.

Tenth Man, The (11/5/59, Booth, 623)

The tenth man is a suicidally despondent

agnostic who is shanghaied off the streets and into a shabby synagogue to complete a *minyon* (a quorum of ten Jewish men). When the synagogue's elders attempt to banish a demon from the body of one of the member's granddaughters, they discover instead that they have exorcised the evil spirit from the bedeviled tenth man. He, in turn, is forced to acknowledge that faith can sometimes effect miracles beyond the reach of science. Paddy Chayefsky's seriocomic fable—a reworking of the Hebrew legend of the Dybbuk—was staged with great theatrical flair by Tyrone Guthrie. A fascinating blend of farce and mysticism, the play was marred only slightly by an unconvincing, O. Henryesque trick ending. C: Jacob Ben-Ami, Lou Jacobi, Jack Gilford, Arnold Marle, David Vardi, George Voskovec, Donald Harron, Risa Schwartz, Gene Saks. P: Saint Subber and Arthur Cantor. SD: David Hays.
R: (11/8/67, City Center, 23). C: John Kerr, Boris Tumarin, Muni Seroff. D: Arthur Cantor.

Tenting Tonight (4/2/47, Booth, 46)

Complications ensue when some ex-GI's take lodgings in a college professor's overcrowded cottage. ". . . a clamorous and exhausting comedy" *(Sun)*. C: Jackie Kelk, Joshua Shelley, Jean Muir, Dean Harens, June Dayton, Richard Clark. A: Frank Gould. P: Saul Fischbein. D: Hudson Faussett.

Terrible Swift Sword, The (11/15/55, Phoenix, 8)

Cruelty and barbarism in a boys' ROTC prep school in Georgia. ". . . horrifying, brutish, sadistic, blood-curdling and abominable in general" *(New York Times)*. Presented O/B by the Phoenix Theatre; staged by Fred Sadoff. C: Conrad Janis, Bob Heller, John Fiedler. A: Arthur Steuer.

Thank You (10/3/21, Longacre, 257)

The tribulations of an underpaid small-town parson (Harry Davenport). Unpretentious, wholesome comedy by Winchell Smith (D) and Tom Cushing. P: John Golden.

Thank You, Svoboda (3/1/44, Mansfield, 6)

Simple-minded Czech handyman (Sam Jaffe) outwits the Nazi invaders. ". . . slow-moving and unconvincing" *(Sun)*. A: H. S. Kraft b/o a novel by John Pen. P: Milton Baron. D: H. S. Kraft and Moe Hack.

That Awful Mrs. Eaton (9/29/24, Morosco, 16)

Middling biographical drama by Stephen Vincent Benet and John Farrar dealing with Peggy Eaton (Katherine Alexander), the notorious belle of Washington during the administration of President Andrew Jackson (Frank McGlynn). P/D: William A. Brady.

That Championship Season (9/14/72, Booth, 700)

Searing examination of the competitive aspect of the American success story, and the wounds it can inflict on those who compete. The scene is the reunion of four high school basketball players and their coach, in celebration of the state championship they won twenty years before. High-spirited friends as the evening begins, a seemingly secure group of mature men, liquor loosens their tongues and unties inhibitions as the reunion progresses. They show themselves to be far different from the successes they appear. The coach, a subscriber to the winning-is-everything ethic, is a brutal fool. His players are an alcoholic cynic, a crooked politico, a leching mining boss, and an unethical school administrator. Despite material comforts, life has defeated them all, and they hearken back to their sports success as the one pure victory of their lives. That the championship itself was unfairly won is an irony that only the alcoholic can face up to. For the others, such an admission would be a trauma too devastating, and as the curtain falls, they are snapping a picture of the coach holding their silver trophy. Though not a likable group, they are arrestingly human, and the author's study of their lives is conducted with compassion, insight, and great technical skill. "Wow! ... It is gorgeous and triumphant" (Clive Barnes, *New York Times*). ". . . a triumph of ensemble acting" (T. E. Kalem, *Time*). ". . . engrossing theater. The cast is matchless" (Douglas Watt, *New York Daily News*). *That Championship Season* opened 5/2/72 at the O/B Newman Theater, part of the New York Shakespeare Festival Public Theater complex. It played 144 performances before moving to Broadway on 9/14/72 for another 700 performances. The play was awarded the Pulitzer Prize and the New York Drama Critics Circle award for Best Play. It won the Tony for Best Play, and A. J. Antoon received a Tony for Best Director. A: Jason Miller. C: Charles Durning, Paul Sorvino, Richard A. Dysart, Walter McGinn, Michael McGuire. D: A. J. Antoon. SD: Santo Loquasto. P: Joseph Papp.

That Ferguson Family (12/22/28, Little, 129)

Another domineering mother (Jean Adair) comedy-drama. Third-rate on all counts. A: Howard Chenery. P/D: Gustav Blum.

That Old Devil (6/5/44, Playhouse, 16)

Dull comedy about a senior citizen who masquerades as a philanderer. C: J. C. Nugent (A/D), Luella Gear, Matt Briggs. P: Lodewick Vroom.

That Summer—That Fall (3/16/67, Hayes, 12)

A wife develops a fatal passion for her handsome stepson. Murky updating of the Phaedra tragedy seldom cast its intended spell; written by Frank D. Gilroy, author of *The Subject Was Roses* (1964). C: Irene Pappas,* Jon Voight,* Richard Castellano. P: Edgar Lansbury. CD: Theoni V. Aldredge. SD: Jo Mielziner. M: David Amram.

---

*Broadway debuts.

That's Gratitude (9/11/30, Golden, 197)

When a stranger saves his life, a traveling salesman is so overwhelmed with gratitude that he insists on taking the good samaritan home with him, only to find the samaritan has no intention of leaving. He prolongs his stay indefinitely, much to the consternation of his now put-upon host. Breezy comedy by Frank Craven (A/D). C: Frank Craven, George Barbier, Ross Alexander. P: John Golden.

R: (6/16/32, Waldorf, 204) with Taylor Holmes and J. C. Nugent in the leads.

SV: Col, 1934, Frank Craven.

That's the Woman (9/3/30, Fulton, 29)

Keen-witted lawyer saves innocent man from the electric chair. Hackneyed courtroom melodrama by Bayard Veiller. C: Gavin Muir, Lucile Watson, A. E. Anson, Effie Shannon, Phoebe Foster. P: Charles Dillingham. D: Lester Lonergan.

Theodora, the Quean (1/31/34, Forrest, 6)

Three acts purporting to show that the Byzantine empress was really a "quean" (a harlot) at heart. Trash. C: Elena Miramova, Minor Watson, Horace Braham, Rex Ingram, Lina Abarbanell. A: Jo Milward and J. Kerby Hawkes. P/D: Jo Graham.

There Was a Little Girl (2/29/60, Cort, 16)

Jane Fonda made her Broadway debut in this melodrama about an eighteen-year-old girl who is raped by a hoodlum and thereafter, instead of being an object of sympathy, becomes a marked figure in her affluent suburban community. "A tawdry tale . . . adolescent and malodorous" *(New York Times)*. ". . . a resplendent young woman with exceptional style and assurance . . . Jane Fonda has a fine future but not, regrettably, in this play" *(Journal-American)*. Also making their Broadway debuts in this 1960 production were Joey Heatherton (as Miss Fonda's pert little sister), Dean Jones (as her boyfriend), and Sean Garrison (as her assailant). C: Ruth Matteson, Gary Lockwood, Whitfield Connor, Phillip Pruneau. A: Daniel Taradash* b/o a novel by Christopher Davis. P: Fryer and Carr. D: Joshua Logan. SD: Jo Mielziner. M: Lehman Engel.

---

*Hollywood screenwriter *(From Here to Eternity, Picnic, Hawaii,* etc.).

There Shall Be No Night (4/29/40, Alvin, 181)

Robert E. Sherwood's timely and eloquent portrait of a beleaguered country (Finland), and its desperate, hopeless stand against Russian invasion, opened on Broadway in the spring of 1940 to "a visibly moved and tremendously appreciative" first-night audience. In the roles of a renowned Finnish scientist and his American-born wife, Alfred Lunt and Lynn Fontanne underplayed with greater skill and dexterity than ever. They were

There Shall Be No Night. **Scene of toast-drinking (1939–40).** *Courtesy Museum of the City of New York Theatre and Music Collection.*

ably supported by an excellent company headed by Montgomery Clift, Sydney Greenstreet, and Richard Whorf (SD). "No one can complain about the theatre's being an escapist institution when it conducts a class in current events at once as touching, intelligent, and compassionate as *There Shall Be No Night*" (John Mason Brown, *Post*). "At a time of national pussy-footing, Mr. Sherwood vigorously takes a stand against the forces of aggression. . . . At a time when isolationist idiots talk of soothing the savage, Mr. Sherwood, with a glowing pen, writes the words that say, 'there are times when a man must fight' " (Arch Oboler).* Sherwood won his third Pulitzer Prize—his first two were for *Idiot's Delight* (1936) and *Abe Lincoln in Illinois* (1938)—with *There Shall Be No Night*. However, when the Finns threw in their lot with Hitler, Sherwood was forced to completely revamp the play. As recounted by George Freedley in his book, *The Lunts*, the illustrious acting team decided to take the Sherwood drama to wartime London. "Since Russia at this time was England's ally against the Nazis," Freedley pointed out, " a play in which she was exposed as an aggressor nation would not be fitting, so Sherwood transposed the situation to the German invasion of Greece." The play proved as big a hit in England as it had been in America. C: Maurice Colbourne, Elisabeth Fraser, Phyllis Thaxter, Brooks West, Ralph Nelson, Robert Downing. P: The Playwrights Company i.a.w. The Theatre Guild. D: Alfred Lunt.

---

*Noted radio dramatist and Hollywood writer-director, in a letter to this editor.

There's Always a Breeze (3/2/38, Windsor, 5)

Mistaken for a murderer, a meek suburbanite thrives on the attention and publicity. Lacklustre 30's comedy with a capable cast: William Lynn, Blanch Sweet, Anne Baxter, Cecilia Loftus, Hume Cronyn, Leona Powers, Otto Hulett, Curtis Cooksey. A: Edward Caulfield. P: Hyman and Cooper. D: Harry Wagstaff Gribble.

There's Always Juliet (2/15/32, Empire, 109)

The three-day romance and whirlwind courtship of an American architect (Herbert Marshall) and an English debutante (Edna Best). "It amuses you royally" *(New York Times)*. This four-character comedy by Anglo-American author John Van Druten could have enjoyed a much longer Broadway run. However, Paramount Pictures was so anxious to obtain the services of Herbert Marshall (for the 1932 Ernst Lubitsch film *Trouble in Paradise*) that they paid Gilbert Miller (P) a substantial sum to close the play ahead of time. C: Dame May Whitty, Cyril Raymond. D: Auriol Lee.

SV: Par, 1941, *One Night in Lisbon*, Fred MacMurray, Madeleine Carroll, Patricia Morison, Billie Burke, John Loder.

There's Wisdom in Women (10/30/35, Cort, 46)

Humdrum comedy about a woman-chasing concert pianist (Walter Pidgeon) and his understanding wife; first play by Joseph Kesselring, author of *Arsenic and Old Lace* (1941). C: Ruth Weston, Glenn Anders, Betty Lawford, Frances Maddux. P: D. A. Doran. D: Harry Wagstaff Gribble.

Therese (10/9/45, Biltmore, 96)

A mother (Dame May Whitty) learns that her beloved son was murdered by his faithless wife (Eva Le Gallienne) and her lover (Victor Jory). The shock turns the old lady into a mute paralytic, but she finally finds a way to communicate her knowledge of the crime to the police. This slow-moving, melodramatic period piece, set in nineteenth-century Paris, was adapted by Thomas Job from the novel *Therese Raquin* by Emile Zola. "*O Zola Mio*" (George Jean Nathan). P: Payne-Jennings and Klawans. D: Margaret Webster. CD/SD: Raymond Sovey.

These Days (11/12/28, Cort, 8)

Schoolgirl crushes and other problems at a fashionable finishing school. Tepid 20's drama. Standout in a cast of a dozen unknown girls was a gangling nineteen-year-old redhead who spoke her few lines in a Bryn Mawr accent and made the audience sit up and take notice every time she appeared. Her name: Katharine Hepburn. A: Katharine Clugston. P/D: Arthur Hopkins.

SV: RKO, 1934, *Finishing School*, Frances Dee, Ginger Rogers, Billie Burke, Bruce Cabot.

These Modern Women (2/13/28, Eltinge, 24)

When a bored wife (Chrystal Herne) has an affair with a visiting author (Alan Mowbray), her novelist-husband (Minor Watson) leaves her. Soporific comedy by Lawrence Langner, directed by Rouben Mamoulian. P: Macgowan and Rockmore.

They All Come to Moscow (5/11/33, Lyceum, 19)

American engineer falls in love with his married Russian secretary. Dawdling 1933 comedy set in the Soviet Union during the days of the first five-year plan. C: Tamara, Jack Davis, Cornel Wilde (deb.), Clifford Odets, Boris Marshalov. A: John Washburne and Ruth Kennell. P: The Players Theatre. D: William J. O'Neill.

They All Want Something (10/12/26, Wallack's, 63)

Insufferably arch comedy about a young millionaire (tennis pro Bill Tilden) who masquerades as a tramp. A: Courtenay Savage. P: Herman Gantvoort. D: Alonzo Price.

They Knew What They Wanted (11/24/24, Garrick, 192)

Pulitzer Prize drama by Sidney Howard. In California's Napa Valley, an elderly Italian winegrower (Richard Bennett) courts a lonely San Francisco waitress (Pauline Lord) by mail, using the photograph of his handsome young overseer (Glenn Anders) to inspire confidence. The consequences of the inevitable love affair between the two young people, and the reactions of the husband to his wife's pregnancy, constitute the core of the drama. In the end, the genial cuckold forgives his wife and accepts the baby with philosophical equanimity. Beautifully acted by its three stars, *They Knew What They Wanted* was one of the memorable productions of the American theatre. P: The Theatre Guild. D: Philip Moeller.

R: (10/2/39, Empire, 24) by Leonard Sillman. C: Giuseppe Sterni, June Walker, Douglass Montgomery. D: Robert Ross.

R: (2/16/49, Music Box, 61) by John Golden. C: Paul Muni, Carol Stone, Edward Andrews. D: Robert Perry.

Musicalized by Frank Loesser as *The Most Happy Fella* (1956) with Robert Weede, Jo Sullivan, Art Lund, Susan Johnson, Shorty Long.

SV: MGM, 1930, *A Lady to Love*, Edward G. Robinson, Vilma Banky, Robert Ames; RKO, 1940, Charles Laughton, Carole Lombard, William Gargan, Harry Carey, Frank Fay.

Note: A silent version entitled *Secret Hour* (Par, 1928) starred Pola Negri and Jean Hersholt.

They Shall Not Die (2/21/34, Royale, 62)

Powerful, splendidly acted drama based on the notorious Scottsboro case in which nine black youths were indicted in

They Knew What They Wanted **Richard Bennett and Pauline Lord (1924–25).** *Courtesy Museum of the City of New York Theatre and Music Collection.*

Alabama on charges of having raped two white girls. In John Wexley's 1934 dramatization, one of the girls (Ruth Gordon) later admits she has given false testimony, but the trumped-up charges remain. Despite the excellent work of a Jewish defense lawyer (Claude Rains), the play ends with little hope for anything but a guilty verdict. C: Linda Watkins, Hugh Rennie, Thurston Hall, Dean Jagger, Helen Westley, Erskine Sanford, Frank Wilson, Tom Ewell (deb.), Ralph Theadore, William Lynn. P: The Theatre Guild. D: Philip Moeller. SD: Lee Simonson.

They Should Have Stood in Bed (2/13/42, Mansfield, 11)

Small-time hoodlums try to rig a championship fight. Former lightweight world champion, Tony Canzoneri, made his acting debut in this 1942 farce. ". . . absolutely and inexpressibly terrible" *(PM)*. C: Jack Gilford, Sanford Meisner, Grant Richards, Martin Ritt. A: Leo Rifkin, Frank Tarloff, and David Shaw. P: Sam H. Grisman i.a.w. Alexander H. Cohen. D: Luther Adler.

Thieves (4/7/74, Broadhurst, 312)

Episodic comedy about life in the big city and the mores and folkways of its citizens circa 1974. The play wanders amiably among the lives of a group of New Yorkers, examining their frustrations and problems with diverting humor. There is no plot to speak of, and the starring players are often offstage. Loosely connected, the various scenes of the play

are entertaining without being incisive. A number of the characters have fine monologues, and these are the high spots of the production. ". . . a mawkish and ill-constructed comedy . . . radiates as much warmth as the surface of the East River" (Douglas Watt, *New York Daily News*). "Mr. Gardner brings neither the original observation nor the unexpected variation that can freshen a familiar theme" (John Beaufort, *Christian Science Monitor*). As an indication of the skyrocketing costs of mounting a Broadway play, *Thieves* lost a quarter-million dollars despite a run of nine months. A: Herb Gardner. C: Marlo Thomas, Richard Mulligan, Dick Van Patten, Irwin Corey, David Spielberg, Sudie Bond, Sammy Smith, Pierre Epstein, Alice Drummond, Ann Wedgeworth, George Loros, William Hickey, Haywood Nelson. D: Charles Grodin. P: Richard Scanga and Charles Grodin. SD: Peter Larkin. CD: Joseph G. Aulisi.
SV: Par, 1977, Marlo Thomas, Charles Grodin, Irwin Corey, Hector Elizondo, Mercedes McCambridge, Gary Merrill, Ann Wedgeworth, Bob Fosse, John McMartin (directed by John Berry from Herb Gardner's adaptation of his play).

Things That Count, The (12/8/13, Maxine Elliott's, 224)

Domestic didoes at a Christmastime family reunion. Sentimental, gossamer-thin comedy-drama. C: Alice Brady, Edna Wallace Hopper, Florine Arnold, Howard Estabrook. A: Laurence Eyre. P: William A. Brady. D: John Cromwell.

Third Best Sport (12/30/58, Ambassador, 79)

Tepid comedy about the rebellion of a businessman's bride against corporate conformity. C: Celeste Holm, Andrew Duggan, William Prince. A: Eleanor and Leo Bayer. P: The Theatre Guild. D: Michael Howard.

Third Degree, The (2/1/09, Hudson, 168)

An innocent man is forced into a murder confession by police brutality. Absorbing 1909 melodrama by Charles Klein (A/D). C: Edmund Breese, Helen Ware, Wallace Eddinger. P: Henry B. Harris.

Thirteenth Chair, The (11/20/16, 48th Street, 328)

A man is killed during a seance. Despite the fact that all doors and windows to the murder room were locked, no weapon is found. When suspicion falls on the daughter of the medium (Margaret Wycherly), her mother uses mind-reading powers to unmask the real criminal. Written by Bayard Veiller, author of *Within the Law* (1912), *The Thirteenth Chair* remains one of the most suspenseful and ingenious of mystery plays. P: William Harris, Inc. D: Ira Hards.
SV: MGM, 1929, Margaret Wycherly, Conrad Nagel, Bela Lugosi; 1937, Dame May Whitty, Lewis Stone, Elissa Landi, Madge Evans.

Thirty Days Hath September (9/30/38, Hudson, 16)

Silly farce about a doting grandmother (Alison Skipworth) who gets mixed up with wills, legacies, and crooks. A: Irving Gaumont and Jack Sobell. P: Kirby Grant. D: Bertram Harrison.
SV: WB, 1941, *Thieves Fall Out*, Eddie Albert, Joan Leslie, Alan Hale, Anthony Quinn, Minna Gombell, Nana Bryant, John Litel, Edward Brophy, Hobart Cavanaugh.

39 East (3/31/19, Broadhurst, 160)

Fairly diverting Rachel Crothers (A/D) comedy set in a nondescript boardinghouse inhabited by representative boardinghouse types. Leading roles were played by Henry Hull (succeeded by Sidney Blackmer) and Constance Binney (succeeded by 17-year-old Tallulah Bankhead in her first speaking role on Broadway). Also in the cast: Alison Skipworth, Luis Alberni, Blanche Frederici, Albert Carroll. P: Messrs. Shubert.

This Fine-Pretty World (12/26/23, Neighborhood Playhouse, 32)

A Kentucky mountaineer hires a "lie-swearer" to testify that he has had illicit relations with the mountaineer's wife. Thus, the would-be Kentucky playboy will be free to marry a young girl. The plan backfires, however, and the "defamin' attorney" lands in jail. This picturesque, highly amusing O/B comedy by Percy MacKaye was marred by the author's use of overly literal dialect. The result, in the words of one critic, was that during certain crucial scenes "the audience was barely able to follow the play." C: E. J. Ballantine, Aline MacMahon, Joanna Roos, Perry Ivans, Albert Carroll, Danton Walker.

This is New York (11/28/30, Plymouth, 59)

Synthetic comedy by Robert E. Sherwood about the melodramatic things that happen to a conservative senator and his wife when they visit New York to stop their daughter's marriage to a playboy. C: Lois Moran, Geoffrey Kerr, Robert T. Haines, Robert Barrat, Virginia Howell. P/D: Arthur Hopkins.
SV: Par, 1932, *Two Kinds of Women*, Miriam Hopkins, Phillips Holmes.

This Man's Town (3/10/30, Ritz, 9)

Slam-bang gangland nonsense with a capable cast: Pat O'Brien, Eduardo Ciannelli, Walter Glass, Willard Robertson (A), Constance Cummings, Marjorie Main, Sam Levene. P: George Jessel. D: Lester Lonergan.

This One Man (10/21/30, Morosco, 39)

A self-sacrificing weakling (Paul Guilfoyle) takes the blame for a murder committed by his wicked, unregenerate brother (Paul Muni), and goes to the electric chair in his place. "Steadily interesting... Mr. Muni is overpowering and magnificent" *(New York Times)*. This murky 30's melodrama was written by screenwriter Sidney Buchman (*Theodora Goes Wild, Mr. Smith Goes to Washington, Here Comes Mr. Jordan*, etc.). P: Arthur Lubin and Richard W. Krakeur, D: Leo Bulgakov.

This Our House (12/10/35, 58th Street, 2)

Costume drama recounting the oft-told story of the vengeful Beatrice Cenci, executed in 1599 for the murder of her nobleman-father. A flawed reworking of Shelley's closet-drama, *The Cenci* (1820), *This Our House* closed after its second performance. The play was written by theatrical producer Joel W. Schenker and Allan Fleming. C: Edith Atwater, Ian MacLaren, Ben Starkie. P: Christopher Noel. D: James Light.

This Rock (2/18/43, Longacre, 36)

Class-conscious Britisher (Billie Burke) is forced to shelter a group of children from the London slums. In so doing, she learns the virtues of democracy and ends by endorsing the marriage of her heiress-daughter (Jan Sterling) to a cockney (Zachary Scott). "... creaky claptrap" *(World-Telegram)*. "... has about it a coy and cloying quality we might expect if Pollyanna had written *War and Peace*" *(Journal-American)*. This "comedy of England during the blitz" was written by Walter Livingston Faust, a Standard Oil of New Jersey vice-president. C: Nicholas Joy, Joyce Van Patten, Gene Lyons. P/D: Eddie Dowling.

This Side of Paradise (2/21/62, Sheridan Square, 87)

Portrait of disillusioned Jazz Age youth Amory Blaine (Paul Roebling) who, lacking moral purpose, flits aimlessly from one love affair to another. By the time he reaches his early twenties, Amory finds his life blighted by regret, cynicism, and world weariness. Imaginative O/B adaptation of the famous postwar novel (1920) that established F. Scott Fitzgerald's reputation. A: Sydney Sloane. D: Herbert Berghof.

This Thing Called Love (9/17/28, Maxine Elliott's, 138)

To test their marriage, newlyweds agree to a strictly platonic three-month arrangement. Bright 20's comedy; deftly written, acted and staged. C: Violet Heming, Minor Watson. A: Edwin Burke. P: Patterson McNutt. D: Howard Lindsay.
SV: Pathé, 1929, Constance Bennett, Edmund Lowe, ZaSu Pitts; Col, 1941, Rosalind Russell, Melvyn Douglas, Binnie Barnes, Lee J. Cobb, Allyn Joslyn, Gloria Dickson.

This, Too, Shall Pass (4/30/46, Belasco, 63)

Anti-semitic mother tries to prevent the marriage of her daughter to a Jewish soldier. "It is a very crude and unorganized drama, and also quite a dull one" *(Sun)*. C: Sam Wanamaker, Jan Sterling, Kathryn Givney, Ralph Morgan, Walter Starkey. A/D: Don Appell. P: Krakeur and Shay.

Thoroughbreds (11/6/33, Vanderbilt, 24)

Romantic mixups among Long Island's horsy set. Plodding 30's comedy. C: Florence Reed, Thurston Hall, Harry Ellerbe, Claudia Morgan. A: Doty Hobart. P: Theodore Hammerstein (D) and Denis Du-For.

Those Endearing Young Charms (6/16/43)

Wartime romance between a lecherous aviator and a wholesome young miss. She gives herself willingly to the cad, but manages to lead him to the altar before the final curtain. ". . . confused and talky" *(New York Times)*. This four-character comedy-drama was written by Edward Chodorov (A/D). C: Zachary Scott, Virginia Gilmore, Blanche Sweet, Dean Harens. P: Max Gordon.
SV: RKO, 1945, Robert Young, Laraine Day, Ann Harding.

Those That Play the Clowns (11/24/66, ANTA, 4)

Pretentious costume piece about the band of strolling players invited by Prince Hamlet to perform at Elsinore. Written by musical-comedy librettist Michael Stewart *(Bye, Bye, Birdie, Carnival!, Hello, Dolly!,* etc.). C: Alfred Drake, Joan Greenwood. P: David Black i.a.w. Nathan Friedman. D: Robin Midgley.

Those We Love (2/19/30, Golden, 77)

Because of his infidelities, a composer (Armina Marshall) leaves her writer-husband (George Abbott); eventually they reconcile for the sake of their child. Dreary soap opera by George Abbott (D) and S. K. Lauren. C: Josephine Hull, Percy Kilbride, Helen Flint, Charles Waldron, Joseph Crehan. P: Philip Dunning.
SV: World Wide, 1932, Mary Astor, Kenneth MacKenna, Lilyan Tashman, Hale Hamilton.

Thou Desperate Pilot (3/7/27, Morosco, 8)

Melancholia, gambling fever, and suicide in the mad, glittering, heartless world of Monte Carlo; as florid and pretentious as its title. Written by Zoe Akins, author of *The Old Maid* (1935). C: Miriam Hopkins, Helen Ware. P: Rachel Crothers (D) and Mary Kirkpatrick. SD: Livingston Platt.

Thousand Clowns, A (4/5/62, O'Neill, 428)

A cheerful nonconformist (Jason

Robards, Jr.) is forced to reexamine his values when a welfare agency threatens to take away the twelve-year-old nephew he's been rearing in his own image. "Sunny and wistful . . . and above all, unfailingly amusing" *(New York Times)*. C: Sandy Dennis, A. Larry Haines, William Daniels, Barry Gordon, Gene Saks. A: Herb Gardner. P: Fred Coe (D) and Arthur Cantor. SD: George Jenkins.

SV: UA, 1965, Jason Robards, Jr., Barbara Harris, Martin Balsam, Barry Gordon, William Daniels, Gene Saks (directed by Fred Coe).

Thousand Summers, A (5/24/32, Selwyn, 47)

Young artist (Franchot Tone) falls in love with glamorous older woman (Jane Cowl). Stagy teacup drama set in England. C: Osgood Perkins, Josephine Hull, Thomas Findlay. A: Merrill Rogers. P: Arch Selwyn and Shepard Traube (D).

Thousand Years Ago, A (1/6/14, Shubert, 87)

When a group of Italian strolling players visit China, they become involved in intrigue, adventure, and a star-crossed romance. Colorful, poetic spectacle play by Percy MacKaye. C: Henry E. Dixey, Jerome Patrick, Rita Jolivet, Fania Marinoff. P: Messrs. Shubert. D: J. C. Huffman.

3 Bags Full (3/6/66, Henry Miller, 33)

Uneven but frequently hilarious farce about a tight-fisted merchant (Paul Ford) in turn-of-the-century New York, and of the madcap complications that ensue when one of his employees embezzles a half-million dollars from the merchant's sporting goods firm. A: Jerome Chodorov b/o a play by Claude Magnier. P: Leonard S. Field. D: Gower Champion. CD: Freddy Wittop. SD: Will Steven Armstrong.

Three Faces East (8/13/18, Cohan and Harris, 335)

Helene (Violet Heming), a beautiful English girl, inveigles her way into the German Secret Service which sends her to England and into the home of a cabinet minister with whom she falls in love. Clever, highly successful espionage drama moved at a rapid pace. C: Emmett Corrigan, Cora Witherspoon. A: Anthony Paul Kelly. P: Cohan and Harris. D: Sam Forrest.

SV: WB, 1930, Constance Bennett, Erich von Stroheim; 1940, *British Intelligence*, Margaret Lindsay, Boris Karloff.

Three Men on a Horse (1/30/35, Playhouse, 812)

Hilarious farce about a timid greeting card writer who picks winning horses with such unerring success that he is shanghaied by a trio of racetrack touts and forced to select winners for them. When he personally places a bet for the first time, the spell is broken, and he is allowed to return home to his loving wife. *Three Men on a Horse* proved to be not only the comedy sensation of its season, but a minor work of art in the escapist *genre* and one of the true classics of the popular American theatre. Brilliantly directed by George Abbott, the play also benefited from the ensemble work of an excellent cast: William Lynn, Sam Levene, Shirley Booth, Teddy Hart, Millard Mitchell, Joyce Arling, Edith Van Cleve, Garson Kanin. A: John Cecil Holm and George Abbott. P: Alex Yokel. SD: Boris Aronson.

R: (10/16/69, Lyceum, 100) by Gaston, Goldberg and Filippo. C: Jack Gilford, Sam Levene, Dorothy Loudon, Hal Linden, Al Nesor, Paul Ford, Rosemary Prinz, Butterfly McQueen, Leon Janney. D: George Abbott.

Musicalized by Quillan, Elinson, La Touche, Adamson and Duke as *Banjo*

Eyes (1941) with Eddie Cantor, Virginia Mayo, Audrey Christie, Lionel Stander, June Clyde, Bill Johnson, The De Marcos, Tommy Wonder, and Jacqueline Susann; musicalized by Ginnes, Livingston and Evans as *Let It Ride!* (1961) with George Gobel, Sam Levene, Barbara Nichols, Paula Stewart, Larry Alpert, and Albert Linville.

SV: WB, 1936, Frank McHugh, Joan Blondell, Sam Levene, Teddy Hart, Allen Jenkins, Guy Kibbee, Carol Hughes, Eddie Anderson, Edgar Kennedy.

Three of Us, The (10/17/06, Madison Square, 227)

Plucky Nevada mining camp heroine (Carlotta Nillson) protects the interests of her two younger brothers. Minor, well-crafted comedy-drama; first play by Rachel Crothers, author of *Let Us Be Gay* (1929), *When Ladies Meet* (1932), *Susan and God* (1937), etc. P: Walter Lawrence. D: George Platt.

Three Times the Hour (8/25/31, Avon, 16)

Banker (Robert Strange) is threatened by unknown murderer. Gimmicky melodrama by future screenwriter Valentine Davies (*The Glenn Miller Story*, *Bridges at Toko-Ri*, etc.); codirected by Antoinette Perry and Brock Pemberton (P).

Three Wise Fools (10/31/18, Criterion, 316)

Into the humdrum lives of three crusty bachelors (Harry Davenport, Claude Gillingwater, William Ingersoll) comes the daughter (Helen Menken) of the woman all three had loved in earlier years. Shortly thereafter the young girl is seemingly involved in a plot to rob the three aging bachelors, but she is cleared of suspicion, marries the nephew of one of her guardians, and promises to continue to keep a watchful eye on her lovable "three wise fools." This sentimental comedy-drama by Austin Strong was one of the big hits of the 1918 season. P: Winchell Smith (D) and John Golden. R: (3/1/36, Golden, 9) by John Golden. C: William Gillette, Charles Coburn, James Kirkwood. D: Austin Strong.

SV: MGM, 1946, Margaret O'Brien, Lionel Barrymore, Thomas Mitchell, Edward Arnold, Lewis Stone, Cyd Charisse.

Three-Cornered Moon (3/16/33, Cort, 76)

Members of a screwball Brooklyn family try to combat the effects of the Depression with a flippant, devil-may-care approach to life and love. The daughter (Ruth Gordon) develops a more realistic attitude, however, and bids farewell to her ineffectual poet-lover (Richard Whorf) in order to wed a dependable young doctor (Brian Donlevy). This frequently hilarious comedy was written by a twenty-five-year-old Brooklynite named Gertrude Tonkonogy. Shortly after her play was successfully launched, the authoress married a young medic and gave up the drama. C: Cecilia Loftus, Ben Lackland, John Eldredge, Elisha Cook, Jr. P: Richard Aldrich and Alfred de Liagre, Jr. (D).

SV: Par, 1933, Claudette Colbert, Mary Boland, Richard Arlen, Hardie Albright, Wallace Ford, Lyda Roberti.

Three's A Crowd (12/4/19, Cort, 12)

Former army captain (Alan Dinehart) makes his way to Stratford–on–Avon to rescue a damsel (Phoebe Foster) in distress. Tedious farce-comedy by Earl Derr Biggers and Christopher Morley. P: John Cort.

Three's a Family (5/5/43, Longacre, 497)

Hectic wartime farce about three pregnant mothers, plus assorted relatives and friends, crowded into one small New

York apartment because of the housing shortage. Highlight: the performance of fifty-year stage veteran William Wadsworth as a doddering, half-blind medic who has been called back into service thanks to the doctor shortage. "Mild entertainment" (*Journal-American*). Coauthored by the husband-wife writing team of Phoebe and Henry Ephron (D), whose Hollywood credits include *The Jackpot; Take Her, She's Mine*, etc. C: Doro Merande, Ruth Weston, Robert Burton, Katharine Bard. P: John Golden.

SV: UA, 1944, *Three Is a Family*, Charlie Ruggles, Fay Bainter, Helen Broderick, Arthur Lake, Marjorie Reynolds, Hattie McDaniel, Walter Catlett, Jeff Donnell.

Thunder on the Left (10/31/33, Maxine Elliott's, 31)

A ten-year-old boy is granted his wish to look into the future and see what life will be like twenty hears hence. Engaging fanatasy b/o Christopher Morley's novel of the same name; staged by Anton Bundsmann (Anthony Mann), future Hollywood director. C: Frank Thomas, Jr., James Bell, Hortense Alden, Otto Hulett, Louis Jean Heydt. A: Jean Ferguson Black. P: Henry Forbes. SD: Aline Bernstein.

Thunder Rock (11/14/39, Mansfield, 23)

Disillusioned by the stupidity and brutality of a world threatened by war, a writer retreats to a deserted lighthouse in search of isolation. For company he has the ghosts of seven people drowned ninety years before, emigrants from Europe to the New World who died believing that everything they had fought for was in vain. In showing them that many past battles had indeed been won, the writer renews his faith in the present and reclaims his rightful place in the world. Directed by Elia Kazan, this intriguing fantasy by Robert Ardrey was a Broadway failure. Produced in wartime England with Michael Redgrave in the leading role, the play scored a great success and later became a memorable British film. C: Luther Adler, Myron McCormick, Morris Carnovsky, Lee J. Cobb, Frances Farmer, Art Smith, Roman Bohnen, Ruth Nelson, Robert Lewis. P: The Group Theatre. SD: Mordecai Gorelik.

SV: British, 1942, Michael Redgrave, James Mason, Lilli Palmer, Barbara Mullen, Frederick Valk.

Thy Name Is Woman (11/15/20, Playhouse, 127)

After an elusive smuggler (Jose Ruben) kills his wife (Mary Nash), authorities manage to trap him in the Spanish Pyrennees. Claptrap. A: Carl Schoner and Benjamin F. Glazer. P: William A. Brady. D: Jose Ruben.

Tide Rising (1/25/37, Lyceum, 32)

Bungled 30's drama revolving around the efforts of a well-meaning sheriff to settle a milltown strike organized by his communist daughter-in-law. C: Grant Mitchell, Tamara, Clyde Fillmore, Cameron Prud'homme. A: George Brewer, Jr. P: Aldrich and Myers. D: Arthur Sircom.

Tiger Cats (10/21/24, Belasco, 48)

A neglected wife (Katharine Cornell) taunts her neurologist-husband (Robert Loraine) with her infidelities until he shoots her. Unpleasant, pseudo-Strindbergian melodrama produced and directed by David Belasco. (Years later Miss Cornell explained the failure of her solitary venture with Belasco by saying merely: "He didn't understand me and I didn't understand him.") A: Karen Bramson, based on a play by Michael Orme.

Tiger Rose (10/3/17, Lyceum, 384)

Mountie pursues man wanted for murder in the Great Northwest. Trite, action-packed David Belasco (P/D) melodrama. C: Lenore Ulric, William Courtleigh, Willard Mack, Pedro de Cordoba. A: Willard Mack.

SV: WB, 1930, Lupe Velez, H. B. Warner, Monte Blue, Grant Withers, Rin Tin Tin.

Tiger! Tiger! (11/12/18, Belasco, 183)

A member of Parliament (Lionel Atwill) jeopardizes his career by becoming involved with a Welsh slut (Frances Starr). Flashy, synthetic sex drama from the David Belasco (P/D) atelier. C: O. P. Heggie, Auriol Lee, Whitford Kane. A: Edward Knoblock.

Tiger, Tiger, Burning Bright (12/22/62, Booth, 33)

Beautifully acted tale of a Negro matriarch and her troubled New Orleans family. "A taut, arresting drama . . ." *(News)*. ". . . overpoweringly depressing . . ." *(Journal-American)*. C: Claudia McNeil, Diana Sands, Cicely Tyson, Alvin Ailey, Al Freeman, Jr., Ellen Holly, Roscoe Lee Browne, Bobby Dean Hooks. A: Peter S. Feibleman b/o his novel *A Place Without Twilight*. P: Oliver Smith (SD) and Roger L. Stevens i.a.w. Austin and Samrock. D: Joshua Logan.

Tight Britches (9/11/34, Avon, 23)

Ornery mountain girl seduces would-be preacher. Meandering hillbilly melodrama. C: Shepperd Strudwick, Joanna Roos, Kathleen Comegys. A: John Taintor Foote and Hubert Hayes. D: Miriam Doyle.

Tightwad, The (4/16/27, 49th Street, 9)

Boy turns miserly to win budget-conscious girlfriend. Humdrum 20's comedy by actor Robert Keith. C: King Calder, Lucile Nikolas. P: Messrs. Shubert. D: A. H. Van Buren.

Time for Elizabeth (9/27/48, Fulton, 8)

Comedy by Groucho Marx and Norman Krasna (D) about an executive who elects to retire to Florida, finds that middle-aged leisure isn't much fun, and gets a better job in good old New York. ". . . a childish charade . . . a strangely callow jest to emanate from two of the theatre's maturest workers" *(New York Times)*. C: Otto Kruger, Katherine Alexander, Harlan Briggs. P: Lewis and Young. *Time for Elizabeth*, a surprisingly mild, sentimental and uneventful comedy, was Groucho Marx's only Broadway play. Groucho later essayed the leading role in summer stock. The title, incidentally, refers not to a woman's name, but to the town of Elizabeth, New Jersey.

Time Limit! (1/24/56, Booth, 127)

Steadily engrossing melodrama concerning the trial of an American major (Richard Kiley) suspected of collaborating with the enemy while a P.O.W. in North Korea. The case against him is so airtight, in fact, that the prosecuting attorney (Arthur Kennedy) begins to ask some disturbing questions, specifically: at what point is a brave man's crackup under enemy torture and brainwashing forgivable? "A taut and striking topical melodrama . . . an extremely moving and upsetting play" *(Post)*. A: Henry Denker and Ralph Berkey. P: The Theatre Guild. D: Windsor Lewis. SD: Ralph Alswang.

SV: UA, 1957, Richard Widmark, Richard Basehart, Rip Torn (directed by Karl Malden).

Time of the Cuckoo, The (10/_ /52, Empire, 263)

An American spinster (Shirley Booth) falls in love with an Italian shopkeeper while vacationing in Venice. When he freely admits he is a contented husband and father, the lady comes to realize the difference between European and American morality, and must choose between a short-term love affair or none at all. Despite mixed reviews, Arthur Laurents' romantic comedy had a successful Broadway run. C: Dino DiLuca, Geraldine Brooks, Donald Murphy, Lydia St.

Clair. P: Whitehead and Fried. D: Harold Clurman. CD: Helene Pons. SD: Ben Edwards.

R: (10/27/58, Sheridan Square, 105). C: Kathleen Maguire, Robert Pastene. D: Jack Ragotzy.

Musicalized by Richard Rodgers, Stephen Sondheim, and Arthur Laurents as *Do I Hear a Waltz?* (1965) with Elizabeth Allen, Sergio Franchi, Carol Bruce, Madeleine Sherwood, Jack Manning, Stuart Damon, and Julienne Marie.

SV: UA, 1955, *Summertime,* Katharine Hepburn, Rossano Brazzi, Darren McGavin, Isa Miranda (directed by David Lean).

Time of Your Life, The (10/25/39, Booth, 185)

William Saroyan's prize-winning 1939 comedy set in a waterfront dive grandly titled "Nick's Saloon, Restaurant, and Entertainment Palace," modeled after an actual San Francisco spot called Izzy Gomez's where the author was fond of hanging out. A bizarre assortment of characters frequent Nick's dingy but hospitable barroom. Among them: a mysterious big spender ("I believe in dreams sooner than statistics"), a couple of hookers ("We wuz formerly models at Magnin's"), a pure-in-heart streetwalker, a hoofer who wants to make people laugh, a singing newsboy, and a pinball addict. Also, an old Arab who keeps shaking his head solemnly and muttering to himself ("No foundation, all the way down the line"), a sadistic vice squad cop, a pair of Nob Hill slummers, and a teller-of-talltales named Kit Carson ("Did you ever fall in love with a midget weighing 39 pounds?"). Essentially plotless, this modern morality play was a paean to the joy of life, a declaration of faith in mankind. Reviewers labeled it " a cosmic vaudeville show," "a goofy binge," "a prose poem in ragtime." "No modern play has given me more pure immediate pleasure," critic-essayist Carl Van Doren

Time of Your Life. **Scene of man at "American Destiny" machine (1939–40).** *Courtesy Museum of the City of New York Theatre and Music Collection.*

noted in a letter to this editor. Saroyan wrote *The Time of Your Life* in six days, holed up in a hotel room. It was a Broadway hit and it was awarded the Pulitzer Prize which, characteristically, Saroyan turned down. "Now if it had been the Nobel," he said, "I'd have taken it—that's worth money." In addition to the Pulitzer Prize, *The Time of Your Life* also received the Critics Circle Award— the only play to win both these honors until *A Streetcar Named Desire* (1947). C: Eddie Dowling, Julie Haydon, Gene Kelly (CH), Celeste Holm, William Bendix, Edward Andrews, Len Doyle Tom Tully, Reginald Beane, Ross Bagdasarian. P: The Theatre Guild i.a.w. Eddie Dowling. D: William Saroyan, Eddie Dowling, Lawrence Langner. SD: Watson Barratt.

R: (1/19/55, City Center, 15). C: Franchot Tone, Myron McCormick, Harold Lang, Lenka Peterson, Lonny Chapman, Biff McGuire,

John Carradine, Mike Kellin, Gloria Vanderbilt, John Randolph, Paula Laurence. D: Sanford Meisner.
R: (11/6/69, Lincoln Center, 52). C: James Broderick, Philip Bosco, Susan Tyrrell, Biff McGuire. D: John Hirsch.
SV: UA, 1948, James Cagney, William Bendix, Wayne Morris, Broderick Crawford, Jeanne Cagney, James Barton, Ward Bond, Paul Draper, Gale Page, James Lydon, Reginald Beane, Natalie Schafer, Howard Freeman (directed by H. C. Potter).

Time Out for Ginger (11/26/52, Lyceum, 248)

Complications ensue when the tomboyish daughter of a staid banker (Melvyn Douglas) insists on trying out for the high-school football team. ". . . fresh, warm-hearted and funny" *(New York Times)*. ". . . about as exciting as a banana split" *(News)*. C: Nancy Malone, Polly Rowles, Philip Loeb, Conrad Janis. A: Ronald Alexander. P: Shepard Traube (D) and Gordon Pollock i.a.w. Don Hershey. SD: Eldon Elder.
SV: UA, 1965, *Billie*, Patty Duke, Warren Berlinger, Jim Backus, Jane Greer, Billy De Wolfe.

Times Have Changed (2/25/35, National, 32)

In order to improve their financial status in the community, grasping New Englanders force the pretty daughter of the family to wed a wealthy psychopath. Garbled melodrama, extensively revised by Louis Bromfield from a play by Edouard Bourdet. C: Robert Loraine, Thais Lawton, Cecilia Loftus, Elena Miramova, Moffat Johnston, Owen Davis, Jr., Eric Wollencott, Fania Marinoff. P: Feodor Rolbein. D: Auriol Lee.

Tin Pan Alley (11/1/28, Biltmore, 77)

Ho-hum drama about the problems of an alcoholic tunesmith (Norman Foster) and his loyal wife (Claudette Colbert). C: John Wray, Constance McKay, Sam Levene. A: Hugh Stanislaus Stange. P: Lang and Forbes. D: Lester Lonergan.
SV: UA, 1930, *New York Nights*, Norma Talmadge, Gilbert Roland, Lilyan Tashman, John Wray (directed by Lewis Milestone).

Tiny Alice (12/29/64, Billy Rose, 167)

A fabulously wealthy woman named Miss Alice (Irene Worth) bequeaths the sum of two billion dollars to the Roman Catholic church on the condition that a tremulous lay brother named Julian (John Gielgud) be sent to accept the gift. When Julian arrives at Alice's vast and vaulted castle (which houses an intricately detailed model of itself), his faith is severely tested. Before the play has run its course, the devoutly Christ-like lay brother has been seduced by Alice, marries her, and, martyr-fashion, is delivered to his death. This wildly abstruse "metaphysical mystery play" by Edward Albee became the conversation piece of its season. The author described his symbolic allegory as "an examination of the relationship between sexual hysteria and religious ecstasy," and cautioned the critics "not to give away the secret of the play." "Give away Mr. Albee's secret?" wrote one critic. "He doesn't have to worry. I don't even know what the secret is!" The *Christian Science Monitor* smartly led off: "It may be that *Tiny Alice* will have a sequel, *A Guide to Tiny Alice*." The *National Observer* thought it "a complex, baffling, and possibly fraudulent theatrical brew . . . all metaphysical sound and fury signifying only that spirituality is *in* once more." The *Daily News* quoted Tallulah Bankhead's famous quip: "There may be less to this than meets the eye." C: John Heffernan, William Hutt, Eric Berry. P: Barr and Wilder. D: Alan Schneider. CD: Mainbocher. SD: William Ritman.

Revived on Broadway by San Francisco's American Conservatory Theatre. (9/29/69, ANTA, 10). C: Paul Shenar, DeAnn Mears, Ray Reinhardt. D: William Ball.

Tired Business Man (6/3/29, Waldorf, 31)

Naïve businessman (Harlan Briggs) gets into one scrape after another when he runs for mayor. Anemic farce. A: Lyle Weaver Hall. P: Regent Productions, Inc. D: Marion Gering.

To Be Continued (4/23/52, Booth, 13)

A mistress tries to provoke her lover's wife into a divorce action in hopes that he will then marry her. When the two ladies finally meet, however, they form a mutual admiration society. As the comedy ends, it appears that the longtime design-for-living arrangement is to be continued. Dorothy Stickney played the mistress, Jean Dixon the wife, Neil Hamilton the husband, and Grace Kelly (in her last New York stage appearance) the daughter in this 1952 production. *To Be Continued*, a failure, marked the Broadway debut of author William Marchant. He subsequently was represented on Broadway by *The Desk Set*, a hit of the 1955 season. C: Luella Gear, Mary Gildea, John Drew Devereaux. P/D: Guthrie McClintic. CD: Motley. SD: Donald Oenslager.

To Bury a Cousin (5/16/67, Bouwerie Lane, 5)

Flashback drama examining the life (and death) of a potentially gifted and loving man blighted by the domination of his narrow-minded parents and frigid wife. Poignant O/B drama by Gus Weill. P: David Lawlor. D: Philip Oesterman, Jr.

To Have and to Hold (3/4/01, Knickerbocker, 40)

The villainous Lord Carnal pursues virtuous Jocelyn Leigh from England all the way to the Colonies. Gimcrack melodrama laid in seventeenth-century Virginia, based on the novel by Mary Johnston. C: Robert Loraine (deb.), Isabel Irving, Holbrook Blinn, Cecil B. De Mille. A: E. F. Boddington. P: Charles Frohman. D: Edward E. Rose.

To Quito and Back (10/6/37, Guild, 46)

Ben Hecht's play about an American novelist (Leslie Banks) who elopes with his secretary (Sylvia Sidney) to Ecuador, and becomes embroiled in a communist revolution for which he eventually gives up his life. ". . . melodramatic absurdity . . . a small, undignified monument of social and intellectual terror" (Mary McCarthy, *Partisan Review*). According to one reviewer, *To Quito and Back* was "carved into a turkey" by grievous miscasting and incessant tinkering on the part of The Theatre Guild (P) and director Philip Moeller. C: Joseph Buloff, Evelyn Varden, Walter Greaza, Francis Compton, Eugenia Rawls, Henry Levin.

To Tell You the Truth (4/18/48, New Stages, 15)

Moldy retelling of the Adam and Eve legend; produced O/B by New Stages, Inc. C: Tony Randall, Jean Gillespie, Raymond Edward Johnson. A: Eva Wolas. D: Ezra Stone.

To the Ladies (2/20/22, Liberty, 128)

George S. Kaufman-Marc Connelly comedy success of 1922. A young wife (Helen Hayes) saves her conceited piano-salesman husband (Otto Kruger) from making a fool of himself in his efforts to get ahead. When he becomes tongue-tied at a company banquet, she even delivers his speech for him. Agreeable fluff with some neat satiric flourishes. P: Tyler and Erlanger. D: Howard Lindsay.

SV: Par, 1934, *Elmer and Elsie*, George Bancroft, Frances Fuller.

Tobacco Road, scene from Act III. Del Hughes, Eddie Garr, Edwin Walter, Kate Morgan, Ann Ere, Vinnie Phillips, and Robert Rose (1933–34). *Courtesy Museum of the City of New York Theatre and Music Collection.*

Tobacco Road (12/4/33, Masque, 3,182)

The long-run Broadway hit about the bold and bawdy doings of the Lesters, a family of mental defectives living in a Georgia backwoods hovel. Jeeter Lester (Henry Hull), head of the clan, sells his daughter for seven dollars, encourages his son to wed a lustful female evangelist, and reacts to his mother's death in the fields with total indifference. "A play that achieves the repulsive and seldom falls below the faintly sickening." (Richard Lockridge, *Sun*). "It isn't the sort of entertainment folks buy in the theatre, nor ever have bought within my memory." (Burns Mantle, *News*). Despite almost unanimously negative reviews, the play gradually found its public and, to the amazement of Broadway showmen, ran on and on for seven-and-a-half years with a total of 3,182 performances, a record surpassed only by *Life With Father* (3,224) and the musical play, *Fiddler on the Roof* (3,242). The phenomenal run of *Tobacco Road* can be attributed in large measure to its profanity, countrified sexuality, and scatological humor. The play catered to an audience wanting to be shocked and willing to be amused, in the words of Professor Arthur Hobson Quinn, by "the spectacle of humanity in disgrace." A big factor in the play's initial success was the excellent performance by Henry Hull in the role of Jeeter Lester. Others who played Jeeter during the New York run included James Barton, James Bell, Eddie Garr, and Will Geer. C: Sam Byrd, Dean Jagger, Mar-

Today. **Edwin Arden, Marie Wainwright, and Emily Stevens (October 6, 1913).**
Courtesy Museum of the City of New York Theatre and Music Collection.

garet Wycherly, Ruth Hunter, Maude Odell. A: Jack Kirkland b/o the novel by Erskine Caldwell. P/D: Anthony Brown. SV: Fox, 1941, Charley Grapewin, Marjorie Rambeau, Gene Tierney, Dana Andrews, William Tracy, Elizabeth Patterson (directed by John Ford from a screenplay by Nunnally Johnson).

Toby's Bow (2/10/19, Comedy, 144)

George Marion (in blackface) as an Uncle Tom servant who lords it over a visiting Japanese valet. Syrupy comedy filled with unpleasant racial slurs and stereotypes. C: Norman Trevor, Merle Maddern, Doris Rankin. A: John Taintor Foote. P: John D. Williams. D: Norman Trevor.

Today (10/6/13, 48th Street, 280)

Luxury-loving woman (Emily Stevens) is discovered in a bordello by her own husband (Edwin Arden). Sleazy melodrama by George Broadhurst and A. S. Schomer. P: Manuscript Producing Company. D: Edward Elsner.

Tom Paine (3/25/68, Stage 73, 295)

Clever, somewhat fictionalized account of the life and times of Tom Paine (Kevin O'Connor), the 18th-century liberal and libertine, famous for his activities in behalf of the American Revolution and French Revolution. Typically eruptive production by off-Broadway's experimental La Mama Troupe. Written by Paul Foster; directed in effective if frenetic fashion by Tom O'Horgan.

Tommy (1/10/27, Gaiety, 232)

To win back his girl, a young paragon of virtue pretends to be considerably less than perfect. Cute 20's comedy of adolescent growing pains. C: William Janney, Sidney Toler, Peg Entwhistle, Alan Bunce. A/P/D: Howard Lindsay and Bertrand Robinson.

SV: RKO, 1930, *She's My Weakness,* Arthur Lake, Sue Carol.

Tomorrow (12/28/28, Lyceum, 10)

1928 sci-fi piece about life in the year 1982. According to the authors, what with "radiovision," air buses, and heliports on every rooftop, life will be both joyous and exciting. The play, alas, was neither. A: Hull Gould and Saxon Kling. P: John Ashley. D: Philip Bartholomae.

Tomorrow and Tomorrow (1/13/31, Henry Miller, 206)

A childless wife turns to a psychologist for help. From their clandestine union, a child is born. Years later, when the boy suffers an emotional trauma, the mother sends for his real father, who cures the child. But when he would take mother and son away with him, the wife decides she must remain loyal to the devoted, unsuspecting man she married. "A play wrought handsomely in the author's best powers" *(Journal).* Helen Hayes expressed interest in playing the wife in this Philip Barry play, but when producer Arthur Hopkins relinquished his option on the script, newcomer Zita Johann inherited the role. The play was the surprise hit of the 1931 season. C: Herbert Marshall, Harvey Stephens, Osgood Perkins. P/D: Gilbert Miller.

SV: Par, 1932, Ruth Chatterton, Paul Lukas.

Tomorrow the World (4/14/43, Barrymore, 500)

This 1943 drama dealt with an American family's adoption of a twelve-year-old German boy and their efforts to transform the diminutive Nazi into a decent human being. The brainwashed little monster disrupts the entire household before being shown the error of his fascist ways. "A strong, interesting and thoughtful play, extraordinarily well acted" *(Sun).* C: Ralph Bellamy, Shirley Booth, Dorothy Sands, Skippy Homeier, Joyce Van Patten, Nancy Nugent, Edit Angold. A: James Gow and Arnaud d'Usseau. P: Theron Bamberger. D: Elliott Nugent.

SV: UA, 1944, Fredric March, Betty Field, Agnes Moorehead, Skippy Homeier, Joan Carroll.

Tomorrow's a Holiday (12/30/35, Golden, 8)

Hopelessly muddled drama, directed by George S. Kaufman, about a nobleman (Joseph Schildkraut) afflicted with gambling fever. *Tomorrow's a Holiday* was an eight-performance disaster. C: Doris Dalton, Curt Bois, Donald Foster, King Calder. A: Romney Brent b/o a play by Perutz and Adler. P: John Golden i.a.w. Joseph Schildkraut. SD: Woodman Thompson.

Tonight at 12 (11/13/28, Hudson, 56)

Trying to discover which of the women guests is her husband's mistress, a suspicious wife turns a dinner party into an inquisition. Contrived Owen Davis drama produced by Herman Shumlin. C: Ann Shoemaker, Spring Byington, Owen Davis, Jr., Viola Frayne. D: Melville Burke.

SV: U, 1929, Madge Bellamy.

Too Hot for Maneuvers (5/2/45, Broadhurst, 5)

Massage parlor, frequented by military school cadets, is mistaken for a house of prostitution. Hollywood's Richard Arlen made his Broadway debut in this smutty, short-lived 40's farce. A/D: Les White and Bud Pearson. P: James S. Elliott.

Too Late the Phalarope (10/11/56, Belasco, 36)

Driven by loneliness, a South African police lieutenant has an affair with a native girl despite strict laws prohibiting sexual relations between the races. When his dereliction becomes known, he is expelled from society. The play ends as he is carted off to jail, his ears ringing with the sound of his stern Dutch-African father nailing shut the family house against him. This dramatization of Alan Paton's novel suffered from a rambling first two acts, but built to a stunning climax in its third act. C: Barry Sullivan, Finlay Currie (deb.), Ellen Holly, Alan Napier, Paul Mann, Estelle Hemsley, Geoffrey Horne, George Tyne, Ann Dere, Laurinda Barrett. A: Robert Yale Libott. P: Mary K. Frank. D: John Stix. SD: George Jenkins. M: Josef Marais.

Too Many Boats (9/11/34, Playhouse, 7)

Army captain falls in love with his commanding officer's wife. Trite, lugubrious World War I melodrama set in the Philippines. C: Earle Larimore, Horace Braham, Helen Flint. A: Owen Davis b/o a novel by Charles L. Clifford. P/D: William A.Brady, Jr.

Too Many Cooks (2/24/14, 39th Street, 223)

Nosy in-laws threaten the happiness of a young suburbanite and his fiancée. Cute comedy by Frank Craven. C: Frank Craven, Inez Plummer, John Cromwell. P: William A. Brady. D: Craven and Cromwell.
Musicalized by Harry Tierney as *Up She Goes* (1922) with Donald Brian and Gloria Foy.
SV: RKO, 1931, Bert Wheeler, Dorothy Lee.

Too Many Heroes (11/15/37, Hudson, 16)

First play by screenwriter-producer Dore Schary, author of *Sunrise at Campobello* (1958). *Too Many Heroes* examined the effects of mob violence in a factory town. A peace-loving millhand defies a lynching party, becomes involved in an accidental murder, and finally pays with his life for his stand against injustice. This 1937 drama was directed by Garson Kanin and produced by Carly Wharton. After a reasonably strong and effective first act, *Too Many Heroes* went to pieces. In the words of *New York Times* critic Brooks Atkinson: "Neither Mr. Schary nor Mr. Kanin can make much out of the vacillation of the last half of the play." C: James Bell, Shirley Booth, Elspeth Eric, Joseph Sweeney, Anthony Ross, James (Jim) Backus. SD: Jo Mielziner.

Too Much Party (3/5/34, Masque, 8)

A social worker finds that her real work begins at home. Tedious farce-comedy by actor Hiram Sherman, presented by a nondescript acting group billed as the Metropolitan Players, under the direction of William B. Friedlander.

Top o' the Hill (11/26/29, Eltinge, 15)

Contemplating marriage to a Nob Hill scion, a seven-thousand-dollar-a-week film star tries to conceal her past as a former San Francisco prostitute. Trite 20's drama by Charles Kenyon.* C: Katherine Wilson, Lester Vail, Charles D. Brown, Claudia Morgan. P: Felix Young. D: Worthington Miner.

---

*Author of *Kindling* (1911) and such screenplays as *The Petrified Forest, The Road Back, 100 Men and a Girl*, etc.

Torch Bearers, The (8/29/22, 48th Street, 128)

Devastatingly funny satire on amateur theatrical groups by George Kelly (A/D). During rehearsals of a Little Theatre production, Paula Ritter (Mary Boland) and her gullible friends are exploited in the interests of art by their director, the shallow and tyrannical Mrs. J. Duro

Pampinelli (Alison Skipworth). On the night of the play, everything that can conceivably go wrong does, but the actors believe the evening was a veritable triumph. However, Paula's long-suffering husband (Arthur Shaw) finally rebels and demands that his wife give up amateur acting, which she reluctantly agrees to do. ". . . moments of real wit. . . . The chances are that Mr. Kelly, if he remembers what is joyous, will be our best writer of comedy" (Stark Young, *New Republic*). P: Stewart and French.

SV: Fox, 1935, *Doubting Thomas,* Will Rogers, Billie Burke, Alison Skipworth.

Torch Song (8/27/30, Plymouth, 87)

Traveling salesman lures Salvation Army lass away from her calling. Pulp fiction stuff, cleverly staged by Arthur Hopkins (P/D). C: Mayo Methot, Reed Brown, Jr., Guy Kibbee (deb.), Russell Hicks, Dennie Moore. A: Kenyon Nicholson.

SV: MGM, 1931, *Laughing Sinners,* Joan Crawford, Clark Gable, Neil Hamilton, Guy Kibbee, Marjorie Rambeau, Cliff Edwards.

Tortilla Flat (1/12/38, Henry Miller, 5)

Poor dramatization of John Steinbeck's novel dealing with a colony of pleasure-loving Spanish-Americans in Monterey, California. The basic storyline relates how one of these *paisanos* discovers that becoming a small property-owner interferes with the good life of wine, women and indolence. *Tortilla Flat* lasted a mere five performances on Broadway. C: Robert Keith, Erin O'Brien-Moore, Edward Woods. A/P/D: Jack Kirkland.

SV: MGM, 1942, Spencer Tracy, Hedy Lamarr, John Garfield, Frank Morgan, Akim Tamiroff, Allen Jenkins, Donald Meek.

Touch of Brimstone, A (9/22/35, Golden, 96)

Egomaniacal theatrical producer (Roland Young) alienates everyone with whom he comes in contact including, finally, his long-suffering wife. Literate, well-acted comedy. C: Mary Philips, Cora Witherspoon, Reginald Carrington. A: Leonora Kaghlan and Anita Phillips. P: John Golden. D: Frank Craven.

Touch of the Poet, A (10/2/58, Hayes, 284)

Four-act drama by Eugene O'Neill. Set in a gloomy tavern outside Boston in 1828, the play centers on ill-tempered Cornelious (Con) Melody (Eric Portman), a boastful, debt-ridden Irish immigrant-innkeeper who clings to illusory memories of European gentility. While his loyal drudge-wife (Helen Hayes) and spirited daughter (Kim Stanley) struggle to keep the tavern going, Con spends his time carousing, and sneering at his merchant-class Yankee neighbors. When his daughter is snubbed by a local family, Con rides forth swaggeringly on his Thoroughbred mare to avenge the insult. Beaten and humiliated, he returns home and shoots the beloved mare, thereby severing all ties with his prideful past. ". . . not one of Eugene O'Neill's great plays, but even as one of his lesser ones it proves again that he is majestically alone in the American theatre" *(Journal-American)*. C: Betty Field, Curt Conway, Art Smith. P: Robert Whitehead. D: Harold Clurman. SD: Ben Edwards.

Revived (5/2/67, ANTA, 5) with Denholm Elliott as Cornelius Melody; directed by Jack Sydow.

Note: This was one of two plays that O'Neill did not destroy in a projected eleven-play cycle dealing with 175 years in the life of an American family. The Theatre Guild had wanted to produce *A Touch of the Poet* in 1947, but O'Neill asked the Guild to defer the production because of his ill health. "The Guild reluctantly acceded to O'Neill's wishes," according to the playwright's biographers, Arthur and Barbara Gelb, "even though Robert Edmond

Jones had already drawn preliminary sketches for the sets and plans had been formulated to have either Spencer Tracy or Laurence Olivier portray Cornelius Melody." *A Touch of the Poet*, like *Long Day's Journey Into Night*, was produced on Broadway posthumously.

Touchstone (2/3/53, Music Box, 7)
Conflicts erupt between the forces of faith and reason in a southern community when a Negro lad professes to see miraculous visions. "Earnest and sometimes perceptive. . . . but it lacks the passion which might have made it thoroughly compelling" (*Herald Tribune*). C: Ian Keith, Josh White, Jr., Ossie Davis, Patty McCormack (deb.), Paul McGrath, Evelyn Ellis, Ann Dere. A: William Stucky. P: Elaine Perry. D: Hale McKeen. SD: George Jenkins.

Tough to Get Help (5/4/72, Royale, 1)
An awkward combination of comedy and social criticism. A wealthy suburban family, ostentatiously liberal, employs a pair of black servants. They all get along splendidly until the militant son of the blacks arrives with his girl friend. He is being hunted by the police for a bank bombing in New York and needs money to flee the country. For the father it is a moment of truth. He holds up his employer and gets his son the necessary cash. Despite many good jokes and bits of humor, the script demeans, rather than illuminates, the racial problem it examines. The cast was generally admired, particularly John Amos as the black servant, and Dick O'Neill as his employer. "If *Tough to Get Help* had been a serious drama this might have been powerful and striking, but it is intended as a comedy, and it doesn't work" (Richard Watts, *New York Post*). A: Steve Gordon. C: John Amos, Dick O'Neill, John Danelle, Billie Lou Watt, Lillian Hayman, Chip Fields, Abe Vigoda, Jimmy Pelham, Anthony Palmer, Ralph Carter. D: Carl Reiner. P: Sandy Farber and Stanley Barnett i.a.w. Jules Love and Roy Rubin. SD: Ed Wittstein.

Tovarich (10/15/36, Plymouth, 356)
A royal but impoverished Russian couple take jobs as servants in the home of a Parisian banker. Pursued by Soviet agents, they eventually are forced to surrender the Czar's funds entrusted to them for the good of Mother Russia. After which they continue happily in service. Delightful hokum, adapted and extensively revised by Robert E. Sherwood from a play by Jacques Deval. C: Marta Abba, John Halliday, Margaret Dale, Jay Fassett, Cecil Humphreys, Ernest Lawford, Frederic Worlock. P/D: Gilbert Miller. SD: Raymond Sovey. *Tovarich* was highly popular throughout the world; it ran eighteen months in London with Eugenie Leontovich and Cedric Hardwicke in the leading roles. In America, Miss Leontovich headed a successful west coast production with a cast that included Osgood Perkins, Melville Cooper, and Bela Lugosi.

R: (5/14/52, City Center, 15). C: Uta Hagen, Herbert Berghof, Luther Adler, Julia Adler, Romney Brent, Paula Laurence, Pat Crowley, Sudie Bond. D: Harry Horner.

Musicalized (1963) by Shaw, Pockriss and Crosswell with Vivien Leigh, Jean-Pierre Aumont, Alexander Scourby, George S. Irving.

SV: WB, 1937, Claudette Colbert, Charles Boyer, Basil Rathbone, Anita Louise, Melville Cooper, Isabel Jeans, Morris Carnovsky, Montagu Love (directed by Anatole Litvak).

Town House (9/23/48, National, 12)
Three young couples try to live compatibly together in an old New York mansion. Negligible comedy staged by George S. Kaufman and adapted by Gertrude Tonkonogy* from John Cheever's *New*

Yorker magazine stories. C: Mary Wickes, Hiram Sherman, June Duprez, James Monks, Peggy French, Reed Brown, Jr., Margaret Dale, Henry Jones, Edwin Jerome. P: Max Gordon. SD: Donald Oenslager.

---

*Author of *Three-Cornered Moon* (1933).

Toymaker of Nuremberg, The (11/25/07, Garrick, 24)

Elderly toymaker interferes in his son's romance. Clumsy fantasy-drama by Austin Strong. C: Archibald Rosamund, Grant Mitchell, Raymond Hackett (deb.). P: Charles Frohman. D: William Seymour.

Toys in the Attic (2/25/60, Hudson, 556)

Julian Berniers returns to the New Orleans home of his adoring old-maid sisters with a childlike bride and—for the first time in his scapegrace life—a lot of money. The two sisters (one of whom has incestuous desires toward Julian) have spent their lives bailing this charming ne'er-do-well out of trouble. His dependence had given them a reason for living. The obsession to get him back with them on the old terms alienates his featherbrained bride, drives the sisters apart and, ultimately, destroys Julian. "Although *Toys in the Attic* is not the greatest play in the world, it is head and shoulders above the level of the season, and it provides opportunities for some extraordinary acting" (*New York Times*). This 1960 drama by Lillian Hellman won the Drama Critics Circle Award as best play of the year. C: Jason Robards, Jr., Maureen Stapleton, Anne Revere, Irene Worth, Rochelle Oliver, Percy Rodriguez (deb.). P: Kermit Bloomgarden. D: Arthur Penn. SD: Howard Bay.

SV: UA, 1963, Dean Martin, Geraldine Page, Wendy Hiller, Yvette Mimieux, Gene Tierney, Nan Martin (directed by George Roy Hill).

Trail of the Lonesome Pine, The (1/29/12, New Amsterdam, 32)

Northerner finds himself caught up in a bloody feud between the trigger-happy Tollivers and the hot-tempered Falins in the Blue Ridge Mountains of Virginia. Routine adaptation of the popular John Fox novel. C: William S. Hart, Charlotte Walker, Berton Churchill, Willard Robertson. A: Eugene Walter. P: Klaw and Erlanger. D: Herbert Gresham.

SV: Par, 1936, Fred MacMurray, Henry Fonda,* Sylvia Sidney, Fred Stone, Beulah Bondi, Nigel Bruce.

---

*This film, the first outdoor picture in Technicolor, provided Henry Fonda with one of his most rewarding early screen roles. His performance as a gangling backwoods mountaineer gave Al Capp the inspiration for Li'l Abner. Indeed, according to Fonda biographer John Springer, "in the early Capp drawings, they [Henry Fonda and Li'l Abner] looked remarkably alike."

Traitor, The (4/4/49, 48th Street, 67)

Herman Wouk's lively and ingenious espionage melodrama in which an idealistic American scientist altruistically turns over atomic bomb secrets to a Soviet spy. When the traitor ultimately turns patriot, he leads the Russian mastermind into a trap, and is himself shot and killed. "... proves that a melodrama can be both exciting and intelligent ... held a first-night audience spellbound" (*Mirror*). Despite almost unanimous critical acclaim, *The Traitor* failed at the box office. It marked novelist Wouk's debut as a dramatist. C: Lee Tracy, Walter Hampden, Wesley Addy, Richard Derr (deb.), Louise Platt, Jean Hagen, Philip Coolidge, John Wengraf. P/D: Jed Harris. SD: Raymond Sovey.

Trapped (9/11/28, National, 15)

Daughter of prominent banker (William Ingersoll) is kidnaped and held for ransom. Mediocre 20's melodrama by Samuel Shipman and Max Marcin (P/D).

Traveling Lady, The (10/27/54, Playhouse, 30)

A young Texas wife (Kim Stanley) tries to effect a reconciliation with her ex-convict husband (Lonny Chapman). When she discovers he has no intention of mending his ways and, in fact, is headed back to jail, she turns to a sober widower (Jack Lord) for comfort and affection. "The basal metabolism of *The Traveling Lady* is low [but] Miss Stanley is magnificent (*New York Times*). A: Horton Foote. P: The Playwrights Company. D: Vincent J. Donehue.

SV: Col, 1965, *Baby, the Rain Must Fall*, Steve McQueen, Lee Remick, Don Murray, Josephine Hutchinson, Paul Fix, Ruth White (directed by Robert Mulligan).

Traveling Salesman, The (8/10/08, Liberty, 280)

Bound home for the holidays at Christmastime, a passenger (Frank McIntyre) on a derailed train is stranded with some other unfortunate knights of the road in a rundown hostelry. There he meets a pretty telephone operator and vanquishes the village skinflint who would rob her of her property. Tenuous but amusing comedy by James Forbes (A/D). C: Gertrude Coghlan, Arthur Shaw, Edward Ellis. P: Henry B. Harris.

Treasure Island (12/1/15, Punch and Judy, 205)

Flavorful adaptation of Stevenson's classic pirate yarn of eighteenth-century England. C: Mr. and Mrs. Charles Hopkins, Oswald Yorke. A: Jules Eckert Goodman. P/D: Charles Hopkins.

SV: MGM, 1934, Wallace Beery, Jackie Cooper, Lionel Barrymore, Lewis Stone, Otto Kruger, Nigel Bruce; RKO, 1950, Robert Newton, Bobby Driscoll; British, 1972, Orson Welles, Walter Slezak, Kim Burfield, Lionel Stander.

Treat 'Em Rough (10/4/26, Klaw, 24)

Italian cabaret owner (Alan Dinehart) tames spirited Irish lass (Genevieve Tobin). Dull comedy by Frederic and Fanny Hatton. C: Walter Connolly, Nedda Harrigan. P: Richard Herndon. D: Alan Dinehart.

Tree, The (4/12/32, Park Lane, 7)

A black boy in the deep South is hanged for the rape of a white girl. The real culprit (Barton MacLane) later confesses to the crime, and is likewise lynched. Shrill, unconvincing 1932 drama was written by future screenwriter-producer Richard Maibaum,* directed by Robert Rossen.** P: Ira Marion.

The Great Gatsby, The Big Clock, Dr. No and subsequent James Bond films, etc.
**Hollywood writer-producer-director (*All the King's Men, The Hustler*, etc.).

Trial Honeymoon (11/3/47, Royale, 8)

Eileen Heckart made her Broadway debut in this stale and amateurish farce about the tribulations of two young honeymooners. "So witless and cheap it wouldn't have gotten by in a high school auditorium . . ." (*PM*). A: Conrad S. Smith. P: Harry Rosen. D: Edward Ludlum.

Trial of Lee Harvey Oswald, The (11/5/67, ANTA, 9)

Static semidocumentary courtroom drama setting forth the theory that John F. Kennedy's alleged murderer was innocent. Good performance by Peter Masterson in the leading role; the production closed after its ninth performance at a loss of $100,000. C: Clifton James, Ralph Waite. A: Amram Ducovny and Leon Friedman. P: Gene Persson. D: Tunc Yalman.

Trial of Mary Dugan, The (9/19/27, National, 437)

One of the most popular courtroom melodramas ever written. A *Follies* girl (Ann Harding), accused of murdering her paramour, is defended—and ultimately exonerated—by her young brother. (She had put him through law school by living in sin.) Though the play's story was patently absurd, veteran melodramatist Bayard Veiller bolstered his script by treating the courtroom procedure material with minute realism. Also, *The Trial of Mary Dugan* was the first play in which all the action took place in a courtroom. The novelty of this device helped ensure the play's success. C: Arthur Hohl, Rex Cherryman, Leona Maricle, Merle Maddern, Louis Jean Heydt, Oscar Polk, Cyril Keightley, Barton MacLane, Dennie Moore. P: A. H. Woods. D: A. H. Van Buren.

SV: 1929, MGM, Norma Shearer, Lewis Stone, Raymond Hackett, Lilyan Tashman, H. B. Warner. This was Metro's first all-talking drama. It was directed by its author, Bayard Veiller. For her talking-picture debut, Miss Shearer was coached by famed Belasco star Mrs. Leslie Carter. The play was remade by MGM in 1941 as a low-budget programmer. The cast included Robert Young, Laraine Day, Tom Conway, Frieda Inescort, John Litel, Marsha Hunt, Marjorie Main.

Trial of the Catonsville Nine, The (6/2/71, Lyceum, 29)

An O/B hit but a disappointment on Broadway, this is a dramatization of the trial of nine persons who stole and burned draft board files in Catonsville, Maryland, in May 1968. The most prominent defendants were two Roman Catholic priests, Daniel and Philip Berrigan. They and their codefendants were found guilty and sentenced to terms of two to three and one-half years in prison. A timely play, *Trial* was produced when public antagonism to the Vietnam war was strongest. The display of public frustration and sense of helplessness is mirrored in the drama. All the participants, on both sides of the law, are presented as caught up in events they cannot control nor order, their acts the result of irresistible momentum. If there is a villain, it is the United States of America. The writing, sometimes moving, sometimes maudlin, is a combination of blank verse by Daniel Berrigan, S.J., and naturalistic dialogue by Saul Levitt, who was earlier responsible for *The Andersonville Trial*. The play opened O/B 2/7/71 at the Good Shepherd Faith Church and ran 130 performances. The Berrigan brothers were played by Ed Flanders and Michael Kane. Others in the cast included Richard Jordan, David Spielberg, Nancy Malone, William Schallert, Leon Russom, Gwen Arner, and Mary Jackson. When the play moved to Broadway the Berrigans were played by Colgate Salisbury and Biff McGuire, with James Woods, Jacqueline Coslow, Michael Moriarty, Ronnie Claire Edwards, Josef Sommer, Mason Adams, and Helen Stenborg in support. Davis Roberts, Sam Waterston, Barton Heyman, Joe Ponazecki appeared in both casts. A: Daniel Berrigan, S.J., i.a.w. Saul Levitt. D: Gordon Davidson. P: Phoenix Theater and T. E. Hambleton i.a.w. Leland Hayward.

Trick for Trick (2/18/32, Harris, 70)

Spiritualist solves murder during a seance. Better-than-average thriller. C: James Rennie, Henry O'Neill. A: Vivian Crosby, Shirley Warde and Harry Wagstaff Gribble (D). P: Robert Newman.

SV: Fox, 1933, Ralph Morgan, Victor Jory.

Trigger (12/6/27, Little, 50)

A hot-tempered Ozark tomboy bewitches

a couple of dam-building engineers with her religious fervor—and sex appeal. Feared because of her faith-healing powers, the girl is cursed, stoned, and finally exiled by her superstitious neighbors. She leaves, but vows to return to her mountain cabin, and to the engineer who loves her, within a year's time. Interesting story and theme handled in commonplace manner. C: Claiborne Foster, Walter Connolly, Minor Watson, Sara Haden, Natalie Schafer. A: Lula Vollmer. P: Richard Herndon. D: George Cukor.

SV: RKO, 1934, *Spitfire*, Katharine Hepburn, Robert Young, Ralph Bellamy, Sara Haden, Martha Sleeper, Sidney Toler, High Ghere (Bob Burns).

Trimmed in Scarlet (2/2/20, Maxine Elliott's, 14)

A mother (Maxine Elliott) returns home after twenty years and tries to shield her son (Sidney Blackmer) from blackmail. Feeble comedy-drama by William Hurlbut; Miss Elliott's last New York stage appearance.

Trio (12/29/44, Belasco, 69)

Barred from most New York theatres because of its subject matter, *Trio* finally secured a booking at the Belasco theatre and premiered to an audience that expected a titillating treatment of "abnormal erotic passions." What they got was a restrained and honest play without a trace of sensationalism. *Trio* dealt with an adolescent girl (Lois Wheeler) who falls under the mental and sexual domination of an older woman (Lydia St. Clair), and of her liberation from the woman's influence through the intervention of a young college student (Richard Widmark).* The triangular conflict is resolved by the older woman's suicide. "The play is unpleasant but it is tense, dramatic and very moral" *(World-Telegram)*. Well-acted, sensitively produced and directed, *Trio* was treated with respect by the press and public. However, after a brief two-month run, New York City's License Commissioner informed the Belasco theatre management that its license would be revoked unless the "morally offensive exhibit" was withdrawn immediately, which it was. A: Dorothy and Howard Baker, b/o the novel by Dorothy Baker.** P: Lee Sabinson. D: Bretaigne Windust. SD: Stewart Chaney.

---

*Succeeded by Kirk Douglas.
**Author of the novel, *Young Man with a Horn* (1938), based on the life of jazz musician "Bix" Beiderbecke.

Trip to Bountiful, The (11/3/53, Henry Miller, 39)

Browbeaten by her shrewish daughter-in-law, an aging widow (Lillian Gish) runs away to the small town where she had once been happy. She soon learns that the friends of her youth have all died or scattered, that her old house is now a ruin, and that her only recourse is to return to the apartment of her spineless son (Gene Lyons) and his nagging wife (Jo Van Fleet). Despite fine performances by the Misses Gish and Van Fleet and, in a smaller role, Eva Marie Saint (deb.), this Horton Foote drama remained "a small play . . . lacking in sustained vitality" *(Herald Tribune)*. P: The Theatre Guild and Fred Coe. D: Vincent J. Donehue.

Truckline Café (2/27/46, Belasco, 13)

Hopelessly jumbled hodgepodge set in a roadside diner between Los Angeles and San Francisco. Into this highway café come a multitude of characters trying, generally unsuccessfully, to adjust to a variety of psychological postwar problems. Highlights: Marlon Brando's galvanizing portrayal of a young soldier who murders his unfaithful wife; Karl Malden's amusing characterization of a drunken sailor on the prowl. "A scrambled piece of theatricalism . . . sorely disappointing . . . a soggy Roman candle" (Howard Barnes, *Herald Tribune*). "The worst play I have seen since I have been in the reviewing business" (John Chapman, *News*). Stung by the brutally unfavorable reviews, author Maxwell Anderson bought advertising space in the daily newspapers to castigate the critics. He called them a Jukes family of journalism, made up of incompetents and irresponsibles, "who bring nothing to the theatre but their hopelessness, recklessness and despair." The public, he asserted, is far better qualified to judge plays than are the reviewers. The ads stirred much controversy in theatre circles, but did nothing to change the fate of the play. *Truckline Café* was sent to the storehouse after thirteen performances. C: David Manners, Virginia Gilmore, Kevin McCarthy, June Walker, Ralph Theadore, Frank Overton, Ann Sheperd, Irene Dailey, Robert Simon, Leila Ernst, Richard Waring, Joseph Adams (Joseph Anthony). P: Harold Clurman (D) and Elia Kazan i.a.w. The Playwrights Company. SD: Boris Aronson.

Trumpet Shall Sound, The (12/10/26, Laboratory Theatre, 30)

Thornton Wilder's first play; curious fable of a wealthy, Christ-like figure who turns his Manhattan mansion over to a group of down-and-outers. The critics were not impressed by this experimental O/B production: "Murky . . . sophomoric . . . very symbolic and quite uninteresting." C: Robert H. Gordon, Arthur Sircom, George Macready. P: American Laboratory Theatre. D: Richard Boleslawski.*

---

*Hollywood director (1930-1937); films included *Rasputin and the Empress*, *Les Misérables*, *Theodora Goes Wild*.

Truth, The (1/7/07, Criterion, 34)

In trying to conceal an innocent flirtation from her husband, a pathological liar (Clara Bloodgood) almost destroys her marriage. Probably the best of the fifty-five plays written by Clyde Fitch (A/D), one of the most prolific and successful of

The Truth. Sydney Booth and Grace George (revival production 1914). *Courtesy Museum of the City of New York Theatre and Music Collection.*

native dramatists and the first American playwright to gain prestige and critical recognition in Europe. *The Truth* scored a triumph in London with Marie Tempest in the leading role, but was unsuccessful both in New York and on the road in the United States. Perhaps attributing the play's failure to her own performance in the central role, star Clara Bloodgood created a front-page sensation by committing suicide in her Baltimore hotel room while on tour with the play. P: Charles Frohman.

R: (4/14/14, Little, 55) by Winthrop Ames. C: Grace George, Conway Tearle, Isabel Irving, Ferdinand Gottschalk, Zelda Sears, Guthrie McClintic, Sydney Booth.

Try and Get It (8/2/43, Cort, 8)

Malodorous farce about a couple of two-timing gold diggers. A: Sheldon Davis. P: A. H. Woods. D: Frank Merlin.

Try It with Alice (6/23/24, 52nd Street, 8)

The time is the future. A new law states that all bachelors must marry. To circumvent this fate, a couple of gay blades invite a clever female impersonator to their digs. Complications, as they say, ensue. Putrescent farce, one of the most odious, painfully unfunny exhibits in Broadway history, with a no-name cast and a bargain-basement production. A: Allen Leiber. P: A. J. Malby. D: Claude Archer.

Tubstrip (10/31/74, Mayfair, 22)

Comedy about life among homosexuals in a bathhouse. The bathhouse is called Boys Town but Spencer Tracy is nowhere in sight. Neither is writing skill nor wit. The leading actor, Calvin Culver, is a star of all-male films, often billed as Casey Donovan. In *Tubstrip* he plays the bathhouse attendant and gets to keep his clothes on. During a pre-Broadway tour *Tubstrip* enjoyed a modest success in San Francisco. A: A. J. Kronengold. C: Calvin Culver, Jade McCall, Walter Holiday, Jake Everett, Gerald Grant, Michael Kearns, Edward Rambeau, John Bruce Deaven, Dick Joslyn. D: Jerry Douglas. P: K.G. Productions, Ltd., i.a.w. Mark Segal. SD: Leo B. Meyer. CD: Jim Faber.

Tunnel of Love, The (2/13/57, Royale, 417)

Wisecracking farce about a married suburbanite who sires a baby out of wedlock and then sneaks it home as an adopted child. "Long on running time and short on taste..." (*Mirror*). C: Tom Ewell,* Nancy Olson (deb.), Darren McGavin, Elisabeth Fraser, Sylvia Daneel, Elizabeth Wilson. A: Joseph Fields (D) and Peter DeVries b/o Mr. DeVries' novel. P: The Theatre Guild. SD: Ralph Alswang.

SV: MGM, 1958, Richard Widmark, Doris Day, Gig Young, Gia Scala (directed by Gene Kelly).

---

*Johnny Carson (debut) succeeded Tom Ewell in the leading role on Broadway and, subsequently, in the national touring company. Mr. Carson in turn was succeeded by Larry Parks during the national tour.

Turn to the Right! (8/18/16, Gaiety, 435)

Ex-cons are regenerated when they foil a dastardly deacon's plot to swindle a sweet old lady's farm. The Old Hokum Bucket, but immensely popular. C: Forrest Winant, Lucy Cotton. A: Winchell Smith (D) and John E. Hazzard. P: Smith and John Golden.

Tweedles (8/13/23, Frazee, 96)

Winsora Tweedles (Ruth Gordon), a waitress, falls in love with the scion (Gregory Kelly) of a snobbish Philadelphia family. Whimsical, rickety comedy by Booth Tarkington and Harry Leon Wilson. C: Donald Meek, Cornelia Otis Skinner, Wallis Clark. P: Robert McLaughlin.

Twelve Miles Out (11/16/25, Playhouse, 188)

Two rival gangs of rumrunners double-cross each other off Fire Island. Slam-bang melodrama by William Anthony McGuire (A/P/D). C: Warren William, Frank Shannon, John Westley, Albert Hackett. Co-director: Ira Hards.

Twentieth Century (12/29/32, Broadhurst, 154)

Temperamental actress Lilly Garland and egomaniacal producer Oscar Jaffe (her former lover) engage in the battle of the sexes aboard the titular train. To lure Lilly into signing a contract, the destitute producer promises to present the Passion Play with La Garland as the Magdalen—only to discover that his principal backer

Twentieth Century. **Scene in club car (1932–33).** *Courtesy Museum of the City of New York Theatre and Music Collection.*

is an escaped lunatic. This durable farce by Ben Hecht and Charles MacArthur was based on an unproduced play, *The Napoleon of Broadway,* by Charles Bruce Milholland. The character of Oscar Jaffe was said to have been a composite of producers Morris Gest, David Belasco, and Jed Harris. C: Eugenie Leontovich, Moffat Johnston, William Frawley, Etienne Girardot, Roy Roberts, Joseph Crehan, Dennie Moore, Matt Briggs. P: George Abbott (D) and Philip Dunning.
R: (12/24/50, ANTA, 218) by ANTA. C: Gloria Swanson, Jose Ferrer (D), Robert Strauss, William Lynn, Robert Carroll, Werner Klemperer.
SV: Col, 1934, John Barrymore, Carole Lombard, Walter Connolly, Roscoe Karns, Ralph Forbes, Edgar Kennedy (directed by Howard Hawks).

$25 an Hour (5/10/33, Masque, 21)

Plain sprite (Jean Arthur) wins handsome music teacher (Georges Metaxa) away from glamorous *femme fatale* (Olga Baclanova). Nicely acted but plodding 30's comedy. A: Gladys Unger and Leyla Georgie. P: Alfred Aarons and Thomas Mitchell (D).

Twilight Walk (9/24/51, Fulton, 8)

Sympathetic reporter (Nancy Kelly) and cynical detective (Walter Matthau) stalk a sex murderer in New York's Central Park. ". . . a slow-moving, prolix case-history with little dramatic suspense" (*New York Times*). C: Ann Shoemaker, Charles Proctor. A: A. B. Shiffrin. P: Richard W. Krakeur. D: Paul Stewart. SD: Paul Morrison.

Twin Beds (8/14/14, Fulton, 411)

The lives of a young married couple are constantly interrupted by a wacky, lecherous neighbor. Flimsy bedroom farce, helped to popularity by uncommonly shrewd press agentry. C: Madge Kennedy, John Westley, Charles Judels. A: Salisbury Field and Margaret Mayo (D). P: William Harris, Jr.
SV: WB, 1929, Patsy Ruth Miller, Jack

Mulhall; UA, 1942, Joan Bennett, George Brent, Mischa Auer, Glenda Farrell, Una Merkel, Margaret Hamilton, Ernest Truex.

Two Blind Mice (3/2/49, Cort, 157)

Melvyn Douglas returned to the stage, after a fourteen-year absence in Hollywood, to star in this Samuel Spewack (A/D) satire on Washington bureaucracy. Learning that a small government office is still functioning years after Congress officially abolished it, a prankish newspaperman pretends that the two prim old ladies who run the bureau are engaged in top-secret herbological warfare experiments. By the time he is through, he has succeeded in fooling the Army, Navy, Air Force, and State Department, and, in the bargain, recaptured his ex-wife (Jan Sterling). "There is no great wit in the offering, but it is good-humored and funny" (*Herald Tribune*). C: Mabel Paige, Laura Pierpont, Geoffrey Lumb, Howard St. John, Robert Webber, Elliott Reid. P: King and Woodhull.

Two by Two (2/23/25, Selwyn, 16)

When Mama, a merry widow type, loses her young fiancé to her own daughter, she wastes little time rekindling an affair with an older admirer. Sluggish comedy. C: Charlotte Walker, Howard Lindsay, Lawrence D'Orsay, Beatrice Herford, Una Merkel (deb.), Lucille Lortel (deb.). A: John Turner and Eugenie Woodward. P: Jessy Trimble, Inc.

Two Fellows and a Girl (7/19/23, Vanderbilt, 132)

Two young men (John Halliday and Alan Dinehart) vie for the affections of a pretty girl (Ruth Shepley). Innocuous fluff. A: Vincent Lawrence. P: George M. Cohan.

Two for the Seesaw (1/16/58, Booth, 750)

William Gibson's two-character comedy-drama that gained stardom for Anne Bancroft (deb.) in the role of a kooky Jewish girl who lets herself fall in love with a midwestern lawyer (Henry Fonda) even though she knows he is destined to leave her. "An absorbing, affectionate and funny delight" (*News*). P: Fred Coe. D: Arthur Penn. SD: George Jenkins.

Musicalized by Michael Bennett, Cy Coleman, and Dorothy Fields as *Seesaw* (1973) with Ken Howard, Michele Lee, and Tommy Tune.

SV: UA, 1962, Robert Mitchum, Shirley MacLaine, Edmon Ryan, Elisabeth Fraser (directed by Robert Wise).

Two Girls Wanted (9/9/26, Little, 324)

Girl takes job as maid in home of her snooty rival. Guess who captures the hero by the final curtain. Featherweight 20's comedy. C: Nydia Westman, William Hanley. A: Gladys Unger. P: John Golden. D: Winchell Smith.

200 Were Chosen (11/20/36, 48th Street, 35)

In 1935 the United States government resettled farmers from the midwestern drought area in Alaska's Matanuska Valley. The adventures of three of these pioneer families, and their battles with substandard living conditions, governmental red tape, and a fever epidemic, furnished the basis for this interesting play by drama professor E. P. Conkle. C: Anthony Ross, Will Geer, Paula Bauersmith. P: Sidney Harmon. D: Worthington Miner and J. Edward Shugrue.

Two Married Men (1/13/25, Longacre, 16)

Two bored wives fall in love with the same "eligible bachelor." Wispy romantic comedy by Vincent Lawrence. C: Ann Andrews, George Gaul, Minor Watson, James Dale, Frances Carson. P: William Harris, Jr. D: Clifford Brooke.

Two Mrs. Carrolls, The (8/3/43, Booth, 585)

Homicidal artist (Victor Jory) plots to do away with his unsuspecting spouse (Elisabeth Bergner). When poison fails, he tries to strangle her, is outwitted, and commits suicide. ". . . a sprawling thriller [which] packs quite a jolt in its final scenes" (*Herald Tribune*). This long-run melodrama was written by "Martin Vale" (pseud. of Mrs. Bayard Veiller). It was first presented in London in 1935 with Elena Miramova and Leslie Banks in the leads. C: Irene Worth (deb.), Vera Allen, Margery Maude, Philip Tonge. P: Robert Reud and Paul Czinner. D: Reginald Denham.

SV: WB, 1947, Humphrey Bogart, Barbara Stanwyck, Alexis Smith, Nigel Bruce, Isobel Elsom.

Two on an Island (1/22/40, Broadhurst, 96)

Multiscened comedy by Elmer Rice (A/D) about a boy and girl who come to New York in search of theatrical careers. Their paths frequently cross, but they meet (and fall in love) only at the end of the play. ". . . an immensely skillful compilation of irrelevancies" (*Sun*). C: Betty Field, John Craven, Luther Adler, Howard da Silva, Martin Ritt, Dora Weissman, Ann Thomas, Whit Bissell, Adele Longmire, Joan Wetmore, Alvin Childress. P: The Playwrights Company. SD: Jo Mielziner.

Two Seconds (10/9/31, Ritz, 68)

A workingman's sordid life flashes before him in the two seconds before he is executed for the murder of his cheating wife. Somber, offbeat melodrama with an intriguing premise. C: Edward Pawley, Preston Foster, Blyth Daly, Harold Huber, Paul Stewart. A: Elliott Lester. P: Lande and Stephens. D: Egon Brecher and Alexander Leftwich.

SV: WB, 1932, Edward G. Robinson, Preston Foster, Vivienne Osborne, J. Carrol Naish, Guy Kibbee, Berton Churchill.

U

Ulysses in Nighttown (6/10/58, Rooftop, 206)

Ambitious, uneven O/B dramatization of the "Nighttown" sequence from James Joyce's *Ulysses*. The play concentrates on the erotic hallucinations of Leopold Bloom and Stephen Dedalus as they explore Dublin's red-light district in the year 1904. As in the novel, the evening concludes with Molly Bloom's famous stream-of-consciousness soliloquy. C: Zero Mostel, Robert Brown, Carroll O'Connor, Beatrice Arthur, Belita, Swen Swenson, Pauline Flanagan, Anne Meara, John Astin. A: Marjorie Barkentin. P: Rooftop Productions. D: Burgess Meredith. CH: Valerie Bettis.

Revived on Broadway (3/10/74, Winter Garden, 69) by Alexander H. Cohen and Bernard Delfont. C: Zero Mostel, Tom Lee Jones, Fionnuala Flanagan, Danny Meehan, Swen Swenson, Beulah Garrick. D: Burgess Meredith. CD: Pearl Somner. SD: Ed Wittstein. CD: Swen Swenson.

Note: Published in Paris in 1922, *Ulysses* draws a series of Homeric parallels between the events in the novel and those presented in the *Odyssey*. Charged with obscenity and prevented from public sale, *Ulysses* was legally admitted into the United States only after a long court battle that ended in 1934. This epic work is considered by many critics to be one of the greatest works of fiction of all time.

Unchastened Woman, The (10/9/15, 39th Street, 193)

Predatory wife (Emily Stevens) seeks to ensnare young architect (Hassard Short), but is outwitted by his clearsighted wife (Christine Norman). Threatened with exposure and divorce by her husband (H. Reeves Smith), she withdraws from the affair, beaten but still unchastened. Emily Stevens scored a substantial success as the bored, neurotic wife in this comedy-drama that was considered ultra-bold in 1915. A: Louis K. Anspacher. P: Oliver Morosco. D: Anspacher and T. D. Frawley.

R: (2/15/26, Princess, 31) by The Stagers. C: Violet Kemble Cooper, Morgan Farley, Josephine Hutchinson, Margaret Douglass. D: Margaret Wycherly and Edward Goodman.

Uncle Harry (5/20/42, Broadhurst, 430)

Bullied for years by his old-maid sisters (Eva Le Gallienne and Adelaide Klein), a mild-mannered bachelor (Joseph Schildkraut) executes the perfect crime by poisoning one sister and pinning the murder on the other. "An admirably sinister murder play" *(Sun)*. This skillful melodrama was written by Yale University-Carnegie Tech professor, Thomas Job. In it, Eva Le Gallienne gave an exceptional performance as the vengeful spinster who goes to the gallows rather than allow her conscience-stricken brother to expiate his crime. C: Beverly Roberts, Leona Roberts, Karl Malden. P: Hayman and Hatten. D: Lem Ward. SD: Howard Bay.

SV: U, 1945, *The Strange Affair of Uncle Harry,* George Sanders, Geraldine Fitzgerald, Ella Raines,

Sara Allgood, Moyna MacGill.

Uncle Willie (12/20/56, Golden, 141)

Formula comedy about a heart-of-gold Bronx peddler (Menasha Skulnik) who plays Mr. Fixit in turn-of-the-century New York. C: Norman Feld, Edith Fellows, Nita Talbot. A: Julie Berns and Irving Elman. P: Albert Lewis and Samuel Schulman i.a.w. I. B. Joselow. D: Robert Douglas.

Unconquered, The (2/13/40, Biltmore, 6)

Ayn Rand, militant champion of *laissez-faire* capitalism, penned this heavily plotted, sketchily characterized melodrama about the evils of communism in Stalinist Russia. Brought to Broadway by, of all people, George Abbott (P/D), the show frequently verged on the ridiculous. In addition, it was very badly acted. "Should be played, if at all, with the audience at tables, drinking vodka" *(Post)*. "Not so much anti-Bolshevik as anticlimax" *(World-Telegram)*. C: Dean Jagger, John Emery, Helen Craig, Arthur Pierson, Howard Freeman, Lea Penman, Ludmilla Toretzka. SD: Boris Aronson.

Note: Dismayed but not defeated by the failure of *The Unconquered*, Ayn Rand returned to her typewriter. Three years later the Russian-born authoress startled the literary world with a blockbuster of a novel, *The Fountainhead*.

Under Cover (8/26/14, Cort, 349)

A woman becomes involved with diamond smugglers and is forced to choose between her sister and the man she loves. Slick melodrama liberally seasoned with "comic relief." C: Lily Cahill, Lucile Watson, Ralph Morgan, William

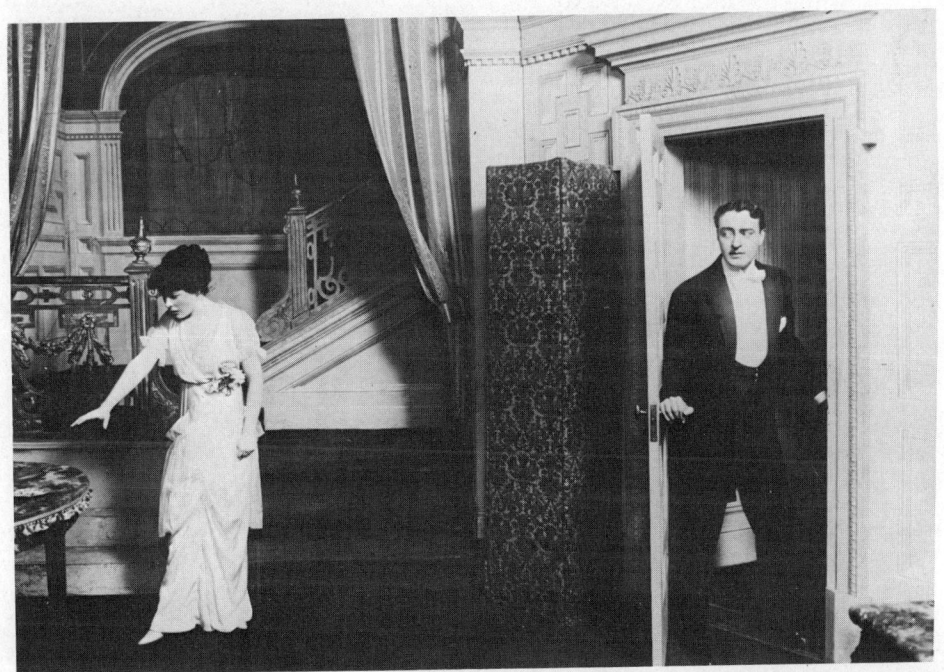

Under Cover. **Lily Cahill and William Courtenay (August 26, 1914).** *Courtesy Museum of the City of New York Theatre and Music Collection.*

Courtenay, Phoebe Foster, Lola Fisher. A: Roi Cooper Megrue. P: Selwyn and Co. D: Felix Edwards.

Under Fire (8/11/15, Hudson, 129)

Action-filled behind-enemy-lines spy melodrama with a stellar cast: William Courtenay, Violet Heming, Frank Craven, Frank Morgan, Edward G. Robinson, McKay Morris, Phoebe Foster, Henry Stephenson, Felix Krembs, Walter Kingsford. A: Roi Cooper Megrue. P: Selwyn and Company. D: Courtenay and Megrue.

Under Orders (8/20/18, Eltinge, 167)

Poignant World War I tale of two officers (one German, the other American) and their respective wives, with all four characters admirably portrayed by Shelly Hull and Effie Shannon. A: Berte Thomas. P: A. H. Woods. D: W. H. Gilmore.

Under Sentence (10/3/16, Harris, 55)

An unscrupulous Wall Street giant (George Nash) sends an innocent man to jail. The scapegoat's wife (Janet Beecher) vows revenge and finally succeeds in placing the financier behind bars. "Utterly lacking [in realism or truth]. . . . Theatrical through and through" *(New York Times)*. *Under Sentence* was written by Roi Cooper Megrue, author of *Under Cover* (1914) and *Under Fire* (1915), in collaboration with Irvin S. Cobb. C: Edward G. Robinson, Frank Morgan, Thomas Mitchell. P: Selwyn and Company. D: Megrue.

Under the Sycamore Tree (3/7/60, Cricket, 41)

Wry, leisurely O/B satirical fantasy about life in an ant colony. To poke fun at the foibles of the human race, the author presented as his leading character an ant-scientist who has learned enough of the ways of man to equip his fellow multipedes with speech and mechanization, as well as enough D.D.T. to preserve the balance of power. In the words of one writer, the play was "a jumble of unresolved revue sketches," but it had its entertaining and provocative moments. C: David Hurst, Margaret Phillips, David Doyle, Thomas Barbour, Wayne Tippit, Gaby Rodgers. A: Sam Spewack. D: Philip Minor.

Note: *Under the Sycamore Tree* was presented in London (1952) with a cast headed by Alec Guinness, Diana Churchill, Ernest Thesiger, Peter Bull, Eric Porter, and Daphne Anderson. The production was staged by Peter Glenville.

Under the Yum-Yum Tree (11/16/60, Henry Miller, 173)

Lecherous San Francisco landlord (Gig Young) schemes to deflower a nubile Berkeley student who is sharing an apartment (platonically) with her high-minded fiancé. "A gay and frothy comedy" *(New York Times)*. ". . . tasteless vulgarity . . . makes sex incredibly trying" *(Post)*. C: Sandra Church, Dean Jones, Nan Martin. A: Lawrence Roman. P: Frederick Brisson and Roger L. Stevens. D: Joseph Anthony. SD: Oliver Smith.

Revived O/B for six performances (5/28/64, Mayfair) with Bill Bixby, Ted Brown, and Marian Hailey heading the cast under the direction of Michael Ferrall.

SV: Col, .1963, Jack Lemmon, Carol Lynley, Dean Jones, Paul Lynde, Imogene Coca, Edie Adams, Robert Lansing.

Under This Roof (2/22/42, Windsor, 17)

Undramatic chronicle play tracing three decades (1846–1873) in the lives of a New England family. "A slow parade of good intentions . . ." *(Sun)*. C: Russell Hardie, Barbara O'Neil, Harlan Briggs, Howard St. John. A: Herbert Ehrmann.

Under Two Flags. Scene in Act IV (1901). *Courtesy Museum of the City of New York Theatre and Music Collection.*

P: Russell Lewis (D) and Rita Hassan.

Under Two Flags (2/5/01, Garden, 135)

Reasonably faithful adaptation of the purple-prose novel by Ouida dealing with love and adventure in the Foreign Legion. C: Blanche Bates, Maclyn Arbuckle, Grace Elliston. A: Paul Potter. P/D: David Belasco.
SV: Fox, 1936, Ronald Colman, Claudette Colbert, Victor McLaglen, Rosalind Russell, Nigel Bruce, Gregory Ratoff.

Undercurrent, The (3/3/25, Cort, 24)

A blow on the head changes a tyrannical father into a paragon of kindliness. Grade C stuff. C: Harry Beresford, Lee Patrick. A: William H. McMasters. P: Barrie, Inc. D: Frank McCormack.

Undesirable Lady, An (10/9/33, National, 24)

Murderess (Nancy Carroll) flees to the frozen north, falls in love with an undercover agent of the law, ends by taking her life. Dreary hokum by Leon Gordon (A/P/D).

Unexpected Husband (6/2/31, 48th Street, 120)

Young man and his girl-friend pass out after a heavy night of drinking, awaken to find themselves in the same bed. Lackluster sex comedy. C: Mary Howard, Arthur Aylesworth, Josephine Hull, Hugh Cameron. A: Barry Conners. P: Richard Herndon. D: Milton Stiefel.

Unknown Purple, The (9/14/18, Lyric, 273)

Gimmicky, entertaining sci-fi yarn of a man who discovers the secret of invisibility and proceeds to revenge himself upon his faithless wife and her lover. C: Richard Bennett; Helen MacKellar, Edward Van Sloan. A/P: Roland West. D: Charles H. Smith and Ira Hards.

Unwritten Chapter, The (10/11/20, Astor, 24)

Biography of Haym Salomon (Louis Mann), one of the heroes of the American Revolution, who extended large cash advances to the United States Treasury, was imprisoned by the British, but escaped to give substantial financial aid to his adopted country. The play's 1776 sequences were framed by a stilted modern-day prologue and epilogue dealing with the evils of anti-semitism. Fascinating historical subject merited a better-written drama. C: Lucile Watson, Clarence Derwent, Robert Barrat. A: Samuel Shipman and Victor Victor. P: A. H. Woods. D: Robert Milton.

Up and Up, The (9/8/30, Biltmore, 81)

Racetrack comedy about a bookie (Pat O'Brien) and his problems. Nice performance by the zestful Mr. O'Brien, but the script had too many holes in it. C: Sylvia Field, Donald MacDonald, William Foran, Percy Kilbride. A: Eva Kay Flint and Martha Madison. P: Blatt and Nicholas. D: Howard Lindsay.

Up in Mabel's Room (1/15/19, Eltinge, 229)

Flustered husband tries to retrieve incriminating memento from his old flame. Harum-scarum bedroom farce, quite funny at times. C: Enid Markey, Hazel Dawn, John Cumberland, Adele Rowland. A: Wilson Collison and Otto Harbach. P: A. H. Woods. D: Bertram Harrison.

SV: UA, 1944, Dennis O'Keefe, Marjorie Reynolds, Gail Patrick, Mischa Auer, Charlotte Greenwood, Lee Bowman.

Up Pops the Devil (9/1/30, Masque, 146)

Carefree Greenwich Village couple find their relationship threatened when they legitimatize their union. Brightly written comedy by Albert Hackett and Frances Goodrich. C: Roger Pryor, Sally Bates, Brian Donlevy, Albert Hackett. P: Lee Shubert. D: Worthington Miner.

Musicalized by Harold Atteridge as *Everybody's Welcome** (1931) with Harriet Lake (Ann Sothern), Oscar Shaw, Frances Williams, Ann Pennington, the Ritz Brothers, and Jimmy Dorsey's orchestra.

SV: Par, 1931, Carole Lombard, Norman Foster, Stuart Erwin, Skeets Gallagher, Lilyan Tashman.

---

*The principal song in this show was "As Time Goes By," a ballad by Herman Hupfeld which finally caught on a decade later when used as the theme in the movie *Casablanca,*

Up the Ladder (3/6/22, Playhouse, 120)

To gain social acceptance, a jazz-age couple (Doris Kenyon and Paul Kelly) join the hard-drinking roadhouse set and soon lose both their self-respect and their money. Flaccid drama by Owen Davis. C: Albert Hackett, Mary Brandon (Mrs. Robert E. Sherwood). P: William A. Brady. D: Lumsden Hare.

Up the Line (11/22/26, Morosco, 24)

Effie (Florence Johns), a ranch girl, falls in love with Slug (Louis Calhern), a harvest worker with itchy feet. Their life together is miserable. So was this play. A: Henry Fisk Carlton. P: Richard Herndon. D: Alan Dinehart.

Upstairs and Down (9/25/16, Cort, 320)

During a weekend house party on Long Island, two sisters—each coveting the same man—engage in a battle of wits to win him. "Entertaining comedy with languid intervals" (*New York Times*). "The play is as clever as the cast" (*Journal*). C: Leo Carrillo, Mary Servoss, Christine Norman, Paul Harvey, Roberta Arnold, Ida St. Leon, Juliette Day. A: Frederic and Fanny Hatton. P: Oliver Morosco. D: Robert Milton.

UTBU (1/4/66, Hayes, 7)

Novelist James Kirkwood (*P.S. Your Cat is Dead!*) made his Broadway playwriting debut, and comedian Nancy Walker her directorial debut, with this zany farce about a murder organization dedicated to righting the world's ills by systematic extermination of all the nasty people in it. *UTBU* (Unhealthy To Be Unpleasant, as per the organization's name) was dismissed by the critics as "wild and wacky. . . . but too often just silly." C: Tony Randall, Thelma Ritter, Alan Webb, Margaret Hamilton, Constance Ford. P: Lyn Austin.

V

Valley Forge (12/10/34, Guild, 58)

Maxwell Anderson's account of the dark winter of 1778 when the American Revolution seemed near collapse. The play's greatest strength was in the vigorously humanized portrayal of George Washington as a rebellious, short-tempered leader struggling valiantly to hold a ragged army together in the snows of Valley Forge, and compelled to fight not only the complacent English, but the treachery, stupidity, and greed of his own countrymen. The play's greatest weakness lay in the romantic episodes involving Washington's first love, Mary Philipse. Highlight: Washington surveying his cold and hungry army as they bury their dead, and grimly reflecting, "This liberty will look easy by and by when nobody dies to get it." Despite generally laudatory reviews, a seven-week run was all that *Valley Forge* could muster, and then it disappeared from the boards. C: Philip Merivale, Margalo Gillmore, Reginald Mason, John Hoysradt, George Coulouris, Stanley Ridges, Alan Bunce, Erskine Sanford, Victor Kilian. P: The Theatre Guild. D: Herbert Biberman and John Houseman. CH: Martha Graham. SD: Kate Lawson.

Valley of Content, The (1/13/25, Apollo, 40)

Country wife (Marjorie Rambeau) has many adventures in the big city, awakens to find it was all merely a dream. Old-hat even for 1925. A: Blanche Upright. P: Tom Wilkes.

Vampire, The (1/18/09, Hackett, 24)

A writer with an absorptive mentality preys on the minds of other artists in hypnotic fashion and drains them of their creative ideas. The poor wretch doesn't really mean any harm. His dark powers, he explains, are involuntary and have brought more misery to him than to his victims. "A highly effective theatrical idea . . . immaturely developed . . . full of crudities and contradictions" (*New York Times*). C: Warner Oland, John E. Kellerd, John Westley. A: Edgar Allan Woolf and George Sylvester Viereck. P: Sam S. and Lee Shubert. D: Albert Cowles.

Note: Co-author Viereck was sentenced to prison (1942) for failure to register as a German agent. He was released in 1947.

Varying Shore, The (12/5/21, Hudson, 66)

Portrait of a worldly, warmhearted harlot (Elsie Ferguson) at the age of forty, then thirty, and finally as a tremulous and trusting girl of sixteen. Sentimental, dramatically unconvincing story wedded to an interesting theatrical device, that of tracing a life backward through the years. This retrogressive method of storytelling also was employed by Kaufman and Hart in their play, *Merrily We Roll Along* (1934). A: Zoe Akins. P: Sam H. Harris. D: Sam Forrest.

Vegetable, The (4/10/29, Cherry Lane, 13)

F. Scott Fitzgerald's only play, a disjointed satiric fable about a young railroad clerk who dreams himself into the presidency and out of it again. "Both the theme and the manner sound sophomoric" (*New York Times*). Presented O/B by the Lenox Hill Players with a nondescript cast; staged within an inch of its life by Lee Strasberg.

Veils (3/13/28, Forrest, 4)

When a disillusioned nun renounces convent life, her prostitute twin sister takes her place in the nunnery. Horrendous tripe. C: Elsa Shelley, Warren William. A: Irving Kaye Davis. P: Donald Heywood. D: Edward Elsner.

Velvet Glove, The (12/26/49, Booth, 152)

The Mother Superior (Grace George) of a Roman Catholic girls' school gently blackmails a stern bishop into rescinding his dismissal of a faculty member. "... an arch, sporadically amusing comedy ... light and innocuous as eiderdown" (*Herald Tribune*). C: Walter Hampden, John Williams, Jean Dixon, Barbara Brady (deb.). A: Rosemary Casey. P/D: Guthrie McClintic.

Veneer (11/12/29, Harris, 31)

Charlie (Henry Hull) is a braggart, liar, and drifter. He soon tires of the girl (Joanna Roos) who was fool enough to love him. When he walks out on her, she takes her life. Compelling 20's drama made few concessions to popular taste. A/D: Hugh Stange. P: Cort and Abramson.
SV: RKO, 1932, *Young Bride*, Eric Linden, Helen Twelvetrees, Arline Judge, Polly Walters, Cliff Edwards, Roscoe Ates.

Venus (12/26/27, Masque, 8)

Futuristic sci-fi whatzit by Rachel Crothers (A/D) in which a new kind of pill makes men more feminine and women more masculine with predictably ribald results. Amusing for perhaps ten minutes, no more. C: Tyrone Power, Sr., Patricia Collinge, Katherine (Kay) Francis, Cecilia Loftus. P: Carl Reed.

Note: Thorne Smith appropriated much the same idea in his 1931 novel, *Turnabout,* subsequently adapted for the stage as *If I Were You* (1938).

Venus at Large (4/12/62, Morosco, 4)

Marilyn Monroe, here called Olive Ogilvie (Joyce Jameson), walks out on her two-timing Hollywood agent (David Wayne) and domineering studio boss (Ernest Truex), comes to New York, becomes infatuated with an Arthur Miller-type playwright (William Prince), and enrolls as a student at The Actors Studio. Stale satirical comedy seldom hit the mark; written by Henry Denker, author of *Time Limit!* (1956), *A Far Country* (1961), *A Case of Libel* (1963), etc. C: Sally Gracie, Boris Tumarin, Leon Janney, Jack Bittner, Robert Yuro. P: Joel Schenker. D: Rod Amateau. SD: Donald Oenslager.

Vermont (1/9/29, Erlanger, 16)

Problems mount for an old New England family when they become involved with hijackers and bootleggers. Old-fashioned, melodramatic antiprohibition tract by A. E. Thomas. C: Allyn Joslyn, Phyllis Povah, John T. Doyle. P: George M. Cohan. D: Sam Forrest.

Veronica's Room (10/25/73, Music Box, 75)

Ira Levin, author of such straightforward thrillers as *A Kiss Before Dying* and *Rosemary's Baby,* came to Broadway with a murky exercise in Gothic mystery that was too mysterious to be satisfying, and ultimately so cryptic that it baffled audiences and critics alike. A young girl is persuaded to impersonate the long-dead Veronica as a charitable act to benefit Veronica's sick sister. This lands the obliging miss in a highly atmospheric bedroom in a mansion outside Boston, and her troubles begin. Nothing is what it seems to be, and the persons about her change disconcertingly. The homey caretakers of the estate (Eileen Heckart and Arthur Kennedy) who inveigled her to agree to their scheme become handsomely dressed aristocrats. Her boyfriend turns into a doctor—perhaps. The proceedings grow ever more bizarre, finally involving incest, murder, and necrophilia. Though she fared badly in the play, Regina Baff as the heroine fought so valiantly against her fate that she was rewarded with a Tony nomination for Best Supporting Actress. ". . . a pretty slick thriller. . . . But in the second act, [Levin's] got to work his way out of the puzzle and he can't. Not satisfactorily, anyway" (Douglas Watt, *New York Daily News*). ". . . not only devoid of credibility but sick besides. . . . Miss Heckart and Mr. Kennedy are giving it their all, and that is quite a lot" (Edwin Wilson, *Wall Street Journal*). C: Eileen Heckart, Arthur Kennedy, Regina Baff, Kipp Osborne. P: Morton Gottlieb. D: Ellis Rabb. SD: Douglas Schmidt CD: Nancy Potts.

Very Rich Woman, A (9/30/65, Belasco, 28)

A pair of heartless daughters scheme to have their wealthy, fun-loving mother (Ruth Gordon) committed to a sanitarium. In the end, the spirited widow triumphs over her avaricious offspring. "Has heart and humor in abundance . . ." (*Journal-American*). C: Ernest Truex, Ethel Griffies, Raymond Walburn, Diana Muldaur, Madge Kennedy, Katharine Houghton, Stefan Schnabel, Joan Wetmore, Carrie Nye, Peter Turgeon. A: Ruth Gordon b/o a play by Phillipée Heriat. P/D: Garson Kanin. CD: Audre. SD: Oliver Smith. SV: U, 1967, *Rosie!*, Rosalind Russell,

Brian Aherne, Sandra Dee, James Farentino, Audrey Meadows, Vanessa Brown, Leslie Nielsen, Margaret Hamilton, Reginald Owen, Virginia Grey, Dean Harens, Richard Derr (directed by David Lowell Rich from a screenplay by Samuel Taylor).

Very Special Baby, A (11/14/56, Playhouse, 5)

Encouraged by his spinster sister (Sylvia Sidney) and an army buddy (Jack Klugman), an amiable thirty-four-year-old lout (Jack Warden) finally finds the confidence to leave the home of his tyrannical Italian-American father (Luther Adler) and strike out on his own. "A quite moving one-act drama which stubbornly refused to be stretched into a full evening in the theatre" (*Journal-American*). *A Very Special Baby*, an expanded version of a television play, was written by novelist and TV playwright-producer Robert Alan Aurthur, whose screenwriting credits include *Edge of the City*, *Warlock*, *Lilith*, etc. P: David Susskind. D: Martin Ritt.

Vickie (9/22/42, Plymouth, 48)

Jose Ferrer and Uta Hagen (Mrs. Ferrer) in a strident wartime farce poking fun at women in uniform. The two stars were badly miscast. ". . . loud, sprawling and tasteless . . . and acted, for the most part, with very little skill" (*PM*). C: Red Buttons (deb.), Mildred Dunnock, Taylor Holmes, Margaret Matzenauer, Sara Seegar. A: S. M. Herzig. P: Frank Mandel. D: Jose Ferrer and Frank Mandel.

Victory Belles (10/26/43, Mansfield, 85)

Imbecilic farce about a couple of husband-hunting gold diggers (Barbara Bennett and Mabel Taliaferro). ". . . the absolute, irreducible zero in the way of entertainment" (*World-Telegram*). ". . . has to be seen to be depreciated"

(*Journal-American*). A: Alice Gerstenberg. P/D: Henry Adrian. Despite the worst reviews received by any Broadway play in several seasons, this 1943 exhibit unaccountably managed a run of 85 performances.

Viet Rock (11/10/66, Martinique, 62)

Protest play satirizing contemporary (1966) attitudes toward the Vietnam war in a series of brief, incisive vignettes. Avant-garde O/B drama used cinematic-styled techniques to hammer home its antiwar message. A/D: Megan Terry.

View From the Bridge, A (9/29/55, Coronet, 149)

Arthur Miller's play about Eddie Carbone (Van Heflin),* a Brooklyn stevedore driven near insanity by repressed desire for his nubile niece. When she falls in love with a Sicilian lad of her own age, Eddie insinuates that the handsome youth is a homosexual. When this ploy fails, the jealous longshoreman informs the immigration authorities that the boy has entered the country illegally and must be deported, and is thereupon killed by the boy's vengeful older brother. All this is told in flashbacks by an elderly neighborhood lawyer (J. Carrol Naish), who attempts to draw a parallel between the melodramatic deeds onstage and the tragic myths of ancient Greece. *A View From the Bridge* was dismissed by the critics as "self-consciously arty" and "lacking in any particular freshness of viewpoint or insight." The author later revised and lengthened the play (it had originally been written as a long one-act drama). The revised script was successfully produced O/B (see below) under the direction of Ulu Grosbard, with Dustin Hoffman serving as assistant director and Jon Voight cast in the role of the Sicilian youth. The 1955 Broadway production was staged by Martin Ritt. The cast included: Eileen Heckart, Jack Warden, Tom Pedi, Gloria Marlowe, Richard Davalos, and Russell Collins. P: Bloomgarden-Whitehead-Stevens. SD: Boris Aronson.

R: (1/28/65, Sheridan Square, 780). C: Robert Duvall, Mitchell Jason, Jon Voight, Susan Anspach, Ramon Bieri, Richard Castellano, Jeanne Kaplan.

SV: Continental, 1962, Raf Vallone, Maureen Stapleton, Carol Lawrence, Jean Sorel (directed by Sidney Lumet).

---

*One controversial scene in the play called for Van Heflin to kiss Richard Davalos on the lips. Said Heflin: "That kiss always got gasps from the audience. We got away with it, I suppose, because neither of us looked effeminate."

Village Green (9/3/41, Henry Miller, 30)

Comedy about a small-town judge (Frank Craven) who becomes involved in a local scandal. "Regrettably tame" (*Post*). A: Carl Allensworth. P: Dorothy and Julian Olney and Felix Jacoves (D).

Vinegar Tree, The (11/19/30, Playhouse, 233)

Flighty matron (Mary Boland) mistakes a suave houseguest (Warren William) for an artist with whom she had once enjoyed a brief but torrid extramarital fling some years earlier. Delightful comedy by Paul Osborn provided Miss Boland with one of her best roles. P: Dwight Deere Wiman. D: Winchell Smith.

SV: MGM, 1933, *Should Ladies Behave?*, Alice Brady, Lionel Barrymore.

Violet (10/24/44, Belasco, 23)

Obstreperous brat sets out to untangle the love life of her much-married father. ". . . a depressingly synthetic comedy" (*Post*). C: Pat Hitchcock,* Harvey Stephens, Helen Claire, Doro Merande, Paula Trueman. A/D: Whitfield Cook. P: Albert Margolies.

---

*Daughter of Alfred Hitchcock.

Virgin, The (2/22/26, Maxine Elliott's, 57)

Simpleton mistakes pretty girl for a reincarnation of the Virgin Mary, attempts to throttle her when he discovers she has feet of clay. Witless 20's melodrama. C: Lee Baker, Phyllis Povah, Jessie Ralph. A: Arthur Corning White and Louis Bennison. P: Jules Hurtig. D: Sam Forrest.

Virgin Man, The (1/18/27, Princess, 64)

Innocent Yale youth is pounced upon by three man-hungry females, but spurns all offers of illicit sex and returns to New Haven as pure as when he left. Smutty 20's comedy was raided by the Police. Its author-producer-director, one William Francis Dugan, was fined and jailed. C: Don Dillaway, Dorothy Hall.

Virginian, The (1/5/04, Manhattan, 138)

Handsome, laconic cowboy (Dustin Farnum) imposes law and order in Wyoming community. Classic, oft-quoted ("When you say that, pardner, smile") western, the prototype of literally thousands of subsequent "horse opera" scenarios. A: Adapted from Owen Wister's novel by Wister and Kirke La Shelle (P). D: John Stapleton.
SV: Par, 1929, Gary Cooper, Walter Huston, Mary Brian, Chester Conklin; 1946, Joel McCrea, Sonny Tufts, Brian Donlevy, Fay Bainter, Barbara Britton, William Frawley.

Visit to a Small Planet (2/7/57, Booth, 388)

Gore Vidal's witty and cogent satiric comedy about an impish creature from outer space who lands on Earth to study the ways of earthlings. Enchanted by hydrogen bombs and other such twentieth-century playthings, the interplanetary visitor sees no reason why they can't be used for his own amusement. It takes the combined efforts of the entire cast to persuade the visitor to abandon his plans for global war. Splendidly acted by Cyril Ritchard (D) as the visitor and Eddie Mayehoff as a cliché-sputtering general, *Visit to a Small Planet* was one of the hits of 1957. The play was an expanded version of a previously produced television script by Mr. Vidal. C: Philip Coolidge, Sibyl Bowan, Sarah Marshall, Conrad Janis. P: George Axelrod and Clinton Wilder.
SV: Par, 1960, Jerry Lewis, Fred Clark, Joan Blackman, Earl Holliman, Lee Patrick, Gale Gordon (directed by Norman Taurog).

Visitor, The (10/17/44, Henry Miller, 23)

A boy who disappeared under mysterious circumstances returns home three years later. Is he the same fellow—or an imposter? Tedious psychological melodrama produced and directed by Herman Shumlin. "It is diffuse, cluttered and exhausting—and very badly acted" *(Sun).* C: Richard Hylton, Ralph Forbes, Walter Greaza, Thomas Chalmers. A: Kenneth White b/o a novel by Leane Zugsmith and Carl Randau.

Viva Madison Avenue! (4/6/60, Longacre, 2)

Flimsy farce about a screwball prankster (Buddy Hackett) who blossoms into an advertising agency genius. C: Fred Clark, William Windom, Lee Krieger, Paul Richards, Jan Miner, Frances Sternhagen. A: George Panetta. P: Tamber and Poll. D: Aaron Frankel.

Voice in the Dark, A (7/28/19, Republic, 134)

The only witnesses in a murder case are a blind newsstand attendant and a deaf old lady. Contrived, wildly implausible melodrama. C: Florine Arnold, William Boyd, Olive Wyndham. A: Ralph E. Dyar. P: A. H. Woods. D: W. H. Gilmore.

Voice of the Turtle, The (12/8/43, Morosco, 1,557)

A GI comes to New York City on a weekend pass. Stood up by his date, he spends the weekend instead with a budding young actress. By the time the curtain falls, their casual affair has blossomed into love. This immensely popular three-character comedy by John Van Druten (A/D) was played with charm and seasoned comic assurance by Margaret Sullavan as the naïve actress, Elliott Nugent as the lonely soldier, and Audrey Christie as the heroine's wisecracking friend. Also applauded was Stewart Chaney's ingenious setting, a cross-section of a three-room apartment in New York's East Sixties. "A romantic comedy that is at once witty, tender and wise" *(Herald Tribune)*. "Mr. Van Druten has written the best light comedy of his career, as winningly gay in spirit as it is superlatively adroit in craftsmanship; and what goes for the play goes equally for the production" *(PM)*. Van Druten wrote *The Voice of the Turtle* in three weeks. He sent it to producer Alfred de Liagre, Jr. who read it immediately, optioned it within twenty-four hours, and cast it within the week. The play was a runaway hit from the rising of its first curtain.

SV: WB, 1948, Ronald Reagan, Eleanor Parker, Eve Arden, Wayne Morris, Kent Smith, John Emery, Erskine Sanford.

Voices (4/3/72, Ethel Barrymore, 8)

A weak ghost story about illusion and reality. The setting is that dependable standby: the deserted, country mansion. It's been newly inherited by a New York matron who arrives with her husband in the middle of a blizzard. She is a neurotic type and it is not long before she is hearing voices, and seeing people who aren't there. Then the husband begins to suffer the same affliction. There is a trick ending, but the surprise has been too long coming, its effect dulled by the soporific dialogue and dim humor that's preceded it. *Voices* is never frightening, though the eerie quality of Jo Mielziner's stage set was highly praised. Despite this asset, and a first-rate cast, the play is a disappointment. A: Richard Lortz. C: Richard Kiley, Julie Harris, Patricia Wheel, Lisa Essary, Scott Firestone. D: Gilbert Cates. P: Jerry Schlossberg, Jerry Hammer, Adela Holzer. SD: Jo Mielziner.

Voltaire (3/20/22, Plymouth, 16)

The efforts of the wily, elderly Voltaire (Arnold Daly) to save a young atheist from the Bastille. Melodramatic hodgepodge billed as "a romantic comedy." A: Leila Taylor and Gertrude Purcell. P/D: Arthur Hopkins.

W

W.P.A. Federal Theatre

See *Federal Theatre Project*.

Wake Up, Darling (5/2/56, Barrymore, 5)

A virginal playwright tries to seduce a stagestruck wife. Dull sex comedy by screenwriter-producer Alex Gottlieb (*Hollywood Canteen, Romance on the High Seas, The Blue Gardenia*, etc.). Song: "Li'l Ol' You and Li'l Ol' Me" by Jule Styne and Leo Robin. C: Barry Nelson, Barbara Britton, Russell Nype, Kay Medford, Paula Trueman. P: Gordon Pollock i.a.w. Segall and Cook. D: Ezra Stone.

Wake Up, Jonathan! (1/17/21, Henry Miller, 105)

Minor Elmer Rice-Hatcher Hughes comedy about a clever wife (Mrs. Fiske) who effects a reconciliation with her blustering businessman-husband (Charles Dalton). Originally intended as a vehicle for Belasco star David Warfield, rewritten to fit the talents of Mrs. Fiske. P: Sam H. Harris. D: Harrison Grey Fiske.

Walk Hard (3/27/46, Chanin, 7)

Straggling tale of a contentious black prizefighter (Maxwell Glanville) and his battles with race prejudice. Former boxing champ Mickey Walker made his stage debut in this play which was originally produced O/B (11/30/44) by the American Negro Theatre. A: Abram Hill b/o the novel by Len Zinberg. P/D: Gustav Blum.

Walk Into My Parlor (11/19/41, Forrest, 29)

Problems of a poverty-stricken Italian family in Chicago; a blurred carbon copy of Odets' *Awake and Sing*. Most interesting character: a goldfish-eating racketeer-son (Nicholas Conte),* who makes passes at his brother's wife and persuades his doting mother to pass counterfeit money to unsuspecting tradesmen. A: Alexander Greendale. P/D: Luther Greene.

---

*Hollywood changed this actor's name to Richard Conte.

Walking Gentleman, The (5/7/42, Belasco, 6)

Deranged actor strangles any woman who reminds him of his former wife. As the homicidal gentleman of the title, Belgian-born Victor Francen (deb.) offered an exceedingly mannered performance. "... oppressive melodrama ... an evening by no means devoid of snickers" *(Post)*. Written by mystery writer Fulton Oursler (Anthony Abbott) and Grace Perkins (Mrs. Oursler). C: Arlene Francis, Richard Gaines, Clay Clement, Arnold Korff, Clarence Derwent, David Stewart, Oscar Polk. P: Albert Lewis and Marion Gering (D).

Wall, The (10/11/60, Billy Rose, 167)

Harrowing chronicle of the horrors inflicted on Warsaw's Jewish community by the Nazis during World War II. Central character: a cynical Jewish ne'er-do-well (George C. Scott) who wishes at first only to survive, but who returns to his people in the ghetto for the final resistance against the German invaders. ". . . combines shattering power with searing compassion" *(New York Times)*. ". . . it is truth that has not been made art. . . . [The play] is scattered, fragmentary, too patly arranged . . ." *(Herald Tribune)*. C: Yvonne Mitchell (deb.), Joseph Buloff, David Opatoshu, Marian Seldes, Vincent Gardenia, Leila Martin, Robert Drivas. A: Millard Lampell b/o the novel by John Hersey. P: Kermit Bloomgarden and Billy Rose. D: Morton Da Costa. SD: Howard Bay.

Wall Street (4/20/27, Hudson, 21)

Unconvincing melodrama about an unscrupulous brokerage clerk who claws his way to the top of the Wall Street jungle. C: Arthur Hohl, Margaret Douglass, Sam Levene (deb.). A: James N. Rosenberg. P/D: Edward Goodman. SD: Cleon Throckmorton.

Wallflower (1/26/44, Cort, 192)

Snickering sex comedy about two adolescent stepsisters, one pretty and the other plain, who vie for the same boy. ". . . an ocean of tedium" *(New York Times)*. C: Mary Rolfe, Sunny O'Dea, Walter Greaza, Kathryn Givney. A: Mary Orr and Reginald Denham (D). P: Meyer Davis.
SV: WB, 1948, Robert Hutton, Joyce Reynolds, Janis Paige, Edward Arnold, Jerome Cowan, Ann Shoemaker.

Waltz in Goose Step (11/1/38, Hudson, 7)

Contrived anti-Nazi melodrama about the efforts of a dictator (Leo Chalzel) to quell a revolution. Written by screenwriter Oliver H. P. Garrett *(Manhattan Melodrama, Night Flight, The Man I Married,* etc.). P: Julien Chaqueneau. D: Arthur Hopkins. SD: Norris Houghton.

War President (4/24/44, Shubert, 2)

Civil War drama dealing with the conflict between President Lincoln and General George Brinton McClellan, pro-slavery advocate and Democratic candidate for president (1864). Interesting historical stage exhibit; presented as an Experimental Theatre (P) offering for two scheduled performances. C: Joel Ashley, Alexander Scourby, Joanna Roos, Russell Collins, Paul Ford, Morton Da Costa. A: Nat Sherman. D: Wendell K. Phillips.

War Song, The (9/24/28, National, 80)

Somber, dispirited account of the problems facing a World War I soldier (George Jessel) and his unmarried, pregnant sister (Shirley Booth). First play by Bella and Samuel Spewack. C: Lola Lane, Raymond Guion (Gene Raymond), William Gargan, Eda Heinemann, Edwin Jerome. P: Albert Lewis (D) and Sam H. Harris.

Warm Body, A (4/15/67, Cort, 1)

Tepid talkfest about the attempted seduction of a career girl (Lois Markle) by a man-about-town (Kevin McCarthy). A: Lonnie Coleman. P: Jeff Britton. D: Porter Van Zandt.

Warm Peninsula, The (10/20/59, Hayes, 86)

A plain Jane (Julie Harris) and her more glamorous roommate (June Havoc) make the mistake of falling in love with a pair of kept Miami beach boys (Farley Granger and Larry Hagman). "Extremely tepid . . . a ramshackle vehicle" *(Post)*. A: Joe Masteroff. P: Manning Gurian. D: Warren Enters. SD: Frederick Fox.

Warp I: My Battlefield, My Body (2/14/73, Ambassador, 7)

Warp I is a science fiction melodrama presented within the stylized conventions of a comic strip. True to the form, the plot is direct and nonchalantly epical. Wholesome young bank teller David Carson is in love with the bank president's daughter and seemingly destined for a life of conventional success. Abruptly, he is spirited off to another dimension in space where if he can only concentrate the cosmic energy dormant in his brain he can save the universe from Prince Chaos. Fearlessly pursuing this worthy enterprise, he encounters militant Amazons, spider women, an evil seductress, and faceless soldiers. The proceedings are augmented by spectacular audio and visual displays, including projections, spurts of fire and smoke, and electronic sound effects. The nine members of the cast play twenty parts with awesome energy. "*Warp* is high camp . . ." (Edwin Wilson, *Wall Street Journal*). ". . . an ill-conceived cross between Superman and science fiction" (Douglas Watt, *New York Daily News*). *Warp I* is the first part of a trilogy. A *Warp II* and a *Warp III* await production. A: Bury St. Edmund and Stuart Gordon. C: John Heard, Carolyn Gordon, William J. Norris, Cordis Fejer, Jane Fire, Richard Fire, Tom Towles, Andre De Shields, Keith Szarabajka. D: Stuart Gordon. SD: Robert Guerra. CD: Laura Crow and Cookie Gluck. Art Director: Neal Adams. P: Anthony D'Amato i.a.w. The Organic Theater Company.

Warrens of Virginia, The (12/3/07, Belasco, 190)

Interesting cast—Cecil B. De Mille, Mary Pickford, Frank Keenan, Emma Dunn, Charlotte Walker, Willard Robertson, Charles Waldron, Ralph Kellard—in a paltry, utterly predictable Southern-girl-loves-Northern-boy Civil War melodrama. A: William C. de Mille. P/D: David Belasco.

Warrior's Husband, The (3/11/32, Morosco, 83)

A gangling, boyish, seventy-five-dollar-a-week actress named Katharine Hepburn took Broadway by storm in this farcical costume romp set in Asia Minor in mythological times. In the play, the sexes are reversed. The Amazon women are the warriors. The effeminate men stay at home to primp, cook, and keep house. This topsy-turvy state of affairs is righted only when a band of Greeks invade the island to recover the girdle of Diana, the source of the women's physical prowess. "Miss Katharine Hepburn comes into her own as Antiope the royal Amazon. . . . It's been many a night since so glowing a performance has brightened the Broadway scene" (*World-Telegram*). C: Romney Brent, Colin Keith-Johnston, Irby Marshal, Bertha Belmore, Porter Hall, Don Beddoe, Alan Campbell. A: Julian Thompson. P: Harry Moses. D: Burk Symon. Musicalized by Rodgers and Hart as *By Jupiter* (1942) with Ray Bolger, Constance Moore, Benay Venuta, Vera-Ellen, Ronald Graham, and Bertha Belmore.

SV: Fox, 1933, Elissa Landi, David Manners, Ernest Truex, Marjorie Rambeau.

Washington Heights (9/29/31, Maxine Elliott's, 7)

Under the influence of a sex-obsessed neighbor, a frustrated genius attacks his niece who is killed resisting his advances. Drab Depression-era drama. C: William Harrigan, Joanna Roos, Clay Clement, Constance McKay. A: Vincent Lawrence. P/D: Philip Goodman.

Washington Jitters (5/2/38, Guild, 24)

Mistaken for an influential bureaucrat, a lowly sign painter reorganizes the United States government, and ends by running for president. Weak satire on Washington bureaucracy by John Boruff and Walter

Hart b/o a novel by Dalton Trumbo. C: Fred Stewart, Will Geer, Anthony Ross, Robert Porterfield. P: The Theatre Guild. D: Walter Hart and Worthington Miner.

Watch on the Rhine (4/1/41, Martin Beck, 378)

A German resistance leader and his exiled family find refuge in the luxurious Washington home of his American wife's mother. One of the house guests, a dissolute Rumanian count, recognizes the hunted fugitive and threatens to expose him to the German ambassador. To protect his cause, the anti-fascist agent is forced to kill the blackmailing count. The play ends with the agent returning to Germany alone to carry on his work. Paul Lukas gave the performance of his career as the gallant and resourceful hero of this stirring anti-Nazi melodrama by Lillian Hellman. Mady Christians, Lucile Watson, and George Coulouris excelled in other roles, while John Lodge (soon to forsake playacting for politics) and twelve-year-old Ann Blyth (destined to desert Broadway for Hollywood) also acquitted themselves admirably. C: Peter Fernandez, Eric Roberts, Helen Trenholme, Eda Heinemann, Frank Wilson. P/D: Herman Shumlin. SD: Jo Mielziner.

SV: WB, 1943, Bette Davis, Paul Lukas, Geraldine Fitzgerald, Lucile Watson, George Coulouris, Beulah Bondi, Donald Woods, Henry Daniell, Kurt Katch, Donald Buka, Eric Roberts, Frank Wilson (directed by Herman Shumlin from a screenplay by Dashiell Hammett).

Watering Place, The (3/12/69, Music Box, 1)

Short-lived (one performance) drama about a Vietnam War veteran and his relationship with the anxiety-ridden family—father, mother, wife—of a dead buddy. C: William Devane, Shirley Knight, Ralph Waite, Vivian Nathan. A: Lyle Kessler. P: Persson/Walsh. D: Alan Schneider.

Waterloo Bridge (1/6/30, Fulton, 64)

Robert E. Sherwood's drama about the ill-fated love affair of a young American soldier and a London streetwalker. "The sophomore's story of the Fallen Woman and the Nice Young Man" *(The Nation)*. "Rubbish, but well-scrutinized rubbish" *(New Republic)*. C: June Walker, Glenn Hunter, Cora Witherspoon. P: Charles Dillingham. D: Winchell Smith.

SV: U, 1931, Mae Clarke, Kent Douglass (Douglass Montgomery), Bette Davis, Doris Lloyd, Ethel Griffies; MGM, 1940, Vivien Leigh, Robert Taylor, Lucile Watson, Virginia Field, C. Aubrey Smith, Maria Ouspenskaya; MGM, 1956, *Gaby,* Leslie Caron, John Kerr, Cedric Hardwicke.

Wayward Stork, The (1/19/66, 46th Street, 5)

Tasteless farce tried for laughs on the subject of artificial insemination—and failed to get them. *The Wayward Stork* was the first Broadway play by screenwriter Harry Tugend (*King of Burlesque, Poor Little Rich Girl, Wake Up and Live, Sing, Baby, Sing,* etc.). C: Robert Cummings, Lois Nettleton, Arlene Golonka, Art Lund, Bernie West. P: Garrick Productions and Martin Lee. D: Dan Levin.

We Americans (10/12/26, Sam H. Harris, 120)

Sentimental comedy-drama about a pair of Jewish parents who attend night school in order to keep pace with their up-to-date, Americanized daughter. Making his Broadway debut as the elderly, white-haired father was thirty-one-year-old Yiddish Theatre alumnus Muni Weisenfreund (Paul Muni). He mimed the role so expertly that one critic expressed outrage that "this old man should have spent a lifetime waiting for a chance to appear on Broadway." A: Milton Herbert Gropper and Max Siegel. P: Sam H. Harris. D: Sam Forrest.

We Bombed in New Haven (10/16/68, Ambassador, 85)

First theatre effort by novelist Joseph Heller *(Catch-22)* used a play-within-a-play technique to satirize the surrealist insanity of the U.S. Air Force bombing missions. Despite several strikingly comic and effective moments, the play as a whole seemed labored and heavy-handed. C: Jason Robards, Diana Sands, William Roerick, Ron Leibman. P: Bonfils/Gottlieb/Stein. D: John Hirsch.

We Comrades Three (12/20/66, Lyceum, 11)

Plodding semibiographical drama dealing with events in the life of poet Walt Whitman. Produced in repertory by APA with a cast that included Clayton Corzatte, Will Geer, Rosemary Harris, and Helen Hayes. A: Richard Baldridge. D: Ellis Rabb and Hal George.

We Have Always Lived in the Castle (10/19/66, Barrymore, 9)

Did the young mistress of Blackwood Manor poison four of her relatives, or was someone else responsible? Unconvincing melodrama by Anglo-American author Hugh Wheeler, b/o the novel by Shirley Jackson. C: Shirley Knight, Alan Webb, Heather Menzies. P: David Merrick. D: Garson Kanin. SD: David Hays.

We Never Learn (1/23/28, Eltinge, 24)

Lawyer commits murder, must then defend client charged with the crime. Old-hat plot handled in commonplace fashion. C: Charles Trowbridge, Elizabeth Risdon, Estelle Winwood. A: Daisy Wolf. P/D: William B. Friedlander.

We, the People (1/21/33, Empire, 50)

Forceful, frequently stirring propaganda play by Elmer Rice (A/P/D) dramatizing the tragic and unjust effects of the Depression upon a factory foreman and his family. The story was told against "a kaleidoscopic background" showing bankers, businessmen, university trustees, senators, and judges tacitly united in an alliance for the preservation of the status quo. "An angry, headlong and disturbing attack upon social complacence. . . . A rude, grim, lumbering drama that can stimulate a mixed audience into choosing sides" *(New York Times)*. The communist press was displeased with *We, the People*. Though the author painted a bitter picture of Depression misfortunes, his solution was a return to democratic ideals rather than Marxist revolution. It was an expensive production requiring twenty-one scenes, fifteen sets, twenty-four stagehands, and a cast of fifty-four actors. Because of its high production cost, *We, the People* was withdrawn after a tempestuous run of six weeks. C: Eleanor Phelps, Blaine Cordner, Herbert Rudley, Ralph Theadore, Walter Greaza, House Jameson, Harry Bellaver, Katherine Emmett, William Ingersoll, Sam Byrd, Frank Wilson, Carol Ashburn, Grace Mills. SD: Aline Bernstein.

Weak Link, The (3/4/40, Golden, 32)

Gangsters kidnap a meek little genius (Hume Cronyn) and force him to plot the perfect crime. Moderately engaging farce along the lines of *Three Men on a Horse* and *Whistling in the Dark*. A: Allan Wood. P/D: Chester Erskine.

Weak Sisters (10/13/25, Booth, 31)

Tasteless farce about a couple of small-town bluenoses (Osgood Perkins and Spring Byington) who try to shut down a local house of prostitution. Produced by Jed Harris (his first Broadway produc-

tion), written and directed by Lynn Starling.
SV: WB, 1930, *Dumbbells In Ermine*, Robert Armstrong, James Gleason, Beryl Mercer.

Weather Clear—Track Fast (10/18/27, Hudson, 63)

Doddering racetrack yarn with Joe Laurie, Jr., William Courtleigh, Joseph Sweeney, and the great vaudeville team of (Joe) Buck and (Jim) Bubbles. A/P/D: Willard Mack.

Web, The (6/27/32, Morosco, 24)

Scientist (William Ingersoll) creates a giant man-eating spider. Boo! A: Frederick Herendeen. P: Abramson and Smith. D: Frank McCormack.

Wedding Bells (11/10/19, Harris, 168)

Reggie (Wallace Eddinger) is about to be married when Rosalie (Margaret Lawrence), his ex-wife, appears on the scene determined to break up the wedding and win back the groom for herself. She does. Sprightly farce-comedy with an excellent performance by Miss Lawrence. A: Salisbury Field. P: The Selwyns. D: Edgar Selwyn.

Wedding Breakfast (11/20/54, 48th Street, 113)

A Greenwich Village intellectual (Lee Grant) tries to remake a hardware salesman (Anthony Franciosa) into the image of her former lover and, in the process, almost loses him. A parallel plot concerns the romance of the heroine's salesgirl-sister (Virginia Vincent) and her bookkeeper-boyfriend (Harvey Lembeck). The critics found this four-character comedy-drama by Theodore Reeves "hilarious and poignant" in its lighter comedy scenes, but "unconvincing and contrived" during its more serious moments. P: Kermit Bloomgarden. D: Herman Shumlin. SD: William and Jean Eckart.

Wednesday's Child (1/16/34, Longacre, 56)

Problems of a ten-year-old boy whose divorced parents remarry. Poignant, understated drama, skillfully acted and well-staged. C: Frank M. Thomas, Jr., Walter Greaza, Katharine Warren, Walter Gilbert. A: Leopold Atlas. P: Potter and Haight. D: H. C. Potter.
SV: RKO, 1934, Edward Arnold, Karen Morley, Frankie Thomas; 1946, *Child of Divorce*, Regis Toomey, Sharyn Moffett.

Week-End (10/22/29, Golden, 12)

Alcoholism, melancholia, and tangled love affairs among the wealthy American set sojourning bibulously in Barbizon, France. "It never comes into clear focus as a study of character under the pressure of calamity. From all the confusion of plot no single meaning rises" *(New York Times)*. C: Warren William, Vivienne Osborne, Hugh O'Connell. A: Austin Parker. P: Bela Blau. D: Worthington Miner. SD: Robert Edmond Jones.

Weekend (3/13/68, Broadhurst, 21)

Gore Vidal's play about a Republican presidential candidate whose son pretends he is engaged to a negress in order to embarrass and blackmail his opportunistic father. *Weekend* was dismissed by the critics as a generally strained, tedious, and tasteless comedy; definitely one of Mr. Vidal's lesser theatre efforts. C: John Forsythe, Rosemary Murphy, Kim Hunter, Marco St. John, Carol Cole, Gene Blakely, Staats Cotsworth, Eleanor Wilson, John Marriott. P: Saint Subber and Lester Osterman. D: Joseph Anthony. SD: Oliver Smith.

Weep for the Virgins (11/30/35, 46th Street, 9)

The efforts of a lower middle-class family to escape their environment, in this case a drab San Diego fish cannery. Sluggish slice-of-life drama, produced by The

Group Theatre. C: Evelyn Varden, Art Smith, J. Edward Bromberg, Alexander Kirkland, Ruth Nelson, Paula Miller, Phoebe Brand, Jules (John) Garfield. A: Nellise Child. D: Cheryl Crawford. SD: Boris Aronson.

Welcome Stranger (9/13/20, Cohan and Harris, 307)

Jewish merchant (George Sidney) settles in New England, battles anti-semitism. finally wins town's trust and affection. Sentimental, engaging comedy-drama by Aaron Hoffman. P: Sam H. Harris.

Welded (3/17/24, 39th Street, 24)

Minor, unsuccessful Eugene O'Neill drama dealing with the inability of a moody playwright (Jacob Ben-Ami) and a temperamental actress (Doris Keane) to separate "in spite of the torments resulting from their bondage of passion." "Ineffective drama, uninspiringly repetitious and not particularly well done" (Burns Mantle, *News*), P; Macgowan, Jones, and O'Neill, i.a.w. The Selwyns. D: Stark Young.

Werewolf, The (8/25/24, 49th Street, 112)

A flighty duchess (Laura Hope Crews) believes that a shy young professor (Leslie Howard) is Don Juan reincarnated and, accordingly, arranges a midnight rendezvous with him. She soon learns she was mistaken—that, in fact, her handsome butler is the real Don Juan. Originally called *Spanish Nights,* this audacious comedy suffered from general miscasting, a ridiculous title, and a poor adaptation by Gladys Unger of the original Rudolph Lothar script. C: Vincent Serrano, Edwin Nicander, Marion Coakley. P: George B. McLellan.

Western Waters (12/28/37, Hudson, 7)

Fiery young rebel (Van Heflin) boards Ohio River flatboat, takes over the lives of the assorted passengers. Cardboard costume piece was written by actor Richard Carlson. C: Thomas Gomez, Jimmy Lydon, Mabel Paige, Joan Wheeler, Thomas Chalmers. D: Elsa Moses (P) and Richard Carlson. CD/SD: Boris Aronson. M: Lehman Engel.

What a Life (4/13/38, Biltmore, 538)

Henry Aldrich (Ezra Stone) is a high-school lad with an infinite capacity for getting into trouble. The son of a Phi Beta Kappa father, Henry is expected to make Princeton, but can't even make the Spring Dance. Eventually, with the help of a sympathetic girlfriend (Betty Field) and an understanding teacher (Arthur Pierson), Henry's problems at home and school are resolved. This George Abbott (P/D) comedy hit was the springboard for the popular Henry Aldrich (*"Coming, Mother"*) radio and film series. C: Eddie Bracken, Vaughan Glaser, Ruth Matteson, Joyce Arling, Edith Van Cleve, Lea Penman, Butterfly McQueen. *What a Life* was written by nutritionist and high school lecturer Clifford Goldsmith.

SV: Par, 1939, Jackie Cooper, Betty Field, Lionel Stander, Hedda Hopper, Lucien Littlefield.

What a Wife! (10/1/23, 49th Street, 72)

To claim an inheritance, a young couple must divorce and then remarry. Foolish farce, also known as *What's Your Wife Doing?* C: Glenn Anders, Dorothy Mackaye. A: Herbert Hall Winslow and Emil Nyitray. P: Arthur Klein.

Musicalized by Con Conrad and William B. Friedlander as *Mercenary Mary* (1925) with Allen Kearns, Winnie Baldwin, John Boles.

What Ann Brought Home (2/21/27, Wallack's, 106)

Ineffectual bridegroom shows his in-laws that he's really a go-getter. Insipid 20's comedy. C: Mayo Methot, William Hanley, Peggy Shannon. A: Larry E. Johnson. P/D: Earl Carroll.

What Big Ears! (4/20/42, Windsor, 8)

Complications ensue when Hollywood mistakenly signs a transvestite to star in the title role of Whistler's Mother. "... struggles hard and long without managing to be funny even once" *(PM)*. C: Edwin Philips, Ruth Weston, Taylor Holmes. A: Jo Eisinger* and Judson O'Donnell. P: Blank and Silberman. D: Arthur Pierson.

---

*Hollywood screenwriter (*Gilda, Night and the City,* etc.).

What Did We Do Wrong? (10/22/67, Hayes, 48)

Lightweight farce about a middle-aged suburbanite (Paul Ford) who decides to rebel against the system and become a hippie. A: Henry Denker. P: Michael Myerberg and Donald Flamm. D: Sherwood Arthur.

What Price Glory? (9/3/24, Plymouth, 435)

Trailblazing World War I drama by Maxwell Anderson and Laurence Stallings, the first contemporary play to deal with the subject of war in forthright, unromantic terms. The play caused a sensation with its profanity, brutality, and hard-boiled cynicism and is credited with having inaugurated the "new" realism of the American stage. The story revolves around the long-standing feud between Captain Flagg (Louis Wolheim) and Sergeant Quirt (William Boyd), two hard-bitten regular Army men, and their rivalry for the favors of the French slut, Charmaine (Leyla Georgie). In the end, Charmaine forgotten, the friendly enemies return to the front lines, Quirt calling out to the captain who has gone ahead, "Hey, Flagg, wait for baby!" "No war play written in the English language

... has been so true, so alive, so salty, and so richly satisfying. ... The first audience gave the play such a welcome as we have seldom seen matched in these many years of Broadway" (Alexander Woollcott, *Sun*). C: Brian Donlevy, George Tobias, Luis Alberni. P/D: Arthur Hopkins.

R: A noteworthy revival of *What Price Glory?*, staged by film director John Ford to raise money for the Military Order of the Purple Heart, toured the West Coast during the 1948–49 theatrical season. Such stars as John Wayne, Gregory Peck, Wallace Ford, and William Lundigan appeared in supporting roles, while Ward Bond was cast as Captain Flagg, Pat O'Brien was Sergeant Quirt, and Maureen O'Hara was Charmaine.

SV: Fox, 1952, James Cagney, Dan Dailey, Corinne Calvet, Robert Wagner (directed by John Ford).

Note: The extremely popular silent version (Fox, 1927) starred Victor McLaglen, Edmund Lowe, and Dolores Del Rio. The amorous antics of Flagg and Quirt proved so successful that audiences were treated to more of their adventures in subsequent films, including one of the biggest hits of all time, *The Cockeyed World* (Fox, 1929) with McLaglen, Lowe, Lili Damita, El Brendel, Stuart Erwin.

Whatever Goes Up (11/25/35, Biltmore, 24)

Grafters and confidence men attempt to part a sweepstake winner (Ernest Truex) from his sudden windfall. Innocuous 30's comedy. A: Milton Lazarus. P: Crosby Gaige. D: Arthur Sircom.

What's Your Wife Doing?

See *What a Wife!*

When Knighthood was in Flower (1/14/01, Criterion, 176)

"Say to the King my brother that I will see him and his Kingdom sunk in hell before I'll marry Louis of France!" cried Mary Tudor (Julia Marlowe) as the curtain fell on Act II of *When Knighthood Was in Flower,* one of the most successful historical romantic plays of its time. The story, adapted from a bestselling novel by Indiana lawyer Charles Major, dealt with the spirited younger sister of lusty Henry VIII and her love affair and marriage to a commoner. "Many felt that *Knighthood* was not a worthy vehicle for me," said Shakespearean star Julia Marlowe, "but I left splitting hairs to the philosophers. . . . My first season of *Knighthood* made me a fortune sufficient to render me independent for the rest of my life. The second season I more than doubled it. Freedom was mine." A: Paul Kester. P: Charles Frohman.

Musicalized by Ludwig Englander as *A Madcap Princess* (1904).

SV: RKO, 1953, *The Sword and the Rose,* Glynis Johns, Richard Todd.

When Knights Were Bold (8/20/07, Garrick, 100)

Silly, knockabout costume farce set in Merrie England,. C: Francis Wilson, Pauline Frederick, Augustin Duncan. A: Charles Marlowe. P: Charles Frohman. D: William Seymour.

SV: British, 1935, Jack Buchanan.

When Ladies Meet (10/6/32, Royale, 203)

A publisher's wife and mistress meet without either being aware of the other's identity. In the end, both women leave the philandering publisher to make new lives for themselves. "As rich in its humor as it is warm in its sympathy" *(Post).* C: Selena Royle, Frieda Inescort, Herbert Rawlinson, Walter Abel, Spring Byington. A/D: Rachel Crothers. P: John Golden.

SV: MGM, 1933, Ann Harding, Myrna Loy, Robert Montgomery, Alice Brady, Frank Morgan; 1941, Joan Crawford, Greer Garson, Robert Taylor, Herbert Marshall, Spring Byington.

"When the Bough Breaks" (2/16/32, 48th Street, 16)

Domineering mother (Pauline Frederick) almost ruins her son's life. Trite domestic drama. C: William Post, Jr., Louis Jean Heydt. A: Jerome Sackheim. P/D: Arthur Lubin.

When You Comin' Back, Red Ryder? (12/6/73, Eastside Playhouse, 302)

Persons with active memories will have no trouble finding similarities between *When You Comin' Back, Red Ryder?* and Robert Sherwood's *The Petrified Forest.* The action of *Red Ryder* takes place in a seedy diner in the Southwest where patrons and employees are held captive by a sadistic drug smuggler. He subjects them to increasingly unpleasant torments, all focused on the weak spots of each, then leaves, still in command, though presumably to be caught somewhere off stage. Throughout, the title character, Stephen Ryder (Brad Dourif), self-styled Red Ryder after the hero of yesteryear's comics, has done little except meekly tolerate the outrages of the bullying criminal, Teddy (Kevin Conway), but at play's end scrapes up gumption enough to tell off his boss at the diner and head for greater things in Baton Rouge, Louisiana. Where Sherwood's hero, Alan Squier, is a disillusioned idealist who finds a cause for which to die, Red Ryder is a callow, inarticulate nonentity who lives for no particular reason. It would appear that ambition, purpose, innocence are gone from America. The answer to the question posed by the play's title is: Never! *When You Comin' Back, Red Ryder?*

originated off-off Broadway on 11/5/73 at the Circle Repertory Theater, opening its commercial run a month later at the off Broadway Eastside Playhouse. Direction and set design were praised and the actors generally lauded. Brad Dourif's performance landed him the choice role of Billy Bibbitt in the SV of *One Flew Over the Cuckoo's Nest* for which he was unsuccessfully Oscar-nominated as Best Supporting Actor. *Red Ryder's* author, Mark Medoff, took over the part of Teddy during the play's final weeks. C: Brad Dourif, Kevin Conway, Elizabeth Sturges, Addison Powell, Joe Jamrog, Robyn Goodman, James Kiernan, Kristin Van Buren. P: Elliot Martin. D: Kenneth Frankel. SD: Bill Stabile.

Where Do We Go from Here? (11/15/38, Vanderbilt, 15)

Callow fraternity brothers are taught a lesson in good business (and good citizenship) by a Jewish student. Stereotyped, rah-rah college comedy-drama. C: Don DeFore (deb.), Theodore Leavitt, Hugh Martin. A: William Bowers. P: Oscar Hammerstein and Dwight Taylor. D: Anatole Winogradoff.

Where's Daddy? (3/2/66, Billy Rose, 22)

Fearful of parental responsibility, an expectant young couple plan to give their child up for adoption, but change their minds once the baby is born. This generation gap comedy by William Inge (his last Broadway play) contained several humorous and touching scenes, but failed to impress a sufficient number of critics to ensure its success. C: Beau Bridges (deb.), Barbara Dana, Betty Field, Hiram Sherman, Robert Hooks, Barbara Ann Teer. P: Michael Wager. D: Harold Clurman.

Whispering Friends (2/20/28, Hudson, 112)

Newly-married couple bicker all night. Innocuous George M. Cohan (A/P) conversation piece. C: Chester Morris, William Harrigan, Ann Shoemaker, Elsie Lawson. D: Sam Forrest.

Whispering Wires (8/7/22, 49th Street, 356)

Murder by telephone—that was the gimmick of this shivery, cleverly plotted whodunit with Paul Kelly as the stalwart hero, Olive Tell as the understandably terrified heroine. A: Kate McLaurin. P: Messrs. Shubert. D: Huffman and Harwood.

Whistler's Grandmother (12/11/52, President, 24)

An amiable old reprobate (Josephine Hull) is hired to impersonate a pedigreed grandmother. "... violently cute ... relentlessly fey." C: Lonny Chapman, Alan Carney. A: Robert Finch. P: Anthony Parella. D: Eugene O'Sullivan. SD: Leo Kerz.

Whistling in the Dark (1/19/32, Barrymore, 144)

A successful mystery writer (Ernest Truex) and his girl (Claire Trevor) are held captive by a band of crooks until the writer can think up a perfect murder that will defy police detection. Aided by alcoholic stimulants, the writer finally supplies the gang leader (Edward Arnold) with a foolproof blueprint for murder but realizes, of course, that he must immediately dream up *another* plot to prevent his own killing. Delightful melodramatic comedy, first-rate in every department. A: Laurence Gross and Edward Childs Carpenter. P: Alexander McKaig. D: Frank Craven.

SV: MGM, 1933, Ernest Truex, Una Merkel, Edward Arnold; 1941, Red Skelton, Conrad Veidt, Ann Rutherford, Eve Arden, Virginia Grey.

White Cargo (11/5/23, Greenwich Village, 864)

Expatriate Englishman on African rubber plantation goes native when the seductive Tondeleyo slithers into his sun-baked bungalow. "*White Cargo* belongs to a time when men were men and women were women and dialogue was dreadful" (Walter Kerr, commenting on the short-lived 1960 O/B revival of 10 performances at the Players Theatre commencing 12/29/60). The original 1923 production of *White Cargo* ran 864 performances. The play was written by Anglo-American author Leon Gordon (A/D) who came to the United States in his twenties as an actor and later settled in Hollywood as a writer-producer (*Freaks, Mata Hari, Mrs. Parkington, The Green Years*, etc.). C: Richard Stevenson, Annette Margules, A. E. Anson. P: Earl Carroll.

SV: British, 1930, Maurice Evans, Tom Helmore, Gypsy Rhouma. (*Note:* This version was banned by movie czar Will Hays and never released in the United States.) MGM, 1942, Hedy Lamarr, Walter Pidgeon, Frank Morgan, Richard Carlson, Reginald Owen.

White Collars (2/23/25, Cort, 104)

When a wealthy young man offers to give his money away, his socialist-minded in-laws learn the virtues of capitalism. Modestly amusing comedy by Edith Ellis, based on a story by Edgar Franklin. C: Mona Kingsley, Clarke Silvernail, Cornelia Otis Skinner. P: Frank Egan.

SV: MGM, 1929, *Idle Rich*, Conrad Nagel, Bessie Love; 1938, *Rich Man, Poor Girl*, Robert Young, Lana Turner, Lew Ayres, Rita Johnson, Guy Kibbee, Ruth Hussey, Don Castle.

White Desert, The (10/18/23, Princess, 12)

Glum verse tragedy set on the snow-covered North Dakota prairie; Maxwell Anderson's first play. The lonely wife (Beth Merrill) of a moody homesteader (Frank Shannon) is killed by her jealous husband when she confesses an affair with a neighboring Swede (George Abbott). P/D: Brock Pemberton. Anderson's tragedy of marital infidelity shocked some of the more conservative reviewers. "Unclean . . . openly off-color . . . touched up with words we cannot print" reported these gentlemen of the press. Curiously, they took no offense the following season at the equally earthy lingo of Anderson's next play, *What Price Glory?* (1924), written in collaboration with Laurence Stallings.

White House Murder Case, The (2/18/70, Circle in the Square, 119)

A mordant look at America's future by playwright-cartoonist Jules Feiffer. The action alternates between battle scenes in Brazil during a war in which American officers accidentally unleash nerve gas on their own troops, and a screwball White House packed with immoral politicians and scientists. The one voice of integrity belongs to the President's wife, and she is silenced just as she's about to expose the cover-up of the gassing to the *New York Times*. A picket sign reading "Make Love, Not War" is found sticking out of her chest. The task now is not only to cover up the gassing, but the First Lady's murder as well. The playwright's viewpoint being as dour as it is, both crimes are successfully hidden. Presented while the Vietnam war was at its height, *The White House Murder Case* was a biting, bitter indictment of American militarism and the nation's leaders. A topical success in antiwar 1970, subsequent peacetime audiences would find this O/B entry still pertinent. The play's self-righteously corrupt politicos offer a zany preview of those attitudes which would soon produce the Watergate scandals. Comedy can get no blacker than this. Critical response was generally favorable, and the direction by actor Alan Arkin was praised. A: Jules Feiffer. C: Peter Bonerz, Cynthia Harris, J. J. Barry, Anthony Holland, Paul Benedict, Bob Balaban, Andrew Duncan, Paul Dooley, Richard Libertini, Edward J. Moore. D: Alan Arkin. P: Theodore Mann, Paul Libin, Harold Leventhal, Orin Lehman. SD: Marsha Louis Eck.

White Man (10/17/36, National, 6)

Tedious drama by Samson Raphaelson about a North Carolina mulatto trying to pass as white in New York City. C: Sam Byrd (P), Patsy Ruth Miller, Louise Campbell, Sylvia Field, Leigh Whipper. D: Melville Burke. SD: Nat Karson.

White Sister, The (9/27/09, Daly's, 48)

A nun is tempted to forswear her vows when she learns that her fiancée was not killed in the war. Talky, tearful drama by F. Marion Crawford and Walter Hackett. C: Viola Allen, James O'Neill, William Farnum. P: Liebler and Company. D: Hugh Ford. Musicalized (1927) by Clement Giglio.

- SV: MGM, 1933, Helen Hayes, Clark Gable, Lewis Stone, Edward Arnold, May Robson (directed by Victor Fleming).
- Note: A silent version (Metro, 1923) starred Lillian Gish and Ronald Colman (directed by Henry King).

White Wings (10/15/26, Booth, 27)

A family of street cleaners fight a losing battle against the horseless carriage. Philip Barry's "fantastic comedy in four acts" dramatized the eternal conflict between tradition and progress in imaginative, frequently hilarious fashion. The play failed to please the general public, but delighted such critics as Robert Benchley who admitted years later that he "shed salty tears whenever the untimely demise of that comedy is mentioned." *White Wings* collapsed after twenty-seven showings. It deserved a kinder fate.

C: Tom Powers, Winifred Lenihan, J. M. Kerrigan, and George Ali as Joseph (a horse). P/D: Winthrop Ames. SD: Woodman Thompson.

Who Was That Lady I Saw You With? (3/3/58, Martin Beck, 208)

Knockabout farce about a couple of men about town who pose as FBI agents and find themselves involved not only with the real FBI, but with real spies as well. "Antically engaging" (*Herald Tribune*). "An over-elaborate jest" (*News*). C: Peter Lind Hayes, Mary Healy, Ray Walston, Roland Winters, Larry Storch. A: Norman Krasna. P: Leland Hayward. D: Alex Segal. CD: Ruth Morley. SD: Rouben Ter-Arutunian. M: Bernard Green.

- SV: Col, 1960, Dean Martin, Tony Curtis, Janet Leigh, James Whitmore, John McIntire, Larry Storch, Barbara Nichols.

Whole Town's Talking, The (8/29/23, Bijou, 174)

Cute Anita Loos-John Emerson comedy about a small-town braggart (Grant Mitchell) who invents a fictitious affair with a glamorous film star (Catherine Owen). When the movie queen arrives in town unexpectedly, the complications begin. P: A. H. Woods. D: John Emerson.

- SV: U, 1931, *Ex-Bad Boy*, Jean Arthur, Robert Armstrong, Lola Lane, George Brent.

Who'll Save the Plowboy? (1/9/62, Phoenix, 56)

O/B drama of a returning soldier who discovers the life he saved on the battlefield was not worth saving. ". . . a starkly taut, clear-cut drama painful in its insights, poignant in its subtleties" (*Herald Tribune*). First play by Frank D. Gilroy, author of *The Subject was Roses* (1964), *The Only Game in Town* (1968), etc.; expertly directed by Daniel Petrie. C: Gerald O'Loughlin, William Smithers, Tom Sawyer, Dorothy Peterson, Patrick O'Shaughnessy, Rebecca Darke, Burton Mallory.

Who's Afraid of Virginia Woolf?
(10/13/62, Billy Rose, 644)

The play of the decade. Edward Albee's study of a sadomasochistic marriage examines one night in the lives of George, a contemplative history professor, and Martha, his foul-mouthed, explosively antagonistic wife. What starts with a nightcap turns into a harrowing marathon of "fun and games" as George and Martha play host to a young faculty couple and engage in a Strindbergian battle royal to destroy each other. By the time the dusk-to-dawn drinking bout has ended, lacerating self-revelations have been made, the guilty secrets of all four characters have been exposed, and at least one of the married couples have exorcised their personal demons under the influence of alcohol. Critics argued the merits of the evening's denouement; few could deny the relentless intensity, savage humor, and stunning impact of the play as a whole. Blessed with a brilliant production, *Who's Afraid of Virginia Woolf?*—Mr. Albee's first full-length drama—won the Drama Critics Circle Award as best play of the year. C: Uta Hagen, Arthur Hill, George Grizzard, Melinda Dillon (Broadway debut). P: Barr and Wilder. D: Alan Schneider. SD: William Ritman.

SV: WB, 1966, Elizabeth Taylor, Richard Burton, George Segal, Sandy Dennis (directed by Mike Nichols from a screenplay by Ernest Lehman).

Note: Henry Fonda lost out on two chances to play the role of George in this milestone drama. According to biographer John Springer, Edward Albee sent a copy of the script to Mr. Fonda's agent who—without even informing his client—peremptorily rejected it. Then, when Fred Zinnemann was slated to direct the film version, Fonda and Bette Davis were paged to play George and Martha. Later, when Mike Nichols (making his screen directorial debut) replaced Zinnemann, Mr. Fonda and Miss Davis were bypassed in favor of Elizabeth Taylor and Richard Burton.

Why Marry? (12/25/17, Astor, 120)

Why Marry?, which was awarded the first Pulitzer Prize for drama (1918), treated the subject of matrimony lightly and philosophically via a young couple who believe that "love is enough." However, they are finally tricked into marriage because it is "the best we [society] have to offer you." *Why Marry?* was journalist Jesse Lynch Williams' first play. In 1922, Mr. Williams wrote a second comedy, *Why Not?*, which dealt amusingly and effectively with the subject of divorce. C: Nat C. Goodwin, Estelle Winwood, Shelly Hull, Edmund Breese, Lotus Robb, Ernest Lawford. P: Selwyn and Company i.a.w. Roi Cooper Megrue (D).

Why Men Leave Home (9/12/22, Morosco, 138)

Marital mixups of three summer bachelors and their globe-trotting wives. Machine-stitched Avery Hopwood farce with a no-name cast. P: Wagenhals and Kemper. D: Collin Kemper.

Why Not? (12/25/22, 48th Street, 123)

Companion piece (though not a sequel) to Jesse Lynch Williams' Pulitzer Prize play, *Why Marry?* (1917). After fifteen years of marriage, two couples decide to exchange mates and discover firsthand the inanities and eccentricities of America's divorce laws. Bubbling, sophisticated comedy, highly amusing. C: Tom Powers, Margaret Mower, Warburton

Gamble, Jane Grey, Marguerite Churchill, Raymond Guion (Gene Raymond). P: Equity Players, Inc. D: O. P. Heggie and Mrs. Shelly Hull.

Why Worry? (8/23/18, Harris, 27)
Fanny Brice as a Second Avenue waitress who foils a gang of World War I German spies in a lower East Side restaurant. "There is probably no reason why German spy melodrama and Yiddish farce comedy should not mingle to make a thoroughly enjoyable play. . . . And there were times when the result was a pursuing whirlwind of laughter. But as a whole the success of the production is problematical, and probably worse than that. . . . There has seldom been a more puzzling, a more baffling, hodgepodge" (*New York Times*). Highlight: Fanny Brice striding forth to the footlights in burlesque costumes to do a movie *femme fatale* and an Indian Maiden of subway melodrama. C: Smith and Dale, Irving Kaufman, May Boley, Vera Gordon, Edwin Maxwell, George Sidney, Charles Trowbridge. A: Montague Glass and Jules Eckert Goodman. P: A. H. Woods. D: George Marion.

Wicked Age, The (11/4/27, Daly's, 19)
America's voluptuous empress of sex, Miss Mae West, in a campy "exposé" of 1920's bathing beauty contests. High spot: La West, in a one-piece bathing suit, wrenching the cup away from a flat-chested flapper. A/P: Anton Scibilia (pseud. for Mae West). D: Edward Elsner.

Wife Insurance (4/12/34, Barrymore, 4)
Neglected wife flirts with handsome novelist. Vapid triangle comedy. C: Ilka Chase, Kenneth MacKenna, Walter Abel, Harvey Stephens. A: Frederick Jackson. P: Langdon Productions. D: Arthur J. Beckhard.

Wild Birds (4/9/25, Cherry Lane, 44)
Sensitive study of two young misfits—an unhappy farm girl and an escaped convict—who fall in love. The boy is killed and the girl commits suicide. Skillfully written by Dan Totheroh, *Wild Birds* was an O/ *succès d' estime* of the 1925 season. C: Mildred MacLeod, Donald Duff. P: Cherry Lane Players, Inc. D: John Wray.
SV: RKO, 1934, *Two Alone*, Jean Parker, Tom Brown.

Wild Man of Borneo, The (9/13/27, Bijou, 15)
Weak Marc Connelly* (D) and Herman J. Mankiewicz** comedy about a sideshow barker who masquerades as a famous actor. C: George Hassell, Marguerite Churchill, Josephine Hull. P: Philip Goodman.
SV: MGM, 1941, Frank Morgan, Billie Burke, Marjorie Main, Donald Meek, Bonita Granville, Dan Dailey.

---

*Author of *The Green Pastures* (1930).
**Author of many films including *Citizen Kane*.

Wild Waves (2/19/32, Times Square, 25)
Microphone-shy crooner (John Beal) is groomed for stardom by cynical radio station manager (Osgood Perkins). Fair comedy with an interesting setting and some clever lines. C: Betty Starbuck, Horace MacMahon, Edith Van Cleve, Bruce MacFarlane, Anne Revere. A: William Ford Manley. P: Doran, Ray, and Hewes. D: Worthington Miner.
SV: Par, 1932, *The Big Broadcast*, Bing Crosby, George Burns, Gracie Allen, Kate Smith, Stuart Erwin, Leila Hyams, Cab Calloway, The Mills Brothers, Boswell Sisters, Arthur Tracy.

Wild Westcotts, The (12/24/23, Frazee, 25)

Good cast—Claudette Colbert, Vivian Martin, Cornelia Otis Skinner, Helen Broderick, Morgan Farley, Elliott Nugent, Boyd Davis—in a hopeless farce-comedy about a family of screwballs in Greenwich, Conn. A: Anne Morrison. P: Lewis and Gordon.

Wild Westcotts. **Isabel Withers and Vivian Martin (December 24, 1923).** *Courtesy Museum of the City of New York Theatre and Music Collection.*

Wildfire (9/7/08, Liberty, 64)

Minor comedy-melodrama dealing with skullduggery at the racetrack; nicely acted by the beauteous Lillian Russell. C: Thurston Hall, Ernest Truex (deb.), Irving Cummings (a successful film director in later years). P: Joseph Brooks. D: Lawrence Marston.

Will Success Spoil Rock Hunter? (10/13/55, Belasco, 444)

Frequently amusing but disjointed comedy-fantasy by George Axelrod (A/D) about a callow scribbler (Orson Bean) who sells his soul in 10% installments to a satanic Hollywood agent (Martin Gabel). In return, the agent arranges that the self-effacing journalist wins not only an Oscar, but also the love of the screen's reigning goddess. Jayne Mansfield made her Broadway debut as the cinemaland sex symbol, a thinly veiled caricature of Marilyn Monroe. Miss Mansfield, blonde and buxom, made history just standing still. Notable performance: Walter Matthau as a former dramatist ("a playwrote") who helps the hero escape his diabolical agent's clutches in the nick of time. C: Harry Clark, Carol Grace, Tina Louise, Michael Tolan. P: Jule Styne i.a.w. Sylvia Herscher. SD: Oliver Smith.

SV: Fox, 1957, Tony Randall, Jayne Mansfield, Joan Blondell, Betsy Drake, John Williams (directed by Frank Tashlin).

Willow and I, The (12/10/42, Windsor, 28)

Two sisters (Martha Scott and Barbara O'Neil), in love with the same man (Gregory Peck), destroy each other in their efforts to win his affections. One becomes a lunatic; the other lives with the knowledge that she is responsible for this tragedy. Gregory Peck played a dual role (father and son) in this gothic tale of sibling rivalry, revenge, and insanity. ". . . a confused and sometimes embarrassingly inept play, but it has moments that are provocative and affecting" (*Post*). *The Willow and I* was written by John Patrick, author of *The Hasty Heart* (1945), *The Teahouse of the August Moon* (1953), etc. P: Donald Blackwell (D) and Raymond Curtis i.a.w. David Merrick. CD: Aline Bernstein. SD: Lemuel Ayers.

Willow Tree, The (3/6/17, Cohan and Harris, 103)

A wooden statue (Fay Bainter) comes to life and falls in love with the handsome young Englishman (Shelly Hull) who purchased her. Earthbound fantasy, set in Japan, written by J. H. Benrimo (D) and Harrison Rhodes. P: Cohan and Harris. Musicalized by Sigmund Romberg as *Cherry Blossoms* (1927).

Wind Is Ninety, The (6/21/45, Booth, 108)

A dead Air Force captain (Wendell Corey), guided back to his home by the Unknown Soldier (Kirk Douglas), appears to different members of his family as each best remembers him. Mixed reviews greeted this wartime fantasy, a first play by Ralph Nelson, future TV-film director (*Requiem for a Heavyweight, Lilies of the Field,* etc.). C: Blanche Yurka, Bert Lytell, Frances Reid, James Dobson. P: Messrs. Shubert i.a.w. Albert de Courville (D).

Window Shopping (12/23/38, Longacre, 11)

Labored comedy about the problems of a department-store magnate (George Sidney). A: Louis Shecter and Norman Clark. P: Thomas Kilpatrick. D: Arthur Sircom.

Wine of Choice (2/21/38, Guild, 43)

S. N. Behrman's comedy about the efforts of a Jewish socialite (Alexander Woollcott), a New Mexico senator (Leslie Banks), and a wealthy playboy (Donald Cook) to prevent the marriage of their protégée to a fanatical communist. "... dozes agreeably in a state of suspended animation" (*New York Times*). This Theatre Guild production had trouble from the start. Film star Miriam Hopkins played the protégée in the pre-Broadway tryout, but resigned from the cast in a huff. Claudia Morgan replaced her. Director Philip Moeller also abandoned the show. Herman Shumlin took over in his stead. When *Wine of Choice* finally reached Manhattan, its reception was far from dazzling. Even Alexander Woollcott was pummeled by the press. (The *Daily News* dubbed him "a third-rate actor in a fourth-rate play.") The Behrman comedy was a resounding 1938 failure. C: Theodore Newton, Herbert Yost, Paul Stewart. SD: Lee Simonson.

Winesburg, Ohio (2/5/58, National, 13)

An idealistic invalid (Dorothy McGuire), married to an unsuccessful hotel proprietor (James Whitmore), valiantly strives to free her would-be writer-son (Ben Piazza) from the small-town chains she could never break herself. Muddled, discursive adaptation of Sherwood Anderson's classic collection of short stories set in turn-of-the-century Ohio. C: Leon Ames, Claudia McNeil, Sandra Church, Ian Wolfe, Crahan Denton, Lee Kinsolving. A: Christopher Sergel. P: Schumer, Adler, Saba. D: Joseph Anthony. SD: Oliver Smith.

Note: Sherwood Anderson was as shocked by the reviews of *Winesburg, Ohio* as the critics were by his book published in 1919. "It was widely condemned, called nasty and dirty by most of the critics... the work of a perverted mind," Anderson wrote later in his memoirs. Twenty years later his collection of vignettes was being used as a college text, and hailed as a masterwork. "The book became an American classic," Anderson concluded, "and started a kind of revolution in short story writing. And the stories themselves which in 1919 were almost universally condemned as immoral might today almost be published in the *Ladies Home Journal,* so innocent they seem."

Winged Victory (11/20/43, 44th Street, 212)

Moss Hart's Air Corps recruiting poster, tracing the exploits of a group of typical young Americans from induction to graduation, and thence to combat duty in the Pacific. Brilliantly staged by its author, with an enormous cast of uniformed men and civilian colleagues, *Winged Victory* was one of the major theatrical events of the wartime years. "A salute to the Air Forces, it is simple, warmhearted, big—and served up with a rousing Army Band. As a play it never once batters the mind. But as a show it often whops the emotions, as a spectacle often tingles the blood" (*Time*). Space permits only a partial cast listing. Prominent in the company were: Edmond O'Brien, Don Taylor, Mark Daniels, Barry Nelson, Lee J. Cobb, Peter Lind Hayes, Alan Baxter, Philip Bourneuf, Dick Hogan, Rune Hultman, Red Buttons, Kevin McCarthy, Karl Malden, Danny Scholl, George Reeves, Ray Middleton, John Tyers, Whit Bissell, Ed McMahon, Gary Merrill, Anthony Ross, Martin Ritt, Don Beddoe, Michael Duane, Don Hanmer, Ray McDonald, Victor Young, Zeke Manners, Alfred Ryder, Phyllis Avery, Elisabeth Fraser, Olive Deering. P: U. S. Army Air Forces. M: David Rose. SD: Harry Horner.

SV: Fox, 1944, Lon McCallister, Jeanne Crain, Edmond O'Brien, Don Taylor, Judy Holliday, Lee J. Cobb, Red Buttons, Peter Lind Hayes, Barry Nelson, Martin Ritt, Gary Merrill (directed by George Cukor).

Note: Allergic to airplanes, Moss Hart nevertheless flew thousands of miles in Air Force bombers gathering material for his play. In addition, he insisted on waiving all royalties. During its S.R.O. six-month Broadway run, *Winged Victory* grossed more than one million dollars for the Army Emergency Relief fund.

Wingless Victory, The (12/23/36, Empire, 108)

Maxwell Anderson's verse tragedy, a reworking of the Medea legend, starred Katharine Cornell (P) as Oparre, a dark-skinned Malay princess. Transported to Salem, Massachusetts in 1800, Oparre encounters race prejudice and religious bigotry. When her sea captain husband (Kent Smith) deserts her, Oparre turns to her old gods and poisons her children and herself. "It has not any reality at all, of any kind. . . . The play is semitosh from start to finish" (Stark Young, *New Republic*). C: Walter Abel, Myron McCormick, Effie Shannon, Ruth Matteson. D: Guthrie McClintic.

Winkelberg (1/14/58, Renata, 48)

The life and times of Greenwich Village poet Maxwell Bodenheim, here called Jonathan Winkelberg, and of his lifelong rebellion against society. Ben Hecht's O/B whimsey—an unsettled mixture of comedy, fantasy, and drama—proved "increasingly monotonous . . . tiresome and repetitious" (*New York Times*). C: Mike Kellin, James Mitchell, Sorrell Booke, Sondra Lee, Robert Earl Jones. P/D: Lee Falk. SD: Lester Polakov.

Winner, The (2/17/54, Playhouse, 30)

Virtuous cigarette girl inherits a fortune from an elderly admirer, faces a variety of problems when his will is contested in court. Uneven mixture of comedy and melodrama by Elmer Rice (A/D). C: Joan Tetzel, Tom Helmore, Frederick O'Neal, Whitfield Connor, Phillip Pruneau. P: The Playwrights Company.

Winter Soldiers (11/29/42, Studio, 30)

Episodic, multiscened war play dealing with the heroic resistance efforts of the Russian people, and their sympathizers in the occupied countries, to delay (and ultimately defeat) Hitler's first drive on Moscow. This frequently absorbing O/B drama was presented by Erwin Piscator, directed by Shepard Traube. C: Herbert Berghof, Dolly Haas, Guy Sorel, Boris Marshalov, Ronald Alexander, Boris Tumarin, David Alexander, Paula Bauersmith, Lothar Rewalt, Ross Matthew. A: Dan James.

Winterset (9/25/35, Martin Beck, 194)

Maxwell Anderson's verse tragedy; winner of the first annual New York Drama Critics Circle award as best American play of the year. The setting is the New York slums in the shadows of a towering East River bridge. To this place comes Mio (Burgess Meredith), son of an alleged anarchist executed for a crime he did not commit. In effect, Mio has come seeking death, for the gangsters who framed his father will kill again to escape punishment. In search of evidence to prove his father's innocence, the boy finds the now-insane judge (Richard Bennett) who presided at the trial. His quest for revenge is complicated when he falls in love with a young Jewish girl, Miriamne (Margo), whose brother knows the identity of the real murderer but has remained silent for fear of endangering his own life. In the end, Mio is finally slain by the gangster's henchmen, and Miriamne chooses to die with him. *Winterset* was a poetic rendering of the Sacco-Vanzetti case, a theme previously explored by the author in *Gods of the Lightning* (1928). The novelty of a modern play in verse so engaged the attention of the critics that comment concerning the production filled the theatre pages of newspapers and magazines for the entire season. Opinion was by no means unanimous, however, concerning the quality of the verse or the violent subject matter of the play. One critic dismissed Anderson's somber tragedy as "merely a gangster melodrama with pretentious trimmings." ". . . the kind of play, although by no means the actual play, upon which the hope and glory of the future theatre rest," said John Mason Brown in the *New York Post*. Sensitively acted and directed, with magnificent scenic designs by Jo Mielziner, *Winterset* provided an exciting—and at times exalting—evening in the theatre. It was, in every sense, a memorable production. C: Eduardo Ciannelli, Harold Johnsrud, Anatole Winogradoff, Theodore Hecht, Abner Biberman, Ruth Hammond, John Philliber, Billy Quinn, St. John Terrell. P/D: Guthrie McClintic.
SV: RKO, 1936, Burgess Meredith, Margo, Eduardo Ciannelli, John Carradine, Edward Ellis, Mischa Auer.

Wisdom Tooth, The (2/15/26, Little, 160)

A browbeaten clerk (Thomas Mitchell) is transported back in time to his youth. There he meets the boy he used to be, and renews his faith in himself. Charming comedy-fantasy by Marc Connelly. C: Mary Philips, Hugh O'Connell. P: John Golden. D: Winchell Smith.

Wise Tomorrow (10/15/37, Biltmore, 3)

Tempestuous star seeks to control the life and loves of her protégé. Murky backstage drama by Stephen Powys (pseud. for Mr. and Mrs. Guy Bolton). C: Josephine Victor, Gloria Dickson, Edith Barrett, Theodore Newton, Naunton Wayne, Rosemary Ames, Olive Reeves-Smith. P: B. Klawans. D: Hugh Macmullan.

Wisecrackers, The (12/16/25, Fifth Avenue, 13)

Satire comedy by Gilbert Seldes* about an iconoclastic journalist (Russell Hicks) who is forced to choose between domestic bliss and his coterie of wisecracking friends. ". . . lugubrious entertainment, ill-suited to the theatre and commonplace in its dramatic design" (*New York Times*). This short-lived O/B production was staged by Clarence Derwent.

---

*Best-known for his book, *The Seven Lively Arts* (1924).

Wiser They Are, The (4/6/31, Plymouth, 40)

To test each other's constancy, a sophisticated young couple (Ruth Gordon and Osgood Perkins) agree to throw a pre-wedding party to which they invite six of their ex-lovers. Foolish comedy by screenwriter Sheridan Gibney (*I Am a Fugitive from a Chain Gang*, *The Story of Louis Pasteur*, etc.). C: Julia Hoyt, Eduardo Ciannelli. P/D: Jed Harris.

Wisteria Trees, The (3/29/50, Martin Beck, 165)

Helen Hayes in Joshua Logan's (A/D) misguided attempt to transplant Chekhov's *The Cherry Orchard* to the deep south. Set in nineteenth-century Louisiana, the piece was promptly dubbed "A Month in the Wrong Country" by Noel Coward and "Southern Fried Chekhov" by another wit. C: Kent Smith, Walter Abel, Bethel Leslie, Douglas Watson, Peggy Conklin, Ossie Davis, Georgia Burke, Alonzo Bosan. P: Leland Hayward and Joshua Logan. CD: Lucinda Ballard. SD: Jo Mielziner. M: Lehman Engel.

R: (2/2/55, City Center, 15). C: Helen Hayes, Walter Matthau, Bramwell Fletcher, Cliff Robertson, Louis Smith, Ella Raines (deb.), Will Geer, Ossie Davis, Evelyn Davis, Alonzo Bosan. D: John Stix.

Witching Hour, The (11/18/07, Hackett, 212)

By using his occult powers, a professional gambler (John Mason) is able to clear a young man of a murder charge. This vivid, skillfully crafted melodrama successfully utilized such "newfangled" subjects as telepathy and mesmerism. Playwright Augustus Thomas (who once worked for celebrated mind reader Washington Irving Bishop) wrote an earlier version of *The Witching Hour*, but waited twenty years before he felt the time was right to produce the revised version of the script. P: Sam S. and Lee Shubert.

SV: Par, 1934, John Halliday, Guy Standing.

With a Silk Thread (4/12/50, Lyceum, 13)

Retired actress develops a yen for her son's college chum. ". . . vulgar, random and tiresome" (*Herald Tribune*). C: Claire Luce, Philip Huston, Phil Arthur, Lilia Skala, Carole Mathews. A/D: Elsa Shelley. P: Irving Kaye Davis.

Within the Law (9/11/12, Eltinge, 541)

Smash hit melodrama about a poor working girl (Jane Cowl) unjustly convicted of stealing from the shop where she works. Three years later, upon release from prison, she seeks revenge by operating a blackmailing gang that operates just within the law—and by marrying the son of the department store magnate who had arranged her conviction. "Four years ago," she informs him triumphantly, "you took away my name and gave me a number. Now I've given up that number and I've got *your* name!" Audiences reveled in this ringing second-act curtain line because of their sympathy for the plucky heroine—an underpaid ($6 a week), overworked (nine hours a day) clerk, railroaded to prison by a heartless uppercrust society. *Within the Law* was a million-dollar bonanza for its producers (the Selwyns, Lee Shubert, A. H. Woods), but not for its author, Bayard Veiller. He rashly sold the play outright for $3,000 cash. If he had retained his author's rights, his royalties would have exceeded $3,000 weekly. C: Dodson Mitchell, Orme Caldara, Florence Nash, William B. Mack, John Willard. D: Holbrook Blinn. R: (3/5/28, Cosmopolitan, 16) by Chamberlain Brown. C: Violet Heming, Claudette Colbert, Robert Warwick, Conway Wingfield, Charles Ray, Julia Hoyt. D: Clifford Brooke and Mabel Brownell.

SV: MGM, 1931, *Paid*, Joan Crawford, Douglass Montgomery, Robert Armstrong, Polly Moran; 1939, Ruth Hussey, Paul Kelly, Tom Neal, William Gargan.

Without Love (11/10/42, St. James, 110)

A young widow (Katharine Hepburn) and an Irish-American diplomat (Elliott Nugent) enter into a marriage of convenience in wartime Washington. By Act Three, their relationship has ripened into love, and sleeping arrangements are revised accordingly. ". . . club soda masquerading as champagne" (*PM*). *Without Love* was written by Philip Barry, author of *The Philadelphia Story*, Miss Hepburn's great 1939 success. *Without Love* toured a full season before it opened in New York. The star's popularity was so great by this time that her public bought tickets months in advance; each theatre was sold out long before the opening. The play—which dealt at great length with efforts to bring Ireland into the war on the side of the Allies—was staged by Robert Sinclair. When Sinclair was drafted into the armed services, Arthur Hopkins was called in to restage the comedy. P: The Theatre Guild. M: Richard Myers. SD: Robert Edmond Jones.

SV: MGM, 1945, Katharine Hepburn, Spencer Tracy, Lucille Ball, Keenan Wynn, Patricia Morison.

Without Warning (5/1/37, National, 17)

When a hated army man is found murdered, there are suspects galore. Barely tolerable whodunit. C: Jack Roseleigh, Franklyn Fox, Philip Ober. A: Ralph Zink. P: A. L. Jones. D: John Hayden. SD: Nat Karson.

SV: WB, 1938, *The Invisible Menace*, Boris Karloff, Regis Toomey, Marie Wilson; 1943, *Murder on the Waterfront*, John Loder, Warren Douglas, Ruth Ford.

Woman, The (9/19/11, Republic, 247)

A Washington telephone operator (Mary Nash) foils the schemes of a gang of crooked lobbyists. Hack melodrama by William C. de Mille. P/D: David Belasco.

SV: Par, 1931, *The Secret Call*, Peggy Shannon, Richard Arlen.

Woman Bites Dog (4/17/46, Belasco, 5)

Satirical farce by Bella and Samuel Spewack about a family of rabidly reactionary newspaper publishers (Taylor Holmes, Ann Shoemaker, Royal Beal). A young lieutenant (Kirk Douglas) sets out to hoax the biggest Red-baiter of the three by announcing that his (the lieutenant's) hometown has gone completely communistic. Meanwhile, because of a disappointing love affair with her editor (Frank Lovejoy), the paper's star reporter (Mercedes McCambridge) gets drunk and writes up the story as true, thus perpetuating the hoax. Before the play is over, the reporter and lieutenant fall in love, the isolationist publisher gets his comeuppance, and, in brief, the forces of liberalism win the day. ". . . begins rather amusingly. [but] becomes completely unmanageable before it is finished" (*Sun*). C: Dudley Sadler, E. G. Marshall, Eda Heinemann. P: Kermit Bloomgarden. D: Coby Ruskin.

Note: Despite protestations to the contrary by the authors, the newspaper publishing family in *Woman Bites Dog* was obviously patterned after "The Three Furies," namely, Colonel Robert McCormick (*Chicago Tribune*), Cissy Patterson (*Washington Times-Herald*), and Joseph Patterson (*New York Daily News*).

Woman Disputed, The (9/28/26, Forrest, 87)

Soggy World War I melodrama about a noble prostitute (Ann Harding) who outwits a sadistic German captain (Lowell Sherman), thereby saving the life of handsome Lieutenant Yank Trinkard (Louis Calhern) of the Foreign Legion. A: Denison Clift. P: A. H. Woods. D: Crane Wilbur.

Woman in Room 13, The (1/14/19, Booth, 175)

A woman composer is the prime suspect in the murder of a shady male singer.

Convoluted, run-of-the-mill melodrama by Samuel Shipman and Max Marcin. C: Janet Beecher, Lowell Sherman, Gail Kane, Charles Waldron. P: A. H. Woods. D: W. H. Gilmore.

SV: Fox, 1932, Elissa Landi, Myrna Loy, Ralph Bellamy, Neil Hamilton, Gilbert Roland.

Woman in the Case, The (1/31/05, Herald Square, 89)

To save her husband from a false charge of homicide, a woman (Blanche Walsh) insinuates herself into the home of a golddigger involved in the murder. Lively but implausible Clyde Fitch (A/D) melodrama. P: Wagenhals and Kemper.

Woman Is My Idea (9/25/68, Belasco, 5)

Dreary historical "comedy-drama" about Brigham Young and his Mormon followers. C: Hugh Marlowe, David Huddleston, John Heffernan. A/P/D: Don C. Liljenquist.

Woman on the Jury, The (8/15/23, Eltinge, 78)

To convince her fellow jurors to acquit a defendant charged with murder, a woman is forced to reveal her past. Hack melodrama. C: Mary Newcomb, Henry Daniell, John Craig, Frieda Inescort. A: Bernard K. Burns. P: A. H. Woods. D: Lester Lonergan.

SV: WB, 1930, *The Love Racket*, Dorothy Mackaill, Sidney Blackmer.

Woman's a Fool—To Be Clever, A (10/18/38, National, 6)

Actress comes between husband-and-wife playwrights. Torpid comedy, as unwieldy as its title. C: Haila Stoddard, Ian Keith, Vera Allen, Edith Meiser. A: Dorothy Bennett and Link Hannah. P: John J. Wildberg. D: Frank Merlin.

Woman's Way, A (2/22/09, Hackett, 112)

A young wife (Grace George) learns she has a rival for her husband's affections. Agreeable triangle comedy by Thompson Buchanan. P/D: William A. Brady.

Women, The (12/26/36, Barrymore, 657)

Vitriolic gossip overheard in a nightclub ladies' room furnished Clare Boothe with the inspiration for this famous comedy. A wickedly amusing appraisal of feminine mores, the play concerns a coven of Park Avenue matrons whose lives are a deadly round of bridge, beauty rituals, bed, and boredom. The lightweight plot follows the travails of nice Mary Haines (Margalo Gillmore) who loses her husband to a scheming hussy, but wins him back at final curtain. The play's appeal lies in its delectable bitchery, with an all-female cast making the most of the pungent dialogue. ("Are you Catholic or just careless?" a perpetually pregnant wife is asked at one point.) At first ignored by Max Gordon (P), the script was urged on him by Bernard Baruch, friend of the authoress. The hesitant producer soon found he had a tremendous hit on his hands, one that was popular with both sexes, was translated into eighteen languages, and twice transcribed by Hollywood. C: Ilka Chase, Betty Lawford, Phyllis Povah, Audrey Christie, Margaret Douglass, Arlene Francis, Jane Seymour, Adrienne Marden, Ethel Jackson, Charita Bauer, Jessie Busley, Marjorie Main, Ruth Hammond. D: Robert B. Sinclair. CD: John Hambleton. SD: Jo Mielziner.

Revived (1973) under Morton Da Costa's direction with a cast headed by Kim Hunter, Alexis Smith, Rhonda Fleming, Myrna Loy, Dorothy Loudon, Leora Dana, Marian Hailey, Marie Wallace, Jan Miner, Doris Dowling, Mary Louise Wilson, Polly Rowles.

SV: MGM, 1939, Norma Shearer, Joan Crawford, Rosalind Russell, Joan

Fontaine, Paulette Goddard, Mary Boland, Lucile Watson, Virginia Weidler, Marjorie Main, Hedda Hopper, Ruth Hussey, Mary Beth Hughes, Virginia Grey (directed by George Cukor); 1956, *The Opposite Sex,* June Allyson, Joan Collins, Dolores Gray, Ann Sheridan, Joan Blondell, Ann Miller, Agnes Moorehead, Carolyn Jones, Charlotte Greenwood (directed by David Miller).

Women Go on Forever (9/7/27, Forrest, 118)

Assorted tribulations of a raffish landlady and her boarders. Mary Boland and James Cagney were the big plus factors in this bleak melodrama which had enough plot for a dozen films and perhaps a couple of dozen radio soap operas. C: Douglass Montgomery, Osgood Perkins, Elizabeth Taylor, Mary Law, Constance McKay. A: Daniel N. Rubin. P: William A. Brady, Jr. and Dwight Deere Wiman i.a.w. John Cromwell (D).
SV: Tiffany, 1931, Clara Kimball Young.

Wonder Boy (10/22/31, Alvin, 44)

Elaborately produced Hollywood satire about a would-be dentist who, briefly and against his will, becomes a movie star. This Jed Harris (P/D) show came in with rave notices from its out-of-town tryouts and a large advance sale, but the opening night performance went badly. *Wonder Boy* collapsed after forty-four performances. The comedy was written by Edward Chodorov* and Arthur Barton. C: William Challee, Hazel Dawn, Gregory Ratoff, Henry O'Neill, Allen Jenkins, Sam Levene, David Burns, Bernard Gorcey, Arnold Moss, Horace MacMahon, Bruce MacFarlane, John Cecil Holm.

---

*Author of *Kind Lady* (1935), *Oh, Men! Oh, Women!* (1953), etc.

Wonderful Journey (12/25/46, Coronet, 9)

Stage version of the 1941 comedy film, *Here Comes Mr. Jordan,* in which a prizefighter, accidentally sent to heaven before his time, returns to earth to find a new body to occupy. "A poky and curiously haphazard blend of realism and fantasy" (*Sun*). C: Donald Murphy, Sidney Blackmer, Philip Loeb. A: Harry Segall. P: Theron Bamberger i.a.w. Richard Skinner. D: Frank Emmons Brown.
SV: Col, 1941, *Here Comes Mr. Jordan,* Robert Montgomery, Claude Rains, Evelyn Keyes, James Gleason, Edward Everett Horton, Rita Johnson, John Emery.

Wonderful Thing, The (2/17/20, Playhouse, 120)

Young bride (Jeanne Eagels) is snubbed by her snooty in-laws. Sentimental, clichéd comedy-drama. A/D: Lillian Trimble Bradley. P: George Broadhurst.

Wooden Dish, The (10/6/55, Booth, 12)

Realizing that he has become a trial and nuisance to his son and daughter-in-law, an old codger finally accepts the inevitable and prepares to enter a home for the aged. ". . . . dreary and unoriginal" (*New York Times*). C: Louis Calhern (D), Polly Rowles, James Westerfield, Barbara Barrie, Edgar Stehli, John Randolph, Gordon Tanner, Jacqueline Scott. A: Edmund Morris. P: Armand Deutsch. SD: Donald Oenslager.

Wooden Kimono, The (12/27/26, Martin Beck, 201)

Three mysterious murders have taken place in The Red Owl Tavern. Now a gang of dope smugglers has taken over the jinxed hostelry. Who will be wiped out next? "It bears all the marks of a successful mystery play" (*New York Times*). C: Alden Chase, Jean Dixon. A: John Floyd.

P: Frederick Stanhope (D) and Jacques Froehlich.

Wooden Slipper, The (1/3/34, Ritz, 5)

Would-be actress settles for marriage instead of a career. Heavy-handed comedy by Samson Raphaelson (A/D) set in Budapest. C: Dorothy Hall, Ross Alexander, Montagu Love, Cecilia Loftus, Lionel Stander. P: Dwight Deere Wiman.

Wookey, The (9/10/41, Plymouth, 134)

The Luftwaffe's bombing of London turns an anti-war cockney (Edmund Gwenn) into a pro-war patriot. ". . . one of the most effective pieces of anti-Hitler propaganda New York has yet experienced" *(Post)*. This 1941 production was immeasurably aided by fifteen thousand dollars worth of sound effects recorded on the spot by the B.B.C. during the blitzkrieg of London in 1940. *The Wookey* was written by Hollywood screenwriter Frederick Hazlitt Brennan. C: Carol Goodner, Norah Howard, Heather Angel, Horace (Stephen) McNally. P: Edgar Selwyn. D: Robert Sinclair. SD: Jo Mielziner.

Note: The title of the play referred to the protagonist's surname.

Work Is for Horses (11/20/37, Windsor, 9)

A loafer (Robert Keith) lets his hard-working wife (Connie Gilchrist) support him. Humdrum comedy-drama had little to recommend it. A: Henry Myers. P/D: Anthony Brown.

World of Suzie Wong, The (10/14/58, Broadhurst, 508)

Elaborately mounted fiction of a high-minded Canadian artist who falls in love with a heart-of-gold Hong Kong prostitute. ". . . the corniest tear-jerker imaginable" *(News)*. "Like the Belasco production of *Lulu Belle, Suzie Wong* is flaring in style and sophomoric in viewpoint and on the artistic level of a comic book" *(New York Times)*. C: William Shatner, France Nuyen (deb.), Ron Randell, Sarah Marshall. A: Paul Osborn b/o the novel by Richard Mason. P: David Merrick, Seven Arts and Mansfield Productions. D: Joshua Logan. SD: Jo Mielziner.

SV: Par, 1960, William Holden, Nancy Kwan, Sylvia Syms, Michael Wilding, Laurence Naismith (directed by Richard Quine).

World Waits, The (10/25/33, Little, 29)

Conflicts and crises galore among members of an Antarctic expedition commanded by an egomaniacal, publicity-seeking explorer. A thinly veiled attack on Admiral Byrd (here called Commander Hartley), this adventure saga with an all-male cast proved too downbeat for Depression era audiences. C: Blaine Cordner, Reed Brown, Jr., Millard Mitchell, Charles Quigley. A: George F. Hummel. P/D: Frank Merlin.

World We Make, The (11/20/39, Guild, 80)

A mental patient (Margo) escapes from a sanitarium, finds a job in a steam laundry, and discovers love and emotional security by living and working in the outside world. Staged with meticulous realism, *The World We Make* nevertheless lacked "the lift of first-rate dramatic writing" *(Herald Tribune)*. The play was adapted from Millen Brand's novel, *The Outward Room,* by Sidney Kingsley (A/P/D). The excellent settings were designed by Harry Horner. C: Herbert Rudley, Joseph Pevney, Harold J. Stone.

World's Full of Girls, The (12/6/43, Royale, 9)

Play by Nunnally Johnson,* based on a novel by Thomas Bell. This short-lived comedy-drama dealt with the visit of a young marine to the disagreeable Brooklyn family with whom he had once lived, and his resumption of a love affair with a former girlfriend. "... full of pleasant things [but] too diffuse and underdeveloped" *(PM)*. C: Berry Kroeger, Virginia Gilmore, Harry Bellaver, Julie Stevens. P/D: Jed Harris.

---

*Noted screenwriter-producer-director. *The World's Full of Girls* was Nunnally Johnson's only Broadway play.

Wren, The (10/10/21, Gaiety, 24)

A pretty young boardinghouse manager (Helen Hayes) and a Canadian artist (Leslie Howard), spending his summer vacation in New England, meet and fall in love. Humdrum, uneventful comedy-drama by Booth Tarkington. P: Tyler and Erlanger. D: Howard Lindsay.

Writing on the Wall, The (4/26/09, Savoy, 32)

Shrill, inconclusive 1909 melodrama on a vital theme—slum-dwelling fire hazards and the need for reform in city building laws. C: Olga Nethersole, Frank Craven, Robert T. Haines, William Morris. A: William J. Hurlbut. D: Walter Lawrence.

Wuthering Heights (4/27/39, Longacre, 12)

Bloodless dramatization of Emily Brontë's novel. Don Terry played Heathcliff in spiritless fashion, while Edith Barrett was somnambulistic as the willful Catherine who married for spite and lived to rue her folly. A: Randolph Carter. P: Robert Henderson and Harry Young. D/SD: Stewart Chaney.

SV: The Brontë novel was filmed (UA, 1939) with Laurence Olivier, Merle Oberon, David Niven, Geraldine Fitzgerald, Flora Robson, Donald Crisp, Leo G. Carroll, Hugh Williams, and Cecil Kellaway heading the cast. A remake (American-International, 1971) featured Timothy Dalton, Anna Calder-Marshall, Harry Andrews, and Hugh Griffith.

X, Y, and Z

Xmas in Las Vegas (11/4/65, Barrymore, 4)

Overblown comedy-drama about the problems of a compulsive gambler (Tom Ewell). A: Jack Richardson. P: Fred Coe (D) and David Karr.

Yankee Point (11/23/42, Longacre, 24)

Typical American family, living on the Eastern seaboard, captures a Nazi saboteur. Hackneyed wartime comedy-melodrama; good cast. C: Edna Best, John Cromwell (D), Elizabeth Patterson, John Forsythe (deb.), K. T. Stevens, Arthur Aylsworth. A: Gladys Hurlbut. P: Choate and Elkins.

Year Boston Won the Pennant, The (5/22/69, Forum, 36)

A crippled baseball player (Roy R. Scheider) struggles to make a comeback. Steadily absorbing symbolic drama by John Ford Noonan. Produced by The Repertory Theater of Lincoln Center; directed by Tim Ward.

Years Ago (12/3/46, Mansfield, 206)

Ruth Gordon's autobiographical comedy about her youthful yearnings for a stage career and her Massachusetts family's reactions to same. This period piece (c. 1913) was produced by Max Gordon (no relation), and was staged by Garson Kanin, Miss Gordon's husband. "A warm and tender little comedy.... But it is also slight, slender and uneventful" (*Post*). C: Fredric March, Florence Eldridge, Patricia Kirkland. SD: Donald Oenslager.

SV: MGM, 1953, *The Actress*, Spencer Tracy, Teresa Wright, Jean Simmons, Anthony Perkins, Mary Wickes (directed by George Cukor).

Years of Discretion (12/25/12, Belasco, 190)

Small-town widow shocks her family and friends by going to the big city and living it up. Flimsy David Belasco (P/D) farce. C: Effie Shannon, Herbert Kelcey, Bruce McRae, Grant Mitchell, Lyn Harding. A: Frederic and Fanny Hatton.

Yellow (9/21/26, National, 132)

Well-acted but contrived melodrama about a callous heel. The first-rate cast included Chester Morris, Spencer Tracy, Selena Royle, Hale Hamilton, Harry Bannister, Shirley Warde, and Helen Mack. A: Margaret Vernon. P: George M. Cohan. D: John Meehan.

Yellow Jack (3/6/34, Martin Beck, 79)

Frequently gripping, if declamatory, documentary-drama depicting the heroic sacrifices of Walter Reed and his associates in Cuba, 1900, while searching for the source of the deadly yellow fever microbe. Written by Sidney Howard in collaboration with bacteriologist Paul de Kruif, *Yellow Jack* received generally laudatory reviews but proved of limited popular appeal. Spendidly acted by a

YES, MY DARLING DAUGHTER 533

Years of Discretion. **Grant Mitchell and Camilla Dalberg (Belasco Theatre, December 25, 1912).** *Courtesy Museum of the City of New York Theatre and Music Collection.*

predominantly male cast, the play was performed for two hours without an intermission. C: John Miltern, Geoffrey Kerr, James Stewart, Sam Levene, Myron McCormick, Eddie Acuff, Barton MacLane, Eduardo Ciannelli, Robert Keith, Millard Mitchell, Whitford Kane, Lloyd Gough, George Nash, Katherine Wilson. P/D: Guthrie McClintic. SD: Jo Mielziner.

R: (2/27/47, International, 21) by American Repertory Theatre. C: Raymond Greenleaf, Victor Jory, Philip Bourneuf, Alfred Ryder, Efrem Zimbalist, Jr., Anne Jackson, Eli Wallach, William Windom, Arthur Keegan, D: Martin Ritt.

SV: MGM, 1938, Robert Montgomery, Lewis Stone, Charles Coburn, Virginia Bruce, Henry Hull, Sam Levene, Stanley Ridges, Andy Devine.

Yellow Jacket, The (11/4/12, Fulton, 80)

The most successful attempt to employ the conventions of Chinese drama to the American stage. As the life of Wu Hoo Git unfolds, from his birth until he attains the yellow jacket of emperor, a chorus explains the action to the audience, while a supposedly invisible property man changes the settings and props. A unique and charming play that has caught the fancy of American audiences whenever it has been done. C: George Relph, Juliette Day, Schuyler Ladd, Grace Valentine, Reginald Barlow, Chamberlain Brown. A: George C. Hazleton and J. Harry Benrimo (D). P: Harris and Selwyn.

R: (11/9/16, Cort, 172) by and with Mr. and Mrs. Charles Coburn.

Yellow Ticket, The (1/20/14, Eltinge, 183)

Russian prostitute, forced to wear the yellow badge of prostitution, is hounded by lustful, predatory baron. Fine cast—John Barrymore, Florence Reed, John Mason, Julian L'Estrange, Emmett Corrigan—in lurid, moth-eaten melodrama. A: Michael Morton. P: A. H. Woods. D: Hugh Ford.

SV: Fox, 1931, Laurence Olivier, Lionel Barrymore, Boris Karloff, Elissa Landi, Mischa Auer.

Yes, My Darling Daughter (2/9/37, Playhouse, 404)

Bright, sophisticated comedy about a progressive mother whose Greenwich Village past catches up with her when her twenty-two-year-old daughter insists upon her own right to sexual freedom. *Yes, My Darling Daughter* was the surprise hit of 1937. C: Lucile Watson, Peggy Conklin, Violet Heming, Boyd Crawford, Nicholas Joy, Charles Bryant. A: Mark Reed. P/D: Alfred de Liagre, Jr.

SV: WB, 1939, Priscilla Lane, Fay Bainter, Jeffrey Lynn, Roland Young, May Robson, Genevieve

Tobin, Ian Hunter, George Tobias.

Note: This film created a mild furor by being banned by the New York Board of Censors. After a few minor cuts were made by the censors, the movie opened concurrently at *two* first-run Manhattan theatres. Thanks to nationwide front page publicity, business was exceedingly brisk.

Yes or No (12/21/17, 48th Street, 147)

Contrived drama paralleled the lives of two women—one rich but miserable, the other poor but happy. C: Willette Kershaw, Byron Beasley, Andriene Morrison. Robert Kelly. A: Arthur Goodrich. P: G. M. Anderson (D) and L. Lawrence Weber.

You and I (2/19/23, Belmont, 174)

Philip Barry's first play, an intriguing tragi-comedy studded with epigrammatic wit. A frustrated businessman (H. B. Warner) decides to take a year's sabbatical and devote himself to painting. He discovers that he lacks a first-rate talent ("There's no such hell on earth as that of the man who knows himself doomed to mediocrity in the work he loves") and relinquishes his dream for the sake of his son (Geoffrey Kerr). C: Lucile Watson, Frieda Inescort, Reginald Mason, Ferdinand Gottschalk. P: Richard G. Herndon. D: Robert Milton

SV: WB, 1931, *The Bargain*, Lewis Stone, Doris Kenyon, Charles Butterworth, Una Merkel, Evelyn Knapp.

You Can't Take It With You (12/14/36, Booth, 837)

Pulitzer Prize play by Moss Hart and George S. Kaufman (D); one of the great comedies of the American stage. Tempering elements of wild farce with an underlying warmth and tenderness, the play takes us into the Vanderhof home in New York City, a Depression-era commune inhabited by some of the most delightful eccentrics in theatrical literature. Here everyone does his own thing with a vengeance. The patriarch of the family is a wise old man who walked out on his job thirty-five years earlier and never went back. His philosophy—life is best when people do as they like rather than as they should—is practiced with endearing single-mindedness by his family and friends. The play's climax is reached when the granddaughter of the house falls in love with the son of a wealthy Wall Street tycoon, and the boy's stuffy parents arrive unexpectedly for dinner. Before the final curtain falls, this family of amiable lunatics has converted the tycoon to their way of thinking. "A gallimaufry of gambols and the best comedy these authors have written" *(New York Times)*. Written in six weeks, *You Can't Take It With You* was a fabulous money-maker. Kaufman and Hart reputedly earned twenty-five thousand dollars a week apiece from royalties and production profits. In addition, the play was sold to Columbia Pictures for the then-unprecedented sum of two hundred thousand dollars. The film won the Oscar as best picture of the year. C: Henry Travers, Josephine Hull, Paula Trueman, Frank Wilcox, Margot Stevenson, Jess Barker, George Tobias, Mitzi Hajos, Hugh Rennie, William J. Kelly, Virginia Hammond. P: Sam H. Harris. SD: Donald Oenslager.

R: (3/26/45, City Center, 17) with Fred Stone in the leading role. P/D: Frank McCoy.

R: (11/23/65, Lyceum, 255) by A.P.A. C: Donald Moffat, Rosemary Harris, Clayton Corzatte. D: Ellis Rabb.

SV: Col, 1938, Jean Arthur, James Stewart, Lionel Barrymore, Edward Arnold, Spring Byington, Mischa Auer, Ann Miller, Donald Meek, Halliwell Hobbes, Harry

Davenport, H. B. Warner, Eddie Anderson (directed by Frank Capra from a screenplay by Robert Riskin).

You Touched Me! (9/25/45, Booth, 109)

An early play by Tennessee Williams b/o a short story by D. H. Lawrence. Written in collaboration with Donald Windham, this "romantic comedy" concerned the love affair between a Canadian Air Force lieutenant (Montgomery Clift) and a timid English spinster (Marianne Stewart). The romance is frustrated by the girl's prudish maiden aunt (Catherine Willard) and by the youngsters' own sexual inhibitions. All ends happily, however, thanks to the intervention of a bibulous, life-loving old sea dog (Edmund Gwenn) who happens to be not only the girl's father, but the boy's foster-father as well. Set in rural England, this curious blend of sex and symbolism failed to impress the critics: "A flickering entertainment, saved time and again by adroit acting" *(Herald Tribune)*. "An elaborate and intensely literary version of *Snow White*." *(The New Yorker)*. Written before *The Glass Menagerie, You Touched Me!* was produced six months after the former play's triumphant Broadway premiere (3/31/45). Tennessee Williams apparently prefers to forget this rambling and fragmentary comedy. It is one of the few Williams plays that has not been rewritten or reprinted. P: Guthrie McClintic (D) i.a.w. Lee Shubert. SD: Motley.

Young Alexander (3/12/29, Biltmore, 7)

Alexander the Great (Henry Hull) decrees that henceforth his legions must forswear the opposite sex. Then he meets a seductive female (Jessie Royce Landis) masquerading as a boy, and changes his mind. Puerile costume fable. C: A. E. Anson, Gladys Lloyd. A: Hardwick Nevin. D: Ira Hards.

Young America (8/28/15, Astor, 105)

Innocuous folderol about the reformation of a pugnacious schoolboy by a small-town druggist and his wife. Otto Kruger and Peggy Wood were the adult stars of this George M. Cohan-Sam H. Harris production, Percy Helton was the kid star, but the real star (according to the press) was a handsome dog actor named Jasper who barked on cue, never missed an entrance, and never failed to show up for a performance. A: Fred Ballard. D: Sam Forrest.

SV: Fox, 1932, Spencer Tracy, Ralph Bellamy, Doris Kenyon.

Young American, A (1/17/46, Blackfriars, 26)

Impressed by a symphony sent to him through the mails, a celebrated orchestra conductor invites the composer to stay in his home while the work is in process of revision. The composer turns out to be a young Negro, and the play thereupon revolves around the minor embarrassments and open prejudices that he encounters in the white household. Billed as "a tragedy of manners," this 1940's play by Edwin Bronner* was presented O/B by the prestigious Blackfriars Guild to generally laudatory reviews: "A pungent play . . . a work of fine dramatic unity. Mr. Bronner knows the ins and outs of his craft. He writes easily and interestingly" *(New York Times)*. "A creditable new drama . . . solid . . . electric . . . eloquent indeed" *(Herald Tribune)*. "This may be a shock to you, but to my mind *A Young American* is the best drama I have seen dealing with racial discrimination against the Negro. . . . A poignant and instructive drama written with utter honesty and truth. It is a beautiful play" *(World-Telegram)*. C: Louis Peterson,** Martha Jean, Alex Wilson, Liam Dunn, Murray Stewart, Marion Douglas, Harry Bolden, Joan Field. D: Dennis Gurney.

*Editor of this volume. *A Young American* subsequently toured under the auspices of the Messrs. Shubert and Albert de Courville.
**Author of *Take a Giant Step* (1953).

Young and Beautiful, The (10/1/55, Longacre, 65)

Incapable of genuine emotion, a narcissistic adolescent discards her Jazz Age suitors the moment she wins their love. Set in 1915 Chicago, this comedy-drama by Sally Benson was b/o a series of short stories by F. Scott Fitzgerald. ". . . written with a shrewd and unsparing hand, and I think that Scott Fitzgerald might well have been pleased with it" *(Herald Tribune).* C: Lois Smith, Douglas Watson, Peter Brandon, James Olson. P: Robert Radnitz i.a.w. Lawrence Baker, Jr. D: Marshall Jamison. CD: Motley. SD: Eldon Elder.

Young and Fair, The (11/22/48, Fulton, 40)

Blackmail, espionage, anti-Semitism, and kleptomania in a fashionable junior college for girls. ". . . overwrought, plot-heavy, frantic, but well acted and far from boring . . ." *(Post).* Standout in an all-female cast was newcomer Julie Harris, whose portrayal of a hapless kleptomaniac in the throes of hysteria stopped the first-night performance dead in its tracks with a near ovation. C: Mercedes McCambridge, Frances Starr, Patricia Kirkland, Lois Wheeler, Doe Avedon, Rita Gam, Lenka Peterson, Frieda Altman. A: N. Richard Nash. P: Vinton Freedley i.a.w. Richard W. Krakeur. D: Harold Clurman.

Young Blood (11/24/25, Ritz, 72)

Nice girl (Helen Hayes) exposes a conniving flapper (Florence Eldridge), thereby winning the boy of her dreams. Tolerable 20's drama with a good cast: Eric Dressler, Norman Trevor, Monroe Owsley. A/D: James Forbes. P: The Dramatists Theatre, Inc.

Young Couple Wanted (12/24/40, Maxine Elliott's, 13)

The tribulations of two newlyweds (Arlene Francis and Hugh Marlowe) in the big city. ". . . a dull play about dull people in dull situations" *(Herald Tribune).* A: Arthur Wilmurt. P: Jerome Mayer i.a.w. Carly Wharton and Martin Gabel (D).

Young Go First, The (5/28/35, Park, 39)

Twenty-six-year-old Elia Kazan made his directorial debut with this straggling comedy about the misadventures of some tough city boys at a rural C.C.C. camp during the Depression. The play was codirected by Alfred Saxe, with settings by Mordecai Gorelik. C: Philip Robinson, Mitchell Grayson, Earl Robinson, Perry Bruskin, Curt Conway. A: Peter Martin, George Scudder and Charles Friedman. P: Theatre of Action.

Young Love (10/30/28, Masque, 87)

An engaged couple grow increasingly cynical about marriage as they become involved in a variety of mate-swapping experiments. George Cukor directed this bold (by 1928 standards) comedy by Samson Raphaelson. The play proved far more successful in Europe than in America. D: Dorothy Gish, Tom Douglas, Catherine Willard, James Rennie. P: Macgowan and Ross.

Young Man's Fancy, A (10/15/19, Playhouse, 13)

A lonely recluse (Philip Merivale) falls in love with a shop-window dummy and then with the girl (Jeanne Eagels) who posed for the model. Offbeat, imaginative comedy-drama, marred by top-heavy, literal production. C: Howard Lindsay, Mary Kennedy, Morgan Farley, J. M. Kerrigan. A: John T. McIntyre. P: George C. Tyler.

Young Man's Fancy, A (4/29/47, Plymouth, 335)

High jinks at a Connecticut summer camp for boys and girls. "A witless comedy" *(News)*. C: Bill Talman, Lenore Lonergan, Ronnie Jacoby. A: Harry Thurschwell and Alfred Golden. P: Henry Adrian. D: Robert E. Perry.

Young Mr. Disraeli (11/10/37, Fulton, 6)

Florid biographical drama dealing with the early life and rise to political fame of Benjamin Disraeli; written by American historical novelist Elswyth Thane, wife of naturalist William Beebe. C: Derrick de Marney, Sophie Stewart, Selena Royle, Ben Webster, Molly Pearson, Lora Baxter, Edgar Kent. P: Alex Yokel. D: Margaret Webster. CD/SD: David Ffolkes.

Young Sinners (11/28/29, Morosco, 229)

Millionaire playboy gets moral fervor and refuses to bed down with an attractive seventeen-year-old girl until they can be properly wed. Cheap 20's sex comedy by Elmer Harris, author of *Johnny Belinda* (1940). C: Raymond Guion (Gene Raymond), Dorothy Appleby. P: Messrs. Shubert. D: Stanley Logan.

SV: Fox, 1931, Hardie Albright, Dorothy Jordan, Thomas Meighan.

Young Wisdom (1/5/14, Criterion, 56)

Two girls (Mabel and Edith Taliaferro) flirt with the idea of trial marriage, but end up with their respective swains at the altar instead. Innocuous Rachel Crothers comedy-drama. P: Joseph Brooks. D: Robert Milton.

Young Woodley (11/2/25, Belmont, 267)

A bashful schoolboy (Glenn Hunter) falls in love with his headmaster's wife (Helen Gahagan). Sensitive, skillfully written comedy-drama; Anglo-American author John Van Druten's first play. P: George C. Tyler and Basil Dean (D).

SV: British, 1930, Frank Lawton, Madeleine Carroll.

Note: The British production of *Young Woodley* was attacked by the censor on the grounds that the play "reflected discreditably" upon the English school system because of its "frank treatment" of adolescent sex problems. The script finally was approved by the censor, with cuts and changes, and had its successful premiere in 1928, three years after the opening of the American production. The British cast was headed by Frank Lawton, Jack Hawkins, and Kathleen O'Regan.

Youngest, The (12/22/24, Gaiety, 100)

A browbeaten teenager (Henry Hull) finally achieves dominance over his impossible family when he discovers that he is the legal owner of the family's business and estate. Arch, mildly amusing domestic comedy by Philip Barry. C: Genevieve Tobin, Verree Teasdale, Effie Shannon, Katherine Alexander, Robert Strange. P/D: Robert Milton.

Your Humble Servant (1/3/10, Garrick, 72)

Fairly amusing comedy about a "ham" actor (Otis Skinner) touring the country in a rickety stage vehicle. A: Booth Tarkington and Harry Leon Wilson. P: Charles Frohman. D: Skinner.

Your Loving Son (4/4/41, Little, 3)

Precocious adolescent reunites his nitwit parents. "Squalid wholesomeness" *(New York Times)*. C: Frankie Thomas, Jessie Royce Landis, Jay Fassett. A: Abby Merchant. P: Jay Richard Kennedy i.a.w. Bloomingdale and Loewi. D: Arthur Sircom.

Your Uncle Dudley (11/28/29, Cort, 96)

Amiable little 20's comedy about a civic-minded booster who neglects home and business in favor of charitable campaigns. C: Walter Connolly, George Barbier, James Bell. A/D: Howard Lindsay and Bertrand Robinson. P: Erlanger and Tyler.

SV: Fox, 1935, Edward Everett Horton.

Yours, A. Lincoln (7/9/42, Shubert, 2)

Static retelling of the plot to assassinate President Lincoln (Vincent Price). Produced for a limited engagement (two performances) by the Experimental Theatre, Inc. A: Paul Horgan b/o a book by Otto Eisenschiml. D: Robert Ross.

Yr. Obedient Husband (1/10/38, Broadhurst, 8)

Comedy about English essayist-playwright Richard Steele (Fredric March) and his faithful wife Prue (Florence Eldridge). Steele is impulsive, improvident, and undependable. Prue almost loses patience with him entirely, and threatens to leave her rakish spouse, but she doesn't. Written by screenwriter Horace Jackson, *Yr. Obedient Husband* was a calamitous failure. "Mr. Jackson's eighteenth-century pastiche is written without much tingle in the lines or ideas and Mr. March plays it literally" *(New York Times)*. C: Montgomery Clift, Dame May Whitty, Brenda Forbes, Frieda Altman, Martin Wolfson. P: Fredric March and John Cromwell (D). SD: Jo Mielziner.

Note: Better remembered than the play itself was the ad that the Marches inserted in the New York papers following the dismal first-night reviews of *Yr. Obedient Husband*. It was a replica of a cartoon from the *New Yorker*, which showed the man on the flying trapeze missing his partner, who exclaimed: "Oops! Sorry!" Newspapers and magazines throughout the country reproduced the ad and complimented the stars for their gallantry under fire.

Zander the Great (4/9/23, Empire, 162)

Picaresque yarn about a drudge-heroine (Alice Brady) and a five-year-old boy who are held hostage on the Mexican border by a band of bootlegger-cowboys led by George Abbott, Jerome Patrick, and Joseph Calleia. A: Salisbury Field. P: Charles Frohman, Inc. D: David Burton.

Zelda (3/5/69, Barrymore, 5)

Contemporary retelling of the Noah story in which a retired Brooklyn druggist tries to convince his family that the world is coming to an end that very weekend. Uneasy mixture of domestic comedy and parable play. C: Ed Begley, Lilia Skala, Nita Talbot. A: Sylvia Regan. P: Hoffe/Isenberg i.a.w. G. B. Seiff. D: Delbert Mann. SD: Will Steven Armstrong.

Zeno (8/25/23, 48th Street, 89)

A psychic joins forces with the police to trap a criminal mastermind. Gaudy melodrama, good fun in its ten-twent'-thirt' fashion. C: Walter Wilson, Hugh O'Connell, William B. Mack, Frederick Bickel (Fredric March). A: Joseph F. Rinn. P: Hampton Play Corp. D: Edward Elsner.

Zeppelin (1/14/29, National, 72)

Murder, adultery, leprosy, poison gas, and heaven knows what else aboard a giant airship. Lurid 20's mystery-melodrama. C: Wallis Clark, Rose Hobart, Raymond Walburn, Paul Guilfoyle, Edward Woods. A: McElbert Moore, Earle Crooker and Lowell Brentano. P: Jimmie Cooper. D: Frank Merlin.

Zira (9/21/05, Princess, 128)

A woman (Margaret Anglin), passing herself off as the niece of a wealthy and influential family, is finally forced to confess her deceit. "Commonplace . . . implausible . . . suffers from too naturalistic handling" *(New York Times)*. This hoary fable was based on Wilkie Collins' story, "The New Magdalen," with the setting transferred to South Africa during the Boer War. Despite generally poor reviews from the critics, *Zira* was a popular success due to the emotion-charged performance of Margaret Anglin in the title role. C: Frank Worthing, Bertram Harrison, Mrs. Thomas Whiffen. A: J. Hartley Manners and Henry Miller. P/D: Henry Miller.

Zombie (2/10/32, Biltmore, 20)

That old black magic in Haiti. Silly horror play with a no-name cast. A: Kenneth Webb. D: George Sherwood.

Zulu and the Zayda, The (11/10/65, Cort, 179)

Gently humorous tale of a Jewish family living in South Africa, and of the friendship that develops between the aged grandfather (Menasha Skulnik) and the native servant (Louis Gossett) hired to look after him. Written by actor Howard Da Silva in collaboration with Felix Leon; b/o a story by Dan Jacobson. Incidental songs by Harold Rome. C: Ossie Davis, Yaphet Kotto, Joe Silver. P: Theodore Mann and Dore Schary (D). SD: William and Jean Eckart.

Appendix I
Theatre Calendar: Notable Premieres of the Century

Note: This compilation includes not only American plays, but also foreign plays, musicals, revivals, etc.

Abbreviations:
    EP (Ensemble Production—No Star Names)
    R   (Revival)

JANUARY

	Title	*Leading Performer(s)*
1	The Milk Train Doesn't Stop Here Anymore (1964–R)	Tallulah Bankhead/Tab Hunter/Ruth Ford.
2	Find Your Way Home (1974)	Michael Moriarty/Lee Richardson/Jane Alexander.
3	The Hasty Heart (1945)	Richard Basehart/John Lund/Anne Burr.
4	Ziegfeld Follies (1934)	Fanny Brice/Jane Froman/Eve Arden/Willie Howard/Buddy Ebsen.
5	The Member Of The Wedding (1950)	Ethel Waters/Julie Harris/Brandon de Wilde.
6	Oliver! (1963)	Clive Revill/Georgia Brown.
7	The Petrified Forest (1935)	Leslie Howard/Humphrey Bogart/Peggy Conklin/Blanche Sweet.
8	Desire Under The Elms (1963–R)	George C. Scott/Colleen Dewhurst/Rip Torn.
9	High Tor (1937)	Burgess Meredith/Peggy Ashcroft.
10	Arsenic And Old Lace (1941)	Boris Karloff/Josephine Hull.
11	The Little Minister (1916–R)	Maude Adams.
12	Show Girl (1961)	Carol Channing.

Title	Leading Performer(s)
13 Darkness At Noon (1951)	Claude Rains/Kim Hunter/Jack Palance.
14 Krapp's Last Tape/The Zoo Story (1960)	Donald Davis/George Maharis/William Daniels.
15 The Shrike (1952)	Jose Ferrer/Judith Evelyn.
16 Hello, Dolly! (1964)	Carol Channing/David Burns/Eileen Brennan/Charles Nelson Reilly
17 The Waltz Of The Toreadors (1957)	Ralph Richardson/Mildred Natwick.
18 Dylan (1964)	Alec Guinness/Kate Reid.
19 No, No, Nanette (1971–R)	Ruby Keeler/Patsy Kelly/Jack Gilford/Helen Gallagher/Bobby Van.
20 The Caine Mutiny Court-Martial (1954)	Henry Fonda/Lloyd Nolan/John Hodiak.
21 Ethan Frome (1936)	Raymond Massey/Ruth Gordon/Pauline Lord.
22 The Crucible (1953)	Arthur Kennedy/Walter Hampden/E. G. Marshall.
23 Lady In The Dark (1941)	Gertrude Lawrence/Danny Kaye/Victor Mature/Macdonald Carey/Bert Lytell.
24 Design For Living (1933)	Alfred Lunt/Lynn Fontanne/Noel Coward.
25 I Never Sang For My Father (1968)	Hal Holbrook/Alan Webb/Lillian Gish/Teresa Wright.
26 Green Grow The Lilacs (1931)	Franchot Tone/June Walker/Helen Westley/Lee Strasberg.
27 Private Lives (1931)	Noel Coward/Gertrude Lawrence/Laurence Olivier/Jill Esmond.
28 A View From The Bridge (1965–R)	Robert Duvall/Jon Voight/Susan Anspach/Ramon Bieri.
29 Sweet Charity (1966)	Gwen Verdon/John McMartin/Helen Gallagher.
30 Strange Interlude (1928)	Lynn Fontanne.
31 The Road To Rome (1927)	Jane Cowl/Philip Merivale/Barry Jones.

FEBRUARY

Title	Leading Performer(s)
1 The Shanghai Gesture (1926)	Florence Reed.
2 Beyond The Horizon (1920)	Richard Bennett.
3 The Rose Tattoo (1951)	Maureen Stapleton/Eli Wallach/Don Murray.
4 Born Yesterday (1946)	Judy Holliday/Paul Douglas/Gary Merrill.
5 The Show-Off (1924)	Louis John Bartels/Helen Lowell/Lee Tracy.
6 Lute Song (1946)	Mary Martin/Yul Brynner/Mildred Dunnock.
7 Visit To A Small Planet (1957)	Cyril Ritchard.
8 The Immoralist (1954)	Louis Jourdan/Geraldine Page/James Dean.
9 The Barretts Of Wimpole Street (1931)	Katharine Cornell/Brian Aherne.
10 Death Of A Salesman (1949)	Lee J. Cobb/Mildred Dunnock/Arthur Kennedy/Cameron Mitchell.
11 The Confidential Clerk (1954)	Claude Rains/Ina Claire/Joan Greenwood/Aline MacMahon.
12 Claudia (1941)	Dorothy McGuire/Donald Cook/Frances Starr/John Williams.

Title	Leading Performer(s)
13 The Last Mile (1930)	Spencer Tracy.
14 Plaza Suite (1968)	George C. Scott/Maureen Stapleton.
15 The Little Foxes (1939)	Tallulah Bankhead.
16 A Majority Of One (1959)	Gertrude Berg/Cedric Hardwicke.
17 Child's Play (1970)	Pat Hingle/Fritz Weaver/Ken Howard.
18 Mister Roberts (1948)	Henry Fonda/David Wayne/Robert Keith/William Harrigan.
19 Picnic (1953)	Ralph Meeker/Janice Rule/Paul Newman/Kim Stanley/Eileen Heckart.
20 Mrs. McThing (1952)	Helen Hayes/Brandon de Wilde.
21 They Shall Not Die (1934)	Claude Rains/Ruth Gordon/Dean Jagger/Helen Westley.
22 Come Blow Your Horn (1961)	Hal March/Lou Jacobi/Pert Kelton.
23 The Dark Is Light Enough (1955)	Katharine Cornell/Tyrone Power/Christopher Plummer/John Williams.
24 Dodsworth (1934)	Walter Huston/Fay Bainter.
25 Toys In The Attic (1960)	Jason Robards/Maureen Stapleton/Anne Revere/Irene Worth.
26 The Green Pastures (1930)	Richard B. Harrison.
27 Truckline Cafe (1946)	Marlon Brando/Karl Malden/Kevin McCarthy/Virginia Gilmore.
28 A Hole In The Head (1957)	Paul Douglas/Lee Grant/Kay Medford/David Burns.

MARCH

Title	Leading Performer(s)
1 This Was Burlesque (1962)	Ann Corio.
2 Bus Stop (1955)	Kim Stanley/Albert Salmi/Elaine Stritch.
3 The Lion In Winter (1966)	Robert Preston/Rosemary Harris.
4 Strike Me Pink (1933)	Jimmy Durante/Lupe Velez.
5 The Girl In Pink Tights (1954)	Jeanmaire/Charles Goldner/Brenda Lewis.
6 Over Here! (1974)	The Andrews Sisters.
7 The Autumn Garden (1951)	Fredric March/Florence Eldridge.
8 Mary, Mary (1961)	Barbara Bel Geddes/Barry Nelson/Michael Rennie/John Cromwell.
9 The Hairy Ape (1922)	Louis Wolheim.
10 Sweet Bird Of Youth (1959)	Paul Newman/Geraldine Page.
11 A Raisin In The Sun (1959)	Sidney Poitier/Claudia McNeil/Ruby Dee/Diana Sands.
12 Golden Boy (1952–R)	John Garfield/Lee J. Cobb.
13 Enter Laughing (1963)	Alan Arkin/Sylvia Sidney/Alan Mowbray/Vivian Blaine/Michael J. Pollard.
14 Dark Of The Moon (1945)	Richard Hart/Carol Stone.
15 My Fair Lady (1956)	Rex Harrison/Julie Andrews.
16 1776 (1969)	Ken Howard/William Daniels/Howard Da Silva/Virginia Vestoff.
17 Kiss And Tell (1943)	Joan Caulfield/Richard Widmark/Jessie Royce Landis/Robert Keith.
18 Tovarich (1963)	Vivien Leigh/Jean-Pierre Aumont.
19 Camino Real (1953)	Eli Wallach/Jo Van Fleet/Hurd Hatfield.
20 Murder In The Cathedral (1936)	Harry Irvine.
21 Orpheus Descending (1957)	Maureen Stapleton/Cliff Robertson.
22 Journey's End (1929)	Colin Keith Johnson.

THEATRE CALENDAR 543

	Title	Leading Performer(s)
23	Detective Story (1949)	Ralph Bellamy.
24	Cat On A Hot Tin Roof (1955)	Barbara Bel Geddes/Ben Gazzara/Burl Ives/Mildred Dunnock/Pat Hingle.
25	Liliom (1940–R)	Burgess Meredith/Ingrid Bergman/Elia Kazan.
26	Funny Girl (1964)	Barbra Streisand/Sydney Chaplin/Kay Medford/Jean Stapleton/Danny Meehan.
27	The Grass Harp (1952)	Mildred Natwick/Russell Collins.
28	The Philadelphia Story (1939)	Katharine Hepburn/Joseph Cotten/Van Heflin/Shirley Booth/Frank Fenton.
29	The King And I (1951)	Gertrude Lawrence/Yul Brynner.
30	Applause (1970)	Lauren Bacall.
31	The Glass Menagerie (1945)	Laurette Taylor/Eddie Dowling/Julie Haydon/Anthony Ross.

APRIL

	Title	Leading Performer(s)
1	Watch On The Rhine (1941)	Paul Lukas/Mady Christians/Lucile Watson/George Coulouris/Ann Blyth.
2	Small Craft Warnings (1972)	EP
3	Justice (1916)	John Barrymore.
4	Follies (1971)	Alexis Smith/Dorothy Collins/Yvonne de Carlo/John McMartin/Gene Nelson.
5	A Thousand Clowns (1962)	Jason Robards/Sandy Dennis.
6	Don Juan In Hell (1952–R)	Charles Boyer/Charles Laughton/Cedric Hardwicke/Agnes Moorehead.
7	South Pacific (1949)	Mary Martin/Ezio Pinza.
8	Follow The Girls (1944)	Gertrude Niesen/Jackie Gleason/Irina Baranova/Frank Parker.
9	Diamond Lil (1928)	Mae West.
10	George M! (1968)	Joel Grey.
11	On Your Toes (1936)	Ray Bolger/Tamara Geva/Monty Woolley.
12	The Searching Wind (1944)	Dennis King/Cornelia Otis Skinner/Dudley Digges/Montgomery Clift.
13	What A Life (1938)	Ezra Stone/Betty Field.
14	Bye Bye Birdie (1960)	Dick Van Dyke/Chita Rivera/Paul Lynde/Kay Medford/Michael J. Pollard.
15	The Boys In The Band (1968)	Kenneth Nelson/Cliff Gorman/Laurence Luckinbill/Leonard Frey.
16	The Playboy Of The Western World (1921)	Thomas Mitchell.
17	No Time For Comedy (1939)	Katharine Cornell/Laurence Olivier/John Williams/Margalo Gillmore/Robert Flemyng.
18	Call Me Mister (1946)	Betty Garrett/Jules Munshin.
19	Waiting For Godot (1956)	Bert Lahr/E. G. Marshall.
20	The Golden Apple (1954)	Kaye Ballard/Priscilla Gilette/Stephen Douglass/Jack Whiting.
21	Inherit The Wind (1955)	Paul Muni/Ed Begley/Tony Randall.
22	Jumpers (1974)	Brian Bedford.
23	Kind Lady (1935)	Grace George/Henry Daniell.
24	Peter Pan (1950–R)	Jean Arthur/Boris Karloff.
25	Little Murders (1967)	Elliott Gould/Barbara Cook/David Steinberg.

Title	Leading Performer(s)
26 Company (1970)	Dean Jones/Elaine Stritch.
27 Candida (1942–R)	Katharine Cornell/Burgess Meredith/ Raymond Massey/Dudley Digges/ Mildred Natwick.
28 The Play's The Thing (1948–R)	Louis Calhern/Faye Emerson.
29 There Shall Be No Night (1940)	The Lunts/Sydney Greenstreet/Richard Whorf/Montgomery Clift.
30 The Little Show (1929)	Clifton Webb/Libby Holman/Fred Allen/ Portland Hoffa/Romney Brent.

MAY

Title	Leading Performer(s)
1 The Medium (1947)	Marie Powers.
2 That Championship Season (1972)	Richard Dysart/Charles Durning/Paul Sorvino/Walter McGinn/Michael McGuire.
3 The Fantasticks* (1960)	Jerry Orbach/Kenneth Nelson/Rita Gardner.
4 The Blacks (1961)	EP
5 The Visit (1958)	The Lunts.
6 Henry IV (1946–R)	Laurence Olivier/Ralph Richardson/ Margaret Leighton/George Relph.
7 Can-Can (1953)	Lilo/Peter Cookson/Gwen Verdon/Hans Conried/Erik Rhodes.
8 A Funny Thing Happened On The Way To The Forum (1962)	Zero Mostel/David Burns/Jack Gilford.
9 Romeo and Juliet (1940–R)	Laurence Olivier/Vivien Leigh/Edmond O'Brien/Dame May Whitty/Cornel Wilde.
10 The Lovers (1956)	Darren McGavin/Joanne Woodward.
11 Once Upon A Mattress (1959)	Carol Burnett.
12 The Nervous Set (1959)	EP
13 The Pajama Game (1954)	John Raitt/Janis Paige/Eddie Foy, Jr.
14 New Girl In Town (1957)	Gwen Verdon/Thelma Ritter.
15 The Brig (1963)	EP
16 Annie Get Your Gun (1946)	Ethel Merman.
17 Godspell (1971)	EP
18 Scapino (1974–R)	Jim Dale.
19 Room Service (1937)	Sam Levene/Eddie Albert/Donald MacBride/Betty Field.
20 Uncle Harry (1942)	Joseph Schildkraut/Eva Le Gallienne.
21 Gypsy (1959)	Ethel Merman/Jack Klugman/Sandra Church.
22 Othello (1945–R)	Paul Robeson/Jose Ferrer/Uta Hagen.
23 Abie's Irish Rose (1922)	EP
24 Mame (1966)	Angela Lansbury.
25 The Subject Was Roses (1964)	Jack Albertson/Irene Dailey/Martin Sheen.
26 Lenny (1971)	Cliff Gorman.
27 The Knack (1964)	George Segal/Brian Bedford.
28 Louisiana Purchase (1940)	William Gaxton/Victor Moore/Zorina/ Irene Bordoni/Carol Bruce.
29 Top-Notchers (1942)	Gracie Fields/Zero Mostel/Argentinita.

*Longest-running production in the history of the American theatre.

Title	Leading Performer(s)
30 Brigadoon (1962–R)	Peter Palmer/Farley Granger/Sally Ann Howes/Edward Villella.
31 Around The World (1946)	Orson Welles/Arthur Margetson/Mary Healy.

JUNE

Title	Leading Performer(s)
1 Concert Varieties (1945)	Jerome Robbins/Zero Mostel/Imogene Coca/Katherine Dunham/Deems Taylor.
2 Snapshots (1921)	Nora Bayes/Lew Fields/Gilda Gray.
3 The Band Wagon (1931)	Fred & Adele Astaire/Frank Morgan/Helen Broderick/Tilly Losch.
4 Uncle Vanya (1973–R)	George C. Scott/Julie Christie/Nicol Williamson/Lillian Gish/Cathleen Nesbitt.
5 Lysistrata (1930–R)	Violet Kemble Cooper/Miriam Hopkins/Sydney Greenstreet/Ernest Truex/Albert Dekker.
6 Hitchy-Koo (1918)	Raymond Hitchcock/Leon Errol/Irene Bordoni.
7 Grease (1972)	EP
8 Garrick Gaieties (1925)	EP
9 Baby Mine (1927–R)	Humphrey Bogart/Roscoe ("Fatty") Arbuckle/Lee Patrick.
10 Ulysses In Nighttown (1958)	Zero Mostel/Beatrice Arthur/Carroll O'Connor/Belita/Swen Swenson/John Astin.
11 Henry IV (1968–R)	Stacy Keach.
12 Ziegfeld Follies (1917)	W. C. Fields/Will Rogers/Eddie Cantor/Fanny Brice/Bert Williams.
13 Shangri-La (1956)	Dennis King/Carol Lawrence/Jack Cassidy/Alice Ghostley/Harold Lang.
14 New Faces (1956)	T. C. Jones/John Reardon/Maggie Smith/Inga Swenson/Jane Connell.
15 Ziegfeld Follies (1908)	Nora Bayes/Jack Norworth/Mae Murray.
16 The Cradle Will Rock (1937)	EP
17 Oh, Calcutta! (1969)	EP
18 The Cage (1970)	EP
19 Streets of Paris (1939)	Abbott & Costello/Carmen Miranda/Jean Sablon/Bobby Clark/Luella Gear/Gower Champion.
20 Hamlet (1972–R)	Stacy Keach/Colleen Dewhurst/James Earl Jones/Sam Waterston/Barnard Hughes.
21 The Wind Is Ninety (1945)	Kirk Douglas/Wendell Corey.
22 The Three Sisters (1964–R)	Kim Stanley/Geraldine Page/Shirley Knight.
23 Shakespeare Chronicles (1970–R)	EP
24 Star And Garter (1942)	Gypsy Rose Lee/Bobby Clark.
25 Wish You Were Here (1952)	Jack Cassidy/Sheila Bond/Pat Marand.
26 Ziegfeld Follies (1911)	Fanny Brice/Leon Errol/Bessie McCoy/Bert Williams/Dolly Sisters.
27 Ten Little Indians (1944)	Estelle Winwood/Halliwell Hobbes/Michael Whalen/Claudia Morgan.

Title	Leading Performer(s)
28 Peep Show (1950)	EP
29 A Midsummer Night's Dream (1967–R)	EP
30 Steambath (1970)	Anthony Perkins/Conrad Bain/Mitchell Jason.

JULY

	Title	Leading Performer(s)
1	Vanities (1930)	Jack Benny/Jimmy Savo/Patsy Kelly.
2	Show Girl (1929)	Ruby Keeler/Jimmy Durante/Eddie Foy, Jr./Frank McHugh/Harriet Hoctor.
3	The Defender (1902)	Blanche Ring/Harry Davenport.
4	This Is The Army (1942)	EP
5	Padlocks (1927)	Texas Guinan/Lillian Roth/Jay C. Flippen/George Raft.
6	Yokel Boy (1939)	Buddy Ebsen/Judy Canova/Phil Silvers.
7	Cabalgata (1949)	EP
8	Peer Gynt (1969–R)	Stacy Keach/Estelle Parsons.
9	Yours, A. Lincoln (1942)	Vincent Price.
10	John Ferguson (1933–R)	Augustin Duncan.
11	Africana (1927)	Ethel Waters.
12	The Midnight Rounders (1920)	EP
13	Patience (1896–R)	Lillian Russell.
14	The Mikado (1902–R)	EP
15	Miss Liberty (1949)	Eddie Albert/Allyn McLerie/Mary McCarty/Ethel Griffies.
16	Sweeney Todd (1924)	Robert Vivian.
17	The American Way (1939–R)	Fredric March/Florence Eldridge.
18	Marinka (1945)	Joan Roberts/Harry Stockwell.
19	Two On The Aisle (1951)	Bert Lahr/Dolores Gray.
20	Ti-Jean And His Brothers (1972)	EP
21	Shoot The Works (1931)	Heywood Broun/Imogene Coca/George Murphy.
22	Two Gentlemen of Verona (1971)	EP
23*	— — — — — — — — — —	
24	Parisienne (1950)	Francis Lederer/Faye Emerson/Helmut Dantine/Romney Brent.
25	Lovers (1968)	Art Carney.
26	King Lear (1973–R)	James Earl Jones.
27	Poor Little Ritz Girl (1920)	Eleanor Griffith/Charles Purcell.
28	A Voice In The Dark (1919)	William Boyd.
29	The Gay Hussars (1909)	EP
30	Opportunity (1920)	Nita Naldi.
31	Judy Garland At Home At The Palace (1967)	Judy Garland/John Bubbles/Jackie Vernon, Lorna & Joey Luft.

---

*A black day in the history of the American theatre—no openings on this date. . . . Birthdate (1915) of Vincent Sardi, Jr. in whose restaurant Broadway opening nights have long been traditionally celebrated.

AUGUST

	Title	Leading Performer(s)
1	School For Brides (1944)	Roscoe Karns/Yolande Donlan.
2	Catherine Was Great (1944)	Mae West.
3	The Two Mrs. Carrolls (1943)	Elisabeth Bergner/Victor Jory/Irene Worth.
4	The Merry Widow (1943–R)	Jan Kiepura/Marta Eggerth/Melville Cooper/David Wayne/Gene Barry.
5	Dancing Partner (1930)	Lynne Overman/Irene Purcell/Henry Stephenson.
6	It's A Wise Child (1929)	Humphrey Bogart.
7	The Lady From The Sea (1950–R)	Luise Rainer/Herbert Berghof/Anne Jackson/Steven Hill/Jeff Morrow.
8	Shore Leave (1922)	Frances Starr/James Rennie.
9	Tangerine (1921)	Frank Crumit/Julia Sanderson.
10	Much Ado About Nothing (1972–R)	Sam Waterston/Kathleen Widdoes.
11	Dancing Mothers (1924)	Helen Hayes/Mary Young/John Halliday.
12	Cymbeline (1971–R)	EP
13	Dulcy (1921)	Lynn Fontanne/Elliott Nugent/Howard Lindsay.
14	The Front Page (1928)	Lee Tracy/Osgood Perkins.
15	Tenth Avenue (1927)	Frank Morgan/William Boyd/Edna Hibbard/Frank McHugh/Gregory Ratoff.
16	Maytime (1917)	Peggy Wood.
17	The Man From Home (1908)	William Hodge.
18	Gay Paree (1925)	Chic Sale/Winnie Lightner/Jack Haley.
19	On Trial (1914)	EP
20	The Dream Girl (1924)	Fay Bainter.
21	Song Of Norway (1944)	Lawrence Brooks/Irra Petina.
22	Everything (1918)	Houdini/DeWolf Hopper.
23	The Bat (1920)	Effie Ellsler/May Vokes.
24	The Girl From Utah (1914)	Julia Sanderson/Donald Brian.
25	Six-Cylinder Love (1921)	Ernest Truex/June Walker/Hedda Hopper/Donald Meek/Berton Churchill.
26	Lightnin' (1918)	Frank Bacon.
27	Life Begins At 8:40 (1934)	Bert Lahr/Ray Bolger.
28	Scandals (1939)	The Three Stooges/Ann Miller/Ella Logan/Willie & Eugene Howard/Ben Blue.
29	The Torch Bearers (1922)	Mary Boland/Alison Skipworth.
30	Anna Lucasta (1944)	EP
31	Rosemary (1896)	Maude Adams/John Drew/Ethel Barrymore.

SEPTEMBER

	Title	Leading Performer(s)
1	Burlesque (1927)	Barbara Stanwyck/Hal Skelly/Oscar Levant.
2	Rose Marie (1924)	Dennis King/Mary Ellis.
3	What Price Glory? (1924)	William Boyd/Louis Wolheim.
4	The Prisoner Of Zenda (1895)	E. H. Sothern.
5	A Flag Is Born (1946)	Paul Muni/Marlon Brando.
6	Good News (1927)	John Price Jones/Mary Lawlor/Zelma O'Neal.

548 THEATRE CALENDAR

	Title	Leading Performer(s)
7	Machinal (1928)	Zita Johann/Clark Gable.
8	Murder At The Vanities (1933)	Bela Lugosi/Olga Baclanova/James Rennie.
9	Forever After (1918)	Alice Brady/Conrad Nagel.
10	The Wookey (1941)	Edmund Gwenn.
11	Hold On To Your Hats (1940)	Al Jolson/Martha Raye.
12	The Circle (1921)	Mrs. Leslie Carter/John Drew.
13	The Chocolate Soldier (1909)	EP
14	Scandals (1931)	Ethel Merman/Rudy Vallee/Ray Bolger/Willie & Eugene Howard.
15	End As A Man (1953)	Ben Gazzara/Pat Hingle/Anthony Franciosa/Paul Richards/Albert Salmi.
16	Broadway (1926)	Lee Tracy.
17	Much Ado About Nothing (1959–R)	John Gielgud/Margaret Leighton.
18	The Awful Truth (1922)	Ina Claire.
19	At Home Abroad (1935)	Beatrice Lillie/Ethel Waters/Eleanor Powell.
20	Clarence (1919)	Alfred Lunt/Helen Hayes/Mary Boland.
21	The Vagabond King (1925)	Dennis King.
22	Fiddler On The Roof (1964)	Zero Mostel.
23	Fine And Dandy (1930)	Joe Cook.
24	Once In A Lifetime (1930)	Hugh O'Connell/Jean Dixon/Grant Mills/Spring Byington/George S. Kaufman.
25	Winterset (1935)	Burgess Meredith.
26	West Side Story (1957)	Carol Lawrence/Larry Kert/Chita Rivera.
27	Vanities (1932)	Milton Berle/Helen Broderick/Will Fyffe/Harriet Hoctor/Robert Cummings.
28	Night Must Fall (1936)	Emlyn Williams/Dame May Whitty.
29	The Heiress (1947)	Wendy Hiller/Basil Rathbone.
30	Tea And Sympathy (1953)	Deborah Kerr.

OCTOBER

	Title	Leading Performer(s)
1	Command Decision (1947)	Paul Kelly/James Whitmore.
2	Ah, Wilderness! (1933)	George M. Cohan.
3	The Great White Hope (1968)	James Earl Jones/Jane Alexander.
4	The Caretaker (1961)	Alan Bates/Robert Shaw/Donald Pleasence.
5	The Diary Of Anne Frank (1955)	Joseph Schildkraut/Susan Strasberg.
6	Summer And Smoke (1948)	Margaret Phillips/Tod Andrews.
7	One Touch Of Venus (1943)	Mary Martin/John Boles/Kenny Baker.
8	Hamlet (1936–R)	John Gielgud/Judith Anderson/Lillian Gish.
9	The Iceman Cometh (1946)	James Barton/Dudley Digges.
10	Porgy And Bess (1935)	Todd Duncan/Anne Brown.
11	Where's Charley? (1948)	Ray Bolger.
12	Call Me Madam (1950)	Ethel Merman.
13	Who's Afraid Of Virginia Woolf? (1962)	Uta Hagen/Arthur Hill/George Grizzard/Melinda Dillon.
14	How To Succeed In Business Without Really Trying (1961)	Robert Morse/Rudy Vallee.
15	Abe Lincoln In Illinois (1938)	Raymond Massey.
16	The Man Who Came To Dinner (1939)	Monty Woolley.
17	Personal Appearance (1934)	Gladys George.

	Title	Leading Performer(s)
18	A Shot In The Dark (1961)	Julie Harris/Walter Matthau/William Shatner.
19	The Miracle Worker (1959)	Anne Bancroft/Patty Duke/Patricia Neal.
20	No Time For Sergeants (1955)	Andy Griffith/Myron McCormick/Roddy McDowall.
21	The Merry Widow (1907)	Ethel Jackson/Donald Brian.
22	Take Me Along (1959)	Jackie Gleason/Walter Pidgeon/Eileen Herlie/Robert Morse/Una Merkel.
23	Barefoot In The Park (1963)	Robert Redford/Elizabeth Ashley/Kurt Kasznar/Mildred Natwick.
24	Equus (1974)	Anthony Hopkins/Peter Firth.
25	The Time Of Your Life (1939)	Eddie Dowling/Julie Haydon/Celeste Holm/Gene Kelly/William Bendix.
26	Mourning Becomes Electra (1931)	Alice Brady/Nazimova.
27	Beyond The Fringe (1962)	Peter Cook/Dudley Moore/Jonathan Miller/Alan Bennett.
28	Dead End (1935)	EP
29	Hair (1967)	EP
30	Panama Hattie (1940)	Ethel Merman/James Dunn/Betty Hutton/Arthur Treacher/Rags Ragland.
31	More Stately Mansions (1967)	Ingrid Bergman/Colleen Dewhurst/Arthur Hill.

NOVEMBER

	Title	Leading Performer(s)
1	Harvey (1944)	Frank Fay/Josephine Hull.
2	I'd Rather Be Right (1937)	George M. Cohan.
3	Elizabeth The Queen (1930)	The Lunts.
4	Fanny (1954)	Ezio Pinza/Walter Slezak/Florence Henderson.
5	Blithe Spirit (1941)	Clifton Webb/Mildred Natwick/Peggy Wood/Leonora Corbett.
6	Counsellor-At-Law (1931)	Paul Muni.
7	Long Day's Journey Into Night (1956)	Fredric March/Florence Eldridge/Jason Robards/Bradford Dillman.
8	Life With Father (1939)	Howard Lindsay/Dorothy Stickney.
9	A Hatful Of Rain (1955)	Ben Gazzara/Shelley Winters/Anthony Franciosa.
10	The Country Girl (1950)	Uta Hagen/Paul Kelly/Steven Hill.
11	The Prisoner Of Second Avenue (1971)	Peter Falk/Lee Grant.
12	Sleuth (1970)	Anthony Quayle/Keith Baxter.
13	Grand Hotel (1930)	Eugenie Leontovich/Henry Hull/Sam Jaffe.
14	State Of The Union (1945)	Ralph Bellamy/Ruth Hussey.
15	Li'l Abner (1956)	Peter Palmer/Edith Adams/Stubby Kaye.
16	Hamlet (1922–R)	John Barrymore.
17	The Lark (1955)	Julie Harris/Boris Karloff/Christopher Plummer.
18	The Skin Of Our Teeth (1942)	Tallulah Bankhead/Fredric March/Florence Eldridge/Montgomery Clift.
19	Twelfth Night (1940–R)	Helen Hayes/Maurice Evans.
20	Cabaret (1966)	Joel Grey/Jill Haworth/Bert Convy/Lotte Lenya/Jack Gilford.

	Title	Leading Performer(s)
21	Anything Goes (1934)	Ethel Merman/William Gaxton/Victor Moore.
22	Man Of La Mancha (1965)	Richard Kiley.
23	Of Mice And Men (1937)	Wallace Ford/Broderick Crawford.
24	Guys And Dolls (1950)	Robert Alda/Sam Levene/Vivian Blaine.
25	The Pirate (1942)	The Lunts.
26	The Corn Is Green (1940)	Ethel Barrymore.
27	Mary Of Scotland (1933)	Helen Hayes.
28	Look Homeward, Angel (1957)	Anthony Perkins/Jo Van Fleet/Hugh Griffith/Arthur Hill
29	Bells Are Ringing (1956)	Judy Holliday/Sydney Chaplin/Jean Stapleton.
30	All The Way Home (1960)	Colleen Dewhurst/Arthur Hill/Lillian Gish/Aline MacMahon.

DECEMBER

	Title	Leading Performer(s)
1	Lady, Be Good (1924)	Fred and Adele Astaire/Cliff Edwards.
2	Carmen Jones (1943)	EP
3	A Streetcar Named Desire (1947)	Jessica Tandy/Marlon Brando/Kim Hunter/Karl Malden.
4	Tobacco Road (1933)	Henry Hull.
5	Angel Street (1941)	Vincent Price/Judith Evelyn/Leo G. Carroll.
6	DuBarry Was A Lady (1939)	Ethel Merman/Bert Lahr/Betty Grable.
7	Seven Lively Arts (1944)	Beatrice Lillie/Bert Lahr/Anton Dolin/Alicia Markova/Benny Goodman.
8	The Voice Of The Turtle (1943)	Margaret Sullavan/Elliott Nugent/Audrey Christie.
9	Major Barbara (1915)	Grace George/Louis Calvert/Conway Tearle.
10	In Praise Of Love (1974)	Rex Harrison/Julie Harris/Martin Gabel.
11	J.B. (1958)	Pat Hingle/Raymond Massey/Christopher Plummer.
12	Biography (1932)	Ina Claire.
13	Hamlet (1945–R)	Maurice Evans.
14	You Can't Take It With You (1936)	Henry Travers/Josephine Hull.
15	Two's Company (1952)	Bette Davis.
16	Lend An Ear (1948)	Carol Channing/William Eythe/Gene Nelson.
17	Oh, Men! Oh, Women! (1953)	Franchot Tone/Gig Young/Larry Blyden/Betsy von Furstenberg/Anne Jackson.
18	Coco (1969)	Katharine Hepburn.
19	The Music Man (1957)	Robert Preston.
20	Romeo And Juliet (1934–R)	Katharine Cornell/Basil Rathbone/Edith Evans/Brian Aherne/Orson Welles.
21	The Three Sisters (1942–R)	Katharine Cornell/Judith Anderson/Ruth Gordon.
22	Outward Bound (1938–R)	Laurette Taylor/Vincent Price/Florence Reed.
23	Dear Brutus (1918)	William Gillette/Helen Hayes.
24	Twentieth Century (1950–R)	Gloria Swanson/Jose Ferrer.
25	Pal Joey (1940)	Gene Kelly/Vivienne Segal.

	Title	Leading Performer(s)
26	Of Thee I Sing (1931)	William Gaxton/Victor Moore.
27	Show Boat (1927)	Norma Terris/Howard Marsh/Helen Morgan/Charles Winninger/Edna May Oliver.
28	The Night Of The Iguana (1961)	Bette Davis/Margaret Leighton/Alan Webb/Patrick O'Neal.
29	A Moon For The Misbegotten (1973–R)	Colleen Dewhurst/Jason Robards/Ed Flanders.
30	Kiss Me, Kate (1948)	Alfred Drake/Patricia Morison/Harold Lang/Lisa Kirk.
31	Caprice (1928)	The Lunts.

Appendix II
Debuts: Actors

The following appendix highlights the New York stage debuts—the first significant (speaking) roles—of approximately one thousand contemporary actors. Though the list features a sprinkling of illustrious names of the past, the emphasis is on twentieth-century performers—including a sizable contingent of Hollywood stars who, at one time or another, braved Broadway. This compilation, it might be noted, is the most comprehensive of its kind ever published.—E.M.B.

Abbreviations:
    OB: Off-Broadway
    R: Dramatic or Musical Revue
    TR: Title Role

ADAMS, MAUDE	Suzanne in The Masked Ball	1892
ADLER, LUTHER	Leon Kantor in Humoresque	1923
ADLER, STELLA	Baroness Creme de la Creme in The Straw Hat	1926
AHERNE, BRIAN	Robert Browning in The Barretts Of Wimpole Street	1931
ALBERT, EDDIE	Bing in Brother Rat	1936
ALBERTSON, JACK	Meet The People (R)	1940
ALBERTSON, FRANK	Billy in Brother Rat	1936
ALDA, ALAN	Telephone Man in Only In America	1959
ALDA, ROBERT	Sky Masterson in Guys And Dolls	1950
ALEXANDER, JANE	Eleanor in The Great White Hope	1968
ALLEN, ELIZABETH	Juliet in Romanoff And Juliet	1957
ALLEN, FRED	The Passing Show (R)	1922
ALLEN, STEVE	Jerry in The Pink Elephant	1953
ALLEN, WOODY	Allan in Play It Again, Sam	1969
ALLGOOD, SARA	Widow Quin in The Playboy Of The Western World	1911
ALLYSON, JUNE	Minerva in Best Foot Forward	1941
AMECHE, DON	Steve Canfield in Silk Stockings	1955
ANDERS, GLENN	Harry Wattles in Just Around The Corner	1919
ANDERSON, JUDITH	Mrs. Bellmore in On The Stairs	1922

ANDREWS, DANA	Jerry in Two For The Seesaw	1958
ANDREWS, JULIE	Polly in The Boy Friend	1954
ANDREWS SISTERS, THE	Pauline and Paulette in Over Here!	1974
ANGLIN, MARGARET	Madeleine West in Shenandoah	1894
ARBUCKLE, ROSCOE ("FATTY")	Jimmy Jenks in Baby Mine	1927
ARDEN, EVE	Ziegfeld Follies (R)	1934
ARKIN, ALAN	The Singer in Heloise (OB)	1958
ARLISS, GEORGE	Cayley Drummle in The Second Mrs. Tanqueray	1902
ARNAUD, YVONNE	Mrs. Pepys in And So To Bed	1927
ARNAZ, DESI	Manuelito in Too Many Girls	1939
ARNOLD, EDWARD	Charles in She Would And She Did	1919
ARTHUR, BEATRICE	Lucy Brown in The Threepenny Opera (OB)	1954
ARTHUR, JEAN	Ann in Foreign Affairs	1932
ASHCROFT, PEGGY	Lise in High Tor	1937
ASHLEY, ELIZABETH	Abigail in The Crucible (OB)	1959
ASNER, EDWARD	Mr. Peachum in The Threepenny Opera (OB)	1955
ASTAIRE, ADELE	Over The Top (R)	1919
ASTAIRE, FRED	Over The Top (R)	
ASTOR, MARY	Cynthia in Many Happy Returns	1945
ATWILL, LIONEL	The Lodger (TR)	1917
AUBERJONOIS, RENE	The Fool in King Lear	1968
AUMONT, JEAN-PIERRE	Pierre in My Name Is Aquilon	1949
AYLMER, FELIX	General Canynge in Loyalties	1922
BACALL, LAUREN	Charlie in Goodbye Charlie	1959
BACON, FRANK	William Carr in Stop Thief	1912
BADDELEY, HERMIONE	Helen in A Taste Of Honey	1960
BADEL, ALAN	Hero in The Rehearsal	1963
BAILEY, PEARL	Butterfly in St. Louis Woman	1946
BAINTER, FAY	Celine in The Rose Of Panama	1912
BAKER, CARROLL	Ruth in All Summer Long	1954
BALL, LUCILLE	"Wildcat" Johnson in Wildcat	1960
BALLARD, KAYE	Three To Make Ready (R)	1946
BALSAM, MARTIN	Mr. Blow in Ghost For Sale	1941
BANCROFT, ANNE	Gittel in Two For The Seesaw	1958
BANKHEAD, TALLULAH	Penelope Penn in 39 East	1919
BARA, THEDA	Ruth Gordon in The Blue Flame	1920
BARRYMORE, DIANA	Caroline Bronson in The Romantic Mr. Dickens	1940
BARRYMORE, ETHEL	Julia in The Rivals	1894
BARRYMORE, JOHN	Corley in Glad Of It	1903
BARRYMORE, LIONEL	Organ Grinder in The Mummy and the Hummingbird	1902
BARTHELMESS, RICHARD	Frank in The Postman Always Rings Twice	1936
BARTON, JAMES	The Passing Show (R)	1919
BASEHART, RICHARD	Weiler in Counterattack	1943
BATES, ALAN	Cliff in Look Back In Anger	1957
BATES, BLANCHE	Bianca in The Taming Of The Shrew	1897
BAXTER, ANNE	Elizabeth in Seen But Not Heard	1936
BAXTER, WARNER	Ricardo in Lombardi, Ltd.	1917
BEAN, ORSON	Edgar in Men Of Distinction	1953
BEATTY, WARREN	Kenny in A Loss of Roses	1959
BEDFORD, BRIAN	Clive Harrington in Five Finger Exercise	1959
BEGLEY, ED	Von Obermann in Land Of Fame	1943
BELAFONTE, HARRY	Almanac (R)	1953
BEL GEDDES, BARBARA	Dottie in Out Of The Frying Pan	1941
BELLAMY, RALPH	Ben in Town Boy	1929

BENDIX, WILLIAM	Krupp in The Time Of Your Life	1939
BENJAMIN, RICHARD	Norman in The Star-Spangled Girl	1966
BENNETT, CONSTANCE	Elsa in A Date With April	1953
BENNETT, JOAN	Daisy in Jarnegan	1928
BENNETT, RICHARD	Jake in The Limited Mail	1891
BENNY, JACK	Great Temptations (R)	1926
BERG, GERTRUDE	Molly in Me And Molly	1948
BERGEN, POLLY	Almanac (R)	1953
BERGMAN, INGRID	Julie in Liliom	1940
BERGNER, ELISABETH	Gemma in Escape Me Never	1935
BERLE, MILTON	Vanities (R)	1932
BERNARDI, HERSCHEL	Cockeye Johnny in Bajour	1964
BEST, EDNA	Pamela in These Charming People	1925
BICKFORD, CHARLES	Owen in Dark Rosaleen	1919
BLACK, KAREN	Olivia in Twelfth Night (OB)	1963
BLACKMER, SIDNEY	Will Crosby in The Thirteenth Chair	1916
BLAINE, VIVIAN	Miss Adelaide in *Guys And Dolls*	1950
BLINN, HOLBROOK	Corporal Ferry in The New South	1893
BLONDELL, JOAN	Etta in Maggie The Magnificent	1929
BLOOM, CLAIRE	The Queen in Richard II	1956
BLORE, ERIC	Bertie Bird in Little Miss Bluebeard	1923
BLYDEN, LARRY	Ensign Pulver in Mister Roberts	1948
BLYTH, ANN	Babette in Watch On The Rhine	1941
BOGART, HUMPHREY	Ernie Crockett in Drifting	1922
BOLAND, MARY	Dorothy in Strongheart	1905
BOLES, JOHN	Paul Revere in Little Jessie James	1923
BOLGER, RAY	The Merry World (R)	1926
BONDI, BEULAH	Maggie in One Of The Family	1925
BOONE, RICHARD	Mr. Stephens in The Man	1950
BOOTH, SHIRLEY	Nan in Hell's Bells	1925
BORDONI, IRENE	Broadway To Paris (R)	1912
BORGNINE, ERNEST	Nelson in Mrs. McThing	1952
BOSLEY, TOM	Fiorello LaGuardia in Fiorello!	1959
BOYER, CHARLES	Hoederer in Red Gloves	1948
BRACKEN, EDDIE	Bill in What A Life	1938
BRADY, ALICE	Olga in The Balkan Princess	1911
BRANDO, MARLON	Nels in I Remember Mama	1944
BRENNAN, EILEEN	Little Mary Sunshine (TR/OB)	1959
BRENT, GEORGE	The Chauffeur in Love, Honor And Betray	1930
BRENT, ROMNEY	Tommy Todd in The Lucky One	1922
BRICE, FANNY	Ziegfeld Follies (R)	1910
BRIDGES, LLOYD	Tom in Suzanna And The Elders	1940
BRODERICK, HELEN	Miss Winston in Jumping Jupiter	1911
BROOK, CLIVE	Josiah Bolton in Second Threshold	1951
BROWN, JOE E.	Phillip in Jim Jam Jems	1920
BROWN, PAMELA	Gwendolyn in The Importance Of Being Earnest	1947
BROWNE, CORAL	Zambina in Tamburlaine The Great	1956
BROWNE, IRENE	Stella in The Happy Husband	1928
BROWNE, ROSCOE LEE	Archibald in The Blacks (OB)	1961
BRUCE, CAROL	Beatrice in Louisiana Purchase	1940
BRUCE, NIGEL	Major Evelyn Bathurst in This Was A Man	1926
BRUCE, VIRGINIA	Miss Mulligan in America's Sweetheart	1931
BRYNNER, YUL	Fabian in Twelfth Night	1941
BUCHANAN, JACK	Charlot's Revue (R)	1924
BUCHOLZ, HORST	Frederick in Cheri	1959
BURKE, BILLIE	Julia in My Wife	1907

BURNETT, CAROL	Princess Winnifred in Once Upon A Mattress	1959
BURNS, DAVID	Mr. B in Polly Preferred	1923
BURSTYN, ELLEN	Susan Hammarlee in Fair Game	1957
BURTON, RICHARD	Richard in The Lady's Not For Burning	1950
BUTTERWORTH, CHARLES	Americana (R)	1926
BYINGTON, SPRING	Miss Hey in Beggar On Horseback	1924
CAESAR, SID	Make Mine Manhattan (R)	1948
CAGNEY, JAMES	Little Red in Outside Looking In (OB)	1925
CALDWELL, ZOE	Sister Jeanne in The Devils	1965
CALHERN, LOUIS	Eugene in Roger Bloomer	1923
CAMBRIDGE, GODFREY	The Butler in Nature's Way	1957
CAMPBELL, MRS. PATRICK	Magda (TR)	1902
CANNON, DYAN	Kathy in The Fun Couple	1962
CANNON, J. D.	Dogberry in Much Ado About Nothing (OB)	1955
CANOVA, JUDY	Calling All Stars (R)	1934
CANTOR, EDDIE	Ziegfeld Follies (R)	1917
CAREY, HARRY	Ed in Heavenly Express	1940
CAREY, MACDONALD	Charley in Lady In The Dark	1941
CARLISLE, KITTY	Prince Orlofsky in Champagne Sec	1933
CARLSON, RICHARD	Lawrence in Now You've Done It	1937
CARMICHAEL, IAN	Robert in Boeing-Boeing	1965
CARNEY, ART	James in The Rope Dancers	1957
CARNOVSKY, MORRIS	Magistrate in The Failures	1923
CARRADINE, DAVID	Atahuallpa in The Royal Hunt Of The Sun	1964
CARRADINE, JOHN	The Cardinal in The Duchess of Malfi	1946
CARRILLO, LEO	Giovanni in Fads And Fancies	1915
CARROLL, DIAHANN	Ottilie in House Of Flowers	1954
CARROLL, LEO G.	Dick in Rutherford And Son	1912
CARROLL, MADELEINE	Agatha in Goodbye, My Fancy	1948
CARROLL, NANCY	Jane in Mayflowers	1925
CARSON, JACK	Wintergreen in Of Thee I Sing	1952
CARSON, JOHNNY	Augie Poole in The Tunnel of Love	1957
CARTER, MRS. LESLIE	Kate in The Ugly Duckling	1890
CASS, PEGGY	Touch And Go (R)	1949
CASSIDY, JACK	Small Wonder (R)	1948
CATLETT, WALTER	Artie in The Prince Of Pilsen	1910
CHANNING, CAROL	Steve in Proof Through The Night	1942
CHAPLIN, GERALDINE	Alexandra in The Little Foxes	1967
CHAPLIN, SYDNEY	Jeff in Bells Are Ringing	1956
CHASE, ILKA	Sister Francesca in The Red Falcon	1924
CHATTERTON, RUTH	Isolde in The Great Name	1911
CHRISTIANS, MADY	Liza in A Divine Drudge	1933
CHRISTIE, AUDREY	Olive in Follow Thru	1929
CHRISTIE, JULIE	Luciana in The Comedy Of Errors	1964
CILENTO, DIANE	Helen in Tiger At The Gates	1955
CLAIRE, INA	Molly in Jumping Jupiter	1911
CLARK, BOBBY	Chuckles (R)	1922
CLARK, DANE	Dominic in The Number	1951
CLARK, FRED	Robert in Schoolhouse On The Lot	1938
CLIFT, MONTGOMERY	Harmer in Fly Away Home	1935
COBB, LEE J.	Koch in Crime And Punishment	1935
COBURN, CHARLES	Dudley in The Coming Of Mrs. Patrick	1907
COCA, IMOGENE	Garrick Gaieties (R)	1930
COCO, JAMES	Tabu in Hotel Paradiso	1957
COHAN, GEORGE M.	Algy in The Governor's Son	1901

COLBERT, CLAUDETTE	Sybil in The Wild Westcotts	1923
COLLIER, CONSTANCE	Anne-Marie in Samson	1908
COLLINGE, PATRICIA	Joyce in The Thunderbolt	1910
COLMAN, RONALD	Temple Priest in The Green Goddess	1921
COMPTON, FAY	Victoria in Tonight's The Night	1914
CONNOLLY, WALTER	Sylvius in As You Like It	1910
CONRIED, HANS	Boris in Can-Can	1953
CONROY, FRANK	Menelaus in Helena's Husband	1915
CONTE, RICHARD	Julio in Heavenly Express	1940
CONVY, BERT	Billy Barnes Revue (R)	1959
COOK, BARBARA	Sandy in Flahooley	1951
COOK, DONALD	John in Seed Of The Brute	1926
COOK, ELISHA	Felix in The Crooked Friday	1925
COOK, JOE	Hitchy-Koo (R)	1919
COOPER, GLADYS	Marietta in The Shining Hour	1934
COOPER, JACKIE	Andy in Magnolia Alley	1949
COOPER, MELVILLE	Bernard in Laburnum Grove	1935
COREY, WENDELL	Joe in Comes The Revelation	1942
CORNELL, KATHARINE	Eileen in Nice People	1921
COTTEN, JOSEPH	Larry in Absent Father	1932
COULOURIS, GEORGE	Friar Peter in The Novice And The Duke (Measure For Measure)	1929
COURTNEIDGE, CICELY	By The Way (R)	1925
COWARD, NOEL	Nicky Lancaster in The Vortex	1925
COWL, JANE	Octavis in The Music Master	1904
CRAVEN, FRANK	Walter in Artie	1907
CRAWFORD, BRODERICK	George in Point Valaine	1935
CREWS, LAURA HOPE	Rosie in Merely Mary Ann	1903
CROMWELL, JOHN	John in Little Women	1912
CRONYN, HUME	The Janitor in Hipper's Holiday	1934
CULP, ROBERT	Alan in The Prescott Proposals	1953
CUMMINGS, CONSTANCE	Carrie in This Man's Town	1930
CUMMINGS, ROBERT	Reggie in The Roof	1931
CUMMINGS, VICKI	June in Here Goes The Bride	1931
CURRIE, FINLAY	Jakob in Too Late The Phalarope	1956
DAILEY, DAN	The Husband in Catch Me If You Can	1965
DAILEY, IRENE	"Shotput" in Nine Girls	1943
DALY, JAMES	Hobe in Virginia Reel	1947
DANA, LEORA	Irma in The Madwoman of Chaillot	1947
DANA, VIOLA	Gwendolyn in The Poor Little Rich Girl	1913
DANIELL, HENRY	Prince Charles in Clair de Lune	1921
DANIELS, WILLIAM	Clarence in Life With Father	1943
DARNELL, LINDA	Marion in Harbor Lights	1956
DARVAS, LILI	"Peter" in Soldier's Wife	1944
DA SILVA, HOWARD	Scaevola in The Green Cockatoo	1930
DAUPHIN, CLAUDE	Cradeau in No Exit	1946
DAVIS, BETTE	Floy Jennings in The Earth Between (OB)	1929
DAVIS, OSSIE	Jeb (TR)	1946
DAVIS, SAMMY, JR.	Charlie in Mr. Wonderful	1956
DAWN, HAZEL	The Pink Lady (TR)	1911
DEAN, JAMES	Wally Wilkins in See The Jaguar	1952
DEE, RUBY	Libby in Jeb	1946
DE HAVILLAND, OLIVIA	Juliet in Romeo And Juliet	1951
DENNIS, SANDY	Millicent in Burning Bright (OB)	1960
DERN, BRUCE	Maguire in The Shadow Of A Gunman	1958

DEBUTS: ACTORS   557

DEWHURST, COLLEEN	Kate in The Taming Of The Shrew (OB)	1956
DE WILDE, BRANDON	John Henry in The Member Of The Wedding	1950
DICKINSON, ANGIE	Janet in The Perfect Setup	1962
DIGGES, DUDLEY	The Policeman in The Rising Of The Moon	1908
DILLMAN, BRADFORD	Richard in The Scarecrow (OB)	1953
DIXON, JEAN	Mary in Wooden Kimono	1926
DONAT, PETER	Prince Leopold in The First Gentleman	1957
DONLEVY, BRIAN	Corporal Gowdy in What Price Glory?	1924
DOUGLAS, KIRK	Messenger Boy in Spring Again	1941
DOUGLAS, MELVYN	Ace Wilfong in A Free Soul	1928
DOUGLAS, PAUL	Radio Announcer in Double Dummy	1936
DOWLING, EDDIE	Ziegfeld Follies (R)	1919
DRAKE, ALFRED	Marshall in Babes in Arms	1937
DRESSLER, MARIE	Cunigonde in The Robber Of The Rhine	1892
DRIVAS, ROBERT	Rameses in The Firstborn	1958
DUKE, PATTY	Helen Keller in The Miracle Worker	1959
DULLEA, KEIR	Timmie in Season Of Choice (OB)	1959
DUMBRILLE, DOUGLAS	Banquo in Macbeth	1924
DUMONT, MARGARET	Madame Ovieda in The Fan	1921
DUNAWAY, FAYE	Faith in But For Whom Charlie	1964
DUNCAN, SANDY	Zaneeta Shinn in The Music Man	1965
DUNN, JAMES	Nick in Panama Hattie	1940
DUNN, MICHAEL	Major Armstrong in Here Come The Clowns (OB)	1960
DUNNE, IRENE	Tessie in The Clinging Vine	1922
DUNNOCK, MILDRED	Miss Pinty in Life Begins	1932
DURANTE, JIMMY	Show Girl (R)	1929
DURYEA, DAN	Bob Johnson in Missouri Legend	1938
DUVALL, ROBERT	Frank in Mrs. Warren's Profession (OB)	1958
EAGELS, JEANNE	Ruth in Daddies	1918
EBSEN, BUDDY	Flying Colors (R)	1932
ELDRIDGE, FLORENCE	Margaret in Ambush	1921
ELLIOTT, MAXINE	Felicia in The Middleman	1890
ERICKSON, LEIF	John in All The Living	1938
ERROL, LEON	Ziegfeld Follies (R)	1910
EVANS, EDITH	Florence Nightingale in The Lady With A Lamp	1931
EVANS, MADGE	Mimsey in Peter Ibbetson	1917
EVANS, MAURICE	Romeo in Romeo And Juliet	1935
EVELYN, JUDITH	Bella Manningham in Angel Street	1941
EWELL, TOM	Red in They Shall Not Die	1934
EYTHE, WILLIAM	Lt. Tondor in The Moon Is Down	1942
FABRAY, NANETTE	Meet The People (R)	1940
FAIRBANKS, DOUGLAS	Glen in Her Lord And Master	1902
FALK, PETER	Sagnarele in Don Juan (OB)	1956
FARENTINO, JAMES	Pedro in The Night Of The Iguana	1961
FARMER, FRANCES	Lorna Moon in Golden Boy	1937
FARRELL, GLENDA	Marion in Skidding	1928
FAY, FRANK	Stephen in The Redemption Of David Corson	1906
FAYE, ALICE	Professor Kenyon in Good News	1974
FERGUSON, ELSIE	Ella in The Earl Of Pawtucket	1903
FERRER, JOSE	Second Policeman in A Slight Case Of Murder	1935
FIELD, BETTY	Reporter in Page Miss Glory	1934
FIELDS, W. C.	The Ham Tree (R)	1905
FINNEY, ALBERT	Luther (TR)	1963

FITZGERALD, BARRY	Phil Noonan in Things That Are Caesar's	1932
FITZGERALD, GERALDINE	Ellie in Heartbreak House	1938
FOCH, NINA	Mary in John Loves Mary	1947
FONDA, HENRY	New Faces (R)	1934
FONDA, JANE	Toni in There Was A Little Girl	1960
FONDA, PETER	Oglethorpe in Blood, Sweat and Stanley Poole	1961
FONTAINE, JOAN	Laura in Tea and Sympathy	1953
FONTANNE, LYNN	Olive in The Harp Of Life	1916
FORD, PAUL	Foreman in Steel (OB)	1939
FORD, RUTH	Jane in The Shoemaker's Holiday	1938
FORSTER, ROBERT	Frankie in Mrs. Dally	1965
FORSYTHE, JOHN	Cootes in Vickie	1942
FOSTER, GLORIA	In White America (R/OB)	1963
FOY, EDDIE, JR.	Show Girl (R)	1929
FRANCIOSA, ANTHONY	Ferdinand in Yes Is For A Very Young Man (OB)	1949
FRANCIS, ARLENE	Soror in La Gringa	1928
FRANCIS, KAY	Player Queen in Hamlet	1925
FREDERICK, PAULINE	Titania in A Princess Of Kensington	1903
FREEMAN, AL, JR.	Fishbelly in The Long Dream	1960
FROMAN, JANE	Ziegfeld Follies (R)	1934
GABEL, MARTIN	Hunk in Dead End	1935
GABLE, CLARK	The Man in Machinal	1928
GARFIELD, JOHN	Bill in Lost Boy	1932
GARRETT, BETTY	Of V We Sing (R)	1942
GARSON, GREER	Auntie Mame (TR)	1958
GAXTON, WILLIAM	Music Box Revue (R)	1922
GAZZARA, BEN	Jocko de Paris in End As A Man	1953
GEER, WILL	Pistol in The Merry Wives Of Windsor	1928
GEORGE, GLADYS	Jalline in The Betrothal	1918
GEORGE, GRACE	Juliette in The Turtle	1898
GHOSTLEY, ALICE	New Faces (R)	1952
GIELGUD, JOHN	Grand Duke Alexander in The Patriot	1928
GILFORD, JACK	Meet The People (R)	1940
GILLMORE, MARGALO	Laurel in The Scrap Of Paper	1917
GILPIN, CHARLES	The Emperor Jones (TR/OB)	1920
GINGOLD, HERMIONE	Almanac (R)	1953
GISH, DOROTHY	Gillie in Dion O'Dare	1907
GISH, LILLIAN	Marjanie in A Good Little Devil	1913
GLEASON, JACKIE	Hellzapoppin (R)	1938
GLEASON, JAMES	George in Pretty Mrs. Smith	1914
GORDON, RUTH	Nibs in Peter Pan	1915
GORMAN, CLIFF	Peter Boyle in Hogan's Goat (OB)	1965
GOULD, ELLIOTT	Earl in Say, Darling	1958
GOULET, ROBERT	Lancelot in Camelot	1960
GRABLE, BETTY	Alice Barton in DuBarry Was A Lady	1939
GRANGER, FARLEY	The Actorman in The Carefree Tree (OB)	1955
GRANT, CARY	Anzac in Golden Dawn	1927
GRANT, LEE	Mildred in Joy To The World	1948
GRAY, DOLORES	Seven Lively Arts (R)	1944
GREENE, LORNE	Elliott in The Prescott Proposals	1953
GREENSTREET, SYDNEY	Sir Toby Belch in Twelfth Night	1907
GREENWOOD, CHARLOTTE	The Passing Show (R)	1912
GREENWOOD, JOAN	Lucasta in The Confidential Clerk	1954
GREGORY, JAMES	Jerry in Key Largo	1939
GREY, JOEL	The Littlest Revue (R)	1956

GRIFFIES, ETHEL	Alice in Havoc	1924
GRIFFITH, ANDY	Will Stockdale in No Time For Sergeants	1955
GRIFFITH, HUGH	The Father in Legend Of Lovers	1951
GRIMES, TAMMY	Cherie in Bus Stop	1955
GRIZZARD, GEORGE	Hank in The Desperate Hours	1955
GRODIN, CHARLES	Robert Pickett in Tchin-Tchin	1962
GUARDINO, HARRY	Chuck in A Hatful Of Rain	1955
GUINNESS, ALEC	Teddy in Flare Path	1942
GWENN, EDMUND	Sir Leslie in A Voice From The Minaret	1922
GWYNNE, FRED	Stinker in Mrs. McThing	1952
HACKETT, BUDDY	Dan Cupid in Lunatics And Lovers	1954
HACKETT, JOAN	Ginna in A Clearing In The Woods (OB)	1959
HACKMAN, GENE	Dan in Chaparral (OB)	1958
HAGEN, UTA	Nina in The Sea Gull	1938
HALEY, JACK	Gay Paree (R)	1926
HAMILTON, MARGARET	Helen in Another Language	1932
HAMILTON, MURRAY	Ensign Pulver in Mister Roberts	1949
HAMILTON, NEIL	Henry in Many Happy Returns	1945
HAMPDEN, WALTER	Silvio in The Comtesse Coquette	1907
HARDING, ANN	Madeline in Inheritors (OB)	1921
HARDWICKE, CEDRIC	Emile in Promise	1936
HARPER, VALERIE	Story Theatre (R)	1971
HARRIGAN, NEDDA	Clio in Josephine	1918
HARRIGAN, WILLIAM	Jimmy in Artie	1907
HARRIS, BARBARA	From The Second City (R)	1961
HARRIS, JULIE	Atlanta in It's A Gift	1945
HARRIS, ROSEMARY	Mabel in The Climate Of Eden	1952
HARRISON, REX	Tubbs in Sweet Aloes	1936
HARTMAN, DAVID	Rudolph in Hello, Dolly!	1964
HARVEY, LAURENCE	Angelo in Island Of Goats	1955
HATFIELD, HURD	Kirilov in The Possessed	1939
HAVOC, JUNE	Rozsa in Forbidden Melody	1936
HAWKINS, JACK	Hibbert in Journey's End	1929
HAYDON, JULIE	Hope Blake in Bright Star	1935
HAYES, HELEN	Little Mimi in Old Dutch	1909
HECKART, EILEEN	Eva McKeon in The Traitor	1949
HEFLIN, VAN	Junior in Mr. Moneypenny	1928
HENREID, PAUL	Dr. Walther in Flight To The West	1940
HEPBURN, AUDREY	Gigi (TR)	1951
HEPBURN, KATHARINE	Veronica Sims in These Days	1928
HERLIE, EILEEN	Mrs. Molloy in The Matchmaker	1955
HESTON, CHARLTON	Proculeius in Antony And Cleopatra	1947
HILL, ARTHUR	Cornelius Hackl in The Matchmaker	1955
HILLER, WENDY	Sally in Love On The Dole	1936
HINGLE, PAT	Koble in End As A Man	1953
HODIAK, JOHN	Sheriff Hawes in The Chase	1952
HOFFMAN, DUSTIN	Zoditch in Journey Of The Fifth Horse (OB)	1966
HOLBROOK, HAL	Mark Twain Tonight! (TR)	1959
HOLLIDAY, JUDY	Alice in Kiss Them For Me	1945
HOLM, CELESTE	Lady Mary in Gloriana	1938
HOLMAN, LIBBY	Garrick Gaieties (R)	1925
HOMOLKA, OSCAR	James in Grey Farm	1940
HOPE, BOB	Huckleberry Haines in Roberta	1934
HOPKINS, MIRIAM	Juliet in Little Jessie James	1923
HORNE, LENA	The Quadronne Girl in Dance With Your Gods	1934

HORTON, EDWARD EVERETT	Joseph in The Cheater	1910
HOWARD, KEN	Karl Kubelik in Promises, Promises	1968
HOWARD, LESLIE	Calverton In Just Suppose	1920
HULBERT, JACK	By The Way (R)	1925
HULL, HENRY	Henry in Green Stockings	1911
HULL, JOSEPHINE	Mrs. Hicks in Neighbors	1923
HUNT, MARSHA	Ann in Joy To The World	1948
HUNT, MARTITA	Countess Aurelia in The Madwoman Of Chaillot	1948
HUNTER, KIM	Stella in A Streetcar Named Desire	1947
HUNTER, TAB	Flanders in The Milk Train Doesn't Stop Here Anymore	1964
HUSSEY, RUTH	Mary in State Of The Union	1945
HUSTON, WALTER	Mr. Pitt (TR)	1924
HUTTON, BETTY	Two For The Show (R)	1940
HYDE-WHITE, WILFRID	Sir Alec in Under The Counter	1947
HYLAND, DIANA	Heavenly in Sweet Bird Of Youth	1959
HYMAN, EARLE	Rudolf in Anna Lucasta	1944
INGRAM, REX	Satan in Ol' Man Satan	1932
IVES, BURL	The Tailor in The Boys From Syracuse	1938
JACKSON, ANNE	Alice in Signature!	1945
JACKSON, GLENDA	Charlotte Corday in Marat/Sade	1965
JACOBI, LOU	Van Daan in The Diary Of Anne Frank	1955
JAFFE, SAM	Trask in The Clod	1915
JAGGER, DEAN	Lov Bensey in Tobacco Road	1933
JANIS, ELSIE	When We Were 41 (R)	1905
JEFFREYS, ANNE	Rose in Street Scene	1947
JENKINS, ALLEN	Scott in Florodora	1920
JENS, SALOME	Miss Ferguson in Sixth Finger In A Five Finger Glove	1956
JESSEL, GEORGE	Gaieties (R)	1919
JESSEL, PATRICIA	Romaine in Witness For The Prosecution	1954
JOHNS, GLYNIS	Gertie (TR)	1952
JOHNSON, RICHARD	Clive Root in The Complaisant Lover	1961
JOHNSON, VAN	New Faces (R)	1936
JOLSON, AL	Erastus in La Belle Paree	1911
JONES, ALLAN	Carl Linden in Bitter Sweet	1934
JONES, BARRY	An Officer in Man And The Masses	1924
JONES, CHRIS	Pancho in The Night Of The Iguana	1961
JONES, DEAN	Stan in There Was A Little Girl	1960
JONES, HENRY	Reynaldo in Hamlet	1938
JONES, JAMES EARL	Edward in Sunrise At Campobello	1958
JONES, JENNIFER	Isabel Archer in Portrait Of A Lady	1954
JONES, SHIRLEY	Sue in South Pacific	1947
JORY, VICTOR	Geoffrey in The Two Mrs. Carrolls	1943
JOURDAN, LOUIS	Michel in The Immoralist	1954
KAHN, MADELINE	New Faces (R)	1968
KANIN, GARSON	Tommy in Little Ol' Boy	1933
KARLOFF, BORIS	Jonathan in Arsenic And Old Lace	1941
KARLWEIS, OSCAR	Keppler in Cue For Passion	1940
KASZNAR, KURT	Zebulon in The Eternal Road	1937
KAYE, DANNY	Straw Hat Revue	1939
KAYE, STUBBY	Nicely-Nicely in Guys And Dolls	1940
KAZAN, ELIA	Louis in Chrysalis	1932

KEACH, STACY	MacBird! (TR/OB)	1967
KEANE, DORIS	Rose in Whitewashing Julia	1903
KEEL, HOWARD	Billy Bigelow in Carousel	1945
KEELER, RUBY	Ruby in Bye-Bye Bonnie	1927
KEITH, IAN	Captain Belgrave in The Silver Fox	1921
KEITH, ROBERT	Ralph in The Triumph Of X	1921
KELLY, GENE	One For The Money (R)	1939
KELLY, GRACE	The Daughter in The Father	1949
KELLY, NANCY	Buteus in Give Me Yesterday	1931
KELLY, PATSY	Revels (R)	1927
KELLY, PAUL	George in Seventeen	1918
KELTON, PERT	The Maid in Sunny	1925
KENNEDY, ARTHUR	The Reporter in Merrily We Roll Along	1934
KERR, DEBORAH	Laura in Tea And Sympathy	1953
KERR, JOHN	Arthur in Bernardine	1952
KERT, LARRY	Tickets, Please! (R)	1950
KIBBEE, GUY	Cass Wheeler in Torch Song	1930
KILBRIDE, PERCY	Harry Keene in The Buzzard	1928
KILEY, RICHARD	Percival in Misalliance	1953
KING, ALAN	Nathan Detroit in Guys And Dolls	1965
KING, DENNIS	The Marquis in Clair de Lune	1921
KIRK, LISA	Emily in Allegro	1947
KITT, EARTHA	New Faces (R)	1952
KLUGMAN, JACK	Frank in Golden Boy	1952
KNIGHT, JUNE	Dorothy in Hot-Cha!	1932
KNIGHT, SHIRLEY	Katherine in Journey To The Day (OB)	1963
KNOX, ALEXANDER	Friar Laurence in Romeo And Juliet	1940
KOHNER, SUSAN	Emily in Love Me Little	1958
KRUGER, OTTO	Jack in The Natural Law	1918
LAHR, BERT	Revels (R)	1927
LAMAS, FERNANDO	The Duke of Granada in Happy Hunting	1956
LAMPERT, ZOHRA	Mashenka in Diary Of A Scoundrel (OB)	1956
LANCASTER, BURT	Sgt. Joseph Mooney in A Sound Of Hunting	1945
LANCHESTER, ELSA	Winnie Marble in Payment Deferred	1931
LANDI, ELISSA	Catherine Barkley in A Farewell To Arms	1930
LANDIS, JESSIE ROYCE	Flora in The Honor Of The Family	1926
LANG, HAROLD	Three To Make Ready (R)	1946
LANGELLA, FRANK	Michel in The Immoralist (OB)	1963
LANSBURY, ANGELA	Marcelle in Hotel Paradiso	1957
LANSING, ROBERT	Dunbar in Stalag 17	1948
LARIMORE, EARLE	Bill in Made In America	1926
LARRIMORE, FRANCINE	Sylvia in Some Baby	1915
LAUGHTON, CHARLES	William Marble in Payment Deferred	1931
LAURIE, PIPER	Candy in The Alligators (OB)	1960
LAVIN, LINDA	Izzy in Oh, Kay! (OB)	1960
LAWRENCE, CAROL	New Faces (R)	1952
LAWRENCE, GERTRUDE	Charlot's Revue	1924
LAWRENCE, STEVE	Sammy in What Makes Sammy Run?	1964
LAYE, EVELYN	Sarah in Bitter Sweet	1929
LEARNED, MICHAEL	Masha in Three Sisters	1969
LEDERER, FRANCIS	Andreas in Autumn Crocus	1932
LEACHMAN, CLORIS	Muriel in Sundown Beach	1948
LEE, CANADA	Blacksnake in Stevedore	1934
LEE, GYPSY ROSE	Claire in Melody	1933
LEE, MICHELE	Vintage 60 (R)	1960

LE GALLIENNE, EVA	Rose in Mrs. Boltay's Daughters	1915
LEIGH, VIVIEN	Juliet in Romeo And Juliet	1940
LEIGHTON, MARGARET	Lady Percy in Henry IV	1946
LEMMON, JACK	Leo in Room Service	1953
LENYA, LOTTE	Miriam in The Eternal Road	1937
LEONARD, SHELDON	Arthur Nathan in Hotel Alimony	1934
LEONTOVICH, EUGENIE	Revue Russe (R)	1922
LEVENE, SAM	Bill in Wall Street	1927
LILLIE, BEATRICE	Charlot's Revue	1924
LINDEN, HAL	Jeff in Bells Are Ringing	1956
LINDFORS, VIVECA	Inez in I've Got Sixpence	1952
LINDSAY, HOWARD	Valentine in Twelfth Night	1914
LITTLE, CLEAVON	Muslim Witch in MacBird! (OB)	1967
LOCKHART, GENE	Gustav in The Riviera Girl	1917
LOCKHART, JUNE	Janet in For Love Or Money	1947
LODEN, BARBARA	Myra in Compulsion	1957
LOFTUS, CECILIA	Bettina in The Mascot	1900
LOGAN, ELLA	Calling All Stars (R)	1934
LOGAN, JOSHUA	Mart in Carry Nation	1932
LORD, JACK	Slim Murray in The Traveling Lady	1954
LORD, PAULINE	Ruth in The Talker	1912
LOVEJOY, FRANK	Jorga in Judgment Day	1934
LOWE, EDMUND	Steven in The Brat	1917
LOY, MYRNA	Mrs. Banks in Barefoot In The Park	1964
LUCE, CLAIRE	Clair in Dear Sir	1924
LUGOSI, BELA	Fernando in The Red Poppy (OB)	1922
LUKAS, PAUL	Dr. Rankin in A Doll's House	1937
LUMET, SIDNEY	Dead End Kid in Dead End	1935
LUND, JOHN	New Faces (R)	1942
LUNT, ALFRED	Claude Estabrook in Romance And Arabella	1917
LYNDE, PAUL	New Faces (R)	1952
LYNLEY, CAROL	Anne in The Potting Shed	1957
LYNN, DIANA	Hedvig in The Wild Duck	1951
LYNN, JEFFREY	Joe in The Long Days	1951
LYTELL, BERT	Robert in A Mix-Up	1914
MACARTHUR, JAMES	Aaron in Invitation To A March	1960
MACDONALD, JEANETTE	Kate in Tangerine	1921
MACGRATH, LEUEEN	Eileen in Edward, My Son	1948
MACMAHON, ALINE	Laura in The Madras House (OB)	1921
MACMAHON, HORACE	Reporter in Wonder Boy	1931
MACNEE, PATRICK	Andrew Wyke in Sleuth	1972
MAGEE, PATRICK	Marquis de Sade in Marat/Sade	1965
MAHARIS, GEORGE	Green Eyes in Deathwatch (OB)	1958
MAIN, MARJORIE	Anna In Music In The Air	1932
MALDEN, KARL	Barker in Golden Boy	1937
MANSFIELD, JAYNE	Rita Marlowe in Will Success Spoil Rock Hunter?	1955
MARCH, FREDRIC	The Promoter in Deburau	1920
MARGO	Miriamne in Winterset	1935
MARLOWE, HUGH	Donald in Arrest That Woman	1936
MARSHALL, E. G.	Henry in Prologue To Glory	1938
MARSHALL, HERBERT	Ernest in Grumpy	1915
MARTIN, MARY	Dolly in Leave It To Me	1938
MARVIN, LEE	Hallam in Billy Budd	1951
MARX BROTHERS, THE	I'll Say She Is	1924

MASON, JAMES	David in Bathsheba	1947
MASON, MARSHA	Bobby in The Deer Park (OB)	1967
MASSEY, ANNA	Jane in The Reluctant Debutante	1956
MASSEY, DANIEL	Frederick in Small War On Murray Hill	1957
MASSEY, ILONA	Ziegfeld Follies (R)	1943
MASSEY, RAYMOND	Hamlet (TR)	1931
MATTHAU, WALTER	Sam in Twilight Walk	1951
MATTHEWS, A. E.	Saunders in Love Amongst The Lions	1910
MATURE, VICTOR	Randy Curtis in Lady In The Dark	1940
MCCALLUM, DAVID	Julian in The Flip Side	1968
MCCAMBRIDGE, MERCEDES	Mary in A Place Of Our Own	1945
MCCARTHY, KEVIN	Phil in Abe Lincoln In Illinois	1938
MCCORMICK, MYRON	Campbell in Carry Nation	1932
MCCOWEN, ALEC	The Messenger in Antony And Cleopatra	1951
MCDOWALL, RODDY	Bentley in Misalliance	1953
MCGAVIN, DARREN	Joe in Cock-A-Doodle-Dandy (OB)	1949
MCGIVER, JOHN	General De Courcelles in Little Glass Clock	1956
MCGRATH, PAUL	Dr. Green in In The Near Future	1925
MCGUIRE, DOROTHY	Emily in Our Town	1938
MCHUGH, FRANK	Dan in The Fall Guy	1925
MCKENNA, SIOBHAN	Miss Madrigal in The Chalk Garden	1955
MCMARTIN, JOHN	Billy Jester in Little Mary Sunshine (OB)	1959
MCNALLY, STEPHEN	Dr. Davidson in Johnny Belinda	1940
MCNEIL, CLAUDIA	Mamie in Simply Heavenly	1957
MCQUEEN, BUTTERFLY	Lucille in Brown Sugar	1937
MCQUEEN, STEVE	Johnny Pope in A Hatful Of Rain	1956
MEDFORD, KAY	Madame Cherry in Paint Your Wagon	1951
MEEKER, RALPH	Chuck in Strange Fruit	1945
MENKEN, HELEN	Blanche in Major Pendennis	1916
MERANDE, DORO	Sophie in Loose Moments	1935
MERCOURI, MELINA	Illya in Illya, Darling	1967
MEREDITH, BURGESS	Peter in Romeo And Juliet	1930
MERIVALE, PHILIP	Henry Higgins in Pygmalion	1914
MERKEL, UNA	Lenore in Pigs	1924
MERMAN, ETHEL	Kate in Girl Crazy	1930
MERRILL, GARY	Don in Brother Rat	1936
MILLAND, RAY	Simon Crawford in Hostile Witness	1966
MILLER, ANN	Scandals (R)	1939
MILLER, MARILYN	The Passing Show (R)	1914
MILLS, JOHN	Ross (TR)	1961
MILLS, JULIET	Pamela in Five Finger Exercise	1959
MINEO, SAL	Salvatore in The Rose Tattoo	1951
MINNELLI, LIZA	Ethel in Best Foot Forward (OB)	1963
MIRANDA, CARMEN	Streets Of Paris (R)	1939
MITCHELL, CAMERON	The Nephew in Jeremiah	1939
MITCHELL, MILLARD	Tremper in A Holy Terror	1925
MITCHELL, THOMAS	Trinculo in The Tempest	1913
MONTALBAN, RICARDO	Chico in Seventh Heaven	1956
MONTGOMERY, DOUGLASS	Tommy in God Loves Us	1926
MONTGOMERY, ELIZABETH	Janet in Late Love	1953
MONTGOMERY, ROBERT	Tito in The Mask And The Face	1924
MOORE, GRACE	Hitchy-Koo (R)	1920
MOORE, VICTOR	Kid Burns in Forty-Five Minutes From Broadway	1906
MOOREHEAD, AGNES	Donna Anna in Don Juan In Hell	1951
MORENO, RITA	Iris Brustein in The Sign In Sidney Brustein's Window	1964

MORGAN, FRANK	Remi in The Beautiful Adventure	1914
MORGAN, HELEN	Scandals (R)	1925
MORGAN, RALPH	Lind in Love's Comedy	1908
MORIARTY, MICHAEL	Octavius Caesar in Antony And Cleopatra (OB)	1963
MORISON, PATRICIA	Helen in Growing Pains	1933
MORLEY, ROBERT	Oscar Wilde (TR)	1938
MORRIS, CHESTER	Sam in The Copperhead	1918
MORRIS, WAYNE	The Duke in The Cave Dwellers	1957
MORSE, ROBERT	Barnaby in The Matchmaker	1955
MOSTEL, ZERO	Keep 'Em Laughing (R)	1942
MOWBRAY, ALAN	Almedy in The Play's The Thing	1926
MUNI, PAUL	Morris in We Americans	1926
MURPHY, GEORGE	Sonny Jim Brooks in Hold Everything	1929
MURPHY, ROSEMARY	Helen Gant in Look Homeward, Angel	1957
MURRAY, DON	Jack in The Rose Tattoo	1951
NAGEL, CONRAD	Ted in Forever After	1918
NATWICK, MILDRED	Mrs. Noble in Carry Nation	1932
NAZIMOVA, ALLA	Hedda Gabler	1906
NEAL, PATRICIA	Regina In Another Part Of The Forest	1946
NELSON, BARRY	Bobby in Winged Victory	1943
NELSON, GENE	This Is The Army (R)	1942
NELSON, KENNETH	Willie Baxter in Seventeen	1951
NESBITT, CATHLEEN	Molly Byrne in The Well Of The Saints	1911
NETHERSOLE, OLGA	Sylvia Woodville in The Transgressor	1895
NETTLETON, LOIS	Laurie in The Biggest Thief In Town	1949
NEVILLE, JOHN	Richard II (TR)	1956
NEWLEY, ANTHONY	Cranks (R)	1956
NEWMAN, PAUL	Alan Seymour in Picnic	1953
NEWMAN, PHYLLIS	Sarah in Wish You Were Here	1953
NEWMAR, JULIE	Vera in Silk Stockings	1955
NIESEN, GERTRUDE	Calling All Stars (R)	1934
NIVEN, DAVID	Gerard in Nina	1951
NOLAN, DORIS	Karen in Night Of January 16	1935
NOLAN, LLOYD	Cape Cod Follies (R)	1929
NUGENT, ELLIOTT	Tom in Dulcy	1921
O'BRIAN, HUGH	Destry in Destry Rides Again	1959
O'BRIEN, EDMOND	Pylades in Daughters Of Atreus	1936
O'BRIEN, PAT	Charlie in A Man's Man	1925
O'CONNELL, ARTHUR	The Postman in Anna Christie	1952
O'CONNOR, CARROLL	Buck Mulligan in Ulysses In Nighttown (OB)	1958
O'CONNOR, UNA	Jessie in The Shewing-Up Of Blanco Posnet	1911
O'HARA, MAUREEN	Christine (TR)	1960
OLIVER, EDNA MAY	Penelope in Oh, Kay!	1917
OLIVIER, LAURENCE	Hugh Bromilow in Murder On The Second Floor	1929
O'LOUGHLIN, GERALD	Stanley Kowalski in A Streetcar Named Desire	1956
OLSON, NANCY	Isolde in The Tunnel Of Love	1957
O'MALLEY, REX	Prince Myshkin in The Strange Prince	1926
O'NEAL, FREDERICK	Frank in Anna Lucasta	1944
O'NEAL, PATRICK	Walter Schwarz in Lulu (OB)	1958
O'NEAL, ZELMA	Flo in Good News	1927
O'NEIL, BARBARA	The Sporting Girl in Carry Nation	1932
O'NEIL, NANCE	Alice Dunning in True To Life	1896
OPATOSHU, DAVID	The Blind Man in Night Music	1940

DEBUTS: ACTORS

ORBACH, JERRY	Mack the Knife in The Threepenny Opera (OB)	1955
O'SULLIVAN, MAUREEN	Edith in Never Too Late	1962
OUSPENSKAYA, MARIA	Paris Pigeons in The Saint (OB)	1924
OVERMAN, LYNNE	Billy in Fair And Warmer	1916
OWEN, REGINALD	Manderville in The Carolinian	1924
PACINO, AL	Murph in The Indian Wants The Bronx (OB)	1968
PAGE, GERALDINE	Alma Winemiller in Summer And Smoke (OB)	1952
PAIGE, JANIS	Jody in Remains To Be Seen	1951
PALANCE, JACK	Boutourlinsky in A Temporary Island (OB)	1948
PALMER, LILLI	Christiane in My Name Is Aquilon	1949
PARKER, JEAN	Loco (TR)	1946
PARKS, LARRY	Jeff in Bells Are Ringing	1957
PARSONS, ESTELLE	Mary Mills in Happy Hunting	1956
PATRICK, LEE	Elsie in The Green Beetle	1924
PATTERSON, ELIZABETH	Hermia in A Midsummer Night's Dream	1910
PATTERSON, NEVA	Brenda in The Druid Circle	1947
PAXINOU, KATINA	Hedda Gabler (TR)	1942
PEARCE, ALICE	New Faces (R)	1943
PECK, GREGORY	Cliff in The Morning Star	1942
PEPPARD, GEORGE	Mickey Argent in Girls Of Summer	1956
PERKINS, ANTHONY	Tom in Tea And Sympathy	1953
PERKINS, OSGOOD	Homer in Beggar On Horseback	1924
PERRY, ANTOINETTE	Rachel Arrowsmith in Mr. Pitt	1924
PETERS, BERNADETTE	Cinderella in The Penny Friend (OB)	1966
PETTET, JOANNA	Roxane in The Chinese Prime Minister	1964
PHILLIPS, MARGARET	Sue in Proof Through The Night	1942
PIAZZA, BEN	George in Winesburg, Ohio	1958
PICKENS, JANE	Ziegfeld Follies (R)	1936
PICKFORD, MARY	Betty in The Warrens Of Virginia	1907
PICON, MOLLY	Becky in Morning Star	1940
PIDGEON, WALTER	Puzzles (R)	1925
PINZA, EZIO	Emile de Becque in South Pacific	1949
PITTS, ZASU	Belinda Pryde in Ramshackle Inn	1944
PLEASENCE, DONALD	Major-Domo in Caesar And Cleopatra	1951
PLESHETTE, SUZANNE	Ruth in Compulsion	1957
PLOWRIGHT, JOAN	The Old Woman in The Chairs (OB)	1958
PLUMMER, CHRISTOPHER	George in The Starcross Story	1954
POITIER, SIDNEY	Polydorous in Lysistrata	1946
POLLARD, MICHAEL J.	Joe in Comes A Day	1958
PORTMAN, ERIC	Boulanger in Madame Bovary	1937
POWELL, ELEANOR	Molly in Follow Thru	1929
POWELL, JANE	Irene (TR)	1974
POWELL, WILLIAM	Javier in Spanish Love	1920
POWER, TYRONE	Benvolio in Romeo And Juliet	1935
PREMINGER, OTTO	Karl Baumer in Margin For Error	1939
PRESTON, ROBERT	Oscar Jaffe in Twentieth Century	1950
PRICE, VINCENT	Prince Albert in Victoria Regina	1935
PRINCE, WILLIAM	Richard in Ah, Wilderness!	1941
QUAYLE, ANTHONY	Mr. Harcourt in The Country Wife	1936
QUINN, ANTHONY	Stephen in The Gentleman From Athens	1947
RAINER, LUISE	Miss Thing in A Kiss For Cinderella	1942
RAINS, CLAUDE	Roberto in The Constant Nymph	1926
RAITT, JOHN	Billy Bigelow in Carousel	1945

RAMBEAU, MARJORIE	Mary in So Much For So Much	1914
RANDALL, TONY	Scarus in Antony And Cleopatra	1947
RATHBONE, BASIL	Count Alexei Czerny in The Czarina	1922
RATOFF, GREGORY	Revue Russe (R)	1922
RAYE, MARTHA	Calling All Stars (R)	1934
REARDON, JOHN	New Faces (R)	1956
REDFIELD, WILLIAM	Hank in Swing Your Lady	1936
REDFORD, ROBERT	Myers in Tall Story	1959
REDGRAVE, LYNN	Carol Melkett in Black Comedy	1967
REDGRAVE, MICHAEL	Macbeth (TR)	1948
REDMAN, JOYCE	Doll Tearsheet in Henry IV	1946
REED, FLORENCE	Anne in Seven Days	1909
REILLY, CHARLES NELSON	Mr. Henkel in Bye, Bye Birdie	1960
REINER, CARL	Call Me Mister (R)	1946
REMICK, LEE	Lois in Be Your Age	1953
RENNIE, MICHAEL	Dirk Winsten in Mary, Mary	1961
REVERE, ANNE	Katie in The Great Barrington	1931
REVILL, CLIVE	Sam Weller in Mr. Pickwick	1952
REYNOLDS, BURT	Reber in Mister Roberts	1956
REYNOLDS, DEBBIE	Irene (TR)	1973
RHODES, ERIK	Pedro in A Most Immoral Lady	1928
RICHARDSON, RALPH	Mercutio in Romeo And Juliet	1935
RICHMAN, HARRY	Henry in Queen Of Hearts	1923
RICHMAN, MARK	Corger in End As A Man	1953
RIGG, DIANA	Cordelia in King Lear	1964
RITCHARD, CYRIL	Puzzles (R)	1925
RITT, MARTIN	Sam in Golden Boy	1937
RITTER, THELMA	Miss Batterson in The Shelf	1926
RIVERA, CHITA	Fifi in Seventh Heaven	1955
ROBARDS, JASON	Ed In American Gothic (OB)	1953
ROBERTI, LYDA	Fanny in You Said It	1931
ROBERTS, ANTHONY	The Air Cadet in Something About A Soldier	1962
ROBERTSON, CLIFF	Matthew in Late Love	1953
ROBESON, PAUL	Jim in Taboo	1922
ROBINSON, BILL	Blackbirds (R)	1928
ROBINSON, EDWARD G.	Andre in Under Fire	1915
ROBINSON, JAY	Archie in The Shop At Sly Corner	1949
ROBSON, FLORA	Ellen in Ladies in Retirement	1940
ROGERS, BUDDY	Jack Whitney in Hot-Cha!	1932
ROGERS, GINGER	Babs Green in Top Speed	1929
ROGERS, PAUL	Macbeth (TR)	1956
ROGERS, WILL	Hands Up (R)	1915
ROMERO, CESAR	John in The Street Singer	1929
ROSAY, FRANCOISE	Catherine the Great in Once There Was A Russian	1961
ROSE, GEORGE	Peto in Henry IV	1946
ROTH, LILLIAN	Flossie in The Inner Man	1917
ROWLANDS, GENA	The Girl in The Seven Year Itch	1952
ROYLE, SELENA	Guinevere in Launcelot And Elaine (OB)	1921
RUGGLES, CHARLES	Jack Scott in Help Wanted	1914
RULE, JANICE	Madge in Picnic	1953
RUSSELL, JANE	Joanne in Company	1971
RUSSELL, ROSALIND	Garrick Gaieties (R)	1930
RUTHERFORD, MARGARET	Lady Bracknell in The Importance Of Being Earnest	1947
RYAN, IRENE	Berthe in Pippin	1972
RYAN, ROBERT	Joe in Clash By Night	1941

SAINT, EVA MARIE	Thelma in The Trip To Bountiful	1953
SAKS, GENE	Joxer in Juno And The Paycock (OB)	1947
SALMI, ALBERT	Gatt in End As A Man	1953
SAND, PAUL	From The Second City (R)	1961
SANDS, DIANA	Juliet in An Evening With Will Shakespeare (OB)	1953
SAVO, JIMMY	Vanities (R)	1923
SCHELL, MAXIMILIAN	Paul in Interlock	1958
SCHILDKRAUT, JOSEPH	Richard in Pagans	1921
SCOFIELD, PAUL	Sir Thomas More in A Man For All Seasons	1961
SCOTT, GEORGE C.	Richard III (TR/OB)	1957
SCOTT, MARTHA	Emily in Our Town	1938
SCOTT, ZACHARY	Neil in The Damask Cheek	1942
SEGAL, GEORGE	Ollie in Leave It To Jane (OB)	1959
SEGAL, VIVIENNE	Gaby in The Blue Paradise	1915
SELDES, MARIAN	Dounia in Crime And Punishment	1947
SHATNER, WILLIAM	Usumcasane in Tamburlaine The Great	1956
SHAW, ROBERT	Aston in The Caretaker	1961
SHEEN, MARTIN	Mike in Never Live Over A Pretzel Factory	1964
SHERMAN, HIRAM	Robbin in Horse Eats Hat	1936
SHERWOOD, MADELEINE	Abigail in The Crucible	1953
SIDNEY, SYLVIA	Prunella (TR)	1926
SILVERA, FRANK	Joe in Anna Lucasta	1944
SILVERS, PHIL	"Punko" Parks in Yokel Boy	1939
SIM, ALISTAIR	Cardinal di Medici in The Venetian	1931
SKALA, LILIA	Margarethe in Letters To Lucerne	1941
SKINNER, CORNELIA OTIS	Dona Sarasate in Blood And Sand	1921
SKINNER, OTIS	His Grace de Grammont (TR)	1894
SKIPWORTH, ALISON	Mrs. Ware in The Princess And The Butterfly	1897
SKULNIK, MENASHA	Max in The Fifth Season	1953
SLEZAK, WALTER	Eric in Meet My Sister	1930
SLOANE, EVERETT	Bosetti in Boy Meets Girl	1935
SMITH, ALEXIS	Phyllis in Follies	1971
SMITH, C. AUBREY	Sir Marcus Ordeyne in The Morals Of Marcus	1907
SMITH, KATE	Tiny Little in Honeymoon Lane	1926
SMITH, KENT	Lieut. Chase in Men Must Fight	1932
SMITH, MAGGIE	New Faces (R)	1956
SONDERGAARD, GALE	Edith in What's Your Wife Doing?	1923
SOTHERN, ANN	Geraldine March in America's Sweetheart	1931
STADLEN, LEWIS J.	Groucho Marx in Minnie's Boys	1970
STAMP, TERENCE	Alfie (TR)	1964
STANDER, LIONEL	The First Fairy in him (OB)	1928
STANLEY, KIM	Denise in Yes Is For A Very Young Man (OB)	1949
STANWYCK, BARBARA	Dot in The Noose	1926
STAPLETON, JEAN	Mother in American Gothic (OB)	1953
STAPLETON, MAUREEN	Sara in The Playboy Of The Western World	1946
STARR, FRANCES	Juanita in The Rose Of The Rancho	1906
STEELE, TOMMY	Kipps in Half A Sixpence	1965
STEIGER, ROD	Rosenberger in Night Music	1951
STEINBERG, DAVID	Kenny in Little Murders	1967
STERLING, JAN	Chris Faringdon in Bachelor Born	1938
STERLING, ROBERT	Charley in Gramercy Ghost	1951
STEVENS, CRAIG	Fred in Here's Love	1963
STEVENS, INGER	Maria in Debut	1956
STEVENS, MARK	Val in Mid-Summer	1953
STEWART, JAMES	Gano in Carry Nation	1932
STICKNEY, DOROTHY	Anita in The Squall	1926

STOCKWELL, DEAN	John Thornton in The Innocent Voyage	1943
STOCKWELL, GUY	Edward Thornton in The Innocent Voyage	1943
STONE, EZRA	Parade (R)	1935
STONE, FRED	Grunt in The Girl From Up There	1901
STONE, LEWIS	Paul in The Bird of Paradise	1912
STONE, MILBURN	The Confederate Soldier in Jayhawker	1934
STRAIGHT, BEATRICE	Lisa in The Possessed	1939
STRASBERG, LEE	Garrick Gaieties (R)	1925
STRASBERG, SUSAN	The Diary Of Anne Frank (TR)	1955
STREISAND, BARBRA	Another Evening With Harry Stoones (OB/R)	1961
STRITCH, ELAINE	Pamela in Loco	1946
STRUDWICK, SHEPPERD	Wu-Hu-Git in The Yellow Jacket	1928
SULLAVAN, MARGARET	Teddy in A Modern Virgin	1931
SULLIVAN, BARRY	Capt. Lynch in I Want A Policeman	1936
SULLIVAN, FRANCIS L.	Stanley Rosel in Many Waters	1929
SWANSON, GLORIA	Katherine in A Goose For The Gander	1945
SWENSON, INGA	New Faces (R)	1956
SWENSON, SWEN	Boylan in Ulysses In Nighttown (OB)	1958
TAMIROFF, AKIM	Roubeau in Miracle At Verdun	1931
TANDY, JESSICA	Tony in The Matriarch	1930
TAYLOR, LAURETTE	Flossie in From Rags To Riches	1903
TEARLE, GODFREY	Silvo Steno in Carnival	1919
TEMPEST, MARIE	Kitty in The Red Hussar	1890
TETZEL, JOAN	Renie in Lorelei	1938
THAXTER, PHYLLIS	Lempi in There Shall Be No Night	1940
THOMAS, MARLO	Sally Cramer in Thieves	1974
THOMPSON, SADA	Mrs. Heidelberg in The Clandestine Marriage (OB)	1954
THORNDIKE, SYBIL	Shakespearean Repertory	1907
THULIN, INGRID	Inga in Of Love Remembered	1967
TIERNEY, GENE	Molly O'Day in Mrs. O'Brien Entertains	1939
TOBIAS, GEORGE	Lipinsky in What Price Glory?	1924
TODD, ANN	Davina in Four Winds	1957
TONE, FRANCHOT	Newland in The Age Of Innocence	1928
TORN, RIP	Brick in Cat On A Hot Tin Roof	1955
TRACY, LEE	Joe in The Show-Off	1924
TRACY, SPENCER	Holt in A Royal Fandango	1923
TRAVERS, HENRY	"Sally" in The Pipes Of Pan	1917
TREACHER, ARTHUR	Great Temptations (R)	1926
TREVOR, CLAIRE	Toby in Whistling In The Dark	1932
TRUEX, ERNEST	Chappie Raster in Wildfire	1908
TUCKER, SOPHIE	Vanities (R)	1924
TUTIN, DOROTHY	The Hollow Crown (R)	1963
TYSON, CICELY	Stephanie Virtue in The Blacks (OB)	1961
ULLMAN, LIV	Nora in A Doll's House	1975
ULRIC, LENORE	Dorothy in The Mark Of The Beast	1915
URE, MARY	Alison in Look Back In Anger	1957
USTINOV, PETER	The General in Romanoff And Juliet	1957
VACCARO, BRENDA	Gloria in Everybody Loves Opal	1961
VALLEE, RUDY	Scandals (R)	1931
VAN DYKE, DICK	The Girls Against The Boys (R)	1959
VAN FLEET, JO	Dorcas in The Winter's Tale	1946
VARDEN, EVELYN	Elsie in Alley Cat	1934
VELEZ, LUPE	Conchita in Hot-Cha!	1932

VERA-ELLEN	Minerva in By Jupiter	1942
VERDON, GWEN	Claudine in Can-Can	1953
VEREEN, BEN	Judas Iscariot in Jesus Christ Superstar	1971
VOIGHT, JON	Rodolpho in A View From The Bridge (OB)	1965
WALBURN, RAYMOND	Skiddy in Manhattan	1922
WALKER, CHARLOTTE	Virginia in The Crisis	1902
WALKER, JUNE	Roselle in The Betrothal	1918
WALKER, NANCY	The Blind Date in Best Foot Forward	1941
WALLACH, ELI	The Crew Chief in Skydrift	1945
WALSTON, RAY	Schwartz in The Front Page	1946
WALTER, JESSICA	Georgia Hands in A Severed Head	1964
WANAMAKER, SAM	Lester in Cafe Crown	1942
WARDEN, JACK	Mickey in Golden Boy	1952
WARFIELD, DAVID	Levi in The Auctioneer	1901
WARFIELD, WILLIAM	Aneas in Set My People Free	1948
WARNER, H. B.	Lancelot in Merely Mary Ann	1907
WATERS, ETHEL	Africana (R)	1927
WATERSTON, SAM	Jonathan in Oh Dad, Poor Dad	1963
WATSON, DOUGLAS	Don in The Iceman Cometh	1946
WATSON, LUCILE	Mrs. Wuthering in The Wisdom Of The Wise	1902
WAYNE, DAVID	Harvey in Dance Night	1938
WEAVER, FRITZ	Fainall in The Way Of The World (OB)	1954
WEBB, ALAN	Tonight at 8:30 (R)	1936
WEBB, CLIFTON	Bisco in The Purple Road	1913
WEBSTER, MARGARET	The Countess in Richard Of Bordeaux	1933
WELLES, ORSON	Tybalt in Romeo And Juliet	1934
WEST, MAE	Maggie O'Hara in A La Broadway	1911
WESTLEY, HELEN	The Oyster in Another Interior (OB)	1915
WESTON, JACK	Michael Lindsey in Season In The Sun	1950
WHITING, JACK	Ziegfeld Follies (R)	1922
WHITMORE, JAMES	Evans in Command Decision	1947
WHITTY, DAME MAY	Florence in There's Always Juliet	1932
WIDDOES, KATHLEEN	Teusret in The Firstborn	1958
WIDMARK, RICHARD	Lenny Archer in Kiss And Tell	1943
WILDE, CORNEL	Dimitri in They All Come To Moscow	1933
WILDER, GENE	Frankie Bryant in Roots (OB)	1961
WILLIAM, WARREN	Sir John Gotch in The Wonderful Visit	1924
WILLIAMS, BERT	In Dahomey (R)	1903
WILLIAMS, EMLYN	The Boy in And So To Bed	1927
WILLIAMS, JOHN	Clifford in The Fake	1924
WILLIAMSON, NICOL	Bill Maitland in Inadmissible Evidence	1965
WILSON, ELIZABETH	Christine Schoenwalder in Picnic	1953
WINNINGER, CHARLES	Rudolph Schnitzel in The Yankee Girl	1910
WINTERS, SHELLEY	Flora in The Night Before Christmas	1941
WINWOOD, ESTELLE	Lucilla in Hush!	1916
WISEMAN, JOSEPH	The Beggar in Journey To Jerusalem	1940
WISDOM, NORMAN	Will in Walking Happy	1966
WITHERS, GOOGIE	Mary Rhodes in The Complaisant Lover	1961
WOLFIT, DONALD	King Lear (TR)	1947
WOLHEIM, LOUIS	Yank in The Hairy Ape (OB)	1922
WOOD, PEGGY	Vera in The Three Romeos	1911
WOODWARD, JOANNE	Douane in The Lovers	1956
WOOLLEY, MONTY	Sergei Alexandrovitch in On Your Toes	1936
WORTH, IRENE	Cecily in The Two Mrs. Carrolls	1943
WRAY, FAY	Nikki (TR)	1931

WRIGHT, TERESA	Mary in Life With Father	1939
WYATT, JANE	Freda in Give Me Yesterday	1931
WYCHERLY, MARGARET	Everyman (TR)	1902
WYNN, ED	Ziegfeld Follies (R)	1914
WYNN, KEENAN	The Reporter in Remember The Day	1935
WYNYARD, DIANA	"Paul" in The Devil Passes	1932
YORK, MICHAEL	Felice in Out Cry	1973
YOUNG, GIG	Arthur in Oh, Men! Oh, Women!	1953
YOUNG, ROLAND	Alan in Hindle Wakes	1912
YURKA, BLANCHE	Helen Hoyt in Is Matrimony A Failure?	1909
ZIMBALIST, EFREM, JR.	Gil in The Rugged Path	1945
ZORINA, VERA	Angel in I Married An Angel	1938
ZUCCO, GEORGE	Lord Beaconsfield in Victoria Regina	1935

Appendix III
Debuts: Playwrights

Following are the names of one hundred American and Anglo-American playwrights, past and present, with the titles and dates of their first-length dramatic (nonmusical) New York stage productions.

Author	Play	Year
ABBOTT, GEORGE	The Fall Guy	1925
ADE, GEORGE	The County Chairman	1903
AKINS, ZOE	Papa	1919
ALBEE, EDWARD	Who's Afraid of Virginia Woolf?	1962
ANDERSON, MAXWELL	White Desert	1923
ANDERSON, ROBERT	Come Marching Home	1946
ARDREY, ROBERT	Star Spangled	1936
AXELROD, GEORGE	The Seven Year Itch	1952
BARRY, PHILIP	You and I	1923
BEHRMAN, S. N.	The Second Man	1927
BOOTHE, CLARE	Abide With Me	1935
CHASE, MARY	Now You've Done It	1937
CHAYEFSKY, PADDY	Middle Of The Night	1956
CHODOROV, EDWARD	Wonder Boy	1931
CHODOROV, JEROME	Schoolhouse On The Lot	1938
COHAN, GEORGE M.	Popularity	1906
CONNELLY, MARC	Dulcy	1921
CROTHERS, RACHEL	The Three Of Us	1906
CROUSE, RUSSEL	Life With Father	1939
CROWLEY, MART	The Boys In The Band	1968
ELIOT, T. S.	Murder In The Cathedral	1936
FEIFFER, JULES	Little Murders	1967
FERBER, EDNA	Our Mrs. McChesney	1915
FIELDS, JOSEPH	Schoolhouse On The Lot	1938
FRANKEN, ROSE	Another Language	1932
FRIEDMAN, BRUCE JAY	Scuba Duba	1967
GALE, ZONA	Miss Lulu Bett	1920
GELBER, JACK	The Connection	1959
GIBSON, WILLIAM	Two For The Seesaw	1958

Author	Play	Year
GILROY, FRANK D	Who'll Save The Plowboy?	1962
GLASPELL, SUSAN	The Verge	1921
GOETZ, RUTH and AUGUSTUS	One-Man Show	1945
GORDON, RUTH	Over 21	1944
GORDONE, CHARLES	No Place To Be Somebody	1969
GREEN, PAUL	In Abraham's Bosom	1926
GUARE, JOHN	The House Of Blue Leaves	1971
HACKETT, ALBERT and FRANCES	Up Pops The Devil	1930
HANLEY, WILLIAM	Slow Dance On The Killing Ground	1964
HANSBERRY, LORRAINE	A Raisin In The Sun	1959
HART, MOSS	Once In A Lifetime	1930
HECHT, BEN	The Egotist	1922
HELLMAN, LILLIAN	The Children's Hour	1934
HERBERT, F. HUGH	Quiet Please	1940
HOPWOOD, AVERY	Clothes	1906
HOWARD, SIDNEY	Swords	1921
HUGHES, HATCHER	Wake Up, Jonathan	1921
INGE, WILLIAM	Come Back, Little Sheba	1950
KANIN, GARSON	Born Yesterday	1946
KAUFMAN, GEORGE S.	Some One In The House	1918
KELLY, GEORGE	The Torch Bearers	1922
KERR, JEAN	The Song Of Bernadette	1946
KINGSLEY, SIDNEY	Men In White	1933
KOPIT, ARTHUR	Oh Dad, Poor Dad	1962
KRAMM, JOSEPH	The Shrike	1952
KRASNA, NORMAN	Louder, Please	1931
LAURENTS, ARTHUR	Home Of The Brave	1945
LAWSON, JOHN HOWARD	Roger Bloomer	1923
LINDSAY, HOWARD	Tommy	1927
LOOS, ANITA	The Whole Town's Talking	1923
MACARTHUR, CHARLES	Lulu Belle	1926
MACLEISH, ARCHIBALD	Panic	1935
MAYER, EDWIN JUSTUS	The Firebrand	1924
MCCULLERS, CARSON	The Member Of The Wedding	1950
MCNALLY, TERRENCE	And Things That Go Bump In The Night	1965
MILLER, ARTHUR	The Man Who Had All The Luck	1944
MILLER, JASON	Nobody Hears A Broken Drum	1970
ODETS, CLIFFORD	Awake And Sing	1935
O'NEILL, EUGENE	Beyond The Horizon	1920
OSBORN, PAUL	Hotbed	1928
PATRICK, JOHN	Hell Freezes Over	1935
POLLOCK, CHANNING	The Pit	1904
RABE, DAVID	The Basic Training Of Pavlo Hummel	1971
RAPHAELSON, SAMSON	The Jazz Singer	1927
RICE, ELMER	On Trial	1914
RIGGS, LYNN	Big Lake	1927
SACKLER, HOWARD	The Great White Hope	1968
SAROYAN, WILLIAM	My Heart's In The Highlands	1939
SCHARY, DORE	Sunrise At Campobello	1958
SCHISGAL, MURRAY	Luv	1964
SHAW, IRWIN	Siege	1937
SHELDON, EDWARD	Salvation Nell	1908

Author	Play	Year
SHERWOOD, ROBERT E.	The Road To Rome	1927
SIMON, NEIL	Come Blow Your Horn	1961
SMITH, WINCHELL	Brewster's Millions	1906
SPEWACK, BELLA and SAMUEL	The War Song	1928
STALLINGS, LAURENCE	What Price Glory?	1924
STURGES, PRESTON	The Guinea Pig	1929
TAYLOR, SAMUEL	Sabrina Fair	1953
VAN DRUTEN, JOHN	Young Woodley	1925
VAN ITALLIE, JEAN-CLAUDE	America Hurrah	1966
VIDAL, GORE	Visit To A Small Planet	1957
WHEELER, HUGH	Big Fish, Little Fish	1961
WILDER, THORNTON	The Trumpet Shall Sound	1926
WILLIAMS, JESSE LYNCH	The Stolen Story	1906
WILLIAMS, TENNESSEE	The Glass Menagerie	1945
WILSON, LANFORD	The Rimers Of Eldritch	1967
ZINDEL, PAUL	A Dream Of Swallows	1964

Appendix IV
The Golden 100
The Hundred Longest-Running Broadway Productions, 1900-1975

Note: An asterisk indicates the production was still playing June 1, 1974, when this list was compiled.

Title	Performances	Ranking Number
Abie's Irish Rose	2,327	7
Angel Street	1,295	24
Anna Lucasta	957	47
Annie Get Your Gun	1,147	34
Any Wednesday	982	44
Applause	896	54
Arsenic And Old Lace	1,444	17
Barefoot In The Park	1,530	15
Bat, The	867	61
Bells Are Ringing	924	51
Born Yesterday	1,642	12
Butterflies Are Free	1,128	36
Cabaret	1,165	32
Cactus Flower	1,234	28
Call Me Mister	734	88
Camelot	873	60
Can-Can	892	55
Carnival	719	95
Carousel	890	56
Claudia	722	92
Comedy In Music	849	66
Damn Yankees	1,019	42
Death Of A Salesman	742	84
Diary of Anne Frank, The	717	96
Don't Bother Me, I Can't Cope*	914	52

Title	Performances	Ranking Number
Fanny	888	58
Fiddler On The Roof	3,242	1
Finian's Rainbow	725	91
Fiorello!	795	74
First Year, The	760	81
Follow The Girls	882	59
Forty Carats	780	77
Funny Girl	1,348	22
Funny Thing Happened On The Way To The Forum, A	964	45
Gentlemen Prefer Blondes (1949)	740	86
Gold Diggers, The	720	93
Grease*	957	48
Guys And Dolls	1,200	31
Hair	1,750	11
Harvey	1,775	10
Hats Off To Ice	889	57
Hello, Dolly!	2,844	4
Hellzapoppin	1,404	20
High Button Shoes	727	90
How To Succeed In Business Without Really Trying	1,417	19
I Remember Mama	714	97
Inherit The Wind	806	72
Jesus Christ Superstar	720	94
Junior Miss	710	99
King And I, The	1,246	27
Kiss And Tell	956	49
Kiss Me, Kate	1,070	39
La Plume De Ma Tante	835	69
Ladder, The	789	76
Last Of The Red Hot Lovers	706	100
Life With Father	3,224	2
Lightnin'	1,291	25
Luv	901	53
Mame	1,508	16
Man Of La Mancha	2,328	6
Man Who Came To Dinner, The	739	87
Mary, Mary	1,572	13
Mister Roberts	1,157	33
Moon Is Blue, The	924	50
Music Man, The	1,375	21
My Fair Lady	2,717	5
My Sister Eileen	864	62
Never Too Late	1,007	43
No, No, Nanette (1971)	861	63
No Time For Sergeants	796	73
Odd Couple, The	964	46
Oh! Calcutta!	1,314	23
Oklahoma!	2,212	8
Oliver!	774	79
Pajama Game, The	1,063	40
Pins And Needles	1,108	37
Plaza Suite	1,097	38
Prisoner of Second Avenue, The	780	78
Promises, Promises	1,281	26
Seven Year Itch, The	1,141	35

Title	Performances	Ranking Number
1776	1,217	30
Sleuth	1,222	29
Song Of Norway	860	64
Sons O'Fun	742	85
Sound Of Music, The	1,443	18
South Pacific	1,925	9
State Of The Union	765	80
Streetcar Named Desire, A	855	65
Subject Was Roses, The	832	71
Tea And Sympathy	712	98
Teahouse Of The August Moon, The	1,027	41
That Championship Season	844	67
Three Men On A Horse	835	70
Tobacco Road	3,182	3
Two For The Seesaw	750	83
Voice Of The Turtle, The	1,557	14
West Side Story	732	89
Where's Charley?	792	75
You Can't Take It With You	837	68
You Know I Can't Hear You When The Water's Running	755	82

Record Long Run Off-Broadway Productions

Title	Performances	Ranking Number
Blacks, The	1,408	5
Boys In The Band, The	1,000	10
Fantasticks, The*	5,863	1
Godspell*	1,270	6
Jacques Brel Is Alive And Well And Living In Paris	1,847	3
Little Mary Sunshine	1,143	8
One Flew Over The Cuckoo's Nest (1971)	1,025	9
Premise, The	1,255	7
Threepenny Opera, The	2,611	2
You're A Good Man Charlie Brown	1,597	4

Additional Long Run New York Productions Playing As of June 1, 1974:

El Grande De Coca-Cola (O/B) ....668 performances
Irene (1973) ....590 performances
Little Night Music, A ....527 performances
Pippin ....669 performances

Appendix V
Statistical Record
(Broadway Productions)

Season	Plays	Musicals	Revivals	Total
1899-1900	63	14	10	87
1900-1901	50	26	20	96
1901-1902	49	21	20	90
1902-1903	55	27	16	98
1903-1904	68	30	20	118
1904-1905	63	29	35	127
1905-1906	62	32	17	111
1906-1907	67	34	28	129
1907-1908	57	37	16	110
1908-1909	77	33	8	118
1909-1910	95	36	13	144
1910-1911	80	34	17	131
1911-1912	85	39	16	140
1912-1913	98	36	28	162
1913-1914	74	37	17	128
1914-1915	92	24	17	133
1915-1916	70	26	19	115
1916-1917	85	25	16	126
1917-1918	100	38	18	156
1918-1919	104	32	13	149
1919-1920	99	43	2	144
1920-1921	94	51	7	152
1921-1922	142	37	15	194
1922-1923	125	41	8	174
1923-1924	130	41	15	186
1924-1925	162	46	20	228
1925-1926	178	48	29	255
1926-1927	188	49	26	263
1927-1928	183	53	28	264
1928-1929	162	43	20	225
1929-1930	169	35	34	233

Season	Plays	Musicals	Revivals	Total
1930-1931	130	29	28	187
1931-1932	146	27	34	207
1932-1933	124	27	23	174
1933-1934	124	15	12	151
1934-1935	123	19	7	149
1935-1936	108	14	13	135
1936-1937	94	11	13	118
1937-1938	82	16	13	111
1938-1939	68	18	12	98
1939-1940	62	18	11	91
1940-1941	49	14	6	69
1941-1942	58	16	9	83
1942-1943	47	18	15	80
1943-1944	59	19	19	97
1944-1945	62	19	11	92
1945-1946	48	16	12	76
1946-1947	48	14	17	79
1947-1948	44	12	20	76
1948-1949	43	18	9	70
1949-1950	28	17	12	57
1950-1951	46	14	21	81
1951-1952	44	9	19	72
1952-1953	34	11	9	54
1953-1954	42	9	8	59
1954-1955	34	13	11	58
1955-1956	35	8	13	56
1956-1957	37	10	15	62
1957-1958	37	11	8	56
1958-1959	37	12	7	56
1959-1960	38	15	5	58
1960-1961	33	15	0	48
1961-1962	34	17	2	53
1962-1963	36	11	7	54
1963-1964	42	15	6	63
1964-1965	39	17	11	67
1965-1966	38	15	15	68
1966-1967	30	15	24	69
1967-1968	47	12	15	74
1968-1969	34	13	20	67
1969-1970	26	17	22	62
1970-1971	16	17	13	46
1971-1972	26	20	10	56
1972-1973	22	18	17	57
1973-1974	21	12	15	48

Appendix VI
Awards

Following are listings of the four major theatre awards: the Pulitzer Prizes, the New York Drama Critics Circle Awards, the off-Broadway Obie Awards, and the Antoinette Perry (Tony) Awards.

Pulitzer Prizes

For an American play, preferably original and dealing with American Life.

1918—Jesse Lynch Williams, Why Marry?
1920—Eugene O'Neill, Beyond the Horizon.
1921—Zona Gale, Miss Lulu Bett.
1922—Eugene O'Neill, Anna Christie.
1923—Owen Davis, Icebound.
1924—Hatcher Hughes, Hell-Bent for Heaven.
1925—Sidney Howard, They Knew What They Wanted.
1926—George Kelly, Craig's Wife.
1927—Paul Green, in Abraham's Bosom.
1928—Eugene O'Neill, Strange Interlude.
1929—Elmer Rice, Street Scene.
1930—Marc Connelly, The Green Pastures.
1931—Susan Glaspell, Alison's House.
1932—George S. Kaufman, Morrie Ryskind and Ira Gershwin, Of Thee I Sing.
1933—Maxwell Anderson, Both Your Houses.
1934—Sidney Kingsley, Men in White.
1935—Zoe Akins, The Old Maid.
1936—Robert E. Sherwood, Idiot's Delight.
1937—George S. Kaufman and Moss Hart, You Can't Take It With You.
1938—Thornton Wilder, Our Town.
1939—Robert E. Sherwood, Abe Lincoln in Illinois
1940—William Saroyan, The Time of Your Life.
1941—Robert E. Sherwood, There Shall Be No Night.
1943—Thornton Wilder, The Skin of Our Teeth.
1945—Mary Chase, Harvey.
1946—Russel Crouse and Howard Lindsay, State of the Union.
1948—Tennessee Williams, A Streetcar Named Desire.
1949—Arthur Miller, Death of a Salesman.
1950—Richard Rodgers, Oscar Hammerstein II, and Joshua Logan, South Pacific.
1952—Joseph Kramm, The Shrike.
1953—William Inge, Picnic.
1954—John Patrick, Teahouse of the August Moon.
1955—Tennessee Williams, Cat on a Hot Tin Roof.
1956—Frances Goodrich and Albert Hackett, The Diary of Anne Frank.
1957—Eugene O'Neill, Long Day's Journey Into Night.
1958—Ketti Frings, Look Homeward, Angel.
1959—Archibald MacLeish, J. B.

1960—George Abbott, Jerome Weidman, Sheldon Harnick and Jerry Bock, Fiorello.
1961—Tad Mosel, All the Way Home.
1962—Frank Loesser and Abe Burrows, How To Succeed In Business Without Really Trying.
1965—Frank D. Gilroy, The Subject Was Roses.
1967—Edward Albee, A Delicate Balance.
1969—Howard Sackler, The Great White Hope.
1970—Charles Gordone, No Place to Be Somebody.
1971—Paul Zindel, The Effect of Gamma Rays on Man-in-the-Moon Marigolds.
1973—Jason Miller, That Championship Season.
1975—Edward Albee, Seascape.

New York Drama Critics Circle Awards

Listed below are the annual Drama Critics Circle Awards, classified as follows: (1) Best American Play, (2) Best Foreign Play, (3) Best Musical, (4) Best regardless of category.

1935-36—(1) Winterset
1936-37—(1) High Tor
1937-38—(1) Of Mice and Men, (2) Shadow and Substance
1938-39—(1) No award, (2) The White Steed
1939-40—(1) The Time of Your Life
1940-41—(1) Watch on the Rhine, (2) The Corn Is Green
1941-42—(1) No award, (2) Blithe Spirit
1942-43—(1) The Patriots
1943-44—(2) Jacobowsky and the Colonel
1944-45—(1) The Glass Menagerie
1945-46—(3) Carousel
1946-47—(1) All My Sons, (2) No Exit, (3) Brigadoon
1947-48—(1) A Streetcar Named Desire, (2) The Winslow Boy
1948-49—(1) Death of a Salesman, (2) The Madwoman of Chaillot, (3) South Pacific
1949-50—(1) The Member of the Wedding (2) The Cocktail Party, (3) The Consul
1950-51—(1) Darkness at Noon, (2) The Lady's Not for Burning, (3) Guys and Dolls
1951-52—(1) I Am a Camera, (2) Venus Observed, (3) Pal Joey (Special citation to Don Juan in Hell)
1952-53—(1) Picnic, (2) The Love of Four Colonels, (3) Wonderful Town
1953-54—(1) Teahouse of the August Moon, (2) Ondine, (3) The Golden Apple
1954-55—(1) Cat on a Hot Tin Roof, (2) Witness for the Prosecution, (3) The Saint of Bleecker Street
1955-56—(1) The Diary of Ann Frank, (2) Tiger at the Gates, (3) My Fair Lady
1956-57—((1) Long Day's Journey Into Night, (2) The Waltz of the Toreadors, (3) The Most Happy Fella
1957-58—(1) Look Homeward, Angel, (2) Look Back in Anger, (3) The Music Man
1958-59—(1) A Raisin in the Sun, (2) The Visit, (3) La Plume de Ma Tante
1959-60—(1) Toys in the Attic, (2) Five Finger Exercise, (3) Fiorello!
1960-61—(1) All the Way Home, (2) A Taste of Honey, (3) Carnival
1961-62—(1) The Night of the Iguana, (2) A Man for All Seasons, (3) How to Succeed in Business Without Really Trying
1962-63—(4) Who's Afraid of Virginia Woolf? (Special citation to Beyond the Fringe)
1963-64—(4) Luther, (3) Hello, Dolly! (Special citation to The Trojan Women)
1964-65—(4) The Subject Was Roses, (3) Fiddler on the Roof
1965-66—(4) Marat/Sade, (3) Man of La Mancha
1966-67—(4) The Homecoming, (3) Cabaret
1967-68—(4) Rosencrantz and Guildenstern Are Dead, (3) Your Own Thing
1968-69—(4) The Great White Hope, (3) 1776
1969-70—(4) Borstal Boy, (1) The Effect of Gamma Rays on Man-in-the-Moon Marigolds, (3) Company
1970-71—(4) Home, (1) The House of Blue Leaves, (3) Follies
1971-72—(4) That Championship Season, (2) The Screens, (3) Two Gentle-

men of Verona (Special citations to Sticks and Bones and Old Times)
1972-73—(4) The Changing Room, (1) The Hot 1 Baltimore, (3) A Little Night Music
1973-74—(4) The Contractor, (1) Short Eyes, (3) Candide

Obie (Off-Broadway) Awards

1956

Best Over-All Production: Uncle Vanya
Best Director: Jose Quintero (The Iceman Cometh)
Best Actor: Jason Robards, Jr. (The Iceman Cometh), tied with George Voskovec (Uncle Vanya)
Best Actress: Julie Bovasso (The Maids)
Best New Play: Absalom (by Lionel Abel)

1957

Best Over-All Production: Exiles
Best Director: Gene Frankel (Volpone)
Best Actor: William Smithers (The Seagull)
Best Actress: Colleen Dewhurst (The Taming of the Shrew, The Eagle Has Two Heads, and Camille)
Best New Play: A House Remembered (by Louis A. Lippa)

1958

Best Over-All Production: No Award
Best Director: No Award
Best Actor: George C. Scott (Richard III, As You Like It, and Children of Darkness)
Best Actress: Anne Meacham (Suddenly Last Summer)
Best New Play: Endgame (by Samuel Beckett)

1959

Best Over-All Production: Ivanov
Best Director: William Bell (Ivanov) tied with Jack Ragotzy (Time of the Cuckoo and A Clearing in the Woods)
Best Actor: Alfred Ryder (I Rise in Flame, Cried the Phoenix)
Best Actress: Kathleen Maguire (Time of the Cuckoo)
Best New Play: The Quare Fellow (by Brendan Behan)

1960

Best Over-All Production: The Connection
Best Director: Gene Frankel (Marchinal)
Best Actor: Warren Finnerty (The Connection)
Best Actress: Eileen Brennan (Little Mary Sunshine)
Best New Play: The Connection (by Jack Gelber)

1961

Best Over-All Production: Hedda Gabler
Best Direction: Gerald A. Freedman (The Taming of the Shrew)
Best Actor: Khigh Dhiegh (In the Jungle of Cities)
Best Actress: Anne Meacham (Hedda Gabler)
Best New Play: The Blacks (by Jean Genêt)

1962

Best Over-All Production: No Award
Best Direction: John Wulp (Red Eye of Love)
Best Actor: James Earl Jones (N.Y. Shakespeare Festival, Clandestine on the Morning Line, The Apple, and Moon on a Rainbow Shawl)
Best Actress: Barbara Harris (Oh Dad, Poor Dad, Mamma's Hung You in the Closet and I'm Feelin' So Sad)
Best New Play: No Award

1963

Best Over-All Production: Six Characters in Search of an Author (Play), The Boys From Syracuse (Musical)
Best Direction: Alan Schneider (The Pinter Plays)
Best Actor: George C. Scott (Desire Under the Elms)
Best Actress: Colleen Dewhurst (Desire Under the Elms)
Best New Play: No Award

1964

Best Over-All Production: The Brig (Play), What Happened (Musical)
Best Director: Judith Malina (The Brig)
Best Actor: (No Award)
Best Performance: Gloria Foster (In White America)
Best New Play: Play (by Samuel Beckett)

1965

Best Play: The Old Glory
Best Musical Production: The Cradle Will Rock
Best Director: Ulu Grosbard (A View From the Bridge)
Best Performances: Roscoe Lee Browne, Frank Langella, Lester Rawlins (The Old Glory)

1966

Best Play: The Journey of the Fifth Horse
Best Actor: Dustin Hoffman (The Journey of the Fifth Horse)
Best Actress: Jane White (Coriolanus and Love's Labor's Lost)

1967

Distinguished Plays: Futz (by Rochelle Owens), Eh? (by Henry Livings), La Turista (by Sam Shepard)
Best Actor: Seth Allen (Futz)
Best Director: Tom O'Horgan (Futz)

1968

Best Actress: Billie Dixon (The Beard)
Best Actor: Al Pacino (The Indian Wants The Bronx)
Best Director: Michael A. Schultz (Song of the Lusitanian Bogey)
Best Musical: In Circles
Best Foreign Play: The Memorandum

1969

Off-Broadway Excellence; categories unspecified. *The Living Theater* (Frankenstein), *Jeff Weiss* (International Wrestling Match), *Julie Bovasso* (Gloria & Esperanza), *Judith Malina* and *Julian Beck* (Antigone), *Arlene Rothlein* (The Poor Little Match Girl), *Nathan George* and *Ron O'Neal* (No Place To Be Somebody), *Theater Genesis* (sustained excellence), *Jules Feiffer* (Little Murders), *Ronal Tavel* (Boy on the Straight-Back Chair), *Israel Horovitz* (The Honest-To-God Schnozzola), *Open Theater* (The Serpent), *Performance Group* (Dionysius in '69), and *Boston Om Theater* (Riot).

1970

Best Play: The Effect of Gamma Rays on Man-in-the-Moon Marigolds
Tied with: Approaching Simone
Best Foreign Play: What The Butler Saw
Best Musical: The Last Sweet Days of Isaac
Tied with: The Me Nobody Knows
Best Performance: Sada Thompson (The Effect of Gamma Rays on Man-in-the-Moon Marigolds)

1971

Best Play: The House of Blue Leaves
Distinguished Foreign Plays: Boesman and Lena; AC/DC; Dream on Monkey Mountain
Distinguished Production: Trial of Catonsville Nine
Special Citation: Orlando Furioso

1972

Best Theater Piece: The Mutation Show
Special Citation: Free the Army
Best Music and Lyrics: Micki Grant (Don't Bother Me, I Can't Cope)
Best Score: Elizabeth Swados (Medea)
Best Visual Effects: Allen Ginsberg (Kaddish)

1973

Best Plays: The River Niger, The Hot L Baltimore

1974

Best Play: Short Eyes
Best Foreign Play: The Contractor

The Antoinette Perry (Tony) Awards

Beginning in 1947, the Tony Awards have been given yearly for "Distinguished Achievement in Theatre." The awards are named "Tony's" after Antoinette Perry (1888–1946), noted American actress-producer-director.

1947

Director: Elia Kazan (All My Sons)
Actor, Dramatic Star: Jose Ferrer (Cyrano de Bergerac), Fredric March (Years Ago)
Actress, Dramatic Star: Ingrid Bergman (Joan of Lorraine), Helen Hayes (Happy Birthday)
Actor-Featured or Supporting: David Wayne (Finian's Rainbow)

Actress-Featured or Supporting: Patricia Neal (Another Part of the Forest)

1948

Play: Mister Roberts (Authors, Thomas Heggen and Joshua Logan; Producer, Leland Hayward)

Actor, Dramatic Star: Henry Fonda (Mister Roberts), Paul Kelly (Command Decision), Basil Rathbone (The Heiress)

Actress, Dramatic Star: Judith Anderson (Medea), Katharine Cornell (Antony and Cleopatra), Jessica Tandy (A Streetcar Named Desire)

1949

Play: Death of a Salesman (Author, Arthur Miller; Producers, Kermit Bloomgarden and Walter Fried)

Director: Elia Kazan (Death of a Salesman)

Actor, Dramatic Star: Rex Harrison (Anne of the Thousand Days)

Actress, Dramatic Star: Martita Hunt (The Madwoman of Chaillot)

Actor-Featured or Supporting: Arthur Kennedy (Death of a Salesman)

Actress-Featured or Supporting: Shirley Booth (Goodbye, My Fancy).

1950

Play: The Cocktail Party (Author, T. S. Eliot; Producer, Gilbert Miller)

Director: Joshua Logan (South Pacific)

Actor, Dramatic Star: Sidney Blackmer (Come Back, Little Sheba)

Actress, Dramatic Star: Shirley Booth (Come Back, Little Sheba)

1951

Play: The Rose Tattoo (Author, Tennessee Williams; Producer, Cheryl Crawford)

Director: George S. Kaufman (Guys and Dolls)

Actor, Dramatic Star: Claude Rains (Darkness at Noon)

Actress, Dramatic Star: Uta Hagen (The Country Girl)

Actor-Featured or Supporting: Eli Wallach (The Rose Tattoo)

Actress-Featured or Supporting: Maureen Stapleton (The Rose Tattoo)

1952

Play: The Fourposter (Author, Jan de Hartog; Producer, Playwrights Company)

Director: Jose Ferrer (The Shrike, Stalag 17, and The Fourposter)

Actor, Dramatic Star: Jose Ferrer (The Shrike)

Actress, Dramatic Star: Julie Harris (I Am a Camera)

Actor-Featured or Supporting: John Cromwell (Point of No Return)

Actress-Featured or Supporting: Marian Winters (I Am a Camera)

1953

Play: The Crucible (Author, Arthur Miller; Producer, Kermit Bloomgarden)

Director: Joshua Logan (Picnic)

Actor, Dramatic Star: Tom Ewell (The Seven Year Itch)

Actress, Dramatic Star: Shirley Booth (Time of the Cuckoo)

Actor-Featured or Supporting: John Williams (Dial "M" for Murder)

Actress-Featured or Supporting: Beatrice Straight (The Crucible)

1954

Play: The Teahouse of the August Moon (Author, John Patrick: Producers, Maurice Evans and George Schaefer)

Director: Alfred Lunt (Ondine)

Actor, Dramatic Star: David Wayne (The Teahouse of the August Moon)

Actress, Dramatic Star: Audrey Hepburn (Ondine)

Actor-Featured or Supporting: John Kerr (Tea and Sympathy)

Actress-Featured or Supporting: Jo Van Fleet (The Trip to Bountiful)

1955

Play: The Desperate Hours (Author, Joseph Hayes; Producers, Howard Erskine and Joseph Hayes)

Director: Robert Montgomery (The Desperate Hours)

Actor, Dramatic Star: Alfred Lunt (Quadrille)

Actress, Dramatic Star: Nancy Kelly (The Bad Seed)

Actor-Featured or Supporting: Francis L. Sullivan (Witness for the Prosecution)

Actress-Featured or Supporting: Patricia Jessel (Witness for the Prosecution)

1956

Play: The Diary of Anne Frank (Authors

Frances Goodrich and Albert Hackett; Producer, Kermit Bloomgarden)
Director: Tyrone Guthrie (The Matchmaker)
Actor, Dramatic Star: Paul Muni (Inherit the Wind)
Actress, Dramatic Star: Julie Harris (The Lark)
Actor-Featured or Supporting: Ed Begley (Inherit the Wind)
Actress-Featured or Supporting: Una Merkel (The Ponder Heart)

1957

Play: Long Day's Journey into Night (Author, Eugene O'Neill; Producers, Leigh Connell, Theodore Mann and Jose Quintero)
Director: Moss Hart (My Fair Lady)
Actor, Dramatic Star: Fredric March (Long Day's Journey into Night)
Actress, Dramatic Star: Margaret Leighton (Separate Tables)
Actor-Featured or Supporting: Frank Conroy (The Potting Shed)
Actress-Featured or Supporting: Peggy Cass (Auntie Mame)

1958

Play: Sunrise at Campobello (Author, Dore Schary; Producers, Lawrence Langner, Theresa Helburn, Armina Marshall, Dore Schary)
Director: Vincent J. Donehue (Sunrise at Campobello)
Actor, Dramatic Star: Ralph Bellamy (Sunrise at Campobello)
Actress, Dramatic Star: Helen Hayes (Time Remembered)
Actor-Featured or Supporting: Henry Jones (Sunrise at Campobello)
Actress-Featured or Supporting: Anne Bancroft (Two for the Seesaw)

1959

Play: J. B. (Author, Archibald MacLeish; Producer, Alfred de Liagre, Jr.)
Director: Elia Kazan (J. B.)
Actor, Dramatic Star: Jason Robards, Jr. (The Disenchanted)
Actress, Dramatic Star: Gertrude Berg (A Majority of One)
Actor-Featured or Supporting: Charles Ruggles (The Pleasure of His Company)
Actress-Featured or Supporting: Julie Newmar (Marriage-Go-Round)

1960

Play: The Miracle Worker (Author, William Gibson; Producer, Fred Coe)
Director: Arthur Penn (The Miracle Worker)
Actor, Dramatic Star: Melvyn Douglas (The Best Man)
Actress, Dramatic Star: Anne Bancroft (The Miracle Worker)
Actor-Featured or Supporting: Roddy McDowall (The Fighting Cock)
Actress-Featured or Supporting: Anne Revere (Toys in the Attic)

1961

Play: Becket (Author, Jean Anouilh (Translated by Lucienne Hill); Producer, David Merrick)
Director: John Gielgud (Big Fish, Little Fish)
Actor, Dramatic Star: Zero Mostel (Rhinoceros)
Actress, Dramatic Star: Joan Plowright (A Taste of Honey)
Actor-Featured or Supporting: Martin Gabel (Big Fish, Little Fish)
Actress-Featured or Supporting: Colleen Dewhurst (All the Way Home)

1962

Play: A Man for All Seasons (Author, Robert Bolt; Producers, Robert Whitehead and Roger L. Stevens)
Director: Noel Willman (A Man for All Seasons)
Actor, Dramatic Star: Paul Scofield (A Man for All Seasons)
Actress, Dramatic Star: Margaret Leighton (The Night of the Iguana)
Actor-Featured or Supporting: Walter Matthau (A Shot in the Dark)
Actress-Featured or Supporting: Elizabeth Ashley (Take Her, She's Mine)

1963

Play: Who's Afraid of Virginia Woolf? (Author, Edward Albee; Producers, Theatre '63, Richard Barr, and Clinton Wilder)
Director: Alan Schneider (Who's Afraid of Virginia Woolf?)
Actor, Dramatic Star: Arthur Hill (Who's Afraid of Virginia Woolf?)
Actress, Dramatic Star: Uta Hagen (Who's Afraid of Virginia Woolf?)
Actor-Featured or Supporting: Alan Arkin (Enter Laughing)

Actress-Featured or Supporting: Sandy Dennis (A Thousand Clowns)

1964

Play: Luther (Author, John Osborne)
Producer: Herman Shumlin (The Deputy)
Director: Mike Nichols (Barefoot in the Park)
Actor, Dramatic Star: Alec Guinness (Dylan)
Actress, Dramatic Star: Sandy Dennis (Any Wednesday)
Actor-Featured or Supporting: Hume Cronyn (Hamlet)
Actress-Featured or Supporting: Barbara Loden (After the Fall)

1965

Play: The Subject Was Roses (Author, Frank D. Gilroy; Producer, Edgar Lansbury)
Director: Mike Nichols (Luv, The Odd Couple)
Actor, Dramatic Star: Walter Matthau (The Odd Couple)
Actress, Dramatic Star: Irene Worth (Tiny Alice)
Actor-Featured or Supporting: Jack Albertson (The Subject Was Roses)
Actress-Featured or Supporting: Alice Ghostley (The Sign in Sidney Brustein's Window)

1966

Play: Marat/Sade (Author, Peter Weiss; Producer, David Merrick Arts Foundation)
Director: Peter Brook (Marat/Sade)
Actor, Dramatic Star: Hal Holbrook (Mark Twain Tonight!)
Actress, Dramatic Star: Rosemary Harris (The Lion in Winter)
Actor-Featured or Supporting: Patrick Magee (Marat/Sade)
Actress-Featured or Supporting: Zoe Caldwell (Slapstick Tragedy)

1967

Play: The Homecoming (Author, Harold Pinter; Producer, Alexander H. Cohen)
Director: Peter Hall (The Homecoming)
Actor, Dramatic Star: Paul Rogers (The Homecoming)
Actress, Dramatic Star: Beryl Reid (The Killing of Sister George)
Actor-Featured or Supporting: Ian Holm (The Homecoming)
Actress-Featured or Supporting: Marian Seldes (A Delicate Balance)

1968

Play: Rosencrantz and Guildenstern Are Dead (Author, Tom Stoppard; Producer, David Merrick Arts Foundation)
Director: Mike Nichols (Plaza Suite)
Actor, Dramatic Star: Martin Balsam (You Know I Can't Hear You When the Water's Running)
Actress, Dramatic Star: Zoe Caldwell (The Prime of Miss Jean Brodie)
Actor-Featured or Supporting: James Patterson (The Birthday Party)
Actress-Featured or Supporting: Zena Walker (A Day in the Death of Joe Egg)

1969

Play: The Great White Hope (Author, Howard Sackler; Producer, Herman Levin)
Director: Peter Dews (Hadrian VII)
Actor, Dramatic Star: James Earl Jones (The Great White Hope)
Actress, Dramatic Star: Julie Harris (Forty Carats)
Actor-Featured or Supporting: Al Pacino (Does a Tiger Wear a Necktie?)
Actress-Featured or Supporting: Jane Alexander (The Great White Hope)

1970

Play: Borstal Boy (Author, Frank McMahon adapting Brendan Behan's autobiography; Producers, Michael McAloney and Burton C. Kaiser in association with the Abbey Theater of Dublin)
Director: Joseph Hardy (Child's Play);
Actor, Dramatic Star: Fritz Weaver (Child's Play)
Actress, Dramatic Star: Tammy Grimes (Private Lives)
Actor-Featured or Supporting: Ken Howard (Child's Play)
Actress-Featured or Supporting: Blythe Danner (Butterflies Are Free)

1971

Play: Sleuth (Author, Anthony Schafer; Producers, Helen Bonfils, and Michael White)
Director: Peter Brook (A Midsummer Night's Dream)
Actor, Dramatic Star: Brian Bedford (The School for Wives)
Actress, Dramatic Star: Maureen Stapleton (The Gingerbread Lady)
Actor-Featured or Supporting: Paul Sand (Story Theater)

Actress-Featured or Supporting: Rae Allen (And Miss Reardon Drinks a Little)

1972

Play: Sticks and Bones (Author, David Rabe; Producer Joseph Papp)
Director: Mike Nichols (Prisoner of Second Avenue)
Actor, Dramatic Star: Cliff Gorman (Lenny)
Actress, Dramatic Star: Sada Thompson (Twigs)
Actor-Featured or Supporting: Vincent Gardenia (Prisoner of Second Avenue)
Actress-Featured or Supporting: Elizabeth Wilson (Sticks and Bones)

1973

Play: That Championship Season (Author, Jason Miller; Producer, Joseph Papp)
Director: A. J. Antoon (That Championship Season)
Actor, Dramatic Star: Alan Bates (Butley)
Actress, Dramatic Star: Julie Harris (The Last of Mrs. Lincoln)
Actor-Featured or Supporting: John Lithgow (The Changing Room)
Actress-Featured or Supporting: Leora Dana (The Last of Mrs. Lincoln)

1974

Play: The River Niger (Author, Joseph A. Walker; Producer, Negro Ensemble Company)
Director: Jose Quintero (A Moon for the Misbegotten)
Actor, Dramatic Star: Michael Moriarty (Find Your Way Home)
Actress, Dramatic Star: Colleen Dewhurst (A Moon for the Misbegotten)
Actor-Featured or Supporting: Ed Flanders (A Moon for the Misbegotten)
Actress-Featured or Supporting: Frances Sternhagen (The Good Doctor)

Index

Aarons, Alex, 216
Aarons, Alfred E., 13, 209, 290, 493
Abarbanell, Lina, 466
Abba, Marta, 486
Abbott, Anthony, 508
Abbott, Bud, 545
Abbott, George, 16, 23, 28, 56, 62, 67, 68, 69, 77, 88, 105, 114, 115, 136, 137, 151, 166, 174, 175, 190, 196, 209, 210, 214, 217, 233, 241, 255, 257, 259, 266, 272, 282, 311, 323, 324, 332, 341, 343, 361, 377, 382, 383, 397, 402, 414, 428, 430, 431, 437-38, 449, 457, 458, 460, 473, 474, 493, 497, 514, 518, 538, 538, 571, 580
Abbott, John, 29, 245, 315
Abbott, Judith, 16
Abbott, Michael, 235, 265
Abbott, Philip, 206, 439, 440
Abbott-Dunning, Inc., 209
Abdullah, Achmed, 67, 192
Abel, Lionel, 581
Abel, Walter, 48, 52, 109, 127, 132, 136, 137, 144, 159, 202, 223, 239, 257, 279, 306, 307, 310, 320, 335, 338, 363, 374, 426, 428, 440, 516, 521, 524, 526
Abeles, Edward, 63
Abelson, Hope, 141, 389
Abraham, F. Murray, 426
Abraham, Saul, 383
Abrams, Leon, 209
Abramson, Charles, 503, 513
Achard, Marcel, 227, 422
Ackley, Gene, 75
Ackroyd, David, 169
Acosta, Mercedes de, 409
Actor's Theatre, Inc., The, 248, 410
Actor-Managers, Inc., 231, 283
Actors Studio, The, 40, 59
Acuff, Eddie, 198, 209, 245, 533
Adair, Jean, 34, 47, 49, 56, 111, 128, 148, 191, 309, 312, 318, 333, 348, 371, 400, 423, 442, 453, 466
Adair, Ronald, 462
Adair, Yvonne, 174
Adams, Don, 205
Adams, Edie, 49, 498
Adams, Edith, 327, 549
Adams, Franklin P., 137, 282
Adams, John T., 210
Adams, Joseph, 491
Adams, Lee, 186
Adams, Leslie, 401-2
Adams, Mason, 238, 461, 489
Adams, Maude, 251, 369, 540, 547, 552
Adams, Neal, 510
Adams, Nick, 314, 340, 371
Adams, Samuel Hopkins, 395
Adams, William P., 382

Adamson, Harold, 474
Addinsell, Richard, 19
Addy, Wesley, 267, 363, 453, 487
Ade, George, 98, 107, 154, 253, 571
Adelson, Leonard, 303
Adler, Celia, 160
Adler, Charles, 223
Adler, Hans, 392, 483
Adler, Hyman, 426
Adler, Jerry, 169, 314
Adler, Julia, 486
Adler, Lutha (Luther), 19, 38, 46, 83, 102, 138, 160, 186, 202, 225, 305, 315, 337, 363, 364, 400, 406, 452, 470, 476, 486, 495, 504, 552
Adler, Richard, 424
Adler, S. L., 523
Adler, Stella, 38, 53, 174, 186, 222, 296, 337, 338, 346, 363, 381, 435, 452, 454, 552
Admire, Jere, 443
Adoree, Renee, 115
Adoue, Tad, 436
Adrian, 151, 233, 323
Adrian, Henry, 505, 537
Adrian, Iris, 150, 344
Adrian, Max, 122
Afinogenov, Alexander, 273
Afton, Effie, 50, 264, 308, 327, 393
Agee, James, 23
Ahearne, Tom, 216, 390
Aherne, Brian, 167, 327, 428, 431, 435, 504, 541, 550, 552
Aidman, Charles, 81
Ailes, Roger, 220
Ailey, Alvin, 76, 81, 477
Akins, Claude, 236
Akins, Zoe, 110, 114, 125, 163, 170, 197, 205, 317, 323, 344, 347, 404, 473, 502, 571, 579
Albee, Edward, 22, 42, 126, 147, 292, 336, 397, 479, 520, 571, 580, 584
Alberg, Mildred Freed, 276
Alberni, Luis, 472, 515
Albert, Eddie, 68, 72, 167, 173, 339, 344, 368, 402, 463, 471, 544, 546, 552
Albert, Edward, 72, 165
Albert, Harry, 145
Albert, Katherine, 278
Albertson, Frank, 68, 265, 318, 320, 402, 418, 439, 552
Albertson, Jack, 368, 450, 451, 455, 544, 552, 585
Albertson, Lillian, 361, 461
Albertson, Mabel, 43, 172, 368
Albright, Hardie, 23, 46, 197, 246, 373, 475, 537
Albright, Lola, 232
Alcalde, Mario, 69, 129, 161, 284
Alda, Alan, 75, 150, 354, 360, 385, 552
Alda, Robert, 168, 205, 325, 550, 552

INDEX

Alden, Hortense, 71, 157, 193, 211, 476
Alderman, John, 85
Aldredge, Theoni V., 32, 59, 98, 159, 287, 466
Aldredge, Tom, 145, 445
Aldrich, Dorrough, 383
Aldrich, Henry, 514
Aldrich, Richard, 17, 74, 112, 122, 166, 179, 191, 241, 298, 316, 325, 370, 373, 385, 475, 476
Aldrich, Robert, 167
Aldrich, Thomas Bailey, 252
Alen, Fred, 552
Aletter, Frank, 208
Alexander, Chris, 327
Alexander, Cris, 36
Alexander, David, 158, 204, 525
Alexander, Irene, 197
Alexander, Jane, 196, 425, 426, 540, 548, 552, 585
Alexander, John, 23, 34, 135, 214, 257, 309, 318, 332, 358, 392, 459, 463
Alexander, Katherine, 49, 61, 85, 124, 173, 202, 218, 220, 240, 248, 257, 267, 269, 274, 356, 364, 386, 441, 444, 445, 452, 465, 477, 537
Alexander, Leon, 250
Alexander, Ronald, 97, 133, 193, 217, 271, 274, 341, 479, 525
Alexander, Ross, 16, 33, 218, 220, 258, 269, 291, 340, 364, 410, 466, 530
Alfasa, Joe, 367
Alfred, William, 216
Ali, George, 519
Ali, Mohammad, 52
Alicoate, Jack, 149
Allan, Gene, 54
Allan, Elizabeth, 305
Allan, Jed, 362
Allardice, James B., 35
Allen, A. J., 267
Allen, Adrianne, 381
Allen, Billie, 55, 110, 463
Allen, Elizabeth, 295, 396, 478, 552
Allen, Ernie, 75
Allen, Fred, 112, 376, 433, 544
Allen, Gracie, 321, 522
Allen, Jay, 165, 382
Allen, John, 72
Allen, Jonelle, 398, 430
Allen, Kelcey, 415
Allen, Lee, 297
Allen, Lewis, 24, 42, 52, 259
Allen, Martha-Bryan, 344
Allen, Rae, 27, 586
Allen, Rita, 113, 194, 327
Allen, Robert, 101
Allen, Seth, 582
Allen, Steve, 372, 552
Allen, Vera, 70, 142, 228, 259, 316, 370, 425, 446, 495, 528
Allen, Viola, 234, 519
Allen, Walter, 107
Allen, Woody, 134, 373, 552
Allenby, Peggy, 26, 102
Allensworth, Carl, 505
Allentuck, Max, 412
Allgood, Sara, 88, 552
Alliot, Beatrice, 68
Allister, Claude, 309
Allwyn, Astrid, 421
Allyson, June, 277, 393, 423, 529, 552
Almeida, Louis d', 301
Alpert, Larry, 475
Alsberg, Arthur, 204
Alswang, Ralph, 15, 44, 46, 99, 150, 167, 169, 218, 219, 224, 259, 268, 283, 290, 390, 417, 436, 446, 477, 492

Altman, Frieda, 82, 120, 131, 171, 263, 298, 363, 371, 419, 439, 536, 538
Altman, Richard, 89, 430
Altman, Robert, 236
Altman, Ruth, 428
Alton, Maxine, 34
Alvardo, Don, 130
Alwynn, Astrid, 449
Amateau, Rod, 503
Amato, Pasquale, 180
Ameche, Don, 217, 257, 392, 552
American Actors Theatre, 355
American Civic Theatre, 68
American Laboratory Theatre, 53, 491
American National Theater and Academy, 264
American Negro Theatre, 508
American Place Theater, 216, 249, 250, 258, 363
American Producing Company, 285
Ames, Adrienne, 46
Ames, Ed, 353
Ames, Leon, 65, 198, 221, 224, 262, 270, 274, 307, 379, 406, 429, 523
Ames, Michael, 323, 384
Ames, Paul, 198
Ames, Robert, 56, 100, 212, 217, 229, 242, 271, 329, 333, 392, 415, 469
Ames, Rosemary, 302, 525
Ames, Stephen, 198
Ames, Winthrop, 90, 234, 310, 491, 519
Amos, John, 486
Amram, David, 16, 71, 365, 398, 466
Amyx, Hurst, 324
Anamark Productions, 204
Anania, John, 367
Anderman, Maureen, 264, 317
Anders, Glenn, 31, 50, 81, 126, 138, 151, 153, 175, 176, 210, 220, 228, 271, 301, 309, 317, 342, 349, 352, 393-94, 428, 432, 447, 468, 469, 514, 552
Anderson, Alan, 43, 247, 442
Anderson, Daphne, 498
Anderson, Donna, 236
Anderson, Eddie (Rochester), 64, 198, 303, 475, 535
Anderson, Edmund, 45
Anderson, G. M., 342, 534
Anderson, Garland, 32
Anderson, Gwen, 124, 244
Anderson, Hans Christian, 172
Anderson, Hugh, 328
Anderson, Judith, 47, 97, 100, 103, 132, 135, 137, 142, 152, 234, 266, 320, 347, 349, 447, 548, 550, 552, 583
Anderson, Mary, 198, 286
Anderson, Maxwell, 11, 30, 42, 43, 60, 69, 78, 91, 119, 124, 142, 147, 158, 185, 187, 199, 213, 217, 247, 250, 255, 300, 337, 347, 354, 359, 410, 442, 445, 491, 502, 515, 518, 524, 525, 571, 579
Anderson, Richard, 214, 421
Anderson, Robert, 22, 29, 99, 100, 227, 424, 462, 571
Anderson, Sara, 290
Anderson, Sherwood, 523
Anderson, Walt, 303
Anderson, Warner, 67, 393
Andersson, Bibi, 169
Andes, Keith, 94
Andrews Sisters, The, 542, 553
Andrews, Ann, 81, 87, 116, 117, 121, 130, 220, 312, 348, 384, 392, 393, 404, 438, 494
Andrews, Charlton, 58, 176, 259
Andrews, D. H., 136

Andrews, Dana, 80, 266, 332, 482, 553
Andrews, Edward, 15, 47, 142, 172, 226, 323, 432, 463, 469, 478
Andrews, Harry, 531
Andrews, Herbert, 326
Andrews, James J. C., 151
Andrews, Julie, 542, 553
Andrews, Lyle, 224
Andrews, Marie, 268
Andrews, Tod, 179, 452, 548
Angel, Heather, 48, 530
Angelis, Jefferson De, 33, 129, 404
Angelou, Maya, 279
Anglin, Margaret, 38, 194, 261, 538, 539, 553
Angold, Edit. 483
Angus, Bernadine, 371
Angus, Bernie, 28, 69
Ankrum, Morris, 166, 184, 185, 234, 328
Annabella, 242, 243, 261
Anouilh, Jean, 584
Anson, A. E., 79, 90, 170, 293, 310, 396, 401, 432, 466, 518, 535
Anspach, Susan, 28, 373, 505, 541
Anspacher, Louis K., 115, 396, 496
Anthony, Carl, 450
Anthony, Joseph, 49, 69, 78, 80, 81, 95, 107, 157, 161, 203, 263, 269, 299, 300, 302, 351, 374, 389, 421, 429, 491, 498, 513, 523
Anthony, Stuart, 99
Antonio, Lou, 42, 69, 172, 190, 391
Antoon, A. J., 466, 586
Aoki, Rocky H., 169, 235
Appel, Anna, 101, 190, 303, 306
Appell, Don, 81, 133, 179, 285, 473
Appleby, Dorothy, 537
Apstein, Theodore, 237
Arbuckle, Maclyn, 107, 404, 499
Arbuckle, Roscoe (Fatty), 40, 64, 545, 553
Arcaro, Flavia, 386
Archer, Claude, 492
Archer, Daniel, 321
Archer, John, 344, 354, 373, 446
Archibald, H. A., 97
Archibald, Jean, 77
Archibald, William, 79, 237, 378
Ardell, Franklyn, 152
Arden, Edwin, 482
Arden, Eve, 108, 116, 135, 191, 208, 270, 420, 441, 507, 517, 540, 553
Ardrey, Robert, 83, 224, 245, 419, 425, 441, 476, 571
Arena Stage Productions, 317
Arent, Arthur, 155
Argentinita, 544
Arkin, Alan, 145, 264, 276, 287, 455, 519, 542, 553, 584
Arlen, Richard, 20, 49, 475, 483, 527
Arlen, Steve, 216
Arling, Joyce, 28, 62, 312, 474, 514
Arliss, George, 118, 201, 202, 267, 333, 359, 361, 375, 452, 553
Arliss, Mrs. George, 361
Armen, Kay, 421
Armitage, Buford, 133, 324
Armont, Paul, 167, 187, 385
Armstrong, Charl (Charlotte), 203, 397
Armstrong, Louis, 220, 302, 370, 372
Armstrong, Paul, 18, 125, 198, 408
Armstrong, R. G., 196-97, 279
Armstrong, Robert, 240, 331, 428, 455, 513, 519, 526
Armstrong, Will Steven, 28, 87, 104, 273, 341, 365, 391, 413, 462, 474, 538
Armus, Sidney, 98, 205, 208, 344
Arnaud, Yvonne, 553
Arnaz, Desi, 553
Arner, Gwen, 489
Arno, Owen G., 350
Arno, Sig, 98
Arnold, Edward, 33, 50, 55, 101, 102, 123, 140, 193, 212, 230, 244, 248, 252, 257, 307, 332, 342, 445, 475, 509, 513, 517, 519, 534, 553
Arnold, Florine, 304, 471, 506
Arnold, Louise, 316
Arnold, Roberta, 13, 89, 159, 501
Arnold, Seth, 227, 297
Arnold, Victor, 169
Aronson, Alvin, 375
Aronson, Boris, 35, 38, 43, 44, 55, 59, 71, 75, 98, 107, 109, 111, 128, 129, 151, 168, 172, 173, 177, 182, 209, 216, 226, 241, 242, 259, 281, 306, 327, 334, 351, 356, 363, 381, 403, 406, 413, 430, 436, 456, 474, 491, 497, 505, 514
Arrick, Lawrence, 212, 250, 325
Arrighi, Mel, 83, 355
Art Theatre, 138, 430
Arthur, Beatrice, 37, 330, 418, 496, 545, 553
Arthur, Daniel V., 223
Arthur, Hartney, 267-68
Arthur, Jack, 248
Arthur, Jean, 33, 60, 64, 113, 164, 282, 295, 377, 493, 519, 534, 543, 553
Arthur, Julia, 359
Arthur, Lee, 36
Arthur, Maureen, 434
Arthur, Phil, 47, 375, 526
Arthur, Sherwood, 375, 515
Artmart Productions, 140
Arts Foundation, 358
Arzoomanian, Ralph S., 104
Ashburn, Carl, 139
Ashburn, Carroll, 28, 121, 464, 512
Ashcroft, Peggy, 22, 213, 419, 540, 553
Ashley, Edward, 205
Ashley, Elizabeth, 43, 397, 460, 549, 553, 584
Ashley, Joel, 84, 453, 509
Ashley, John, 483
Ashton, Herbert, Jr., 68, 277
Askin, Harry, 69
Asner, Edward, 150, 553
Associated Players, 212
Astaire, Adele, 97, 545, 550, 553
Astaire, Fred, 97, 114, 374, 421, 545, 550, 553
Astar, Ben, 102, 196, 380
Asther, Nils, 336
Astin, John, 461, 496, 545
Astor, Gertrude, 84
Astor, Mary, 26, 35, 117, 133, 164, 217, 231, 277, 292, 297, 329, 361, 386, 388, 392, 396, 452, 473, 553
Astredo, Humbert Allen, 268
Ates, Roscoe, 503
Atherton, William, 221
Atkinson, Brooks, 161, 198, 252, 270, 284, 326, 357, 484
Atkinson, Mrs. Brooks, 252
Atkinson, Oriana, 252
Atlas, Leopold, 71, 513
Attaway, Ruth, 324
Atterbury, Malcolm, 353
Atteridge, Harold, 500
Attles, Joseph, 264
Atwater, Edith, 66, 67, 173, 249, 294, 308, 363, 394, 456, 472
Atwell, Roy, 224, 349
Atwill, Lionel, 28, 100, 133, 191, 192, 256, 261, 295, 329, 417, 435, 440, 451, 477, 553
Auberjonois, Rene, 111, 157, 553
Aubrey, James, 240

Aubuchon, Jacques, 322
Audley, Eleanor, 456
Audre, 350, 504
Auer, Mischa, 19, 64, 113, 284, 494, 500, 525, 533, 534
Auerbach, George, 53
Aulisi, Joseph G., 185, 443, 471
Aumont, Jean-Pierre, 78, 214, 327, 486, 542, 553
Aurthur, Robert Alan, 82, 504
Austen, Jane, 381
Austin, Lyn, 20, 57, 76, 90, 149, 153, 168, 236, 300, 309, 378, 460, 477, 501
Avedisian, Edward, 219
Avedon, Doe, 327, 536
Avery, Phyllis, 269, 274, 524
Avery, Stephen Morehouse, 269
Axelrod, George, 190, 351, 418, 442, 506, 522, 571
Axelson, Mary Macdougal, 270
Ayer, Frederick, 143, 364
Ayers, Ann, 223
Ayers, Lemuel, 78, 142, 206, 366, 372, 373, 415, 522
Aylesworth, Arthur, 26, 499
Aylmer, Felix, 380, 553
Aylsworth, Arthur, 89, 532
Ayre, Robert, 322
Ayres, Lew, 15, 101, 140, 217, 249, 439, 518
Azenberg, Emanuel, 185, 273, 434, 455
Azertis, Lorenzo de, 82

Babbin, Jacqueline, 397
Bacall, Lauren, 75, 190, 197, 248, 255, 543, 553
Bach, Reginald, 217, 410
Bacher, John, 184
Backer, George, 218
Backus, Jim, 110, 216, 454, 479, 484
Baclanova, Olga, 95, 291, 493, 548
Bacon, Catherine, 367
Bacon, Frank, 93, 271, 310, 445, 547, 553
Bacon, Lloyd, 271
Baddeley, Hermione, 203, 309, 553
Badel, Alan, 553
Baff, Regina, 165, 504
Bagdasarian, Ross, 478
Bagley, Henrietta, 220
Bagnold, Enid, 416
Bailey, Le Roy, 113
Bailey, Oliver, 108, 194
Bailey, Pearl, 256, 302, 341, 385, 553
Bain, Conrad, 15, 111, 117, 216, 230, 412, 426, 440, 443, 546
Bainter, Fay, 34, 91, 133, 140, 144, 162, 172, 245, 247, 310, 319, 320, 333, 356, 357, 368, 384, 476, 506, 522, 533, 542, 547, 553
Baird, John, 269
Baker, Benny, 108, 168
Baker, Carroll, 13, 22, 100, 553
Baker, Diane, 118, 129
Baker, Dorothy, 490
Baker, Edythe, 418
Baker, Elliott, 367
Baker, George Pierce, 88
Baker, Howard, 490
Baker, Joe Don, 59, 297
Baker, Kenny, 548
Baker, Lawrence, Jr., 536
Baker, Lee, 25, 210, 275, 320, 334, 365, 388, 424, 440, 464, 506
Baker, Lenny, 453
Baker, Melville, 228
Baker, Phil, 175
Baker, Robert, 34
Baker, Word, 111
Bakos, John, 170
Balaban, Bob, 519
Balderston, John, 48, 136, 393
Balding, Ivor David, 111, 178, 412, 443
Baldridge, Richard, 512
Baldwin, Faith, 192
Baldwin, James, 24, 59
Baldwin, Winnie, 514
Balf, Miriam, 454
Balin, Ina, 102, 291
Ball, Jessica, 446
Ball, Lucille, 37, 110, 208, 215, 402, 405, 421, 441, 527, 553
Ball, William, 480
Ballantine, E. J., 19, 316, 364, 365, 45, 109, 394, 472
Ballantyne, Paul, 191, 457
Ballard, Frederick, 47, 260, 535
Ballard, Kaye, 303, 543, 553
Ballard, Lucinda, 31, 95, 116, 181, 202, 204, 228, 239, 248, 273, 280, 281, 292, 316, 324, 327, 356, 449, 526
Ballou, David R., 79
Balsam, Martin, 78, 262, 308, 403, 454, 474, 553, 585
Bamberger, Theron, 162, 293, 483, 529
Bamman, George, 328
Banbury, Frith, 117
Bancroft, Anne, 111, 275, 311, 383, 494, 549, 553, 584
Bancroft, George, 480
Banghart, Kenneth, 119
Bankhead, Tallulah, 31, 94, 113, 117, 122, 146, 147, 148, 163, 164, 246, 275, 307, 308, 309, 333, 389, 393, 427, 428, 429, 434, 439, 448, 449, 471, 479, 540, 542, 549, 553
Banks, Leslie, 434, 439, 480, 495, 523
Banks, Nathaniel, 413
Banky, Vilma, 469
Banner, John, 52, 365
Bannister, Albert, 33, 45, 196, 440, 444
Bannister, Harry, 44, 165, 180, 187, 248, 283, 395, 450, 532
Banzie, Brenda de, 437
Bara, Theda, 58, 163, 553
Baragrey, John, 160, 194, 352, 382, 396
Baragwanath, John, 23
Baranova, Irina, 543
Barasch, Norman, 292, 415
Barber, Ellen, 151
Barbier, George, 13, 43, 46, 53, 62, 168, 262, 280, 295, 333, 347, 367, 409, 466, 538
Barbour, A., 97, 148, 240
Barbour, Oliver, 59
Barbour, Thomas, 273, 412, 498
Barclay, Patricia, 62, 394
Bard, Katharine, 201, 227, 278, 289, 476
Barillet, Pierre, 75, 165
Barkentin, Marjorie, 496
Barker, Albert, 69, 193, 294
Barker, Edwin, 69, 294
Barker, Jean, 462
Barker, Jess, 24, 162, 534
Barker, Margaret, 37, 83, 186, 222, 259, 305, 415
Barlow, Reginald, 90, 347, 358, 386, 533
Barnard, Harold, 133
Barnard, Henry, 218
Barnard, Julie, 430
Barnes, Binnie, 165, 176, 217, 428, 473
Barnes, Clive, 22, 66, 91, 141, 151,

184, 185, 204, 220, 256, 264, 268, 283, 337, 367, 373, 463, 466, 1155
Barnes, Howard, 318, 490
Barnes, Howard McKent, 212
Barnes, Joanna, 37, 190, 462
Barnes, Margaret Ayer, 16, 131, 245
Barnett, Stanley, 486
Barney, Jay, 23
Barnstead, Margaret, 124
Barnum, George W., 94
Baron, Milton, 97, 273, 465
Baron, Sandy, 173, 351, 462
Baron, William Le, 434
Barr, Geoffrey, 118
Barr, Jeanne, 278
Barr, Richard, 22, 62, 126, 148, 241, 249, 264, 292, 336, 397, 413, 479, 520, 584
Barrangon, Eloise, 438
Barrat, Robert, 88, 272, 300, 433, 472, 500
Barratt, Watson, 83, 258, 261, 285, 370, 401, 478
Barrett, Edith, 24, 232, 317, 364, 368, 372, 459, 525, 531
Barrett, Irving, 55
Barrett, Laurinda, 362, 484
Barrett, Maurice, 347
Barrie, Barbara, 111, 203, 256, 383, 529
Barrie, Elaine, 215
Barrie, Inc., 499
Barrie, James, 170
Barrie, Leslie, 410
Barrie, Mona, 429
Barrie, Wendy, 121
Barrier, Edgar, 58, 60, 230, 281, 300, 305, 365, 374
Barrison, Mabel, 59
Barron, Bobby, 26
Barry, Gene, 84, 368, 385, 547
Barry, J. J., 169, 519
Barry, Leonard, 335, 410
Barry, Patricia, 372
Barry, Philip, 28, 29, 66, 97, 163, 211, 217, 220, 233, 240, 247, 251, 269, 327, 363, 370, 414, 438, 483, 519, 527, 534, 537, 571
Barry, Tom, 107
Barry, Wesley, 367
Barry, William E., 205
Barrymore, Diana, 205, 262, 401, 553
Barrymore, Ethel, 79, 80, 93, 105, 125, 142, 176, 239, 251, 256, 357, 404, 411, 454, 461, 547, 550, 553
Barrymore, John, 47, 93, 105, 106, 124, 130, 165, 182, 193, 215, 246, 255, 298, 314, 325, 369, 395, 493, 533, 543, 549, 553
Barrymore, Mrs. John, 255
Barrymore, Katherine Harris, 51
Barrymore, Lionel, 18, 41, 104, 105, 130, 167, 193, 222, 246, 255, 258, 263, 265, 273, 349, 356, 369, 371, 389, 395, 407, 418, 426, 475, 488, 505, 533, 534, 553
Barrymore, Mrs. Lionel, 105
Bart, Frederick, 222
Bart, Jean, 295, 440
Bartels, Louis John, 422, 541
Bartenieff, George, 315
Barter, Theodore, 261
Barthelmess, Mary, 269
Barthelmess, Richard, 269, 379, 430, 437, 553
Bartholomae, Philip, 43, 360, 483
Bartlett, Martine, 172, 440, 457
Bartlett, Michael, 431
Bartlett, Peter, 59
Barton, Arthur, 293, 529
Barton, James, 229, 347, 424, 479, 481, 548, 553
Baruch, Bernard, 11, 216, 228, 276, 528
Basehart, Richard, 106, 119, 207, 212, 263, 314, 378, 456, 460, 477, 540, 553
Baseleon, Michael, 250, 355
Basquette, Lena, 240
Basserman, Albert, 143, 413, 419
Basshe, Em Jo, 400, 425
Bataille, Nicolas, 266
Bates, Alan, 377, 548, 553, 586
Bates, Blanche, 87, 118, 152, 156, 180, 289, 315, 324, 331, 341, 499, 553
Bates, Esther Willard, 44
Bates, Florence, 67, 228, 266, 271
Bates, Granville, 272
Bates, Sally, 190, 500
Batiste, John, 455
Batson, George, 119, 291, 390
Bauer, Charita, 190, 528
Bauer, M. K., 44
Bauersmith, Paula, 494, 525
Baum, Vicki, 132, 193, 453
Baumann, Kathryn, 367
Baumer, Marie, 109, 274, 415
Baumer, Max, 367
Baumgarner (Garner), James, 76
Bavier, Frances, 56, 246, 257, 290, 298, 330, 375
Baxley, Barbara, 78, 161, 168, 359, 362, 368
Baxter, Alan, 56, 186, 201, 218, 246, 305, 524
Baxter, Anne, 113, 147, 198, 289, 415, 437, 440, 468, 553
Baxter, Billy, 296
Baxter, George, 167, 368
Baxter, Keith, 37, 549
Baxter, Lora, 29, 56, 101, 151, 160, 537
Baxter, Warner, 35, 108, 114, 195, 278, 441, 553
Bay, Howard, 37, 51, 53, 68, 84, 88, 99, 104, 113, 126, 127, 147, 156, 193, 194, 214, 240, 249, 273, 275, 296, 309, 315, 326, 332, 336, 365, 413, 423, 455, 487, 496, 509
Bayer, Eleanor, 471
Bayer, Leo, 471
Bayes, Nora, 545
Baylies, Edmund, 122
Bayne, Beverly, 112, 227, 278
Beach, Gertrude, 299
Beach, Lewis, 191, 307, 440
Beach, Rex, 437
Beach, Stewart, 268
Beadle, Spofford J., 27, 414
Beahan, Charles, 69
Beal, John, 31, 54, 76, 78, 79, 207, 227, 266, 269, 299, 312, 339, 357, 406, 420, 433, 521
Beal, Royal, 62, 136, 201, 340, 363, 527
Beall, Alex, 184
Bean, Orson, 228, 305, 314, 330, 332, 420, 522, 553
Beane, Reginald, 293, 478, 479
Beasley, Byron, 256, 293, 534
Beaston, Frank, 394
Beaton, Cecil, 194, 378
Beatty, Roberta, 67, 167, 254, 338, 378
Beatty, Warren, 281, 354, 553
Beaufort, John, 471
Beaumont, Gerald, 135
Beavers, Louise, 105
Becher, John C., 42, 89
Bechet, Sidney, 209
Beck, Julian, 32, 65, 582
Beck, Martin, 92
Beck, Thomas, 464
Beck, Walter, 20
Beckett, Samuel, 581

Beckett, Scotty, 429
Beckhard, Arthur J., 26, 31, 65, 82, 101, 190, 206, 228, 371, 521
Beddoe, Don, 55, 158, 293, 428, 510, 524
Bedelia, Bonnie, 327, 373
Bedford, Brian, 280, 417, 543, 544, 553, 585
Beebe, Stuart, 324
Beebe, William, 537
Beecher, Janet, 77, 84, 107, 150, 257, 265, 281, 305, 321, 341, 348, 356, 429, 498, 528
Beerbohm, Max, 235
Beers, Francine, 257, 426
Beers, Robert, 219
Beery, Noah, 119, 129, 135, 415, 437
Beery, Wallace, 18, 41, 130, 193, 360
Begley, Ed, 15, 22, 175, 236, 263, 357, 381, 419, 457, 538, 543, 553, 584
Behan, Brendan, 581, 585
Behrman, S. N., 11, 54, 63, 64, 71, 98, 138, 227, 243, 280, 283, 299, 308, 340, 364, 372, 389, 391, 413, 414, 416, 461, 523, 571
Beich, Albert, 294
Bein, Albert, 209, 263, 268, 276
Bein, Mary, 263
Bel Geddes, Barbara, 125, 147, 157, 228, 274, 300, 316, 323, 338, 358, 553
Bel Geddes, Edith Lutyens, 177
Bel Geddes, Norman, 146, 240, 248
Belack, Doris, 212
Belafonte, Harry, 553
Belasco, David, 13, 14, 36, 40, 53, 60, 67, 77, 78, 82, 100, 114, 116, 118, 119, 135, 137, 140, 153, 157, 180, 186, 189, 192, 205, 209, 212, 241, 255, 265, 272, 286, 289, 293, 298, 310, 312, 325, 331, 341, 351, 356, 375, 395, 403, 417, 419, 421, 434, 457, 476, 477, 489, 493, 499, 510, 527, 530, 532
Belasco, Leon, 162, 351
Belita, 496, 545
Bell, C. W., 363
Bell, F. G., 211
Bell, James, 41, 69, 71, 159, 167, 191, 221, 255, 263, 272, 285, 319, 355, 385, 409, 476, 481, 484, 538
Bell, Rex, 107, 152
Bell, Robert, 203
Bell, Thomas, 530
Bell, William, 581
Bellamy, Francis R., 73
Bellamy, Madge, 483
Bellamy, Ralph, 38, 57, 62, 128, 168, 198, 381, 391, 399, 442, 454, 483, 490, 528, 535, 543, 549, 553, 584
Bellaver, Harry, 86, 249, 406, 512, 531
Bellew, Kyrle, 174
Bellow, Saul, 263
Bellwood, Pamela, 157
Bellwood, Peter, 142
Belmont, Mrs. August, 234
Belmore, Bertha, 178, 329, 510
Beloin, Edmund, 233
Bemelmans, Ludwig, 342
Ben-Ami, Jacob, 55, 247, 421, 465, 514
Benchley, Nathaniel, 168
Benchley, Robert, 67, 103, 193, 207, 244, 257, 358, 368, 406, 431, 432, 440, 447, 519
Bender, A., 134
Bendix, William, 47, 128, 201, 312, 405, 478, 479, 549, 554
Benedek, Laslo, 124
Benedict, Paul, 519
Benelli, Sem, 246
Benet, Stephen Vincent, 331, 411, 412, 465

Benjamin, Richard, 442, 455, 554
Bennett, Alan, 549
Bennett, Barbara, 504
Bennett, Belle, 107
Bennett, Constance, 36, 101, 119, 140, 157, 473, 474, 554
Bennett, Dorothy, 162, 528
Bennett, High, 261
Bennett, Jean, 441
Bennett, Joan, 47, 98, 233, 277, 283, 290, 295, 298, 327, 332, 385, 408, 494, 554
Bennett, Michael, 185, 494
Bennett, Richard, 50, 51, 125, 164, 191, 212, 273, 356, 404, 433, 445, 469, 500, 524, 541, 554
Bennett, Wilda, 189
Bennison, Louis, 506
Benny, Jack, 175, 303, 455, 546, 554
Benoit, Patricia, 63, 208
Benrimo, J. Harry, 109, 403, 405, 523, 533
Benson, E. F., 292
Benson, Sally, 252
Bentham, Josephine, 244
Bentley, Beverly, 126, 212
Bentley, Eric, 161
Bercovici, Leonardo, 171, 217, 451
Berenson, Marisa, 226
Beresford, Harry, 133, 348, 420, 499
Berg, Gertrude, 122, 291, 303, 542, 554, 584
Berg, Harold K., 372
Berg, Nancy, 314
Bergen, Edgar, 228
Bergen, Polly, 35, 86, 381, 554
Berger, Bill, 424
Bergerac, Jacques, 178
Berghof, Herbert, 28, 46, 237, 295, 384, 393, 406, 464, 473, 486, 525, 547
Bergman, Herbert T., 30
Bergman, Ingmar, 169
Bergman, Ingrid, 75, 247, 256, 318, 543, 549, 554, 582
Bergner, Elisabeth, 112, 159, 495, 547, 554
Berini, Mario, 160
Berkeley, Busby, 79
Berkeley, Martin, 402, 415
Berkley, Ralph, 477
Berle, Milton, 191, 227, 298, 414, 548, 554
Berlin, Alexandra, 204
Berlin, Irving, 97, 414, 421, 435
Berlinger, Warren, 30, 48, 58, 99, 460, 479
Berman, A. L., 182
Berman, Shelley, 49
Bernard, Barney, 71, 215
Bernard, Bern, 68, 330
Bernard, Joseph, 297
Bernard, Sam, 167
Bernard-Luc, Jean, 151
Bernardi, Herschel, 554
Bernauer, Rudolph, 172
Bernay, Lynn, 206
Berneis, Peter, 297
Berney, William, 117, 126, 384
Bernhardt, Curtis, 317
Bernhardt, Melvin, 27, 141, 154, 256
Bernie, Ben, 196
Berns, Julie, 163, 497
Bernstein, Aline, 28, 70, 91, 155, 205, 206, 251, 292, 413, 476, 512, 522
Bernstein, Leonard, 327
Bernstein, Munsell, 282
Bernstein, Shirley, 240
Berrigan, Daniel (S. J.), 489
Berry, Eric, 177, 479

Berry, John, 24, 111, 159, 268, 330, 471
Berry, Noah, Jr., 236, 345
Berry, Wallace, 290, 299, 321, 348, 488
Berton, Eugene, 109
Besch, Betty Ann, 221
Besch, Bibi, 151
Bessie, Alvah, 383
Best, Edna, 117, 158, 210, 243, 259, 265, 532, 554
Best, Willie, 240
Bettger, Lyle, 115, 158, 162, 182, 248, 316, 453
Bettis, Valerie, 496
Betz, Carl, 279
Bevan, Donald, 441
Bevan, Frank, 197
Bevans, Phillippa, 322
Bey, Turhan, 96
Beyea, Basil, 84
Beymer, Richard, 107, 129, 281
Bianco, Tony Lo, 191, 338, 346
Biberman, Abner, 146, 363, 402, 423, 525
Biberman, Herbert J., 197, 295, 502
Bickel (March), Frederick, 266, 538
Bickerton, Joseph P., Jr., 305
Bickford, Charles, 29, 56, 83, 88, 101, 154, 184, 185, 203, 223, 249, 253, 339, 345, 359, 361, 403, 435, 441, 554
Biddle, Cordelia Drexel, 203
Bidwell, Martin, 285
Bieri, Ramon, 365, 505, 541
Bigbee, North, 153
Bigelow, Otis, 104
Biggers, Earl Derr, 112, 238, 254, 417, 475
Bikel, Theodore, 75, 403
Bill, Tony, 99
Billetdoux, Francois, 462
Billings, Andrew, 81
Bilowit, Ira, 345
Bing, Herman, 246, 321
Bingham, Amelia, 96
Binney, Constance, 471
Binns, Edward, 101, 128, 454
Birabeau, Andre, 114, 274
Bird, Richard, 132
Birell, Tala, 325, 349, 355
Birney, David, 86, 453
Biro, Lajos, 113, 317
Bisch, Louis E., 102
Bishop, Julie, 85, 240
Bishop, Richard, 228, 312
Bishop, Stuart, 79
Bisoglio, Val, 257
Bissell, Whit, 26, 75, 112, 171, 442, 457, 495, 524
Bittner, Jack, 213, 341, 503
Bixby, Bill, 362, 498
Bjurman, Susan, 23
Black, David, 157, 232, 280, 330, 391, 473
Black, Jean Ferguson, 367, 476
Black, Karen, 195, 203, 373, 554
Black-Eyed Susan, 219
Blackburn, Clarice, 25
Blackfriars' Guild, 85, 100, 139
Blackman, Joan, 81, 506
Blackmar, Beatrice, 296
Blackmer, Sidney, 41, 63, 82, 99, 162, 194, 241, 282, 310, 317, 319, 342, 356, 378, 381, 404, 432, 439, 445, 457, 471, 490, 528, 529, 554, 583
Blackwell, Donald, 132, 185, 274, 338, 405, 522
Blackwell, Earl, 33
Blackwood, George, 431
Blaine, Martin, 143
Blaine, Vivian, 145, 329, 542, 550, 554

Blair, Betsy, 31, 45, 126, 150, 256
Blair, Eugenie, 29
Blair, Janet, 67, 179, 327
Blair, John, 349
Blair, Mary, 20, 109, 130, 201
Blake, Robert (actor), 206
Blake, Robert (producer), 384
Blakely, Colin, 111
Blakely, Gene, 76, 513
Blandick, Clara, 426
Blane, Sally, 312
Blaney, H. Clay, 221, 266, 303
Blank, L. Daniel, 515
Blankenchip, John, 28
Blankfort, Dorothy, 315
Blankfort, Michael, 307, 315, 444
Blasco-Ibanex, Vicenter, 57
Blatt, Edward A., 205, 452, 500
Blatty, William Peter, 422
Blau, Bela, 148, 158, 208, 288, 421, 513
Blechman, Burt, 326
Bleckner, Jeff, 414, 445
Bledsoe, Jules, 232
Bleezarde, Gloria, 332
Blinn, Holbrook, 41, 60, 86, 135, 311, 315, 408, 480, 526, 554
Blitzstein, Marc, 31, 155, 275
Bloch, Bertram, 117, 184, 250
Bloch, Charles B., 279
Block, Anita Rowe, 282
Block, Bertram, 246, 438
Blocki, Fritz, 49
Blondell, Gloria, 240
Blondell, Joan, 24, 127, 186, 190, 197, 290, 297, 307, 329, 366, 367, 384, 403, 458, 475, 522, 529, 554
Bloodgood, Clara, 96, 181, 491
Bloom, Claire, 390, 554
Bloomfield, Harry, 166, 297
Bloomgarden, Kermit, 31, 37, 91, 101, 111, 124, 125, 129, 171, 209, 220, 268, 280, 293, 315, 326, 336, 374, 412, 487, 505, 509, 513, 527, 537, 583, 584
Bloomingdale, Alfred, 397, 457, 537
Blore, Eric, 12, 195, 253, 275, 392, 404, 405, 419, 554
Blossom, Roberts, 42, 104, 133, 443
Blue, Ben, 354, 547
Blue, Monte, 477
Blue, Samual, Jr., 86
Blum, Edward, 226
Blum, Gustav, 134, 175, 211, 328, 429, 466, 508
Blyden, Larry, 206, 208, 258, 346, 550, 554
Blyth, Ann, 31, 48, 179, 257, 511, 543, 554
Blyth, E. M., 411
Blythe, Betty, 384
Boardman, Eleanor, 114
Boaz, Charles, 56, 263
Bob Banner Associates, 327
Bobrick, Sam, 339, 341
Bock, Jerry, 173, 332, 580
Boddinton, E. F., 480
Bodeen, DeWitt, 206, 228
Bodenheim, Maxwell, 524
Boehm, David, 425
Bogart, Humphrey, 15, 24, 40, 76, 86, 92, 107, 108, 117, 121, 127, 136, 160, 210, 227, 239, 241, 255, 303, 309, 327, 332, 357, 369, 370, 407, 410, 428, 459, 495, 540, 545, 547, 554
Bogdanoff, Rose, 88, 403
Bogdanovich, Peter, 351, 453
Bogert, William, 256
Bogue, Galen, 386

Bohnen, Roman, 35, 53, 38, 83, 160, 173, 175, 186, 335, 363, 476
Boileau, Pierre, 315
Bois, Curt, 483
Bois, Raoul Pene du, 233, 269, 361
Bois, William Du, 227, 308, 361
Boland, Mary, 13, 18, 94, 107, 210, 285, 303, 326, 355, 381, 385, 405, 423, 475, 484, 505, 529, 547, 548, 554
Bolden, Harry, 279, 405, 444, 535
Boldman, Byron, 317
Boles, John, 16, 89, 108, 114, 277, 403, 514, 548, 554
Boleslavsky, Natasha, 441
Boleslawski, Richard, 42, 251, 321, 408, 491
Boley, May, 521
Bolger, Ray, 510, 543, 547, 548, 554
Bolin, Shannon, 354
Bolt, Robert, 584
Bolton, Guy, 13, 89, 198, 216, 375, 525
Bolton, Mrs. Guy, 525
Bolton, Lawrence, 48
Bolton, Lois, 323
Bonanova, Fortunio, 131
Bond, Lillian, 276, 444
Bond, Rudy, 337, 363
Bond, Sheila, 121, 208, 277, 286, 545
Bond, Sudie, 205, 326, 471, 486
Bond, Ward, 121, 247, 314, 479, 515
Bondi, Beulah, 98, 132, 214, 265, 319, 347, 349, 353, 357, 389, 410, 449, 487, 511, 554
Bondio, J. H. Del, 222, 452
Bonerz, Peter, 519
Bonfils, Helen, 69, 99, 197, 263, 361, 365, 429, 453, 512, 585
Bonfils-Seawell Enterprises, 45
Bonime, Abby, 37, 415
Bonnelli, Richard, 145
Bonstelle, Jessie, 151, 277, 343
Booke, Sorrell, 81, 249, 330, 385, 524
Boone, Pat, 48, 190
Boone, Richard, 284, 293, 398, 554
Booraem, Hendrik, 428
Boorman, John, 254
Boosey, William, 383
Booth, Carol, 45
Booth, John Hunter, 254, 301, 340
Booth, Shirley, 73, 97, 99, 127, 148, 191, 210, 213, 262, 263, 281, 283, 302, 305, 306, 327, 370, 474, 477, 483, 509, 543, 554, 583
Boothe, Clare, 11, 257, 298, 528, 571
Boothe, Earle, 33, 240, 249, 377, 420, 456
Bordages, Asa, 68
Borden, Ethel, 30
Borden, Olive, 171
Bordoni, Irene, 167, 275, 331, 544, 545, 554
Borell, Louis, 78
Boretz, Allen, 219, 345, 397, 402
Borg, Veda Ann, 28
Borgnine, Ernest, 323, 554
Bori, Lucrezia, 369
Borodin, Alexander, 257
Boroff, George, 351
Borough, Margaret, 210
Boruff, John, 65, 85, 119, 281, 365, 510
Bosan, Alonzo, 198, 279, 417, 526
Bosco, Philip, 479
Bosley, Tom, 84, 318, 330, 554
Bostwick, Barry, 98
Bostwick, E. F., 40, 242
Boswell Sisters, 522
Boswell, Connee, 257
Bosworth, Francis, 156

Bosworth, Hobart, 311
Bosworth, Patricia, 224, 430
Bottomley, Roland, 429
Boucicault, Aubrey, 119, 314
Boulle, Pierre, 150
Boulton, Milo, 113, 326, 340, 365
Bourbon, Ray, 84
Bourdet, Edouard, 81, 356, 479
Bourne, Whitney, 83, 344
Bourneuf, Philip, 20, 121, 160, 303, 316, 330, 337, 464, 524, 533
Bova, Joseph, 239
Bovasso, Julie, 59, 130, 184, 581, 582
Bow, Clara, 255, 275, 282
Bowan, Sibyl, 506
Bowden, Charles, 336, 413
Bowers, John, 269
Bowers, William, 517
Bowes, Edward, 256
Bowhan, Gustave, 195
Bowie, John, 253
Bowles, Jane, 234
Bowles, Paul, 115, 141, 183, 234, 243, 269, 285, 309, 326, 436, 453, 457
Bowman, Lee, 208, 290, 500
Boxill, Roger Evan, 187
Boxleitner, Bruce, 443
Boyd, Hutcheson, 368
Boyd, Lawrence, 46
Boyd, William, 100, 261, 357, 437, 445, 464, 506, 515, 546, 547
Boyer, Charles, 43, 158, 179, 205, 256, 280, 299, 486, 543, 554
Boyer, Monica, 453
Boyle, Peter, 419
Boyt, John, 284
Brachita, John, 117
Bracken, Eddie, 68, 224, 240, 358, 407, 432, 514, 554
Brackett, Charles, 129, 386, 398
Bradbury, Lane, 297, 336
Bradbury, Ray, 314
Braddell, Maurice, 234
Bradford, Roark, 197
Bradley, Alice, 192
Bradley, Grace, 240
Bradley, Harry, 12
Bradley, Lillian Trimble, 100, 462, 529
Bradna, Olympe, 85, 209
Brady, Alice, 13, 56, 62, 64, 136, 152, 164, 261, 277, 282, 319, 320, 346, 369, 420, 425, 436, 447, 471, 505, 516, 538, 548, 549, 554
Brady, Barbara, 503
Brady, William A., 35, 40, 41, 47, 60, 61, 75, 86, 97, 136, 152, 164, 167, 174, 188, 194, 231, 256, 266, 267, 269-270, 270, 277, 284, 294, 302, 343, 355, 360, 372, 409, 425, 449, 465, 471, 484, 500, 528
Brady, William A., Jr., 86, 116, 128, 203, 222, 240, 245, 246, 251, 285, 301, 319, 332, 356, 386, 399, 415, 484, 529
Bragdon, Guy, 110
Braggiotti, Stiano, 143, 256
Braham, Horace, 87, 185, 186, 250, 267, 393, 411, 440, 449, 466, 484
Braidwood, Margaret, 281
Brain, Mary, 57
Bramson, David, 52
Bramson, Karen, 476
Brand, Millen, 530
Brand, Neville, 335
Brand, Phoebe, 38, 53, 83, 186, 305, 337, 338, 514
Brando, Jocelyn, 87, 158, 187, 313, 320
Brando, Marlon, 87, 160, 228, 356, 448, 449, 463, 490, 542, 547, 550, 554

Brandon, Mary, 500
Brandon, Peter, 213, 536
Brandt, George W., 296
Brandt, Frances, 424
Brandt, Harry, 133
Brandt, Max, 169
Brandt, William, 133, 432
Branon, John, 165
Brash, Arthur F., 343
Brasselle, Keefe, 25
Bratsburg, Harry, 334
Brazzi, Rossano, 478
Brecher, Egon, 166, 237, 443, 495
Brecher, Irving, 457
Breen, Robert, 148, 184
Breese, Edmund, 58, 92, 155, 273, 301, 410, 432, 471, 520
Breit, Harvey, 131, 199
Brendel, El, 264, 426. 437, 515
Brennan, Eileen, 302, 453, 541, 554, 581
Brennan, Frederick Hazlitt, 44, 444, 530
Brennan, George H., 94
Brennan, Walter, 79, 319
Brenner, Carolyn, 99
Brent, Evelyn, 67, 142, 220, 282, 361
Brent, George, 79, 117, 190, 247, 272, 282, 347, 494, 519, 554
Brent, Romney, 44, 125, 247, 282, 288, 334, 352, 440, 483, 486, 510, 544, 546, 554
Brentano, Felix, 156, 295
Brentano, Lowell, 152, 437, 538
Bressart, Felix, 52
Breuer, Bessie, 454
Brewer, George, 117, 476
Brian, David, 160
Brian, Donald, 43, 224, 484, 547, 549
Brian, Mary, 79, 162, 255, 290, 404, 506
Brice, Carol, 194
Brice, Fanny, 97, 428, 521, 540, 545, 554
Brickert, Carlton, 114
Bricusse, Leslie, 403
Bridgers, Ann Preston, 105
Bridges, Beau, 92, 517
Bridges, Jeff, 230
Bridges, Lloyd, 121, 218, 389, 457, 554
Brieux, Eugene, 13
Briggs, Don, 332
Briggs, Harlan, 53, 133, 159, 162, 164, 172, 182, 241, 341, 446, 477, 480, 498
Briggs, Matt, 56, 201, 252, 255, 292, 298, 431, 458-459, 466, 493
Bright, John, 68
Brightower, Daniel, 66
Brill, Marty, 75
Brinckerhoff, Burt, 58, 75, 409
Brisson, Frederick, 159, 172, 173, 374, 498
Bristol, W. D., 394
Briton, Sherry, 136
Brittan, Robert, 390
Britten, Bill, 23
Britton, Barbara, 224, 303, 358, 437, 506, 508
Britton, Jeff, 12, 83, 509
Britton, Kenneth, 223
Britton, Mozelle, 24, 416
Britton, Tony, 75
Broad, Jay, 256
Broadhurst, George, 61, 100, 266, 294, 381, 445, 462, 482, 529
Broadhurst, Kent, 117
Broadhurst, Thomas W., 146
Brockmeyer, John D., 219
Broderick, Helen, 261, 347, 476, 522, 545, 548, 554
Broderick, James, 249, 269, 479
Brodie, Steve, 218
Brodkin, Herbert, 424

Bromberg, J. Edward, 24, 38, 53, 61, 164, 186, 222, 237, 243, 261, 305, 337, 338, 404, 514
Bromfield, Louis, 223, 479
Bromley, Harald, 29, 121, 182, 270, 415
Bronesky, Leon J., 165, 224
Bronner, Edwin, 535
Bronson, Betty, 47, 424
Bronston, Samuel, 366
Bronte, Charlotte, 243
Bronte, Emily, 531
Brook, Clive, 269, 299, 307, 356, 414, 424, 436, 554
Brook, Faith, 269
Brook, Peter, 585
Brooke, Clifford, 24, 82, 140, 199, 223, 224, 261, 278, 324, 369, 372, 384, 494, 526
Brooke, Eleanor, 256
Brooks, Alan, 374
Brooks, Alfred, 345
Brooks, Donald, 43, 129, 264, 337
Brooks, George S., 438
Brooks, Geraldine, 66, 477
Brooks, Helen, 34, 228, 249, 348
Brooks, Hildy, 204, 238
Brooks, Jan, 243
Brooks, Jean, 207
Brooks, Joseph, 215, 326, 404, 521, 537
Brooks, Lawrence, 401, 547
Brooks, Louise, 282, 360
Brooks, Martin, 15, 70, 226, 336, 410
Brooks, Norman A., 167
Brooks, Phyllis, 334, 404, 419, 441
Brooks, Richard, 255, 457
Brooks, Wilson, 15, 99
Brophy, Edward, 19, 429, 471
Brotherson, Eric, 174, 219, 351
Brotherton, Thomas, 357
Broun, Heywood Hale, 276, 283, 326, 372
Broun, Heywood, 21, 48, 55, 94, 140, 171, 198, 333, 411, 422, 452, 453, 546
Brown, Alice, 90
Brown, Anne, 293, 548
Brown, Anthony, 65, 158, 223, 249, 298, 436, 460, 482, 530
Brown, Arvin, 278
Brown, Barry, 453
Brown, Beth, 46
Brown, Calvin, 282
Brown, Chamberlain, 196, 232, 526, 533
Brown, Charles D., 134, 211, 213, 361, 438, 484
Brown, Clarence, 18, 255, 401
Brown, Edward Sargent, 239
Brown, Elmer, 222
Brown, Frank Emmons, 529
Brown, George Carleton, 411
Brown, Georgia, 540
Brown, Graham, 398
Brown, Harry Joe, 71
Brown, Harry, 436
Brown, James, 188
Brown, Joanna, 112
Brown, Joe E., 37, 72, 79, 98, 142, 207, 377, 554
Brown, John Mason, 33, 38, 284, 300, 313, 316, 468, 525
Brown, Johnny Mack, 105, 442
Brown, Johnny, 82
Brown, Josephine, 178
Brown, Katharine, 452
Brown, Kenneth H., 65
Brown, Louise, 79
Brown, Martin, 97, 116, 148, 261
Brown, Max, 72, 317
Brown, Oscar, Jr., 52
Brown, Pamela, 554
Brown, Phil, 449

Brown, Porter Emerson, 41
Brown, Reed, Jr., 67, 156, 247, 308, 485, 487, 530
Brown, Robert, 496
Brown, Rowland, 249
Brown, Russ, 52
Brown, Susan, 179
Brown, Ted, 498
Brown, Tom, 240, 297, 299, 341, 363, 420, 452, 521
Brown, Vanessa, 210, 265, 418, 504
Brown, William F., 179
Browne, Coral, 37, 554
Browne, Irene, 48, 243
Browne, Porter Emerson, 163
Browne, Roscoe Lee, 42, 104, 172, 477, 554, 582
Brownell, Atherton, 408
Brownell, John C., 343
Brownell, Mabel, 232, 526
Browning, Peaches, 441
Browning, Robert, 79
Browning, Susan, 282
Bruce, Carol, 478, 544, 554
Bruce, Nigel, 88, 456, 487, 488, 495, 499, 554
Bruce, Virginia, 243, 258, 321, 383, 533, 554
Bruckner, Ferdinand, 184
Bruning, Albert, 331, 396
Bruning, Francesca, 26, 65, 145, 252, 354, 394, 439, 453
Bruno, Jean, 273
Bruns, Philip, 440
Bruskin, Perry, 115, 303, 536
Brustein, Robert, 16
Bryan, Gertrude, 386
Bryan, Jane, 68, 347, 429
Bryan-Allen, Martha, 266
Bryant, A., 97, 148, 240
Bryant, Charles, 116, 533
Bryant, Nana, 53, 157, 158, 299, 471
Bryant, Willie, 293
Bryden, Eugene S., 283
Brydon, W. B., 273
Brynner, Yul, 316, 351, 541, 543, 554
Bubbles, Jim, 513
Bubbles, John, 546
Buchanan, Frank, 163
Buchanan, Jack, 64, 207, 554
Buchanan, Thompson, 35, 93, 269, 425, 528
Buchholz, Horst, 88, 299
Buchman, Harold, 431
Buchman, Sidney, 472
Bucholz, Horst, 554
Buchwald, Art, 420, 421
Buck, Gene, 397
Buck, Inez, 311
Buck, Joe, 513
Buck, Pearl, 126, 188
Buck, Richard, 66
Buckler, Hugh, 45, 103, 231, 258, 396, 404
Buckley, Hal, 282
Buckner, Robert, 15, 382
Buell, Tait, 278
Bufano, Remo, 19, 384, 428
Bufman, Zev, 150, 247, 309, 310, 362, 437
Bujold, Genevieve, 30
Buka, Donald, 65, 277, 511
Bulgakov, Barbara, 185
Bulgakov, Leo, 26, 31, 100, 185, 268, 337, 354, 449, 472
Bulifant, Joyce, 362
Bull, Peter, 498
Bullock, Ridgely, 348, 413
Bullock, Turner, 261
Bullock, Walter, 321

Buloff, Joseph, 77, 134, 197, 293, 319, 323-324, 438, 480, 509
Bunce, Alan, 53, 55, 89, 104, 121, 136, 162, 187, 256, 262, 270, 383, 405, 454, 483, 502
Bunde, Irene, 79
Bundsmann, Anton, 432, 476
Bunker, Ralph, 211, 351
Bunyan, John, 92
Buono, Victor, 78
Burbridge, Edward, 133, 443
Burby, Jane, 405
Burch, Ramsey, 28
Buren, A. H. Van, 24, 47, 49, 56, 211, 238, 240, 276, 320, 338, 477, 489
Buren, Kristin Van, 517
Burfield, Joan, 339
Burfield, Kim, 488
Burgess, Dorothy, 171
Burgess, Grover, 53, 298, 337, 425
Burgin, Jon, 350
Burk, Frank, 53
Burke, Billie, 108, 130, 137, 152, 164, 239, 246, 288, 295, 323, 347, 364, 403, 468, 469, 472, 485, 521, 554
Burke, Claire, 189
Burke, Edwin, 473
Burke, Georgia, 30, 124, 194, 293, 296, 526
Burke, Melville, 13, 22, 42, 99, 145, 148, 212, 221, 253, 274, 309, 345, 368, 380, 383, 386, 394, 409, 429, 483, 519
Burke, Peggy, 194
Burleigh, Alston, 405
Burlingame, Lloyd, 283
Burman, Howard, 203
Burnet, Dana, 41, 61, 166, 200
Burnett, Carol, 168, 544, 555
Burnett, Frances Hodgson, 119, 276
Burnett, Murray, 212
Burns, Bernard K., 528
Burns, Bob, 19, 490
Burns, David, 216, 226, 294, 302, 305, 375, 421, 463, 529, 541, 542, 544, 555
Burns, George, 433, 455, 522
Burns, Katherine, 335
Burns, William J., 33
Burnside, R. H., 224
Burr, Anne, 207, 225, 330, 540
Burr, Courtney, 21, 44, 83, 173, 187, 203, 243, 259, 274, 334, 359, 407, 413, 416, 418, 430, 437
Burr, Raymond, 25, 103
Burr, Robert, 130, 284
Burrell, John, 322
Burroughs, Don, 167
Burroughs, Edgar Rice, 462
Burrows, Abe, 75, 165, 187, 339, 381, 392, 433, 580
Burrows, James, 83
Burrows, Jonathan, 157
Bursten, Mike, 238
Burstyn, Ellen, 150, 555
Burt, Frederic, 310
Burton, David, 55, 261, 285, 366, 404, 538
Burton, Marion, 223
Burton, Martin, 67, 155
Burton, Philip, 238
Burton, Richard, 30, 309, 336, 520, 555
Burton, Robert, 204, 428, 476
Burton, Wendell, 165
Busch, Mae, 133
Bush-Fekete, L., 19, 52, 142, 143, 151, 259, 261
Bush-Fekete, M., 19
Bushar, George, 109, 288, 317, 319, 355, 464
Bushkin, Joe, 391

Busley, Jessie, 114, 528
Bussiere, Tadema, 175
Butler, Frank, 203
Butler, Fred, 195
Butler, Rachel Barton, 293
Butterworth, Charles, 66, 70, 164, 297, 420, 434, 534, 555
Button, Dick, 314
Button, Jeanne, 288
Buttons, Red, 504, 524
Buzzell, Eddie, 140, 332
Byington, Spring, 44, 46, 88, 133, 158, 247, 249, 260, 270, 277, 340, 350, 372, 384, 396, 426, 483, 512, 516, 534, 548, 555
Byrd, Sam, 75, 87, 190, 250, 295, 344, 481, 512, 519
Byrne, Dolly, 145
Byrne, Donn, 203
Byrne, Francis, 338
Byron, Arthur, 56, 60, 109, 160, 176, 213, 257, 291, 396, 421, 445, 463
Byron, Edward, 131
Byron, Marcia, 358
Byron, Michael, 66

Cabot, Bruce, 371, 405, 456, 469
Cabot, Eliot, 20, 105, 177, 194, 233, 247, 324, 413, 424
Cabot, Sebastian, 257
Cacoyannis, Michael, 28
Caesar, Arthur, 345
Caesar, Irving, 342, 376
Caesar, Sid, 555
Cagney, James, 62, 67, 85, 290, 314, 354, 359, 360, 366, 367, 479, 515, 529, 555
Cagney, Jeanne, 227, 230, 373, 449, 479
Cahill, Lily, 19, 26, 35, 79, 92, 158, 283, 304, 355, 385, 389, 432, 497
Cahn, Sammy, 136
Cahn, William, 129, 227
Cain, James M., 379, 449
Caine, Georgia, 40, 75, 218, 429
Calbes, Eleanor, 463
Caldara, Orme, 101, 110, 236, 272, 404, 431, 526
Calder, King, 56, 63, 75, 160, 413, 477, 483
Calder-Marshall, Anna, 531
Caldwell, Erskine, 250, 482
Caldwell, Gladys, 130
Caldwell, Zoe, 98, 108, 109, 382, 555, 585
Calhern, Louis, 65, 97, 116, 117, 130, 131, 157, 186, 194, 199, 210, 233, 238, 242, 290, 307, 332, 370, 393, 396, 400, 410, 435, 453, 456, 500, 527, 529, 544, 555
Calhoun, Rory, 197, 437
Call, John, 306
Callahan, James, 90
Callahan, Margaret, 112
Callaway, Kirk, 453
Calleia, Joseph, 67, 68, 168, 186, 191-92, 193, 218, 263, 430, 538
Calloway, Cab, 522
Calthrop, G. E., 148
Calvert, Catherine, 57, 125
Calvert, Louis, 14, 550
Calvert, Patricia, 15, 341
Calvert, Phyllis, 256
Calvet, Corinne, 392, 407, 515
Cambridge, Edmund, 86

Cambridge, Godfrey, 330, 385, 460, 555
Cameron, Donald, 20, 138
Cameron, Hugh, 26, 499
Cameron, John, 109
Cameron, Kenneth, 363
Cameron, Mitchell, 197
Cameron, Rod, 188, 336, 391
Cameron, Rudolph, 158
Cameron, William, 20
Camp, Wadsworth, 264
Campanella, Frank, 122, 314, 341, 393, 426, 441
Campanella, Joseph, 80, 177
Campbell, Alan, 60, 170, 251, 411, 510
Campbell, Colin, 358
Campbell, Douglas, 177, 314
Campbell, Flora, 182, 250, 297, 354
Campbell, Kane, 143
Campbell, Lawton, 232, 433
Campbell, Louise, 198, 221, 519
Campbell, Maurice, 92, 176
Campbell, Mrs. Patrick, 279, 555
Campbell, Shawn, 89
Canary, David, 194
Canfield, Mary Cass, 30
Canfield, Mary Grace, 45
Cannon, Alice, 194
Cannon, Dyan, 169, 338, 555
Cannon, J. D., 194, 195, 302, 555
Cannon, John, 397
Canova, Judy, 420, 546, 555
Cantor, Arthur, 23, 165, 177, 344, 365, 465, 474
Cantor, Eddie, 332, 475, 545, 555
Cantor, Lew, 23, 107, 297, 306, 373, 432
Cantor, Nat, 286
Canzoneri, Tony, 470
Capalbo, Carmen, 85, 416
Capell, Peter, 224, 262
Capers, Virginia, 390
Caplan, Arthur, 271
Caplin, Gertrude, 426
Capote, Truman, 193, 237
Capra, Frank, 34, 56, 134, 216, 442, 535
Carb, David, 386
Carew, Helen, 244, 357
Carewe, Edwin, 209
Carey, Harry, 18, 71, 209, 437, 469, 555
Carey, Joyce, 245, 246, 399
Carey, Macdonald, 30, 58, 136, 194, 541, 555
Cariou, Len, 337
Carlett, Walter, 389
Carlin, Thomas, 104, 194, 217
Carlin, Tom, 293
Carlino, Lewis John, 149
Carlisle, Alexandra, 107
Carlisle, Kitty, 30, 420, 555
Carlisle, Mary, 307
Carlo, Monte, 109
Carlo, Yvonne De, 543
Carlson, Linda, 169
Carlson, Richard, 176, 177, 274, 275, 343, 514, 518, 555
Carlton, Henry Fisk, 500
Carlton, Rex, 355
Carlyle, Richard, 217, 359
Carmichael, Ian, 555
Carminati, Tullio, 450
Carmines, Al, 192
Carnegie, Hattie, 360
Carney, Alan, 517
Carney, Art, 344, 383, 402, 460, 546, 555
Carnovsky, Morris, 38, 61, 75, 83, 98, 106, 142, 175, 186, 220, 222, 251, 284, 298, 305, 327, 331, 335, 337, 338, 363, 400, 452, 457, 476, 486, 555
Carole, Joseph, 416

INDEX

Caron, Leslie, 114, 178, 299, 511
Carpenter, Carleton, 65, 81, 138, 290, 446
Carpenter, Carol, 154
Carpenter, Constance, 235
Carpenter, Edward Childs, 39, 40, 42, 93, 103, 355, 384, 517
Carr, Alexander, 71, 306, 364, 379
Carr, Cora Gay, 452
Carr, Lawrence, 15, 37, 127, 410, 467
Carradine, David, 555
Carradine, John, 57, 112, 266, 300, 479, 525, 555
Carraway, Robert, 187
Carricart, Robert, 403
Carrillo, Leo, 68, 135, 180, 199, 290, 312, 408, 501, 555
Carrington, Elaine, 337
Carrington, Frank, 226, 363
Carrington, Katherine, 146
Carrington, Reginald, 485
Carroll, Albert, 283, 472
Carroll, David, 75
Carroll, Diahann, 555
Carroll, Earl, 262, 418, 515, 518
Carroll, Harry, 59, 391
Carroll, Helena, 430
Carroll, Joan, 483
Carroll, John, 154, 371, 382, 392, 456
Carroll, Leo G., 30, 132, 137, 142, 210, 246, 265, 277, 301, 327, 349, 370, 380, 410, 437, 531, 550, 555
Carroll, Lewis, 20
Carroll, Madeleine, 191, 363, 468, 537, 555
Carroll, Marie, 12, 432
Carroll, Mary, 380
Carroll, Nancy, 12, 70, 89, 100, 163, 227, 499, 555
Carroll, Robert, 28, 327, 424, 493
Carroll, Vinnette, 249, 430
Carroll, Walter, 279
Carson, Frances, 41, 220, 494
Carson, Jack, 19, 29, 34, 109, 135, 224, 248, 292, 334, 349, 354, 426, 555
Carson, Jean, 55, 63
Carson, Johnny, 555
Carson, Mindy, 130
Carstarphen, Frank E., 47
Carter, Arthur, 343
Carter, Daniel D., 301
Carter, Jack, 378, 444
Carter, Jean, 450
Carter, Mrs. Leslie, 14, 137, 419, 489, 548, 555
Carter, Louise, 426
Carter, Marian T., 214
Carter, Oscar M., 315
Carter, Ralph, 390, 486
Carter, Randolph, 146, 171, 531
Cartwright, Veronica, 91
Caruso, Enrico, 180
Cary, Joyce, 313
Caryl, William, 368, 460
Casey, Rosemary, 265, 503
Casey, Stuart, 392
Cash, Rosalind, 86
Cashman, Barney, 264
Cason, Barbara, 337
Caspary, Vera, 57, 175, 266
Cass, Peggy, 36, 48, 90, 168, 277, 555, 584
Cassel, Milton, 113
Cassella, Alberto, 124
Casselle, Jeanne, 132
Cassidy, Jack, 208, 351, 545, 555
Cassini, Oleg, 110
Castellano, Richard, 421, 466, 505
Castillo, 327

Castle, Agnes, 457-58
Castle, Alice, 381
Castle, Don, 518
Castle, Edgerton, 382, 457-58
Castle, John, 273
Castle, William, 140, 269, 303, 339, 442
Casto, Jean, 23, 124, 372
Cates, Gilbert, 227, 507
Catlett, Walter, 97, 190, 220, 310, 476, 555
Cauley, Harry, 269, 362
Caulfield, Betty, 227
Caulfield, Edward, 26, 69, 468
Caulfield, Joan, 44, 123, 257, 542
Cava, Gregory La, 441
Cavanaugh, Hobart, 35, 220, 294, 332, 342, 361, 394, 458, 471
Cavanaugh, Paul, 131, 445
Cavett, Frank, 164
Cellini, Benvenuto, 157
Cerf, Bettina, 143
Chaliapin, Feodor, 173
Challee, William, 529
Challenger, Rudy, 412
Chalmers, Thomas, 23, 24, 42, 51, 124, 146, 256, 277, 318, 320, 388, 394, 506, 514
Chalzel, Leo, 211, 230, 509
Chambers, Haddon, 461
Chambers, Norma, 160
Champion, Gower, 13, 326, 399, 474, 545
Champion, Marge, 13, 399
Champlin, Charles, 222
Chan, Charlie, 187
Chancel, A., 383
Chandler, Helen, 109, 136, 158, 217, 293, 299, 316, 367, 377, 381, 380, 408
Chandler, Jeff, 55, 437
Chandler, Joe, 323
Chandler, Joan, 265, 327
Chaney, Creighton, 55
Chaney, Frances, 415
Chaney, Lon, 258, 311
Chaney, Lon, Jr., 55, 60
Chaney, Stewart, 17, 64, 126, 138, 143, 165, 213, 221, 227, 241, 243, 265, 270, 277, 316, 327, 347, 354, 364, 381, 384, 421, 453, 457, 490, 507, 531
Chanin, John Morris, 100, 290
Channing, Carol, 302, 384, 540, 541, 550, 555
Channing, Stockard, 339
Chapereau, Albert, 292
Chapin, Anne Morrison, 340
Chapin, Brian, 89
Chaplin, Charles, Jr., 342
Chaplin, Geraldine, 555
Chaplin, Sydney, 190, 234, 543, 550, 555
Chapman, John, 72, 236, 277, 491
Chapman, Lonny, 69, 87, 97, 99, 172, 183, 259, 297, 478, 488, 517
Chapman, Marguerite, 106
Chapman, Robert, 54
Chappell, Delos, 119
Chaqueneau, Julien, 509
Charig, Philip, 253, 342, 375
Charisse, Cyd, 475
Charles Frohman, Inc., 31, 38, 49, 57, 81, 113, 442, 444, 538
Charles, Keith, 204
Charles, Theodore, 245
Charney, Jordan, 206
Charnin, Martin, 161
Chase Productions, 445
Chase, Alden, 393, 529
Chase, Ilka, 29, 31, 49, 50, 53, 106, 120, 164, 233, 349, 363, 430, 521, 528, 555
Chase, Mary Ellen, 263

Chase, Mary, 48, 206, 323, 333, 342, 343, 571, 579
Chase, Stanley, 85
Chatfield-Taylor, Otis, 161
Chatterton, Ruth, 87, 100, 114, 133, 137, 267, 272, 317, 389, 413, 483, 555
Chatzel, Leo, 325
Chayefsky, Paddy, 177, 308, 364, 465, 571
Cheever, John, 486
Chekhov, Michael, 12
Chenery, Howard, 466
Cheng, Stephen, 205
Cherry Lane Players, Inc., 521
Cherry, Charles, 21, 359, 461
Cherryman, Rex, 341, 489
Chester, George R., 176
Chevalier, Maurice, 53, 178, 299, 307, 348, 383, 392
Chief Deer, 209
Chief White Hawk, 41
Child, Nellise, 514
Childress, Alice, 30, 104
Childress, Alvin, 30, 69, 495
Chiles, Lois, 195
Chilton, Eleanor, 160
Chinley, Jeannette C., 396
Choate, Edward, 19, 102, 124, 162, 228
Chodorov, Edward, 102, 112, 124, 256, 346, 473, 529, 571
Chodorov, Jerome, 30, 57, 135, 167, 172, 252, 292, 327, 377, 411, 474, 571
Chorpenning, Ruth, 197
Chotzinoff, Samuel, 218
Christensen, Lew, 269
Christian, Linda, 205
Christians, Mady, 22, 132, 228, 262, 395, 410, 511, 543, 555
Christie, Audrey, 24, 37, 73, 175, 217, 271, 330, 395, 407, 475, 507, 528, 550, 555
Christie, Julie, 545, 555
Christmas, David, 72
Christmas, Eric, 351
Chrysler, Walter P., Jr., 78
Church, Sandra, 217, 498, 523, 544
Churchill, Berton, 13, 19, 42, 82, 87, 93, 103, 107, 153, 160, 215, 233, 307, 339, 342, 361, 395, 426, 487, 495, 547
Churchill, Diana, 498
Churchill, Marguerite, 130, 152, 222, 238, 426, 521
Churchill, Sarah, 192
Churchill, Winston, 396
Ciannelli, Eduardo, 109, 128, 163, 168, 250, 291, 395, 472, 525, 526, 533
Cilento, Diane, 190, 555
Cimber, Matt, 456
Cimino, Leonardo, 129, 202, 315, 335
Cioffi, William, 177
Ciolli, Augusta, 257
Circle Repertory Theater, The, 220, 412
Cirker, Ira, 145, 224, 460
Clair, Rene, 167
Claire, Helen, 50, 156, 227, 247, 257, 386, 505
Claire, Ina, 38, 43, 54, 58, 95, 144, 154, 186, 197, 198, 340, 375, 392, 404, 461, 541, 548, 550, 555
Clanton, Ralph, 86, 264
Clark, Alexander, 76
Clark, Barrett, 213
Clark, Bobby, 97, 545, 555
Clark, Dane, 107, 121, 167, 309, 343, 363, 555
Clark, Dort, 285
Clark, Edward, 121, 393
Clark, Fred, 12, 37, 160, 224, 271, 314, 332, 420, 433, 506, 555
Clark, Harry, 208, 522
Clark, Kendall, 127, 218
Clark, Marguerite, 40
Clark, Maurice, 73
Clark, Norman, 523
Clark, Richard, 465
Clark, Roger, 98, 192, 428
Clark, Ron, 339, 341
Clark, Stephen, 58
Clark, Wallis, 137, 369, 420, 492, 538
Clarke, Gage, 247, 297, 453
Clarke, J. I. C., 383
Clarke, Mae, 117, 151, 341, 511
Clary, Robert, 418
Clay, Cassius, 52
Clay, Louise, 220
Clayton, Jack, 237
Clein, John, 457
Clemens, LeRoy, 19, 24
Clement, Clay, 112, 222, 251, 272, 393, 405, 508, 510
Clements, Colin, 182, 206, 446
Clements, Dudley, 134
Cleve, Edith Van, 23, 25, 28, 67, 87, 191, 397, 474, 514, 521
Cleveland, Phyllis, 165
Clifford, Charles L., 484
Clift, Denison, 527
Clift, Montgomery, 25, 114, 149, 162, 166, 210, 312, 357, 413, 427, 468, 535, 538, 543, 544, 549, 555
Clifton, Burt, 191
Cline, Edward F., 209
Clive, Colin, 243, 359
Clive, E. E., 47, 392
Clive, Madeleine, 375, 448
Clork, Harry, 310, 414
Clovely, Cecil, 143
Cluchey, Rick, 75
Clugston, Katharine, 469
Clurman, Harold, 22, 37, 38, 46, 55, 71, 98, 120, 127, 143, 173, 186, 259, 304, 335, 356, 363, 395, 400, 406, 422, 478, 485, 491, 517, 536
Clyde, June, 475
Coakley, Marion, 43, 79, 107, 242, 303, 388, 439, 514
Cobb, Bruce, 221
Cobb, Buff, 90, 332
Cobb, Elisabeth, 305
Cobb, Humphrey, 365
Cobb, Irvin S., 498
Cobb, Lee J., 13, 55, 57, 94, 99, 124, 143, 156, 173, 186, 316, 435, 473, 476, 524, 541, 542, 555
Coburn, Charles, 13, 34, 107, 113, 158, 174, 175, 202, 230, 253, 279, 347, 357, 360, 374, 394, 420, 453, 475, 533, 555
Coburn, Mrs. Charles, 533
Coburn, Helen, 53
Coburn, James, 237, 417
Coca, Imogene, 149, 181, 438, 439, 498, 545, 546, 555
Cochran, Mabel, 131
Cochran, Steve, 129, 212, 310
Coco, James, 147, 173, 264, 555
Cody, Lew, 72, 196, 304
Coe, Fred, 23, 177, 250, 311, 337, 474, 490, 494, 532, 584
Coe, John, 154
Coffee, Lenore, 152
Coffin, Frederick, 59
Cogan, David J., 234, 390
Coghlan, Gertrude, 488
Cohan, George M., 13, 17, 25, 37, 40, 51, 67, 74, 80, 122, 142, 165, 168, 169, 171, 176, 195, 216, 218, 222,

241, 277, 281, 289, 303, 310, 311,
331, 345, 349, 359, 371, 383, 395,
396, 417, 432, 434, 435, 445, 460,
462, 474, 494, 503, 517, 523, 532,
535, 548, 549, 555, 571
Cohan, Georgette, 289
Cohen, Jay J., 149
Cohen, Alexander H., 44, 169, 246, 276,
280, 283, 290, 426, 470, 496, 585
Cohen, Harold D., 341
Cohen, Judith, 165
Cohen, Octavus Roy, 100
Cohn, A., 410, 431
Cohn, Sam, 410
Colbert, Claudette, 43, 53, 58, 138,
154, 216, 252, 257, 258, 261, 299,
307, 311, 324, 365, 394, 415, 428,
475, 479, 486, 499, 522, 526, 556
Colbourne, Maurice, 26, 468
Cole, Beatrice, 283
Cole, Carol, 513
Cole, David, 237
Cole, Dennis, 23
Cole, Mrs. Nat King, 25
Coleman, Cy, 122, 494
Coleman, Emil, 122
Coleman, Lonnie, 249, 373, 509
Coleman, Nancy, 55, 127, 269, 317, 320
Coleman, Patricia, 316
Coleman, Robert, 274
Colette, Sidonie Gabrielle Claudine,
88, 98, 177, 178
Coletti, Frank, 448
Coley, Thomas, 203, 357
Collidge, Philip, 357, 487
Collier, Constance, 33, 44, 130, 248,
369, 416, 441, 456, 556
Collier, John, 284
Collier, William, 84, 130, 220, 332,
342, 349, 426, 444, 449
Collier, William, Jr., 149, 304
Collinge, Patricia, 31, 114, 210, 241,
253, 275, 376, 422, 503, 556
Collins, Dorothy, 543
Collins, Frank J., 417
Collins, Ray, 103, 134, 148, 330
Collins, Russell, 53, 61, 76, 150, 159,
175, 186, 193-94, 203, 209, 211, 230,
235, 312, 316, 318, 322, 363, 407,
442, 452, 456, 505, 509, 543
Collins, Stephen, 317
Collison, Wilson, 176, 179, 392, 500
Collyer, June, 202
Colman, Ronald, 255, 257, 265, 301,
499, 519, 556
Colodny, Lester, 169
Colon, Alex, 178
Colon, Miriam, 303
Colonna, Jerry, 420
Colpitts, Cissy, 59
Colt, Alvin, 45, 81
Colt, Ethel Barrymore, 411
Colt, John Drew, 276
Colton, John, 136, 338, 388, 408, 419
Colvan, Zeke, 102
Combs, Frederick, 62
Comden, Betty, 37, 174, 327
Comegys, Kathleen, 92, 158, 177, 280,
281, 293, 311, 378, 424, 477
Comingore, Dorothy, 46, 201
Como, Perry, 329
Compson, Betty, 208, 238
Compton, Betty, 165
Compton, Fay, 348, 556
Compton, Francis, 178, 230, 243, 261,
315, 323, 333, 430, 456, 480
Compton, Joyce, 231
Comstock, Howard Warren, 133, 444
Comstock, Nanette, 84
Comstock, Ray, 13, 375

Conant, Oliver, 157
Condon, Eva, 97
Condon, Richard, 305
Cone, Rhett, 362
Conforti, Gino, 332
Congdon, David, 225
Congdon, James, 281, 311
Conkle, E. P., 155, 494
Conklin, Chester, 506
Conklin, John, 412
Conklin, Peggy, 19, 83, 106, 155, 177,
208, 212, 215, 220, 224, 289, 312,
321, 347, 364, 369, 371, 385, 526,
533, 540
Conlon, Noel, 79
Conlow, Peter, 18
Connell, Jane, 37, 545
Connell, Leigh, 278, 584
Connell, Louise Fox, 386
Connelly, Hubert, 110
Connelly, Marc, 46, 125, 137, 148, 154,
162, 197, 198, 203, 208, 219, 285,
307, 357, 359, 446, 461, 480, 521,
525, 571, 579
Conners, Barry, 32-3, 181, 210, 365,
432, 499
Connolly, George, 264
Connolly, Thomas, 397
Connolly, Walter, 32, 46, 55, 100, 158,
188, 259, 265, 307, 378, 439, 444,
488, 490, 493, 538, 556
Connor, Whitfield, 131, 148, 467, 524
Connors, Chuck II, 374
Conor, Harry, 59
Conover, Theresa Maxwell, 373, 444
Conquest, Ida, 396
Conrad, Barnaby, 51
Conrad, Con, 514
Conrad, Eugene, 219
Conried, Hans, 461, 544, 556
Conroy, Frank, 22, 41, 63, 76, 102,
114, 150, 163, 172, 177, 209, 233,
256, 275, 344, 348, 354, 375, 403,
404, 556, 584
Considine, Tim, 454
Constant Productions, Inc., 104
Constantine, Michael, 101, 102, 236, 311
Conte, John, 385
Conte, Nicholas (Richard), 151, 209,
326, 335, 508
Conte, Richard, 47, 437, 508, 556
Converse, Frank, 159, 221
Convy, Bert, 168, 226, 282, 549, 556
Conway, Bert, 115
Conway, Curt, 209, 485, 536
Conway, Kevin, 317, 516, 517
Conway, Tom, 41, 186, 207, 321, 489
Coogan, Richard, 19, 129, 389
Cook, Barbara, 194, 276, 543, 556
Cook, Donald (Donn), 25, 65, 87, 95,
163, 201, 256, 283, 289, 301, 316,
333, 339, 363, 378, 391, 415, 422,
428, 523, 541, 556
Cook, Elisha, Jr., 17, 92, 99, 109,
175, 281, 297, 307, 383, 418, 475, 556
Cook, Fielder, 104
Cook, George Cram, 143, 202
Cook, Joe, 345, 548, 556
Cook, Madge Carr, 96, 324
Cook, Peter, 549
Cook, Richard, 237, 508
Cook, Thomas Coffin, 252
Cook, Whitfield, 505
Cooksey, Curtis, 45, 99, 129, 166, 209,
223, 277, 309, 357, 392, 406, 468
Cookson, Peter, 166, 210, 237, 274, 544
Cooley, Dennis. 109
Cooley, Isabelle, 279
Cooley, Leslie John, 430
Coolidge, Philip, 43, 111, 118, 152,

235, 236, 243, 268, 306, 457, 506
Cooney, Dennis, 264, 273, 282
Cooper, Anthony Kemble, 17, 387
Cooper, Ben, 403
Cooper, Frank Kemble, 206, 358
Cooper, Gary, 20, 58, 153, 272, 274, 307, 354, 363, 369, 437, 506
Cooper, Giles, 147
Cooper, Gladys, 12, 203, 372, 435, 556
Cooper, Irving, 208, 343, 468
Cooper, Jackie, 256, 290, 314, 393, 418, 488, 514, 556
Cooper, James, 417
Cooper, Jane, 94
Cooper, Jimmie, 58, 538
Cooper, Lew, 405
Cooper, Marilyn, 463
Cooper, Maury, 184
Cooper, Melville, 57, 157, 486, 547, 556
Cooper, Violet Kemble, 94, 204, 288, 496, 545
Coote, Robert, 122, 264
Coots, J. Fred, 87
Cope, John, 12, 241
Cope, Patricia, 273
Copeland, Joan, 128, 161, 202
Coppel, Alec, 172, 173, 226
Coppel, Myra, 172
Coppin, Grace, 166
Corbett, Gretchen, 165
Corbett, Leonora, 549
Corbin, John, 246, 333, 388, 393
Corby, Ellen, 228
Cordner, Blaine, 58, 64, 151, 158, 417, 512, 530
Cordoba, Pedro de, 158, 265, 298, 331, 334, 415, 477
Cordova, Fred de, 50, 142, 459
Corey, Irwin, 323, 471
Corey, Jeff, 88, 218
Corey, Wendell, 46, 53, 71, 100, 108, 136, 159, 249, 296, 336, 389, 450, 523, 545, 556
Corio, Ann, 542
Corle, Edwin, 294, 433
Corley, Pat, 414
Cormack, Bartlett, 388
Cornelius, Henry, 226
Cornell, Katharine, 16, 17, 19, 82, 131, 161, 162, 233, 247, 333, 340, 380, 447, 476, 524, 541, 542, 543, 544, 550, 556, 583
Cornell, Ted, 340
Corri, Adrienne, 243
Corrigan, Emmett, 18, 77, 125, 192, 331, 474, 533
Corrigan, Lloyd, 211
Corsaro, Frank, 40, 208, 218, 335, 336
Corsia, Ted De, 411
Cort, Harry L., 503
Cort, John, 319, 475
Cortez, Ricardo, 41, 117, 207, 240, 297, 349
Corthell, Herbert, 169, 224, 371, 417, 444
Corwin, Norman, 398
Corzatte, Clayton, 423, 512, 534
Cosentino, Nicholas, 316
Coslow, Jacqueline, 489
Cossart, Ernest, 12, 82, 128, 241, 248, 298, 300, 428
Cossart, Valerie, 83
Costa, Morton Da, 136, 198, 340, 428, 509, 528
Costa, Patti, 165
Costello, Dolores, 98
Costello, Lou, 545
Costello, Mariclare, 16
Coster, Nicolas, 204
Costigan, James, 40, 276

Cotes, Peter, 213
Cotsworth, Staats, 15, 236, 289, 445, 513
Cotten, Joseph, 76, 126, 247, 280, 351, 370, 379, 407, 543, 556
Cotter, Jayne, 258
Cotton, Lucy, 492
Cotton, Will, 64
Cottrelly, Mathilde, 12, 380
Coulouris, George, 45, 57, 112, 265, 289, 300, 464, 502, 511, 543, 556
Courtenay, William, 79, 205, 238, 266, 323, 362, 391, 401, 497-98
Courtland, Jerome, 257
Courtleigh, Stephen, 150
Courtleigh, William, 145, 160, 163, 209, 264, 339, 432, 477, 513
Courtneidge, Cicely, 556
Courville, Albert de, 406, 523, 536
Cover, Franklin, 256
Cowan, Irene, 359
Cowan, Jerome, 28, 61, 62, 167, 173, 198, 253, 259, 297, 327, 347, 365, 394, 509
Coward, Noel, 309, 404, 526, 541, 556
Cowen, Ron, 453
Cowen, William Joyce, 152
Cowl, Jane, 101, 110, 120, 132, 158, 171, 192, 236, 245, 272, 306, 325, 347, 389, 397, 398, 403, 431, 458, 474, 526, 541, 556
Cowles, Albert, 502
Cowles, Chandler, 54, 153, 305
Cowles, Matthew, 292
Cowles, Virginia, 282
Coxe, Louis O., 54
Coy, Walter, 145, 160, 263, 297, 335, 337, 363
Coyle, J. J., 338
Crabtree, Paul, 230, 277, 305, 309, 424, 428, 446
Craft, Paddy, 278
Craig, Helen, 129, 249, 263, 406, 497
Craig, James, 167, 257, 312
Craig, John, 47, 528
Craig, Michael, 118
Craig, Walter, 354
Crain, Jeanne, 524
Crandall, Edward, 210, 215, 430
Crane, James, 20, 355, 395
Crane, Norma, 81, 240
Crane, Vernon, 281, 412, 432
Crane, William H., 119, 154
Craven, Frank, 37, 61, 64, 71, 130, 159, 162, 164, 323, 338, 357, 396, 408, 417, 437, 466, 484, 485, 498, 505, 517, 531, 556
Craven, John, 33, 203, 357, 495
Crawford, Alice, 48
Crawford, Bobby, 416
Crawford, Boyd, 44, 184, 453, 533
Crawford, Broderick, 60, 67, 334, 344, 429, 458, 479, 550, 556
Crawford, Cheryl, 23, 31, 53, 78, 97, 98, 100, 152, 162, 182, 188, 218, 222, 279, 313, 346, 368, 398, 403, 457, 514, 583
Crawford, Clifton, 326
Crawford, F. Marion, 234, 519
Crawford, Joan, 108, 160, 164, 166, 191, 193, 225, 311, 389, 439, 456, 485, 516, 526, 528
Crawford, Kathryn, 96
Crawford, Michael, 302
Crehan, Joseph, 272, 307, 349, 473, 493
Crews, Laura Hope, 69, 73, 87, 151, 153, 194, 212, 227, 230, 295, 348, 349, 369, 377, 389, 401, 410, 424, 514, 556

Crews, Laurie, 340
Crichton, Kyle, 203
Crimmins, A., 148, 240
Crisp, Donald, 24, 142, 162, 247, 255, 300, 347, 364, 392, 451, 531
Crist, Judith, 300
Cromwell, John, 11, 35, 50, 61, 65, 95, 128, 136, 152, 153, 171, 174, 177, 206, 240, 266, 270, 277, 285, 294, 296, 298, 300, 316, 333, 346, 347, 375, 386, 388, 407, 420, 424, 425, 462, 471, 484, 529, 532, 538, 542, 556, 583
Cromwell, Richard, 110, 222, 247, 432
Cronyn, Hume, 52, 126, 141, 145, 213, 214, 218, 288, 289, 293, 321, 342, 345, 379, 394, 402, 429, 454, 456, 468, 512, 556, 585
Crooker, Earle, 152, 239, 538
Crosby, Bing, 13, 107, 203, 290, 370, 420, 522
Crosby, Gary, 217
Crosby, Juliette, 88, 339, 422
Crosby, Vivian, 489
Crosby, William, 319
Crosman, Henrietta, 90, 92, 108, 314, 404, 457
Crosswell, Anne, 486
Crothers, Rachel, 35, 59, 85, 147, 149, 262, 269, 275, 296, 300, 319, 333, 347, 358, 456, 471, 473, 475, 503, 516, 537, 571
Crouse, Russel, 34, 128, 174, 196, 207, 270, 352, 380, 393, 442, 450, 461, 571, 579
Crow, Laura, 510
Crowe, Gordon, 412
Crowley, Ann, 418
Crowley, Mart, 62, 571
Crowley, Matt, 124, 147
Crowley, Pat, 166, 436, 486
Crowther, Bosley, 175
Crowther, John, 434
Crumit, Frank, 547
Crump, John, 134, 214
Crump, Owen, 436
Cukor, George, 31, 60, 116, 130, 167, 170, 194, 199, 217, 277, 370, 404, 449, 456, 490, 524, 532, 536
Cullinan, Ralph, 81
Cullum, John, 24
Culp, Robert, 95, 380, 454, 556
Culver, Calvin, 492
Cumberland, John, 179, 211, 259, 363, 380, 500
Cummings, Constance, 12, 109, 231, 278, 354, 472, 556
Cummings, E. E., 214
Cummings, Irving, 521
Cummings, R. F., 319
Cummings, Robert, 151, 420, 511, 548, 556
Cummings, Vicki, 72, 73, 164, 219, 224, 241, 286, 309, 323, 346, 362, 556
Cummins, Peggy, 265
Cunningham, Cecil, 240
Cunningham, Robert, 99
Cunningham, Zamah, 201
Curci, Gennaro, 163
Curran, Homer, 245, 393
Current Productions, 348
Currie, Finlay, 129, 484, 556
Curtis, Donald, 32
Curtis, Francis, 182, 228
Curtis, Jack, 47, 373, 379, 444
Curtis, John, 288
Curtis, Keene, 98, 337
Curtis, Margaret, 214
Curtis, Raymond, 274, 405, 522
Curtis, Tony, 190, 385, 391, 519

Curtiz, Michael, 270, 327
Curzon, George, 216, 364
Cushing, Catherine Chisholm, 141, 246, 258, 301, 376
Cushing, Tom, 57, 128, 258, 265, 465
Cusick, Peter, 392
Cutler, Lester, 291
Cypher, Jon, 131, 295
Czinner, Paul, 112, 360, 495

d'Almeida, Louis, 301
D'Amato, Anthony, 510
D'Annunzio, Gabriele, 113
D'Elia, Marie, 184
D'Lugoff, Burton, 379, 423
Da Costa, Morton, 37, 136, 198, 340, 428, 509, 528
da Silva, Howard, 11, 15, 19, 20, 56, 70, 83, 102, 122, 186, 194, 195, 197, 234, 327, 385, 390, 453, 495, 539, 542, 556
Daab, Hyatt, 397
Dabney, Augusta, 374, 457
Daffi, 184
Dahl, Roald, 218
Dailey, Dan, 70, 84, 88, 137, 346, 347, 515, 521, 556
Dailey, Irene, 312, 338, 439, 451, 491, 544, 556
Dalberg, Camilla, 533
Dale, Alan, 411, 456
Dale, Charles, 306, 420, 428, 521
Dale, Esther, 26, 31, 74, 82, 206, 371, 439
Dale, Frances, 280
Dale, James, 494
Dale, Jim, 544
Dale, Margaret, 49, 87, 107, 117, 120, 130, 265, 347, 349, 486, 487
Daley, Cass, 391
Dalio, Marcel, 419
Dall, John, 31, 86, 123, 210
Dalrymple, Jean, 66, 70, 219
Dalton, Charles, 90, 194, 252, 293, 300, 303, 508
Dalton, Doris, 58, 150, 226, 271, 305, 370, 406, 418, 483
Dalton, Timothy, 273, 531
Daly, Arnold, 267, 291, 301, 349, 383, 462, 507
Daly, Blyth, 64, 87, 259, 495
Daly, James, 15, 54, 183, 202, 368, 556
Daly, Tyne, 72
Damita, Lili, 64, 331, 515
Damon, Cathryn, 373
Damon, Stuart, 145, 478
Damone, Vic, 257, 421
Damrosch, Gretchen, 364, 370
Damrosch, Walter, 364, 370-71
Dana, Barbara, 145, 517
Dana, Kenneth, 59
Dana, Leora, 45, 49, 205, 234, 264, 375, 528, 556, 586
Dana, Royal, 151, 230, 309, 380, 443
Dana, Viola, 377, 556
Dandridge, Dorothy, 393
Daneel, Sylvia, 126, 492
Danelle, John, 486
Danielewski, Tad, 68, 126
Daniell, Henry, 38, 94, 120, 142, 217, 245, 256, 280, 327, 370, 416, 511, 528, 543, 556
Daniels, Bebe, 106, 266
Daniels, Billy, 186, 341

Daniels, Carolan, 354, 429
Daniels, J. B., 57, 68, 135, 212
Daniels, Jack, 19, 294, 365
Daniels, Marc, 121, 179
Daniels, William, 116, 122, 267, 353, 474, 541, 542, 556
Dann, Roger, 380
Danner, Blythe, 72, 453, 585
Dano, Royal, 166, 308, 323
Danson, Ted, 443
Dante, Ron, 54
Dantine, Helmut, 369, 546
Danton, Ray, 291
Darby, Kim, 173
Darden, Severn, 361
Darke, Rebecca, 520
Darlan, Jean Francois, 35
Darnell, Linda, 57, 205, 556
Darrid, William, 28, 104, 131, 236
Darro, Frankie, 285
Darvas, Lili, 63, 88, 153, 159, 213, 219, 268, 326, 432, 556
Darwell, Jane, 89, 108, 209, 228, 421, 452, 459
Dash, Thomas, 300
Dassin, Jules, 159, 240, 251, 303
Daudet, Alphonse, 409
Daugherty, Richard, 150
Dauphin, Claude, 122, 177, 205, 244, 556
Davalos, Richard, 505
Davenport, Charles, 68
Davenport, Harry, 44, 158, 205, 245, 271, 320, 334, 393, 439, 465, 475, 534-35, 546
Davenport, Nigel, 237
Daver, Minoo, 380
David Merrick Arts Foundation, 367
David, Benjamin, 15
David, Jean, 45
David, Mack, 303
David, Thayer, 81, 187, 313, 384
Davidson, Gordon, 489
Davidson, John, 203, 240
Davies, Hubert Henry, 359
Davies, Margaret, 59
Davies, Marion, 40, 137, 184, 365, 366, 375
Davies, Valentine, 58, 254
Davis, Allen, 94
Davis, Ann, 283, 299, 420
Davis, Bette, 67, 110, 117, 139, 142, 245, 247, 275, 295, 297, 336, 347, 359, 369, 433, 511, 520, 550, 551, 556
Davis, Blevins, 250
Davis, Boyd, 522
Davis, C. T., 401
Davis, Cherry, 430
Davis, Christopher, 467
Davis, Clifton, 144
Davis, Donald, 134, 142, 146, 188, 320, 541
Davis, Dorrance, 33, 261, 421
Davis, Edgar B., 258
Davis, Evelyn, 526
Davis, Fay, 222
Davis, Garry, 441
Davis, Gwen, 48
Davis, Humphrey, 157
Davis, Irving Kaye, 22, 129, 264, 431, 503, 526
Davis, J. Frank, 258
Davis, Jack, 469
Davis, James, 204
Davis, Luther, 258
Davis, Marion, 241, 361
Davis, Meyer, 116, 405, 435, 509
Davis, Ossie, 198, 245, 267, 385, 393, 404, 431, 486, 526, 539, 556

Davis, Owen, 35, 50, 82, 128, 134, 140, 146, 152, 164, 173, 188, 194, 228, 247, 253, 266, 321, 332, 339, 340, 355, 409, 425, 431, 439, 483, 484, 500, 579
Davis, Owen, Jr., 215, 247, 339, 433, 479, 483
Davis, Peter, 133
Davis, Richard Harding, 130
Davis, Richard, 258
Davis, Sammy, Jr., 30, 186, 556
Davis, Sheldon, 139, 492
Davis, Susan, 104
Davison, Bruce, 37
Dawn, Hazel, 126, 176, 500, 529, 556
Dawn, Isabel, 297
Dawson, Forbes, 119
Dawson, Hal K., 133, 259
Dawson, Mark, 397
Day, Alice, 234, 304
Day, Clarence, 270
Day, Doris, 367, 416, 456, 492
Day, Edith, 37
Day, Edmund, 404
Day, Juliette, 501, 533
Day, Laraine, 41, 473, 489
Day, Lillian, 98, 357
Dayan, Assaf, 159
Daykarhanova, Tamara, 69, 143
Dayton, June, 241, 465
Dayton, Katharine, 158, 410
Dazey, Frank, 55, 459
de Acosta, Mercedes, 409
De Angelis, Jefferson, 33, 129, 404
de Azertis, Lorenzo, 82
de Banzie, Brenda, 437
de Carlo, Yvonne, 543
de Cordoba, Pedro, 158, 215, 265, 298, 331, 334, 415, 477
de Cordova, Fred, 50, 142, 459
De Corsia, Ted, 411
de Courville, Albert, 406, 523, 536
De Foe, Louis, 448
de Forest, Marian, 145, 277
de Gaw, Boyce, 297
de Hartog, Jan, 583
De Haven, Gloria, 18, 402, 418, 456
de Havilland, Olivia, 142, 177, 210, 292, 317, 354, 556
De Koven, Reginald, 452
De Koven, Roger, 35, 102
de Kruif, Paul, 532
De La Traz, Jean, 362
De Leath, Vaughn, 265
De Leon, Walter, 285
de Liagre, Alfred, Jr., 35, 74, 137, 181, 226, 244, 274, 282, 306, 321, 330, 370, 385, 475, 507, 533, 584
De Marcos, The, 475
de Mario, Paul, 316
de Marney, Derrick, 537
de Maupassant, Guy, 87
De Mille, Cecil B., 146, 382, 395, 441,' 480, 510
de Mille, William C., 94, 201, 510, 527
de Neergaard, Beatrice, 133, 277
de Reeder, Pierre, 230
De Santis, Joe, 119, 168, 214, 233, 250, 413
De Shields, Andre, 510
de Sica, Vittorio, 153
de Silva, Frank, 386, 425
de Vise, Peter, 250, 424
de Wilde, Brandon, 58, 100, 143, 304, 305, 323, 388, 540, 542, 557
De Wilde, Frederic, 262
De Witt, Paul, 414
De Wolfe, Billy, 123, 479
de Wolfe, Elsie, 356

Deacon, Richard, 145
Dean, Basil, 537
Dean, James, 232, 415, 541, 556
Dean, Julia, 61, 266, 375, 404
Deane, Christopher, 92
Deane, Gregory, 77
Deane, Hamilton, 136
Deane, Katherine, 149
Deaven, John Bruce, 492
Dee, Frances, 25, 277, 333, 414, 469
Dee, Ruby, 245, 279, 385, 390, 431, 460, 542, 556
Dee, Sandra, 221, 378, 460, 504
Deems, Mickey, 187
Deer, Chief, 209
Deering, Olive, 86, 106, 119, 128, 146, 168, 297, 303, 412, 428, 524
Deering, William, 358
Deeter, Jasper, 143, 232
DeFore, Don, 136, 292, 354, 443, 517
Dehner, John, 110
Deighton, Marga Ann, 453
Dekker, Albert, 28, 55, 66, 102, 150, 158, 162, 250, 258, 286, 298, 365, 545
Del Bondio, J. H., 222, 452
Del Grande, Louis, 165
Del Rio, Dolores, 55, 135, 146, 515
Delancey Productions, 303
Deland, Margaret, 38
Delany, Maureen, 347
Delbert, Robert, 367
DeLeath, Vaughn, 140
Delf, Harry, 152
Delfont, Bernard, 426, 496
Dell, Claudia, 458
Dell, Dorothy, 196
Dell, Floyd, 97, 274
Dell, Gabriel, 121, 169, 297, 423, 434
Delmar, Vina, 40, 309, 396
Delorme, Daniele, 178
Delroy, Irene, 415
Demarest, William, 142, 158
DeMille, Katherine, 24
Demongeot, Mylene, 111
Dempsey, Clifford, 35, 42, 191, 266, 355, 419
Dempsey, Jack, 51, 336
Dempsey, Mrs. Jack, 51
Denham, Reginald, 42, 44, 116, 119, 192, 198, 244, 245, 250, 309, 338, 378, 404, 421, 464, 495, 509
Denison, Leslie, 184
Denison, Michael, 12
Denker, Henry, 82, 153, 477, 503, 515
Dennis, Patrick, 37
Dennis, Sandy, 29, 32, 116, 150, 474, 520, 543, 556, 585
Denniston, Reynolds, 267, 371
Denny, Reginald, 33, 85, 255, 363
Denton, Crahan, 69, 71, 167, 356, 523
der Vlis, Diana van, 100, 422
Derby, Joan, 268
Dere, Ann, 265, 484, 486
Dermer, Bob, 165
Dern, Bruce, 195, 457, 556
Derr, Richard, 97, 193, 239, 302, 487, 504
Derwent, Clarence, 24, 66, 67, 121, 151, 200, 221, 226, 237, 246, 256, 264, 265, 266, 372, 373, 386, 416, 425, 500, 508, 525
Derwent, Elfrida, 256
DeSales, Francis, 233
DeSeta, William F., 79
Destinn, Emmy, 180
DeSylva, B. G., 167, 275. 362
Deutsch, Armand, 529
Deval, Jacques, 486
Devane, William, 86, 288, 353, 368, 511
Devere, Trish Van, 255

Devereaux, John Drew, 177, 270, 480
Devine, Andy, 154, 332, 533
Devine, Jerry, 90, 332
Devlin, John, 54
DeVonde, Chester, 258
DeVries, Peter, 437, 492
Dewhurst, Colleen, 22, 23, 42, 90, 127, 194, 318, 320, 540, 545, 549, 550, 551, 557, 581, 584, 586
Dewing, E. B., 134
Dews, Peter, 585
DeYoung, Cliff, 445
Dhiegh, Khigh, 581
di Cosmi, Bruno, 350
Diamond, David, 403
Diamond, I. A. L., 75
Diaz, Rosita, 463
Dick, Douglas, 218, 413
Dickey, Annamary, 148
Dickey, Paul, 34, 68, 176, 271, 311, 420
Dickinson, Angie, 87, 368, 557
Dickinson, Emily, 20
Dicks, Joseph, 81
Dickson, Gloria, 142, 310, 473, 525
Diener, Joan, 216, 257, 413
Dieterle, William, 413
Dietrich, Dena, 383
Dietrich, Marlene, 257, 435, 437
Dietz, Eileen, 443
Dietz, Howard, 389
Dietz, John, 110
Digges, Dudley, 13, 138, 143, 175, 176, 200, 202, 229, 273, 283, 296, 298, 299, 301, 333, 348, 361, 367, 413, 433, 440, 543, 544, 548, 557
Dillaway, Don, 154, 217, 506
Diller, Phyllis, 14, 302
Dillingham, Charles, 35, 211, 212, 239, 276, 285, 321, 324, 444, 466, 511
Dillman, Bradford, 102, 169, 230, 278, 394, 549, 557
Dillon, Melinda, 520, 548
DiLuca, Dino, 477
Dinehart, Alan, 24, 32, 58, 63, 86, 87, 109, 148, 181, 264, 266, 303, 299, 311, 339, 365, 386, 403, 416, 425, 475, 488, 494, 500
Dinelli, Mel, 293
Dingle, Charles, 23, 25, 83, 120, 232, 268, 275, 432, 442, 459
Dishy, Bob, 108, 109, 191, 434
Ditrichstein, Leo, 141, 195, 385
Dix, Beulah Marie, 388, 399
Dix, Richard, 158, 274, 319, 342, 404
Dixey, Henry E., 299, 348, 383, 474
Dixon, Beverly, 339
Dixon, Billie, 582
Dixon, Ivan, 85, 390
Dixon, Jean, 40, 47, 66, 125, 171, 175, 209, 210, 217, 252, 350, 440, 480, 503, 529, 548, 557
Dixon, Lee, 197, 458
Dixon, Thomas, 94, 239, 294
Dmytryk, Edward, 76
D'Orsay, Fifi, 154
D'Orsay, Lawrence, 139, 404, 432, 441, 494
d'Usseau, Arnaud, 125, 259, 268, 483
Dobbs, Randolph, 75
Dobson, James, 320, 446, 523
Dodd, Claire, 142, 160, 297
Dodd, Lee Wilson, 87, 215, 362
Dodson, J. E., 311
Dohanos, Peter, 254
Dolan, Michael, 33
Dolan, Robert Emmett, 281, 342
Dolin, Anton, 115, 550
Doll, Bill, 421
Dolley, Sara, 184

Dolly Sisters, The, 214, 545
Donahue, Troy, 164
Donald, James, 150
Donald, Peter, 385
Donaldson, Ted, 92, 435
Donaldson, Walter, 332
Donat, Peter, 37, 557
Donath, Ludwig, 122, 166, 354
Donehue, Vincent J., 84, 92, 119, 280, 312, 326, 454, 488, 490, 584
Donen, Stanley, 256, 351
Donlan, Yolande, 411, 547
Donleavy, J. P., 178
Donlevy, Brian, 62, 101, 238, 309, 340, 386, 397, 421, 432, 475, 500, 506, 515, 557
Donnell, Jeff, 338, 476
Donnelly, Dorothy, 396, 435
Donnelly, Leo, 220, 293, 309
Donnelly, Ruth, 37, 57, 87, 190, 209, 231, 246, 272, 303, 372, 383, 397, 404, 409, 410, 420, 429, 435
Donner, Clive, 287
Donoghoe, Dennis, 267
Donovan, Casey, 492
Donovan, King, 181
Doolar, James, 367
Dooley, Paul, 344, 519
Doran, D. A., 175, 186, 415, 455, 468, 521
Doran, Johnny, 89
Doren, Carl Van, 478
Dorfman, Nat, 145, 461
Dorn, Philip, 52, 228, 369
Doro, Marie, 94, 272
Dors, Diana, 323
Dorsey, Jimmy, 500
Dortner, Fritz, 31
Doubleday, Kay, 130
Doucet, Catherine, 35, 60, 91, 128, 138, 149, 259, 264, 312, 380, 404
Douglas, Diana, 214
Douglas, Gilbert, 213
Douglas, Jerry, 492
Douglas, Kirk, 19, 46, 128, 180, 183, 257, 320, 352, 353, 365, 438, 523, 527, 545, 557
Douglas, Margaret, 142, 345, 358
Douglas, Marion, 535
Douglas, Melvyn, 40, 49, 54, 55, 68, 106, 121, 167, 171, 182, 227, 236, 274, 317, 319, 339, 343, 357, 392, 437, 461, 473, 479, 494, 557, 584
Douglas, Michael, 453
Douglas, Paul, 60, 94, 134, 216, 433, 541, 542, 557
Douglas, Robert, 15, 64, 92, 281, 319, 377, 497
Douglas, Sharon, 28
Douglas, Mrs. Stephen, 398
Douglas, Tom, 417, 536
Douglas, Wallace, 282
Douglas, Warren, 527
Douglass, Kent, 511
Douglass, Margaret, 114, 154, 282, 406, 496, 509, 528
Douglass, Stephen, 389, 543
Dourif, Brad, 516, 517
Dove, Billie, 125, 356
Dowd, Harrison, 131, 318
Dowdy, Helen, 293, 324
Dowling, Constance, 269, 355
Dowling, Doris, 528
Dowling, Eddie, 28, 53, 182, 183, 211, 229, 285, 296, 305, 357, 444, 472, 478, 543, 549, 557
Dowling, Robert W., 381, 382, 421
Downey, Morton, 148
Downing, David, 86

Downing, Joseph, 110, 121
Downing, Robert, 468
Downing, Todd, 84
Downs, Johnny, 190, 198, 388
Doyle, Conan, 421
Doyle, David, 45, 228, 434, 498
Doyle, John T., 503
Doyle, Len, 373, 478
Doyle, Miriam, 56, 306, 385, 477
Doyle, William R., 82
Drake, Alfred, 178, 197, 251, 257, 280, 283, 358, 473, 551, 557
Drake, Betsy, 522
Drake, Donna, 31
Drake, Ervin, 209
Drake, Frances, 341
Drake, Stuart, 434
Drake, William A., 146, 193, 207
Drama Craftsmen, 416
Dramatists' Theatre, 191, 358, 536
Draper, Paul, 479
Drayton, Mary, 124, 374
Dreiser, Theodore, 25, 83, 202
Dresser, Louise, 119, 271, 380, 444
Dressler, Eric, 21, 33, 42, 46, 109, 110, 148, 191, 251, 334, 358, 366, 536
Dressler, Marie, 29, 130, 265, 269, 344, 365, 557
Drew, Ellen, 336, 357
Drew, John, 84, 120, 291, 396, 547, 548
Drew, Sidney, 254
Drew, Mrs. Sidney, 254
Drey, Walter, 296
Dreyfuss, Arthur, 24
Dreyfuss, Richard, 72
Driscoll, Bobby, 205, 488
Driscoll, Lawrie, 151
Drivas, Robert, 28, 130, 280, 509, 557
Driver, Donald, 247, 309, 357, 443
Drouet, Robert, 181
Dru, Joanne, 12, 121, 424
Druce, Hubert, 204, 261, 299, 301, 359, 461
Druce, Olga, 316
Druli, Sylvia, 171
Drummond, Alice, 58, 471
Drury, Allen, 15
Druten, John Van, 15, 47, 114, 131, 132, 137, 162, 226, 228, 241, 267, 292, 306, 319, 347, 364, 433, 468, 507, 537, 573
du Bois, Raoul Pene, 233, 269, 324, 361
Du Bois, William, 227, 308, 361
Du Maurier, George, 369
Du-For, Denis, 67, 224, 377, 473
Duane, Michael, 524
Duckworth, Dortha, 373
Ducovny, Amram, 488
Dudley, Doris, 144, 211, 325, 413, 444
Duel, Peter, 173
Duerrenmatt, Friedrich, 122
Duff, Donald, 521
Duff, Howard, 22
Duff-MacCormick, Cara, 317, 358
Duffey, Vincent, 197, 328
Duffy, Henry, 387
Dufour, Val, 194
Dugan, William Francis, 506
Duggan, Andrew, 30, 167, 403, 471
Duggan, Thomas, 42
Dukakis, Olympia, 12, 154
Duke, Patty, 30, 240, 311, 479, 549, 557
Duke, Vernon, 389, 474
Dullea, Keir, 72, 135, 413, 557
Dumbrille, Douglas, 89, 250, 369, 557
Dumont, Margaret, 332, 342, 429, 557
Duna, Steffi, 135
Dunaway, Faye, 71, 216, 557
Dunbar, Janet, 278

606 INDEX

Duncan, Andrew, 519
Duncan, Augustin, 128, 159, 206, 210,
    254, 294, 360, 421, 516, 546
Duncan, Isadora, 129
Duncan, Jesse, 21
Duncan, Mary, 26, 324, 419
Duncan, Sandy, 86, 270, 283, 442, 557
Duncan, Todd, 548
Dundy, A., 64
Dunham, Clarke, 288, 373
Dunham, Katherine, 545
Dunn, Emma, 57, 67, 133, 192, 221, 252,
    347, 425, 510
Dunn, Isabel, 124
Dunn, James, 41, 207, 215, 432, 549, 557
Dunn, Josephine, 79, 296
Dunn, Liam, 65, 535
Dunn, Michael, 42, 224, 309, 557
Dunn, Ralph, 350
Dunne, Irene, 16, 38, 165, 228, 253,
    261, 270, 360, 424, 557
Dunne, Philip, 58, 214
Dunning, Philip, 67, 137, 176, 255,
    272, 335, 361, 394, 405, 411, 473, 493
Dunnock, Mildred, 31, 79, 84, 89, 98,
    124, 163, 201, 214, 234, 245, 266,
    270, 309, 355, 382, 457, 504, 541,
    543, 557
Dunphy, Jack, 410
DuPont, Paul, 381
Dupree, Minnie, 87, 96, 97, 147, 215,
    263, 264, 272, 325, 348, 363, 399,
    416, 419
Duprez, June, 487
Durante, Jimmy, 176, 295, 542, 546, 557
Durkin, James, 92
Durkin, Junior, 107, 198, 261
Durning, Charles, 59, 89, 225, 236,
    239, 466, 544
Durning, Dan, 184
Duryea, Dan, 31, 121, 275, 297, 312, 557
Duse, Eleonora, 113
Duser, Jane Van, 308
Duvall, Robert, 76, 87, 120, 505, 541,
    557
Dvorak, Ann, 57, 209, 392
Dwyer, Ethel, 462
Dyar, Ralph E., 506
Dyas, James, 416
Dyer, William, 277
Dyer-Bennet, Richard, 413
Dyke, Dick Van, 543, 568
Dysart, Richard A., 275, 466, 544

Eagels, Jeanne, 114, 201, 245, 388,
    421, 529, 536, 557
Eagle, Oscar, 223, 253, 324, 429
Eames, Clare, 158, 285, 331, 382, 459
Eames, Kathryn, 262
Earl, Marshall, 97
Eason, Myles, 252
Eaton, Charles, 42, 426
Eaton, Walter Prichard, 157, 386
Ebb, Fred, 88, 205, 226
Eberhart, Mignon G., 142
Ebsen, Buddy, 180, 332, 540, 546, 557
Eburne, Maude, 362
Ecco Productions, 430
Eck, Marsha Louis, 519
Eckart, Jean, 313, 332, 341, 346, 378,
    460, 513, 539
Eckart, William, 313, 332, 341, 346,
    378, 460, 513, 539
Eckstein, Gustav, 92
Eddinger, Wallace, 37, 60, 79, 84, 94,
    208, 291, 345, 417, 471, 513
Eddy, Nelson, 180
Edelman, Herb, 43, 280, 344
Edelman, Maurice, 77
Edelstein, Ray, 79
Edeson, Robert, 94, 96, 396, 425
Edison, Arthur, 202
Edmonds, Beulah, 69
Edmonds, Walter D., 154, 285
Edney, Florence, 43, 2334
Edwards, Bart, 209
Edwards, Ben, 42, 52, 55, 116, 131,
    143, 150, 152, 157, 206, 218, 243,
    268, 279, 318, 377, 385, 388, 394,
    422, 454, 478, 485
Edwards, Blake, 422
Edwards, Cliff, 85, 97, 180, 285, 420,
    444, 485, 503, 550
Edwards, Felix, 238
Edwards, James, 218, 305
Edwards, Ronnie Claire, 273, 489
Edwards, Rowland, 377
Edwards, Ben, 308
Edwards, Felix, 498
Efird, Mel, 459
Efron, Marshall, 196
Egan, Frank, 442, 518
Egan, Jenny, 42, 111
Egan, Michael, 235
Egan, Richard, 376
Egbert, Leslie Floyd, 62
Eggerth, Marta, 547
Ehrmann, Herbert, 498
Eigsti, Karl, 221, 238
Eikenberry, Jill, 317
Eilers, Sally, 41, 71, 420
Einhorn, Abe, 16
Eisenschiml, Otto, 538
Eisinger, Jo, 375, 515
Elcar, Dana, 188, 218, 357
Elder, Eldon, 89, 170, 198, 479, 536
Elder, Lonne III, 86
Eldredge, John, 251, 475
Eldridge, Florence, 15, 24, 26, 31, 37,
    50, 83, 87, 120, 194, 218, 236, 266,
    278, 300, 342, 345, 384, 394, 426,
    427, 532, 536, 538, 542, 546, 549, 557
Eldridge, Frank, 24
Eldridge, John, 237
Eldridge, Paul, 239
Elias, Alix, 221, 263, 346
Elias, Hector, 445
Elinson, Izzy, 474
Eliot, T. S., 155, 571, 583
Eliscu, Davie, 206
Eliscu, Edward, 140, 314, 388
Elizondo, Hector, 443, 471
Elkins, Hillard, 48, 100
Elkins, Marie Louise, 19, 57, 68, 212,
    308, 532
Ellerbe, Harry, 155, 164, 288, 294,
    346, 352, 370, 372, 428, 473
Ellin, David, 457
Elliott, Arthur, 87
Elliott, Clyde, 428
Elliott, Denholm, 315, 485
Elliott, Francis Perry, 362
Elliott, Harold, 62
Elliott, James S., 284-85, 483
Elliott, James W., 63, 220, 256, 402,
    410
Elliott, James, 44, 216, 420
Elliott, Jimmy, 159
Elliott, Maxine, 211, 212, 490, 557
Elliott, Stephen, 101, 108, 109, 111
Elliott, Sumner Locke, 73
Elliott, William, 149, 192, 218, 258
Ellis, Charles, 126, 130, 408
Ellis, Edith, 281, 299, 442, 518
Ellis, Edward, 44, 88, 98, 132, 137,

176, 238, 356, 393, 395, 451, 488, 525
Ellis, Evelyn, 125, 330, 378, 404, 486
Ellis, Mary, 82, 90, 110, 153, 246,
    447, 547
Ellis, Maurice, 279, 305, 312, 372
Ellis, Michael, 12, 15, 45, 86, 99,
    179, 246, 362
Ellis, Patricia, 35, 67, 98, 142
Ellison, James, 259
Elliston, Grace, 107, 273, 358, 499
Ellsler, Effie, 44, 179, 547
Elman, Irving, 63, 159, 497
Elmore, Lee, 167, 425
Elmslie, Kenward, 194
Elser, Frank B., 154, 285, 321
Elsner, Edward, 61, 265, 319, 342, 419,
    420, 482, 503, 521, 538
Elsom, Isobel, 25, 46, 95, 162, 202,
    237, 324, 367, 495
Elson, Charles, 87, 284
Elston, Robert, 187, 461
Eltz, Theodore von, 90
Elviry, 459
Ely, Ron, 394
Elzy, Ruby, 69
Emerson, Faye, 384, 544, 546
Emerson, Geraldine, 71
Emerson, Hope, 88, 112, 290, 459
Emerson, John, 93, 174, 432, 519
Emerson, Lillian, 34, 294, 342, 373, 375
Emery, Dorothy, 374
Emery, Edward, 215, 299, 308, 324
Emery, Gilbert, 86, 92, 145, 212, 223,
    282, 305, 363, 386, 462
Emery, John, (Ian), 47, 162, 175, 364,
    366, 394, 404, 410, 497, 507, 529
Emery, Katherine, 82, 91, 148, 384, 402
Emhardt, Robert, 181, 188, 244, 270,
    293, 330, 372, 418
Emmerson, Dorothy, 341
Emmet, Katherine, 91, 202, 246
Emmett, Katherine, 176, 179, 211, 317,
    367, 376, 512
Emmett, Robert, 289, 309
Enck, Gary, 270
Endrey, Eugene, 448
Endust, 219
Engel, Alexander, 58, 116
Engel, Lehman, 30, 148, 152, 209, 308,
    449, 467, 514, 526
Englander, Ludwig, 516
Englund, Patricia, 45, 279
Enters, Warren, 318, 362, 509
Entrikin, Knowles, 64, 415, 430
Entwhistle, Peg, 483
Ephraim, Lee, 82
Ephron, Henry, 307, 325, 460, 476
Ephron, Phoebe, 224, 325, 460, 476
Epstein, Alvin, 187, 364, 379
Epstein, Julius, 27, 72, 88, 299
Epstein, Philip, 27, 88
Epstein, Pierre, 169, 422, 471
Equity Players, Inc., 386, 400, 521
Eric Productions, 353
Eric, Elspeth, 121, 298, 430, 484
Erickson, Leif, 23, 108, 258, 298, 342,
    394, 400, 407, 463, 557
Ericson, John, 441
Erlanger, A. L., 33, 107, 159, 187, 201,
    204, 206, 233, 239, 241, 257, 260,
    289, 338, 359, 361, 366, 367, 376,
    383, 391, 404, 423, 448, 480, 487,
    531, 538
Erlanger Productions, 432
Ernst, Jessie, 392
Ernst, Leila, 491
Errol, Leon, 20, 140, 545, 557
Ersi, Elsa, 409
Erskine, Chester, 121, 187, 205, 263,
    316, 385, 393, 423, 444, 452, 512

Erskine, Howard, 32, 76, 127, 203, 310,
    583
Erskine, Marilyn, 148, 177, 191, 338,
    357, 381, 382, 397
Ervine, St. John, 138
Erwin, Stuart, 72, 85, 140, 307, 311,
    322, 364, 372, 426, 500, 515, 522
Esler, Lemist, 161
Esmond, Carl, 166
Esmond, Jill, 541
Essary, Lisa, 507
Essex, Harry, 434
Estabrook, Howard, 69, 277, 471
Estry, Joseph, 133
Ethier, Alphonz, 246
Etting, Ruth, 332
Eunson, Dale, 198, 278, 384
Evans, Edith, 265, 550, 557
Evans, Estelle, 460
Evans, Evans, 116, 131, 165
Evans, Greek, 149
Evans, Harvey, 357
Evans, Julius, 136, 462
Evans, Larry, 433
Evans, Madge, 21, 114, 130, 197, 211,
    365, 369, 370, 423, 471, 557
Evans, Maurice, 256, 284, 340, 463,
    518, 549, 550, 557, 583
Evans, Michael, 178
Evans, Monica, 344
Evans, Ray, 475
Evans, Reynolds, 102, 153, 265, 280,
    308, 358
Evelyn, Judith, 108, 214, 241, 396,
    423, 541, 550, 557
Everest, Barbara, 30
Everett, Chad, 232
Everett, Edward, 20
Everett, Jake, 492
Everett, Tim, 98, 116, 297
Everhart, Henry, 75
Evslin, Bernard, 443
Ewell, Tom, 32, 121, 146, 152, 158,
    175, 248, 268, 269, 306, 418, 441,
    457, 470, 492, 532, 557, 583
Ewing, Marjorie, 212
Experimental Theatre, 464, 509
Eyre, Laurence, 153, 311, 471
Eythe, William, 113, 147, 316, 435,
    550, 557

Faber, Jim, 492
Fabian, Olga, 99, 226
Fabray, Nanette, 108, 142, 339, 385, 557
Fagan, Myron C., 247, 276, 329, 393
Faggen, Jay, 431
Fair, Joyce, 137
Fairbanks, Douglas, Sr., 97, 174, 294,
    372, 384, 418, 422, 557
Fairbanks, Douglas, Jr, 132, 208, 240,
    274, 280, 452
Fairchild, Charlotte, 23
Fairfax, Marion, 322, 461
Fairman, Austin, 130, 261, 416
Falana, Lola, 186
Falk, Henri, 331
Falk, Lee, 524
Falk, Peter, 287, 364, 383, 549, 557
Falk, Sawyer, 277
Falkenburg, Jinx, 338
Fallon, Thomas F., 264
Fanning, Gene, 430
Fant, Roy, 32, 117, 415
Faragoh, Francis Edwards, 455

Farber, Sandy, 152, 486
Farentino, James, 234, 284, 336, 449, 504, 557
Farley, Morgan, 25, 87, 192, 300, 364, 418, 461, 496, 522, 536
Farmer, Frances, 186, 476, 557
Farnsworth, William P., 53, 159
Farnum, Dustin, 77, 277, 440, 441, 506
Farnum, William, 31, 69, 137, 208, 277, 383, 437, 519
Farrand, Jan, 378
Farrar, John, 331, 465
Farrell, Anthony B., 28, 54, 279
Farrell, Brian, 264
Farrell, Charles, 16, 159, 294, 324, 408, 418
Farrell, Glenda, 72, 165, 209, 270, 282, 286, 301, 308, 323, 360, 392, 416, 456, 458, 494, 557
Farren, George, 386
Farrow, Mia, 195
Fassett, Jay, 35, 54, 101, 134, 252, 278, 357, 406, 486, 537
Fauchois, Rene, 265
Faulk, John Henry, 49
Faulkner, Virginia, 241
Faulkner, William, 394, 449
Faussett, Hudson, 465
Faust, Walter Livingston, 472
Faversham, William, 42, 155, 211, 267, 382, 440
Fawcett, George, 266, 294, 440
Fay, Frank, 206, 207, 469, 549, 557
Fay, Mary Helen, 52, 143, 151
Faye, Alice, 276, 377, 392, 557
Faye, Joey, 450, 464
Faylen, Frank, 310
Fazenda, Louise, 20, 108, 158, 280, 347, 351, 459
Fazio, Dino, 15
Fears, Peggy, 89, 132, 341
Feder, 179, 350
Federova, Nina, 151
Feibleman, Peter S., 477
Feiffer, Jules, 276, 518, 519, 571, 582
Feigay, Paul, 263, 303
Feilbert, Edward, 221, 362
Feinstein, Ashley, 58
Fejer, Cordis, 510
Feld, Fritz, 43, 48
Feld, Morris, 126
Feld, Norman, 497
Feld, Rose C., 435
Feldman, Gladys, 106, 307, 416
Feldman, Laurence, 179
Felix, Hugo, 258, 366
Fell, Norman, 236
Fellows, Don, 173, 297, 354
Fellows, Edith, 109, 497
Felton, Francis J. (Happy), 160
Felton, Verna, 371
Fennelly, Parker, 111, 112, 169, 277, 278, 322, 357, 430, 436
Fenton, Frank, 370, 445, 543
Fenton, Leslie, 363
Fenwick, Irene, 152, 265, 372, 435
Ferber, Edna, 63, 130, 262, 310, 357, 404, 441, 571
Ferguson, Elsie, 44, 223, 317, 359, 371, 410, 448, 452, 502, 557
Ferleger, Alvin, 412
Fernandez, Peter, 114, 284, 511
Ferrall, Michael, 498
Ferrell, Conchata, 220, 412
Ferrer, Jose, 28, 68, 76, 87, 141, 145, 224, 233, 247, 255, 293, 312, 327, 389, 423, 424, 429, 439, 441, 444, 446, 493, 504, 541, 544, 550, 557, 582, 583
Ferrer, Mrs. Jose, 504
Ferrer, Melchor (Mel), 112, 256, 446
Ferris, Walter, 124, 251
Fetchit, Stepin, 42, 77, 119
Fetter, Ted, 109, 297, 299
Feuer, Cy, 191
Ffolkes, David, 305, 537
Fickett, Mary, 227, 282, 454
Fiedler, John, 205, 224, 344, 352, 390, 425, 465
Field, Betty, 22, 28, 71, 136, 156, 161, 194, 231, 259, 281, 333, 341, 345, 361, 371, 382, 390, 397, 402, 418, 447, 483, 485, 495, 514, 517, 543, 544, 557
Field, Joan, 535
Field, Joseph, 135
Field, Leonard, 189, 474
Field, Salisbury, 493, 513, 538
Field, Sylvia, 13, 55, 67, 71, 72, 73, 85, 103, 132, 228, 252, 253, 276, 298, 302, 324, 346, 380, 404, 434, 444, 500, 519
Field, Virginia, 135, 136, 248, 271, 368, 511
Fielding, Edward, 378
Fields Productions, 57
Fields, Chip, 486
Fields, Dorothy, 108, 385, 494
Fields, Gracie, 544
Fields, Herbert, 108, 304, 385
Fields, Joseph, 30, 127, 167, 174, 226, 252, 295, 327, 377, 411, 492, 571
Fields, Lew, 304, 315, 332, 545
Fields, W. C., 20, 290, 545, 557
Fields, William, 224, 267, 383
Figaro, Inc., 440
Figman, Max, 255, 311
Filippo, Bud, 474
Fillmore, Clyde, 28, 45, 121, 151, 253, 283, 380, 382, 459, 476
Fillmore, Russell, 387
Finch, Flora, 84
Finch, Robert, 517
Findlay, Ruth, 382
Findlay, Thomas, 109, 132, 158, 222, 255, 345, 361, 434, 437, 474
Fingar, Thelma, 426
Finkel, Bella, 166
Finklehoffe, Fred F., 68, 210
Finn, Jonathan, 86
Finnerty, Warren, 59, 581
Finney, Albert, 557
Finney, Mary, 218, 244
Fiore, Frank, 92
Fire, Jane, 510
Fire, Richard, 510
Firestone, Eddie, 401
Firestone, Scott, 157, 507
Firth, Peter, 549
Fischbein, Saul, 465
Fischer, Robert C., 207
Fisher, Alice, 410
Fisher, Bob, 232
Fisher, Lola, 22, 42, 188, 357, 498
Fisher, Robert, 204
Fisher, Steve, 456
Fiske, Dwight, 117
Fiske, Harrison Grey, 145, 155, 213, 241, 257, 260, 311, 322, 333, 408, 508
Fiske, Minnie Maddern ("Mrs. Fiske"), 241, 260, 267, 289, 311, 322, 333, 408, 508
Fitch, Clyde, 58, 59, 79, 93, 96, 179, 181, 182, 211, 212, 222, 284, 291, 409, 491, 528
Fitz-Allen, Adelaide, 156
Fitzgerald, Barry, 558
Fitzgerald, Edith, 296
Fitzgerald, F. Scott, 131, 194, 473, 503, 536

Fitzgerald, Geraldine, 85, 117, 270, 278, 435, 496, 511, 531, 558
Fitzgerald, Neil, 22, 456
Fitzgibbons, Dorothy, 282
Fix, Paul, 488
Flamm, Donald, 63, 515
Flanagan, Fionnuala, 235, 496
Flanagan, Hallie, 155
Flanagan, Neil, 414, 421
Flanagan, Pauline, 443, 496
Flanagan, William, 42, 292
Flanders, Ed, 489, 551, 586
Flavin, James, 168
Flavin, Martin, 13, 34, 67, 90, 110, 262, 461
Fleet, Jo Van, 78, 97, 161, 279, 346, 403, 490, 542, 550, 568, 583
Fleischer, Richard, 102, 205, 296
Fleischmann, Julius, 122, 166, 179, 238, 316, 394
Fleming, Allan, 472
Fleming, Eric, 327, 378, 441
Fleming, Rhonda, 528
Fleming, Victor, 247, 519
Flemyng, Robert, 340, 378, 543
Fletcher, Allen, 60
Fletcher, Bramwell, 142, 284, 298, 393, 445, 526
Fletcher, Lawrence, 212, 289, 295, 313, 327, 405
Fletcher, Lucille, 337
Fletcher, Robert, 316
Flexner, Anne Crawford, 17, 22, 311, 324
Flint, Eva Kay, 452, 500
Flint, Helen, 203, 299, 453, 473, 484
Flippen, Jay C., 87, 418, 546
Flood, Ann, 217
Flournoy, Peter, 237
Flournoy, Richard, 100, 162, 259
Flower, Gene, 321
Floyd, John, 386, 529
Fluellen, Joel, 196
Flynn, Errol, 142, 243, 382
Flynn, Gertrude, 247
Flynn, Joe, 164
Flynn, Thomas F., 221
Foch, Nina, 57, 103, 248, 558
Fodor, Laszlo, 246, 445
Foe, Louis De, 448
Fogelson, E. E., 365
Fokine, Leon, 115
Foley, Paul, 62
Folfe, Mary, 115
Fonda, Henry, 15, 49, 57, 58, 76, 110, 154, 172, 177, 227, 247, 285, 292, 313, 314, 357, 375, 424, 487, 494, 520, 541, 542, 558, 583
Fonda, Jane, 32, 43, 87, 169, 239, 368, 447, 454, 461, 467, 558
Fonda, Peter, 57, 558
Fontaine, Joan, 243, 339, 462, 528, 558
Fontaine, Robert, 205
Fontanne, Lynn, 29, 79, 137, 142, 196, 204, 227, 230, 233, 308, 340, 358, 372, 395, 413, 433, 446, 447, 458, 467, 541, 547, 558
Foote, Horton, 87, 355, 488, 490
Foote, John Taintor, 477, 482
Foran, Dick, 62, 224, 369
Foran, Edward, 383
Foran, William, 500
Forbes, Brenda, 162, 381, 410, 452, 538
Forbes, Henry, 238, 476, 479
Forbes, James, 92, 102, 152, 191, 302, 358, 380, 422, 488, 536
Forbes, Kathryn, 228
Forbes, Ralph, 32, 40, 100, 214, 238, 272, 275, 300, 413, 441, 493, 506
Forbes, Scott, 219

Ford, Clebert, 268
Ford, Constance, 124, 187, 341, 415, 501
Ford, Frank, 84
Ford, Glenn, 172, 433, 463
Ford, Gwyllyn, 433
Ford, Harriet, 33, 137, 166, 174, 291, 349, 376
Ford, Harry Chapman, 140
Ford, Helen, 356
Ford, Henry, 48
Ford, Hugh, 18, 44, 69, 77, 119, 125, 129, 166, 293, 307, 379, 408, 519, 533
Ford, John, 63, 85, 263, 300, 314, 482, 515
Ford, Montgomery, 364
Ford, Paul, 15, 31, 63, 101, 124, 160, 168, 169, 188, 244, 259, 285, 302, 332, 463, 474, 509, 515, 558
Ford, Ruth, 130, 194, 240, 309, 338, 394, 527, 540, 558
Ford, Wallace, 190, 199, 305, 311, 343, 344, 371, 389, 475, 515, 550
Ford, William, 454
Forde, Hal, 223
Foreman, Milos, 353
Forest, Marian de, 145, 277
Forman, Norman, 101
Forrest, Anne, 82, 87, 167
Forrest, George, 257
Forrest, Sam, 13, 37, 40, 80, 87, 107, 123, 142, 152, 169, 171, 173, 176, 192, 195, 212, 222, 229, 241, 276, 277, 281, 333, 338, 345, 349, 371, 393, 395, 396, 417, 426, 445, 460, 474, 502, 503, 506, 512, 517, 535
Forsslund, Louise, 347
Forster, Robert, 449, 558
Forsyth, Rosemary, 284
Forsythe, Henderson, 85, 126, 207, 292, 312
Forsythe, John, 241, 314, 463, 513, 532, 558
Fosse, Bob, 226, 327, 351, 471
Foster, Claiborne, 57, 87, 146, 169, 179, 199, 259, 356, 365, 380, 381, 401, 425, 490
Foster, Donald, 19, 103, 113, 189, 483
Foster, Frances, 398
Foster, Gloria, 558, 581
Foster, Harry, 410
Foster, Lillian, 103, 363
Foster, Norman, 26, 43, 82, 135, 174, 241, 252, 253, 335, 388, 455, 479, 500
Foster, Paul, 482
Foster, Phoebe, 25, 26, 79, 93, 134, 158, 179, 213, 321, 466, 475, 498
Foster, Preston, 13, 43, 103, 133, 142, 158, 209, 263, 270, 404, 417, 495
Foster, Susanna, 96
Fowkes, Conrad, 23
Fowler, Gene, 196
Fowler, Mary, 400
Fowler, Pat, 360
Fox, Dorothi, 264
Fox, Franklyn, 527
Fox, Frederick, 30, 68, 95, 118, 150, 187, 191, 197, 248, 252, 256, 263, 286, 296, 332, 355, 392, 418, 437, 509
Fox, Harry, 391
Fox, James, 87
Fox, John, 487
Fox, Maxine, 27
Fox, Paul Hervey, 164, 231, 432
Fox, Sidney, 241, 307, 309, 333, 351, 426, 450
Fox, Susan, 453
Foxe, Earle, 79, 100
Foxworth, Robert, 111

610 INDEX

Foxx, Redd, 341
Foy, Eddie, Jr, 142, 154, 234, 544, 546, 558
Foy, Gloria, 484
Francen, Victor, 508
Franchi, Sergio, 478
Franchot Productions, 112
Francine, Anne, 299
Franciosa, Anthony, 81, 143, 207, 208, 368, 513, 548, 549, 558
Francis, Anne, 18, 456
Francis, Arlene, 22, 23, 28, 45, 59, 112, 130, 135, 167, 250, 265, 274, 308, 327, 351, 360, 462, 508, 528, 536, 558
Francis, Ivor, 280, 390
Francis, Kay (Katherine, 107, 109, 133, 142, 158, 162, 174, 246, 503, 558
Francis, Robert, 76
Franck, Edward, 309
Francke, Caroline, 165, 221
Frank, Mary K., 463, 484
Frank, Melvin, 257, 383
Frank, Pat, 320
Frankel, Aaron, 506
Frankel, Doris, 283
Frankel, E. M., 192
Frankel, Gene, 111, 145, 236, 273, 288, 351, 581
Frankel, Kenneth, 517
Franken, Rose, 31, 95, 133, 201, 359, 432, 571
Frankenheimer, John, 230
Franklin, Edgar, 518
Franklin, Hugh, 227, 422
Franklin, Nancy, 69, 332
Franklin, Pamela, 237, 382
Franklin, Sidney, 137
Franklin, Walter, 153
Franz, Arthur, 101, 219, 274, 305, 316, 436
Franz, Eduard, 52, 69, 75, 104, 141, 143, 159, 218, 238, 245, 290, 312, 359, 406
Fraser, Bryant, 92
Fraser, Elisabeth, 151, 240, 295, 320, 406, 468, 492, 494, 524
Frawley, T. D., 137, 211, 237, 439, 496
Frawley, William, 152, 177, 196, 342, 493, 506
Frayne, Viola, 439, 483
Frazee, H. H., 137, 169, 326, 342, 362, 391
Frederici, Blanche, 92, 383, 472
Frederick, Pauline, 166, 223, 301, 350, 432, 516, 558
Fredrik, Burry, 279
Freed, Bert, 106, 251
Freed, Donald, 238
Freedley, George, 85, 148, 468
Freedley, Vinton, 13, 284, 312, 536
Freedman, Gerald, 98, 109, 235, 239, 581
Freedman, David, 306
Freeman, Al, Jr, 59, 104, 135, 279, 477, 588
Freeman, Arny, 75
Freeman, Charles K., 129, 202, 227, 319
Freeman, Don, 45
Freeman, Helen, 223, 293, 408
Freeman, Howard, 98, 112, 160, 269, 284, 320, 340, 442, 457, 479, 497
Freeman, Max, 296, 387
Freeman, Mona, 123, 252
Freeman, Morgan, 135
Freeman, Stan, 463
Freezer, Robert, 129
French, Arthur, 86
French, Bert, 304, 422, 485
French, Peggy, 487
Frey, Leonard, 46, 62, 543

Frey, Nathaniel, 205, 344
Freyer, Nathaniel, 202
Friebus, Florida, 19, 20, 98, 382
Fried, Franklin, 379
Fried, Martin, 104, 107, 116, 330, 363
Fried, Walter, 12, 22, 55, 124, 156, 259, 379, 478, 583
Friede, Donald, 25
Friedkin, William, 62
Friedlander, Jane, 280
Friedlander, William B., 45, 84, 110, 190, 277, 333, 396, 412, 416, 421, 431, 437, 484, 512, 514
Friedman, Bruce Jay, 412, 443, 571
Friedman, Charles, 55, 536
Friedman, Edward, 296
Friedman, Leon, 488
Friedman, Nathan, 473
Friend, Philip, 243
Frierson, Monte, 69
Friml, Rudolph, 55, 440, 458
Frings, Ketti, 279, 322, 579
Frisco, Joe, 191
Frizzell, Lou, 194
Frobe, Gert, 237
Froehlich, Jacques, 530
Frohman, Bert, 248-9
Frohman, Charles, 31, 38, 40, 49, 57, 79, 81, 84, 93, 94, 113, 119, 120, 125, 130, 154, 179, 181, 182, 209, 210, 222, 235, 246, 253, 257, 275, 312, 323, 331, 356, 357, 359, 382, 396, 404, 442, 444, 454, 461, 480, 487, 491, 516, 537, 538
Frohman, Daniel, 437
Froman, Jane, 540, 558
Fromkes, Harry, 198
Frost, Alice, 402
Frost, Walter Archer, 79
Frye, Ben, 172
Frye, Dwight, 128, 136, 237, 254, 296, 384, 386, 432
Frye, Peter, 165
Fryer, Robert, 15, 37, 127, 467
Fulda, Ludwig, 372
Fuller, Albert C., 394
Fuller, Frances, 29, 75, 148, 160, 168, 212, 227, 354, 441, 480
Fuller, John G., 283, 372
Fuller, Lester, 164
Fuller, Rosalinde, 166
Fulton, Maude, 63
Funk, Larry, 394
Funt, Julian, 115, 290
Furness, Betty, 13, 186, 321, 325, 348
Furniss, Grace L., 381
Fursman, Georgia, 189
Furstenberg, Betsy von, 37, 89, 122, 178, 300, 330, 346, 362, 413, 414, 550
Furth, George, 49, 104
Fyffe, Will, 548

Gabel, Martin, 35, 52, 90, 108, 190, 213, 274, 293, 303, 305, 351, 392, 398, 421, 428, 456, 464, 522, 536, 550, 558, 584
Gabel, Ruby, 219
Gabel, Zac, 219
Gable, Clark, 13, 101, 140, 151, 164, 167, 208, 230, 263, 282, 305, 311, 364, 375, 392, 447, 485, 519, 548, 558
Gabor, Eva, 178, 205
Gabrielson, Frank, 318, 444

Gadd, Renee, 26
Gagliano, Frank, 154, 336
Gahagan, Helen, 27, 86, 143, 158, 267, 296, 317, 319, 537
Gaige, Crosby, 13, 57, 72, 144, 146, 188, 207, 221, 227, 274, 337, 349, 388, 420, 421, 424, 515
Gaige, Russell, 30, 112
Gaines, Richard, 235, 508
Gaites, Joseph M., 295, 315, 393, 395
Gaither, Gant, 108, 122, 172
Gale, Joan, 343
Gale, Zona, 312, 322, 571, 579
Galik, Denise, 157
Gallagher, Francis, 240
Gallagher, Helen, 216, 541
Gallagher, Skeets, 20, 55, 100, 142, 165, 259, 275, 311, 500
Gallaher, Donald, 107, 187, 191, 304, 349, 408, 419, 429, 432
Galland, Bertha, 381
Gallaudet, John, 281
Gallienne, Eva Le, 18, 19, 20, 122, 140, 237, 289, 304, 322, 342, 380, 409, 468, 496, 544, 562
Gallo, Ray, 368
Galloway, Louise, 285
Galphin, Martha, 66, 367
Gam, Rita, 464, 536
Gamble, Warburton, 520-21
Ganthony, Richard, 308
Gantt, Cora Dick, 462
Gantvoort, Herman, 210, 382, 469
Garbo, Greta, 29, 151, 193, 401, 409, 442
Garde, Betty, 16, 140, 197, 382
Gardenia, Vincent, 98, 119, 185, 276, 288, 354, 383, 415, 509, 586
Gardiner, Becky, 115
Gardiner, Reginald, 29, 95, 137, 295, 298
Gardner, Ava, 336, 392
Gardner, Dorothy, 140
Gardner, Ed, 97
Gardner, Herb, 191, 471, 474
Gardner, Rita, 544
Gare, Maryanna, 28
Garen, Leo, 126, 178
Garfein, Jack, 144, 182, 424
Garfield, John (Jules), 38, 53, 83, 162, 173, 186, 187, 208, 209, 225, 281, 365, 379, 410, 448, 485, 514, 542, 558
Garfield, Kurt, 421
Garfinkle, Louis, 303
Gargan, William, 24, 29, 208-9, 231, 264, 389, 394, 469, 509, 526
Garland, Judy, 372, 546
Garland, Robert, 228
Garner, James, 76, 91
Garner, Martin, 165
Garner, Peggy Ann, 158, 243, 252, 293, 404
Garon, Jay, 254
Garr, Eddie, 481
Garrett, Betty, 179, 327, 543, 558
Garrett, Charlcie, 428
Garrett, Joy, 79
Garrett, Oliver H. P., 428, 509
Garrick Productions, 272, 511
Garrick, Beulah, 496
Garrison, Sean, 45, 467
Garson, Barbara, 288
Garson, Greer, 36, 203, 381, 454, 516, 558
Garson, Harry, 233
Gary, Harold, 381
Gaskill, William, 122
Gassel, Sylvia, 238

Gassner, John, 335
Gaston, Ken, 474
Gaston, William, 115
Gates, Eleanor, 377
Gates, Larry, 47, 81, 82, 104, 214, 425, 463
Gates, Nancy, 207, 305
Gateson, Marjorie, 29, 35, 75, 196, 212, 272, 432
Gaul, George, 24, 138, 262, 356, 368, 418, 494
Gaumont, Irving, 471
Gavin, John, 348
Gaw, Boyce de, 297
Gaxton, William, 95, 544, 550, 551, 558
Gaye, Gregory, 70, 130, 133, 158
Gaynes, George, 327, 344, 419
Gaynor, Janet, 48, 114, 154, 159, 222, 294, 418
Gaynor, Mitzi, 30
Gazzara, Ben, 143, 144, 208, 335, 447, 543, 548, 549, 558
Gazzo, Michael V., 78, 208, 335
Gear, Luella, 166, 186, 362, 371, 407, 466, 480, 545
Gearon, John, 121
Geddes, Barbara Bel, 70, 125, 147, 157, 177, 228, 274, 300, 316, 323, 338, 358, 424, 453, 542, 543, 553
Geddes, Edith Lutyens, 177
Geddes, Norman Bel, 121, 146, 240, 248, 423, 435
Geddes, Virgil, 139
Geer, Will, 15, 160, 221, 249, 250, 268, 316, 318, 344, 350, 377, 389, 412, 481, 494, 511, 512, 526, 558
Geiger, Milton, 141
Geist, Richard, 443
Gelb, Arthur, 485
Gelb, Barbara, 485
Gelber, Jack, 32, 103, 111, 440, 571, 581
Geld, Gary, 385
Gellhorn, Martha, 282
Genet, Jean, 581
Genn, Leo, 31, 128, 150, 314, 320, 354, 430
Gensler, Lewis E., 79, 110, 361, 362, 400, 415, 453
Gentles, Avril, 130
Gentry, Minnie, 455
George, Geo W., 32, 138, 195, 203, 337
George, Gladys, 131, 160, 166, 270, 298, 309, 368, 386, 428, 548, 558
George, Grace, 97, 153, 256, 298, 302, 333, 420, 438, 491, 503, 528, 543, 550, 558
George, Hal, 512
George, Nathan, 340, 582
George, Susan, 296
Georgie, Leyla, 227, 493, 515
Gerald, Ara, 113, 211
Geraldy, Paul, 420
Gerard, Ben, 89
Gerard, Rosemond, 189
Gerber, Ella, 126
Gerbidon, Marcel, 167, 187
Gericke, Eugene, 455
Gering, Marion, 41, 67, 373, 426, 461, 480, 508
Gerken, Ted, 323
Gernhardt, Willard, 24
Gerringer, Robert, 28
Gershe, Leonard, 72
Gershwin, George, 97, 167, 275, 378, 386
Gershwin, Ira, 97, 157, 378
Gerstad, John, 22, 23, 117, 124, 135, 224, 292, 367, 418
Gersten, Berta, 161

Gerstenberg, Alice, 505
Gerton, Philip, 60
Gerussi, Bruno, 314
Gessner, Adriene, 228
Gest, Morris, 375, 493
Gethers, Steven, 104
Geva, Tamara, 132, 230, 332, 366, 382, 392, 543
Geyra, Zvi, 141
Ghere, High, 490
Ghostley, Alice, 45, 302, 423, 545, 558, 585
Gibbons, Arthur, 462
Gibbs, Wolcott, 11, 326, 413
Gibney, Sheridan, 526
Gibson, Henry, 326
Gibson, William, 111, 130, 186, 311, 494, 571, 584
Gibson, Wynne, 149, 171, 342, 435
Gide, Andre, 232
Gielgud, John, 22, 52, 463, 479, 548, 558, 584
Gierasch, Stefan, 178, 240
Giglio, Clement, 519
Gilbert, Edward, 224, 308, 360
Gilbert, Edwin, 187
Gilbert, John, 166, 348
Gilbert, Lou, 109, 128, 196
Gilbert, Ruth, 18, 230, 384
Gilbert, Walter, 153, 277, 281, 371, 411, 428, 513
Gilbert, Willie, 84
Gilchrist, Connie, 37, 148, 224, 259, 324, 530
Gildea, Mary, 127, 154, 480
Gilder, Jeannette L., 387
Gilette, Priscilla, 275, 543
Gilford, Jack, 129, 136, 145, 226, 277, 465, 470, 474, 541, 544, 549, 558
Gilkey, Stanley, 16, 120, 125, 402
Gill, Brendan, 119
Gill, Frank, Jr., 411
Gillespie, Christina, 235
Gillespie, Jean, 480
Gillette, Anita, 134
Gillette, William, 94, 418, 452, 475, 550
Gillian, Kay, 336
Gillingwater, Claude, 14, 137, 331, 475
Gillmore, Margalo, 18, 48, 117, 152, 162, 200, 256, 259, 296, 298, 331, 340, 359, 414, 424, 448, 502, 528, 543, 558
Gillmore, Ruth, 339
Gilman, Sam, 224
Gilman, Toni, 305
Gilmore, Frank, 452
Gilmore, Virginia, 110, 123, 473, 491, 531, 542
Gilmore, W. H., 5', 58, 167, 176, 182, 262, 275, 331, 356, 396, 399, 498, 506, 528
Gilmore, W. L., 400
Gilpin, Charles, 143, 558
Gilroy, Frank D., 354, 451, 466, 519, 572, 580, 585
Gingold, Hermione, 47, 178, 346, 381, 558
Ginn, Asa, 445
Ginnes, Abram S., 137, 475
Ginsberg, Allen, 582
Ginsbury, Norman, 30
Ginty, Elizabeth B., 312
Girardot, Etienne, 189, 267, 311, 493
Gish, Dorothy, 64, 66, 74, 140, 164, 194, 290, 293, 312, 318, 446, 536, 558
Gish, Lillian, 23, 112, 189, 227, 251, 322, 338, 442, 490, 519, 541, 545, 548, 550, 558

Gist, Robert, 104
Givens, Charles, 322
Givney, Kathryn, 162, 203, 281, 337, 473, 509
Givot, George, 104
Glad, Gladys, 332
Glancy, A. R., Jr., 308, 312
Glanville, Maxwell, 508
Glaser, Michael, 72
Glaser, Vaughan, 62, 514
Glaspell, Susan, 20, 101, 236, 572, 579
Glass, George, 363
Glass, Montague, 215, 254, 364, 379, 380, 521
Glass, Walter, 104, 472
Glassman, Stephen, 54, 453
Glazer, Benjamin, 156, 453, 476
Gleason, Jackie, 18, 134, 334, 543, 549, 558
Gleason, James, 34, 70, 72, 87, 95, 125, 151, 167, 240, 241, 377, 420, 456, 513, 529, 558
Gleason, Mrs. James, 420
Gleason, Lucile, 72, 347, 420
Gleckler, Robert, 67, 209
Glendinning, Ernest, 40, 46, 74, 179, 197, 276, 320, 417, 420, 429, 435
Glenny, Peter, 333
Glenville, Peter, 112, 138, 148, 237, 243, 358, 390, 424, 453, 462, 498
Glick, Joseph B., 386
Glickman, Will, 323
Glover, Bruce, 206
Glover, John, 195, 217
Gluck, Cookie, 510
Gluck, Stephen Van, 375
Glyn, Elinor, 146
Gobel, George, 475
Goddard, Charles W., 68, 176, 311
Goddard, Paulette, 30, 84, 176, 342, 529
Goetz, Augustus, 210, 213, 232, 354, 572
Goetz, E. Ray, 167, 262, 275
Goetz, Ruth, 210, 213, 232, 354, 572
Goff, Ivan, 378
Gold, Michael, 156
Gold, Robert, 69
Goldberg, Leonard, 474
Goldberg, Dan, 77, 293
Golden, Alfred, 98, 261, 537
Golden, Eleanor, 438
Golden, Harry, 354
Golden, I. J., 380, 393
Golden, John, 13, 16, 35, 55, 71, 85, 88-9, 95, 106, 122, 132, 146, 159, 166, 192, 217, 250, 269, 271, 289, 292, 335, 340, 371, 373, 396, 408, 416, 418, 428, 437, 456, 465, 466, 469, 475, 476, 483, 485, 492, 494, 516, 525
Golden, Raymond, 428
Goldin, Al, 100
Goldina, Miriam, 214
Golding, Samuel Ruskin, 355, 385
Goldman, Byron, 72
Goldman, Harold, 106
Goldman, James, 57, 273
Goldman, Robert, 381
Goldman, William, 57
Goldner, Charles, 542
Goldreyer, Michael, 264
Goldschmidt, Lena, 83
Goldsmith, Clifford, 514
Goldsmith, Jack, 268
Goldsmith, Lester M., 204
Goldsmith, Milton, 274
Goldstein, Jennie, 78
Goldwasser, Lawrence, 364
Goldwyn, Samuel, 81, 441, 449
Golonka, Arlene, 18, 99, 335, 353, 391,

511
Gombell, Minna, 42, 152, 247, 322, 329, 349, 444, 471
Gomez, Thomas, 162, 230, 255, 400, 421, 514
Gompers, Samuel, 251
Gonzales, Marcial, 220
Goodhart, William, 173
Goodman, Arthur, 231, 415
Goodman, Benny, 550
Goodman, Dody, 168, 325, 327, 390
Goodman, Eckert, 297
Goodman, Edward, 25, 85, 296, 340, 496, 509
Goodman, James, 56, 283
Goodman, Jules Eckert, 71, 86, 215, 266, 294, 297, 364, 488, 521
Goodman, Martin, 121, 283
Goodman, Paul, 249
Goodman, Philip, 26, 97, 510, 521
Goodman, Randolph, 279
Goodman, Robyn, 517
Goodner, Carol, 37, 63, 125, 151, 194, 219, 223, 294, 530
Goodrich, Arthur, 79, 250, 368, 374, 432, 534
Goodrich, Frances, 18, 64, 129, 148, 194, 386, 426, 500, 579, 584
Goodwin, Nat C., 520
Gorcey, Bernard, 12, 109, 254, 529
Gorcey, David, 121
Gorcey, Leo, 121, 173
Gordon, Barry, 474
Gordon, Bruce, 129, 372
Gordon, C. Henry, 246, 258, 271, 322, 384, 408, 419
Gordon, Carolyn, 510
Gordon, Charles K., 79
Gordon, Don, 348
Gordon, Gale, 119, 506
Gordon, Gavin, 73, 85, 108, 173, 261, 308, 401
Gordon, Grant, 368
Gordon, Irving, 56, 444
Gordon, J. M., 121
Gordon, Kilbourn, 83, 103, 258
Gordon, Leon, 342, 372, 499, 518
Gordon, Mack, 414
Gordon, Mark, 295
Gordon, Max, 26, 60, 63, 133, 135, 140, 146, 152, 154, 208, 212, 245, 252, 262, 265, 308, 312, 327, 332, 333, 360, 381, 410, 430, 433, 439, 473, 487, 522, 528, 532
Gordon, Michael, 29, 31, 87, 121, 152, 214, 218, 232, 284, 290, 292, 352, 415, 435, 445, 464
Gordon, Pamela, 248
Gordon, Richard, 321
Gordon, Robert H., 122, 491
Gordon, Ruth, 11, 82, 146, 151, 190, 211, 220, 224, 266, 267, 301, 302, 306, 324, 326, 360, 410, 416, 418, 428, 431, 470, 475, 492, 504, 525, 532, 541, 542, 550, 558, 572
Gordon, Stanley, 397
Gordon, Stephanie, 220
Gordon, Steve, 486
Gordon, Stuart, 510
Gordon, Vera, 521
Gordone, Charles, 339, 572, 580
Gorelik, Mordecai, 21, 22, 53, 83, 131, 175, 186, 208, 276, 305, 316, 335, 339, 383, 400, 424, 452, 476, 536
Gorman, Cliff, 62, 216, 543, 544, 558, 586
Gorman, Mari, 220
Gorme, Eydie, 216
Gosch, Martin, 173

Gose, Carl, 372
Goss, Barry, 90
Gossett, Louis, 82, 127, 327, 390, 398, 460, 539
Gottfried, Martin, 59, 66, 169, 358
Gottlieb, Alex, 416, 508
Gottlieb, Morton, 99, 145, 214, 361, 504, 512
Gottschalk, Ferdinand, 13, 79, 96, 110, 250, 289, 373, 445, 491, 534
Goudal, Jetta, 212, 375
Gough, Lloyd, 17, 22, 42, 84, 102, 112, 125, 177, 284, 375, 393, 401, 533
Gould, Bruce, 296
Gould, Elliott, 276, 543, 558
Gould, Frank, 411, 465
Gould, Harold, 221
Gould, Hull, 483
Gould, Morton, 385
Gould, Stanley, 63
Goulding, Edmund, 116, 117, 193, 402, 406
Goulet, Robert, 205, 558
Goulston, Andre, 169-70
Gow, James, 125, 268, 483
Grable, Betty, 70, 74, 87, 154, 197, 302, 420, 421, 550, 558
Grace, Carol, 98, 351, 522
Gracie, Sally, 35, 72, 131, 150, 503
Graff, William, 280
Graff, Wilton, 300
Grafton, Gloria, 255
Graham, Carroll, 386
Graham, Garrett, 386
Graham, Jo, 177, 209, 234, 373, 466
Graham, Joseph, 274
Graham, Joseph H., 432
Graham, Martha, 140, 363, 502
Graham, Ronald, 510
Graham, Ronny, 302, 373, 464
Graham-Brown, W., 404
Grahame, Gloria, 197, 307
Granach, Alexander, 47
Granat, Frank, 32, 138, 195, 203
Grande, Louis Del, 165
Granger, Farley, 81, 111, 381, 509, 545, 558
Grant, Alberta, 282
Grant, Cary, 34, 38, 129, 145, 168, 217, 256, 258, 289, 331, 370, 558
Grant, Gerald, 492
Grant, James Edward, 373
Grant, Kirby, 471
Grant, Lee, 24, 80, 128, 216, 277, 308, 383, 513, 542, 549, 558
Grant, Micki, 582
Granville, Bernard, 59
Granville, Bonita, 91, 107, 521
Granville, Charlotte, 42, 116, 132, 173, 196, 211, 269, 294, 431
Grapewin, Charley, 188, 369, 426, 482
Grattan, Lawrence, 192
Grau, Dorothy, 12
Grauer, Ben, 367, 383
Gravers, Steven, 72
Graves, George, 222
Graves, Peter, 80, 393, 441
Graves, Ralph, 19, 408
Gravet, Fernand, 45, 159
Gray, Coleen, 267
Gray, David, 49
Gray, Dolores, 257, 294, 529, 546, 558
Gray, Dulcie, 12
Gray, Gilda, 24, 545
Gray, Joan, 446
Gray, Lawrence, 37, 282, 435
Grayson, Bette, 186, 335
Grayson, Mitchell, 536
Greaza, Walter, 20, 71, 85, 234, 251,

343, 401, 455, 464, 480, 506, 509, 512, 513
Greco, Jose, 217
Gredy, Jean-Pierre, 75, 165
Greeley, Dana Watterson, 237
Green, Adolph, 37, 174, 327
Green, Bernard, 519
Green, Diana, 119, 309, 312
Green, Harry, 35, 100, 132, 151, 182, 196, 255, 372
Green, Howard J., 50
Green, Isaac, 109
Green, Marion, 44
Green, Martyn, 89, 230, 235
Green, Mawby, 221, 362
Green, Millicent, 56, 216
Green, Mitzi, 100
Green, Morris, 61, 90, 113, 283, 361, 367, 394, 400, 440
Green, Nigel, 322
Green, Paul, 156, 221, 232, 330, 400, 572, 579
Green, Phil, 158
Greendale, Alexander, 508
Greene, Bertram, 453
Greene, James, 28, 397
Greene, Lorne, 121, 141, 380, 437, 558
Greene, Luther, 142, 375, 508
Greene, Patterson, 363
Greene, Reuben, 62
Greene, Richard, 276
Greene, Will, 397
Greener, Dorothy, 326
Greenfield, Josh, 94
Greenleaf, Raymond, 20, 124, 533
Greenough, Walter, 148, 199
Greenstreet, Sydney, 48, 160, 188, 230, 252, 261, 298, 372, 468, 544, 545, 558
Greenwald, Joseph, 379
Greenwald, Robert, 368
Greenwood, Charlotte, 197, 228, 290, 363, 378, 444, 500, 529, 558
Greenwood, Jane, 221, 268, 279, 318, 367, 417, 421
Greenwood, Joan, 473, 541, 558
Greenwood, Rosemund, 302
Greer, Jane, 479
Greer, Michael, 164, 165
Greet, Maurice, 234
Gregg, Jess, 422
Gregorio, Rose, 120, 247, 250, 257
Gregory, Andre, 20, 361
Gregory, James, 98, 121, 127, 131, 136, 167, 182, 235, 250, 255, 296, 558
Gregory, Paul, 76, 280, 299, 332
Gresham, Herbert, 383, 404, 487
Grew, William A., 326, 333, 409
Grey, Clifford, 257
Grey, Jane, 121, 255, 331, 521
Grey, Joel, 68, 226, 543, 549, 558
Grey, Katherine, 191
Grey, Nan, 299
Grey, Virginia, 13, 230, 347, 504, 517, 529
Gribble, George Dunning, 301
Gribble, Harry Wagstaff, 17, 30, 187, 223, 232, 249, 293, 314, 346, 347, 396, 405, 434, 468, 489
Gribbon, Harry, 191, 303, 321
Griem, Helmut, 226
Griffen, Edan, 189
Griffies, Ethel, 20, 37, 109, 137, 201, 261, 266-67, 268, 330, 404, 444, 504, 511, 546, 559
Griffin, Arthur, 11
Griffin, Eleanor, 303-4
Griffis, William, 216
Griffith, Andy, 340, 549, 559
Griffith, Corinne, 40, 125, 272, 410

Griffith, D. W., 94, 294
Griffith, Eleanor, 546
Griffith, Hugh, 279, 346, 531, 550, 559
Griffith, Robert, 68, 77, 414
Griggs, John, 12
Grimes, Tammy, 354, 559, 585
Griscom, Lloyd, 464
Grisman, Sam H., 65, 116, 470
Grismer, Joseph R., 174, 294
Grissmer, John, 79
Grizzard, George, 15, 52, 107, 108, 109, 127, 131, 150, 183, 203, 238, 462, 520, 548, 559
Grodin, Charles, 12, 462, 471, 559
Groody, Louise, 149, 421
Gropper, Milton Herbert, 51, 190, 199, 260, 311, 333, 512
Grosbard, Ulu, 120, 381, 451, 505, 582
Gross, Edward, 88
Gross, Laurence, 517
Gross, Shelly, 84, 238
Gross, Stephen, 218, 353
Grossmann, Suzanne, 273
Group Theatre, The, 38, 53, 83, 221, 305, 335, 337, 338, 363, 395, 400, 476, 514
Grove, F. C., 163
Gruenberg, L. S., 102
Gruenberg, Louis, 143
Grunwald, Alfred, 116
Guardino, Harry, 143, 208, 330, 403, 417, 559
Guardino, Jerome, 422
Guare, John, 221, 572
Guber, Lee, 84, 238
Guerdon, David, 266
Guernon, Charles, 149
Guerra, Robert, 510
Guest, Christopher, 317
Guetary, George, 385
Guilfoyle, Paul, 62, 109, 162, 182, 245, 297, 367, 383, 396, 443, 472, 538
Guinan, Texas, 546
Guinness, Alec, 138, 291, 498, 541, 559, 585
Guion, Raymond, 107, 282, 311, 380, 460, 509, 521, 537
Guitry, Sacha, 100, 192
Gunn, Bill, 460
Gunn, Moses, 197, 230
Gurian, Manning, 436, 509
Gurney, Dennis, 85, 100, 139, 535
Gussow, Mel, 219, 412
Guthrie, Tyrone, 130, 177, 302, 365, 465, 584
Gwenn, Edmund, 55, 266, 270, 303, 381, 530, 535, 548, 559
Gwynne, Fred, 168, 273, 323, 559

Haade, William, 240
Haas, Dolly, 133, 525
Haas, Hugo, 158, 307
Haas, Roland, 464
Haase, John, 169
Hack, Moe, 465
Hackett, A., 304
Hackett, Albert, 18, 64, 129, 194, 253, 311, 321, 332, 345, 492, 500, 572, 584
Hackett, Buddy, 286, 506, 559
Hackett, Frances, 572
Hackett, James K., 184, 359, 381, 397
Hackett, Joan, 76, 95, 337, 369, 559
Hackett, Raymond, 13, 83, 103, 105, 107, 137, 146, 337, 338, 372, 487, 489

Hackett, Walter, 79, 239, 355, 356, 519
Hackman, Gene, 32, 87, 90, 227, 330, 377, 390, 559
Haden, Sara, 158, 159, 181, 214, 266, 358, 426, 490
Hagan, James, 199, 211, 309, 354
Hagen, Jean, 31, 454, 487
Hagen, Reigh, 184
Hagen, Uta, 107, 203, 233, 255, 290, 449, 486, 504, 520, 544, 548, 549, 559, 583, 584
Haggart, John, 288
Haggott, John, 166, 449
Hagman, Larry, 45, 81, 100, 509
Hague, Albert, 23, 75
Haigh, Kenneth, 144
Haight, George, 73, 134, 190, 256, 378, 458, 513
Hailey, Marian, 48, 83, 302, 498, 528
Hailey, Oliver, 155, 159, 212
Haines, Larry, 173, 339, 344, 474
Haines, Robert T., 24, 97, 118, 134, 187, 201, 234, 311, 349, 472, 531
Haines, William Wister, 101
Haines, William, 18, 116, 176, 296, 394, 439, 460
Haislip, Captain Harvey, 279
Hajos, Mitzi, 75, 321, 452, 534
Hakim, Raphael, 205
Hakim, Robert, 205
Hale, Alan, 151, 244, 285, 349, 354, 369, 382, 409, 471
Hale, Chester, 366
Hale, Creighton, 84
Hale, Frank J., 179, 309
Hale, Georgia, 195
Hale, Louise Closser, 31, 33, 97, 130, 149, 206, 312, 333, 353, 405
Hale, Randolph, 51, 349
Hale, Richard, 101, 185, 197
Hale, Walter, 33
Haley, Jack, 207, 377, 547, 559
Hall Johnson Choir, 198, 405
Hall, Adrian, 356
Hall, Alexander, 327
Hall, Clay, 22
Hall, Cliff, 280
Hall, Dorothy, 46, 89, 102, 181, 197, 272, 356, 361, 380, 385, 437, 506, 530
Hall, Ellen, 145
Hall, Grayson, 336, 422
Hall, Howard, 294
Hall, Huntz, 121
Hall, James, 282
Hall, Jon, 24
Hall, Juanita, 372, 377, 407, 459
Hall, Lois, 114
Hall, Lyle Weaver, 480
Hall, Mark, 92
Hall, Mary, 134
Hall, Natalie, 431
Hall, Peter, 403, 585
Hall, Porter, 117, 168, 194, 241, 257, 282, 335, 369, 392, 510
Hall, Thurston, 22, 29, 47, 73, 92, 93, 102, 148, 167, 324, 370, 389, 393, 439, 445, 470, 473, 521
Hall, Zooey, 165
Halle, Abe, 357
Haller, Tobias, 264
Halliday, Heller, 428
Halliday, John, 55, 79, 110, 115, 216, 225, 245, 329, 369, 370, 389, 410, 436, 437, 486, 526, 547
Halliday, Richard, 119, 494
Hallow, John, 346
Halloway, Sterling, 176
Halop, Billy, 86, 121
Halton, Charles, 350

Hambleton, John, 528
Hambleton, T. Edward, 158, 227, 289, 382, 400, 489
Hamilton, Ann, 356
Hamilton, Hale, 122, 165, 176, 195, 311, 321, 362, 372, 380, 444, 452, 473, 532
Hamilton, Jane, 451
Hamilton, Jeffery, 367
Hamilton, John F., 210, 344-45, 345
Hamilton, Lynn, 104, 150, 354
Hamilton, Mahlon, 114
Hamilton, Margaret, 31, 117, 153, 154, 198, 228, 305, 348, 349, 357, 359, 429, 442, 494, 501, 504, 559
Hamilton, Murray, 12, 87, 110, 165, 212, 314, 340, 446, 461, 559
Hamilton, Nancy , 381
Hamilton, Neil, 29, 83, 125, 195, 265, 285, 305, 354, 480, 485, 528, 559
Hamlin, Fred, 33
Hamlin, Mary, 201
Hammer, Jerry, 235, 507
Hammerstein, Arthur, 121, 199, 295
Hammerstein, James, 12, 58, 362
Hammerstein, Oscar, 146
Hammerstein, Oscar II, 70, 199, 204, 205, 228, 248, 333, 517, 579
Hammerstein, Theodore, 67, 224, 377, 409, 473
Hammerstein, William, 15, 99, 177
Hammett, Dashiell, 511
Hammond, Edward, 42
Hammond, Henry, 245, 276
Hammond, Kay, 349
Hammond, Percy, 58, 66, 91, 137, 171, 176, 304, 388, 411, 424
Hammond, Ronald, 37
Hammond, Ruth, 270, 410, 525, 528
Hammond, Virginia, 534
Hampden, Walter, 13, 26, 79, 93, 111, 175, 188, 232, 253, 269, 271, 358, 365, 370, 416, 417, 487, 503, 541, 559
Hampton Play Corp., 538
Hampton, Hope, 186
Hancock, John, 144
Handley, Alan, 150
Handy, John, 92
Handzlik, Jan, 36, 37
Haney, Carol, 281
Hanley, Millicent, 102, 164, 367
Hanley, William, 384, 429, 494, 514, 572
Hanmer, Don, 293, 377, 454, 524
Hanna, Mark, 258
Hannah, Link, 528
Hannen, Nicholas, 12
Hansberry, Lorraine, 268, 390, 423, 572
Hansen, Waldemar, 172
Hansen, William, 43, 119, 280, 315, 326, 463
Hanson, Gladys, 192, 246, 252, 386
Hanson, Lars, 442
Harbach, Otto, 500
Hardie, Russell, 28, 45, 70, 104, 109, 177, 190, 205, 206, 218, 265, 283, 308, 326, 361, 382, 394, 402, 408, 431, 432, 453, 498
Harding, Ann, 12, 29, 54, 143, 172, 180, 217, 237, 244, 290, 338, 363, 369, 461, 473, 489, 516, 527, 559
Harding, June, 460
Harding, Lyn, 358, 532
Harding, Warren G., 171
Hards, Ira, 34, 44, 55, 57, 136, 216, 239, 290, 362, 392, 410, 471, 492, 500, 535
Hardwicke, Cedric, 24, 179, 219, 228, 265, 266, 291, 316, 349, 486, 511,

616 INDEX

542, 543, 559
Hardy, Joe, 314
Hardy, Joseph, 89, 92, 249, 336, 373, 585
Hardy, Sam, 87, 255
Hardy, Sarah, 90
Hare, Lumsden, 31, 142, 215, 500
Hare, Will, 138, 355
Harens, Dean, 44, 465, 473, 504
Harfod, Burton, 281
Hargrave, Roy, 51, 57, 84, 122, 223, 241, 270, 370, 402, 424, 428, 437
Haring, Forrest, 33
Harling, Frank, 363
Harlow, Jean, 130, 392
Harmon, Joy, 456
Harmon, Sidney, 57, 59, 71, 305, 310, 380, 400, 494
Harnick, Jay, 452
Harnick, Sheldon, 332, 580
Harper, H. H., 401
Harper, Marguerite, 401
Harper, Ray, 196
Harper, Ron, 426
Harper, Valerie, 18, 559
Harrigan, Nedda, 35, 85, 136, 207, 235, 307, 488, 559
Harrigan, William, 13, 22, 26, 61, 117, 120, 135, 195, 203, 235, 237, 254, 304, 313, 314, 364, 365, 370, 375, 402, 409, 411, 419, 431, 510, 517, 542, 559
Harriman, Borden, 322
Harrington, John, 429
Harrington, Kate, 318
Harrington, Pat, 168, 190, 204, 205, 259, 277, 391, 454
Harris, Barbara, 346, 367, 474, 559, 581
Harris, Cora, 112
Harris, Cynthia, 48, 519
Harris, Elmer, 196, 249, 295, 299, 314, 444, 537
Harris, Henry B., 33, 92, 94, 102, 107, 273, 371, 381, 410, 452, 461, 471, 488
Harris, Mrs. Henry B., 57, 271-72, 341
Harris, Herbert H., 22, 167, 226, 295
Harris, Jed, 32, 66, 89, 105, 111, 168, 210, 271, 278, 282, 321, 354, 357, 404, 416, 438, 487, 493, 512, 526, 529, 531
Harris, John, 37
Harris, Jonathan, 160, 194, 396
Harris, Julie, 20, 27, 136, 165, 226, 264, 275, 290, 297, 304, 305, 315, 421-22, 454, 507, 509, 536, 540, 549, 550, 559, 583, 584, 585, 586
Harris, Katherine, 47, 255
Harris, Mark, 434
Harris, Mildred, 106
Harris, Robert, 17
Harris, Robert H., 68, 310
Harris, Rosemary, 95, 131, 238, 273, 449, 462, 512, 534, 542, 559, 585
Harris, Sam H., 26, 37, 51, 67, 79, 80, 87, 88, 103, 117, 130, 140, 150, 152, 158, 165, 169, 173, 175, 176, 195, 211, 212, 220, 222, 229, 233, 241, 245, 252, 253, 266, 276, 277, 294, 299, 307, 310, 311, 316, 333, 345, 347, 349, 450-51, 388, 393, 402, 410, 417, 426, 437, 441, 445, 460, 474, 502, 508, 509, 512, 514, 523, 533, 534, 535
Harris, Sylvia, 292
Harris, William, Jr., 34, 41, 42, 58, 109, 131, 140, 158, 197, 233, 238, 273, 311, 312, 436, 451, 471, 493, 494
Harrison, Bertram, 34, 46, 73, 126,
176, 210, 215, 220, 236, 257, 259, 266, 277, 312, 363, 364, 392, 426, 439, 459, 471, 500, 539
Harrison, Kathleen, 323
Harrison, Nell, 330
Harrison, Rex, 30, 47, 542, 550, 559, 583
Harrison, Richard B., 198, 542
Harrison, Seth, 89
Harrison, Susan, 85
Harron, Donald, 147, 465
Hart, Anita, 234
Hart, Bernard, 30, 92, 95, 123, 271, 414, 456
Hart, Dolores, 312, 374
Hart, Edward, 152
Hart, Everett, 56
Hart, Frances Noyes, 47
Hart, Harvey, 165
Hart, Lorenz, 158, 304, 434, 510
Hart, Moss, 25, 30, 92, 95, 123, 143, 150, 167, 175, 233, 252, 271, 294, 295, 306, 350, 351, 414, 502, 523, 534, 572
Hart, Richard, 117, 205, 267, 355, 372, 542
Hart, Teddy, 318, 402, 414, 474, 475
Hart, Walter, 307, 380, 382, 510-11, 511
Hart, William S., 440, 487
Harte, Bret, 408
Hartford, Edward, 239
Hartford, Huntington, 133, 243
Hartley, Neil, 309
Hartman, David, 302, 559
Hartman, Don, 21
Hartman, Elizabeth, 357
Hartman, Paul, 136, 236, 287
Hartog, Jan de, 583
Hartwig, Walter, 231, 280
Hartzell, Rachel, 49, 218
Harvey, Anthony, 273
Harvey, Elwyn, 148, 421
Harvey, Georgette, 69, 115, 218, 293, 319, 364, 365, 378, 380, 433, 444
Harvey, Helen, 330
Harvey, Laurence, 226, 337, 390, 453, 559
Harvey, Paul, 38, 65, 130, 131, 134, 192, 248, 312, 501
Harvey, Peter, 62
Harvey, Ross, 319
Harwood, John, 517
Hasenclever, Walter, 211
Hassan, Rita, 428, 499
Hassell, George, 521
Hasso, Signe, 182
Hast, Walter, 274
Hastings, Griffith P., 171
Haswell, Percy, 102
Hatch, Cutler, 231
Hatch, Eric, 275
Hatch, Frank, 94, 164, 270, 355
Hatcher, Tom, 239
Hatfield, Hurd, 69, 78, 241, 284, 542, 559
Hatfield, Lansing, 389
Hathaway, Joan, 412
Hatten, Lennie, 496
Hatton, Fanny, 116, 195, 215, 278, 282, 439, 488, 501, 532
Hatton, Frederic, 116, 195, 215, 278, 282, 439, 488, 501, 532
Hatton, Raymond, 20
Haupt, Ulrich, 386
Haven, Gloria De, 18, 402, 456
Haver, Phyllis, 88
Havilland, Olivia de, 142, 177, 210, 292, 317, 354, 556
Havoc, June, 64, 70, 130, 138, 297,

327, 389, 406, 509, 559
Hawkes, Kerby, 466
Hawkins, Jack, 537, 559
Hawkins, Louis (Goldi), 233
Hawkins, Maxwell, 109
Hawkins, Trish, 220
Hawkins, William, 433
Hawks, Howard, 108, 168, 174, 493
Hawn, Goldie, 72, 75
Haworth, Jill, 226, 549
Hawthorne, Nathaniel, 144, 410
Hawthorne, Ruth, 386
Hawtrey, Charles, 307
Hayakawa, Sessue, 254
Hayden, John, 11, 32, 143, 210, 258,
  281, 307, 336, 384, 409, 527
Hayden, Terese, 131
Haydn, Richard, 265
Haydon, Julie, 16, 66, 182, 357, 365,
  426, 478, 543, 549, 559
Haye, Helen, 15
Hayes, Alfred, 180, 250
Hayes, Barbara, 363
Hayes, Bernadene, 292, 411
Hayes, Bernardine, 33, 57, 319
Hayes, Helen, 31, 39, 78, 94, 105, 115,
  153, 168, 183, 187, 204, 206, 207,
  259, 285, 300, 321, 323, 367, 423,
  428, 434, 442, 480, 483, 485, 512,
  519, 526, 531, 536, 542, 547, 548,
  549, 550, 559, 582
Hayes, Hubert, 477
Hayes, Joseph, 76, 127, 203, 267, 583
Hayes, Maggie, 150
Hayes, Margaret, 355, 443
Hayes, Peter Lind, 418, 519, 524
Hayman, Clifford, 159, 227, 404
Hayman, H. M., 159, 496
Hayman, Lillian, 486
Hays, David, 23, 111, 129, 135, 177,
  178, 237, 278, 280, 302, 335, 369,
  398, 401, 454, 465, 512
Hays, H. R., 303
Hays, Will, 378, 518
Hayward, Brooke, 296
Hayward, Grace, 212
Hayward, Leland, 30, 47, 190, 314, 375,
  380, 391, 393, 422, 442, 489, 519,
  526, 583
Hayward, Louis, 328
Hayward, Susan, 118, 201, 299, 358
Hayworth, Rita, 57, 354, 389, 443, 456
Hazard, Lawrence, 259
Hazleton, George C., 314, 533
Hazzard, John E., 188, 223, 492

Head, Edith, 141, 374
Healy, Eunice, 173, 415
Healy, Mary, 102, 519, 545
Healy, Ted, 21, 348
Heard, John, 510
Hearn, Lew, 49
Hearst, William Randolph, 409
Heath, Gordon, 125
Heatherton, Joey, 467
Hecht, Ben, 62, 141, 160, 168, 174,
  196, 259, 272, 445, 457, 480, 493,
  524, 572
Hecht, Harold, 53
Hecht, Jenny, 309
Hecht, Theodore, 525
Heckart, Eileen, 28, 42, 71, 72, 116,
  141, 147, 214, 233, 239, 371, 488,
  504, 505, 542, 559
Hector, Louis, 112, 226, 236, 318, 322,
  349, 393
Hedman, Martha, 60, 158, 164, 216, 235
Heffernan, John, 239, 292, 379, 385,
  479, 528
Heflin, Frances, 21, 228, 427

Heflin, Van, 64, 82, 83, 144, 309, 321,
  337, 370, 505, 514, 543, 559
Heggen, Thomas, 313, 583
Heggie, O. P., 67, 163, 172, 204, 309,
  310, 358, 359, 454, 477, 521
Hegira, Anne, 454
Heidt, Charles P., 267, 349
Heilbron, Adelaide, 434
Hein, Silvio, 130
Heinemann, Eda, 18, 67, 85, 88, 132,
  133, 175, 177, 239, 242, 264, 282,
  294, 312, 326, 327, 385, 411, 424,
  444, 509, 511, 527
Helburn, Theresa, 92, 274, 300, 584
Heldabrand, John, 232, 315
Heller, Bob, 465
Heller, Claire, 144
Heller, George, 125
Heller, Joseph, 512
Heller, Rhodelle, 384
Heller, Robert, 297
Heller, Trude, 374
Hellinger, Mark, 134
Hellman, Lillian, 31, 37, 87, 90, 91,
  120, 121, 275, 315, 326, 412, 487,
  511, 572
Helmond, Katherine, 195, 221
Helmore, Tom, 15, 124, 268, 352, 373,
  518, 524
Helpmann, Max, 314
Helton, Percy, 535
Heming, Violet, 22, 26, 50, 92, 121,
  122, 160, 246, 432, 453, 473, 474,
  498, 526, 533
Hemingway, Ernest, 156
Hemsley, Estelle, 324, 460, 484
Hemsley, Sherman, 385
Henderson, Albert, 273
Henderson, Charles, 146
Henderson, Florence, 208, 299, 549
Henderson, Robert, 159, 531
Henkle, Carl, 124
Hennequin, Maurice, 257
Henning, Ted, 184
Henreid, Paul, 156, 161, 217, 245, 559
Henry, Charlotte, 017, 19, 20
Henry, Martha, 111
Henry, O., 18
Hepburn, Audrey, 91, 177, 178, 407,
  559, 583
Hepburn, Katharine, 29, 53, 118, 124,
  126, 127, 217, 243, 273, 277, 278,
  300, 335, 336, 370, 389, 441, 442,
  469, 478, 490, 510, 527, 543, 550, 559
Hepple, Jeanne, 337
Herbert, F. Hugh, 163, 164, 179, 257,
  316, 386, 572
Herbert, Henry, 34, 262, 265, 393
Herbert, Hugh, 35, 67, 190, 274, 419
Herbert, John, 164
Herbstman, Harold, 250
Herendeen, Frederick, 377, 513
Herford, Beatrice, 98, 405, 494
Heriat, Phillipee, 504
Herk, I. H., 40
Herlie, Eileen, 18, 302, 549, 559
Herlihy, James Leo, 58
Herman, Jerry, 37, 302
Herman, John, 15
Hermant, Abel, 442
Hernandez, Juano, 56, 69, 365, 407,
  417, 446, 459
Herndon, Richard, 44, 63, 81, 87, 109,
  181, 199, 225, 254, 365, 380, 421,
  425, 488, 490, 499, 500, 534
Herne, Chrystal, 13, 35, 108, 149, 260,
  291, 376, 396, 401, 402, 407, 426,
  440, 469
Herne, James A., 407

Herne, Julia, 407
Herrick, Robert, 301
Herrmann, Edward, 317
Herscher, Sylvia, 522
Hersey, John, 47, 89, 509
Hershey, Burnet, 69
Hershey, Don, 479
Hersholt, Jean, 12, 19, 96, 130, 151, 193, 240, 265, 285, 305, 418, 469
Hervey, Harry, 103
Hervey, Irene, 264, 340
Herz, Ralph, 405
Herz, William, 448
Herzig, S. M., 504
Hess, John D., 198
Heston, Charlton, 126, 267, 284, 314, 559
Heusen, James Van, 136
Hewes, 521
Hewes, Henry, 103
Hewes, Margaret, 24, 159, 338, 400
Hewitt, Alan, 26, 124, 173, 187, 284, 301, 316
Hewitt, Raymond, 156
Heyburn, Weldon, 190, 228, 328
Heydt, Louis Jean, 22, 45, 66, 76, 204, 223, 380, 450, 476, 489, 516
Heyer, Bill, 130
Heyer, Georgette, 306
Heyer, Walter, 177
Heyman, Barton, 236, 489
Heyman, Edward, 420
Heyn, Ernest, 119
Heyward, Dorothy, 293, 351, 378, 417, 436
Heyward, DuBose, 63, 143, 293, 378
Heywood, Donald, 223, 503
Hibbard, Edna, 41, 174, 240, 378, 464, 547
Hickerson, Harold, 185
Hickey, William, 204, 312, 320, 430, 443, 471
Hickman, Alfred, 162
Hickman, Darryl, 463
Hicks, Leonard, 184
Hicks, Russell, 185, 340, 341, 485, 525
Higgins, Michael, 81, 111, 130
Higgins, Robert, 36
Higginson, Girvan, 149
Higley, Philo, 394
Hiken, Gerald, 85, 165, 284
Hilary, Jennifer, 37
Hildreth, Carleton, 103
Hill, Abram, 508
Hill, Arthur, 23, 171, 279, 302, 318, 520, 548, 549, 550, 559, 584
Hill, Chandler, 117
Hill, George Roy, 171, 280, 368, 487
Hill, Lucienne, 584
Hill, Phyllis, 156, 435
Hill, Steven, 107, 153, 160, 314, 454, 547, 549
Hill, Wesley, 198
Hillary, Ann, 117
Hiller, Wendy, 210, 487, 548, 559
Hillerman, John, 58
Hilliard, Harriet, 421
Hilliard, Mack, 407, 461
Hilliard, Robert, 33, 163, 180
Hinckley, Alfred, 443
Hindman, Earl, 273
Hines, Elizabeth, 87
Hingle, Pat, 23, 59, 91, 92, 116, 122, 143, 144, 156, 179, 183, 242, 249, 381, 447, 542, 543, 548, 550, 559
Hinkley, Eleanor Holmes, 122
Hinnant, Bill, 340
Hinsdale, Harriet, 457
Hinton, Jane, 245, 303

Hirsch, John, 46, 479, 512
Hirsch, Judd, 220, 412
Hirsch, Louis A., 37
Hirschfeld, Ludwig, 83
Hirson, Roger O., 250
Hitchcock, Alfred, 433, 505
Hitchcock, M., 119
Hitchcock, Pat, 433, 505
Hitchcock, R., 119
Hitchcock, Raymond, 253, 409, 545
Hoagland, Carleton, 444
Hoare, J. E., 393
Hobard, Rick, 368
Hobart, Doty, 134, 147, 473
Hobart, George V., 58, 149, 151, 357
Hobart, Rose, 107, 108, 124, 132, 227, 285, 321, 342, 357, 358, 382, 395, 423, 456, 538
Hobbes, Halliwell, 44, 245, 285, 292, 378, 534, 545
Hobble, John L., 114
Hobbs, Bertram, 280
Hobbs, Peter, 270
Hock, Robert D., 60
Hocker, David, 325
Hoctor, Harriet, 546, 548
Hodge, Edwin, 175
Hodge, Martha, 84, 269, 393, 439
Hodge, William, 112, 163, 252, 293, 324, 347, 407, 547
Hodges, Eddie, 15, 110, 203, 216
Hodges, Horace, 454
Hodges, Joy, 344
Hodges, William, 460
Hodiak, John, 47, 87, 101, 541, 559
Hoey, Dennis, 143
Hoffa, Portland, 544
Hoffe, Arthur, 538
Hoffenstein, Samuel, 298
Hoffman, Aaron, 167, 182, 342, 514
Hoffman, Bill, 15
Hoffman, Dustin, 104, 247, 250, 505, 559, 582
Hoffman, Ferdi, 28, 122, 150
Hoffman, Louis, 21
Hogan, Dick, 524
Hogan, James, 42
Hogan, Jonathan, 220
Hogarth, Leona, 25, 195, 198, 217, 266, 440
Hohl, Arthur, 132, 240, 489, 509
Holbrook, Hal, 11, 133, 196, 227, 298, 541, 559, 585
Holbrook, Walter, 153
Holden, Fay, 426
Holden, Gloria, 164
Holden, John, 426
Holden, Phyllis, 32
Holden, Ruth, 299
Holden, William, 33, 57, 60, 107, 123, 153, 186, 316, 357, 358, 371, 407, 441, 530
Holiday, Walter, 492
Holland, Anthony, 326, 519
Holland, Joseph, 430
Hollander, Jack, 238, 250
Holliday, Judy, 60, 136, 433, 524, 541, 550, 559
Holliman, Earl, 389, 453, 506
Holloway, Baliol, 298
Holloway, Sterling, 20, 194, 312
Holly, Ellen, 150, 460, 477, 484
Hollywood, Daniel, 23, 28, 332
Holm, Celeste, 29, 31, 88, 114, 142, 184, 197, 214, 238, 239, 325, 363, 370, 395, 462, 464, 471, 478, 549, 559
Holm, Eleanor, 271
Holm, Ian, 585

INDEX 619

Holm, John Cecil, 15, 57, 66, 165, 192, 300, 308, 309, 436, 474, 529
Holman, Libby, 544, 559
Holmes, Lois, 367
Holmes, Phillips, 25, 109, 130, 261, 472
Holmes, Reverend John Haynes, 232
Holmes, Taylor, 102, 119, 159, 192, 196, 215, 293, 342, 466, 504, 515, 527
Holmes, Terry, 296
Holofcener, Lawrence, 46
Holsman, Mary, 337, 354
Holt, David, 328
Holt, Henry, 267
Holt, Jack, 134, 277, 452
Holt, Tim, 135
Holzer, Adela, 507
Homeier, Skippy, 483
Homeric Productions, Inc., 252
Homolka, Oscar, 30, 63, 153, 228, 237, 390, 418, 559
Hooks, Bobby Dean, 477
Hooks, David, 430
Hooks, Robert, 417, 517
Hooper, Dennis, 296
Hope, Bob, 44, 84, 108, 110, 176, 196, 256, 332, 342, 405, 559
Hope, Edward, 420
Hopkins, Anthony, 273, 549
Hopkins, Arthur, 29, 58, 66, 67, 69, 70, 84, 87, 97, 101, 103, 114, 146, 152, 155, 158, 179, 188, 201, 202, 209, 217, 223, 233, 246, 251, 288, 289, 290, 294, 348, 349, 363, 364, 365, 369, 374, 377, 392, 394, 400, 404, 408, 418, 439, 442, 452, 469, 472, 483, 485, 507, 509, 515, 527
Hopkins, Charles, 128, 228, 259, 408, 488
Hopkins, Mrs. Charles, 488
Hopkins, F. Richard, 177
Hopkins, Miriam, 25, 49, 87, 91, 92, 148, 161, 171, 210, 215, 246, 247, 283, 347, 355, 356, 368, 384, 394, 397, 420, 428, 472, 473, 523, 545, 559
Hopper, DeWolf, 142, 315, 547
Hopper, Edna Wallace, 471
Hopper, Hedda, 26, 130, 132, 215, 217, 269, 426, 514, 529, 547
Hopper, William, 355
Hopton, Russell, 351
Hopwood, Avery, 44, 49, 97, 126, 150, 172, 176, 179, 186, 205, 259, 275, 331, 341, 417, 436, 520, 572
Horgan, Paul, 538
Horine, Charles, 303
Hornblow, Arthur, Jr., 81
Horne, Geoffrey, 144, 447, 484
Horne, Lena, 115, 559
Horner, Richard, 124
Horner, Charles, 218
Horner, Harry, 23, 92, 145, 152, 224, 240, 251, 272, 293, 486, 524, 530
Horner, Jacqueline, 457
Horner, Jed, 97, 301
Hornish, Ruth, 151
Horovitz, Israel, 582
Horrigan, Jack, 89
Horst, Julius, 59
Horton, Claude, 235
Horton, Edward Everett, 26, 34, 35, 37, 55, 142, 168, 184, 207, 212, 217, 220, 329, 409, 426, 452, 529, 538, 560
Horton, Kate, 42, 206
Horton, Louisa, 22
Horton, Robert, 389
Horwin, Jerry, 325
Houdini, 547
Houghton, Katharine, 168, 504

Houghton, Norris, 54, 115, 189, 224, 233, 289, 445, 509
House, Henry Arthur, 164
Houseman, John, 26, 107, 155, 251, 269, 330, 363, 502
Houston, George, 314, 421
Houston, Norman, 393
Houston, Philip, 292
Housum, Robert, 179
Hovis, Joan, 283
Howard, Bette, 86
Howard, Cy, 445
Howard, Eleanor Harris, 302
Howard, Eugene, 547, 548
Howard, Frances, 49, 239
Howard, Harry, 411
Howard, Jennifer, 454
Howard, John, 370
Howard, Ken, 91, 92, 494, 542, 560, 585
Howard, Leslie, 28, 29, 32, 48, 167, 253, 369, 370, 416, 431, 514, 531, 540, 560
Howard, Mary, 11, 499
Howard, Mel, 351
Howard, Michael, 471
Howard, Norah, 89, 122, 243, 530
Howard, Sidney, 11, 19, 50, 82, 133, 176, 201, 265, 285, 288, 299, 331, 348, 365, 408, 424, 459, 469, 532, 572, 579
Howard, Willie, 49, 403, 540, 547, 548
Howe, George, 322
Howell, Margaret, 117
Howell, Virginia, 472
Howells, William Dena, 397
Howes, Basil, 322
Howes, Sally Ann, 545
Howland, Jobyna, 130, 186, 275, 344, 358, 405, 444
Hoysradt (Hoyt), John, 160, 294, 301, 502
Hoyt, Julia, 396, 403, 416, 526
Hubbard, Elizabeth, 89, 365
Hubbard, John, 231, 357
Hubbard, Lulu Mae, 179
Huber, Gusti, 129, 161
Huber, Harold, 35, 153, 307, 429, 495
Huber, Paul, 232, 322
Hubert, Marcie, 232
Huddleston, David, 206, 528
Hudson, Robert, 349, 433
Hudson, Rochelle, 129, 266, 321
Hudson, Rock, 153, 416
Huey, Richard, 69, 378, 433
Huff, Grace, 444
Huff, Louise, 300
Huffman, David, 430
Huffman, J. C., 58, 184, 253, 256, 287, 366, 399, 439, 474, 517
Hughes, Arthur, 232, 320
Hughes, Barnard, 15, 131, 216, 228, 291, 341, 421, 463, 545
Hughes, Carol, 475
Hughes, Gareth, 138
Hughes, Hatcher, 210, 241, 280, 405, 422, 508, 572, 579
Hughes, Howard, 370, 386
Hughes, Langston, 324, 390, 449
Hughes, Mary Beth, 529
Hughes, Richard, 237
Hughes, Rupert, 84, 148
Hughes, Tresa, 15, 122, 128, 216, 263, 383
Hugo, Larry, 124
Hugo, Laurence, 55, 135, 441
Hugo, Victor, 93
Hugo-Vidal, Victor, 26
Hulbert, Jack, 560
Hulett, Otto, 86, 283, 322, 325, 326, 369, 400, 464, 468, 476

620 INDEX

Hull, Elizabeth, 214
Hull, Henry, 47, 64, 83, 87], 103, 147, 163, 164, 193, 233, 259, 286, 294, 296, 300, 309, 356, 374, 400, 471, 481, 503, 533, 535, 537, 549, 550, 560
Hull, Josephine, 16, 25, 34, 46, 74, 108, 114, 132, 187, 200, 207, 220, 239, 309, 349, 417, 432, 473, 474, 499, 517, 521, 534, 540, 549, 550, 560
Hull, Shelly, 93, 246, 498, 520, 522
Hull, Mrs. Shelly, 521
Hull, Warren, 67, 98
Hultman, Rune, 524
Human, Mac, 340
Hume, Benita, 95
Hummel, Carolyn, 228
Hummel, George F., 530
Humphreys, Cecil, 142, 239, 364, 365, 486
Humphreys, Joseph, 404
Hunnicutt, Arthur, 32, 46, 284, 285, 322
Hunt, Carl, 62, 224
Hunt, Marsha, 58, 205, 251, 268, 362, 381, 384, 489, 560
Hunt, Martita, 117, 560, 583
Hunt, Peter, 412
Hunt, Randy, 219
Hunt, William, 55
Hunter, Alberta, 293
Hunter, Evan, 388
Hunter, Glenn, 47, 94, 143, 307, 511, 537
Hunter, Harrison, 381
Hunter, Ian, 137, 276, 348, 359, 534
Hunter, Kenneth, 345
Hunter, Kim, 87, 91, 118, 367, 448, 449, 464, 513, 528, 541, 550, 560
Hunter, Mary, 355
Hunter, Ruth, 482
Hunter, Tab, 309, 374, 540, 560
Huntington, John, 413, 436
Huntley, G. P., 366
Huntley, G. P., Jr., 48
Huntley, Hugh, 435
Hurlbut, Gladys, 74, 253, 270, 397, 532
Hurlbut, William, 64, 92, 157, 212, 272, 349, 363, 382, 401, 448, 490, 531
Hurley, Arthur, 68, 134, 141, 162, 210, 252, 274, 335, 409
Hurst, David, 68, 498
Hurst, Fannie, 40, 225, 240
Hurtig, Jules, 42, 253, 506
Husmann, Ron, 463
Huson, Albert, 327
Hussey, Ruth, 13, 194, 357, 370, 371, 404, 439, 442, 456, 518, 526, 529, 549, 560
Hussung, Will, 66
Huston, John, 24, 234, 235, 255, 336, 364, 405
Huston, Martin, 341, 388
Huston, Philip, 84, 177, 526
Huston, Walter, 18, 32, 41, 43, 101, 109, 126, 127, 133, 140, 142, 162, 165, 174, 258, 261, 284, 322, 364, 389, 411, 419, 506, 542, 560
Hutchins, Will, 340
Hutchinson, Arthur, 147
Hutchinson, Josephine, 19, 20, 122, 237, 291, 296, 488, 496
Hutner, Glenn, 239
Hutt, William, 479
Hutton, Betty, 108, 136, 407, 549, 560
Hutton, Brian, 337
Hutton, Jim, 187, 332-33, 368
Hutton, Robert, 244, 509
Hutty, Leigh, 222
Huxley, Aldous, 173, 179, 381
Hyams, Leila, 26, 176, 319, 356, 522
Hyde-White, Wilfrid, 560

Hyer, Martha, 87, 407
Hyland, Diana, 87, 457, 560
Hyland, Frances, 279, 314
Hylton, Richard, 506
Hyman, Earle, 30, 95, 268, 313, 340, 560
Hyman, Elaine, 89
Hyman, Joseph M., 30, 92, 95, 123, 150, 271, 322
Hyman Productions, 241
Hyman, Robert, 81
Hyman, Walter, 130, 232, 273, 434
Hymer, John B., 19, 24, 109, 140, 154, 205, 261, 410
Hymer, Warren, 437

Ide, Leonard, 397
Igo, Harold, 443
Illington, Margaret, 256, 323
Inches, Howard, 365
Independent Theatre, Inc., The, 140, 419
Indig, Otto, 64
Inescort, Frieda, 102, 151, 282, 300, 306, 432, 489, 516, 528, 534
Ingalls, Albert, Jr., 136, 412
Inge, William, 71, 99, 116, 281, 330, 371, 517, 572, 579
Ingersoll, William, 18, 132, 158, 220, 240, 271, 338, 356, 386, 461, 475, 487, 512, 513
Ingram, Rex, 30, 115, 198, 223, 298, 444, 466, 560
Ingrassia, Anthony J., 151
Inlender, Avraham, 348
Irby, Dean, 398
Ireland, John, 106, 121, 133, 214, 333
Irish, Annie, 96, 311
Irish, Richard, 219
Irvine, Harry, 30, 122, 213, 247, 542
Irving, George S., 174, 190, 486
Irving, Harry, 33
Irving, Isabel, 480, 491
Irwin, Edward, 454
Irwin, Will, 28
Isenberg, Charles, 538
Isham, Frederick, 342
Isherwood, Christopher, 226
Isler, Lloyd, 98
Isquith, Louis, 213
Israel, Irving, 208
Itallie, Jean-Claude Van, 573
Ivans, Perry, 472
Ives, Burl, 127, 135, 209, 319, 543, 560
Ives, George, 413

Jackson, Anne, 149, 238, 283, 287, 290, 308, 332, 346, 424, 453, 461, 533, 547, 550, 560
Jackson, Captain Andrew, 158
Jackson, Delmar, 113
Jackson, Ethel, 133, 432, 528, 549
Jackson, Frederick, 55, 122, 169, 216, 429, 521
Jackson, Glenda, 560
Jackson, Helen Hunt, 66
Jackson, Horace, 538
Jackson, Mahalia, 49
Jackson, Mary, 489
Jackson, Shirley, 512
Jackson, T. E., 174
Jacobi, Lou, 99, 129, 134, 276, 341,

465, 542, 560
Jacobs, Irving L., 48, 436
Jacobs, Morris, 37
Jacobson, Dan, 539
Jacobson, Helen, 12, 415
Jacobson, Irving, 145
Jacoby, Ronnie, 537
Jacoby, Scott, 216
Jacoves, Felix, 256, 505
Jaeckel, Richard, 99
Jaeger, C. P., 112
Jaffe, Henry, 233
Jaffe, Sam, 64, 75, 146, 173, 193, 245, 377, 405, 465, 549, 560
Jagger, Dean, 48, 69, 133, 142, 148, 187, 312, 470, 481, 497, 542, 560
Jahre, J. I., 423
Jakobs, Ned, 223
Jamerson, Pauline, 155, 346
James, Benedict, 274
James, Clifton, 23, 28, 85, 104, 194, 242, 279, 488
James, Dan, 525
James, Henry, 48, 89, 146, 210, 232, 237, 378, 453
James, Ida, 224
James, Mary, 32, 81
James, Millie, 182, 276
James, Sidney, 433
Jameson, House, 235, 251, 332, 365, 512
Jameson, Joyce, 503
Jameson, Storm, 213
Jamison, Marshall, 314, 349, 536
Jamrog, Joe, 517
Janis, Conrad, 63, 168, 297, 333, 339, 431, 454, 465, 479, 506
Janis, Elsie, 560
Janney, Leon, 107, 147, 161, 172, 262, 263, 289, 341, 351, 419, 474, 503
Janney, Russell, 42
Janney, Sam, 280, 315
Janney, William, 483
Jannings, Orin, 106, 209
Jansen, Neil, 169
Janssen, David, 173
Janssen, Werner, 290
Jaray, Hans, 31
Jarrett, Arthur L., 326
Jarrett, Dan, 53, 254, 408
Jarrett, Jerry, 303
Jason, Mitchell, 177, 443, 505, 546
Jason, Rick, 342
Jasper, Zina, 409
Jay, William, 86
Jean, Martha, 535
Jeanmaire, 542
Jeans, Isabel, 178, 292, 348, 486
Jedd, Gerry, 195
Jeffers, Robinson, 122
Jefferson, Marc, 264
Jeffreys, Anne, 401, 402, 560
Jeffreys, Ellis, 383
Jeffries, Lionel, 323, 346
Jelin, Max, 285
Jenkins, Allen, 24, 56, 57, 72, 121, 160, 168, 184, 220, 361, 419, 429, 459, 475, 485, 529, 560
Jenkins, Butch, 18
Jenkins, Dorothy, 112
Jenkins, George, 42, 47, 84, 102, 110, 112, 117, 127, 167, 173, 203, 228, 232, 249, 337, 351, 443, 446, 461, 474, 484, 486, 494
Jenkins, Megs, 237
Jennings, Talbot, 339
Jens, Salome, 16, 71, 131, 153, 159, 335, 419, 426, 560
Jergens, Adele, 57

Jerome, Ben, 342
Jerome, Edwin, 289, 487, 509
Jerome, Helen, 381
Jessel, George, 245, 249, 405, 411, 472, 509, 560
Jessel, Patricia, 315, 560, 583
Jessy Trimble, Inc., 494
Jewell, Isabel, 56, 248, 369
Jewison, Norman, 416
Job, Thomas, 43, 263, 469, 496
Joffe, Charles, 134, 373
Johann, Zita, 67, 70, 288, 362, 417, 483, 548
John, Mary W., 98
Johns, Florence, 90, 282, 500
Johns, Glynis, 516, 560
Johns, Mervyn, 351
Johns, Pierce, 428
Johnson, Albert, 87, 97, 153, 277, 335, 384, 428
Johnson, Arnold, 86, 409
Johnson, Ben, 391
Johnson, Bill, 475
Johnson, Celia, 382
Johnson, Colin Keith, 542
Johnson, Geoffrey, 368
Johnson, Chic, 414, 415, 431
Johnson, Georgann, 110, 136, 392
Johnson, Greer, 324
Johnson, Hall, 198, 405
Johnson, Haven, 69
Johnson, Jack, 196
Johnson, Kay, 20, 46, 109, 167, 340, 353, 442
Johnson, Lamont, 368
Johnson, Larry E., 213, 241, 515
Johnson, Nunnally, 346, 482, 530, 531
Johnson, Owen, 101
Johnson, Raymond Edward, 365, 480
Johnson, Richard, 560
Johnson, Richard T., 23
Johnson, Rita, 103, 169, 368, 392, 518, 529
Johnson, Rosamond, 293
Johnson, Susan, 469
Johnson, Van, 76, 95, 100, 101, 193, 302, 393, 442, 560
Johnsrud, Harold, 146, 525
Johnston, Agnes Christine, 459
Johnston, Mary, 480
Johnston, Moffat, 15, 98, 137, 162, 251, 320, 433, 479, 493
Johnstone, Anna Hill, 23, 161, 213, 457, 463
Johnstone, Tom, 149, 431
Johnstone, Williamm S., 214
Jolivet, Rita, 257, 322, 474
Jolson, Al, 245, 367, 548, 560
Jones, A. L., 61, 90, 282, 283, 367, 394, 440, 527
Jones, Allan, 420, 560
Jones, Barry, 26, 43, 85, 399, 541, 560
Jones, Brutus, 143
Jones, Buck, 89
Jones, Carolyn, 81, 216, 418, 464, 529
Jones, Chris, 560
Jones, Christine, 23
Jones, Christopher, 336
Jones, Dean, 32, 463, 467, 498, 544, 560
Jones, Earl, 153, 207, 313, 446
Jones, Elinor, 98
Jones, Gloria, 129
Jones, Gordon, 327, 387
Jones, Henry, 15, 20, 42, 223, 244, 308, 333, 433, 446, 454, 487, 560, 584
Jones, J. Paul, 202
Jones, James Earl, 32, 94, 104, 196, 230, 268, 361, 398, 454 545, 546, 548, 560, 581, 585

Jones, Jennifer, 107, 153, 378, 435, 560
Jones, John Price, 140, 547
Jones, Lauren, 133
Jones, Marcia Mae, 91, 338
Jones, Margo, 116, 183, 236, 247, 350, 436, 453
Jones, Martin, 324
Jones, Robert Earl, 524
Jones, Robert Edmond, 18, 29, 117, 127, 148, 166, 188, 195, 198, 230, 246, 251, 288, 289, 300, 320, 337, 338, 360, 363, 370, 408, 416, 453, 459, 485, 513, 514, 527
Jones, Shirley, 142, 197, 560
Jones, Stephen, 79
Jones, T. C., 545
Jones, Tom, 389
Jones, Tom Lee, 496
Jones, Walter, 340
Jonsson, Judyann, 86
Jordan, Bobby, 107, 121, 429
Jordan, Dorothy, 439, 460, 537
Jordan, Richard, 489
Jory, Victor, 158, 227, 311, 356, 368, 468, 489, 495, 533, 547, 560
Joselow, I. B., 497
Joseph, Edmund, 416
Joseph, Robert L., 150, 240
Joslyn, Allyn, 23, 34, 62, 98, 108, 157, 252, 261, 316, 327, 328, 340, 409, 473, 503
Joslyn, Dick, 492
Jostyn, Jay, 121
Jourdan, Louis, 55, 178, 205, 232, 541, 560
Joy, Edward, 309
Joy, Leatrice, 47, 319
Joy, Nicholas, 64, 122, 189, 230, 250, 314, 323, 340, 370, 430, 472, 533
Joyce, Alice, 414, 440
Joyce, James, 496
Joyce, Peggy Hopkins, 262, 429
Joyce, Stephen, 149
Judd, Edward, 430
Judels, Charles, 109, 493
Judge, Arline, 110, 196, 503
Judge, James P., 440
Julia, Raul, 83, 236
Julien, Jay, 169, 208, 335
June, 376
Jurgens, Curt, 164, 195, 243
Justin, John, 275
Jutte, William B., 41

K. G. Productions, Ltd., 492
Kabatchnik, Ammon, 83
Kaelred, Katherine, 163
Kaghlan, Leonora, 485
Kahn, Gus, 332
Kahn, Madeline, 59, 161, 560
Kahn, Michael, 397
Kahn, Otto, 48
Kaiser, Burton C., 585
Kalem, T. E., 22, 455, 466
Kalich, Bertha, 396
Kallen, Lucille, 302
Kallesser, Michael, 68
Kallman, Dick, 156, 418
Kamen, Milt, 365
Kamp, Irene, 195

Kamsler, B. F., 153, 164
Kandel, Aben, 220
Kandel, Judith, 373
Kander, John, 88, 205, 226, 332
Kane, Carol, 397
Kane, Gail, 206, 266, 310, 528
Kane, Helen, 342
Kane, Michael, 128, 489
Kane, Michael J., 204
Kane, Whitford, 81, 90, 142, 148, 158, 263, 295, 303, 316, 400, 412, 477, 533
Kanin, Fay, 191, 390
Kanin, Garson, 59, 60, 62, 82, 100, 129, 177, 190, 215, 216, 224, 228, 259, 267, 276, 302, 390, 402, 405, 430, 431, 439, 441, 454, 474, 484, 504, 512, 532, 560, 572
Kanin, George, 277
Kanin, Michael, 191, 214, 390, 416
Kantor, Lenard, 121
Kapen, Ben, 367
Kapilow, Susan, 219
Kaplan, Henry, 32, 361
Kaplan, Jeanne, 505
Kaplan, Saul, 308
Karin, Rita, 221, 367
Karlan, Richard, 100
Karloff, Boris, 34, 41, 96, 160, 349, 474, 527, 533, 540, 543, 549, 560
Karlweis, Oscar, 112, 227, 242, 351, 560
Karnilova, Maria, 178
Karns, Ad, 135, 443
Karns, Roscoe, 20, 94, 196, 240, 411, 493, 547
Karr, David, 374, 532
Karson, Nat, 218, 250, 519, 527
Karweis, Oscar, 243
Kasha, Lawrence, 155, 339
Kass, Jerome, 409
Kass, Peter, 335, 379, 423
Kastner, Peter, 373
Kasznar, Kurt, 43, 146, 153, 205, 251, 292, 315, 327, 418, 549, 560
Katch, Kurt, 228, 349, 511
Katselas, Milton, 72, 76, 78, 165, 172, 348, 403
Katz, Peter, 32, 369
Katzell, William R., 251
Katzka-Berne, Inc., 28
Kaufman, Beatrice, 132
Kaufman, David, 208
Kaufman, George S., 25, 26, 46, 63, 72, 87, 117, 125, 130, 135, 137, 150, 153, 158, 168, 175, 188, 211, 233, 250, 252, 262, 265, 294, 295, 306, 307, 308, 310, 321, 327, 329, 333, 345, 350, 351, 360, 404, 428, 430, 433, 441, 449, 480, 483, 486, 502, 534, 548, 572, 579, 583
Kaufman, Mrs. George S., 132
Kaufman, Irving, 521
Kaufman, Jay, 267
Kaufman, Millard, 284
Kaufman, William, 372
Kauser, Benjamin, 455
Kawans, B., 525
Kay, Beatrice, 47
Kay, David, 163
Kay, Geraldine, 443
Kaye, A. P., 100
Kaye, B. M., 349, 420
Kaye, Benjamin, 113
Kaye, Danny, 108, 161, 243, 310, 332, 392, 414, 541, 560
Kaye, Stubby, 147, 549, 560
Kazan, Elia, 16, 22, 71, 75, 78, 83, 92, 116, 124, 125, 138, 141, 159, 161, 173, 186, 206, 242, 243, 305, 335, 363, 375, 427, 449, 454, 457,

INDEX 623

462, 476, 491, 536, 543, 560, 582, 583, 584
Kazan, Molly, 141
Keach, Stacy, 235, 278, 288, 545, 546, 561
Kean, Betty, 453
Keane, Charles, 295
Keane, Doris, 113, 120, 401, 442, 514, 561
Keane, George, 283
Keane, Robert Emmett, 67
Kearney, Eileen, 397
Kearney, Patrick, 25, 142, 296, 347
Kearns, Allen, 26, 514
Kearns, Michael, 492
Keathley, George, 183, 232, 440, 443
Keating, Fred, 21, 122, 164
Keating, Joseph, 43
Keaton, Buster, 363
Keaton, Diane, 373
Keats, John, 16
Keats, Viola, 30, 131
Kedrova, Lila, 237
Keefe, Willard, 85, 383
Keefer, Don, 161
Keegan, Arthur, 533
Keel, Howard, 257, 399, 561
Keeler, Marion, 441
Keeler, Ruby, 186, 319, 541, 546, 561
Keenan, Frank, 180, 452, 510
Keene, Richard, 418
Keener, Suzanne, 366
Kees, John David, 430
Keighley, William, 198, 238, 253, 367
Keightley, Cyril, 22, 275, 419, 435, 489
Keim, Betty Lou, 402
Keith, Brian, 121
Keith, Ian, 28, 113, 141, 194, 203, 265, 266, 300, 301, 386, 400, 486, 528, 561
Keith, Robert, 51, 91, 162, 173, 187, 191, 195, 244, 257, 259, 340, 365, 373, 401, 425, 438, 477, 485, 530, 533, 542, 561
Keith, Robert, Jr., 359
Keith-Johnston, Colin, 37, 48, 115, 364, 375, 381, 510
Kelcey, Herbert, 90, 296, 532
Kelk, Jackie, 64, 107, 190, 339, 368, 465
Kell, Michael, 59
Kellard, Ralph, 140, 391, 420, 510
Kellaway, Cecil, 71, 188, 207, 247, 336, 379, 531
Keller, Helen, 336
Kellerd, John E., 502
Kellerman, Sally, 264
Kellin, Mike, 35, 55, 143, 479, 524
Kellogg, Marjorie, 256
Kelly, Anthony Paul, 474
Kelly, Gene, 95, 165, 236, 302, 372, 478, 492, 549, 561
Kelly, George, 47, 73, 108, 114, 125, 154, 268, 290, 370, 393, 422, 423, 484, 572, 579
Kelly, Grace, 107, 268, 370, 392, 480, 550
Kelly, Gregory, 42, 72, 137, 257, 418, 492
Kelly, Harry, 419
Kelly, Jack, 152, 335
Kelly, John Walter, 358
Kelly, Kitty, 40, 92
Kelly, Nancy, 42, 53, 107, 167, 173, 177, 271, 309, 398, 413, 456, 493, 561, 583
Kelly, Patsy, 102, 192, 361, 541, 546, 561
Kelly, Paul, 13, 40, 46, 86, 101, 107, 196, 216, 223, 253, 321, 367, 412, 418, 435, 500, 517, 526, 548, 549, 561, 583
Kelly, Paula, 135
Kelly, Robert, 51, 360, 388, 449, 534
Kelly, Walter C., 61, 245, 268
Kelly, William J., 52, 534
Kelton, Dorrit, 23, 159, 318, 413
Kelton, Pert, 99, 198, 228, 261, 310, 437, 542, 561
Kemble-Cooper, Anthony, 215, 300
Kemper, Collin, 44, 97, 198, 283, 361, 396, 415, 417, 436, 520, 528
Kenan, Dolores, 256
Kendall, Henry, 331
Kendall, Kay, 351
Kendrick, Richard, 134, 187, 401, 439, 441
Kennedy, Adam, 397
Kennedy, Arthur, 22, 111, 124, 127, 142, 183, 209, 239, 281, 307, 317, 381, 415, 477, 504, 541, 561, 583
Kennedy, Aubrey, 47, 415
Kennedy Center Productions, Inc., 358
Kennedy, Charles Rann, 416
Kennedy, Edgar, 209, 475, 493
Kennedy, Harold, 294, 316
Kennedy, Harold J., 168, 191, 235
Kennedy, Jay Richard, 537
Kennedy, John, 159
Kennedy, Madge, 50, 64, 106, 150, 282, 363, 437, 439, 493, 504
Kennedy, Mary, 234, 251, 324, 342, 536
Kennell, Ruth, 469
Kenneyd, Charles O'Brien, 130
Kent, Barbara, 163
Kent, Carl, 267
Kent, Edgar, 537
Kent, Guy, 308
Kent, Walter, 418
Kenward, Allan R., 384
Kenwith, Herbert, 303
Kenyon, Charles, 256, 484
Kenyon, Doris, 179, 202, 500, 534, 535
Kercheval, Ken, 154, 155, 203, 434
Kerman, Sheppard, 113
Kermoyan, Michael, 199
Kern, Jerome, 98, 148, 165, 293, 403
Kernell, William, 418
Kerr, Deborah, 237, 336, 387, 462, 463, 548, 561
Kerr, Elaine, 337
Kerr, Geoffrey, 13, 40, 87, 163, 227, 233, 253, 445, 472, 533, 534
Kerr, Jean, 110, 157, 246, 256, 299, 377, 435, 572
Kerr, John, 22, 23, 48, 112, 462, 463, 465, 511, 561, 583
Kerr, Sophie, 53
Kerr, Walter, 16, 73, 76, 78, 110, 141, 178, 185, 236, 256, 283, 435, 518
Kerrigan, J. M., 43, 71, 204, 358, 519, 536
Kershaw, Willette, 107, 534
Kert, Larry, 548, 561
Kerz, Leo, 517
Kesey, Ken, 352
Kesselring, Joseph, 34, 110, 166, 468
Kessler, Lyle, 511
Kester, Paul, 261, 458, 516
Kester, William, 179
Kettering, Ralph Thomas, 97, 140
Key, Leonard, 351
Keyes, Daniel, 373, 412
Keyes, Evelyn, 338, 418, 529
Kibbee, Guy, 13, 35, 53, 186, 220, 250, 272, 291, 299, 357, 389, 475, 485, 495, 518, 561
Kibbee, Roland, 13

Kiehl, William, 337
Kiepura, Jan, 547
Kiernan, James, 517
Kilbourn, Fannie, 103
Kilbride, Percy, 112, 175, 191, 196, 272, 274, 282, 378, 445, 455, 473, 500, 561
Kilburn, Terence, 421
Kilcullen, William, 65
Kiley, Richard, 15, 235, 257, 425, 436, 453, 477, 507, 550, 561
Kilgour, Joseph, 202, 391
Kilian, Victor, 51, 64, 171, 177, 196, 280, 293, 337, 365, 433, 502
Kilpatrick, Thomas, 56, 208, 234, 356, 523
Kilty, Jerome, 168, 279
Kim, Willa, 412
Kimbrough, Clinton, 71, 78, 280, 314, 357
Kimmel, Jess, 130
Kindl, Charles, 22
King, Alan, 130, 232, 273, 434, 561
King, Andrea, 393
King, Archer, 494
King, Cameron, 339
King, Charles, 150, 394, 415, 421
King, Dennis, 15, 54, 93-94, 138, 197, 213, 286, 310, 364, 369, 370, 412, 543, 545, 547, 548, 561
King, Dennis, Jr., 258
King, Edith, 70, 88, 185, 188, 201, 219, 326
King, Henry, 47, 519
King, Louise, 446
King, Perry, 296
King, Rufus, 228, 240
King-Wood, David, 213
Kingsberry, Jack, 199
Kingsford, Walter, 15, 22, 56, 90, 109, 185, 331, 209, 291, 498
Kingsley, Herbert, 372
Kingsley, Mona, 518
Kingsley, Sidney, 118, 121, 127, 286, 305, 335, 365, 464, 530, 572, 579
Kinkead, Cleves, 101
Kinoy, Ernest, 216, 434
Kinsky, Leonid, 419
Kinsolving, Lee, 523
Kipness, Joseph, 24, 44, 72, 155, 208, 339, 442
Kirby, Durward, 303
Kirk, Lisa, 551, 561
Kirk, Phyllis, 68, 327
Kirkland, Alexander, 83, 107, 152, 186, 252, 297, 299, 305, 358, 431, 432, 447, 514
Kirkland, Jack, 65, 163, 167, 227, 296, 316, 320, 457, 482, 485
Kirkland, Muriel, 11, 98, 197, 236, 261, 267, 358, 445, 450
Kirkland, Patricia, 163, 404, 431, 532, 536
Kirkley, Donald, 203
Kirkpatrick, John, 13, 59, 344
Kirkpatrick, Mary, 147, 473
Kirkwood, James, 107, 141, 162, 260, 417, 475, 501
Kirland, Jack, 452
Kirshner, M., 286
Kiser, Terry, 83, 164, 185, 336
Kitch, Kenneth, 75
Kitt, Eartha, 30, 249, 324, 561
Klauber, Adolph, 132, 338
Klauber, Marcel, 326
Klavun, Walter, 318
Klaw, Marc, 33, 107, 201, 204, 206, 210, 257, 289, 359, 361, 367, 376, 383, 391, 404, 423, 448, 487

Klawans, Bernard, 203, 293, 469
Klein, Adelaide, 68, 134, 232, 297, 496
Klein, Arthur, 514
Klein, Charles, 36, 171, 273, 290, 325, 471
Klein, Robert, 360
Kleiner, Harry, 428
Klemperer, Werner, 122, 209, 493
Kline, A., 358
Kling, Saxon, 108, 483
Klugman, Jack, 186, 344, 452, 462, 504, 544, 561
Knapp, Dorothy, 67
Knapp, Evelyn, 220, 367, 452, 534
Knight, Esmond, 143
Knight, Jack, 443
Knight, June, 561
Knight, Raymond, 405
Knight, Shirley, 116, 250, 457, 511, 512, 545, 561
Knighton, Willis, 172
Knoblock, Edward, 155, 230, 257, 285, 298, 324, 326, 351, 361, 437, 477
Knopf, Edwin H., 53, 172
Knotts, Don, 340
Knowles, Patric, 37, 136
Knox, Alexander, 97, 360, 561
Knox, Mrs. Alexander, 97
Kober, Arthur, 208, 303, 309
Kobi, Michi, 463
Koch, Howard, 88, 182, 196, 234, 235
Koenig, John, 211
Koenig, Laird, 135
Koestler, Arthur, 118
Kohlmar, Lee, 380
Kohn, Rose Simon, 372
Kohner, Frederick, 45
Kohner, Susan, 283, 561
Kolker, Henry, 198, 217
Komack, Jimmie, 426
Kondolf, George, 156, 165, 203, 210, 319, 402
Kopit, Arthur, 236, 346, 572
Korda, Alexander, 125
Korda, Zoltan, 106
Korff, Arnold, 16, 17, 31, 54, 145, 151, 235, 267, 325, 348, 404, 410, 413, 461, 508
Korkes, Jon, 276, 367
Kornfeld, Lawrence, 192, 249
Kornfeld, Robert, 255
Kosleck, Martin, 437
Kosta, Tessa, 258
Kostant, Anna, 106
Koster, Henry, 207
Kotto, Yaphet, 55, 539
Koud, Billy, 450
Kovack, Nancy, 131
Kovacs, Ernie, 47
Koven, Reginald De, 452
Koven, Roger De, 35, 102
Kovens, Edward, 165
Kraft, Beatrice, 257
Kraft, H. S., 75, 112, 174, 377, 465
Kraft, Jill, 122
Krakeur, Richard W., 151, 208, 281, 301, 349, 428, 472, 473, 493, 536
Kraly, Hans, 387
Kramer, Lloyd, 92
Kramer, Stanley, 218, 236
Kramer, Wright, 234
Kramm, Joseph, 122, 177, 250, 295, 423, 572, 579
Krasna, Norman, 123, 248, 256, 282, 296, 430, 454, 477, 519, 572
Krauss, Paul, 99
Krellberg, Sherman S., 252, 277
Krembs, Felix, 87, 271, 438, 498
Kreuger, Kurt, 437

Krieger, Lee, 506
Krimsky, J., 233
Kroeger, Berry, 247, 392, 531
Kroll, Jack, 108, 358, 412
Kronberg, Virginia, 299
Kronenberger, Louis, 78, 116, 146, 269, 456
Kronengold, A. J., 492
Kroopf, Milton, 409
Kruger, Alma, 20, 91, 114, 305, 381, 399
Kruger, Hardy, 379
Kruger, Otto, 13, 18, 21, 35, 61, 80, 106, 140, 194, 266, 273, 286, 305, 316, 332, 404, 417, 418, 431, 448, 477, 480, 488, 535, 561
Krumschmidt, E. A., 52
Krupa, Gene, 196
Krutch, Joseph Wood, 452
Kubly, Herbert, 305
Kubrick, Stanley, 365
Kugel, Lee, 347, 455
Kuluva, Will, 69, 118, 327
Kummer, Clare, 26, 42, 188, 212, 297, 319, 376-377, 400, 439, 452
Kurnitz, Harry, 351, 392, 422
Kurosawa, Akira, 390
Kurty, Lee, 12
Kurtz, Swoosie, 141
Kusell, Daniel, 364
Kwan, Nancy, 530
Kyne, Peter B., 79

L'Estrange, Julian, 533
La Cava, Gregory, 157, 441
La Mama Troupe, 482
La Plante, Laura, 33, 84, 304
La Rocque, Rod, 269, 424
La Rosa, Julius, 257
La Rue, Grace, 122, 444
La Rue, Jack, 129, 153, 156, 166, 309
La Shelle, Kirke, 33, 139, 506
La Touche, John, 474
La Tourneaux, Robert, 62
La Verne, Lucille, 56, 93, 94, 100, 187, 321, 367, 417, 455
Lackaye, Wilton, 44, 187, 213, 260, 266, 282, 315, 346, 372
Lackland, Ben, 434, 475
Lacy, Jerry, 373
Ladd, Alan, 194
Ladd, Diane, 82, 356
Ladd, Margaret, 421
Ladd, Schuyler, 533
Lahr, Bert, 45, 70, 306, 543, 546, 547, 550, 561
Laire, Judson, 15, 23, 158
Lait, Jack, 218, 353
Lake, Arthur, 108, 476
Lake, Harriet, 500
Lamarr, Hedy, 131, 485, 518
Lamas, Fernando, 167, 561
Lamb, Gil, 391
Lambert, George, 333
Lambert, Harry, 274
Lamkin, Speed, 100
Lamos, Mark, 109
Lamour, Dorothy, 24, 70, 286, 391, 407
Lampell, Millard, 509
Lampert, Zohra, 16, 280, 298, 302, 330, 561
Lancaster, Burt (Burton), 22, 46, 99, 142, 389, 403, 436, 561
Lanchester, Elsa, 47, 266, 561
Landau, David, 405
Landau, Jack, 73, 81, 122, 397

Lande, Irving, 82, 495
Landi, Elissa, 32, 116, 143, 145, 153, 227, 261, 301, 461, 471, 510, 528, 533, 561
Landis, Carole, 231
Landis, Frederick, 105
Landis, Jessie Royce, 45, 69, 98, 110, 115, 257, 273-74, 284, 290, 299, 307, 312, 363, 369, 380, 425, 433, 451, 535, 537, 542, 561
Landis, William, 384
Lane, Cherry, 72
Lane, Lenita, 60, 366-67
Lane, Lola, 51, 162, 437, 509, 519
Lane, Lupino, 383
Lane, Priscilla, 34, 68, 162, 224, 303, 533
Lane, Rosemary, 72, 162
Lane, Rusty, 285, 314
Lanella, Frank, 111
Lang, Harold, 478, 545, 551, 561
Long, Harry, 479
Lang, Howard, 12, 60, 133, 245, 259, 411, 453
Lang, Matheson, 82, 385
Lang, Monica, 30
Lang, Pearl, 338
Lang, Walter, 127, 338
Langan, Glenn, 47, 153, 182
Langdon Productions, 521
Lange, Hope, 365
Langella, Frank, 232, 561
Langford, Frances, 87, 385
Langham, Michael, 382
Langner, Lawrence, 92, 211, 349, 385, 457, 469, 478, 584
Langner, Ruth, 64
Langsner, Clara, 166
Langton, Basil, 425
Langton, Paul, 205
Lansbury, Angela, 22, 37, 116, 256, 348, 385, 393, 442, 544, 561
Lansbury, Bruce, 159
Lansbury, Edgar, 145, 159, 354, 451, 466, 585
Lansing, Robert, 66, 112, 113, 157, 195, 284, 498, 561
Lanvin-Castillo, 299
Larabee, Louise, 28, 343
Lardner, Ring, 142, 252, 283
Larimer, Robert, 101
Larimore, Earle, 11, 54, 117, 120, 220, 296, 298, 320, 331, 339, 414, 424, 447, 484, 561
Larkin, John, 432
Larkin, Peter, 17, 58, 102, 188, 236, 268, 269, 297, 340, 354, 384, 412, 421, 463, 471
Larrie, Jack, 140, 429
Larrimore, Francine, 64, 88, 215, 269, 284, 333, 363, 421, 439, 561
Larson, John, 28, 279
LaRue, Jack, 109, 280, 394
Lascoe, Henry, 342
Lasky, Jesse, 351, 387, 441
Lasky, Zane, 220
Lasswell, Mary, 452
Latham, S. L., 21
Lathem, Fred, 285
Latimer, Louise, 215
LaTour, Nick, 185
Laudati, Anthony, 223
Laughlin, Sharon, 352
Laughton, Charles, 15, 76, 203, 266, 405, 469, 543, 561
Lauren, S. K., 305, 473
Laurence Rivers, Inc., 370
Laurence, Paula, 208, 252, 413, 479, 486
Laurents, Arthur, 55, 95, 218, 239,

477, 478, 572
Laurie, Joe, Jr., 231, 459, 513
Laurie, Piper, 183, 561
Lavery, Emmet, 158, 173, 290
Lavin, Linda, 144, 264, 276, 397, 434, 561
Lavren, Christine, 151
Law, Mary, 529
Lawes, Lewis, 86
Lawford, Betty, 174, 182, 261, 468, 528
Lawford, Ernest, 12, 69, 150, 189, 265, 291, 294, 303, 323, 333, 344, 486, 520
Lawford, Peter, 15, 277
Lawler, Anderson, 164, 211, 346, 384
Lawler, Jerome, 110, 251, 302
Lawlor, Andrew, Jr., 367
Lawlor, David, 480
Lawlor, Mary, 69, 362, 547
Lawren, Jules, 239
Lawrence, Beverly, 48
Lawrence, Carol, 335, 505, 545, 548, 561
Lawrence, D. H., 535
Lawrence, Gertrude, 183, 271, 428, 456, 541, 543, 561
Lawrence, Jack, 302
Lawrence, Jerome, 37, 77, 129, 171, 235, 236, 354
Lawrence, Lawrence Shubert, 103
Lawrence, Marc, 46, 57, 456
Lawrence, Margaret, 46, 209, 233, 266, 360, 378, 463, 513
Lawrence, Mark, 365
Lawrence, Pegeen, 150
Lawrence, Reginald, 232, 267, 305
Lawrence, Robert, 355, 368
Lawrence, Steve, 216, 561
Lawrence, Vincent, 26, 131, 176, 233, 360, 439, 494, 510
Lawrence, Walter, 475, 531
Lawrence, Warren F., 102
Lawson, Elsie, 517
Lawson, Howard, 174, 297
Lawson, John Howard, 106, 238, 281, 339, 383, 385, 400, 452, 572
Lawson, Kate, 502
Lawson, Lee, 16, 325
Lawson, Leigh, 37
Lawson, Wilfrid, 375, 380
Lawton, Frank, 226, 537
Lawton, Thais, 55, 148, 185, 314, 339, 370, 404, 479
Laye, Evelyn, 561
Layton, Joe, 369
Lazarus, Milton, 147, 228, 453, 515
Le Baron, William, 434
Le Gallienne, Eva, 18, 122, 140, 237, 289, 304, 322, 342, 380, 409, 436, 468, 496, 544, 562
Le Massena, William, 45, 372
Le Noire, Rosetta, 59, 166, 313
Le Roy, Warner, 419
Leachman, Cloris, 122, 256, 277, 301, 446, 453, 454, 561
Lean, David, 478
Learned, Michael, 561
Leath, Vaughn De, 265
Leavitt, Theodore, 517
Lebowsky, Stanley, 142
Leder/Michael Productions, 116
Lederer, Francis, 186, 385, 546, 561
Lee, Auriol, 15, 131, 227, 267, 319, 347, 348, 362, 468, 477, 479
Lee, Bernard, 231
Lee, Bryarly, 453
Lee, Canada, 30, 52, 69, 293, 330, 350, 407, 417, 436, 561
Lee, Carl, 86
Lee, Dai-Keong, 463
Lee, Dorothy, 377, 484

Lee, Gypsy Rose, 281, 329, 545, 561
Lee, James, 81
Lee, Jessica, 143
Lee, Leonard, 121
Lee, Lila, 23, 33, 57, 141, 191, 194
Lee, Martin, 511
Lee, Michele, 494, 561
Lee, Ming Cho, 239, 276, 316
Lee, Peggy, 13, 245
Lee, Robert E., 37, 77, 129, 171, 235, 236, 354
Lee, Sondra, 302, 454, 524
Lee, Will, 126, 263
Lee, William A., 136
Leech, Margaret, 132
Leeds, Andrea, 441
Leeds, Phil, 130, 238, 276, 302, 341
Leftwich, Alexander, 304, 416, 435, 495
Lehman, Ernest, 520
Lehman, Orin, 141, 339, 412, 452, 519
Lehr, Wilson, 345
Leiber, Allen, 492
Leiber, Fritz, 31, 156
Leibman, Ron, 122, 512
Leigh, Janet, 277, 327, 450, 519
Leigh, Mitch, 216, 332
Leigh, Rowland, 132, 171, 395
Leigh, Vivien, 449, 486, 511, 542, 544, 562
Leighton, Isabel, 438
Leighton, Margaret, 49, 75, 275, 336, 462, 544, 548, 551, 562, 584
Leisen, Mitchell, 124, 136
Leiter, Edward, 408
Leland, Gordon, 62
LeMassena, William, 104
Lembeck, Harvey, 314, 441, 513
Lemmon, Jack, 37, 47, 150, 168, 287, 314, 327, 344, 383, 402, 498, 562
Lenard, Mark, 177, 326
Lengsfelder, H. J., 209
Lengyel, Melchior, 31, 113
Lenihan, Winifred, 57, 61, 164, 332, 519
Lennart, Isobel, 368
Lenny, Jack, 443
LeNoire, Rosetta, 30, 94, 111, 185, 460
Lenox Hill Players, 503
Lenox, Cosmo, 383
Lenrow, Bernard, 102, 171
Lenya, Lotte, 43, 78, 146, 157, 226, 549, 562
Leo, Carl, 332
Leon, Felix, 539
Leonard, Charles, 429
Leonard, Robert Z., 193, 381
Leonard, Sheldon, 208, 257, 337, 423, 429, 562
Leonard, William, 405
Leontovich, Eugenie, 77, 85, 193, 245, 486, 493, 549, 562
Lepane Amusement Company, 335
Lerner, Alan Jay, 178
LeRoy, Mervyn, 42, 277, 291, 300, 314, 340
LeRoy, Warner, 187, 462
Lescoulie, Jack, 461
Lesley, Carole, 64
Leslie, Aleen, 429
Leslie, Bethel, 63, 72, 84, 223, 236, 431, 526
Leslie, Joan, 292, 471
Lester, Barbara, 249
Lester, Elliott, 324, 460, 495
Lester, Will, 384
Levant, Oscar, 26, 70, 225, 257, 547
Leve, Samuel, 100, 131, 202, 322, 436
Levene, Sam, 72, 75, 128, 130, 150, 186, 190, 209, 219, 263, 271, 291, 298, 402, 415, 436, 439, 455, 472,

474, 475, 479, 509, 529, 533, 544,
    550, 562
Leventhal, Harold, 72, 147, 191, 195,
    261, 315, 423, 519
Leverett, Lewis, 53
Leversee, Loretta, 69, 145, 188
Levey, Harold, 100, 285
Levi, Stephen, 116
Levin, Dan, 511
Levin, David, 129
Levin, Henry, 112, 182, 380, 480
Levin, Herman, 196, 585
Levin, Ira, 110, 135, 172, 238, 340,
    503, 504
Levin, Jack, 190
Levin, Meyer, 102
Levine, Joseph E., 28, 52, 230
Levine, Roy, 288
Levitt, Amy, 141
Levitt, Saul, 28, 489
Levy, Benn W., 13, 231, 268
Levy, Jacques, 258, 412
Levy, Leo, 240
Levy, Melvin, 186, 221
Lewers, William, 96
Lewis, Al, 335
Lewis, Albert, 51, 134, 140, 152, 208,
    245, 311, 326, 332, 345, 363, 402,
    437, 497, 508, 509, 522
Lewis, Brenda, 75, 275, 542
Lewis, Edward, 353
Lewis, Fred Irving, 103, 314
Lewis, George, 157
Lewis, Jerry, 35, 103, 176, 407, 506
Lewis, Joe E., 102
Lewis, John, 330
Lewis, Michael, 430
Lewis, Milton, 115
Lewis, Monica, 249
Lewis, Philip, 160
Lewis, Robert, 83, 87, 160, 186, 194,
    202, 205, 209, 213, 222, 263, 305,
    313, 326, 363, 463, 476
Lewis, Russell, 112, 245, 446, 477, 499
Lewis, Sinclair, 51, 112, 133, 142,
    155, 190, 245, 291
Lewis, Windsor, 477
Lewisohn, Ludwig, 146
Lexington Productions, 464
Liagre, Alfred de, Jr., 35, 74, 137,
    181, 226, 242, 244, 274, 282, 306,
    321, 330, 370, 385, 414, 475, 507,
    533, 584
Libertini, Richard, 519
Libin, Paul, 192, 519
Libott, Robert Yale, 484
Lichterman, Marvin, 443
Lieber, Paul, 27
Lieberman, Herbert, 302
Lieberman, Leo, 80
Lieberson, William & Martin, 439
Liebler and Company, 18, 44, 77, 119,
    172, 174, 234, 293, 324, 383, 408,
    440, 519
Liebler, Theodore, 125
Liebman, Max, 37, 345
Liebman, Ron, 402
Liff, Samuel, 314
Light, James, 21, 56, 130, 139, 156,
    214, 281, 363, 400, 405, 472
Light, Karl, 236
Lightner, Frances, 384
Lightner, Winnie, 186, 420, 547
Ligon, Tom, 283
Liljenquist, Don C., 528
Lilley, Edward Clarke, 103, 109, 259,
    303, 357, 453
Lillie, Beatrice, 36, 306, 548, 550, 562
Lilo, 544

Limon, Jose, 338
Lincoln, Elmo, 462
Lincoln, Joseph C., 420
Lincoln, Victoria, 382
Linden, Eric, 18, 110, 253, 259, 270,
    307, 348, 426, 503
Linden, Hal, 474, 562
Linder, Jack, 129, 441
Linder, Mark, 441
Lindfors, Viveca, 68, 187, 241, 379, 562
Lindley, Audra, 209
Lindo, Olga, 389
Lindsay, Howard, 13, 34, 74, 89, 128,
    137, 188, 196, 207, 208, 254, 270,
    347, 352, 364, 377, 380, 393, 420,
    429, 442, 450, 458, 473, 480, 483,
    494, 500, 531, 536, 538, 547, 549,
    562, 572, 579
Lindsay, Margaret, 247, 350, 437, 474
Lindsay, Powell, 52
Lindsay-Hogg, Michael, 85
Lindsey, Gene, 325
Linger, Louis J., 357
Linley, Betty, 210
Linn, Bambi, 20, 197
Linn, Margaret, 221, 397
Linville, Albert, 475
Linville, Joanne, 119
Lipman, Clara, 142
Lippa, Louis A., 581
Lippin, Renee, 169
Lipton, George, 275
Lipton, James, 37, 294
Lipton, Martha, 89
Lipton, Michael, 238, 425
Lister, Francis, 131, 392, 451
Lister, Walter B., 438
Litel, John, 15, 45, 85, 86, 107, 158,
    201, 210, 260, 271, 272, 350, 429,
    446, 471, 489
Lithgow, John, 586
Little, Betty Greene, 436
Little, Cleavon, 247, 288, 385, 412, 562
Littlefield, Lucien, 84, 514
Littler, Emile, 215
Litvak, Anatole, 24, 180, 486
Liveright, Horace, 25, 55, 136, 157
Living Theatre, The, 32
Livings, Henry, 582
Livingston, Jay, 475
Livingston, Jerry, 303
Livingston, Robert L., 87
Livy, A., 339
Lloyd, Doris, 511
Lloyd, George, 202
Lloyd, Gladys, 32, 160, 211, 535
Lloyd, Harold, 207, 310
Lloyd, John Robert, 137, 217, 295, 441
Lloyd, Norman, 35, 148, 269, 289, 303
Lloyd, Rollo, 15, 81, 97, 240, 261,
    420, 456
Lo Bianco, Tony, 191, 338, 346
Loan, H. H. Van, 57
Loane, Mary, 412
Lochbiler, Don, 293
Locke, Edward, 82, 96, 115
Locke, Katherine, 92, 94, 156, 208,
    224, 384
Locke, Ralphe, 112
Locke, Sam, 150
Lockhart, Calvin, 104
Lockhart, Gene, 11, 18, 33, 148, 168,
    203, 218, 396, 455, 458, 562
Lockhart, June, 164, 193, 562
Lockridge, Frances, 321
Lockridge, Richard, 45, 316, 321, 481
Lockwood, Gary, 467
Loden, Barbara, 16, 71, 102, 107, 279,
    562, 585

Loder, John, 29, 131, 164, 201, 272, 347, 468, 527
Lodge, John, 511
Loeb, Harold, 82
Loeb, Lee, 428
Loeb, Philip, 69, 102, 209, 252, 303, 326, 331, 335, 360, 383, 402, 457, 479, 529
Loesser, Frank, 351, 469, 580
Loew, Arthur, 249
Loewe, Frederick, 178
Loewi, Joseph F., 537
Loftus, Cecilia, 11, 217, 347, 392, 468, 475, 479, 503, 530, 562
Logan, Ella, 547, 562
Logan, Joshua, 58, 71, 82, 204, 208, 210, 228, 248, 256, 299, 308, 313, 314, 319, 348, 371, 391, 402, 424, 461, 467, 477, 526, 530, 562, 583
Logan, Lyn, 371
Logan, Stanley, 35, 98, 211, 215, 299, 314, 432, 537
Loggia, Robert, 59
Lom, Herbert, 422
Lombard, Carole, 49, 65, 70, 203, 241, 331, 469, 493, 500
Lombard, Michael, 178
London, Julie, 144
Lonergan, Lenore, 123, 370, 537
Lonergan, Lester, 41, 58, 167, 291, 319, 341, 399, 466, 472, 479, 528
Long, Avon, 198, 324
Long, Huey P., 157
Long, Jesse, 152
Long, John Luther, 14, 119, 289
Long, Shorty, 469
Long, Sumner Arthur, 332
Long, Tamara, 174
Longfellow, Henry W., 146
Longhi, V. J., 273
Longmire, Adele, 11, 338, 347, 359, 495
Longo, Billy, 165
Loos, Anita, 88, 151, 174, 177, 432, 456, 519, 572
Loquasto, Santo, 59, 414, 445, 466
Loraine, Robert, 120, 301, 476, 479, 480
Lord, Barbara, 95
Lord, Jack, 488, 562
Lord, Marjorie, 179, 274, 424
Lord, Pauline, 29, 132, 146, 265, 408, 409, 428, 447, 461, 469, 541, 562
Loren, Sophia, 127, 348
Lorenz, Herbert Richard, 304
Lorimer, Louise, 460
Loring, Eugene, 45
Loring, Kay, 208
Loros, George, 471
Lorraine, Lillian, 59
Lorre, Peter, 34
Lorring, Joan, 37, 38, 95, 99, 121
Lortel, Lucille, 494
Lortz, Richard, 507
Losch, Tilly, 188, 545
Losey, Joseph, 245, 276, 309, 455
Lothar, Rudolph, 392, 514
Louden, Thomas, 87
Loudon, Dorothy, 474, 528
Louis Isquith, Inc., 213
Louise, Anita, 33, 79, 107, 158, 192, 220, 274, 276, 298, 338, 486
Louise, Tina, 522
Love, Bessie, 146, 518
Love, Elizabeth, 280, 393
Love, Jules, 486
Love, Montagu, 40, 55, 170, 202, 203, 257, 486, 530
Love, Phyllis, 71, 107, 131, 141, 394, 403
Lovejoy, Frank, 49, 86, 153, 191, 197, 431, 436, 527, 562
Lowe, David, 284, 378, 436
Lowe, Edmund, 63, 130, 240, 311, 396, 399, 406, 434, 437, 473, 515, 562
Lowe, Florence, 165
Lowe, Isabelle, 115
Lowe, Kaye, 371
Lowell, Helen, 184, 241, 281, 324, 422, 541
Lowell, Robert, 144
Lowenthal, Jean, 425
Lowry, Judith, 141
Loy, Myrna, 16, 29, 33, 77, 194, 305, 312, 364, 370, 392, 440, 516, 528, 562
Lubin, Arthur, 198, 211, 472, 516
Lubitsch, Ernst, 52, 113, 468
Lucas, Karl, 393
Lucas, Nick, 186
Lucasta, Anna, 29
Luce, Claire, 344, 378, 410, 432, 526, 562
Luce, Clare Boothe, 137, 154, 159
Luce, Henry, 11
Luckenbach, Edgar, 305, 378
Luckey, Susan, 18
Luckinbill, Laurence, 45, 62, 543
Ludlam, Charles, 219
Ludlum, Edward, 278, 488
Ludwig, Salem, 38, 78, 236, 336
Luescher, Mark, 301
Luft, Joey, 546
Luft, Lorna, 546
Lugosi, Bela, 34, 83, 128, 135, 136, 191, 355, 471, 486, 548, 562
Lukas, Paul, 57, 114, 133, 161, 176, 277, 450, 483, 511, 543, 562
Luke, Keye, 188
Lumb, Geoffrey, 119, 494
Lumet, Baruch, 351
Lumet, Sidney, 68, 92, 121, 146, 250, 278, 319, 326, 336, 351, 356, 411, 415, 417, 455, 505, 562
Lummis, Dayton, 84
Lumpkin, Grace, 268
Lund, Art, 345, 469, 511
Lund, John, 207, 370, 540, 562
Lundell, Kert, 83, 144, 216, 455
Lundigan, William, 85, 131, 209, 234, 347, 515
Lunsford, Beverly, 403
Lunt, Alfred, 42, 78, 79, 94, 142, 159, 196, 227, 230, 239, 298, 308, 331, 372, 395, 401, 413, 458, 467, 468, 541, 548, 562, 583
Lunts, The, 92, 395, 544, 549, 550, 551
Lupino, Ida, 53, 173, 293, 317, 369, 372
Lutyens, Edith, 111
Luxembourg, Ella, 184
Lawrence, Gertrude, 340
Lydon, Jimmy, 203, 270, 396, 455, 479, 514
Lynd, Helen, 44, 218
Lynde, Paul, 416, 498, 543, 562
Lyndon, Barre, 24
Lynley, Carol, 58, 217, 281, 498, 562
Lynn, Amy, 280
Lynn, Diana, 103, 219, 562
Lynn, Eleanor, 55, 64, 99, 171, 187, 296, 400, 450
Lynn, Jeffrey, 77, 130, 162, 224, 270, 277, 278, 533, 562
Lynn, William, 168, 259, 269, 276, 424, 444, 468, 470, 474, 493
Lyon, Ben, 300
Lyon, Sue, 336
Lyon, Wanda, 97
Lyons, E. D., 174
Lyons, Gene, 95, 301, 472, 490
Lyons, Ruth, 335

INDEX 629

Lyons, Warren, 221
Lytell, Bert, 41, 68, 158, 227, 298,
   350, 395, 523, 541, 562

Mabley, Edward, 182, 464
MacArthur, Charles, 62, 168, 174, 249,
   259, 286, 408, 457, 493, 572
MacArthur, Mrs. Charles, 105
MacArthur, James, 92, 239, 437, 562
MacBride, Donald, 135, 402, 544
MacColl, James, 62, 267
MacDonald, Donald, 56, 164, 176, 211,
   267, 276, 282, 349, 383, 500
MacDonald, Jeanette, 180, 188, 342,
   383, 404, 431, 562
MacFadden, Hamilton, 69, 185, 258
MacFarlane, Bruce, 47, 168, 175, 258,
   263, 327, 361, 387, 407 444, 521, 529
MacFarlane, George, 218, 285, 359, 395,
   408
MacFayden, Harry, 343
Macgowan, Kenneth, 90, 166, 184, 195,
   360, 469, 514, 536
MacGrath, Leueen, 152, 153, 430, 562
MacGregor, Edgar, 42, 135, 169, 201,
   277, 335, 339, 349, 362, 371, 423, 444
Machiz, Herbert, 146, 233, 309, 449
MacHugh, Augustin, 303, 345
Mack, Helen, 92, 265, 395, 430, 452, 532
Mack, Nila, 146
Mack, Russell, 440
Mack, Willard, 51, 78, 102, 135, 153,
   167, 171, 185, 202, 213, 255, 272,
   324, 341, 410, 477, 513
Mack, William B., 395, 433, 526, 538
Mackaill, Dorothy, 24, 194, 260, 528
Mackall, Lawton, 73
Mackay, Elsie, 94, 100, 375
Mackaye, Dorothy, 415, 514
MacKaye, Percy, 175, 410, 472, 474
MacKellar, Helen, 40, 50, 61, 188, 291,
   324, 355, 401, 417, 445, 460, 500
Mackendrick, Alexander, 150, 346
MacKenna, Kenneth, 17, 53, 74, 106,
   213, 233, 301, 307, 331-332, 346,
   355, 367, 373, 473, 521
Mackenzie, Will, 412, 421
Mackintosh, Robert, 301
MacLaine, Shirley, 81, 91, 302, 494
MacLane, Barton, 85, 185, 203, 218,
   361, 394, 443, 451, 488, 489, 533
MacLaren, Ian, 201, 472
MacLean, Peter, 92
MacLeish, Archibald, 242, 362, 411,
   412, 572, 579, 584
MacLendon, Rose, 378
MacLeod, A., 82
MacLeod, Gavin, 80
MacLeod, Mildred, 59, 461, 521
MacMahon, Aline, 18, 23-4, 51, 53, 103,
   147, 148, 160, 173, 186, 198, 209,
   211, 231, 256, 270, 299, 306, 351,
   438, 472, 541, 550, 562
MacMahon, Horace, 44, 128, 258, 293,
   407, 521, 529, 563
MacMichael, Florence, 358, 384, 431
MacMillan, Louis, 296
Macmullan, Hugh, 525
MacMurray, Fred, 70, 76, 203, 276, 468,
   487
Macnee, Patrick, 562
Macollum, Barry, 234
Macrae, Barclay, 269
MacRae, Gordon, 68, 72, 197, 367

Macrae, Michael, 269
Macready, George, 25, 69, 106, 306,
   365, 410, 491
Macy, Bill, 27, 38
Macy, Carleton, 426
Macy, Gertrude, 203, 226, 241
Madden, Donald, 86, 233, 352, 443
Madden, Harry, 255, 324
Maddern, Merle, 34, 124, 143, 149, 155,
   156, 160, 234, 257, 263, 267, 289,
   322, 333, 344, 425, 482, 489
Maddux, Frances, 468
Madison, Guy, 214, 271
Madison, Martha, 337, 452, 500
Magee, Patrick, 411, 412, 562, 585
Magnani, Anna, 356, 403
Magnier, Claude, 474
Maguire, Kathleen, 49, 397, 478, 581
Maharis, George, 541, 562
Maibaum, Richard, 55, 414, 458, 488
Mailer, Norman, 125, 126
Mailey, Frederick, 394
Main, Marjorie, 121, 140, 231, 347,
   408, 411, 456, 472, 489, 521, 528,
   529, 562
Mainbocher, 136, 163, 196, 256, 267,
   342, 375, 479
Mainman, 151
Mainoff, Fania, 474
Majestic Productions, 212
Major, Charles, 516
Malby, A. J., 492
Malden, Karl, 22, 35, 106, 127, 141,
   161, 173, 186, 224, 250, 255, 312,
   376, 435, 448, 449, 453, 477, 490,
   496, 524, 542, 550, 562
Malina, Judith, 32, 6255, 5, 103, 581,
   582
Malina, Luba, 156, 283
Mallory, Burton, 424, 520
Mallory, Jack, 219
Malone, Dorothy, 176, 224, 354
Malone, Nancy, 479, 489
Maltz, Albert, 56, 307, 365
Maltz, Maxwell, 133, 213
Mamoulian, Rouben, 18, 103, 153, 186,
   267, 298, 378, 385, 389, 433, 449, 469
Manchester, Joe, 122
Mandel, Frank, 157, 326, 339, 445, 504
Mandel, Loring, 15
Mander, Miles, 382
Maney, Richard, 440
Manheimer, Wallace A., 67, 314
Manhoff, Bill, 360
Mankiewicz, Herman, 56, 188, 307, 404,
   521
Mankiewicz, Joseph L., 20, 265
Manley, William Ford, 521
Mann, Anthony, 432, 476
Mann, Daniel, 99, 232, 281, 403, 463
Mann, Delbert, 116, 308, 437, 538
Mann, Gubi, 318
Mann, Iris, 91, 112, 237
Mann, Louis, 142, 167, 182, 500
Mann, Paul, 161, 187, 262, 484
Mann, Theodore, 28, 172, 194, 263, 278,
   305, 320, 519, 539, 584
Mann, Thomas, 171
Mannering, Mary, 184, 244, 296
Manners, David, 136, 257, 491, 510
Manners, J. Hartley, 183, 204, 206,
   225, 330, 353, 358, 366, 458, 539
Manners, Zeke, 524
Mannes, Marya, 75
Mannheimer, Albert, 45
Manning, Irene, 135, 349, 369
Manning, Jack, 54, 464, 478
Manoff, Arnold, 24
Manoussi, Jean, 385

Mansfield, Jayne, 258, 522, 562
Mansfield Productions, 530
Mansfield, Rankin, 354
Mansfield, Richard, 44
Manson, Alan, 28, 177, 339, 373
Mantle, Burns, 225, 251, 307, 360, 422, 481, 514
Manton, Maria, 163
Manulis, Martin, 289, 305, 382, 423
Manuscript Producing Company, 482
Mapes, Victor, 60, 220
Marais, Josef, 484
Marand, Patricia, 208, 545
Marasco, Robert, 92
Marbury, Jane, 243, 424
Marceau, Felicien, 190
March, Charles, 459
March, Fredric, 26, 31, 37, 47, 92, 124, 127, 128, 137, 157, 177, 201, 206, 218, 230, 236, 245, 266, 278, 300, 304, 307, 308, 342, 363, 384, 404, 427, 431, 456, 483, 532, 538, 542, 546, 549, 562, 582, 584
March, Hal, 99, 542
March, Jo Anna, 312
March, Liska, 68, 173
March, William, 42
Marchand, Nancy, 27, 165, 462
Marchant, William, 127, 480
Marcin, Max, 42, 51, 86, 88, 115, 149, 222, 225, 281, 424, 487, 528
Marcus, Frank, 240
Marcy, George, 54
Marden, Adrienne, 26, 528
Marechal, Judy, 120
Maren, Greta, 250
Margetson, Arthur, 83, 274, 323, 341, 409, 545
Margo, 47, 300, 530, 562
Margolies, Abe, 309
Margolies, Albert, 505
Margolin, Janet, 119, 145
Margolis, Henry, 213, 351, 392
Margules, Annette, 518
Maricle, Leona, 117, 159, 206, 316, 332, 350, 429, 489
Marie, Julienne, 478
Marinoff, Fania, 64, 77, 212, 251, 462, 479
Marion, George, 29, 71, 98, 107, 148, 163, 482, 521
Marion, Ira, 488
Markey, Enid, 18, 42, 43, 50, 73, 148, 204, 264, 318, 322, 323, 324, 354, 371, 405, 431, 434, 436, 457, 462, 500
Markey, Melinda, 349
Markham, Marcella, 230
Markle, Lois, 509
Markova, Alicia, 550
Marks, Joe E., 205, 326
Marks, Richard L., 233
Marks, Walter, 216, 369
Marle, Arnold, 465
Marley, John, 102, 131, 192, 425
Marlow, Brian, 40, 190
Marlow, David, 339
Marlowe, Charles, 516
Marlowe, Faye, 437
Marlowe, Gloria, 233, 505
Marlowe, Hugh, 34, 126, 161, 241, 257, 262, 266, 424, 528, 536, 562
Marlowe, Julia, 516
Marmont, Percy, 24
Marney, Derrick de, 537
Marquand, John P., 265, 375
Marquis, Don, 116, 148, 348, 358
Marquis, Marjorie, 18, 116
Marre, Albert, 156, 188, 216, 274, 332, 390
Marriott, John, 198, 223, 230, 377, 413, 513
Marrow, Macklin, 127, 408
Mars, Kenneth, 48
Marsala, Marty, 209
Marsh, Howard, 551
Marsh, Marian, 160
Marshal, Alan, 55, 163, 185, 349, 364
Marshal, Irby, 510
Marshall, Armina, 64, 296, 349, 385, 457, 473, 584, 2232
Marshall, Bette, 23
Marshall, Brenda, 209
Marshall, E. G., 46, 76, 87, 102, 111, 171, 230, 243, 275, 308, 428, 456, 527, 541, 543, 562
Marshall, George, 172
Marshall, Herbert, 13, 275, 468, 483, 516, 562
Marshall, Marion, 407
Marshall, Mort, 351
Marshall, Peter, 136, 224
Marshall, Robert, 404
Marshall, Sarah, 99, 190, 243, 322, 377, 506, 530
Marshall, Tully, 84, 93, 307, 361, 392, 461
Marshall, William, 198, 279, 417
Marshalov, Boris, 252, 469, 525
Marson, Ann, 264
Marston, Don, 443
Marston, Joel, 152, 190, 299
Marston, John, 47
Marston, Lawrence, 12, 110, 124, 149, 205, 257, 262, 304, 315, 383, 391, 521
Martin, Ernest H., 191
Martin, Allan Langdon, 431
Martin, Dean, 35, 81, 103, 176, 407, 487, 519
Martin, Dewey, 127
Martin, Dophe, 400
Martin, Elliot, 302, 318, 332, 341, 416, 517
Martin, Helen, 125, 279, 326, 330, 385
Martin, Helen R., 145
Martin, Hugh, 517
Martin, Leila, 509
Martin, Lewis, 11, 101, 247
Martin, Mary, 95, 256, 257, 428, 541, 543, 548, 562
Martin, Nan, 78, 195, 242, 410, 446, 487, 498
Martin, Paul, 241
Martin, Peter, 536
Martin, Quinn, 304
Martin, Ron, 92
Martin, Tony, 421
Martin, Townsend, 319
Martin, Vivian, 253, 345, 384, 445, 522
Martineau, Stanley, 304
Martinetti, Ignacio, 39
Martini, Eaurto, 265
Martins, Frank, 385
Marvin, Lee, 54, 76, 167, 230, 254, 436, 562
Marvin, Mark, 350
Marx Brothers, The, 219, 402, 562
Marx, Arthur, 232
Marx, Groucho, 13, 477
Marx, Harpo, 295
Marye, Donald, 235
Mason, A. E. W., 311
Mason, Ann, 152, 162, 248, 354, 387
Mason, Florence, 157
Mason, Jackie, 463
Mason, James, 92, 296, 299, 476, 562
Mason, John, 35, 51, 101, 235, 267, 333, 435, 526, 533

Mason, Marsha, 126, 204, 563
Mason, Marshall W., 220, 412
Mason, Mary, 33, 191, 411
Mason, Reginald, 13, 30, 87, 93, 120, 151, 210, 232, 234, 311, 366, 502, 534
Mason, Richard, 86, 530
Mason, Ruth, 156
Massen, Osa, 190
Massena, William Le, 45, 372
Massey, Anna, 563
Massey, Daniel, 178, 430, 563
Massey, Edward, 48, 62, 308, 316, 385
Massey, Ilona, 563
Massey, Raymond, 11, 34, 146, 223, 230, 242, 320, 541, 544, 548, 550, 563
Massey, Valgene, 87
Mast, Jane, 418
Masteroff, Joe, 226, 380-81, 509
Masterson, Peter, 196, 488
Matalon, Zack, 280
Matchabelli, Princess, 109
Mather, Aubrey, 163, 189, 202
Mather, Charles, 126
Mathews, Carmen, 126, 206, 217, 241, 280, 289, 293, 327, 335, 397
Mathews, Carole, 526
Mathews, George, 43, 46, 84, 112, 127, 145, 147, 196, 217, 258, 270, 334, 352, 358, 384, 424, 449, 464
Mathews, Joyce, 175, 305
Mathews, Vera, 292
Matson, Norman, 101
Matteson, Ruth, 43, 233, 364, 439, 459, 467, 514, 524
Matthaei, Konrad, 268, 373
Matthau, Walter, 30, 75, 152, 168, 190, 198, 233, 259, 302, 326, 344, 351, 352, 422, 455, 493, 522, 526, 549, 563, 584, 585
Matthew, Ross, 525
Matthews, A. E., 207, 210, 302, 366, 416
Matthews, Adelaide, 253, 338, 384
Matthews, Billy, 463
Matthews, Hale, 135
Matthews, Inez, 372
Matthews, Ross, 48
Mature, Victor, 419, 541, 563
Matzenauer, Margaret, 504
Mauch, Billy, 382
Mauch, Bobby, 382
Maude, Margery, 129, 495
Maugham, W. Somerset, 243, 388, 389
Maurette, Marcelle, 289
Maurey, Nicole, 243
Maurier, George Du, 369
Maxwell, Edwin, 342, 380, 461, 521
Maxwell, Elsa, 121
Maxwell, Frank, 441
Maxwell, Marguerite, 296
Maxwell, Marilyn, 18, 110, 423
May, Elaine, 145, 287
May, Henry, 35
May, Monica, 224, 330
Mayberry, Robert, 295
Mayehoff, Eddie, 287, 389, 413, 506
Mayer, Edwin Justus, 90, 157, 401, 572
Mayer, J. C., 106, 421
Mayer, Jerome, 189, 285, 536
Mayer, Louis B., 175
Mayer, Ray, 209
Mayes, Wendell, 15
Mayhew, Kate, 154, 250, 251
Mayhew, Stella, 322
Maynard, Mabel, 213
Mayo, Margaret, 40, 215, 375, 415, 493
Mayo, Nick, 419
Mayo, Virginia, 186, 292, 310, 475
Mazo, Joseph, 23, 91
McAloney, Michael, 585

McArdle, Kip, 150, 308
McArther, Avis, 367
McArthur, Jane, 357
McAvity, Helen, 302
McAvoy, May, 245, 273
McBain, Diane, 300
McCall, Jade, 492
McCall, Joan, 388
McCallion, James, 402
McCallister, Lon, 524
McCallum, Charles, 35
McCallum, David, 563
McCalman, Macon, 264
McCambridge, Mercedes, 153, 373, 471, 527, 536, 563
McCarthy, Charles, 39
McCarthy, Kevin, 11, 15, 29, 49, 63, 119, 124, 161, 204, 247, 434, 456, 491, 509, 524, 542, 563
McCarthy, Lin, 95
McCarthy, Mary, 374, 442, 480
McCarty, Mary, 390, 546
McCauley, Jack, 174
McClain, John, 141
McClain, Saundra, 398
McClanahan, Rue, 138, 247, 288
McCleery, William, 219, 363
McClelland, Charles, 62
McClelland, Donald, 154, 271
McClendon, Rose, 56, 222, 232, 324, 332, 363, 400
McClintic, Guthrie, 16, 19, 20, 43, 48, 65, 70, 92, 98, 110, 131, 132, 146, 162, 166, 184, 213, 224, 234, 239, 245, 247, 248, 255, 262, 266, 270, 271, 293, 312, 324, 333, 340, 347, 364, 402, 410, 419, 428, 438, 440, 442, 480, 491, 503, 524, 525, 533, 535
McComas, Carroll, 238, 312, 335, 385, 417
McComb, Kate, 318
McConnell, Frederic, 119
McConnell, Lulu, 434
McConnor, Vincent, 250
McCormack, Frank, 60, 191, 315, 499, 513
McCormack, John, 399
McCormack, Patty, 42, 486
McCormick, Langdon, 445
McCormick, Myron, 82, 108, 114, 190, 210, 223, 224, 228, 233, 251, 272, 292, 340, 349, 365, 430, 432, 442, 445, 451, 476, 478, 524, 533, 549, 563
McCormick, Parker, 464
McCormick, Robert, 527
McCowen, Alec, 563
McCoy, Bessie, 545
McCoy, Frank, 113, 191, 435, 534
McCoy, Mildred, 46, 241
McCracken, Joan, 28, 53, 197
McCrea, Joel, 19, 55, 91, 121, 271, 375, 382, 424, 506
McCullers, Carson, 42, 304, 440, 572
McCullough, Paul, 97
McCutcheon, Bill, 325
McCutcheon, George Barr, 64
McDaniel, Hattie, 175, 476
McDermott, John, 13
McDevitt, Ruth, 12, 49, 153, 158, 191, 303, 371
McDonald, Grace, 318, 414
McDonald, Laetitia, 261
McDonald, Marie, 176, 198, 391
McDonald, Ray, 524
McDonald, Tanny, 273
McDowall, Roddy, 102, 188, 202, 340, 549, 563, 584
McEnroe, Robert, 424
McEvoy, J. P., 184, 380
McFadden, Elizabeth, 134, 424

632 INDEX

McFarland, Nan, 87, 327
McGavin, Darren, 57, 130, 237, 284, 327, 389, 478, 492, 544, 563
McGee, Florence, 91, 455
McGee, Harold, 109
McGinn, Walter, 466, 544
McGiver, John, 37, 97, 104, 136, 168, 172, 204, 368, 460, 563
McGlynn, Frank, 67, 85, 465
McGlynn, Frank, Jr., 167
McGlynn, Thomas, 85
McGoldrick, A. J., 26
McGovern, John, 134, 293, 377, 419
McGowan, John, 148, 210, 261, 334, 464
McGranary, Al, 230
McGrath, Byron, 26, 68, 82, 171, 213
McGrath, Frank, 82
McGrath, Paul, 15, 53, 66, 89, 101, 102, 171, 177, 179, 211, 233, 371, 397, 415, 430, 456, 486, 563
McGrath, Russell, 239
McGuire, Biff, 46, 141, 155, 478, 479, 489
McGuire, Dorothy, 95, 116, 256, 303, 319, 394, 523, 541, 563
McGuire, Michael, 92, 466, 544
McGuire, William Anthony, 231, 426, 492
McHattie, Stephen, 320
McHugh, Frank, 37, 57, 62, 98, 102, 142, 148, 162, 209, 220, 270, 272, 297, 361, 410, 459, 464, 475, 546, 547, 563
McIntire, John, 519
McIntyre, Bill, 414
McIntyre, Frank, 94, 291, 362, 415, 488
McIntyre, John T., 536
McIntyre, Molly, 258
McKaig, Alexander, 115, 117, 388, 433, 517
McKay, Constance, 106, 175, 479, 510, 529
McKay, David, 265
McKay, Norman, 155
McKay, Scott, 31, 47, 158, 277, 330, 350, 394, 407, 457
McKee, Frank, 244, 291
McKee, John, 106
McKee, Wesley, 357
McKeen, Hale, 486
McKenna, Siobhan, 402, 563
McKenney, Eileen, 189
McKenney, Ruth, 281, 327
McKenzie, James B., 27, 179, 414
McKnight, Tom, 134
McLaglen, Victor, 188, 396, 499, 515
McLain, George, 350
McLaughlin, Mignon, 172
McLaughlin, Robert, 172, 366, 492
McLaurin, Kate, 240, 517
McLean, R. D., 14
McLellan, George B., 151, 514
McLellan, M. S, 267
McLeod, Mildred, 231
McLeod, Norman, 20
McLerie, Allyn, 546
McLiam, John, 424
McMahon, Ed, 524
McMahon, Frank, 585
McMartin, John, 57, 90, 195, 351, 390, 471, 541, 543, 563
McMasters, William H., 499
McMurray, Richard, 352
McNally, Horace (Stephen), 249, 295, 530, 563
McNally, Terrence, 28, 572
McNally, William J., 188, 237, 380
McNamara, Edward, 245, 258, 298, 395, 417, 450
McNamara, Maggie, 316, 443

McNaughton, Glen, 109, 280
McNeil, Claudia, 390, 434, 477, 523, 542, 563
McNutt, Patterson, 97, 255, 371, 377, 473
McOwen, Bernard J., 58
McQueen, Butterfly, 69, 168, 474, 514, 563
McQueen, Steve, 187, 208, 488, 563
McQuillan, Thomas, 429
McRae, Bruce, 38, 100, 186, 275, 283, 331, 532
McRae, Ellen, 150
McVey, Patrick, 71, 84
McWade, Robert, 79, 107, 128, 151, 198, 218, 238, 333, 348
Meacham, Anne, 111, 233, 267, 279, 581
Meade, Julia, 135, 168, 401, 464
Meadows, Audrey, 460, 504
Meadows, Jayne, 172
Meara, Anne, 221, 312, 496
Meara, Evy, 178
Mears, DeAnn, 480
Mears, John Henry, 68, 342, 343, 425
Mears, Stannard, 418
Mearson, Lyon, 357, 367
Medcraft, Russell, 73, 107
Medford, Kay, 56, 134, 202, 212, 216, 234, 285, 391, 508, 542, 543, 563
Medina, Patricia, 76
Medoff, Mark, 517
Meehan, Danny, 496, 543
Meehan, John, 43, 56, 218, 261, 303, 331, 397, 432, 435, 462, 532
Meehan, William E., 51
Meek, Donald, 16, 37, 67, 216, 220, 231, 249, 276, 282, 321, 347, 380, 395, 421, 426, 438, 461, 485, 492, 521, 534, 547
Meeker, George, 40, 102, 450
Meeker, Ralph, 16, 71, 97, 314, 365, 371, 434, 446, 542, 563
Megna, John, 23
Megrue, Roi Cooper, 241, 380, 417, 463, 498, 520
Meighan, Thomas, 33, 130, 182, 291, 388, 418, 537
Meiser, Edith, 81, 108, 134, 226, 396, 404, 448, 528
Meisner, Sanford, 23, 25, 38, 55, 83, 98, 143, 166, 186, 227, 273, 305, 335, 337, 363, 383, 470, 479
Melcher, Martin, 368
Mellish, Fuller, 119
Mellish, Vera Fuller, 275
Meloney, William Brown, 133, 201, 359, 432
Melville, Alan, 122
Melville, Herman, 53
Mencken, H. L., 202, 236
Mendelssohn, Edward, 191
Mendelssohn, Eleonora, 119, 161, 406, 414
Menjou, Adolphe, 26, 35, 41, 88, 140, 153, 168, 186, 231, 310, 321, 365, 376, 402, 441, 442
Menken, Helen, 80, 103, 291, 300, 347, 363, 400, 408, 418, 475, 563
Menzies, Heather, 512
Merande, Doro, 28, 32, 50, 166, 168, 169, 172, 219, 277, 280, 284, 318, 329, 357, 370, 391, 393, 418, 424, 476, 505, 563
Mercer, Beryl, 48, 359, 386, 409, 513
Mercer, Marian, 373
Merchant, Abby, 537
Mercier, Mary, 249
Mercouri, Melina, 159, 563
Meredith, Burgess, 15, 19, 44, 59, 161,

168, 213, 214, 228, 230, 274, 276, 308, 344, 345, 359, 393, 413, 420, 437, 439, 442, 496, 524, 525, 540, 543, 544, 548, 563
Meredith, Lee, 463
Meredith, Leo, 455
Meredith, Lois, 211
Meredyth, Bess, 157, 321, 401
Merivale, Herman, 163
Merivale, Philip, 31, 77, 124, 198, 206, 212, 245, 259, 300, 353, 376, 384, 398, 399, 461, 502, 536, 541, 563
Meriwether, Susan, 161
Merkel, Una, 18, 21, 44, 55, 95, 105, 192, 196, 261, 319, 348, 349, 355, 377, 394, 395, 408, 426, 434, 453, 494, 517, 534, 549, 563, 584
Merlin, Frank, 151, 190, 216, 218, 227, 256, 395, 402, 405, 411, 461, 492, 528, 530, 538
Merman, Ethel, 302, 544, 548, 549, 550, 563
Merrick, David, 65, 75, 92, 134, 165, 190, 228, 302, 309, 317, 353, 358, 373, 417, 454, 462, 512, 522, 530, 584, 585
Merrill, Beth, 22, 37, 92, 212, 260, 262, 266, 272, 518
Merrill, Bob, 18, 29
Merrill, Dina, 127, 306
Merrill, Gary, 35, 60, 374, 414, 443, 471, 524, 541, 563
Merrill, Scott, 418
Merrow, Jane, 273
Messager, Andre, 44
Messel, Oliver, 390
Metaxa, Georges, 493
Methot, Mayo, 19, 23, 201, 272, 343, 435, 450, 485
Metropolitan Players, 484
Meyer, Annie Nathan, 56
Meyer, Joseph, 140, 253, 332
Meyer, Leo B., 23, 492
Meyer, Lester, 76, 226, 332
Meyerowitz, Jan, 324
Miano, Robert, 151
Michael, Gertrude, 85, 160, 404
Michaels, Kay, 221
Michaels, Sidney, 138, 462
Michel, Leon, 439
Michel, Scott, 28, 426
Michel, Trudi, 28
Middlemass, Robert, 69
Middleton, Charles, 244
Middleton, George, 13, 53, 57, 216, 289, 356, 375, 399
Middleton, Jane, 271
Middleton, Ray, 524
Middleton, Robert, 127, 393
Midgley, Robin, 473
Miele, Elizabeth, 49, 201, 217
Mielziner, Jo, 11, 13, 16, 23, 30, 31, 43, 46, 52, 54, 70, 71, 74, 78, 89, 92, 98, 106, 108, 117, 119, 121, 124, 128, 132, 133, 134, 136, 146, 147, 155, 161, 162, 163, 171, 172, 183, 202, 204, 213, 227, 228, 237, 245, 250, 255, 256, 262, 280, 293, 307, 308, 309, 312, 314, 318, 321, 324, 327, 340, 348, 358, 360, 363, 368, 371, 374, 375, 379, 381, 385, 402, 405, 410, 417, 424, 433, 440, 442, 447, 449, 453, 456, 457, 461, 463, 466, 467, 484, 495, 507, 511, 525, 526, 528, 530, 533, 538
Mifune, Toshiro, 254, 390
Milan, Frank, 127, 214, 351
Miles, Carleton, 338

Miles, Henry, 218
Miles, Sarah, 111
Miles, Sylvia, 397
Miles, William, 185, 338
Milestone, Lewis, 168, 345, 388, 479
Milholland, Charles Bruce, 493
Miljan, John, 151, 311, 409
Milland, Ray (Raymond), 38, 40, 103, 375, 428, 430, 563
Millay, Edna St. Vincent, 104
Mille, Cecil B. De, 146, 395, 441, 480, 510
Mille, William C. de, 94, 201, 510, 527
Millen, James Knox, 332
Miller, Albert G., 416
Miller, Alice Duer, 87, 100, 439
Miller, Allen C., 133
Miller, Ann, 402, 420, 421, 441, 529, 534, 547, 563
Miller, Arthur, 16, 21, 22, 108, 109, 111, 124, 256, 295, 381, 503, 505, 572, 579, 583
Miller, Ashley, 416
Miller, Betty, 180, 302
Miller, Colleen, 385
Miller, David, 30, 529
Miller, Dennis, 462
Miller, Fred, 32
Miller, George, 62
Miller, Gilbert, 16, 24, 29, 30, 48, 64, 81, 82, 113, 129, 131, 163, 187, 206, 219, 259, 265, 272, 299, 315, 348, 369, 396, 398-99, 403, 428, 468, 483, 486, 583
Miller, Henry, 69, 87, 100, 114, 151, 152, 153, 194, 198, 314, 315, 317, 389, 396, 416, 539
Miller, Hugh, 116
Miller, Jason, 466, 572, 580, 586
Miller, Joe, 259
Miller, Jonathan, 549
Miller, Lorraine, 204
Miller, Marilyn, 563
Miller, Morris, 371
Miller, Patsy Ruth, 37, 151, 220, 409, 493, 519
Miller, Paula, 75, 337, 514
Miller, Robert, 32
Miller, Sigmund, 301, 352
Miller, Warren, 104
Millhauser, Bertram, 388
Millholin, James, 340
Millott, Tom, 422
Mills Brothers, The, 522
Mills, Grace, 512
Mills, Grant, 350, 548
Mills, Hayley, 37, 319, 376
Mills, John, 563
Mills, Juliet, 37, 563
Milner, Martin, 102, 270, 338
Miltern, John, 533
Milton, Ernest, 117
Milton, Robert, 24, 26, 42, 58, 64, 70, 87, 93, 107, 117, 144, 150, 167, 211, 215, 233, 299, 301, 363, 391, 395, 409, 413, 416, 418, 500, 501, 534, 537
Milward, Jo, 466
Mimieux, Yvette, 487
Mindlin, Michael, 223, 264, 457
Mineo, Sal, 131, 164, 403, 434, 563
Miner, Jan, 506, 528
Miner, Peter, 348
Miner, Worthington, 57, 115, 148, 160, 166, 212, 221, 227, 268, 349, 395, 445, 457, 459, 484, 494, 500, 511, 513, 521
Minnelli, Liza, 226, 563
Minnelli, Vincente, 178, 190, 372, 463
Minoff, Lee, 99

Minor, Philip, 498
Mins, Leonard, 464
Minskoff, Jerome, 273
Minter, Mary Miles, 277
Mintz, Eli, 84, 165, 228, 247, 303
Miramova, Elena, 466, 479, 495
Miranda, Carmen, 176, 329, 392, 545, 563
Miranda, Isa, 478
Misrock, Henry R., 65, 152
Mitchell, Basil, 217
Mitchell, Cameron, 124, 266, 268, 436, 541, 563
Mitchell, David, 98, 235, 443
Mitchell, Dodson, 101, 106, 234, 291, 396, 464, 526
Mitchell, Donald J., 48
Mitchell, Grant, 23, 39, 40, 53, 87, 130, 158, 176, 182, 200, 212, 222, 241, 254, 295, 353, 397, 428, 452, 460, 476, 487, 519, 532, 533
Mitchell, James, 381, 524
Mitchell, Kay, 250
Mitchell, Langdon, 291, 333
Mitchell, Millard, 62, 67, 112, 151, 174, 191, 196, 217, 219, 224, 257, 282, 283, 284, 293, 297, 318, 321, 329, 341, 367, 371, 414, 417, 434, 435, 441, 445, 450, 474, 475, 530, 533, 563
Mitchell, Norma, 37, 73, 107, 187, 378
Mitchell, Rena, 330
Mitchell, Thomas, 52, 57, 95, 97, 108, 113, 124, 162, 164, 173, 184, 218, 255, 274, 337, 342, 357, 396, 434, 444, 475, 493, 498, 525, 543, 563
Mitchell, Yvonne, 509
Mitchum, Robert, 388, 494
Mittelholzer, Edgar, 95
Mixon, Alan, 89, 320, 430
Mizner, Wilson, 125, 198
Moberly, Robert, 373
Modern American Theatre, 69
Modern Play Co., 376
Moeller, Philip, 14, 18, 25, 28, 54, 79, 120, 138, 142, 144, 188, 220, 247, 289, 301, 308, 309, 315, 320, 331, 380, 383, 389, 397, 414, 447, 469, 470, 480, 523
Moffat, Donald, 155, 534
Moffet, Harold, 213, 240
Moffett, Cleveland, 44
Moffett, Sharyn, 513
Moffitt, John C., 155
Mohyeddin, Zia, 199
Moiseiwitsch, Tanya, 302
Molineux, Roland Burnham, 293
Moll, Elick, 415
Molnar, Ferenc, 63, 142, 310, 348
Monica, Corbett, 16
Monks, James, 36, 68, 147, 446, 487
Monks, John, Jr., 68, 394
Monroe, Lucy, 376
Monroe, Marilyn, 16, 71, 94, 151, 174, 197, 418, 503, 522
Montague, John, 62
Montague, Lee, 95
Montalban, Carlos, 303
Montalban, Ricardo, 418, 563
Montand, Yves, 111, 394
Monte-Britton, Barbara, 59
Montel, Michael, 217
Monterey, Carlotta, 201, 321, 356, 429
Montgomery, Douglass, 25, 79, 84, 109, 172, 184, 267, 277, 297, 305, 308, 469, 511, 526, 529, 563
Montgomery, Earl, 453
Montgomery, Elizabeth, 265, 563
Montgomery, George, 88, 286
Montgomery, James, 37, 342, 391
Montgomery, Robert, 21, 31, 52, 54-5, 76, 102, 127, 140, 164, 213, 328, 370, 373, 378, 409, 439, 516, 529, 533, 563, 583
Moody, William Vaughn, 151, 194
Mooney, Martin, 177
Mooney, William, 373
Moore, Carlyle, 445
Moore, Carroll, 292, 416
Moore, Charles, 157
Moore, Charles H., 198, 268
Moore, Charlotte, 217
Moore, Colleen, 272, 432, 452
Moore, Constance, 510
Moore, Dennie, 18, 102, 110, 129, 196, 216, 233, 249, 261, 293, 360, 385, 391, 442, 459, 485, 489, 493
Moore, Dickie, 107, 147, 310
Moore, Douglas, 89, 411
Moore, Dudley, 549
Moore, Edward J., 412, 519
Moore, Erin O'Brien, 449
Moore, Eulabelle, 194, 292
Moore, Florence, 363, 420
Moore, Gar, 117
Moore, Grace, 97, 563
Moore, Laurens, 249
Moore, Lucia, 181
Moore, Mabel, 232
Moore, McElbert, 538
Moore, Melba, 385
Moore, Monica, 109
Moore, Raymond, 48, 260
Moore, Robert, 62, 75, 147, 178, 264
Moore, Terry, 48, 99
Moore, Tom, 335
Moore, Vera, 463
Moore, Victor, 95, 140, 261, 349, 391, 418, 458, 544, 550, 551, 563
Moorehead, Agnes, 44, 178, 249, 280, 337, 376, 483, 529, 543, 563
Moores, Clara, 420
Moorhead, Natalie, 39
Mooser, George, 322, 396
Moran, Lois, 437, 472
Moran, Peggy, 19
Moran, Polly, 20, 442, 526
Moray, Mona, 150
Morcom, James, 330
Morea, Gabor, 443
Morehouse, Ward, 174, 312
Moreno, Rita, 142, 423, 453, 563
Morgan, Agnes, 226, 231, 283, 363
Morgan, Al, 310
Morgan, Claudia, 27, 28, 33, 64, 116, 121, 151, 175, 233, 261, 280, 299, 301, 306, 314, 349, 453, 473, 484, 523, 545
Morgan, Dan, 312
Morgan, Dennis, 29, 186, 224, 259, 310, 354
Morgan, Dickson, 113
Morgan, Frank, 18, 26, 49, 71, 74, 143, 157, 174, 274, 285, 299, 326, 328, 362, 395, 418, 452, 464, 485, 498, 516, 518, 521, 545, 547, 564
Morgan, Gary, 101
Morgan, Harry, 236
Morgan, Helen, 167, 551, 564
Morgan, Henry, 22, 47
Morgan, Joan, 281
Morgan, Juliana, 20, 367
Morgan, Ralph, 97, 115, 150, 160, 169, 233, 271, 316, 319, 330, 349, 401, 434, 447, 459, 460, 473, 489, 497, 564
Morgan, Roger, 463
Morganstern, C. W., 419
Moriarty, Michael, 489, 540, 564, 586
Morison, Patricia, 404, 468, 527, 551,

564
Moritz, Al, 218
Morley, Christopher, 475, 476
Morley, Karen, 130, 166, 274, 277, 285, 381, 513
Morley, Robert, 294, 298, 460, 564
Morley, Ruth, 85, 519
Morley, Victor, 40, 454
Morosco, Oliver, 55, 63, 79, 93, 211, 215, 278, 293, 353, 366, 496, 501
Morrill, Katherine, 131
Morris, Aldyth, 81
Morris, Chester, 15, 44, 57, 58, 105, 109, 148, 149, 154, 167, 196, 218, 310, 319, 337, 420, 517, 532, 564
Morris, David, 319
Morris, E. B., 460
Morris, Edmund, 529
Morris, Gordon, 242
Morris, Grant, 51
Morris, Jeremiah, 421
Morris, John, 239
Morris, Lloyd, 114
Morris, Mary, 108, 109, 110, 126, 134, 143, 212, 222, 319, 337, 402
Morris, McKay, 26, 31, 45, 98, 142, 232, 291, 315, 345, 395, 397, 419, 462, 498
Morris, Nelson, 51
Morris, Wayne, 68, 72, 85, 248, 365, 479, 507, 564
Morris, William, 68, 77, 86, 152, 429, 531
Morrison, Andrienne, 534
Morrison, Anne, 249, 371, 522
Morrison, George, 452
Morrison, Joe, 430
Morrison, Mabel, 440
Morrison, Paul, 54, 71, 79, 85, 151, 281, 301, 323, 426, 493
Morrison, Priestly, 19, 23, 43, 49, 107, 140, 145, 245, 372, 385, 386, 431, 446
Morrison, Mrs. Priestly, 294
Morrow, Doretta, 257
Morrow, Jeff, 54, 129, 322, 547
Morrow, Karen, 194
Morrow, Macklin, 166
Morse, N. Brewster, 201
Morse, Robert, 18, 84, 302, 346, 548, 549, 564
Mortman, Mike, 463
Morton, Brooks, 367
Morton, Harold, 411
Morton, Joe, 390
Morton, Martha, 318
Morton, Michael, 533
Mosby, Walter, 372
Moscowitz, Jennie, 106, 148, 435
Mosel, Tad, 23, 35, 580
Moses, Elsa, 514
Moses, Harry, 344, 347, 510
Moses, John, 258, 381
Mosheim, Grete, 76, 269
Moss, Arnold, 156, 168, 250, 262, 529
Moss, John, 185
Moss, Stewart, 415
Mostel, Barbara, 326
Mostel, Zero, 161, 188, 424, 496, 544, 545, 548, 564, 584
Motley, 30, 47, 98, 115, 134, 214, 218, 219, 232, 237, 278, 280, 283, 291, 308, 309, 394, 398, 413, 480, 535, 536
Mottyleff, Ilya, 143
Mowbray, Alan, 26, 135, 145, 202, 246, 300, 307, 332, 333, 366, 469, 542, 564
Mower, Margaret, 159, 262, 520
Mowery, Irl, 285

Muir, Esther, 140, 326
Muir, Gavin, 49, 328, 466
Muir, Jean, 72, 133, 273, 465
Muir, William, 316
Muldaur, Diana, 415, 504
Mulhall, Jack, 72, 106, 151, 234, 260, 377, 493-94
Mulhare, Edward, 128
Mullally, Don, 103, 262, 282, 392
Mullen, Barbara, 476
Mullen, Margaret, 324, 402, 459
Mulligan, Charles, 335
Mulligan, Richard, 302, 341, 354, 397, 471
Mulligan, Robert, 100, 488
Mumford, Ethel Watts, 423
Munday, Penelope, 95
Mundy, Meg, 128, 150, 223, 283, 464
Muni, Paul, 106, 124, 160, 166, 188, 193, 236, 255, 400, 469, 472, 511, 543, 547, 549, 564, 584
Muni, Mrs. Paul, 166
Munker, Ariane, 89, 204
Munn, Frank, 216
Munn, Margaret Crosby, 365
Munn, Tom, 66
Munsell, Warren, 461
Munshin, Jules, 168, 190, 323, 543
Munson, Ona, 37, 158, 160, 370, 419
Murdock, Ann, 148, 362
Murfin, Jane, 120, 236, 272, 431, 451
Murphy, Donald, 102, 122, 163, 424, 477, 529
Murphy, George, 396, 402, 546, 564
Murphy, Michael, 23
Murphy, Owen, 285
Murphy, Ralph, 56, 71, 176, 213, 419, 456
Murphy, Rosemary, 32, 126, 279, 368, 513, 564
Murray, Charlie, 377
Murray, Don, 15, 71, 208, 219, 403, 428, 488, 541, 564
Murray, Gerald M., 81
Murray, J. Harold, 77, 79
Murray, John, 402
Murray, Ken, 261
Murray, Mae, 213, 452, 545
Murray, Vera, 64
Musante, Tony, 336
Muse, Clarence, 405
Musgrove, Gertrude, 445
Musser, Tharon, 337
Myerberg, Michael, 102, 122, 428, 459, 515
Myers, Barbara, 95
Myers, Carmel, 132
Myers, Henry, 158, 201, 303, 356, 530
Myers, Richard, 76, 112, 122, 166, 179, 182, 191, 228, 238, 298, 316, 323, 325, 373, 385, 394, 435, 476, 527
Myers, William, 188
Myles, Meg, 145

Nabokov, Vladimir, 239
Nadzo, Guido, 24, 113, 262, 426
Nagel, Anne, 220
Nagel, Conrad, 23, 24, 44, 80, 158, 164, 166, 191, 201, 258, 361, 456, 471, 518, 548, 564
Nail, Joanne, 412
Naish, J. Carrol, 57, 221, 225, 247, 386, 421, 495, 505
Naismith, Laurence, 54, 392, 530

Naldi, Nita, 233, 355, 386, 546
Napier, Alan, 201, 484
Napier, John, 147
Narayan, R. K., 199
Narcejac, Thomas, 315
Narizzano, Dino, 339, 384
Nash, A., 421
Nash, Florence, 262, 311, 425, 526
Nash, George, 84, 109, 130, 140, 171, 177, 224, 310, 312, 341, 345, 347, 369, 498, 533
Nash, Johnny, 460
Nash, Mary, 51, 79, 93, 129, 261, 262, 286, 294, 333, 370, 476, 527
Nash, N. Richard, 182, 202, 205, 389, 413, 415, 536
Nash, Ogden, 46
Nasser, Sam, 274
Nassif, Fred, 23
Natanson, Jacques, 228
Nathan, Adele, 451
Nathan, George Jean, 17, 21, 32, 37, 84, 138, 190, 226, 230, 279, 282, 290, 298, 308, 320, 325, 359, 419, 436, 449, 456, 469
Nathan, Paul, 135
Nathan, Vivian, 69, 78, 284, 315, 403, 511
Nathanson, Julius, 262
Natter, Dorothy, 425
Natwick, Mildred, 26, 43, 82, 92, 110, 119, 131, 144, 179, 190, 193, 262, 265, 312, 357, 442, 453, 541, 543, 544, 549, 564
Naughton, James, 278
Nazimova, Alla, 57, 101, 133, 188, 320, 549, 564
Neal, Patricia, 31, 91, 207, 248, 311, 402, 410, 451, 549, 564, 583
Neal, Tom, 119, 439, 526
Neame, Ronald, 382
Nederlander, David, 338
Neergaard, Beatrice de, 133, 277
Negri, Pola, 250, 469
Negro Ensemble Company, 398
Negro Playwrights Company, 52
Negro Theatre Guild, 223
Neill, Terrence, 136
Neilson, Francis, 276
Neilson, James, 203
Nelson, Barry, 75, 144, 147, 271, 300, 316, 354, 391, 508, 524, 542, 564
Nelson, David, 394
Nelson, Gene, 72, 186, 197, 292, 543, 550, 564
Nelson, Haywood, 471
Nelson, Jack T., 394
Nelson, Kenneth, 62, 418, 463, 543, 544, 564
Nelson, Mervyn, 241, 431
Nelson, Ozzie, 232
Nelson, Ralph, 294, 468, 523
Nelson, Ruth, 194, 337, 338, 400, 452, 476, 514, 2325
Nemerov, Howard, 461
Nemiroff, Robert, 268, 379, 390, 423
Nesbitt, Cathleen, 132, 178, 378, 407, 545, 564
Nesor, Al, 474
Nestor, Mitchell, 107, 164
Nethersole, Olga, 409, 531, 564
Nettleton, Lois, 52, 118, 368, 424, 449, 511, 564
Neville, John, 54, 564
Nevin, Hardwick, 535
New Phoenix Repertory Company, 216
New Playwrights Theatre, 238, 282, 375
New Stages, Inc., 69, 262, 453, 480
New Theatre, 334

New York Repertory Company, 64
New York Shakespeare Festival Lincoln Center, 59
New York Shakespeare Festival Public Theater, 256
Newcomb, Mary, 140, 335, 528
Newcombe, Caroline, 405
Newcombe, Jean, 360
Newcombe, Jessamine, 169
Newland, John, 193
Newley, Anthony, 453, 564
Newman, Barry, 302, 330, 335
Newman, Howard, 68
Newman, Paul, 40, 127, 141, 371, 390, 457, 542, 564
Newman, Phyllis, 208, 351, 371, 381, 564
Newman, Robert, 40-41, 345, 347, 409, 489
Newmar, Julie, 299, 351, 564, 584
Newport, Beatrice, 284
Newton, Robert, 266, 488
Newton, Theodore, 12, 25, 53, 121, 251, 263, 294, 404, 457, 523, 525
Ney, Richard, 265
Niblo, Fred, 216, 387
Nicander, Edwin, 155, 188, 324, 346, 423, 514
Nicholas, Denise, 86
Nicholas, M. J., 56, 426, 500
Nicholas, Ron, 454
Nichols, Alberta, 404
Nichols, Anne, 12, 224, 253, 380, 384
Nichols, Barbara, 475, 519
Nichols, Dudley, 99, 300, 320, 447
Nichols, George, 342
Nichols, Mike, 43, 275, 287, 344, 383, 520, 585, 586
Nicholson, Jack, 353
Nicholson, Kenyon, 32, 43, 46, 115, 162, 283, 359, 407, 444, 459, 485
Nicholson, Leta Vance, 58
Nichtern, Claire, 247, 287
Nicol, Alex, 395, 454
Nicolai, George, 409
Nielsen, Leslie, 504
Niesen, Claire, 112
Niesen, Gertrude, 543, 564
Niki, Mariko, 463
Nikolas, Lucile, 53, 477
Nillson, Carlotta, 475
Nimoy, Leonard, 169
Nissen, Timothy, 256
Niven, David, 30, 58, 133, 232, 316, 338, 346, 368, 531, 564
Nixon, Marian, 16, 107, 391, 410
Nizer, Louis, 82
Noah, Robert, 15
Noble, Robert, 339
Noble, Sheldon, 354
Noble, William, 58
Noe, Yvan, 293
Noel, Christopher, 472
Noire, Rosetta Le, 59, 166, 313
Nolan, Doris, 34, 84, 97, 112, 135, 217, 336, 464, 564
Nolan, Kathleen, 282
Nolan, Lloyd, 76, 174, 208, 333, 353, 354, 378, 388, 395, 459, 541, 564
Nolan, Mrs. Lloyd, 459
Noland, Nancy, 102
Nolte, Charles, 54, 132
Noonan, John Ford, 532
Noonan, Tom, 305
Noonan, Tommy, 224
Norcross, Hale, 245, 263
Norcross, Richard, 68
Norden, Christine, 412
Nordenson, Lars, 55
Nordstrom, Clarence, 391

Norman, John G., 45
Norman, Christine, 110, 366, 496, 501
Norris, Edward, 192, 350
Norris, Frank, 372
Norris, Richard, 12
Norris, William, 189, 234
Norris, William J., 510
North, Alex, 124, 237
North, Caroline, 33
North, Clyde, 20, 234, 297, 394
North, Sheree, 420
North, Wilfred, 120
Norton, Cliff, 101
Norton, Dean, 201, 359
Norton, Elliot, 375
Norworth, Jack, 150, 545
Novak, Kim, 47, 308, 371
Novarro, Ramon, 33, 434
Novotna, Jarmila, 421
Noyes, Thomas, 168, 378, 460
Nugent, Eddie, 47, 404, 414, 431, 442, 448
Nugent, Elliott, 21, 33, 52, 63, 73, 74, 137, 197, 254, 292, 323, 337, 341, 373, 377, 401, 418, 483, 507, 522, 527, 547, 550, 564
Nugent, Frank, 314
Nugent, J. C., 53, 63, 73, 74, 136, 184, 254, 292, 314, 318, 337, 373, 377, 428, 431, 466
Nugent, Judy, 367
Nugent, Nancy, 483
Nugent, Ruth, 152, 162, 254, 321
Nuyen, France, 530
Nye, Carrie, 504
Nye, Louis, 281
Nyitray, Emil, 326, 514
Nype, Russell, 68, 179, 275, 350, 508

O. Henry, 18, 399
O'Brian, Hugh, 159, 564
O'Brien, Adale, 83
O'Brien, Edmond, 31, 119, 241, 267, 442, 524, 544, 564
O'Brien, Eugene, 107, 258
O'Brien, George, 240
O'Brien, Joe, 362
O'Brien, Liam, 394
O'Brien, Margaret, 243, 277, 475
O'Brien, Pat, 62, 67, 85, 168, 175, 211, 224, 291, 312, 361, 472, 500, 515, 564
O'Brien, Virginia, 307
O'Brien-Moore, Erin, 214, 305, 396, 485
O'Casey, Mercer, 138
O'Connell, Arthur, 29, 66, 71, 100, 186, 224, 286, 371, 433, 564
O'Connell, Hugh, 42, 162, 174, 309, 350, 388, 405, 409, 455, 513, 525, 538, 548
O'Connor, Carroll, 496, 545
O'Connor, John J., 91
O'Connor, Kevin, 184, 482
O'Connor, Tim, 172
O'Connor, Una, 354, 406, 564
O'Dea, Denis, 385
O'Dea, Sunny, 509
O'Donnell, E. P., 194
O'Donnell, Jack, 409
O'Donnell, Judson, 515
O'Flaherty, Liam, 321, 385
O'Flynn, Damian, 43, 69, 143
O'Hara, Maureen, 515, 564
O'Herlihy, Dan, 241, 385

O'Higgins, Harvey, 33, 137, 291, 349, 376
O'Horgan, Tom, 170, 482, 582
O'Keefe, Dennis, 19, 64, 131, 176, 329, 332, 500
O'Keefe, Michael-Raymond, 256
O'Loughlin, Gerald S., 76, 104, 203, 206. 353, 449, 520, 564
O'Malley, J. Pat, 71
O'Malley, Rex, 40, 128, 288, 297, 302, 306, 329, 339, 392, 564
O'Neal, Frederick, 30, 460, 524, 564
O'Neal, Patrick, 153, 178, 336, 551, 564
O'Neal, Ron, 340, 582
O'Neal, Zelma, 547, 564
O'Neil, Barbara, 82, 106, 133, 164, 319, 378, 413, 464, 498, 522, 564
O'Neil, George, 25
O'Neil, Nance, 162, 223, 252, 260, 348, 386, 564
O'Neil, Peggy, 160
O'Neil, Sally, 63
O'Neill, Carlotta Monterey, 278
O'Neill, Dick, 486
O'Neill, Eugene, 17, 20, 21, 29, 38, 50, 51, 120, 126, 127, 130, 138, 143, 159, 165, 166, 185, 186, 195, 200, 229, 278, 298, 318, 319, 360, 395, 443, 446, 448, 485, 514, 572, 579, 584
O'Neill, Henry, 103, 160, 163, 166, 227, 263, 347, 440, 489, 529
O'Neill, James, 304, 519
O'Neill, Maire, 321, 347
O'Neill, Standish, 316
O'Neill, William J., 285, 469
O'Rear, James, 281
O'Regan, Kathleen, 537
O'Shaughnessy, John, 101, 113, 148
O'Shaughnessy, Patrick, 520
O'Shea, Eddie (Michael), 147
O'Shea, Kevin, 136
O'Shea, Milo, 14, 323
O'Sullivan, Eugene, 517
O'Sullivan, Maureen, 55, 168, 299, 332, 381, 439, 447, 462, 565
O'Toole, Peter, 273
Oakie, Jack, 20, 70, 87, 137, 142, 196, 307, 351, 391, 409
Oakland, Simon, 196, 208, 271
Ober, Philip, 108, 133, 149, 214, 252, 257, 271, 321, 358, 369, 420, 439, 527
Oberon, Merle, 91, 392, 531
Oboler, Arch, 336, 468
Ocasio, Jose, 426
October Productions, 279
Odell, Maude, 482
Odets, Clifford, 38, 53, 94, 102, 107, 161, 186, 222, 243, 305, 309, 335, 337, 338, 363, 400, 406, 469, 508, 572
Odetta, 394
Oenslager, Donald, 26, 37, 60, 77, 82, 115, 122, 127, 132, 150, 153, 154, 158, 159, 162, 166, 181, 186, 191, 214, 219, 224, 226, 244, 247, 262, 267, 270, 277, 282, 289, 291, 294, 299, 312, 327, 330, 345, 352, 374, 378, 381, 395, 400, 402, 406, 407, 414, 419, 430, 431, 434, 437, 438, 439, 441, 459, 461, 464, 480, 487, 503, 529, 532, 534
Oesterman, Philip, Jr., 480
Oesterreicher, Rudolph, 172
Oestreicher, Gerard, 72, 179
Offner, Mortimer, 402
Oland, Warner, 35, 245, 381, 434, 502
Olcott, Chauncey, 141, 359
Oliver, Edna May, 20, 107, 229, 233,

260, 277, 282, 364, 381, 551, 564
Oliver, Gordon, 84
Oliver, Rochelle, 203, 205, 487
Oliver, Roland, 335
Oliver, Shirling, 459
Olivier, Laurence, 278, 340, 381, 404, 436, 486, 531, 533, 543, 544, 564
Olney, Dorothy, 505
Olney, Joseph, 148
Olney, Julian, 505
Olsen, Charles, 81
Olsen, Moroni, 300
Olsen, Ole, 414, 415, 431
Olson, James, 242, 344, 424, 536
Olson, Nancy, 13, 153, 416, 492, 564
Ongley, Byron, 64, 101, 255, 435
Onstott, Kyle, 296
Opatoshu, David, 133, 145, 161, 280, 303, 335, 392, 509, 564
Operti, Le Roi, 26, 303
Oppenheim, David, 263
Oppenheimer, George, 211, 309
Oppenheimer, Jacob, 253
Orbach, Jerry, 330, 412, 425, 426, 544, 565
Orbok, Attila Von, 215
Organic Theater Company, The, 510
Orkow, B. Harrison, 442
Orlandi, Felice, 302
Orme, Michael, 476
Ornitz, Samuel, 175
Orr, Forrest, 76, 281, 295, 303, 334, 370
Orr, Mary, 44, 92, 116, 404, 421, 509
Ortega, Santos, 245
Orzazewski, Kasia, 452
Osborn, Paul, 47, 220, 237, 267, 318, 348, 375, 505, 530, 572
Osborne, Hubert, 421
Osborne, John, 585
Osborne, Kipp, 504
Osborne, Vivienne, 24, 35, 162, 223, 270, 299, 333, 355, 404, 395, 513
Osmun, Leighton, 296
Osterman, Georg, 219
Osterman, Lester, 104, 150, 240, 281, 312, 513
Osterman, Martin, 130
Osterwald, Bibi, 279, 290
Ostrov, Dmitri, 33, 133, 261
Ostrow, Stuart, 412
Ottiano, Rafaella, 129, 193
Otto, Linda, 368
Oursler, Fulton, 23, 47, 409, 437, 508
Oursler, Mrs. Fulton, 508
Ouspenskaya, Maria, 11, 119, 133, 246, 359, 364, 408, 419, 511, 565
Overman, Lynne, 24, 69, 73, 88, 102, 116, 145, 192, 253, 367, 435, 547, 565
Overton, Frank, 116, 491
Owen, Catherine, 519
Owen, Catherine Dale, 78, 205, 319, 321, 348
Owen, Reginald, 44, 89, 328, 370, 371, 372, 426, 431, 504, 518, 565
Owens, Rochelle, 45, 170
Owsley, Monroe, 65, 217, 297, 536

Pacino, Al, 78, 133, 565, 582, 585
Page, Anita, 140, 274
Page, Gale, 24, 86, 162, 270, 479
Page, Geraldine, 195, 203, 232, 237, 279, 309, 361, 389, 447, 453, 457, 487, 541, 542, 545, 565
Page, Mann, 271

Page, Patti, 142
Page, Paul, 437
Paget, Debra, 55
Pagnol, Marcel, 299
Paige, Janis, 354, 393, 509, 544, 565
Paige, Mabel, 188, 192, 281, 358, 494, 514
Paige, Robert, 299
Pakula, Alan, 100
Palance, Jack (Walter), 52, 53, 118, 167, 449, 464, 541, 565
Paley, Paul K., 396
Pallette, Eugene, 88, 292, 383, 402
Palmer, Anthony, 486
Palmer, Betsy, 15, 193, 314
Palmer, Lilli, 13, 47, 327, 374, 476, 565
Palmer, Peter, 174, 545, 549
Palmer, Rose A., 79
Panama, Norman, 257
Panetta, George, 101, 257, 309, 506
Pangborn, Franklin, 137, 175, 231
Pape, Joan, 414
Papp, Joseph, 59, 225, 239, 256, 340, 445, 466, 586
Pappas, Irene, 466
Paramore, Edward E., 397, 416
Parella, Anthony, 205, 517
Parent, Gail, 174
Parfrey, Woodrow, 15
Park, Samuel John, 56
Parker, Austin, 513
Parker, Barnett, 179, 185, 392
Parker, Cecil, 256
Parker, Cecilia, 18, 426
Parker, Dorothy, 96, 117, 125, 152, 179, 211, 221, 246, 259, 360, 431, 434
Parker, Eleanor, 128, 216, 507
Parker, Frank, 224, 543
Parker, Gilbert, 371
Parker, Joan, 60, 70, 271, 277, 278, 521, 565
Parker, Lew, 168
Parker, Suzy, 258
Parker, Willard, 249, 429
Parks, Hildy, 44, 290
Parks, Larry, 106, 282, 565
Parone, Edward, 135
Parrish, Claire, 291
Parrish, Judith, 160, 257, 268
Parrish, Judy, 203
Parsons, Estelle, 27, 134, 227, 234, 292, 391, 417, 546, 565
Parsons, Eugene, 46
Parsons, Kate, 101
Parsons, Milton, 342
Partridge, Bellamy, 244
Parver, Michael, 280
Pascal, Ernest, 26, 226, 299, 366
Pashalinski, Lola, 219
Pasquin, John, 317
Passos, John Dos, 316
Pastene, Robert, 91, 234, 250, 478
Paton, Alan, 484
Patrick, Dennis, 89
Patrick, Gail, 64, 124, 240, 441, 500
Patrick, Jerome, 298, 474, 538
Patrick, John, 112, 147, 188, 207, 210, 277, 283, 370, 446, 463, 572, 579, 583
Patrick, Lee, 11, 37, 40, 56, 102, 109, 168, 190, 240, 252, 257, 258, 337, 383, 410, 421, 441, 499, 506, 545, 565
Patrick, Nigel, 37
Patson, Doris, 178
Patten, Dick Van, 26, 72, 146, 405, 428, 471
Patten, Dorothy, 214
Patten, Joyce Van, 127, 216, 472, 483
Patterson, Cissy, 527

Patterson, Elizabeth, 59, 62, 71, 82, 199, 212, 214, 239, 257, 266, 270, 290, 296, 299, 327, 363, 369, 394, 402, 433, 439, 482, 532, 565
Patterson, James, 104, 585
Patterson, Joseph Medill, 166, 527
Patterson, Lee, 361
Patterson, Neva, 135, 241, 278, 418, 437, 565
Paul, Eugene, 372
Paul, Isaac, 67
Paul, Louis, 112
Paul, Steven, 204
Paulsen, Albert, 354, 363
Pavan, Marisa, 403
Pavey, Marie, 277
Pawley, Edward, 132, 142, 495
Paxinou, Katina, 172, 320, 435, 565
Paxton, Glenn, 381
Payne, Barbara, 125
Payne, Iden, 143, 291
Payne, John, 133, 394
Payne, Virginia, 27
Payne-Jennings, Victor, 203, 435, 469
Payton, Lew, 64, 247, 332, 433
Payton-Wright, Pamela, 141, 247, 320
Peaker, E. J., 302
Pearce, Alice, 122, 194, 308, 565
Peardon, Patricia, 218, 252
Pearl, Barry, 463
Pearl, Jack, 182
Pearlman, Nan, 145
Pearson, Anne, 95
Pearson, Beatrice, 175, 306, 360
Pearson, Bud, 483
Pearson, Burke, 220
Pearson, Malcolm, 11, 216, 228, 276, 359, 413
Pearson, Molly, 410, 537
Peaslee, Richard, 111
Peck, Gregory, 271, 314, 435, 515, 522, 565
Pedi, Tom, 46, 68, 101, 124, 216, 230, 257, 326, 446, 505
Peel, Eileen, 421
Pegler, Westbrook, 82
Pelham, Jimmy, 196, 486
Pelish, Thelma, 202
Pelletier, Gilles, 361
Pelletier, Louis, Jr., 224
Pember, Clifford, 81
Pemberton, Brock, 85, 86, 112, 145, 182, 185, 207, 220, 244, 257, 258, 280, 283, 301, 312, 321, 322, 342, 358, 369, 372, 384, 393, 450, 459, 475, 518
Pemberton, Murdock, 425
Pemberton, Virginia, 81
Pen, John, 465
Pendleton, Austin, 275, 346
Pendleton, Nat, 166, 326, 331, 349, 459
Pendleton, Wyman, 89, 292
Penman, Lea, 28, 50, 84, 101, 222, 239, 271, 372, 431, 497, 514
Penn, Arthur, 23, 87, 234, 280, 311, 326, 487, 494, 584
Penn, Leo, 131, 180, 345
Penn, Leonard, 365
Penner, Joe, 87
Pennington, Ann, 186, 397, 500
Penrose, Gibbs, 154
Peple, Edward, 277, 362, 382
Peppard, George, 144, 182, 374, 565
Percival, Walter, 433
Percyval, T. Q., 454
Percyval, T. Wigney, 172
Peregrine Productions, 46
Perelman, Laura, 21, 334
Perelman, S. J., 21, 45, 334
Perez, Jose, 133, 303
Perez, Lazaro, 133
Perez, Susan, 165
Perkins, Anthony, 127, 205, 279, 302, 442, 443, 456, 461, 462, 532, 546, 550, 565
Perkins, Grace, 508
Perkins, Kenneth, 109, 115
Perkins, Millie, 129
Perkins, Osgood, 46, 85, 92, 144, 164, 168, 190, 280, 282, 301, 349, 377, 408, 438, 456, 458, 474, 483, 486, 512, 521, 525, 529, 547, 565
Perley, A., 349
Perlman, William J., 67
Peron, Eva, 129
Perry, Albert, 331
Perry, Antoinette, 85, 86, 112, 138, 149, 182, 185, 192, 220, 244, 257, 258, 301, 310, 322, 342, 358, 369, 372, 393, 450, 475, 565, 582
Perry, Elaine, 182, 256, 388, 486
Perry, Frederick, 212, 213, 294, 296, 299, 309, 333, 349, 410, 435, 463
Perry, Joan, 57
Perry, Margaret, 15, 16, 85, 197, 283, 321, 343
Perry, Robert, 117, 129, 469, 537
Persoff, Nehemiah, 78, 315, 354, 392, 454
Persson, Gene, 452, 488, 511
Perutz, Leo, 250, 483
Peter, Rene, 331
Peterkin, Julia, 411
Peters, B., 26, 337, 354
Peters, Bernadette, 249, 565
Peters, Leo, 268
Peters, Paul, 444
Peters, Rollo, 16, 75, 358
Petersen, Don, 133, 144
Peterson, Dorothy, 136, 184, 377, 451, 520
Peterson, Lenka, 23, 182, 194, 206, 454, 478, 536
Peterson, Louis, 145, 357, 460, 535
Peterson, Marjorie, 109
Petina, Irra, 547
Petrie, Daniel, 118, 258, 390, 419, 520
Petrova, Olga, 225
Pettet, Joanna, 377, 565
Pettitt, Wilfred H., 338
Pevney, Joseph, 106, 218, 219, 272, 330, 457, 530
Pfeiffer, Jules, 291
Pfoutz, S. F., 76
Phelps, Eleanor, 512
Phelps, Pauline, 192, 420
Philips, Edwin, 158, 276, 412, 432, 515
Philips, Lee, 308
Philips, Mary, 21, 61, 88, 100, 221, 307, 347, 348, 379, 428, 462, 485, 525
Philips, Wendell, 319
Philliber, John, 213, 312, 322, 442, 525
Phillips, Albert, 11
Phillips, Anita, 485
Phillips, David Graham, 151
Phillips, Howard, 263
Phillips, Margaret, 31, 178, 210, 265, 414, 452, 498, 548, 565
Phillips, Mary, 272, 332, 353
Phillips, Murray, 162, 261, 314, 328
Phillips, Peggy, 273
Phillips, Rufus, 261, 397
Phillips, Sidney, 57
Phillips, Wendell K., 11, 30, 509
Phipps, Sallie, 258
Phipps, Thomas W., 166
Phoenix Theatre, Inc., The, 11, 81, 289, 363, 425, 465, 489
Piazza, Ben, 169, 254, 523, 565

Picard, Andre, 255
Pickup, Ronald, 278
Pickens, Jane, 275, 565
Pickford, Jack, 171
Pickford, Mary, 105, 114, 141, 189, 255, 377, 384, 510, 565
Picon, Molly, 99, 163, 168, 318, 565
Pidgeon, Walter, 15, 18, 37, 101, 125, 130, 180, 191, 193, 203, 319, 336, 421, 434, 458, 468, 518, 549, 565
Pierce, Betty, 252
Pierce, Noel, 421
Pierpont, Laura, 431, 494
Pierson, Arthur, 67, 84, 281, 497, 514, 515
Pinchot, Rosamond, 146
Pincus, Irvin, 187, 318
Pincus, Norman, 187, 318
Pinter, Harold, 585
Pinto, Effingham A., 96, 269
Pinza, Ezio, 299, 450, 543, 549, 565
Pious, Minerva, 122, 263
Pirandello, Luigi, 163
Piscator, Erwin, 83, 264, 525
Pitkin, William, 45, 85, 239
Pitoeff, Ludmilla, 221
Pitou, Augustus, 141
Pitt, Addison, 332, 440
Pitts, ZaSu, 33, 44, 108, 125, 137, 270, 274, 307, 347, 351, 368, 390, 405, 408, 440, 473, 565
Plante, Laura La, 33, 84, 304
Platt, George, 272, 401, 475
Platt, Jean (Louise), 357
Platt, Joseph B., 233
Platt, Livingston, 222, 240, 410, 473
Platt, Louise, 30, 160, 233, 402, 439, 487
Platt, Marc, 197
Play Producing Co., 137
Players Company, Inc., 409, 455
Players Theatre, The, 285, 469
Playshop, The, 342
Playwright and Players Company, 265
Playwrights Company, The, 11, 22, 25, 30, 42, 43, 49, 78, 88, 112, 118,, 136 172, 193, 202, 224, 234, 247, 250, 255, 284, 322, 333, 340, 342, 351, 365, 372, 374, 377, 403, 405, 407, 424, 430, 431, 445, 461, 463, 468, 488, 491, 495, 524
Pleasence, Donald, 548, 565
Pleshette, Suzanne, 98, 102, 187, 565
Plohn, Edmund, 461
Plowright, Joan, 565, 584
Plummer, Christopher, 242, 336, 542, 549, 550, 565
Plummer, Inez, 68, 484
Pockriss, Lee, 486
Pohl, Frederick, 66
Pohle, Lawrence, 24
Pointer, Priscilla, 453
Poitier, Sidney, 82, 390, 542, 565
Polakov, Lester, 143, 194, 274, 304, 324, 524
Polan, Lou, 71, 109, 173
Polesie, Herbert, 210
Polk, Oscar, 110, 198, 321, 341, 350, 385, 489, 508
Poll, Martin, 506
Pollak, Joseph, 22
Pollard, Michael J., 100, 145, 281, 319, 357, 542, 543, 565
Pollick, Teno, 443
Pollitt, Josephine, 66
Pollock, Allan, 119, 246, 417, 452
Pollock, Channing, 97, 110, 144, 162, 221, 321, 372, 399, 424, 452, 572
Pollock, Gordon, 56, 237, 479, 508

Pollock, Nancy R., 86, 208, 234, 308, 453
Ponazecki, Joe, 489
Pons, Helene, 217, 224, 378, 478
Poole, Daniel, 230
Poole, Robert, 75
Poole, Roy, 150, 314, 342, 412
Poor, Henry Varnum, 454
Pope, Peggy, 257
Porcasi, Paul, 67, 346
Pordes-Milo, L., 82
Porter, Cole, 95, 108, 294, 414
Porter, Don, 31, 37, 168
Porter, Eleanor, 376
Porter, Eric, 498
Porter, Gene Stratton, 146
Porter, H. T., 409
Porter, Neil, 120
Porter, Rose Albert, 92
Porter, Stephen, 207
Porterfield, Robert, 148, 214, 268, 511
Portman, Eric, 243, 244, 382, 485, 565
Post, Guy Bates, 291, 296, 301, 334, 348
Post, W. H., 332
Post, William, 76, 297
Post, William, Jr., 18, 289, 321, 327, 516
Poston, Richard, 441
Poston, Tom, 72, 136, 187, 193
Potter, H. C., 30, 47, 73, 134, 256, 375, 378, 407, 479, 513
Potter, Paul, 499
Potts, David, 412
Potts, Nancy, 504
Potts, Nell, 141
Povah, Phyllis, 30, 57, 67, 106, 123, 220, 229, 262, 271, 310, 329, 393, 503, 506, 528
Powel, Robert Hare, 132
Powell William, 314
Powell, Addison, 144, 187, 517
Powell, Dawn, 53, 247
Powell, Dick, 57, 76, 184, 186, 220, 224, 361, 391, 456, 458
Powell, Eleanor, 548, 565
Powell, Elmer, 440
Powell, Jane, 72, 421, 565
Powell, William, 167, 195, 197, 220, 246, 261, 270, 396, 436, 565
Power, Tyrone, 14, 48, 57, 298, 314, 542, 565
Power, Tyrone, Sr., 92, 274, 503
Powers, Charles, 65
Powers, Eugene, 90, 145, 232, 246, 269, 393
Powers, James T., 359, 417
Powers, Leona, 17, 53, 136, 145, 187, 316, 322, 326, 350, 371, 392, 395, 468
Powers, Mala, 12
Powers, Marie, 544
Powers, Tom, 64, 67, 144, 158, 160, 184, 221, 222, 232, 271, 282, 288, 385, 397, 447, 462, 519, 520
Powys, Stephen, 525
Prager, Stanley, 47, 99, 134, 402, 428
Pransky, John, 16
Pratt, Stanley, 400
Premice, Josephine, 313
Preminger, Otto, 15, 49, 50, 110, 112, 113, 166, 168, 169, 235, 266, 298, 316, 318, 325, 441, 565
Prentice, Keith, 62
Prentiss, Paula, 187, 264
Pressman, David, 131, 401, 453
Pressman, Lawrence, 332
Preston, James, 81
Preston, Robert, 23, 37, 92, 116, 213, 214, 244, 273, 290, 292, 305, 336, 340, 464, 542, 550, 565

INDEX 641

Prevost, Marie, 106, 260, 285, 388
Price, Alonzo, 323, 469
Price, Dennis, 47, 48, 237
Price, George N., 238
Price, Georgie, 435
Price, Lorin, 316, 330
Price, Paul B., 269
Price, Stanley, 99
Price, Vincent, 44, 56, 113, 142, 147, 261, 266, 435, 538, 546, 550, 565
Prideaux, James, 264
Primrose, Alek, 273, 397
Primus, Barry, 109, 225
Prince, Frank, 280
Prince, Harold, 77, 195, 460
Prince, Robert, 346
Prince, William, 18, 42, 147, 165, 198, 214, 226, 248, 275, 372, 447, 471, 503, 565
Princess Matchabelli, 109
Prine, Andrew, 60, 131, 173, 311
Pringle, Aileen, 110, 397, 432, 452
Pringle, Jessie, 271
Printzlau, Olga, 40
Prinz, Rosemary, 474
Prior, Allan, 441
Proach, Henry, 421
Proctor, Charles, 493
Proctor, Elita, 198
Proctor, Wynn, 410
Producers Theatre, Inc., The, 98, 294, 346, 378, 443
Proser, Monte, 24
Prouty, Jed, 26, 130, 209
Provincetown Players, 109, 130, 202, 232
Prud'homme, Cameron, 29, 126, 136, 389, 415, 476
Prumbs, Lucille S., 159, 160, 227
Pruneau, Phillip, 85, 467, 524
Prussing, Louise, 45, 106, 425
Pryor, Roger, 19, 33, 56, 314, 404, 410, 412, 415, 420, 500
Puck, Eva, 304
Puget, Claude-Andre, 205
Pulitzer, Ralph, 132
Punsley, Bernard, 121
Purcell, Charles, 546
Purcell, Dick, 365
Purcell, Gertrude, 404, 461, 507
Purcell, Irene, 12, 110, 116, 157-58, 196, 258, 367, 547
Purdon, Edmund, 89
Purdum, Ralph, 90, 268
Purdy, James, 292
Pygmalion Productions, 213
Pyzel, Robert, 32

Qualen, John, 106, 154, 168, 173, 449
Quayle, Anthony, 549, 565
Queen, Murray, 221, 406
Questel, Mae, 133, 291
Quigley, Charles, 129, 151, 411, 530
Quigley, Jack, 113
Quigley, Rita, 456
Quillan, Joe, 474
Quilley, Dennis, 278
Quine, Richard, 47, 327, 346, 433, 530
Quinn, Anthony, 57, 173, 176, 237, 334, 378, 449, 462, 471, 565
Quinn, Arthur Hobson, 481
Quinn, Billy, 437, 525
Quintero, Jose, 25, 78, 90, 127, 129, 180, 193, 194, 230, 234, 237, 278, 280, 298, 302, 318, 357, 378, 417,
447, 453, 581, 584, 586
Quintus Productions, 274

Rabb, Ellis, 249, 449, 462, 504, 512, 534
Rabe, David, 59, 445, 572, 586
Raceward, Thomas, 454
Rachel, Annie, 443
Raddock, Charles, 290
Radice, Ronald, 220
Radnitz, Robert, 168, 536
Rado, James, 273
Rae, Charlotte, 45, 59
Raft, George, 41, 67, 92, 104, 165, 546
Ragland, Rags, 549
Ragotzy, Jack, 95, 101, 478, 581
Rahn, Muriel, 324, 372
Raine, Jack, 421
Raine, Norman Reilly, 203
Rainer, Luise, 188, 400, 547, 565
Raines, Ella, 384, 496, 526
Rains, Claude, 25, 118, 162, 184, 188, 245, 295, 336, 358, 382, 410, 470, 529, 541, 542, 565, 583
Raisbeck, Kenneth, 400
Raitt, John, 544, 565
Rall, Tommy, 75, 216, 327
Ralph, Jessie, 89, 188, 211, 215, 381, 383, 399, 405, 421, 452, 506
Ramage, Jack, 256
Rambeau, Edward, 492
Rambeau, Marjorie, 31, 67, 88, 114, 140, 149, 158, 187, 253, 335, 382, 399, 409, 424, 482, 485, 502, 510, 566
Rambova, Natacha, 109, 416
Ramondetta, John, 356
Ramsay, Remak, 421
Ramsey, Logan, 457
Rand, Ayn, 336, 497
Randall, Bob, 426
Randall, Dick, 224, 351
Randall, Tony, 236, 346, 416, 480, 501, 522, 543, 566
Randau, Carl, 506
Randell, Ron, 226, 530
Randolph, Amanda, 292
Randolph, Clemence, 388
Randolph, John, 82, 99, 104, 187, 289, 303, 357, 402, 479, 529
Randolph, Robert, 32, 339, 463
Rankin, Doris, 92, 105, 172, 212, 415, 482
Rankin, Mckee, 252
Ranson, Herbert, 116
Raphael, Frederic, 453
Raphael, John, 369
Raphaelson, Samson, 12-13, 214, 245, 368, 428, 519, 530, 536, 572
Rapp, William Jourdan, 205, 217, 451
Rapper, Irving, 109, 183
Rasch, Albertina, 385
Rascoe, Burton, 243
Rathbone, Basil, 80, 102, 113, 179, 210, 243, 245, 251, 256, 283, 327, 421, 486, 548, 550, 566, 583
Rathbone, Mrs. Basil, 421
Rathbone, Ouida, 421
Ratoff, Gregory, 56, 156, 338, 351, 418, 464, 499, 529, 547, 566
Raucher, Herman, 206
Rawlings, Margaret, 364
Rawlins, Lester, 78, 89, 233, 582
Rawlinson, Herbert, 516

Rawls, Eugenia, 91, 196, 295, 446, 480
Rawson, Ruth, 101, 257
Ray Productions, 222
Ray, 521
Ray, Aldo, 38, 327, 389
Ray, Andrew, 346
Ray, Charles, 526
Ray, James, 22
Raye, Martha, 302, 332, 548, 566
Rayfiel, David, 361
Raymond, Cyril, 468
Raymond, Gene, 49, 65, 108, 249, 282, 297, 380, 392, 417, 419, 421, 431, 460, 509, 521, 537
Raymond, Helen, 444
Rea, Oliver, 304
Readick, Bobby, 21, 175
Readick, Robert, 52
Reading, Bertice, 394
Reagan, Ronald, 41, 62, 68, 72, 85, 117, 207, 220, 224, 248, 292, 459, 507
Reardon, John, 89, 545, 566
Reardon, Marian, 89, 312
Reardon, Nancy, 151
Redfield, Billy (William), 69, 135, 148, 252, 308, 315, 357, 431, 445, 459, 566
Redford, Robert, 43, 87, 195, 214, 275, 454, 549, 566
Redgrave, Lynn, 417, 566
Redgrave, Michael, 237, 320, 463, 476, 566
Redgrave, Vanessa, 382
Redman, Joyce, 30, 111, 566
Reed Producers, Inc., The, 102
Reed, Alan, 219, 284, 372
Reed, Carl, 24, 48, 82, 374, 410, 432, 503
Reed, Daniel, 43, 99, 283, 411
Reed, Florence, 162, 167, 285, 311, 320, 375, 399, 417, 419, 420, 473, 533, 541, 550, 566
Reed, Joseph Verner, 90
Reed, Luther, 122
Reed, Lydia, 323
Reed, Mark, 370, 428, 533
Reed, Philip, 13, 24, 325, 393
Reed, Rex, 444
Reed, Robbie, 92
Reed, Robert, 37
Reeder, Pierre de, 230
Reeves, George, 67, 354, 524
Reeves, Theodore, 46, 513
Reeves-Smith, H., 186, 253, 366
Reeves-Smith, Olive, 371, 525
Regan, Sylvia, 156, 319, 538
Regent Productions, Inc., 480
Rehan, Ada, 458
Reicher, Frank, 24, 162, 381, 410
Reid, Beryl, 585
Reid, Carl Benton, 164, 211, 230, 275, 363, 392-93, 446, 455
Reid, Elliott, 236, 277, 494
Reid, Frances, 214, 442, 523
Reid, Kate, 126, 138, 381, 541
Reilly, Charles Nelson, 136, 185, 302, 541, 566
Reilly, Frank C., 373
Reilly, Hugh, 122, 150, 332
Reilly, Walter, 282
Reiner, Carl, 30, 145, 172, 173, 434, 486, 566
Reiner, Ethel, 78, 302
Reiner, Ethel Linder, 389, 401
Reiner, Rob, 145, 453
Reines, Bernard, 165
Reinhardt, Max, 146, 306, 435
Reinhardt, Ray, 480
Reinheart, Alice, 267

Reizenstein, Elmer L., 349
Relph, George, 179, 533, 544
Remarque, Erich Maria, 168
Remick, Lee, 44, 126, 394, 488, 566
Renavent, George, 31
Rendel, Robert, 445
Rennick, Nancy, 81
Rennie, Hugh, 187, 190, 251, 280, 349, 371, 393, 470, 534
Rennie, James, 11, 19, 41, 49, 64, 79, 92, 106, 109, 132, 166, 180, 194, 258, 289, 297, 312, 317, 324, 421, 436, 439, 489, 536, 547, 548
Rennie, Michael, 48, 266, 300, 402, 542, 566
Repertory Theater of Lincoln Center, The, 16, 71, 453, 532
Resnik, Muriel, 32
Reud, Robert, 344, 390, 495
Revel, Harry, 414
Revelle, Hamilton, 79, 137, 150, 257, 403
Revere, Anne, 25, 91, 112, 134, 166, 194, 249, 303, 336, 347, 394, 435, 487, 521, 542, 566, 584
Revill, Clive, 37, 235, 294, 322, 540, 566
Rewalt, Lothar, 525
Rey, Antonia, 165
Reynolds, Burt, 280, 314, 566
Reynolds, Debbie, 164, 172, 190, 300, 374, 391, 421, 456, 464, 566
Reynolds, James, 119
Reynolds, Joyce, 244, 509
Reynolds, Marjorie, 476, 500
Reynolds, Quentin, 82, 160
Rhau, Lee Von, 62
Rhodes, Erik, 98, 224, 544, 566
Rhodes, Harrison, 174, 211, 321, 405, 523
Rhouma, Gypsy, 518
Rhue, Madlyn, 291
Ribman, Ronald, 206, 250
Ricardel, Molly, 227
Rice, Alice Hegan, 324
Rice, Elmer, 11, 13, 14, 25, 49, 56, 96, 97, 103, 106, 112, 136, 161, 164, 193, 240, 250, 251, 267, 333, 341, 349, 415, 449, 451, 461, 495, 508, 512, 524, 572, 579
Rice, Florence, 252, 384, 420
Rich, David Lowell, 504
Rich, Irene, 108, 331, 417, 432
Richardon, Jack, 532
Richards, Addison, 158
Richards, Ann, 413
Richards, Beah, 24, 196, 311, 385, 460
Richards, Grant, 470
Richards, Jon, 133
Richards, Lex, 122, 172
Richards, Lloyd, 141, 279, 316, 390
Richards, Paul, 143, 208, 234, 351, 506, 548
Richards, Stanley, 299
Richardson, Abby Sage, 381
Richardson, Anna S., 53
Richardson, Claibe, 194
Richardson, Don, 208
Richardson, Howard, 117, 126, 266, 384
Richardson, Jack, 280, 384
Richardson, Lee, 267, 280, 540
Richardson, Ralph, 210, 278, 541, 544, 566
Richardson, Tony, 126, 309, 330, 394
Richardson, Wells, 215
Richen, Neville, 398
Richman, Arthur, 20, 24, 31, 38, 210, 221, 342, 384, 413, 416
Richman, Charles, 28, 49, 54, 61, 211,

234, 237, 247, 283, 425
Richman, Harry, 566
Richman, Mark, 143, 144, 301, 566
Richmond, Charles, 403
Rickles, Don, 145
Rideout, Ransom, 185
Ridges, Stanley, 25, 118, 120, 158, 238, 300, 329, 502, 533
Ridiculous Theater Company, The, 219
Riewerts, J. P., 58
Rifkin, Leo, 470
Rigg, Diana, 566
Riggs, Lynn, 53, 108, 400, 406, 572
Rigsby, Howard, 436
Riley, Edna, 45
Riley, Edward P., 45
Riley, James, 437
Riley, Janet, 464
Riley, Lawrence, 369, 395
Rin Tin Tin, 477
Rinehart, Mary Roberts, 39, 44, 417, 436
Rinehart, Patricia, 199
Ring, Blanche, 121, 196, 223, 239, 289, 546
Ring, Frances, 176
Rinn, Joseph F., 538
Rio, Dolores Del, 55, 135, 147, 515
Ripley, Arthur, 147, 295
Risdon, Elizabeth, 53, 143, 163, 261, 283, 384, 424, 439, 512
Rising, Lawrence, 215
Riskin, A., 56, 261, 420
Riskin, R., 261, 324, 420
Riskin, Robert, 56, 296, 535
Risser, Marguerite, 315
Ritchard, Cyril, 73, 147, 243, 292, 374, 506, 541, 566
Riter, Joseph, 401
Ritman, William, 126, 133, 148, 185, 264, 292, 317, 336, 367, 426, 479, 520
Ritt, Martin, 147, 161, 186, 197, 293, 305, 322, 390, 417, 470, 495, 504, 505, 524, 533, 566
Rittenhouse, Florence, 419
Ritter, Tex, 319, 404
Ritter, Thelma, 29, 154, 216, 234, 259, 421, 501, 544, 566
Ritz Brothers, The, 191, 500
Rivera, Chita, 88, 418, 543, 548, 566
Rivers, Joan, 169
Rivers, Laurence, 198, 290, 306, 307, 349, 385, 393
Rivers, Pamela, 246, 370
Rives, Amelie, 282, 382
Rivkin, Allen, 258
Rizer, Elsie, 51
Roache, Viola, 40, 47, 131, 202, 226, 292, 293, 381, 457, 459
Robards, Jason, Jr., 16, 25, 32, 51, 71, 107, 131, 230, 278, 473-74, 474, 487, 512, 542, 543, 549, 551, 566, 581, 584
Robards, Jason, Sr., 131, 233, 350, 437, 452
Robb, Lotus, 26, 42, 254, 520
Robbins, Barbara, 16, 45, 252, 340
Robbins, Carrie F., 414
Robbins, Jerome, 102, 346, 545
Robbins, R. N., 62, 224
Robbins, Rex, 412
Roberti, Lyda, 475, 566
Roberts, Anthony, 134, 263, 373, 434, 566
Roberts, Ben, 378
Roberts, Beverly, 41, 160, 220, 365, 496
Roberts, Cledge, 428
Roberts, Davis, 489
Roberts, Doris, 264, 414

Roberts, Edward, 164, 261
Roberts, Eric, 511
Roberts, Eve, 351
Roberts, Joan, 197, 546
Roberts, Leona, 19, 20, 122, 441, 496
Roberts, Les, 398
Roberts, Meade, 356
Roberts, Paul, 150
Roberts, Pernell, 95, 284
Roberts, R. A., 244, 273
Roberts, Roy, 67, 238, 254, 380, 493
Roberts, Stephen, 394
Roberts, Theodore, 33, 47, 440
Roberts, Tony, 373, 442
Roberts, Walter Charles, 393
Robertson, Cliff, 49, 265, 355, 371, 454, 526, 542, 566
Robertson, Dale, 154
Robertson, Willard, 56, 128, 168, 229, 266, 312, 388, 402, 412, 440, 472, 487, 510
Robeson, Paul, 20, 21, 55, 143, 544, 566
Robin, Dany, 180
Robin, Leo, 174, 253, 508
Robins, Edward H., 253
Robinson, A. L., 460
Robinson, Bartlett, 31, 123, 271, 306, 375, 380
Robinson, Bertrand, 109, 347, 483, 538
Robinson, Bill, 277, 566
Robinson, Charles, 32, 162, 291, 407, 459
Robinson, Earl, 384, 536
Robinson, Edward G., 14, 22, 24, 42, 117, 118, 121, 140, 157, 158, 160, 211, 216, 255, 277, 308, 331, 334, 369, 375, 388, 390, 404, 429, 469, 495, 498, 566
Robinson, Jay, 73, 172, 566
Robinson, Judith, 116
Robinson, Philip, 536
Robinson, Phyllis, 216
Robinson, Roger, 133
Robinson, Thomas P., 44
Robles, Emmanuel, 315
Robson, Eleanor, 33, 119, 174, 234, 408
Robson, Flora, 21, 30, 114, 531, 566
Robson, Mark, 218
Robson, May, 20, 88, 130, 162, 166, 395, 447, 519, 533
Robson, Stuart, 348
Roc, John, 157
Roche, Emeline, 172, 191
Roche, Gene, 154
Roche, John, 288
Rockmore, Robert, 115, 405, 469
Rocque, Rod La, 269, 424
Rodale, J. I., 145
Rodd, Marcia, 264
Rodgers, Gaby, 213, 313, 498
Rodgers, Richard, 37, 70, 161, 204, 205, 228, 248, 304, 434, 478, 510, 579
Rodriguez, Domingo A., 365
Rodriguez, Percy, 59, 487
Roducers Theatre, 120
Roe, Patricia, 16, 71, 131, 336
Roe, Raymond, 21, 415
Roebling, Paul, 126, 309, 472
Roerick, William, 203, 512
Rogers, Buddy, 12, 57, 191, 290, 566
Rogers, Earl, 167
Rogers, Emmett, 340, 363, 397, 461
Rogers, Ginger, 72, 88, 103, 121, 173, 186, 193, 208, 259, 302, 346, 362, 382, 402, 409, 421, 441, 469, 566
Rogers, Jean, 152
Rogers, Lela, 173
Rogers, Mary, 109
Rogers, Merrill, 211, 474

Rogers, Paul, 566, 585
Rogers, Will, 17, 107, 109, 119, 154, 271, 307, 375, 432, 485, 545, 566
Roker, Roxie, 398
Roland, Gilbert, 129, 135, 270, 479, 528
Roland, Norman, 117
Rolbein, Feodor, 479
Rolf, Frederick, 216
Rolfe, Mary, 147, 277, 414, 509
Rollins, Jack, 134, 373
Romain, Gary, 159
Roman, Lawrence, 361, 498
Roman, Murray, 335
Romberg, Hugo W., 392
Romberg, Sigmund, 386, 401, 405, 523
Rome, Harold, 208, 299, 539
Romero, Cesar, 88, 130, 276, 566
Romero, Ramon, 457
Romson, Adele, 212
Ronkel, Alford Van, 380
Rooftop Productions, 496
Rooney, Mickey, 18, 19, 107, 175, 263, 426
Roos, Joanna, 56, 119, 270, 356, 363, 371, 472, 477, 503, 509, 510
Roos, William, 244, 270
Root, John, 106, 197, 210, 214, 342
Root, Lin S., 353
Root, Lynn, 56, 309, 445
Rork, Ann, 152
Rorke, Hayden, 271, 410
Rosa, Julius La, 257
Rosamund, Archibald, 487
Rosay, Francoise, 243, 351, 566
Rose Marie, 169
Rose, Billy, 94, 107, 156, 196, 232, 271, 395, 509
Rose, David, 524
Rose, Edward E., 18, 79, 119, 244, 367, 382, 396, 480
Rose, George, 429, 566
Rose, Norman, 81, 263
Rose, Philip, 133, 212, 338, 341, 360, 385, 390
Rose, Reginald, 55
Rose, Robin Pearson, 217
Roseleigh, Jack, 51, 365, 527
Rosen, Al, 259, 353
Rosen, Albert, 129, 332
Rosen, Carol, 341
Rosen, Harry, 488
Rosen, Martin, 317
Rosenberg, Edgar, 169
Rosenberg, James N., 509
Rosendahl, Henry, 451
Rosener, George, 230, 353, 420, 437
Rosenfeld, Jerome, 35
Rosenthal, Andrew, 67, 70, 219
Rosenthal, Harry, 252
Rosenthal, Laurence, 294, 390
Rosica, Tom, 184
Rosqui, Tom, 273
Ross, Anthony, 34, 56, 71, 83, 107, 112, 143, 148, 162, 168, 182, 197, 241, 259, 267, 413, 454, 456, 484, 494, 511, 524, 543
Ross, Elizabeth, 435, 446
Ross, Frank, 296
Ross, George, 76, 137, 435
Ross, Herbert, 360, 373, 455
Ross, J. A., 203
Ross, Katharine, 278, 302
Ross, Robert, 20, 33, 92, 132, 154, 237, 256, 349, 375, 406, 469, 538
Ross, Shirley, 196
Ross, Sidney, 283, 536
Ross, Thomas W., 192, 213, 357
Rossen, Carol, 145, 440
Rossen, Robert, 55, 59, 104, 488

Rostand, Maurice, 189
Rosten, Herman, 100
Rosten, Norman, 159, 313
Roth, Ann, 131, 150, 155, 330
Roth, Lillian, 100, 367, 383, 418, 420, 546, 566
Roth, Wolfgang, 122
Rothenberg, David, 164
Rothier, Leon, 47
Rothlein, Arlene, 582
Rothstein, Arnold, 12
Rotsten, Herman, 290
Rotter, Fritz, 269
Rouleau, Raymond, 111, 178
Rounds, David, 92, 264
Roussin, Andre, 338, 361
Rouverol, Aurania, 198, 241, 373, 426
Rowan, Frank, 297
Rowland, Adele, 80, 176, 259, 500
Rowland, Jeffrey, 39
Rowlands, Gena, 308, 566
Rowles, Polly, 36, 48, 165, 187, 309, 430, 479, 528, 529
Roy, Warner Le, 419
Royal, Edwin Milton, 212
Royce, Jessie, 257
Royle, Edwin Milton, 265, 440
Royle, Josephine, 265, 440
Royle, Selena, 26, 113, 120, 187, 191, 265, 301, 329, 349, 363, 516, 532, 537, 566
Royston, Roy, 87, 366
Rozakis, Gregory, 330
Rubber, Violla, 336
Ruben, Jose, 75, 115, 137, 159, 160, 267, 289, 302, 389, 451, 459, 476
Rubin, Daniel N., 128, 320, 335, 396, 529
Rubin, Roy, 486
Rubinstein, Eva, 129
Rubio, Emery, 454
Rublee, J. B., 316
Ruby, Toby, 285
Rudd, Enid, 369
Ruderman, Mikhail, 106
Rudley, Herbert, 11, 31, 142, 146, 224, 435, 512, 530
Rudley, Sarett, 224
Rue, Grace La, 122, 444
Rue, Jack La, 129, 166
Ruggles, Charles, 20, 80, 126, 135, 167, 174, 179, 184, 190, 191, 211, 259, 275, 289, 299, 307, 331, 340, 362, 368, 374, 385, 405, 476, 566, 584
Rule, Janice, 81, 87, 161, 191, 335, 371, 542, 566
Ruman, Sig, 351, 441
Rumann, Siegfried, 19, 87, 154, 193, 201, 272
Runyon, Damon, 429
Rupert, Gene, 157
Rush, Barbara, 99, 346
Ruskin, Coby, 355, 527
Ruskin, Leonard, 104
Russell, Annie, 179, 334, 404
Russell, Evelyn, 373
Russell, Franklin L., 194
Russell, Jane, 174, 566
Russell, Lillian, 521, 546
Russell, Robert, 18
Russell, Rosalind, 36, 37, 47, 102, 108, 164, 168, 291, 320, 327, 328, 340, 346, 371, 473, 499, 504, 528, 566
Russo, James, 26, 246, 384
Russom, Leon, 489
Rutherford, Ann, 381, 517
Rutherford, Margaret, 433, 566

Ruymen, Ann, 178
Ryan, Edmon, 101, 119, 136, 268, 280, 299, 330, 378, 494
Ryan, Elaine, 342
Ryan, Irene, 566
Ryan, Mabel, 201, 339
Ryan, Mary, 165, 222, 277, 349, 393, 424, 445
Ryan, Nancy, 164
Ryan, Robert, 54, 94, 168, 230, 278, 293, 312, 388, 566
Rydell, Mark, 202
Ryder, Alfred, 23, 149, 153, 212, 234, 296, 303, 357, 428, 524, 533, 581
Ryerson, Florence, 182, 206, 446
Ryley, Madeleine, 396
Ryskind, Morrie, 279, 441

Saari, Charles, 116
SABA Company, 523
Sabine, Lillian, 397
Sabinson, Lee, 52, 106, 490
Sablon, Jean, 545
Sackheim, Jerome, 516
Sackler, Howard, 196, 572, 580, 585
Sadler, Dudley, 295, 527
Sadoff, Fred, 78, 465
Safian, L. A., 196
Sagalyn, Robert, 168
Sagan, Leontine, 344
Sagar, Lester W., 32
Saidenberg, Eleanore, 28, 104, 131, 219
Saint, Eva Marie, 208, 256, 273, 308, 490, 567
Saint-Gaudens, Homer, 22, 51, 186
Saint-Subber, Arnold, 43, 82, 116, 135, 178, 194, 264, 280, 281, 318, 327, 344, 383, 440, 442, 465, 513
Sakall, S. Z., 67, 396
Saks, Gene, 24, 37, 43, 75, 145, 173, 224, 264, 341, 344, 383, 421, 422, 465, 474, 567
Sale, Chic, 310, 547
Sales, Soupy, 99
Salisbury, Colgate, 489
Salkow, Sidney, 56, 152, 175, 428
Salmi, Albert, 71, 143, 224, 351, 389, 542, 548, 567
Salt, Jennifer, 155
Salvio, Robert, 38, 54, 336
Sammis, Edward, 119
Samrock, Victor, 90, 224, 267, 309, 477
Sand, Paul, 250, 567, 585
Sanders, Alma, 109
Sanders, Byron, 127
Sanders, George, 256, 399, 422, 496
Sanders, Kevin, 337
Sanderson, Julia, 547
Sands, Diana, 59, 390, 477, 512, 542, 567
Sands, Dorothy, 85, 201, 250, 297, 350, 363, 400, 483
Sanford, Erskine, 25, 320, 330, 397, 470, 502, 507
Sanford, Jane, 184
Sankowich, Lee D., 138, 353
Santis, Joe De, 119, 168, 233, 250, 413
Santley, Joseph, 210, 253, 261, 270
Santoni, Reni, 145
Sardi, Vincent, Jr., 46, 301, 546
Sargent, Alvin, 141
Sargent, Anne, 227
Sargent, Brent, 359
Saroyan, William, 44, 85, 159, 160, 175, 284, 285, 326, 430, 478, 572, 579
Sartre, Jean-Paul, 111
Saul, Oscar, 303
Saunders, Pamela, 204
Sauvajon, Marc-Gilbert, 122
Savage, Courtenay, 134, 280, 469
Savage, Henry W., 98, 106, 107, 148, 299, 420
Savo, Jimmy, 546, 567
Savoir, Alfred, 42, 58
Savory, Gerald, 202, 274
Sawyer, Ivy, 253
Sawyer, Joseph, 83
Sawyer, Tom, 520
Sax, Carol, 393
Saxe, Alfred, 536
Saxon, John, 164, 378
Sayers, Jo Ann, 327
Sayre, Theodore Burt, 141, 296
Scala, Gia, 492
Scanga, Richard, 471
Scanlon, Edward J., 431
Scarborough, George, 35, 209, 286, 317, 434
Scardino, Don, 249, 325
Schaal, Richard, 276
Schachtel, Irving, 113
Schaefer, George, 173, 195, 210, 264, 436, 463, 583
Schaefer, Louis, 264
Schafer, Anthony, 585
Schafer, Natalie, 131, 135, 165, 191, 194, 214, 250, 343, 368, 396, 431, 479, 490
Schaffner, Franklin, 15, 49, 281, 284
Schallert, William, 489
Schapiro, Seth L., 27
Schary, Dore, 66, 128, 214, 282, 291, 352, 434, 454, 484, 539, 572, 584
Schary, Jeb, 434
Schauffler, Elsie, 364
Scheff, Fritzi, 63
Scheider, Roy R., 532
Schell, Maximilian, 238, 567
Schenck, Mary Percy, 84, 428
Schenker, Joel, 80, 82, 153, 236, 279, 398, 416, 472, 503
Schildkraut, Joseph, 19, 44, 49, 94, 122, 129, 157, 230, 261, 298, 483, 496, 544, 548, 567
Schirmer, Gus, 270
Schisgal, Murray, 247, 287, 572
Schlatter, George, 341
Schlesinger, M. S., 277
Schlick, Frederick, 57
Schlossberg, Jerry, 507
Schmidlapp, W. H., 395
Schmidt, Harvey, 389
Schmidt, Douglas, 151, 504
Schnabel, Stefan, 182, 263, 342, 430, 504
Schnebbe-Bacon, Inc., 326
Schnee, Charles, 32
Schnee, Thelma, 333, 384
Schneider, Alan, 22, 42, 126, 133, 179, 183, 227, 238, 254, 279, 292, 312, 317, 394, 428, 445, 479, 511, 520, 581
Schneider, Benno, 71, 446
Schneir, Miriam, 238
Schnitzler, Heinrich, 161
Schochen, Seyril, 316
Schoeffel, John, 252
Schoenberg, Edgar, 328, 367
Schoenfeld, Bernard C., 215, 421
Scholl, Danny, 524
Schomer, A. S., 482
Schoner, Carl, 476
Schooler, Dave, 66

Schorr, William, 310, 397, 445
Schrank, Joseph, 189, 361
Schrapps, Ernest, 84
Schubert, Bernard S., 134
Schulberg, Budd, 131, 461
Schulman, Arnold, 99, 216
Schulman, Joseph, 439
Schulman, Samuel, 497
Schultz, Michael, 133, 582
Schulz-Breiden, Eugene, 433
Schumer, Lee, 144
Schumer, Yvette, 523
Schunzel, Reinhold, 53, 315, 464
Schuyler, M. Van R., 201
Schwab, Laurence, 50, 115, 157, 339, 361, 362, 445
Schwanneke, Ellen, 83
Schwartz, Arthur, 214, 420
Schwartz, Kenneth, 351
Schwartz, Risa, 465
Schwartz, Sid, 434
Schweid, Mark, 67
Scibilia, Anton, 521
Scimonelli, Glenn, 302
Scofield, Paul, 126, 567, 584
Scott, Allan, 190, 233, 251
Scott, Bobby, 443
Scott, Bruce, 273
Scott, Cyril, 34, 217, 281, 349, 365, 382
Scott, George C., 28, 90, 100, 127, 135, 172, 194, 243, 275, 509, 540, 542, 545, 567, 581
Scott, Harold, 179, 268
Scott, Jacqueline, 529
Scott, Lizbeth, 46, 176, 388, 428
Scott, Martha, 97, 126, 131, 165, 241, 292, 343, 357, 393, 432, 522, 567
Scott, Pippa, 89, 312
Scott, Randolph, 369, 421, 437, 452
Scott, Walter, 191
Scott, Zachary, 18, 47, 114, 160, 390, 394, 472, 473, 567
Scourby, Alexander, 118, 128, 486, 509
Scudder, George, 536
Seagram, Wilfrid, 15, 47, 393, 404
Searle, Jackie, 20
Sears, Lucille, 285
Sears, Zelda, 80, 179, 182, 285, 422, 491
Seaton, George, 71, 107, 282, 374
Seawell, Donald, 263, 429
Sebastian, Dorothy, 68
Sebastian, John, 247
Sebree, Charles, 324
Sedgwick, Anne Douglas, 461
Seegar, Sara, 35, 504
Seeley, James, 161
Seff, Manuel, 56, 330, 457
Seff, Richard, 118
Segal, Alex, 24, 102, 249, 353, 519
Segal, Ben, 153
Segal, George, 177, 357, 360, 520, 544, 567
Segal, Mark, 492
Segal, Morton, 351
Segal, Vivienne, 550, 567
Segall, Bernardo, 78, 85
Segall, Harry, 46, 281, 344, 529
Segall, Lee, 508
Segasture, Jack, 126
Seger, Richard, 72
Seidelman, Arthur, 38, 86
Seiden, Stan, 150, 362
Seiff, G. B., 538
Seiler, Conrad, 86
Seitz, George B., 216
Selby, David, 445
Selden, Albert, 198, 214, 273

Seldes, Gilbert, 525
Seldes, Marian, 45, 126, 130, 154, 177, 178, 309, 509, 567, 585
Self, Edwin B., 131, 253
Sellers, Peter, 68, 422
Selser, Maxwell, 149
Selwart, Tonio, 78, 213, 385, 415, 464
Selwyn and Company, 120, 150, 236, 272, 422, 463, 498, 520
Selwyn, Arch, 164, 172, 474
Selwyn, Edgar, 32, 33, 43, 106, 110, 116, 146, 148, 174, 272, 311, 331, 356, 371, 378, 384, 410, 418, 434, 513, 530, 533
Selwyns, The, 86, 364, 431, 513, 514, 526
Selzer, Milton, 69
Selznick, Irene M., 47, 161, 449
Semple, Lorenzo, Jr., 187
Sergel, Christopher, 523
Serlin, Oscar, 46, 67, 151, 270, 316, 450
Seroff, Muni, 419, 465
Serrano, Vincent, 33, 121, 286, 323, 514
Servoss, Mary, 115, 449, 501
Seven Arts, 353, 360, 530
Seyfferitz, Gustav Von, 33, 312, 376
Seymour, Anne, 454
Seymour, Jane, 61, 206, 227, 308, 316, 394, 415, 423, 456, 457, 528
Seymour, John, 271
Seymour, Jonathan, 44
Seymour, Louise, 401
Seymour, William, 154, 234, 253, 454, 487, 516
Shaber, David, 177
Shah, Krishna, 398
Shain, Carl, 291
Shakar, Martin, 337
Shaktman, Ben, 440
Shaler, Anna, 426
Shalleck, Joseph, 190
Shane, Margaret, 321
Shannon, Effie, 43, 71, 90, 128, 222, 233, 293, 296, 307, 318, 356, 364, 365, 376, 466, 498, 524, 532, 537
Shannon, Frank, 29, 492, 518
Shannon, Harry, 324
Shannon, Mark, 164
Shannon, Peggy, 40, 110, 191, 361, 432, 515, 527
Shapiro, C. M., 246
Shapiro, Mel, 221
Shapiro, Stanley, 144
Sharaff, Irene, 19, 26, 262, 315, 430
Sharmat, S. W., 315
Sharon, Fran, 332
Sharpe, Stanley, 102
Shatner, William, 390, 422, 530, 549, 567
Shattuck, Richard, 431
Shaw, Arthur, 485, 488
Shaw, David, 470, 486
Shaw, George Bernard, 163, 279
Shaw, Irwin, 35, 90, 173, 394, 423, 435, 456, 572
Shaw, Oscar, 261, 371, 500
Shaw, Reta, 241, 371
Shaw, Robert, 142, 548, 567
Shawhan, April, 388
Shawn, Dick, 369
Shay, David, 81, 473
Shea, Gloria, 148
Shea, Joseph, 92, 142, 349
Shea, Patrick, 92
Shean, Al, 133, 303, 361, 377
Shearer, Norma, 167, 230, 269, 298, 431, 447, 489, 528
Shecter, Louis, 523

Sheean, Vincent, 238-39
Sheehan, Jack, 261
Sheehan, John, Jr., 342
Sheekman, Arthur, 321
Sheen, Martin, 332, 451, 544, 567
Sheiner, David, 344
Sheldon, Edward, 50, 60, 113, 131, 172,
    213, 246, 286, 334, 369, 401, 408,
    435, 572
Sheldon, Sidney, 19, 400
Shelle, Kirke La, 33, 139, 506
Shelley, Carole, 344
Shelley, Elsa, 81, 166, 370, 503, 526
Shelley, Gladys, 316
Shelley, Joshua, 99, 166, 465
Shelton, Hall, 62, 241, 374
Shelton, James, 324
Shenar, Paul, 480
Shepard, Joan, 163
Shepard, Sam, 258, 582
Sheperd, Ann, 491
Shepherd Productions, 283
Shepherd, Cybill, 453
Shepley, Ruth, 13, 60, 79, 123, 241, 494
Sheppard, John R., Jr., 163, 291
Sher, Ben, 226
Sher, Jack, 368
Sheridan, Ann, 29, 135, 175, 190, 224,
    295, 529
Sheridan, Frank, 147
Sherin, Edwin, 150, 426
Sherman, Arthur, 144
Sherman, Charles, 290
Sherman, George L., 199, 276
Sherman, Henry, 351
Sherman, Hiram, 166, 168, 300, 461,
    484, 487, 517, 567
Sherman, Lowell, 26, 82, 162, 208, 209,
    213, 252, 260, 267, 414, 424, 439,
    442, 527, 528
Sherman, Nathan, 157, 509
Sherman, Vincent, 56, 251, 363
Sherry, John, 12
Sherwin, Louis, 349, 366
Sherwood, Bobby, 209
Sherwood, George, 539
Sherwood, Madeleine, 22, 111, 172, 212,
    239, 457, 478, 567
Sherwood, Robert E., 11, 206, 230, 283,
    369, 386, 395, 398, 405, 414, 430,
    467, 468, 472, 486, 511, 516, 573,
    579
Sherwood, Mrs. Robert E., 500
Shesgreen, A., 253
Shevelove, Burt, 72, 148
Shields, Andre De, 510
Shields, Sydney, 155, 392
Shiffrin, A. B., 28, 56, 227, 283, 493
Shimkus, Joanna, 309
Shipman, Samuel, 24, 46, 87, 109, 140,
    142, 154, 158, 167, 261, 266, 339,
    410, 420, 487, 500, 528
Shirley, Anne, 109, 319, 410
Shirley, Peg, 23
Shockley, Marian, 123
Shoemaker, Ann, 18, 56, 73, 133, 136,
    195, 341, 384, 396, 418, 437, 454,
    493, 509, 517, 527
Shore, Dinah, 332
Shore, Lois, 146
Shore, Viola Brothers, 372
Short, Bobby, 335
Short, Hassard, 26, 140, 158, 182, 340,
    366, 433, 496
Short, Marion, 187, 192, 420
Showalter, Max, 194, 248
Shubert, John, 249, 252
Shubert, Lee, 20, 112, 124, 141, 145,
    158, 163, 209, 211, 252, 299, 300,
    334, 339, 384, 385, 393, 399, 411,
    439, 440, 449, 455, 500, 502, 526, 535
Shubert, Lee and J. J., 35, 93, 104,
    115, 117, 128, 149, 151, 184, 185,
    187, 205, 206, 215, 226, 250, 253,
    262, 275, 281, 287, 291, 296, 309,
    314, 342, 358, 366, 369, 382, 398,
    405, 406, 429, 434, 439, 472, 474,
    477, 517, 523, 536, 537
Shubert, Milton, 83, 459
Shubert, Sam S., 502, 526
Shugrue, J. E., 250, 494
Shulberg, B. P., 461
Shulman, Max, 464
Shumlin, Herman, 51, 52, 64, 73, 85,
    91, 95, 120, 122, 193, 194, 236, 245,
    258, 263, 275, 276, 292, 306, 354,
    413, 437, 458, 483, 506, 511, 513,
    523, 585
Shurtlett, Michael, 76
Shuta, Ethel, 332
Shyre, Paul, 89, 130, 150
Sica, Vittorio de, 153
Sickle, Raymond Van, 49, 276, 353, 453
Sidney, Basil, 246
Sidney, George, 182, 220, 306, 391,
    422, 514, 521, 523
Sidney, Sylvia, 13, 25, 36, 40, 63,
    109, 110, 121, 145, 173, 185, 266,
    289, 296, 307, 310-311, 311, 333,
    413, 440, 449, 480, 487, 504, 542, 567
Siebert, Charles, 98, 178, 445
Siegel, Max, 326, 512
Sienkiewicz, Henry, 387
Sifton, Claire, 309, 338
Sifton, Paul, 48, 309, 338
Signore, Don, 45
Signoret, Simone, 111
Sil-Vara, 79
Silberman, David, 515
Sillings, John, 436
Sillman, Leonard, 152, 282, 324, 469
Sills, Milton, 192, 266, 293, 437
Silone, Ignazio, 55
Silva, Frank de, 386, 425
Silva, Henry, 78, 208
Silva, Howard da, 11, 15, 19, 20, 56,
    70, 83, 102, 122, 186, 194, 195, 197,
    234, 327, 385, 390, 453, 495, 539,
    542, 556
Silver, Joe, 212, 330, 539
Silver, Lee, 141
Silver, Milton, 328
Silvera, Frank, 25, 78, 207, 243, 428,
    567
Silvernail, Clarke, 333, 342, 441, 518
Silvers, Phil, 88, 546, 567
Silverstein, Elliot, 302
Sim, Alistair, 567
Simak, Clifford, 224
Simmons, Bartlett, 282
Simmons, Jean, 23, 142, 214, 532
Simms, Don, 23
Simms, Hilda, 30, 104
Simon, Louis M., 190
Simon, Neil, 43, 99, 169, 178, 185,
    264, 344, 383, 442, 455, 573
Simon, Peter, 255
Simon, Richard, 270
Simon, Robert, 406, 491
Simon, Simone, 418
Simone, Deirdre, 184
Simonov, Konstantin, 406
Simonson, Lee, 14, 25, 120, 138, 142,
    144, 166, 188, 230, 247, 298, 301,
    380, 389, 393, 397, 449, 470, 523
Simpson, Ivan, 65, 172, 292
Simpson, Kenneth, 23
Sinatra, Frank, 99, 216, 370, 402, 464

Sinclair, Arthur, 153, 321, 347
Sinclair, Betty, 235
Sinclair, Hugh, 211, 356, 392, 416, 434
Sinclair, Robert, 133, 250, 270, 365, 370, 379, 381, 435, 527, 530
Sinclair, Robert B., 115, 327, 332, 410, 528
Sinclair, Upton, 425
Sinden, Donald, 392
Singer, Campbell, 76
Singer, Louis J., 183, 454
Singer, Mort, Jr., 45
Singer, Raymond, 79
Singleton, Penny, 459
Sircom, Arthur, 21, 44, 83, 119, 182, 228, 305, 323, 344, 367, 383, 390, 401, 415, 464, 476, 491, 515, 523, 537
Sirovich, William Irving, 411
Sitgreaves, Beverly, 440
Skala, Lilia, 269, 526, 538, 567
Skelly, Hal, 69, 70, 100, 177, 386, 423, 547
Skelton, Red, 208, 307, 423, 517
Skinner, Cornelia Otis, 57, 233, 374, 413, 492, 518, 522, 543, 567
Skinner, Otis, 257, 417, 537, 567
Skinner, Richard, 152, 227, 424, 529
Skipworth, Alison, 20, 73, 143, 159, 172, 196, 220, 252, 272, 280, 282, 291, 299, 333, 359, 382, 404, 435, 471, 472, 485, 547, 567
Skirball, Jack, 243
Sklar, George, 266, 307, 365, 444
Skulnik, Menasha, 161, 165, 497, 539, 567
Slade, Susan, 330, 391
Slaiman, Marjorie, 236
Slater, Barton, 67
Slatery, Richard X., 104
Sleeper, Martha, 92, 108, 130, 134, 189, 227, 262, 405, 406, 410, 444, 490
Slevin, James, 224
Slezak, Walter, 172, 274, 299, 327, 372, 488, 549, 567
Sloan, Edward Van, 124, 136, 394, 500
Sloane, Everett, 23, 47, 53, 55, 56, 62, 115, 223, 330, 402, 567
Sloane, Robert, 224
Sloane, Sydney, 473
Small, Jack, 24, 70
Small, Victor, 23
Smart, Jack, 416
Smight, Jack, 165
Smiley, Brenda, 412
Smith and Dale, 428
Smith, Albert, 124
Smith, Alexis, 29, 92, 135, 164, 495, 528, 543, 567
Smith, Art, 23, 29, 38, 83, 186, 209, 222, 326, 333, 335, 337, 338, 400, 452, 476, 485, 514
Smith, Beaumont, 348
Smith, Ben, 28, 115, 120, 217, 389
Smith, C. Aubrey, 33, 40, 375, 438, 511, 567
Smith, Charles H., 500
Smith, Conrad S., 488
Smith, Esther, 446
Smith, Ethel, 413
Smith, G. Albert, 87
Smith, Gladys, 141
Smith, H. Reeves, 496
Smith, Hardy, 390
Smith, Harry James, 277, 460
Smith, Helen Zenna, 444
Smith, Howard, 30, 123, 124, 171, 270, 290, 296, 309, 322, 340, 372, 393, 442
Smith, Howard K., 49

Smith, Jess, 42, 513
Smith, Joe, 306, 420, 428, 521
Smith, Kate, 522, 567
Smith, Kent, 37, 70, 92, 133, 137, 224, 239, 305, 347, 415, 442, 446, 507, 524, 526
Smith, Lillian, 446
Smith, Lois, 141, 183, 356, 536
Smith, Loring, 30, 44, 182, 203, 248, 250, 270, 301, 360, 433
Smith, Louis, 526
Smith, Maggie, 382, 545, 567
Smith, Mildred Joanne, 165, 279, 305, 417
Smith, Milton, 156, 231
Smith, Muriel, 357
Smith, Oliver, 20, 37, 43, 45, 88, 90, 95, 100, 119, 138, 146, 149, 190, 234, 236, 264, 280, 287, 300, 303, 330, 336, 344, 368, 377, 429, 477, 498, 504, 513, 522, 523
Smith, Patricia, 224, 302, 375
Smith, Philip J., 336
Smith, Queenie, 147
Smith, Robert, 36
Smith, Robert Paul, 464
Smith, Robinson, 145, 364
Smith, Roger, 37
Smith, Sammy, 471
Smith, Sarah B., 372
Smith, Stanley, 56, 362
Smith, Thorne, 231, 503
Smith, Winchell, 19, 60, 64, 89, 122, 159, 165, 217, 271, 335, 345, 375, 418, 465, 475, 492, 494, 505, 511, 525, 573
Smithers, William, 143, 440, 520, 581
Smithson, Frank, 218
Smollett, Tobias, 101
Smyth, A., 349
Sneider, Vern, 463
Snow, Davis, 278
Snyder, Arlen Dean, 66, 79
Snyder, Drew, 445
Snyder, William, 120, 177
Sobell, Jack, 471
Sobol, Eddie, 439
Sobol, Louis, 213
Soboloff, Arnold, 45, 363
Sokal, Dennis, 184
Sokol, Marilyn, 195
Sokoler, Bob, 254
Sokoloff, Vladimir, 162
Solin, Harvey, 336
Solms, Kenny, 174
Solomon, Louis, 431
Solt, Andrew, 247
Sommer, Edith, 402
Sommer, Elke, 422
Sommer, Josef, 89, 169, 489
Somner, Pearl, 496
Somnes, George, 69, 197, 260, 263, 365, 394, 453
Sondergaard, Gale, 20, 25, 84, 96, 112, 133, 239, 255, 332, 418, 447, 567
Sondergaard, Hester, 326
Sondheim, Stephen, 182, 239
Sonino, Max, 339
Sordi, Alberto, 153
Sorel, Felicia, 148, 372
Sorel, Guy, 177, 365, 525
Sorel, Jean, 505
Sorel, Louise, 280
Sorel, Sonia, 279, 403
Sorin, Louis, 98, 182, 254, 281, 334, 411
Sorvino, Paul, 302, 466, 544
Sothern, Ann, 49, 137, 151, 364, 384, 392, 500, 567

Sothern, E. H., 13, 547
Sothern, Georgia, 329
Sovey, Raymond, 23, 34, 114, 155, 178,
    196, 210, 306, 359, 360, 369, 393,
    420, 469, 486, 487
Spad Producing Co., Inc, 103
Spark, Muriel, 382
Sparks, Ned, 19, 20, 57, 87, 151, 186,
    311, 342, 422
Sparks, Robert, 315, 332
Spaull, Guy, 54
Spears, Patti, 448
Specter, Edward, 32, 416
Spector, Joel, 292
Spelvin, George, Jr., 438
Spence, Ralph, 191
Spence, Wall, 222
Spencer, R. E., 262
Spencer, T. J., 249
Spengler, Thomas, 168
Spewack, Bella, 62, 95, 156, 187, 327,
    377, 439, 509, 527, 573
Spewack, Samuel, 62, 95, 156, 187, 312,
    327, 351, 377, 439, 494, 498, 509,
    527, 573
Speyer, Wilhelm, 207
Spielberg, David, 471, 489
Spigelgass, Leonard, 122, 291
Spiller, Leslie J., 26, 218, 337, 354
Spina, Anthony, 165
Spinetti, Victor, 344
Spong, Hilda, 296
Spottswood, James, 97
Springer, John, 520
Squire, Jack, 285
Squire, Katherine, 190
Squires, Irving, 172
St. Clair, Lydia, 477-78, 490
St. Clair, Mal, 174
St. Denis, Ruth, 137, 271
St. Edmund, Bury, 510
St. Jacques, Raymond, 104, 335
St. John, Adela Rogers, 167
St. John, Howard, 112, 154, 191, 214,
    243, 244, 254, 265, 494, 498
St. John, Jill, 99, 217, 394
St. John, Marco, 28, 165, 513
St. John, Theodore, 132, 215
St. Joseph, Ellis, 364
St. Leon, Ida, 501
St. Polis, John, 304
Stabile, Bill, 517
Stadlen, Lewis J., 455, 567
Stafford, Hanley, 134
Stagers, The, 296
Stahl, John, 364
Stahl, Rose, 92, 290
Stahl, William, 56
Stallings, Laurence, 21, 69, 153, 158,
    449, 515, 518, 573
Stambler, Bernard, 111
Stamp, Terence, 54, 567
Stander, Lionel, 64, 68, 137, 214, 221,
    298, 310, 361, 425, 453, 475, 488,
    514, 530, 567
Standing, Guy, 35, 124, 132, 245, 341,
    526
Stang, Arnold, 21, 168
Stange, Hugh, 16, 151, 209, 319, 503
Stange, Hugh Stanislaus, 162, 387, 418,
    479
Stanhope, Frederick, 47, 94, 103, 246,
    361, 376, 383, 420, 433, 445, 530
Stanley, Florence, 383, 414
Stanley, Kim, 71, 87, 88, 95, 153, 330,
    371, 485, 488, 542, 545, 567
Stanley, Martha, 338, 384
Stanley, Pat, 58, 454
Stanwyck, Barbara, 56, 69, 70, 94, 186,
    260, 297, 337, 341, 495, 547, 567
Stapleton, Jean, 25, 234, 543, 550, 567
Stapleton, John, 506
Stapleton, Maureen, 98, 107, 128, 143,
    178, 183, 312, 341, 355, 356, 403,
    414, 487, 505, 541, 542, 567, 583,
    585
Starbuck, Betty, 521
Starcke, Walter, 226, 241
Starett, Charles, 404
Stark, Leslie, 149
Starkey, Walter, 306, 473
Starkie, Ben, 143, 472
Starling, Lynn, 50, 157, 233, 304, 426,
    513
Starr, Ben, 152
Starr, Frances, 82, 95, 140, 160, 187,
    191, 232, 259, 278, 298, 317, 351,
    403, 421, 477, 536, 541, 547, 567
Starr, Sally, 67
Starrett, Charles, 49
Stavis, Barrie, 262, 295, 453
Stebbins, Rowland, 160, 198, 281, 365,
    370, 385, 393
Steckler, R., 266
Steckler, S., 266
Steele, Bernard, 15
Steele, Bob, 345
Steele, Richard, 538
Steele, Tommy, 203, 567
Steele, Vernon, 233, 258
Steele, Wilbur Daniel, 223, 378
Steell, Susan, 289
Steffens, Lincoln, 60
Stehli, Edgar, 34, 55, 58, 63, 69, 87,
    109, 119, 149, 166, 197, 205, 258,
    309, 364, 443, 529
Steiger, Rod, 53, 197, 314, 335, 390,
    567
Stein, Ben, 49, 56, 240
Stein, Joseph, 18, 145, 323, 512
Stein, Sol, 419
Steinbeck, John, 70, 316, 344, 449, 485
Steinberg, David, 82, 276, 543, 567
Steinbrenner, George, 338
Steiner, Max, 414
Steiner, Robert, 145
Stenborg, Helen, 220, 489
Stephani, Frederick, 212
Stephens, William, 495
Stephens, Harvey, 11, 29, 49, 131, 356,
    360, 364, 483, 505, 521
Stephens, Martin, 237
Stephens, Robert, 382
Stephenson, Henry, 29, 110, 115, 116,
    162, 236, 238, 258, 261, 307, 420,
    431, 498, 547
Stephenson, James, 85, 224, 347, 350
Sterling Productions, 243
Sterling, Ford, 20, 151
Sterling, Jan, 138, 168, 249, 350, 368,
    405, 430, 472, 473, 494, 567
Sterling, Philip, 453
Sterling, Richard, 19, 106, 149, 434
Sterling, Robert, 124, 192, 400, 567
Stern, Alfred, 130
Stern, Nancy, 140, 342
Stern, Philip Van Doren, 295
Sternberg, Josef von, 25, 419
Sterne, Morgan, 415
Sterne, Stephen, 219
Sternhagen, Frances, 81, 194, 506, 586
Sterni, Giuseppe, 374, 469
Sterns, Roger, 164
Steuer, Arthur, 465
Stevens Productions, 129, 377, 390
Stevens, Ashton, 408
Stevens, Connie, 332, 442
Stevens, Craig, 135, 225, 240, 567

Stevens, Emily, 60, 163, 172, 267, 311, 333, 482, 496
Stevens, George, 25, 129, 228, 354
Stevens, Inger, 124, 400, 567
Stevens, Jeremy, 151, 463
Stevens, Jerry, 87
Stevens, Julie, 384, 431, 531
Stevens, K. T., 262, 266, 338, 532
Stevens, Leslie, 69, 87, 284, 299
Stevens, Mark, 309, 567
Stevens, Morton L., 230
Stevens, Nat, 268
Stevens, Onslow, 70, 95, 115, 140, 308, 351, 366, 411, 441
Stevens, Paul, 15, 172
Stevens, Roger, 159, 236, 394
Stevens, Roger L., 45, 51, 57, 71, 76, 82, 85, 90, 95, 147, 153, 157,, 159, 236, 252, 263, 300, 308, 309, 346, 394, 421, 424, 443, 477, 498, 505, 584
Stevens, Warren, 128, 431, 454
Stevenson, Burton, 234
Stevenson, Charles A., 14
Stevenson, Janet, 106
Stevenson, Margot, 534
Stevenson, Philip, 106
Stevenson, Richard, 97, 98, 518
Stevenson, Robert Louis, 488
Stewart, Charles, 283
Stewart, David J., 16, 43, 78, 232, 403, 508
Stewart, Donald Ogden, 137, 217, 223, 270, 281, 370, 391, 392
Stewart, Fred, 111, 148, 161, 171, 181, 263, 290, 335, 400, 511
Stewart, Grant, 34, 84
Stewart, James, 21, 47, 82, 132, 190, 207, 250, 340, 361, 370, 418, 460, 533, 534, 567
Stewart, Johnny, 48, 194, 205
Stewart, Marianne, 456, 457, 535
Stewart, Michael, 302, 473
Stewart, Murray, 535
Stewart, Paul, 330, 425, 493, 495, 523
Stewart, Paula, 475
Stewart, Ray, 273
Stewart, Rosalie, 47, 108, 114, 143, 304, 380, 422, 485
Stewart, Sophie, 537
Stewart, Thomas A., 217
Stickney, Dorothy, 31, 88, 107, 168, 218, 227, 256, 270, 348, 370, 394, 397, 430, 440, 480, 549, 567
Stiefel, Milton, 219, 499
Stiller, Jerry, 81
Stillman, Henry, 138, 341, 355, 430, 455
Stine, Gayle, 87, 284
Stix, John, 460, 484, 526
Stockwell, Dean, 102, 237, 278, 568
Stockwell, Guy, 88, 237, 284, 568
Stockwell, Harry, 546
Stoddard, Haila, 121, 133, 168, 182, 227, 316, 352, 414, 457, 528
Stoddard, Lorimer, 234
Stoker, Bram, 136
Stokowski, Leopold, 269
Stokowski, Sonya, 136, 269
Stollery, David John, 349
Stone, Carol, 117, 127, 245, 261, 288, 469, 542
Stone, Ezra, 35, 68, 219, 244, 303, 344, 414, 480, 508, 514, 543, 568
Stone, Fred, 221, 245, 271, 310, 487, 534, 568
Stone, George E., 160
Stone, Harold, 12, 106, 218, 355, 397, 402
Stone, Harold J., 47, 319, 530

Stone, Lewis, 55, 63, 193, 238, 285, 311, 401, 409, 426, 434, 442, 450, 471, 475, 488, 489, 519, 533, 534, 568
Stone, Milburn, 34, 245, 310, 568
Stone, Peter, 136, 161, 168
Stone, Sid, 150
Stone, W. Clement, 348, 397
Stoppard, Tom, 585
Storch, Arthur, 48, 143, 144, 165, 182, 232, 279-280, 335, 360
Storch, Larry, 519
Stork, Clifford, 253
Storm, A., 134
Storm, Howard, 169
Storm, Joan, 62
Stothart, Herbert, 199, 375
Stowe, Harriet Beecher, 458
Stradner, Rose, 57
Straight, Beatrice, 111, 140, 147, 193, 237, 263, 425, 568, 583
Strange, John Stephen, 448
Strange, Michael, 93
Strange, Robert, 61, 158, 188, 191, 210, 233, 297, 417, 475, 537
Strasberg, Lee, 23, 32, 53, 83, 94, 97, 115, 156, 166, 175, 186, 197, 222, 297, 305, 337, 338, 383, 402, 436, 452, 453, 503, 541, 568
Strasberg, Susan, 129, 371, 548, 568
Strasser, Robin, 107
Stratton Productions, 68
Stratton, Chester, 393, 411, 421
Straus, Barnard, 135, 164, 167, 337, 464
Straus, Sylvie, 238
Strauss, Robert, 83, 84, 128, 167, 441, 493
Strawn, Arthur, 428
Stream, Eloise, 67, 72, 363
Street, Julian, 107
Street, William, 301
Streger, Paul, 246, 363, 459
Streisand, Barbra, 302, 306, 360, 543, 568
Stribling, T. S., 402
Strickland, Gail, 443
Stricklyn, Ray, 95, 394
Stritch, Elaine, 71, 153, 278, 424, 430, 542, 544, 568
Stroheim, Erich von, 34, 474
Strombert, Hunt, Jr., 168
Strong, Austin, 189, 373, 418, 475, 487
Strong, Michael, 16, 71, 128, 143, 305
Stroock, Bianca, 154
Strouse, Charles, 186, 426
Strouse, Irving, 158, 295
Strozzi, Kay, 24, 110, 210, 237, 297
Strudwick, Shepperd, 44, 61, 92, 126, 144, 247, 259, 261, 268, 335, 354, 392, 477, 568
Struthers, James, 142
Stuart, Gloria, 410
Stuart, Jonathan, 75
Stuart, Maxine, 35
Stuart, Norman, 439
Stuart, Patricia, 111
Stucky, William, 486
Sturges, Elizabeth, 517
Sturges, Preston, 89, 199, 220, 299, 392, 450, 573
Sturm, Justin, 124, 227, 351, 352
Styne, Jule, 174, 233, 312, 403, 508, 522
Sudermann, Hermann, 435
Sues, Alan, 463
Sues, Leonard, 249, 435
Suesse, Dana, 187, 241, 418
Sullavan, Margaret, 41, 92, 205, 231, 244, 314, 384, 407, 441, 442, 507,

550, 568
Sullivan, Barry, 23, 176, 194, 228, 249, 321, 397, 484, 568
Sullivan, Brad, 430
Sullivan, Charles, 162
Sullivan, Elliott, 102
Sullivan, Francis L., 117, 247, 568, 583
Sullivan, Jean, 369
Sullivan, Jo, 345, 469
Sullivan, Joseph, 410
Sullivan, Maxine, 220
Sullivan, Sheila, 373
Sully, Ruby, 219
Summerville, Slim, 154, 209, 347, 408
Sundberg, Clinton, 50, 129, 228, 293, 308, 405
Sunderland, Nan, 39, 133, 140, 142, 261, 400
Sundgaard, Arnold, 148, 158, 344
Sundsten, Lani, 59
Sundstrom, Florence, 280
Sundstrom, Frank, 35, 214
Sunshine, Marion, 37, 79
Susann, Jacqueline, 283, 326, 475
Susskind, David, 202, 390, 504
Sutherland, Donald, 276
Sutherland, E. G., 399
Sutherland, Evelyn Greenleaf, 44
Sutton, Dolores, 172, 288
Sutton, Frank, 28
Swados, Elizabeth, 582
Swan, Mark, 224, 363
Swann, Francis, 358
Swanson, Gloria, 72, 191, 338, 389, 493, 550, 568
Swarthout, Gladys, 403
Sweeney, Joseph, 16, 32, 61, 111, 120, 154, 216, 233, 249, 259, 268, 306, 312, 316, 391, 429, 446, 484, 513
Sweet, Blanche, 33, 335, 468, 473, 540
Sweet, Dolph, 15, 54, 86, 367, 423
Swenson, Inga, 15, 311, 389, 545, 568
Swenson, Karl, 214, 295
Swenson, Swen, 496, 545, 568
Swerling, Jo, 255, 353
Swete, E. Lyall, 94
Swetland, William, 60
Swift, Madeleine, 59
Swinnerton, Frank, 341
Swope, Herbert, Jr., 150, 167, 443
Sydney, Basil, 90, 110, 117, 246, 409
Sydow, Jack, 111, 485
Sylva, B. G. De, 167
Sylvester, William, 313
Symington, Donald, 179
Symon, Burk, 341, 393, 510
Symonds, Robert, 111
Syms, Sylvia, 78, 129, 530
Syrjala, S., 91, 445
Szabo, Sandor, 346
Szarabajka, Keith, 510
Szczepkowska, Marja M., 133

Tabbert, William, 299
Taber, Richard, 397
Tabori, George, 68, 143, 161
Tabori, Mrs. George, 68
Tabori, Kristoffer, 111, 367
Tait, 278
Talbot, Hayden, 240
Talbot, Lyle, 209, 361, 369, 416
Talbot, Nita, 156, 332, 497, 538
Taliaferro, Edith, 80, 181, 218, 319, 391, 537
Taliaferro, Mabel, 175, 324, 375, 439, 504, 537
Tallmer, Jerry, 398
Talmadge, Constance, 137
Talmadge, Norma, 135, 137, 255, 431, 479
Talman, Bill, 537
Talman, William, 50, 388, 438
Tamara, 95, 469, 476, 543
Tamber, Selma, 368, 506
Tamblyn, Russ, 421
Tamiris, Helen, 186
Tamiroff, Akim, 390, 485, 568
Tandy, Jessica, 22, 30, 78, 126, 179, 214, 218, 288, 293, 448, 550, 568, 583
Tannen, Julius, 380
Tanner, Gordon, 529
Tanner, W. P., 367, 405
Taradash, Daniel, 467
Tarbell, Ida, 60
Tarkington, Booth, 44, 77, 94, 98, 107, 224, 239, 290, 293, 312, 367, 374, 375, 403, 418, 492, 531, 537
Tarloff, Frank, 212, 470
Tashlin, Frank, 522
Tashman, Lilyan, 43, 83, 108, 167, 186, 473, 479, 489, 500
Tattersall, Viva, 397
Taurog, Norman, 189, 506
Tavaris, Eric, 273
Tavel, Ronald, 192, 582
Taylor, Clarence, 57, 68
Taylor, Deems, 14, 46, 82, 369, 545
Taylor, Mrs. Deems, 324
Taylor, Don, 167, 441, 524
Taylor, Douglas, 452
Taylor, Dwight, 517
Taylor, Elizabeth (film actress), 25, 167, 243, 270, 277, 309, 337, 354, 396, 520
Taylor, Elizabeth (stage actress), 384, 529
Taylor, Estelle, 51, 449
Taylor, Holland, 98
Taylor, Kent, 119, 124, 134, 203, 240
Taylor, Laurette, 18, 55, 170, 182, 183, 203, 206, 225, 233, 330, 353, 358, 359, 366, 458, 543, 550, 568
Taylor, Leila, 507
Taylor, Mabel, 359
Taylor, Matt, 445
Taylor, Merlin, 203
Taylor, Noel, 100, 194, 234, 259, 264, 297, 302, 336, 463
Taylor, Rebecca, 443
Taylor, Renee, 16, 130, 264
Taylor, Richard, 240
Taylor, Robert, 101, 307, 387, 511, 516
Taylor, Rod, 454
Taylor, Rosemary, 88
Taylor, Ruth, 174
Taylor, Sam, 445
Taylor, Samuel, 37, 45, 159, 205, 338, 374, 407, 504, 573
Taylor, Valerie, 179, 369, 393
Teal, Ben, 458
Tearle, Conway, 77, 130, 142, 186, 333, 491, 550
Tearle, Godfrey, 81, 82, 568
Teasdale, Verree, 73-4, 133, 158, 197, 231, 299, 301, 310, 333, 347, 380, 404, 432, 537
Tedrow, Irene, 357
Teer, Barbara Ann, 517
Teichmann, Howard, 181, 252, 312, 390, 433
Telfer, Ronald, 346
Tell, Alma, 151, 240, 291, 439
Tell, Olive, 93, 331, 517
Tellegen, Lou, 195
Tempest, Marie, 404, 416, 491, 568

Temple, Shirley, 114, 257, 276, 277, 377, 391
Tennant, Dorothy, 98
Tennent, H. M., 338
Tenuta, Antony, 220
Ter-Arutunian, Rouben, 15, 22, 519
Terrell, St. John, 251, 525
Terris, Norma, 77, 431, 551
Terry, Beatrice, 90, 212, 247, 300, 411
Terry, Don, 531
Terry, Megan, 368, 505
Terry, Nigel, 273
Terry, Philip, 417
Terry, Ruth, 19
Terry, William, 53, 227, 290
Tetzel, Joan, 114, 205, 206, 228, 353, 366, 381, 446, 524, 568
Texas, Temple, 241
Thacker, Russ, 194
Thacker, Rusty, 270
Thane, Elswyth, 537
Thatcher, Torin, 54, 213, 311
Thaxter, Phyllis, 193, 292, 454, 460, 468, 568
Thayer, Sigourney, 64, 115, 254
Theadore, Ralph, 262, 446, 470, 491, 512
Theatre 200, 15, 280
Theatre 1965, 133
Theatre Assembly, 267
Theatre Guild, The, 14, 15, 18, 24, 25, 28, 54, 71, 78, 79, 80, 89, 99, 112, 115, 120, 122, 138, 214, 219 220, 227, 230, 232, 237, 239, 243, 247, 249, 277, 285, 291, 292, 296, 300, 301, 302, 308, 320, 322, 327, 331, 355, 363, 370, 371, 372, 378, 380, 383, 389, 394, 395, 397, 398, 406, 414, 416, 417, 424, 434, 447, 454, 468, 454, 468, 469, 470, 471, 477, 478, 480, 485, 490, 492, 502, 511, 527
Theatre of Action, 536
Theatre Union, The, 55, 56, 365, 444
Thesiger, Ernest, 498
Thirkfeld, Rob, 220
Thom, Robert, 51
Thomajan, Guy, 78, 205
Thomas, A. E., 53, 87, 100, 167, 211, 253, 306, 339, 503
Thomas, Ann, 88, 90, 133, 160, 208, 281, 289, 333, 445, 495
Thomas, Augustus, 33, 35, 105, 120, 139, 235, 323, 331, 348, 349, 356, 445, 526
Thomas, Bernard, 283
Thomas, Berte, 498
Thomas, Calvin, 11, 416
Thomas, Danny, 245
Thomas, David, 275
Thomas, Dylan, 138
Thomas, Edna, 405
Thomas, Frank M., 24, 222, 267, 303, 393, 396
Thomas, Frank M., Jr., 276, 476, 513
Thomas, Frankie, 158, 394, 415, 513, 537
Thomas, Marlo, 471, 568
Thomas, Richard, 147, 148, 373, 447
Thomas, Robert, 84
Thompson, Beatrice, 31
Thompson, Charlotte, 38, 391
Thompson, Dorothy, 31, 112
Thompson, Frank, 178, 373
Thompson, Frederic, 64, 163, 375
Thompson, Hal, 249
Thompson, Harlan, 57
Thompson, Julian, 211, 510
Thompson, Marshall, 179
Thompson, Rex, 235
Thompson, Robert E., 443
Thompson, Ronnie, 340

Thompson, Sada, 81, 141, 249, 568, 582, 586
Thompson, Woodman, 483, 519
Thomson, Archie, 250, 327
Thomson, Barry, 230, 413
Thomson, Beatrix, 358
Thomson, Virgil, 194
Thorley, Victor, 335
Thorndike, Sybil, 119, 131, 134, 568
Thorne, Olive Harper, 152
Thorne, Worley, 104
Thorpe, Richard, 187
Three Stooges, The, 547
Throckmorton, Cleon, 19, 55, 92, 116, 130, 328, 360, 365, 378, 509
Thulin, Ingrid, 344, 568
Thuna, Lee, 330
Thuna, Leonora, 269
Thurber, J. Kent, 140
Thurber, James, 292
Thurman, Wallace, 205
Thurschwell, Harry, 537
Thurston, Katherine Cecil, 301
Tiano, Lou, 367
Tibbett, Lawrence, 143, 324
Tierney, Gene, 15, 47, 266, 292, 324, 392, 397, 419, 482, 487, 568
Tierney, Harry, 484
Tiffany, Lylah, 23
Tiffin, Pamela, 130, 453
Tilden, Bill, 134
Tilton, George, 164, 432
Timberg, Herman, 411
Tiomkin, Dmitri, 254
Tippit, Wayne, 498
Titheradge, Dion, 206, 269
Titheradge, Madge, 404
Tobias, Fred, 142
Tobias, George, 56, 67, 173, 189, 210, 238, 327, 349, 354, 365, 410, 441, 515, 534, 568
Tobin, Dan, 370
Tobin, Genevieve, 35, 74, 190, 201, 276, 339, 340, 369, 375, 391, 452, 488, 533-34, 537
Tobin, Vivian, 182, 253, 349, 460
Todd, Ann, 166, 568
Todd, James, 57, 64, 98, 344
Todd, Michael, 77, 84, 244, 277, 293, 329, 370
Todd, Richard, 207, 516
Todd, Thelma, 106, 125
Tolan, Michael, 173, 291, 522
Toler, Sidney, 78, 187, 241, 255, 265, 322, 349, 375, 397, 433, 483, 490
Tolkan, James, 165, 169
Tolkin, Mel, 302
Tombes, Andrew, 342
Tompkins, Joan, 381
Tone, Franchot, 15, 16, 48, 51, 110, 156, 166, 173, 197, 219, 220, 221, 238, 296, 337, 338, 346, 355, 361, 477, 452, 474, 478, 541, 550, 568
Tonge, Philip, 47, 112, 142, 292, 431, 495
Tonkonogy, Gertrude, 475, 486
Toohey, John Peter, 249
Toombs, Alfred, 188
Toomey, Regis, 148, 233, 255, 513, 527
Toos, Audrey, 437
Toos, William, 437
Torchiana, Frances, 299
Toretzka, Ludmilla, 129, 219, 245, 261, 339, 403, 455, 497
Torn, Rip, 59, 87, 107, 110, 111, 119, 126, 127, 279, 457, 477, 540, 568
Torrence, Ernest, 458
Torres, Raquel, 13
Toser, David, 196, 443

INDEX   653

Totero, Charles, 177
Totheroh, Dan, 132, 277, 317, 412, 521
Totten, Joe Byron, 284
Totter, Audrey, 71, 379
Touche, John La, 474
Tourneaux, Robert La, 62
Towers, Constance, 144,145
Towers, Susan, 422
Towles, Tom, 510
Towne, Walker, 425
Towner, Wesley, 83
Townes, Harry, 192, 322
Townsend, K. C., 353
Towse, Ranken, 186
Tozere, Frederic, 112, 119, 158, 171, 233, 250, 255, 289, 359, 392, 396, 424, 444
Tract, Jo, 84
Tracy, Arthur, 522
Tracy, Lee, 49, 57, 59, 66, 67, 95, 130, 133, 147, 168, 184, 240, 282, 310, 312, 321, 346, 422, 423, 487, 541, 547, 548, 568
Tracy, Spencer, 39, 102, 127, 236, 263, 334, 404, 405, 423, 426, 432, 442, 485, 486, 492, 527, 532, 535, 542, 568
Tracy, William, 216, 482
Trahey, Jane, 397
Traube, Shepard, 71, 90, 179, 193, 217, 315, 339, 365, 407, 474, 479, 525
Travers, Bill, 12, 104
Travers, Henry, 41, 86, 117, 124, 188, 298, 316, 349, 371, 382, 395, 397, 410, 430, 534, 550, 568
Travis, June, 85, 218
Travis, Richard, 295
Traz, Jean De La, 362
Treacher, Arthur, 98, 184, 276, 549, 568
Treadwell, Sophie, 219, 259, 288, 344, 374
Trebitsch, Paul M., 335, 454
Tree, Dorothy, 217
Tremayne, Les, 128, 209
Trenerry, Walter, 238
Trenholme, Helen, 24, 511
Trent, Sheila, 121
Trevor, Claire, 24, 52, 121, 255, 281, 364, 429, 435, 517, 568
Trevor, Edward, 119
Trevor, Hugh, 208, 397
Trevor, Norman, 20, 81, 191, 240, 272, 296, 482, 536
Triangle Productions, 379
Tricorn Productions, 255
Tripp, Paul, 415, 464
Tripp, Peter, 220
Trollope, Anthony, 43
Troobnick, Gene, 45
Troubetzkoy, Princess, 155
Trowbridge, Charles, 46, 61, 68, 100, 108, 227, 259, 260, 264, 285, 317, 512, 521
Troy, Louise, 422
Trueman, Paula, 155, 257, 260, 283, 295, 505, 508, 534
Truesdell, Frederick, 98, 349
Truex, Ernest, 67, 113, 137, 151, 166, 175, 187, 189, 190, 218, 247, 274, 333, 346, 377, 391, 397, 426, 456, 464, 494, 503, 504, 510, 517, 521, 545, 547, 568
Trumbo, Dalton, 52, 511
Tryon, Glenn, 43, 67
Tryon, Tom, 208
Trzcinski, Edmund, 441
Tubby, Gertrude Ogden, 62
Tucci, Maria, 275, 403
Tucker, Forrest, 37, 150, 224

Tucker, Richard, 440
Tucker, Sophie, 95, 568
Tuerk, John, 40, 75, 109, 131, 170, 288, 317, 319, 353, 355, 401, 464
Tufts, Sonny, 418, 506
Tugend, Harry, 511
Tully, Jim, 55
Tully, Richard Walton, 55, 160, 254, 301, 348, 377, 403
Tully, Tom, 18, 76, 86, 316, 335, 453, 478
Tumarin, Boris, 128, 262, 315, 380, 453, 465, 503, 525
Tunbridge, Joseph, 342
Tune, Tommy, 494
Tuotti, Joseph Dolan, 52
Tupou, Manu, 236
Turenne, Louis, 204, 235, 397
Turgenev, Ivan, 250
Turgeon, Peter, 277, 504
Turman, Glynn, 390, 398
Turnbull, Margaret, 94
Turner, Douglas, 86
Turner, Holly, 173
Turner, John, 215, 494
Turner, Justin, 279
Turner, Lana, 193, 378, 379, 518
Turner, Linda, 279
Turner, Robert, 119
Turney, Catherine, 325
Turney, Robert, 414
Turpin, Ben, 307, 383
Tutin, Dorothy, 568
Tuttle, Day, 152, 270
Tuttle, Lurene, 191
Twain, Mark, 382
Twain, Norman, 131, 187, 369
Tweddell, Frank, 230
Twelvetrees, Helen, 42, 83, 503
Twomey, Neil, 339
Tyers, John, 524
Tyler, Beverly, 157
Tyler, George C., 18, 29, 39, 47, 94, 98, 107, 125, 137, 163, 164, 187, 201, 204, 206, 223, 241, 260, 304, 307, 322, 330, 349, 353, 358, 359, 361, 367, 375, 376, 433, 448, 480, 531, 536, 537, 538
Tyler, Richard, 92
Tynan, Brandon, 101, 291, 304, 331, 337
Tynan, Kenneth, 103, 141, 242
Tyne, George, 415, 484
Tyner, Charles, 316, 457
Tyrrell, Susan, 78, 111, 239, 479
Tyson, Cicely, 58, 82, 104, 398, 477, 568

Udell, Peter, 385
Ullman, James R., 57, 134, 305, 310, 432, 445
Ullman, Liv, 165, 568
Ulric, Lenore, 156, 205, 211, 255, 285, 310, 341, 361, 432, 434, 477, 568
Underwood, Franklin, 463
Underwood, Franklyn, 88, 93
Unger, Gladys, 187, 260, 341, 442, 493, 494, 514
United Producers, 439
Upham, T. C., 281
Upright, Blanche, 502
Urban, Joseph, 172
Ure, Mary, 358, 568
Usseau, Arnaud d', 259, 268, 483
Ustinov, Peter, 54, 327, 387, 568

654 INDEX

Vaccaro, Brenda, 75, 90, 147, 155, 191, 330, 453, 568
Vague, Vera, 431
Vail, Amanda, 283
Vail, Lester, 33, 47, 60, 64, 88, 199, 207, 219, 241, 322, 329, 484
Vajda, Ernest, 110, 198, 205
Valando, Tommy, 16
Vale, Eugene, 129
Vale, Martin, 495
Vale, Michael, 165
Vale, Rita, 185, 269
Valente, Jack, 367
Valentina, 191, 327, 368
Valentine, Grace, 29, 150, 204, 278, 533
Valentine, Paul, 208
Valentino, Mrs. Rudolph, 416
Valenty, Lili, 112, 262, 342
Valk, Frederick, 476
Vallee, Rudy, 210, 228, 548, 568
Vallone, Raf, 505
Van Buren, A. H., 24, 47, 49, 56, 109, 154, 211, 238, 240, 276, 320, 338, 477, 489
Van Buren, Kristin, 517
Van Cleve, Edith, 23, 25, 28, 67, 87, 191, 397, 474, 514, 521
van der Vlis, Diana, 100, 203, 309, 348, 422
Van Devere, Trish, 255
Van Doren, Carl, 478
Van Druten, John, 15, 47, 114, 131, 132, 137, 162, 226, 228, 241, 267, 306, 319, 347, 364, 433, 468, 507, 537, 573
Van Duser, Jane, 308
Van Dyke, Dick, 543, 568
Van Fleet, Jo, 78, 97, 161, 279, 346, 403, 490, 542, 550, 568, 583
Van Gluck, Stephen, 375
Van Heusen, James, 136
Van Itallie, Jean-Claude, 573
Van Loan, H. H., 57
Van Patten, Dick, 26, 72, 146, 405, 428, 471
Van Patten, Joyce, 127, 216, 472, 483
Van Ronkel, Alford, 380
Van Sickle, Raymond, 49, 276, 353, 453
Van Sloan, Edward, 124, 136, 394, 500
Van Volkenburg, Ellen, 140
Van Vooren, Monique, 30
Van Zandt, Philip, 208
Van Zandt, Porter, 509
Van, Billy, 129
Van, Bobby, 541
Vance, Vivian, 108, 241, 325, 358, 428
Vanderbilt, Gloria, 479
Vandis, Titos, 199
Vane, Norman, 205
Vanoff, Nicholas, 344
Varconi, Victor, 88, 406
Varden, Evelyn, 24, 42, 78, 119, 136, 151, 152, 214, 259, 262, 271, 343, 357, 380, 395, 406, 480, 514, 568
Vardi, David, 465
Varesi, Gilda, 90, 145, 246, 275, 401
Varesi, Elena, 145
Vassar, Queenie, 382
Vath, Richard, 362
Vaughan, Stuart, 11, 195
Vaughn, Denis, 453
Vaughn, Hilda, 175, 184, 243, 355, 415
Vaughn, Robert, 367
Veasey, William, 357
Veber, Pierre, 257
Vehr, Bill, 219
Veidt, Conrad, 517
Veiller, Anthony, 441
Veiller, Bayard, 115, 466, 471, 489, 526

Veiller, Mrs. Bayard, 495
Velez, Lupe, 68, 140, 258, 441, 445, 477, 542, 568
Venable, Evelyn, 119, 124, 134
Venable, Virginia, 156
Venuta, Benay, 257, 510
Vera-Ellen, 310, 510, 569
Verdi, Francis M., 238
Verdon, Gwen, 29, 88, 89, 541, 544, 569
Vereen, Ben, 569
Vermilyea, Harold, 121, 125, 169, 171, 184, 243, 280, 309
Verne, Lucille La, 56, 93, 94, 100, 187, 321, 367, 417, 455
Verneuil, Louis, 245, 302, 346
Vernon, Frank, 326
Vernon, Jackie, 546
Vernon, Margaret, 532
Vernon, Wally, 192
Vershinin, Ilya, 106
Verwayne, Percy, 378
Vestoff, Virginia, 542
Vichman, Theodore, 147
Victor, Dee, 89
Victor, Josephine, 44, 133, 251, 253, 525
Victor, Victor, 161, 433, 500
Vidal, Gore, 48, 417, 506, 513, 573
Vidor, Doris, 227
Vidor, Florence, 291
Vidor, King, 365, 366, 449
Viereck, George, 502
Viertel, Joseph M., 432
Viertel, Peter, 456
Vigoda, Abe, 486
Vilan, Demetrios, 243
Villechaize, Herve, 184
Villella, Edward, 545
Vincent, Allen, 269, 438
Vincent, Virginia, 513
Vincent, Walter, 209
Vinson, Helen, 35, 48, 124, 246, 280
Vinton, Arthur, 51, 437
Vise, Peter de, 250, 424
Vitale, Joseph, 102
Vittes, Louis, 100
Viva, 373
Vivian, Robert, 546
Vivian, Ruth, 294
Vlis, Diana van der, 100, 203, 309, 348, 422
Voelpel, Fred, 27, 141
Voight, Jon, 466, 505, 541, 569
Vokes, May, 44, 169, 188, 547
Volkenburg, Ellen Van, 140
Vollmer, Lula, 138, 214, 419, 455, 490
von Eltz, Theodore, 90
von Furstenberg, Betsy, 37, 89, 122, 178, 300, 330, 346, 362, 413, 414, 550
Von Orbok, Attila, 215
Von Rhau, Lee, 62
Von Seyfferitz, Gustav, 33, 142, 312, 376
von Sternberg, Josef, 25, 419
von Stroheim, Erich, 34, 474
Vonnegut, Kurt, Jr., 204
Vonnegut, Walter, 193
Vooren, Monique Van, 30
Voskovec, George, 22, 52, 77, 156, 214, 230, 256, 367, 465
Voss, Grace, 211
Voutsinas, Andreas, 170
Vroom, Lodewick, 34, 116, 466
Vroom, Paul, 135, 167, 253, 332, 343
Vuolo, Tito, 47
Vye, Murvyn, 277, 343

Wadsworth, William, 146, 476
Wagenhals, Lincoln A., 44, 97, 198, 283, 361, 396, 415, 417, 436, 520, 528
Wager, Michael, 48, 111, 394, 430, 517
Wagg, Kenneth, 166
Wagner, Charles L., 43, 237, 282, 317, 319, 439
Wagner, Robert, 515
Wagner, Robin, 145, 169, 196
Wagner, Thomas, 273
Wagstaff, Joseph, 67
Wainwright, Lennal, 398
Waissman, Kenneth, 27
Waite, Ralph, 59, 216, 256, 297, 488, 511
Wakeman, Frederic, 258
Walburn, Raymond, 38, 64, 69, 196, 221, 231, 293, 296, 342, 385, 423, 425, 442, 460, 504, 538, 569
Walden, William, 308
Waldron, Charles, 19, 25, 105, 114, 115, 125, 162, 166, 209, 213, 226, 324, 385, 459, 473, 510, 528
Walken, Christopher, 273, 403
Walken, Ken, 95
Walker, Betty, 391
Walker, Charlotte, 77, 174, 230, 487, 494, 510, 569
Walker, Clint, 416
Walker, Danton, 472
Walker, Helen, 64, 188
Walker, Johnnie, 292
Walker, Joseph A., 398, 586
Walker, June, 22, 40, 58, 92, 154, 164, 174, 184, 197, 201, 203, 259, 283, 306, 308, 318, 326, 332, 355, 357, 383, 397, 404, 426, 469, 491, 511, 541, 547, 569
Walker, Laura, 26, 133, 176
Walker, Mickey, 508
Walker, Mildred, 436
Walker, Nancy, 148, 165, 501, 569
Walker, Polly, 67
Walker, Ray, 104, 205
Walker, Stuart, 187, 192, 418
Walker, Zena, 585
Wall, Mildred, 201
Wallace, Coley, 296
Wallace, David, 261, 402
Wallace, General Lew, 383
Wallace, George, 29
Wallace, Jean, 330
Wallace, Lee, 414, 463
Wallace, Marie, 341, 528
Wallace, Mike, 392
Wallace, Morgan, 103, 278
Wallace, Ramsey, 51, 376, 385
Wallace, Regina, 189, 422
Wallace, Richard, 72
Wallach, Eli, 20, 78, 98, 287, 403, 410, 428, 533, 541, 542, 569, 583
Wallach, Ira, 12, 137
Wallach, Michael, 458
Wallach, Roberta, 141
Wallach, Samuel, 19, 240, 446
Waller, Jack, 342
Walling, Roy, 213, 262, 296
Walliser, Blair, 372
Wallsten, Robert, 142
Walpole, Hugh, 256
Walsh, Blanche, 528
Walsh, *, 126, 511
Walsh, Joseph Lee, 143
Walsh, Mary Jane, 108
Walsh, Raoul, 389
Walston, Ray, 16, 258, 323, 378, 391, 453, 456, 461, 519, 569
Walten, William, 308
Walter, Eugene, 86, 99, 139, 245, 253, 361, 487
Walter, Jessica, 335, 569
Walters, Charles, 339, 357, 370, 432, 447, 464
Walters, Polly, 59, 270, 420, 503
Walters, Sidney, 303
Walthall, Henry B., 79, 194
Walther, Gretchen, 434
Walton, Douglas, 300
Walton, Georgina Jones, 271
Walton, Tony, 351
Wanamaker, Sam, 75, 82, 90, 106, 153, 173, 191, 247, 473, 569
Waram, Percy, 30, 31, 42, 79, 142, 202, 265, 306, 315, 371, 381, 392
Ward, Douglas Turner, 398
Ward, Janet, 87, 312, 344
Ward, Lee, 384
Ward, Lem, 68, 147, 496
Ward, Richard, 86
Ward, Robert, 111
Ward, Theodore, 52, 357
Ward, Tim, 532
Ward, Tom, 273
Ward, Tommy, 191
Warde, Shirley, 290, 489, 532
Warden, Jack, 285, 425, 453, 504, 505, 569
Wardwell, Geoffrey, 35
Ware, Helen, 359, 381, 408, 471, 473
Warfield, David, 36, 192, 325, 395, 508, 569
Warfield, Marlene, 196
Warfield, William, 275, 417
Waring, Richard, 19, 20, 122, 141, 192, 295, 491
Warner, H. B., 18, 24, 33, 44, 160, 170, 176, 359, 408, 424, 434, 477, 489, 534, 535, 569
Warren, Chandler, 325
Warren, Gloria, 162
Warren, Jennifer, 412, 426
Warren, Joseph, 249, 273
Warren, Julie, 163
Warren, Katharine, 513
Warren, Lesley Ann, 203
Warren, Michael, 341
Warren, Mike, 72
Warrick, Ruth, 198, 312
Warriner, Frederic, 81
Warwick, James, 57
Warwick, Robert, 87, 133, 136, 182, 215, 262, 333, 382, 386, 526
Washburn, Charles, 20
Washburne, John, 469
Washington, Fredi, 224, 279, 293, 405, 457
Wasserman, Dale, 352, 353
Waterman, Willard, 37
Waters, Ethel, 293, 304, 540, 546, 548, 569
Waterston, Sam, 173, 195, 236, 258, 346, 489, 545, 547, 569
Watkin, Lawrence Edward, 348
Watkins, Linda, 17, 107, 128, 182, 226, 244, 252, 309, 367, 459, 470
Watkins, Maurine, 88, 395
Watling, Jack, 64
Watson, Bobs, 349
Watson, Douglas, 63, 127, 203, 267, 378, 410, 413, 454, 526, 536, 569
Watson, Leona, 96
Watson, Lucile, 44, 93, 108, 130, 147, 151, 155, 181, 182, 215, 265, 283, 317, 339, 345, 378, 380, 381, 429, 466, 497, 500, 511, 529, 533, 534, 543, 569
Watson, Minor, 100, 132, 144, 168, 224, 241, 385, 395, 442, 461, 466, 469,

473, 490, 494
Watson, Susan, 46
Watt, Billie Lou, 486
Watt, Douglas, 59, 66, 91, 108, 155, 157, 165, 169, 178, 184, 273, 358, 373, 430, 444, 455, 466, 471, 504, 510
Watters, George Manker, 70
Watts, Richard, 11, 59, 72, 78, 79, 89, 109, 116, 155, 157, 165, 167, 169, 229, 264, 268, 273, 337, 412, 423, 430, 486
Waxman, Philip, 442, 446
Wayne, David, 26, 71, 115, 145, 197, 205, 281, 298, 313, 366, 377, 411, 416, 463, 464, 503, 542, 547, 569, 582, 583
Wayne, John, 33, 85, 437, 515
Wayne, Naunton, 525
Wayne, Paula, 186, 335
Wead, Frank (Commander "Spig"), 85
Weatherford, Earl, 146
Weatherly, Tom, 274
Weaver Brothers, 459
Weaver, Dennis, 359
Weaver, Fritz, 91, 92, 195, 280, 312, 384, 542, 569, 585
Weaver, H. A., 348
Weaver, John V. A., 282
Weaver, Marjorie, 426
Webb, Alan, 173, 277, 336, 419, 501, 512, 541, 551, 569
Webb, Clifton, 27, 217, 266, 294, 303, 394, 424, 544, 549, 569
Webb, Kenneth, 223, 353, 539
Webber, Robert, 150, 196, 281, 340, 356, 368, 404, 494
Weber, Bernard M., 463
Weber, Joseph, 96
Weber, Karl, 262, 453
Weber, L. Lawrence, 97, 110, 129, 152, 211, 261, 295, 333, 342, 397, 401, 412, 451, 534
Weber, Lawrence, 431
Webster, Ben, 383, 537
Webster, H. M., 272
Webster, Jean, 114
Webster, Lucille, 72, 73, 420
Webster, Margaret, 20, 106, 152, 289, 355, 469, 537, 569
Webster, Nicholas, 385
Webster, Tony, 197
Wedgeworth, Ann, 59, 263, 471
Wee, O. E., 147, 195, 315, 423
Weede, Robert, 216, 469
Weenolsen, Robert, 218, 268
Weidler, Virginia, 319, 328, 370, 396, 529
Weidman, Jerome, 580
Weill, Gus, 480
Weill, Kurt, 146, 157, 160, 289, 449
Weiman, Rita, 13
Weiner, Leslie, 234
Weiner, Robert, 461
Weinstein, Arnold, 392
Weinstock, Elias, 258
Weinstock, Jack, 84
Weisenfreund, Muni, 166, 511
Weiser, Jacob, 67, 90, 157, 262
Weiser, Mel, 66
Weisgal, Meyer W., 146
Weiskopf, D. K., 207
Weiss, George, 381
Weiss, Jeff, 582
Weiss, Noel, 199
Weiss, Peter, 585
Weissberger, Felix, 459
Weissman, Dora, 216, 296, 495
Weissman, Henry, 433

Weissmuller, Johnny, 462
Weitzenkorn, Louis, 159, 160
Welch, Charles, 443
Welch, Jack, 409
Welch, Mary, 251, 454
Welch, Phyllis, 429
Welch, William, 224
Weld, Sylvia, 25, 160, 226
Weldon, Charles, 398
Welford, Nancy, 186
Weller, Michael, 317
Weller, Peter, 169
Welles, Halsted, 158, 400, 464
Welles, Orson, 102, 155, 243, 314, 330, 362, 464, 488, 545, 550, 569
Wellman, Emily Ann, 142
Wells, Charlotte E., 396
Wells, Emma, 74
Wells, Jacqueline, 205
Wells, Leigh Burton, 24
Welsh, Robert, 21
Welty, Eudora, 377
Wendel, Beth, 173
Wendell, Dorothy Day, 464
Wengraf, John, 78, 167, 487
Wentworth, William, 162
Werba, Louis, 43, 142, 301
Werfel, Franz, 143, 146, 243, 435
Werker, Alfred, 312
Wertenbaker, Lael Tucker, 177
Wesson, Dick, 68
West, Bernie, 45, 90, 463, 511
West, Brooks, 468
West, Jennifer, 129
West, Mae, 84, 103, 104, 129, 146, 369, 374, 418, 419, 521, 543, 547, 569
West, Morris L., 119, 128
West, Nathanael, 189, 312
West, Roland, 500
Westbay, Annette, 209
Westcott, Edward, 119
Westerfield, James, 113, 128, 529
Westervelt, Conrad, 135, 342, 401
Westheimer, David, 327
Westley, Helen, 13, 25, 124, 138, 197, 247, 261, 382, 395, 397, 447, 470, 541, 542, 569
Westley, John, 73, 137, 215, 229, 331, 415, 492, 493, 502
Westman, Nydia, 13, 69, 131, 143, 249, 306, 308, 322, 371, 446, 494
Weston, Betty, 304
Weston, Jack, 75, 187, 413, 569
Weston, Jay, 133
Weston, Ruth, 26, 175, 329, 334, 339, 358, 365, 392, 405, 417, 468, 515
Wetmore, Joan, 106, 148, 256, 430, 495, 504
Wetzel, Donald, 22
Wexler, Norman, 296
Wexley, John, 24, 263, 443, 470
Weyman, Stanley J., 174
Whale, James, 202, 299
Whalen, Michael, 435, 545
Wharton, Carly, 35, 108, 303, 484, 536
Wharton, Edith, 16, 146, 222, 347
Wheatley, Jane, 24
Wheatley, Tom, 83
Whedon, John, 271
Wheel, Patricia, 507
Wheeler, Bert, 142, 171, 207, 484
Wheeler, Gary James, 398
Wheeler, Hugh, 52, 280, 512, 573
Wheeler, Joan, 198, 514
Wheeler, Lois, 22, 131, 156, 237, 490, 536
Whelan, Arleen, 135
Whiffen, Mrs. Thomas, 191, 194, 253, 291, 539

Whipper, Leigh, 223, 224, 303, 332, 345, 378, 417, 444, 519
Whipple, Sidney B., 294
Whitaker, Grenna, 398
Whitaker, James, 93
White Hawk, Chief, 41
White, Alfred, 409
White, Alice, 130, 160, 174, 336
White, Arthur Corning, 506
White, Betty, 15
White, Christine, 279
White, Corning, 252
White, David, 267, 372, 402
White, Eddie, 152
White, Edmund, 58
White, F. F., 69
White, Henry C., 454
White, Hugh, 274
White, Irving, 162
White, J. J., 222
White, Jane, 95, 111, 243, 446, 460, 582
White, Jesse, 168, 207, 323, 435
White, Josh, 224, 279
White, Josh, Jr., 224, 354, 486
White, Kenneth, 262, 506
White, Les, 483
White, Marjorie, 140
White, Michael, 585
White, Miles, 88, 146, 372
White, Peter, 62
White, Ruth, 12, 52, 87, 241, 276, 280, 292, 377, 488
White, Sammy, 304
White, Tommy, 216
Whitehead, O. Z., 245, 312, 344
Whitehead, Robert, 71, 109, 143, 157, 161, 216, 304, 308, 321, 356, 381, 382, 394, 421, 428, 478, 485, 505, 584
Whitelaw, Arthur, 72, 89
Whitelaw, Billie, 337
Whiteside, Walker, 274, 408
Whiting, Barbara, 252
Whiting, Jack, 149, 179, 285, 342, 360, 439, 543, 569
Whitman, Ernest, 57
Whitman, Lawrence, 112
Whitman, Walt, 512
Whitman, William, 243
Whitmore, James, 101, 197, 238, 519, 523, 548, 569
Whitney, Eleanore, 307
Whitney, F. C., 387
Whittington, Alease, 104
Whitty, May, 468, 471, 538, 544, 548, 569
Whorf, Richard, 71, 151, 156, 161, 163, 173, 230, 252, 315, 347, 362-63, 393, 404, 413, 439, 468, 475, 544
Whytal, Russ, 172
Whyte, Jerome, 37
Wickes, Mary, 32, 116, 216, 294, 295, 439, 441, 487, 532
Wickwire, Nancy, 12, 95, 193, 415
Widdoes, Kathleen, 547, 569
Widmark, Richard, 138, 175, 257, 258, 477, 490, 492, 542, 569
Wiess, Rudolf, 257
Wiggin, Kate Douglas, 319, 391
Wigreen Company, 198
Wiklin, Stan, 169
Wilbraham, Edward, 356
Wilbur, Crane, 33, 60, 64, 85, 153, 154, 166, 201, 203, 315, 320, 339, 356, 402, 435, 527
Wilck, Laura D., 161, 175, 176
Wilcox, Collin, 78, 119, 152, 280, 413
Wilcox, Frank, 460, 534
Wilcox, Nina, 461

Wildberg, John, 30, 528
Wilde, Brandon de, 58, 100, 143, 304, 305, 323, 388, 540, 542, 557
Wilde, Cornel, 119, 208, 315, 365, 469, 544, 569
Wilde, David, 338
Wilde, Frederic De, 262
Wilde, Hagar, 198, 289
Wilde, Percival, 158, 276
Wilder, Alec, 55, 415
Wilder, Billy, 37, 168, 407, 418, 441
Wilder, Clinton, 126, 148, 464, 506, 584
Wilder, Duane, 179, 249, 292, 336, 397, 479, 520
Wilder, Gene, 353, 569
Wilder, Robert, 160, 457
Wilder, Sally, 160
Wilder, Thornton, 301, 306, 357, 427, 428, 491, 573, 579
Wilderman, William, 275
Wilding, Michael, 530
Wile, Everett, 160
Wilk, Max, 97
Wilke, Hubert, 96
Wilkes, Alton, 122
Wilkes, Tom, 502
Wilkinson, Kate, 264, 397
Willa, Suzanne, 338
Willard, Catherine, 125, 148, 194, 226, 283, 292, 431, 535, 536
Willard, Dorothy, 424
Willard, Fred, 276
Willard, John, 15, 58, 83, 162, 526
William Harris, Inc., 471
William, Warren, 133, 149, 153, 186, 190, 218, 269, 341, 363, 369, 444, 492, 503, 505, 513, 569
Williams, Alan, 214, 241
Williams, Allen, 22
Williams, Ann, 309
Williams, Bert, 545, 569
Williams, Billy Dee, 58, 86, 104
Williams, Christola, 69, 407
Williams, Clarence III, 195, 279, 429
Williams, Dick, 52
Williams, Emlyn, 119, 265, 315, 419, 548, 569
Williams, Esther, 399
Williams, Florence, 24, 251, 275
Williams, Frances, 53, 83, 175, 500
Williams, Fritz, 438
Williams, Guinn (Big Boy), 51
Williams, Herb, 154
Williams, Herschel, 244, 305
Williams, Hope, 21, 217, 363, 364, 391
Williams, Hugh, 161, 531
Williams, Jesse Lynch, 283, 520, 573, 579
Williams, John, 30, 43, 95, 133, 152, 257, 305, 312, 340, 407, 433, 503, 522, 541, 542, 543, 569, 583
Williams, John D., 22, 51, 105, 164, 186, 291, 361, 388, 410, 482
Williams, Malcolm, 290, 375
Williams, Margaret, 359
Williams, Ralph, 280
Williams, Rex, 277, 296, 351, 391
Williams, Rhys, 52, 88, 206, 322
Williams, Robert, 12, 148, 247, 268
Williams, Tennessee, 78, 116, 160, 168, 182, 183, 233, 267, 304, 309, 330, 336, 355, 356, 358, 366, 368, 403, 413, 417, 429-30, 448, 452, 457, 535, 573, 579, 583
Williams, Tom Emlyn, 160
Williams, Valentine, 48
Williams, Wes, 184
Williamson, Nicol, 545, 569
Willingham, Calder, 143

Willis, Harold, 436
Willison, Walter, 341
Willman, Noel, 45, 240, 273, 390, 584
Wills, Chill, 41
Wilmer, Sidney, 209
Wilmurt, Arthur, 536
Wilson, Alex, 535
Wilson, Alma, 102
Wilson, Dolores, 216
Wilson, Don, 404
Wilson, Dooley, 448
Wilson, Dorothy, 110
Wilson, Edmund, 109, 274
Wilson, Edwin, 16, 398, 504, 510
Wilson, Eleanor, 424, 513
Wilson, Elizabeth, 30, 52, 127, 276, 371, 383, 414, 421, 445, 492, 569, 586
Wilson, Ethel, 211
Wilson, Forrest, 57
Wilson, Francis, 40, 516
Wilson, Frank, 53, 57, 198, 224, 232, 378, 400, 417, 457, 460, 470, 511, 512
Wilson, Harry Leon, 77, 215, 224, 293, 307, 405, 492, 537
Wilson, John C., 146, 148, 163, 227, 233, 265, 338, 372, 449
Wilson, Katherine, 25, 26, 223, 282, 484, 533
Wilson, Lanford, 220, 397, 573
Wilson, Lionel, 167, 190, 351
Wilson, Lois, 153, 170, 195, 306, 310, 350
Wilson, Marie, 62, 142, 527
Wilson, Mary Louise, 528
Wilson, Perry, 350, 372
Wilson, Scott, 195
Wilson, Walter, 149, 152, 212, 272, 538
Wiman, Dwight Deere, 15, 41, 53, 107, 114, 116, 128, 131, 132, 203, 222, 245, 246, 251, 267, 269, 285, 301, 318, 319, 347, 348, 356, 386, 399, 402, 415, 420, 433, 446, 505, 529, 530
Wiman, Nancy, 269
Winant, Forrest, 106, 140, 152, 255, 322, 435, 492
Wincelberg, Shimon, 254
Winchell, Walter, 56, 91
Windham, Donald, 535
Windom, William, 20, 179, 193, 506, 533
Windsor, Claire, 62
Windust, Bretaigne, 34, 131, 151, 181, 196, 207, 228, 230, 233, 270, 276, 348, 363, 393, 442, 450, 490
Wingfield, Conway, 217, 526
Winkler, Henry, 165
Winkler, Mel, 367
Winninger, Charles, 79, 167, 285, 342, 420, 431, 432, 551, 569
Winogradoff, Anatole, 517, 525
Winslow, Herbert Hall, 514
Winston, Harold, 63, 356
Winter, Keith, 317
Winter, William, 137
Winters, Charlotte, 94
Winters, Jonathan, 346
Winters, Lawrence, 279
Winters, Marian, 36, 136, 165, 226, 302, 341, 425, 461, 583
Winters, Roland, 76, 104, 107, 519
Winters, Shelley, 25, 53, 129, 145, 181, 195, 207, 226, 334, 549, 569
Wintz, George, 420
Winwood, Estelle, 32, 69, 131, 164, 170, 189, 228, 275, 315, 322, 372, 411, 437, 452, 512, 520, 545, 569
Wisdom, Norman, 569
Wise, Robert, 494
Wise, Thomas A., 79, 174, 321, 362, 382, 435
Wiseman, Alfred, 12
Wiseman, Joseph, 11, 78, 128, 186, 247, 250, 263, 298, 569
Wishengrad, Morton, 403
Wister, Owen, 506
Witbeck, B. F., 247, 276
Withers, Googie, 569
Withers, Grant, 40, 67, 367, 410, 432, 477
Withers, Isabel, 522
Withers, Jane, 63, 154
Witherspoon, Cora, 38, 117, 121, 151, 164, 246, 247, 272, 288, 348, 370, 380, 421, 474, 485, 511
Witt, Paul De, 414
Wittop, Freddy, 474
Wittstein, Ed, 28, 145, 204, 390, 397, 486, 496
Wolas, Eva, 480
Woldin, Judd, 390
Wolf, Daisy, 512
Wolf, Eugene, 83
Wolf, Jay, 397
Wolfe, Billy De, 479
Wolfe, Edwin, 156
Wolfe, Elsie de, 356
Wolfe, Ian, 523
Wolfe, Karin, 178
Wolfe, Thomas, 279, 405
Wolferman, Barbara, 58
Wolff, William Almon, 67
Wolfington, Iggie, 297, 323, 352
Wolfit, Donald, 569
Wolfson, Martin, 56, 68, 84, 106, 112, 171, 298, 538
Wolfson, Victor, 25, 55, 106, 148, 365, 382
Wolheim, Louis, 68, 200, 246, 388, 515, 542, 547, 569
Wolin, Donald, 63
Wolkowitz, Morton, 144
Wollencott, Eric, 28, 119, 228, 251, 479
Wolper, Dave, 305
Wolsk, Eugene V., 87, 185, 273, 434, 455
Wonder, Tommy, 475
Wong, Anna May, 378
Wontner, Arthur, 81
Wood, Allan, 512
Wood, Douglas, 201
Wood, Eugene R., 196
Wood, G., 304-5
Wood, Judith, 130
Wood, Maxine, 350
Wood, Natalie, 88
Wood, Peggy, 136, 181, 203, 261, 307, 312, 347, 373, 409, 535, 547, 549, 569
Wood, Peter, 377
Wood, Philip, 268
Wood, Roland, 216
Wood, Sam, 101
Woodbury, Clare, 32, 152, 162
Woodgate, Herbert, 462
Woodhull, Harrison, 494
Woodruff, Eleanor, 395
Woodruff, Henry, 69
Woods, A. H., 11, 20, 34, 40, 51, 58, 71, 82, 86, 88, 101, 103, 109, 126, 149, 153, 154, 160, 167, 176, 179, 188, 213, 215, 238, 245, 255, 257, 259, 261, 266, 277, 282, 320, 324, 338, 339, 356, 363, 364, 372, 379, 380, 392, 393, 399, 410, 419, 424, 435, 439, 489, 492, 498, 500, 506, 519, 521, 526, 527, 528, 533
Woods, Al, 336
Woods, Donald, 352, 387, 425, 511
Woods, Edward, 437, 485, 538
Woods, James, 157, 317, 489

Woods, Richard, 264
Woodward, Charles, 62, 249, 264
Woodward, Edward, 48
Woodward, Eugenie, 494
Woodward, Joanne, 40, 141, 281, 284, 356, 544, 569
Woolf, Edgar Allan, 502
Woollcott, Alexander, 29, 41, 46, 51, 64, 81, 87, 92, 93, 94, 117, 130, 136, 137, 159, 199, 200, 225, 237, 294, 298, 304, 330, 353, 399, 411, 416, 427, 435, 448, 515, 523
Woolley, Monty, 257, 294, 295, 332, 543, 548, 569
Worlock, Frederic, 24, 30, 102, 133, 163, 170, 197, 247, 317, 349, 486
Woronov, Mary, 59
Worth, Harry, 128
Worth, Irene, 479, 487, 495, 542, 547, 569, 585
Worthing, Frank, 96, 97, 289, 331, 539
Wouk, Herman, 76, 330, 487
WPA Federal Theatre, 384
WPH Nut Crackers, 394
Wray, Fay, 88, 133, 157, 298, 321, 354, 569
Wray, John, 13, 133, 337, 409, 479, 521
Wren, Sam, 64
Wright, Frank Lloyd, 415
Wright, Haidee, 404, 461
Wright, Ivan L., 333
Wright, Mark, 179
Wright, Richard, 279, 330
Wright, Robert, 257, 461
Wright, Teresa, 116, 227, 270, 274, 275, 532, 541, 570
Wright, William H., 294
Wrightson, Earl, 157
Wrixon, Maris, 234
Wulp, John, 392, 581
Wyatt, Jane, 37, 55, 103, 219, 251, 281, 288, 333, 335, 387, 410, 570
Wycherly, Margaret, 14, 31, 122, 316, 321, 384, 416, 471, 481, 496, 570
Wyckoff, Evelyn, 248
Wyler, William, 91, 106, 121, 127, 128, 133, 210, 247, 275, 408, 445
Wyman, Jane, 29, 38, 68, 72, 135, 183, 190, 217, 249, 334, 349, 376, 458
Wyman, Joel, 131
Wyndham, Olive, 130, 506
Wyngarde, Peter, 237, 358
Wynn, Ed, 129, 570
Wynn, Keenan, 56, 71, 193, 216, 249, 256, 289, 318, 394, 450, 527, 570
Wynter, Dana, 56
Wynyard, Diana, 112, 395, 436, 570

Xanrof, A., 383

Yacht Club Boys, The, 249
Yaffe, James, 122
Yalman, Tunc, 488
Yokel, Alex, 219, 431, 435, 474, 537
Yordan, Philip, 30
York, Dick, 236, 327, 336, 463
York, Michael, 226, 358, 570
York, Susannah, 243
York, Vincent, 66

Yorke, John, 346
Yorke, Oswald, 488
Yorkin, Bud, 99, 333
Yost, Herbert, 84, 243, 318, 360, 523
Youmans, Vincent, 115, 421, 431
Young, Alan, 88, 179
Young, Clara Kimball, 529
Young, David, 255
Young, Elizabeth, 23
Young, Felix, 484
Young, Gig, 127, 167, 346, 347, 463, 492, 498, 550, 570
Young, Harry, 355, 531
Young, Howard, 112, 245, 446, 477
Young, Howard Irving, 137, 208, 342
Young, Joe, 455
Young, Loretta, 67, 101, 106, 132, 257, 270, 280, 368, 440
Young, Mary, 47, 115, 547
Young, Noel, 169
Young, Rida Johnson, 69, 80, 184, 276, 281
Young, Robert, 16, 21, 95, 107, 191, 222, 285, 413, 447, 473, 489, 490, 518
Young, Roland, 32, 35, 46, 125, 132, 137, 179, 188, 212, 254, 331, 361, 370, 386, 400, 405, 439, 452, 485, 533, 570
Young, Stanley, 35, 65, 400
Young, Stark, 284, 405, 408, 424, 485, 514, 524
Young, Victor, 418, 524
Youngstein, Max, 374
Your Theatre, Inc., 209
Yurka, Blanche, 42, 81, 82, 101, 120, 130, 184, 236, 243, 266, 412, 440, 464, 523, 570
Yuro, Robert, 503

Zaltzberg, Charlotte, 390
Zandt, Philip Van, 208
Zandt, Porter Van, 509
Zanetta, Tony, 151
Zaneville, Bernard, 121, 363
Zara, Lee, 443
Zerbe, Anthony, 85
Ziegfeld, Florenz, 239, 246, 369, 403
Zimbalist, Efrem, Jr., 533, 570
Zimmerman, J. F., Jr., 362
Zinberg, Len, 508
Zindel, Paul, 27, 37, 141, 414, 573, 580
Zink, Ralph, 527
Zinnemann, Fred, 208, 305, 520
Zipprodt, Patricia, 171, 312, 346
Zola, Emile, 469
Zorich, Louis, 169
Zorina, Vera, 464, 544, 570
Zucco, George, 28, 404, 570